National Intelligencer Newspaper Abstracts 1866

Joan M. Dixon

HERITAGE BOOKS
2009

HERITAGE BOOKS
AN IMPRINT OF HERITAGE BOOKS, INC.

Books, CDs, and more—Worldwide

For our listing of thousands of titles see our website
at
www.HeritageBooks.com

Published 2009 by
HERITAGE BOOKS, INC.
Publishing Division
100 Railroad Ave. #104
Westminster, Maryland 21157

Copyright © 2009 Joan M. Dixon

All rights reserved. No part of this book may be reproduced or transmitted in any form or by any means, electronic or mechanical, including photocopying, recording or by any information storage and retrieval system without written permission from the author, except for the inclusion of brief quotations in a review.

International Standard Book Numbers
Paperbound: 978-0-7884-4790-7
Clothbound: 978-0-7884-8108-6

NATIONAL INTELLIGENCER NEWSPAPER
WASHINGTON, D C
1866

TABLE OF CONTENTS

Daily National Intelligencer, Washington, D C, 1866: pg 1

Analostan Mansion: 437
Appointments by the President: see index page 602
Appointments in the Regular Army: 24; 32; 99-105; 171; 263; 343-344
Appointments to the Naval Academy: 259
Arlington and Nat'l Cemeteries: 216; 218; 519; 521
Army and Navy Union Meeting: 392
Asbury Methodist Church: 351
Assassination of President Lincoln: 83; 147; 162; 170
Bills Affecting the District of Columbia: 325-326
Columbia Hospital for Women: 207

Commencements: Columbian College: 253; 281; 356
                 Columbian College-Law School: 253; 255
                 Georgetown College: 290-291
                 Gonzaga College: 292
                 St Vincent's, Washington: 282-284
                 Visitation Academy: 288
                 West Point: 267

Conspiracy Awards for the capture of Booth and Herold: 159
Convention of Soldiers and Sailors, Lancaster, Pa: 342
Cooper, Wm Ringgold-arrested for forgery: 349
Death bed marriage: 54

Death of Ah-moose, Indian Chief: 93
Death of Bishop Alexander Campbell: 78
Death of Gen Lewis Cass: 260; 262-263; 296
Death of Hon Henry Winter Davis: 1
Death of Hon Daniel S Dickinson: 145
Death of Philip Embury: 164
Death of Rt Rev John B Fitzpatrick: 52
Death of Admr French Forrest: 539
Death of Chester Harding: 132
Death of Maj Arnold Harris: 131

Death of Hon Jas Humphrey: 261; 225-226
Death of Maj Henry Hungerford: 184
Death of Lt Cmder M Patterson Jones: 142
Death of Lt Col Jas McElhone: 389
Death of Dr Eliphalet Nott: 37
Death of Gen Chas H Peaslee: 427
Death of Wm Winston Seaton: 259
Death of Lt Gen Winfield Scott: 225-226; 227-228; 234
Death of Mrs Sophia Harwood Seney: 149
Death of Cmder Albert N Smith, U S N: 398
Death of Jared Sparks: 88
Death of Brig Gen W H Trapier: 24
Death of Hon John Van Buren: 461; 464
Death of Wm M Walker: 532
Dept of the Potomac: 544

Effects of Tobacco: 54
Execution of Dr John W Hughes: 49
Fast Driving-Gen Grant: 134
Female Bookkeeper: 450
Fenian prisoners-Buffalo: 287
Festival of St Valentine: 51
Fire Dept, Washington: 358-359
Fire destroys St Patrick's Cathedral, N Y C: 447
Five cent coin: 232
Ford Theatre: 21; 162; 238; 242; 369; 500
Funeral of Col Jas Duncan Graham: 4
Funeral of Gen Hickey: 12
Funeral of Jos Libbey: 376
Funeral of John Ross, Chief of the Cherokee Nation: 349

General Orders-Dept of Washington: 475
Generals & the Regular Army: 24; 99-105
Georgetown building improvements: 472
Grand Jury, Norfolk, Va: 196
Grocers-Washington: 176
Honorably discharged soldiers of Harrisburg: 345-346
Hotels and Restaurants-Washington: 35
House in which President Lincoln died: 83
Income $2,000 and Upwards for Washington: 332-338
Indian outrage on the Plains: 373
Joseph Jefferson, actor: 534-535
Jumel will case: 506; 514
Jury-Washington City: 59; 196; 287
Lands for sale in Allegany Co, Md: 588

Letters of Gen Washington: 58
Life of James Madison: 291
Local Board of Nat'l Soldiers and Sailors Orphan Home: 73
Marriage of Miss Lane, niece of ex-Pres Buchanan: 22
Medical Association of the District of Columbia: 336-337
Military Academy Graduates: 331-333
Military Road condemned: 478
Miss Clara Barton: 211
Murder of Christopher Deering and Family: 130-131; 135
Murder of Mr Wm Lyles, Piscataway, Md: 293
Mustered out of Service: 15; 102; 154; 256-258; 277; 282; 342; 361
Naval Hospital Site: 338
Navy Bulletin: see index page 618
Navy Officers commissioned: 294
Oak Hill Cemetery: 299-303
Obsequies of the ex-Queen of the French: 145
Obsequies of Hon Henry May: 398
Ofc of Claims Commision: 363-365; 402-405; 462-464; 529-532
Officers paid for captures during the war: 98-100
Officers of the 12th U S Infty: 534
Officers of Customs: 66-67
Oldest Inhabitants-Washington: 7; 41; 72; 128; 169; 242; 244; 411; 472
Oldest man: 44
Oldest newspaper: 247
Organization of new regiments: 525-527
Paymasters, U S Navy: 308-309; 392
Post Ofc appointments: 356; 384; 389; 482-483; 494; 497; 504-505; 539; 552
Property sold for Taxes, Washington: 116-119
Providence Hospital-New: 112; 272
Public School Awards-Washington: 279-281; 282-284; 286-288; 289-291
Public School Teachers-Washington: 344
R R Accident, Chicago: 349
R R Accident, Cleveland: 216
R R Accident, Erie, Pa: 490
R R Accident, Richmond: 232
R R Accident, Rochester, N Y: 372
Rhinehart, Wm H, sculptor: 278
Saint Aloysius Catholic Church bells: 316-317; 371; 372
Saint Lawrence's Catholic Church, Jessup's Cut, Md: 385
Secretaries of the Treasury Dept: 229

Steamer European disaster: 165
Steamer Kelso disaster: 571
Steamer Gen Lytle: 362
Steamer Miami disaster: 38
Steamship Constitution disaster: 6
Steamship Evening Star disaster: 453
Sunday Herald Newspaper: 133
Suicide of Hon Jas H Lane: 288; 412
Telegraph Line: 114
Thanksgiving: 450
The See of Balt, Md: 443
Trial of Paymaster Edmund E Paulding: 206
Troops in the Dept of Virginia: 202
Washington City Improvements: 366; 375; 452; 466; 468; 471; 474; 485; 500; 536
Washington Gas Light Co: 169
Wedding of Princess Mary: 273
Weat Point appointments: 354-355
West Point Graduates: 432-433
Will of the Late Col Samuel Colt: 199
Woman candidate for Congress: 459

Index: pg 601

Dedicated to our second Va Tech grandchild: Jarret Andrew Dixon
Born: April 19, 1988
Columbia, Howard Co, Md

PREFACE
Daily National Intelligencer Newspaper Abstracts
1866
Joan M Dixon

The National Intelligencer & Washington Advertiser is hereafter the Daily National Intelligencer. It was the first newspaper printed in Washington, D C; Samuel H Smith, the originator. The same was transferred to Jos Gales, jr on Aug 31, 1810; on Nov 1, 1812, the paper was under the firm of Jos Gales, sr, & Wm W Seaton. The Library of Congress has microfilm of the paper from the first issue of Oct 31, 1800 thru Jan 8, 1870, the final paper. The Evening Star Newspaper of Jan 10, 1870 reports: The Intelligencer is discontinued: the proprietor, Mr Alex Delmar, says that having lost several thousand dollars, & being in poor health, he has resolved to discontinue its publication.

Included in the abstracts are advertisements; appointments by the President; Hse o/Rep petitions; passed Acts; legal notices; marriages; deaths; mscl notices; social events; military promotions; court cases; deaths by accident; & maritime information-officers-crews. Items or events which might be a clue as to the location, age or relationship of an individual are copied.

No attempt has been made to correct the spelling. Due to the length of some articles, it was necessary to present only the highlights of same. Chancery and Equity records are copied as written.

The index contains all surnames and *tracts of lands/places*. **Maritime vessels** are found under barge, boat, brig, frig, schn'r, ship, sloop, steamboat, tugboat, yacht or vessel.

ABBREVIATIONS:

AA CO	ANNE ARUNDEL COUNTY
CMDER	COMMANDER
CMDOR	COMMODORE
ELIZ	ELIZABETH
ELIZA	ELIZA
MONTG CO	MONTGOMERY COUNTY
PG CO	PRINCE GEORGE'S CO
WASH, D C	WASHINGTON, DISTRICT OF COLUMBIA

BOOKS IN THE NATIONAL INTELLIGENCER NEWSPAPER SERIES: 1800-1805/1806-1810/1811-1813/1814-1817/1818-1820/1821-1823/1824-1826/1827-1829/1830-1831/1832-1833/1834-1835/1836-1837/1838-1839/1840/1841/1842/1843/1844/1845/1846/1847/1848/1849/1850/1851/1852/1853/1854/1855/1856/1857/1858/1859/1860/1866/1867/1868/1869-Jan 8, 1870. SPECIAL: CIVIL WAR 2 VOLS, 1861-1865

DAILY NATIONAL INTELLIGENCER NEWSPAPER WASHINGTON, D C 1866

MON JAN 1, 1866

Hon Henry Winter Davis died at his home in Balt, on Sat, of pneumonia, after a very brief illness. He was born in 1817 at Annapolis, Md, & was educated at Hampden Sidney College, in Va; graduated with uncommon honors at the Law Dept of the Univ of Va, with a degree of LL D. His demise will be mourned by a large circle of personal & political friends. His funeral will be on Tues next at 1 o'clock P M.

Snow, Coyle & Co, publishers & proprietors, ofc-Intell Bldg, D st, Wash City. One year ago today the Intelligencer made its first appearance under the present proprietorship.

Orphans Court-Judge Purcell, Dec 30, 1865. 1-The will of Valentine Blanchard, deceased, was filed, fully proven, & admitted to probate & record. Mrs Frances Blanchard, widow of deceased, qualified as executrix of the estate of said deceased by giving bond in the sum of $20,000, with Messrs Richd R Mohun & Saml A Peugh as sureties. 2-Annie Tunion qualified as admx of Comfort Tunion, deceased, by giving bond in the sum of $600, with Palmer Briscoe & John Bell as sureties. 3-Wm N Fendall qualified as adm of Chas A Henderson, deceased, by giving bond in the sum of $10,000, with Philip R Fendall & John P Fendall as sureties. 4-John W Hodgson qualified as adm of Eleanor P Goods, deceased, by giving bond in the sum of $600, with Saml E Douglass & Jeremiah Hepburn as sureties. 5-Annie Tunion qualified as guardian to Wm H Tunion, orphan of Wm Tunion, deceased, by giving bond with

Palmer Briscoe & John Bell as sureties. 6-Susan Clark qualified as admx of Otho Clark, deceased, by giving bond, Richd Vigle & Saml Payne as sureties. 7-The will of Eliz Herbert was exhibited & fully proven. 8-The final accounts of W N Dalton, guardian of the orphans of Wm Dalton, deceased, & the second accounts of Margaret Bayley, guardian of the orphans of W E Bayley, deceased, were approved & passed.

Henry Chatham died at his residence in this city last night. The deceased was one of our oldest & most highly respected citizens. He was thought to be the oldest native of Alexandria at the time of his death. –Alexandria Journal

The residence of Mr H M Lindon, on I st, between 10th & 11th sts, was on Sat partially destroyed by fire. Loss, $2,500. Insurance on the bldg, $1,400.

Geo & John Lee, & Geo & John Patterson, all negroes, were arrested yesterday on charge of having attempted to murder the son of Mr H Portfield Taylor, who resides on the Meadow Bridge road, about 3 miles from town. Mr Taylor, jr, is about 18 years old, was standing in his father's yard playing with a dog, when 2 shots were fired, one killing the dog, & the second wounding Mr Taylor in the shoulder. The negroes were arrested & brought to the city.
–Richmond Exam, Dec 30th

Edw B Ketchum, the forger, was today sentenced in the Court of General Sessions to confinement in the State prison for 4 years & 6 months.
[Jan 2nd newspaper: Edw B Ketchum's father, Morris Ketchun, was with him in the court room & his grief was intense. The younger sons of Morris Ketchum were visibly affected.]

Mrd: on Oct 31 in Wash City, by Rev W M D Ryan, Capt Frank Munroe, U S Marine Corps, to Alice, daughter of the late Jas Broom.

Died: on Dec 29, in Gtwn, D C, John Wm Smoot, son of Mrs Mary B & the late John W Smoot, in his 25th year.

Obit-died: on Dec 30, in her 64th year, Mrs Eliza Duvall, late of PG Co, Md.

Valuable Fairfax land for sale. Pursuant to a decree of the County Court of Fairfax, rendered in the case of Jackson vs Jackson, I will sell, on Feb 16 next, at Drainesville, Fairfax Co, the valuable hotel at Dranesville, formerly kept by Geo W Jackson; also, the farm of which Geo W Jackson died seized, about 2 miles north of Dranesville, containing about 300 acres, with a comfortable dwlg-house & barn. –Jas T Jackson, Com'r of sale

Orphans Court of Wash Co, D C. Letters testamentary on the personal estate of Valentine Blanchard, late of Wash, deceased. –Frances Blanchard, excx

Orphans Court of Wash Co, D C. Letters of administration on the personal estate of Chas A Henderson, late of Wash, deceased. –W Y Fendall, adm

Information is wanted of Jas T Smull, son of Jacob Smull, deceased. When last heard from he was in Nebraska Territory. It is thought that he has since moved to Colorado. Any information respecting him will be thankfully received. Address Chas Champion, Navy Yard, Wash, D C

Wanted-a tutor in a private family. –W O Reeder, Oakville, St Mary's Co, Md.

TUE JAN 2, 1866
New Year's reception. Mrs Pres Johnson was too ill to undergo the fatigues of the ceremonies of the day, but her place was supplied by Mrs Patterson & Mrs Stover, daughters of the Pres.

Copartnership existing between Z M P King & N W Burchell dissolved by mutual consent, I have this day associated with me my son Rudolph A King, under the name of Z M P King & Son, as Wholesale & Retial dealers in Fine Teas & Choice Family Groceries, at the old stand Vt & 15th sts. –Z M P King & Son

The clothing store of Mr A Schmidt, Wash & Bridge sts, was entered by burglars on Fri last & clothing, valued at $400, was stolen. Lewis White, Wm Smith, Jonathan H Payton, Martha White, & Edw Beatty have been arrested on the charge of the robbery.

Thos McKnight, age 78 years old, died on Nov 29, at his home in Dubuque, Iowa. Fifty years ago he became a subscriber to the Intelligencer. Thos McKnight settled at St Louis in 1809; in 1835 he married, in Dubuque, Miss Hempstead, now his widow, & in 1835 commenced living in the house where he has ever since resided, & in which he died.

WED JAN 3, 1866

The first prayer made in the old Continental Congress, in 1777, was by Rev Jacob Duchet, then rector of Christ Church, Phil.

On Fri last, in Worcester, Mass, Artemus Ward & his wife, residing at 91 Main st, were found dead in their room from inhaling coal gas, as there was a hot coal fire in the room. Two children & a servant girl in another room were not effected.

Mrd: on Dec 19, in Cleveland, Ohio, at the residence of the bride's father, by Rev A H Strong, J W Krafft, of Wash, D C, to Lizzie M, daughter of H D Pheatt.

Mrd: Dec 6, 1865, in Balt, by Rev Geo A Leakin, Mr Danl D Tompkins, of N Y, to Miss Mattie J Jewell, of Wash City.

Orphans Court-Jan 2. 1-Letters testamentary were issued to Asbury Lloyd & J W Boteler as excs of the estate of the late Eliz Herbert, the will being fully proven; to Mrs Frances Blanchard, as excx of the estate of Valentine Blanchard; & to Abraham Blakely, as exc of the estate of the late Eliz Miles, the will being fully proven. In the last case the real estate in Phil & the personal property in this District are willed to Eliz L Griffith, an adopted daughter of her late husband. 2-Letters of adm were issued, with the will annexed, to Susan Clarke, on the estate of Otho Clarke, deceased, & to Johanna Hickey, on the estate of Morris Hickey, deceased. 3-First accounts of the guardian to the orphans of R Jones, & the 2nd individual & 3rd general accounts of the guardian to the orphans of John Shreve, were approved & passed.

Jas M Tyler, of the police force of Richmond, was shot there on Sunday by a desperado named Ennis, alias Curley, whom he attempted to arrest. Some hopes were entertained for the recovery of Mr Tyler.

Appointments recently made: Maj J P Sherburne, A A G, U S A, to be Adj Gen of the Dept of the Missouri; Capt Richd Butler, 54th U S colored troops, to be Acting Assist & Inspector Gen of the Dept of Arkansas; & Maj E Jones, Assist Inspector Gen U S A, to be Assist Inspector Gen of the Military Dept of the Mississippi.

Boston, Jan 2. The commutation of the sentence of Edw W Greene, the Walden murderer, to imprisonment for life was decided at a meeting of the executive council today, in the negative. The vote stood 3 for imprisonment, & 6 for hanging.

Died: on Jan 2, in Wash City, John C Kilby, aged 35 years. He was acting chief engineer of the Senate ventilating apparatus for several years, & has been connected with that work from its commencement. Mr Kiley was one of the first to volunteer his services in the defence of Wash City at the breaking out of the rebellion. The members of the Wash Light Infty, & members of Lebanon Lodge, & of Royal Arch Chapter, No 16, are invited to attend his funeral from his late residence, on First st & Delaware ave, Capitol Hill, this afternoon at 3 o'clock.

Robt Mitchell, mate of the schnr **John Boynton**, lying at anchor in East river, near Riker's Island, was murdered early Sat by a burglar who boarded the vessel for the purpose of plundering it. The ball from his pistol passed directly through the heart of Mr Mitchell, who dropped upon the floor & died without a groan.

The funeral of Col Jas Duncan Graham, of the U S Engineer Corps, took place Sat in St Paul's Church; Rev Wm R Nicholson, D D, officiated in the burial service; pallbearers: Rear Adm Silas H Stringham, U S Navy, commandant at Charlestown Navy Yard; Maj Gen Henry W Benham, U S engineers; Brig Gen Schouler, Adj Gen of Mass; Col John M Fessenden; Brig Gen Thos H Neill, U S Army; Col John M Macomb, U S engineers; Capt B F Sands, U S Navy, exc ofcr Charlestown Navy Yard; Maj Chas E Blunt, U S engineers. The remains were deposited in the tomb beneath the church, to await the disposition of the relatives of the deceased. –Boston Post

Mrs Hannah F Lee, widow of the late Geo Gardiner Lee, died in Boston on Wed, aged 85 years. She was the author of "Three Experiment in Living," & other popular works.

A Hartford papers states that Mr J Dickinson Ripley, a nephew of Govn'r Buckingham, of Conn, was burned to death on the steamer **Commonwealth**. He was asleep in his stateroom & could not be aroused.

John Campbell, died in Cecil Co, Md, lately at the great age of 98 years. He was very deaf & almost blind. His friends never informed him of the existence of the war.

A young man, Richd Owens, a landscape painter, shot himself dead with a pistol, on Sat, in Boston. He had recently manifested symptoms of insanity.

THU JAN 4, 1866
Personal: 1-Hon D R Ashley, Nevada; Jas G Blount, Kansas, are at the Metropolitan. 2-Hon J A J Creswell & family, Md, are at the National. 3-Hon Richd Busteed, Ala; Hon Rufus F Andrews, N Y; Hon John B Steele, N Y; Capt Wm M Leverett, U S A; Col Elias M Greene, N Y, are at Willard's. 4-Capt Morris, U S A; Gen S Bronson, Ill; Hon Geo Thompson, N J; Col Pritchard, Mich, are at the Owen House.

John Moore, a restaurant-keeper on Md ave, was arrested by Ofcr Weoden on Tue for shooting Frank Strong with a pistol. The shooting was accidental.

Last night the steamship **Fairfax**, of the Atlantic steamship line, was discovered to be on fire at the G st wharf. She arrived here yesterday from N Y, & fortunately all her freight had been taken off. Capt Winters, the cmder of the vessel, could not tell how the fire originated.

Thos Dignan, a discharged soldier, late of the 2nd btln Veteran Reserve Corps, was found by Ofcr O'Callahan in a frozen condition, in an outbldg on N J ave. He was taken to the station-house & properly cared for, or life would have been extinct. Dignan is from Boston.

Brvt Brig Gen Wm G Mank, who was some days ago arrested on a charge of adultery, was yesterday held to bail in the sum of $600 to answer the charge at court.

The bark **B Sewell**, of Richmond, Maine, was driven ashore on the coast of Texas, 12 miles from Galveston, on Dec 26. Capt T A Hussey & daughter reached Galveston in safety, after 12 hours' exposure in an open boat. The mate & crew were probably saved.

Died: on Jan 1, at Rochester, N Y, Mrs Mary L Tyler, aged 37 years, daughter of the late Mrs Mary Smith. Her funeral is tomorrow at 10 o'clock A M, from the residence of her brother, John McNerhany, 6th & P sts.

Died: Jan 3, after a protracted illness, Eugene Bonnet, civil engineer & architect, formerly of France, in his 61st year. His funeral will be Jan 5 at 2 P M, from 261 F st. Friends of the family & of the late Dr Gaburri are invited to attend.

N Y, Jan 3. Wm H Russ, who attempted to murder Miss Dayton on Dec 23rd, & then attempted to commit suicide, died today.

N Y, Jan 3. Capt Campbell, of the steamer **Britannia**, was lost over-board in a gale on the passage from Glasgow.

Capt Greenman, late master of the steamship **Constitution**, wrecked on Cape Lookout Shoals, arrived at N Y on Tue from Morehead City, N C, in the steamer **Louisa Moore**. On Dec 26 the **Constitution** struck the outer shoals of Cape Lookout. Passengers lost as near as ascertained: Miss Land, residence unknown; Capt Sherwood, of Savannah; Capt French, of N Y; Capt Lane, of brig___; Mr Fitzgerald, of the Savannah Daily Herald; Danl Biggs, of Phil; Anthony French, engineer of steamer **Indian River**; Mr Haydon, of Hartford. List of the crew supposed to be lost: C W Greenman, mate; Wm Tilts, chief engineer; W I Crocheron, purser; Capt King, Savannah pilot; Edw Bailey, oiler; Wm Elkinton, coal-passer; Henry McNeil, cook; Danl McNeal & John Fitzgerald, seamen; Andrew Burk, second steward; Edw Read, pantryman; ___ Read, waiter, bother to Edw, Patrick Brown. Passengers & crew saved: Passengers: W P Long, of N Y; Ralph Lewis, engineer of steamer **Indian River**. Crew: Wm Greenman, master; Edw Cotter, second mate, of Boston; Robt L Ray, steward, N Y; Caleb P Borley, second engineer, N Y; John Borley, third engineer, N Y; Lewis Samson, carpenter, N Y; Peter Murphy & Robt Erwin, firemen; Chas Lewis, C Wright, John Wilson, & Benj Bush, seamen.

Died: on Dec 29, at Rockville, Montg Co, Md, Wm O'Neale, after a lingering disease, in his 71st year. He was one of the oldest citizens of the county, having been born & reared in the county. He was a consistent member of the Baptist Church. He leaves a wife & 4 children. His remains were interred in the family burying-ground near Rockville.

Cloudland for sale, with desirable residence & out-bldgs, with 9 acres, overlooking the town of Bladensburg, Md. Inquire of J B Wheeler & Co, Real Estate Brokers, 500 7th st, between D & E sts.

Supreme Court of D C, in Equity, No 554. John Ellis against Mathew Hagan & his wife, & Thos, John, Sarah, & Michl Callahan, heirs of John Callahan. On Jan 13 in City Hall, statement of the personal estate of said John Callahan.
--W Redin, auditor

Supreme Court of D C, in Equity. Johns et al vs Darrell et al. The trustee reported he has sold parts of lots 6 & 7 in square 367, to John Murphy, for $6,525, & purchaser has complied with the terms of sale. --Geo P Fisher
-R J Meigs, clerk

Phil, Jan 3. Hon Jacob K McKenly died today at Douglassville, Berks Co. He represented Berks District in 1860 & 1861, having been elected to fill the vacancy caused by the death of Hon John Swartz.

Large sale of Gov't bldgs & other property at ***Point Lookout***, Md: auction on Jan 18, 1866: the general hospital; prison camp; quartermaster's dept; & mscl bldgs.
-M I Ludington, Col & Chief Quartermaster, Dept of Wash.

Dr Hammond, who was removed from the Surgeon Generalship of the army, goes to Europe, it is stated, with a son of John Jacob Astor, getting $10,000 & his expenses for the first 6 months, & $3,000 for each additional month.

FRI JAN 5, 1866
The Sec of War has ordered the muster-out of Brvt Lt Cols Wm Tillman, Stephen W Crosby, Jas A Farrish, W B Mendenhall, Saml E Adams, & Majors S A Safford, C W Campbell, Jas Mann, John B Cravens, Henry McFarland, N M Knapp, W H McAllister, C S Chase, Z Voorhies, Fred'k Kelly, Wm Arson, & W H Stewart, Additional Paymasters, U S A.

Dept of the Interior, U S Patent Ofc, Wash, Dec 29, 1865. Ptn of Saml Fox, of Deepear, near Sheffield, Kingdom of Great Britain, praying for the extension of a patent granted to him May 17, 1853, for the improvement in Umbrellas & Parasols, for 7 years from the expiration of said patent, which takes place on Apr 6, 1866. –T C Theaker, Com'r of Patents

St Albans, Vt, Jan 4. The singular disappearance of Mr Hubbell, cashier of the Missouri Bank, at Sheldon, Vt, turns out to be a defaulter in the amount of as high as $75,000. His embezzlements began a year ago. His whereabouts is still unknown.

Trustee's sale of vale flour mill & machinery, Feb 5 next, by decree of the Supreme Court of D C, in Equity, passed in cause wherein heirs of Chas L Coltman et al are cmplnts, & Robt L Coltman & Jas Adams, excs, are dfndnts, we shall sell lot 2 in square 295, with Flouring Mill 4 stories high, on Ohio ave, between 12th & 13th sts, known as the ***Metropolitan Mills***. Reputation of the mill is unsurpassed. –Robt Coltman, Jas Adams, excs -Jas C McGuire & Co, aucts

Dept of the Interior, U S Patent Ofc, Wash, Dec 27, 1865. Ptn of Jonathan S Turner, of Fair Haven, Conn, praying for the extension of a patent granted to him Jul 13, 1852, for an improvement in Alarm Clocks, for 7 years from the expiration of said patent, which takes place on July 13, 1866.
–T C Theaker, Com'r of Patents

Chancery sale of improved property on 12th st between F & G sts, by decree of the Supreme Court of D C, passed in a cause wherein Beall et al are cmplts & Tilley et al are dfndnts, No 579 Equity Docket. I shall sell on Jan 11 next lot 6 in square 320, improved by a small brick house. –Robt Beall, trustee
-Jas C McGuire & Co, aucts

N Y, Jan 4. 1-Gerald Halleck, founder & for many years proprietor of the N Y Journal of Commerce, died at his residence today. He had been suffering from complication of disorders for the last 6 months, but was not confined to his residence until 2 weeks past. He was 66 years of age.
2-Rev Dr Cummings, of St Stephen's Catholic Church, died suddenly today.

The Oldest Inhabitants meeting was held yesterday in the room of the School Board, City Hall, Wash. The following gentlemen have connected themselves with the association since the last meeting, viz:
John B Blake, born in Va, Aug 12, 1802
Wm Jones, born in Montg Co, Md, Apr 12, 1790, came to Wash in 1815.
Ulysses Ward, born in Montg Co, Md, in 1792, came to Wash in 1811.
Saml Crown, born in Wash, Jan 15, 1805.
R C Weightman, born Jan, 1787.
J A Kenedy, born in Phil, Sep 26, 1795, came to Wash in 1801.
John P Pepper, Edw Mattingly, E J Middleton
Peter Grayson, born in Wash, Aug 31, 1798.
David Hines, born Oct 13, 1803
Chas Newton, born in St Mary's Co, Md, May 8, 1788, came to Wash in 1810. In the absence of the president, Mr Peter G Washington was called upon to preside; the secretary was Dr A McD Davis. The following were proposed & elected members, viz:
Thos Havenner, born in Chas Co, Md, 1785, came to Wash in 1811.
Randolph Coyle, born Oct 8, 1812
Butler Baker, born in Westmoreland Co, Va, Jul, 1800.
Richd Walach, Wm Thompson, John Sessford, Michl Nash, Jenkin Thoma, Edw Simms, Lewis Johnson, Saml H Taylor, M L Galt, W W Seaton, & Amos Green. The names of those to whom no date or place of birth is attached were not present when elected, & have not signed the consitution. Mr Clephane offered a resolution declaring that no person should be a member of the association who had not arrived at the age of 50 years & been 40 years a resident of Wash prior to the year 1866. The resolution was laid over. A resolution was adopted that each member contribute his photograph to be preserved among the archives of the association.

John Q Willson, s e corner of 9th & D sts, is now offering his excellent stock of furniture at cost, until Feb 1, having determined to reduce his stock before taking inventory.

Mrd: on Dec 25, by Rev A D Gillett, D D, Chas H Ingram to Anna Louisa McGill, all of Wash City.

Died: on Jan 4, in Wash City, Teresa A, wife of Wm E Morcoe, 2nd daughter of the late R J Culverwell, aged 36 years, after a long & painful illness. Her funeral will be on Sat at 3 o'clock, from 421 8th st, between G & H sts. Balt Sun please copy.

Died: on Jan 4, of consumption, in his 29th year, Jas Handley. His funeral will be on Jan 5, at 2 o'clock P M, from the residence of his brother-in-law, S R Sylvester, 6th & H sts.

Died: on Jan 3, Jacob Staub, in his 75th year. His funeral is today at 3 o'clock, from his late residence, 83 Market, between 3rd & 4th sts, Gtwn, D C.

Died: on Dec 18, in Northumberland, Pa, at the residence of her niece, in her 64th year, after an illness of 2 months, Miss Ann E Beall, formerly of PG Co, Md, but for the last 25 years a resident of Wash City. The deceased at the age of 11 years dedicated herself to the service of her Saviour, & united with the Methodist Church, of which she continued a member until her death. Balt Sun, & Mt Carmel, Ill, papers please copy.

Died: on Jan 4, Kate Hellas Kemon, aged 22 years. Her funeral will be from the residence of her father, 393 9th st, at I, on Jan 6, at 2 P M.

SAT JAN 6, 1866
Gen Wm Hickey, Chief Clerk of the U S Senate, died at his residence, in Bladensburg, yesterday. He had been sick for some months past, & unable to be present in the Senate.

Mrd: by Rev A D Gillette, D D, Jas W Newman, of Montreal, Canada, to Miss Mary A Platt, of Wash City. [No marriage date given-current item.]

Mobile, Ala, Dec 18, 1865. Benefit for Mrs Thos I Jackson, wife of the late Gen Stonewall Jackson, who is in reduced circumstances, next Sat. A tribute to the widow & orphan of a Christian soldier & gentleman, who was respected alike, during his life, by both sections of the country. –C Forsyth

On New Years' Day, Mrs Scripps, wife of the postmaster of Chicago, while engaged in receiving visits from her friends at her residence, fell back suddenly in her chair, & died instantly, without a struggle or a word.

Jas C McGuire & Co, aucts, sold the lot at the s w corner of 10th st west & L st south, to Mr B Wheeler for .60 per foot.

Meeting of the Plasterers' Association in GermanHall, 11th st, on Thu. Mr C Saunders, president; Robt F Muir, sec. Ofcrs elected to serve during the next 6 months: Jas Barrett, pres; Chas L Phillips, vice pres; Robt F Muir, rec sec; David Mohoney, financial sec; Jas S Lynch, treasurer; & Jos Parris, doorkeeper.

Seman Crumfels, a German, having imbibed too much lager, on Thu, lay down to rest on the 7th st road, where he was found by Ofcrs Boose & Crown, & saved from freezing to death. His arms & legs were badly frozen, & he suffered much pain when restored to consciousness.

Buffalo, Jan 5. Carrington was executed at noon today for the murder of policeman Dill last winter. He was not quite 20 years of age.

The copartnership of Barbour, Semmes & Co having been dissolved by the death of John F Semmes, the undersigned, surviving partners, will continue the business from this date under the name of Barbour & Hamilton. –Jas L Barbour, John A Hamilton, Jan 1, 1866

The Haverhill Gaz announces that Geo Peabody, the London banker, is to erect a new church edifice in Gtwn to accommodate the church & society lately formed in that place to sustain the faith of their fathers, in opposition to the new divinity introduced there by Rev Chas Beecher.

MON JAN 8, 1866
On Sat a butcher at the Northern Liberty market, John Fielder, while cutting a piece of meat, accidentally cut an artery in his left thigh. Medical assistance was procured but he died in a short time. He was a resident of Gtwn, & leaves a wife & several children.

Orphans Court, Jan 6. 1-Inventory of the personal estate of Powell Hess, deceased, returned by admx. 2-Inventory of the personal estate of Comfort Trunion, deceased, returned by admx. 3-Balance & distribution of the personal estate of Nicholas Snyder, deceased, by Sarah Synder, admx, approved & passed. 4-First general account of Sarah A Snyder, guardian to Mary E Franklin, Chas N, Catharine A, Agnes M, & Ananette A Snyder, orphans of Nicholas Snyder, deceased, approved & passed. 5-Inventory of the personal estate of Eliz Miles, deceased, returned by exc. 6-Appraisement of the annual value of the real estate of orphans of Wm Trunion, deceased, sworn to.

An affair at Offutt's Cross Roads on Monday last resulted in the death of John Henley, a resident of that county. Henley had been playing cards in the house of his mother with a negro named Jake, who formerly belonged to Mr Nicholas D Offutt, of this place, but for 2 or 3 years past has been living in the District. A brother of Henley & a young man named Magruder state that the negro won ten cents worth of apples & ten cents worth of whiskey from Henley; that the negro took Henley's gun. When Henley tried to get it back, the negro shot him in the face & he died the next day. The negro's statement is that he won what little money the white men had, that Henley then put up his gun against twenty-five cents; that he won that also; the he was carrying the gun home when he was attacked by all three, & he shot Henley in self defence. He came voluntarily & made this statement; but afterwards when a warrant was issued he could not be found. The verdict of the jury was"Killed by a shot from a gun in the hands of negro Jacob Diggs." -Rockville Sentinel, Jan 6.

Orphans Court of Wash Co, D C. In the case of Eliza M L Boucher & John J Bogue, adms of Theodore F Boucher, deceased, the administrators & Court have appointed Jan 30th next, for the final settlement of the personal estate of the said deceased, of the assets in hand. -Z C Robbins, Reg/o wills

Obit-died: on Jan 5, Wm Hickey, born Aug 3, 1801; for 65 years occupied in public & private life a prominent place in the eyes of his fellow-citizens; prior to 1824 held a clerkship in the War Dept; since then was engaged, without intermission, for 42 years in the ofc of the Sec of State. Until his death he commanded as Brig Gen the militia forces of the District. In the bosom of his family he was a model of the Christian gentleman. Married in 1826 to Miss C A Plowden, of St Mary's Co, Md, he educated his children to heed his precepts & walk in his footsteps.

Mr Beales, the publisher of the Boston Post, has entered upon his 81st year, & is still hale & hearty.

An old man, Simon Nelson, Prussian by birth, who kept a second hand clothing store in Detroit, was murdered on Sat by 2 negroes, Joshua Williams & Jas Knox, who entered his store & shot him through the head. Knox is in jail, but Williams escaped.

Phil, Jan 6. A woman named Mary Watts was found with her throat cut, on the floor of her residence, in Germantown, this morning. She was over 70 years of age, & lived alone. The murder was believed to have been committed by burglars. The house was stripped of much valuable property.

Trustee's sale of land, by decree of the Circuit Court for PG Co, Md, in Equity; public sale at Broad Creek, near the premises, on Jan 28th next, that piece of land which P Henry Brooke, late of Chas Co, died seized & possessed, containing 50 acres, between the roads of Augustus & Robt W Brooke. –John W Mitchell, trustee

TUE JAN 9, 1866
The friends of Capt Tappan & lady called upon him last evening with tin presents to celebrated the 10th anniversary of his wedding.

A life-size bust portrait of Govn'r Morton, painted by T Buchanan Read, was on Fri presented to the city of Cincinnati by the citizens who ordered it as a token to the Govn'r for the great service rendered that city when threatened by rebels in Kentucky.

A young man, Julius Meritt, at Cambria, Mich, accidentally shot himself last Friday night blowing into the muzzle of his gun. Mr Frink, a neighbor, aged 60 years, was so overcome by the occurrence that he dropped dead at the gate before reaching the scene.

Gtwn: Last night a man named Chalmers fell from a tug boat lying at the Gtwn wharf, into the river, & was drowned.

The subscriber will sell the farm on which he now resides, containing 130 acres of land in D C, within 4 miles of the City Markets; improvements are a frame dwlg, with back bldgs; 3/4th of a mile from Rock Creek Church. Price moderate; possession can be given within 2 weeks or before. –C H Wiltberger

The funeral of the late Gen Hickey, took place at St Aloysius Church yesterday. The pallbearers were: Hon Senator Wilson, Messrs Simms, Murray, Fenwick, J C Brent, & Queen. Fr Roccoford said the requiem mass, Rev B F Wiget said the burial service, & Rev Fr Stonestreet preached the sermon. The choir was lead by Mrs Kretschmar. Among the mourners was Rev Fr Hickey, formerly of Wash City, but now of Balt. The funeral cortege proceeded to *Mount Olivet Cemetery*, where the remains were interred.

WED JAN 10, 1866
Mrd: on Jan 4, at Trinity Rectory, by Rev R J Keeling, Mr Wm W, Edilin to Miss Julia Ann Swain, both of Upper Marlboro, Md.

Mrd: on Jan 9, in Trinity Church, by Rev R J Keeling, rector, H Skipworth Gordon, of Balt, to Miss Mary T Wheeler, of Wash City.

Died: on Jan 8, Miss Sarah Behethlen Burch, daughter of Eliz & the late Jos A Burch, aged 49 years. Her funeral will take place from the residence of her brother-in-law, Mr John H Cook, corner of 4½ & G sts, Island, today at 3 o'clock.

Orphans Court of Wash Co, D C. In the case of Eliz E Abbott, excx of Jos Abbott, deceased, the executrix & Court have appointed Feb 3 next, for the final settlement of the personal estate of the said deceased, of the assets in hand.
-Z C Robbins, Reg/o wills

Trust sale of Va farm, under a deed of trust from Robt Coles, deceased, for the benefit of Tucker S Coles, executed & recorded in Apr, 1860, I will offer at public auction, on Feb 1 next, one of the finest farms in Albemarle Co, adjoining the lands of Dr B F Randolph, P S Coles, & others, containing about 900 acres; with a large dwlg-house, comparatively new, with the usual necessary out-bldgs. This is a *Green Mountain Farm*. –E R Watson, Charlottesville, Va, Or address Edw Coles, jr, 432 Walnut st, Phil.

For sale: a beautiful country residence on Elk Ridge, Howard Co, Md, only 1 mile from a railway station & peat ofc at Ellicott's Mills, adjoining the residence of Maj Geo W Peters, & within a mile of the Patapsco Female Institute; includes about 200 acres; the residence is of granite of modern construction. The owners propose to leave the country for several years, & would prefer to sell the entire property together, including the furniture, stock, & implements. –Jas Mackubin, Atty, Ellicott's Mills, Md

Died:Jan 8, in Balt, John M, eldest child of John & Ellanora L Harrison, in his 4th year.

Orphans Court of Wash Co, D C. Letters of administration on the personal estate of Eliza Cassin, late of Wash, deceased. –Edw C Dyer

I offer at private sale my farm, *Rockburne*, on which I now reside; contains 108 acres; comfortable frame dwlg & numerous out-bldgs. Apply to T M Hanson, Intelligencer Bldg, 7th st, ofc No 9, or to my son, on the premises.
–A Addison, Wash Co, D C

THU JAN 11, 1866
Hon Thos L Tullock, of Portsmouth, N H, was married yesterday to Mrs Miranda Swayne, of Wash City. The wedding took place at the residence of Matthew G Emery, of Wash City, in whose family the bride has for sometime had her home. The nuptial ceremonies were performed by Dr Nadal, & Mr Wm Beveridge & his lady officiated as bridegroom & bridesmaid on the occasion. Among the guests were Senator Clark & lady, Hon E H Rollins & lady, Hon Jas W Patterson & lady, Hon E A Rollins & lady, Assist Postmaster Gen Hon A M Zevely & lady, & Hon John M Brodhead & lady. The bridal party left in the evening train for Phil

N Y, Jan 10. Prof Jas L Mapes, a distinguished agriculturist, died today at his residence in Newark, N J, aged 60 years.

Savannah, Ga, Jan 10. Hon Peter Cone, for many years State Senator, & a prominent citizen of Bullock Co, died at his home on Jan 6.

Louisville, Jan 10. Rev Jos Fisher, one of the most eminent divines of Ky, had his skull fractured by a slungshot on Monday. He has been insensible every since. Physicians report no hope of his recovery. There is no clue to his assassin.

Orphans Court of Wash Co, D C. Letters of administration on the personal estate of Ann E Beall, late of Wash City, D C, deceased. –R F Morsell, adm

Mrd: on Jan 4, by Rev A D Gillette, D D, Thos S Hopkins to Carrie W Eastman, all of Wash, D C.

Mrd: on Jan 10, at Trinity Church, by Rev Mr Lowrie, Miss Sue Beall, daughter of J E S Hollyday, of PG Co, Md, to Mr Wm T Wallis, of Kent.

Died: on Jan 8, after a long & painful illness, Eliz L Barlow, the beloved wife of H N Barlow. Her funeral is on Jan 12 at 2 o'clock P M, from her late residence, P st, west of 14th st, to proceed to *Congressional Cemetery*. Phil papers please copy.

Died: on Jan 9, Jane Frances Castell, wife of Edw O Castell, & daughter of the late Benj Bean, in her 42nd year. Her funeral will take place from her late residence, 4th & I sts, on Jan 12 at 9 o'clock A M. Her remains will be carried to St Peter's Church; services to commence at 10 o'clock A M.

Died: on Jan 9, Isaac B Iglehart, after a protracted illness. His funeral sermon will be preached at 10 o'clock, at his late residence on 7th st, near the Navy Yard. Balt papers please copy.

Brvt Major Thatcher, of the 14th U S Infty, who was on mustering & disbursing duty in Indianapolis during a part of 1864, & recently tried in that city by court martial for defalcation of $24,000, has been found guilty & fined $18,000 & sentenced to the penitentiary for 5 years, as well as to be dismissed from the service. Gen Ord, however, remitted the fine & imprisonment.

The Houston Telegraph announces the death of Hon C W Buckley by accidental drowning in the Brazos river on Dec 19th, 1865.

FRI JAN 12, 1866
Orphans Court-Judge Purcell, Jan 9.
1-Eliza J Stewart renounced all claim to administer on the estate of Eliza Cassin, deceased, & requested that E C Dyer be appointed administrator e t a.
2-The will of Eliza Cassin was proven & admitted to probate & record.
3-Wm H McCoy qualified as guardian to the orphan children of Patrick O'Brien, deceased, & gave bond in the sum of $1,500, with Rosa O'Brien & John F Ennis as sureties.
4-Dores De Schiele qualified as administrator of the personal estate of Henry De Schiele, deceased, & gave bond in the sum of $500 with Wm Bergen & Chas Hogeman as sureties.
5-Richd T Morsell qualified as administrator of the personal estate of Ann E Beall, deceased, by giving bond in the sum of $4,000, with Benj F Morsell & John W Morsell as sureties.

Col Benj F Dill, proprietor of the Memphis Appeal, died on Jan 4.

Pottsville, Pa, Jn 11. Henry H Dunne, coal inspector & superintendent of the N Y & Schuylkill Coal Co, was brutally murdered by 3 men last night on his way home to Pottsville. The murder was committed on a public highway. No arrests made.

Phil, Jan 11. Christopher Berger, aged 27 years, has been arrested for the murder of Miss Mary L Watts in Germantown last Sat. He had made a partial confession. Money appears to have been the incentive to the deed. The razor with which he committed the murder has been found.

Mrd: on Jan 9, in Gtwn, by Rev W B Edwards, Jas W Deeble to A America Meem, both of Gtwn.

The *Sisters of Mercy* held a fair last night; a fine band played at Gonzaga Hall; refreshment table was under the charge of Miss Alice Herbert; a beautiful opera cloak was on display upon Mrs Clare's table; Mrs Griffith's table had a splendid piece of tapestry work, " The Monk blessing game after a chase."

Died: on Jan 10, after a short but painful illness, Louisa Benner, aged 54 years. Her funeral is on Jan 12, at 3 o'clock, from the residence of her son-in-law, Jos Gawler, No 182 Pa ave, between 17th & 18th sts.

Died: on Jan 8, after a long & painful illness, Eliz L Barlow, the beloved wife of H N Barlow. Her funeral will take place on Jan 12 at 2 o'clock P M, from her late residence, P st, west of 14th, to proceed to *Congressional Cemetery*. Phil papers please copy.

Died: on Jan 9, Jane Frances Castell, wife of Edw O Castell, & daughter of the late Benj Bean, in her 42nd year. Her funeral will take place from her late residence, 4th & I sts, on Jan 12, at 9 o'clock A M. Her remains will be carried to St Peter's Church, services to commence at 10 o'clock A M.

Appointments of Com'rs & Assist Com'rs of Musters & Mustering Ofcrs recently made by the Sec of War: Lt Wm O Douglass, U S A, for the District of Northern & Western N Y; Capt Thos C J Bailey, U S A, District of Maine; Brvt Lt Col Clinton H Meneely, U S Vols, to be Commissary of the Dept of Ky; Lt Saml C Williamson, U S A, Dept of Missouri; Capt Jos W Chamberlain, 10th U S colored heavy artil, Dept of Texas; Capt T T Brand, U S A, Indianapolis, Indiana; Maj A T Lee, U S A, Albany, N Y.

The Pres commuted the sentence of John Kile, jr, 31st Tenn [Confederate] cavalry, to be hung to imprisonment during & for the term of his natural life, at the State penitentiary at Columbus, Ohio. The sentence of Wm Jones, an employe of the Fred Gov't, to be shot, has also been commuted by the Pres to imprisonment at hard labor for 10 years.

The Sec of War has approved the findings & sentence in the case of 1st Lt Thos Keif, 4th Mass cavalry, who was recently tried by a court-martial at Richmond, Va, of which Brvt Maj Gen John W Turner, U S volunteers, was president. Lt Keif was found guilty of murder in the 2nd degree, in wilfully & maliciously killing Dr Geo Martin, a citizen of Albemarle Co, Va, by shooting him through the head with a revolver, on Oct 3 last, at the residence of Mr Jesse L Heiskill, Nelson Co, Va. The sentence is to be dismissed the service, with loss of all pay & emoluments now due, or that may hereafter become due, & to be confined for 20 years in the State prison at Concord, N H.

By direction of the Pres, the 25th army corp is to be discontinued as an organization. This corp is at present serving in the Dept of Texas, & is composed of colored regts.

Supreme Court of D C, Jan 11, 1866. No 567 Equity Docket 7. Alice Jordan vs Patrick Jordan. The subpoena issued to compel the dfndnt's appearance having been returned to the Clerk's ofc by the marshal on Nov 30, 1865, "not found," & the dfndnt having failed to enter his appearance on the first rule day, occurring 20 days afterwards, & the cmplnt having filed an affidavit that he is out of the District, so that the process cannot be served on him, it is, on motion of the cmplnt, this 11th day of Jan, 1866, ordered by the Court, that the dfndnt cause his appearance to be entered in this suit on or before the first Tue of Mar next, otherwise the bill may be taken for confessed. –R J Meigs, clerk

The Pres has accepted the resignation of Brvt Maj Geo A Chapman. He formerly commanded a brigade of cavalry in the Army of the Potomac, & afterwards served under Sheridan in the Shenandoah Valley.

Trustee's sale of val property on Capitol Hill, by decree of the Supreme Court of D C, dated Nov 10, 1865, passed in a cause wherein John Grinder is cmplnt, & Jacob B Gardner & others are dfndnt, No 327 equity, I will auction on Jan 12, on the premises, lots 17 & 18 in square 688; also lot 13 in square 761, in Wash City, with all & singular appurtenances. –Edw Swann, trustee -K F Page & Co, aucts

List of volunteer organizations which have been, or are ordered to be, **mustered out** of service, not included in previous circulars: Illinois Infty, 8th, 21st, 47th, 147th, 149th, 150th, detachment 25th. This completes the muster out of the regiment. Indiana Infty: 26th, 31st, 35th, 51st, 145th.
Ky Infty: 7th, 21st. Kansas Infty: 8th.
Minnesota Cavalry: Co D, 2nd. Maine Infty: 8th.
Missouri Infty: 11th, 2 companies 49th. This completes the muster out of the regiment.
Ohio Infty: 15th, 19th, 26th, 49th, 51st, 64th, 71st, 187th, 48th, detachment.
Pa Infty: 77th. Artl-2nd heavy, independent battery B.
Wash Territory Infty: Co I, 1st. Wisconsin Infty: 13th.

SAT JAN 13, 1866
Exhumation & **re-interment** of bodies of Unions soldiers buried during the War- John R Hynes, Assist Quartermaster, U S V, has lately exhumed some 13,000 bodies of Union soldiers, that were buried at different times during the war on farms & in private cemeteries throughout the States of Va & Md & the District of Columbia. The bodies, as fast as they are exhumed, are re-intered in the Arlington, Va, **Military Cemetery**, by Col Jas A Moore.

The resignation of Brvt Maj Gen Henry A Barnam, recently tendered, was accepted by the Pres on Jan 9th.

Under the provisions of Genr'l Orders of the War Dept, No 79, dated May 1, 1865, the following named surgeons & assist surgeons are ordered to be mustered out of service: Surgeon Silas A Holman, brvt col U S V; Surgeon Jas F Baucher, brvt col U S V; Surgeon David Stanton, brvt lt col U S V; Surgeon Clayton A Cowgill, U S V; Assist Surgeons G H Porter, A Delancy, Augustus P Williams, brvt majors Saml Kitchen, & Frank A Utter, U S V.

Brvt Col & late Maj Gen Geo L Hartsuff has been assigned to duty as Assist Adj Gen on the staff of Maj Gen P H Sheridan, commanding the Military Division of the Gulf.

Dept of the Interior, U S Patent Ofc, Wash, Jan 2, 1866. Ptn of Ebenezer W Phelps, of Eliz, N J, praying for the extension of a patent granted to him Apr 6, 1852, for an improvement in Moth Traps to Bee Hives, for 7 years from the expiration of said patent, which takes place on Apr 6, 1866.
–T C Theaker, Com'r of Patents

Mrs Harriet Lane, niece of ex-Pres Buchanan, was on Thu, married to Henry E Johnston, of Balt, at *Wheatland*, the residence of Mr Buchanan. The bridal party at once started on a Northern tour.

The Police Com'rs have appointed John McGraw an additional policeman at Willard's, & have recomissioned R T Taylor at special patrolman on Pa ave, between 9th & 10th sts, & Michl French a special patrolman on the square bounded by 6th & 7th sts & Pa ave & C st.

Died: on Jan 12, of pneumonia, Arthur, son of Arthur J & Adeline McGuiggan, aged 6 months.

Four large paintings by Mr John R Key, of Wash City, are now on exhibition for a few days at Galt & Bros jewelry establishment. Three are pictures of *Fort Sumter*; another represents the gorge of Cheat Mountain.

Died: Jan 11, Dr Reinhold Solger, late Assist Register of the U S Treasury. His funeral will be from his residence on 11th st, between M & N sts, Jan 13, 10 A M.

The following gentlemen have been elected board of directors of the Merchants' Nat'l Bank for the ensuing year: C W Boteler,jr, Wm Bayne, Zeph English, J W Maury, B R Mayfield, Oscar King, & Ly Huyck.

N Y, Jan 12. The Associated Press have heard with deep regret of the death of Gerard Hallock late a proprietor of the Journal of Commerce, & for many years President of the Associated Press; copy of resolutions to the family of the deceased.

Holmes' Hole, Jan 12. The schnr **Christiana**, of Yarmouth, Maine, sunk near Cape Page. Her mate, Chas Tullman, was taken off yesterday with his feet & hands badly frozen. Capt Leach & the remainder of the crew were frozen to death. Their bodies were recovered.

Valuable timber & wood land for sale, the estate of John H T Magruder, in PG Co, Md; contains about 553 acres; with a frame bldg, 2 stories high, with 7 rooms, & all necessary out-bldgs. –Fendall Marbury, Atty for the Proprietor, T B Post Ofc, PG Co, Md

Augusta, Ga, Jan 12. The negro Isaac, convicted of the murder of Henry Amos, of Hancock Co, was executed today. He died protesting his innocence, though previously repeatedly confessing his guilt.

Louisville, Jan 11. Rev Thos J Fisher died today from the wounds received from his assassins on Monday night.

Supreme Court of D C, Jan 9, 1866, in Equity, No 415. Toulmin A Poe & others vs Fernando Poe & others. The trustee reported he sold the west 25 feet, from front to rear, of lot 2 in square 318, to Jos W Nairn, for $3,425, & that he has complied with the terms of sale. –R J Meigs, clerk

Orphans Court of Wash Co, D C, Jan 9, 1866, in the case of John A Baker, adm of Jos B Towers, deceased, the administrator & Court have appointed Feb 6 next, for the final settlement of the personal estate of the said deceased, of the assets in hand. -Z C Robbins, Reg/o wills

MON JAN 15, 1866
Orphans Court-Judge Purcell, Jan 13, 1866.
1-The inventory & personal estate of Jos Cross, deceased, was entered & filed.
2-Alethea F F Potter gave bond in the sum of $1,000 as guardian to the orphans of Thos L Potter, deceased.
3-Catharine A Tallburt was appointed admx of the estate of Geo W Tallburt, deceased. She also qualified as guardian to the orphans of said deceased by giving bond in the sum of $7,000.
4-The will of Danl Rowland, deceased, was filed & partially proven.
5-The final account of the administrator c t a of the estate of Jos Bryan, deceased, was approved & passed.

The numerous friends of Henry Toomey, U S Consul at Munich, & his wife, who is a native of Wash City, will be gratified to learn of the birth of a son to them on Dec 16 last.

Messrs Brady & Co's Nat'l Photographic Gallery, 332 Pa ave, is the prettiest establishment in town. Call & examine their pictures; they have a large supply.

Saturday ofcr Thos H Robinson discovered that the cigar store of Mr Emanuel Hoffman, on Pa ave, was on fire, & ran to the box & gave the alarm. The engines promptly responded, but the fire had communicated to an adjoining room, occupied by Mr Genan as a shoemaker's shop. Mr W Grupe, the owner of the bldg, occupied the upper portion as a residence, & the rooms were completely burnt out. His family, who was asleep at the time, narrowly escaped. Mr Hoffman's stock was destroyed; Mr Genan lost all his tools, & Mr Grupe a portion of his furniture. [Nov 8th newspaper: Mr Hoffman returned to Wash City after being absent since the fire; he was arrested on charges of arson in firing his bldg & of perjury in swearing to a false statement before Justice Walter. He was held to bail in $5,000 for a hearing today.]

Thos Hudson, house carpenter for the past 2 years at Willard's Hotel, was arrested yesterday by Patrolman John Magraw, on the charge of robbing the hotel of silverware, sheeting, napkins, liquors, glass goblets, & register books; the stolen goods were found at Hudson's residence, 317 7th st, corner of I. He was committed to jail for court, in default of $500 bail.

Wash Corp, Jan 8, 1866. 1-Ptn of J W Drane & others, to open, grade, & pave an alley in square 369: referred to the Cmte on Improvements. 2-Ptn of Solomon J Fague; & of Maria Anna Sarkint; asking the remission of fines: referred to the Cmte on Claims.

Mr Darwin Stewart, of Memphis, on Sat last, about 3 miles from there, enroute to his mother's plantation, was shot by a negro, in the uniform of a soldier, the ball piercing through the right lung. He was then approached by the negro, & robbed of all his money & a fine gold watch, after which he made off. No hopes are entertained of the recovery of Mr Stewart.

On Sat last Chas Gilpin, about 12 years of age, son of Col Chas Gilpin, of Cumberland, Md, while skating broke through the ice & was drowned.

Mr B P Garrison, a highly esteemed citizen of Memphis, was accidentally killed on Sunday last, while at a fire, by a guard who fired at a negro who was stealing goods.

Supreme Court of D C, Equity Docket 7, No 539. Lucy M Johns, H Howard Young & Florence E his wife, Virginia E Darrell, & Armsted M Darrell against Mary Darrell, Wm B Darrell, & Benj V Darrell. On Jan 31 next, I shall state the trustee's account & the distribution of the fund in his hands to the parties entitled. If there be any creditors of the late Lucy Ann Brooke, they will file their claims with me on or before said day. -W Redin, auditor, City Hall, Wash, D C

San Francisco, Jan 12. The steamer **Colorado** from N Y on Dec 21 has arrived here. She reports the death of Capt R W Scott, late commanding the U S steamer **Saginaw** at Acapulco on Jan 5, after 3 weeks' sickness from fever.

Supreme Court of D C, Equity Docket 7, No 495. Danl C Barrand & Mary L his wife, John W Young & Indiana E his wife, John O Payne & Catharine his wife, Chas D Willard & Lucy A his wife, Thos C Hanford & Mary his wife, Wm A Niemeyer & Sarah H his wife, Leonidas Rosser & Martha W his wife, Henry Harwood & Virginia J his wife, Henry F Woodhouse & Georgiana his wife, & Mary Eliza Hill against Eliz W Ransone, Geo H Mitchell, & Geo A Hanson. On Jan 25, at City Hall, Wash, D C, I shall state the trustee's account & the distribution of the fund in his hands to the parties entitled. If there be any creditors of the late Thos Lawson, they will file their claims with me on or before said day. –W Redin, auditor

On Friday last Mr John Kussmaul, residing in the township of Caldwell, N J, woke up & found that his wife, who had been confined to her bed by illness for several days, was missing. His son & neighbor found her tracks in the snow & found her at the foot of a hill, lying on her back, in her night clothes, frozen to death. No satisfactory explanation can be discovered of this strange & melancholy affair.

Dept of the Interior, U S Patent Ofc, Wash, Jan 4, 1866. Ptn of Joel Whiting, of Winchester, Mass, praying for the extension of a patent granted to him Apr 13, 1852, for an improvement in Feed Apparatus for Planting Machines for 7 years from the expiration of said patent, which takes place on Apr 13, 1866. –T C Theaker, Com'r of Patents

Absconded. N Y Herald of yesterday: Mr Chas H Carr, engaged in brokerage transactions for many years past, at 30 Broad st, absconded to Europe, having previously drawn from the bank $17,000, the property of the firm of which he was a member. Rumors found credence that Mr Carr had fled to Europe & forsaken his wife & family for the purpose of joining a young actress, who left the country a few days before; but as yet these stories rest on no positive foundation.

Dept of the Interior, U S Patent Ofc, Wash, Jan 4, 1866. Ptn of Chas F Grilley, of New Haven, Conn, praying for the extension of a patent granted to him Apr 20, 1853, for improvement in Capping of Screws, for 7 years from the expiration of said patent, which takes place on Apr 20, 1866. –T C Theaker Com'r of Patents

Dept of the Interior, U S Patent Ofc, Wash, Dec 15, 1865. Ptn of Saml T Thomas, of Laconia, N H, & Eliza A Adams, admx of the estate of Edw Everett, of Townsend, Mass, praying for the extension of a patent granted to the said Edw Everett Mar 16, 1852, for an improvement in Pattern Cards for Jacquard Looms, for 7 years from the expiration of said patent, which takes place on Mar 16, 1866. –T C Theaker, Com'r of Patents

Admx's sale of household & kitchen furniture at auction on Jan 15, by order of the Orphans Court of , of the personal effects of the late Wm Ford, deceased, on G st, between 3rd & 4th sts. –Green & Williams, aucts

Dept of the Interior, U S Patent Ofc, Wash, Jan 4, 1866. Ptn of Danl Shaw, of Elkhart, Indiana, praying for the extension of a patent granted to him Apr 6, 1852, for an improvement in Smut Mill & Grain Separator for 7 years from the expiration of said patent, which takes place on Apr 6, 1866. –T C Theaker, Com'r of Patents

Dept of the Interior, U S Patent Ofc, Wash, Jan 4, 1865. Ptn of Wm Baker, of Utica N Y, praying for the extension of a patent granted to him Apr 13, 1853, for an improvement in Hinges, for 7 years from the expiration of said patent, which takes place on Apr 13, 1866. –T C Theaker, Com'r of Patents

TUE JAN 16, 1866
Board of ofcrs to examine into the merits of volunteer ofcrs serving in the Dept of the Columbia: Surgeon B G S Ten Broeck, U S A, Medical Dir of the Dept of the Columbia; Capt T J Eckerson, U S A; Capt J W Hopkins, Commissary of Subsistence, & Capt W M Knox, Commissary of Musters, has been ordered to convene at *Fort Vancouver*, Wash Territory, for the purpose of examining into the relative merits & fitness for position of the volunteer ofcrs serving the Dept of the Columbia.

The following assignment of staff ofcrs has just been made: Capt W J Sambour, to be Assist Adj Gen of the Dept of Columbia; Capt J W Hopkins, to be Chief Commissary of Subsistence of the Dept of the Columbia, & Lt Col W R Smedberg, to be Inspector Gen of the Dept of the Columbia.

Died: Jan 3, at his residence, in Richmond Co, Va, A Oscar Yerby, in his 49th yr.

Special Agent Geo C Whiting details to Com'r Cooley, of the Indian Bureau, interesting particulars of a recent visit to the Miami & Eel river Indians, under date of Jan 15, 1866: The Indians whom I visited in Indiana & Michigan are far advanced in civilization, & are orderly, industrious, & good citizens. In the main they live comfortably & are doing well, though some of them are very poor & destitute. Many of them are professing Christians, & all speak the English language intelligibly, & some few read & write. I was informed that nearly four-fifths of the men capable of bearing arms had been in the service of the U S in the late war for the Union.

Ford Theatre. According to a contract made by the Gov't, the theatre bldg & the 2 adjoining bldgs, [one in front, the other in the rear,] are to be purchased, with the ground, for $100,000, by Feb 1, 1866, or the property restored as it was to Mr Ford. The Gov't has entirely destroyed the theatrical part of the bldgs, & by the carpenters of the Quartermaster's Dept & by contractors about $35,000 have been expended upon the property. To restore the property to Mr Ford now will involve a loss to the Gov't nearly if not fully equal to the full amount of the purchase money, as all the present improvements must be removed & the theatre reconstructed.

Mrs Grinder, the Pittsburgh poisoner, who will expiate her crime on Jan 19, remains in bed the greater part of the time, & seems to care for nothing but morphine & opium, using all that she can procure. She has the benefit of a clergyman, & says that she derives great consolation from his visits. In the same jail are Marschall & Frecke, who will be hung for the murder of a German emigrant, just arrived in the country, last August.

$10 reward for return of strayed Pointer Dog, answers to the name of Joe.
–C Theo Griffith, 67 Louisiana ave, between 6th & 7th sts.

Senate: 1-Resolved, That Jas J Wheeler, of Ky, now a cadet in the Naval Academy, & formerly in the military service of the so-called Confederate States, be dismissed from the academy; & no one shall be appointed as a cadet in the Naval or Military Academy of the U S who shall have rendered aid or assistance to said rebellion: referred to the Cmte on Naval Affairs.

WED JAN 17, 1866
Orphans Court-Judge Purcell, Jan 16, 1866
1-Henry G Ayer qualified as guardian of Saml E Shields, orphan of Jas W Shields, dec'd, by giving bond in the sum of $1,000, with John T Given & Jas V A Shields as sureties.
2-John T Cochrane & John Carter Marbury, adms c t a of the personal estate of Jos Bryan, deceased, returned the assets of the estate of said dec'd, amounting to $59,421.63, & the court ordered that the amount be turned over to Henry H Cumming, trustee under the will of said deceased.
3-Maria L Dommer qualified as guardian to the orphan child of Garrett Smith, dec'd, & gave bond in the sum of $300, with Wm E Chaffee & Jos Whitcomb as sureties.
4-A certificate was received from Israel Lawton, Surrogate of Albany Co, N Y, certifying that Jos P Wilkes had been appointed guardian of Wm V Wilkes, minor son of the late Hattie Wilkes, & that he had given bond in the sum of $3,000 for the faithful performance of his duty.
5-Morris Adler appointed guardian to Wm V Mason, minor child of Maynadier Mason & legatee under the will of Mary Ann Clark, dec'd, & qualified by giving bond in the sum of $2,000, with Wm H Dougal & Morris J Adler as sureties.
6-Mary Horraghan qualified as administratrix of the personal estate of John Horraghan, dec'd, by giving bond in the sum of $500, with Patrick Donney & Michl Donney as sureties.
7-The answer of Sarah K Boswell, widow of Otho Boswell, dec'd, to the petition of E V Boswell, adm, requiring her to show cause why the profits of the business should not be applied to the payment of debts before a distribution was made, was filed.

Henry A DeSaussure, senior member of the Charleston Bar, died a few days since, aged 77 years.

Died: on Sunday last, at Plattsburg, N Y, Col H M Judah, U S A, late Brig Gen of Volunteers, aged 40 years. -Calif papers please copy.

The 49th annual meeting of the American Colonization Society was held yesterday in the Colonization Rooms, Pa ave & 4½ st, Mr J H B Latrobe presiding, & Rev Mr Coppinger, sec. Delegates were present from nearly every State. Prayer by Rev Mr Clark, of N J; vice presidents: David Hunt, Jas Reiley, Danl Turnbull, & Hon Thos Corwin, have been removed by death. Friends of the society who have died are Hezekiah Huntington, Sec of the Conn Colonization Society; Dr Lyndam A Smith, Sec of the N J Colonization Society; Mrs Lydia H Sigourney, Gerald Hallock, & President Lincoln. A handsome tribute is paid to the memory of Pres Stephen A Benson, of Liberia. Aiding emigrants from Barbadoes to Liberia: the zealous financial sec of the society, Rev Wm McLain, D D, embarked at Phil, Feb 24, & arrived at Bridgetown, the port of entry of that island, on Mar 11, after a pleasant voyage of 15 days. Henry W Johnson, formerly a barber of Canandaigua, N Y, is now an eminent lawyer in Liberia, a man of most gifted & eminent legal attainments.

Died: on Christmas day, at **Chatham**, his residence in Westmoreland Co, Va, John Brokenbrough, after a short illness. In a few days after, Mrs Brokenbrough, wife of John Brokenbrough. In the space of a few days God saw right to remove father & mother. Star & Balt Sun copy.

Brvt Maj John Vanzant, Assist Surgeon, U S Army, has been relieved from duty in the Military Division of the Gulf, & ordered to report for duty to the commanding general of the Dept of Arkansas.

On Friday last Ofcr Crown was informed by a colored man, John H Francis, that in 1864 his sister-in-law, Martha Forrest, had murdered two of her children, one in Apr, 1864, & the other in Jun, 1864, & had buried both in a yard on 3rd st, between L st & N Y ave. Sgt Johnson & Ofcr Crown, accompanied by Francis, disinterred the bodies, & arrested Martha Forrest, her sister Adelaide, [wife of Francis,] & their mother, Maria Forrest. Justice Walter investigated the case, & Francis charged Martha with the murder of the children & the others with aiding & abetting her. The wife of Francis then charged him with being concerned in the murder, & all parties were held for further hearing.

Annual renting of pews in <u>Plymouth Church</u>; the pews in Mr Beecher's church were rented for the year 1866 Tuesday night. Mr Beecher was absent, & Mr Freeland, was master of ceremonies. Mr Pillsbury, auctioneer, sold the first choice to Mr H B Claflin, pew 89, at $400, the regular rental raising the sum of $520. Mr Jos P Howard obtained the next choice for $300; Mr R S Benedict the third for $320; Mr H C Bowen took the fourth of $315. This is an increase of $2,736 over the amount obtained in 1865.

Wash Society: on Monday Mrs Sec Harlan & daughter received a numerous & distinguished company.

Orphans Court of D C. Letters of administration on the personal estate of Geo W Talburtt, late of Wash City, deceased. –Catharine A Talburtt, admx

The marriage of Miss Lane, niece of ex-Pres Buchanan, to Henry E Johnston, transpired at **Wheatland**, Mr Buchanan's residence, near Lancaster, at 1 o'clock P M on Thu last. The ceremony was performed by Rev E Y Buchanan, [brother of the ex-President,] pastor of the Trinity Church, Oxford, near Wash City, & the fair bride was given away by her uncle. Invited guests: Rev E Y Buchanan & lady & 4 daughters; Mr J Buchanan Henry, private sec of the Pres for 2 years from 1857; Mr & Mrs Thos E Franklin; Dr Henry Carpenter; Mrs Jas B Lane; Rev B Keenan, of the Catholic Church; Rev Mr Powell, of the Presbyterian Church, all of Lancaster; Mr & Mrs Brinton; Dr & Mrs Nevin & the Misses Nevin; Capt Nevin, late of the U S army; Mr & Misses Johnston, of Balt, brother & sisters of the groom; & Chas Macalester, of Wash City; & Augustus Schell, of N Y. Mr Johnston is a gentleman of large fortune in Balt, & a banker by avocation.

The Charleston papers announce the sudden death of Brig Gen W H Trapier, of the late Confederate army. He was a graduate of S C College, & afterward entered West Point. He was in the same class with Gen Beaureard, & graduated with high honor; served in the U S army for 14 years; was promoted to Capt of Engineers; resigned & returned home to take charge of his estate near Gtwn; at the breaking out of the war he received the State appointment of Chief of Ordnance; afterwards took charge of the defences of Charleston; after the bombardment of **Fort Sumter** he accepted the ofc of Major of Engineers in the Confederate service; was promoted to Brig Gen in the Confederate service, ordered to Fla; afterward to Gen Johnston's army in Mississippi, &, finally, was placed in command of Gtwn, S C, which post he retained till the close of the war.

THU JAN 18, 1866
Assist Surgeons K J Marsh, Thos C Brainard, & Chas K Winne, U S Army, have been ordered to report to the Pres of the Army Medical Examining Board, now in session in N Y C, for examination for promotion.

The Sec of the Navy has ordered a board of ofcrs of the Marine Corps, consisting of Maj C R Graham, Lt R S Colburn, & H C Cochrane, recorder, to convene in Wash City to examine the applicants for appointment as 2nd lts. There are only 6 vacancies to be filled, for which there are over 500 candidates.

Senate: 1-The highest in rank in the regular army are as follows: Lt Gen Grant, Maj Gens Holleck, Sherman, Meade, Sheridan, & Thomas. The Brig Gens are: Irvin McDowell, Wm S Rosecrans, Philip St Geo Cooke, John Pope, Jos Hooker, W S Hancock, John M Schofield, O O Howard, A H Terry, & J S Rawlins.

Incendiary fires. On Tuesday the stable belonging to Mr J Coburn, 13th & I sts, was fired; the carpenter shop on K & 11th st, owned by J B Williamson was discovered to be on fire yesterday; as was the family residence of Benj Williamson which was slightly damaged; & a two story house at 6th & E sts, owned & occupied by Michl Kelly was also discovered to be on fire.

Fortress Monroe, Jan 17. 1-Rev W C Blunt, of Portsmouth, was shot by a negro yesterday. 2-Arrived-schnr **Rhodella** & schnr **Americus**, from Richmond; ship S H **Sharp**, from N Y; & steamer **L J Cannon**, from Balt.

Died: on Jan 16, in Wash City, at the residence of her son, Rev C S Spencer, Mrs E A Spencer, relict of the late Matthew Spencer, of Talbot Co, Md. Her funeral is this morning at 11 o'clock.

Died: on Jan 17, Chas W Boteler, sr, in his 68th year. His funeral is Jan 19, 2:30 o'clock, from Wesley Chapel Methodist Episcopal Church, corner of 5th & F sts.

Recent mail brings news of the death of the celebrated artist, Sir Chas Lock Eastlake, at Pisa, Italy, on Dec 24, aged 72 years. He was the son of a solicitor of Plymouth; studied his art under Fuseli; about 1820 he took up residence at Rome; in 1830 he was made a Royal Academician; in 1850 was elected president of the Royal Academy, & was at that time knighted. He married, late in life, Miss Rigby, who enjoys considerable reputation as a writer.

Died: on Tue, after a brief illness, at *Poplar Hill*, his residence in PG Co, Md, Henry Daingerfield, son-in-law of Hon Reverdy Johnson. In all relations of life he was exemplary, & his death to his immediate family is irreparable.

Supreme Court of D C, No 1,800, in Equity. Cassin vs Williams. The trustee reported he sold lot 16 in square 5, & the east 7 feet 8 inches of lot 15, in said square, being the real estate mentioned in the above cause, to John Williams, & that John Williams subsequently assigned his said purchase to Michl C Hart, who has complied with the terms of sale. –R J Meigs, clerk

Household & kitchen furniture at auction on Jan 26, by order of the Orphans Court of D C., sale of the personal effects of the late Jos Cross, deceased, at his late residence, Va ave & 2nd st, Island. –R H Laskey, exc -Green & Williams, aucts

FRI JAN 19, 1866
Wash City Ordinance: 1-Act for the relief of Mrs McCarthy, widow of Eugene McCarthy, deceased, to be paid the sum of twenty & ninety-three one hundredths dollars, being the amount of taxes on lots 6 & 7 in square 341, paid by her in error during the years 1863 & 1864. –Wm W Moore, Pres of the Board of Common Council Thos E Lloyd, Pres of the Board of Aldermen. Approved Dec 23, 1865. –Richd Wallach, Mayor

Terre Haute, Jan 18. Hon John G Davis, a member of Congress for a long time from this district, died of apoplexy this A M.

Mrd: on Jan 16, in Wash City, by Rev Fr McNally, Mr John F Boyle to Miss Joann Ellen Ball, of Montg Co, Md.

Mrd: on Jan 18, by Rev Dr Sunderland, Dr C I Wilson, U S Army, to Miss Gertrude L, daughter of John H Houston, of Wash City.

The country residence of Hon Wm Izard Bull, near Charleston, was fired by an incendiary a few days ago & the clothing therein consumed. The Col & sons then resorted to a small cottage on his plantation. While the Col was preparing for bed, on last Monday night, with a bright light in his room, a shot entered the window & narrowly missed his head. The track of the feet of 2 negroes was discovered near the window next morning, but the Col has not yet obtained any other satisfaction.

At Savannah, on Jan 9, Gazaway B Lamar made a plea in his own defence before the military court which is trying him on charges of cotton stealing. My nephew & myself acted in endeavoring to secure my own cotton & that of the company, which was being illegally seized. The case is still on.

Court-martial of a Colonel of Colored Infty. Col H N Frisbie, 92nd U S colored troops, having been found guilty of neglect of duty to the prejudice of good order & military discipline, has been sentenced to foreit to the U S his pay & allowances for the period of one month.

Supreme Court of D C, in Equity, No 1,415. Augusta M Blair vs Wm Gadsby et al. The trustee reported he has sold lot 39 in square 167 to Wm J Albert for $10,423.12 , & lot 30 in the same square to Geo Schaffer for $4,152.50, & that the purchasers have complied with the terms of sale. –R J Meigs, clerk

The report that Gen Hooker is a hopeless invalid is contradicted by O V Barnard, his brother-in-law, who says the Gen is rapidly recovering from his recent illness, is looking well, & would be out in a few days. –Cincinnati Commercial

The death of Dr Reinhold Solger occurred in Wash last Sat. He was a German scholar of great erudition. –Boston Transcript

SAT JAN 20, 1866
Savannah, Jan 19. The trial of Gen Mercer, late of the Confederate army, charged with murder, in shooting 7 Union soldiers who had joined the rebel army, for desertion, was finished today. The testimony is favorable for Mercer, & it is believed he will be acquitted.

Pittsburgh, Jan 19. Mrs Martha Grinder was executed today. She made a confession, admitting the murder of Mary Caruthers & Jas Buchanan, but denied the other charges of poisoning. Her demeanor on the scaffold was calm & collected.

N Y, Jan 19. Gonzales, the murderer of Senor M Otero at Brooklyn some months since, was yesterday convicted of murder in the first degree.

Cincinnati Commercial: defaulting is becoming common in Iowa. The private sec of the Govn'r is said to be a defaulter to the extent of $25,000 in State bonds. H C Ohrt, county judge of Des Moines Co, has left for unknown parts, with $30,000 belonging to his German fellow-citizens.

Among the hardest working men in Washington is Gen Spinner, of the Treasury Dept. He works early & late, very frequently eats his meals in the Treasury bldg, & always sleeps there. –Exchange
+
Gen Spinner is almost as busy as he is handsome. And you may judge how handsome he is from his having been, as he says, mistaken almost every day for us. –Louisville Journal

A very large swindle, implicating Dectective Lafayette C Baker, is alleged by a N Y paper. Some $300,000, it is said, were fingered.

The subscriber offers for sale 60 acres, more or less, about one-half mile east of Benning's Bridge. Will be sold for cash at the low price of $45 per acre. Apply at the premises, to Selby B Scaggs, or to John Borland, Master Carpenter, Treasury Extension.

Orphans Court of Wash Co, D C, Jan 19, 1866. In the case of John D McPherson, adm of Thos P Wilson, deceased, the administrator & Court have appointed Feb 10 next, for the final settlement of the personal estate of the said deceased, of the assets in hand. -Z C Robbins, Reg/o wills

MON JAN 22, 1866
The Spanish Admiral, Pareja, committed suicide in the harbor of Valparaiso, on Nov 29, by shooting himself with a revolver. His body was put up in guano on board one of the Spanish, or, as others say, a French ship, to be sent home.

N Y, Jan 21. John A Cook, late cashier of the Catskill [N Y] Nat'l Bank, is reported to be a defaulter to the amount of $90,000.

Died: on Jan 20, Mrs M L C, beloved wife of Poinsett Mechlin. Her funeral will take place on Monday at 4 o'clock P M, from her late residence, West st, Gtwn.

Orphans Court-Judge Purcell, Jan 20, 1866.
1-The ptn of Wm J Hickey & Cecilia P Hickey, eldest son & daughter of Wm Hickey, deceased, for letters of administration on his personal estate, was filed.
2-Letters of administration on the estate of Clement Smith, deceased, were issued to Walter S Cox, he giving bond in the sum of $1,800.
3-John Jackson was appointed guardian to the orphans of Michl Short, by giving bond in the sum of $300.
4-In relation to the ptn of E V V Boswell, adm w a, the Court ordered that the said administrator do pay to Mrs Sally R Boswell, widow of the deceased, one half of the net proceeds of the apothecary store from the time of the death of the testator, retaining to himself the other half until the further order of the Court.
The case of Wm E Horton, 8th U S Veteran Volunteers, charged with defrauding the Gov't by dealing in horses & disposing of rations unlawfully, before the court of which Capt Kirkman is judge advocate, has been concluded, & the proceedings & finding, which cover 300 pages, have been forwarded to the Sec of War.

Mrs Eliz Akers Allen [recently Mrs Akers] began writing many years ago under the signature of Florence Percy & has published a large number of beautiful poems, which give her a high rank among the poetesses of America. In Mrs Swisshelm's "Reconstructionist," lately commenced in Wash, she gives the credit of the fine poem of "Rock Me to Sleep, Mother," to a Miss Lizzy Alger, of N Y C. If she investigates the matter she will see that she has done Mrs Allen a great wrong. The true history of the poem may be given in a few words. It was written by Mrs Akers in Rome, during her visit to that city a few years since, & sent to a friend in this city, who caused it to be published in the Phil Evening Post, in which paper it first appeared in print.

Col Harvey Craven has been appointed Assessor of Internal Revenue for the 11th District of Indiana, vice Wm Peiree, resigned.

Cincinnati, Jan 21. A difficulty last night between Col Knoll & Capt Hines, proprietors of the Planter's Hotel, about the character of a lady boarder at the house, resulted in the fatal stabbing of Knoll by Hines.

Orphans Court of Wash Co, D C. In the case of Jas G Smith, adm of Peter A Brinsmade, deceased, the administrator & Court have appointed Feb 13 next, for the final settlement of the personal estate of the said deceased, of the assets in hand. –A C Robbins, Reg/o wills

Orphans Court of Wash Co, D C. In the case of Wm S Graham, adm w a of Eliz Graham, deceased, the administrator & Court have appointed Feb 27th next, for the final settlement of the personal estate of the said deceased, of the assets in hand. –Z C Robbins, Reg/o wills

I wish to employ a Music & French Teacher in my school. Liberal salary.
-Jas S Hallowell, Sandy Spring P O, Montg Co, Md.

TUE JAN 23, 1866

A S Haskins, member of the Lower House of the Ohio Legislature, from Wash Co, died suddenly at Lafayette, Indiana, on Friday night.

Soldiers' & Sailors' Nat'l Convention assembled yesterday & the following were appointed ofcrs: for Pres, Maj Gen John A Logan; 1st Vice Pres, Gen A C Parry; 2nd Vice Pres, Gen E W Hinks; Secs, Maj J E Doughty & Capt Jas Cross; Treasurer, Col Chas Houghtling; Sgt-at-Arms, John M Powers.

Rev W C Blount, paster of the Dinwiddie st Methodist Church in Portsmouth, Va, was on last Tue morning, accidentaly shot by a colored boy, Chas H Nelms, from the effects of which he died on Wed. It appears the colored boy, about 12, purchased a musket & ammunition from a member of the 9th Vt regt, & was firing at a mark on the fence which enclosed the residence of Mr Blount, when the latter suddenly came out of his house into the yard, & was shot in the breast.

John O Butler, a young mulatto, was arrested by Detectives Clarvoe & McDevitt for burglary last evening. The amount of his robberies is estimated at $3,700.

Orphans Court of Wash Co, D C. In the case of Mary H Schoolcraft, excx of Henry R Schoolcraft, deceased, the executrix & Court have appointed Feb 13 next, for the final settlement of the personal estate of the said deceased, of the assets in hand. -Z C Robbins, Reg/o wills

Raleigh, Jan 22. W S Henrahan, a member of the Legislature, who was in his seat on Sat in the House, died suddenly last night.

N Y, Jan 22. Two men named David *Schff & Geo Boyce, were arrested & identified as the robbers of the messenger of the Farmers' & Citizens' Nat'l Bank of Wmsburg on Fri. *Copied as written.

Margaret Gantt, a woman who cleans out Grover's Theatre, was arrested yesterday on the charge of stealing from the theatre a curtain valued at $75.00. Detectives Clarvoe & McDevitt search the house & found the curtain.

A son of Mr Jas Skidmore, aged about 13 years, broke through the ice at 11th st wharf, yesterday, & was drowned. The body has been recovered.

Balt, Jan 22. A clerk in the Balt post ofc, Alonzo Hutchins, has been arrested for robbing the mails by a special agent of the Post Ofc Dept. This makes the second arrest in this office in two months.

Died: on Jan 21, Capt Jas White, aged 75 years. His funeral is this evening, at 2 P M, from his residence, B st south.

$20 reward for return of strayed Pointer Dog. –C Theo Griffith, 67 Louisiana ave, between 6th & 7th sts.

WED JAN 24, 1866
Law Cards: 1-Black, Lamon & Co: 468 14th st.
–Jeremiah S Black, Ward H Lamon, G F Black
2-Brent & Merrick: north side of La ave, at 5th st: Robt J Brent, of Balt, & Richd T Merrick, of Chicago, Ill, have formed a partnership, Wash City, D C.
3-Wm A Monroe: 227 Pa ave, Wash, D C.
4-S F Glenn: ofc 136 Gravier st, between Camp & St Chas, New Orleans.
5-Browning & Ewing: ofc & residence, 12 north A st, Capitol Hill, Wash, D C.
–C H Browning, of Ill, Thos Ewing, jr, of Kansas.
6-Ould & Carrington: Govn'r st, near Broad, Richmond, Va. –Robt Ould & Isaac H Carrington.
7-Mygatt, Thompson, & Hackett: 221 Pa ave, Wash, D C. Chas Mygatt, late of the 2nd Auditor's Ofc; Geo A Thompson, of Ill; Isaac Hackett, late of the 4th Auditor's Ofc.

Last evening Gen Robt Williams, U S A, was married to Mrs S A Douglas, at her residence, **Douglas Place**, by Rev Fr Lynch, in the presence of the immediate friends of the bride & groom.

Yesterday Mr Jas Hines, employed in the Naval Ordnance Yard, fell through the main hatch of the steamer **Marblehead**, & was so injured that death ensued about 5 o'clock. He resided on the Island & is reported to have left a wife & 5 children.

A reception was given by Mrs Chas Knapp, at her beautiful residence on I st. The elegance & taste of this hospitable mansion are too well known in Wash & to the elite of our visitors to require any encomium.

Died: on Jan 22, James Claude, only son of Jas & Cornelia Skidmore. His funeral is on Wed at 3 o'clock, from his parents' residence on 10th, between Md ave & C sts. [Balt Sun copy.]

N Y, Jan 23. The bark **Diadem**, of Liverpool, with refined petroleum, capsized on Jan 9 during a gale. The capt's wife & 2 boys were lost. The capt, cook, & 3 seamen died on Jan 12. The remainder of the crew were taken off by the bark **M and E Robbins** & brought to this port.

Phil, Jan 23. Hon Oswald Thompson, the present Judge of the Court of Common Pleas, & one of Phil's most brilliant lawyers, died this morning, from a second stroke of paralysis, which happened a few days since. The Courts adjourned at once.

Raleigh, Jan 23. Brvt Lt Col R A Coolidge, Surgeon, U S A, Medical Director of this Dept, died here this morning.

Chancery sale of a val improved real estate on 12th st west, between G & H sts north, by decree of the Supreme Court of D C, dated Oct 16, 1865, passed in a cause wherein Geo Fitzhugh & Martha L Smith are cmplnts, & Wm Bell, exc & others, are dfndnts, No 1,229, in Equity: public auction on Jan 16, of lot 23 in square 288, with a brick dwlg-house. –A Thos Bradley, turstee
-Jas C McGuire & Co, aucts

THU JAN 25, 1866
To be mustered out: Capts Jesse E Scott, Dard W Porter, P B Johnson, & Lyne S Metcalf, Assist Quartermasters, U S Vols, ordered to be mustered out of the service of the U S.

Lt Col Jas M Moore, A Q M, U S Vols, has recently sold a number of Gov't frame bldgs, at public auction, which netted the sum of $1,276.94.

Lewis Fisher, a fresco painter, fell 25 feet in one of the Chelsea, Mass, Churches, while at work a few weeks ago, & received injuries which have disabled him for life. The trustees of the church lately sent him a bill of $7.60 for damage sustained by the pews on which he fell! So says the Springfield Republican.

Died: on Jan 24, of consumption, John H C Sheckels, aged 15 years, 9 months & 5 days. His funeral will take place from the residence of his father, Theodore Sheckels, 8th st west, between M & N sts north, on Jan 26, at 10 o'clock, & proceed to St Aloysius Church, where the funeral services will take place, & the remains removed to Carroll's Church, [Catholic,] Montg Co, Md.

Died: at the residence of his parents, **Wareland**, Montg Co, Md, John Dorsey Read, infant son of Wm & Eliza Read, aged 9 months & 20 days. His funeral will be from the residence of his grandmother, Mrs Emily Beale, North Capt st, this morning, at 12 o'clock. [No death date given.]

Died: on Jan 20, in Gtwn, D C, after suffering a lingering disease for nearly 2 years, Ella Lee, daughter of D W & Alverda J Whiting, in her 4th year.

Ashland, so long the home of Henry Clay, has been purchased by the trustees of the Ky Univ, at a cost of $90,000. The farm contains about 325 acres of the best land in the Blue Region region. The greater portion of the farm will be devoted to experimental farming.

Dissolution of the partnership existing between Gerard Bancker & Wm Penn Flasson, & known as Bancker & Flasson, at the Clarendon Hotel, Pa ave, & 6th st, Wash, this day, Jan 21, by mutual consent. –Gerard Bancker, Wm Penn Flasson -Wm Lilly, atty

Napoleon III has presented a complete set of his works to the N H Historical Society, with his imperial autograph upon the fly leaves.

Imported Fruits, Malaga Grapes, Canton Ginger, & Crown Raisins, in very beautiful bunches; &, West India Oranges. All received today.
–N W Burchell, 14th & F sts.

The School in my family, conducted by Miss Nellie C Kerfoot, can take an additional 4 students. The next session will commence Feb 1 next. Board & Tuition for 10 months: $175 in specie, or its equivalent. –Thos E Hunton, near New Balt, Fauquier Co, Va.

FRI JAN 26, 1866
Dismissed. Capt R D Pettit, 12th Veteran Reserve Corps, & Lt Henry Mente, 42nd U S colored troops, have been dismissed the service.

Jas B Simpson, Plumber, Steam & Gasfitter, 344 C st, near Nat'l Hotel. All work done promptly & on the most reasonable terms. Country work also attended to. [Ad.]

The Pinckneys of South Carolina. By a lady of this city, a relative of the distinguished family concerning which we recently published a long historical sketch under the title of The Last of the Pinckneys, we have been courteously informed that a Mr Henry L Pinckney, son of the former Mayor of Charleston, is now residing in Sumter District, S C, & was very well a few weeks ago. He married a daughter of Rev Dr Post, late of Charleston, & formerly of this city, & as he has a large family of children the name is not likely to become soon extinct.

Died: on Jan 23, at Raleigh, N C, Brvt Lt Col Richd H Coolidge, Surgeon U S A. His friends are requested to attend his funeral, from the residence of Mrs Cmdor Morris, 322 H st, corner of Vt ave, on Jan 27 at 2 o'clock P M.

Pittsburgh, Jan 25. Rev John Barrett Kerfoot, Bishop elect of the new diocese of Pittsburgh of the Protestant Episcopal Church, was consecrated today, in the Trinity Church. Bishop Hopkins, of Vt, presided, assisted by Bishops McIlvains, of Ohio; Whttingham, of Md; Williams, of Conn; Talbert,of Indiana; Clarkson, of Nebraska, & Coxe of Western Pa.

Senate: 1-Ptn of Paul L Forbes, asking relief from a contract for bldg a war vessel: referred to the Cmte on Naval Affairs.

Headquarters Dept of N C, Raleigh, N C, Jan 23, 1866. General Orders, No 7. Announcement of the death of Brvt Lt Col R H Coolidge, Surgeon U S Army, director of this dept, who died in this city this morning. Col Coolidge was one of the oldest Surgeons of the regular army, having served in the medical corps for more than 25 years. He was a loving husband & father.
–J C Campbell, Assist Adj Genr'l.

N Y, Jan 25. Foreign papers announce the death of Frederika Bremer, of Stockholm.

Hardware Dealers: 1-John D Edmond & Co, 513 7th st, between D & E sts. Dealers, blacksmiths, household & general hardware & cutlery. 2-John R Elvans & Co, 27 La Ave, & 303 C st, Wash, D C. Dealers in iron & steel. 3-J P Barthlomew: 353 7th st, below Pa ave, Wash, D C. Builders & house-furnishing hardware. Agents for Herring's Fire & Burglar-Proof Safes. Sole agent for Fairbanks' Standard Scales, Safes, & Scales.

One of the richest lady in the world, perhaps, is Miss Burdett Coutts, of London, England, who became the heiress of Mrs Coutts, who had been Miss Mellon, the actress. Her fortune has been computed at thirteen tons of gold. This money has been handed down from heir to heir many times, & increases in value.

For sale: the house & lot in square 258, n e corner of D st north & 13½ st west. The premises has been occupied for many years as a successful stand for the grocery business by Mrs Bevans. —Thos P Simpson, 4 La ave.

SAT JAN 27, 1866
General Land Agents: 1-Dowman & Green: Ofc No 18 Intelligencer Bldg, 7th st, Wash, D C. —R W Downman, T Ritchie Green. 2-S Surbrug & Co, Nat'l Military & Naval Agency: Ofc E & 7th sts. 3-East Tenn Land Agency: Cockrill & Seymour, Knoxville, Tenn. 4-P McCracken & Bro, Commerce st, Fredericksburg, Va. 5-Nicholas Callan, jr, Ofc 480 15th st, corner of F st.

Last night Elmore Van Yassel was shot at near the 8th Precinct station-house, the ball passing through his clothing & just grazing the skin near the heart. Samson, the son of a fortune teller, has been arrested & held for examination this morning.

Trustee's sale of valuable Market Farm, by decree of the Circuit Court for PG Co, Md, in Equity, in a cause in which Francis A Kerby & others were cmplnts & Catharine Taylor & others are dfndnts: public sale of *Grimes' Tavern*, on the Wash road, in said county: sale on Feb 7. Also the farm formerly occupied by John Taylor, deceased, containing about 110 acres; adjoins the lands of Dr John H Bayne & Thos E Berry, & others. Comfortable dwlg-house & kitchen, & all necessary out-bldgs. —Edw W Belt, Danl Clarke, trustees

Orphans Court of Wash Co, D C. Letters of administration on the personal estate of Wm Hickey, late of Wash City, D C, deceased. —Wm J Hickey, Cecilia P Hickey, admx

The Pres has appointed Nicholas Smith Minister Resident at Greece, to reside at Athens.

Amon Duvall, deputy warden of the jail, was today removed from ofc by order of Warden Brown.

The firm of Wm H Godey & John A Rheem, trading under the firm of Godey & Rheem, is this day dissolved by mutual consent. The business will be conducted as heretofore by Wm H Godey. –Wm H Godey, J A Rheem

Orphans Court for PG Co, Jan Term, 1866. In the matter of the ptn of Richd S Blackburn, adm of David Craufurd, for leave to pass final account, & make distribution of the personal estate of his intestate. On the within ptn, it is ordered by said Court, Jan 23, 1866, that the said Richd S Blackburn, adm of David Craufurd, pass his final account & make distribuition of the personal assets of the deceased among the heirs at law & next of kin of said deceased, if any; & the said Richd S Blackburn, adm, has with the approbation of this Court, this day, appointed Feb 20 next for the final settlement & distribution of the personal estate of said deceased, of the assets in hand, when & where all of the creditors & heirs at law & next of kin of the said deceased [other than Geo T Crawfurd & his sisters, or those representing or claiming through them, & those who have heretofore claimed or do now claim under an alleged marriage between the lat Thos R Craufurd & one Eliz Taylor] are notified to attend at said Court, previous to Feb 20 next. –Geo W Wilson, Wm B Hill, trustees -A H Lambert, Reg/o Wills

MON JAN 29, 1866
Orphans Court, Jan 27, 1866. 1-The will of Chas B Fisk was fully proven & admitted to probate & record, & Mary E Fisk qualified as excx by giving bond in the sum of $12,000, with Saml V Niles & Thos P Morgan as sureties. 2-John Fagan was appointed adm of the personal estate of Patrick McNeal, deceased, & gave bond in the sum of $300, with Jas Keenan & Leonard Kean as sureties.

N Y, Jan 27. Gonzales & Pellicer, the murderers of Otego, were today sentenced to be hung on Mar 9th. They received their sentences without emotion.

Mrs J S Allen, late of Nat'l Hotel, N Y, has just opened & refurnished her large & commodious Boarding House, 439 Pa ve, between 3rd & 4½ sts, Wash, D C.

On Friday Mr Henry Rheam, a driver of one of the wagons of Adams' Express Co, fell from the wagon at the depot & was run over, the wheels passing over him & breaking 2 ribs. He was attended by Dr Todd.

Wash Society-Jan 29. Mrs Lt Gen Grant had one of the largest & most distinguished receptions of the season. The roll of carriages to the door was incessant, & the calls continued until 6 o'clock.

Yesterday fire was discovered in the bakehouse of Mr John Voight, on H st, between 12th & 13th sts. Loss about $50.

Hotels & Restaurants:
1-Metropolitan Hotel, late Brown's Hotel, Pa ave, Wash.
–A R Potts, proprietor
2-U S Hotel, Pa ave, Wash, D C. –M H Bean & Co, proprietors.
3-Rodier's White House Restaurant. Steamed Oyster & Billard Saloon: 32 & 33 High st, next to the Canal, Gtwn, D C.
4-Thompson's Dining Rooms & Saloon, 360 C st, between 4½ & 6th sts.
5-Owen House, [late Marsham's Hotel] the European Plan, 212 Pa ave, Wash, D C. -Thos P Jacks, proprietor
6-Waverly House, 451 8th st, furnished rooms & board by day or week, Wash, D C. -S G Langley, proprietor
7-Green's Restaurant, corner 8th & E sts. –Wm Klein, C Eber, proprietors.
8-The Woodbine, David R Smith, proprietor, 17 4½ st, corner of C st, Wash, D C.
9-Intelligencer Restaurant & Ale Vaults, corner of 7th & D sts, Wash.
–John Harrison, proprietor
10-Spotswood Hotel, 8th & Main sts, Richmond, Va.
–Corkery & Millward, proprietors
11-Jarratt's Hotel, Terminus Weldon Railroad, Petersurg, Va.
–Platt & Simmons, proprietors.
12-Monumental Hotel, corner 9th & Grace sts, Richmond, Va.
–D T Norris & Co, proprietors.
13-Exchange Hotel, Richdmond, Va. –J L Carrington & Co, proprietors.
14-Ballard House, Richmond, Va. –M D Maine & Co, proprietors.
15-Orange House, Lynchburg, Va. –Houston Rucker, proprietor.

Mrd: on Jan 24, at St Paul's [Protestant Episcopal] Church, Balt, Md, by Rev Dr Mahan, Rector of St Paul's, Miss Mattie V Gordon, of Miss, to Col J T Ward, of Louisiana. Jackson, Miss, & New Orleans papers will please notice.

Mrd: on Jan 17, at the residence of the bride's father, in Liberty, Bedford Co, Va, by Rev John A Wharton, Mr Jas Warwick Smith to Miss Annie Howard, daughter of Mr Alfred A Bell.

TUE JAN 30, 1866
Fred'k Hudson, the well know managing editor of the N Y Herald, has been compelled at last, by his gradually failing health, to relinquish the position he has held for many years. He has received leave of absence for 2 years, & will spend the time in travelling.

Gov Jacobs, of Ky, is dangerously ill of congestion of the brain.

Yesterday, John Simpson, employed at the 6th st wharf, found the body of a colored man floating in the Potomac. No one knew the deceased, although a mark over his eye indicated that he had suffered violence.

Wallace W Whittlesey, who was arrested some months since on the charge of abstracting bonds from the U S Treasury, has been removed from the jail to the residence of his wife on 9th st. Whittlesey is in a dying condition, & Judge Fisher humanely granted permission for his removal upon the representation of his physician, Dr N S Lincoln. Whittlesey was not able to furnish the bail required, & in order that the Court may be advised of his condition, his physician will make written reports twice each day.

Supreme Court of D C, No 1,445, in Equity. McBlair & others against Gadsby & others. The parties & trustees are notified that on Feb 6 next, I shall state the trustees account & the shares of the parties in the new funds in his hands for distribution. –W Redin, auditor

Schnectady, Jan 29. Dr Nott died here this morning.

Obit-died: on Jan 24, at his residence, in the vicinity of Chestertown, Hon Jas R Ricaud, in his 57th year. He was born in the city of Balt, but removed to Kent in his boyhood; studied law with Judge Chambers; at a later period was elected to the Congress of the U S for 2 successive terms; was elected to the Senate of Md; was appointed Judge, by Gov'r Bradford, of the Circuit Court, composed of Kent, Queen, Ann, & Caroline Counties. In the early part of the present year he was stricken with a paralysis of motion, but recovered enough to attend to professional business. For the past two months he was unable to leave his home. As a husband, parent, brother, & friend, he was affectionate & true. –V

Wm Pettit, of this place, whilst out hunting yesterday endeavoring to get his dog off the track was struck violently by the passing train & died in the course of 2 hours. He leaves a destitute family, who reside at the north end of Wash st. –Alexandria Gaz, Jan 27

Sales of real estate-Wash. W L Wall & Co, aucts, sold on Thu, house & lots in square 769, on 3rd st, between L & M sts; house & lot on 3rd st, to J G Carrol, $1,045, lot adjoining, to W H McGinnis, 14 cents per foot, lot in rear, on Canal sts, to J G Carrol, 5¾ cents; lot on corner Canal & M sts, to A N Thompson, 7¼ cents; lot adjoining, to same, 3½ cents; lot adjoining, to Jos Gordon, 3 3/8 cents. Also, in front of the premises, on Jan 27, house & lot, square No 905 L st south, near 8th st, to Mr Edw Gatton, for $600.

Wm A Hall, arrested for the larceny of articles from the Navy Yard, was released on Sat by giving $1,000 for his appearance at court. In consideration of his family, who are all exemplary members of society, Mr Geo A Gulick became his bondsman.

WED JAN 31, 1866
Orphans Court of Wash Co, D C. Letters of administration on the personal estate of Louisa Collins, late of Wash, D C, deceased. –John H Semmes, adm

Grocery & Liquor Stores:
1-Z M P King & Son, King Pl, corner of Vt ave & 15½ st, Wash. 2-J B Bryan & Bro, 345 Pa ave, Wash. 3-Richd J Ryon, 481 9th st, between D & E sts, Wash. 4-N W Burchell, corner of 14th & F sts, under Ebbitt House, Wash. 5-Stone & Pugh, Commission Merchants, 277 D st, between 6th & 7th sts.

Dr Eliphalet Nott, D D, L D, Pres of Union College, at Schenectady, N Y, died at that place on Jan 26. His illness was long known to be fatal. He was born in Windham Co, Conn, Jun 25, 1773, & having studied theology at home, went as a missionary to central N Y in 1794. In 1797 he emigrated to Albany, where his preaching at once became celebrated. He was chosen Pres of Union College in 1804, & has sustained that relation the long period of 60 years. He was the oldest of American college presidents. For some years he has been withdrawn from active service in the presidency by the appointment of an assistant.

The citizens of *Ellicott's Mills*, in anticipation of that thriving village being incorporated the title of Ellicott City, have selected municipal ofcrs. They have designated E A Talbott for mayor, & J Groves, Wm B Collier, S Radcliffe, of Howard Co, & Wm H Gibbons, Jas Piper, Jos Leishear, of Balt Co, for councilmen, whose names are to be inserted in the act of incorporation.

Orphans Court of Wash Co, D C. In the case of Abraham F Kimmell, adm of John E Foulkes, deceased, the administrator & Court have appointed Feb 24 next, for the final settlement of the personal estate of the said deceased, of the assets in hand. -Z C Robbins, Reg/o wills

Orphans Court of Wash Co, D C. In the case of David L Shoemaker, adm of Geo Thompson, deceased, the administrator & Court have appointed Feb 24 next, for the final settlement of the personal estate of the said deceased, of the assets in hand. -Z C Robbins, Reg/o wills

Orphans Court of Wash Co, D C. In the case of Abraham F Kimmell, adm of Eliz A Foulkes, deceased, the administrator & Court have appointed Feb 24 next, for the final settlement of the personal estate of the said deceased, of the assets in hand. -Z C Robbins, Reg/o wills

Cincinnati, Jan 30. The steamer **Missouri** exploded her boilers this A M at the mouth of Green river. Her ofcrs & crew numbered about 100. Reports from Newburg say only 20 survivors have been taken off, including wounded.

New Orleans, Jan 29. Ex-Govn'r Rollins died here today. Both houses of Legislature adjourned in honor of his memory.

Mrd: on Jan 30, at St Aloysius Church, by Rev John McNally, Francis B Mohun to M Virginia, daughter of John Y Laub, all of Wash City.

Memphis, Jan 30. The steamer **Miami** blew up & burned on Sunday last, 6 miles above the mouth of the Arkansas river. 130 lives were lost. [Feb 5th newspaper: 91 soldiers of Co B, 33rd C S regulars were on board. Mr John Lusk, 2nd clerk of the boat, along with Chas J Johnston, his assistant, were either killed by the explosion or burned to death; John Lusk's wife & child, his sister-in-law, & a German lady, just from her native soil, were in the ladies' cabin. The former three were lost & the latter was saved. Miss J E Rankin last saw Mrs Lusk with her child on a state-room floor. Capt Thos L Crawford, of the steamer **Henry Ames**, repaired with haste to the scene. Gen Ashley's band of Little Rock were aboard, 3 of whom were lost. Pilots Levy & Wherry, the head engineer, & the first mate, Saul Franklin, are safe. Clerk Harrinway luckily remained behind.]

Mr E H Fuller died suddenly yesterday, in the midst of his family. Mr Fuller came to Wash City near 2 generations since, with his father. He leaves a sorrowing family.
+
Died: on Jan 29, Edward H Fuller, of Wash City, in his 49th year. His funeral will be on Wed at 2 o'clock, from his late residence, 357 Mass ave, between 10th & 11th sts.

Died: on Jan 30, Ernest Gilman, son of Wm H & Cornelia G Baldwin, aged 10 years & 6 months. His funeral is on Jan 31 at 2 o'clock.

Died: on Jan 30, after a lingering illness, in her 60th year, Mrs Eliz Taylor Craufurd formerly of PG Co, Md. Her funeral will be from the residence of her daughter, Mrs Danl Wall, G st, between 5th & 6th sts, this afternoon at 3 P M.

Died: on Jan 30, at his late residence, in Wash City, David Harper. His funeral services will be today at 3 P M, in the Seventh Presbyterian Church.

THU FEB 1, 1866
Died: Jan 30, at **Colebrooke**, PG Co, Md, Walter D Addison, in his 73rd year, the eldest son of the late John Addison. His funeral is today at 12 o'clock.

Died: Jan 31, Mrs Eliz Hassler, wife of the late Scipio Hassler, of the U S Coast Survey, & daughter of the late Wm Hebb. Her funeral is on Feb 2 at 2:30 P M, from her late residence.

Hartford, Jan 31. Starkweather was convicted of murder in the first degree, & will be sentenced on Feb 3 next.

N Y, Jan 31. 1-The steamship **New York**, from Bremen, via Southampton, Jan 18, has arrived. 2-The steamship **London**, for Melbourne, foundered at sea, & 270 lives were lost. Only 16 of the crew & 3 passengers were saved. 3-Prince Christian & Princess Helena will not be married until July.

Orphans Court of Wash Co, D C. In the case of Chas M Matthews, adm of Chas W Bennett, deceased, the administrator & Court have appointed Feb 24 next, for the final settlement of the personal estate of the said deceased, of the assets in hand. -Z C Robbins, Reg/o wills

FRI FEB 2, 1866
The sculptor Gibson is dead. [No death date given-current item.]

The trial of Lafayette C Baker, late a detective in the employ of the War Dept, was concluded yesterday, in the Criminal Court, Judge Fisher presiding. Verdict of the jury: guilty of false imprisonment, but not guilty of extortion.

The steamer **London**, which foundered at sea, had a cargo valued at L305,000. Rev Dr Wooley, Bishop of Sidney, & G V Brooke, the actor were among her passengers.

Loss of the steamer **Missouri**: among the saved, there is a passenger from Lowell, Mass, connected with the Freedmen's Bureau, & his family, Capt Stewart, & Engineers Shroder & Cox, of New Albany. The cabin register being lost, the names of the passengers could not be ascertained.

Orphans Court of Wash Co, D C. Letters testamentary on the personal estate of Richd H Coolidge, late a Surgeon in the U S Army, deceased. –Harriet B Coolidge

SAT FEB 3, 1866
Jurors selected to serve as at the next term of the Circuit Court, commencing on the first Tuesday of Feb, 1866:

Fred'k Bates	W C Harper
Perry C Brown	Perry Sherwood
Henry C Mitchell	Geo Klotz
John F Ballenger	Philip Otterback
John P Murphy	Henry Walker
P H Hauptan	W E Chandler
Wm Keefe	Henry Wingate
Jas Curtain	Jas Mannoghue
Wm O Holt	Wm M Davis
Richd Sheckelford	Jas W Barker
John F Bridge	Wm Goods
Henry Birch	Geo C Henning
Nicholas Acker	B F Swart

In the Criminal Court yesterday Albert G Clark, indicted for the forgery of the name of Capt E M Camp, whereby he obtained $550 from the bank of Lewis Johnson & Co, plead guilty to that charge. There is another indictment for forgery pending against Clark.

New Orleans, Feb 1. An engine exploded on the Jackson railroad, near Amite City, killing three, including Col Forney, ex-chief of police, & wounding 4. The engine is a total wreck.

Phil, Feb 2. Christian Berger was convicted today of murder in the first degree. He killed an old lady named Miss Watt, at Germantown, on Jan 6. He received the verdict with no apparent emotion.

Wm R Collins, who has been chief clerk in the ofc of the Chief Quartermaster, Dept of Wash, for 3 years past, has resigned to accept the position in the ofc of the Evening Star, of Wash City, vacated by Mr S M Carpenter, who has gone to Chili as special agent of the N Y Herald.

Notice is given that Bond No 206, dated Feb 1, 1848, for $216.57, & issued by the Chesapeake & Oio Canal Co in favor of my brother, the late Wm J Goszler, has been lost or mislaid, & that it is my intention to apply for a renewal of said bond. -Jas Goszler

Maj Gen J W Fessenden, who has just been mustered out of the service, has accepted the position of Superintendent of the New England division of the Nat'l Express Co of which Gen Jos E Johnston is president. Gen Fessenden's headquarters will be at Boston.

Died: on Feb 2, Charles Ives, only child of Dr C M & Hattie A Ford, aged 21 months. His funeral is next Sunday at 2½ o'clock P M.

MON FEB 5, 1866
A desirable bldg lot on F st, between 6th & 7th sts, was sold by J C McGuire & Co, on Sat, for $1.89 per square foot. Mr A Pollak was the purchaser.

Orphans Court-Judge Purcell, Feb 3, 1866.
1-The will of Harriet Butler was fully proven & admitted to probate.
2-Letters of administration were issued to Euphemia B Riley.
3-Letter of administration on the estate of David Atkins were issued to Geo & Matilda Atkins.
4-Helen Bates was appointed guardian to the orphans of Wm Crawford.
5-Letters of administratin on the estate of Geo McGuire were issued to Patrick White.
6-The inventory of the person estate of Eliza Reeves was filed by the executor.
7-Also, the inventory of the goods & chattels of Henry Lehne.
8-Letters of administration on the estate of Wm Long were issued to Catharine Long.

Mr Chas S Taft, chemist & druggist, has opened a new drug store at 467 9th st, between E & F sts, Wash.

Mr Edw Deeble, one of our oldest & most esteemed citizens, has some articles valuable for the historical memories that invest them, a tea kettle, a coffee urn, & a cream pitcher, a portion of Washington's camp utensils which he carried with him throughout the Revolutionary struggle. At the expiration of the war these articles were given by Washington to his gardener, an old German by the name of Ellis, who presented them to his daughter, now surviving in Alexandria, Va, & who furnishes a written certificate on the subject. This daughter married the brother of the present owner of the articles.

New Orleans, Feb 3. The steamer **W R Carter** exploded her boilers this afternoon at Island 98. A large number of lives were lost. The boat & cargo are a total loss. The following are known to be lost: Mrs Dr Richardson & 3 children, New Orleans; Mrs Gibbons, Mrs Wolf, & Mrs Rice, for Cincinnati; Mrs Osterman, Texas; Mrs Norse, Mrs Norris, Columbus; & Mrs Howland. She was commanded by Capt Hurd, a brother to the cmder of the steamer **Missouri**.

Hon Jos Allison has been appointed to fill the vacancy occasioned by the death of Judge Oswald Thompson, & Hon W S Peirce has been appointed to fill the place of Judge Allison in the Court of Common Pleas of Phil.

Orphans Court of Wash Co, D C-Feb 3, 1866. In the case of Alex'r Hay, adm of Jas McCullough, deceased, the administrator & Court have appointed Feb 27th next, for the final settlement of the personal estate of the said deceased, of the assets in hand. -Z C Robbins, Reg/o wills

Hon Luther Eaton, of Tolland, Conn, died on Feb 1, in his 81st year.

Orphans Court of Wash Co, D C-Jan 9, 1866. In the case of John Van Riswick & Wm A Fenwick, excs of Philip Fenwick, deceased, the executors & Court have appointed Feb 27 next, for the final settlement of the personal estate of the said deceased, of the assets in hand. -Z C Robbins, Reg/o wills

TUE FEB 6, 1866
Residences of the Judges of the Supreme Court of the U S.
Mr Chief Justice Chase, corner of E & 6th sts.
Mr Justice Wayne, 2 Franklin pl, I st, btwn 13th & 14th sts.
Mr Justice Nelson, Nat'l Hotel.
Mr Justice Grier, 6 north A st, Capitol Hill.
Mr Justice Clifford, D Taylor's, s w corner C & 3rd sts.
Mr Justice Swayne, 244 F st.
Mr Justice Miller, Nat'l Hotel.
Mr Justice Davis, Taylor's, corner C & 3rd sts.
Mr Justice Field, 6 north A st, Capitol Hill.
Reporter, John Wm Wallace, Nat'l Hotel.
Marshal, D S Gooding, 463 E st.
Clerk, D W Middleton, 568 N J ave.

Senate: 1-Bill for the relief of Paymaster Rittenhouse, of the Pacific squadron, to indemnify him for the loss of Gov't funds stolen from his safe. Mr Wilson stated that the Govn't had lost not less than a quarter of a million dollars through the negligence of the paymasters since the commencement of the war. He thought it best to hold everyone of them to a strick accountability, & not set a bad precedent at this time, when there were so many settlements with paymsters being made.

Died: on Sunday, of consumption, Mrs Unice N Smith, widow of the late C F Smith, formerly of N H. Her funeral will be from the residence of her son, 383 9t^h st, between I & N Y ave, on Feb 6 at 2 o'clock.

The case against Mr Gilbert Vanderwerken, who is indicted for an assault & battery with intent to kill Mr Geo Hill, jr, by shooting him, was postponed until Feb 19, on account of the serious illness of the accused. The alleged act was perpetrated over 4 years ago, & was tried once but the jury failed to agree upon a verdict, & it has been continued from term to term for causes stated.

Trustee's sale, by virtue of a decree passed by the Supreme Court of D C, in Chancery, cause No 463, wherein Eliz Sibley is cmplnt & Ellen Edes et al are dfndnts: public auction, on the premises, on Feb 22, all that part of lot 5 in square 401, in Wash City, on 9th st west, near L st, with a small dwlg.
–Wm F Mattingly, trustee -Jas C McGuire & Co, aucts

Dept of the Interior, U S Patent Ofc, Wash, Jan 27, 1866. Ptn of John M Earls, of Troy, N Y, praying for the extension of a patent granted to him on Apr 27, 1852, for an improvement in Smut Machines for 7 years from the expiration of said patent, which takes place on Apr 27, 1866. –T C Theaker, Com'r of Patents

Dept of the Interior, U S Patent Ofc, Wash, Jan 26, 1866. Ptn of Thos J Woolcocks, & Wm Ostrander, of N Y, N Y, praying for the extension of a patent granted to them on May 4, 1852, for an improvement in Speaking Tubes, for 7 years from the expiration of said patent, which takes place on May 4, 1866.
–T C Theaker, Com'r of Patents

Mrs Col John S Mosby, who has been in this city several days seeking for her husband, from the authorities in Wash, the privileges accorded to other paroled prisoners of war, has returned to her home in Warrenton, having succeeded in obtaining from Gen Grant the object of her visit. The papers given to the Colonel hold good until revoked by the Pres. -Alexandria Gaz

Hon J M Curry has been elected president of Howard College, Alabama.

WED FEB 7, 1866
Mrd: on Feb 6, at St Patrick's Church, by Rev Dr Norris, of Wisc, Mr John L Joyce to Miss Mary A, eldest daughter of Mr Wm H Ward, all of Wash.

Orphans Court-Judge Purcell, Feb 6, 1866.
1-The will of Chas W Boteler, sr, deceased, was fully proven & admitted to probate & record, & letters of administration c t a were granted to Chas W Boteler, jr, & John W Boteler, who gave bond in the sum of $30,00, with John Q Willson & Wm H Falconer as sureties.
2-The first & final account of Wm O Shreeve, guardian to Chas S Shreeve, was approved & passed.
3-Susan Dalton was appointed admx of the estate of John Dalton, deceased, & gave bond in the sum of $200, with Hugh Divine & Robt Rollings as sureties.
4-Sarah C West was appointed admx of the estate of Clement L West, deceased, & gave bond in the sum of $20,000, with Anthony Addison & Wm S Huntington as sureties.
5-The balance & distribution of the personal estate of Victor Ciroux, deceased, by Danl E Groux, adm, was entered & filed, & the first & final account of the same was approved & passed.
6-Martha Ann Cotes was appointed guardian to the orphans of John Churn, deceased, & gave bond in the sum of $300, with Hillary Cotes, Wm Hodges, & Lorenzo Coyle as sureties.

Mrd: on Feb 6, at St Patrick's Church, by Rev Dr Norris, of Wisc, Mr John L Joyce to Miss Mary A, eldest daughter of Mr Wm H Ward, all of Wash.

Died: yesterday, in Gtwn, Mr Peter W Magruder, in his 76th year. His funeral will take place from the residence of Dr H Magruder, 44 Third st, today at 3 o'clock.

Association of the Oldest Inhabitants regular monthly meeting was held at the City Hall. In the absence of the pres & vice pres, Peter G Washington, was called to preside, & Dr A McD Davis was at his post as secretary. The following were elected members: Christopher Andrews, born in Ireland 1790, came to Wash in 1800; Gen Timothy P Andrews, born in Ireland 1794, came to Wash 1800; Geo W Young, born in Md 1796, came to Wash 1814; John Hollingshead, Wm B Magruder, & Chas Calvert. Messrs J C Brent, Thos Havenner, & C Andrews were appointed the cmte to act in conjunction with the chairman & secretary. Mr Thos H Havenner, jr, was elected a member of the association, to take effect Sep 1866, when he will have arrived at the age required by the constitution of the association. Mr Saml Wells, the acknowledged oldest citizen of Wash, entered the room, & was elected a member of the association unconditionally. He was born in Fairfax Co, Va, Aug 28, 1780, & came to what is now the city of Wash in 1790. He assisted in carrying the chains for the survey of D C & the city of Wash, & was present at the laying of the foundation stone of the city.

Clinton M Sears, Druggist, corner of 11th & E sts. This Store is always open, day & night, for the prompt & careful dispensing of physicians' prescriptions. All the standard & patent preparations are sold here.

Deuel & Wells, Dentists, 448 Pa ave, between 4½ & 3rd sts.

Orphans Court of Wash Co, D C. Letters of administration on the personal estate of Clement L West, late of Wash, D C, deceased. –Sarah C West

The co-partnership existing under the firm of Blanchard & Mohun was dissolved on Dec 21, by the death of Mr V Blanchard. –Richd R Mohun, surviving partner
+
The Book & Stationery business under the firm of Blanchard & Mohun, will be continued at 11th st & Pa ave. –Richd B Mohun, Frances Blanchard

Orphans Court of Wash Co, D C. Letters of administration on the personal estate of John McGuire, late of Wash, D C, deceased. –Patrick White

THU FEB 8, 1866
Gen Grant & Gen Sherman paid a visit to Admiral Porter, at the Naval School, Annapolis. The marine guard presenting arms as they entered the grounds; the midshipmen, in full uniform, were drawn up in front of the recitation hall & were reviewed by the Generals. At 10 o'clock they left for Washington.

Hon Asbury Hull, of Ga, died at Athens on Jan 25. His death was sudden, while in the enjoyment of his usual health. It was his custom at morning to devote a short time to the study of the Bible which had been the constant companion of his long & useful life. On being called to breakfast, his failure to attend, a servant was sent to summon him when he was found in his chair, & the spark of life had flown.

Died: on Feb 7, Margaret Catherine, the beloved wife of B D Hyam, & daughter of the late Francis Masi, of Wash City. Her funeral will take place on Friday, at 9:30 o'clock, from the residence of her brother, S Masi, 461 9th st. A solemn requiem mass will be celebrated at St Patrick's Church at 10 o'clock.

Died: on Feb 7, Sallie M, wife of Aaron H Bradley. Her funeral is on Feb 9 at 2 o'clock P M, from the residence of her brother-in-law, T H Phillips, 276 B st, near 3rd st.

Orphans Court of Wash Co, D C. Letters of administration on the personal estate of Harriet Butler, late of Wash, D C, deceased. –Euphemia B Reily

FRI FEB 9, 1866
Stone Works, constantly on hand, & manufactured to order at the shortest notice & lowest cash prices. –Nicholas Acker, N J ave & E st, near the Balt Depot.

Wanted-information of A J Kendall, late of the 2nd Ohio volunteer cavalry, & formerly a printer in Cincinnati. Persons seeing him will know by his having the left arm off at the elbow. Any one knowing of his whereabouts will confer a great favor to his wife & children, by sending the desired information to Mrs Mary Kendall, Box 2, 6sl, Post Ofc, Cincinnati, Ohio.

A large & very fashionable audience filled the Church of the Epiphany yesterday to witness the marriage ceremonies of Miss Helmick, daughter of Hon Wm Helmick, ex-M C, of Ohio, to Mr D P Moore, of Ohio. At 2 o'clock P M the house of the bride's father was thrown open to receive the invited guests; the party adjourned to the church to witness the solemn ceremony performed by the Rector, Dr Hall. The bridal party left last evening for the North, to return soon & become permanent citizens of this community.

+

Mrd: on Feb 8, at the Church of the Ephphany, by Rev C H Hall, D D, D P Moore, of Carrollton, Ohio, to Miss Jennie R Helmick, daughter of Hon Wm Helmick, of Ohio. [Feb 10th newspaper: Correction: substitution of the name of Rev Dr Hall for that of Rev Dr Gurley, who officiated on the occasion.]

For sale-market farm, containing 60 acres, within 8 miles of Annapolis, Md; bldg new; & neighborhood healthy. –M E McKnew, Real Estate Agent, 7th & La ave.

Wm M Sampson, Chief Justice of Ky, died on Feb 5, after a painful & protracted illness.

Newark, Feb 8. A train from Mount Clair, on the Bloomfield railroad, ran off the track this morning, due to the bridge being rotten, & a man, Wilton Holt, of Mount Clair, was killed, & 5 were severely injured.

Guardian's sale by order of the Orphans Court of D C, ratified by the Supreme Court of D C, valuable improved real estate at Va ave & C st, Island, at auction, on Feb 21. I shall proceed to sell, as guardian of the orphan children of John A Cassell, deceased, the interest of said orphans in lot 2 in square numbered south of square 463; & part of said lot & square, beginning on Va ave. On the first lot is a nearly new 3 story brick dwlg, with back bldg, containing 13 rooms. On the other lot is a frame dwlg containing 8 rooms. The title has been perfected, & is now indisputable. –Alfred C Cassell, guardian -Green & Williams, aucts

Orphans Court of Wash Co, D C. In the case of Richd H Laskey, exc of Jos Cross, deceased, the executor & Court have appointed Mar 3 next, for the final settlement of the personal estate of the said deceased, of the assets in hand.
-Z C Robbins, Reg/o wills

Pittsburg paper: loss of life on Friday at the Mechanics' Factory, on Swift creek, when the boiler exploded. Mr Stephens, aged 45, was blown away, & at last accounts, his body had not been recovered. He leaves a wife & 6 children entirely unprovided for; Frank Stephens, a boy aged 10, son of the above, was killed; also, Wm Grubbs, aged 22, & Chas Tatum, aged 25, both single. Among the wounded were Richd Roberts, aged 45, engineer of the establishment, mortally; John Norris, aged 20, fireman, supposed mortally; Jas Daniel, aged 9, badly; Ross Scott, severely; John Stephens, aged 14, badly; Mr & Mrs Gall, slightly; Emily Ferguson, Mrs Scott, & Jane Smith, all slightly.

SAT FEB 10, 1866
Metropolitan Police Com'rs. On Thu the complaints against Patrolmen J W Davis & Wm C Adler, of the 8th Precinct; Roundsman B F Barker, & Patrolmen W H Evans & Z H Whitemore, of the 10th Precinct, were dismissed. Patrolman Patrick Doyle, of the 6th Precinct, was fined $5 for receiving a reward without the consent of the Board, & the reward was ordered to be returned to the donor. Patrolman W Leonard, 10th Precinct, was dismissed the force, with loss of all pay, for intoxication, & John Fainter was appointed a patrolman in his stead. Richd Spencer was appointed an additional patrolman for square bounded by D & E, & 14th & 15th sts.

Heavy defalcation in the ofc of the U S sub-Treasurer in San Francisco, committed early in Jan by Wm Macy, cashier in the ofc. So far the defalcation amounts to about $30,000. The defaulter has absconded to parts unknown. Wm Macy is a young man not over 22 years of age, & a brother-in-law of Mr Cheeseman, the Treasurer, who for 2 or 3 months has been in the east.

Judge Radcliff, an old & respected citizen of Albany died on Wednesday.

Died: on Feb 9, Mrs Ellen Sullivan, aged 72 years, formerly of Gtwn, but for the last 6 years a resident of Wash. Her funeral will be on Feb 11 at 2 o'clock, from the residence of her son, Jos P Sullivan, 4th & I st.

Died: on Feb 9, of consumption, Louisa M, beloved wife of Terrence Drury, in her 30th year. Her funeral will be this day, at 2 o'clock, from her late residence, 372 19th st, between G & H sts.

Died: on Jan 29, in St Louis, of paralysis, Mrs Hannah Keane, in her 70th year, relict of Stephen Keane.

Wheeling, W Va, Feb 9. Gregan & Boyce, who were convicted of the murder of Adam Deems, were executed at Parkersburg today. The rope broke on the first attempt, & both men were again mounted to the scaffold, stronger ropes were applied & they were hanged separately.

The Benton [Ill] Standard of Jan 31 gives an account of the trial of Mr David Williams, of that place, for murder. A skeleton was found near his father's house & was supposed to be the remains of a man named Henry Mahorn, who had been lost sight of for some time previous, & the circumstances pointed conclusively to Mr Williams as guilty of his murder. But on Jan 15th, while the trial was going on, Mr Mahorn turns up again & came into court to the surprise of all & the relief of the accused, who was acquitted at once.

Judge Brayton has declined the ofc of Justice of the Supreme Court of Rhode Island, to which he was elected on Wednesday.

Accident on Thu on the Bloomfield Railroad killed Mr Milton B Holt, passenger, & injured Mr Theron Sandford, slightly. Mr Holt was a single man aged about 30 years. Also injured: Jos A Davis, jr, of Newark, quite severely; Jos Doremus, of N Y; Mr Brantigam, a merchant of N Y; Saml Arbuthnot, conductor, quite severely; Owen Conlin, paper boy; Jas Robby, of Newark; & V W Graham, paying-tell of Phoenix Bank, N Y.

Hon A J Glossbrenner has retired from the proprietorship of the Phil Age.

Balt, Feb 9. The Mount Hope Insane Asylum case progresses slowly today. Miss Mary Fleming, who has been for many years an inmate of the asylum, was called. The defence denies that she is a competent witness.

Orphans Court of Wash Co, D C. In the case of Caroline H Skirving & John T Given, excs of Jas Skriving, deceased, the executors & Court have appointed Mar 3 next, for the final settlement of the personal estate of the said deceased, of the assets in hand. -Z C Robbins, Reg/o wills

St Mary's C W, Feb 9. Mr Phelps, agent of the American Express Co, has absconded, taking $12,000. He has gone to Europe.

Some weeks since Col King, of the 13th Missouri regt, arrived at Jefferson City, Mo, from the plains, bringing with him a white boy about 12 years of age, who wandered into his camp on the plains among the Sioux. He could speak little or no English, & knew nothing of his birthplace. Is has since been discovered that he was the son of a Mr Sylvester, & was stolen on the plains while his parents were on their way to Oregon in the summer of 1860. An uncle, residing in Quincy, Ill, hearing of Col King's discovery, made inquiries which resulted in his identifying the boy as his nephew. The latter, however, has become quite an Indian, has forgoten all about his parents, who are now living in Oregon, & is strongly attached to wild life.

Rev John J Williams has been appointed Coadjutor Bishop of Boston, with the right of succession in the event of the death of Rt Rev Bishop Fitzpatrick, who is in ill health.

The Portago [Wis] Register announces the death of Jos Crele, the aged veteran of 141 years, which occurred on Jan 27, after a brief illness, at the residence of his grand- daughter, Mrs Brisbois, in Caledonia, about 4 miles from Portage. He was born near the city of Detroit, in 1725, as shown by the records of the Catholic Church of that city, & was probably the **oldest man** in the world.

MON FEB 12, 1866
In conformity to the will of the late Lambert Suydam, his real estate was sold at auction, in N Y, on Thu. Upwards of 51 houses, stores, & lots were sold, realizing about $450,000.

Military trials in Alexandria; Feb 9. The Commission for the trial of parties charged with assault & battery & murder on Christmas reassembled, the evidence for the defence was resumed. Mrs Johnson testified she lived on King st, & saw Oscar Mankin pass her door; heard 2 shots fired; not long enough for him to get to the corner. Mrs Keniston testified that she was at the house of her mother, Mrs Johnson, on Christmas, & saw a colored man shaking his fist at Mr Noland. Saw 2 men run up & shoot him on Gregg's corner. Witness knows Oscar & John Mankin, but did not see either of them there. Mrs Willie A Briscoe testified that she lives on King st; testified the same at Mrs Keniston. Eliza Campbell, colored, was at the Virginia House, & saw some colored soldiers throwing stones. Thos Dutcher testified that while in his door, on King st, he saw a colored man shaking his fist in a white man's face. Robt Alexander, colored, testified for the prosecution as the man who had been knocked down at King & Alfred sts; testified that he went with Mr Willoughby & Thos Jackson to the place where he was beaten. Thos Jackson, colored, testified that Robt Armstrong pointed out to him the place where he was hurt. Alexander was hurt after the man was shot. Saml Baggett testified he was across the street when the man was killed. Huntington was not there at the time. Jas Claridge testified he saw from Mr Cook's store, on Alfred st, a colored man lying in the street. E Fields was with him trying to get him away. Capt Saml Baker & Wm D Massey were called, & testified as to the good character of Messrs Horseman & F Travis for peace, quietness, & order. Jas M Stewart testified that he knew John Mankin & that his reputation is very good as a peaceful, quiet, & orderly citizen. Jas Noland testified that he saw Geo Huntington pass King & Paine sts about 5 minutes after the firing. Huntington was going in the direction of the firing.
[Feb 13th newspaper: Fred Knapp testified that he was in Dukehart's saloon with Mr Childs; heard shots & saw a man lying on the ground. Chas A Ware testified that he is Mayor of Alexandria; complaint was made by John Mankin against Jane Grey for keeping a disorderly house & being disorderly; complaint was proven, & witness imposed a fine & discharged her; arrested a second & third time on the complaint of Mankin, again fined. Capt Jesse Childs testified that he belonged to the 1st Md volunteer infty & on Christmas day was at 352 King st; heard a noise & went to the door & saw a colored man going up the street. Wm Allen recalled: Travis & Horseman were standing at Cox's tavern when the guard came up. Capt Hambrick, provost judge, Freedman's Bureau, testified: Simpson & Huntington voluntarily surrendered themselves. Ferdinand Mankin testified: saw Travis on Christmas. John W Horseman testified: met his brother Jos, & took him home. Gen Well announced that the evidence for the defence was concluded.]
[Feb 19th newspaper: In relation to the killing of Anderson, Gen Wells stated that no murder had been committed, as there was no malice prepense or forethought.]

J N Washington was elected Mayor of Newbern, N C, on Thursday.

Died: on Feb 7, at Sandy Hill, N Y, Mrs Olivia F Martindale, widow of the late Henry C Martindale, & daughter of the late Dr Jas Ewell, formerly of Wash City.

Dept of the Interior, U S Patent Ofc, Wash, Jan 31, 1866. Ptn of Wm Southwell, of West Cambridge, Mass, praying for the extension of a patent granted to him on May 4, 1852, for an improvement in Machinery for Grinding or Polishing Saw Blades, etc, for 7 years from the expiration of said patent, which takes place on May 4, 1866. -H C Theaker, Com'r of Patents

Personal: Geo H Chickering, of Chickering & Sons, Boston, & his bride are on a visit to Wash City, the guests of our fellow-citizen, John F Ellis.

Dept of the Interior, U S Patent Ofc, Wash, Jan 29, 1866. Ptn of Peter Dorsch, of Schenectady, N Y, praying for the extension of a patent granted to him on Jun 15, 1852, for an improvement in Cast-Iron Car Wheels, for 7 years from the expiration of said patent, which takes place on Jun 15, 1866.
-H C Theaker, Com'r of Patents

Dept of the Interior, U S Patent Ofc, Wash, Jan 29, 1866. Ptn of Moses G Farmer, of Salem, Mass, praying for the extension of a patent granted to him on May 4, 1852, for an improvement in Electro Magnetic Alarm Bells, for 7 years from the expiration of said patent, which takes place on May 4, 1866.
-H C Theaker, Com'r of Patents

Orphans Court of Wash Co, D C. Letters of administration on the personal estate of Chas W Boteler, sr, late of Wash City, D C, deceased. –C W Boteler, John W Boteler, admx

It is 18 years since a man with a **middle name** occupied the Presidential chair.

TUE FEB 13, 1866
Mrs Stonewall Jackson has written a letter stating that the contributions that are called for in her behalf are given under a false impression, & it is inconsistent with her ideas of rectitude & honor to receive them. She begs that all efforts made to raise funds for her "relief" will be immediately stopped.

The execution of Dr John W Hughes, the murderer of Miss Tanza Parsons, of Bedford, Ohio, took place last Friday, in the jail at Cleveland, Ohio. He was confined in our county jail for some time during last winter on the charge of bigamy & adultery. The prosecutrix in the case was Miss Tanza Parsons, of Bedford, Ohio. He was convicted of the crimes charged against him & sentenced to 1 year in the penitentiary. He was released after a short time through executive clemency. On his release he went immediately to Cleveland, where he met his legal wife, whom he induced to return to her friends on the Isle of Man, & after her departure he began to pay his attentions to his former victim, who received him very coldly. This infuriated him & he shot her in the neck & head instantly killing her. He was convicted of murder in the first degree.

Wash Corp-Feb 12, 1866. 1-Ptn of Henry Dimond for the remission of a fine: referred to the Cmte on Claims. Same for M Lucas. 2-Bill for relief of Patrick HcHugh: passed. 3-Ptn for relief of J W Studley: referred to Cmte on Claims.

Died: on Jan 31, [at his uncle's, Dr T Nevitt,] in Fairfax Co, Va, Chas W, son of Robt K Nevitt, of Richmond Co, Va, late of Wash Co, D C, [from the effects of a pistol wound accidentally received,] aged 18 years. He was a pious youth & from the moment of the fatal accident to his death, a period of 12 days, he expressed, in the most calm & hopeful manner, a preparation for & resignation to the Divine will.

Dedication of a new Catholic colored Chapel, on 15th st, between L & M sts, which has been erected under the auspices of St Matthew's Church, & especially under the exertions of Fr White, was formally opened yesterday for religious purposes. In the second story is a fine colored school, & Miss Mary Smith, a colored teacher of Gtwn, will instruct there.

WED FEB 14, 1866

A petition has been received here for presentation to the Pres asking for the pardon of John C Breckinridge. It is signed by upwards of 70 members of the Ky Legislature.

The Chicago Republican says, that Miss Ellen O'Mahony, Head Centress of the Fenian Sisterhood, is not the wife, daughter, or sister of the Irish chief, John O'Mahony. For many years she was principal of the High School at Quincey, & added to her reputation as a teacher by her essays & other productions, presented to the Teachers' State Conventions. In 1863 she went to Chicago, & was made assistant of the Kinzie School.

Diffulty at Gtwn, Ky, Wed, between 2 students of the Baptist College, named Hayden & Theodore Hughes. The latter died yesterday from a pistol shot received.

Mrs Deborah Baxter, residing in Warren Co, Ohio, wife of D W Baxter, deceased, committed suicide some days since. Her husband died in July last, since which time she has been inconsolable for his loss, & had attempted on several occasions to put an end to her life, which she at last succeeded doing, being found dead in her carriage-house, hanging by the neck.

Wm Carll, keeper of a restaurant at the corner of Washington & Courtlandt sts, N Y, was shot on Tue by a party of ruffians.

A coroner's inquest was held on Friday upon the body of Mr Holt, killed by the railroad accident near Bloomfield, N J. The jury censured the company for culpable neglect as to the state of the bridge, the unsoundness of which caused the accident.

Festival of St Valentine. St Valentine was a holy priest of Rome, who, with St Marius & his family, assisted the martyrs in the persecution under Claudius II, in the 3rd century. He was apprehended, & sent by the Emperor to the Prefect of Rome, who, on finding all his efforts to make him renounce his faith ineffectual, commanded him to be beaten with clubs, & afterwards beheaded; & this occurred on Feb 14. About the year 270 Pope Julius is said to have built a church near Ponte Mole to his menory, which for a long time gave name to the gate afterwards called Porta del Populo. The greatest part of the relics are preserved in the Church of St Praxedes. Some have conjectured that the custom of devoting the day to Cupid is traceable to the ancient Romans, whose festivals, called Lupercalia, were celebrated in this month.

Hon Jonathan E Whipple died on Friday last, at Lansingburgh, NY. He has been engaged for the last 35 years in the manufacture of oilcloth.

Wm B Astor, who owns some 1,500 houses in N Y, is said to have started the movement for the great advance in rents in that city.

Mrd: on Feb 13, at the E st Baptist Church, by Rev Dr Gray, Mr Elisha R Reed, of Ray Co, Mo, to Miss Isabella O Brown, only surviving daughter of Edmund F Brown, of Wash City.

Two boys, Saml Higgins & John Perkins, found the body of an identified man floating in the Eastern Branch yesterday

Died: on Feb 13, Mrs Eliza V Thaw, widow of the late Jos Thaw, sr, of Wash City, in her 80th year. Her funeral will be from her late residence on 9th st, near L, on Feb 15 at 2 o'clock.

A man named Jas Kennedy, who resided on N Y ave, between 4th & 5th sts, committed sucide yesterday by shooting himself through the head with a navy revolver. He formerly kept a grocery on N Y ave, but sometime ago failed in business & lost much of what he was worth. He has been unable to find employment. He went home & collected his family, his wife & 4 children, & locked them in a room. He went to his bedroom & shot himself. He was about 35 years of age.

Mrd: on Feb 13, at the Church of the Ascension, by Rev Dr Pinkney, Miss Mary M, daughter of John Y Bryant, of Wash City, to Mr Jos P Myers, of Balt, Md.

Meeting of the Corp of the Chesapeake Bay & Potomac River Tidewater Canal Co will be held at the Banking house of Mr Jay Cooke & Co, on 15th st, Wash City, on Feb 19, 1866. -Henry D Cooke, Wm E Spalding, Gideon S Walker, Saml F Dickinson, Jas Higgins, Thos Landsdale, Wm Thompson of R, Wm H Tuck, Andrew J Hull

Murder of a wife by an old man of 60, & his suicide afterward, took place in the township of Rockport, Ohio, on Wed last. Fred'k Oden, A German gardener, living with his wife, aged 55, on his place, about 4 miles from Rockport. On Wed one of the daughters, Adeline, who slept in a chamber, was awakened by her father & mother quarelling. Soon after he left the house. She found her mother in the bedroom, on the floor, in a pool of blood dead. She had a gash down her face made by an axe. In the front yard of Mr John N West is a pond. Oden chopped a hole in the ice & drowned himself. His body was recovered.

The death of Geo R Cinnamond, a member of the Balt bar, is announced.

Boston, Feb 13. Rt Rev John B Fitzpatrick, Catholic Bishop of Boston, died late night after a lingering illness. [Feb 16th newspaper: Rev Fitzpatrick was in his 53rd year; born in Boston; was sent to the Sulpician College in Montreal, where he remained 8 years; 3 years at the Sulpician Seminary in France, where he was ordained a priest, & returned to Boston in 1840; on Mar 24, 1844, was consecrated Bishop of the diocese of Mass.]
[Feb 19th newspaper: The funeral of Rt Rev John B Fitzpatrick took place in Boston, in the Cathedral Chapel of the Holy Cross; a richly silver mounted casket was provided by the <u>Sisters of Charity</u>; the lid on the coffin bore the following inscription:
Right Rev Bishop,
John B. Fitzpatrick,
Born November 15, 1812,
Died February 13, 1866.
Aged 53 years and 3 months.
The remains were buried in *St Augustin's Cemetery*, in South Boston.]

The Powhatan House, Richmond, Va, is for rent or lease from Apr 1 next. Apply to P Johnston, sr, exec of J McKildoe.

THU FEB 15, 1866
Court of Appeals of Md, Annapolis, Feb 14, 1866. No 58: Mary E Myers, excx of Chas Myers vs Jas Forbes et al. This argument of this cause was commenced by B F Horwitz for the appellant & W W Frick for the appellees.

<u>Court of Claims</u>, Feb 14, 1866.
1-Julian J Alexander, of Balt, Md, was appointed a com'r of the Court.
2-Thos W Peirce vs The U S. Chief Justice Casey deliver the opinion of the Court in this case, adverse to the claim.
3-Arabella Riley, excx of Bennet Riley, dec'd, vs the U S. Judge Peck delivered the opinion of the Court in this case, finding due to the claimant $4,425.52. Judge Loring read a separate opinion, concurring with the majority, except as to the amount of the judgment.

Mrd: on Feb 13, at the Church of the Epiphany, by Rev Dr Hall, Howard Edmunds, of Pottsville, Pa, to Mary E Owen, daughter of S W Owen, of Wash City.

On Friday last, 2 soldiers, W F Tewksberry & G G Harding, belonging to the 147th Ill vols, who had recently been mustered out of the service in Texas, arrived in Chicago, & took a room at the Briggs House. On retiring for the night, Harding, instead of turning off the gas, blew out the light, & they went to sleep. The next morning Harding was found lifeless, & Tewksberry was in agony. Restoratives were applied, & he recovered.

Mrd: on Feb 7, at the residence of the bride-groom's father, at Tarrytown, N Y, by Rev J Selden Spencer, rector of Christ Church, John D Maynard to Miss Sarah Maynard, eldest daughter of Butler Maynard, of N Y.

Mrd on Tue, at the Church of the Ascension, by Rev Dr Pinkney, rector, Miss Mary Bryant, daughter of Capt John Y Bryant, of Wash City, to Mr Jos P Myers, of Balt. First bridesmaid, Miss Abbott, of Gtwn; second was Miss Moulder, of Wash; third, Miss Walters, of Alexandria; fourth, Miss Franks, of Wash. Groomsmen, Messrs Miller, of Cumberland; Bryant, of Wash; Duncanson, of Wash, & Thomas, of Balt. The newly married couple left by train on a bridal tour North.

Died: on Feb 12, Alex'r Clements, in his 38th year. His funeral will be from his late residence, 20th & N sts, Feb 16, at 2 o'clock. Port Tobacco Times please copy.
+
Alex'r Clements, a roundsman of the Metropolitan Police force, lately on duty in the First Ward, died yesterday after a long & painful illness. He has been a member of the police force since its organization, & was one of its most faithful & efficient officers.

John Smith. If John Smith, who emigrated from Linnhall, Parish of Tundergarth, Scotland, to Canada, about 32 years ago, will communicate with Rev Walter Smith, Half Morton, by Canonbie, Scotland, he will hear of something to his advantage.

Excx's sale of very valuable farm within 2 miles of Wash, fronting on the new road to Bladensburg, & the road from said farm to **Mount Olivet Cemetery**, which is divided into 11 sections, ranging from 7 to 15 acres, that beautiful farm, belonging to the estate of Mrs Mary E Fenwick, deceased, being a part of **Youngsborough**, in Wash Co, D C, containing 105 acres, 2 roods & 36 perches in all. There is a fine frame dwlg & out bldgs on Section 11. Two other lots have houses on them. –M E Smith, excx -Green & Williams, aucts

Knoxville, Tenn, Feb 14. A negro yesterday was hung by a mob for shooting Lt Col Ayer of the 1st Tenn cavalry.

FRI FEB 16, 1866
Effects of tobacco. The immoderate use of tobacco, & more especially of the pipe, produces a weakness of the brain & the spinal marrow, which causes madness.

A gentleman, Mr Pettit, a clerk in the Genr'l Land Ofc, was killed at 7th & H sts, by being run over by a horse ridden by a colored boy, Amos Hamer, who was committed to jail to await trial for murder. The case was tried yesterday in the Criminal Court, & the jury returned a verdict of not guilty.

Chas Ripley, one of the most eminent lawyers of Ky, died at Louisville on Monday.

A baby boy, abandoned at Williard's Hotel, was found by a private watchman, on the curbstone, on F st. He was taken to St Ann's Infant Asylum, where a card was found saying he was Frank Leroy Palmerston. –E P. The parents said they were unable to raise him.

Death-bed marriage now pending in the Circuit Court. Some years since a prominent citizen Mr Andrew Fuqua, died possessed of considerable property. By his will his wife by his second marriage came into possession of all his property, which she has to hold during her life, in case she remained a widow. At her death, if unmarried, the property would revert to her husband's relatives. If she married one half the property was to be hers, to be disposed as she might think proper. Mrs Fuqua, 2 days before her death, was induced by her brother to marry, that she might thus acquire the title in fee simple to half the property, which she could then deed to her own relatives, instead of allowing her husband's heirs to inherit it. Her brother had been a captain in one of the Indiana regts, & induced one of his men to play the role of husband in the death bed marriage, for $500 paid down. The dying woman was married in her bed by a minister. The "husband" left immediately after the ceremony & never returned again. The action was brought by Mr Fuqua's relatives, to test the validity of the marriage. The case will prove to be one of great interest. –Indianapolis Journal

Metropolitan Police Com'rs. Patrick Kearney was appointed a patrolman for the 5th Precinct, vice Jas C Taylor, resigned. Jos Straub appointed additional patrolman for duty at the Balt & Ohio railroad depot. W H Sherwood & Robt Sutton, appointed additional patrolmen near 11th & 12th sts.

Mrd: on Feb 15, at the First Presbyterian Church, 4½ st, by Rev Byron Sunderland, D D, Mr Frank S Altemus, of Phil, to Hannah A, daughter of Wm M Ellis, of Wash City.

Mrd: on Feb 13, at Fourth Presbyterian Church, by Rev John C Smith, Oscar R Hough to Marion V Creaser, both of Wash, D C. Richmond & Petersburg papers please copy.

Mrd: on Feb 13, in Bridge St Church, Gtwn, by Rev Dr Tustin, Dr Chas McCormick to Miss Mittie L, daughter of the late Jas C Wilson, all of Gtwn.

Mrd: on Feb 8, at the E St Baptist Church, by Rev Dr Gray, Mr Chas N Simms, of Wash City, to Miss Mary A Burr, of the same place.

Died: on Feb 15, at her residence, Rebecca Howle Riley, wife of Dr John C Riley, & daughter of the late Maj Park G Howle. Her funeral will take place at St Matthew's Church, 15th & H sts, on Feb 17 at 10 o'clock, where the Holy Sacrifice of the Mass will be offered for the repose of her soul.

Capt Burnett, an ex-Confederate ofcr, has been sentenced at Nashville, Tenn, to 3 years in the penitentiary for killing Sgt Pollard, of the 108th Ohio regt, at Shell Mound, on Jul 4 last. Pollard & Burnett simultaneously fired at one another. Burnett's wound was slight. Pollard was killed.

SAT FEB 17, 1866
Dr Jos H Levering, who resides on the Lancaster turnpike, near Rosemount Station, about 9 miles from Phil, was murdered on his own premises, on Tue, just after dark. He was leading his horse into the stable, when he was shot through the heart & instantly killed by some person unknown. Mrs Levering found him near the stable door, already dead.

Andrew McArthur, an Englishman, known as the "Old Book Dealer," of Cincinnati, died there on Feb 13, in his 72nd year.

Mr Geo W Hatch, who died on Monday, in his 62nd year, was one of the oldest engravers in the country. He was for a great many years a member of the firm of Rawdon, Wright & Hatch, who, 40 years ago, & for a long time after, did the large part of the bank-note engraving of the U S. He was a gentleman of intelligence & genial manners.

A young man named Benj Luckett was stabbed last night in the right breast by Milburn Hunter, in front of J Aberdeeser's restaurant, 321 7th st, near L. Luckett has been a soldier throughout the war in the Union army, having served as a member of the 3rd Pa cavalry. He was enlisted by Capt Wm J Gary, at the outbreak of the rebellion. His brother, Ashmun Luckett, also met a violent death, having been killed some years ago in a riot. Hunter is a young man, 21 or 22 years of age, carpenter by trade, & was but recently married. It is feared his wound will prove fatal.

Alex'r M Porter, a well known & wealthy citizen of Nashville, Tenn, died on Wed of an epileptic fit.

Mrd: on Feb 15, in Phil, at the residence of J W Dallam, by Rev John W Todd, of Tarrytown, N Y, Capt Wm Budd, late of U S Navy, to Fannie, daughter of the late David English, of Gtwn, D C.

A man named Bowling, & 6 of his confederates, all horse-thieves, were recently executed near Saltillo, Miss, by a party composed of the best citizens. The outrages of Bowling & gang compelled the citizens to the action.

Clark & Tristran were found guilty in the heavy robbery of the Adams Express Co on the New Haven railroad on Jan 6, & were on Wed sentenced to the Conn Penitentiary.

MON FEB 19, 1866
An inhuman wretch, Chas Carter, colored, was arrested on Friday by Ofcr Calhoun, on a charge of unmercifully beating his mother, who is over 60 years of age. He was committed for trial at the Criminal Court.

Frank E Wherren was arrested on Sat by Ofcr Johnson, charged with an attempt to pass a $20 counterfeit greenback on Mr Jas Cottingham, at a cigar store on Pa av.

The wife of J A Gaylor, a banker of St Louis, died on Thu from the effects of burns received the day previous, her clothes having caught fire while passing before a grate.

Mrd: on Feb 14, by Rev S D Finckel, Mr Jesse Jenkins, of Pa, to *Mrs/Miss Mary A V Winemiller, of D C. *Ink spot on Mrs or Miss.

The venerable Robt Cary, the father of Alice & Phoebe Cary, died in Cincinnati on Feb 11. Mr Cary was nearly 80 years of age, & was one of the first settlers of Cincinnati.

Muster out of Paymasters on Sat: Rowland G Usher, Mass; Jas B Sheridan, Pa; Justus M Phelps, Va; Stephen A Walker, Vt; Eli Van Valkenburg, Mich; John M Doddridge, Pa; Orloff M Dorman, Mass; Geo W De Costa, Kan; W S Pope, Ill; Jas L Cramer, N Y; Wm H Nichols, Pa; Jacob Sallade, Pa; Edw H Gratiot, Wis; Wm L Fleming, N Y.

Premptory Chancery sale of valuable improved property on H near 9th st, by decree passed by the Supreme Court of D C, on Nov 17, 1865, in a cause No 538-Equity, in which Wm A Hyland is cmplnt & Christopher H Hyland & others are dfndnts: public auction on Mar 13 next, of part of lot 1 in square 374, with 2 comfortable brick houses. –Richd T Merrick, trustee
-Jas C McGuire & Co, aucts

Robbery yesterday at the store of Mr Geo F Allen, 8th & Market Space, articles valued at $50.

Circuit Court for Talbot Co, in Equity, Feb 15, 1866. Thos B Quigly & Anna S Quigly his wife, vs Jas Valliant & others. The object of this suit is to procure a decree for the sale of certain real estate in Dorchester & Talbot Counties, of which Rigby Valliant, late of Talbot Co, died seized & possessed, & a division of the proceeds thereof between the parties. This bill states that Jas Valliant, Thos R Vallaint, Mary R Valliant, Geo W W Valliant, Sarah F Valliant, Edwin S Valliant, John Valliant, & the complnts are seized as tenants in common in fee of certain lands therein named, in said counties, of which Rigby Vallient died seized & possessed; & prays a sale of said lands & division of the proceeds, & that Thos R Valliant resides out of the State of Md. Absent dfndnt to appear in this court, in person or by solicitor, on or before Jul 2nd next. –Henry H Goldsborough -Saml T Hopkins, clerk

Orphans Court of Wash Co, D C. Letters of administration on the personal estate of Edw H Fuller, late of Wash, D C, deceased. –Emily Fuller, John E Fuller

Orphans Court of Wash Co, D C. Letters testamentary on the personal estate of Rachel Harrison, late of Wash, D C, deceased. –Jas S Harvey, exc

TUE FEB 20, 1866
Wash Corp-Feb 19, 1866. 1-Bill granting certain privileges to John Bontz: referred. 2-Ptn of M Donelly, referred to the Cmte on Claims. 3-Ptn of J P Purdy: referred to the Cmte on Police. 4-Bill for the benefit of Edw O'Connor: passed. 5-Bill for the relief of J W Studley: passed. 6-Adverse report on the ptns of M Zange, John Holzshire, & Thos Boursh. 7-Bill for the relief of Henry Dramond: passed.

On Sat, as the Franklin hose carriage was returning from the fire in Gtwn, Thos Martin, the fireman of the Franklin, was thrown from the seat of the hose-carriage & the wheels passed over his arms & thighs. His head was badly cut by being dragged on the street. Dr Borrows is attending his injuries.

The children of a German woman, Anastina Schetz, living in a tenement in 27th st, near Broadway, N Y, aged 1, 2, & 6 years, were on Sat found dead from the supposed effects of suffocation. The woman was found in an insensible state, having afterwards attempted to destroy her own life.

Mrd: on Feb 13, at the Church of the Ascension, by Rev Wm Pinkney, D D, Armistead M Darrell to Nannie E Brooke, both of Wash, D C.

Roofs! Roofs! Improved fire & water-proof. Thos Fahey, 10th & Canal st.

Dry & Fancy Goods: John S Yates, Store-515 9th st, corner of D, under Seaton Hall.

Supreme Court of D C, Feb 14, 1866, No 528, in Equity. Margaret A Moore, cmplnt vs Thos Moore, dfndnt. The subpoena issued to compel the dfndnt's appearance having been returned into the Clerk's ofc by the Marshal, on Dec 11, 1865, endorsed "non est," as to the above named dfndnt, Thos Moore; & the said dfndnt having failed to enter his appearance at the first rule day; it is, on the motion of the cmplnt, that the said dfndnt cause his appearance to be entered in this suit on or before the first Tue of Apr next; otherwise the bill may be taken for confessed. -Andrew Wylie, a Justice of said Court. -R J Meigs, clerk

Rev N O Preston, a professor in the Arkansas Agricultura College, died while sitting in his chair at the college at Manhattan, on Wednesday last.

Brutal murder in East Balt on Sat night, during a difficulty between 20 persons-2 rival clubs, the Fountain Rackers & the Stay Lates, resulting in a young man, John Finch, being struck on the head by a billy, by a man named Fred'k Smith, & a moment later stabbed in the breast by Thos Barnes. Finch died while being conveyed to the station house. Jury verdict: dec'd came to his death at the hands of Thos Barnes. Fred'k Smith guilty as an accessory to the murder. Both were committed to jail to await the action of the Grand Jury.

WED FEB 21, 1866
Col Sherman, late of the Confederate army, & said to be a relative of Gen Sherman, died at St Augustine, Fla, on Feb 3, of consumption.

The elegant residence of Mr Howard Potter, at Astoria, L I, was burned on Sunday. The furniture was all saved, but the bldg was totally destroyed. Loss $50,000, on which there is an insurance of $14,000.

New Orleans, Feb 16. Gen Clay Crawford last night escaped from the fort where he was confined. The remainder of the Bagdad filibusters were today released on parole.

Mrd: on Jan 9, by Rev R J Keeling, rector of Trinity Parish, Wash City, Col Lambert A Whitely to Miss Clara Bel, only daughter of Col Wm R Bradford, all of Wash City.

Died: on Feb 20, in Wash City, Rev Rufus Buel, in his 53rd year. His funeral will take place at the Cavalry Baptist Church, H & 8th sts, on Feb 22 at 3 P M.

THU FEB 22, 1866
Died: on Feb 21, aged 81 years, Mary, widow of the late Philip Johnson, of St Mary's Co, Md. Her funeral will be from the residence of her daughter, Mrs Wimsatt, 321 G st, Friday at 10 o'clock.

Mrs Hough, well known for many years as a popular boarding-house keeper, on Pa ave, between 3rd & 4½ sts, died very suddenly yesterday of apoplexy. Mrs Hough retired to her chamber in usual health Tue night.
+
Died: on Feb 21, of asthma, Mrs Harriet R Hough, in her 62nd year. Her funeral will be from her late residence, 452 Pa ave, on Feb 23, at 11 o'clock.

Criminal Court-Wash-Jury of the Criminal Court, March Term:
Grand Jury:
Thos A King
Michl Green
John H Grant
Wm H Barbour
John Keller
Adam Gaddis
A Nailor, jr
Jas McCarthy
W J Dyer
Peter Taltavull
Richd E Booth
Jas D Benjamin

Richd M Devine
John King
Wm Harrover
Henry Thorn
H Kaiser
G P Fenwick
J H D Richards
Josiah Ray
Peter Dill
Michl Conner
Jerome Callaghan

Petit Jury:
Saml H Donaldson
John T Webster
John M Ray
Arthur Proby
Wm Arnold
Edw J Shoemaker
Wm R Simmons
J Y Davis
Walter Godey
John Adamson
Lambert T Follansbee
Wm Kitchan
C B Bayley

John Corcoran
John T Givens
Jos R Burch
Wm Wilson
Z M P King
Jonathan Kirkwood
Wm P Boyd
John Davidson
Enoch Heard
Jas M Darnell
Washingtoon Berry
Geo H Turton
John H Baker

Benj W Luckett, who was badly wounded by Milburn Hunter, at Ardeeser's restaurant, on Friday last, died last evening at his residence, 583 G st.

N Y, Feb 21. This morning an alleged defaulter from Jacksonville, Morgan Co, Ill, named Edw L Dawson, was arrested on board the Calif steamer **New York**. The prisoner was collector & supervisor in Jacksonville, & it is alleged, that he decamped on Feb 7 with $7,000 of the public funds. About $4,000 were found in his possession. He is held to await requisition from the Illinois authorities.

N Y, Feb 21. Dr John H Boyle, formerly of Md, died yesterday at the Fifth Ave Hotel, N Y, of congestion of the lungs.

Willard P Hall, age 14 years, son of ex-Govn'r Hall, of St Jos, Mo, received a few days since a severe wound by the accidental discharge of a gun. He was on a horse, & the horse stumbled & fell, discharging the load into the boy's thigh. His condition is critical.

Edw Miller, a notorious colored thief & burglar, was shot & killed yesterday by Mr Chas T Stewart, who resides on 15th st, between K & L sts. About 3 o'clock in the morning Mr Stewart heard glass breaking & discovered a man on the porch, the upper part of his body extended through the window. Mr Stewart fired 2 shots as the burglar ran. The jury returned a verdict: shooting was justifiable.

John Essinger, a German, committed suicide, at the Pa House, 3rd & Pa ave, on Monday, by shooting himself with a pistol, the ball having entered at the mouth & come out through the skull, scattering the brains all about the bed. The deceased is a short, stout man, with black hair & moustache, aged about 40 years. He has been in the army 15 years & was but recently honorably discharged.

FRI FEB 23, 1866
Sigston & Crocker [late Fussell] Confectioners: 12th& F sts, Wash.

Nagle & Co will give their personal attention to the sale of Real Estate & Household furniture, at the residence of families declining housekeeping. Sales rooms 267 Pa ave, corner of 11th st., Wash.

Carpenters' & Bldg Depot, H W Hamilton, 292 C st, between 9th & 10th sts.

T Lubey, Commission Merchant for sale of Produce, Provisions, & Fruits. Sole agent for sale of Wm Clagett & Co's Balt Ale & Porter, 361 D, btwn 8th & 9th sts.

Brady & Co: Nat'l Photograph Gallery, 352 Pa ave, Wash, D C.
–M R Brady, Jas F Gibson

N W Burchell, corner of 14th & F sts, [under Ebbitt House,] Importer of Mediterranean Goods; Dealer in Fine Teas; Pickles & Sauces.

Md Fire Ins Co of Balt, Home ofc in their new Marble Bldg on 2nd st, Balt. Thos E Hambleton, Pres; Jos K Milnor, Sec. –Nathl Pope Causin, Agent at Wash. Ofc: No 5, first floor, Intelligencer Bldg, 7th st.

Fire Ins-Potomac Ins Co, Gtwn, D C; chartered by Congress 1831. Re-chartered 1861. Ofc: High st, 4th door north from Bridge st, Gtwn, D C. –John Marbury, Pres -J W Deeble, sec

Nat'l Union Ins Co of Wash, chartered by Congress. Ofc: 424 15th st Branch Ofc: at John H Johnson's Law Ofc, 64 La ave. Directors: Chas Knap, Pres;
G W Riggs, Vice Pres
Thos Berry
Geo S Gideon
Marshall Brown
Richd Wallach
Danl Dodd
H C Fahnestock
Wm Dixon
Noble R Larner, Sec

Lewis Johnson & Co: Bankers & Dealers in Foreign Exchange, corner of 10th & Pa ave, Wash City.

Maury & Co, Bankers, 517 7th st.

Rittenhouse, Fowler & Co, Bankers, 352 Pa ave.

Nat'l Bank of the Metropolis, U S Depositary & Loan agency: 432 15th st, Wash, D C. -J R Hutchinson, Cashier

Jay Cooke & Co, Bankers, 15th st, opposite the Treasury, Wash City.

First Nat'l Bank of Wash: 15th st. H D Cooke [of Jay Cooke & Co] Pres. Wm S Huntington, Cashier

Merchants' Nat'l Bank of Wash, 7th & D sts. L Huyck, Pres; C W Boteler, Vice Pres; C A Sherman, Cashier.

The anniversary of the birthday of Washington was celebrated yesterday by a grand demonstration at Grover's Theatre; Wm L Hodge called the assembly to order; Mr Hodge then announced the following as the ofcrs of the meeting, & the nominations were confirmed: Philip R Fendall, Pres. Vice Presidents, Wash:

R Wallach
W B Magruder
Wm A Bradley
W L Hodge
G W Riggs
Chas Knap
Wm B Todd
G H Plant
Wm Flinn
J B Blake
C Wendell
Jas Sykes
W E Spalding
John Purdy
M W Galt
John H Semmes

Jos H Bradley
P G Washington
L Huyck
J C McGuire
J W Nairn
A Green
A P Hoover
P F Bacon
Wm Jones
Wm S Mitchell
I F Clarke
J H Wheeler
W F Purcell
C W Boteler
Jas Maguire
H Addison

Peter Force
J G Berret
R C Weightman
Amos Kendall
B Ogle Tayloe
Geo Parker
Jerome Digges
J F Haliday
J D Hoover
A Provest
J F Coyle
Evan Hughes
H Polkinhorn
T E Lloyd
C Alexander
Gtwn:
Jas Dunlop
E M Linthicum
Esau Pickrell
J L Kidwell
R R Crawford
C M Matthews
Wash Co: T A McLaughlin; B T Swart
Secretaries: Wash:
John F Ennis
P W Browning
D C Lawrence
Louis Schade
S L Phillips
W J Gary
C A Sherman
S R Sylvester
C H Snow
E F Queen
W M Wallington
B B Curran
John Morris
Chas Kloman
Gtwn:
Wm D Beall
H Dodge
G Hill, jr

T A Tolson
Fitzhugh Coyle
Ward H Lamon
Wm Howard
J B Turton
B L Jackson
A E Perry
S W Owen
Saml Fowler
D R McNeir
Jas Y Davis
Wm Selden
Wm Forsyth
Chas Allen
E C Dyer

Anthony Hyde
J M Stake
Hugh Caperton
Saml Cropley
B B Williams

John E Norris
N Callan
J W Clampitt
Thos J Galt
Geo Savage
S S Parker
J W Maury
T C Clayton
C H Anderson
A T Gray
WW J Duhamel
M Marceron
John Thomas

Jenkin Thomas
J Goddard
R A Edmonston

The band played "Columbia, the Gem of the Ocean," after which Mr Philip R Fendall addressed the assembly.

S Goldstein & Co: Licensed Pawnbrokers, 34 4½ st, Wash. Business strictly private.

Letter of Gen Washington elicited considerable local interest in the Supreme Court of N Y C on Wed. It was an action brought by the Mayor & Commonalty of N Y for the recovery of an autograph letter from Geo Washington, written by him on May 2, 1785, addressed to the Mayor & Common Council of N Y. The letter purports to be an answer to an invitation tendered to Washington to come to N Y, the Mayor promising to give him the "freedom of the city." The plntfs in their complaint demanded the letter or its value, which they averred was $2,500. Two or three years ago an antiquarian, John Allan, died leaving this autograph letter & about $10,000 worth of books & papers, & valuable relics of olden time. Mrs Stewart, daughter of Allan, & excx of his estate, placed the letter with his other effects in the possession of Bangs & Merwin, to be sold at public auction. At the sale the letter was bid off at the sum of $2,050 by the dfndnt, a Mr Lent. He kept it 2 days & returned it to the auctioneers, & asked to have the contract rescinded, which request was refused. Meantime the city authorities learned of its whereabouts, & made a demand of it from the auctioneers, on the ground that it was their property, & had been wrongfully taken from their possession. The jury, after a long deliberation, rendered the following verdict:"We find for the plntfs, & assess their damages for the detention at six cents, & assess the value of the letter at $2,050.

Wanted: a small unfurnished house of 6 or 8 rooms, between 16th & 20th sts, north of Pa ave. Possession desired immediately. –Mrs Clement L West, 287 H st.

Mrd: on Feb 22, by Rev C H Hall, D D, Brvt Maj J R Edie, Ordnance Corps, U S Army, to Julia, daughter of Cmdor McCauley, U S Navy.

Died: on Feb 22, Mrs Mary Curtis, in her 60th year. Her funeral is tomorrow at 10:30 o'clock, from her late residence, 8th st, between L & M sts.

Died: Feb 21, Mr Beniah W Luckett, aged 24 years, 4 mos & 7 days. His funeral is today at 3 PM, from the residence of his brother, 583 G st, btwn 1st & 2nd.

SAT FEB 24, 1866

Richd T McLain, 2nd son of R T McLain, of north A st, was on Wed last run over & so seriously injured that he died yesterday. He had left his home after school to join the boys of Prof Wight's school, near 3rd & Indiana ave, & as car No 8, of the Metropolitan line, approached the boys, on the down grade, they made an effort to jump on the front platform, when Richd fell upon the track, the car wheel cutting the flesh entirely from the outside of the right leg, & passing over & almost severing the left, near the ankle. He was attended by Drs Todd, Johnson, Norris, Baxter, & Pancoast, & survived until Friday. Before he died he said the driver did not know that he had fallen under the car. The accident has most seriously affected his parents & friends.

Senate: 1-Ptn of Dr Evans, of Colorado, recommending strict quarantine as a preventive of the spread of cholera in this country.

Miss Mollie Stone, employed at the Gov't Printing Ofc, was engaged at one of the presses, when she dropped a roller, & in picking it up her arm was caught in one of the wheels of the press & painfully crushed. She was taken to her residence, on G st, between 1st & 2nd sts, & medical aid was summoned.

N Y, Feb 23. 1-John R Person, who murdered Walter Gregory, in Coalkill, Orange Co, last Sept, was executed at Goshen today. 2-In the case of John Cashill, for the murder of Policeman Duryea, the jury returned a verdict of guilty of murder in the 2nd degree. Judge Russell sentenced the prisoner at once to imprisonment at Sing Sing for life.

Rev M M Campbell, of Princeton College, has been called to become pastor of the First Presbyterian Church of Alexandria.

New Orleans Picayune. Isaac Edw Morse, so long in Congress, died suddenly, on Feb 11, of pneumonia, in his 57th year. He graduated at Harvard in 1829.

Died: on Feb 22, at Lower Giesboro, Wash Co, D C, of pneumonia, Arthur Dominic, aged 8 months & 16 days, infant son of J Fenwick & Nora Young. His funeral will take place at St Dominic's Church, [Island] on Feb 24 at 10 AM..

Spring Goods: S W Owen, 212 Pa ave, Wash. [Ad]

High-colored silks, for evening dresses. White alpacas, white cashmere, & white shalleys; white & 8 colored kid gloves. Dry Goods. —Wm R Riley & Bro, 36 Central Stores, between 7th & 8th sts.

MON FEB 26, 1866
Geo Wallace & Alex'r Powell, leaders of a gang of thieves who have been engaged for a long time in robbing the freight cars on the Erie railway, were arrested at Elmira on Wed last, having been detected in the commission of a robbery their. They were released from State Prison about 2 years ago, & since then have been engaged in robberies.

Orphans Court-Judge Purcell, Feb 24, 1866.
1-Thos Brown was appointed adm of the estate of Chas Williams, deceased, & qualified by giving bond in the sum of $500, with Stephen T Brown & Wm R Woodward as sureties. 2-The first & final account of Walter S Cox, adm d b n, c t a, of the estate of Clement Smith, deceased, was approved & passed. 3-The first & final account of Jos Beasly, exc of the estate of Ellen Pumphrey, deceased, was approved & passed. 4-Adelia Brothers was appointed guardian to Geo W Brown, & gave bond in the sum of $300.

Wash Corp, Feb 19, 1866. 1-Ptn of M Donnelly: referred to Cmte on Claims. 2-Ptn of H A Raw: referred to Cmte on Claims. 3-Ptn of John Purdy & others: referred to Cmte on Police. 4-Ptns of A Henderson & Frank E Middleton for remission of fines: referred to Cmte on Claims.

Chas W Delius committed suicide by shooting himself through the head, in Brooklyn, on Friday last. Disappointment in love was the cause of this rash act.

The residence of Mr D Logan, in St Louis, was entered by burglars on Tue last & robbed of $9,000 in gold & $1,200 worth of silver plate.

On Sat, as Mr Patrick Clark was driving along south B st, his horse took fright & running off, threw him & a friend from the carriage. Mr Clark had his arm broken.

Crime & Police matters. 1-The shoe store of Mr H Aue, on D st, between 6th & 7th sts, was burglariously entered on Sat & robbed of 10 pair of boots, valued in all at $110. 2-Lewis Butler & Annie Stewart were each muleted in a fine of $20.90 by Justice Handy for carrying concealed weapons. 3-Bernard Bryan, of the 6th Ward, & Thos Boland, of the 7th Ward, were fined $20 each for selling liquor in violation of the ordinances of the Corp in such cases made & provided. 4-Nicholas Taylor, colored, was arrested by Ofcr Crump for stealing lumber, the property of Mr Dennis. He was committed to jail. 5-Wm Smith, having a warlike turn in mind, by force of arms took possession of a valuable revolver belong to Hugo Kandler. He was arrested & committed to jail for court.

Loudoun land & valuable Mill-seat for sale: by decree of the Circuit Court of Loudoun Co, Va, rendered on Oct 22, 1860, in the case of Israel Warner & others, plntfs, against Geo Kephart & others, dfndnts, & by the consent of the said Geo Kephart, given in writing: sale of the land & Mill-seat containing 51 acres. This is the tract on which the *Elizabeth Mills*, now burned down, formerly stood, on Goose Creek. The Cotton Farm containing about 843 acres; the improvements are comfortable. Dwlg-house, new Switzer barn, corn house, dairy, smoke-house, & carriage house. Also, a tract of land on the east side of Goose Creek, containing 42 acres, 3 roods & 29 perches. Mr Dove, residing on the tract of 843 acres, or Geo Kephard, at Belmont, adjoining the land offered for sale, will show the same. –Chas B Tebbs, Matthew Harrison, John Janney, Com'rs
-John L Rinker, aucts

Died: on Feb 24, of croup, at the residence of her parents, in PG Co, Md, Hattie Boardman, aged 5 years & 8 months, eldest daughter of Robt S & Alice A Widdicombe. Her funeral is on Feb 26 at 1 o'clock, from the residence of her grand-parents, 352 G st.

Pianos, Melodeons, & Organs, restored equal to new, at Geo L Wild & Bro's, Pianoforte Manufactory, 497 11th st, near north side of Pa ave, Wash.

Cincinnati, Feb 24. The steamer **Hillman** collided with the steamer **Nannie Byers** this morning, near Madison, Ind, sinking the latter almost immediately. Thirty lives are reported lost. Second despatch: some say 25 & others report between 60 & 70 were lost. The collision occured while every one was asleep. The **Hillman** picked up about 30 persons & brought them to Cincinnati.

Criminal Court, on Sat, the jury in the case of the U S against Barthold J Dresser, Wm Rabe & Herman Grossman, charged with conspiracy to defraud the U S, returned a verdict of guilty as to all of the accused, but recommended Dresser to the mercy of the court. [Feb 28th newspaper: Dresser, Rabe, & Grossman were yesterday, sentenced to imprisonment in the common jail, the first for 1 yr, & the others for 2 yrs.]

On Thu last a large portrait of Gen Scott was presented to Lt Gen Grant at the Union League Rooms in N Y, as an expression of the admiration which we have always entertained of your character & career. We remain, yours devotedly, Hamilton Fish, C E Detmold, Leonard W Jerome, Effingham H Nichols, Chas B Collins, R Bayard, C Butler, H G Stebbins, Richd Butler, H C Smith, Peter Cooper, Henry A Smythe, Horace B Clafflin, Moses H Grinnell, Willis Gaylord, Henry Clews, Edwin Hoyt, Jas Wadsworth, Geo Opdyke, Wm E Dodge, Marshall O Roberts, E S Sanford, Simeon Draper, Ben Holladay, Geo Griswold, E A Quintard, Wilson G Hunt, R D Lathrop, John H Hall, J Butler Wright.
+
Gentlemen: The notice of your intention to present me with Page's portrait of Lt Gen Winfield Scott was duly received. –U S Grant, Lt Gen, U S A

Died: on Feb 25, Mrs Eliz Jewell, relict of the late Wm Jewell, in her 78th year. Her funeral is on Feb 27 at 11 o'clock, from her late residence, Gay & High sts, Gtwn.

Died: on Feb 23, in her 64th year, Mrs Margaret D P Wise, widow of the late Tully R Wise, sister of Henry A Wise, sr, & the mother of 7 sons, who survive to mourn her loss.

Household & kitchen furniture at auction on Mar 1, at the late residence of Saml Harkness, deceased, No 7, north K, between 8th & 9th sts.
–Green & Williams, aucts

Trustee's sale of valuable property fronting on Mass ave running through to north I st, between 4th & 5th sts, by decree of the Supreme Court of D C, in a cause wherein O'Brien & others are cmplnts, & Fortune & others are dfndnts: sale on Mar 14 next, of the east 18 feet of lot 12 in square south of square 516, with a good 2 story frame dwlg & other out-bldgs. –John F Ennis, trustee
-Green & Williams, aucts

TUE FEB 27, 1866
On Sat, in Balt, Mr Henry Hanna, sr, his son Henry, & his wife & infant, & 2 sisters of Mrs Hanna, Anna & Lina Highland, aged 18 & 10 years, met with an untimely death in a house on Fayette & Ann sts. The house was owned by a German, John Bohnner, who, with his wife, occupied a portion of the bldg, the remainder being occupied by the persons above mentioned. Mr Henry Hanna, jr, was the foreman of the pyrotechnic manufactory of Mr John W Bond. Mr Hanna made a fire in the cooking-stove, & laid down by the stove & went to sleep. He awoke with a sensation of suffocation. He at once knew the house was on fire, & knowing the danger of a box nearby containing the combustible materials of which fire-works are made, he seized it with the intention of throwing it out of the window; before reaching it, he fell from exhaustion, & the contents of the box exploded. Messrs Geo W Deal & Wm Tudor, who were passing by, seeing the flames, went to the house & woke up Bohnner. Mr Hanna, horribly burned, expired on Sunday. The two girls & Mrs Hanna were but little burned, but bore evidence of having been suffocated. Verdict of the jury: we believe John Bohnner & wife ought to be held amenable for the death of the parties, on account of negligence & refusal in saving the lives of the deceased. John Bohnner, who is a German, scarcely able to speak English, & his wife, were taken into custody by order of the Coroner, & held in their own recognizances to appear before the grand jury. Mr Bohnner thought that when he was approached by the parties telling him about smoke, he thought they wanted to rob him, & paid no attention to their information. The bodies of the 6 unfortunate victims were on Sunday placed in a vault at the *Loudoun Park Cemetery*.

Obit-died: on Feb 25, in Bedford Co, Va, his native state, Harvey Michel, about 68 years of age, late draughtsman in the Gen Land Ofc in Wash City, but better known in the Southern States as an artist, & in Boston, in the art & literary circles of the past generation, as the gifted but eccentric pupil & friend of Washington Allston. He was truly a Christian gentleman. No cleaner soul ever went to its God.

Died: on Feb 24, Miss Lydia S English, in her 64th year. Her funeral is this afternoon at 4 o'clock, from her late residence, corner of Washington & Gay sts, Gtwn, D C.

Burning of the steamboat **Winchester**, near East Liverpool, Ohio, on Friday, ignited by a spark or cinder from the furnace. Those known to be lost are Michl Fragrett, of Sewickley, Pa; Jas Aldeo & wife, & Mrs A M Sheets, all of Matamoras, Ohio; John Vanmeter, & 4 children, of Woodland, W Va; Geo Young, of Rochester, Pa, a barkeeper on the boat; Ebenezer Martin, of Sistersville, brother-in-law of Col Johnson, of the House of Delegates of W Va; & a man named Walters, with one child, were burned. The **Winchester** was a new boat, valued at $80,000, & was on her first trip, many of the passengers having been invited by the owners to accompany her on this occasion.

Some weeks ago Hattie Bell, a white woman of notoriously bad character, who resided on D st, between 13th & 13½ sts, placed her son, a child between 6 & 7 years of age, in charge of a colored woman residing in Wash alley. The child became sick with small-pox, & for want of proper attention, died, & the parties in charge being unable to bury him, the corpse remained in the alley until Sunday, when the police procured an order for its burial.

Wash Corp, Feb 26, 1866. 1-Ptn of Wm Sauntry for the remission of a fine: referred to the Cmte on Claims. 2-Ptn of Patrick McHugh & others for a gravelled sidewalk on the south side of K st south: referred to the Cmte on Improvements. 3-Ptn of J R Zimmerman & others: referred to the Cmte on Improvements. 4-Cmte on Claims: adverse report on the ptn of J A Rau for the remission of a fine. Favorable upon a bill for the relief of M Donnelly: passed.

WED FEB 28, 1866
Orphans Court-Judge Purcell, Feb 27, 1866.
1-John D McPherson qualified as adm of the personal estate of Robt B Carter, late of Norfolk, Va, deceased, & gave bond in the sum of $4,000, with Christopher T Brown & Jas M Carlisle as sureties.
2-Jerome C Berry, of Howard Co, Md, qualified as adm of the estate of Tramel H Cloud, deceased, by giving bond in the sum of $300, with Francis Mohun & Francis B Mohun as sureties.
3-Margaret J West was appointed admx of the estate of Arthur J West, deceased, & gave bond in the sum of $600, with John I Turner & Mary Ann Turner as sureties.

John O Butler was convicted on Monday in the Criminal Court of larceny & burglary, & sentenced to an imprisonment of 6 years in the Albany Penitentiary.

Sale of the <u>Wm Tell Hotel</u>, by a writ of distraint: public auction on Mar 2 next, the furniture, fixtures, license & good will of the hotel with the bar & fixtures. Located on Pa ave, between 4½ & 6th sts. The Hotel has always done an excellent business. -C W E Oye, Bailliff, for John P Pepper. –Nagle & Co, aucts

Louisville, Feb 27. A writ of habeas corpus was issued today by Judge Ballard for the bodies of Capt Reed & Lemmon, who were lately fined & committed to jail in Campbell Co, for protecting the polls at the last election. The cases are important, & will present the whole subject of the powers of the military where the national law prevails.

Boston, Feb 27. Ed S Owing, cashier in the Boston post ofc for nearly 36 years, & much esteemed in Boston, died yesterday, aged 71 years.

Mrd: on Feb 24, at Norfolk, Va, by Dr Leroy M Lee, Col Franklin A Stratton, of Mass, to Mrs Geo Griffith, of Norfolk.

Supreme Court, D C, in Equity, No 1,822. Francis Wheatley against Jas A Johnson, Mary & Anthony Wagoner, Mary A McCarthy, & Allen Burch. The parties above & the creditors of the late Mildred Johnston are to attend at my room, City Hall, Wash, on Mar 20th next, for distribution of the fund.
–W Redin, auditor

Dissolution of the copartnership under the firm of Chapin & Matlock, this day by mutual consent. The business will be continued by J G Matlock.
–R M Chapin, J G Matlock, Wash, Feb 26, 1866

THU MAR 1, 1866
Maggie Mitchell's house in N Y was robbed last week, & a large quantity of silver-ware was taken, including the vase presented to her at the close of her last engagement here.

Dept of State, Wash, Feb 24, 186. Information has been received from Mr Wm W Murphy, the Consul Gen of the U S at Frankfort-on-the Main, of the death in Jan, in the Duchy of Nassau, of Mr Senec, or Senac, or Senack, a native of Florida. The legal reps of the deceased can obtain futher information by addressing this Dept.

Equity Court-Judge Wylle, Feb 27, 1856. 1-Sarah McIntosh et al vs Ann C McIntosh et al. The bill shows the parties to the suit to be the heirs at law of Thos McIntosh, who died intestate & possessed of certain real estate described in the bill, & that the same cannot be divided without loss to the parties interested, & Jas Lynch, Thos Scrivener, John Dudley, Ammon Green, & Florian Hitz were appointed com'rs to sell the estate in order that the proceeds may be distributed according to the respective rights of the parties. -M Thompson solicitor for cmplnts. 2-Gwynn Harris et al vs Mary A Jones. The bill in this cause shows that the parties are heirs at law of Peter Jones, deceased, & that he died intestate, seized, etc, of the real estate described in the bill, & that the same cannot be divided consistently with equality, etc; & that the Court appointed Chas Wilson, Lewis Thomas, Thos W Riley, John A Stephenson, & David McQueen com'rs to sell the estate & to divide the proceeds between the parties.
-M Thompson solicitor for cmplnts.

Senate: 1-Bill to incorporate the Pharmaceutical Association of D C: referred to the District Cmte. The incorporators named are Valentine Harbaugh, John L Kidwell, Jos W Nairn, Francis S Walsh, John A Milburn, Jos B Moore, Jas N Callan, & Saml E Tyson.

Judge Underwood asked to resign. The resolutions reported by the joint cmte appointed by the Gen Assembly of Va, requesting him to resign his position as Senator from Va in the U S Senate, have been adopted by the House of Delegates: Yeas 42; Nays 1.

Died: on Jan 2 last, at **Haw Hill**, in King Geo Co, Va, Benj Hales, in his 53rd year. For more than 30 years a member & communicant of the Baptist Church, the deceased, by his life, ever illustrated the virtues & graces which adorn the Christian character.

Died: on Feb 29, in her 63rd year, Mrs Mary Mattingly, wife of Geo Mattingly, of Wash City. An exemplary wife, a devoted mother, & an affectionate friend. Her memory will long be cherished by her children & grandchildren. She died in the full exercise of her faculties, & with all the consolations of religion. Her funeral is on Sat at 10 o'clock, from St Dominick's Church, when a Grand Requeim Mass will be celebrated.

Mr C W Boteler, auct, has sold part of lots 1, 18, 19, & 20, in square 165, at $1.86 & $1.41 per square foot. Hon Hugh McCulloch was the purchaser.

Wm S Teel, Merchant Tailor, 358 Pa ave, under Metropolitan Hotel. [Ad]

Geo W Smythe, one of the ablest statesmen of Texas, is dead. His funeral was attended by all members of the Texas State Convention, in session in Galveston, to which he was a delegate. [No death date given-current item.]

Mrs Catherine Fay, an old lady residing in Rochester, N Y, was burned to death on Feb 23. She laid down on a lounge to sleep with matches in her pocket, & in moving about they ignited.

Mr Thos Swift, or Morrisania, was killed at Melrose, N Y, yesterday, by a switch-tender in the employ of Harlem railorad. Mr Swift entered the ladies saloon of the station at Melrose to wait for a train. The switch-tender, who is a powerful Irishman, followed Mr Swift, & told him to leave the saloon. Mr Swift answered that he would not go except by the direction of the station agent. On receiving this reply, the switch-tender struck Mr Swift two heavy blows on the head. One broke his nose, & Mr Swift fell to the floor, never spoke again, & died.
-N Y Post, Feb 28.

Brightwood, D C. The partnership exiting under the firm of A G Osborn & Co is this day dissolved by mutual consent. Alfred G Osborn will continue the business at the old stand, known as Brightwood Stores. –Alfred G Osborn, John M McChesner, Brightwood

Mrs Rufus F Buel will re-open her School for Young Ladies on Mar 5: 369 8th st at H. st.

FRI MAR 2, 1866
I have this day sold my entire stock of lumber to my two sons, Jos Libbey, jr, & Edw Libbey, who will hereafter carry on the business under the name of Jos & J E Libbey. Lumber Business, ofc at 27 Water st, Gtwn, D C.
–Jos Libbey, jr; J Edw Libbey

Gen Stephen Elliott, jr, of the rebel army, died in Aiken, S C, on Feb 21. He will be remembered as the brave & stubborn defender of *Fort Sumter*. He had recently accepted the appointment of agent of transportation on the Augusta branch of the S C railroad, & had taken up his residence at Aiken.

Mrs Bigelow, wife of the American Minister at Paris, is seriously ill.

Apr 13 next has been appointed for the execution of Edw__, for the murder of young Converse, assist cashier of the Malden Bank, Boston, some 2 years ago. [Apr 11th newspaper: Green will be executed at East Cambridge, Mass, jail, on Apr 13. He has no parents except for a step-mother. A Boston paper states that a new rope has been manufactored by a cordage company in that city expressly for the occasion.] [Apr 14th newspaper: Boston, Apr 13. Edw W Greene, the murderer of young Converse at the Malden Bank about 2 years ago, was executed this forenoon in the jail-yard at East Cambridge. He behaved with great calmness & composure, & died with hardly a struggle.] [Apr 27th newspaper: Autopsy held on the body of Greene revealed his brain was found perfect & of medium size; the twisting of the knot of the rope to the back of the neck alleviated, rather than increased, the agonies of death. –Boston Transcript]

Pres Johnson yesterday signed the commissions of the following ofcrs of customs:
Collector of Customs:
Wm L Adams, District of Oregon
John F Miller, San Francisco, Calif
Wm G Isbell, Detroit, Mich
Jos Lemby, Dist of Minn
Jas F Webb, Dist of Vienna, Md
John Young, Sandusky, Ohio
John W McMath, Machilemackinac, Mich
Israel S Adams, Egg Harbor, N J
Thos Wilkens, Erie, Pa
Thos E Rodney, Dist of Delaware
John L Boggs, Perth Amboy, N J
David M Chapin, Oswegatchie, N Y
Jarvish L Bartlett, Little Egg Harbor, N J
Chas D Norton, Buffalo Creek, N Y
Franklin Spalding, Niagara, N Y
Thos Loring, Plymouth, Mass
Geo M Abell, Dunkirk, N Y
W S Havens, Sag Harbor, N Y

John M Ingalls, Cape Vincent, N Y
Lawrence Grinnell, New Bedford, Mass
Enoch G Carrier, Newburyport, Mass
Wm Standley, Marblehead, Mass
Jas Brady, jr, Fall River, Mass
Alfred Macy, Nantucket, Mass
John Vinson, Edgartown, Mass
Silas C Booth, Fairfield, Conn
Edw Prentis, New London, Conn
Seth W Masy, Newport, R I
Chas Anthony, Providence, R I
Origen Utley, Middletown, Conn
Erastus Foote, Wiscasset, Maine
Seth K Devereaux, Penobscot, Maine
Wm Clapp, Dist of Vt
Jeremiah S Putnam, York, Maine
Owen B Chadbourne, Saco, Maine
Wshington Long, Passmaquoddy, Maine
Wm P Wingate, Bangor, Maine
Truman Harmon, Belfast, Maine
Wm H Cresswell, Genessee, N Y
Luther Haven, Chicago, Ill
Hannibal Hamlin, Boston & Charlestown, Mass

Surveyors of Customs:
Thos Hornbrook, at Wheeling W Va
Clark Denham, Burlington, Iowa
John B Henton, Dubuque, Iowa
Danl Arter, Cairo, Ill
Adin B Underwood, Boston, Mass
Wm C Mumford, Snow Hill, Md
Chas W Bachelor, Pittsburgh, Pa
Reuben Daniels, Ipswich, Mass
Chas J Talbott, Portland, Maine

Naval Ofcrs:
Noah Brooks, at San Francisco, Calif; Danl W Booch, Boston, Mass;
Geo J L Colby, Newburyport, Mass;
Wm M Reese, Balt, Md; Thos B Bush, Newport, R I

The residence of Hon Reverdy Johnson, on Vt ave, was burglariously entered yesterday by 2 negro burglars. Their operations were overheard by the family, & one of the burglars was seized by Mr Johnson, who could not hold him, but had sufficient time to recognize the man as one formerly in his employ, named Wm Davis. Ofcr Britt & Markwood arrested him, & he is held for a hearing.

The friends & acquaintances of Mr Geo Messer are invited to attend the funeral of his deceased wife, Hannah Patterson, at the Presbyterian Church on 7th st, Island, on Mar 2nd at 2 o'clock P M.

Wash City Ordinance: 1-Joint resolution for the relief of J A W Clarvoe: permission to open 7th st west, between E & F sts south, for the purpose of introducing gas into his house; any act of the Corp to the contrary notwithstanding. Approved: Feb 24, 1866.

Reese Nesbit, alias Matt Doyle, a colored thief, was released from the Albany penitentiary about 2 weeks ago, after having served 2 years there. While passing through N Y C on his way to Washington, he robbed Jas Monroe of $225 & a suit of clothing. He is held in custody until the arrival of Detective Coyle of N Y.

Died: on Jan 4, at St Augustine, Fla, Chas K Sherman, of Wash City, [late an ofcr of the Confederate army,] aged 33 years. He leaves a wife & children & a large circle of relatives & friends to lament his early death. He was born in the State of Florida, & it was his desire that he should exchange time for eternity in the land of his birth. Richmond & Mobile papers please copy.

Died: on Mar 1, in her 81st year, Mrs Isabella Cridier/Cridler, formerly of Leesburg, Va. Her funeral will take place from the residence of her son-on-law, Thos Rich, 467 9th st, on Sat, at 11 o'clock. [*Ink spot on part of name.]

House of Reps: 1-Bill incorporating the Nat'l Safe Depository Co of the City of Wash: incorporators are A R Shepherd, Wm W Huntington, S P Brown, G W Riggs, Nathan Wilson, & G H Plant: capital stock is $200,000. Referred to the Cmte on the District of Columbia. 2-Bill to incorporate the Nat'l Capital Ins Co, the incorporators being Erastus Poulson, Green Adams, Robt Leech, F M Blair, John B Clarke, jr, J J Combs, G H Chandler, P M Moriarty, & J P Reynor. Referred to the Cmte on the District of Columbia.

SAT MAR 3, 1866
We, who have known Col Wm A Browning from boyhood, feel deeply poignant grief on hearing of his early decease. Besides the soothing administrations of mother & father, & other dear relatives during his sickness, the frequent attendance of the Pres at his bedside served to lighten those sorrow that are the inseparable concimitants of human life.
+
Died: on Feb 2, Col Wm A Browning, the oldest son of P W & Margaret A Browning, in his 31st year. His funeral will be next Sunday afternoon at 3 o'clock, from the residence of his father, 52 Missouri ave. Nashville & Memphis papers please copy.

Reward for lost black Scotch Terrier Pup. Return to C Ingle, 143 Wash st, Gtwn.

Died: on Mar 2, after a short but painful illness, Mary A Daly, aged 42 years, beloved wife of Jas Daly, leaving an affectionate husband & 8 children to mourn her loss. Her funeral will be from her late residence, Vt ave & L st, Mar 4, 2 PM.

Died: on Mar 2, at his residence in Montg Co, Md, Wm Edw Stubbs, formerly of Wash, in his 42nd year. His funeral will take place on Mar 4, at Carroll Chapel, 7 miles out the 7th st road, at 3 o'clock P M.

Died: on Mar 2, at the residence of her sister, Mrs Henreitta A Ely, in Fairfax Co, Va, Ann Foote, wife of Richd W Wallace, of Wash City, & daughter of the late Col Gerrard Alexander, of Campbell Co, Va. Lynchburg, Va, & Louisville, Ky, papers please copy.

MON MAR 5, 1866
Orphans Court-Judge Purcell, Mar 3, 1866.
1-The appraisement of the annual value of the real estate of the orphans of Henry & Eliz Jane Filson, deceased, was returned by the guardian, Harriet A Lee, & the inventory of the personal estate of the above was returned by the administrator.
2-The following appointments were made, viz: Augusta Brown, excx of the estate of Jane Raymond, deceased. Bond, $1,000. Sureties: Peter Parker & Z C Robbins.
3-John B Adams, guardian to the orphans of John Wills, deceased. Bond, $1,400. Sureties,
Alex T Gray & Geo Cottingham.
4-Joshua A Ritchie, adm of the estate of Artemesia Carberry, deceased. Bond, $150. Sureties, E A Eliason & Washington L Baldwin.
5-Caroline W Bradley True, admx c t a, of the estate of Chas Coleman, deceased. Bond, $200. Sureties, M Thompson & Wm P Partello.
6-John P Hurley, adm of the estate of Jeremiah Hurley, deceased. Bond, $500. Sureties, Wm Johnson & Cecelia V Hurley.
7-Laura V C Whiton, admx of the estate of Albert G Whiton, deceased, was directed to increase her administration bond in the sum of $10,000.
8-The following accounts were approved & passed, viz:
2nd account of Helen Weaver, [now Chapin,] guardian to orphan of Danl Weaver, deceased.
1st & final account of Abraham F Kimmell, adm of estate of Eliz Foulkes, deceased.
1st & final account of Abraham F Kimmell, adm d b n of estate of John E Foulkes, deceased.
1st account of Mary W Spignul, guardian to the orphans of Wm B Spignul, deceased.
Account of Mary W Spignul, admx of the personal estate of Wm B Spignul, deceased.

Providence, R I, Mar 4. Rev Dr E B Hall, for 43 years pastor of the first Congregational Unitarian Church in this city, died suddenly Sat aged 65 years.

Savannah, Ga, Mar 3. J W Duncan, late an ofcr of the Commissary Dept at Andersonville, was arraigned before a military commission yesterday, charged with murder, robbery, & cruel treatment of Union prisoners. Several of the former prisoners at Andersonville, who were witnesses in the Witz case, have already arrived.

Funeral of Col W A Browning. The Pres, accompanied by Deputy Marshal O'Beirne, Judge Patterson, Mrs Patterson, & Mrs Stover, nearly all the members of the Wash bar, a number of members of Congress, & a very large concourse of citizens, were present during the solemn ceremonies. Rev A Rolte of the Episcopal Church officiated. Pall bearers: Col W Rives, Col W Moore, & Majors Long & Morrow, of the Pres' household; Dr Thos Young, E Welles, [Sec Welles' son;] Dr Duhamel, & Jos H Bradley, jr.

Military prisoners. After 65 days' confinement in the military prison, five of the citizens of this city, A D Warfield, John Mitchell, Geo Huntington, J L Hick, & H E Smith, of the 11 who were arrested on Christmas for alleged participation in the distrubances which occurred here on that day were released yesterday evening. Messrs Horseman, Travis, Simpson, John & Oscar Mankin, & Lawler are still in prison. –Alexandria Gaz

Died: on Mar 3, in Gtwn, Frank Marie, infant son of Mr Deles & Eleanor Clements.

Died: on May 4, J H Clay Mudd, in his 45th year. His funeral is on Mar 6 at 10 o'clock A M, at the residence of his sister, Mrs Thompson, 616 Md ave, Island.

Mr McGuire & Co sold a small frame house & lot on south P st, near **Greenleaf Point**, to John V Kehl, for $855. Frame house & lot on 9th st, between L & M sts, to Geo Turnburke, for $1,600.

Obit-died: on Feb 16, in Winchester, Va, at the residence of his mother, Mrs Col Tuley, Westel Willoughby Jackson, son of the late Dr Jackson, U S Army. In his last painful illness, his sufferings were soothed & alleviated by that peace of the soul which the world can neither give nor take away.

Pauline T Barnum, the youngest daughter of P T Barnum, was married at Bridgeport, Conn, on Thu last, to Mr Nathan Seeley, of the firm of Seeley & Stevens, N Y.

The Pres has nominated Gen Asboth as Minister to Venezuela.

Rev Lawrence P Hickok, D C, was on Thu elected president of Union College. Dr Hickok has acted as vice president of the college since 1849. During the late years of Dr Nott's life he acted as acting president.

Dr Isaiah P Lynn, a well known physician of Chicago, died on Wed last, from the effects of 9 grains of morphine. He had been visiting his patients as usual, & on reaching his ofc in the evening took 5 grains of morphine, to ease pains from which he was suffering. Finding no relief, he took 4 grains more, when he relapsed & could not be restored.

Orphans Court of Wash Co, D C. Letters of administration on the personal estate of Jeremiah Hurley, late of Wash, D C, deceased. –John T Hurley

TUE MAR 6, 1866
Jas Dillon, a hack driver, was seriously injured yesterday by his horses running off near 4th st & Indiana ave & throwing him from his seat.

Murder in Montg Co, Md. Mr Wm Pierce, a farmer residing 8 miles north of Wash City, was brutally murdered, as was supposed, by robber. He was found lying upon the floor of his house with his skull crushed in. He was yet alive when found, but all efforts to save him were unavailing. He expired in a very short time. Plunder was no doubt the object of the assassins, as the deceased was known to have money. He was highly esteemed in Wash City.

Mr John Henry Clay Mudd breathed his last on Mar 4, at his sister's residence, [Mrs Thompson's,] on Md ave, Island, in his 45th year of his age. He died of consumption, under which he had been suffering many months. His last moments were cheered by the tender attentions of his affectionate sister, & by the warm solicitude of Rev Fr Bogle, of the Catholic Church.

Died: on Mar 2, at the residence of Rt Rev Bishop Whipple, Faribault, Minn, Wm Wilkins Davis, in his 24th year, only son of Allen Bowie Davis, of Montg Co, Md.

N Y, Mar 5. Gen Scott was somewhat injured, though not seriously, by falling from his berth on his recent trip from Key West to New Orleans. He recovered slowly & attended church on Feb 25, though still feeble.

Notice. Francis Fred'k Viale, alias Pennington, formerly of the Island of Corsica, France, who married Mary C J Ellmyer, of Gtwn, D C, is notified to answer, by counsel or in person, to a claim of said Mary C J Ellmyer, within 3 months from this date. –Chris C Callan, Atty, Gtwn, D C

Phil, Mar 5. Dr David Jayne died this afternoon, in his 67th year of his age.

Notice. The undersigned, in continuing the Coal & Wood Business of the late Edw H Fuller, informs the Public that she has on hand a quantity of Superior Coal, which will be sold at reduced rates, at the Yard, 14th & K sts.
–Mrs Emily Fuller

For sale: one of the most desirable Farms in Md, **Marshall Hall**, containing 377 acres, with a large brick dwlg-house, barn, & stables. Apply to J M Hanson & Co, Real Estate Brokers, 64 La ave, Bank of Wash Bldg.

Giesboro Point for sale; known as **Great Cavalry Depot of the U S**; sits upon the banks of the Potomac; contains 625 acres in the tract, with a river front of 1½ miles. Inquire at 435 6th st, between E & F sts. –Geo Washington Young

Sale: 2 bldg lots, by decree of the Supreme Court of this District, passed in the cause of Frederica Roemmele & others against Jos Roemmele & others: auction of lot 16 in square 126, now divided into 2 parcels, each fronting 20 feet on 18th st, between I & K sts. –Andrew Noerr, John A Rheem, Geo A Lane, Wm J Williams, John Keiler, Com'rs -Jas C McGuire & Co, aucts

WED MAR 7, 1866
Col T S Bowers, of Lt Gen Grant's staff, was instantly killed yesterday at a station called Garrison's, opposite West Point, N Y, on the railroad, by being crushed between 2 cars while in the act of mounting the train.

Mrd: on Mar 6, at Alexandria, Va, at the resident of the bride's father, J N Harper, by Rev Fr Robt K Andrews, of Richmond, Albert T Skinner, of N Y, to Miss Mary L Harper, of Alexandria. No cards.

Orphans Court-Judge Purcell, Mar 6, 1866.
1-The will of Miss Lydia S English, deceased, was filed. The bulk of the property is bequeathed to Dr Chas G English, of Tallahassee, Fla, the brother of the testatrix, & her sister, Mrs Eliz A B Henderson, of Jefferson Co,
W Va. Mrs Sarah S Dougherty is named as executrix.
2-John H Goddard qualified as adm of the estate of Marshall Dowling, deceased. Bond, $600. Sureties, Valentine Harbaugh & Theodore Sheckels.
3-Washington L Baldwin qualified as adm of the estate of Ludem Bailey, deceased. Bond, $150. Sureties, Joshua Pierce & Pierce Shoemaker.
4-Laura V T Whiton gave an additional bond in the sum of $10,000 as admx of the estate of Albert G Whiton, deceased, with Geo R Barnard as surety.
5-John D Buckley qualified as adm of the estate of Mary D Buckley, deceased. Bond, $1,200. Sureties, John J Sullivan & Mark McIntee.
6-Robt J Campbell qualified as adm of the estate of John Foster, deceased. Bond, $3,000. Sureties, Jas Moffit & Albert W Jackson.
7-The first & final account of Thompson Ragan, adm of the estate of Danl Ragan, deceased, was approved & passed as was also the account of the personal estate of said deceased.

Died: on Mar 6, after a brief but painful illness, Myra Rosalie, 2nd daughter of Edw A & Sarah N Gallaher, & grand-daughter of John S Gallaher & Isaac N Carter, aged 4 years, 11 months & 1 day. Her funeral will take place from St Dominick's Church, at 3:30 o'clock P M, today, Wednesday.

Supreme Court of D C, in Equity, No 1,229. Fitzhugh & Smith vs Wm Bell, exc, & others. Ordered that the report of a sale, this day filed by the trustee in the above cause, be ratified & confirmed. –R J Meigs, clerk [No details given.]

Yesterday at the residence of Mr Clark, 437 10th st, a little girl, daughter of Mr Clark, was burned so badly that death ensued in a short time after the accident. Mr Geo R Herrick, property clerk of the Metropolitan Police force, was passing down 10th st on his way to his ofc, when he heard screams issuing from Mr Clark's residence. With another gentleman, he entered the house & in the far corner of a room he saw a little girl about 3 years old enveloped in flames. Seizing some garments at hand, Mr Herrick enveloped the child in them & soon extinguished the fire, but the little sufferer expired within a few hours. Mr Herrick had his hands badly burned in his efforts. The mother of the child was necessarily absent at the time of the accident. A sister, but just a little older, can give no account of the distressing occurrence. It is supposed she went too near the stove.

Madame Murat, of Tallahassee, Fla, widow of the late Col Archie Murat, & first cousin to the Emperor of France, has received as a gift from Louis Napoleon of a life annuity of 50,000 francs, in consideration of her losses by the results of the war.

Chancery sale of valuable property, by decree of the Supreme Court of D C, passed in the cause of Ball & others against Dyer & others: public auction on Mar 28, of lot 13 in square 564, & lot E, of Ball's Subdivision of Dyer's Subdivision of lots in said squares. Lot 13 is on 3rd st west; lot E fronts on G st north.
–Robt Ball, trustee -Green & Williams, aucts

Edw Newmeister & E H Johnson, two of the 5 thieves who robbed the U S express messenger at St Louis 2 weeks ago, have been arrested, & $19,214 recovered. The remainder of the $40,000 stolen is supposed to be in the possession of the other 3 robbers, who are still at large.

Bishop Alex'r Campbell, generally known as the founder of the Disciple denomination of Christians, & eminent as a theologian, died at his residence at Bethany, near Wheeling, Va, on Sunday, in his 78th year. [Mar 26th newspaper: Alex'r Campbell died in his 80th year; for month past he had been in failing health. He was born in the county of Antrim, Ireland, in 1786; educated, as was his father before him, at the Univ of Glasgow, Scotland, both of them as Presbyterian clergymen. Thos Campbell, the poet, was a relative & classmate of his father; on the one side is ancestry was of Scotch origin, & on the other Huguenot French. He immigated to this country in 1809, two years after his father, bringing with him his mother & younger brothers & sisters, & settled at first in Wash Co, Pa, on which spot he has lived continually. That spot, now the village of Bethany, was then a wild & secluded locality.

N Y, Mar 6. Gen Grant ordered the remains of Col Bowers to be taken to West Point under the charge of Major Hill.

THU MAR 8, 1866
Regular monthly meeting of the Association of Oldest Inhabitants was held yesterday in City Hall; B Ogle Tayloe presided, J C Brent was sec pro tem. Present: Col J S Williams; Mr Carusi; Dr Blake. The following gentlemen were proposed & elected members, viz: Peter F Bacon, Robt Widdecombe-born in England in 1799,came to Wash in 1825, Edw M Drew, Martin King, Robt Beall, Wm H Prentiss-born Oct 12, 1796; John M Young, Henry Ould, Thos Young, Wm Kumles-born in Mass in 1787, came to Wash in 1802, & Jas H Birch-came to Wash in 1804. At the next meeting Jas Clephane will give his reminiscences of Wash City. The association then adjourned.

C W Boteler, auct, sold lot 12 in square 54 on 22nd st, between Pa ave & I st, to Mr Franklin Etchison for $1,750. The lot is improved by a small frame house.

Col S W Owen, military & naval merchant tailor, 212 Pa ave, between 14th & 15th sts, Wash City. [Ad]

Concert of the Female Intermediate School for the Third District last night. Solos by M Williss, S Thompson, M Castel, Isabel Kelser, Sallie Thomson, Josephine Easton, Annie Taltavull, Lillie Evans, Mary Langley, Mary Sanderson, Master Geo Mantz. Marion Wetherell, Sallie Locke, Annie Young, & Jeannette Russell & Master Frank Dixon-duet

<u>Ladies comprising the local board of the Nat'l Soldiers' & Sailors' Orphan Home:</u>

Mrs Lt Gen Grant	Mrs Atty Gen Speed
Mrs Gen Sherman	Mrs Wm B Todd
Mrs Gen Williams	Mrs John C Smith
Mrs Henry D Cooke	Mrs Capt C V Morris
Mrs H C Fahnestock	Mrs David A Hall
Mrs J C Carlisle	Mrs Robt Farnham
Mrs Charlotte Taylor	Mrs J C Lewis
Mrs Secretary Harlan	Mrs Sarah Wood
Mrs Senator Patterson	Miss L Howard
Mrs Secretary Welles	

Gen Howard & Hon John Sherman addressed the meeting.

Mrd: on Feb 22, at Faribault, Minn, by Rt Rev Bishop Whipple, Wm Wilkins Davis to Nellie W, daughter of Bishop Whipple.
+
Died: on Mar 2, at the residence Rt Rev Bishop Whipple, Faribault, Minn, Wm Wilkins Davis, in his 24th year, only son of Allen Bowie Davis, of Montg Co, Md.

Large stock of tobacco & cigars: Mr Jas Tharp, 509 7th st. [Ad]

FRI MAR 9, 1866
Mrs Rosa Fitzgerald, the wife of Capt Fitzgerald, of Wash City, has written, for the N Y Ledger, a delightful story just commenced in that paper, & which we advise you to read. Robt Conway, a soldier of Hancock's corps, was robbed in the Smithsonian grounds yesterday of $24. He was very intoxicated & 2 boys, Chas Fanning & Wm Simms, noticed that he was being followed by notorious thieves. Conway was choked by the thieves & robbed of his money. Mr John T Lacey, a lumber dealer at 12th st & the canal, saw the transaction & told Ofcrs Sneed & Walker, who overtook the thieves. The parties secured are John Lambert & Martin Welsh, 20 & 27, both well known to the police. Sgt Skippon later arrested Bernard Adamson, the third robber. [Mar 10th newspaper: Lambert & Welsh were committed to jail for court. Adamson was dismissed.]

Mrs Mary Callahan was arrested yesterday by Ofc Brosnan for attempting to set fire to her house on North Capitol st. Being drunk & crazy she was sent to the work-house.

Supreme Court of D C, in Equity. Isaac Talks et al vs Isaac S Hollidge. Ordered that the sale reported by Wm Kilgour, trustee, be ratified & confirmed. –R J Meigs, clerk

Louisville, Mar 8. Gen Palmer has commuted the death of 17 guerillas, including Jas Harvey Wells, alias Wm Henry, & Saml Q Berry, to 10 years at Albany, subject to the approval of the President.

Boston, Mar 6. The schnr **West Wind**, of Portland, Capt Harrington, sunk off Chatham, Cape Cod, today. Crew saved & went on board the schnr **Emeline**, G Sawyer.

Gov Vance, of N C is at his home, stricken with paralysis on one side, & with poor hopes of recovery.

SAT MAR 10, 1866
Pianoforte & household & kitchen furniture at auction on Mar 13, at the residence of Mr H Miller, 512 M st, between 9th & 10th sts. –Green & Williams, aucts

Criminal Court, D C-Judge Fisher, Mar 9, 1866: Hon E C Carrington, Dist Atty, prosecuting. 1-Richd Rivers, who was convicted on Wed of stealing a coat from John Holloran, was sentenced to 10 weeks in the county jail. 2-U S vs Richd Rivers: larceny; verdict not guilty. 3-U S vs Henry O Wright, indicted for passing counterfeit money, the District Atty entered a nolle pros. 4-U S vs Jane Williams: larceny, guilty of stealing 2 shirts of the value of $2 & one pair of corsets of the value of $2: sentenced to one week in the county jail. 5-U S vs Jas Nagle, alias Jas Bouch; larceny; convicted on Wed. Mr Gooding made a motion for a new trial; trial granted. The Dist Atty entered a nolle pros.

The wife of Gen Eli Long, whose trunk rolled off the boiler deck of a Louisville steamer during the careening caused by a sudden gale, has recovered, in the Supreme Court of Cincinnati, $1,380.60 for its loss, being a little over half the amount for which suit was brought.

Boston, Mar 9. Chas Anson Dodge has been arrested for the murder of the Joyce children. He confesses the crime. He is a native of Mass, but served in the rebel army, & was captured during Morgan's raid. He then enlisted in the Federal army, & again deserted & joined the Federal navy.

Alfred J Fitzpatrick was last night sent to jail for court by Superintendent Richards to answer the charge of robbing Mr J Herzberg some weeks ago. Mr Herzberg was violently assaulted during the robbery. Fitzpatrick admitted he was the depredator.

Mrd: on Mar 8, at Gerardstown, Berkeley Co, West Va, by Rev D M Hair, John L Underwood, of Cambridge City, Indiana, to Miss Bettie S Hair, of the former place.

Messrs O O'Hare & T V Noonan, plumbers, steam & gas-fitters, 501 9th st, between D & E sts, under Seaton Hall. [Ad.]

Chancery sale, by decree of the Supreme Court of D C, in Equity, No 356, in the cause of Williams et al vs Mattingly et al. Auction on Apr 5, on the premises, a 2 story brick dwlg on 4½ st, south of the property of Geo Parker, being part of lot 27 in reservation 10. -Walter S Cox, R T Merrick, trustees
-Jas C McGuire & Co, aucts

Supreme Court of D C, in Equity, No 1,617. Catherine Hill against Henry Hill, Sarah A Taylor, Permilla Kidwell, Geo W Smith & Henrietta his wife, John F Parker & Mary A his wife, John S Hill & Geo Hill. The parties above are to meet in my room, in City Hall, Mar 23, for the distribution of the fund raised by the sale of property described in the bill. -W Redin, auditor

MON MAR 12, 1866
Equity Court-Judge Wylie, Mar 10, 1866. Jos R Dailey vs The American Colonization Society. Dailey is a merchant of Liberia, & he claims from the Colonization Society $1,452, claimed to be due him on account of provisions, etc furnished recaptured Africans in Liberia. Judge Wylie expressed the opinion that the plntf had no equitable claim against the society & dismissed the rule.
[Mar 16th newspaper: The only point decided by the Court was, that upon the showing made, there was not adequate ground for requiring the respondent to pay into the court, to abide the result of the suit, the money in question. The suit itself is yet to pass upon.]

Died: on Mar 10, Chas F A Coltman, aged 55 years. His funeral will take place this day at 3 o'clock, from his former residence, No 597 12th st.

Engine belonging to the New Haven railroad exploded in N Y on Friday, killing Jas McGuire, the fireman, & dangerously injured Danl S Olds, the engineer.

Orphans Court-Judge Purcell, Mar 10, 1866.
1-The will of Basil Patterson, deceased, was exhibited & proven. 2-The first & final account of Hudson Taylor exc of the estate of Eleanor Lindsley, deceased, was approved & passed; as were also the first & final account of Richd H Laskey, exc of the estate of Jos Cross, deceased; first & final account of Chas M Mathews, adm of the estate of Chas W Bennett, deceased; & second balance & distribution account of the personal estate of Jas M Minor, deceased. 3-In re: petition of Thos R Brayton against Laura V T Whilton, admx of Albert G Whiton, deceased. In this cause on motion of counsel for the petitioner citation ordered & issued against said admx, requiring her to appear on Mar 17, & show cause why an attachment should not issue

As Mr Michl Coomes passed St Joseph's Asylum, 10th & G sts, he heard the cries of an infant & found a basket on the steps with a female, about 1 month old, dressed in neat & costly clothing. The little sranger was handed over to the Third Ward police, & taken to St Ann's Infant Asylum where it was received by the kind sisters there.

Wash Corp-Mar 5, 1866. 1-Ptn of Henry Bayley: referred to the Cmte on Claims. 2-Bill for Julius Veidt, for repairs in the Aldermen's Chamber: referred to the Cmte on Finance. 3-Bill for the relief of J B Studley: passed. 4-Bill for the relief of M Donnely, widow of John Donnelly: referred to the Cmte on Claims.

N Y Commercial of Sat: The safe of Mr Rufus Lord, in Exchange Place, was robbed sometime last night of Gov't & other securities amounting to one million & a half dollars. The securities were in 2 tin boxes. A reward of $200,000, the largest ever offered in this country, will be given to any party who may trace out & cause the arrest of the perpetrators of this stupendous robbery. Mr Lord is a private capitalist, & owner of the late Stock Exchange.

John Dugan, about 12, was taken to the 2nd Police Precinct yesterday. He says he was born in Ireland, where he lived with his father & stepmother. His home was not a happy one, & an uncle, John Donoho, who resides in Alexandria, had him come to this country, where he arrived about 8 months ago. He immediately went to his uncle in Alexandria, & while the soldiers were about that city, the uncle employed him to peddle to them. When the soldiers left, the boy says his uncle's wife objected to keeping him longer, & he was turned adrift to look out for himself. He is utterly alone in this country, & seems anxious to get a good home. He appears to be a healthy & intelligent boy.

Wm H Belcher, a well-known sugar refiner, died in Chicago on Thu.

Albany, Mar 10. A horrible murder was committed in Albany on Mar 8. Jonathan J Osbon, who resided at 73 Union st, in that city, was found in his stable with his head broken by a club, which had been used with great violence by his assailant. One Horace G Paddock, who has been in the State Prison for rape, is under arrest for this crime. Revenge is supposed to have been the cause of the murder, growing out of the affair in which Paddock was involved. Mr Osbon was a most worthy citizen, 50 years of age.

Mrs Kasson, wife of Hon John A Kasson, Rep in Congress from Iowa, was granted a divorce from her husband by the Des Moines District Court on Sat last. Mrs Kasson is a daughter of Hon Thos D Eliot, Rep in Congress from the First Dist in Massachusetts.

Farm for sale in PG Co, Md, containing 111¼ acres, with a fine dwlg; adjoins the land of Edw Herbert & Col Irwin. Edw Herbert will show the premises. –W E McKnew, Real Estate Agent, Room No 7, Intellgencer Bldg.

The House in which Pres Lincoln died-card from Mr Peterson: to the Editors of the National Intelligencer. Will you oblige me with a small space in your paper? A Mr Washington Correspondent of the N Y Tribune informs the readers of that journal that the Treasury has finally settled with me for the amount of damages done to my private residence during the fatal night of the assassination of President Lincoln. Mr Correspondent seems to feel considerably chagrined at my modest partiotism in accepting a few dollars at the hands of the Government so justly due. I must confess that the modus operandi in connection with this collection might have been quite a different one. I ought to have entered into a bargain with a Mr Correspondent, by means of which my humble claims would have been heralded from pole to pole; bassooned forth to a sympathizing public- and instead of the small sum awarded me, the so-proposed co-partnership might have recalled several thousand. Under such an arrangement or understanding my modest patriotism would probably not have been questioned. But it is never to late to reform. I have no hesitation in disposing of my residence, for quite a moderate consideration, to any wool-dyed, loyal, patriotic Republican, whose ambition it may be to become the owner of the dwelling where the lamented President breathed his last. And I entertain no doubt that, in the hands of such a party, a handsome revenue could be realized, say from $13 to $15 per day. Will Mr Tribune correspondent give the first bid? W Peterson

Public sale of lot on Bridge st, Gtwn, by deed of trust for Wm Hardy, dated Feb 11, 1850, recorded in Liber J A S, No 11, folios 155 et seq, of the land records of Wash Co: auction on Apr 3 of lot 14 in Holmead's addition to Gtwn, being the lot at the corner of Bridge & Montgomery st, 30 feet on Bridge st, by 120 feet deep, of equal width, with bldgs, improvements, privileges & appurtenances to the same belonging. -A Hyde, Th R Suter, trustees -Thos Dowling, auct

Chancery sale of valuable real estate, by decree of the Supreme Court of D C, rendered on Mar 9, 1866, in a cause, No 615 in Equity, in which Jas W Gibson is cmplnt & Eliz Gibson, John H Gibson, & others are dfndnts: public auction on Apr 3 of lot 5 in square 461, with a good 2 story brick house, fronting on 7th st. Parts of lots 4 & 5 in square 490, on north C st, with large brick house, back bldgs, stable, & carriage house. On Apr 4th: parts of lots 3 & 4 in square 296 on south C, with a good 2 story frame house. Part of lot 6 in square 264 with a good frame dwlg-house. The west 14 feet front of lot 17 in square 496, with a good 2 story frame dwlg-house. –A Green, Joss F Hodgson, E F Queen, J W Barnaclo, Jos Peck, Comr's -J M Thompson, cmplnts' solicitor -Green & Williams, auct

Sale of condemned Medical & Hospital property, at public auction, on Mar 22, consisting of splints, air rubber cushions, slates, clocks, inkstands, water coolers, tin cups & plates, bed covers, water beds, sheepskins dressed, tourniquets, trusses, mortars, knapsacks, iron washstands, bedside tables, mess chests, cooking utensils, bedding, etc. –Chas Sutherland, Surgeon U S A, Medical Purveyor -C W Boteler, auct

Orphans Court of Wash Co, D C. In the case of Wm H Thomas & Jos Beasley, adms of Levi Pumphrey, deceased, the administrators & Court have appointed Apr 5 next, for the final settlement of the personal estate of the said deceased, of the assets in hand. -Z C Robbins, Reg/o wills

Sale of <u>Gov't bldgs</u>, on the premises, Mar 16, 1866, under the direction of Brvt Lt Col Jas M Moore, at Signal Camp of Instruction, on the Tennallytown road, near Gtwn, D C, viz:

One Ofcrs' quarters, 34 by 67 feet One Blacksmith shop, 13 by 39 feet.
One Kitchen, 12 by 14 feet One sink, 5 by 10 feet.
One Guard-house, 20 by 24 feet One Signal stand, 10 by 10 feet
One stable, 20 by 26 feet One Flag Pole, 90 feet long.
One shed, 12 by 96 feet.

The bldgs will be sold singly, & must be removed by the purchaser within 15 days from date of sale. Terms: Cash, in Gov't funds. -D H Rucker, Brvt Maj Gen & Chief Quartermaster, Depot of Washington.

TUE MAR 13, 1866
War Dept. Adj General's Ofc, Wash, Mar 12, 1866. The following ofcrs, having been reported at the headquarters of the army for the offences hereinafter specified, are hereby notified that they will stand dismissed the service of the U S unless, within 15 days from this date they make satisfactory defence in writing to the Adj Gen of the army to the charge of Absence without leave. 1st Lt John W Maddox, 13th Conn volunteers. 2nd Lt H W Kaestner, 12th US Colored heavy artl. –E D Townsend, Assist Adj Gen

Died: Mar 6, in Brooklyn, N Y, Mr Alfred M Sampson, formerly a resident of Wash City.

Yesterday a 32 pound shell exploded in an out bldg attached to the Ordnance Dept, at the Navy Yard, terribly injuring one of the employes of Mr Bowman, the gunners' gang-Mr Thos Holland, who has served as an acting gunner throughout the war & but lately honorably discharged from the navy. Mr Holland had got the fuse out & was attempting to remove the stock, when it exploded. Mr Holland has his left hand completely destroyed, & so injuring his right as to possibly necessitate amputation. It is the first occasion of any accident occurring, although about 200,000 shells have been handled & emptied in this dept since the commencement of the war. [Mar 14th newspaper: Mr Holland died yesterday about 4 P M. His left ankle was also completely shattered beneath the knee & ankle, & would have had to be taken off had he lived. His body was taken in charge by Wash Circle No 3, Brotherhood of the Union, of which he was a member. He will be buried in the ***Congressional Cemetery*** tomorrow.]

Criminal Court, D C-Judge Fisher. 1-U S vs Geo H Lyons, larceny, dfndnt plead guilty. 2-U S vs Wm Chamberlain, larceny, verdict guilty of stealing a $10 Treasury note, but strongly recommended to the mercy of the Court. H C Gooding for defence. 3-U S vs Chas Meyer, larceny, not guilty.

Milburn Hunter, charged with causing the death of Beniah W Luckett, by stabbing him, was brought out of jail yesterday for trial, when it was discovered he had been indicted by the last Grand Jury simply for assault & battery with intent to kill. The Grand Jury, now in session, were advised of the death of Luckett, whereupon the witnesses were sent to them, & the result was a presentment in due form for murder. The prisoner was remanded to jail. Mr J H Bradley, jr, has been retained as counsel for the accused.

Mr Fred'k W Schmidt, a sculptor, was called upon to take a cast of the face of Col Jas R O'Beirne's child, who had just died. While proceeding in a carriage to Maj O'Beirne's residence, at I & 5th sts, Mr Schmidt was suddenly taken ill, & falling back in the carriage expired, as is supposed, from disease of the heart. The deceased was a native of Germany & was about 60 years of age. He leaves a widow, but no children.

Yesterday the horse attached to the business wagon of Messrs Turton & Lowrey, carpenters, on 12th st, ran off, & Mr Jas E Turton was violently thrown from the wagon, causing a fracture of the collar bone. He was conveyed to his residence, 11th st, between I & K sts.

We all know the state of the Canal & the **Tiber creek** now, the result of a few years' increase, viz: the largest & most filthy cesspool of any city known among civilized mankind in its midst, yet nothing of importance is done to abate the nuisance. Sewerage: many of the sewers already made enter the Tiber. Let us all, then-Congress, Corporation, citizens, & residents-strive to accomplish a desirable improvement, without delay. -Jas Crutchett

Mrs J Sanford will open, Mar 15, an elegant assortment of Spring & Summer French Millinery & Fancy Hats, at her new store: 34½ Market Space, Pa ave, between 7th & 8th.

Hon Luther Haven, Collector of Customs at Chicago, died in that city on Friday last. He was one of the oldest & most respected citizens of Chicago.

Supreme Court of D C, Equity Doc, No 6, No 1,617. Catherine Hill vs Henry Hill et al. Report of sale filed this day by the trustee to be ratified & confirmed. By order of the Court, R J Meigs, clerk. [No other information.]

Maj J M Ridenour, a well known citizen of Cincinnati, committed suicide on Thu last by jumping overboard from one of the Covington ferryboats. Bad health is supposed to have been the cause of this rash act.

Dept of the Interior, U S Patent Ofc, Wash, Feb 28, 1866. Ptn of John Rider, of N Y, N Y, praying for the extension of a patent granted to him Jun 1, 1852, for an improvement in Process of Manufacturing Gutta-Percha, for 7 years from the expiration of said patent, which takes place on Jun 1, 1866.
–T C Theaker, Com'r of Patents

Dept of the Interior, U S Patent Ofc, Wash, Feb 27, 1866. Ptn of Rensselaer Reynolds, of Stockport, N Y, praying for the extension of a patent granted to him Jun 1, 1852, for an improvement in Power Looms, for 7 years from the expiration of said patent, which takes place on Jun 1, 1866. –T C Theaker, Com'r of Patents

WED MAR 14, 1866
Orphans Court-Judge Purcell, Mar 13, 1866.
1-Eliz Kraft was appointed guardian to the orphans of Peter Kraft, deceased. Bond $2,000. Sureties, Augustus E L Keese & Wainwright M Preston.
2-Eliz B Thompson was appointed guardian to the orphan of Robt J Donoghue, late of Syracuse, N Y. Bond $1,000. Sureties, Saml E Thomason, Isaac C Nesmith, & Jas R Barr.
3-The will of Lydia S English, deceased, was fully proven
& admitted to probate & record.
4-The first & final account of John Van Riswick & Wm A Fenwick, excx of Philip Fenwick, deceased, was approved
& passed.

The Balt Catholic Mirror announces that the Most Rev Archbishop Spalding has received letters from the Pope of Rome appointing him Apostolic Delegate, with authority to convene a plenary Council of all the Archbishops & Bishops in the U S during the present year, & to preside over them. Archbishop Spalding is to be constituted a Cardinal at no distant day.

The Alexandria Gaz says that on Sat last, while Mrs Mathew O'Brien & her son Edwin were on their way home, they were stopped by 3 negro men dressed in citizens clothes. They asked directions & she kindly informed them the best directions to Wash City. One of them put a pistol at the head of Edwin and fired the ball into the right side of his neck, & he fell backward into the carriage, blood gushing from his mouth. The negroes robbed Edwin of his purse, & rifled the carriage of its contents, threating to kill Mrs O'Brien all the time. Fortunately the negroes saw some men coming in the distance, & made off. Dr J B Johnson was called & found the ball had penetrated his neck cutting the windpipe in its passage, emerging beneath the left jaw, inflicting a severe & dangerous wound, leaving the patient in an exceedingly critical condition.

The commission of Wm Thompson, as a justice of the peace, expired on Sunday. He has for a long time, been the police magistrate for the 3rd Ward, & has ever been recognized as one of our most fearless & impartial justices.

Washington Bonifant was confirmed by the Senate as U S Marshal for the District of Md, on Monday. Mr Bonifant's nomination was a second time presented to the Senate by the President, at the request of the Senate.

On Sunday last, the consecration of Rt Rev Dr Williams, the Bishop elect of Boston, took place in St James' Church, in that city.

John P Crozier, one of the largest manufacturers in Pa, died on Sunday last. He owned extensive factories at Upland, near Chester, & also at Crozierville, both of which villages have grown up under his fostering care.

The manuscript of an elaborate speech in favor of universal suffrage has been found among the papers of the late Henry Winter Davis.

Trustee's sale of a lot of land in the addition to Uniontown, D C. By decree of the Supreme Court of D C, dated Mar 6, 1866, passed in a cause between John Goodrick & Wm Goodrick, cmplnts, & Mary Goodrick, dfndnt: public auction on Apr 4 next, on the premises, part of the tract of land in Wash Co, D C, which was conveyed by Knoch Tucker & wife to John Fox, John W Van Hook, & John Dobler; which said part was afterwards conveyed to John H Goodrick, containing 10 acres & 26 perches, more or less, with improvements. The property is situated in Uniontown, near the s e end of the eastern Branch bridge, opposite Wash City.
–Henry N Young, trustee -Chas W Boteler, auct

THU MAR 15, 1866
Gen Grant has appointed Col Eli Parker to fill the position made vacant by the lamentable death of Col Brown.

Savannah, Mar 14. Henry Low, who last week shot & killed a citizen, but was acquitted by the coroner's jury of accidental shooting, has been re-arrested by order of the military.

Criminal Court, D C-Judge Fisher, Mar 14, 1866.
1-U S vs Wallace W Whittlesey: abstracting bonds from the Treasury Dept: verdict-guilty, but recommended to the mercy of the Court. 2-U S vs John Campbell: larceny: verdict not guilty. 3-U S vs Jacob Watson & Wm Brown: larceny: verdict not guilty to Watson, but guilty to Brown. Sentenced to 2 weeks in jail. 4-U S vs John Johnson: larceny: verdict guilty of stealing a pair of pantaloons valued at $4.75. Sentenced to the county jail for 3 weeks.

Marlboro Gaz: Judge Wm R Barker died in Balt city on Friday last. He was long a citizen of Aquasco district in this county. His estimable wife & himself left a comfortable home last fall in hopes of recuperating their failing health. Alas! In a short space of time both have been consigned to the tomb; & their home, always the abode of hospitality, will know them no more forever. He was a Christian & a gentleman.

Wm Edmonston, Thos Dumbar, & Abraham Myers, were arrested yesterday for robbing the millinery store of Mrs Sanford some time ago. Mary Blake was arrested for receiving the goods, knowing them to be stolen.

Died: on Mar 10, at *Fort Morgan*, N Y, of organic disease of the liver, Brvt Capt Saml T Crowley, 4th U S Infty, aged 27 years. His funeral will take place from the residence of his father, 542 I st, between 4th & 5th, this day at 3 o'clock P M.
[Mar 16th newspaper: Capt Saml T Crowley, who died at *Fort Niagara*, N Y, where he was stationed, was buried in the *Congressional Cemetery* yesterday. In 1861, when the Washington Zouaves were organized, Capt Crowley was chosen 2nd Lt, & held that position during the time the lamented Ellsworth commanded the organization. After the Zouaves were discharged from service Capt Crowley received an appointment at 2nd Lt in the 4th U S Infty, receiving at the battle of the Wilderness a wound in the arm, from which he never recovered. For his bravery on the field he was promoted to a 1st lieutenancy, & subsequently brevetted a captain, which position he held at the time of his death. He was a son of Mr Patrick Crowley, of Wash City.]

Boston, Mar 14. Jared Sparks, the historian, & ex-Pres of Harvard College, died at his residence in Cambridge, this morning, of pneumonia.
[Mar 16th newspaper: Jared Sparks was born at Willington, Conn, May 10, 1789, & nearly reached his 77th birthday. He graduated at Harvard College in 1815; at one time taught in a small school at Havre de Grace, Md; served for a short period in the militia called out to repel an anticipated attack by the British; was a tutor of Mathematics & Natural Philosophy at Harvard College; May, 1819, settled as a Unitarian pastor in Balt; his becoming impaired in 1823, he purchased the North American Review, & continued as its sole proprietor for 7 years; he now gave himself up almost wholly to writing & literary pursuits.]

Messrs J C McGuire & Co sold part of lot 1 in square 372, on H st, near 9th, improved by 2 comfortable brick houses. The east house was bought by Mr John T Lenman for $2,800; & the west house by Mr Thos E France for $2,225.

Rev Martin Moore, for many years editor of the Boston Recorder, died in Boston Sunday, aged 76 years.

Balt, Mar 14. This morning the steamer **Adelaide**, for Norfolk, when off *Sharp's Island*, was run into by a schnr, demolishing the cook room of the steamer. The cook, J Chapman, who for 30 years has been employed on this line, was lost overboard. No blame can be attached to Capt Cannon, of the **Adelaide**.

Yesterday, as Mr J H Wood, son-in-law of John S Blackford, was returning to Gtwn from his wood land, in Md, when a negro approached him, drew a pistol & fired at Mr Wood, the ball passing near his face, badly burning & blackening it. Mr Wood fired at the negro, but was so blinded that he missed & the negro escaped.

A Match at chess is to be played this week at the N Y Chess Club, between Capt Mackenzie, the victor in the recent tournament, & Mr G Richleim, the best player in Phil. The match is to be for the first 7 games, & neither player is to occupy more than an hour over twelve consecutive moves. [Mar 24th newspaper: The chess contest in N Y between Mr Reichhelm, of Phil, & Capt McKenzie, of the former city, was brought to a close on Tue by the resignation of Reichhelm. Six games were played, of which Capt McKenzie won five, & one was drawn.]

FRI MAR 16, 1866
Freedmen's Bureau agent dismissed. Thos W Edwards, of Loudoun Co, Va, having been charged $5.50 by the bureau agent who handed him the order restoring his property, Gen Howard relieved the gentleman from duty.

Criminal Court, D C-Judge Fisher. 1-U S vs Wm Young & Patrick W McCann, alias Patrick W Kennedy. Robbed $10 from Annie Lang. While one held her down & choked her, the other robbed her. Verdict guilty. Sentenced to 3 years each in the Albany Penitentiary. 2-Walter W Whittlesey, convicted on Wed, to pay a fine of $1,000, & stand committed until the sentence be complied with.

Mr Geo Parry, resident secretary of the English capitalists interested in Minnesota railroads, in a speech at St Cloud, said that the English capitalists are now considering the propriety of bldg a railroad from Minnesota to Montana.

Yesterday the horse attached to the milk-wagon of Mr Wm Rowzer, a dairyman, ran off on D st & the wagon upset causing the milk to be very generally distributed in the gutter.

On Tue night Margaret Ragan, Catharine Donovan, [white,] & Henry Butler, colored, went to one of the low dens of infamy on 7th st, near the Park, & assaulted Bridget McMahon, dragging her from the house, & leaving her senseless by the roadside. A few hours later Mrs Donovan, Mrs Ragan, & Hugh Ragan went to the same house & paid their respects to Mathew McIntire in a similar manner. Bridget McMahon recovered & cut Henry Butler badly about the head with a knife. Sgt Johnson arrested the entire party, & all were sent to jail, except McIntire, who, being a deserter from the 5th cavalry regt, was returned to his command. All of the parties are frequently in the hands of police.

On Mar 7, a soldier of the 5th U S Cavalry, John Harnett, went to the residence of J Hume Burnley, 1st secretary of the British Legation, & demanded admittance. He was refused, & Harnett assaulted a man named Middleton, a servant, in the employ of Mr Burnley. Ofcr Campbell arrested Harnett & he was fined $3. Middleton declined to prosecute for the assault. Harnett had committed what is recognized by all nations as a grave offence, assaulting a member of the household of a foreign minister, & Sec Seward had him re-arrested & held to bail for court. The accused pleads he was intoxicated & not aware of what he was doing.

Left Wash City for Indiana last evening, Marshal Gooding, to attend the funeral of John T Sebastian, his brother-in-law, & will be absent about a week or so.

Patrick Henry, the eminent Virginian, left in his will the following important passage: I have now disposed of all my property to my family; there is one thing more I wish I could leave them, and that is, the Christian religion. If they had that, and I had not given them one shilling, they would be rich, and if they had not that, and I had given them all the world, they would be poor.

Messrs J C McGuire & Co sold a lot on N st, between 14th & 15th sts, to Mr Mathew Newbern, at 30¾ cents per square foot. They sold a small frame house on L st, between 18th & Conn ave, to Mr Patrick Conroy for $800.

Americans in Havana-letter dated Mar 9. Among the arrivals at the Hotel Santa Isabel, which seems to have become the American headquarters, I have noticed the niece of ex-Pres Buchanan, late Miss Harriet Lane, now Mrs H E Johnston, & R Patterson Kane, of Phil, brother of the celebrated Dr Kane.

SAT MAR 17, 1866
Duplex Skirt Fashions for 1866: Bradley's Duplex Elliptic [or double] Spring Hoop Skirt. They will not bend or break; each hoop is composed of 2 finely tempered steel springs, braided tightly & firmly together, edge to edge. Their wonderful flexibility adds to the comfort & gives intense pleasure to the wearer. Manufactured exclusively by the Sole Owners of Patent. West, Bradley, & Cary: 97 Chambers & 79 & 81 Reade sts, N Y. For sale in all first-class stores in Wash City.

Thos Skinner, one of the most desperate & notorious negroes outside the walls of a penitentiary, was arrested yesterday on a charge of grand larceny. His most serious of charges is assault & battery with intent to kill Dr Wm Boyd, of the 7th Ward.

About Jan 10th Mr Edw McCormick, a grocer of Gtwn, was robbed of about $2,000 in gold & silver. Suspicion of the robbery was fixed upon Barney McQuade, a canal boatman, who resided in Cumberland, Md, & the evidence against him was sufficient to warrant his arrest. He was indicted & brought to Wash City to stand his trial.

Messrs Wm L Wall & Co sold the ground lease of 3 stores on N Y ave, between 13th & 14th sts to Mr B W Reed, for $575. Lot 2 on square 70, on M st, near N J, was sold to Mr B Curran, at two cents per square foot. Lot 19 in square 163, on L st, between 17th & 18th, improved by a 2 story frame house, was sold to Mrs Mary Barnett for $1,100.

Circuit Court, D C-Chief Justice Cartier. Mar 16, 1866. Fred'k Stein vs The Wash & Gtwn Railroad Co. This is an action for damages sustained by the plntf in Sept last while riding upon one of the cars. While passing through the Capitol grounds one end of a beam, which had been placed upon the same platform, struck against the fence, causing the other end to strike against the legs of the plntf, fracturing the bones. [Mar 21st newspaper: Verdict for the plntf, $3,100. Amount claimed was $10,000.]

On Monday, Dr A R W Barton, a practicing physician of Chicago, was found near the Michigan Southern railroad cattle yards, in that city, nearly lifeless, having attempted to commit suicide by cutting himself with a knife. Little hopes of his recovery.

Died: on Mar 16, Mrs Sarah Jones, in her 78th year. Her funeral is on Sunday at 2 o'clock, from the residence of her son, Z Jones, 333 9th st.

Criminal Court, D C-Judge Fisher, Mar 16, 1866. 1-U S vs Jas Horn, Philip Thom, Jas D McBride, Jos Fay, & Thos G Liber: assault & battery on Geo Seiss: verdict not guilty. 2-U S vs Chas Ford: larceny: verdict guilty. Sentenced to 2 weeks in jail. 3-U S vs Mary Jones, alias Mary Cooper: larceny: jury out. 4-Anthony Schroeder, arrested some time ago in Detroit, Mich, on charge of stealing U S bonds, was indicted by the grand jury, gave security in the sum of $21,000 for his appearance for trial. The prisoner is in very delicate health, & he is to report to the Marshal from time to time. 5-The District Atty entered a nolle pros in each of the following cases, viz: Wm Young & Patrick McCann, alias Patrick Kennedy, larceny; Jas Evans & Lavina Evans, Warren Davis, Julia Jackson & John Graff, receiving stolen property.

Information has been received at the Dept of State, of the death, on Mar 7th, of Jos Scoville, Consul at Prince Edward's Isle.

Leesburg [Va] Mirror. Chaplain Jas J Ferre, who had been serving as agent for the Freedman's Bureau in Loudoun Co for some months past, was last week ejected from his position for malfeasance in ofc. Chaplain Ferree is a Minister of the Gospel! He was paid by the U S Gov't to look after the interests of freedmen. We understand that where "Cuffee" had business with him he was invariably charged a small fee to keep up the ofc. Philanthropic Chaplain Ferree.

Maj W W Rogers, late of the Veteran Reserve Corps, has been appointed Assist Adj Gen on the staff of Brig Gen C H Howard, Assist Com'r of the Freedmen's Bureau for D C. Lt S N Clark, an efficient ofcr of the Bureau, has been appointed Inspector General on the staff of Brig Gen Howard.

The monument of John Bunyan, at Bedford, England, is to take the form of a large & handsome school, to be named after the immortal author of the "Pilgrim's Progress." The cost is estimated at nearly L3,000.

MON MAR 19, 1866
Mrs Eliz Bull was recently sentenced by a military commission, at Raleigh, N C, to 3 years imprisonment for murdering Jas Thomas, a colored man. Her sentence has been mitigated to 1 year by Gen Roger.

Melvin Kurtz & Matthew Elgish, of Phil, were on Friday placed in custody at Lancaster, Pa, on suspicion of having stolen Gov't bonds, a number of which they sold at a sacrifice.

D Stuart McKay, engaged at Springfield, Ill, in the sale of ready-made clothing for some months past, in the employ of Bartlett & Bros, of Chicago, was arrested on Wed last on a charge of having embezzled money to the amount of $10,000, belonging to said firm, & the larceny of clothing of the value of $15,000 belonging to the same parties.

Orphans Court-Judge Purcell, Mar 17, 1866.
1-The will of the late Chas F A Coltman was filed & partially proven.
2-Catherine Barrett was appointed admx of the estate of T J Barrett, deceased.
3-W D Beall was appointed guardian to W D Beall, jr.
4-The third account of W H & O H Morrison, excs of the estate of Wm H Morrison, deceased, was approved & passed.

Mrd: on Mar 17, by Rev Fr Alig, Marcus R Hook to Annie M Lay, daughter of Richd Lay, all of Wash City. [Balt papers please copy.]

Died: on Mar 18, of tetanus, John D Lakeman, in his 45th year. His funeral is this day at 3 P M, from the residence of his family, on 6th st, between E & F sts. The friends of the family & members of Equal Division, S of T, are invited to attend.

Real estate sales by Green & Williams, aucts, in Washington.
1-Lot 14 in square 455, on G st, between 6th & 7th, at $1.08 per foot, to P A Sellhausen.
2-Lot E square 568, 3rd & F sts, to J P Sullivan, at 75 cents; part of lot 12 in square south of square 516, on Mass ave, with a 2 story frame dwlg, to Alfred Falconer, for $1,220.
3-Lot 12 in square 788, A st, between 3rd & 4th sts, 20½ cents per foot, to W J Bradford.
4-Lot B in square 731, with a small frame house, on Pa ave, between 1st & 2nd sts, to August Monterean, for $1,475.

Ah-Moose, or Wasp, or Little Bee, head chief of the Lac de Flambare tribe of Chippewa Indians, whose hunting grounds are on the Wisconsin river, died on Sat, at the rooms temporarily occupied by the delegation now here, on B st, near 3rd, & yesterday his remains received Christian burial at the ***Congressional Cemetery***, Rev Dr Keeling, of Trinity Church, officiating. The deceased & 3 others of the tribe who came here some time ago to talk with their Great Father, were taken sick last week with black measles, a disease peculiar to the Indians. The remains were encased in one of Dr Scollay's deodorizing burial cases, the **dead chieftain**, according to custom of the tribe, being buried with all the clothing in which he died. It is also a custom of this tribe, when the master dies to kill his dog & bury it with him. [Mar 20th newspaper: St Germain, another of the Chippewa Indians, died yesterday of that same disease that carried off his chief, Ah-moose. He was also placed in one of Scolley's deodorizing cases & buried in the ***Congressional Cemetery***. Others of the Indians are yet ill & refuse to obey the orders of their physicians, & use medicines of their own, & indulge in liquor.] [Mar 23rd newspaper: Skau-ba-wis, another of the Lac de Flambare tribe of Chippewa Indians, died yesterday & was buried yesterday from Dr Scollay's, having first been encased in a deodorizing burial case. This is the third of the tribe who has died, but there are others who are sick & convalescing.]

Wm A Wharton, a well known member of the bar of the Supreme Court of this District, died on Sat in his 48th year, after a lingering illness of almost a year, the last month of which he was confined to his room. His funeral was largely attended yesterday from the Lichan House, Messrs E J Middleton, W D Davidge, R H Laskey, E Carusi, G W Campbell, & J F Ennis officiating as pall bearers.

Govn'r Curtin, on Sat, issued warrants for the execution of Houser & Buzer, the murderers of Miss Polly Paul, of Cambria Co, & Christian Berger, the murderer of Miss Mary Watts, of Germantown. The warrants fix the execution of the two former on Apr 20, & the latter on Apr 27.

Indian prisoners at *Fort Abercrombie*. 1-A despatch from St Paul, dated Mar 14. Lt Col Adams, commandant at *Fort Abercrombie*, has returned from an expedition across James river with 126 Indian prisoners, Yanktons & Cutheads. He made the march over 325 miles without loss. 2-Gen Pope has ordered the completion of *Fort Wadsworth* this season, so that it will accommodate 3 infantry & 2 cavalry companies.

Dept of the Interior, U S Patent Ofc, Wash, Mar 6, 1866. Ptn of Christopher C Brand, formerly of New London, Conn, but now of Norwich, Conn, praying for the extension of a patent granted to him on Jun 22, 1852, for an improvement in Bomb Lance for killing Whales, for 7 years from expiration of said patent, which takes place on Jun 22, 1866. -H C Theaker, Com'r of Patents

Dept of the Interior, U S Patent Ofc, Wash, Mar 6, 1866. Ptn of Jas Sharp, of Brooklyn, N Y, praying for the extension of a patent granted to him on Jun 15, 1852, for an improvement in Label Cards, for 7 years from expiration of said patent, which takes place on Jun 15, 1866. -H C Theaker, Com'r of Patents

Miss Spafford, of Rickford, Ill, who was betrothed to Col Ellsworth previous to his death, was married on Mar 7 to a Mr Brett, a gentleman of wealth & position in Boston.

TUE MAR 20, 1866
Criminal Court, D C-Judge Fisher, Mar 19, 1866. 1-U S vs Henry Watson, Martin Parsonins, & Geo M Don: larceny: Watson guilty. Nolle pros entered in the cases of the others. Watson was sentenced to 1 year in the Albany Penitentiary.
2-U S vs John Armstrong: larceny of vest patterns from Mr W Tucker, merchant tailor. Dfndnt plead guilty. Sentence suspended.
3-U S vs Fred'k Warren & Wm Galloway: receiving stolen goods. Verdict guilty. Sentenced to 1 year each in the penitentiary.
4-U S vs Mary Moriatta: larceny. Verdict guilty of stealing goods to the value of $2.50. Sentenced to 1 week in jail.
5-U S vs Thos Armstrong, Robt Sprigg, & John Clark: larceny. Jury out. [Mar 21st newspaper: verdict guilty.]
6-A nolle pros was entered in the case of Patrick J Hawkins, indicted for larceny.
7-Chas Reed, who has been in jail on a charge of larceny, was released upon giving bail for his appearance.

Hon N F Doubleday, father of Maj Gen Abner Doubleday, died at Belvidere, Ill, on Mar 10. He was for many years a resident of Auburn, N Y, & represented that district in Congress several terms. He was a printer by trade, & for 20 years editor of the Cuyahoga County Patriot. At the time of his death he was a citizen of Bloomington, Ill.

On Thu, a 6 year old son of Mr Isaac Sycles, dry goods merchant, in Richmond, was immediately killed by falling from the 3rd story of his father's dwlg on the brick pavment below.

Died: on Mar 18, of tetanus, John D Lakenan, in his 45th year.

Alice, aged 5 years, daughter of Mr Wm F Humphrey, at Melwood, near this village, was burned to death on Sat last. Little Alice & a brother near her age were amusing themselves in the garden by making a fire, when the flames reached her, & before aid could be obtained she was so badly burned that she died immediately. –Marlboro [Md] Gazette

Wm Wetcroft King, of the Interior Dept, died on Monday. He was injured about a month since by an express wagon. Paralysis set in & his death ensued at the advanced age of 70 years. Mr King, when a boy, removed with his family to Wash in 1899, & for the past 35 years had filled a responsible position in the Land Ofc. He leaves a fond, devoted partner to mourn her irreparable loss, his children a loving father, & his friends will miss one of nature's noblemen. His funeral takes place at 3 P M today, from his residence, on F st.

Chas Seibold, a soldier belonging to company E, 4th artl, & who has for some time past has been the mail carrier for the regt, came to Wash City on Sunday for his mail, & after obtaining it went to a house on D st, near 3rd, & complained of being ill. He laid down upon the sofa & expired at an early hour yesterday.

Harrison Taylor, a Com'rs of the Northern Market, died on Sunday at age 69 years. His funeral will be tomorrow.
+
Died: on Sun last, at his residence in Wash City, 375 7th st, after a long & painful illness, Mr Harrison Taylor, in his 69th year. His funeral is tomorrow at 3 P M, at the E st Baptist Church, where for many years he was a consistent member.

Died: on Mar 19, in his 71st year, Wm W King, one of the oldest citizens of Wash, & for many years a clerk in the Gen Land Ofc. His funeral will be this evening at half-past 3 o'clock, from his late residence, 254 F st.

Died: on Mar 17, of consumption, George W, son of Robt & Martha A Clarke, aged 17 years & 23 days. His funeral will be on Mar 21 at 3 o'clock, from the residence of his parents, on K st south, between 8th & 9th sts.

Dr Thos M Busk, formerly of Balt, committed suicide in Richmond, Va, on Wed last, by taking an ounce of the solution of morphine.

Ex-Pres Pierce will build a summer residence at North Hampton this season, & have it completed by July 1. He owns about 40 acres of land there, in one of the finest locations on the Atlantic coast.

Lawrence, Kansas, Mar 12. Despatch that Maj Wyncoop, a few months since collected the hostile bands of Cheyenne Indians & placed them upon the reservations assigned them by the treaty of Oct last. There were about 4,000 Indians at the council yesterday, 800 of whom were warriors. Maj Wyncoop made a long speech setting forth the advantages that would accrue through a resumption of friendly relations. Amanda Fletcher, aged 15 years, was captured near **Fort Halleck**, on Aug 1 last, while en route for Iowa with her parents. Her mother was badly wounded at the time, & may have died, but her father escaped. The family was from Minersville, Henry Co, Ill. She had been subjected to all the cruelties & atrocities incident to a captivity of this degradation, but enjoys now excellent health, & is delighted at her deliverance. She will be taken back to **Fort Larned** & remain in charge of the lady of Maj Dryer until claimed by her relatives.

Dr Henry Maupin, formerly a member of the Va Legislature from Cabell Co, was killed a short time since by Guyandotte by being crushed between 2 boats, from one of which he had accidentally fallen.

On Monday night last Mr McKean Buchanan & his daughter, Virginia, were announced for Hamlet at Terre Haute. Mrs Buchanan was at the time lying dangerously ill at the Terre Haute House, of neuralgia of the heart. Mr Buchanan had not proceeded a half dozen lines when he exclaimed, "My wife is dying-take your money-run down the curtain-I cannot play!" The audience slowly dispersed. Mrs Buchanan was dead when her husband reached the hotel.

WED MAR 21, 1866
Orphans Court-Judge Purcell, Mar 20, 1866.
1-The will of Chas F A Coltman, deceased, was fully proven & admitted to probate & record, & Sophia Coltman qualified as excx of the estate of said deceased by giving bond in the sum of $8,000, with Edw G Handy & John H Reiss as sureties. 2-The will of Jasper M Jackson, deceased, was fully proven & admitted to probate & record. 3-The first & final account of Alfred C Cassell, guardian to the orphans of John A Cassell, deceased, was approved & passed.
4-The following appointments were made, viz:
Eliz O'Keefe, admx of the estate of John O'Keefe, deceased. Bond $500. Sureties, Wm West & Hugh Doran.
John B Adams, guardian to the orphans of Geo Brockerton, deceased. Bond $600. Sureties, Jacob F King & John N Trook.
Martin M V Bogan, guardian to the orphans of John A Johnson, deceased. Bond $800. Sureties, John H Varnell & Mary E Johnson.
Edw M McCook, adm of the estate of Lt M J Miller, late of the 18th Indiana battery. Bond $1,500. Sureties, Louis J Davis & John N Oliver.
Mary B Smoot, admx of the estate of John W Smoot, deceased. Bond $18,000. Sureties, Geo Waters & Wm S Mathews.
Wm A Carter, adm of the estate of Robt W Hamilton, deceased. Bond $2,500. Sureties, David A Burr & Z C Robbins.

Evening Post: A really good concert at Metzerott Hall tonight. Miss Harrison is an American vocalist who has won the warmest commendation from the best critics. Evening Post: Miss Zelda Harrison is a young lady of some 18 summers, modest & comely in apperance, with a child-like witchery of manner & expression which carried captive the young & the old. Her contralto voice is rich & vigorous by nature, with an inonation of seductive plaintiveness as rare as irrestible.

Nashville, Mar 19. Dr Saml Wolfe was brutally assaulted on Sat night & wounded. [Mar 22nd newspaper: Dr Wolfe, over 60 years of age, suddenly fell to the pavement by a terrible blow on the back of the head just as he was issuing from a saloon on Church st in that city. While unconscious his throat was cut, fortunately without severing the wind-pipe of jugular. At last accounts he was not expected to recover.]

Stephen Lawton, a stranger, walked off the abutment of a bridge in Pittsfield, Mar 13, & received injuries from which he died. He's supposed to have belonged in Brandon, Wisc.

The following property belonging to the estate of Peter Jones, deceased, was sold on Monday, by Green & Williams, aucts. 1-Part of lot 4 in square 354, on 11th st, with a 2 story frame house, bought by Capt H White for $1,100. Lot 87 feet 4 inches front on 10th st, between F & G sts, with a 2 story frame house, bought by Wm R Riley, for $1,620. Lot 15 in square 413, on 8th st, with a small frame house, bought by Robt L Amery for $1,000. A vacant lot, 25 feet front on 8th st, with improvements, bought by Giles Worster for $1,000. A vacant lot on 8th st, between F & G sts, bought by John A Stephenson, at 30½ cents per foot. This sale is considered the best that has been made on the Island for several months past. 2-Jas C MrGuire & Co sold yesterday a lot of ground on east side of 18th st, between I & K sts west, at 62½ cents a square foot, bought by Nicholas Eckhardt.

Criminal Court, D C-Judge Fisher, Mar 20, 1866. 1-U S vs Wm White: larceny: verdict guilty. 2-U S vs John Lambert, Martin Welsh, & Edw Magee: robbery; Lambert pleaded not guilty. Jury out.

Died: on Sunday last, at his late residence in Wash City, 375 7th st, Mr Harrison Taylor, in his 69th year. His funeral will be at the E St Baptist Church, today at 3 o'clock P M.

Died: on Mar 17, of consumption, George W, son of Robt & Martha A Clarke, aged 17 years & 25 days. His funeral will be on Mar 21 at 3 o'clock, from the residence of his parents, on K st, between 8th & 9th sts. [The notice of Mar 20 had 23 days, not 25 days.]

Late English advices bring intelligence of the death of Dr Whewell, author of the "History of the Inductive Sciences", & the "Philosophy of the Inductive Sciences." He was master of Trinity College.

Sale of the "Old Capitol" & grounds, by decree of the late Circuit & present Supreme Court of D C, pronounced in causes 164 & 1,006, in equity, wherein Jas Adams & others are cmplnts, & J D Hanson, Ingle, & others are dfndnts: public auction on Apr 26 next, of lot 14 thru 19, in square 728, in Wash City, on which stands the bldg known as the "Old Capitol." This property has a front of 171 feet 3 inches on First st east, & 191 feet 8 inches on north A st. Immediate possession given. –Jas Adams, John H Ingle, W Redin, trustees -Jas C McGuire & Co, aucts

Orphans Court of Wash Co, D C. Letters of administration on the personal estate of John W Smoot, late of Gtwn, D C, deceased. –Mary B Smoot

Orphans Court of Wash Co, D C. Letters of administration on the personal estate of Lt M J Miller, of Indiana Battery, deceased. –Edw M McCook

THU MAR 22, 1866
Criminal Court, D C, Mar 21, 1866. 1-U S vs John Lambert: robbery: verdict guilty. Sentenced to 3 years in the Albany Penitentiary.
2-U S vs John Handley & Patrick Joyce, jr: larceny: jury discharged, being unable to agree upon a verdict.
3-U S vs Jonas Day: larceny: verdict guilty.
4-U S vs Saml Rogers: larceny: verdict guilty.
5-U S vs Henry Scrivener, Chas Lockrey, & Columbus Kidwell: assault & battery. Nolle pros by the District Atty.
6-U S vs Robt Eliason: larceny: verdict guilty. Sentence suspended.

San Francisco, Mar 19. 1-A despatch from Portland today says that Geo Baden, a noted guerilla, was shot dead yesterday, it is supposed, by Michl Gallagher, who is now under arrest. 2-Gen McDowell is on his way back here from Arizona.

N Y, Mar 21. The family of Uriah Townsend, of Tarrytown, consisting of himself, wife, & 4 children, were poisoned by something eaten in their own house. The eldest daughter, aged 19 years is dead, & the others are in critical condition. Mr Townsend is a justice of the peace, & the deed is suspected to have been done in revenge by some unknown parties.

Mr Morrill introduced a bill to incorporate the General Hosital of D C. It names as corporators, Jas Henry, Jas C Hall, Amos Kendall, Thos Miller, Richd Wallach, Geo W Riggs, Grafton Tyler, Henry D Cooks, D W Middleton, Chas Knap, Benj B French, Jas C McGuire, Chas H Nichols, Wm B Todd, Wm Gunton, Ed Simms, & Thos Young. Bill was referred to the Cmte on the District of Columbia.

Died: on Mar 13, after a short illness, in Flushing, L I, N Y, Rev Chas E Pleasants, formerly of Wash City.

Louisville, Mar 21. Sterling King, who confessed himself guilty of the attempted assassination of Sec Seward, endeavored to commit suicide this morning by severing a blood vessel of his arm. His recovery is considered doubtful.

Sale of real estate in the 7th Ward: Wm L Wall & Co, aucts, sold yesterday property on F & G & 6h & 7th sts, known as the *Page property*, comprising all of lots numbered 1 to 30, inclusive, except lot 9, 19 thru 22, as follows, viz: lot 1 to T McCaffery, for 29 cents per foot; lots 2 thru 8 to D D Foley, for 13 cents per foot; lot 10 to Hugh McCaffery, for 51 cents per foot; lot 11 to Hugh McCaffery, for 23½ cents per foot; lots 12 & 13 to Saml Hoover, for 23¼ cents per foot; lot 14 to Mrs Gibson, for 19½ cents per foot; lot 14½ to M Keenan, for 29 cents per foot; lot 15, with a large dwlg house & outbldgs, to M Keenan, for $5,550; lot 16 to M Keenan, for 19¼ cents per foot; lot 17 to John Shehan, for 19¼ cents per foot; lot 18 to Peter Donelly, at 20 cents per foot; lots 24 & 25, for 25 cents; lot 26, to D D Foley, for 37 per foot; lots 27 thru 29 to D D Foley, for 20 cents per foot, & lot 30, to John Fagan, for 20½ cents per foot.

A man named Britton, sentenced to 10 years in the Nashville penitentiary for cotton frauds, recently escaped by jumping from the cars, while en route, from Decatur, Ala, to Nashville.

Despatch from Chicago to the Cincinnati Commercial says: The appointment of Mr Lawson as U S Collector of Customs for this port takes the people by surprise. Lawson is a Norwegian, of but little influence, but he is one of Long John Wentworth's special favortes, & it was through the latter's influence that the appointment was made. The Evening Journal says so long as the Pres appoints such good & through-going Republicans to ofc as is Mr Lawson, no one need question his Republicanism very critically.

<u>Confirmation of appointments in the Regular Army. Yesterday the Senate confirmed the following nominations for 2nd Lt in the regular army made by the Pres. The appointments are dated Feb 23, 1866, except in a few cases:</u>
9th Regt of Infty: Maj Alfred Morton, of the 7th Calif vols, Mar 3, 1866, vice Hardie, promoted.
11th Regt of Infty: Thos D Sheherd, of Ill, Mar 5, 1866, vice Pettee, promoted.
12th Regt of Infty: Assist Surgeon Benj R Davidson, of the 143 Indiana vols, Mar 5, 1866, vice Knox, promoted.
15th Regt of Infty: Gordon Winslow, late capt of the 5th N Y vols, Mar 3, 1866, vice Williams, promoted.
17th Regt of Infty: Chas Garretson, late capt & assist quartermaster of vols, Mar 3, 1866, vice Plummer, promoted.
19th Regt of Infty: Capt Wm Atwood, assist adj gen of vols, Mar 6, 1866, vice Mills, promoted.

5th Regt of Cavalry: Robt S Stockton, jr, of N J, vice Harris, promoted.
16th Regt of Infty: Chas C Drew, late 1st lt of the 26th Mass infty, Mar 8, 1866, vice Ross, promoted.
1st Regt of Cavalry: Wm R Parnell, late lt col of the 4th N Y cavalry, vice Ward, promoted. Greenleaf Cilley, late capt of the 4th Ohio cavalry, vice Carr, promoted. John Madigan, late 1st lt of the 2nd N J cavalry, vice Veil, promoted.
2nd Regt of Cavalry: Jas N Whelan, late lt col of the 1st N Y mounted rifles, vice Lester, promoted. Jas T Peal, late major of the 4th Pa cavalry, vice Lewis, dishonorably dismissed. John A Wanless, late capt of the 15th Kansas cavalry, vice Cahill, promoted. Randolph Norwood, late capt of the 1st Md cavalry, vice Beckman, deceased. Thos I Gregg, late capt of the 8th Pa cavalry, vice McMaster, promoted. Capt Horatio S Bingham, of the 2nd Minn cavalry, vice Egan, promoted.
3rd Regt of Cavalry: Chas H Smith, late col of the 1st Maine cavalry, vice Meinhold, promoted. Peter D Vroom, jr, late major of the 2nd N J cavalry, vice Wall, promoted. Jos Lawson, late major of the 11th Ky cavalry, vice Russell, promoted. L L O'Connor, late capt of the 5th N Y cavalry, vice Harrington, killed by the enemy. Lambert L Mulford, late capt of the 2nd N J cavalry, vice Falvey, promoted. 1st Lt Alstorphius Werninger, jr, of the 6th West Va cavalry, vice Monahan, promoted.
4th Regt of Cavalry: Robt McClermont, late lt of the 11th N Y cavalry, vice Fitzgerald, promoted. Justinian Alman, late major of the 5th Pa cavalry, vice Conway, promoted. Milton L Webster, late capt of the 7th Ill cavalry, vice Fletcher, promoted. Isaac A Taylor, late capt of the 13th Tenn cavalry, vice McCafferty, promoted.
5th Regt of Cavalry: Capt Geo F Price, of the 2nd Calif cavalry, vice Robbins, promoted. Henry Jayne, late capt of the 7th Ill cavalry, vice Fitzgerald, promoted. Edw M Hayes, late capt of the 10th Ohio cavalry, vice Taylor, promoted. Capt Michl V Sheridan, aide-de-camp, U S vols, vice Trevor, promoted.
6th Regt of Cavalry: Lt Col Clarence E Bennett, of the 1st Calif cavalry, vice Whitside, promoted. Jeremiah C Wilcox, late major of the 5th Iowa cavalry, vice Madden, promoted. Gustavus Schreyer, late capt of the 1st Missouri cavalry, vice Nolan, promoted. Moses Wiley, late capt of the 1st Tenn cavalry, vice Irwin, promoted. Theodore Majtheny, late capt of the 1st Indiana cavalry, vice Carpenter, promoted.
1st Regt of Artl: Junius W McMurray, late capt of the 1st Missouri light artl, vice Egan, promoted. Capt John W Dillenbach, of the 10th N Y artl, vice Counselman, promoted. Geo P Thyng, late capt of the 1st N H heavy artl, vice Leahy, promoted. Geo Ashbury, late 1st lt of the 13th regt U S colored artl, vice Maclay, transferred to the Ord Dept. Alonzo E Miltimore, late lt of the 1st Wisc heavy artl, vice O'Brien, promoted.
2nd Regt of Artl: Thos D Maurice, late major of the 1st Missouri light artl, vice Elliott, retired. Cornelius Gillett, late capt of the 1st Conn heavy artl, vice Monteith, promoted. John H Howell, late capt of the 3rd N Y artl, vice Loucks, promoted. B Franklin Ryer, late capt of the 20th N Y independent battery, vice Howell, promoted. Eli L Huggins, late 1st lt of the 1st Minn heavy artl, vice Vose,

promoted. Jas L Mast, late 2nd lt of battery D, 2nd independent Pa artl, vice Petriken, transferred to the 1st artl.

3rd Regt of Artl: Wm Arthur, late major of the 4th N Y artl, vice Floyd, deceased. John F Mount, late major of the 7th N J heavy artl, vice Hunting, promoted. Chas M Callahan, late capt of the 1st Missouri light artl, vice Hamilton, promoted. Geo K Dukin, late capt of the 1st N H heavy artl, vice Lancaster, promoted. Alpheus E Clarke, late commisary of subsistence of vols, vice Bartlett, promoted. Abram G Verplanck, late 1st lt of the 14th N Y artl, vice Smith, promoted. Thos A Porter, late 1st lt of the 1st Dela battery, vice Chestar, promoted.

4th Regt of Artl: Jas Marr, late capt of the 1st Missouri light artl, vice Roder, promoted. Bela P Learned, late capt of the 1s^{t} Conn artl, vice Reilly, promoted. Edw P Newkirk, late 1st lt of the 1st N Y light artl, vice Rugg, dismissed. Jas M Waite, late 2nd lt of the 4th N Y heavy artl, vice Redmond, promoted.

5th Regt of Artl: Edmund L Zalinski, late 2nd lt of the 2nd N Y heavy artl, vice H M Baldwin, deceased.

1st Regt of Infty: 2nd Lt Thos W Cluster, of the 6th Mich cavalry, vice Hynes, dismissed.

2nd Regt of Infty: Chas Harkins, late 1st lt of the 2nd Mass cavalry, vice Butler, promoted. Stephen H Carey, late lt of the 57th Ohio vols, vice Driscoll, transferred to the 1st artl.

3rd Regt of Infty: John W Thomas, late 1st lt of the 9th Vt vols, vice Kaiser, promoted. 1st Lt Stanley A Brown, of the 5th regt U S veteran vols, vice Winebrener, transferred to the Ord Dept. Gustav A Hesselberger, late 1st lt of the 6th Iowa cavalry, vice Mourton, promoted. John P Thompson, late 2nd lt of the 1st N H cavalry, vice Hamilton, promoted.

4th Regt of Infty: Edw Simonton, late capt of the 1st regt U S colored troops, vice Simons, promoted. Jas R Mullikin, late 1st lt of the 25th regt U S colored troops, vice Dost, promoted. 1st Lt Henry C Sloan, of the 48th Wisc vols, vice Luhn, promoted. John T Hendricks, late 2nd lt of the 4th Indian cavalry, vice Hassler, promoted.

5th Regt of Infty: Capt Edwin T Bridges, commissary of subsistence vols, vice Newbold, promoted. Jas Dugan, late 1st lt of the 8th regt U S veteran vols, vice Johnson, promoted. 1st Lt Ephraim Williams, of the 1st regt U S veteran vols, vice Compston, deceased. 1st Lt Wm I Reed, of the 6th Calif vols, vice Taylor, promoted. Edw L Randall, late 1st lt of 1st regt U S colored troops, vice Curtis, promoted.

6th Regt of Infty: 1st Lt Solomon L Hoge, of the 7th regt Veteran Reserve Corps, vice Drake, promoted. 1st Lt Danl H Murdock, of the 1st regt U S colored roops, vice Bickely, promoted. John W Godman, late 1st lt of the 96th Ohio vols, vice Schindel, promoted. 1st Lt Stephen Jocelyn, of the 115th regt U S colored troops, vice Kirby, promoted. R W Ross, late 2nd lt of the 4th Iowa vols, vice McKim, promoted.

7th Regt of Infty: W W Armstrong, late capt of the 92nd regt U S colored troops, vice Sanno, promoted. 1st Lt Richd P Strong, of the Signal Corps, U S vols, vice Williams, promoted. Roswell P Patterson, late Logan, promoted. Wm T Dodge, late 2nd lt of the 16th Maine vols, vice Coolidge, 1st lt of the 9th Ill vols, vice

Robinson, promoted. Chas F Larrabee, late 1st lt of the 30th Maine vols, vice promoted.

8th Regt of Infty: Rollin Perkins, late 1st lt of the 24th regt U S colored troops, vice Cooper, resigned. Burnett E Miller, late lt of the 149th N Y vols, vice Franks, resigned.

9th Regt of Infty: Chas H Shepard, late 1st lt of the 4th N Y provisional cavalry, vice Walker, promoted. John S Bergen, late 1st lt of the 173rd N Y vols, vice Devine, resigned. Wm T Smith, late lt in the 13th Maine voluunteers, vice Connelly, promoted. John D Blaker, late 2nd lt of the 3rd regt U S colored troops, vice Fitzgerald, promoted.

10th Regt of Infty: Chas L Davis, late capt of the Signal Corps U S vols, vice Schwan, promoted. Capt Wm H King, of the 1st regt Veteran Reserve Corps, vice Henry, deceased. Chas M Edwards, late 1st lt of the 18th Ill vols, vice Stanley, promoted. Chas E Jewett, late 1st lt of the 39th Wisc vols, vice French, promoted. John A Schwartz, late 1st lt of the 6th Md vols, vice White, promoted. Freeman E Olmstead, late 2nd lt of the 12th Tenn cavalry, vice Broatch, promoted.

11th Regt of Infty: Frank W Hess, late major of the 3rd Pa cavalry to fill an original vacancy. Wm H Clapp, late capt & assist adj gen of vols, to fill an original vacancy. Henry C Ward, late capt of the 57th Mass vols, to fill an original vacancy. Ogden B Reed, late capt of the 39th regt U S colored troops, to fill original vacancy. Chas O Bradley, late capt in the 13th N H vols, vice Hagan, promoted. Wm N Sage, late capt of 137th N Y vols, vice Pratt, promoted. Ralph Maxwell, late capt of the 57th Pa vols, vice Huntington, promoted. Geo M Fleming, late 1st lt of the 21st Pa cavalry, vice Field, promoted. Stephen K Mahon, late 1st lt of the 36th Iowa vols, vice Guthrie, promoted. Wm I Driggs, late 1st lt of the 1st Michigan sharpshooters, vice Harbach, promoted. Robt G Heiner, late 2nd lt of 22nd regt U S colored troops, vice Rockford, killed in battle. Lt Chas C Hyatt, of the 6th regt Veteran Reserve Corps, vice Robins, promoted. Francis J Dunn, late sgt of the 61st Ohio vols, vice Barber, died of wounds received in battle. Henry D Clarke, late private of the 11th Pa cavalry, vice Staples, promoted. Wm H Vinal, late private of the 7th Ohio battery, vice Farnsworth, dismissed. Capt Herman Schreiner, commissary of subsistence of vols, Feb 21, 1866, vice Nealy, promoted.

12th Regt of Infty: 1st Sgt John W Bubb, of company E, 1st btln, Feb 5, 1866, to fill an original vacancy. Alex'r B MacGowan, late capt of the 6th Calif vols, to fill an original vacancy. Jas H Spencer, late capt of the 20th Mass vols, vice Mimmack, promoted. Capt Wm Crosby, of the 2nd regt U S veteran vols, vice Van Duzer, killed in battle. Alfred S Newlin, late capt of the 11th Pa vols, vice Patterson, promoted. 1st Lt John L Viven, of the 1st New Mexico cavalry, vice Wagner, promoted. Wm E Dove, late 1st lt of the 196th Ohio vols, vice Jackson, promoted. Andrew M Trolinger, late 1st lt of the 10th Tenn vols, vice Alston, promoted. Jos H Hayes, late 1st lt of 142nd N Y vols, vice Meyer, promoted. Alex'r S B Keyes, late 2nd lt of the 1st btln of Mass heavy artl, vice Putnam, promoted. Danl W Applegate, of the 1st Oregon vols, vice May, promoted. John F Cluley, late sgt of 2nd Ill artl, vice Eggemeyer, promoted. Thos E Lawson, late private of the 3rd Ky cavalry, vice Stough, promoted. Private Washington I Henderson, of the 1st Oregon cavalry, vice Tompkins, promoted. 13th Regt of Infty: John Cooley, late major of the 148th N Y vols, to fill an original vacancy. Capt John M Green, of the 58th Ill vols, to fill an original vacancy. Wm S McCaskey, late capt of the 79th Pa vols, to fill an original vacancy. Jas T McGinniss, late capt of the 124th Ohio vols, vice Meagher, promoted. Mott Hooton, late capt of the 1st Pa vols, vice Griffin, promoted. Platt M Thorne, late capt of the 150th N Y vols, vice Bates, promoted. Andrew N Canfield, late 1st lt of the 5th Iowa vols, vice Torrey, promoted. Wm J Reedy, late 1st lt of 1st Dela cavalry, vice Little, promoted. Otto Vermann, late 1st lt of the 41st Missouri vols, vice Sanford, promoted. Philip H Ellis, late 1st lt of the 6th Pa cavalry, vice Newlin, promoted. Thos I Elliott, late 2nd lt of the 2nd Ky vols, vice Humphrey, promoted. Martin O Codding, late quartermaster sgt of the 141st Pa vols, vice Gates, whose appointment has been revoked. Fred'k H Dibble, late sgt of the 15th Ohio artl, vice Nelson, whose appointment has been revoked. Martin E Hogan, late private of the 1st Indiana cavalry, vice Keeling, promoted. Hiram H Ketchum, late private of the 16th N Y vols, vice Roman, promoted. Capt Ellwood Griest, commissary of subsistence of vols, Feb 24, 1866, vice Paschal, resigned. 14th Regt of Infty: Saml McConihe, late colonel of the 93rd N Y vols, vice Lyon, promoted. John H Gallagher, late lt col of the 106th Pa vols, vice Wright, cashiered. Fred'k E Camp, late lt col of the 29th regt U S colored troops, vice Loosley, promoted. Geo W Steele, late major of the 101st Indiana vols, vice Perry, promoted. Capt Azor H Nickerson, of the Veteran Reserve Corps, vice Choisy, promoted. Otis W Pollock, late capt of the 63rd Ohio vols, vice Smedberg, deceased. John C Carroll, late capt of the 15th Ky vols, vice Moroney, promoted. Chas B Western, late capt of the 150th N Y vols, vice Doebler, promoted. Richd I Eskridge, late capt of the 2nd Iowa vols, vice T E Collins, deceased. 1st Lt Orville A Loomis, of the 14th U S colored infty, vice Peck, promoted. Oscar I Converse, late 1st lt of the 1st N H cavalry, vice Clay, promoted. Geo W Chilson, late 1st lt of the 24th Michigan vols, vice Douglass, promoted. F M Gilliland, late 1st lt of the 15th Ky cavalry, vice Bainbridge, promoted. Jos L Jack, late 2nd lt of the 201st Pa vols, vice McKibbin, promoted. David S Hinman, late commissary sgt of the 79th Ohio vols, vice Vernon, promoted. John F Lewis, late sgt of the 107th Ill vols, vice Browning, promoted. Lewis P Derby, late private of the 68th Ohio vols, vice Burgoyne, promoted. Jas F Mays, late private of the 72nd Michigan vols, vice Hartell, whose appointment had been cancelled. Private John R Eschenburg, of Co I, 2nd Calif vols, vice Lord, promoted. 15th Regt of Infty: Eramus C Gilbreath, late major of the 20th Indiana vols, to fill an original vacancy. Capt Jas H Stewart, of the 2nd Calif vols, to fill an original vacancy. Teo Shorkley, late capt of the 51st Pa vols, to fill an original vacancy. John F Conyngham, late capt of the 16th Iowa vols, to fill an original vacancy. Egbert B Savage, late capt of the 47th N Y vols, vice King, promoted. Fred'k W Coleman, late capt of the 151st N Y vols, vice Binckley, resigned. Ira Quinby, late 1st lt of the 1st Colorado cavalry, vice Mallory, resigned. John G S White, late 1st lt of the 5th Mass cavalry, vice Pettit, resigned. Jos G Waters, late 1st lt of the

84th Ill vols, vice Simple, promoted. Frank T Adams, late 1st lt of the 2nd N J cavalry, vice Heilman, promoted. 2nd Lt Ferdinand Bayer, of the 38th regt of U S colored troops, vice Jackson, promoted. Geo W Ballantine, late 1st sgt of the 190th Pa vols, vice Forbes, deceased. Calvin A Anderson, late 1st sgt of the 74th Indiana vols, vice Harrison, promoted. Wm P Schall, late private of the 51st vols, vice Kendall, promoted. John L Churchill, late private of the 7th regt N Y State militia, vice Burness, promoted.

16th Regt of Infty: Sgt Maj Geo I Madden, of the 2nd btln, Jan 24, 1866, vice Power, promoted. Clayton Hale, late lt col of the 59th Ill vols, vice Clarke, promoted. Robt W Bard, late lt col of the 95th N Y vols, vice Arnold, promoted. Chas R Paul, late major of the 15th N J vols, vice Howland, promoted. Capt Saml McKeever, of the Veteran Reserve Corps, vice Kellogg, promoted. Allen Almy, late capt of the 58th Mass vols, vice Mitchell, resigned. Merritt Barber, late capt & assist adj gen of vols, vice Hearn, promoted. Chas S Haley, late capt of the 15th Maine vols, vice Schiffler, promoted. Evarts S Ewing, late commissary of subsistance of vols, vice Mahan, promoted. 1st Lt Wm J Kyle, of the 25th Ohio veteran vols, vice Coenzler, deceased. Jas Miller, late 1st lt of the 4th Mass cavalry, vice Mackey, promoted. Wm M Hudson, late 1st lt of the 92nd Ohio vols, vice Clifford, promoted. 1st Lt Henry Cateley, of the 1st Oregon vols, vice Hotsenpiller, promoted. Wm W Parry, late 2nd lt of the [blank] Pa vols, vice Thompson, promoted. Wm A Miller, late 1st sgt of the 8th Ky vols, vice Parkinson, promoted. Edwin R Parks, late sgt of the 13th U S infty, vice Ingalls, promoted. Chas H Noble, late private of the 1st Indiana cavalry, vice Story, promoted. Henry W Adams, late private of the 98th Ohio vols, vice Totten, promoted.

17th Regt of Infty: Adam G Mallory, late colonel of the 17th Wisc vols, to fill an original vacancy. Sumner H Lincoln, late colonel of the 6th Vt vols, to fill an original vacancy. Geo H Cram, late colonel of the 9th Ky vols, vice Whittemore, promoted. Arthur McArthur, jr, late lt col of the 24th Wisc vols, vice Hargrave, promoted. Wm A Sutherland, late major & assist adj gen of vols, vice Ewing, promoted. Henry H Humphreys, late major & aid-de-camp U S vols, vice Carter, promoted. Wm H W Krebs, late capt & additional aide-de-camp U S vols, vice Lay, promoted. Capt Joel T Kirkman, of the 6th regt U S veteran vols, vice Dowling, promoted. Capt Phineas Stevens, of the 1st regt U S veteran vols, vice Hopkins, promoted Wm M Van Horne, late capt of the 195th Ohio vols, vice Rice, promoted. Capt John P Willard, aide-de-camp U S vols, vice Adams, promoted. 1st Lt John W Eckles, of the 1st regt U S veteran vols, vice Smith, promoted. Edwin O Gibson, late 1st lt of the 114th N Y vols, vice Steelhammer, promoted. Julian R Fitch, late 2nd lt of the Signal Corps, U S vols, vice Black, promoted. Wm W Clemens, late 2nd lt of the Signal Corps U S vols, vice Mitchell, promoted. Robt S Oliver, late 2nd lt of the 5th Mass cavalry, vice McLoughlin, promoted. Thos G Troxel, late 1st sgt of the 25th Iowa vols, vice Bailey, promoted. John B Engle, late corporal of the 86th Indiana vols, vice C P Smith, promoted. Hamilton C Peterson, late private of the 64th Ill vols, vice M McArthur, promoted.

18th Regt of Infty: Sgt Major Edmund F Thompson, of the 1st btln, Dec 14, 1865, vice White, whose appointment has been canceled. Henry M Benson, late major of the 4th Calif vols, vice Madeira, whose appointment has been cancelled. Napoleon H Daniels, late capt of the 18th Indiana vols, vice Townsend, promoted. Capt Wm M Knox, of the 1st Washington Territory vols, vice Whitaker, dismissed. Geo M Templeton, late capt of the 32nd regt U S colored troops, vice Arnold, promoted. Prescott M Skinner, late capt of the 20th Michigan vols, vice Horton, whose appointment has been revoked. Capt Sanford C Kellogg, aide-de-camp U S vols, vice Little, promoted. Chas E Dibble, late 1st lt 11th Conn veteran vols, vice Lind, promoted. Henry H Link, late 1st lt of the 6th West Va cavalry, vice Mitchell, deceased. Oliver B Liddell, late 1st lt of the 68th Indian vols, vice Wilcox, promoted. 1st Lt Orlando F Leman, of the Veteran Reserve Corps, vice Williamson, promoted. Wm D F Landon, late 2nd lt of the 14th Indiana vols, vice Lane, deceased. Jas H Bradley, late sgt of the 45th Ohio vols, vice Pohlman, deceased. Reuben N Fenton, late private of the 9th N Y cavalry, vice Ostrander, promoted. Thos Sletor, jr, late private of the 51st Pa vols, vice Gates, promoted. Geo W Wood, of Maine, vice Bennett, promoted.

<u>19th Regt of Infty:</u> Fred'k W Moore, late colonel of the 83rd Ohio vols, vice Berg, resigned. John Pulford, late colonel of the 5th Michigan vols, vice Bigger, resigned. John E Bennett, late colonel of the 74th Ill vols, vice Culbertson, promoted. Col Ransom Kennicott, of the 37th Ill vols, vice Wheeler, resigned. John S Hammer, late lt colonel of the 16th Ky vols, vice Haines, whose appointment has been cancelled. Lt Col Geo F Towle, of the 4th N H vols, vice Johnston, promoted. Alfred Freddburg, late major & assist adj gen of vols, vice Carpenter, promoted. John E S Cooper, late commissary of subsistencce of vols, vice Edwards, promoted. Oliver Phelps, late capt of the 1st West Va veteran vols, vice Ayres, promoted. Capt Mark Walker, of the 214th Pa vols, vice Gageby, promoted. John Harold, late capt of the 4th Tenn vols, vice Ewers, promoted. Frank D Baldwin, late capt of the 19th Michigan vols, vice Davis resigned. Denis Carolin, late capt of the 155th N Y vols, vice Patterson, promoted. D Mortimer Lee, late 1st lt of the 29th Conn colored infty, vice Baldwin, promoted. Richd Vance, late 1st lt of the 26th Ky vols, vice Ledyard, promoted. Josiah S Styles, late 1st lt of the 32nd Wisc vols, vice Sherman, promoted. Andrew Campbell, late lt of the 13th Tenn cavalry, vice Reid, promoted. Jas M Smith, late 2nd lt of the 29th regt U S colored troops, vice Olmstead, promoted. Jos C Coffman, late 2nd lt of the 173rd Ohio vols, vice Krause, promoted. Jas S Wilson, late 1st sgt of the 42nd Ill vols, vice Garland, promoted.

Improvements on H st. 1-Chas Eames, having purchased the old brick house on the n w corner of H & 14th st, will commence to take down & erect in its place one of the finest residences in Wash City. 2-The Sec of the Treasury has commenced laying the foundation for a fine house on the lot recently purchased by him, between Sec Harlan's house & Cmdor Shubrick's, on H st.

Israel Russell, an old merchant of N Y, died on Monday of paralysis, aged 76 years.

Hon Bannon G Thibodeaux, of the parish of Terrebonne, La, died a few days since. He graduated at Hagerstown College, Md, studied law, & became a distinguished member of the Louisiana bar. He served several sessions in the Legislature, until in 1846 he was elected to Congress as a member of the 5th Rep Dist of that State.

The remains of Betsey Bishop, a prostitute, were found last Sunday in a cave 40 feet deep in the neighborhood of Busheng's Forge, 6 miles south of Bristol, Tenn. She had been missing for a month. The body had received several stabs, one near the heart.

Dept of State: Mr I M Hood, the Consul of the U S at Bangkok Siam, received information on Aug 15, 1865, of the death of Geo G Allen, & of C H Thomas [colored] on Nov 25, 1865, both being American citizens residing at Bangkok. Legal reps of the dec'd can obtain further information by reference to this Dept.

Officers who received $5,000 and upwards, together with the amount received by each:
Vice Admr D G Farragut: $56,270.67
Rear Admr D D Porter: $91,528.98
Rear Admr S F Dupont: $57,003.25
Rear Admr S H Stringham: $15,417/52
Rear Admr J A Dahlgren: $9,938.58
Rear Admr L W Goldsborough: $5,013.07
Cmdor T Bailey: $40,504.29
Cmdor J L Lardner: $36,241.01
Cmdor W W McKean: $33,530.33
Cmdor H H Bell: $13,043.22
Cmdor C H Wilkes: $8,284.03
Cmdor G Van Brunt: $6,712.06
Cmdor H K Thatcher: $5,660.43
Cmdor John Rodgers: $5,137.91
Capt S P Lee: $109,689.60
Capt G H Scott: $8,340.14
Capt H F Sands: $36,806.97
Capt W M Walker: $35,448.40
Capt O S Glisson: $24,906.72
Capt D B Ridgely: $14,441.38
Capt J B Marchant: $12,720.76
Capt T P Greene: $12,503.81
Capt Jos I Greene: $7,483.19
Cmder J J Almey: $54,508.71
Cmder J F Armstrong: $5,299.54
Cmder T M Brasher: $9,944.21
Cmder J P Bankhead: $6,819.61
Cmder John C Beaumont: $5,224.47

Capt P Crosby: $24,312.42
Cmder Napoleon Collins: $15,815.83
Cmder A O Clary: $9,641.82
Cmder Overton Carr: $7,067.30
Cmder J Downes: $10,425.71
Cmder C Hunter: $5,943.12
Cmder Jos Lanman: $14,012.80
Cmder J R M Mullaney: $15,747.23
Cmder J E Parrott: $10,772.05
Cmder Geo W Ranson: $29,193.50
Cmder S D Trenchard: $18,750.40
Cmder R H Wyman: $24,009.56
Lt Cmder: Wm Budd: $38,766.24
Lt Cmder K R Breese: $17,535.28
Lt Cmder R F Bradford: $13,426.20
Lt Cmder F Burgess: $13,034.32
Lt Cmder G S Barnes: $9,834.04
Lt Cmder W B Cheeseman: $29,549.69
Lt Cmder C F B Caldwell: $10,902.68
Lt Cmder E F Devine: $9,859.79
Lt Cmder John C Febiger: $9,551.23
Lt Cmder C H Green: $6,513.97
Lt Cmder J E Jouett: $27,778.76
Lt Cmder E Y McCauley: $6,430.46
Lt Cmder W P McCann: $6,103.67
Lt Cmder S P Quackenboss: $8,240.67
Lt Cmder W C Rodgers: $9,614.30
Lt Cmder R R Wallace: $8,038.63
Lt Cmder P G Watmough: $25,159.54
Lt E A K Benham: $8,945.51
Lt Wm B Cushing: $15,628.76
Lt E Conroy: $9,780.70
Lt Earl English: $21,017.10
Lt W B Eaton: $8,697.65
Lt N F Farquhar: $11,022.30
Lt B Gherardi: $6,940.41
Lt N Goodwin: $5,397.06
Lt S H Hunt: $5,752.99
Lt Louis Kempff: $14,549.06
Lt R H Samson: $11,102.00
Lt F Rodgers: $8,244.03
Lt J P Robertson: $7,265.12
Lt F D Steuart: $16,000.00
Lt B F Smith: $10,556.72
Lt J O Vance: $6,187.06
Lt W H West: $8,686.81

Acting Master:
J F Alcorn: $5,418.39
J H Breck: $9,258.96
F M Bonney: $9,931.09
W T Buck: $5,108.88
C H Crosier: $7,380.11
P N Cruse: $6,059.91
W E Dennison: $20,600.30
L E Degu: $8,086.13
P C Gibbs: $5,100.44
F Hopkins, jr: $15,849.15
J A Hannum: $6,042.17
W O Lundt: $21,209.97
C W Lawson: $5,984.76
W S Martin: $11,920.49
S W Mather: $5,176.81
A W Mildrum: $5,021.71
C Potter: $12,391.64
L H Partridge: $5,393.99
Frank Smith: $7,806.44
W L Tuttle: $6,059.94
E Van Sloe: $6,268.76
A Wallace: $13,249.06
F H Wilkes: $5,801.93
Acting Ensign:
C M Bird: $5,274.95
G H Colby: $5,771.45
C H Coldin: $5,243.95
H H Draper: $6,880.79
A Davis: $5,085.65
T Delano: $5,317.70
C H Frisbee: $5,243.78]
W S Howorth: $9,773.38
S Harding: $8,771.71
C F Hodgkins: $5,771.45
S M Lane: $9,589.67
J O Morse: $6,250.53
Warren Porter: $5,771.45
O E S Roberts: $8,577.05
J M C Reville: $8,061.03
R Rabadon: $5,196.37
Acting Master:
T Stothard: $11,445.99
W M Swazey: $9,035.75
C B Staplis: $5,780.67
O P Thompson: $5,685.60

M E Wandell: $9,736.63
F Wallace: $9,035.75
Geo E Williams: $6,602.14
Acting Surgeon:
A E Emory: $5,133.16
J Hugg: $7,511.08
G D Harris: $6,011l99
G B Higginbotham: $5,402.26
C T Hubbard: $5,047.76
R O Mason: $7,905.31
J D Murphy: $5,704.32
J Poole: $6,878.62
A S Reider: $7,002.83
A Shirk: $15,339.43
P S Wales: $7,548.02
The total amount that had been paid to naval officers for captures made during the war was $4,702,398.12. There were 1,296 officers who received less than $100 each. The aggregate amount paid to this class was $50,426.66. 3,100 officers received $100 and upwards, amounting in the aggregate to $1,711,976.46. Treasury Dept Mar 19, 1866. -H McCulloch, Sec of the Treasury

FRI MAR 23, 1866
Criminal Court, D C-Judge Olin, Mar 22, 1866.
1-U S vs Elias Lawrence, alias Lawrence Lawer: larceny of a horse: verdict guilty, but recommended to the mercy of the Court. Motion for a new trial. Verdict set aside & new trial granted.
2-U S vs Fred'k Thompson: larceny: trial deferred.
3-U S vs Tyler Burk: larceny: verdict guilty.
4-U S vs Wm H Emoss: larceny: verdict not guilty.
5-U S vs same: larceny: verdict guilty, but recommended to the mercy of the Court
6-U S vs Thos Ogleton, alias John Johnson: larceny: verdict guilty.
7-U S vs Jas Barnes, J C Tenbrook, Solomon Quinn, & Wm Greason: larceny: jury not returned a verdict at midnight.
8-U S vs Tyler Burk: larceny: nolle pros by the District Atty.
9-John C Donoho, who has been confined in jail to answer a charge of assault & battery, gave a bond in the sum of $200 for his appearance to answer.
10-Jacob Freeling was discharged from jail upon the recommendation of the grand jury.

Wed night, in the U S Hotel, Wash, Timothy F Heald, a discharged soldier of the 1st Mass infty, committed suicide by cutting his throat. He was discharged from the army on account of insanity, & sent to the Insane Asylum, whence he was discharged in Nov last. The Massachusetts State agent took charge of his remains & effects.

Died: on Mar 19, at Nashville, Tenn, Mrs Mary A, wife of Dr Chas E Goddard, U S A, & daughter of the late Robt M Barr, of Pa. Her remains will be brought to Wash City for interment.

Died: on Mar 22, at *Ingleside*, near Wash City, after a long & painful illness, Frances J, daughter of Maj Gen H Walbridge, & wife of Col A H Jackson, of Omaha City, Nebraska Territory. Her funeral will take place from the residence of the widow of Mr C Walbridge, *Ingleside*, on Mar 24, at half-past one o'clock P M, without further notice.

Died: on Mar 22, Morris Hodgkin, aged 15 months & 12 days, only son of Wm & Martha A Coppinger.

Senate confirmed the nominations of Wm Thompson, Jas Lawrenson, & Jos Peck, as Justices of the Peace for the District of Columbia. Mr Thompson has long filled the ofc of Police Magistrate.

Louisville, Ky, Mar 21. The remains of the Confederate Gen Robt Hatton reached here today, & will be interred at Bebanon by the Odd Fellows, where of he was Grand Master, in Tenn.

Charleston, Mar 21. The steamer **General Hooker**, while on her way from Charleston to Gtwn, when off Sullivan's Island, this morning took fire in her wood-room. She was run ashore & entirely destroyed. Three men & 2 ladies were drowned, including Miss Bush, who had just come from school at the North.

Thos J Musgrove was hung in Macon, Ga, on Friday, for the murder of Isaac N Armstrong, of Co C, 145th Indiana, on Aug 25. He was tried & sentenced by a military commission. The doomed man read a long confession.

Essex Walker was tried before a military court in Augusta, Ga, in Jan, for the murder of Dr Byrne, & sentenced to be hung. Execution ordered to take place on Friday, Mar 23.

Mary Ellen Karney, about 19 years of age, daughter of Patrick Karney, living at 93 Tremont st, Roxbury, was instantly shot dead last evening in her own house, by a man named John Moran, about 21 years of age. She answered the door & Moran shot her right there in the doorway. Moran was involved in a robbery with a man named Malloy, last fall, & Miss Karney read a note about it, that Moran accidentally dropped. He told her not to tell anyone, but it weighed so heavy on her, that she told her father & uncle, who live under the same roof. Moran has been delivered over to the Roxbury authorities. -Boston Transcript, Mar 20

An only son aged 13 years, of Maj Axel Dearborn, of Boston, was a few days since thrown from a carriage against a fence, & so badly injured that he has since died.

Volunteer ofcrs to be mustered out by order of the Sec of War.
Assist Quartermasters: Capts Simon B Brown, Jas Brooks, Greenberry L Fort, [brvt Lt col,] Underhill F Wheeler, Thos Palmer, Richd Perry, Farnaham Lyon, [brvt major,] Sanford Harned, Cyrus K Drew, [brvt lt col,] John R Boyle, Milton Dana, Jos D Treadway, [brvt major,] & Maj Thos F Purnell.
Commissaries of Subsistence: Capts Wm P Cowie, [brvt lt col,] A W Sheldon, Otho W Heiskell, & Levi Ruggles.
Assist Adj Gen: Majors Wm McMichael, [brvet col,] Jas B Sample, Jacob L Green, [brvt lt col,] & Capts Geo H Caldwell & Levant W Burnhart, [brvt maj.]
Additional Aides-de-Camp: Colonel Danl T Van Buren, [brvt brig gen] & Capt John A Pratt. Surgeon Robt R Taylor.

Nominations confirmed by the Senate on Wed:
Edw M McCook, of Colorado, Minister Resident at the Hawaiian Islands.
To be Consuls:
Jas Donaldson Long, of Md, at Montevideo
Hiram R Hawkins, of Nevada, at Tumbeat
Chas A Leas, at Funchal
Andrew J Stevens, of Iowa, at Smyrna
Fred'k F Cavada, of Pa, at Trinidad de Cuba
Wm M Jones, of N Y, at Clifton, Canada
O M Spencer, of Iowa, at Geneva
Saml R Campbell, at Bayonne
A Gregg, of Tenn, Kingston, Jamaica
John C Walker, of Tenn, at St Thomas
E P Smith, of N Y, to be Com'r of Immigration
Lewis Blodgett, Appraiser at the port of Phil
Jas Jones, Surveyor of customs at Town Creek, Md
Chas F Swift, Collector of Customs at Barnstable, Mass
Byrneus Bliss, surveyor of Customs for Tiverton, Rhode Island
Alvin W Chapman, collector of customs at Apalachicola, Fla
Wm E Wells, Collector of Customs for Petersburg, Va
Wm H Barnhart, of Oregon to be the Indian Agent in the Territory of Washington
Isaac Colman, of Indiana, to be Agent for the Choctaw & Chickasaw Indians
Luther E Webb, of Wisc, Agent for the Chippewas of Lake Superior
Franklin H Head, of Utah, to be Superintendent of Indian Affairs for Territory of Utah
Thos Murphy, of Kansas, to be Superintendent of Indian Affairs for the central Superintendency
Edw B Taylor, of Nebraska, to be Superintendent of Indian affairs for the Northern Superintendency
Jos R Hanson, of Dakota Territory, to be Agent for the Upper Missouri river
Chancy H Adams, of Nebraska, to be Agent for the Iowa Sacs & Foxes of Missouri
Danl C Oakes, of Colorado, to be Agent of the Grand river & Wintah bands of Indians

H L Fairfield, of Calif, to be Agent for the Mound Valley Indians
Joab Houghton, of New Mexico, to be Associate Justice of New Mexico
Jas R Drybergh to be Chief Engineer of the revenue cutter **Sirius**

SAT MAR 24, 1866
Criminal Court, D C-Judge Olin, Mar 23, 1866
1-U S vs Jas Barnes, J C Tenbrook, Solomon Quinn, & Wm Greason: larceny: guilty to all but Greason. Sentence: Tenbrook-2 years in prison; Barnes-3 years at Albany; Quinn-1 year at Albany.
2-U S vs John Miller & Kate Miller: larceny: John Miller guilty: Kate Miller not guilty.
3-U S vs John Armstrong: larceny: the accused is 16 years of age, & the court directed a nolle pros to be entered in the case.
4-U S vs John Handley & Patrick Joyce: larceny of a pocket-book & $20 from a soldier named Michl Burns: verdict guilty.
5-U S vs John Howard: larceny: verdict guilty. Sentence:
2 years in the Albany Penitentiary.
Tyler Burke & Thos Ogleton were each sentenced to 1 year in the Albany Penitentiary
Robt A Eliason, convicted of larceny, was sentenced to 2 years at Albany. The prisoner is from PG Co, Md, & belongs to a very respectable family. Judge Olin adverted to that, & also to the fact that none of his family had made their appearance in court to support him in his trouble. They seemed to consider him almost incorrigible, & no doubt thought that the best means to adopt to induce him to alter his course of evil conduct was to incarcerate him in a prison. Judge Olin also adverted to the fact that the prisoner was a man of intelligence, &, therefore, knowing his duty, he deserved greater punishment for a violation of law than ignorant men who hardly knew the criminality of appropriating to their own use the property of another. [Same newspaper: Robt A Eliason attempted to escape from the court-house yesterday. He was recaptured on E st, near 6th.]

Our fellow citizen, Mr T M Harvey, of oyster dealing fame, has purchased the property at the corner of 11th & Pa ave, now occupied as a drug store by Mr Ford, for $30,000. Mr Harvey intends the erection of a large bldg to accommodate his rapidly increasing oyster trade, his present bldg on C st not affording sufficient accommodations.

A German committed suicide in Phil on Sunday last. In his room was found the following farewell: I was a soldier in the 15th N Y heavy artl, U S A, & I got a disease [palsy] in the service, from the effects of which I was obliged to stop work. In consequence I applied for a pension from the U S Gov't. Not receiving any support from the Gov't, this is to inform my friends & acquaintances I have been obliged to kill myself. –John Rabus, from Gotha

The statement recently made that Ives Lawson has been appointed collector of customs for Chicago is incorrect. No appointment has as yet been made by the Pres, but the position is filled by the deputy collector, J T Kinsello.

Died: on Mar 23, Edw Burchell, in his 69th year. His funeral will take place from his residence in Alexandria on Mar 25 at 2 P M.

Col Jas Morgan, one of the early settlers of Texas, is dead. The Galveston Civilian says of him: he died at New Washington, on the bay, a few days since; he had lost his sight; he had been a citizen of Texas 35 years; he commanded the Texas troops on Galveston Island in 1836; & he carried the vessels of the Texas navy into the fight with those of Mexico, off the coast of Yucatan, in 1844.

Brownsville Courier, of Mar 8, records the death, by assassination, of Mr Eben Cobb, a native of Portland, Maine, but a resident of Texas for several years. His body, with bullet-holes in the head, was found 4 or 5 miles below Brownsville, on the Brazos road.

Henry C Atwood, indicted for the murder of his wife at Sycamore, in De Kalb Co, Ill, was on Thu last found guilty of manslaughter & sentenced to 5 years in the penitentiary.

Private teacher wanted-a Protestant gentleman. –Geo McCrone, Hare's Corner, New Castle, Dela.

Mr Levi Whitcomb died at his residence in Boston on Tuesday aged 54 years. He had filled the ofc of janitor to the Lowell Institute from its foundation, a period of service reaching over 30 years.

Jas Lackey, Merchant Tailor, 7th st. [Ad]

MON MAR 26, 1866
Orphans Court-Judge Purcell, Mar 24, 1866.
1-Mrs Eliz Clements filed a caveat to the will of the late Alex'r Clements, deceased.
2-John N Trook qualified as adm of the estate of Philip Evans, deceased, by giving bond in the sum of $10,000.
3-Mrs Laura V T Whiton, an additional bond in the sum of $10,000 as admx of the estate of Albert G Whiton, deceased.
4-In re. Estate of H C Wiltsoff, deceased. Ordered that the adm render a fruther account, retaining $2,000 to meet outstanding claims, & distribute the balance among the heirs.

Two brothers, Geo & Henry Carley, died, the former on Wed & the latter on Sat, in Manchester, N H, of a disease termed cerebro-spinal meningitis.

Twenty-six murder indictments await Mr Quantrell's return to Kansas. Twenty-six hangings are fewer than he deserves.

Criminal Court, D C-Judge Olin, Mar 24, 1866; N Wilson, Assist Dist Atty.
1-U S vs Daml Carter: larceny of $50 from Wm Burley: verdict not guilty.
2-U S vs Wm Samuels: larceny of 72 pounds of bacon: verdict guilty.
3-John Hendley & Patrick Joyce were convicted of robbery & sentenced to 1 year each in the Albany Penitentiary.
4-John Miller, convicted of larceny of dresses & blankets, sentenced to 1 year in the Albany Penitentiary.

The **telegraph line** between Chicago & Lake Superior is completed. The first despatch was sent on the 19th & reported the snow three feet deep on the level.

Navy Yard affairs. 1-Mr Saml Montgomery, a well known engineer, lately attached to the Quartermaster's Dept, is chief engineer of the side-wheel steamer **Coeur de Leon**. 2-Acting Boarswain Wm Allen has reported for duty as foreman of laborers at this yard, relieving Boatswain Geo Smith, who has reported for duty on the U S steamer **Augusta**. 3-Capt M Smith, executive ofcr of the yard, had an alarm of fire rung throughout the yard on Sat for the purpose of testing the efficiency of the yard fire dept; within 3 minutes there were 2 streams of water ready for action.

Rt Rev Bishop Hopkins, of Vt, administered the rite of confirmation on Sunday at the Church of the Ascension, on H st.

Some days past Messrs Michl Phelan, Philip Tieman, Pierre Carme, & Isadore Gayrand, whose superiority in the billard world is very generally acknowledged, have been giving exhibiitions of their skills at the prominent billard saloon of Wash City.

Died: on Mar 9, at *Spring Hill*, near Mobile, Rebecca, daughter of the late Wm Hewett, of Wash City.

Real estate sales by Green & Williams, aucts. Frame house on N H ave to Mr B Morgan, for $900; one house in the same locality to Mr Owen O'Hare, for $625; & 2 houses to the same for $600 each. Also sold lot W in square 492, fronting on Md ave, improved by a 2 story frame dwlg, to Mr G E Noyes for $1,650. John Pendergrass was the purchaser of property on north B st, between 1st & 2nd st, belonging to the McIntosh estate, at 27 cents per foot.
The terms of the above sale all cash.

Malcolm Wallingsford, dealer in butter, eggs, etc. Stands: Centre & Northern Liberty Markets. [Ad]

Supreme Court of D C, in Equity, No 177. Eleanor Lindsley & others vs Jos L Ingle & others. John C Kennedy, trustee, reported that on Oct 9, 1865, he sold at public auction, part of lot 1 in square 681, in Wash City, as belonged to the late Wm Ingle at the time of his decease, to Geo B Patch, as agent for one Moses Kelly, for $2,140.34; & lots 14 thru 17 in square 733, to J H Thompson, for $846.51; & on Dec 13, 1865, he sold lots 18 thru 21 in square 733, to J H Thompson, for $1,116.73; & lots 7 thru 13 in square 733, to J H Thompson, for $896.05; & part of lot 2 in square 681, to J H Thompson, for $639; & part of lot 4 in square 637, to Richd Barry, for $87.60; & lot 2 in square 693, to Richd Barry, for $145.94; & the purchasers have complied with the terms of sale.
–R J Meigs, clerk

TUE MAR 27, 1866
Fred'k Koones, late Chief Clerk of the Navy Agent's Ofc, Wash, D C. Solicitor of claims, Commissioner of deeds, notary public, & real estate agent. Ofc: s w corner of Pa ave & 11th st.

Nicholas Callan, jr, Com'r for the U S Court of Claims, also Agent for the Md Life Ins Co of Balt. Ofc: 460 15th st, corner of F st, opposite the Treasury Dept.

S Surbrug & Co: Nat'l Military & Naval Agent. Ofc: E & 7th st.

Mr Jno E Owens begins an engagement of 2 weeks at the Boston Theatre on Apr 20, & will afterwards make a tour of the New England cities.

A report is going the rounds of the press that Gen J B Hood was to be married to a daughter of Gen Wm Preston, of Louisville. We remarked to him that he had to suffer for his notoriety. "Yes," said he, "and it must be exceedingly annoying to the lady, as we have no acquaintance whatever." -Natchez Democrat

Obit-died: on Thu, at ***Ingleside***, near Wash City, after a long & painful illness, Frances J, daughter of Mrs Gen H Walbridge, & wife of Col A H Jackson, of Omaha City, Nebraska Territory. During 8 weary weeks the deceased suffered without a murmur. The sympathies of the whole community are with her bereft consort, who within 6 years has buried his wife, 4 children, [all he had,] a father, brother & sister. [Nebraska papers please copy.]

Chancery sale of improved property: by decree of the Supreme Court of D C, rendered on Feb 27, 1866, in a cause in which Sarah McIntosh & others are cmplnts, & Ann V McIntosh & others are dfndnts; in Equity, No 605. Public auction on Apr 7, of lot 5 in square 705, with the bldgs thereon, said lot fronting on north B st, between 1st & 2nd sts. -Jas Lynch, Thos Scrivener, A Green, John G Dudley, Florian Hitz, Com'rs -Green & Williams, aucts [M Thompson, S W Williams, cmplts' solicitors.]

Mr Eugene Thayer, the organist, has returned home from an extended foreign tour.

WED MAR 28, 1866

At Cleveland, Ohio, Henry Bansfield & Co's wooden-ware factory was burned on Friday night. Loss $50,000, with partial insurance.

Recovery of quinine stolen from the Medical Purveyor's ofc on Feb 3 last. Quinine & powder of morphine to the value of over $1,000 was stolen. Wm Edmonston, Jas Jecobaman, & Geo Sears, alias Jersey, alias Howard, gang of robbers, have been arrested. [Mar 29th newspaper: W J Edmonston, Jas Jarolomon, & Geo Sears, the parties arrested for stealing quinine, were yesterday committed to jail for court in default of $1,000 bail each.]

Some months ago a woman, Mary A Gatewood came to Wash City, & obtained an introduction to several of our most respectable families. She obtained employment in several families & during her stays she stole valuables from Mrs Geo W Riggs; Mr Jos A Kieffer; & Mrs Abbey. Superintendent Richards committed her to jail for court. The accused is about 35 years of age, originally from Ky, but came here from Phil.

Last night a negro band was passing up the avenue, & the horses of a hackman, Osborn Eckton, whose stand is at 7th st, ran from fright, & Mr Eckton, who is advanced in years, seeking to stop them, was caught under the wheels of the carriage & seriously injured. He was carried to his home at the Navy Yard.

Mr Cornelius Noonan, who has for a long time honorably filled the ofc of clerk in the detective dept of the Metropolitan Police, has been promoted to a clerkship in the immediate ofc of the Superintendent of Police. Members of the detective force presented him with a handsome gold pen & pencil case. Mr Moses Meredith, a patrolman, has been detailed to fill the place vacated by Mr Noonan's promotion.

Died: on Mar 26, in PG Co, Md, in her 78th year, Mrs Maria, wife of John T Whitaker, a native of Truro Co, Cornwall, England, but for many years a resident of Wash, D C. Her funeral will be at Rock Creek Church, on Thu at 12 o'clock.

Died: on Mar 27, Col Wm P Young, aged 73 years. His funeral will be from his late residence, 360 10th st, between L & M sts, on Mar 29, at 4 o'clock P M.

For sale, desirable cottage sites one mile from the capitol: a small tact of land, 21 acres, on the old Bladensburg road, adjoining **Eckington**, the country seat of the late Jos Gales; the estate of the late Washington Berry, & **Brentwood**, the residence of Mrs Pearson. Apply to John Carroll Brent, Atty-at-Law, City Hall or Theodore Mosher, **Nonsuch**, near the NavyYard.

The copartnership existing under the firm of Henry Polkinhorn & Son, is this day, Mar 28, dissolved by mutual consent. –Henry Polkinhorn, Saml Polkinhorn

Balt, Mar 27. Bradley Johnson, who left Md at the outbreak of the rebellion, & returned as a general, commanding a rebel brigade, was arrested yesterday by U S Marshal Bonifant, on a warrant issued for an indictment for treason, found by the grand jury in August last. Judge Giles held Johnson to bail for his appearance in the sum of $10,000.

Mrs O'Brien, a soldier's widow at Montpelier, died in her house last week from cold & exhaustion. She was 22 years old, & left a child, which was nearly dead when found. Have they no "Bureaus" in Vermont? -Exchange

Memphis. During a quarrel at Fayette, Miss, J Terry was shot in the face by Saml Owens, his half-brother, & instantly killed. [No date given-current item.]

Maj Ned Burns & Col T Wyman, both ex-confederate ofcrs, residing in Mississippi, met at Point Cheyatt, Ark, to settle a difficulty of long standing. The weapons were bowie knives. Maj Burns was wounded in the arm, & Col T Wyman was wounded in 3 places in his body, which are thought to be mortal. He was severely injured in the face, his nose being entirely severed, & one of his eyes injured as to greatly interfere with, if not totally, destroy his sight. The Colonel's second was slightly wounded by a thrust from Maj Burns.

THU MAR 29, 1866

The deeply regretted decease, at his residence, No 4 north A st, of Senator Solomon Foot, of Vt, takes from the superior branch of Congress another of the few men of large legislative experience that remained in it. He was the Pater Senatus, & also one of the few relics of the period of gifted American statesmen. His disease was jaundice. On Tue Dr Sunderland administered to him the holy communion. He grasped his wife's hand & said, "Oh! This is my only trouble-leaving my wife." Before he breathed his last he clasped his wife's arm, & kissed her. He was born in Cornwall, Addison Co, Vt, in Nov, 1802; graduated at Middlebury College, Vt, in 1826; was also Pres of the Brunswick & Florida Railroad Co, of Georgia. [Same newspaper: Senator Foot was yesterday embalmed by Dr Scollay, & Messrs Harvey & Co, undertakers, are preparing a handsome burial case for the reception of his remains, which will be conveyed to his native State for interment.] [Mar 30th newspaper: inscription on the lid of the coffin, on a large silver plate: Hon Solomon Foot, U S Senator from Vermont, Died, Mar 28, 1866, in his 63rd year. Among the family & friends at the funeral were Mrs Foot, & [blank] Foot, brother of the deceased, Judge Foot, a cousin, with his lady & 2 daughters; Mr Seward Foot, a nephew, Mr Hodges, & Maj Dana.]

Orphans Court-Judge Purcell, Mar 27, 1866.
1-Mary A Wannall qualified as guardian to the orphans of Jas Cochran, deceased: bond, $300. Sureties, Wm J Miller & Chas H Winder.
2-John N Trook qualified as adm of the personal estate of Philip Evans, deceased: bond, $10,000. Sureties, Michl Thompson & Wm H Clagett.
3-The fourth account of John Handy, guardian to the orphans of John Smith, deceased, was approved & passed.
4-The first & final account of Sophia C Harrison, admx of the estate of Uriah D Harrison, deceased, was approved & passed.
5-Mary O'Shea qualified as admx of the estate of Jas Waterbury, deceased: bond, $2,000. Sureties, Patrick Downs & Lawrence Hogan.
6-The will of Harrison Taylor, deceased, was fully proven & admitted to probate & record. The property of the decid is bequeathed to his children, Richd Taylor, Mrs Rosalie McKnew, & Mrs Mary Spignul. Richd Taylor & John H Yeatman qualified as excs, by giving bonds in sum of $3,500, with Herman L Chapin & Wm F Mattingly as sureties.
7-The will of Alex'r Clements, deceased, was further exhibited, & additional testimony was taken, showing the testator to have been of unsound mind at the time of his death, whereupon the will was set aside as invalid.

Messrs Peter F Bacon & Chas S English, the newly appointed Com'rs of Police, have received their commissions from the Pres, & will enter upon their duties today as members of the Police Board. Gen Bacon qualified yesterday.

Died: on Mar 27, Mrs Ellen Talbott, in her 78th year. Her funeral is this afternoon, at 3 o'clock, from the residence of her son-in-law, Robt Clarke, on K st, between 8th & 9th sts.

We will apply to the Com'r of the Land Ofc of the U S for duplicates of the following pieces of Scrip issued to us: One piece to Chas S Bekem, No 4,700, all dated May 19, 1854, for 80 acres; 4,701 for 17 7/9th acres; 4,689 for 80 acres; 4,690 for 80 acres; 4,691, for 80 acres; 4,592 for 80 acres; 4,693 for 80 acres; 4,694 for 80 acres; 4,695 for 53 1/8th acres; 4,685 for 80 acres; 4,686 for 80 acres; 4,687, for 17 7/9th acres. One piece to Wm & Jas King, No 4,678, all dated May 19, 1854, for 80 acres; 4,979 for 80 acres; 4,680 for 17 7/9th acres; 4,688 for 59 2/27 acres; 4,703 for 59 7/27th acres. One piece to Jane Frances Cosby, [now wife of Edw Zollicoffer,] Virginia E, Chas V, John D, Lewis F, Sarah E, & Wm H Cosby, children & heirs of Jane Eliza Cosby, No 8,164, all dated May 16, 1857, for 53 1/3rd acres; 8,163 for 80 acres; 8,161 for 80 acres; 8,159 for 80 acres; 8,158 for 80 acres; 4,681 for 80 acres; 4,680 for 80 acres; 8,159 for 80 acres; 8,158 for 80 acres; 4,681, all dated May 19, 1854, for 80 acres; 4,682 for 80 acres; 4,683 for 80 acres; 4,864 for 56 8/27th acres; 4,673 for 80 acres; 4,674 for 80 acres; 4,675 for 80 acres; 4,676 for 80 acres; 4,677 for 35 5/9th acres; 4,677 for 35 5/9th acres; 4,696 for 80 acres; 4,697 for 80 acres; 4,697 for 80 acres; 4,698 for 80 acres; 4,699, for 56 8/27th acres. The above pieces were lost by John McCulloch, of Jefferson Co, Iowa. –C S Bekem, & others

Died: on Mar 28, Thos P Trott, aged 66 years. His funeral will take place from his late residence, 586 N J ave, Capitol Hill, at 2 P M on Mar 30.

Supreme Court of D C, in Equity Docket 7, No 487. Fred'k Roemmele et al vs Jas Roemmele et al. Reported the sale made by the com'rs to Nicholas Eckhardt of lot 16 in square 126, for $1,591.67 be ratified & confirmed. –R J Meigs, clerk

Orphans Court of Wash Co, D C. Letters testamentary on the personal estate of Harrison Taylor, late of Wash, D C, deceased. –Richd H Taylor; J H Yeatman

Orphans Court of Wash Co, D C. Letters of administration on the personal estate of Philip Evans, late of Wash Co, D C, deceased. –John N Trook

Dept of the Interior, U S Patent Ofc, Wash, Mar 14, 1866. Ptn of Saml Nye Miller, of West Roxbury, Mass, praying for an extension of a patent granted to him Jun 29, 1852, for an improvement in Compound Anchors for 7 years from expiration of said patent, which take place on Jun 29, 1866.
–T C Theaker, Com'r of Patents

Isaac Chaney, a freedman of Botetourt Co, Va, has been sentenced to be hung, by a military commission, he having been convicted of the murder of John F Geralds, of Rockbridge Co, Va, near the Natural Bridge on Oct 13 last. He has been ordered to be executed on May 4 next, in the city of Richmond.

FRI MAR 30, 1866
Wash: Real estate sale by Messrs Green & Williams, aucts, on Tue. Lots 1 & 2 in square 33, at E & 14th st, to Mr Hugh Cameron, at 11½ & 9½ cents per foot. Lot 12 in square 564, on 3rd st, to F M Dellinger, at 56 cents per foot. Lot E of square 564, with a 2 story frame bldg, to Jas T Ball, for $2,450. Lot 21 in square 568 to Chas Mygatt, at 30 cents per foot. Lot 2 in square 511, on O st, between N J ave & 5th st, to Anna M Jardella, at 15 cents per foot. Lot 45 in square 511, to Jas Wallace, at 19½ cents per foot. Jas C McGuire & Co sold, on Sat, lot 2 in square 220, on H st, near 14th st, to M W Galt, for $1.66 per square foot. Lots 11 thru 13 in square 455, with a brick house, to John Saul, for $8,600. Messrs W L Wall & Co on Wed sold lot 4 in square 37, between 23rd & 24th sts, to Mrs Fannie O'Neal, for 15½ cents per foot. Lot 14 in square 43, on 23rd st, between G & H, sold to Thos O'Neal, at 8 cents per foot.

The resignation of Maj Gen John M Palmer, commanding the Dept of Ky, tendered sometime ago, has been accepted by Pres Johnson.

Gtwn Affairs: 1-Communication from: W D Busey in regard to renting the wharf at the foot of High st. From L W Richie, physician for the poor & work-house, asking for an increase of salary: referred to the Cmte on the Work-house. 2-Mr Edes offered a resolution to pay John Kaiser $51.25 for repairs on pumps: passed.

Casper Martin, formerly a resident of one of the cantons Grisons in Switzerland, during the war a private in the 28th Ohio, & recently a resident of Switzerland, was found murdered a few days since near Lafayette, Indiana. He had $1,500 in deposit, which his murderers, it is presumed, supposed he had on his person.

The following is a list of the passengers for Para by the steamer **Margaret**, which cleared yesterday: Maj L H Hastings, O F Chatlit, Capt W Mathews, S C Sparks, Jas Daniel, sr, Mrs Lydia Daniel, Miss Deneil A Daniel, Miss Lydia Daniel, B H Harrison, Mrs E Harrison, Nancy Harrison, Wm Barr, Mrs Nancy Barr, Lydia Barr, Eliz Barr, Jos Daniel, Mrs Ann H Daniel, Chas Daniel, Jos Perry, Camilla Daniel, Stephen E Daniel, Jas Daniel, jr, Mrs M Daniel, Daniel Lambert, Thos I Carter, Mrs Margaret Carter, Robt J Carter, Wm B Graham, Mrs Mary J Graham, Jane R Graham, Wm A Graham, John H Graham, Augustus Simmons, Wm F Routh. –Mobil Register & Advertiser

On Thu, Mar 22, Mr Jas Burke & wife, & John Kelley, wife & daughter, residing just without the limits of Springfield, Ill, on the Rochester road, in attempting to cross the south fork of the Sangumon river, all were drowned. They had all been to Christian Co to attend the wedding of of a daughter of the party.

Letter from Florence Nightingale, dated London, Feb 23, speaks of her health a even more delicate than it has been. She says: "I am always & entirely a prisoner to my room, & latterly to one position."

A promiment Chicago merchant, Mr Adolph Kramer, was found suffocated in a bed in the house of a brother-in-law in that city on Sat night. Gas was found in the room, which left no doubt of the cause of death.

Orphans Court of Wash Co, D C. In the case of Jane O Mahon, excx of Ann W Smith, deceased, the executrix & Court have appointed Apr 21 next, for the final settlement of the personal estate of the said deceased, of the assets in hand. -Z C Robbins, Reg/o wills

H Koppel, Civil & Military Tailor, corner 15th & Pa ave, Wash. [Ad]

For sale: Beautiful country seat, **Ridgewood**, on Roland ave, near Charles st, 4½ miles from the Balt city limits, 20 acres, with dwlg house-20 rooms, billiard room, gate-lodge, dairy, ice-house, gardener's house, & extensive stabling. Address Box 897 Balt Post Ofc.

SAT MAR 31, 1866
Hon Joshua Hill is being urged as Collector of Customs as Savannah in place of Mr Woodbridge, who wants to resign. The test-oath is said to stand in the way of his appointment, as it is said he cannot take it, he having served as a member of the Confederate Congress.

Died: on Mar 20, Mrs Fanny L Wood, wife of Col H Clay Wood, U S A, aged 30 years. Portland, Me papers please copy.

Prof Augustus W Smith, L L D, Instructor in Mathematics at the U S Naval Academy at Annapolis, died there on Mar 22 at the age of 64, of pneumonia. He was a native of N Y, & a graduate of Hamilton College; & was professor in the Wesleyan Univ of Conn, of which he was president for several years. In 1850 he was appointed to his late post. [Apr 13th newspaper: in the relations of husband & father he was most happy, & in his death we all feal the loss of daily Christian example.]

A new commodious hospital, **Providence Hospital**, is now proposed to be built, under the management of the Sisters of Charity. Staff: Physicians: D R Hagner, M D, 209 H st; John C Riley, M D, 453 14th st; Wm Marbury, M D, 456 H st. Surgeons: J F Thompson, M D, 9th & Mass ave; C M Ford, 582 N J ave; Dr N Lincoln. Advisory & Consulting: Grafton Tyler, M D, Wash & Gay sts, Gtwn; W P Johnston, M D, 7th st. Application can be made at the hospital, or to either of the above-named physicians. No contagious diseases admitted.
–Sister Loretto Riley, superior

Mr Josias Adams, a very worthy citizen, who had been for a number of years intendant at the Wash Asylum & workhouse, died at his rooms there yesterday, from an attack of typhus fever, which yet prevails there in a very malignant form, caused by the over crowded condition of the bldg.
+
Died: on Mar 30, Josias Adams, in his 58th year. His funeral will take place Apr 1 at 3 o'clock, from the Wash Asylum. [Apr 2nd newspaper: The remains of Mr Adams were conveyed to the **Congressional Cemetery** yesterday. The funeral was attended by Mayor Wallach, Collector Dixon, & other municipal ofcrs, & a large number of old citizens of Wash. Rev Mr Leech, of the East Wash M E Church performed the services.]

We learn that Govn'r Dillingham, of Vt, will appoint Mr Hiland Hall as U S Senator in the place of Mr Foot, deceased.

J C McGuire & Co, aucts, sold a 3 story brick dwlg, with back-bldg, fronting on Pa ave, between 20th & 21st sts, to Mrs S Henriques, for $9,100.

John L Flagg, lately chosen mayor of Troy, is the youngest mayor in the country. He is only 24. He is a graduate of Harvard College.

The old family mansion of Maj Gen John Starke, the hero of Bennington, was burned a few days since at Manchester, N H. This bldg was put up by the General in 1765, & was used by him as a homestead until his death in 1822.

Died, of inflammation of the brain, at the residence of his brother-in-law, Chas A Lambard, of Boston, Brvt Maj Gen Seth Williams, Inspector Gen U S army, & during the war Adj General of the Army of the Potomac. [No death date given- current item.] [Apr 2nd newspaper: Kennebec, [Me] Journal: The remains of Gen Williams were brought to this city on Sat by special train; services were held at St Mark's Church, by Rev E E Johnson, rector; the day was inclement; by the desire of the family, there were no military demonstrations, save the usual salute of 15 guns, fired by order of Maj Gilbreth, commandant of the U S arsenal. Pall bearers: Maj Gen J L Chamberlain, [of Brunswick;] Adj Gen J L Hodsdon, Lt Col J W T Gardiner, Maj B H Gilbreth, Capt T C J Baily, & Capt C Boutelle, [of Brunswick.] A despatch was received by Hon Danl Williams, the father of Gen Williams, from Lt Gen Grant, conveying to the family of the deceased expression of his condolence in their deep affliction & the country's loss. Gen Grant, also, in behalf of himself & brother graduates of the Military Academy, expressed a desire for the interment of his remains at West Point, if agreeable to the wishes of his family. We believe, however, it is their desire that his ashes should repose among those of his kindred.]

Mrs Rowley recently died at Tuscarora, Steuben Co, N Y, in her 100th year of her age, leaving nearly 200 direct descendants.

Plumbing, Gas, & Steam Fitting: Arthur Shepherd, agent: D st, near 7th. [Ad]

Chancery sale of land in the county, by decree of the Supreme Court of D C, made on Mar 7, 1866, in Equity, No 466, wherein Wm H Morrison & others were cmplnts, & Emma T Mills & other dfndnts: public auction on Apr 17 next, of land in Wash Co, D C, being that part of **Robert's Choice**, & **Beall's Fancy**, as recorded in Liber No 1, folio 58, adjoining **Kendall Meadow**, & Kitty Savoy's 10 acre lot; containing about 74 acres. -Jno D McPherson, Wm J Mattingly, trustees -Jas C McGuire & Co, aucts

Christian Berger, who was to be hung in Phil on Apr 27, was found dead in his cell, in the county prison, on Thu. A jury summoned by the coroner, who rendered a verdict of death from congestion of the brain.

MON APR 2, 1866
Powerful influences are being brought to bear to induce the Pres to remit the sentence pronounced by a military commission against G B Lamar, for attempts to defraud the Gov't.

Mr Jas Winter, of Phil, has been appointed a special Treasury agent.

Phil, Mar 31. Wm S Pierie, for 20 years past commercial editor of the North American & U S Gaz, formerly a merchant of this city, died this morning, aged 63 years.

Harriet Barker, deceased, of Melboune, Austrailia. If Mrs Wilkie, [late Maria Barker,] will send her address to W Seabright, Sherborne Terrace, Cheltenham, England, she will hear of something to her advantage. If this should meet the eye of Mrs Harriet Cheeklay she will oblige by sending address as above.

Died: on Sat, S Fred'k Arthur Hodgkins, only son of Saml & Mary Ann Hodgkins, after an illness of but a few hours, aged 3 months. His funeral will be from the residence of Mr Cudlipp, 427 Pa ave, today at 4 o'clock.

Died: on Mar 31, Mrs Elivina N Barbour, beloved wife of Wm H Barbour, & eldest daughter of S A H Marks, aged 27 years & 10 months. Her funeral will be this afternoon at 3 o'clock, from the residence of her father, 398 south G st, Navy Yard.

Died: on Apr 1, Joseph Savage, infant son of Brvt Lt Col E S & Martha Allen. His funeral is today at 3 o'clock P M, from 320 Va ave.

Died: on Apr 1, Annie Powell, wife of Thos W Spence. Her funeral is on Apr 3 at 3 P M, from 14th & G st, services at St Aloysius Church.

Obit-died: suddenly, on Monday, at Wyoming, Kate, wife of Fendall Marbury, daughter of A K Marshall, of Va, & grand-daughter of the Chief Justice. She was a filial daughter, devoted wife, & affectionate mother. True to her birthright, she was a Virginian always. She adopted herself with wonderful sincerity to the soil of her adoption.

Died: on Mar 27, at Columbia, Pa, Edw C Dimick, son of Gen Justin Dimick, U S A, in his 19th year.

Dept of the Interior, U S Patent Ofc, Wash, Mar 16, 1866. Ptn of Allen B Wilson, of Waterbury, Conn, praying for the extension of a patent granted to him Jun 15, 1852, for an improvement in Sewing Machines, for 7 years from the expiration of said patent, which takes place on Jun 15, 1866. –H C Theaker, Com'r of Patents

Supreme Court of D C, in Equity Docket 7, No 651. Julia A Van Ness vs Barney Barry. On Oct 22, 1845, Barney Barry entered into a contract with Gen John P Van Ness, now deceased, for the purchase of a certain part of a lot, in Wash City, being lot 12 in square 348, for which part of lot the said Barry agreed to pay the sum of $1,000, in 10 annual payments of $100 each. That the said lot was conveyed & the said notes assigned to Col Eugene Van Ness. That the said Barry failed to pay said notes, & that he is now a non-resident of D C. The object of this suit is to procure a sale of the property to satisfy the said note. Absent dfndnt to appear in this Court on the first Tues of Sep next. -R J Meigs, clerk
-Philip, solicitor for cmplnt

Supreme Court of D C, in Equity, No 654. Danl R Hagner & others vs Nathl B Keen, Wm Mitchell, Chas S Mitchell, Eliz Mitchell, Isabella Mitchell & Margaret Mitchell. In 1837 Nathl B Keen sold to Jas Mitchell, jr, a lot of ground described as part of square 355, in Wash; in Feb, 1838, he the conveyed the lot, but, by mistake decribed it as beginning at a point on said 11th st & F; that said lot is known as lot 11; that said Jas Mitchell, jr, was seized of lot 10 also, being a lot immediately south of, & adjoining the the first lot, also fronting 25 feet on 11th st; that said Jas Mitchell, on May 10, 1847, conveyed lots 10, 11, 13, 14, 15, & 16 in square 355, to Nicholas Callan, in trust to secure a debt; that said numbers 10 & 11 were intended to describe the lots aforesaid, but were as insufficient description thereof, & were were applicable to the original lots in said square, which fronted on F st; said Callan sold under the deed of trust, & made a deed to Jas M Smith, in which the same error was repeated. It further states that the cmplnts are heirs at law of the said Jas M Smith; that said Nathl Keen is a non-resident; that the other dfndnts are children & heirs-at-law of Jas Mitchell, jr, who died intestate seized of said property, & said Wm Mitchell is a non-resident. The object of the bill is to have the error in the deed corrected by new conveyances to the cmplnts from said Keen & heirs of Jas Mitchell, jr. Absent dfndnts to appear in this court, in person or by solicitor, on the first Tue of Sept next.
–A B Olin, Justice -R J Meigs, clerk

Mr Faulkner swallowed the test-oath. Hon Chas Jas Faulkner, quondam lt col in the late Confederate army has been admitted to practise his profession in the Circuit Court of Berkeley by Judge Hall. In order to do this he was obliged to take the strongest West Va test-oath-has had to swear that he has not, since Jun 20, 1863, voluntarily borne arms against the U S, including a declaration that he had never aided or sympathized with rebellion, etc. –Richmond Dispatch

TUE APR 3, 1866
The Sec of War has brevetted Maj Robt Morrow, on the Pres' military staff, to be lt colonel for uniform gallantry & meritorious service during the war, the commission to date Apr 12, 1865, on which day Capt Morrow, [since promoted Major] was badly wounded in a cavalry fight at Salisbury,
N C. Capt Morrow was, at that time, on Gen Stoneman's staff.

It was rumored that Chief Justice Chase, with his daughters, Mrs Sprague & Miss Chase, with the child of the former, had set out for N Y en route to Europe. There is great improbability in this rumor.

The new gunboat **Quinebaug** was launched at the Brooklyn Navy Yard on Sat, christened by Lt Cmder Danl B Harmony. The launch was superintended by Naval Constructor B F Delano & his assistant, Mr Thos Webb.

Hon Heister Clymer, Democratic candidate for Govn'r of Pa, on Friday sent in his resignation as Senator from the 6th Senatorial District of that State.

Died: on Apr 2, at the residence of Robt Widdicombe, 352 G st, Laura Leah, youngest child of John W & Gertrude Leftwich, of Memphis, Tenn, aged 1 year. Her funeral, by Rev Brown, is today at the residence, at 11 A M.

Died: on Apr 2, William Berry, infant son of Zach R & Deborah C Brooke, aged 10 months & 11 days. His funeral will take place from the residence of his grandfather, Jas Mankin, 398 9th st, on Wed at 11 A M. Upper Marlborough papers please copy.

Orphans Court of Wash Co, D C, Mar 31, 1866. In the case of Sarah A Butt, admx of Richd Butt, deceased, the administratrix & Court have appointed Apr 24 next, for the final settlement of the personal estate of the said deceased, of the assets in hand. –Z C Robbins, Reg/o wills

At Portsmouth, R I, on Tue, the wife of Mr Isaac Fish having occasion to leave the house, locked her 2 children in & went out on an errand. While gone the children played with matches & the oldest child took fire & was burned in the most shocking manner. It died during the day. Mr Geo E Anthony, a relative of the family, proceed to the house of Mr Fish to render what assistance he could, & on his return, in the afternoon, found his eldest child, a boy 5 years old, drowned in a pond near his house. –Providence Journal

I have this day associated with me, in the real estate business, John F Hickey, & the business will hereafter be McKnew & Hickey. -Room 7, Intelligencer Bldg.

The copartneship existing under the firm of Wyckoff & Denison is this day, Mar 3, dissolved by mutual consent. W S Wyckoff is retiring. The business will be continued by Lyman Denison, jr.

Supreme Court of D C, in Equity Docket 7, No 463. Eliz Sibley vs Ellen Edes et al. Wm F Mattingly, trustee, sold lot 5 in square 401, on Mar 1, 1866, at public auction, to Geo Turnburke, for $1,600, & Turnburke has complied with the terms of sale. –A B Olin, Justice -R J Meigs, clerk

Supreme Court, D C, in Equity No 463. Eliz Sibley against, Barnes, Edes, Hunt, & others, heirs of Ann Martin & Eliz Vigel. Distribution of the fund on Apr 25 next, at my ofc, City Hall, Wash. –W Redin, auditor

WED APR 4, 1866
Chas Dickens is about to give a series of readings, thirty in number, in London, the provinces, & in Scotland, beginning in Liverpool on Apr 5.

Balt, Apr 3. Gen Bradley T Johnson, of Md, late of the rebel army. The Pres has interposed, ordering his bail to be discharged & the abandonment of the case. Johnson claims exception under the terms of the parole.

Mrd: on Apr 3, at the residence of the bride's father, by Rev Fr McCarthy, Wm L Wall to Mary E Berry, all of Wash City. No cards.

Orphans Court-Judge Purcell 1-Mrs S C Harrison appointed guardian to the orphan of U Harrison. 2-Mrs M A Dukes appointed admx of the estate of Levi Dukes. 3-Mrs R M Steward appointed the admx to the estate of A L Steward. 4-J J Bogus appointed guardian to the orphans of S F Boucher. 5-A decree of court was ordered to sell the estate of John Hines. 6-The first & final account of the admx of J Varden, deceased, & J W Perkins, & the second account of John Crumbaugh, were approved & passed.

Notice is given that the following property was sold for taxes by the Collector May 4, 1864, & if not redeemed at this ofc, [together with interest & cost of advertising,] prior to May 4, 1866. Corp deeds will issue to the purchasers, in accordance with existing law. –Saml E Douglass, Reg. In whose name sold:

Alexander, Columbus
Adams, E A
Adams, John G
Anthony, J B
Adams, Jemima, & others
Ashford, John
Adams, J M
Austin, Wm
Anderson, Wm [colored]
Bayliss, Buckner
Boyle, Cornelius
Bevan, C F & W F
Beall, E A & R J
Bird, Eburn
Berret, J H & J W Arnold
Broadhead, J M & Jas Adams
Burche, John C, in trust
Blackestone, Lewis
Boyle, Lavinia
Briscoe, R G
Beale, Robt
Beall, Richd J
Busey, Saml C
Black, Saml
Burdette, W W
Beall, W D
Cazenove, A C
Cazenove, Peter
Coltman, C C
Cleary, D M
Clements, B H
Carroll, D of D'n

Coon, Eliz
Chancellor, P M
Costigan, Eliza
Colton, Edwin
Custis, G W P
Chaves, G G
Clark, Geo R
Coombs, J W, & others
Casgrove, John
Castigan, Joh
Coombs, J J & J Welsh
Clark, Ignatius
Chandler, M & W S
Callahan, Mary E
Callan, Nicholas
Cazenove, Peter
Clarke, Saml
Cassin, Stephen
Cripps, W & M
Cadman, Walter
Downer, Michl
Dunnington, C W C
Davidson, Elanor
Dainies, Francis
Davis, Gideon
Douglass, Henry
Dickson, John
Drury, John H
De Compte, Joachim
De Voss, P J

Downs, Solomon [colored]
Everett, R F & J F
Emerson, G W
Easby, Wm
Everett, S & R
Etting, Solomon
Easby, Wm, in trust
Elliott, Wm P
Ford, Alex, & others
Fling, Jas W
Fitzgerald, Jas
Fisher, T J, in trust
Gladmon, A B
Golding, Eliz
Garner, G W
Garner, G W, in trust
Gardner, Jacob B
Gaddis, L, in trust
Gunnell, W H
Hyde, A, trustee
Hoffman, E R B
Hobzer, Fred'k
Hay, Henry
Hutton, J G
Hitchcock, J V
Holleran, John
Healy, John
Hart, John
Harrison, H B
Hough, Oscar R
Hauptman, P H
Howell, S H
Hill, S H, trust
Hallinane, Thos
Ingle, C
Johnson, Josiah
Jarboe, John T
Johnson, Jas E
Jarboe, Matthew
Jones, P D
Jewell, Wm
Kubel, Edw
Kenney, F S
Kirk, G E, trust
Kendall, J E
Kibbey, John B

Kennally, Martin
Kelly, Miles
King, Thos
King, Z M P
Lyles, Aaron
Lee, Catherine
Linkins, Danl
Lewis, H H
Larned, Jas
Lockwood, J A
Long, John
Lewis, Saml L
Lee, Saml
Law, Thos
Middleton, Arthur
McWilliams, A T
Mulligan, Ann E
Middleton, E J, trustee
Mason, Henry
Mary, H R
Mitchell, H T
Maloney, John
McWilliams, Jos L
McGill, Mary
Morris, Thos
Mitchell, T A
Marcy, V
Noble, Martha
Nicholls, W S
Nicholls, W S & W W Corcoran
O'Donnell, J & M
Openheimer, L
O'Neale, Rhoda
O'Donnell, W & M
Perkins, D R
Page, Geo
Pomeroy, J W
Prout, Jonathan
Prather, O J
Parker, S A
Platt, S H
Phillips, W H & W B Todd
Phillips, Wm F
Rich, David
Roberts, E, & others
Reese, Hugh

Reeside, J O
Ray, J W, trust
Roche, R J
Reynold, Thos
Ridenour, U H & J F Wollard
Rapley, W W
Shadd, B
Sohl, Conrad
Slicer, C H
Stott, Chas
Serrin, Danl
Swinghammer, Eugene
Smith, Gerret
Simmons, J B
Shannon, John
Shields, J W & M Young
Sweetzer, Mary E
Snyder, Nicholas
Sewall, Robt
Sterling, S H
Shoemaker, T E
Shannon, Timothy
Swann, W T
Stone, W H
Smith, Wm, colored
Thruston, B
Taylor, Geo P

Toll, Isaac D
Thomas, J H
Tobin, Jas
Towers, John T
Turner, J H, trust
Thompson, M
Tate, M A S
Tucker, Thos
Taylor, Tho B
Thompson, W S
Tayloe, W H
Terrett, W H
Todd, W B
Uhlman, C L trust
Vanbiller, A
Venable, C S
Van Patten, C H
Vanarsdale, P H
Venable, W P
Wallach, C S, in trust
Wallach, C S
Wimsatt, E
White, M R & others
Williams, S B
Williams, J B
Yates, Wm

Dissolution of copartnership under the name of Legg & Davidson in Wash City. –G W Legg, John Davidson   The business of the late firm will be conducted by me. -John Davidson

Excellent sale of Rosewood Case Piano, parlor suites, & household & kitchen furniture at auction on Apr 4, at the residence of S M Meyenberg, 359 F st, between 9th & 10th sts, opposite St Patrick's Church. –Green & Williams

THU APR 5, 1866
Mr Ewd Burt, a ship carpenter, was accidentally kocked overboard yesterday, by the entangling of a block & falls, whilst shipping the rudder of the new steamer **Resaca**, now on the railway. His head was badly cut & his side much bruised, by striking on the stage before falling in the water, out of which he was taken in an insensible condition, by Mr Geo Cunningham, who was also thrown overboard, but not hurt. Mr Burt recovered sufficiently to be taken home in the yard carryall.

Criminal Court-Wash.
1-J W Hays, indicted for robbery was found guilty of petty larceny.
2-Thos Taylor, for keeping a disorderly house, found guilty.
3-Eliz Harley, for keeping a bawdy house, found not guilty.
4-A nol pros was entered in the case of E Lawrence, alias Lancet, indicted for the larceny of a horse.
5-R McQuade was ordered to be discharged-no one appearing against him.
6-Martin, alias Reddy, indicted with Lambert & McGee for highway robbery, sent back to jail-the witness against them failing to appear.

Died: on Mar 28, at Newport, R I, Mrs Mary P Newton, mother-in-law of Prof John C Schaad, of Wash, D C.

Dan Rice's circus performed yesterday under the canopy at 6th & Missouri ave. Among the distinguished personages present was Lt Gen Grant, accompanied by his little son, & Senor Romero, the Mexican Minister.

Lt Gen Grant has appointed Maj Geo K Leet, Assist Adj Gen of volunteers, to fill the position which was occupied by the late Col T S Bowers. Maj Leet entered the service as a private in a Chicago battery, & having by meritorious conduct received a commission, was selected for his gallantry & zeal by Gen Grant as an officer of his staff. He has since been associated with the late Col Bowers as Assist Adj Gen on the staff of the Lt Gen, & is now a major in the regular army.

On Monday some thieves entered the house of Mr G Fayman & took goods & money to the amount of $250. No clue has yet been obtained of the robbers.

Thos Rogers, who was held for a hearing in a case of larceny, was yesterday sent to jail in default of bail by Superintendent Richards.

Ann Nolan, Mary A Dumont, & Ellen McMichael were arrested on Tue for robbery of a lot of clothes from D Turner, & were sent to jail for court by Justice Handy.

Mrd: on Easter Sunday, 1866, by Rev Mr Keeling, in the Church of the Holy Trinity, Wash, D C, Wm Maitland Wright, of Mass, to Alice A, adopted daughter of Mr & Mrs H R Schoolcraft.

Mrd: on Apr 3, by Rev Mr Walters, at the pastor's residence, Francis M Girton, of Bloomsburg, Pa, to Margaret J Morrison, of N Y. The parties left in the evening train on their bridal tour for Pa. Bloomsburg papers please copy.

Died: on Apr 4, in Alexandria, Va, Mrs Ann Burchell, relict of the late Edw Burchell, in her 80th year. Her funeral will take place from her late residence, 9 South Royal st, in Alexandria, on Apr 6, at 11 A M.

Died: on Apr 1, at Murrey, Pa, Mrs Mary Wallis, daughter of the late John McClelland, of Wash City. Her end was peace.

Fatal railroad accident at Phil on Apr 4, killing the engineer of the train, whose name is Fennimore, & the fireman, whose name is unknown.

Boston, Apr 3. The Supreme Court this afternoon, in the case of Edw Green, the Malden murderer, decided against the writ of error applied for, & confirmed the previous judgment of the court, appointing him to execution.

N Y, Apr 4. The corner-stone of the new cemetery, *St Charles Borromeo Cemetery*, on Lancaster pike, 5 miles from the city, was laid this afternoon with appropriate ceremonies. Nearly all the Catholic clergy were present, & Bishop Hood laid the corner-stone. This is intended to be one of the largest structures of the kind in the world.

The New Hampshire Historical Society has received, through the ex-Pres Pierce, the "Records in the Court of Sessions" in the province of New Hampshire, from 1692 to 1704.

John Ward, one of the oldest & most esteemed citizens of N Y C, died on Mar 31, in his 69th year. His father was Col Saml Ward, of the Revolutionary army. His mother was a daughter of Govn'r Wm Greene, of Rhode Island. Mr Ward was for many years president of the N Y Stock Exchange. By a resolution of that body on his retiring from business, the sum of $500 was appointed for a portrait of him by Wenzler, which has been lately completed.

Maj W C Manning, commanding the District of Savannah, Ga, on Mar 27 received instructions from the authorities in this city to release Mr Yulee from confinement in *Fort Pulaski*, on his parole to proceed to Fla, there to remain until further others from Wash.

Judge Nathl E Green, principal instructor of the Law Dept of the Cumberland Univ, & formerly one of the Justices of the Supreme Bench of Tenn, died at his home in Lebanon on Thursday morning.

Paris True Kentuckian, 29th. On Tue last, Millie, aged 10 years, a daughter of Thos Dolan, a respectable Irishman, living near Ewalt's Cross Roads, was found by her parents on the ground, with her throat cut, & her bowels protruding from a wound in her abdomen. Her person had been outraged. She died in a few minutes after they found her. Suspicion against a negro man, Burt, formerly a slave of H W Thomas. He was arrested & brought to Paris yesterday. Circumstantial evidence being conclusive against him, the outraged citizens took him from the jail & hanged him on a tree. He said he did not do it. After hanging a while he was let down, & still protested his innocence, when he was finally hanged until he died.

FRI APR 6, 1866
Died: on Apr 5, after a long & painful illness, Ida E, oldest daughter of John W & Eliza E Dick, aged 13 years, 10 months & 22 days. Her funeral will take place from the residence of her parents, 206 N Y ave, between 4th & 5th sts, this day at 3 o'clock P M.

Nashville, Apr 5. David Henderson, of this city, has been arrested, charged with being implicated in heavy frauds against the Gov't, occurring in the management of the horse & mule corrals in this vicinity. Henderson gave bail in the sum of $30,000. Mr Phillips & Green Darling were afterwards arrested, & the latter was held for want of bail. A board of inspection is investigating the matter. It has been recently discovered that the fraud on the Gov't will reach $2,000,000.

Obit-died: on Apr 2, at his residence, Midway, Ky, Maj Arnold Harris. He was appointed to West Point from Montg Co, N Y; graduated in 1834; assigned to the 7th infty, stationed at *Fort Gibson*, Cherokee Nation; resigned in 1837; appointed post sutler in 1847 he contracted to carry the U S mail from Panama to San Francisco for 10 years, at $199,000 per annum. This contract assigned to Mr Wm H Aspinwall, taking stock therefore in the Pacific Mail Steamship Co, & the New Orleans agency. He came to Wash, with his father-in-law, the late Gen Robt Armstrong, when the latter was elected Gov't printer. Maj Harris was a warm supporter of Douglas & spent thousands on the Washington States, advocating his election. Jeff Davis never forgave him for this, & when Harris was taken to Richmond a prisoner, having gone out with Magraw to recover the body of Col Cameron, after the first battle of Bull Run, Davis kept him confined 6 months for spite. Few men were better known in the U S than Major Harris; he was a very genial, exceedingly liberal, & never turned his back on a friend. Having an iron constitution & great good humor, he withstood for years an exhausting disease.

Mrs Senator Sprague & Miss Chase sailed for Europe on Wed in the mail steamer **Cunard**.

Died: on Apr 4, Thos Walker, aged 42 years & 4 months. His funeral will be from his late residence, 236 7th st west today, at 3 o'clock P M.

Jas C McGuire & Co, aucts, sold yesterday a 2 story brick dwlg, lot fronting 22 feet with a depth of 55 feet, in reservation 10, 4½ st, Island, to E H King, for $4,700.

Dept of the Interior, U S Patent Ofc, Wash, Mar 21, 1866. Ptn of Wm O Grover & Wm E Baker, of Boston, Mass, praying for the extension of a patent granted to them on Jun 22, 1852, for an improvement in Sewing Machines, for 7 years from the expiration of said patent, which takes place on Jun 22, 1866. –H C Theaker, Com'r of Patents

Chester Harding, the artist, died Sunday at the Tremont House, in this city, after a few days illness. He was one of the pioneer portrait painters of this country, & excelled in the correctness of his likeness. He was born in Conway, Mass, Sep 1, 1792; served in the war of 1812 & then settled in Caledonia, N Y, but adversity obliged him to leave his wife & infant child & seek a new home in the then pathless West. He reached Pittsburgh, & then returned for his family walking some 200 miles, guided by the blazed trees. In 1823 he went abroad & remained 3 years, & on his return he became a resident of this city, & mainly through his efforts the bldg now being removed, on School st, was erected for the accomodation of artists, & known as Harding's Gallery. Among the distinguished men he painted were Webster, Clay, Madison, Monroe, John Quincy Adams, Allston, of this country, & Saml Rogers, Lord Aberdeen, Dukes of Norfolk, Hamilton, & Sussex, of England. His latest effort was a picture of Gen Sherman, which, though unfinished, was exhibited at a recent Artists' Reception in this city. Mr Harding's latter years have been chiefly passed his home in Springfield, Mass. His remains will be carried there for interment. –Boston Journal

Supreme Court of D C, in Equity Docket 7, No 656. Thos Cogan vs Jane McManus et al. Jas McManus, deceased, was in his lifetime indebted to cmplnt in the sum of $430.47, & that he died leaving him surviving Jane McManus, his widow, [who administered on his personal estate,] Hugh McManus, a half brother, & [blank] McManus, brother, & nearest of kin, & that the two last are non-residents of D C; that deceased left a small personal estate, & was seized & possessed of certain real estate in Wash City. The object of this suit is to have an account of the personal estate, & in the event of the same being insufficient for the purpose to subject the real estate to sale for the payment of cmplnt's demand & the other unsatisfied creditors of deceased. Absent dfndnts to appeear in this court on the first Tues of Jun, 1866. –A B Olin, Justice -R E Meigs, clerk -Jas E Williams, solicitor for cmplnts

SAT APR 7, 1866

J C McGuire & Co, aucts, yesterday sold a lot on 13th st, near Mass ave, with a frame dwgl upon it, for $2,100 to Michl Green.

Capt Raphael Semmes was released on his original parole under the Johnston-Sherman convention, under an order issued by the President, yesterday. Capt Semmes left the Marine Barracks in the evening for Balt, it is presumed, accompanied by Mrs Semmes.

Large collection of superior household & kitchen furniture at auction on Apr 12, at the residence of the late David English, 29 First st west, between High & Potomac sts, Gtwn. –Wardwell & Hays, aucts. –C W Boteler, salesmann

Yesterday the parties implicated in the Alexandria riots were sentenced: Mankin, 5 years; Lawlor, 2 years; Horseman & Simpson, 6 months each, in the Albany Penitentiary.

Criminal Court-Wash.
1-Wm Wood, larceny, found guilty.
2-H Birch, larceny, found guilty.
3-F F Grophard was surrendered over to court by his surety, W A Boss, & was rebailed.
4-Wm Samuels, larceny, found guilty.
5-J Day, larceny, found guilty.
6-C H Tyler, larceny, found guilty.
7-W White, larceny, found guilty.
8-Geo Otto, assault with intent to murder a negro boy. Found guilty.
9-W H Shaw, larceny, found guilty.
10-Henry Short, larceny, found guilty.

New Sunday Paper: The **_Sunday Herald_**, devoted to literature & local & general intelligence. The first number of a Newspaper will be published in Wash City on Apr 1st next. Terms: $3 per annum, in advance. Single copies five cents. For further particulars, address Jno T Halleck & Co, Publishers, 375 D st, Wash.

A stable in West Lake st, Chicago, caught fire on Tue, & an old man named Heinrich Bohler & his daughter, age 13, who were asleep in the loft, were burned to death.

Pere Wilmer, in his 80th year, one of the oldest & wealthiest citizens of Queen Anne's Co, died on Mar 31. The deceased frequently represented his county in the legislature.

Harvey Mansfield, of Bristol, Vt, while filing a saw with his gloves on, stopped to rub his eyes, & so filled them with steel filings that it is feared he will entirely lose his sight.

Died: on Apr 6, of consumption, Dr Henry G Gibbs, of Norwich, N Y, aged 36 years. His funeral is tomorrow at 3 o'clock P M, from the residence of his brother-in-law, Dr S A H McKim, 472 I st south.

Died: on Apr 5, Jas Sheehy, formerly of Alexandria, Va, in his 42nd year. His funeral is this evening at 3 o'clock, from the residence of his mother, 535 I st, near 5th.

John Lee, a highly respected colored man died on last Friday, in his 73rd year. He has been well known in Charleston for the past half century. -Charleston Courier

MON APR 9, 1866
Hon Mathew Harvey, Judge of the U S District Court for N H, died at Concord on Sat, aged 85 years.

Gen Scott was expected to leave New Orleans for N Y on Friday. His health has been gradually improved by his trip.

Alexandria Gaz of Sat: We regret to announce the death of Maj Alfred M Barbour, formerly of Culpeper, but for several years before the war a resident of Jefferson Co, Va, & superintendent of the armory at Harper's Ferry. Maj Barbour served several times in the Va Legislature, & during the late war was chief quartermaster to Gen Jos E Johnston's army. [No death date given-current item.]

Maj Gen A T A Torbert has been granted 6 months' leave of absence, with permission to go beyond the sea.

The steamboat **C H Hayner** exploded her boiler at Troy, N Y, on Sat. Five lives were lost, including the capt, C H Hayner, of West Troy. The boat instantly sunk.

On Friday, Judge Wyhe, in the Equity Court, made a decree divorcing from bed & board Margaret A Moore from Thos Moore, giving cmplnt the custody & management of all property acquired by her since her marriage, & the custody of the children, & directing the dfndnt to pay the costs of the suit & alimony of $30 per month. The ground for the petition is alleged harsh & cruel treatment. –A Lloyd for petitioner.

Wash Corp, Apr 2, 1866. 1-Ptn of Mrs Mary E Murtagh: referred to the Cmte on Improvements. 2-Ptn of John R Murray: referred to the Cmte on Finance. 3-Ptn of Victor Von Briesen for relief: referred to the Cmte on Claims.

On Sat, while Gen Grant was exercising his fast gray nag on 14th st, Ofcrs Bailey & Crown, after a sharp race, arrested him for **fast driving**. Gen Grant offered to pay the usual fine imposed in such cases, which of course, the ofcrs could not receive; but the Gen expressed his doubts of their authority to arrest him, & drove off. The case was reported to Superintendent Richards. It is stated that this street is becoming a common racing ground, & that a large number of arrests for violations of the ordinance prohibiting fast driving are made every pleasant day, when those who delight in speed are out exercising their stock.

Real estate sales by Green & Williams, aucts: lot 5 in square 461, on 7th st, with a 2 story brick house, to Mrs Margaret Golden, for $9,550. Part of lots 3 & 4 in square 296, on C st, with a good 2 story frame house, to John H Gibson, for $2,000. Part of lot 6 in square 264, on 13½ st, to John Shea, for $1,600. Part of lot 17 in square 496, on F, to J W Gibson, for $1,000. A 2 story frame house & lot on M st, near 15th, to Col J S Williams, for $1,000.

Died: on Mar 28, in Chas Co, Md, in her 61st year, Mrs Mary E Wilmer, relict of the late Rev Simon Wilmer.

Died: on Apr 5, in Geneva, N Y, M G Delaney, surgeon U S N, aged 54 years.

Died: at St Augustine, Fla, whither he had gone for the improvement of his declining health, Emund Brick, of Phil, latterly a resident of Wash City, in his 36th year. [No death date given-current item.]

Gtwn affairs. Man shot at Lang's Hotel. Yesterday Benj F Hough, a clerk in one of the depts shot Saml Gaskings, of this place. Hough has been in the hotel & someone pinned a note on his coat which was written "nuisance." He left the hotel, & returned in a short time & said he could whip the man who pinned that note to his coat. Gaskings said, "I did it." Hough drew a pistol & fired, the ball taking effect in the stomach of Gaskings. Hough tried to escape, but was turned over to the police. Gaskings was conveyed to his home on Jefferson st, but it is not known if the wound is dangerous or not. [Apr 12th newspaper: Gaskings was much better yesterday evening at 7 o'clock.] [Apr 13th newspaper: Benj F Hough was held to bail in the sum of $1,000, Mr Wm Boss becoming his surety.]

Mrs Mary A Gatewood, if an innocent woman, is certainly a grievously abused one, for she is known to the police as an old offender. Messrs Clarvoe & McDevitt arrested her yesterday for robbing the house of Senator Sprague. She was sent to her old quarters in the jail by Justice Walter. She is to be tried in the Criminal Court tomorrow.

For sale or rent, the commodious house & grounds located at the n e corner of North Capitol & Boundary sts, lately the residence of Chas J Uhlman. Apply to Mrs Mina Uhlman, on the premises, or to Fred W Jones, Atty-at-Law, 5th st, between D & E sts.

Will be offered at public sale, on Apr 16, the premises known as Cloudland, adjoining the property of Judge Carroll Stephens; within 10 minutes walk of the Bladensburg Depot; the house is comfortable, & contains 10 rooms, with kitchen, carriage-house, & stable. Possession given at any moment. Judge Stephens will show the place, but the owner will be almost constantly in the house till the day of sale. –Thos T Hunter, on the premises, of Mr Hyatt's, Bladensburg Depot.

Mr Reid Bigler, a son of ex-Govn'r Bigler, of Pa, committed suicide a few days since.

TUE APR 10, 1866
On Feb 2, Col Geo W McCook, of Ohio, reported at police headquarters that his room, no 68, Willard's Hotel, had been robbed. Yesterday Chas E Beecher, not yet 19, of N Y C, was found to have McCook's valise in his possession, having offered to sell it to Jas Richardson for $3. His family occupies a highly respectable position in N Y C. He was arrested & was waiting for his brother to arrive, whom he telegraphed, for bail.

Fancy & Theatrical Costumes to be hired from Frank E Rea, Franklin House, corner of 8th & D sts. [Ad]

Criminal Court-Judge Fisher, Apr 9, 1866.
1-Rachel Smith, murder, verdict guilty of manslaughter.
2-Alfred Grimes, who has been confined in jail on a charge of assault & battery was admitted to bail in the sum of $250, Wm H Upperman, becoming his surety.
3-Jas Wills, charged with larceny; Wm F Hartright, charged with obtaining goods by false pretences, & Henry Prince, charged with assault & battery, & who are out on recognizances, were discharged upon the recommendation of the Grand Jury; & by the same authority Dennis Hill & Martha Plant were discharged from jail.
4-Naturalization papers were granted to Henry Dickman, a subject of the Duke of Hesse Darmstadt, & August Dittrich, a subject of the King of Prussia.

Died: on Apr 8, suddenly, Geo McCeney. His funeral will be from his residence, near Wash City, this morning at 10 o'clock.

Died: on Apr 9, Mrs Mary A B, wife of Israel M Jackson, sr, in her 68th year. Her funeral will be from the residence of her son-in-law, T J Barclay, in PG Co, Md, today at 2 P M.

Green & Williams, aucts, yesterday sold lot 12 in square 441, on 7th st, between S & T sts, to Chas M Floyd, at 30 cents per foot. On Sat they sold lot 5 in square 705 to Wm H Marlow, at 20½ cents per square foot.

Criminal Court-Wash-Apr 9. Rachel Smith, colored, was convicted of manslaughter in the death of a child 32 days old, an infant son of Mary Parker, colored. She dropped the child while she was intoxicated.

Mr Henry Shultz died in Balt on Friday last, after an illness of several years. He was a veteran of the war of 1812.

Excellent household & kitchen furniture at auction on Apr 12, at the residence of R A Phillips, 114 Bridge st, near Congress, all of the furniture.
–Thos Dowling, auct

Colt's new pistol factory at Harford will be the most complete establishment of the kind in the world, & will contain an immense & very perfect system of varied & most ingenious machinery. The new Colt's pistol factory, [on the site of the burnt edifice,] will, with the cost of the timber for piling, exceed $60,000. It will have a front of 500 feet, all of beautiful pressed brick with stone caps & facings, & the total cost of the new bldg must be about a quarter of a million.

House for rent with furniture, 16, corner of Pa ave & 21st st, at present occupied by Maj Gen O O Howard, [next house west of Sir Ed Bruce's residence,] contains 15 rooms, with 1 acre of ground. Possession given May 5 next. Apply to Wm Y Steiger at the Gen Land Ofc.

Fashionable 3 story brick house on 11th st, between G & H sts, at public auction,

on Apr 18, contains 8 good rooms. House was formerly occupied by Gen Carrington, U S District Atty, & now occupied by E Kuhl.
–Green & Williams, aucts

Cincinnati Daily Times: M D Potter, of the Daily Commercial, died at his residence in this city, this morning. He was born on Nov 27, 1819, of poor parents, residing in Clinton Co, Ohio, & was 46 years, 4 months & 7 days old at the time of his death. His father died when he was a young child, & his early life was passed under all the disadvantages of orphanage. By some means he was able to attend school for some time in Gtwn, D C. His mother resided for a short time in Vicksburg, Miss, & her son went into the ofc of the Jackson Mississippian, where he learned the printer's trade, under the care of Hon H S Foote. About 22 years ago, after being married, he moved to Cincinnati; & later became the sole proprietor of the Commercial. Richd Henry Lee, of Maysville, Ky, was at one time owner of a portion of the Commercial, but on Mr Lee's death, Mr Potter took back the share of the deceased.

Fashionable 3 story brick house on 11th st, between G & H sts, at public auction, on Apr 18, contains 8 good rooms. House was formerly occupied by Gen Carrington, U S District Atty, & now occupied by E Kuhl.
–Green & Williams, aucts

Chancery sale of improved real estate, by decree of the Supreme Court of D C, rendered on Feb 27, 1866, in a cause in which Sarah McIntosh & others are cmplnts, & Ann V McIntosh & others are dfndnts: public auction on Apr 21, of lot 5 in square 725, with bldgs thereon; the said lot fronting on north B st, between 1st & 2nd sts. –Jas Lynch, Thos Scrivener, A Green, John Dudley, Florian Hitz, Com'rs. –M Thompson, S W Williams, cmplnts solicitors
-Green & Williams, aucts

Supreme Court of D C, No 538, in Equity Docket 7. Wm A Hyland et al vs Christopher Hyland et al. Sale reported by the trustee be ratified & confirmed. By order of the Court: -R J Meigs, clerk [No other information.]

Chancery sale of valuable property on east side of 14th st, between E & F sts, opposite Willard's Hotel; by decree passed by the Supreme Court of D C, in Chancery No 561, Equity Docket No 7, wherein Francis H Espey is cmplnt & Jas W St Clair et al are dfndnts: public auction, on May 21 next, of all those 2 parts of lots 10 & 11 in square 254, in Wash City, with 2 brick bldgs thereon.
–Wm F Mattingly, Jno H Johnson, trustees -Green & Williams, aucts

WED APR 11, 1866
"Our Mutual Friend" brings Dickens between five & ten thousand pounds.

Thos Clowes, postmaster at Troy, N Y, ex-recorder & politician of considerable prominence in times past throughout the State, died Sunday, aged 76 years.

Orphans Court-Judge Purcell, Apr 10, 1866.
1-Mrs Susan G Trott, widow of the late Thos P Trott, deceased, renounced her right to administer on the estate of said deceased in favor of her son, Thos H Trott.
2-Maggie Galvin, a daughter of Mich Galvin, was, with the consent of her father, bound apprentice to Robt Widdicombe until she shall attain the age of 16 years.
3-Priscilla Marshall was appointed guardian to the orphans of Eliz Chew, deceased. Bond $2,500. Sureties, Noah Bias & Philip B Vernon.
4-Susannah Holland was appointed guardian to the orphans of John E Holland, deceased. Bond $5,000. Sureties, Wm W Cox & Wm E Lowry.
5-Thos H Trott qualified as adm of the estate of Thos P Trott, deceased. Bond $5,000. Sureties, Thos M Smith & Selina C Pendleton.

On Apr 3, Peter Penn Gaskill, the head of the lineal descendants of Wm Penn, the founder of Pa, died in Phil, after a short illness, on his 66th birthday.

Mormon obituatry notice: The death of the Mormon bishop is announced in the Salt Lake paper. "He was 37 years old, & leaves an interesting family of 11 wives & 37 small children to mourn his death.:

Criminal Court-Judge Fisher-Apr 10, 1866.
1-Mary A Gatewood: larceny: verdict, not guilty, by reason of insanity.
2-G A Smyth, who is out on bail, & Frank Bell, who is confined in jail, were discharged by order of the Grand Jury.
3-John Thomas, who has been held in custody on a charge of arson, gave bail for his appearance in the sum of $100, Mr Edw Hammond becoming his surety.
4-Wm Williamson, who was held as a witness in the case of John Housewright et al, indicted for keeping a gaming house, gave bail for his appearance in the sum of $1,000.
5-Mary Jones, alias Mary Cooper: larceny: motion for a new trial overruled.
6-John Henry: larceny: motion for a new trial overruled.

Fortress Monroe, Apr 9. A daring escape from the fortress of a prisoner, Michl Foeley, a private of Co H, 5th U S artl, under sentence in main guard-house for mutiny & other misdemeanors, was made night before last, & so far he has eluded the ofcrs. The manner of escape is somewhat involved in mystery. The ball & chain attached to his leg were sawed off by some means, &, forcing the iron bars of one of the windows of the guards, he either precipitated himself into the moat & swam out of the tide gates, or scaled the parapet. A reward of $50 has been offered for his apprehension.

Mrd: on Mar 13, at the Church of Epiphany, by Rev Chas H Hall, D D, Arthur St J Causir, of Wash, to Miss Mary C, 2nd daughter of W W Bruce, of Lexington, Kentucky.

Oldest Inhabitants meeting: date correction. Mr Gurk was executed on Oct 28, 1802. See Cranch's Report, Vol 1, page 72. –Amicus [Note: This does not refer to anything in this paper, but to Cranch's Report. That report was not in the newspaper.]

Dept of State, Wash, Apr 7, 1868. 1-Information received from Mr W P Jones, the Consul of the U S at Amoy, of the death, on Nov 16, 1865, at the hospital in Amoy, of S Peterson, a seaman of the vessel **Wild Gazelle**. 2-Information received from Mr Geo F Seward, the Consul Gen of the U S at Shanghai, China, of the death, on Nov 6, 1865, at Shanghai, of Saml Langford, an American citizen. Also from the same source, information of the death, on Dec 4, 1865, at sea, of Saml Penderson, a seaman on the ship **E W Seyburn**.

Mrd: on Apr 10, at the residence of the bride's father, by Rev Fr Heitzelberger, Horatio Bates, of N Y, to Sophie Diggs, of Wash City.

Executor's sale of **Grassland**, residence of the late Hamilton Loughborough, 2½ miles from Wash, & 1 miles from the limits of Gtwn; will be sold in one tract, 204½ acres, or in subdivisions to suit purchasers. The family mansion is large & substantial, built of brick in the old English style. –A H Loughborough, exc, at 42 Lexington st, Balt. Or Downman & Green, agents, 18 Intelligencer Bldg, Wash, D C.

Chancery sale of lots 1 thru 17 in square 566, in Wash City, one lot improved by a good 2 story frame dwlg. Auction on May 1, by decree of the Supreme Court of D C, pronounced in cause No 618, in Equity, wherein Saml Pumphrey et al are cmplnts, & Wm Downs et al are dfndnts. Suqare 566 is bounded by south M & west 3rd sts & Delaware ave, Island. –Jas E Williams, Wm Jno Miller, trustees -Green & Williams, aucts

Thos Clowes, postmaster at Troy, N Y, ex-recorder & politician of considerable prominence in times past throughout the State, died Sunday, aged 76 years.

Orphans Court of Wash Co, D C. Letters of administration on the personal estate of Thos P Trott, late of Wash, D C, deceased. –Thos H Trott, adm

THU APR 12, 1866
Albany, Apr 11. This afternoon a Frenchman, whose name is not known, & a man named Michl Chestnut, had an angry discussion over political matters, on Broadway, during which Chestnut struck the Frenchman with a powerful blow on the head, killing him instantly. Chestnut has not been arrested.

Fearful tragedy in Ky-Maj Waters, of Ga, killed. In Millersburg, of this county, Henry M Boulden, of this county, about 19 years of age, son of Jesse H Boulden, was being tried before the trustees of Millersburg for a breach of the peace, committed the night before, & during the progress of the trial young Boulden jumped up, drew his pistol, flourished it, & swearing said, "any person who said he fired his pistol the night before told a lie," & he would kill the person who touched him. The marshal attempted to arrest him, & called bystanders to assist, & in the attempt to do so he fired his pistol twice, the first shot killing F E Waters, son of H H Waters, of Columbus, Ga, & formerly auditor of that State. Waters was about 21 years of age, & had lost a leg before Atlanta, during the war, having been a major in the 4th Georgia regt. He was a student in the College of Millersburg & was looked upon as the most brilliant young man in the institution. When Boulden found he had killed Waters he was deeply affected.
–Paris [Ky] True Kentuckian

Criminal Court-Wash-Apr 11, 1866.
1-Henry Short & Geo W Allen, alias John W Wilson: larceny. Nolle pros, as to Short. Verdict, guilty as to Allen: sentenced to 1 year in the Albany penitentiary.
2-Jas Taylor: larceny: accused plead guilty. Sentence: 1 year in the Albany penitentiary.
3-Wm Williams: larceny. Nolle pros by the District Atty.
4-Jacob Stephens, Geo Lawrence, & Asbury H Parry: larceny. The recognizance of Parry forfeited. Verdict, guilty as to Lawrence, not guilty as to Stephens. Sentence: 15 months in the Albany penitentiary.
5-Del Bartlett: larceny. Nolle pros by the District Atty.

Circuit Court-Judge Olin, Mar 11, 1866.
1-Clement Hill vs K H Lambell. Verdict for plntf in the sum of $178.70, with interest from Mar 1, 1864.
2-Benj F Moxley vs Geo W Hopkins & John S Hopkins. Case settled & dismissed.
3-John O'Connell vs Edw S O'Connor. Verdict for plntf in the sum of $143.
4-Jacob H Smith, Franklin L Smith, & Saml F Smith vs David R Smith. Verdict for dfndnt. Motion for new trial withdrawn.
5-Griffith vs Plantz & Lynch. Verdict for plntf for $166.32.
6-Nelson S Easton vs Erwin G Comstock & Jos L Savage. Verdict for plntf for $613.

Real estate sales: J C McGuire & Co, aucts, sold lot 28 in square 107, fronting on 18th st west, between K & L sts, improved by a small frame dwlg-house, to B Curran, at 60 cents per square foot. Mr C W Boteler, auct, sold lot 11 in square 502, on H st, between 2nd & 3rd sts, to John C McKelden, for 33 1/8th cents per foot.

Died: on Apr 10, suddenly, Mr Wm Richards, aged 58 years. His funeral will take place from Christ Church, Navy Yard, on Apr 13 at 3 o'clock P M.

Phil, Apr 11. Horrible crime. A family of 7 persons were murdered. It consisted of Christopher Deering, his wife, niece, & 4 children. Mr Deering's farm is at Point House road & Jones lane. The supposed murder was committed last Friday, by a German laborer on the farm. One of the victims was a baby 10 months old. Deering was a cattle dealer, aged 38 years. Miss Healing, his cousin, was aged 45 years, & his 4 children ranged from 14 months to 8 years. His residence is located in the suburbs, about 1½ miles beflow the Navy Yard. The murderer has not yet been captured.
+
Phil, Apr 11. Mayor McMichael has offered a reward of $1,000 for the apprehension of the murderer of the Deering family. [Apr 13th newspaper: the name of the missing German is Timothy Slomon. Mrs Dolan, the mother of Eliz Dolan, one of the murdered parties, was brought down this monring from Burlington, & an examination made under her direction. It revealed that Slomon carried away with him 2 guns & 2 pistols, a satchel containing several ladies' dresses, a gold locket & chain, 2 rings, 2 fifty dollar compound-interest notes & one twenty dollar ompound interest note. The name of the murderer is Antoine- last name unknown. The name previously telegraphed is an error. He is believed to have been in the army, & was formerly from Brooklyn. He is 5 feet 11 inchess; aged 25 to 30 years, weight about 175 to 180 pounds, loosely made, shuffling gait, & speaks broken English. The bodies were terribly mutilated. The only remaining of the entire family, was a son, who was absent. Mr Deering's family consisted of himself, wife & 5 children, a relation named Eliz Dolan, & a boy who had resided with the family for several years known to the neighborhood as Cornelius. A German was engaged by Mr Deering to do work around the premises, & who, with the boy Cornelius, is missing at the present time. The absent son, William, age 10 years, happened to be paying a visit to a relative, named Duffy, in West Phil. The names of the persons murdered are:
Mr Christopher Deering, aged 37 years.
Mrs Julia Deering, aged 44 years.
John Deering aged 8 years.
Thos Deering, aged 6 years.
Annie Deering, aged 4 years.
Emma Deering, aged 14 months.
Mrs Eliz Dolan, aged [blank] [An elderly lady.]
There is every reason to believe the murders were committed on Saturday. Yesterday a neighbor visited the premises to feed a colt he had charge of & discovered the feet of Mr Deering projecting through the hay. He made a hasty retreat to inform an acquaintance, John Gool. The other bodies were soon found. Chief Detective Benj Franklin, Police Lt Frank Hampton, Detective John Lamon, proceeded at one to the scene of the murder. Phil, Apr 12. An additional victim to the horrible tragedy was discovered this morning. The body of the boy Cornelius Cary was found under a hay-stack, with his head crushed.]
[Apr 16th newspaper: The prisoner said his accomplice, Jacob Gaunter, came to Mr Deering's place on Friday, the day before the murder, & had 5 bottles of whiskey, which they drank while making arrangements for murdering the family.

It was finally agreed between them that he [Probst] was to make away with the boy, & Gaunter the rest of the family. Probst killed the boy with an axe. The family was killed first; when Mr Deering stepped out of the carriage Gaunter knocked him down with the axe. The woman was killed right there. Gaunter was a man about 38 years old, stout, large shoulders, big face, & dark brown hair; came from Switzerland. Antoine Probst, the murderer, reached the county prison yesterday & placed in the cell recently occupied by Berger, the murderer of Miss Watt.] [Apr 19th newspaper: Counsel assigned by the court for Antoine Probst: Messrs John P O'Neil & J C Wolbert. Probst was a bounty jumper who had entered the service several times, & had received large counties. They allege, also, that he shot his thumb off deliberately, in order to gain his discharge. Among his comrades his character was anything but enviable.]

Mrd: on Mar 13, 1866, at the Church of Epiphany, by Rev Chas H Hall, D C, Arthur St J Carrier, of Wash, to Miss Mary C, 2nd daughter of W W Bruce, of Lexington, Ky. Lexington, Ky, Observer & Reporter please copy.

Burgundy for rent: the spacious & elegant residence of Mr Geo D Fowle, with about 5 acres of land, about 3 miles from town. Apply to Hooe & Wedderburn, Alexandria, Va.

Sale of 3 story brick house, 10 rooms, gas, etc, 361 K st, between 12th & 13th sts. Apply to C C Meador, 339 Pa ave.

Died: on Apr 11, Lt Cmder M Patterson Jones, U S Navy. [Apr 27th newspaper: Lt Cmder Jones died suddenly at the late residence of his father, in Fairfax Co, Va; his father, late Cmdor Thomas Ap Catesby Jones, was a highly distinguished ofcr who had served in the war of 1812 & other occasions. His son Patterson, the subject of this notice, entered the naval service in Sep, 1841, & after several years of active service at sea, passed with high honors in 1847, the examination at the Annapolis Academy, then recently established. During out late unhappy civil war he remained true to the flag & served with honor the whole war, his last duty at sea in command of the U S steamer **Pocahontas**, attached to the West Gulf Blockading Squadron. Peace to his ashes. His sorrowing mother & relatives have met with an irreparable loss. He was a modest Christian gentleman & a steadfast friend.]

Richmond, Apr 11. Capt R B Winder, who has been imprisoned here for several months, was discharged today by orders from Washington.

Raleigh, N C, Apr 3, 1866. The trial of Maj John H Gee, the former commandant of the rebel prison at Salisbury, N C, which began here on Feb 21, is still in progress, although the evidence for the prosecution has not been closed. No doubt the trial will be continued throughout the spring, & will cost the Gov't at least $100,000 to $125,000. Not to speak of the witnesses, some of whom have been kept here 3 months on pay not sufficient to meet their ordinary expenses.

Troy Times, Apr 7. Accident today in the river to the tug steamboat **Charles H Hayner**, by the explosion of the boiler. It immediately sunk, & all on board perished. There were 5 on the boat: Chas H Hayner, capt & one of the owners of the vessel; Thos Ryan, engineer; Wm Ward, hand, Walter Myers, cook; & Geo Green, fireman. Other owners of the *Hayner* were Senator Collins & Michl McDonough. It was rumored that Mr A D Collins, engineer of the Osgood fire engine, was on board, but we cannot vouch for that.

Sale of valuable real estate within 1 mile of Wash City, being the residence of the late Washington Berry, called *Metropolis View*: by decree of the Supreme Court of D C, in Chancery, in a cause wherein Middleton et al are cmplnts, & Berry et al are dfndnts: auction on Dec 21, at the auction rooms of C W Boteler, jr, on May 3. *Metropolis* is at the terminus of Lincoln ave, opposite *Glenwood Cemetery*, & binding on what is known as the old Bladensburg road; contains 376 acres. The trustees have had the property carefully surveyed & subdivided into 40 lots, containing from 5 to 31 acres each. Mr T C Magruder, who resides upon the premises, will show the house. –John A Middleton, Thos W Berry, trustees -W D Davidge, Atty. –Chas W Boteler, jr, auct.

Dept of the Interior, U S Patent Ofc, Wash, Apr 4, 1866. Ptn of Asahel G Batchelder, of Lowell, Mass, & Geo O Way, of Claremont, Minn, administrator of the estate of Lafayette F Thompson, deceased, praying for the extension of a patent granted to them on Jul 6, 1852, for an improvement in Railroad Car Brakes, for 7 years from the expiration of said patent, which takes place on Jul 6, 1866. –H C Theaker, Com'r of Patents.

FRI APR 13, 1866
Mr Danl Harris, living in Paris Grove township, Benton Co, Ind, died on Mar 22, from that terrible malady, hydrophobia, after 4 days of intense suffering. About 2 months ago, Mr Harris brought a pup that he was raising into the house, supposing from its actions that it had the distemper. He was bitten on the finger. He then killed the dog. On Sunday he was attacked with all the symptons of hydrophobia. When will people learn that human lives are more valuable than dogs?

Excellent household & kitchen furniture at auction on Apr 12, at the residence of R A Phillips, 114 Bridge st, near Congress, all of the furniture.
–Thos Dowling, auct

The wife of Saml K Rose, a justice of the peace of Chicago, was burned to death on Monday last. Her clothes caught fire while she was working about the stove in the kitchen.

Mr Warren Teaton, a native of Alexandria, Va, & for 8 years past connected with E J Hart & Co, of New Orleans, died in that city on Apr 6.

Appointments: Mr E A Adams, Intendant of the Wash Asylum, made vacant by the death of his father, Josias Adams, & which was lately declined by Mr Wm E Hutchinson, master plumber in the Navy Yard. Mr Adams is a graduate of the Gtwn Medical School, & a practical chemist & druggist.

Criminal Court-Judge Fisher, Apr 12, 1866.
1-Asbury H Parry: larceny: forfeiture of recognizance remitted, & nolle pros entered by the District Atty.
2-Benj F Hough: assault & battery with intent to kill: accused gave bail in the sum of $1,000 for his appearance in court.
3-Jas Housewright, Jas P Ellicott, & Robt Magee: indicted for keeping gaming tables, were admitted to bail in the sum of $1,000 each.
4-Wm H Shaw, convicted of larceny & who escaped from the custody of the marshal,
a capias was issued for the arrest of the accused.
5-Geo Thomas, who is out on bail, was discharged by direction of the grand jury.
6-Isadore Phillips, who was arrested here by the deputy marshal of the State of N Y under a warrant issued by Judge Betts on a charge of forgery, was brought into court, & ordered to be committed to the common jail until he shall be discharged by due course of law.

An old man named Patrick Farley was cruelly murdered on Sunday last at the junction of the Michigan Southern railroad, 6 miles south of Chicago. Farley was paralyzed in his right arm. He permitted John Mollison to sleep in his watch-box, & it is supposed they had a quarrel & Mollison killed Farley by beating him to death with a long iron bolt.

Nashville, Apr 11. 1-Danl Williams, postmaster at Franklin, Tenn, has been committed to jail by the U S com'r, charged with abstracting letters with money enclosures, addressed to parties in Phil 2-Henry Bruner's trial has been postponed until Monday.

Wm Grady was hung at Eliz, N J, on Wed, for the murder of Fergus Collins, in Aug, 1864. His crime: on the evening in question, Grady, with Geo Dixon, returned to Eliz from N Y, after drinking freely, & were noisy & boisterous. They met Collins on 4th st, & he unintentionally shoved against one of them, the result being that he, Collins, was beaten until life was extinct, the body being thrown into a creek. Grady was tracked to Trenton & there lost-having enlisted in the N J volunteers. Grady went to the war, & after remaining there about 12 months was taken suddenly sick while in camp at Goldsboro, N C. He exhibited symptoms of insanity, & while in one of these fits, he made his confession of his guilt. In the meantime Geo Dixon was convicted of murder in the 2nd degree, & sentenced to the State prison for 20 years, where he is now serving his sentence. The Govn'r consented to respite the unhappy man for 2 weeks.

The Senate confirmed the following named brig generals to be major generals by brevet: Thos H Neill, Benj J Spooner, Morgan H Chrysler, & Martin T McMahon.

Fortress Monroe, Apr 9. The schnr **Pacific** arrived today from Pobosko Bar, Mexico, bound to N Y with a cargo of logwood. She brings the capts of the brig **Star of Hope**, Boston, & the schnr **Wm Cousins**, of Prince Edward's Island. Both vessels were totally lost on the coast of Mexico. Th brig wrecked on Feb 16 on the Pobosko bar. The schnr caught fire on Mar 8, & burned to the water's edge. The brig **Cyclone**, of Prince Edward's Island, was also lost in Mar, 22 miles from Tobasko Bar, having gone there to load logwood for NY. The schnr **John C Henry**, reported by telegraph as having arrived here leaking, was from Wash, D C, bound to Norfolk, with a cargo of lime & coal. She encountered heavy weather from the n e in Chesapeake Bay on Sat, & was abandoned. The capt & crew were taken on board the steamer **Liberty**, from Balt, bound for Havana, & were transferred to the schnr **Witch of the Wave**, from N Y, bound to the York river.

Phil, Apr 12. A despatch to the police & fire alarm system says that this evening the gas meter in Simon Gartland's, undertaker, stable, on 17th & Barker sts, exploded under the dead bodies of the Deering family. The damage was slight.

Mrd: on Apr 12, at the Church of the Epiphany, by Rev C H Hall, D D, Capt Robt G Rutherford, Veteran Reserve Corps, to Lizzie M, daughter of the late Wm W King, of Wash, D C. N Y papers please copy.

Died: on Apr 11, Lt Cmder M Patterson Jones, U S Navy. His funeral is today at 10 o'clock A M, from Sharon, Va, the residence of his father, the late Cmdor T Ap Catesby Jones.

Died: on Apr 10, suddenly Mr Wm Richards, aged 58 years. His funeral will take place from Christ Church, Navy Yard, on Apr 13 at 3 o'clock P M.

Mr John E Tilton, senior member of the publishing-house of J E Tilton & Co, Boston, died on Sat of consumption, aged 35 years.

SAT APR 14, 1866

N Y, Apr 13. The Hon Danl S Dickinson died this morning. Mr Dickinson died last night, at the residence of S G Courtney, his son-in-law. His death was occasioned by strangulated hernia. He was down town yesterday attending to business.
+
Birmington, Apr 13. Arrangements have been made for the interment of his body in this place Sunday. The bells are tolling & the stores & public bldgs are being draped in mourning. He was universally beloved, & all feel his death as a personal affliction.
+

Death of Hon Danl S Dickinson: born in Goshen, Litchfield Co, Conn, Sep 11, 1800, was in his 66th year at the time of his death. While yet a mere child his father removed to the village of Chanango, N Y, in what is now known as the town of Guilford. Young Danl went to a common school; worked at a mechanical trade; became a student of law; admitted to the bar in 1826; in 1831 he removed to Binghamton; in 1836 he was elected to the State Senate; elected to the position of lt govn'r in 1842; in 1844 was a member of the convention that named Jas K Polk for the Presidency; in 1844 was elected to the Senate of the U S; in 1852 he was brought forward for the Presidency, but after some ballots, his name, by his own direction, was withdrawn. He was appointed U S District Atty for N Y by Pres Lincoln, & died in that position.

Geo B Lipscomb, a roundsman of the Metropolitan Police force, on duty in the 3rd Police Precinct, Gtwn, died at his residence in Gtwn, yesterday morning. He had been on the police force since its organization, & was a faithful & most efficient ofcr. He also served as a soldier for the Union, being one of the first to repond to Pres Lincoln's first call for troops, & served, we believe, as a lt during the 3 months service. Superintendent Richards, yesterday, issued the porper order announcing Mr Lipscomb's death, & directed a detail of 30 men of the police force to attend the funeral this afternoon.

Circuit Court-Judge Olin, Apr 13, 1866.
1-Geo A Bohrer vs Thos E Clarke: verdict for the plntf in the sum of $727.82 with interest from Apr 6, 1865.
2-John Henney vs Peter Hartenstein. Dfndnt confesses judgment for $432.97, with interest.
3-Peter Henney vs John Keller. Verdict for plntf in the sum of $209.72, with interest.
4-Oliver G Abell vs Wm H Goddard. The death of the plntf was suggested, & on the motion of Mr Mattingly, it was ordered that the suit be revived, in the name of the plntf's executor, Lyman M Green.
5-Oliver G Abell vs Philip H Reinhard & Horace L Skinner. Same order as above.
6-Naturalization papers were granted to Godfrey H Leonard, a subject of the Queen of Great Britain.

N Y, Apr 13. John Lambert, an Englishman, has been arrested here, charged with having stolen $20,500 from W L Adams, U S collector at Astoria, Oregon.

Mary Nepper, age 6 years old, living in Cleveland, Ohio, was so severely burned on Monday, that she died a few hours therafter. She & several little girls had built a small bonfire in the road in front of her father's house. The mother put it out, but the children kindled it again. Mary's clothes caught fire, & her mother, in attempting to rescue her child, was so severely burned, that she is not expected to live.

Criminal Court-Judge Fisher, Apr 13, 1866.
1-Mary A Gatewood: larceny: jury could not agree-jury discharged.
2-Wm P Hanley, Jas Pike, Chas McGuire, & Henry Collins. Assault & battery, with intent to kill Robt Edelin. It is alleged that the crime was committed in Feb last at the residence of Mr John Hogan, beyond Rock Creek bridge. Mr Hogan was in Wash attending market, & it was asserted that the accused went to his home to commit a robbery, & were prevented by Edelin, a colored man in the employ of Mr Hogan; & it is further alleged that the accussed committed an assault upon Mrs Hogan. Verdict, guilty. Sentenced to 2 years in the Albany Penitentiary.
3-Chas E Beecher, under indictment for larceny, gave bail for his appearance in the sum of $150. Mr Wm A Boss becoming his surety.
4-Wm Butler was discharged from jail upon the recommendation of the Grand Jury.

This day one year ago. Assassination of President Abraham Lincoln. The calamitous day on which, one of the kindest hearted rulers that ever governed a great people fell by the hand of a bloody assassin, the President of the U S has directed all unnecessary labor to be suspended in the Depts today. Pres Lincoln & Mrs Lincoln, together with other friends, visited Ford's Theatre for the performance of the "American Cousin.' During the third act, a sharp report of a pistol was heard, which attracted attention, but suggested nothing serious, until a man rushed to the front of the President's box, waving a long dagger in his right hand, & exclaiming "Sic Semper Tyrannis" & immediately leaped from the box, which was of the second tier, to the stage beneath, & ran across to the opposite side, thus making his escape, amid the bewilderment of the audience, from the rear of the theatre, &, mounting a horse, fled. The screams of Mrs Lincoln first disclosed the fact to the audience that the President had been shot. All started to their feet, there being cries that the President was shot, the first intimation of danger was a call for a surgeon, the crowd exclaimed, "Secure the Assassin!" "hang him." Miss Laura Keene appeared on the stage, & with great self possession implored the audience to be silent. The President was seen to turn in his seat, & persons leaped upon the stage & clambered up to the box. His clothes were stripped from his shoulders, but no wound was at first found. He was entirely insensible. Further search revealed the fact that he had been shot in the head. Maj Potter, paymaster in the army, & Maj Rathbone [the latter having been in the box] assisted by others, carried the President from the theatre, the blood from the death wound falling upon the floor, stairway, & side-walks as he was born to the nearest house opposite, which was that of Mr Ulke. Mrs Lincoln was assisted in crossing the street in a frantic condition. She was attended by Miss Laura Keene & others. It was found that Maj Rathbone had received a wound in the arm, which he intentionally concealed to prevent excitement. He then fainted. Drs Hall & Stone arrived. A Common single-barrelled pocket pistol was found on the carpet in the box. The parting of his family with the dying President is too sad for description.

In the Criminal Court yesterday Cordial Storrs was, upon motion of John Jollife, admitted to practise as an atty of the Supreme Court of D C.

Phil, Apr 13. A man was arrested at 23rd & Market sts this morning, who confesses having committed the murder of the Deering family, assisted by a companion, who he has described minutely to the authorities. Search is being made for the accomplice. 2nd Despatch. Mrs Dolan, the grandmother of Deering's children, has fully identified the prisoner as the man employed on the farm, & also articles of clothing he had on when arrested, as belonging to Mr Deering. He confesses the murder of the boy Cornelius Cary, but says his accomplice, Jacob Gaunter, committed the rest of the butchery. Gaunter is 38 or 39 years of age; broad shouldered; heavy black moustache; dark brown hair; wore military pants; had a boil on the left side of his neck; & his weight was about 160 pounds. The prisoner lost his thumb in the cavalry service. 3rd Despatch: Antoine Gauler formerly belonged to the 5th Pa cavalry. He says on Sat he killed the boy, but another man, formerly of the 111th Pa cavalry, killed the rest of the family. A cousin of the murdered family wanted to take summary vengeance, & considerable force was necessary to prevent him. The prisoner was removed in safety to Moyamensing prison.

Pittsburgh, Apr 13. The steamboat **Financier**, bound from Pittsburgh to New Orleans, burned last night at Remington, 20 miles below this city. Those lost: Emmanuell Ralchild, wife & 2 children, of Texas; a daughter of Capt Darrah, Thos Badder, colored, & 2 deck hands. Others were not seriously injured. The fire was occasioned by the explosion of a petroleum lamp, in the hands of Mr Darrah. [Apr 14th newspaper: Those on the steamboat **Financier** who were lost: capt's wife-Mrs Capt John Darrah & daughter-14; Mr Russell-clerk; & Mr Jos Darrah-engineer. Mr Emanuel Rothschilds, wife & 2 children-the family was going to their residence in Texas, having been on a visit to Mr Kauffman, of this city. Thos Bolster, a colored man, a pantryman, was also drowned. The **Financier** was built in Apr, 1864, & was owned by Capt John Darrah, who was in command, Capt Jas Russell, chief clerk, & Jos Darrah, first engineer. The bodies of Mr Rothschilds & Mrs Darrah have been recovered.]

Chancery sale of valuable real estate; by decree passed by the Supreme Court of D C, on Apr 7, 1866, in a cause in Equity No 402, in which Jas R Clayton & wife are cmplnts, & Harriet Williamson et al are dfndnts: public auction on May 2 next, of lot 22 in the subdivision of lots 6 thru 8 in square 342, as made on Mar 17, 1866, recorded in the ofc of the Surveyor; lot 22 fronts on 11th st running back that width 71 feet & 9 inches; part of lot 2 in square 414, on 8th st. On Mar 3: part of lot 7 in square 345 fronting 20 feet on 11th st, between G & H sts; part of said lot 7 in square 345; with a 3 story brick house. -Geo T Langley, Jno T Lenman, Jas W Barker, Geo W Harkness, Wm Choppin, com'rs -H Thompson & Leach, solicitors for cmplnts. -Green & Williams, aucts

Mrs Margaret Kerr, residing at 30 Constitution st, near Monument st, died late on Tue from the effects of poison, partaken of several hours previous. She had called to her daughter to tell her she had swallowed ten cents worth of laudunum & five cents worth of arsenic. She was about 53 years old, & leaves a husband & several children, all of them grown. It is thought that she was laboring under aberration of mind at the time. She was buried yesterday. –Balt Sun, Thu

Mrd: on Apr 12, by Rev Dr Sunderland, Lt Frank A Warthen, late of the 6th West Va cavalry, to Miss Mary McNeal, of N J. Will the Newark papers please copy.

Mrd: on Apr 11, by Rev Louis Hitzelberger, S J, Cmder Danl Ammen, U S N, to Miss Zoe Attocha, daughter of A J Attocha.

Mrd: on Apr 12, at the residence of the bride's father, by Rev Fr J A Walter, Capt Geo H Moore to Miss Lizzie E Heydon, all of Wash City.

Obit-died: at her residence, 53 Franklin st, Balt, Mrs Sophia Harwood Seney, at an advanced age. The name will be recognized at once by those familiar with Dr Sprague's sketches of eminent American clergyman, as being that of a granddaughter of the Rev Thos Bacon, justly esteemed by comtemporaries for his public spiritedness. Mr Bacon, coming from the Isle of Man to Oxford, in Md, in 1745, after being ordained the year before, in London, by Bishop Wilson, devoted the subsequent years of his life to the promotion of the schools he found already established. Under the petitioning act of Wm & Mary for free schools, every county in Md was soon supplied with persons of learning, as teacher, & St John's College, Annapolis, is the Protestant Williams' free school. It is by his Body of Laws of Md, complied with the critical exactness, that Mr Bacon is chiefly remembered, & the recent death of an estimable lady so nearly related to him is fit occasion for recurring to lifetime services giving him a claim to the grateful remembrance of those now urging the self same objects he had so much at heart from 1745 to his death, at Frederick, in 1768, when chaplain to Lord Baltimore. [No death date given-current item.]

Dr Henry R Frost, one of our oldest & most distinguished physicians, & one of the founders of the S C Medical College, died in this city, at his residence on Broad st, after a brief illnes, Sat, aged 70 years & 6 months.
–Charleston Courier, Apr 9th.

Mrs Letitia S Lister, wife of Thos S Lister, whose residence is in 4th st, above German, went with a female acquaintance, yesterday, to the rooms of Mr Slack, dentist, to have teeth extracted. Being delicate, & fearing she would suffer much from the operation, she requested Mr Slack to administer chloroform, which he did. He was proceeding to extract the teeth, when the patient was discovered to be in spasms. An effort was at once made to restore her to consciousness, but it was unsuccessful. She died in a few minutes. -Public Ledger, Apr 9.

Essex Junction, Vt, Apr 13. Accident near Williston, this morning, by the burning of a bridge 20 feet in length. A Frenchman was killed, & Conductor Appleton was seriously injured in the spine, & is in a helpless condition.

Captain, familiarly known in Pawtucket, R I, as "Grandpa" Dexter, died there on Sunday, in his 78th year. He was a native of Grafton, Mass, & in early life, when he acted as clerk to Saml Slater, who originally started cotton manufactures in Rhode Island, Mr Dexter opened & taught himself the first Sabbath school ever established in the U S-the scholars being the children employed in Slater's mill. –Boston Journal

Horrible murder was committed near Warsaw, Richmond Co, Va, on Apr 3. Julius Hall went into the kitchen where a colored woman & her 3 children were, & with an axe killed them all. The children were about 7, 5, & an infant. Hall was arrested & committed to jail for trial. After he had committed the deed he told his wife that he had done it. He went to his father's, 4 miles away, & told his father, that he didn't want to do it, but something told him he must do it. He said this woman had never done anything to cause him to do as he had done. Hall had acted in a strange manner for some time past.

An order was received at Mobile from Gen Thomas on Friday last for all the volunteer organizations in Alabama to be gotten in readiness for muster out. The 86th colored infty, Col Geo Robinson, was mustered out on Friday. The regt goes to New Orleans to be paid off. The negro troops set their shanties on fire as soon as they learned they were to be mustered out.

MON APR 16, 1866
Died: on Apr 12, in Balt, Mary Humphreys Yonge, wife of Geo Yonge, of Augusta, Ga, & youngest daughter of the late Saml Humphreys, of Gtwn, D C. Her funeral will take place from the residence of Gen Humphreys, 19th st, Wash, D C, on Apr 16, at 3 o'clock.

Augusta, Ga, Apr 14. Col Henry H Cummings, an eminent lawyer of this place, died suddenly today.

Despatch from Memphis states that Philip Reeder, a planter of Lauderdale Co, while returning to his home from Ripley with an ox team, last week, was murdered by 2 of his negroes, who broke his skull in with an ax & then threw his body into a creek, after which they ran the oxen & wagon over the bridge to make it appear that his death was accidental. The negroes were arrested & confessed their guilt, but said they had been employed to commit the foul deed by Mrs Reeder, who was anxious to get rid of him for some purpose.

Fatal accident on Friday, on the Erie railway, when a young man, Thos Cunningham, attempted to pass between 2 cars at Provost st, Jersey City, when he fell from the bumper to the track & was almost instantly killed.

At a recent meeting of the stockholders of the Atlantic cable project, Mr Cyrus W Field amused the assembly by several anecdotes of suggestions which had been made to him. One gentleman had gravely proposed to him to sink a hollow tube in which to go down & seek after the cable, & he was so annoyed by continual calls at his hotel that one morning he told his visitor that it should be done, & that the author of the idea should made the attempt. He had not seen him since.

Election at Hagerstown, Md, on Monday: for Mayor: Wm Biershing, Independent, 268; John Cook, Republican, 216; M S Barber, W H Protzman, Wm Hall, T A Boult, & R Sheckles were elected aldermen.

Henry Gardner, a member of the 12th U S Infty, has been convicted at Elmira, N Y, of the murder of an old man named Murlock, in Dec last, & has been sentenced to be hung on Jun 1 next.

The Montreal Gaz reports the death of "Ole Bull," the celebrated violinist, at Quebec, on Apr 10. This distinguished musical genius was born at Bergen, Norway, Feb 5, 1810. His Parisian wife predeceased him. -N Y Post [Apr 18th newspaper: Buffalo, Apr 17. There is no truth in the reported death of Ole Bull, the celebrated violinist. He has not been in Quebec for years.]

N Y, Apr 14. Halifax, Apr 14. The city medical ofcr reports, up to last evening, 170 deaths on board the steamer **England**, including 40 who died on the passage from Liverpool. The disease is probably a severe form of ship fever, with many of the prominent symptoms of cholera. It amounts to a regular plague. The surviving passengers have been removed, some to her Britannic Majesty's receiving ship **Pyramus**, & others to tents on shore at the quarantine grounds. –M M Jackson, U S Consul [Apr 17 newspaper: Epidemic on board the **England** is undoubtedly Asiatic Cholera.]

Nashville, Apr 14. The House of Reps have expelled Jas R Hood, one of the absconding members, charged with wilfully absenting himself to prevent a quorum. Mr Hood will be remembered as a former local reporter in Washington.

Splendid estates in Piedmont, Va, for sale privately: *Locust Shade*, in Rappahannock Co, 1,500 acres of superior land; with a grist mill, a saw mill, & a distillery on the place. In the same neighborhood, *Bleak House*, a tract of 400 acres, with a fine residence & all out-bldgs in superb order. Adjoining the same the *Lodge*, a tract of 300 acres, with good residence & out bldgs. Fairfax Co: *Buena Vista*, a splendid estate of 402 acres, with a fine mansion with 13 rooms, & a variety of out-bldgs. –Shackelford & Spilman, Attys at Law, Warrenton, Va.

Peremptory trustee's sale, on Apr 21, on the farm, 4½ miles from Balt, on the Phil railroad turnpike, the old residence of Gen Tobias Stansbury, containing 500 acres. Apply to: Richd Gettings, trustee, 47 St Paul; M Bannon, Agent, 32 St Paul st, Balt, Md.

Chancery sale, by decree of the Circuit Court of D C, made in the cause of Armand Jardin et al vs Albertine Favier et al, No 1,253 in Equity, dated May 27, 1857, auction on May 8 next, on the premises, in Washington, known as *Favier's Square*, being square 160. -Walter S Cox, trustee -Jas C McGuire & Co, aucts

TUE APR 17, 1866
Mr F Wagner, a wealthy coal dealer, residing at 298 3rd st, N Y, committed suicide Sat by jumping off one of the Houston st ferry boats into the river. No cause for his act.

A car was thrown from the track at Pittsburgh on Sat, & a brakeman, Geo W Johnson, received fatal injuries & died soon after.

Mr Winans, of Balt, presented $25,000 to the managers of the Southern Relief Fair.

A German, Adam Gass, committed suicide in Cincinnati on Fri, by taking laudanum.

Died: on Apr 15, John Newton, only child of the late John D & Anna McKenney, aged 3 years, 7 months & 2 weeks. His funeral will take place at the residence of his grandfather, 213 N Y ave, this evening, at 3 P M.

Circuit Court-Julde Olin, Ar 16, 1866.
1-Isaac Bryant vs John L White, Martin Edmonds, W L Dawson, & Stephen Prentice, trading as Dawson, White & Co. Motion of dfndnts to set aside the judgment by confession, entered on Jan 3 last, denied at the costs of the mover.
2-Geo Lea vs Jos Nathans. Judgment for plntf for $100, with interest from Oct 1, 1865.
3-John Leifried & Reuben A Shetaline, trading as Leifried & Shetaline, vs Thos R Wilson. Judgment for plntf confessed for $375, with interest from Mar 15, 1865.
4-Asbury F Fawsett vs Catharine Crumbaugh, admx of John Crumbaugh, deceased. Jury out.
5-Thos A Stephens vs Wm A Robertson. Judgment by default for plnts for $83,00, with interest from Mar 31.
6-Jas L Barbour & John A Hamilton vs Henry P Parker. Judgment for plntf by default, & value of goods to be ascertained by inquisition of a jury.
7-H Shafer, W H Whitlord, & A T Hamilton, late firm of Shafer, Whitford & Co, vs S P Hanscom. Verdict for plnts by default, & value of goods to be ascertained by inquisition of a jury.

Sebastian Baumgarten & John Bulwinkle were loitering at the depot yesterday & Ofcrs Straub & O'Callahan arrested them as suspicious characters. Papers found upon their persons indicated that they both had been convicted of burglary in Alabama & sentenced to 10 years in the penitentiary.

Criminal Court-Judge Fisher, Apr 16, 1866.
1-Wm P Hanley, Jas Pike, Chas McGuire, & Henry Collins: assault & battery. These parties were convicted of assault & battery with intent to kill, & sentenced to the Albany Penitentiary. This grew out of the same affair, & the Dist Atty entered a nolle pros.
2-Alfred J Fitzpatrick: assault & battery on Isaac Herzberg: verdict guilty: motion for a new trial.
3-Alfred J Fitzpatrick: larceny of money from Isaac Hertzberg in Oct last: verdict guilty: motion for a new trial.
4-Mary A Gatewood: larceny: jury was discharged, the jury failing to agree.
5-John Turner, indicted for larceny, gave bail for his appearance in the sum of $100. Security: Christian Turner.
6-A bench warrant was issued for the apprehension of Benj F Hough, who was released on bail a few days ago, the Court having received information of the death of Gaskins, who Hough is charged with shooting.
7-Mary E Jones, under charge for larceny, gave bail for her appearance, in the sum of $150. Security: Theodosia Herbert.

Equity Court-Judge Wylie, Apr 16, 1866.
1-Given vs Skriving. Order of reference to Auditor to state account of exc & excx. 2-Weaver vs Barnes. Order releasing Weaver as trustee on his filing Barnes' receipt for $4,519.95½. 3-Owen vs Kelley. Order of reference to Auditor. 4-James vs Jones. Order to take testimony.

Sunday night burglars robbed the establishment of M Losano & Co, 9th & D sts, of clothing to be valued at $250. They wire shutters were torn off & a pane of glass broken.

San Francisco, Apr 16. Terrible explosion of what was supposed to be nitra glycerine occurred today, near Wells, Fargo & Co's Express Ofc. Saml Knight, superintendent of the express company, died in half an hour. G W Bell, supervisor & assayer, was instantly killed. Mr Wallbut, assayer; Jos Elliot, John Galliger, Frank Webster, & Wm Justin, were also killed. Louis McLane & Capt Eldridge, of the Pacific Mail Steeamship Co, & Judge Hoffman, were bruised & cut.

The **Greenberry Point Farm** on the Severn river, about 1½ miles from Annapolis, Md: contains 301½ acres, divided & fenced in 6 lots; dwlg house is a large brick bldg, with 10 rooms, & all necessary out-bldgs; vessels of reasonable size approach the wharf on the estate. Henry C Middleton is residing on the estate, & will show it. –Henry O Middleton, Buckhannon, Upshur Co, West Va.

Phil, Apr 16, 1866. The Coroner's jury investigating the murder of the Deering family found a verdict charging Antoine Probst, now under arrest, with the murder of the eight persons.

Louisville, Ky, Apr 15. Tomorrow the military court martial assemblies to investigate frauds in the Quartermaster's Dept during the war. Brig Gen A C Gillen is president, & Capt S P Yots/Yois judge advocate, assisted by Lts Col W H Coyle, Judge Advocate of the Dept of Ky. Henry Bruner's case will be tried first. Maj H C Blakeman is counsel for the defence.

Louisville, Apr 16. The notorious murderers, Terrill & Withers, were rescued from the Spencer Co jail on Fri, by a party of 7 men, who threatened the life of the jailer, on his refusal to unlock their cells.

New Orleans, Apr 16. Letters to the Methodist Conference report that Bishop Soule is dying.

Supreme Court of D C, in Equity, No 662. John T Given & Caroline H Skriving against John J, Saml McE, Wm A, Esther M A, Eliz A, Sarah E, Clara E, & Geo B McL Skirving, & Louis R Humpton, guardian & litem. Statement of the account of the late Jas Skirving, on May 9 next, at my room, City Hall, Wash. –W Redin, auditor

Orphans Court of Wash Co, D C. In the case of Jas L Barbour, adm of John E Leach, deceased, the administrator & Court have appointed May 8 next, for the final settlement of the personal estate of the said deceased, of the assets in hand. -Z C Robbins, Reg/o wills

Atlanta, Ga, Apr 13. 1-A G Chisholm, who shot a personal enemy dead in the streets here a few days ago, has been acquitted on the ground that he acted in self-defence. 2-The remains of Preston Sheldon, who was drowned recently at Jacksonville, have been recovered & brought to Savannah, whence they will be conveyed to his home at the North. 3-J W Duncan, who is on trial before a military commission in Savannah, for maltreating the prisoners at Andersonville, has been removed from the county jail, where he has been confined, & transferred to **Fort Pulaski**. His trial will be resumed on the arrival of witnesses that have been subpoenaed.

The Newbern [N C] Journal of Sat says: yesterday one of the boilerss of the wrecking steamer **Alpha** exploded. It was engaged at the time in pumping water from the wreck of the transport **Thorn**, 3 miles below the city. The engineer of the boat, Henry Crosby, colored, has not since been seen, & is certainly killed. Jas Harris, colored, fireman, was seriously injured, & will probably soon die. The ofcrs & the whites of the crew were at dinner, & were all more or less injured: Jas Orrell, of Wilmington, N C, Chas Bailey, of Maine, John Williams, of Newburyport, Mass, & John Spates, of Balt Md. The cmder of the steamer, Capt Jere Wager, of Troy N Y, was slightly injured.

The merciless slayer of African lions, Mr Gordon Cumming died at Iverness, Scotland, on May 24. He was born on Mar 15, 1820, & was the 2nd son of Sir Wm Gordon Cumming. He early showed a passion for hunting.

Burlington, Vt, Apr 14. In Chittenden Co, the jury returned a verdict of guilty against John Ward, alias Jerome Tavigne, of N Y C, for the murder of Mrs Sally Griswold, of Williston, on Aug 28 last. A verdict of not guilty for Chas H Potter, of Williston, who was tried for the same offence.

On Sunday last Mr Raleigh Moler, an esteemed citizen of this county, died very suddenly, at his residence, near Unionville. He had just risen, & was in the act of dressing himself, when the messenger came, & so sure was he of the sumons that he laid himself down & announced to his wife that his time had come. In a few moments life was extinct. His age was about 58 years.
–Shepherdstown [Md] Register

WED APR 18, 1866
Brig Gen W G Mank, of Hancock's corps, has been appointed by the Pres, U S consul to Matamoras. Gen Mank is from the State of Indian, & entered the service at the beginning of the war as a private.

Messrs Green & Williams, aucts, sold lot 4 in square 495, for $3,000; two of the lots to Emeline West, for $1,500, & two others to John H Bullmand, for $1,500. Two small houses & lots on H st south, between 6th & 7th sts, were sold to Thos Collins, for $760. Sold at private sale: lot 10 in square 562, on H st, between 2nd & 3rd sts, to John C McKelden, for $1,100.

Circuit Court-Judge Olin, Apr 17, 1866.
1-Asbury F Fawsett vs Catharine Crumbaugh, admx of John Crumbaugh, deceased. Verdict for dfndnt.
2-Thos C Magruder, adm of Mary Hughes, deceased, vs Peregrine W Browning. Judgment for plntf confessed for $800, with interest from Jun 1, 1850. Stay of execution for 6 months.
3-Jackson King vs John J Bogue, adm of H C Wiltsof, deceased. Reference to auditor to ascertain whether any, & if any, how much assets which were of the estate of the dfndnt intestate, have or may come to the hands of the dfndnt to be administered, & whether the whole, or only part, or if only part, what part of the plntf's demand against the deceased outght to be levied of said assets.
4-Chas Vinson vs E B Olmstead. Judgment for the plntf confessed for $150, with interest from Jun 1, 1864.
5-Eliz A Bryant vs Wm Williams & Eliz M Williams. Judgment for the plntf for $5,000.
6-Hamilton G Fant vs Thos H Ford. Judgment for plntf confessed for $256.25, with interest from Feb 12, 1861.
7-Naturalization papers were granted to Patrick Donoho, a subject of the Queen of Great Britian.

Orphans Court-Judge Purcell, Apr 17, 1866.
1-Robt White qualified as adm of the estate of Wm Hardy, dec. Bond, $800. Sureties: Francis A Jones & Richd P Jackson.
2-Susan B Young qualified as admx of the estate of Wm P Young, deceased. Bond, $2,000. Sureties, Nathl Wilson & Alex'r R Shepherd.
3-The second account of LeRoy Edwards, guardian to the orphan of Geo S Null, deceased, was approved & passed.
4-The inventory of the personal estate of Thos P Trott, deceased, was retuned & filed.
5-The answer of Mrs Eliz Clements, admx of the estate of A N Clements, deceased, to the exceptions filed, was returned.
6-The will of Bridget d Taylor, deceased, was filed. Thos J Martin, the grandson of the deceased, is named sole exec.
7-Eliza J V Clements was appointed guardian to the orphan child of Alex'r Clements, deceased. Bond, $1,500. Sureties, Chas H Winder & Jas Maguire.
8-Eliza J V Clements qualified as admx of the estate of Alex'r Clements, deceased. Bond, $3,000. Sureties, Chas H Winder & Jas Maguire.

St Louis, Apr 14. Despatch from Wyandotte, Kansas, states that another of the desperadoes that infest this country, Newt Morrison, is hanging from the courthouse railing this morning. One of his accomplices, Harry Johnson, was killed a week since while resisting arrest. They were of the party that robbed a coach on the Leavenworth road & murdered Mr Freeland, of Platte City, about 4 months ago.

Criminal Court-Judge Fisher, Apr 17, 1866.
1-Wm H Faulkner was returned as a petit juror in the stead of Edw J Shoemaker, who was excused.
2-Thos Ford moved the admission to the bar of Mr Jacob Lewenthal, & Messrs Saml L Phillips, Wm J Miller, & Nathl Wilson were appointed to examine the applicant.
3-Robt Bransell & Jas Doyle: larceny: verdict not guilty.
4-John Williams, alias Johnson: larceny: verdict guilty.
5-Geo Edwards, alias Wm H Munroe: burglary: accused was arraigned & plead guilty.
6-Isidore H Phillips: forgery. The accused is charged with forging the name of C S Jones, a paymaster in the U S army, to a check for $892. On Jan 14, 1866. Case on trial.
7-Jacob Thomas, who was committed to jail in Mar last to await the requisition of the Govn'r of Md, was discharged from custody, he not having been demanded by the Md authorities.
8-Geo Otto, convicted of an assault with intent to kill, was sentenced by Judge Olin to 2 years in the Albany Penitentiary.
9-Horace Brent, convicted of larceny, was sentenced to 1 year in the Albany Penitentiary.

In memoriam: died, on Apr 13 last, at his residence, in his 18th year of his age, R W Fort, after a lingering illness of some weeks. He was a devoted son, beloved friend & brother, respected classmate, & pious Christian. –Sophomore Class, Columbian College

Victor Hannet's Street Directory of Washington & Gtwn will be found valuable to citizens & sojourners. Its accompanying map is neat & accurate. It is a pocket edition, recently republished for sale by Hudson Taylor.

Died: on Mar 29 last, at the residence of her father, in Chas Co, Md, Bessie Lee, infant daughter of Ruel Keith & Rachael Compton, aged 1 year, 1 month & 11 days. PG please copy.

Phil: supposed loss of schooner. A Cape May despatch says that a bottle drifted ashore there on Apr 12, containing a paper with the following note: The schnr **J L Diess**, of N Y, lost Mar 16, 1866: all lost but Ned Conkling & Silas Rodgers. Please report if found.

Newark, Apr 17. Capt Ezra Nye, formerly of the Collins line of steamers, died today.

Claremont [Eng] Cor London Times, 2nd. Today the obsequies of the late Marie Amelie, ex-Queen of the French, were celebrated with all the respect that the adherents of the House of Orleans coul show towards the consort of Louis Philippe. Inscription on the name-place on the coffin:
Marie Amelie,
Reine des Francais.
[Nee a Caserte, Deux Siciles]
le 26 Avril, 1782,
Morte a Claremont
[Comte de Surre, Anngleterre.]
Le 24 Mars, 1866
The body of the ex-Queen was interred by the side of her late husband, King Louis Philippe.

Dr W R Spence, surgeon of the post hospital at Richmond, Va, during the rebellion, states, in reply to an inquiry made by the Gov't authorities whether he could furnish any information concerning the Union dead buried near Richmond, that he had induced the undertaker to keep a record of all Federal soldiers that were buried, & to mark their graves, but the object sought was frustrated by the destruction of the records in the great fire that occurred on the evacuation of the city.

Orphans Court of Wash Co, D C. Letters of administration on the personal estate of Wm P Young, late of Wash, D C, deceased. –Susan B Young, admx

London, C W, Apr 16. The supposed accomplice of the eight-fold Phil murderer has been arrested here. He gives his name as Chas McCutcheon. When arrested he turned pale, & nearly fainted. The only discrepancy between the description of the murderer & the appearance of the prisoner is, that instead of having lost a thumb his foreginger is gone. Otherwise there is the closest identity. Further examination to take place.

THU APR 19, 1866
Mr Pearl L Sternbery, a prominent & influential merchant of Buffalo, N Y, died a few days since.

Equity Court-Judge Wylie, Apr 18, 1866.
1-In re. Estate of Jas Johnson, deceased. Order confirming the Orphans Court proceedings.
2-Bean vs Patterson: order dismissing the cause.
3-Means et al vs Murphy et al. Order to cmplnts' solicitor to dismiss the bill.
4-Ball et al vs Dyer et al. Order confirming the trustee's report.
5-Phillips vs The Corp & Collector of Wash. Order for notice of injunction.
6-Hamilton vs Obenchain. Order refusing the prayer for injunction.
7-McGill vs McGill. Order of retification of trustee's report nisi, & reference to auditor.
8-Jones vs Jones. Decree for divorce from bond of matrimony.
9-Columbian College vs Zeph English. Order of reference to auditor.
10-Krake vs Krake. Order for rule to show cause, etc.

Circuit Court-Judge Olin, Apr 18, 1866.
1-Geo H Nicholas vs Ramson S Mairn. Demand of plntf satisfied, & motion for a new trial disallowed.
2-Asbury F Fawsett vs Catharine Crumbaugh, admx of the estate of John Crumbaugh, deceased. Mr Cox, atty for plntf, moved that the verdict rendered on Tue be set aside, & a new trial granted: 1st-because the verdict was against the evidence, & 2nd-because of new-discovered evidence material to the issue.
3-Wm Young vs Simon Bensinger & Chas Ebel. Cause continued till next term, with leave to plntf to amend his declaration.
4-Geo R Adams & others vs Geo F Rider. By argument of counsel the judgment heretofore rendered in this case by default was struck out, & the case placed on the calendar of the present term to be tried in the stead of the case of Adams vs Gibson.
5-Jas Montgomery vs Jos Willard. Case on trial.
6-Fielder M Magurder vs Horace S Johnson. Jury respited.

Malcolm Wallingsford, Dealer in Butter, Eggs, etc. Stands: Centre & Northern Liberty Markets, Wash.

The English papers announce the death of Mr Thos Thornton, who was for 40 years connected with the parliamentary staff of the London Times.

Criminal Court-Judge Fisher, Apr 18, 1866.
1-Isidore H Phillips: forgery. Jury had not returned a verdict.
2-The following persons, who have been confined in jail on charges stated, were released from custody upon giving bail for their appearance, viz: Thos Rogers, larceny: bail $100. Security, Wm A Boss. Thos F Hurst, assault & battery, bail $200. Security, Wm W Laskey. Maurice Brady, receiving stolen property, bail $200. Security Jas Connor. Saml Howard, assault & battery, bail $150. Security, John A Lynch. Patrick Hogan, assault & battery on an ofcr: bail $500. Security, Jas Cunningham.
3-Geo Edwards alias Wm H Munroe, who pleaded guilty to a charge of burglary, was sentenced to 3 years in the Albany Penitentiary.

Conspiracy Awards. Awards for the capture of Booth & Herold.
L C Baker: $3,750.
Capt D P Doherty, 16th N Y Cavalry: $7,500.
E J Conger, detective: $4,000.
Luther B Baker, detective: $4,000.
Sgt Boston Corbett, 16th N Y Cavalry: $2,546.
Adnrew Wendell, sgt: $2,545.
Corporals Chas Zimmer, Michl Uniac, John Winter, Therman Newgarten, John Waltz, Oliver Lonpay, & Michl Hornsly, of the 16th N Y Cavalry, each: $2,290.
The remainder of the reward is distributed amongst 17 privates of the same regt, being $2,037 each.
For the capture of Atzerodt:
Maj Artman, 213th Pa vols: $1,250.
Sgt Gimmill, 1st Delaware Cavalry: $3,598.
The remainder of the $25,000 is distributed amongst 7 others.
For the Capture of Payne:
Brig Gen H H Wells, Provost Marshal: $625.
Col H S Olcott, special commissioner: $625,
Brvt Maj H V Smith, A A G: $2,500.
R C Morgan, assist to Col Olcott: $1,796.
W M Wemerskerch, assist to Col Olcott: $1,436.
Detectives Eli Devoe, C H Rosch, & T Sampson, each: $1,005.75.
Rewards for the capture of Jefferson Davis:
Lt Col B D Pritchard, 4th Michigan cavalry: $10,000.
Captains J C Hathaway & C T Hudson, each: $729.
First Lts: Ripley, Palmer, Boutwell, Bachus, Stanber, Fisk, & Hazleton, & Second Lts: Treat, Bennett, Rickford, Southworth, Purindon, Remington, & Murphy, each: $555.88.
Three others receive $660; one, $555; one, $271; one, $239; one, $229; 61, $250 each; & about 400 receive from $166 to $187.
There are about eighty of the claimants who are adjudged to be entitled to no compensation. The com'rs making the awards were Adj Gen Townsend & Judge Advocate Holt.

John McDermott & Bros, Coach-makers & Carriage dealers: 455 Pa ave, near 3rd.

Fine Oil Paintings, H N Barlow, liner, cleaner, & restorer of oil paintings at Mr F Lamb's, 237 Pa ave, between 12th & 13th sts, Wash, D C.

A lady, Jane Harper, aged 62, while walking on the track of the Cincinnati, Hamilton & Dayton railroad, at the former place, on Monday, was run over & killed by the train.

Dept of the Interior, U S Patent Ofc, Wash, Apr 7, 1868. Four petitions Jesse S Lake & David Lake, of Smith's Landing, N J, praying for the extension of patents granted to them Jul 20, 1852, for an improvement in Grass Harvesters, & reissued for four several divisions, dated Jan 1, 1861, & numbered 9 thru 12, these petitions being for an extension of reissued patents No 9 thru 12, for 7 years from the expiration of said patents, which takes place on Jul 20, 1866.
–H C Theaker, Com'r of Patents

Fort Monroe, Apr 18. C C Clay was released on his parole this morning. [Apr 21st newspaper: It is probable Clay will leave Apr 19, when his wife is expected.]

Mrd: on Apr 17, at Christ Church, Gtwn, D C, by Rev Dr Pinckney, Thos L Hume, of Wash, D C, to Miss A G Pickerell, daughter of A H Pickerell, of Gtwn, D C.

Died: on Apr 17, after a protracted illness, Nicholas M Iardella. His funeral will be from his late residence, 589 Pa ave, Capitol Hill, on Apr 20 at 10 o'clock A M.

Died: on Apr 17, John Larkin, son of L A & Jane E Beall, & grandson of John Sessford, aged 2 years & 6 months. His funeral is this morning at 11 o'clock, from the residence of his uncle, Jos Little, 546 H st, between 6th & 7th sts.

Louisville, Apr 14. On Friday Mr C W Nichols, who lives between Midway & Versailes, sent his son, age 11, to Midway after another son, when the boy's horse threw him. Just then a man named Geo Weeks came up & asked the boy to let him ride. The boy not returning, Mr Nichols went in search of him. He was found with his head & body beaten into a jelly. Weeks was seen near Gtwn riding Nichols' horse, & was arrested. He confessed he murdered the boy for the horse. At 4 o'clock P M the citizens took him to the scene of the murder & hung him to a tree.

FRI APR 20, 1866
Lt Louis Ahrens, V R C, one of Gen Howard's staff, committed suicide yesterday by blowing out his brains with a pistol that he asked to examine in the gun shop of J Kuehling. He was Hungarian, & leaves a wife in the State of Michigan. The cause of his temporary insanity is not known.

Destructive fire in Alexandria on Tue: the dwlg & grocery of Mrs McGinniss was entirely consumed. Unsightly gap on King st: Restaurant & store of Mr Glachett, owned by Mr Wm N Brown, who has insurance of $2,000 on both houses. Mr Berry had a quantity of articles stolen from his store; insured for $5,000. The store belonging to the estate of R Y Cross had just been occupied by Chas Gladke. Mr Moran lost heavily.

Pres Johnson, on Wed, issued a pardon to Wallace W Whittlesey, who was convicted a few months since of abstracting public records. In our Criminal Court, & sentenced to pay a fine of $5,000, & to stand committed in jail till the fine be paid, & he was released from jail. The Pres also pardoned Barthoid J Dresser, who was convicted about 2 months since of a conspiracy to defraud the Gov't, & sentenced to 2 years in the county jail.

On Apr 18, while off Huntington L I, the freight steamer **City of Norwich** was run into by the three-master schnr **General S Van Vliet**-the weather was foggy. In a few minutes the flames rapidly spread over the vessel, enveloping her in fire. Within 30 minutes she sank. Of the 45 on board, 35 were rescued by the capt, ofcrs, & crew of the steamboat **Electra**, Capt J W Nye, of the Neptune Steamship Co. Much praise to Capt Nye, Messrs Crowley, Nye, jr, his mates, Mr Persons, the pilot, & Mr Smith, the steward.

Accident on the Pittsburgh, **Fort Wayne**, & Chicago Railroad Sunday, when the train hit a cow on the track, instantly killed the engineer, Mr Robt Andrews, of Manchester. He was about 38 years of age, & leaves a wife & 3 children.
–Pittsburgh Gaz, Monday

South Royalston, Mass, Apr 15. 1-Mr Anron Sargent, jr, wife & 3 children were returning for home in Baldwinsville, in the evening, when the carriage fell off the bridge into the river, & Mrs Sargent & 2 children drowned. Mr Sargent saved himself & boy aged 8 years. 2-Another accident also occurred in town last Wed, at the mill of Mr Underwood, when Mr Amos Bosworth was at work on a circular saw, when his arm became entangled in the belt, & he was thrown upon the saw & terribly mangled. He lived but a few moments. Mr Bosworth was a retuned soldier & leaves a family.

Supreme Court, D C, in Equity, No 194. Wm W Mac Gill & others, against Emily Mac Gill & others. I shall state the trustee's account at my ofc, City Hall, Wash, on May 12th next; of the estate of the late Thos Mac Gill, deceased.
–W Redin, auditor

Mrd: on Apr 19, by Rev Mr Lewis, at St John's Church, Wash, D C, John R Waller, of N Y, to Mary E Nye, daughter of Hon Jas W Nye, of Nevada.

Mrd: on Apr 17, by Rev Fr A Charlier, Mr Raphael P Thian, of N Y, to Miss Marquerite A Rainey, eldest daughter of the late Saml Rainey, of Gtwn.

The Sec of War said he would not confirm the sale of the magnificent car that bore the remains of Mr Lincoln from Wash City to his final resting place in Ill. The sale took place last Thu, in Alexandria, when the Quartermaster Gen, in pursuance of an order from the War Dept, offered at public auction a lot of Govn't property, in which the car was included, & it was struck off to Ward H Lamon, late U S Marshal for D C, for $6,800. The car cost the Govt something over $15,000 & was manufactured by the Gov't Military Railway Corps, to be used by Mr Lincoln when he should have occasion to travel by railroad. Mr Lamon, a steadfast friend of Mr Lincoln, purchased it to prevent other bidders from getting possession of it for exhibition, & that he coincides with Mr Stanton, who thinks the Gov't should hold the relic & place it among the rebellion archives in the late **Ford Theatre**. –Corr N Y Times [Same newspaper: N Y, Apr 18. The Sec of War has finally consented to the sale of the Presidential funeral car to Thos C Durant, vice president & general manager of the Union Pacific railroad, who tenders its use to his company for the accommodation of officers on special occasions. It will leave N Y in a few days for the West, with several Gov't directors, who go out to examine the condition of the work on the road.]

Mrd: on Apr 19, at St John's Church, Wash, D C, by Rev John Trumble, jr, D D, Dr Oliver A Judson, of Phil, to Eliz, daughter of the late Capt W M Boyce, U S Army.

Died: on Apr 18, 1866, Thomas Taylor, infant son of Thomas Taylor & Maria Bacon Page, aged 11 months & 19 days. His funeral will be from their residence, 438 H st, between 10th & 11th, on Apr 20, at 10 o'clock A M. Papers at St Louis, Mo, & Richmond, Va, please copy.

Died: on Apr 10, of congestion of the brain, by a sudden though not unexpected stroke, at his residence in Wash, aged 59 years, Wm Richards, for many years past a vestryman of Christ Church, Washington Parish, the venerable mother church in this city. He leaves an afflicted family to mourn his loss.

Died: Apr 19, in Wash City, Mrs Alice L Coombs, wife of Jos J Combs, aged 41 years. Her funeral will be from the residence, 249 I st, tomorrow at 11 A M.

Died: on Apr 19, at the residence of Geo W Riggs, in Wash City, in his 31st year, Remus Geo, son of Remus & Catharine Riggs.

Fortress Monroe, Apr 17. Disturbance on Upper Union st, in the suburbs of the city, originated with a number of the rowdy elements, & a few negroes inflamed with liquor. Fire arms were discharged & Robt Whitehurst was killed, & his stepmother mortally wounded. John Whitehurst was dangerously wounded. Wm Masely, a city watchman, was badly beaten, & his son so dangerously injured that his life is despaired of; Lawrence Hampton, colored, seriously wounded by a bayonet. Maj Stanhope, commanding a company of the 12th U S Infty, appeared on the scene & subdued the crowd.

Richmond, Apr 19. Dr T S Maddox & Wm Vernon exchanged shots on Broad st, near 6th, this afternoon. Both were slightly wounded, Maddox in the leg, Vernon in the hand. They were arrested.

N Y, Apr 19, 1866. N Y Car-drivers strike ended. The old drivers have resumed work.

Fr Stromberg, a Catholic priest, of Scott Co, Mo, has been fined $200 by a Radical jury, for solemnizing a marriage without taking the new constitution oath.

SAT APR 21, 1866
Dept of the Interior, U S Patent Ofc, Wash, Apr 10, 1866. Four ptns of Eliakim B Forbush, of Buffalo, N Y, praying for the extension of patents granted to him on July 20, 1852, for an improvement in Grain & Grass Harvesters, & reissued May 23, 1865, in four several divisions, numbered 1972 thru 1975, ptns being for extenion of reissued patents 1972 thru 1975, for 7 years from the expiration of said patents, which takes place on Jul 20, 1866. –H C Theaker, Com'r of Patents

Orphans Court of Wash Co, D C, Oct 17, 1866. In the case of John T Mitchell, exc of Judson Mitchell, deceased, the executor & Court have appointed May 12 next, for the final settlement of the personal estate of the said deceased, of the assets in hand. -Z C Robbins, Reg/o wills

Richmond, Apr 20. 1-Thos Shields has been convicted of deliberate murder by a military commission. 2-Robt Taylor was hung at Libby Prison today. He was impenitent to the last.

The widow of Rev T Starr King, of Boston, was married in N Y last week.

E M Fisher, a banker at Princeton, Ill, committed suicide by shooting himself on Sat, while alone in his banking room. He fired 2 shots into his head. The wounds are believed not to be fatal. Mr Fisher has been in ill health.

Mr Danl Gressman was killed at Grapeville, Westmoreland Co, on the Pa railroad, a few days since. His spirited horse became so frightened when the near the train, he ran at full speed, throwing Mr Gressman & fracturing his skull, causing instant death. He was about 70 years of age, & resided nearby. The accident was witnessed by one of his daughters. The deceased leaves a wife & family to mourn his loss.

Lansing [Iowa] Journal: a few days ago residing on Bear Creek, on the Iowa river, lived a family named McLaughlin, consisting of father, mother, & 5 children. All drowned while escaping from a flood which had surrounded their house while they were asleep.

MON APR 23, 1866
Orphans Court-Judge Purcell, Apr 21, 1866.
1-The order issued on Apr 3 directing J C McGuire & Co to pay to John R Minor, guardian of Ann Maria Minor, the sum of $452.89 was revoked, & they were order to pay to said guardian $352.89.
2-The ptn of Edw Shanahan for the revocation of the appointment of Maria Shanahan as guardian of Sarah Shanahan, orphan of Dennis Shanahan, deceased, was filed.
3-The following accounts were approved & passed: first & final account of Helen Hartman, admx of Ferdinand Hartman, deceased. First & final account of Jas L Barbour, adm of Horace Edelin, deceased. Third account of Christopher Cammack, sr, guardian to the minors of Michl Connington, deceased. First & final account of Susannah Carrico, excx of Jas Carrico, deceased. First account of Susannah Carrico, guardian to the orphan of Peter G & Eliz Carrico.

On Friday last the remains of Philip Embury, the Founder of American Methodism, were conveyed from an obscure graveyard located about 3 miles from Cambridge, on the line of the Rutland & Wash railroad, to *Woodland Cemetery*, near the same village. He was born in Limerick Co, Ireland, in 1728, removed to America in 1760, organized the first Methodist church in this country in his own house, in N Y, in 1766, aided by Mrs Barbara Heck, a zealous woman, who had accompanied him to this country.

Nicholas Quinn, Chas Forbis, Danl Hagerts, & John Beatie were arrested on Fri by Detective Tucker, of the Treasury Dept, & Ofcr Mills, of the 2nd Ward, on the charge of fraud in attempting to pass cancelled drafts of the U S Treasury Dept. Justice Clayton committed Quinn to jail for court, & dismissed the other three.

On Sat a soldier of the 12th U S infty, Michl Meany, was shot at *Kendall Green Park*, by a corporal of his company. Meany refused to do duty, whereupon the corporal fired at him, the charge from the musket taking effect in Meany's stomach. He lingered until yesterday, when he expired. No arrest has been effected. The commanding ofcr of the regt took the corporal into custody. [Apr 25th newspaper: Cpl Geo Metzgher, of Co D, 12th U S Infty, was in command of a detail of men doing guard duty at *Kendall Green*. The deceased was one of that detail, & on Sat he refused to do duty. This being the third & fourth time he had so refused, the cpl took a rifle from the rack & was removing the gun strap for the purpose of tying Meaney with it, when his coat caught the hammer & caused the gun to explode, the ball taking effect in the stomach of the deceased. The cpl hastened immediately to Sherburne Barracks & reported to the colonel, who directed Meany to be brought to the hospital. Metzgher was not aware that the gun was loaded, & he was of a mild, inoffensive disposition. The jury returned a verdict setting forth the facts, but fully exculpating Cpl Metzgher. Meany was not more than 16 years of age, & during the war was engaged in selling newspapers. His parents reside on Capitol Hill.]

Edw Holloway, a promising member of the Balt bar, died in Balt on Friday.

Wm Joyce & Thos Callaghan have been arrested on charges of being concerned in the assault upon Conductor Young, of car #17, of the Wash & Gtwn line, on Friday last. Hearing today before Justice Drury.

Geo Fagan yesterday disappeared from the receiving ofc of the Wash & Gtwn railroad in Gtwn with a tin box containing between $600 & $700, the property of said company. [May 5th newspaper: Geo Fagan was arrested last night, & $500 was found on his person, along with $45 in postage currency.]

Mrd: on Apr 3, in Gtwn, D C, by Rev Dr Pinckney, J W Berry, of Bowieville, PG Co, Md, to Kate Steuart, only daughter of W Brenton Boggs, U S N.

Richmond, Apr 21. Lt Gen Grant & wife, accompanied by Col Badeau & A H Dent, Mrs Grant's father, arrived here this afternoon on a brief visit to Postmaster Sharp & family, Mrs Grant's relatives. The proprietors of the Spottswood Hotel will, tomorrow, give a complitmentary dinner to the distinguished guests.

Explosion of nitro-glycerin on board the British steamer **European**, at Aspinwall, on Apr 3. Sixty-three killed, wounded, & missing. Two clerks on the wharf, Mr Swainson, of the West India & Pacific Steamship Co, & Mr Calvo, of the Panama Railroad Co, were both instantly killed. Known to be killed: Capt Cole, Mr Glass, chief ofcr; Mr Paison, 2nd ofcr; Dr Burrows, surgeon; Edw Davis, carpenter; W Pritchard, sailor; J A Young, sailor; W Beremund, sailor, & Richd, cabin boy.

Trustee's sale of valuable real estate in St Mary's Co: by decree of the Circuit for St Mary's Co, in Equity, passed in the cause of Henry A Didier, adm of Edmund Didier & others, vs Jas T Blackistone, the undersigned, as trustee, will offer at public sale, in Leonardtown, on May 16, all that tract of land on the Patuxent river, containing 504 acres, more or less, owned by Col Jas T Blackistone. The improvements consist of a small but comfortable frame dwlg, meat-house, stable for 8 horses, & 3 barns. Apply to Col Jas T Blackistone, Leonardtown, St Mary's Co, or to J Straaffstockett, trustee, 43 St Paul st, Balt, Md.

TUE APR 24, 1866
The Pres has nominated Gen Danl Sickles as Minister Resident at the Hague, Holland, in place of Jas S Pike, resigned.

Passed at the First Session of the 39th Congress. Public Resolution No 19. A resolution for the restoration of Cmder Wm Reynolds & Cmder Melancton B Woolsey, U S navy, to the active list from the reserved list.

Jesse D Bright claimed about $15,000 for damages due to his farm during the war. The Indiana Military Auditing Cmte has allowed him $9,476.44.

Mr & Mrs Chas Kean sailed on Wed by the steamer **Cuba** for England. Mr Kean's visit to this country has been one of great profit. After paying all the expenses of himself & his company, he has remitted to England over L7,000 sterling during the year he has been in America.

Col J H Taggart has been removed as Collector of Internal Revenue for the First District of Pa. The name of A B Sloanaker was yesterday sent to the Senate for confirmation in his place.

Died: on Apr 23, after a long & painful illness, Eliz, beloved wife of Jos F Downing, in her 73rd year. Her funeral will be from the residence of her husband, 362 8th st, between K & L sts, tomorrow at 10 o'clock A M. Balt Sun & Marlboro papers please copy.

Died: on Apr 20, at Annapolis, Md, Jas Murray, in his 81st year.

Wm C Peters, of Cincinnati, music publisher, died suddenly yesterday, at his residence, on East Walnut Hills. There will be a solemn requien mass celebrated at the Cathedral on Monday.

Obit-died: Apr 22, at Wash City, Judge Thos Pegg, one of the Delegates of the Cherokee Nation now in this city. He was in his 65th year; born in the State of Alabama; one of the "Old Settlers" of the West; has been Pres of the Upper House of their Legislature, & Judge of the Supreme Court. His funeral will take place at 2 o'clock, from Joy's, corner of 8th st & Pa ave. He will be interred in the *Congressional Burying Ground*.

Orphans Court of Wash Co, D C. In the case of Wm Q Force, surviving exc of Jas W Shields, deceased, the executor & Court have appointed May 15th next, for the final settlement of the personal estate of the said deceased, of the assets in hand. -Z C Robbins, Reg/o wills

WED APR 25, 1866
Madison, Wisc. 1-Under the law of last winter, the Govn'r has appointed Hon Stoddard Judd, of Fox Lake, Geo Garry, of Oshkosh, & Danl K Tenney, of Madison, com'rs to revise the laws on the subject of the assessment & collection of taxes. 2-Much indignation is felt here on account of the distribution of the reward money for capturing Jeff Davis. Flagrant injustice has been done to the Wisconsin soldiers, who were as much his captors as Michigan soldiers.

The resignation of Brvt Maj Chas Fletcher, capt 1st U S Infty, has been accepted by the Pres, to take effect Apr 19, 1866.

Died: on Apr 24, at his residence on K st, between 11th & 12th sts, Avery E Smoot, in his 64th year of his age.

Honorably mustered out. Assist Quartermasters: Capts Alonzo S Gear, J R Russell, Geo C Winslow, Alex'r McIntosh, John Power, John H Creswell, H C Lawrence, [brevet major,] Edw P Graven, Chas H Deane, [brevet lt col,] & Edwin B Burrows.
Additional Paymasters: Wm Penn Clark, [brevet lt col,] & J A Sabin.
Aides-de-Camp: Majors H E Tremaine, [brevet brig gen,] Silas Ramsey, [additional,] & Capt Chas Sproul
Assist Adj Gen: Major Fred'k F Wilson, [brevet lt col.]
Commissaries of Subsistence: Capts Marvin, A Daily, [brevet major,] & Sylvester A Ballou. Assist Surgeon: Alex'r Gelong.
The musters-out to take effect on Apr 20, with the exception of Assist Quartermaster Alonzo S Gear, which will date from Apr 27, & [Additional Paymaster] J A Sabin, which is to date from May 1, 1866.

Supreme Court, D C. Apr 24, 1866. 1-The court decreed the divorce of Ann E McCarthy a mensa et thoro from Dennis A McCarthy. Alimony to the amount of $80 per month is to be paid by the cmplnt. The children of the parties, except a boy, are to under the control of the cmplnt. The respondent gets the custody of the boy. 2-Alex'r Gray was appointed an examiner in chancery. 3-Danl H Leckner was appointed a constable for the 1st Ward.

Supreme Court, D C-in Equity. Ratcliffe vs Malone & Ratcliffe. The bill in this case was brought by Mrs Ratcliffe to set aside the proceedings under which certain real estate held by Mr Ratcliffe in trust for his wife was confiscated & sold. Malone, who purchased at the confiscation sale, put in a demurrer to the bill. After argument on the demurrer the Judge stated that the questions raised in the argument were very important, & would require the most careful & deliberate examination, that the case would have to go up to the court in general ther, which meets in May; & that it might go up to that term, he would not postpone it to examine the question, but would give a pro forma decree sustaining the demurrer & reserve his opinion until the case was heard before all the judges. Brent & Merrick for cmplnt, & Riddle for dfndnt. This case involves the constitutionality of the confiscation law & the regularity of the proceedings of the court in condemning property under that law.

Orphans Court-Judge Purcell, Apr 24, 1866.
1-Katharine King filed a protest against the appointment of Otho Holloway as guardian to the minor heirs of Thos King, deceased.
2-The will of Wm W Connor, deceased, was fully proven, & admitted to probate & record. Wm Dixon is named sole executor.
3-The will of Margaret A Granger, deceased, was filed, fully proven, & admitted to probate & record. Jas H Granger is named as executor.
4-L Maria Muneret qualified as admx of the estate of Gabriel Muneret, deceased. Bond, $1,000. Sureties: John C Riley & John W Van Hook.
5-Margaret E Snowden qualified as admx of the estate of Isaac Snowden, deceased. Bond, $300. Sureties: Isaac Boon & Emily Jane Lancaster.

Criminal Court-Judge Fisher, Apr 24, 1866. 1-Patrick Clarey: murder. Verdict: not guilty. 2-John White alias Isaac White: assault & battery with intent to commit rape. Verdict: guilty.

Circuit Court-Judge Olin, Apr 23, 1866.
1-John O'Connell vs Edw S O'Connor. Verdict for plnts for $143.
2-Jas Montgomery vs Jos C Willard. Mr Day, counsel for plntf, filed the following reasons in support of a motion for a new trial: 1st-The verdict has been influenced by the misbehavior of the dfndnt, in this, that he took from the courtroom during the progress of the trial testimony or evidence, which he introduced, to wit: his account book, used in evidence on said trial & said plntf was deprived of the advantage of its use in summing up the case. 2nd-The verdict was palpably unreasonable; & 3rd, new & material facts have come to light since the trial, of which the party was ignorant at the time, & which consequently could not be laid before the jury.
3-Pierce Babbington vs Jas Bowen. Appeal. Verdict for the appellee for $50.
4-Wm G Coffin vs The Washington & Gtwn Railroad Co. Judgment for dfndnt by default.
5-Jos Baugher, trading as P Tiernan & Son, vs Jas B Leach & Jos Smith, partners of Wm Garrish, deceased. The plntf's atty, Mr Ennis, suggests the death of Jas B Leach, & it is ordered that the suit be revived against Louisa Leach, admx of said Jas B Leach.
Tue, Apr 24, 1866.
6-Naturalization papers were granted to Philip Riley, a subject of the Queen of Great Britain & Ireland.
7-John W Lamsden vs Peter McDonough. On motion of Mr Totten, atty for plntf, it is ordered that the plntf have execution as per judgment of May 31, 1865.
8-Wm P Williams for use of John Van Riswick, vs Geo Page. Motion of dfndnt's counsel to set aside the judgment of Oct 21, 1857, refused, & an appeal granted to the Supreme Court in General Term. D D Foley for dfndnt.

Senate: 1-Ptn from Dr Henry Oak, of Phil, to regard to the rinderpest, or cattle plague, & professing to know the means of prevention: referred to the Cmte on Agriculture. 2-Ptn from Sewall H Fessenden, Wm Carleton, Chas H Burgess, Henry G Packard, Wm E Boyden, & John Q Miller, of Sandwich, Mass, & John G Nichols, of N Y C, which represents that on Nov 22 last the schnr **William Carleton**, of which they were owners, sailed from Balt with a full cargo to Sandwich, Mass, & that during the following night the vessel was sunk & totally lost, with cargo & personal effects, by collision with the U S steam ram **Stonewall**. They represent the schnr as staunch & strong, with a brilliant light up, a watch on the lookout, & that the accident resulted from gross negligence of the ofcrs or crew of the steamer & a disregard of the laws of the U S. The schnr's capacity is 180 tons, & its value $28,000, & the freight $1,385.33; her cargo, 291 tons of coal, valued at $2,141.55, owned by the Boston & Sandwich Glass Co. The private property is valued at $579.95. The petitioners pray the U S to reimburse them for their loss.

The Wash Gas Light Co has purchased of Mr Jas Harvey the lot on 10th st, above D, immediately opposite the bldg now occupied by them, & by the Metropolitan police as headquarters, & they propose to demolish it & erect a 2 story brick bldg to be used as offices for the gas company. The lot has a front of 26 feet on 10th st & runs back about 107 feet.

On Monday morning Mary Courtenay, a little girl between 9 & 10 years of age, left home on Captiol Hill to go to school, at Miss Martin's school, on north A st. She was last seen at 12 o'clock on Monday, & since then her friends have no knowledge of her, & it is feared that she has met with foul play. All the police ofcrs have been notified; & her brother-in-law, Mr J W Smoot & others, have been seeking her. She is a very intelligent child, & the worst fears are entertained. These fears are intensified by the recollection of the horrible fate of little Octavie Rousseau, who went to the same school & resided in the same neighborhood. [Apr 26th newspaper: Mary Courtenay was found yesterday & restored to her friends. It is stated that she had been forcibly abducted by one of those moral pests that disgrace humanity.]

Died: on Apr 24, at his residence on K st, between 11th & 12th sts, Avery E Smoot, in his 64th year of his age.

San Francisco, Apr 22. 1-A letter from Lopez, Arizona, dated Apr 19, announces that Maj Miller, of the 14th U S Infty, & 4 men were killed while going from **Fort Grant** to Tuscan. After the murder a company of Maricopas & Pinas went in pursuit of the Apaches, killing 25 & capturing others. 2-Maj Gen Rossecrans arrived at San Diego Mar 10th. The citizens gave him the freedom of the place, fired 100 guns, & delivered an address, to which the General responded.

Charleston, S C, Apr 22. Verdict of the military commission convened for the purpose of trying certain persons who were charged with the murder of the Federal guard last Oct at Anderson, S C, has just been made public. The prisoners Stowers & Kris were declared guilty of murder, & condemned to be executed on Apr 27. The other prisoners were sentenced to life in the N H State Prison.

Richmond, Apr 24. Judge Lucas P Thompson, of the Va Supreme Court of Appeals, died at Staunton on Saturday.

Boston, Apr 23. The charges implicating Dodge, alias Scratch Gravel, in the murder of the Joyce children at Roxbury, some 18 months ago, have been withdrawn, the investigation showing that he was not in Massachusetts at the time the murder was committed.

Galveston, Apr 22. Gen Gregory, of the Freedmen's Bureau, has been dismissed & ordered to Washington.

Criminal Court on Monday: Patrick Clarey was placed on trial for the murder of Jas Smith on Feb 26 last. Clarey was a soldier, a member of 2nd D C volunteers. On his discharge he came home to Wash City to find his wife living intimately with Smith. He ordered Smith to leave his house & a quarrel ensued. Smith beat Clarey with a whip handle. Smith appeared to be intoxicated, left the house, & was followed by Clarey, who stabbed him with a knife, the wound causing death. The case was concluded yesterday, & the jury returned a verdict of not guilty. The verdict is generally approved.

Arthur Hays, a watchman at Winder's Bldg, was arrested on Sunday by Ofcr Stinchcomb, of the 1st Ward, on a charge of the larceny of a pocket book & $28, the property of Jas Eveleth, the superintendent of the bldg; & other articles. Hays confessed to taking the money, but denied he had taken other property. Upon searching his room, the other articles were found there. The accused was committed to jail to answer the charges of forgery & grand larceny.

$10,000 worth of Gentlemen's Furnishing Goods at auction: on Apr 30, at J Baronn's gentlemen's furnishing store, under Willard's Hotel, his entire extensive stock. -C W Boteler, auct

Died: Dr Jos M Smith, a distinguished & learned physician. He was born at New Rochelle, Westchester Co, N Y, Mar 14, 1789, & was the son of the eminent Dr Matson Smith. Dr Smith graduated at the College of Physicians & Surgeons, N Y, in 1815, & in 1826 was appointed Professor in his Alma Mater, a position which he has most ably filled to the time of his death. –N Y Times
[Death date not given-current item.]

Orphans Court of Wash Co, D C. In the case of Jos C Baugher, exc of Geo T Smith, deceased, the executor & Court have appointed May 15th next, for the final settlement of the personal estate of the said deceased, of the assets in hand. -Z C Robbins, Reg/o wills

Orphans Court of Wash Co, D C. Letters of administration on the personal estate of Gabriel Muneret, late of Wash, D C, deceased. –L Maria Muneret, admx

Chicago, Apr 21. There arrived this morning at the Pittsburgh, **Fort Wayne**, & Chicago Railroad Depot the famous Presidential car, which was manufactured especially for the use of Pres Lincoln, & was shortly thereafter used for the conveying of the remains of the assassinated Pres from Wash to Springfield. The car is now owned by the Dirs of the Pacific Railroad Co. The following gentlemen arrived on it this morning, coming direct from Wash by way of Harrisburg & Pittsburgh: Thos C Durant, Vice Pres of the Pacific Railroad Co; Col C O Babcock, of Gen Grant's staff; Springer Harbaugh, Dir for the Gov't of the Pacific railroad; Hon &W B Judd & E Cooke, Dir & Land Com'r of the Pacific railroad.

Chicago, Apr 21. This morning Jacob Saschell, a butcher, was found by his daughter hanging, with life extinct, in a shanty in the rear of Fritz's saloon, South Canal & Farquhar sts. Verdict of the jury: the man had committed suicide while drunk.

Col Otto Burnstenbender has been arrested in NY on the charge of having shipped the nitro-glycerine that exploded in San Francisco.

THU APR 26, 1866
Brevet appointments of the General Officers in the Regular Army. The Board convened on Mar 1, at St Louis, Generals Geo G Meade, W T Shetman, Thomas, & Lt Col L M Dayton as recorder. Recommendations are made as follows for brevet major generals: Irwin McDowell, for the battle of Cedar Mountain; John Pope, for Island No 10; Jos Hooker, Chattanooga; W S Hancock, Spottsylvania; J M Schofield, Franklin; O O Howard, campaign of Atlanta; A H Terry, Wilmington, N C; E O C Ord, *Fort Harrison*; John G Parke, *Fort Steedman*; D S Stanley, Franklin; A A Humphrey, Sailor's Creek; H G Wright, Petersburg; A J Smith, Nashville; John Gibbon, Petersburg; Jeff C Davis Jonesboro; Jos A Mower, Salkehatchie; T J Wood, Nashville; Chas R Woods, Bentonville, N C; & Jas H Wilson, Selma. The list numbers 20, rank in order as named. Recommendations for the brevet rank of brigadier general were made, as follows: David Hunter, for campaign in Valley, of Va; A McD McCook, Perryville; J G Foster, Savannah; C C Augur, Port Hudson; Gordon Granger, Mobile; Geo Stoneman, Charlotte, N C; Geo Sykes, Gettysburg; Frank Steele, Little Rock; G L Hartsuff, surrender of Lee; G K Warren, Bristow Station; A Pleasanton, Missouri campaign; Q A Gillmore, *Fort Wagner*; W F Smith, Chattanooga; Geo Crook, West Va; Godfrey Weitzel, surrender of Lee; W B Hazen, *Fort McAllister*; Wesley Merritt, Five Forks; Geo A Custer, Five Forks; T W Sherman, Port Hudson; H W Benham, surrender of Lee; Wilham F Berry, surrender of Johnston; J G Barnard, surrender of Lee; Seth Williams, surrender of Lee; John Newton, Atlanta; J M Brannan, Atlanta; E W Johnson, Nashville; Z B Lower, Graveton; J W Davidson, Little Rock; Eugene A Carr, Little Rock; W H Emory, Shenandoah Valley; Cuvier Grover, Cedar Creek; T W Crawford, Five Forks; J H Carleton, New Mexico; Absalom Baird, Atlanta; J C Robinson, Spottsylvania; Truman Seymour, Petersburg; Chas Griffin, Five Forks; W S Elliott, Nashville; H J Hunt, Petersburg; G W Getty, Petersburg; Alfred Sully, White Stone Valley; Robt S Granger, Decatur, Ala; John H King, Ruff's Station; Frank Wheaton, Petersburg; Wm P Curlin, Bentonville; R B Ayres, Five Forks; R O Tyler, Cold Harbor; J T A Torbert, Cedar Creek; Adelbert Ames, *Fort Fisher*; Judson Kilpatrick, Fayetteville, N C; A S Webb, surrender of Lee; Kenner Garrard, Nashville; S S Caroll, Spottsylvania; E Upton, Selma; John B McIntosh, Winchester, Va; Eli Long, Selma, Ala; Louis D Watkins, Resaca; Sidney Burbank, Gettysburg; R C Buchannan, Groveton; J C Duane, Petersburg; H F Clarke, Gettysburg; A Beckwith, surrender of Johnston; C B Comstock, Mobile; O M Poe, surrender of Johnston; J H Potter, surrender of Johnston.

Edw P Doherty, the captor of Booth, was, on Sat last, appointed a 2nd Lt in the th Regular Cavalry.

Moses F Odell has been confirmed by the Senate as Navy Officer at N Y.

Mrs John Wood, the actress, has sold her residence in West 20th st, N Y, to a nephew of Mr Geo Peabody, of London, for $24,000, including the furniture. Mrs Wood returns to England about the middle of July.

It is reported in Camden, on the authority of a member of Congress, that R H Lee, Postmaster of Camden, has been removed, & H H Goldsmith, a soldier, [who served all through the war,] & a member of the late Gen Kearney's staff, appointed in his place. -Phil Telegraph

Circuit Court-Judge Olin, Apr 26, 1866.
1-Solomon B Cully vs Henry Xelowski. The was a suit brought by the contestant, contesting the will of Jouseff Bey. The issue was submitted to this Court by order of the Orphans Court, dated Sep 27, 1864. The jury found that the paper propounded for probate was the last will & testament of said Jouseff Bey, deceased. 2-Naturalization papers were granted to Chas Spraul, a subject of the King of Bavaria. 3-Maria J Hutton vs The Wash & Gtwn Railroad Co. This is an action to recover damages claimed of $10,000 sustained by reason of the plntf having been injured on car No 2 at the time of the collision on the tract of the Wash & Alexandria road, [which crosses the track of the other company at right angles near the west gate of the Capitol,] on Nov 16 last, at which time the conductor of the car, Mr Geo J Reedle, was also badly injured. The fact of the injury is not denied; but the question mooted is whether the conductor & driver of the street car, or the engineer of the Wash & Alexandria Railroad Co were to blame for the collision. A G Riddle & R T Merrick for plntf. Bradley & Bradley & Davidge for dfndnts.

Equity Court-Judge Wylie, Apr 25, 1866.
1-Simpson vs Beach. Order of final ratification of auditor's report.
2-Herr et al vs Mahaffy et al. Order suspending writ for injunction until further motion.
3-Hooe et al vs Ingle et al. Order granting leave to amend bill for process.
4-Ward vs Hammack et el. Injunction to stay proceedings at law.

Criminal Court-July Fisher, Apr 25, 1866.
1-John McCoy. Nolle pros by the U S District Atty.
2-Adam Jackson: assault & battery with intent to kill. Verdict: not guilty.
3-Henry Jackson: larceny. Verdict guilty.
4-Matilda Mumford: larceny. Verdict guilty.
5-Wm Smith: receiving stolen property. Verdict not guilty.
6-Louis McPherson, under charge of assault & battery & highway robbery, was admitted to bail in the sum of $500.

The sale of the ***Old Capitol*** & grounds, to take place this evening, on the premises. It offers a rare opportunity for a location for a first-class hotel, or bldg sites for private residences, being immediately opposite the Capitol grounds.

Mrd: on Apr 25, in Wash City, at the residence of Oscar A Stevens, by Rev A I Hitzelberger, S J, of St Aloysius Church, Assist Surgeon Wm R Ramsey, U S Army, to Lucie C, youngest daughter of the late Hon Hector L Stevens, of Michigan.

Nashville, Apr 24. In the Senate today a bill passed tendering the Mansion House at the ***Hermitage*** [Jackson's residence] & 200 acres of ground, on condition that the U S Gov't would establish on it as branch of the West Point Military Academy, or some other public institution. The rest of the estate, about 300 acres, is to be sold, & the proceeds to be applied to payment of the bonds issued by the State in payment for the whole property.

Caution. The public are cautioned against negotiating a note drawn by Geo E Jillard on Wm E Spalding, dated Wash, D C, Apr 19, 1866, for $400, the same having been stolen. –Wm E Spalding

Valuable garden spot, house & 5 acres of ground at auction, on Apr 30, on the premises, we will sell that valuable property formerly owned & occupied by the late Jas Maher, on Boundary st, near the toll-gate & ***Camp Barry***, containing 5 acres of ground, suitable for nursery or garden purposes being one of the best locations in the city for that purpose, improved by a good-sized brick house, containing 10 rooms. –W L Wall & Co, aucts

Bailiff's sale, by order of distrain; sale on Apr 30, the 2 small frame tenements on C st, between 1st & N J ave, in Wash City, to satisfy rent due by Patrick Mann to Geo Wheeler. -John H Hilton, bailiff

Supreme Court, D C-in Equity, No 99. John O'Brien against Ann Fortune & others. Distribution amongst the heirs of the estate of the late Jas O'Brien, deceased, on May 18th next, at City Hall, Wash. -W Redin, auditor

Supreme Court, D C-in Equity, No 518. Isabella Johnston against Johnston, Clayton, Tilden & others. Distribution amongst the heirs of the estate of Thos J Johnston, deceased, at City Hall on May 18, Wash. –W Redin, auditor

Trustee's sale of valuable real estate in Chas Co, Md. By decree of the Circuit Court of said county, in Equity, public sale on May 10 next, the real estate of which the late Thos A Burgess died siezed & possessed, in Nanjemoy; contains about 260 acres, more or less, with a dwlg-house, corn-house, granary & stables. Mr F R Speake, living upon the adjoining farm, or Jas F Owens, residing on the place will show it. -F C Burgess, trustee, Port Tobacco, Md.

Trustee's sale of 60 acres of valuable land in Montg Co, Md. By deed of trust, dated Apr 3, 1865, recorded among the land records of Montg Co, in Liber P B P No 2, folios 121 to 123. Public auction in front of the Court House at Rockville, on May 19, the following property, to wit: *Yorkshire*, being part of *Resurvey on the Grove*, & also part of a tract called *Resurvey on part of the James & Mary*, together with all the bldgs & improvements thereon. –J C Kennedy, trustee

FRI APR 27, 1866
Circuit Court-Judge Olin, Apr 26, 1866.
1-Pierce Babbington vs Jas Bowen. Motion & reasons for a new trial.
2-Maria J Hutton vs the Wash & Gtwn Railroad Co. The trial was continued.

Equity Court-Judge Wylie, Apr 26, 1866.
1-Southal vs Southal. Decree of divorce.
2-Fitzgerald et al vs Fitzgerald. Decree ratifying Orphans Court proceeding.
3-Hoose vs Ingle et al. Decree appointing J D Wilson receiver.
4-Baldwin et al vs Baldwil Order of final ratification of comr's report.
5-Kracke vs Kracke. Order discharging the rule granted Apr 18, 1866.

Criminal Court-Judge Fisher, Apr 26, 1866.
1-Naturalization papers were granted to Fred'k Walter, a subject of the Duke of Saxony; & Chas Donnelly, a subject of the Queen of Great Britain.
2-Wm H Shaw, heretofore convicted of larceny & who has escaped, but was apprehended on Wed, was sentenced to 10 years in the Albany Penitentiary.
3-Chas Longston, alias Evans: larceny. Verdict not guilty.
4-Wm Brent: assault & battery, with intent to kill. Verdict, guilty of assault & battery, but not intent to kill. Sentence: 10 days in jail.
5-Robt R Smith: larceny. Verdict guilty. Sentence: 1 year in the Albany Penitentiary.
6-John Howard: obtaining money by false pretence. Property was wrongly described in the indictment. The jury was discharged, & a nolle pros in the case, but a new indictment will be prepared.
7-Jacob Brown: passing counterfeit coins. Nolle pros, by the District Atty.
8-Eliz Herbert & Theodore Herbert: assault & battery. Verdict: guilty. Sentence: fined $20.
9-Basil Oliver: larceny. Nolle pros, by the U S Atty.
10-Hilman A Hall: assault & battery. Verdict: guilty. Capias issued for the apprehension of the dfndnt.

Mrd: on Apr 24, by Rev R J Keeling, Thos M McRoberts to Nannie H, daughter of the late John W Maury.

Mrd: on Apr 26, by Rev Fr Boyle, Mr Nicholas Phelan to Miss Mary A Higgins, all of Wash City.

Mrd: on Apr 26, at St Aloysius' Church, by Rev B A Maguire, S J, Pres of Gtwn College, assisted by Rev B F Wiget, S J, Geo Courtney to Maggie, 2nd daughter of P Conlan, all of Wash City.

Mrd: on Apr 26, at the Church of the Epiphany, by Rev C H Hall, D D, H A Goldsborough to Ellen, daughter of Alex'r Ray, of Wash City.

Mrd: on Apr 25, in Portsmouth, N H, by Rev Jas De Normandie, Philip R Fendall, jr, of Wash, Capt U S Marines, to Annie C, only daughter of J M Tredick, of Portsmouth.

Mrd: on Apr 24, at the residence of Mrs Dr Sayder, in Gtwn, D C, Gen Thos T Munford, late U S A, to Emma Tayloe, daughter of Wm H Tayloe, all of Va. Balt papers please copy.

Died: on Apr 26, Mary D, wife of Edw W Hale, late of Ogdensburgh, N Y, aged 21 years. Her funeral will be from 71 14th st, between T & U, on Apr 28 at 4 o'clock P M.

J C McGuire & Co, aucts, sold yesterday, lot 20 in square 85, on 19th st, between K & L; divided into 3 smaller lots as follows: one to J O'Leary, 26 cents per square foot; one to G A Lane, at 25½ cents per foot, & the third to John Pfinger, at 25½ cents per foot.

Mrs Mary Sanchez died in Baton Rouge, La, on Apr 11, at the advanced age of 110. She was born at Galveston, in East Baton Rouge, on Aug 16, 1756, & with a few exceptions, has never been beyond the parish lines. She witnessed the elevation of the Spanish, French, English, American, & Confederate flags over the fort & city of Baton Rouge.

Mr Adam M Brown, of Lynchburg, died on Apr 15, from the effects of poison. To cure the itch he had been taking a strong decoction of peach kernels & wild cherry bark, prescribed by a negro woman, & a wine glassful was taken as a dose. Last Sunday he took a double dose which proved fatal. Post mortem revealed the presence of prussic acid, the most deadly of poisons.

Valuable farm for sale; on the Gtwn & Rockville turnpike; containing 65 acres; with a good dwlg-house, barn, stables, & granary, all in good order. Call upon the proprietor on the premises; or Thos A McLaughlin, property agent, at the ofc of Nicholas Callan, Notary Public. -Henry Gingall

Country residence & market garden on the Heights of Gtwn at auction, on Apr 30, now occupied by Diedrich Hieder as a market garden, adjoining the residence of Richd Cox & Henry Kengla; contains 13 acres, with good dwlg-house, large barn & stables, carriage-house, smoke-house, & all necessary outbldgs.
–Thos Dowling, auct

Montreal, Apr 26. Mr Jefferson Davis has obtained permission, & will leave by the first train, to visit her husband.

Sale on May 5, on the premises, of lot 1 in square 740, on N J ave, at I st, improved by a 2 story frame dwlg containing 7 rooms: by decree of the Orphans Court. -Margaret Fitzgerald, guardian -Green & Williams, aucts

The Peoria [Ill] Transcript announces that Isaac Underhill has been nominated by Pres Johnson for postmaster of that city, to supersede Mr Emery, who is the proprietor of the Transcript.

Boston, Apr 26. The Newburyport Herald publishes the statement of Chas H Golden, in jail there on the charge of burglary, in which he claims to have been intimate with Mrs Cunningham & her family, & knew all about the project murder of Dr Burdell in Bond st, N Y, a few years ago. He says that Mrs Cunningham offered him $25,000 & her daughter Augusta in marriage if he would murder Dr Burdell, by whose death Mrs Cunningham would get $100,000. He declined the job, but took Augusta to the theatre & returned with her to Bond st & slept in the house that night, knowing before he went to bed that the murder had been committed.

Cincinnati, Apr 26. Last night a party of 7 or 8 men demanded admittance to John Robinson's circus, at Crittenden, Ky, & on being refused, fired revolvers killing Jas Robinson, & wounding 2 other performers. The murderers made their escape. [Apr 28th newspaper: Jas Robinson was not killed, but dangerously wounded. John Alex'r Robinson & Jas Robinson, jr, were also severely hurt. The attacking party numbered 20 men, who were formerly guerillas.]

Grand Opening: Boots & Shoes by L Heilbrun & Bro, 506 7th st.

Notice: we the undersigned Grocers, do hereby agree to close our respective Stores at 7½ P M, except Saturdays, from May 1 to Oct 1.

Geo Parker & Sons	Barbour & Hamilton
Jos B Bryan & Bro	Wm Bryan
Beall & Baker	Hall & Deming
H Browning	G E Kennedy
S H Bacon	Egan & Perrie
Wm Henry Upperman & Co	A H Young
Sioussa & Enals	McKnew & Bell
J B Wilson	J Russell Barr
Hall & Hume	Rd J Ryon
B F Morsell	S Evans
J C Whitwell & Co	Saml Bacon & Co
E E White	John Keyworth

Information wanted of my sister Mary Names, who formerly lived with Sgt Byram, on Govn'rs Island, N Y, & when last heard from had arrived to Wash City. Any information concerning her will be thankfully received at this ofc, or by Thos Names, Columbus, Ga.

SAT APR 28, 1866
The execution of Jas Glennon, for the murder of his wife, took place at Eliz, N J, Thu, in the presence of several hundred spectators. The condemned admitted he beat his wife, but had no intentions of killing her, & said his wife was a confirmed drunkard, & drove him to the rash act. Glennon was 30 years of age & a native of Brooklyn.

Criminal Court-Judge Fisher, Apr 27, 1866.
1-Robt L McPherson, held to answer a charge of assault & battery, gave bail for his appearance in the sum of $300.
2-John Jones: assault & battery with intent to kill. Nolle pros by the District Atty.
3-Thornton Moore: assault & battery. Dfndnt submitted his case: fined one cent.
4-Naturalization papers were granted to John O Flynn, a subject of the Queen of Great Britain; Augustus Pohler, a subject of the Duke of Saxe Altenberg; & Chas Fisher, a subject of the King of Wurtemburg.
5-Thos Norton: assault & battery. Verdict: guilty.
6-Eliz Brown: larceny. Verdict: guilty. Sentenced to 1 year in the Albany Penitentiary.
7-Beverly Smith & Henry Lee: larceny. Smith's recognizance forfeited. Jury sworn as to Lee. Verdict: guilty of petty larceny. Sentence: 5 days in jail.

Fire yesterday in the 2 story frame house, 22nd & I sts, owned by Dr Boyle, & occupied by Chas Bastapool. The fire is supposed to have been the work of an incendiary.

Wm Geo Krebs, formerly judge of the Circuit Court of Balt, died in that city on Apr 24.

A little daughter of Peter S Poorks, of Westerly, R I, age 4 years, was fatally poisoned on Sunday last, by taking creosote. She was playing with her 6 year old sister when they found the bottle of cresote in a bureau. The younger sister died in 15 minutes.

Rev Laurence McCauley, D D, died on Friday last. His funeral took place yesterday from St Peter's Roman Catholic Church, corner of Popleton & Hollins sts. Rev Archbishop Spalding preached the funeral sermon; grand requien high man was sung by Rev Edw McColgan, pastor of the church, assisted by Revs John Foley & John Dougherty, as deacon & sub-deacon. The remains were interred in *St Peter's Cemetery*, on the old Windsor road. The deceased was about 30 years of age, & had received from the Pope the degree of Dr of Divinity.
–Balt Commercial, Monday.

The Lowell News reports the death in that city, on Monday, of Benj Kaye, an Englishman, who was a recent passenger in a recent steamship. His disease was said to have been cholera, or at least a severe case of ship fever.

Recently Mr Hiram McIntyre, of Illinois, who was visitng a brother at Dover, Dutchess Co, N Y, while practicing with a revolver, fired at a dog-house in which 2 little daughters of his brother were playing, killing one of them instantly.

On Friday, Mr Jas H Coggins, a well known citizen of Nashville, committed suicide by cutting his throat with a razor. The supposed cause was mental derangement, consequent upon financial difficulties.

Mrs Caroline S Schenck, residing at 71 West 14th st, N Y, committed suicide on Friday, by jumping out of a fifth story window, while laboring under a fit of temporary insanity. Her landlord had raised her rent to $4,000 & she had failed to find a substitute for the house she had lived in so many years.

MON APR 30, 1866
Orphans Court-Judge Purcell, Apr 28, 1866.
1-First & final account of Francis W Brent, guardian to the orphans of Jas B Brent, was approved & passed.
2-The will of Wm W Connor, deceased, was admitted to probate & record.
3-Inventory of the personal estate of Gabriel Maneret, deceased, was returned by the admx.
4-Will of Courtney Reeves was fully proven. Mary Jane Reeves named as sole excx.
5-The Court ordered that Thos Thornly, adm of Chas Deviney, dec'd, pay to Ellen Brogan, or her atty in fact, Roland Cromlein, the amount of the balance in hand shown by said adm's first & final account filed in the ofce of the Reg of Wills.
6-The third account of Susan Whitney, guardian to the orphan of Chas S Whitney, deceased, was approved & passed.
7-The first & final account of Sarah A Britt, admx of Richd Britt, deceased, was approved & passed.
8-Wm Brown qualified as guardian to the orphans of Wm G Hunt, deceased: bond, $10,000. Securities, Jas H Hazel & Turner A Ball.
9-Mary Ann Fletcher, qualified as guardian to the orphans of Jas H Fletcher, deceased: bond, $500. Securities, Jos Fletcher & Geo W Benser.
10-Henry Xelowski qualified as adm c t a of Jouseff Bey, deceased: bond, $20,000. Securities, Geo Delly & Chas Just.

J Newton Gotthold: this young American, born in Va, & who bore himself gallantly during the recent conflict as a captain in the 42nd N Y volunteers, has recently returned from a 2 years' absence in London, where, under the able Mr Walter Lacey, he studied for the stage. His debut at the Drury Lane, London, was flattering indeed, as was also his recent debut at the Winter Garden, N Y, where for 3 nights he played Othello.

Railroad appointments: The Board of Directors of the Orange & Alexandria Railroad Co have appointed this week, the following: Anthony McLean, auditor; D R Semmes, bookkeeper; J F Latham, general freight agent; J M Broadus, general ticket agent; John F Dyer, local freight agent at Alexandria; A R Freeman, agent at Gordonsville; J A Evans, general agent at Lynchburg; W E Gaskins, agent at Washington. –Alex Gaz

On Monday last, Blair Laurie, highly esteemed in this community, expired, afrer a brief illness, at his residence on Stockton st. He was the son of a distinguished Presbyterian clergyman, who, for a long period, had charge of a congregation in Wash City. He leaves a widow & one child, a daughter of 6 or 7 years, overwhelmed by his sudden death. -Calif paper

A Nashville despatch states that the rebel Capt Burnett, who killed Sgt Pollard, of the 187th N Y, at Shell Mound last July, & has been unconditionally released by Gen Thomas, on account of the dying declaration of Pollard that he was partly to blame, & he did not want Burnett prosecuted.

Died: Apr 28, in Wash City, suddenly, Mrs Arian Tweedy, in her 78th year, relict of the late Robt Tweedy. Her funeral will be from her late residence today at 4 o'clock P M.

Died: on Apr 26, in Wash City, Geo W Barclay, late of Louisville, Ky, in his 71st year. Louisville, Ky, papers please copy.

Died: on Apr 29, James, aged 1 year, youngest child of Dr S A H & Caroline L McKim. His funeral is today at 4 o'clock P M, from the residence of his parents, 472 I st, between 6th & 7th.

W Rullman's Garden Restaurant, 13th & E sts, will be reopened on May 1.

Orphans Court of Wash Co, D C. In the case of Flodoardo Howard, exc of Rachel Robertson, deceased, the executor & Court have appointed May 21 next, for the final settlement of the personal estate of the said deceased, of the assets in hand. -Z C Robbins, Reg/o wills

Orphans Court of Wash Co, D C. Letters of administration on the personal estate of Jousuff Bey, late of Wash, D C, deceased. –Henry Xelowski, adm c t a -Wm J Miller, atty

Supreme Court of D C, in Equity, No 341, Docket 7. Matilda Grammer vs Todd & Probasco. Sale made by the trustee, to Geo C B Mitchell, of the south half of Lot 16 in square 258, in Wash City, for $2,064.35; & to Saml Norment, lot 1 in Reservation C, in said city, for $1,058 & of the south part of lot 12 in square 533, for $952.20, be ratified & confirmed. –R J Meigs, clerk

TUE MAY 1, 1866

Mrd: on Apr 26, at the residence of the bride's parents, in Fairfax Co, Va, by Rev Jos Packard, D D, Jacob Coleman DeEntron, of Phil, Pa, to Mary Eliz Sherwood, of Fairfax Co, Va.

M Gustave de Beaumont, member of the French Instutute, has just died in Paris, at age 65. In 1831 he came to the U S in company with DeTocqueville. In 1839 he was elected member of the House of Deputies; & in 1848 he was appointed ambassador at Vienna, but soon resigned. He published many books.

The Senate on Tuesday confirmed the nomination of Hon Moses F Odell as Naval Ofcr for the port of N Y. He received his appointed from Mr Lincoln, & stands well with Pres Johnson. –N Y Commercial Adv

Criminal Court-Judge Fisher, Apr 30, 1866.
1-Abraham Myers & John Dunbar: larceny. Verdict: guilty.
2-Eliza Donovan, Margaret Rogers, & Henry Butler, under charges of assault & battery, were released on bail.
3-Geo Parker, alias Robt Parker: larceny. Verdict: guilty.
4-Thos Skinner & Wm Lanum: larceny Verdict: not guilty.
5-Thos Skinner: assault & battery. Verdict: guilty of assault but not of battery.
6-Jas Dixon, Chas Reed, Robt Johnson, & Jas Davis: nolle pros entered as to Johnson & Reed. Verdict guilty as to Dixon & Davis. Sentenced: 3 months in the Albany Penitentiary.
7-Wm C B Thornton: assault & battery. Verdict: guilty of assault only.
8-Chas Ossinger: larceny. Verdict: not guilty.
9-Beverley Smith: larceny. Verdict: guilty of stealing articles of less value than $5. Sentence: fined $5.

Senate: 1-Ptn of Chas K Tucker to be reimbursed for expenses for the colonization expedition to Hayti, under a contract with Sec Usher, in which 453 freedmen were taken to the Isle A'Vache, & returned because of unforseen difficulties, by which the experiment failed. The petitioner asked for $50 per man: referred.

The wife of Wm M Zearing, probate judge of one of the interior counties of Ill, was found dead in her room, at the Briggs House, Chicago, on Friday last. She had been on a visit to her mother, in Louisville, for 2 or 3 weeks, & on Wed came to Chicago & stopped at the hotel on her way to Princeton, awaiting the arrival of her husband, who was to meet her. Mrs Zearing was found in her room on Friday by the chambermaid, with a half full bottle of chloroform in her hand, & a handkerchief still at her nostrils. At the coroner's inquest her brother, Mr Cannon, stated that she had been much affected with neuralgia, & had been in the habit of taking chloroform to allay the pain. The jury returned a verdict that the deceased came to her death from the effect of chloroform administered by her own hands, & administered accidentally.

Ground will be broken this morning at 25th & Pa ave preparatory to the erection there of a splendid new Roman Catholic Church edifice; 52 feet on Pa ave, will run back 125 feet on 25th st; will seat 700 to 800 persons. The style of architecture will be Bysantine, the front of the church to be of pressed brick, & the steeple 140 feet high. The architects are Messrs Cluss & Kammerhueber, & the edifice will be erected under the immediate auspices of Rev Fr White, of St Mathew's Church.

WED MAY 2, 1866
Phil, May 1. Antoine Probst was sentenced this morning to be hung for the murder of the Deering family. He received his sentence unmoved, & made no remarks. The day of his execution will be fixed by the Govn'r of the State.

Criminal Court-Judge Fisher, May 1, 1866.
1-Eliza Boyd & Annie Massie: larceny. Jury sworn as to Annie Massie only. Verdict: not guilty.
2-Jonas Webster & Wm Smith: larceny. Verdict: guilty. Motion for a new trial.
3-Hilman A Hall, heretofore convicted of assault & battery. Sentenced: fined five cents.
4-John Murphy: assault & resisting an ofcr, gave security for his appearance.
5-Eliza Donovan, Margaret Rogan, & Henry Butler: assault & battery. Verdict : not guilty.
6-In another case against Eliza Donovan the Dist Atty entered a nolle pros.
7-Brian Carroll, John Ballenger, & Jas S Williams: robbery. Charged with assaulting & robbing Mr Rudolph Buckley, in Sep last. They were tried in the Dec term, & the jury failed to agree.

Orphans Court-Judge Olin, May 1, 1866.
1-The will of Courtney Reeves, deceased, which was fully proven, was admitted to probate & record, & Mary J Reeves qualified as excx by giving bond in the sum of $5,000. Sureties, Robt B Howison & Peter F Horig.
2-First & final account of John A Baker, adm of Jos B Towers, deceased, approved & passed.
3-The contested will of Edw Wayson, deceased, filed in 1863, was partially proven.
4-Jas E Williams qualified as guardian to the orphans of John A Cassell, deceased. Bond, $1,000. Sureties, John N Oliver & Alfred C Cassell.

Circuit Court-Wash: yesterday the following were drawn to serve as jurors for the May term: Chas H Osborn; W L Nicholson; Wm H N Mack; Chas H Demar; B F Beers; Jas H Stone; Thos P Morgan; Jas G Bowen; Andrew Noerr; John Maden; Addison L Davis; David Cissel; Geo A Barron; Wm Knowles, jr; David Edes; J H Kuchling; Henry B Otterback; Wm Daw; Saml H Sanderson; John Smith; August Schroeder; P White; Jas Fenwick; B H Stinemetz; J H B Jenkins; & Henry H Clark.

Brvt Maj Horatio C King, of Wash City, who served during the war as Quartermaster of the First Cavalry Division in the Army of the Shenandoah, has received the following promotions for faithful & meritorious services: full major, to date from Mar 13, 1865; lt colonel, from May 19, 1865, & colonel, from May 19, 1865. Col King entered the service early, & by a career of long & efficient service with Gen Sheridan & others entitled himself to the recognition which the Gov't has seen fit to grant.

Mrd: on Apr 26, at the residence of the bride's parents, in Fairfax Co, Va, by Rev Jos Packard, D D, Jacob Coleman DePutron, of Phil, Pa, to Mary Eliz Sherwood, of Fairfax Co, Va.

Died: on May 1, after a lingering illness, Lucy, wife of H H Voss, & daughter of Mary A Peters & the late Julius A Peters. Her funeral will be from her late residence, 89 D st, between 21st & 22nd sts, this afternoon at 3 o'clock.

Chancery sale of brick dwlg-house on F st north, between 19th & 20th sts: by decrees of the Supreme Court of D C, in chancery cause No 495, docket 7: Barraud et al vs Ransone et al: public auction on May 19, of parts of lots 8 & 9 in sq 122, with improvements. -W Y Fendall, trustee -Jas C McGuire & Co, aucts

Trustee's sale of valuable Pa ave property, by deed of trust from Robt Keyworth & wife, dated Apr 29, 1866, recorded in Liber W B No 122, folios 131 thru 136, land records of Wash Co, D C: public auction on May 16 next, being part of lot 1 in square 461, being the same property deeded by said Keyworth & wife to Hugh Gilston, of Balt, Md, on Mar 14, 1850, & now in default for both principal & interest due & unpaid. –T P Andrews, trustee -Jas C McGuire & Co, aucts

Dept of the Interior, U S Patent Ofc, Wash, Apr 27, 1866. Ptn of Wm McCord, of Sing Sing, N Y, praying for the extension of a patent granted to him on Jul 27, 1852, for an improvement in Soaps, for 7 years from the expiration of said patent, which takes place on Jul 27, 1866. –H C Theaker, Com'r of Patents

THU MAY 3, 1866
The Senate in executive session yesterday refused to confirm the appointment of Gen Frank P Blair, to be collector of internal revenue at St Louis. T Parker was confirmed as surveyor of the port of New Orleans. The nomination of J V L Findlay, of Balt, was also rejected.

Warren White was arrested yesterday by Detective Kelly & Bigley, & held to bail to answer the charge of obtaining money from Mr A S Cox by false representations. The accused is a clerk in the ofc of the Commissary of Subsistence, & last Dec he gave Mr Cox an order on Capt Potts, disbursing ofcr, for his salary. When Mr Cox presented the order he was informed that White had drawn his pay. Hence the arrest.

Association of the Oldest Inhabitants regular meeting yesterday, B Ogle Tayloe, presiding, & Dr A McD Davis, sec. Mr Randolph Coyle, reported a form for certificates of membership, which was adopted. Messrs Caleb Buckingham, Evan Lyons, Col J Pickett, Lemuel J Middleton, Saml Bacon, & Peter O'Donoghue, were elected honorary members. Messrs W W Seaton, W W Corcoran, Hon Amos Kendall, & Col Pickett, were elected honorary members. Messrs Tayloe, Clephane, & Col Williams related many interesting reminiscences of the early days of Wash.

Died: on May 2, Gabriel Barnhill, in his 92nd year, a native of Ireland, but for nearly 60 years a resident of this District. His funeral will be this morning at 10 o'clock, from his late residence, N st, between 9th & 10th sts.

Toronto, C W, May 1. Dr Gustaff, late of N Y C, who attempted to poison a man named McKivron here several months ago, was tried yesterday, found guilty, & sentenced to 15 years in the penitentiary.

For sale: a valuable stone quarry & 40 acres of land, on the heights of Wash City, bounded by the lands of John Little, Thos P Morgan, & Thos Corcoran.
–Wm Nourse, trustee & agent

Bailiff's sale, by an order of distress for $500 rent, due & in arrears to Hamilton G Fant, from F A Patterson, for 2 months' rent due & in arrears: sale on May 4 of sundry household & kitchen furniture: at the Bazaar of W L Wall & Co, on La ave, between 9th & 10th sts. –A E Allen, bailiff & constable

FRI MAY 4, 1866
Willie Zimmerman, 10 or 11 years of age, son of H F Zimmerman, furniture dealer on 7th st, resides on 12th st, between G & H sts. Yesterday a gentleman rode up to his residence on horseback & dismounted. While the gentleman was inside Willie mounted the horse, which started in a gentle trot down 12th st. The boy becoming frightened, was either thrown or fell from the horse. He was carried into the drug store of Mr Wallace. Dr Turpin & Blanchard were summoned & discovered the spinal column had been broken. Death resulted in 15 minutes. Mrs Zimmerman, who had been summoned to the drug store, fainted time & time again.

Yesterday Green & Williams, aucts, sold lot 10 & 11 on 14th st, with 2 brick bldgs, for $17,645 & $15,000 to H R Witt.

Senate: 1-Ptn of Rear Admiral W S Godon, & the line & staff ofcrs of the Pacific squadron, alleging the insufficiency of their pay, & asking an increase: referred to the Cmte on Naval Affairs. 2-Bill appropriating $13,930 to John Ericsson as additional compensation for bldg the steamer **Princeton** was passed.

Cholera cases in Halifax. The pilot who brought the steamer **England** into Halifax has since died, with 2 members of his family. He said before his death that he did not board the vessel, but merely towed in her wake, whence he gave the necessary directions. [No names were given.]

The schnr **Clara Coward**, Capt Geo White, of Tyaskin, Somerset Co, encountered a whale off Barren Island, in the Chesapeake Bay, Apr 23. The whale was 150 years from the schnr & was observed for about an hour, when it ran up the bay. –Somerset Herald

Died: on May 2, Gabriel Barnhill, in his 92nd year, a native of Ireland, but for nearly 60 years a resident of this District. His funeral is this morning at 10 o'clock, from his late residence, N st, between 9th & 10th sts.

Died: suddenly, at Montrose, Westmoreland Co, Va, Maj Henry Hungerford, in his 78th year. [No death date given-current item.]

Hon D W Voorhees announces in the Terre Haute Journal, that he will not be a candidate, under any circumstances, for re-election to Congress.

Nashville: The first conviction for treason to this State which has ever taken place in Tenn was adjudicated at Danbridge, Jefferson Co, at the last session of the Circuit Court. The man was D C Williams, jr's, whose punishment was fixed at 14 years in the State Penitentiary.

Cleveland Herald of Sat. Jack Cooper, a desperado, convicted of the murder of a man named Rodebaugh, required being subdued in his cell on Sunday night. On Wed chloroform was used to subdue the enraged murderer, & in about 15 minutes he was unable to do further harm. He was executed before some 80 to 100 persons. The spirit of one of the most desperate men & deliberate murderers known in the annals of crime was sent before the Great Judge. His neck was instantly broken, & he did not move a muscle.

On Wed 2 sons of Mr Jos H Buck, who keeps a junkshop at 100 Light st wharf, Balt, undertook to ascertain the contents of an exploded shell. The shell exploded & grazed the upper lip of the younger Bucks, & passed through the window, lodging in a wall.

John D Edmond & Co, 513 7th st, between D & E sts, Nat'l Intelligencer Bldg, dealer in Builders, blacksmiths, household & general hardware & cutlery.

SAT MAY 5, 1866
Hon Lewis D Campbell, of Ohio, who was some time since appointed Minister to the Republic of Mexico, was yesterday confirmed by the Senate.

Criminal Court-Judge Fisher, May 4, 1866..
1-Brian Ballinger, John Carroll, & Jas S Williams: robbery. Jury discharged, having been unable to agree.
2-Barbara Burley: larceny. Verdict: not guilty.
3-Jas Jeralman & Geo Sayres: larceny. Plead guilty. Sentence: 1 year each in the Albany Penitentiary.
4-Thos H Yates & Richd Johnson, alias Jones: larceny. Nolle pros by U S atty.
5-Edw Hammond: arson. Verdict: not guilty.

Mr Alex'r Webb, age about 25, unmarried, residing with his mother on Monument st, committed suicide at an early hour yesterday by shooting himself through the heart with a pistol. He wrote his mother that he had been unable to procure respectable employment & was determined to take his own life.
–Balt Sun, 3rd.

Adam Gurowski died of typhoid fever yesterday, at the residence of Chas Eames, in Wash City. His funeral will take place on Sunday afternoon.
+
Died: on May 4, Adam, Count Gurowski. His funeral is on May 6 at 4 o'clock P M, from the residence of Chas Eames, 451 14th st. [May 7th newspaper: the funeral of Count Gurowski took place yesterday, Rev John Pierpont, officiating. The remains were interred at *Oak Hill Cemetery*, Gtwn.]

Died: on May 3, Willie, aged 10 years, son of Henry F & Sarah V Zimmerman. His funeral will take place from his father's residence, 448 12th st, near H, tomorrow at 3 o'clock.

Died: on May 4, of heart disease, after a lingering illness of several weeks, Susie Rose, wife of Emanuel B Caton, in her 27th year. Her funeral will be from 500 Mass ave, between 4th & 5th sts, on Sunday, May 6, at 3 o'clock.

Obit-died: on Mar 19, Wm W King, of Wash City. Mr King was a gentleman in his appearance, bearing, & cast of mind. His taste was artistic & select. Dear King! I deeply regret your departure, but, according to the common course of nature, I shall soon follow. –Estwick Evans

Fortress Monroe, May 3. Mrs Jefferson Davis, accompantied by 2 servants & her youngest child, a little girl 2 years old, arrived here this morning from Balt, Md, on the steamer **Adelaide**. She brought a large quantity of baggage with her, evidently designing to remain some time, in which event she would probably make her home at the residence of Dr Cooper, the post surgeon of the Fortress. [May 11th newspaper: Mrs Davis is now to remain with her husband till his fate is decided one way or the other. She is said to be in possession of ample means, which will enable her to remain in the Fortress without being an additional burden upon the Gov't.]

Despatch from San Francisco states that Eliz Thorn & Jacob W Balch commenced a suit against Asa S Mercer, of the steamer **Continental**, to recover damages amounting in the aggregate to $3,500, for loss of baggage, detention, & fraud.

Another Swindle. Bangor, Me, May 4. Henry Marsh, a middle-aged man, of gentlemanly address, who opened a brokerage ofc on State st, about 6 weeks ago, yesterday disappeared from the city, leaving worthless checks behind, on which it is said he has realized from seven to ten thousand dollars from various parties.

San Francisco, May 3. The steamer **Constitution**, from Panama, arrived with N Y dates to Apr 11. Edwin Forrest, the tragedian, is a passenger by her.

Phil, May 4. Geo C Bower, jr, a well-known & highly esteemed war correspondent attached to several journals in this city & Wash during the rebellion, died this morning of heart disease.

Memphie, May 3. The tow-boat **Tigress** exploded her boilers when near Fulton, last night, killing the captain's wife, first engineer, carpenter, & 3 deck hands, & scalding other persons. [No names were given.]

Brvt Lt Col J M Hoag, 4th U S colored troops, has been relieved from duty with his regt, & ordered to report to Gen Howard, for duty in the Freedman's Bureau.

The order directing Brvt Brig Gen Jas H Wilson, of the Engineer Corps, to report to the senior engineer of the defences of Delaware river & bay, as his assistant, has been confirmed by the War Dept.

Page & Maury, Attys & Counsellors at Law, Franklin st, between 7th & 8th sts, Richmond, Va. –Lege R Page, W A Maury

Certificate No 47, for 30 shares, at $25 each, of the stock of the Farmers' & Mechanics' Bank of Gtwn, D C, issued to John Harry, late of said town, deceased, has been lost or mislaid. The public are cautioned against purchasing said certificate, as application will be made for its renewal. –Harriet Eliza Harry, excx of John Harry, deceased.

Loudoun Land for sale: by decree of the Circuit Court of Loudoun Co, Va, rendered at the Apr term, 1866, in the case of Heaton vs Heaton & others: public auction on Jun 2 next, in front of Purcells' store, Purcellville, Va, the following tracts of land: *O'Neal Tract*, containing 133 acres; & the *PiggottError! Bookmark not defined. Tract*, adjoining, containing 100 acres. The tracts are about half a mile south of the crossing of the *Snicker's Gap* & Berlin turnpikes. Improvements on *O'Neal Tract* are a comfortable dwlg house, & all necessary out-bldgs, except the barn, the walls of which are standing. –Henry Heaton, Com'r, Leesburg, Va

Chas S Wallach, Atty & Counsellor at Law, having resumed his residence in Wash, tenders his professional services. Ofc: Mr F Callan's Notary Public, La ave.

Trustee's sale: by decree of the Circuit Court of PG Co, Md, in Equity, in the case of Hume vs Hume: public sale, on the premises, on May 31 next, that valuable property of which Chas Hume, died seized, containing about 40 acres; adjoining the village of Bladensburg. The dwlg is of brick & commodious, with all the bldgs in good order. -N C Stephen, trustee

MON MAY 7, 1866
The scriptural readings by Mr Jas E Murdoch, at Grover's Theatre, last evening attracted a thronging house, & the entertainment was worthy alike of the cultivation of the magnificent audience, the personal & professional merits of the reader, & the humane & exalted purposes of the occasion.

Circuit Court-Judge Olin, May 5. 1866. Maria J Hutton vs The Wash & Gtwn Railroad Co. On the question of the right of a married woman to sue in her own name, the theory of the law is that she cannot do this without joining with her husband, but there is an exception to the rule in this; that when a married woman does bring suit in her own name, & might properly sustain the action, but for the fact of coverture, she is entitled to recover in such case unless the dfndnt plead such converture in abatement. The injury, if any, in this case, was to the person of the plntf, & she might therefore bring suit, & if this dfndnt does not plead in abatement her converture, as wife may sue alone. In reference to the claim of $1,000 for expenses incurred for nursing, medical attandance, etc, the Court instructs the jury that if she was a married woman at the time of the injury, she could incur no such liabilties, as such expenses would create an obligation on the part of her husband, but not on her part. If not married at the time of the injury, she is entitled to recover whatever expense she necessarily incurred for board, medical attendance, etc. The relation of marriage may be proved without establishing the fact of a marriage ceremony, if the parties were known to cohabit together or were commonly reputed & represented themselves as man & wife. The Jury was instructed to return a sealed verdict. [The only ground on which the present action can be maintained is negligence on the part of the dfndnt. Negligence means the doing or omitting to do what an ordinarily prudent man would not do, or omit to do, in a matter in which he is engaged or employed. The person who had the management of the horse car ought to have seen the steam train in time to have avoided it, or if it appears that they did see said train, the dfndnt is liable for whatever injury the plntf has sustained. If there was negligence, what damages has the plntf sustained by reason of this negligence?] [May 8th newspaper: Hutton: verdict for plntf; damages $3,000.]

Mrd: on Apr 17, at St Mary's Church, Brooklyn, N Y, by Rev E W Syle, Henry M Oddie to Eleanor Gibson, youngest daughter of Jonathan Prout, formerly of Wash.

Mrd: on May 3, by Rev W V Tudor, at the First Congregational Methodist Chapel, Mr Wm W Graham, of Wmsburg, N Y, to Miss Imogene D Jordan, of Smithfield, Va. N Y papers please copy.

Green & Williams, aucts, sold lot 28 in square 544, on M st, to John Ashford, for 5½ cents per foot; a 2 story frame dwlg, a slaughter-house, etc, on 7th st, at **Mount Pleasant**, to M Menke, for $4,500; lot 23 in square 388, on F st, to J A Stephenson, for 12½ cents per foot; a frame stable on Ohio ave, between 14th & 15th sts, to Auguste Hoach, for $75; 1 part of lots 10 & 11 in square 251, on 14th st, with 2 brick bldgs, one for $17,550 & the other for $15,000, to H R Wilt; lot 22 in square 242, on 11th st, near K, with 2 small brick bldgs, to Jos B Williamson, for $3,000; part of lot 2 in square 414, on 8th st, to John F Yates, for $205; lot 1 in square 596, with a 2 story frame dwlg, on south M, to John C Wiegand, for $690; lot 2, same purchaser; lot 3, to Ellen Hake, & lot 4 to Lawrence McMahan, for 4 cents per foot each.

Died: on May 6, after a few hours' illness, infant daughter of Annie E & Jas L Barbour. Her funeral will be place from 409 D st at 4 o'clock P M, today, May 7.

Died: on May 4, in Upper Marlborough, Md, Martha Ellen Hagner, infant daughter of Sallie A & Michl J Slayman, aged 3 months. Phil papers please copy.

Died: on May 6, after a painful illness, Robt E Warren, aged 42 years. His funeral will be from his late residence, 202 10th st, this evening at 3 o'clock P M.

Died: on May 6, Edward Hall, twin son of Wm & Julia M Linton, aged 1 year & 18 days. His funeral will be from the residence of his parents, 45 La ave, today at 4 o'clock P M.

Batavia, N Y, May 4. Levi Mayherr was executed this afternoon for the murder of Theodore Durham. The condemned man confessed at the gallows.

Cairo, May 3. The towboat **Nick Hughes** exploded her boiler last night, near Randolph, 60 miles above Memphis, killing: Capt Van Dorn & wife, Frank Mentz, & Heal, the engineer, who was asleep. Capt John McLean, formerly captain of the boat **Calumet**, was pilot of the **Hughes**, & escaped with slight injury. Jas Eisley also escaped.

Fort Monroe, May 6. The revenue cutter **Northerner**, with Secretary McCulloch & family, arrived this morning, on a short vist to this fort & Norfolk. They returned to Washington this evening.

Albany, May 5. Geo E Gordon, for the murder of Owen Thompson, at Schoharie, has been found guilty of murder in the 2nd degree, & sentenced to life in prison.

Mr Wm W Clapp, formerly a well-known editor & printer in Boston, died on Wed, aged 83 years.

M Leuven, of the Opera Comique, says the Gazette Musicale, has entrusted 3 libretti to 3 young composers, M M Conte, Saml David, & Massenet-who have all 3 won the grand prize for musical composition.

Dept of the Interior, U S Patent Ofc, Wash, May 1, 1866. Ptn of Jos Guild, of Buffalo, of N Y, praying for the extension of a patent granted to him on Nov 30, 1852, for an improvement in Mortising Machine, for 7 years from the expiration of said patent, which takes place on Nov 30, 1866.
–H C Theaker, Com'r of Patents

Orphans Court of Wash Co, D C, May 5, 1866. In the case of Jas W Carlisle & Jos H Bradley, jr, excs of Richd S Coxe, deceased, the executors & Court have appointed May 29 next, for the final settlement of the personal estate of the said deceased, of the assets in hand. -Z C Robbins, Reg/o wills

Orphans Court of Wash Co, D C, May 5, 1866. In the case of Wm D Nutt, exc of Alex'r Hunter, deceased, the executor & Court have appointed May 29 next, for the final settlement of the personal estate of the said deceased, of the assets in hand. -Z C Robbins, Reg/o wills

Orphans Court of Wash Co, D C, May 5, 1866. In the case of Harriet E Harry, excx of John Harry, deceased, the executrix & Court have appointed May 28 next, for the final settlement of the personal estate of the said deceased, of the assets in hand. -Z C Robbins, Reg/o wills

TUE MAY 8, 1866
Mr Nathan Rice, so long a resident of Wash City, & for more than 30 years connected with the War Dept, has resigned his position in that Dept, & intends to leave Wash City soon to make his future home at the North.

Orphans Court-Judge Purcell, May 5, 1866.
1-The will of the late Adam G Herold was admitted to probate.
2-The will of the late Edw Wayson was partially proven.
3-Letters of administration on the estate of Wm Richards, deceased, were issued to Mrs Harriet R Richards & Jas H Richards; bond, $8,000.
4-Geo E Bernard was appointed guardian to the minor children of Catherine Bernard; bond, $1,000. Henry Mades to the minor children of Eliz Seitz; bond, $4,000. Wm Miller to the orphan of Edw Briscoe, of Md. Eliz Dennis to the orphan of W H Brown, late of Wayne Co, N Y; bond, $8,000.
5-Geo E Moore appointed administrator of estate of Jas H Moore, deceased; bond, $2,000.

Terrific boiler explosion at Riley's saw mill, in Wayne Co, Iowa, a few days since, by which Wm Robinson was killed & 2 men dangerously wounded.

Criminal Court-Judge Fisher, May 7, 1866.
1-Brian Carroll, John Ballenger, Jas S Williams: robbery. Nolle prosequi by U S D A.
2-Same parties: assault & battery. Nolle pros.
3-Jas Pike: assault & battery with intent to kill. Nolle Pros.
4-W H Taylor indicted with Chas Smith: larceny of horses. Verdict: not guilty.
5-Jas Webster: larceny. Not guilty.
6-W C B Thornton convicted of assault & battery. Nominal sentence.
7-Jacob Roth: assault & battery, with intent to kill. Verdict: not guilty.

Atlanta, May 4. The remains of Maj Thos H Clay, of Ky, who died in this city in 1864, were disinterred today & forwarded to Ky. Maj Clay was a distinguished rebel ofcr, a son of Col Clay of Mexican fame, & a grandson of Henry Clay. His remains are to be reinterred beside his father in the **State Cemetery**, at Frankfort. They were escorted to the depot by a number of Kentuckians, who are in the city.

Troy, N Y. Fire broke out May 5 in the Roman Catholic Orphan Asylum, & burned to the ground. The bldg was the private property of Rev Fr Peter Havermans. There were about 172 orphan boys in the asylum, all of whom were saved. The asylum was probably set on fire by a young man originally from Va. He was an inmate of the asylum 5 years ago, when he set fire to the bldg. For this he was sent to the House of Refuge for 4 years, but as he threatened to fire the bldg when he got out, he was kept a year longer. He was set at liberty 2 weeks ago, & a few days ago attempted to set fire to a barn near the asylum. A large Catholic Orphan asylum is now in course of construction in this city. The Troy Catholic Hospital, in close proximity, escaped unharmed. Loss by the fire $10,000; insured for $5,000.

Mrd: on Apr 24, in Trinity Church, Gtwn, D C, by Rev Fr Charlier, Mr T A Poe to Miss Susie Major, youngest daughter of John Major, of N Y.

Died: on May 7, after a short illness, John Ryan, clerk in the ofc of the Sixth Auditor, aged 37 years. His funeral will take place on May 9, at 9 o"lock A M, from his late residence, 6th st, between E & F. The members of St Vincent de Paul & Young Catholic's Friend Society are invited to attend.

Phil, May 7. Probst has made a full confession to his priest of all the murders of the Deering family, commencing with Cornelius Carey, the hired boy. His account of the murders agrees with the general belief that he had no accomplice.

The Sec of War, at the instance of Gen Howard, has assigned Col John Mansfield & Brvt Col R E Johnson, of the Veteran Reserve Corps, to duty in the Freedmen's Bureau.

Letter from *Fortress Monroe:* the interview of Mrs Jefferson Davis with her husband, on May 3. Mr Davis had been apprised of her coming; she was with him in Carroll Hall within 15 minutes of her arrival. Lt Fessenden bore her company. She remained with Mr Davis all day, & took dinner with him. An ofcr has been constantly in the same room. Their meeting was a tender & affecting one. She confesses finding Mr Davis in better health than she had expected, but still avers that he is much feebler than when brought here. To Dr Cooper, his medical attendant & adviser, she is specially thankful. Mrs Davis is accompanied by her younger child, a sprightly girl, 20 months old.

Hon Wm Johnston, late Rep in Congress from the 8th Congressional District of Ohio, died at his residence in Mansfield on May 3, of consumption, occasioned by a cold taken in the political campaign of 1864.

Wm B Shoemaker, sheriff of Gentry Co, Missouri, died suddenly on Tue last, under circumstances that raise the suspicion that he committed suicide. He was found dead in the road, with a pistol-shot in the head. He is said to have become perplexed in his tax accounts, & had for some time been dejected & malancholy.

<u>Cemetery for Union dead</u> at *Seven Pines*. Lt Col Jas M Moore, A Q M, who was lately assigned to duty by the Quartermaster General im laying out & establishing cemeteries, wherein are to be deposited the remains of Union soldiers at present lying unburied on battlefields, has selected a site for a burial ground at *Seven Pines*, on the Peninsula, & workmen are at present engaged in laying it out.

The Pres yesterday pardoned Jos Warner, Jas N Moody, Thos B Graynor, John D Nevell, N G Shelley, J R Jefferson, & Edwin Burt. These parties, who are citizens of Texas, all come under the 13th exception or twenty thousand dollar clause of the amnesty proclamation.

WED MAY 9, 1866

Hon Alex'r G Penn, of Louisiana, died suddenly in Wash City yesterday. Mr Penn has been in Wash City for a short time, but appeared to be much debilitated from age.
+
Died: on May 8, at the residence of Mr John Moore, 347 F st, Wash, Hon A G Penn, ex-member of Congress from Louisiana. His funeral is tomorrow at 12 o'clock noon.

John Ryan, clerk in the ofc of the Auditor of the Post Ofc Dept, has suddenly deceased. He was from Mass, where he was once an editor of a Democratic paper. His life in Wash was illustrated by quiet & unobtrusive acts of kindness to the sick & suffering.

Maj Gen Howard left Wash City last evening on a brief visit to N Y.

Assigned: Majors Wm E Prince & J H McArthur, U S Army, have been ordered to report to Gen Danl Butterfield, at N Y C, for assignment to duty on general recruiting service.

Some vicious persons have been tearing down the posters of Grover's Theatre. Lewis & Anthony Williams, 17 & 18 years of age, have been arrested on this charge. Both were sentenced to 90 days in the Workhouse.

N Y, May 8. All the parties implicated in the Adams Express robbery, in Jan last, have been arrested, & all the money, except $40,000 has been recovered. The originator of the robbery was John Grady, a brakesman on the New Haven railroad, assisted by Martin Allen, Gilbert McGlan, alias Getty McCloug, & Jas Wells. They were all taken to Bridgeport & were committed.

Criminal Court-Judge Fisher, May 8, 1866.
1-Davis Watson: murder of Benj White, in Oct last. On trial.

Orphans Court-Judge Purcell, May 8, 1866. 1-The will of the late Danl Rowland was fully proven & admitted to probate for personalty. 2-Jas W Gibson was appointed guardian to the orphans of Joshua Gibson. Bond, $10,000.

Homicide at the village of Cookstown, Fayette Co. Martin Lutz, a wealthy respectable farmer, left his home a few days ago on a visit to Ohio, expecting to be absent several days. He returned on Friday evening, about 9 o'clock, & knowing that his wife would not be looking for him, he concluded to steal in upon her unawares. He soon discovered that she was absent, & had left the house in the charge of his cousin, a boy about 16 years of age. As Lutz had considerable money in the house he seems to have conceived the idea of testing the courage & fidelity of the boy. He entered the house stealthily, but the boy hearing the noise gave an alarm, & called to a companion begging him to get assistance, as there was a robber in the house. The boy then approached the room, challenged the robber 3 times, & on the third warning, the boy fired with a navy revolver. Lutz up to this time had not spoken, but as he fell to the ground he exclaimed: "You have killed me, but it is all my fault!" He was a victim of his own folly. Lutz was about 40 years of age, & leaves a wife, but no children. –Pittsburgh Gaz, May 7

THU MAY 10, 1866
Last evening at 9 o'clock an interesting marriage ceremony took place at the Calvary Baptist Church, H & 8th sts, Rev T R Howlett officiating. Capt Saml Surburg was married to Miss Nettie I Shedd, & were followed to the altar by J R Shedd & lady, Mr Oliver M & Nettie F Shedd, Mr K W Shedd, & Miss Sarah E Crane, bridesmaids & groomsmen. There was a very large attendance; the church was lighted up; & among the guests we noticed Hon Amos Kendall, the founder of the church. After the services the company repaired to the lecture room, where they found an elegant collation awaiting them. Capt Surburg & lady leave this morning by the 6 o'clock train on their bridal tour.

Mr John Savage, biographer of the President, has been in Wash City for some days, during which time he has had several interviews with Pres Johnson. Mr Savage's Life of Johnson is the only authorized & official work on the subject; & the second edition, now in press, will contain all the vetoes, speeches, & other documents emanating from the President, up to this time. Mr Savage left for N Y last evening.

Mr Geo Peabody is staying with his sister at Gtwn, near South Danvers, Mass. He declined a formal reception which was tendered to him by a cmte of the citizens of South Danvers.

Ex-Pres Pierce was confirmed a member of St Paul's Episcopal Church, by Bishop Chase, at Cocord, N H, on Sunday.

Campaigns of the Army of the Potomac: A critical history of operations in V, Md, & Pa, from the commencement to the close of the war-1861-65. By Wm Swinton, the well known army correspondent of the N Y Times. Published by Chas B Richardson, N Y. For sale by Philp & Solomons.

Gerritt Smith brought a suit against the Rome & Oswego railroad, claiming $60,000 for the damages done to his property. The case was submitted to the arbitration of Hon Jas Platt, Hon Wm F Allen, & Messrs J McWhorter, O H Hastings, & G Mallison. The referee awarded Mr Smith $9,500.

Robt Williams, a discharged soldier, was found dead in his bed yesterday in his room, at Donnelly's restaurant, on 14th st, above K. Justice Morsell held an inquest; & an empty phial of laudanum & one of morphine was found in his room. His improper use of liquor & the laudanum caused his death. He was a native of Wales, & formerly a member of the 1st regt artl. Latterly he was a member of the 17th company, 1st btln. Veteran Reserve Corps: he was discharged by reason of expiration of term of service. He was about 35 years of age. He had told a female friend that his love had not been reciprocated by someone to whom he was attached.

Guardian's sale of very valuable brick house & lot, & frame house & lot on the Island: on May 21, in front of the premises, the interest of the orphan children of John A Cassel, deceased, in part of lot 2 in square south of square 463, with 3 story brick house; at Va & Md aves; & an 8 room frame dwlg, with private alley to back entrance, on Va ave, 308 7th st. Indisputable title. –Jas E Williams, guardian -Green & Williams, aucts

Died: on May 8, in Balt, at **Bolton**, the residence of her mother, Eliz Gwynn, wife of Capt Thornton A Jenkins, U S Navy, Chief of the Bureau of Navigation & Ofc of Detail, & daughter of the late Paymaster Francis A Thornton, U S Navy, in her 38th year.

Chancery sale of valuable tavern & garden farm at Tennally Town, D C: by decree of the Supreme Court of D C, in Equity, passed on Jul 5, 1865, in the chancery cause No 447, docket 7, J R Keene et al vs A L Keene et al: auction on May 29 next, on the premises, **Conrad's Tavern** & enclosure containing 10 acres, one rood & 30 perches of land, beginning at a boundary stone standing on the south side of the River road 60 feet s w of a boundary of the original tract, **Friendship**; with improvements thereon. Title perfect.
–Jos R Keene, trustee -Thos Dowling, auct

Supreme Court of D C, in Equity, docket 7, No 614. John Goodrick et al vs Mary Goodrick. Henry N Young, trustee, reported that on May 3, 1866, he sold the said real estate to C H Lieberman for the sum of $930. –A B Olin, Justice of the Supreme Court, D C -R J Meigs, clerk

Chancery sale of very valuable improved & unimproved real property in Wash City, under a decree of the Supreme Court of D C, in Equity No 56, in which John H Ingle & others are cmplnts, & Eliza B Ingle & others are dfndnts: sale on Thu: lots 16 thru 18 in Reservation B, on Pa ave, near 6th. Lot 25 in reservation B, on Pa ave, between 4½ & 6th sts, with a brick house. Lot 30 in Reservation B, on Pa ave; with a substantial brick house. On Friday, Jun 1: lot 1 in square 458, on La ave, near 6th st, with a brick house. Part of lot 2 in square 458, on La ave. Lot 1 in square 5_8, on H st; also a lot on 4th st, near H. Also, the interest of the heirs of the late John P Ingle in lot 5 of John P Ingle's subdivision of lot 7 in square 5_8. On Sat, Jun 2: on the premises, the residence of the late John P Ingle, & ground attached; property in square 690, fronts on N J ave, between B & C sts, handsomely improved. Lot 1 in square 690, at 2nd & A st. On Monday, Jun 4: east half of lot 3 in Reservation 11, on B st. Lots 4 thru 12, 35, 37, 38, & 39 in square 782. On Tue, Jun 5: lot 1 in square 971. Lots 1 thru 3, 9 thru 13, in square 1059. Other lots noted at the auction rooms of J C McGuire & Co. –John C Kennedy, Wm B Webb, trustees -Jas C McGuire & Co, aucts

London journals: the wife of Mr Thos Carlyle died on the 24th. She was taking her usual drive in Hyde Park when her little favorite dog, which was running by the side of the brougham, was run over by a carriage. She lifted the dog into the carriage & the man drove on. When he stopped the carriage, he discovered her, as he thought, in a fit or ill, & drove to St George's Hospital. When there it was discovered she must have been dead some little time. Mrs Carlyle's health had been for several months feeble, but not in a state to excite anxiety or alarm. Mr Carlyle is still in Scotland.

Col J W Burke, formerly colonel of the 10th Ohio, has published a statement of the sufferings of the people for food in North Alabama which is truly heartrending. He says the destitution is not confined to Marshall Co, but extends through Blount, Winston, Walker, those counties south of the Tenn river.

Died: on Apr 28, at Walnut Hills, Ohio, after a most painful illness of 4 months, Lizzie M Ballantine, daughter of Rev E Ballantine, aged 21 years. To her" dying was but going home."

FRI MAY 11, 1866
Israel Hutchinson, an old & esteemed citizen of Phil, died in that city on Wed, in his 77th year.

W M Fleming, a well-known actor, died in N Y on Monday.

Ex-Senator D L Yulee has been elected Pres of the Florida railroad.

St Louis despatch: adultery case had a tragic end today. The parties accused pleaded guilty & were fined $100. Mrs Bright left the court-room to pay the fine, when her husband drew a pistol upon her & shot her in the right cheek. She hurriedly went towards the door, when he shot her again. Mr Bright was caught by John Gilford & John Ortell, & was disarmed. The woman was removed to a hospital, where she shortly after died.

Dr E D Fenner, an eminent physician & resident for the last 25 years of New Orleans, died on Sat last. He was an editor of a medical journal published in that city before the war, & was one of the founders of the New Orleans School of Medicine, & professor at the time of his death in that institution.

San Francisco, May 6. A special messenger arrived yesterday at Los Angelos bearing a despatch from the Cmder of ***Fort Grant*** to Gen Mason, announcing that ***Fort Goodwin***, Arizona, had been attacked by 2,000 Indians, & the garrison, numbering 124 men, massacred, with one exception, & the fort burned. The man who escaped was out hunting & witnessed the commotion from a distance. He saw the fort burning & heard the firing of guns during the fight, which lasted nearly an hour. It is supposed that the Indians gained admission into the fort under pretext of entering into a treaty of peace, which Gen Mason had instructed the Cmder to make.
Later: San Francisco, May 8. A letter dated Maricoha Wells, Arizona, Apr 18, received here, states that Brvt Maj Jas T Mullen, Capt Co B, 14th U S Infty, & Acting Assist Surgeon Toppon, U S A, were fired upon by a band of Apaches at Cottonwood Springs, on Mar 22, wich resulted in Mullen being killed & Toppon badly wounded.

Boston, May 10. Fatal explosion of a shell in the iron foundry of Davis & Farnham, at Waltham, yesterday, killed Wm H Howard & 2 boys, & wounded the foreman.

Exc's sale of 2 brick dwgl house & lots on N J ave, near L st on May 22, on the premises, lots 1 & 3 in square 556. –Jas Fitzpatrick, exc Dominic Conroy.
-Jas C McGuire & Co, aucts

Mrd: on May 9, in Wash, at the residence of the bride's father, by Rev Dr Gillette, John W Lord, of West Lebanon, Maine, late Capt & Brvt Major 8th U S Vet Vols, 1st A C, to Henrietta O'Brien, of Wash, D C. Maine papers please copy.

Died: on May 10, after a long & painful illness, John I Kidwell, in his 39th year. His funeral will take place from the residence of his mother, Mrs Fletcher, 600 I st, today, May 11, at 11 o'clock A M.

Died: on May 10, Eliz A White, relict of the late Jas C White, in her 74th year. Her funeral is today at 4 o'clock P M, from her late residence, 474 9th st, between D & E.

A sailboat upset on Sunday, on the Jersey flats. Jas Mountford, Robt J Collins, Jos Clement, & Henry Tossell, employes in the Atlantic & Great Western Railway Locomotive Works, in Warren st, Jersey City, hired a sailboat for an excursion to Staten Island. A sudden flaw of wind caused the boat to capsize. Mountford, Collins, & Clement were drowned. Tossell clung to the boat & was rescued. Mountford leaves a wife & 4 children, & Collins a wife & 5 children. Clement was unmarried. -N Y World

John J Davies, Grand Master of the Independent Order of Odd Fellows of the State of N Y, died on Wed in Brooklyn. He was also at the time of his death Grand Scribe of the Grand Encampment, & a rep of that body in the Grand Lodge of the U S. He had been a member of the Order a quarter of a century.

<u>U S District Court in Norfolk, Va; the Grand Jury-charge of Judge Underwood.</u>
The following are the names of the jurors:

J R Bigelow, of Alexandria	John T Daniels, of Norfolk
Isaac Snowden, of Fairfax	John B Borume, of Norfolk
John Taylor, of Alexandria	Wm G Webber, of Norfolk
C Gillingham, of Fairfax	C K Cole, of Norfolk
Geo C Hens, of Norfolk	Wm Harrison, of Norfolk
D Hodgkins, of Norfolk	Wm N Tinsley, of Richmond
L D Harmon, of Norfolk	Wm Fay, of Richmond
C W Nowland, of Alexandria	Burnham Wardwell, of Richmond
F Deeordy, of Norfolk	T Dudley, jr, of Richmond
Geo W Singleton, of Norfolk	Burnham Davis, of Richmond

The Judge appointed Mr Gillingham foreman. Mr Wm H Barry, clerk, administered the usual oaths.

Dept of the Interior, U S Patent Ofc, Wash, May 4, 1866. Ptn of Thos Castor, of Phil, Pa, for the extension of a patent granted to him on Aug 3, 1852, for an improvement in Dumping Wagon, for 7 years from expiration of said patent, which takes place on Aug 3, 1866. –H C Theaker, Com'r of Patents

Mrd: on May 9, by Rev Dr Gurley, Edwin Downing, of Mich, to M A Carter, of New Orleans, La.

Powder-mill explosion at Enfield, Conn, Monday killed: Edw Burke, aged 40; John Keeshan, aged 37; Wm Agnue, aged 44; & Patrick Bailey, aged 22. All except Bailey were married. Keeshan leaves one child, Burke three, & Agnue four. The funeral services will take place tomorrow, & will be conducted by Rev Fr Tully, of Thompsonville. The bodies were blown to fragments, of which but few have been found & of course any idenfication will be impossible. They will therefore be put in a coffin together, & buried in a single grave.
-Hartford Times of Tue.

SAT MAY 12, 1866

Gen Danl E Sickles was yesterday confirmed by the Senate as Minister Resident to the Hague, Holland. Simon Stone, of Norfolk, to be Collector of Internal Revenue, & John M Dunn to be Assessor of the 2nd District of Va. Thos L Sandborn, of Alexandria, to be Collector of Internal Revenue for the 7th District of Va. John H Hudson, of Richmond, Va, to be Assessor of the 3rd District of Va.

Homicide in Balt: yesterday an affray took place between 2 young men in the slaughter house of Lewis L Barranger, jr, on Pa ave, near Hoffman, which resulted in the death of one of them, a young German, Henry Misnering, aged about 23 years. Jas Gibbons & deceased are both butchers at the slaughter house, in the employ of Mr Barranger, who is brother-in-law of Gibbons. An altercation arose between them, Misnering striking Gibbons with his fist, Gibbons seized a butcher knife & cut Misnering. As Misnering started to flee he plunged the knife into his back. Misnering ran out of the slaughter-house crying murder, which attracted the attention of Sgt Cadwallader & Ofcr Childs, who ran to Misnering just as he fell & died. The mother of the accused showed signs of great grief & horror at the situation of her son, & asked him to finish the affair by plunging the knife into her bosom. –Balt

Balt, May 11. Yesterday Jefferson Davis was indicted for treason against the U S by the grand jury in session at Norfolk. The trial of the prisoner it is supposed will take place in June.
+
Norfolk, May 11. Late yesterday the grand jury of the U S Circuit Court, in session here, brought in a true bill of indictment against Jeff Davis for treason, & adjourned until the first Tue in June, to meet in Richmond.

I would respectfully inform my friends & the public that I have secured the services of Mr J C Fill, a practical pharmaceutist, to take charge of my Drug Store, La ave & 7th st, hoping in the future, as in the past, to merit the patronage of the citizens of Wash. –Mrs S B Waite

Thurlow W Brown, a well-known lecturer on temperance, & editor of the Wisconsin Chief, died at his residence at **Fort Atkinson**, Wisc, last Friday.

Accident befell the steamer **City of Washington** on her last passage from N Y to Liverpool. The screw steamer **Propontis**, from N Y, arrived at Queenstown, having the purser, Mr Main, & passengers of the **City of Washington** on board. They fell in with her on Apr 18, with loss of rudder & mainshaft. Captain & crew still on board.

Nashville, May 8. Lyman Brodie, an Adams Express messenger, was killed on the hither Louisville train, this morning, between Cave City & Glasgow Junction. He was leaning down to see if the wheel under the car needed oiling, when his head struck a projection beside the truck. He lived only a short time.

Real estate known as the **Meadows**, in Beltsville, PG Co, Md, at public sale on May 17. Valuable farm on which Edw Herbert now resides; contains about 200 acres; with a new dwlg house & out bldgs. Mr Edw Herbert will show the premises. –Danl Clarke, atty

Supreme Court of D C, in Chancery, No 500. John A Middleton et al vs Eliza T Berry et al. Ordered that the sale reported by John A Middleton & Thos W Berry, trustees, for the sale of the real estate of Washington Berry, deceased, be ratified & confirmed. The amount of sales was $7,189.62. –R J Meigs, clerk

Mrd: on May 9, in Chester, Pa, by Rev Henry Brown, Rector of St Paul's Church, Ben B French, jr, Engineer U S Capitol Extension, to Abbie M, daughter of Chas F Thomas, formerly of Wash City.

Died: on May 10, Lizzie Wirt, daughter of Rear Admiral Louis M Goldsborough, U S Navy & Eliz W Goldsborough. Her funeral is today at 4 o'clock P M, from St John's Church.

Died: on May 8, at the residence of his brother-in-law, T A Toldon, East Washington, Henry W Arnold, aged 24 years. But passed through death to eternal life.

Died: on May 11, Thos Gally Drinkard, son of Wm R & Mary T Drinkard, of Wash City. His funeral will take place from the M-street Methodist Church, between 9th & 10th sts, this afternoon at 2½ o'clock P M.

Shooting affray in Balt yesterday. John Price, a notorious outlaw, shot his cousin, a young man, Clinton James, with a revolver. Price has been tried 4 times for murder, & been charged with killing 8 persons during his life, & served 15 years in the Md Penitentiary. He is about 50 years old. He is now in prison. James still survives, but cannot live over night.

Union Base-Ball Club, Wash, May 11, 1866. Members of the club are requested to meet at the residence of Mr Drinkard, at 2 o'clock P M, punctually, for the funeral of the late Thos Gally Drinkard. —W E Urell, Pres

Despatch to the Chicago Tribune from Memphis says: Lt Blanding, adj of the Freedmen's Bureau, while walking the streets of Meridian, Miss, in company with a Mrs Woodruff, the other night, was shot at by some unknown persons from behind & pierced with bullets, which caused his death in about 2 hours.

On May 8th, Mr F C Kelton, of the firm of Kelton, Bancroft & Co, wholesale druggists, merchants of Columbus, Ohio, fell from the rear window in the 3rd story of their store. He will live only a few hours. He had recently been to Mississippi for the remains of his son, Lt Kelton, of the 95th Ohio, & while there met with a severe accident to his head, & frequently complained of dizziness.

Sale of celebrated trotting horse Dexter, realizes $14,000. Mr Louis Petter, [the owner of the famous trotting mare Lady Emma,] who bought him for Mr Geo Alley, of Astoria, L I, his former part owner, was the purchaser. —N Y Times

A letter from Madrid states that ex-Pres Millard Fillmore & wife arrived there on the 22nd of last month.

A final decision by the Supreme Court Judges on the contested will of the late Col Saml Colt was made yesterday at New Haven. It is decided that the interest of Col Colt's brother, Judge Colt, in the stock of the Colt's Arms Manufacturing Company is a life estate, & not an absolute one; that he takes 574 shares of the stock, & that, besides the back dividends, he takes interest on the dividends, so far as the Arms Company has used the money & made interest. The Court distributes the residuum of the stock, which is found to be 5,346 shares, as follows:
To Mrs Colt: 1,149 shares
To Jas B Colt [for life:] 574 shares.
To Saml C Colt: 574 shares.
To Caldwell H Colt: 574 shares.
To Henrietta Colt, deceased: 574 shares
To Eliz E Colt, deceased: 574 shares.
To Saml J Colt, deceased: 574 shares.
To Christopher Colt's children: 450 shares.
To R D Hubbard, R W H Jarvis, & Mrs Colt, as excs, each: 57 shares.
To L P Sargent: 57 shares.
To E K Root: 57 shares.
A dividend, we believe, of about 150% on these shares is now due from the time of Col Colt's death. It would give $86,000 as Judge Colt's share. It will be seen that a very large amount goes into the hands of Mrs Colt for herself & children, living & deceased.
-Hartford Times, 8th

MON MAY 14, 1866

Jefferson Fowler, of the Indian Bureau, has just put in force practical sympathy for soldiers, by resigning his position, & thus making room for the appointment of one of that class.

It is stated that Gen Fisk has ordered the negro schools & churches recently destroyed at Memphis to be immediately rebuilt at the expense of the city.

Tragedy in Montg Co, Ga on Sunday of last week. Alfred Morrison plunged a knife into the bosom of Seaborn Hall, inflicitng a mortal wound. Levi Hall, a brother of Seaborn, ran to separate them, but was too late. Levi drew a pistol & sent a bullet into the brains of Morris, killing him instantly. The affair took place at Bell's Ferry, on Occo river. All the parties were respectably connected, Morris' father being a member of the Legislature.

J W Kellogg, a defaulter in the sum of $40,000, late a treasury agent at San Antonio, Texas, with his accomplice, was arrested at Memphis recently on his way up the river.

Yesterday Mr & Mrs Thos Hines were passing along H st in a buggy, when a dog bit the horse, causing him to take fright & run off. They were both thrown from the buggy, & Mrs Hines leg was fractured.

Real estate sales: -Green & Williams, aucts: lots 5 & 6 in square 566, to J C Sthelon, at 5 cents per foot; lot 7 to Wm Downs, for 5¾ cents; lot 8 to Jas Downs for 5½ cents; lots 9 thru 11 to R Jacobs for 5¾ cents; lots 13, 14, & 16 to R Barry for 4½ cents; lot H in square 398, on O st, to Thos Lewis for $2,200; part of lot 7 in square 345, on 11th st, to John Alexander for $6,525; part of same lot, improved with a 3 story brick dwlg, for $9,560; part of lot 3 in square 523, on 4th st, to Eliza Drane for 43 cents per foot; part of lot 5 in square 140 on L st, with 2 story frame house, to Michl Caffay for $920; lot 5 in square 537, to John McKenney for 17½ cents per foot; a 3 story brick house, on 11th st, to John Alexander, for $3,625. C W Boteler, auct, sold part of lot 13 in square 5, with a brick stable, for $768.50, to Luke Conner; part of lot 14 in square 5, on K st, 45 cents per foot, to Dennis Burns; 10 acres of land near Uniontown, $930, to Dr Leiberman; lots 24 & 25, opposite **Glenwood Cemetery**, $225 per acre; lots 26 & 27, same tract, $217.50 per acre; lot 14, same tract, $150 per acre, to T McGuire; part of lot 6 in square 629, 9 cents per foot, to S Cook.

On Sat a colored boy, Jas M Robbins, who resided in the alley between M & N sts, fell into the creek & drowned, while collecting drift wood. His body was recovered.

Died: on May 12, Marian Jenifer, youngest daughter of H S & Mary E Davis, aged 6 years & 5 months. Her funeral will be from the parents' residence, 59 9th st, this morning at 10 o'clock A M.

Orphans Court-Judge Purcell, May 12, 1866.
1-The will of the late Saml Gates, bequeathing his estate to his aunt, Sarah Jane Gates, was filed.
2-The will of the late Francis M Strother, executed Nov 9, 1864, bequeathing his estate to his heirs-at-law, & revoking a former will which left the estate to the widow, was brought into court by the widow & fully proven. The widow filed a caveat against the will, & also renounced any bequeath made, agreeing to take her legal share in the estate. Letters testamentary were issued to Jas Nicholson, who is named executor under the last will.
3-The will of the late Adam Geo Harold was admitted to probate.
4-The inventory of the personal estate of Jas H Moore, deceased, was returned by the administrator.
5-Jas J Kane was appointed guardian to the minor children of their mother, Mary Eliz Kane: bond, $2,000.
6-Catherine Herbert obtained letters of administration on the estate of the late Anton Herbert; bond $1,000, & was also appointed guardian of the minor children.
7-Mrs Sophia Douglas was appointed guardian of the minor children of Wm Douglas, deceased; bond $5,000.
8-The first acount of the admx of Stephn R Wilson; the 15th & final account of the guardian of the orphan of Horatio Barnes, deceased; & the 4th general account of the guardian to the orphans of Benj Bean, were approved & passed.

The **Greenberry Point Farm**, 301 acres, opposite Annapolis, Md, will be offered at public auction on May 22, at the City Hotel, in Annapolis.
–Henry O Middleton

The wife of Thos Chadwick, of East Waterloo township, arose from her bed in the middle of the night, without the knowledge of her husband, went to the room of her little son, kissed him; proceeded to the grave of her child she had buried but a few weeks previous, then went to the Cedar river & threw herself in. Her dead body was found in the water. Mrs Chadwick was a lady of high esteem, & never manifested any evidences of insanity, although she had been much distressed by the death of her child.

On Wed night a party of 4 negroes broke into the house of Miss Mahala Palmer, near Broad Creek Church, in this county, & robbed the house of a lot of silverware, all the money in the house, carried off a wagon & horse, & 2 horses from the adjoining place. Miss Palmer & her aged sister are the only inmates of the house. An arrest is said to have been made. –Marlborough Gaz

Raphael Semmes was, on Tue last, elected judge of probate for Mobile Co, Ala.

For rent: 5 rooms suitable for ofcs, N Y & 14th st. Rent moderate. Apply to Francis Lamb, 237 Pa ave, near 13th st.

The following exhibits the distribution of troops in the Dept of Va:
District of Henrico: R S Granger, brvt brig gen, U S army, lt col 11th U S infty, companies C & G, 2nd btln 12th U S infty.
Battery F, 5th U S artl, 1st & 2nd btlns 11th U S infty, Co H, 3rd btln 11th U S infty, cos C & G, 2nd btln 12th U S infty.
District of **Fort Monroe**: N A Miles, major gen, U S vols, commanding. Headquarters 5th U S artl. Batteries A, B, C, & H, 5th U S artl; Cos A, B, C, D, & G, 1st btln U S infty.
Post of Petersburg: T M Anderson, capt 12th U S infty, & brvt lt col, U S army, commanding.
Post of Norfolk: P W Stanhope, capt 12th U S infty, & brvt maj, U S army, commanding.
Post of City Point: Thos S Dunn, capt 12th U S infty, & brvt maj, U S army, commanding.
Post of Fredericksburg: Henry A Hambright, capt 11th U S infty, brvt lt col, U S army, commanding.
Companies E & G, 3rd btls 11th U S infty.
Post of Lynchburg: Alfred E Latimer, capt 11th U S infty, & brvt maj, U S army, commanding.
Post of Danville: Chas E Farrand, capt 11th U S infty, commanding.
Co C, 3rd btln 11th U S infty.
Post of Charlottesville: Geo E Head, capt 11th U S infty, & brvt maj, U S army, commanding.
Co B, 3rd btln 11th U S infty.
Post of Bristol: H L Chipman, capt 11th U S infty, & brvt lt col, U S army, commanding.
Co D, 3rd btln 11th U S infty.

Supreme Court of D C, in Equity, No 698: in the matter of the division of the real estate of Louisa Collins, deceased. Fred'k Foote et al vs Wm H Phillips. To all Concerned: meet at the ofc of A Lloyd, 20 La ave, on May 17 at 4 o'clock. –Wilson, Levy, & Carrington, for Com'rs.

Cincinnati, May 10. Sterling King, who asserted that he was an accomplice of Booth in the assassination of Pres Lincoln, & that Booth was yet alive, has confessed that the story about Booth was a hoax. Failing in this ruse, he refused to eat anything, & for the past 2 weeks has not eaten a particle of food. King was yesterday transferred from the Louisville jail to the mail-boat to be brought to this city, but only living until reaching this port, when death ensued. –Chicago Times [May 15th newspaper: Sterling King, the self accused assassin, whose death at Cincinnati was announced yesterday by telegram, was indicted by the Grand Jury a few days ago for stealing a horse from Mr Allison Nailor, of Wash City, some months ago. The proof against him was of a clear & positive character, & the authorities at Louisville had been telegraphed to hold him in custody until he should be required for trial here.]

The friends of Hon D C Littlejohn, at Oswego, N Y, on Sat last, presented him with a magnificent dinner service of silver, worth $4,120.

TUE MAY 15, 1866
Hon Geo E Badger, of Raleigh, N C, died in that city on Friday last, in his 72nd year. He was born in Newbern, N C; graduated at Yale College in 1813; studied & practised law, & was elected to the Legislature in 1816; in 1820 elected a Judge of the Supreme Court, which he resigned in 1825; was appointed Sec of the Navy by Pres Harrison in 1841; elected a Senator in Congress in 1846, & re-elected in 1848 for a term of 6 years. Of late years he has devoted his time to the practise of his profession.

Rear Admiral Dahlgren, Capt W H Walker, & Cmder Ammen, are to be examiners at the annual exhibition at the Naval School, now at hand.

Fortress Monroe, May 14. Pres Johnson has directed the surgeon of the post to make a special report of the health of Jeff Davis, & it is confidently said that during the past 12 months the unceasing tramping & changing of the guard around his cell has prevented him from enjoying, at any one time, more than 2 hours unbroken sleep, & that his health is failing rapidly. He expressed extreme pleasure when the news of his indictment reached him, confident that speedy action in his case will soon follow.

Mr Robt Tyler, of Va, has replied to the recent letter of Cmdor Maury, in the London Herald, estimating the losses of the South in the late war at a total of seven billions of dollars. Mr Tyler entirely dissents from this statement, & says the item of three billions loss in emancipated slaves is excessively high, at least 50% above actual damages. According to his own premises, the total loss of the South was $3,000,000,000.

On Sat, on Eutaw st, near German, Rudolph Hagins shot his own child, a little girl about 5 years of age. Hagins & his wife had been for some time separated, the latter having taken up her residence with her brother-in-law, J Henry Maenner, 53 German st. Hagins appeared at the residence, & seizing his child, hurried & placed her in hack 86, which was standing in the street. Maenner pusued him & jumped into the hack; Hagins attempted to shoot Maenner, when the latter seized the barrel of the pistol, a Sharps four-shooter, when it discharged, striking the child in the thigh. The child was at once carried to Mr Maenner's residence, & Dr Claude Bexley called; while Hagins was arrested by Sgt Handy & Policeman Tipton. Hagin attempted to commit suicide by hanging himself with two handkerchiefs, which he had tied together, fastened to a bar of iron at the top of the window of his cell. He was taken down & restored to consciousness. He was committed to jail by Justice Showacre, to answer the charge of shooting. The condition of the little girl is not regarded as dangerous. –Balt Gaz, Mon

Died: on May 14, Dr Richd Gudgen. His funeral will take place at 3 o'clock from his late residence, 300 10th st, between N & O. [Must be today.]

Boston Journal of Thu: sad affair yesterday at the iron foundry of Messrs Davis & Farnum. Mr Augus McMillan, employed in the foundry, tried experimenting with a pile of shells that appearded loaded. He inserted a rod of iron heated at one end in the aperture of the shell, & it soon burnt out. Capt Howard spoke to him & told him it was a dangerous undertaking. At this moment the shell exploded, fragments flying in all directions, & instantly killing Capt Howard, 2 little boys, who were near by, named Robt Flynn & Edmund Casey, & dangerously wounding McMillan in the leg, so that amputation may be necessary, & slightly injuring Mr Chas C Bean, foreman for Messrs Davis & Farnum. Capt Howard served with distinction during the war, in 2 different regts. He was universally respected by the community in which he lived & was a member of the Methodist Church in Waltham. He leaves a widow & 3 children. Robt Flynn was 8 years of age, one of 5 children of a widowed mother, who lost her husband in the war. Edmund Casey, about 11 years old, was the son of Cornelius Casey, & resided with his parents a short distance from the foundry. Coroner E W Fiske summoned a jury of inquest to investigate the whole affair.

WED MAY 16, 1866
N Y Commercial Advertiser of Monday. The body of John Preston King, who disappeared from a Hoboken ferry-boat on Nov 13, 1865, was found this morning floating into the gap from Buttermilk Channell. Some school children stated that they saw a man jump overboard, & from the description it became evident that the man was Mr King. Mr Lydecker & a nephew of the deceased, Mr Preston King Webster, both positively identified him. Mr King had remarkably small feet for so large a man, another evidence of identification. Mr King had been ill for some time & on the morning of Nov 13th, he rose at an unusually early hour & left the Astor House, saying he was going out for a short walk. The remains will be conveyed tomorrow to St Lawrence Co, where the funeral will take place.

Orphans Court-Judge Purcell.
1-This morning the will of the late Edw Wayson was admitted to probate, the caveat filed having been dismissed.
2-Letters of administration were issued to John Van Riswick on the estate of Benj Easby, of Ga, who died in Richmond in 1861: bond, $40,000.
3-Catherine Herbert was appointed guardian to the orphan of Amos Herbert: bond, $800.
4-The first & final account of the exec of Judson Mitchell, deceased; the first account of the guardian of the orphans of Thos Corcoran, deceased; the first & final account account of the admx of Max Mayer; & the first general account of the orphans of Emanuel Crampton were approved & passed.

Mr Anthony Gardner is about to erect at the intersection of Va ave, Dela ave, & First st, a market-house bldg, 176 feet front on Va ave, & 91½ feet on Delaware ave, which will contain 100 stalls; ready for occupancy by Jul 1st.

On Monday the Senate confirmed the following nominations: Richd H Rousseau, of Ky, to be Minister resident at Honduras. Consuls: Edw Maynard, of Tenn, at Turk's Island; John Henry, at Quebec; Chas Yates Roosevelt, of N Y, at Copenhagen; Geo F Kettell, of N Y, at Carlsruhe. The Senate also confirmed Morris B Brown as Indian Agent for Utah; E C Carrington as District Atty for District of Columbia; H H Henry as marshal for the District of Vt; & John Blevins, as marshal for the Northern District of Miss.

The holy rite of confirmation will be administered at St John's Church, Gtwn, D C, by Rt Rev Bishop Whipple, of Minn, this night at 8 o'clock. The Bishop is expected to preach.

New Orleans, May 14. Advices from Mexico confirm the death of ex-Govn'r Allen, of Louisiana.

Orphans Court of Wash Co, D C. Letters of administration on the personal estate of Benj Easley, late of Dale Co, Ga, deceased. –John Van Riswick, adm

Montpelier, Vt, May 18. By fire at North Regallin, Vt, last night, the house of Mr Burbank was destroyed, & himself, daughter, & another young lady perished in the flames. The barn, containing a large number of cattle, was also consumed.

Louisville, May 15. In the case of Col Jacques, of Ill, whose trial on an indictment for murder has been for some days in progress, the jury returned a verdict of not guilty, without leaving their seats.

Mr Geo Peabody, who is now sojourning with his friends in Essex Co, has been notified to make a return of his income since Sep, 1862, for the purpose of taxation under the revenue laws of the U S.

Mr C W Jordon, clerk of the steamer **Clinton**, returning from Eliz City to Norfolk, Va, a few days since, accidentally fell overboard & was drowned before he could be rescued.

Prof W Byrd Powell died in Cincinnati on Sunday.

On Monday, in Richmond, Mr John G Moss, baggage-master on the Richmond & Fredericksburg railroad, was stabbed by Mr Wm S Phillips, superintendent of the city poorhouse. The quarrel was over some insulting language addressed by a servant of Mr Moss to the wife of Mr Phillips. Mr Moss was stabbed in the side, the knife penetrating the lung, which renders his recovery doubtful.

E T Armstrong, formerly of Chappel, Bance & Co, of Cincinnati, was killed at Paris, Ky, on Sat, by a man named Muriwell.

THU MAY 17, 1866

Lt Col E E Paulding, Paymaster U S Army, who, at the time of the failure of the Merchants' Nat'l Bank of this city, had on deposit a large amount in Gov't funds, was yesterday arrested by orders from the Sec of War. Lt Col Paulding asks for the suspension of public opinion until the facts of the case are elicited by the com'r now investigating the affairs of the bank referred to.

Accident at Foundry Church, yesterday, when a portion of the scaffolding used in the painting of the audience-room of this Church, with 3 men at work on, fell, precipitating them over 30 feet to the floor. Mr Geo Adams, who resides at 288 C st, was dangerously injured in the head & side, & it is feared internally. Mr Isaac McConnell, who resides next door to Mr Adams, was seriously injured in the head & back. Mr Chas Kahlert, who resides on Capitol Hill, was injured in nearly the same manner. Mr McConnell & Mr Kahlert have large families dependent on them for support. Mr B Polglass, a carpenter, was working directly under the scaffold, & made a narrow escape, being slightly injured.

The contract for the erection of a new **naval magazine** near the ***Congressional Cemetery***; for the removing & erecting a new keeper's house; repairing the old brick storehouse, & for about 23,000 feet of fencing, was yesterday awarded to Messrs Wise, Callihan & Co, whose bid was $8,634.71 for magazine; $3,217 for keeper's house; $682.86 for repairing storehouse; & $1,824 for fencing-making a total of $17,832.

San Francisco, May 16. A letter from Chas Hamilton, dated Williams' Ford, Ariz, Apr 30, seems to confirm the massacre at ***Fort Goodwin***. He states that of 2 companies of regulars, belonging to the 3rd btln of the 11th regt, consisting of 100 men, only 7 escaped. The remainder were murdered & scalped. The Apaches reaped a rich harvest, carrying off arms, ammunition, & commissary stores. A number of supposed friendly Indians were admitted into the fort, & surprised the garrison. A tribe called the Huolapes had murdered one man & committed other outrages in the vicinity. Lt Cervantes, Co D, with 26 men, attacked the Apaches 40 miles east of ***Camp Lincoln*** about Mar 24, killing 22, wounding 50, & capturing 2. The same day the party was planning an attack upon large ranches in the vicinity.

Died: on May 15, Mrs Augusta E M McKim, in her 71st year. Her funeral will be from the residence of her husband, John McKim, 563 8th st, this afternoon, at 4 o'clock.

Died: on May 16, after a lingering illness, Thos Baker, aged 70 years. His funeral is on May 18 at 3 o'clock, from his late residence, 495 H st.

Fire at Syracuse, N Y, on Tue, destroyed a wooden bldg, owned & occupied by the Sisters of Charity, & 2 outhouses owned by Rev Mr O'Harra. The main bldg, belonging to the Sisters, was saved. Loss $2,000, probably insured.

Columbia Hospital for Women & Lying-in Asylum, 14th st, [Circle] corner of M st. Terms of admission: $6 to $10 per week, in accordance with the room required, payable in advance. This includes board, medicines, medical & surgical attendance. Medical Staff: surgeon in Charge: J H Thompson, M D, 184 I st, between 10th & 21st sts.
Consulting physicians & surgeons:
Jos K Barnes, M D, Surgeon Gen U S A
Jos Riley, M D, Gtwn
Thos Miller, M D, F st, Wash
A Y P Garnett, N Y ave
W P Johnston, Wash
Grafton Tyler, Gtwn
Applications for admission can be made to any of the Medical Staff or to the Matron of the Hospital. Orders for admission to the free beds of this institution can be obtained of Rev C H Hall, rector of the Epiphany Church; of Rev A D Gillette, pastor of the First Baptist Church; & of the Surgeon in Charge, at his residence. Orders for the admission of wives & widows of soldiers of the U S army can be procured through the Surgeon Gen U S A. –C H Hall, D D, sec

A new singer is expected in Paris, who is said to eclipse even Jenny Lind & Malibran. Her name is Marie Taskatt, & she hails from Stockholm.

Civil Rights case in Balt, on May 5. Two colored woman, Mary J C Anderson & Ellen G Jackson, entered the Pres st Depot bldg of the Phil, Wilmington, & Balt Railroad Co, & proceeded to the room set apart for the use of ladies while waiting for the starting of trains. Special Ofcr Mr Adam Smyzer, gave them the information that the room was not intended for their accommodation. They were compelled to go out. They are teachers, one living at Havre de Grace & the other at Port Deposit. The railroad company has a separate room & special cars on each or certain trains, for the use of colored persons. Whether the matter will be decided here or at Annapolis is uncertain. -Balt American, May 16

Mrs Hatting, of Cincinnati, on Sat last, cut her throat with her husband's cutlass, causing death almost instantly. She has contemplated self-destruction heretofore.

Mrs Rencher, of Cincinnati, on Fri last, was badly burned when coal oil, on igniting kindling, produced an explosion in the can, scattering the burning fluid over herself & her little boy. Both suffered intensely & have both since died.

FRI MAY 18, 1866
Miss Adelina Patti has given 1,000f to be distributed among the chorus singers of the Italian Opera, Paris.

On Wed Jas C McGuire & Co, aucts, sold lots 1, 17 & 18 in square 160, to J C Noerr, for 21 cents per square foot; lots 2 to 10 in square 160 to W H Philip, at 15¼ cents per foot. Above property is known as *Favier's Square*, bound by Rhode Island ave, 17th & M st.

Dr Benj Newland, recently on trial at New Albany, Ind, for the murder of Prof Evans, whom he charged with seducing his daughter, has been acquitted on the ground of insanity.

A few days since Mr Edwin H King, an undertaker, took up the body of the late Wm B Talley, buried in the *old Foundry burial-ground*, & reinterred it in the *Congressional Cemetery*. It has been 16 years since the interment was made, & the pine case & mahogany coffin were found in a perfect state of preservation. Some curiosity being expressed as to the state of the body, the coffin was opened. The body & shroud were found to be in a perfect state of preservation. The body was found to have almost the hardness & consistency of stone, showing that petrifaction was rapidly going on.

Caution. As my name has been forged to checks, I have determined to issue no checks, & the public is therefore cautioned against receiving checks purporting to be mine. -Johnson Hellen

Richmond Examiner of yesterday: interview with Mrs Davis. We observed Mr Davis taking his customary walk upon the ramparts of the fort; [*Fortress Monroe*] & from a distance he looked weak & emaciated, & used a cane for support. His suit was the old familiar gray in which he so often appeared to the citizens of Richmond, as his erect form strided back & forth through Capitol Square to & from the Presidential mansion & his ofc in the Custom house. The interviewer found Mrs Jefferson Davis, at the residence of Dr Cooper, the post surgeon. She was in an apartment comfortably though not elegantly furnished, & she did not seem to want for anything. Though weak from long confinement & want of change of air, she thought Mr Davis' general health was good, & his spirit had revived since she had been permitted to visit & be nearby. Her youngest, Georgie, a beautiful child, was with her, with sadness in her eyes & face. The other children, Jeffy & an older daughter, are in Montreal, Canada. Mrs Davis' old dining-room servant, Frederick, who waited at the President's mansion, is also with her. [May 22nd newspaper: *Fortress Monroe*, May 18. The health of Jeff Davis is now on the mend. About a week since he was attacked by a severe diarrhoea, which has yielded under medical treatment. His is allowed abundance of liquors & cigars, & many little luxuries are extended him through the courtesy of the ofcrs of the garrison. Mrs Davis is allowed uninterrupeed access to his cell at certain hours of the day. She has been assigned a casement such as the wives & families of the ofcrs occupy. This privilege she has not availed herself of.]

New Orleans, May 16. Senator Gwin has arrived. He was released on parole without other conditions. He refused to take the oath or to leave the country. He is visiting his friends today.

Comrs' sale of valuable real estate on the Jas River, in Rockbridge Co, Va: by decree in a cause pending in the Circuit Court for said county, dated Apr 12 last, in which John M Yuille & wife are plntfs, & Thos G Burks & others are dfndnts: public auction on Jun 23 next, of a tract of 820 acres in said county. The bldg are large with a well-furnished 2 story brick-frame dwlg, & all necessary out-bldgs. –E Pendleton, John Letcher, com'rs

Dr B L Suago, assist editor of the Atlanta [Ga] Era, was found dead in his bed at the Southern Hotel in St Louis, on Tue, he having committed suicide. Letters found in his room indicate poverty, sorrow, & disappointment were the causes of the rash act.

SAT MAY 19, 1866
John Porterfield, of Nashville, formerly a banker & an old resident, has been arrested & lodged in the penitentiary, it is rumored, in consequence of implication with the conspirators in Canada some time previous to the death of Pres Lincoln.

Gen T W Sherman arrived at St Paul on Sunday last, & was cordially welcomed by his friends in that city.

Headquarters Dept of Ala, May 17, 1866. Raphael Semmes not to be permitted to exercise the functions of Probate Judge of Mobile Co, or any other civil or policitcal ofc of trust, while he remains unpardoned by the Pres. By order of the Brvt Maj Gen Chas R Woods, A Ramsey Ninninger, Assist Adj Gen.

Mrd: on Apr 30, 1866, by Rev Jos Gordon, Wm T Goodrich to Mary Catharine, 2nd daughter of John S Bogan, all of Mount Vernon, Jefferson Co, Ill.

Died: on Apr 23, at **Tudor Hall**, Montg Co, Md, in his 41st year, Mr D T White, son of the late Dr S N C White.

Died: on May 11, at Salem City, N J, Emeline, wife of Isaac Hackett, of Wash City.

Wm Carpenter, of the firm of A W & W Carpenter, jewellers, of Burlington, Iowa, was killed suddenly at the Agency, on Friday last, by a gunshot, whether by accident or design is not known. He took a gun to kill some rabbits, & his dead body was discovered soon after. He was occasionally much depressed. He left no word indicating a determination to commit suicide. He had been successful in business & was highly esteemed.

Providence, May 18. Information received of the death of Rt Rev Geo Bergess, D D, Bishop of Maine, while returning from the West Indies, where he had been for his health.

Trustee's sale of two valuable farms in Howard Co, Md, & limestone quarries; by decree of the Circuit Court for Howard Co, Md: public sale on Jun 9, at the Tavern in Clarksville, Howard Co, the following: 1-The **Home Place** of the late A J Adams, now the residence of Mrs Adams, on the road leading from Ellicott's Mills to Sandy Spring, adjoining the lands of G S Hopkins, Jas Morris, B G Cissell, & others. Contains about 254 acres; with a handsome frame dwlg house, lately built, a barn, ice house, blacksmith shop, & other out-bldgs. 2-A farm of 109 acres, part of the estate of the late A J Adams, on the Patuxent river, adjoining the lands of Chas Cissell, Philip Smallwood & others.
3-Two limestone quarry lots, near the last named farm containing about one-quarter of an acre each, known as **Cissell's Quarries**. –Thos Donaldson, trustee

Supreme Court, D C-in Equity, No 250. Isaac Talks & others against Isaac S Hollidge & others. Statement of the estate of the late Jas Hollidge on Jun 11th next, at my ofc, City Hall. –W Redin, auditor

Supreme Court, D C-in Equity, No 198. Wm J Downing et al against Andrew J Wallace et al. Distribution of the fund of the late Richd Brown, on Jun 11, at my ofc, City Hall. -W Redin, auditor

The pews in Calvary Baptist Church, the new & magnificent edifice, H & 8th st, are now for rent. A Trustees will be in attendance daily for one week at 6 P M at the Church to wait upon applicants. –Henry Beard, David Haynes, Wm Stickney, C S Butts, trustees

The eccentric Lord Holland, of the reign of Wm III, used to give his horses a weekly concert in a covered gallery specially erected for the purpose. He maintained that it cheered their hearts & improved their tempers, & an eye-witness says that "they seemed delighted with it."

A new opera, "Loretta l'Indovina," has been produced at the Teatro Bellini, in Naples. The music is by Sig Francesco, & the libretto by Sig Almerindo Spadetta. The composer was called on ten times.

Yesterday, as the canal boat **W J Shreve** was coming up to the lock, the mules attached to it took fright, & turning around, started fown the tow-path at full speed, catching the driver, Geo Hoffman, in the rope & dragging him a distance of more than a mile. His body was found at the canal bridge, terribly manageld, & life extinct. Hoffman was 17 years of age, & a native of Hollidaysburg, Pa.
–Cumberland Civilian

Arrangements have been made to have all the remains of the Union soldiers, buried along the line of the Tenn & Ala railroad, removed to one ***national cemetery***, to be established for that purpose.

MON MAY 21, 1866

Gen Solomon Meredith has been appointed Collector of the 5th collection district of Indiana, vice Cheney, removed. Gen Meredith is an earnest supporter of Pres Johnson's policy.

The 200th anniversary of the settlement of Newark, N J, was celebrated on Thu by a gathering of the citizens, & public addresses & other exercises by the N J Historical Society.

Rev F E Boyle, the esteemed pastor of St Peter's Catholic Church, Capitol Hill, contemplates having erected at once, in the vicinity of the Church, a commodious bldg for the accommodation of the many children of the parish who are now deprived of proper moral & intellectual training for the want of such facilities as will be accorded by the new school. A handsome & eligible lot, on E st south, between 3rd & 4th sts, has already been donated for the purpose by Thos Bayne, of the 5th Ward. The bldg cmte consists of Rev F E Boyle, Thos Bayne, John H Russell, & Jas Marceron. Upwards of 600 children are now awaiting admission into the school.

The Flannery Brothers, of Wash City, are now engaged on a statuette of Lt Gen Grant, which will be completed in time to furnish duplicates for the fair of the Ladies' Nat'l Soldiers' & Sailors' Orphans' Home Association.

The late Moses Ward, father of Govn'r Ward, of N J, bequeathed $15,000 for the completion of the Newark Orphan Asylum.

Notice. There will be a reunion of the former pupils of Nazareth Hall, on Jun 8. All who purpose attending will please address Rev Edw H Reichel, Principal, Nazareth, Northampton Co, Pa.

The Planing & Sawing business conducted in the name of N C Draper & Co, 13th & C sts, is this day mutually dissolved. –N C Draper, H S Davis

Died: on May 10, in Wash City, Mrs Lucy E N Florence, wife of Hon Thos B Florence. Her remains will be taken to Phil for interment on Tuesday.

For sale-beautiful country seat on Piney Branch road, 2 miles from the termination of the railroad on 14th st; with a house that is new & built under my own supervision; contains about 24 acres, has the best kind of water. As business requires me to go to Europe for one or two years, I offer it at private sale, with all the furniture, stocks, & farming implements. –B Jost, Brightwood P O, D C, or Mr B Hart, 181 Pa ave, Wash, D C.

The Shaw & Clark $20 sewing machines. Come & see for yourself. Room 5, No 234 Pa ave, over Mr Stinemetz's Hat Store. Miss M H O'Connor, Agent for Md, D C, & Va.

Ogdensburg Journal of May 17, says: the remains of Preston King, in charge of Preston K Webster & Martin Thatcher, arrived here Wed; they were conveyed to the late residence of the deceased; the next day the funeral took place at 2 P M, Rev Dr Peters officiating & performing the rites of the Episcopal Church. The remains of Mr King were deposited in the *Ogdensburg Cemetery*, by the side of the father & mother & other friends of Mr King, & lowered in the tomb, at his native home.

Boston, May 19. The suit of John M Way, in the Supreme Court, for $20,000 damages, has resulted in a verdict giving him $100. The ground for the suit was the plntf being compelled to raise a flag & make a loyal speech by some of his neighbors, who thought him disloyal.

TUE MAY 22, 1866
The President Fully Endorsed: grand mass meeting on Sat at Carroll Co, Westminster, Md. The meeting numbered from 2,500 to 3,000 persons, & was called to order about
12 o'clock, by the election of the following ofcrs, all of whom were & have been Union men: Pres, Geo Jacobs. Vice presidents: Sterling Galt, Jacob Koontz; Capt Geo W Shull; Mordecai G Cockey; John T Ways; Phanuel Wentz; David Fowble; John W Murray; Somerset R Waters; Thos F Cover; John Deihl. Secretaries: Jos M Parke, Edwin F Reese, & Chas F Reifsnider.

Mr Henry Duke, of Richmond, while walking on Broad st, on Sat last, fell to the pavement & expired almost immediately. His death was probably occasioned by an affection of the heart, or apoplexy.

Obit-died: on May 18, Theodore Von Kamecke, a son of Gen Von Kamecke, commanding the Prussian artl, died at the residence of Baron de Witzieben, in this city. Von Kamecke came to the U S previous to the breaking out of the late war with the South, & soon obtained a commission as an engineer capt in the 23rd Brooklyn regt, N Y vols, in which capacity he rendered signal service to his adopted country. The term of service of the Capt having expired he accepted a position as a topographer, under Arthur de Witzieben, with whom he completed a survey of the grounds where the famous battles of South Mountain & Antietam were fought. Capt Von Kamecke remained in the Topographical Bureau until the latter part of 1865, when physical disability severed him from his labors. He was a courteous gentleman, with a heart overflowing with goodness.

New Orleans, May 19. Bishop Lay has been rejected & Dr Wilmer chosen Bishop of the diocese of Louisiana.

Poughkeepsie, May 20. At Port Ewell, on the Hudson, on Sat, Thos Pinkerton, while in a quarrel with his wife, knocked her from her chair & kicked her in the breast with such violence as to cause her death, 3 of her ribs being broken. Pinkerton was immediately arrested, & is now confined in the Kingston jail.

Va Military Institute, Lexington, Va. The Board of Visitors will meet on Jun 27 to make appointments of cadets. They must be exempt from bodily disease, & of ages 16 & 25 years; able to read & write well. Apply to Francis H Smith, Superintendent.

We offer for private sale that elegant & commodious Brown Stone House, on the south side of H st north, between 14 & 15th sts, late the residence of his Excellency M Berrada, the Peruvian Minister. Apply to J C McGuire & Co, aucts.

WED MAY 23, 1866

Albany Argus of Monday: yesterday a well-known printer, Robt J Martin, in the employ of Luther Tucker, fell from the 3rd story of the Commercial Bldg, on Dean st, which resulted in his death in an hour. While sitting on a high stool, near the window, he was seized with an epileptic fit, & fell from the window. He was in his 37th year, a large, heavy built man; unmarried, & lived with his mother on Clinton Ave. He had been subject to fits for quite a while, occurring every 6 weeks to 2 months.

The Pres has pardoned Gilbert Simpson, John Travis, & Jos Horseman, who were sent to the Albany Penitentiary, for participation in the Alexandria riots on Christmas day. These are all young men, one being only 17, & it is stated, took no active part in the disturbances at Alexandria. Pardons were forwarded to Albany on Monday night for their release.

The Sec of War has ordered the release from **Fort Delaware**, of Mr Saml Trunnell, formerly a private of Co C, 5th U S Cavalry, who was tried by General Court Martial in Mar last, & sentenced to be dismissed the service & suffer imprisonment one year. The sentence in his case has been remitted, his friends will be glad to learn.

Christopher C Callan was admitted an attorney & counsellor of the Supreme Court of the District of Columbia. [No date-current item.]

Died: on May 21, in Wash City, Mr J Harry Heath, in his 35th year. His funeral is today at 3 o'clock from the church of Rev Dr Smith, on 9th st.

Bethlehem, Pa, May 21. Dr Wm Wilson, an enterprising & distinguished citizen of Bethlehem, died at his residence this afternoon.

Orroway, C W, May 21. Mr John Galt, brother of Hon H F Galt, the Finance Minister, dropped dead, of apoplexy, while visiting the Parliament bldg.

Rochester, May 22. Lemuel Cook, one of the last Revolutionary heroes, died on Sunday night at Clarendon, Orleans Co, aged 102 years.

B L Seago, assistant editor of the Atlanta Era, committed suicide at the Southern Hotel, St Louis, by taking morphine & chloroform. Disappointed love, poverty, & misanthropy appear to have been the inciting cause. He left several letters to relatives & others. He asked that his body be sent to Atlanta, & that it be buried by the Masons. Her name is Delia. Send this note to Delia, through my uncle H R Seago.

Maj Gen Halleck, at San Francisco, has telegraphed to Lt Gen Grant, saying that there is no foundation for the **Fort Goodwin** massacre story, & that it was a newspaper sensation account, gotten up for the benefit of certain contractors.

Judge Danl S Bacon, of Monroe, Mich, a promising citizen of that State, & father-in-law of Gen G A Custer, died on Friday.

Wm Tripp nominated Surveyor Gen of Dakota Territory, vice Geo D Hill, resigned.

The steamboat **Lion**, formerly the steamer **St Andrew**, on May 17, after having had a new boiler & engine put in & sundry repairs, invited a number of guests to make a trip with her. On leaving Hochelaga wharf the boiler exploded, breaking in two pieces. Known dead: Alexis Charbonnean. Slightly scalded, Marquerite Etien, a cook; the owners of the boat-Messrs William & Robt Standish, the latter scalded & otherwise hurt; the captain, Capt Lee, was scalded, his son, Jeff Lee, is missing. Antoine Larocque, pilot, from Rigand, had both legs broken, & Benj Jerome, of Rigand, capt of the barge **Rose** is missing; Tourville Mallette had his leg broken; & Xavier Lafebvre was so injured about the head that it is doubtful whether he will survive. A passenger was drowned, & Poitevin, engineer, was scalded. Chief McLaughlin, of the Water Police, & 2 of his men were in attendance, but a number of petty thefts were committed, such as taking away part of the wreck. A boy, Chas Graham, a plumber, was on board, & is missing.

The wife of Rev Thos F King & mother of Rev T Starr King, died in Charlestown, Mass, at the age of 60 years.

THU MAY 24, 1866
Mrd: on May 17, in Brooklyn, by Rev Jas Eells, D D, Chas W Hassler, Paymaster, U S N, to Clara Brace, only daughter of D Walter Smith.

Died: on May 22, Otho Boswell, sr, in his 62nd year. His funeral is this afternoon at 3 o'clock, at his late residence, 623 7th st, between D & E sts.

Hon W Wright, U S Senator from N J, died yesterday after a long & severe illness. He was a native of Rockland Co, N Y, & removed to N J in 1794. Firm in his convictions, he came to Washington to vote, his vote being relied upon to sustain the Pres' veto of the civil rights bill, at the risk of his life. [Nov 6th newspaper: The remains were deposited in the family vault at *Mount Pleasant Cemetery*. The pall bearers were Gov'r Marcus L Ward, Edwin A Stevens, Jos A Halsey, Beach Vanderpool, Jos P Bradley, J C Garthwaite, J H Stephens, M Hitchcock, Edwin Van Antwerp, Wm S Faltoute, & ex-Chancellor Williamson.]

It is just one year ago yesterday, May 23, since Jefferson Davis entered *Fortress Monroe* as a prisoner.

The Com'r of Pensions yesterday received intelligence of the death of Lemuel Cooke, the late Revolutionary pensioner in N Y C, on May 22. Mr Cooke was originally from N H, & died at the advanced age of 101 years.

Lr Gen Grant's pay under the law establishing the full rank of General will be about $15,000 per annum.

Orphans Court-Judge Purcell.
1-Robt R Pywell & Atwell Cowling gave bill in the sum of 6,000, as excs of Richd Gudgin, & letters of adm were issued to them.
2-The court passed an order requiring the admx of Arthur J West to give additional security in the sum of $3,400, on or before Jun 23.
3-Thos Henry Norris, a colored boy, was bound as an apprentice to Wm H Hill, colored, until he attains the age of 21 years-his mother giving her consent thereto.
4-The inventory of the personal estate of Rose _ Harte was returned by the exc.
5-The will of Richd Godgin was filed, fully proven & admitted to probate & record. He leaves one-third of his property to his wife, & the remaining portion to his 5 childern.

FRI MAY 25, 1866
By direction of the Pres, so much of Special Orders, No 220, May 11, 1866, from this ofc, as dishonorably mustered out of the service Brvt Brig Gen H H Heath colonel 7th Iowa cavalry, is hereby revoked, the charges against him having been satisfactorily explained. By order of the Sec or War, E D Townsend, Assist Adj Gen. May 24, 1866.

Supreme Court, D C, in Equity, No 559. John Purdy agt Isaac D Surratt & others. Statement of the personal estate of John H Surratt, deceased, at my ofc, City Hall, on Jun 2nd next. –W Redin, auditor

N Y, May 24. The U S Com'r ordered the discharge of Otto Burnstenbinder, declaring that he could not be held for trial, not having been personally engaged in the shipping of nitro-glycerine to San Francisco, being absent from the city at the time, & cannot be held guilty of crime constructively.

Arlington & the Nat'l Cemetery. The estate came to Geo Washington Parke Custis from his own father, & was called *Arlington* in memory of his great grandfather, Hon John Custis, a king's counsellor, & whose estate on the Eastern Shore, in Northampton Co, was known as *Arlington.* Henry Earl of *Arlington,* whose daughter was the wife of the son of Charles II, by Lady Castlemaine, & who was regarded as the best bred gentleman at the royal court, was granted by that lavish & profligate Sovereign of England, in 1673, in connection with Lord Culpeper, all the dominion of land & water in Va, for the full term of 31 years. Arlington transferred his interest to Culpeper, whose rule there was so intolerable that the grant was recalled in 1684. Culpeper, though held in infamy in Va history, has been honored in the name of a county, while Arlington, whose name was never in disgrace in the State, has been perpetuated in the names of two estates. Geo Washington Parke Custis, & his sister, Nelly, were adopted by Geo Washington & reared at *Mount Vernon,* the former being 6 months old & the later 2½ years old when thus adopted & placed in the care of their grandmother, Mrs Washington, in 1781. Their father, Col John Parke Custis, was an aide-de-camp to Gen Washington, & died at the ancestral home of his wife, Eleanor Calvert, at Mount Airy, Md, of camp fever contracted at the siege of Yorktown. He was 27 years of age at his death & his wife 23, having been married 8 years, & Washington, hastening to his dying bed, was so much affected at the scene as to take the younger of the 4 children in his arms with the following language to the mother: "I adopt these 2 children as my own." Their father was the last surviving child of Mrs Washington by her first husband. Hon John Custis, the great grandfather of G W P Custis, died at Wmsburg, Va, leaving immense landed estates & L30,000 in money to his heirs. His remains were carried to *Arlington,* on the Eastern Shore; the tomb enclosing his remains, is regarded as one of the curiosities of the Eastern Shore. The inscription which his son, the first husband of Mrs Washington, was compelled by the conditions of the will to place upon the tomb is still to be seen, as follows: "Under this marble tomb lies the body of Hon John Curtis, of the city of Williamsburg, & the parish of Bruton. Formerly of Hunger's parish, on the Eastern Shore of Va, & county of Northampton, aged 71 years, & yet lived but 7 years, which was the space of time he kept a bachelor's home at *Arlington,* on the Eastern Shore of Virginia." On the opposite side is the following: "This inscription put on his tomb was by his own positive orders." G W P Custis had no brother, & his sisters who all preceded him to the grave, were Eliz Parke, the wife of Thos Law, brother of Lord Ellenborough, & son of Edmund Law, the celebrated Bishop of Carlisle. When he married Miss Custis Mr Law was possessed of great wealth. He invested $160,000 in city lots soon after this city was founded. The lots, for which he paid an average $400 each, were all located east of the Capitol, long occupied by the Coast Survey. Bishop Carlisle was not the author of Law's Serious call, as has been often times in this connexion erroneously stated. Martha Parke was the wife of Thos Peter, & Eleanor Parke became the wife of Maj Lawrence Lewis, Washington's favorite nephew. Nelly & her husband inherited by the will of Washington a magnificent seat, more than 2,000 acres from the *Mount Vernon* estate, on which they erected a spacious brick mansion, at a cost of $20,000, in 1802, & made it their elegant home for nearly half a century. About 1846 they sold this home & removed to Clark Co upon another inheritance. In that seclusion, Mrs Lewis, once the beautiful & accomplished Nelly, the pride & captivation of *Mount Vernon*, died in her 74th year, & her remains slumber by the side of the *Mount Vernon* tomb, & near the remains of her husband, Maj Lewis, who died a few years later while on a visit to *Arlington House*. Mr Custis was married soon after he was of his majority to Miss Mary Lee Fitzhugh, of Chatham, Va, leaving *Mount Vernon* immediately after the death of Mrs Washington, took up his residence on Arlington Heights with his youthful & cultivated wife, & there kept a hospitable & delightful home for more than 50 years, Mrs Custis dying in 1853, & Mr Custis in 1857. The fruits of Mr Custis' marriage were 4 daughters, all of whom died in infancy, except Mary Custis, the wife of Gen Robt E Lee. Mrs Custis' mother was a Miss Randolph, of Chatham, & the ancient grave in the brick enclosure near the Arlington House, with the stone inscribed Mary Randolph, marks the resting place of the member of that family, whose name is borne by Mrs Lee as it was by her mother. "The Washington treasures of Arlington" were taken South by Gen Lee, in 1861. Among them were the original three-quarter length portrait of Mrs Washington, by Woolaston, from which the engraving in Sparks' Life of Washington was made; the original portraits of Washington by Trumbull; of Martha Custis & Danl Parke Custis, Mrs Washington's two children; also the portrait by Stuart of Nelly Custis, & the portrait, by Kneller, of Hon John Custis; crayon profile sketches of Washington & his lady; & several others. The mansion is now occupied by the ofcr in charge of the cemetery, & by the chaplain on duty there, with his family, & is altogether a dilapidated & desolate habitation. By Mr Custis' will, all his servants, some 200 in number, were freed Oct 10, 1862. Of these about 50 are now about the premises. Robt E Lee was born in 1808; son of Maj Gen Henry Lee, known as Light-Horse Harry, of the Revolution, a gallant ofcr, the author of 'Memoirs of the War in the South." Govn'r of Va in 1791, an advocate of the Federal Constitution in the Va Convention, who originated the classic word: "First in war, first in peace, & first in the hearts of his countrymen." Gen Harry Lee's mother was the beautiful Miss Grimes, Washington's first love. [There is not the remotest blood relation between Light-Horse Harry Lee, the gallant soldier & patriot, with that of Maj Gen Chas Lee, the trailor.] The mansion has externally been brushed up, as also the out-bldgs. The farm is cultivated by contrabands at Freedmen's Village, located half a mile down the river. Each able-bodied negro hires 5 acres, paying a rent of a dollar for each acre, & those being able to take care of themselves pay each a monthly rent of $3 for the small house furnished them by the Gov't. There are 60 of these 5 acre lots thus rented. There are upwards of 200 of these houses at Freedmen's Village, a portion of them occupied by those not able to pay rent. The *Nat'l Cemetery* is filling up at the rate of some 25 bodies daily! There have already been deposited within its enclosure the remains of 6,958 white soldier, & 2,570 colored persons, a part of them soldiers. The remains of the colored people occupy one corner of the grounds, & those of the white soldiers the corner diagonally opposite. From one headboard we copied, "Right leg of John Harron, 8th Pa cavalry; another-Left arms of G S Schmidt, 49th & F Hughes, 64th N Y infty. In the midst of these soldiers' graves stands a small wooden enclosure, painted white, within which rise the 2 unpretending marble columns marking the resting place of George Washington Parke Custis, & of his wife, Mary Lee Fitzhugh. The ***Nat'l Cemeteries*** are under the charge of Brvt Lt Col Jas M Moore, assist quartermaster, whose ofc is 151 G st, near 21st st, in Wash City. All the remains of soldiers scattered within a radius of 30 to 40 miles of this city are to be gathered into this ***Arlington Cemetery***, & all those finding interments on their premises will confer a humane favor by informing this ofc. The remains of Confederate soldiers are buried with precisely the same care & tenderness as are the remains of our own dead. The cemetery connected with the Old Soldiers' Home was exhausted last autumn, when that at Arlington was selected. The ***Harmony Cemetery*** lies northwesterly of Eckington Hospital, where all soldiers dying of infectious diseases & contrabands are buried. This cemetery now contains the remains of 566 white & 3,072 colored persons. There is another national cemetery, ***Union Burial Ground***, just beyond the northern bounds of Wash City, & ***Battle Cemetery***, on 7th st, near ***Fort Stevens***. The cemetery at Alexandria contains 3,372 white & 229 colored bodies; that at Bull Run has over 2,000 bodies; at ***Point Lookout*** 440 Union soldiers; Spottsylvania, 535; Wilderness, 180; & Coal Harbor, 1,930. The largest national cemetery is at Andersonville, Ga, containing 12,912 bodies. There is a cemetery also at ***Fortress Monroe***, at Hampton, at Petersburg, at Richmond, & at Winchester, in Va. There are 3 burying parties at work around Richmond, one in front of Richmond, & one at each of the following places: Coal Harbor, front of Petersburg, at Antietam, a private party, to which the Gov't has already furnished 6,000 coffins, in the Valley, near Winchester, at Bull Run, a party traversing the country between this city & Bull Run, & a party has just been sent to Cedar Mountain. The coffins for all these parties are made by the Gov't in this city. The records of the dead soldiers in these cemeteries throughout the country are kept with great care & system at the Death & Burial Bureau, under Col Moore, from which the brief history of any buried soldier can be found in a few minutes up to the very day on which information is sought.

Dept of the Interior, U S Patent Ofc, Wash, ptn of Luther C White, of Waterbury, Conn, praying the extension of a patent granted to him on Sep 7, 1852, for an improvement in Method of making Lamp Tops, Rivets, etc, for 7 years from the expiration of said patent, which takes place on Sep 7, 1866. –H C Theaker, Com'r of Patents

May 24 will be the 47th anniversary of the birthday of Queen Victoria, Queen of England. Her Majesty is now in the 29th year of her reign, having ascended the throne on the demise of her uncle, William the Fourth, in June, 1837. This is a long time for the reign of a British sovereign, the greatest longevity having been attained by her grandfather, who reigned 60 years. Queen Victoria's popularity has been somewhat impaired by her long seclusion from public life in consequence of the death of her husband, Prince Albert of Coburg. She has a numerous family of 9 children, 5 sons & 4 daughters, all of whom are living.

Supreme Court of D C, in Equity 574, docket 7. Herman G Lorch vs Maria Lorch. The subpoeina issued to compel the dfndnt's appearance having been returned into the Clerk's ofc by the Marshal on Dec 14, 1866, endorsed "not found", & the dfndnt having failed to enter her appearance; said dfndnt to appear in this suit on or before the first Tue of Aug next; otherwise the bill may be taken for confessed. –Andrew J Wylie. R J Meigs, clerk

Gen Fremont has purchased the Southwestern Pacific Railroad, of Missouri, for $1,300,000. The road is to be finished to Springfield in 2½ years, & to the State line in 3 years.

Mr Merrill, of Memphis, agent for Appleton's New American Cyclopaedia, was found dead in a bayou near Grenada, Miss, a fortnight ago. It appears he was accidentally drowned in attempting to cross the bayou. His horse was found without a rider & his saddle bags disclosed his name.

On Sat last Mr L L Barrell, a resident for 30 years of St Louis, rode out into the country in his private carriage with his daughter, Mrs Henry R Hall, & his daughter-in-law, Mrs Wilbur F Barrell. When west of *Bellefontaine Cemetery*, Mr Barrell amused himself in firing at a five cent mark with a pocket pistol, a revolver. He restored it to his pocket, when the pistol discharged lodging in the abdomen, & he died on Monday.

Obit-died: May 10, after a long & painful illness, Lizzie Wirt Goldsborough, only daughter of Admiral Lewis & Eliz W Goldsborough, 23 years of age. Unselfish love was the element of her life. At a very early age she dedicated herself to God. Her mortal remains repose near the body of her illustrious grandfather, the late Wm Wirt, whose rare eloquence is embalmed in the brightest memories of the past.

SAT MAY 26, 1866
Supposed suicide of Washingtonian. Advices from our Pacific squadron report the death of Boatswain Jas Polly, at Valparaiso, by being shot through the head. A note found in his pocket seems to indicate that he committed suicide. His family, who reside near the Navy Yard, where he was well known, are much sympathized with.

Fortress Monroe, May 25. Instructions from Washington were received this morning by Maj Gen Miles to give Jeff Davis, on his parole, the freedom of the fort, retiring to his room in Carroll Hall, at night. Messrs Shea & O'Connor, his counsel, have been allowed access to the fort & private interviews with him at any time. Mrs Davis left here on May 23, & was in Washington yesterday, the date of the instructions sent Gen Miles.

Boston, May 25. Dr Bowditch has been mulcted in $1,000 for branding a man with the letter D, [deserter] while examining him during the war.

Frankfort, Ky, May 23. Mr Van Winkle, the Sec of State, died this afternoon.

Yesterday intelligence reached the Coroner's ofc that Mr Thos W Birdsall, the Pres of the Security Fire Ins Co, whose ofc is at 119 Broadway, had committed suicide by taking poison. Coroner Nanmann proceeded to the ofc & found the information was correct. It was stated that he had engaged in several private speculations which had terminated disastrously, by which he had lost considerably. He leaves a wife & several children, who reside in Yonkers, Westchester Co. Deceased was age 42 years. N Y Tribune, 24th

Died: on May 25, in Wash City, after a long & painful illness, Mary Eliz Topping, eldest daughter of Mary Ann & the late R Cuiverwell, in her 37th year. Her funeral will take place from the residence of her mother, 413 L st, between 9th & 10th sts, today at 12 o'clock.

St Aloysius' Academy, under the care of the **Sisters of Mercy**, Loretto, Cambria Co, Pa, will commence on Sep 1 & Feb 1.

Orphans Court of Wash Co, D C, May 23, 1866. In the case of Lucy E Mattingly, excx of Nancy Mattingly, the executrix & Court have appointed Jun 16 next, for the final settlement of the personal estate of the said deceased, of the assets in hand. -Z C Robbins, Reg/o wills

Miscellaneous Items:
1-Charlotte Cushman's mother died in England on May 7.
2-Gov Sutter, the first discoverer of gold in Calif, is supported by a pension from the State.
3-John G Whittier refuses to be a candidate for Congress from the 5th Dist of Mass.
4-Mrs Anna Cora Mowatt Ritchie has become the London correspondent of the N Y News.
5-The Pres has nominated John Logan, father of Gen Logan, Marshal for the Southern District of Illinois.
6-Mr John White, of Nashville, was drowned on Sunday last while bathing in the Cumberland. A young colored boy who attempted to rescue him was also drowned.
7-The corner stone of the magnificent monument to be erected over the remains of Stephen A Douglas will be laid on Jun 13.
8-Wm G Ewing, jr, adopted son of the late Wm G Ewing, committed suicide by shooting himself with a revolver through the head, at **Fort Wayne**, Indiana, a few days since.
9-A few days since Thos L Jones, a fireman, belonging to the Franklin Engine Co No 3, of Brooklyn, was knocked from the apparatus he was riding & run over & killed.

10-Mrs Abbey Lester, a much respected lady, 69 years old, residing in Parma, 11 miles from Rochester, N Y, committed suicide by cutting her throat with a razor on Tue last.
11-Geo W Pridham, of Portland, Maine, a painter at the repair shop of the Grand Trunk railroad, while painting the inside of a tender, fell, & appeared to be intoxicated. He was taken home, went into convulsions, attended by lockjaw, from inhaling the poisonous vapor from the napththa in the paint.
12-Jacob Desohart, 2 years old, playing with other children, was found by his mother with life extinct. His neck was in the loop of a window-shade cord over a door knob. They were playing "horse," the boy fastented there by his sister.

Richmond Whig of yesterday says that Mrs Martin, wife of Mr Martin, of the firm of Martin & Finney, Main & 17th sts, it is feared was mortally wounded yesterday. Mrs Martin was in the store behind the counter, when her son entered & removed his pistol & holster from his waist, & reaching over the counter handed them to his mother, when the pistol fell & exploded, the ball entering her abdomen. She is lying in a critical condition.

Com'rs sale of the real estate of the late Thos Sylvester; by order of the Supreme Court of D C, dated May 23, 1866, to divide the real estate of Thos Sylvester, late of Wash Co, deceased: sale at public auction, on Jun 11 next, lot 7 in square 517, in Wash City, with 2 frame tenements thereon, on north H st. –H B Sweeney, Thos W Busch, Jas English, John E Neale, WmWm Nalley, Com'rs
-Green & Williams, aucts

Public sale of valuable real estate, by decree of the Circuit Court of PG Co, Md, in Equity: sale on Jun 19 next, a part of the real estate of which the late Jas F Brown died seized & possessed: 201½ acres in Spalding's district, PG Co, adjoining the lands of Jas L Addison, Nathan Masters, & others: divided into 2 lots. Lot 1 contains 105 ½ acres; lot 2 contains 96 acres.
–C C Magruder, jr, trustee

MON MAY 28, 1866
Orphans Court-Judge Purcell, May 26, 1866.
1-The will of Hannah Wilson, which beqeathes her estate to her sister, Harriet Wilson, who is also nominated as excx, was filed & fully proven.
2-Will of Wm W Conner, which has been fully proven, was admitted to probate, & letters issued to Wm Dixon, the exc named in the will. Bond, $1,000.
3-Letters testamentary were issued to Mary Heald, the excx named on the estate of Adam Geo Herold. Bond, $6,000.
4-Letters of administration were issued to Orry Duckery on the estate of Henry Frazier, late of the army. Bond, $200.

Mrd: on May 24, in Phil, by Rev Edmund C Bittinger, U S Navy, Wm Lowler, Surgeon U S Navy, to Eliz, daughter of the late Edw Ingersoll, of the above city.

Mrd: on May 24, at the residence of the bride's father, by Rev Dr Minsingerode, E W Wade to Miss Mattie J. daughter of G A Schwarzman, both of Wash, D C.

Chas J Saxton, from Boston, attempted to commit suicide on Sat, at the Nat'l Hotel, by cutting himself with a razor. When found he was in a dangerous state. Dr Pancoast, who was stopping at the hotel dressed the wound. A friend of Mr Saxton took charge of him.

Thos Jenkins, one of the station hands on the railroad at Beaver Dam, Va, was killed on Tue upon the arrival of the freight train there. The deceased was in the habit of getting drunk & slipped off the car & fell between the wheels, the train passing over his body.

Lemuel Cook, the Revolutionary soldier, who died in Clarendon, N Y, Sunday night, was not the last of the heroes of the war for independence. There are two others still living, Mr Saml Downing, of N H, & Jas Burham, of Missouri.

Extensive sale of rosewood furniture, silver-plated ware, rich cut glass ware, etc, at the well known establishment of Mr C Gautier, Pa ave, between 12th & 13th sts. -C W Boteler, auct

The defence of Jeff Davis, it is said, has been entrusted to Chas O'Conor, Jas T Brady, of N Y; W B Reed, of Phil; Mr Brown, of Balt; Mr Pugh, of Ohio, & Geo Shea, of N Y.

Miscellaneous Items:
1-The nomination of Wm H Purnell as postmaster at Balt has been rejected by the Senate.
2-Gen Robt Anderson is still seriously ill in N Y C.
3-John C Beck, one of the men engaged in the forging of certificates to the amount of $300,000, on bonded warehouses in N Y, was arrested at Rochester on Wed.
4-It is said that Mr Gran has paid Madame Ristori $50,000 in advance upon her contract to play in this country. She is to arrive in Sept next, & bring with her a troupe of 50 actors & actresses.
5-Ex-Gov Ryland Fletcher, of Vt, was thrown from his carriage a few days since, & from the effects of his injuries, he is now lying, it is feared past recovery, at his residence in Cavendish, Vt.
6-Surrogate Webster, of Essex Co, N J, has within a few days admitted to probate several wills, the value of the property devised amounting in the aggregate to nearly half a million dollars. Among them is the estate of the late Moses Ward, valued at $200,000; Elias Tompkins, $146,000; Ellis Dunn, $63,000; Thos Francisco, $50,000. Except a bequest to the Orphan Asylum by Mr Ward, the property is all given to private parties.
7-The Montpelier [Vt] Journal states that a person named Fox, in Tunbridge, reported to have murdered his wife & burned the body in a barn. The fire was

discovered, the body rescued & the murderer arrested. They had parted, & Fox persuaded her to meet him.

8-The very valuable leases held by Wm B Astor, of Trinity Church, N Y, will terminate on May 31, & put the church into full control of property worth at least $6,000,000. Mr Astor held possession of 336 lots, which were let in 1767, at a very low rate of interest, for the term of 99 years. His income out of the houses built on them reached, in one year, the sum of $1,300,000.

9-Jonathan Burr, one of the oldest & most prominent citizens of Chicago discovered on Thu that he had been robbed of U S & Cook Co bonds to the value of $18,000. A gardener, Wm Brown, recently in Mr Burr's employ, is suspected.

10-Geo W Sage, the murderer of a little child 2 years of age, belonging to Wm Todd, near Paris, Indiana, was hung at Mount Vernon, Ind, on Fri. He made a confession on the scaffold, saying that while he was stealing some money belonging to Mr Todd three children of the latter came in & discovered him in the act. He determined to kill them, but only succeeded in killing the baby. The others recovered & informed against him, & he was arrested. He died firmly, & almost without a struggle.

11-Boston Herald of Friday states that the case of Jas Mulcheary vs Dr H I Bowditch, has just been finished, the action is one in which the plntf sought to recover damages for being branded upon his breast the letter D, in 1865, by the surgeon in the 4th District. The plntf was going through the process necessary to make him a cavalryman. The dfndnt did not deny the act of marking a letter D, in the belief the plntf was a deserter. At the present trial the jury found a verdict for the plntf & assessed damages at $1,000.

TUE MAY 29, 1866

Robt P Price, of Galveston, Texas; John M Boyd, Knox Co, Tenn, & Gen Guest, of Va, were pardoned by the Pres yesterday.

Richd Pollard, age 24 years, a native of Ireland, was found murdered on Sat in the apartments occupied by Wm McCormick, 166 East 4th st, N Y. MrCormick surrendered himself Sunday, stating he had a quarrel with the deceased, & stabbed him in self defence.

Benj S Beard, a Councilman of Louisville, Ky, has absconded. He is said to be guilty of forgery & frauds.

Rev Dr Chas Constantine Pise, of Brooklyn, died in that city on Sat. He was one of the most learned & eloquent divines of the Catholic Church in America. He was born in Annapolis, Md, in 1802, age 64 at the time of his death. His father was an Italian, & his mother a native of Phil; began his theological studies at Gtwn College, & finished them at Rome; in 1825 he was ordained priest & began his labors in Fred'k, Md, then located in Balt & Washington, where he was the intimate friend of Henry Clay, through whose influence he was appointed chaplain in the Senate. In 1849 he removed to Brooklyn. -Balt Sun

Capt Thos F T Wingate, a well-known & respected shipmaster of Balt, died in that city, on Sat, in his 61st year.

Accident on the Balt & Ohio railroad on Wed, near Cranberry Summit, when a portion of a freight train broke loose, coming in contact with another freight train. Mr Millsager, engineer on the locomotive of the last train, had both of his arms broken & the fireman had one of his legs severely crushed. –Wheeling Reg

Three attempts have been made recently to shoot Col Hart, one of the editors of the Memphis Commercial.

Criminal Court, yesterday, Judge Wylie presiding, Milburn Hunter, who is indicted for the murder of Beniah W Luckett, was placed on trial. The affair occurred on Feb 16 last, in front of Ardeeser's restaurant, 321 7th st. Luckett & Hunter were quarrelling, & the former was stabbed. Hunter was much intoxicated at the time. He said that Luckett had threatened to kill him. Luckett died 5 days after he was stabbed. Juror sworn in yesterday: John W Mead, Wm P Boyd, Michl French, John Tretler, Enoch Heard, Jos R Burch, Jas Coleman. John Corcoran, on his voir dire, stated that he had formed an opinion to get off from serving on the case, & the Court fined him $40, which was paid.

Chicago: 1-John H Woster, committed suicide in Green township, near South Bend, Ind, by shooting himself. The young lady to whom he was engaged to be married, & to whom he was devotedly attached, refused to consummate the engagement. 2-Benj F G Ross was run over by the cars on the Michigan Southern railroad, at Salem Crossing, near Laporte, last evening, & died from the effect of his legs being cut off. He was from Decatur, Ill, on his way to Goshen, Ind.
3-Jas P Luce, late postmaster at Lafayette, Ind, & editor of the Lafayette Journal, it is reported, succeeds Chas A Dana as editor of the Chicago Republican.
4-Dr J M Shaffer, Sec of the Iowa State Agricultural Society, has been appointed by Gov'r Stone Com'r for Iowa to the Paris Exposition.

Mrs Pumphrey, who resides near 3rd west & F st south, yesterday swallowed laudanum for the purpose of committing suicide. Dr Amery immediately applied restoratives, & succeeded in restoring her. Jealousy was the cause that prompted the act.

Louisville, May 27. Perrell, the murderer, was captured by citizens of Shelbyville yesterday & sent here tody. He received 33 shots before being captured, & it is supposed they will prove mortal. A man named Baker was captured after him.

Died: on May 16, at Lynnhaven, Princess Ann Co, Va, Lavinia, aged 4 months daughter of Dr Cornelius & Fannie R Boyle, of Wash City.

Orphans Court of Wash Co, D C. Letters of administration on the personal estate of Chas B Wilder, late of Wash, D C, deceased. –W H Freer, adm

Obit-died on Apr 29, in the village of Montross, Westmoreland Co, Va, Maj Henry Hungerford, in his 78th year. As a husband, kind & affectionate; as a father indulgent to a fault; as a man, honest & honorable. Descended from a stock of Revolutionary patriots, he distinguished himself in the war of 1812 as capt in the 111th Va militia by his gallant repulse of an English force foraging up Mattox creek. At one time he was a member of the Va Legislature; 30 years ago he moved to Wash, where he resided until the beginning of the late war, when he returned to his native county. He was in the full possession of his faculties, & conscious of his approaching change. His remains now rest by the side of his ancesters on the banks of the Rappannock. Peace to his ashes. The old flag-bearers of '98 & '99 are being numbered among the things that were, & those we have loved & revered, we can know here no more. –Montross

In Norwich rose the world famous firm of Overend & Co, the oldest house in existence that attempted bill brokering in its present form. The firm was a direct offshoot of the Norwich Bank, established by Mr Henry Gurney, in 1770. The founder of the bank was succeeded by his son, Mr Bartlett Gurney, who, in 1803, took into partnership his cousin, Mr John Gurney, & several other members of this family. Mr John Gurney had previously been a wool stapler & spinner of worsted yard. The founders of the firm were Mr John Overend, Mr Saml Gurney, [21 year of age, the 2nd son of Mr John Gurney, previously a clerk to Mr Fry, who had married his sister, the celebrated Mrs Fry,] & Mr Thos Richardson, [a clerk in the banking house of Messrs Smith, Wright, & Gray, afterwards Esdaile & Co.] Mr Richardson soon retired, Mr Overend died not long after, leaving Mr Saml Gurney sole rep of the firm. Mr Gurney died in 1856, & was succeeded by Mr David Barclay Chapman, who retired from the firm on Dec 21, 1857.

WED MAY 30, 1866
Executive Mansion, May 29, 1866. The Pres with profound sorrow announces to the people of the U S the death of Winfield Scott, the late Lt Gen of the army. On the day which may be appointed for his funeral the several Executive Depts of the Gov't will be closed. Lt Gen Winfield Scott died at West Point yesterday morning, at the age of 80. He was born near Petersburg, Va, in 1786; chose the law; was admited to the bar in 1806; appointed capt of artl in the army of the U S in 1808; in 1812 war was actualy declared, took his station at Black Rock, on the Niagara river; was distinguished in the battle of Quebec; was taken prisoner & sent to Quebec, but was exchanged in 1813; in 1814 he made brig genr'l, & on Jul 5 fought the battle of Chippewa; twenty days later was the battle of Lundy's Lane, in which Gen Scott's brig for some time bore the brunt of the contest; Gen Scott was appointed major general by brevt; wounded severely in the action, was for some time an invalid. On the conclusion of peace he was offered the post of Sec of War, but declined on the score of youth. In 1833 Gen Scott was summoned to Washington by Pres Jackson, upon an occasion of very delicate & important nature. The Pres was determined to avert nullification. He had issued his celebrated proclamation, & it was not an empty threat. The Gov't was not to be taken by surprise, whatever might happen & sent Gen Scott to S C to take

precautionary measures. He executed his difficult task with great prudence. Next he was called to the command in the Seminole war, in Fla; then he conducted the operations against the Creeks. For the closing month of Mr Buchanan's administration, & the accession of Mr Lincoln, Gen Scott was in command in Washington, at his headquarters. He resigned his command Feb 1, 1861. Ex-Pres Pierce spoke of the name alone of Gen Scott, in the Valley of Mexico, as equal to more men than the force he had under his command.
+
West Point, May 29. Gen Scott began failing quite fast on Sunday, though none of his physicians expected he would expire at such an early day. He was perfectly conscious up to the moment of his death, though he lost his voice some 2 hours previous. He recognized the chaplain of the post ten minutes before he expired, & clasped his hands in silence.

Lewis Rhinehardt, employed in Mr Herman's clothing store, 4½ st, Island, attempted suicide by shooting himself after being accused of stealing some clothes. The real thief was Jacob Burwanger, & he was aware that Ofcr Wallingsford was following him. Yesterday his body was seen floating near the wharf. He has a brother & some other relatives living in Gtwn, but we believe he came here from Balt. He was about 18.

John S Hollingshead, Notary Public; Com'r of Deeds for Calif, N Y, Pa, etc. Corner of 8th & E sts.

The subscriber offers for sale his Farm, on which he resides, lying in Pomonkey Neck, Chas Co, Md: contains about 382 acres, more or less, with a comfortable dwlg-house & all necessary out-bldgs. –H R V Cawood, Pomonkey, Md

Public sale of stock & other property, at auction, at Barnesfield, King Geo Co, Va, on Jun 28. –Abram B Hooe

On Sat in Rose township, F L Shellman was killed & his two sons, Frank 14, & Edw 16, injured when proceeding down a hill with lumber, a board slipped forward & struck one of the horses. The animal became frightened & started at full speed. All were thrown from the wagon. Mr Shellman was killed, Frank was severely injured & it is doubtful he will recover, & Edw was injured, but not dangerously. The deceased was about 47 years of age, & leaves a wife & 8 children. –Pittsburgh [Pa] Gaz

Died: on May 11, in Phil, Dr Chas Pendleton Tutt, aged 33 years, only son of the late Col Chas Pendleton & Ann Mason Tutt, of Loudoun Co, Va. He was an accomplished gentleman. He died a martyr to his profession. Va papers please copy.

Died: on May 20th, in Chas Co, Md, at the residence of Richd W Bryan, Mrs Mary E Briscoe, relict of Gerrard Briscoe, deceased, & daughter of the late Richd Dement, of Wash City, D C.

Miscellaneous Items:
1-Bishop Duggan, of Chicago, has gone to Europe for his health, to be absent 4 months.
2-Gen Ferrero appointed deputy collector of customs at N Y.
3-The trial of Maj Gee is still progressing at Raleigh, N C.
4-Gen J B Hood is at the head of a stock company, which is forming in New Orleans, with a capital of $250,000, for draining & sweeping the streets of the city by machinery.
5-John T Naylor, late clerk of Burlington Co, N Y, was robbed of $5,100, in Phil, Tue.
6-Mrs Annie M Moreland, a young actress performing at the Olympic Theatre, New Orleans, committed suicide on Wed last by taking chloroform. She was a native of Birmingham, near Pittsburgh, Pa.

A card-on account of my bad health, I have appointed my son, Jos Libbey, jr, General Agent, to attend to all my business. –Jos Libbey, sr, Gtwn, May 29, 1866

THU MAY 31, 1866
War Dept, Adj Gen Ofc, Wash, D C, May 30, 1866. Special Orders, No 256. Extract.
The following ofcrs are detailed to proceed to West Point, N Y, to attend the funeral of the late Lt Gen Winfield Scott, on Friday, Jun 1, at one o'clock:
Brvt Maj Gen L Thomas, adj gen.
Brvt Maj Gen E Schriver, inspector gen.
Brvt Maj Gen J Holt, Judge advocate gen
Brvt Maj Gen M C Meigs, quartermaster gen
Brvt Maj Gen A B Eaton, commissary gen of subsistence.
Brvt Maj Gen J K Barnes, surgeon gen.
Brvt Maj Gen B W Brice, paymaster gen
Brvt Maj Gen R Delafield, chief engineer U S A
Brvt Maj Gen A B Dyer, chief of ordnance.
Maj Gen O O Howard, chief of Bureau of Refugees, Freedmen, & Abandoned Lands.
Maj Gen E A Hitchcock, U S volunteers.
Brvt Maj Gen A E Shivas, assist commissary general of subsistence.
Brvt Maj Gen E D Townsend, assist adj gen, late chief of staff to Lt Gen Scott.
By order of the Sec of War, E D Townsend, Assist Adj Gen
+
During the night Gen Scott slept soundly, & on Sunday morning seemed much refreshed; but he kept to his bed for most of the day, in obedience with the physician, the assist surgeon of the post, Dr Marsh. On Monday, his daughter, Mrs Hoyt, who came up on a visit from the city on Sat, returned to N Y, leaving

her father, as she supposed, on a fair way to recovery. During Monday night he experienced a chill; this morning he was known to be very ill; Rev J A French was at his bedside. Gen Scott was unable to speak, but signified by look & motion, that he was conscious that he was soon to die.

Miss Clara Barton, whose name has become familiar to the world & dear to the American people by her noble work in obtaining, classifying, & imparting information respecting soldiers killed in battle, & those who died in hospitals & prisons, has just issued roll No 3, in which she requests information to be furnished her concerning any soldier whose name is mentioned, & also solicits letters of inquiry. The following is the list of soldiers from this District whose fate is unknown: Walter Blanchard, co F, 1st cavalry; Edwin R Blodgett, sgt, co G, 1st cavalry; Patrick Burrows, co A, 2nd infty; Walter D Daniels, co E, 1st cavalry; Gorham P Fassett, co F, 1st cavalry; Jos W Fletcher, co [blank,] 1st cavalry; Adalbert J Friend, co G, 1st cavalry; Jesse L Gilpatric, co H, 1st cavalry; Henry A Hamlin, co [blank,] 1st cavalry; Michl Hayes, co H, 1st cavalry; Henry J Hurd, co G, 1st cavalry; Jas R Hussey, co H, 1st cavalry; Alonzo L Johnson, co F, 1st cavalry; John H McComb, Co G, 1st cavalry; Albert S McKenney, co F, 1st cavalry; Morris L Moons, co K, 1st cavalry; Albert P Monroe, co K, 1st cavalry; Elijah Morrill, co L, 1st cavalry; Jos Richardson, co G, 1st cavalry; Francis E Robinson, co I, 1st cavalry; Stephen P Rowell, co G, 1st cavalry; John H Rollins, co [blank,] 1st cavalry; Thos Royell, co E, 1st cavalry; Ansil T Sylvester, co G, 1st cavalry; Wm H Thurlow, co H, 1st cavalry; Richd Vance, co F, 1st cavalry; Danl Walton, co K, 1st cavalry; Nathan B Wiggins, jr, co M, 1st cavalry.

Eleven years since Hiram Tucker, of Boston, patented a Spring Bed of his own invention, which has steadily increased in popularity since that time, & today stands unrivaled. For sale by Jas C McGuire & Co, Pa ave & 10th st.

On Sunday at the dwlg of Mr Jos Anderton, a coal miner, residing in Rochester township, near New Brighton, Beaver Co, his daughter, Mary, about 14 years, was kindling a fire in the cooking stove & poured some oil from a large can upon the fire. The flames communicated to the can & it exploded. The unfortunate girl was enveloped in flames & her father & mother hastened to put the fire out. She was terribly burned & died yesterday, after most intense agony. Mrs Anderton was burned so severely that her recovery is doubtful. Mr Anderton received minor burns.

In the matter of the division of the real estate of Benj Bean, deceased, No 197, in Equity. On consideration of the ptn filed in the above cause against David & Henry Jones, defaulting purchasers of a portion of said property, it is ordered by the Court that said David Jones & Henry Jones show cause, on or before the first Tues in July next, why the said property should not be resold at their cost & expense, & at their risk, to pay & satisfy the balance of the purchase money.
—R J Meigs, clerk

The following persons were pardoned on Mon & Tue, by the President, under the provisions of the amnesty proclamation, 1st & 13th exceptions: Jas E Carter & Wm Morrow, of Tenn; T A Harris, of Texas; Albert Sears, & Hammond Marshall, of Ga; W A Townes, of S C, & Bernard Avego, of New Orleans, La.

Miscellaneous Items:
1-A woman, Jennie Mitchell, committed suicide in New Orleans, on Thu last, by taking laudanum.
2-Hon Wm A Graham has been invited to deliver an address on the life & character of the late Hon Geo E Badger, of N C.
3-Robt McGowan committed suicide by jumping from the steamer **Herman Livingston** on the last trip of that steamer from Savannah to N Y.
4-Naval Ofcr Lynch, of Charleston, having declined to take the oath, the Sec of the Treasury will not sign his pay warrants.
5-Col Edw Parrott, Speaker of the Ohio House of Reps, announced himself a candidate for Congress against Gen Schenck.
6-Mr Jas M Scovell, it is said, will run as an independent candidate for Congress in the First District, in N J, in the coming election-the Democracy having agreed to make no nomination.
7-Mr Chas S Leader, the despatcher of the Reading railroad at Schuylkill Haven, was instantly killed on Fri, by being rum over by a passing train. He was in the Mexican war, & commanded a company for State defence during the rebellion.
8-At the last meeting of the Board of Health, of N Y: interesting history of a woman named Mary Ann Bastine, who died in the alms house a few days ago. At the date of her death she was nearly 119 years old. She was a native of N Y, & was admitted on Dec 14, 1807, aged 59, by Gideon Ostrander, for destitution.

Mr Robt F Price, of Balt Co, was accidentally killed on Sat last, on the Northern Central railroad, at Cockeysville, as he was returning to his home. The engine struck his horse that he was riding & had to be killed. Mr Price was taken up from the cow-catcher, apparently dead. His body was put on a board & carried to the warehouse. On Sunday, the body was found in a sitting posture in another part of the room, with his head resting on a piece of iron. John Willis held an inquest rendering a verdict that Mr Price, from a wound in his leg, had bled to death. –Balt Sun, 25th

FRI JUN 1, 1866
Mr Geo W Morgan, the acknowledged leader of the organists of this country, will remain & perform once more upon the grand organ recently erected in the new Cavalry Baptist Church, H & 8th sts. The Pres & Sec of State & their families intend on being presen

Fortress Monroe, May 31. Mrs Davis arrived here this morning from Balt, in the steamer **James T Brady**, from her prolonged visit to Washington.

Gardiner, Me, May 30. The funeral ceremonies over the remains of the late Bishop Burgess took place this afternoon at Christ Church.

Supreme Court of D C holding a District Court of the U S for said District. Notice: on Nov 8, 1866, the rebel privateer **Royal Yacht** was attacked, burned, sunk, & destroyed in Galveston Bay, Texas, by an expedition under command of Lt Cmder Jas E Jouett, of the U S steamer **Santee**, whereby an award of bounty inured to the ofcrs & men of said expedition; & therefore they prosecute in this Court, in the name of the U S, for the reasons in the libel stated; & that said cause will stand for trial at the City Hall, Wash City, on the first Monday of July next, when & where all persons are warned to appear to show cause why condemnation should not be decreed, & to intervene for their interests. -R J Meigs, clerk

Mrd: on May 31, by Rev Dr Smith, Mr John D Bayne to Miss Jennie V Davis, 3rd daughter of the late Mr Jas Davis.

Mrd: on May 29, in Wesley Chapel, in Wash City, by Rev F S De Hass, Mr Jas A Booth, of Kent Co, Md, to Miss Mary C Lashhorn, of Martinsburg, Va. Balt & Martinsburg papers please copy.

Mrd: on May 31, at Mrs Heydon's, 381 Pa ave, by Rev R B Williamson, Geo Isaacs to Miss Jennie Jones, all of Orange Co, Va.

Mrd: on May 31, at the residence of the bride's father, by Rev Wm B Evans, Mr Fred'k Brackett, of Maine, to Miss Narcissa A Shryock, of Balt, Md. Balt papers please copy.

Died: on Thu, at the residence of A E Perry, Miss Mary Ann Sexton, aged 23 years, a native of Cavan Co, Ireland, daughter of Michl & Rosina Sexton. Her funeral is today at 10 o'clock at St Patrick's Church, F st. Her mortal remains will repose at **Mount Olivet Cemetery** awaiting the resurrection. Freeman's Journal & Boston Pilot please copy.

Chancery sale of property near the Navy Yard; by decree of the Supreme Court of D C, dated May 29, 1866, in equity, No 678, in which A C Winn & another were cmplnts, & Mary Winn & others were dfndnts: public auction on Jun 19 of Lot 6 & 7 in square 974; lot 6 has a brick dwlg with all necessary out bldgs, at 10th & I sts. Lot 7 unimproved. –John D McPherson, Jas A Buchanan, trustees -Jas C McGuire & Co, aucts

SAT JUN 2, 1866
The body of Andrew Kepler, aged 7 years, was found in the Eastern branch, near the Navy Yard bridge, yesterday. He went to a picnic on last Monday & was lost. A diligent search was made for him, but he was not found until yesterday. He had drowned.

Memphis, May 31. The steamer **City of Memphis**, from New Orleans for St Louis, exploded at the foot of Buck Island, 40 miles below here, this morning. The following are lost: Mr Smith, Evansville, Ill; Mrs Donne, of Deagle's Varieties; Pilot Frank Perdue, Geo Britton, steersman; Geo Hanger, St Louis; 1st Engineer Harrison Fox, 2nd Steward C A Hambleton, Cabin boy Jas Robinson. The following were scalded: Mrs Selden, Jefferson, Texas; Saml Harris, 2nd Mate, leg broken; 2nd Engineer Burns, leg broken; 3rd Engineer Smith, slightly. The steamboat **St Patrick** brought up the survivors.

Mrd: on May 23, by Rev Dr McCabe, Lewis Clark, of Balt, to Kate Middleton, of Hyattsville, all of Md.

Mrd: on May 31, by Rev Dr Fall, Rector of the Church of the Epiphany, Benj C Card, U S Army, to Miss Isabel L Hunter.

St Louis, May 29. Jas A Rodgers, well known in this city as an ice man, & driver of a dray, was arrested on the levee this morning, on a charge of murder committed in St Louis some 13 years ago. His arrest at this time, so long after the murder, is not easily accounted for.

Chicago, May 29. 1-Feud of long standing at Alexandria, Mo, between two farmers, Miller & Heacock, resulting in the instant death of Miller & the mortal wounding of Heacock. 2-Maj Gen C S Hamilton, of the volunteer army, was shot last night at Fond Du Lac, Wisc, by R A Baker, cashier of the Mechanics' & Farmers' Bank, in a personal altercation. The Gen received 2 wounds, neither of which is thought to be life threatening. He fell at the first fire, & was shot the second time when he was down. Baker is under arrest. 3-The beautiful adopted daughter of Mr Bursher, of Springfield, Ill, was shot dead in her father's house last evening. A couple of boys were amusing themselves with an old pistol, when one pointed the gun at the ladies' head & fired. She lingered for about an hour. She was beloved by the family. [Her name was not given.]

Hon W D McIndoe, rep in Congress from Wisc, is at Stevens' Point, suffering from a second attack of erysipelas. He is getting better.

Detroit, May 29. Hon John A Brooks, died at Newaygo, on Sat. He was one of the most prominent men in the northern part of this State; founder of Newaygo village.

The estate of M D Potter, lately deceased proprietor of the Cincinnati Commercial, proves unexpectedly, worth $500,000.

Cincinnati Commercial: Jas P Luce, late Postmaster at Lafayette, Ind, & editor of the Lafayette Journal, has succeeded Chas A Dana as editor of the Chicago Republican.

Alexander Gaz of Wed: Mr Robt Collingsworth, of this city, a brakesman on the Orange & Alexandria railroad train, was very seriously injured yesterday, by being caught between 2 cars & mashed. The accident happened near Culpeper Court House.

St Joseph, May 28. Yesterday, at Sac Prairie, two young men, Stephen Woodson & Lafayette Farris, were returning from church, when they became involved in a difficulty. Woodson drew a revolver & shot Farris, & lived but a short time. Woodson was arrested.

For sale: the valuable estate of John H T Magruder, in PG Co, Md; in Lower Md; contains about 553 acres; with a frame bldg, 2 stories high, with 7 rooms, & all necessary out-bldgs. –Fendall Marbury, Atty for Proprietor, T B Post Ofc, PG Co, Md, or to M E McKnew, Rm 7, Intelligencer Bldg.

MON JUN 4, 1866
Corner-stone laid yesterday for the new Catholic church on 25th st & Pa ave; the stone was lowered by Fr White; a vessel containing the usual enclosures of documents, newspapers, etc, was inserted in the corner stone; discourse was by Rev Fr Maguire.

Leonard Huyck, late Pres of the Merchants' Nat'l Bank, was arrested on Sat by Ofcr Coomes, charged with having taken & misapplied $200,000 of the funds by paying them into the hands of L P Bayne & Co, of Balt, Md, unlawfully, & without authority.

Alleged disorderly house on 7th st, between F & G sts. Mary Ann Siskut, proprietress, & 21 persons at a dance, were arrested. Siskut gave bail, the others were each fined $5.

Dr Henry G Cox, a well known & highly esteemed member of the medical profession, died Tue in N Y C. About 2 years ago he met with a painful & serious accident, which confined him to his bed for many months. Three weeks since he was attacked with paralysis, which terminated in his death.

The new *five cent coin* being issued, will be of the same size as the three dollar gold coin, & is very nearly eight-tenths of an inch in diameter, & three of them will weigh a half ounce, thus being very convenient as a postage weight.

Sydney Howard Gay, for some years managing editor of the Tribune, has resigned his position, but still retains his connection with that journal as a leading writer.

Mrd: on May 23, at the residence of Rev John Vaughan Lewis, rector of St John's Church, Edw K Springer, of Wash, D C, to Anna R Gosnell, of Balt.

Died: on Jun 2, at the residence of Miss Bates, Charlotte Ward, wife of Thos Ward, aged 44 years. Her funeral is today at 3 o'clock.

Died: on Jun 2, Hellen, aged 2 years & 7 months, only daughter of Jas & Hellen Martin. Her funeral will take place from the residence of her parents at 3 o'clock, this afternoon.

Died: on May 2, 1866, in Wash, D C, Mrs Mary S Williams, in her 62nd year, a native of Dumfries, Va. Her funeral will be this evening at 2 o'clock from her late residence.

Railroad accident at Cleveland on Friday. The train from Sandusky was stopped on the track by the breaking of a rod of the engine. A flagman was sent back to flag the train approaching from Toledo, but the grade being very heavy, & the train at full speed, it could not be stopped. Mr John Allen, engineer of the Toledo train, jumped off; Mr Sawyer, fireman, also jumped. Mrs Atwater escaped injury, but her little boy was bruised about the head, & her little girl, about 5, received some fearful internal injuries, & will probably die today. Mrs Atwater was of Castalia, & with her 2 children & sister, Mrs Charlott Swift. They were taken to Mr Robt Allen's residence. Mrs Swift lives on Detroit st, & had been on a visit to her sister at Monroeville. Killed & wounded: Mrs Hannah Lynch, of Berea, was killed. Mrs E W Greenwood, of Olmsted Falls, & her little girl, injured. Mrs Jackson, of Cleveland, slightly injured, & her child probably fatally injured. Mr Philip Lynch, Berea, son of Mrs Lynch, who was killed, was severely injured. Widow Sarah Litchfield, of Berea, badly bruised. Mr Bridget Daly, of Olmsted, severely injured. Mrs Ann Thornton, of Olmsted, leg badly broken; Mr W B Dimick, of Bellevue, servere contusions about the head & shoulders; Mrs Eliz Wright, of Olmsted, severely injured; Mrs Sarah Watson, Berea, bruised; Mrs Ann Kelly, Berea, bruised; Mrs Mary Curtain, Berea, bruised; Mrs Geo Kent, Olmsted, slightly injured; Mr Geo Hall, Olmsted, slightly injured; Mr Robt Mathews, Olmsted, badly bruised; Chas Flynn, newsboy on the Toledo train, slightly hurt. Dr J H Lamphere, of Brunswick, Medina Co, who was on the Sandusky train, being an experienced traveller, left the train when it stopped.
+
Mrs Charlotte M Swift lies in an unconscious state, & her recovery is doubtful. Mrs Atwater & her boy are doing well, the little girl died about 5 P M.

State of Md: $1,000 reward for the apprehension of Jas K Harper, of Easton, Talbot Co, Md, who murdered a quiet, inoffensive colored man, Edw Sherwood, without any provocation, on May 20, in Easton. –Thos Swann, Govn'r of the State of Md

There was an immense gathering at St Chas Borromeo Church, in Brooklyn, to witness the funeral obsequies of the late Rev Dr Pise. A silver plate surmounted the coffin, with the following inscription: Rev Charles C Pise, D D /Born November 22, 1801 /Died May 22, 1866. Solemn requiem mass was celebrated by Fr J Malone as celebrant, & F Friel, deacon; Rev Fr Goodman, sub-deacon; & Rev Dr Gardner as master of ceremonies. Rt Rev Archbishop McCloskey delivered the sermon.

Funeral of Lt Gen Winfield Scott, at West Point, on Friday. Gen Schuyler Hamilton, formerly Gen Scott's private secretary, was present. The guard of honor, who marched on each side of the coffin: Col Black, Lt Col Hildt, Capt Francis Davies, Lt Col Piper, 3rd artl; Maj McMillan & Capt Arnold, 5th cavalry. Following the coffin were Gen Callum, commandant, & Capt Bush, 10th infty; the servants of the deceased-Geo Gibson, his valet; Jas Allen, his coachman; Peter Egenolf, a former coachman of Gen Scott. The coffin was preceded by Mr John Harper, the assistant of Mr Brown, the undertaker of Grace Church. The body was received at the door of the chapel by Maj Leighton, Engineer corps, who had charge of the chapel & its decorations. The lid of the coffin was removed, & the deceased presented a more natural appearance; the lower portion was somewhat contracted, owing to the removal of his false teeth. The Gen was dress in a plain black suit. When the body was laid in the church, Mrs Col Black, wife of the commandant of the Cadet corps; Mrs Grabel, whose husband was killed at Big Bethel, & Miss Princeton, were completing the last crape adorments required for the bier. On board the steamer **C W Thomas** were Gens Van Vliet, Delafield, Anderson, Alden, Loomis, Ingalls, Brice, Andrew Porter, Ruggles, Satterlee, & Clarke, Admirals Farragut, Palmer, Powell, Cmdor Worden, Cols Patten & Stinson, Mr Hoyt, Gen Scott's son-in-law, & his two boys, Messrs Stone & Gebhard, Senator Nesmith, of Oregon, & others. Rev Dr French, chaplain of the post, assisted by Bishop Potter, & Rev D F Warren, pastor of the church at Eliz, N J, where Gen Scott worshipped for many yers, & Rev Dr Hollman, of St Philip's Church, at Garrison's, officiated at the services. All that lives of Winfield Scott will find a befitting shrine in the memory of the American people. Gen Scott's own pew, where he sat unconspicuously, with his hands crossed on his knees, was occupied by the son-in-law of Gen Scott, Gould Hoyt, & his two sons, Gould Hoyt, jr, & Winfield Scott Hoyt, fine, intellectual-looking boys, apparently about 14 & 10 years of age. Mrs Hoyt had taken a long & last farewell of the beloved remains in the morning, wholly secluded in the room with the remains, & was prevailed upon to absent herself from the public ceremony.

TUE JUN 5, 1866
Orphans Court-Judge Purcell, Jun 2, 1866.
1-Will of the late Danl Rowland, heretofore fully proved, was admitted to probate & record, & letters testamentary were issued to Geo Mattingly: bond, $4,000.
2-The first & final accounts of the adms of Betsey Kennedy; the second of the administrator of Lewis J Kennedy; the third of the guardian of the orphans of Saml Atkins; & the 4th of the orphans of Thos Scanlon. were proved & passed.

Trial of Paymaster Edmund E Paulding, brevet Lt Col U S Army was yesterday arraigned for trial before a general court martial in Wash City, of which Gen Augur is president, & Capt W K Haviland judge advocate. Three charges against Col Paulding. 1-Disobedience of orders in transferring $75,000, Apr 13, 1866, from the Nat'l Bank of the Metropolis to the Merchants' National Bank, whereas such transfers are prohibited by the circular of the Paymaster Gen of May, 1865. 2-The second charge recounts the same transactions as misappropriation of public money. 3-The third charge alleges that it was a neglect of duty, Col Paulding having been warned that the Merchants' Nat'l Bank was in a critical condition, as was soon proved. The accused plead not guilty to all the charges & specifications. Gen N P Chipman, of Chipman & Hosmer, appeared as counsel for Col Paulding. John B Hutchinson, cashier of the Nat'l Bank of the Metropolis, T M Meline, chief book-keeper of the Treasurer's ofc, U S Treasury Dept, & Wm S Huntington, were examined.

Board of Trade: meeting last night, Saml Bacon, 1st vice pres, in the chair. R B Mohun tendered his resignation as secretary, which was accepted, & Mr N Sardo, on motion, was elected secretary.

Phil, Jun 4. The friends of Col O'Neil, especially those who served with him in the Union army in the West, & assisted in the capture of Col Morgan, sympathize with him in his capture. Col O'Neil was a gallant soldier in the Union army & not a rebel officer, as has been reported.

E P Hastings, one of the oldest citizens of Detroit, died on Friday.

Fatal accident occurred to Jos Reno, brakeman on the Prairie du Chien railroad, on Thu. He was standing upon the top of a car as the train was passing under a bridge near Wanwatoss, Wis, when he was struck on the forehead & killed instantly.

Died: on Jun 3, Dudley, son of Geo A & Sarah Digges, aged 8 years. His funeral will take place on Jun 5, at 10 o'clock A M, from the residence of his father, 651 Pa ave.

Died: on Jun 4, at his residence, 129 Beall st, Gtwn, D C, Capt Geo Edw Curtis, late of the U S steam transport **Star**, in his 33rd year, after a protracted illness of 3 months, contracted during the late war. His funeral will take place from his late residence on Wed next at 5 P M. Balt & N Y papers please copy.

John D Williams, celebrated as the best Ornamental Penman & Teacher of Business Writing in the U S, has been secured in the Writing Dept of the Wash Business College. Everybody is invited to call, S W corner of 7th & H sts.
–Bryant, Stratton, Church & Co

Miscellaneous Items:
1-Mr Bayard Taylor & Mr Geo Boker about to make an overland journey to Calif.
2-The father of Romisarow, who saved the life of the Emperor Alexander, had been transported to Siberia in 1866 & set to hard labor for some political offence. Letter from St Petersburgh states that the Czar has ordered him to be set at liberty.
3-The Hartford Courant says the monument to Col Saml Colt, the revolver man, about to be placed in *Cedar Hill Cemetery*, in that city, will cost about $25,000. It is of Scotch granite, 40 feet hight, & surmounted by a beautiful figure-"The Angel of Resurrection." 4-Cmdor Vanderbilt has received from the Gov't the gold medal voted him for his gift to the nation of the steamship **Vanderbilt** during the war. He received a history of the circumstances under which the vessel was presented to the Gov't, & sent to Hampton Roads to run down the rebel ram **Merrimack** if she should venture out.

John D Williams, celebrated as the best Ornamental Penman & Teacher of Business Writing in the U S, has been secured in the Writing Dept of the Wash Business College. Everybody is invited to call, S W cor 7th & H sts.
–Bryant, Stratton, Church & Co

Fulton market-house & grocery, with lease of ground, 14th & E sts, at auction: on Jun 8, known as *Fulton Market*; with every convenience for the business for which it was erected. Ground rent $50 per month. Did a business of $50,000 annually. -D L Well & Co, aucts

WED JUN 6, 1866
John Ross, of the Cherokee Nation, has been confined by a severe illness to his bed for the last 12 weeks. His numerous friends will be gratified to learn that Dr Hall, of Wash City, his attending physician, considers his symptoms for recovery more favorable.

Mrd: on Jun 5, by Rev T F McCarthy, Mr Henry Hodges to Miss Mary C Bailey, both of Montg Co, Md. [Rockville papers please copy.]

Died: on Jun 5, of paralysis, in Gtwn, Rev Chas B Mackie, in his 75th year, & the 45th of his ministry. His funeral will be from the Bridge St Presbyterian Church at 3 o'clock this afternoon. His friends & those of his son, Jas S Mackie, late of the Dept of State, are invited. [Balt & Rochester, N Y papers please copy.]

Rev Francis Mohony, known throughout Great Britain & Ireland as "Father Prout," one of the most accomplished scholars, one of the wittiest & most brilliant writers, died in Paris, on May 19. He was born in Ireland about 1805, & educated in Jesuit colleges in France & the Univ of Rome, Mahony was a Roman Catholic Irishman of the old school.

Died: on May 30, at Butler Place, near Germantown, Pa, Annie N, wife of Lamar W Fisher, & daughter of the late Jos Parker Norris, of Phil.

On Sat a well-dressed man, about 30, stepped into the pistol gallery of Mr Werne, 66 West Fayette st, & after firing some 20 rounds aimed the pistol at his own head & fired, the ball passing clear through it. Drs Richard & Reed were summoned, but to no avail, the man expired. His name was Chas Springer, & he was from Bangor, Maine; three letters were found among his papers, one to his mother residing in Bangor; another to Sec Stanton resigning his position as clerk under that ofcr; the other letter was directed to a party in Wash, in which he stated that he had been robbed of $1,400, though he did not state as to where the robbery occurred.

Jacksonville]Fla] Times: on Sat, May 26, a party consisting of Mr D J Mickler & family, Mr Alonzo A Brave, wife & daughter, Miss Ratila Liambias, Miss Antonia Liambias, Mr Jos Liambias, Mr Jerome Liambias, a daughter of Mr Jas A Mickler, & a colored girl left St Augustine on a pleasure visit to the farm of Mr Jas A Mickler, on North River, & the boat capsized, drowning Mr A A Bravo, his daughter Anna, Miss Rafilia Liambias, Melanie, daughter of Mr Jas A Mickler, & an infant son of Mr D J Mickler. The remainder of the party clung to the boat & were rescused 3 hours afterwards, by Mr Jos F Liambias, who swam to shore & secured a boat & returned to the unfortunate party, whom he brought to the shore. The bodies of Mr A A Bravo & his daughter were recovered & taken to St Augustine, for burial.

Miscellaneous items: 1-The wife of Wm Cullen Bryant is dangerously ill at her husband's residence, in Roslyn, N J. 2-Ex-Gov Allen, of Louisiana, at his own request, was buried in full Confederate uniform. 3-BrighamYoung's 65th birthday was celebrated in N Y C on Friday last by the Mormons now stopping there, in a dinner at the Metropolitan Hotel.

The Boston Herald states that at the military parade in Lawrence, on Wed, Col Beal ordered the uniform to be stripped from a non-commissioned ofcr who was intoxicated. The order was carried out, & the man went home in disgrace, wearing a pair of overalls that had been loaned him.

Hon Chas Wells, ex-Mayor of Boston, died on Sunday, aged 80 years.

Despatch from Cairo, Ill, says: Capt G W Gordon, at one time an ofcr on Kirby Smith's staff, was drowned in Pearl river, where he was bathing.

Valuable improved property in Gtwn at auction, on Jun 12, the large & desirable frame dwlg in which I reside, on Prospect st, Gtwn, with adjoining lot; house contains 15 rooms, including bath-room & water-closet supplied with Potomac water. The house is supplied throughout with gas, built in the best manner & of the best materials, & is covered with a tight, painted tin roof. –Thos Jewell, Thos Dowling, auct, Gtwn, D C

Supreme Court, D C. Benj F Morsell against Eliz O'Keefe & others. The creditors of the late John O'Keefe are notified to file their claims with me, at my room, City Hall, on or before Jun 12 next. —W Redin, auditor

Chief Quartermaster's Ofc, Depot of Wash. Wash, D C, May 28, 1866. Sealed proposals will be received at this ofc until Jun 12, 1866, for the heating by steam, [direct radiation,] the bldg in this city known as **_Ford's Theater_**, & the 2 small bldgs connected therewith. -D H Rucker, Brvt Maj Gen & Chief Quartermaster, Depot of Wash.

THU JUN 7, 1866
Thos Mackenzie, an old & esteemed citizen of Balt, died in that city on Sat, aged 73 years.

Orphans Court-Judge Purcell.
1-On Tue the will of the late Phebe Mitchell, bequeathing her estate [personal & real] to her daughter, Margaret Ann Smith, was filed & fully proved. 2-The will of the late Wm Barbour, of Gtwn, bequeathing his property to D Rittenhouse Shuman, in trust for his wife & children, was filed & partially proven. 3-Letters of administration were issued to Emily B Bidwell on the estate of the late Gen Danl D Bidwell, U S army, & to Anna G Gaston on the estate of Albert G Gaston. 4-The first & final account of the excx of John Harry, deceased, was approved & passed.

Nashville, Jun 5. A despatch has been sent to Pres Johnson for a suspension of action upon the application of the British Govn't for Col O'Neil & others, until the petition from citizens of Nashville had been received.

West Point: the annual examination of the cadets of the U S Military Academy commenced on Tues at West Point. The most noticeable feature of the day was the arrival of Gen Grant's son, a bright-looking youth of about 16 years of age. He reported himself early in the morning to Gen Cullum, was at once assigned quarters, & finally enrolled a cadet of the Military Academy at West Point.

Personal:
1-Amos Kendall proposes to pass a pleasant year in Europe & will sail Jun 27.
2-Chas F Browne [Artemus Ward] sailed for England on Sat.
3-Capt W L Herdon's widow has received from Congress the exclusive right to publish for 14 years her husband's book on the Amazon.
4-Mr & Mrs Barney Williams, after one of the most successful theatrical engagements on record, have retired for the summer to their country seat at Bath.

A little son of Mr Wm H Wales, cashier of the Merchants' & Mechanics' Savings Bank in Norfolk, was crushed to death by a train of cars at the depot of the Norfolk railroad on Friday.

Miscellaneous Items:
1-Last Monday Fanny S Hubbell, daughter of Mr Wm L Hubbell, of Brooklyn, fell from a 3rd story window while leaning over the sill, & was immediately killed. 2-Judge Story's son, Wm W Story, now in Rome, is one of the most promising of the American sculptors. An English nobleman lately offered him L3,000 for one of his works. 3-Albert C Perham, between 3 & 4 years of age, died at Mass Gen Hospital, Boston, on Monday. About a week ago a bean lodged accidentally in the air passages, causing inflammation of the lungs, from the effects of which he died. 4-Gen Wm F Barry, now in command of the U S forces between Buffalo & the Niagara river, is colonel of artl in the regular army, & brig gen by brevet. He was at one time chief of artl of the Army of the Potomac, & occupied the same position in Sherman's army during the famous march.

Chancery sale of a large & commodious brick house on 12th st, between N Y ave & I st, on Jun 26, by decree of the Supreme Court of D C, in equity, in the cause of Roche vs Smith et al, No 174, equity, part of lot 12 & 13 in square 986, with improvements. -Asbury Lloyd, trustee

Dept of the Interior, U S Patent Ofc, Wash, Jun 2, 1866. Ptn of Edw A Palmer & Adolphus J Simmons, of Clayville, N Y, praying for the extension of a patent granted to them on Sep 7, 1852, for an improvement in Whiffletree Hook, for 7 years from the expiration of said patent, which takes place on Sep 7, 1866.
–T C Theaker, Com'r of Patents

Dept of the Interior, U S Patent Ofc, Wash, Jun 2, 1866. Ptn of Horace T Robbins, of Boston, Mass, praying for the extension of a patent granted to him on Sep 14, 1852, for an improvement in Shuttleguides to Looms, for 7 years from the expiration of said patent, which takes place on Sep 14, 1866.
–T C Theaker, Com'r of Patents

Dept of the Interior, U S Patent Ofc, Wash, Jun 2, 1866. Ptn of Robert Knight, of Cleveland, Ohio, praying for the extension of a patent granted to him on Sep 21, 1852, for an improvement in Machinery for Bevelling the edges of Skelps or Metallic Strips, etc, for 7 years from the expiration of said patent, which takes place on Sep 21, 1866. –T C Theaker, Com'r of Patents

FRI JUN 8, 1866
Gen Santa Anna arrived at N Y on Wed, accompanied by his staff & suite, & took up his quarters at the mansion in West Twenty-eighth st, near 5th ave, which has been carefully prepared for the accommodation of the General.

J C White, the present Mayor of Portsmouth, Va, was pardoned by the Pres yesterday. Mayor White held a petit ofc under the rebel gov't, & was pardoned as coming under the first section of the amnesty proclamation. Having been elected mayor, he was not permitted to assume the duties of the ofc until pardoned.

Boston, Jun 7. A special from St Albans says: Gen Sweeny was arrested by order of Maj Gibson, cmder of the regulars. Gen Sweeny was in bed at the Tremont House, & offered no resistance. He is now in the ofcrs' quarters.

N Y, Jun 7. Col Roberts was arrested today, under direction of Marshal Murray. The warrant was issued by U S Com'r Betts, & served by the deputy marshal, at the Fenian headquarters, Roberts having declined a request from Marshal Murray to come to his ofc. It is rumored that Col Kerrigan was also arrested, but released, & is now keeping out of sight.

Cincinnati, Jun 6. Capt Menter, of the celebrated Menter's Band, was mortally wounded by a pistol ball fired by a burglar who entered his house at Newport, Ky, this morning, for the purpose of robbery. Menter's son afterwards shot the burglar, fatally wounding him.

Balt, Jun 7, Wm S Sherwood, proprietor of the principal printing establishment in this city, died today.

Mrd: on Jun 7, at the Parsonage of Wesley Chapel, by Rev F S Dehass, Mr John A Perkins, of Brooklyn, N Y, to Miss Mollie A Merrilat, of Wash, D C.

For rent: near Wash City, *Eckington House*, formerly the residence of the late Hon Jos Gales; immediate grounds 15 or 20 acres; within 20 minutes drive of the Capitol. Inquire of J C McGuire & Co.

Trustee's sale of valuable real estate on the Heights of Gtwn, D C, by deed of trust recorded in the land records of said District, in Liber R M H, No 4, folios 151 etc; public auctionon Jun 25, all that real estate, fronting 170 feet on the east side of Congress st, & 107 on Road st, adjoining the residence of Brook B Williams, & opposite Mr Edw Linthicum's & *Tudor Place*. The property will be sold in 3 lots. –Hugh Caperton, trustee -Thos Dowling, auct

Supreme Court of D C, No 495 Equity, Docket 7. Danl C Barrand et al vs Eliz W Ransone et al. Wm Y Fendell, trustee, reported he sold parts of lot 8 & 9 in square 122, for $4,000 to John F Webb, the purchaser, who has complied with the terms of sale. -R J Meigs, clerk

Supreme Court of D C, in Equity 661, docket 7. Adelaide E Allen vs Wm C Allen. The subpoena issued to compel the dfndnt's appearance having been returned into the Clerk's ofc by the Marshal on Apr 26, 1866, endorsed "not found", & the dfndnt having failed to enter his appearance; said dfndnt to appear in this suit on or before Jun 7, 1866, otherwise the bill may be taken for confessed. –R J Meigs, clerk

Miscellaneous Items:
1-Edw Brady was shot in Louisville on Monday by N P Tutweiler, & died soon after. 2-Edw Simons, aged 10 years, was drowned in the Troy river, N Y, Tuesday. 3-Danl Robinson, editor of the Maine Farmers Almanac, died at Hallowell, in that State, on May 16th, & his wife on the day following. 4-Miss Sallie H Polk, daughter of the late Rt Rev Leonidas Polk, [General C S A,] was married on Jun 1st to Capt F D Blake, of Charleston, S C. 5-Dr G R Swetting, of Berlin, Wisc, died May 30, from the effects of a slight puncture in the finger with a needle, received while sewing up a body after a post mortem examination. 6-Franz Jos Christ was killed by injuring his spine, while attempting to turn a somersault, in Pittsburgh, Pa, on Monday last. He fell upon his head, & lay senseless, with his lower extremities paralyzed, for 48 hours, when he expired. 7-Dr Saml Wolfe, formerly of Cincinnati, where he has a family living, committed suicide on Monday at Nashville, by drowning in the Cumberland. He attempted to commit suicide, by cutting his throat, some months ago. 8-A despatch from Nashville: In disinterring the Federal dead near Resaca, a body, exciting attention from its small feet, was found to be that of a woman, shot through the head. The supposed name was Chas Jonesboro, co E, 60th Missouri volunteers.

SAT JUN 9, 1866

Despatch from St Louis: the steamer **Ida Handy**, steamer **Bostona**, & the steamer **James Raymond**, the two latter dismantled, burned at the upper part of the levee Sat. The **Ida Handy** was owned by the Atlantic & Mississippi Steamship Co, & valued at $75,000; insured for $56,000 in Cincinnati ofcs. The value of the other boats is small.

St Albans, Jun 8. Gen Sweeny & Col Meehan were arraigned before a civil tribunal at the Weldon House this morning. The proceedings were private, no reported being admitted.

Phil, Jun 8. The Monster Probst executed. Sheriff Howell drew the cord, the drop fell, & life was extinct in 2 or 3 minures. Probst wrote a letter to his parents yesterday; many prayers are offered up for me; the clergyman will send you all the particulars of my death. Have the holy sacrifice of mass offered up frequently for the repose of my poor soul. I trust to meet you all in eternity, in a happier & better place. –Antoine Probst

Phil, Jun 8. Fatal accident on the Reading Railroad yesterday, when the mail train from Pottsville ran off the track at Valley Forge, caused by a switch being left open. Thos Dornan, mail conductor, died shortly afterwards. The fireman was instantly killed.

Supreme Court, D C, in Equity, No 554. Ellis against Hagan & Callahan. I shall state the trustee's account; & distribute the fund of the late John Callaghan, on Jun 30 next, at my ofc, Court House. –W Redin, auditor

John Dyott, the well-known actor, arrived here yesterday to join the comedy combination which opens at Grover's Theatre on Monday. The last half of a character which Mr Dyott played in this city was that of Abel Mercott, in Our American Cousin. He never finished that performance, the pistol of John Wilkes Booth ended the mirth of the audience, sending woe through the land. The old actor, on his arrival yesterday, walked from the train straight to *Ford's Theatre*, & standing inside, simply exclaimed, "Crazy John, crazy John!"

Mrd: on Jun 7, at the residence of Col Jacob M Long, Harlem, N Y, by Rev Mr Bourne, Geo W Cochran, of Wash, D C, to Rose M Long, of Reading, Pa.

Mrd: on Jun 7, at the English Lutheran Church, by Rev J Geo Botler, Wm B Reed to Miss Katie A, eldest daughter of A Schneider, all of Wash City.

Died: on Jun 8, of consumption, Robt M Beale, aged 26 years. his funeral will be from the residence of his father, Robt Beale, on Jun 10 at 4 P M.

Died: on Jun 4, at his late residence, in PG Co, Md, John Higgins, in his 84th year.

Boston Traveller, referring to the recent reinterment of the late Wm B Tulley, of this city: a similar instance occurred many years ago, in the case of Judge Fuller, father-in-law of Gen Hull, who died in Newton about 1790, & was buried in a tomb of the old burying ground on the road from Newton Corner to Newton Centre. Judge Fuller was a prominent actor in the scenes of the Revolution, & highly esteemed. When it was examined, during the early part of the present century, the body had not decayed, but had become petrified, assuming the color of bacon. Many flocked to the tomb from all parts of the country, & some even from England. Public exhibition was stopped by the heirs about a quarter of a century ago. The body has been removed to another burial ground. The body of Gen Hull remains in this tomb, with a stone with his name & that he was an ofcr in the Revolutionary war. By his side are the remains of his faithful black servant, who followed him through all his wars, survived him several years, & died in Newton not a great many years ago, at the advanced age of nearly 100 yrs.

Summer Boarding at *Granby Farm*, on the old Bladensburg Road, 3 miles from Washington. –Mrs McElroy

Trustee's sale of valuable bldg lots near the Navy Yard, with one comfortable dwlg house of 7 rooms, also bldg lots on Capitol Hill; by decree of Chancery, in the case of Little vs Little, No 672 upon the Equity Docket of the Supreme Court of D C: sale on Jul 2 next of part of lot 2 in square south of square 853, on 5th st. Also the northern portion of said lot fronting 14 feet on 5th st running back to Canal st. Also, part of lot 6 in square 849, on Va ave, with a frame house. On Jul 3, all of lot 3 in square 970, on 10th st. Also part of lot __ in square 970, fronting on 11th st. Lot 3 on 10th st, will be subdivided into 2 lots.
-David A Burr, trustee -Jas C McGuire & Co, aucts

Supreme Court, D C, in Equity No 356. Eliza R Williams et al against Mattingly, Williams, Widdicombe, et al. The above parties & creditors of the late Jas Williams are notified to meet on Jun 30 next, at my ofc, Court House. I shall state the trustee's account & the distribution of the funds. —W Redin, auditor

A Phil papers says that the life-boat used by Dr E K Kane in escaping from the perils of the Arctic seas has been presented to the Com'rs of City Property by Mr Geo W Childs. It will be placed between 2 trees at Fairmount Park near Gen Grant's cabin, & will be protected by a light shed.

The Cincinnati Commercial has an account of a family meeting of the Kumlers, in Millville, Ohio. It was held on the estate of Mrs Susan Kumler, whis is now in her 87th year. She has now living 230 descendants of blood: 11 children, 84 grandchildren, 132 great grandchildren, & 3 great great grandchildren, with 52 marriages, making a total of 282. Of this number 204 were present.

The first bank established in the U S was the Bank of North America, of Phil, founded in Dec, 1781, by Robt Morris, with a capital of $100,000, divided into shares of $400 each, & its management was placed in the hands of 12 directors, chosen by the shareholders.

Dr Manning, of Palmer, Mass, has brought a suit against W S Nichols, of Monson, to recover $200 for medical attendance upon his daughter, who for several years has been unable to walk or talk. Dr Manning says he commenced treating her in Jan last, & agreed to charge nothing for his services unless he could make her walk & talk before May 1. The young lady did recover previous to that time, & her friends decline paying the doctor's bill, claiming that her remarkable cure was effected by the prayers of the church, & not by any medicine of the doctor's.

Perry Sloan, a young man, jumped out of the 4th story of the Merchants' Hotel, at St Louis, Sunday, while intoxicated, & was almost instantly killed.

On Tue a party of young men went to Curtis Creek & while there, one of them, Henry Rufus Burnham, about 23, member of the U S marine corps, an expert swimmer, while diving, struck his head violently upon the hard bottom of the creek. He was rescued in an insensible condition & was placed upon the receiving ship for medical attention. His injuries were such that he died at midnight. His neck bone being dislocated. He was from the State of N Y, but had made many acquaintances in Balt. He was buried yesterday with appropriate ceremonies. —Balt Gaz, Thu

MON JUN 11, 1866
Hon Horace Greeley, of the N Y Tribune, has been in Wash City for the last 2 days, endeavoring, we understand, to obtain the release, either on parole or bail, of Jefferson Davis. Mr Greeley left last evening.

Equity Court, Jun 7, 1866, before Judge Wylie. Jas W Gibson, cmplnt, vs Eliz Gibson et al, dfndnts. This is a proceeding for the sale of the real estate of Joshua Gibson, deceased, for the purpose of distribution amongst the widow & children of the deceased, & the court ratified the sale of said estate as made & reported to the court by the com'rs appointed by the court in that behalf. Mr Thompson solicitor for cmplnt.

Mary Foley, who resides in Murder Bay, on Ohio ave, between 13th & 14th sts, having had a difficulty with her landlord, attempted to end her earthly troubles by committing suicide with a razor, the sharp edge of which she applied to her throat. She was arrested by Ofcr Roth, but yesterday was released, her husband taking charge of her.

Dr Mary E Walker was at the police headquarters in Mulberry st, to enter a complaint against a policeman for illegally arresting her. It seems that on Tue the woman was walking in Canal st, dressed in a long black coat & black pantaloons, when a policeman took her into custody for wearing men's attire. The woman convinced the sgt that she ought not to have been arrested, & that ofcr discharged her. Dr Walker was well known during the war as "Major" Walker. She served as surgeon in the army during the war. [Jun 8th newspaper: Mrs Dr Mary Walker, formerly an assist surgeon in the Army of the Cumberland, was arrested yesterday for disorderly conduct in appearing on the streets in partially male attire. She was required to give bail in $300 to keep the peace. –N Y Herald, Sunday.]

Died: on Jun 8, near Leesburg, Loudoun Co, Va, after a short illness, Robt J Drane, of Dranesville, Va, aged 39 years.

Mrd: on Jun 7, at the Church of the Ascension, by Rev Dr Pinckney, Sallie A, daughter of Wm H Harrover, to J M Duncanson, all of Wash City.

Mrd: on Jun 7, at the residence of the bride's mother, by Rev Dr S Ridout, Wm Laird, jr, to Nannie Key, daughter of the late Wm G Ridgely, all of Gtwn.

Prof W Byrd Powell, who died in Covington, Ky, a few days ago, bequeathed his head to Mrs F H Kinzie, of Cincinnati, to be used for scientific purposes; in accordance with this, a surgeon cut off the professor's head, & it is now in the possession of the lady. [Jul 6th newspaper: The head of Dr Powell was delivered on May 15 to the residence of Prof Keckeler, 152 Broadway. The Dr's cranium is threatened with legal process to compel his restoration to the grave of that portion of the late Dr Powell legally his, under the testator's will, but demanded by Kentucky as part of her sacred soil. How this will turn out remains to be seen.]

Cincinnati Gaz: The House Judiciary Cmte will not, for some days to come, report upon the evidence in the matter of the alleged complicity of Jeff Davis in the plot to assissinate President Lincoln.

Sale of house & lot in Franklin Row, by decree passed by the Supreme Court of D C, in chancery cause No 691, wherein John D & Annie L Wells are cmplnts, & Chas G Baylor et al are dfndnts: public auction on Jun 27, all that part of square 284, in Wash City; corner of 12th & K sts. –Wm F Mattingly, trustee -Green & Williams, aucts

The trial of Mrs Haviland & Dr Baker, at Marshall, Mich, for the murder of the woman's children, at Battle Creek, some time since, resulted Thu in a verdict of guilty for both.

Charleston [S C] Courier: On Tue at the village of Bamberg, on the Augusta branch of the S C railroad, in a two story frame bldg known as Allen Lodge of Freemasons, lately used as a school house by Mr Robt Seabrook & his sister, the bldg was struck by a gale of wind or a tornado. The chimney was carried away at the same time the roof was rent asunder. Geo W Patrick, one of the older boys, found the door impossible to open; Chas Stewart proposed to escape by the window, when the whole bldg fell, killing young Stewart. The following were killed: Master Angus M Brabbham, aged 15 years, son of Maj J J Brabbham; Miss Hattie Brabbham, aged 14 years, daughter of Hampton Brabbham; Master Chas Stewart, 16, son of Hansford Stewart; Miss Urbanna Rentz, aged 10, daughter of Mrs Emma Rentz, lately removed from Orangeburg; Miss Uprasia Hoffman, aged 15 years, daughter of E G Hoffman; Master Elmore Sanders, 16, son of Jabez Sanders; Master Chas Simmons, age 6, son of A E Simmons. The following were wounded: Geo W Patrick, severely; Jas Renett, severely; Miss Annie Rennett, severely; Miss Sallie Brabbham, severely; Miss Julia Salter, severely; Miss Hoffman, severely; Thos Rivers, severely. Miss Urbanna Rentz, who was carried home in a dying condition, told her mother that she was going to Heaven & requested that her body might be taken to Orangeburg & deposited alongside of her father, who had died a few months before.

Montg Co land at trustee's sale: by decree of the Circuit Court for Montg Co, as Court of Equity, passed in a cause wherein Martha R Shaw, Wm E Shaw, & others are cmplnts, & Helen L Shaw, Benj F Shaw, Mary E Shaw, & Ellen R Shaw are dfndnts: public auction at Colesville, Montg Co, Md. On June 23, the real estate of which Elbert Shaw died seized & possessed: farm on the **Burnt Mills & Colesville** road, adjoins the farms of Dr Washington Duvall, E L Parker, Alpheus Middleton, & John T Parker; contains 175 acres of land, with a small frame dwlg house contianing 4 rooms. –Wm Veirs Bouic, trustee

Bailiff's sale on Jun 21, public auction, for cash, of furniture & sundry articles, taken as the property of Fred'k Aiken & John W Clampitt, under order of distrain, to satisfy arrears of rent due to Spalding & Rapley. –Jos H Hilton, Bailiff

Rossini has petitioned the Pope to allow women to sing in Italian church choirs.

Dept of the Interior, U S Patent Ofc, Wash, Jun 8, 1866. Ptn of Henry Smith, of Cleveland, Ohio, for the extension of a patent granted to him on Sep 28, 1852 for an improvement in Lath Machine, for 7 years from the expiration of said patent, which takes effect on Sep 28, 1866. –T C Theaker, Com'r of Patents

TUE JUN 12, 1866
At Elk Ridge bridge, which is a small wooden affair, the passage over was only allowed upon the payment of toll, a private structure owned by a man named Dennis, & the bridge keeper's house was on the Balt Co side of the stream. The toll collector, David White, aged about 65 years, has been in charge of the bridge. On Sunday he & other members of his family retired to bed at the usual hour, & were asleep, when the premises were visited by 2 men, doubtless intent upon robbery, as the following particulars, furnished by Messrs Smith & Gray, regular police detectives, will attest: the particulars they learned were furnished by a grandson of White. Persons entered the chicken house, which was in the cellar, & awoke his grandfather, who went to see what was wrong. He heard the cry of murder & found his grandfather hanging on a porch rail lifeless. His mother was beaten over the head with clubs, & he was attacked, but not fatally. [His mother's recovery is doubtful.] The two men robbed the old man & his daughter, an old silver watch & $46 in Gov't notes, $40 of which belonged to the daughter. Since writing the above, Michl Carmichael has gone out to the place, with the intention of eliciting such information as will lead to the arrest & punishment of the guilty parties. –Balt American of last evening

Fortress Monroe, Jun 9. Dr Cooper, surgeon attending Jeff Davis, said he was improving. Mrs Davis is almost daily in receipt of money, sent her by sympathizing friends, through Adams Express. The Express agent says that these contributions sometimes amount to $500 & $1,000 per day. She has been called upon by nearly all the ladies of the fort.

Titusville, Pa, Jun 10. This morning, a young man, named John Dall, left here in a wagon to be married to Miss Hattie Mathison, living about 6 miles north of here. About 2 miles on the road he received a rifle ball through his body. He fell from the wagon & turned the horse loose. Two gentlemen passing by, carried him to a friend's house, & he died. A rival for the hand of the young lady threatened to shoot him, & he is supposed to be the guilty party. He has not yet been arrested, but probably will be before morning.

Dr Chas H Stutman, a well-known physician of Boston, died on Friday, aged 60 years.

Catharine M Peat, a Phil lady, has volunteered as a nurse in the cholera hospital at Staten Island.

The Treasury Dept was created by act of Congress approved Sep 2, 1779. List of the Secretaries from the creation of the Dept:
[Date of appointment, birth & death.]

Alex'r Hamilton, N Y, Sep 11, 1789	Born 1757, died 1804.
Oliver Wolcott, Conn, Feb 3, 1795.	Born 1759, died 1833
Saml Dexter, Mass, May 31, 1800.	Born 1761, died 1816.
Albert Gallatin, Pa, Jan 26, 1802	Born 1761, died 1849.
Geo W Campbell, Tenn, Feb 9, 1814.	Born 1768, died 1848.
Alex'r J Dallas, Pa, Oct 6, 1814.	Born 1760, died 1817.
Wm H Crawford, Ga, Mar 5, 1817.	Born 1772, died 1836.
Richd Rush, Pa, Mar 7, 1825	Born 1780, died 1860.
Saml D Ingham, of Pa, Mar 6, 1829.	Born 1779, died 1860.
Louis McLane, Del, May 6, 1833.	Born 1786, died 1856.
Wm J Duane, Pa, May 29, 1833.	Born 1780, died ____
Roger B Taney, Md, not confirmed by The Senate,] Sep 23, 1833.	Born 1777, died 1864.
Levi Woodbury, N H, Jun 28, 1834.	Born 1789, died 1851.
Th Ewing, Ohio, Mar 5, 1841.	Born 1789, died ____
Walter Forward, Pa, Sep 13, 1841.	Born 1786, died 1852.
John M Spencer, N Y, Mar 3, 1843.	Born 1787, died 1855.
Geo M Bibb, Ky, Jun 15, 1844.	Born 1784, died ____
Robt J Walker, Miss, Mar 6, 1845.	Born 1801, died ____
W M Meredith, Pa, Mar 8, 1849.	Born ____, died ____
Thos Corwin, Ohio, Jun 23, 1850	Born 1794, died 1865.
Jas Guthrie, Ky, Mar 7, 1853.	Born 1793, died ____
Howell Cobb, Ga, Mar 6, 1857.	Born 1815, died ____
Philip F Thomas, Md, Dec 12, 1860.	Born 1810, died ____
John A Dix, N Y, Jan 11, 1861.	Born 1798, died ____
Salmon P Chase, Ohio, May 5, 1861.	Born 1808, died ____
Wm P Fessenden, Me, Jul 1, 1864.	Born 1806, died ____
Hugh McCulloch, Ind, May 7, 1865, a native of Maine.	Born ____, died ____

The body of Anton Probst, the murderer, was dissected at Jefferson College, Phil, on Sat. The brain of the dead criminal was found to be in a healthy condition, weighing 36 ounces. The result of the examination will, it is expected, be given in a fitting form soon to the medical fraternity.

Worcester, Mass, Jun 10. A drunken man was being conveyed to the Police ofc tonight, from a melee at East Worcester, a stone was thrown at one of the ofcrs, hitting him in the head, whereby the ofcr fired at the crowd. He hit a man named H T Weikel, a cigar manufacturer, near the eye, passing through the skull. He can survive but a short time. He was a mere spectator. Great excitement prevails.

Cincinnati, Jun 10. The second trial of Saml Covert, for the murder of the Roosa family, at Lebanon, Ohio, yesterday resulted in a verdict of murder in the first degree. Harrison McNeal, brother-in-law of Covert, is to be tried as an accessory.

Albany, Jun 10. A yacht containing 3 young men, while on the way from Cozzens' to Peekskill, collided with the steamer **Dean Richmond**, & was capsized. The steamer stopped & John Best, pilot, went to their assistance, & rescued two of them, one of whom was a son of John C Fremont. The third, named Marvin, from Pa, was drowned.

St Louis, Jun 9. The examination of W W Hogan before the U S District Court closed today. Judge Treat decided to hold the gentleman in $5,000 bond for a probable violation of the neutrality law. The case of A L Morrison, of Chicago, was then commenced.

Yesterday workmen were digging a connection with the main sewer on 14th st, when suddenly the earth gave way & Patrick Diggins was buried. He was dead when extricated from the dirt. He resided on the Island.

Mr Wm Waller, one of the sufferers by the accident at the Treas bldg, on May 28, died at his residence on G st, between 23rd & 24th sts, on Friday last, & was buried on Sunday. Mr Waller, with Mr Chas Burch, were severely scalded by the blowing out of the man hole plate of a boiler in the Printing Division of the Treasury, while they were repairing the boiler. Mr Burch has almost entirely recovered from his injuries.

Died: on Jun 10, at the Agricultural College of Md, Anna Ridgely, wife of John D Perryman, of Memphis, Tenn, in her 44th year. Her funeral services will take place at 9 o'clock this morning at the college. Memphis, Murfreesboro, & Jackson, Tenn, papers please copy.

Reopening of Columbia Garden, 12th & Ohio ave. This popular & pleasant resort having been refitted up in fine style, is now open to the public. Popular Artists, nightly performances, talented musicians; the bar is supplied with choice brands of liquors & cigars. –Jos Nathans

Supreme Court, D C, No 615 in Equity. Jas W Gibson against Eliz, John H, Margaret A, Susan A, Robt, & Martha E Gibson, widow & heirs of Joshua Gibson. The parties above & com'rs are to appear at my ofc, in the Court-house, where I shall state the account of the said com'rs of the sales made by them, the proper allowance to the widow for her dower in the premises sold, & the shares of the heirs in the surplus of the purchase-money. If there be an creditors of said Joshua Gibson whose claims are unpaid, they are warned to present the same to me forthwith. –W Redin, auditor

Supreme Court, D C, No 711 Equity, Docket 8. Robt McDuell et al vs John McDuell et al. The object of this bill is to procure a decree for the sale of part of square 369, in Wash City, described in the bill of cmplnt, & distribution of the proceeds among the heirs of Henry McDuell, deceased. Henry McDuell, late of Fred'k Co, Md, died intestate on or about Mar 12, 1866, seized in fee of the premises aforesaid, leaving a widow named Magdalena, & the following heirs at law, viz: John McDuell, brother of the intestate, now married to Eliz McDuell; Jane, a sister of intestate, now married to Michl Early; & the following children of Geo McDuell, a brother of intestate, who died in intestate's lifetime, viz: Ann S Smallwood, a widow; Eliz S, now married to Geo E Kennedy; Sarah J, now wife of Wm Kay; & John McDuell, who married [blank] McDuell; also cmplnt, brother of intestate, to whom said premises & real estate descended. The bill further states that, since the death of intestate, said estate has been in the possession of one Wm Y Newton, who claims to hold as tenant of one Sarah Ann McDuell, widow of said Geo McDuell, deceased, who claims to have an interest in said real estate, but whose claim is denied by cmplnts, & they call for an account of rents & profits received by her since the death of intestate. The bill further states that the said widow of said intestate is willing to have her dower estate in said premises sold & commutation thereof had out of the purchase money. Magdalena McDuell, Sarah McDuell, Wm Kay & Sarah J his wife, John L McDuell & ___ his wife; & Michl Early & Jane Early his wife, do not reside in this District. Said absent dfndnts are to appear in the Court on or before the first Tue of Nov, 1866. –R J Meigs, clerk. –Fendall & Ashford, solicitors for cmplnts

Mr C N Lovejoy, residing at 110 Princeton st, East Boston, went into the jewelry store of N G Woods, 11 Hanover st, yesterday, to purchase a watch. Before he completed his purchase he asked Mr Woods if he had some water, as he felt thirsty. Mr Woods referred him to the back room. Instead of getting water out of the faucet, he took a dipper full from a jar. He had taken a deadly poison, used for cleaning silver & in spite of all remedies, he died at 6 o'clock, one hour from the time he swallowed the poison. -Boston Herald, Thu

Early May measures were taken in Brownsville, Texas, to inflict the death penalty on Rodgers, who had killed the assist surgeon of his regt, 77th Ohio. The gallows were ready but Rodgers was not to be found. He had spent 28 days under ground, in a hole he had hollowed out with his hands. Hunger led to his recapture.

Supreme Court, D C. Jos Walsh against Mary A, Adelaide, & John Fletcher, widow & heirs of Jas H Fletcher. The parties above & creditors of Jas H Fletcher are to meet at my ofc, Court-house, for an account of the personal estate of said Jas H Fletcher, on Jun 18 next. -W Redin, auditor

Supreme Court, D C. Equity, No 513. Wm N Dalton against Susan Dalton, John R Dalton et al. The parties above & creditors of late John Dalton are to meet at my ofc, City-Hall, for an account of the personal estate of said John Dalton, on Jun 20 next. -W Redin, auditor

WED JUN 13, 1866
A day or two since a marriage license was issued to an old colored couple, Henry & Ann Dixon, who have been living together as man & wife for about 50 years past, they desiring to be legally wedded, to legitimatize their children. The expense of the marriage license might have been saved by a delay of a few days, for it will be perceived that in a bill passed by the House of Reps yesterday, the difficulty above indicated to legitimacy of children is obviated.

Augusta, Jan 12. Edgar M Lazarus & J R W Walter, U S collectors, have resigned, because they were unable to subscribe to the test-oath.

Orphans Court-Judge Purcell, Jun 12, 1866.
1-The will of the late Thos Baker, bequeathing his estate to his wife & children & nominating his brother, John A Baker, exec, was fully proven, & letters testamentary were issued to the exc; bond $4,000; & letters of guardianship were issued to the widow, bond in the same amount. 2-The will of the late Geo E Curtis was further partially proven. 3-Margaret A Dukes was appointed guardian to the orphans of Levin Dukes, of Gtwn: bond $12,500. 4-Letters of adm were issued to Jas La Fontaine on the estate of Jos D La Fontaine: bond $1,000. 5-Letters of adm to Mary S Smith, on the estate of John F Smith, deceased: bond $400. 6-The first & final account of the admx of Patrick O'Brien,; & account of the personal estate of Lewis J Kennedy, were approved & passed. 7-The Supreme Court of the District having certified the finding of the jury on the issues from this court in the case of the estate of Tillotson P Brown that Emily F Wiley is the child of the late Tillotson P Brown, the court passed an order declaring that as such child she is entitled to two-thirds of the amount in the hands of the administratrix, & requiring the latter to pay that amount over to her.

Richmond, Jan 12. Railroad accident on the Danville road, near Coalfield, today, caused by the breaking of a switch-rod. The ladies' car was precipitated over an embankment, & Mrs Trotler, of the vicinity of Danville, was instantly killed, & 13 others injured, among them Bishop Early, of the Methodist Church, & Isaac Overly, of Charlotte. [Jun 14th newspaper: Richmond Despatch: Mr E Vickers, railroad conductor, was standing on the platform & escaped by jumping off. The body of Mrs Trotter, of Swanson, Pittsylvania Co, was found, she was the mother-in-law of Mr Green T Pace, formerly of Danville, & now of this city, & was returning to Lynchburg, her home. Mrs S E Hayward, wife of Capt Wm H Hayward, of this city, had her left arm broken. Bishop John Early, of the Episcopal Methodist Church, received such severe injuries about the face & internally that it was not deemed safe to bring him on the train to the city, & he was removed to the house of Mr Cunliff, near the accident. His friends fear that his age & with infirm health, his wounds may prove fatal. His symptoms are very unfavorable, accompanied with spitting of blood. Miss Newman, of Orange, who had been teaching school in Prince Edward, was returning to her home, & was seriously injured, & had to be left in the care of some ladies near Coalfield. Isaac Overby was severely injured about the breast, & will be taken to his home near

Mossingford, Charlotte Co, on the train this morning. Mrs G T Pace, the daughter of Mrs Trotter, was badly injured, & brought to her home in this city. Mrs L H Dance, of Nottoway, the widow of Capt L H Dance, formerly of this city, was badly bruised, & suffering great pain. Mrs John C Hobson, of this city, was injured. Her wounds are painful, but are not believed to be serious. Miss M B Anderson, daughter of Gen Jos R Anderson, was badly stunned & slightly bruised, but not otherwise hurt. Robt D Green; & Mrs K A Denier, both of this city, were both slightly injured. Mr & Mrs J C Harkness, of Wash City, slightly injured. C Edw Melcher, of Blanning, Germany, slightly injured.]

Galveston, Jun 9. 1-The body of Dr Morse, who was murdered near Brownsville, has been sent to Ohio. 2-Fletcher, the colored soldier who was accused of killing Helfstean, has been acquitted.

Boston, Jun 11. A man named Conness, living in Bridgewater, was shot dead last night by Geo H Morse, a deputy State constable. The latter was called to quell a row in Conness' house, when he was savagely assaulted & fired in self-defence. Morse was not prosecuted.

N Y, Jun 12. 1-The Court of Appeals has confirmed the sentence of death of Gonzales & Pellicer for the murder of Senor Otero in Brooklyn a short time since. 2-Gen Strong, whose illness we noticed yesterday, is much better.

Orphans Court of Wash Co, D C. Letters testamentary on the personal estate of Thos Baker, late of Wash City, D C, deceased. –John A Baker, exc

The copartnership existing under the style of L J Hawley & Co is this day dissolved by mutual consent. –L J Hawley, Wm H Myers, Jun 12, 1866, Wash.

Miscellaneous Items:
1-Mrs Teresa Yelverton has withdrawn her suit for libel against the conductors of the London Sat Review. 2-Queen Victoria has given a sitting for the portrait which she intends to present to Mr Peabody. 3-It is reported that M Victor Hugo has lost 370,000f by one of the recent failures in London. 4-Jos Higgins, a brakeman on the Chicago & Northwestern railroad, was run over by the cars & instantly killed near Galena Junction Friday night. 5-Boston papers announce the death of Rev Warren Burton, at Salem, on Wed, after a protracted illness of 2 yrs. He was connected with the Unitarian Ministry & the ministry at large among the poor. His latter years have been devoted to the cause of home education.

Capt Menter, who was shot by a burglar at Newport, Ky, on Wed, is dead.

Guardian's sale, by an order of the Orphans Court of D C, dated May 19, ratified by the Supreme Court of D C, May 30, 1866: sale on Jul 3 next, of lot 2 & part of lot 3 in square 553, on O st. –Eliz Kraft, guardian -Green & Williams, aucts

Henry Wayne, colored, has been committed to jail at Rockville, Md, charged with having murdered his father in Fairfax Co, Va, last summer. The crime was lately disclosed by a boy, the grandson of the murdered man, but was deterred from giving information by the threats of the murderer. The fiend cut off his father's head & buried it & the body in separate places, which were pointed out by the boy. The negro was arrested on the farm of Mr A Nailor, between Rockville & Gtwn, where he had been living quietly & peaceably for sometime. He will await requisition of the Govn'r of Va.

N Y Express of Mon: Gen Wm K Strong, of this city, was last evening prostrated by a paralytic shock, which was so violent as to leave but faint hopes of his recovery. He had just returned to this city from the bedside of his son, who lies dangerously ill at Palmyra, N Y, & was conversing with his family at home on the subject when he was stricken down.

Notice is given that Louis F Perry, has by deed, dated the 2nd & recorded Jun 7, 1866, conveyed to me, in trust for his creditors, all his stock in trade, debts, books of account etc, & all his personal estate whatsoever. All persons indebted to him are to call & settle with me. My acquittances alone are a sufficient discharge.
–E T Morsell, trustee.

Letters by the ship **Africa**, from ex-Pres Fillmore, in Paris, state that he will not return home until after the World's Exhibition. He has promised to make an address on behalf of America on that occasion.

Mrd: on Jun 12, at the Ninth st Presbyterian Church, by Rev Dr Smith, Mr R A Walker to Miss S R Allen, all of Wash City.

Mrd: at the Church of the Epiphany, by Rev C C Adams, of N Y, assisted by Rev Dr Hammond, of St Anne's Church, Annapolis, Md, Brvt Maj Saml Adams, assist surgeon U S A, son of the officiating clergyman, to Miss Ruth Clagett, eldest daughter of Mr J W Clagget, of Wash, D C. Church papers will please copy. [No marriage date given-current item.]
+
Mrd: on Jun 12, at the Church of the Epiphany, by Rev Chas C Adams, Dr Saml Adams, U S A, son of the officiating clergyman, & Miss Ruth, daughter of H R Clagett, of Alexandria, Va. Balt & Alexandria papers please copy.
[See Jun 14th newspaper.]

Died: on Jun 3, at the residence of her brother, at Annington, Montg Co, Md, Miss Sarah Maria Smoot, a native of Chas Co, & recently of Gtwn, D C, leaving a large circle of relatives & friends to mourn her loss. Her health had been delicate for some time. [Rockville Journal & Port Tobacco Times will please copy.]

Died: on Jun 12, Florence, infant daughter of Francis D & K G Shoemaker, aged 4 months & 5 days. Her funeral is this afternoon at 6 o'clock, from the residence of her parents, 11 First st, Gtwn, D C.

Died: on Jun 12, in his 23rd year, Robt Wm Godey. His funeral will take place from the residence of his father, Walter Godey, Green & Dumbarton sts, Gtwn, D C, at 4 o'clock P M, on Jun 14th.

THU JUN 14, 1866
Michael O'Brien & Thos Norton, alias Simpson, were arrested yesterday for robbing the store of Mr Barr, on 9th st, the night before. They had forced open a window.

In Equity, Jun 11, 1866, before Judge Wylie. Jas R Clayton & wife vs Harriet Williamson et al. The bill in this case was filed to procure the sale of the real estate of Benj Williamson, dec'd, for the purpose of distribution amongst the heirs, & the Court ratified the sale of the said estate as made & reported to the Crt by the Com'rs appointed by the Crt. M Thompson, solicitor for the cmplnts.

Annual commencement of Columbian College Law School last evening by an intelligent audience, who could only have been induced to endure the almost suffocating atmosphere of the over crowded, ill-ventilated hall, by the interesting nature of the entertainment. The order of exercises was as follows: Music, Prayer, Oration, by Hon Horace Maynard, of Tenn. Address by Hon Wm M Merrick. The graduating class consisted of the following named gentlemen:

Jas F Allen, N H
M Bailey, Wash, D C
Henry M Baker, Bow, N H
Wm D Blackford, Lawrence, Kansas
Geo Burgess, Lockport, N Y
J Irving Burns, N Y C
Geo S Coleman, Bloomsburg, Pa
John Cruikshank, Gtwn, D C
John Deering, jr, Boston, Mass
Theodore A Dodge, Wash, D C
J Monroe Donnell, Wash, D C
Adams Emerson, Wash, D C
Wm A D Gordon, jr, Gtwn, D C
Chas V Harmon, Albemarle Co, Va
J H Hobbs, Wakefield, N H
Arnold B Johnson, Rochester, Mass
Geo G Kimball, Portsmouth, N H
E De Witt Kinne, Syracuse, N Y

Ben G Lovejoy, Wash, D C
Geo Mason, Oxford, Mass
J O McClellan, Chicago, Ill
Wm S Mills, Lexington, Mich
Thos J Miller, Wash, D C
J C Normile, Normonville, Kansas
M D O'Connell, Plattsburg, N Y
J Van Offenbacher, Urbana, Ohio
Chas H Patterson, Hanover, N H
Thos Raftery, Wash, D C
Gilbert J Raynor, East Moriches, L I
Geo B Sherman, **Fort Dodge**, Iowa
Frederic H Smith, Wanpaca, Wis
Myron L Story, Claremont, N H
Edw R Tyler, New Haven, Conn
J Kendrick Upton, Manchester, N H
W Frank Warren, Phil, Pa
A H Wright, Boston, Mass

N Y, Jun 13. 1-Hon Moses F Odell, naval officer of this port, died today. 2-Jas C Gallagher, U S consul at Ponce, died on May 28 in an apoplectic fit.

Sentenced & Pardoned. Yesterday Judge Fisher, in the Criminal Court, sentenced Benj F Hough, convicted of manslaughter on Sat last, to 2 yrs in the penitentiary. Hough was tried for the murder of Saml E Gaskins, in Gtwn, on Apr 8 last. A petition for his pardon had been presented to the Pres, & one was issued immediately.

The Pres yesterday granted executive clemency to Thos Mcmanue, convicted of an aggravated assault & battery in the Criminal Court of this District, at the Nov term of 1865, & sentenced to 1 year in prison. Because of his good conduct his pardon was recommended by a large number of the citizens of this District. Judge Wylie recommends that the remaining portion of his imprisonment, 5 months, be remitted.

Mrd: on Jun 12, at Church of the Epiphany, by Rev Chas C Adams, of N Y, assisted by Rev J P Hammond, of St Ann's Church, Annapolis, Md, Assist Surgeon Saml Adams, U S A, son of the officiating clergyman to Miss Ruth, daughter of Mr H B Clagett, of Alexandria, Va. [See Jun 13th newspaper.]

Died: on Jun 12, at Cloverdale, near Wash, in her 42nd year, Martha L, wife of Peria Shoemaker, & daughter of the late Lewis Carbery, of Gtwn. Her funeral will take place today at 10 A M, from Trinity Church, Gtwn, D C.

Died: on Jun 13, after a long & painful illness, Mrs Harriet Eliz Nailor, in her 77th year. Her funeral is Fri at 4 o'clock, from the residence of her son, Allison Nailor, 441 13th st.

Died: on Jun 13, Harry, youngest son of Patrick & Eliz C Sweeny, aged 3 months.

In Memoriam: the city of N Y, on Jun 7, the Great Architect of the Universe called unto himself the pure soul of Rebecca E Noah, consort of the late Judge M M Noah, so long favorable known & distinguished as the veteran editor of the U S. During her earthly career of but 45 years, this fair daughter in Israel labored zealously & effectively to do good. –Semi-Occasional, Wash, D C, Jun 10, 1866.

Supreme Court, D C, No 641-Equity Docket No 7. Clarke et al vs Clarke et al. Wm Y Fendall, trustee, reported he sold parts of lots 5 & 6 in square 786 to Michl Phelan, for $937.40, & he has complied with the terms of sale. –R J Meigs, clerk

Chancery sale of desirable dwlg house on H st, between 6th & 7th sts, by decree of the Supreme Court of D C, passed in cause 559, Equity Docket 7, Purdy vs Surratt et al: public auction on Jun 26 next, of the eastern part of lot 20 in square 454 in Wash City, on H with, with dwlg house. –W Y Fendall, trustee -Jas C McGuire & Co, aucts

FRI JUN 15, 1866
Yesterday, in the Circuit Court, the following gentlemen, who graduated on Wed from the Columbian College Law School, were admitted members of the bar:

Maurice D O'Connell	J Kendrick Upton
Thos Raftery	Chas H Patterson
Geo S Coleman	Geo S Kimball
Myron L Story	A H Wright
Ed D Kinnie	Gilbert J Raynor
Jas O McClellan	J Irving Burns
Geo B Sherman	John Deering, jr
Geo Burgess	Jas C Normile
Adams Emerson	Geo Mason
Henry M Baker	
W Frank Warren	

Wm Page has finished his historical painting of Admiral Farragut. It represents the Admiral lashed to the shrouds of the ship **Hartford**, as he appeared during the great naval fight in Mobile Bay on Aug 5, 1864. The picture will shortly be on exhibition at the Mercantile Library in N Y C.

The richest men & estates in Boston are reported as follows: Estate of Aug Hemenway, $2,406,000; Nathl Thayer, $2,362,500; estate of John Bryant, $1,500,000; Sears' estate: $1,742,500; David Sears, $1,401,600; Moses Williams, $1,271,500; & estate of E Frances, $1,010,700.

The Richmond Despatch states that Cmdor John Randolph Tucker, late of the Confederate navy, has received the appointment of the supreme command of the Peruvian navy, with the title of Admiral, & he departed on Jun 1st from N Y for Peru. Capt D P McCorkle, of Va, & Lt Butt, of N Y, accompanied him. Capt McCorkle is to take command of one of the vessels, & Lt Butt is to be flag lt to the Admiral.

Police Commissioners: meeting yesterday: ofcrs dismissed the force: David Cudden, Jos Harbour, & John Carey. Appointments for patrolmen: Jas T Turnburke, vice Carey. Peter A Becker, vice Harbour. Edw Hughes, vice Cudden. S S Lester, vice Noonan, promoted. Appointed additional patrolmen: Jas F Marr, Benj R Norwood, & Thos R Newman.

Boston, Jun 13. Mr Robt N Corning, postmaster at Concord, N H, died today, after an illness of several weeks.

Judge Lane, late Chief Justice of the Supreme Court of Ohio, died on Tue.

Geo S Goodall, a young man employed in the Commissary Dept at **Fortress Monroe**, as a night watchman, fell overboard a few nights ago from one of the wharves & drowned.

Orphans Court of Wash Co, D C. In the case of Chas Walter, adm of Hugh McMahon, deceased, the administrator & Court have appointed Jul 7 next, for the final settlement of the personal estate of the said deceased, of the assets in hand. - Z C Robbins, Reg/o wills

Mr Saml Hanson committed suicide yesterday, in his room in Mrs Smith's boarding house, corner of Pa ave & 4½ st. The pistol he used to shoot himself in the right temple was a large sized Colt. Death was instant. The deceased was about 35 to 40 years of age, born & raised in Wash City, where he resided until he went South, & took a position in the rebel post ofc dept at Richmond. He had been at Mrs Smith's about 6 weeks. He had difficulty obtaining employment, coupled with the fact that his brother had recently been dissipated, & failing to do anything to support his mother, who is now on a visit near Marlboro. An unfinished manuscript stated the circumstances which had reduced him to almost absolute want.
+

Died: on Jun 14, Saml Hanson, in his 42nd year. His funeral will take place from the residence of Miss Rebecca Smith, corner of 4½ st & Pa ave, today at 3 P M.

Fortress Monroe: On Sunday J I Crenshaw of the firm of blockade rummers during the war, was with Mr & Mrs Davis, remaining in the fort until this morning, when he left for Richmond on the mail steamer **John Sylvester**. The object of his visit has not been made known, but rumor says it only in a pecuniary point of view, looking forward to the anticipated release of Mr Davis. Mrs Davis accompanied Mr Crenshaw to the wharf, & the lively & pleasant conversation which ensued between them showed her to be in good spirits.

Boston paper: Mr Chas S Vining, General Agent of the New Gloucester Society of Shakers, has been arrested & brought to Portland, Me, charged with misappropriating & retaining funds belonging to the Society to the amount of $15,000. It was reported that he was about to leave the Society & take to himself a wife.

Supreme Court, D C, No 641-Equity. Eleanor Clarke et al vs Alice R Clarke et al. Distribution of the fund among the heirs of Thos Clarke, at my ofc, Court House, on Jul 7 next. –W Redin, auditor

Mr Chauncey Loomis, of Bloomfield, Conn, recently found a box turtle on his farm, which is probably a centenarian. His father, Mr Jacob Loomis, 73 years ago carved his intitials & the date: J L, 1793, upon the lower shell of this same animal, & then let him go. In 1817, he was captued by Harry Cornish, of Bloomfield, & the initials B C, 1817, are cut underneath those of Mr Loomis.

SAT JUN 16, 1866
Brvt John B Summers, U S army, has been appointed Medical Director of the Dept of the Cumberland.

The marriage of Mr Cushing, of Boston, with Miss Grinnell, daughter of Moses H Grinnell, of this city, took place yesterday. A special train was engaged for the occasion, which left the Hudson railroad depot at 2:15 P M; was comprised of 6 cars, all loaded with guests; & Wall street was well represented. When the train arrived at Mr Grinnell's mansion, between Irvington & Tarrytown, it was halted at the platform erected specially for the occasion, & under the direction of Ofcr Teichman, despatched to preserve order, the entire company disembarked to enjoy themselves with the nuptial festivities. –N Y Herald, 15th

Brvt Lt Col D S Magruder, surgeon U S army, has been relieved from duty as Medical Director of the Dept of the Platte, & Brvt Lt Col E H Alexander, now serving in the Dept of the Missouri, has been assigned to that duty.

Brvt Col Ebenezer Swift, surgeon U S army, has been relieved from duty in Louisville, Ky, & assigned to duty as port surgeon at the Jefferson Barracks, at St Louis, Mo.

Board for the examination of Cadets at West Point, to consist of: Brvt Lt Cols A N McLauren, & L F Head, surgeons U S Army; Brvt Maj E J Marsh, surgeon U S army; to assemble at West Point on the 15th instant.

Free railroad excursion & great auction sale of 100 beautiful bldg lots in the new town of **Centralia**, [**Centre City**] Annapolis Junction, on the Wash Branch of the B & O R R, Anne Arundel Co, Md, on Jun 18, 1866, on the premises. The lots vary in size from 33 to 100 feet front by from 110 to 300 feet deep, & cover that gentle & beautiful elevation to the south & immediately at Annapolis Junction, [recently occupied as a military camp.] The private sale price is affixed on the plot to each lot, varying from $100 to $200, & none will be sold for less at private sale; but each lot, when put up at auction, will be sold to the highest bidder regardless of price. Title fee simple & perfect. Deeds furnished free of expense to the purchasers. No one under 21 years of age will be allowed on the trains. No tickets required. –Saml H Gover, auct

On Thu Gustave A Jung, about 27, who served in the 3rd Pa regt, & afterwards established himself in the confectionary business in Gtwn, committed suicide by taking laudanum. It appears he had become financially embarrassed.

Patrick Sheehan, aged 70, residing at 54 Cherry st, N Y, an emigrant who arrived her 5 weeks ago, died Wed at 9 o'clock, of what was pronounced cholera.

Mrd: on Jun 14, at Christ Church, Gtwn, D C, by Rev Walter W Williams, Warren C Benton, of Hudson, N Y, to Miss Mary M Hepburn, daughter of late John M Hepburn, of Gtwn.

Died: on Jun 15, William H, 2nd son of Fred'k & Louisa Schneider, aged 14 years. His funeral will take place on Sunday at 3 o'clock, from the residence of his parents, on H st, between 18th & 19th sts.

Boston Post: The golden wedding of the venerable Presiding Bishop of the U S, Bishop Hopkins, of Vt, & his estimable lady, took place at the episcopal & family homestead, at Rock Point, Vt, on the borders of Lake Champlain, last week, & continued from Wed evening to Fri morning. The issue of the marriage consisted of 9 sons & 4 daughters, of these 7 sons & 2 daughters are living. Members of the family are settled in Buenos Ayres, Calif, New Orleans, N Y, & Burlington, Vt, besides other places. Five sons & sons-in-law are clergymen, 3 editors, 1 physician, one [Casper] stands at the head of the marine insurance business on the Pacific coast, & one [Jerome] has devoted himself to the art of music, with a passion for which he seems to have been born. The eldest son [John Henry] is proprietor & editor of the Church Journal, one of the most able religious papers in the country. The family dinner took place on Thu, & on Friday there was a Holy Communion service in the chapel of the Episcopal Institute, near to the Bishops' house, after which the partings & adieus took place. There was a representation of nearly 50 at the family dinner, all but 2 of the children being unmarried, Henry & Jerome.

The trial of Maj Gee, at Raleigh, N C, was concluded on Wed last. The proceedings were forwarded for revision to the proper authorities in Wash City.

Supreme Court of D C, 696 Equity, docket 7. Jas W Gibson vs Riley A Shinn, Eliz Blount, Alice K Blount, Louisa K Blount, Margaret E Blount, Wm B Blount, Charlotte C Blount, Saml Bootes & Mary R his wife, Amariah Storrs & Annie J Storrs his wife. The cmplnt, by deed of indenture, dated Jan 11, 1864, conveyed to Thos M Blount all his estate, right, etc, in & to parts of lots 4 & 5 in square 490, upon which the Exchange Hotel is situated, on C st, in Wash City, D C, in trust to secure the payment of a debt described in the said deed, due & owing to the said Riley A Shinn; that the said Thos M Blount has since departed this life intestate, leaving the said Eliz Blount, his widow, & the said Alice K, Louisa K, Margaret E, & Charlotte C Blount, & Mary B Bootes & Annie J Storrs, his daughters, & the said Wm R Blount, his son, & only heirs at law of him, the said Thos M Blount, deceased; that the said debt is still due & owing to the said Shinn; that cmplnt is willing & desirous to pay the same, & to have the said deed of trust thereupon released & discharged; & the bill prays that a trustee may be appointed in the place of the said Thos M Blount, deceased, with power to release & discharge the said deed of trust upon the payment of said debt. The said Margaret E Blount, Charlotte C Blount, Wm R Blount, Amariah Storrs, & Annie J Storrs are non-residents & cannot be found within the jurisdiction of this court. Absent dfndnts are to appear in this court, in person or by solicitor, on or before the first Tue in Nov next. –R J Meigs, clerk -M Thompson, solicitor for cmplnt

Louisville, Ky. Prof E W Gunter, organist of St Paul's Church, was thrown from a rockaway wagon today, breaking his neck, & dying instantly. His family, in the same vehicle with him, were not injured.

The following appointments to the Naval Academy at Annapolis have been made by the Pres: At Large:
Wm Kelley, Ky   Thos S Plunkett, Tenn
Willie M Belcher, Ill   R A Page, D C
Sons of Ofcrs:
Jas M Gow, Ky   Wm S Long, Pa
Walter Frazier, Md   Walter H Donaldson, jr, N Y
Danl Whipple, N H   Thos C Spinner, Ohio
Frank H Harbuck, Iowa   Frank Ellery, jr, Vt
John M Robinson, N Y   Ellis B Bliss, Mich

Miscellaneous Items:
1-Rev Dyer Ball, a missionary since 1838, of the American Board, died in China Mar 27th. 2-Rev Dr Peabody, chaplain of Harvard College, sailed for Europe to make a tour on the continent & pay a visit to the Holy Land. 3-Edw Cline, age 12 years, fell from one of the Hudson River railroad cars, in N Y, while stealing a ride on Thur, & was fearfully injured that he will probably die. 4-Mr Thos McElrath, of the N Y Tribune, has been appointed a deputy collector in the N Y Custom House, in the place of Mr Embree, who is now a deputy at large.

New Haven, Jun 13. 1-The second game of baseball between the Yale College nine & the Charter Oak nine, of Hartford, resulted in another victory for the Charter Oaks. The score stood 21 to 10. The Charter Oaks still hold the championship. Jun 14. 2-Geo Knight, a colored man, a freedman, was murdered last night, in this city, by some unknown party. 3-Leman W Cutler was today elected by the Legislature to the ofc of State Comptroller, vice Batelle, resigned.

MON JUN 18, 1866
Wm Winston Seaton departed this life at his residence, in Wash City, on Saturday, at the age of 81 years. His death was caused by a canerous affection of the face, which was so terribly afflicting as to affect his mind at its latest stages. Death came, almost on an errand of mercy. He survived by 2 years the cherished partner of his life, the mother of an excellent & gifted family. His funeral will take place from his late residence this afternoon at half-past four o'clock.
+
Sketch of the life of Wm W Seaton. Born Jan 11, 1785, on the paternal estate in King Wm Co, Va, one of a family of 4 sons & 3 daughters. He betook himself with his whole family to Richmond, & with his brothers & sisters, Wm was taught, through an ascending series of schools, until he arrived at the academy of Ogilive, the Scotchman. A very solid teacher he was not. Young Seaton became acquainted with the art of printing, in an ofc where he became the companion & friend of the late Thos Ritchie. He took sole charge of a respectable paper in

Petersburg, the Republican, the editor & proprietor of which, Mr Thos Field, was about to leave the country for some months. He then became the proprietor & editor of the North Caroline Journal, published at Halifax, the former capital of that State, & the only newspaper there. He made his way to Raleigh, the new State capital, & became connected with the Register. This connection was drawn yet closer by his happy marriage with the lady who became a shining charm of his household & of the society of Wash. He came to the metropolis to join all his fortunes with those of his brother-in-law. From the time of their coming together, down to the year 1820, Gales & Seaton were the exclusive reporters, as well as editors, of their journal. The Nat'l Intellgencer newspaper was the first newspaper printed in Wash, D C, Aug, 1800, Saml H Smith, the originator. It was transferred to Jos Gales jr, on Aug 31, 1810; on Nov 1, 1812, it was under the firm of Jos Gales, sr, & Wm W Seaton. [Jun 20th newspaper: W W Seaton was born in New Kent Co, Va, descended from one of the noblest families of that time-honored & illustrious Commonwealth.]

Detroit, Jun 17. Gen Lewis Cass died here at 4 A M this morning, aged 83 years.

The U S District Court grand jury for the Southern District of Ala, Judge Busteed's district, has found a bill of indictment against Geo M Gayle, on the joint charge of murder & conspiracy to overthrow the U S Gov't. Gayle has been arrested & held to answer in the sum of $15,000. He will be remembered as the man who advertised in the Selma papers for contributions to a fund of $1,000,000 to procure the assassination of Mr Lincoln, who was brought here under arrest last summer, but finally released & allowed to return.

Memphis, Jun 15. 1-A telegram from Little Rock, last night, states that Dr Webb, a wealthy citizen of that place, & his son, were murdered in their beds by an unknown assassin. 2-A posse of men today attempted to bring into the city two men, S A Boyett & Frank Wingate, arrested for the murder of a man named Payne, on Tue night. The guilty parties were informed by E N Bank, an accomplice, who hunted them out near the city. They were met by a Mr Henderson, a relative of Payne, who shot all 3, killing Bank, & mortally wounding Bayett. The leader of the posse ordered Henderson to desist, & on refusing, the latter was shot & killed. The man who killed Henderson was his own uncle.

Richmond, Jun 16. 1-Dr Maddox was tried today at the Hustings Court for shooting at W H Vernon, on Broad st a few days ago. Fined $100 & committed to jail for 6 months. 2-The Hanna-Ogden shooting affair was continued until the next term of the court.

Cincinnati, Jun 16. 1-Walter B Watson, the murderer of Capt Menter, was tried at Newport, Ky, yesterday, & found guilty. 2-Mortimer Gibbony, one of the murderers of Abraham Durns, was hung at Parkersburg, West Va, yesterday.

Boston, Jun 16. The mother of Senator Sumner, of Mass, died yesterday, aged about 81 years.

Frank Arthur, about 22 years of age, employed for many months past as solicitor & collector for the Evening Transcript, decamped on Monday with upwards of $300 belonging to his employer, Mr Wm H Neilson, which he had collected at various times from the patrons of the establishment. Arthur resided with his mother & sisters, neither of whom have any knowledge of his whereabouts. He is below the medium stature, about 5 feet 2 inches in height; well formed; blue eyes; brown hair, rather short & has a scar under his left eye. –Balt Transcript

Cholera, Schenectady, N Y. The first victim was Jas Laden who died on Tues. The second victim was Wm H Snyder, about 30 years of age, who died on Wed. The third case is that of Mr John W Evans, whose decease was sudden. He died on Thu. Dr A M Vedder was the attending physician in two of the cases.

Lt Gen Grant & wife were entertained at a soiree & banquet at the Southern Hotel, St Louis, Tue night. The Gen was expected to be in Louisville on Sat last.

Masonic: member of the Grand Lodge of Free & Accepted Masons of D C, are to meet at the Masonic Hall, D & 9th sts, on Jun 18, at 3 o'clock, to attend the funeral of the late Most Worshipful Past Grand Master, Wm W Seaton. –Geo C Whiting, Grand Master. Notice of the same given by the: 1-Knights Templar: W M Smith, recorder; E L Stevens, Em Cmder. 2-Columbia Typographical Society: to attend the funeral of Col Wm W Seaton, -E Mac Murray, R S. 3-Associated Soldiers of the War of 1812: J S Williams, V P; Jas Lawrenson, sec. 4-Oldest Inhabitants: -Alex McD Davis, recording sec.

Death of Hon Jas Humphrey, M C from Brooklyn. Hon Jas Humphrey died at his residence, corner of Columbia & Pierrepont sts, last night. He was a member of Congress from the Third Congressional District, & came home from Washington upon some private business. Although an invalid for years, he did not feel worse than usual, & left Brooklyn again on Wed to return to Wash. He was taken ill on the cars, & when the train reached Wilmington, Dela, his friends found it necessary to remove him. He remained in Wilmington until yesterday, & as he appeared to be growing worse, he was brought home reaching there last evening. Shortly before 12 o'clock he breathed his last. Mr Humphrey, age 54, was born in Fairfield, Conn, & was the son of the late Heman Humphrey, D D, pres of Amherst College, where Mr Jas Humphrey graduated with honor & distinction. He removed to Brooklyn in 1839, & became a prominent member of the bar. In 1848 he was elected alderman; re-elected again in 1849; served as Corp counsel 1850-51; in 1858 elected to Congress; in 1860 was defeated by Moses F Odell; in 1862 he was again defeated by Odell; in 1864 Mr Humphrey was elected by a large majority. Mr Humphrey was a member of the Church of the Pilgrims, of which Dr Storrs is pastor. -N Y Express, [Sat]

The funeral of Moses F Odell, late naval ofcr at N Y, took place in Brooklyn, at 4 o'clock on Fri. The pall-bearers were Henry B Smythe, collector of the port of N Y; Abram Wakeman, surveyor of the port; Saml Booth, Mayor of Brooklyn; David G Farragut, admiral U S Navy; John J Studwell, supervisor Third Ward, Brooklyn; Mr Guthrie, of the Treas Dept; Alex'r T Stewart; C T Cobb; J M Franklin, deputy naval agent; S Crowell; J W Harper, C C Smith; Ira Perego; Schureman Halstead, C C Clinch, of N Y. The officiating clergy were Bishop Janes, Rev Chas Fletcher, & Rev L M Vincent. The remains of Mr Odell will be taken to White Plains for interment in the family burying ground.

TUE JUN 19, 1866
Robt M Magraw died last evening at the N Y Hotel, N Y C, attacked with paralysis on Sat last & was not conscious thereafter. He had been in poor health for some time, & was attended in his last moments by his brother, Henry Magraw, now residing in Cecil Co, & by a son of the latter. R M Magraw was for many years a well known citizen of Balt; & was a native of West Nottingham, Cecil Co, Md. –Balt Sun

Association of Oldest Inhabitants meeting yesterday, vice pres Mr Lewis Johnson presiding; Dr A McDonald Davis, sec. Cmte: Messrs J F Callan, J C Brent, & Ulysses Ward. Tribute to Col Wm Weston Seaton, one of our number.

Funeral of Mr Wm W Seaton, Jun 18: the remains were arrayed in a black suit with a white vest, & were encased in a mahogany coffin, lined with satin, & a massive silver plate had the simple inscription: William Winston Seaton, Born January 11, 1785; Died Jun 16, 1866. Drs Hall & Pinckney, of the Episcopal Church, & Rev Mr Augur, of the Unitarian Church, commenced the religious services. Burial was in the **_Congressional Cemetery_**. There were over 50 carriages in line, all along the route the sidewalk was crowded with spectators, which faces peered from windows & doorway at all points.

Gen Lewis Cass died on Jun 18; born at Exeter, N H, Oct 9, 1782, & was 84 at the time of his death; sprang on both his parents' sides from N H Puritan stock. His father, Jonathan Cass, at 19 years, marched to the field immediately after the battle of Lexington, & was at the battle of Bunker Hill, & serving through the war; rose from private to capt, & was retained in the service after the war, & rose to the rank of major. In 1799 the father was on duty at Wilmington, Dela, & Lewis, who had been at Exeter Academy from the age of 10 years up to this time, went with his parents & taught school in that vicinity. In 1800 Maj Cass resigned his commission, & accompanied by the son, the family emigrated to the West, descending the Ohio from Pittsburgh in a flatboat, & arriving at the pioneer settlement of Southeastern Ohio in Oct of that year. The family took up their home on a tract of land near Zanesville, which had fallen to Maj Cass as a military bounty, but the son remained at Marietta & entered upon the study of law, coming to the bar in Dec, 1802. In 1806 he married Eliz Spencer, whose parents, emigrating from Lansingburg, N Y, had settled on the Va side of the

Ohio. In 1812 the troubles with the Indians & the exasperated feeling towards Great Britain led the State to organize 3 regts of volunteers, of which Mr Cass was made the colonel of the 3rd regt. These volunteers, 1,200 in all, together with 300 regulars under Col Miller, after a march of more than 200 miles, arrived at Detroit in Jul, & on the 11th of that month marched into Canada under Gen Hull. The retreat of Hull & the surrender of his whole force ignominiously on Aug 16, at Detroit, is well known. Col Cass, temporarily absent for the relief of a provision train at the time of the surrender, was with his command, included in the capitulation, & when returning & learning the result, he indignantly broke his sword & flung it away. His regt was dismissed on parole, & he went to Washington to vindicate himself. Col Cass was exchanged in Feb 1813, & commissioned colonel in the regular army; soon promoted to be brig gen, he joined Gen Harrison's army in Jul & shared in the pursuit of Proctor & the victory of the Thames. Gen Cass was put in command in Detroit & appointed Govn'r. In Jun, 1815, he moved his family to that place, which was ever after his home. In 1816 he purchased 500 acres of land for $12,000, a tract upon which much of the city now stands. He was superintendent of Indian affairs: in 1831 appointed Sec of War by Gen Jackson; in 1836 transferred from that post to that of Ambassador at the French court; in 1842 he resigned & returned home; elected to the U S Senate & took his seat in Dec, 1845; in 1851 he again came into the Senate; in 1856 he was appointed Sec of State; he resigned his ofc at Sec of State on Dec 12, 1860; Gen Cass retired to his home in Detroit

Died: on Jun 17, C Ellsworth son of Dr M Tucker, aged 5 years. His funeral is today at 3 o'clock P M from the residence of his aunt, Mrs Walleron, H st, between North Capitol & First sts.

Died: on Jun 16, after a painful illness, Frances Elizabeth, aged 8 years, 8 months & 5 days, daughter of John & Hester J Eagleston.

Prof Wm Baer died on Jun 7 at his residence in Fred'k, Md, in his 79th year. Prof Baer was born in Fred'k City, but resided in Balt & near Sykesville until last year. He was for many years the director of the Md Chemical Works. In agricultural chemistry he was, perhaps the most intelligent man in the U S.

A fatal case of cholera in Balt, on Jun 17: Wm Howard Mann, aged 41 years. His father resides in the western section of the city. The deceased contracted the disease in N Y, his room mate having died of it. He was sick when he left N Y, & on arriving here, on Sunday, he was taken to the Infirmary. He was too far gone to arrest the disease.

Chancery sale by decree of the Supreme Court of D C, in Equity No 708, Docket 8, Cazenove et al vs Cazenove et al: sale on Jun 28 next, at public auction, lots 2 & 17 in square 568. Lot 2 fronts on F st; lot 17 fronts on N J ave. –W Y Fendall, trustee -Jas C McGuire & Co, aucts

Trustee' sale by deed of trust from Philip Wagner, duly executed & recorded: public auction on Jun 29 next, of lots 14 & 15 in square south of square 915, located at the intersention of 8th st & Md ave, improved by a large, commodious, & well built brick house, containing a large storeroom & dwlg apartments. After the above sale will be sold all said Wagner's interest & estate in & to lot 8 & 9, according to W B Todd's subdivision of square 893: fronts on Md ave, with 3 newly built 2 story frame houses. –Chas H Utermehle, Fred'k Schmidt, Saml L Phillips, trustees -Green & Williams, aucts

Supreme Court, D C, No 697, Equity. Patrick White against Maria McGuire & others, widow & heirs of John McGuire. Statement of the personal estate of John McGuire, at my ofc, Court House, on Jun 27. –W Redin, auditor

Supreme Court, D C, No 527, Equity, Docket 7. Ira W Clatlin et al vs Benj F Dyer. The subpoena issued to compel the dfndnt's, Jas Owner, jr's appearance, has been returned by the marshal on Sep 28, 1865, endorsed "not found." He is to cause his appearance on or before the first Tue of Oct next, otherwise the bill may be taken for confessed against him. –R J Meigs, clerk

WED JUN 20, 1866
On Monday the corner stone of the new Episcopal Church, 12th & N sts, was laid. Service by Rev Mr Williams, the new rector of Christ Church, Gtwn. The stone was laid by the rector of the congregation, Rev R W Lowrie. Rev Mr J E Brown, of Grace Church, Gtwn, read the anthem. Rev Mr Chew, of St Alban's followed with prayer. An address was delivered by Rev J V Lewis, rector of St John's Church, West End. The depositing of the contents of the stone, one of the wardens, Mr J Dille, announced them.

Capt J V Meigs, of Wash City, has invented a new device for changing the common musket into a breech-loader, which can be attached to the U S arms with little difficulty.

Mrd: on Jun 14, at St Paul's Church, Balt, by Rev Dr Pinckney, Chas B Calvert, of PG Co, Md, to Miss Eleanor Mackubin, of Annapolis.

Died: on Jun 17, at Memphis Tenn, Abby G, widow of Robt E Clary, jr, & daughter-in-law of Brvt Brig Gen A E Clary, U S Army.

The Wash Orphan Asylum bldg, fronting 99 feet 11 inches on north H st, has recently been sold by Messrs Todd, Harkness, & Blagden, trustees of the asylum, to Mr Wm M Galt, for $25,000; & the Grammer Property, at 4½ & north C sts, has been sold to Mr Francis A Lutz, for $17,500.

Orphans Court of Wash Co, D C. Letters testamentary on the personal estate of Lydia S English, late of Gtwn, D C. –Sarah T Daugherty, excx

Trustee's sale of val lots by decree of the Supreme Court of D C, in the cause of Jas Lynch & Jane Lynch vs Ann Phillips, No 431 Equity, dated May 17, 1865: auction on Jul 10 next, of the east half of lot 3 in square 687, fronting on North A, between First st & Dela ave. Also, lot 4 in square 730, fronting on 2nd st, between Pa ave & South A st. -Walter S Cox, trustee -Green & Williams, aucts

Dept of the Interior, U S Patent Ofc, Wash, Jun 15, 1866. Ptn of Saml Hulbert, of Ogdensburg, N Y, praying for an extension of a patent granted to him Sep 20, 1853, & ante-dated Sep 20, 1852, for an improvement in Ploughs, for 7 years from the expiration of said patent, which takes place on Sep 20, 1866. -H C Theaker, Com'r of Patents.

Dept of the Interior, U S Patent Ofc, Wash, Jun 14, 1866. Ptn of Wm Moore, of Brooklyn, praying for the extension of a patent granted to Jas Carman, assignee of the said Wm Moore, on Sep 14, 1852, for an improvement in Door Locks, for 7 years from the expiration of said patent, which takes place on Sep 14, 1866. -H C Theaker, Com'r of Patents

Supreme Court, D C, No 532 Equity, docket 7. Geo Presburg vs Nannie Haw, adm et al. The subpoena issued to compel the apprearance of the dfndnt, Geo Preston, returned by the Marshal, on Oct 28, 1865, endorsed "not found." Preston to cause his appearance on or before the first Tue of Sep next, otherwise the bill may be taken for confessed. -R J Meigs, clerk -John F Ennis, solicitor for cmplnt

Supreme Court, D C Saml Pumphrey et al agt Wm Downs & others, widow & heirs of Wm Downs, deceased. I shall state the account of Messrs Williams & Miller, trustees in the cause, & distribute the funds of said Wm Downs, on Jul 12 next, at my ofc, in the Court House. -W Redin, auditor

Supreme Court, D C. Keene, Conrad, Robinson et al agt A L & J S Keene. I shall state the account of Jos R Keene, the trustee & distribute the funds of the late Godfrey Conrad. -W Redin, auditor

THU JUN 21, 1866
Phil, Jun 20. Geo Squibbs, aged 72 years, & his grand-daughter, were butchered last Sunday near Rossville, York Co. Miss Squibbs was in a dying condition at last accounts. The weapon used is supposed to have been a hatchet. An Irishman named Conovan was arrested on suspicion. Money is believed to have been the object of the murder.

Oldest newspaper in this country. The Newport Mercury, was established in 1758. Gen Peter Force's library contains files of this paper, commencing in 1762. The N H Gaz, which still survives in Portsmouth, N H, was established in 1756. The earliest file of this paper in Gen Force's library is for the year 1770. It is well known that the first newspaper printed in this country was the Boston News Letter, established in 1704. Gen Force's library earliest volume is for 1762.

New Orleans, Jun 19. Bob Jamison, the nortorious gambler, was murdered last night by a man named Duffie, in a gambling-house. Jamison received 9 balls & 6 stabs.

Died: on Jun 11, after a very short illness, at Brooklyn, N Y, Theodore Kolecki, formerly topographer of the Water Board in Wash City.

Died: on Jun 20, after a brief illness of 12 hours, Harry Milton, son of Lemuel & Leonora Gaddis, aged 2 years, 7 months & 19 days. His funeral will be from the residence of his father, Ga ave, between 10th & 11th sts, [Navy Yard,] this afternoon at 4 o'clock.

Died: on Jun 20, at Hyattsville, Ellenor May, daughter of F B & Maggie Guy, aged 13 months. Her funeral will take place from the residence at 4 o'clock P M, today. To be interred at *Oak Hill Cemetery*, Gtwn.

Circuit Court for PG Co, in Equity, No 545. C C Magruder & Saml H Berry, trustees for the sale of the real estate of Saml B Fowler, & Thos E Williams vs Rebecca Bowie & C C Magruder, adms of Fielder Bowie & Rebecca Bowie et al. The suit is to procure a sale of the real estate of which Fielder Bowie, of PG Co, died seized & possessed, for the payment of his debts; & also for a decree to assign & allot Rebecca Bowie, his widow, her dower in said real estate. The bill states that Fielder Bowie, late of PG Co, Md, departed this life in May, 1866, being possessed of a valuable personal & real estate; that he died indebted to the cmplnts & divers other persons; that he owed at the time of his death to the said C C Magruder & Saml H Berry, trustees for the sale of the real estate of the Saml B Fowler, three judgments recovered in the Circuit Court for PG Co, each for the sum of $2,096, rendered at the Apr term of this Court, 1866, with interest on each from Oct 2, 1861, & costs. That he owed to the said Thos E Williams upon his single bill dated Sep 10, 1862, $249.38, payable on demand; & that he was indebted, as aforesaid, to divers other persons in large amounts; that the said Fielder Bowie died intestate, & at the time of his death left a widow, Rebecca Bowie, & the following persons, his only heirs-at-law, to wit: Mary Reed Grayson, Beverly Grayson, Wm Spence Grayson, & Letitia Grayson, the children of Chas Grayson, deceased, who was a half-brother to the said Fielder Bowie, all of whom are minors, non-residents, & beyond the jurisdiction of this Court. The bill further states that the said Fielder Bowie died seized & possessed of a tract of land lying & being in PG Co, containing about 230 acres, which he purchased of the said cmplnts, C C Magruder & Saml H Berry, trustees for the sale of the real estate of Saml B Fowler, as aforesaid, & for the purchase money of which real estate the 3 judgments were recovered as aforesaid; & also of the following tracts & parcels of land lying in the county aforesaid, called *Eversfield's Map of Italy*, containing about 327 acres; *Page's Rest*, containing 50 acres; & a part of *Red House Field*, containing 40 acres; that letters of administration on the personal estate of the said Fielder Bowie have been granted by the Orphans Court of PG Co, Md, to the said Rebecca Bowie & C C Magruder, who have possessed

themselves of the same. It futher charges that the personal estate of the said Fielder Bowie is insufficcient for the payment of his debts, & prays that the said administrators may account for said personal estate in said court & apply the same to the payment of the debts of the said intestate; that a decree may be passed by the court to assign & allot dower to the widow as aforesaid, in the said real estate of the said deceased, by com'rs, to be appointed by the court, & that a decree may be passed for a sale of the residue of said real estate or as much thereof as may be necessary for the payment of the creditors of the said Fielder Bowie, according to their respective rights, privities, & liens, & for general relief. Absent dfndnts are to appear in this Court in person, or by solicitor, on or before Nov 6 next.
–Fred'k Sasscer, Clerk for PG Co.

Pension Ofc, Jul 25, 1865. Application having been made under the act approved Jun 23, 1860, for the re-issue of Land Warrants, described therein, which are alleged to have been lost or destroyed, notice is given that at the date following the description of each warrant, a new certificate or warrant of like tenor will be issued, if no valid objection should then appear. No 40,400, for 40 acres, issued under the act of Sep, 1850, in the name of Jane Agnew, widow of Saml Agnew, & was granted Feb 12, 1852. Aug 11, 1866. No 95,290, for 160 acres, issued under the act of Mar 3, 1855, in the name of Judith, widow of David Fuller, & was granted Oct 20, 1860. Jul 14, 1866. -Jos H Barrett, Com'r

The class at West Point for the year 1866 was graduated on Monday. Class according to general merit, Jun 18, 1866:

1-Adams, H M
2-Mercur
3-Davis, C E L B
4-Green
5-Weeden
6-Wheelen, G M
7-Woodruff
8-Quinn
9-Lockwood
10-Butler
11-Soule
12-Wright
13-Churchill
14-Smith, C S
15-Herr
16-O'Hara
17-Kilbourne
18-Merrill
19-Dunwood
20-Craig

21-Dixon
22-King
23-Eastman
24-Webster
25-Upham
26-Orr
27-Hills, E R
28-Swift
29-Hills
30-Webster, G O
31-Brown
32-Payne
33-Campbell
34-Stretch
35-Neff
36-Fleming
37-Umstaetter
38-Moberly
39-Thompson, J C

Ice-Cream: G Brengle, 373 D st, between 8th & 9th sts. Manufactured from Pure Country Cream, received fresh every day, the purest & best, $1.50 per gallon.

Dr L Draper [late assist surgeon U S navy,] has removed from 430 Carroll Pl, to 122 Pa ave, between 19th & 20th sts. Dr Draper will attend to calls in the country, as well as in any part of the city.

Orphans Court of Wash Co, D C. In the case of Rebecca S Gillis, admx of Jas M Gillis, deceased, the administratrix & Court have appointed Jul 14 next, for the final settlement of the personal estate of the said deceased, of the assets in hand. -Z C Robbins, Reg/o wills

U S District Court at Montgomery, on Jun 11, an indictment for treason was read against Judge Wm G Jones. The indictment sets forth that the accused did, in Dec, 1860, in connection with Jeff Davis, Judah P Benjamin, & divers others, conspire to obstruct the execution of the laws of the U S, & attempt to overthrow said Gov't, by inciting to & organizing armed resistance & insurrection, etc. Other indictments were also found for conspiracy, & a true bill was also found against G W Gayle, T S Casswell, & J A Works, for complicity in the assassination of Pres Lincoln.

Edgar Welles, a son of Sec Welles, has been appointed Chief Clerk of the Navy Dept, in place of Mr Faxon, recently appointed Assist Sec of the Navy.

FRI JUN 22, 1866
Mr Mitchell H Miller, late Trustee of Public Schools, who had been ill for some months past, & who had just started for Texas on a tour for his health, died at Matagordas, whence his body will be brought to this city, & the funeral services will take place at Dr Smith's church this afternoon. [Board of Trustees: Sympathy to his widow.] The funeral of Mr M H Miller will take place at 4:30 P M, from the Ninth St Presbyterian Church. [No death date given-current item.]

Mrd: on Jun 20, at the parsonage of the M P Church, Navy, in Wash City, by Rev Jas Thompson, Mr T Theodore Frazier, formerly of Balt, Md, to Miss M Isidore Darnall, formerly of Alexandria, Va.

Mrd: on Jun 21, at the residence of the bride's mother, by Rev C H Hall, Wm H Grevemeyer, of York, Pa, to Miss Bertha McPherson, daughter of the late H H McPherson, of Wash City.

Died: on Jun 20, Rebecca, widow of the late John L Fowler, in her 65th year. Her funeral is this afternoon at 3 o'clock, from her late residence, 600 7th st, between D & E, Island.

Died: on Jun 21, Sallie M, infant daughter of Wm H & Anna E Johnson, aged 2 years, 7 months & 21 days. Her funeral will take place from the residence of her parents, 353 5th st, this afternoon at 4 o'clock.

Navy Yard Affairs. 1-Yesterday, Mr Chas Osborn, a wheelwright, whilst using a circular saw, had his left hand struck & so mutilated that he has lost 3 entire fingers & the 2 first joints of the index finger. 2-Shortly after noon, Mr John Neenan, whilst engaged handling goods in the naval store, made a misstep & fell through the hatchway about 12 feet to the next floor. Although able to stand up & walk with some assistance, it is feared he is severely injured internally. 3-The fine steamer **Swatara**, Lt Cmder Jeffries commanding, having been fully fitted out, has left for service in the Gulf squadron

Phil, Jun 21. Madame Julie de Marguerrites, a well known dramatic critic, & authoress of various works, died suddenly this morning of heart disease. She was for many years a writer for various journals in N Y & elsewhere. Her daughter recently made her debut on the stage in Balt.

SAT JUN 23, 1866
Hon Anson Burlingame has purchased a tract of land near San Mateo, containing 1,100 acres, & purposes to become a resident of Calif as soon as his mission to China is ended.

Dick Turner, the turnkey of Libby Prison, who has been in confinement since the fall of Richmond, was released on Monday by order of the Sec of War.

Fire last night in the cellar of the store of John T Foster & Co, on 8th, near Pa av. The fire was undoubtedly the work of an incendiary.

Fortress Monroe, Jun 20. On Jun 16, a Mr Woodward, while riding to Edenton, N C, was met on the road by a negro highwayman, who demanded his money & valuables, fired a pistol 3 times at him, shattering his arm & wounding him in the breast, after which he was badly beaten on the head. The negro obtained only $10. Mr Woodward, recovering so far as to return home, the negro was soon arrested & lodged in jail.

Executor's sale on Jul 26 of the private residence of the late Dr Benj B Hodges, adjoining the lands of Greenbury Watkins, Saml B Anderson, & Jos H Bradley. The farm is in the lower part of Montg Co, Md, a short distance from the District line, immediately upon the 14th st road, 4 miles out of Wash. The farm contains 180 acres of land; the dwlg house contains 6 rooms; all necessary out bldgs in good order. Inquire of Wm R Riley & Bro, Wash, D C, or to S T Hodges, Rockville, Md. [If not disposed of by private sale prior.]

Died: on Jun 4, at Floradale Plantation, Morengo Co, Ala, in his 61st year, Geo D Spencer, formerly of Wash, D C. Balt Gaz please copy.

Died: on Jun 23, in Gtwn, Lilly A, only daughter of C T & M A Edmonston, aged 1 month & 16 days. Her funeral will take place today at 5 o'clock, from the residence of her father, on Lingan st.

The Philodermic Society of Gtwn College having heard of the death of its old & distinguished member, Rev Dr Pise, sincerely condole with his bereaved family. -Chas C Homer, Arthur Lee, Chas S Abell, cmte

Orphans Court of Wash Co, D C. In the case of Chas H Poor & Wm A Poor, excs of Charlotte Poor, deceased, the executors & Court have appointed Jul 14 next, for the final settlement of the personal estate of the said deceased, of the assets in hand. -Z C Robbins, Reg/o wills

Augusta, Jun 22. 1-Wm Burns, a citizen, & John Jackson, a freeman, were hung here today in accordance with the sentence of a court martial for the murder of Chas H Tew, near Marieta, Ga, last Oct. 2-Lafayette Laws, who was a general in the Confederate army, recently elected clerk of the Superior & Inferior Court of Richmond Co, has received an order from Gen Tillson, commanding the post, forbidding him to hold or exercise any civil or political office. The order is similar to that served on Capt Semmes, received from the Sec of War.

John Augustine, of Carondelet, Mo, was brutally murdered on Jun 17 by a desperado, John Lane, who was arrested & sent under strong guard to Waterloo. The citizens became infuriated over the murder, & incited by the fact that Lane had murdered a woman & child 2 years ago near the same place, overtook the guard, & taking Lane out of the wagon, hung him to a tree, dug a hole in the ground near by, & when he had died, hastily cut him down, & threw the body into it, covering it with earth & a pile of stones.

MON JUN 25, 1866
Springwood Select Home School for Young Ladies, located near Leesburg, Loudoun Co, Va, reopens Oct 1, 1866. Apply to G Washington Ball, Springwood, Loudoun Co, Va.

Orphans Court of Wash Co, D C. Letters testamentary on the personal estate of Geo E Curtis, late of Gtwn, D C. —Chas M Matthews, exc

Supreme Court of D C, No 585 Equity Docket 7. Robt Ball, jr, et al vs Francis E Dyer et al. Robt Ball, trustee, reported sales in the above entitled cause, & the same to be ratified & confirmed. –R J Meigs, clerk [No other information.]

David Adams & his son, age 18, were indicted for assault & battery at the recent term of the Court of Common Pleas of Wood Co, Ohio. After the finding Adams & the boy returned home, went to the woods, & a neighbor saw them suspended to a tree, cut the bodies down, & after much effort brought the boy to life. The father was dead.

Died: on Jun 24, Andrew Johnson, aged 2 months, son of Emeline & J C Baum. His funeral is this afternoon at 4 o'clock.

Died: on Jun 24, Abraham Kendall Bohrer, the son of Geo A & Catharine Bohrer, aged 15 years. His funeral is on Tue next at 4 P M, from his father's residence, 11th & G sts.

Died: in Jun 22, at his late residence, in the Forest, PG Co, Md, Grafton Tyler, in his 79th year. His remains were followed to the grave on Sat, by his family & a large concourse of friends & neighbors.

Obit-died: on Jun 23, at the residence of her grandson, Goodwin Yorke At Lee, near Wash City, Mrs Margaret Snyder, widow of the late Edwin Augustus AtLee, M D, of Phil, in her 87th year. Her remains will be buried in Phil. She was the mother of S York AtLee, of Wash City, & a niece of Simon Snyder, formerly Gov'r of Pa, & a native of Lancaster Co, Pa.

TUE JUN 26, 1866
Hon W Dennison, Postmaster Gen, is absent from Wash City, on a visit to Ohio, where he will remain 8 to 10 days. The excessive labors of his ofc have been so fatiguing that a period of rest is an absolute necessity to his health.

John Cruikshand was yesterday admitted an atty & counsellor in the Supreme Court of D C, having obtained a certificate of graduation of the Columbian College Law School.

Miscellaneous Items:
1-Isaac Scholfield, a well-known merchant of Boston, died on Monday, aged 56 years. 2-Francis Bush, of the firm of Bent & Bush, hatters, Boston, was drowned on Thu night by the upsetting of a boat off South Boston Point. 3-Dr F N Burke, a well-known Irish born physician, of Cincinnati, has just returned from a protracted visit to his native land.

Mrd: on Jun 21, at the residence of & by Rev E H Gray, chaplain U S Senate, W L Cowan to Mary E N Cross, both of Wash City.

Mrd: on Jun 24, at the pastor's residence, St Peter's, Capitol Hill, by Rev Fr Boyle, Thos B Cross, jr, to Kate M Taltavull, both of Wash City.

Died: on Jun 19, in Port Huron, Mich, Jennie, wife of Col Geo Clendenin, jr, in her 22nd year.

Died: on Jun 25, John M Maher, son of P Maher, aged 8 years & 11 months. His funeral will take place from Va ave, near 22nd st, today at 4 o'clock.

Died: on Jun 25, in Norfolk, Va, at the residence of his grandfather, Mr John M Donn, Ernest, infant child of Edw W & Laura J Donn, aged 16 months & 1 week. His funeral will be from the residence of his parents, 8th st, between K & L sts, this evening at 5 P M.

Orphans Court of Wash Co, D C. In the matter of the ptn for sale of real estate of orphans John A Cassell, deceased. Jas E Williams, guardian, who was authorized to execute the unexecuted part of a decree passed authorizing Alfred C Cassell, the former guardian to sell certain real estate, having on Jun 12, 1866, reported the sale on May 21, 1866, of all the right, title, & estate of Washington F J & Wm M Cassell, orphans as aforesaid, in & to the unsold portion of lot 2 in square 463, in Wash City, to John H D Richards, for $2,806, that being the proportion of said wards in the said estate, & that the purchaser has complied with the terms of sale. –Wm F Purcell, Judge of Orphans Court -Z C Robbins, Reg/o wills

Recently on the Norwich, Conn railroad, a high wind blew a car from one track onto another causing a freight train to collide with it, Tyler Peck, a fireman was killed, & Frank Greenwood, another employee, was terribly scalded. The train was smashed up.

WED JUN 27, 1866

At Hudson, Mich, on Jun 14, a girl name Josephine Smith, 13 years of age, made an attempt upon the life of her father by putting arsenic in his tea. She says she was persuaded to give the poison to her father by her brother & sister-in-law; that her sister-in-law told her that her father had money, & that she could put the old man out of the way & marry a young man to whom the old man was opposed; that her brother gave her the money, & that she bought the poison at a drugstore.

The funeral of Gen Cass took place at Detroit on Jun 20. The pall-bearers were Hon Robt McClelland, Hon Rose Wilkins, Hon John Owen, E Chapston, Hon B F H Witherell, Hon Shubael Conant, & Hon Geo E Hand. Sermon by Dr Duffield. The body was placed in a stone sarcophagus at *Elmwood Cemetery*, by the side of his wife & daughter. Masonic ceremonies were performed over the grave by Hon S C Coffinberry, grand master of the State.
+
It is stated that Gen Cass' large fortune of four or five millions of dollars had its origin in his fortunate investment in real estate in what is now the heart of the city of Detroit; & the heirs of the deceased statesman may thank the late Mrs Cass, who died in 1855, for the great wealth they inherit. Repeatedly, when the property was rising in value years ago, the Gen was anxious to sell, & was only restrained by the earnest advice & remonstrance of his wife.]

A monument in memory of the late Hon Owen Lovejoy, has just been erected over his grave at Princeton, Ill. The cube contains on the front side, [besides other inscriptions of members of the family,] Owen Lovejoy, born January 6, 1811; died March 25th, 1864.

On Jun 12, the Princess Mary, one of the popular princesses of the royal family, was married at the village church at Kew to his Serene Highness Francis Lewis Paul Alex'r Prince von Teck, a prince among the nobility of Hungary, & lately an ofcr in the Austrian service. The ceremony was unattended by any kind of State pageantry or pomp. Except for the presence of the illustrious visitors who graced it. The Queen arrived, leaning on the arm of the Duke of Cambridge. She was attired in the very deepest mourning, not a speck of white relieved its sombreness.. With her Majesty came their Royal Highnesses Prince Arthur, Princess Helena, & Princess Louisa. Both princesses were dress in blue silk trimmed with white. The four bridesmaids were Lady Georgiana Susan Hamilton, 5th daughter of the Marquis of Abercorn, K G; Lady Cornelia Henrietta Maria Churchill, eldest daughter of the Duke of Marlborough; Lady Cecilia Maria Charlotte Molyneux, only daughter of Lady Sefton, & Lady Agueta Harriet York, youngest daughter of Lord Hardwick.

Mrs Herron, in Noble Co, Ohio, a few days since gave birth to 4 children within as many hours, the four weighing 12 pounds. They died shortly after their birth. One hundred & fifty dollars has been raised to erect a monument over their graves.

The Tallahassee [Fla] Sentinel states that Maj John E Gee, who has been on trial at Raleigh, N C, has been acquitted. Telegram to his wife: Raleigh, N C, Jun 16, 1866. Mrs Mary Holland: he is triumphantly aquitted. About 3 weeks yet before official order for discharge can come from Washington. D P Holland.

Indianapolis, Jun 24. 1-On Fri at Edinburg, Johnson Co, Martha Bennett, a married lady, was shot 5 times with a pistol, then beat over the head, & the fiendish murderer finished his horrible deed by setting fire to her clothes. 2-A young man named John Kerns was arrested last night at Buffalo, & brought here, who had embezzled $800 from his employer, C F Schmidt, brewer, of this city.

Jas M Winslow, of St Paul, Minn, offers to build a hotel costing $200,000 in that city, if the citizens will furnish a site & $20,000 bonus.

Orphans Court-Judge Purcell. 1-J B Adams has been appointed guardian to the orphans of Dennis Dennbond $2,200. 2-Letters of administration have been issued to Catherine E Ryan on the estate of John Ryan, deceased-bond $1,000.

Died: on Jun 25, in Gtwn, D C, Charles, infant son of Charles & Kate B Sutherland, aged 6 months.

Died: on Jun 25, Katherine Sandford, infant daughter of J E & Kate S Hilgard, aged 8 months. Her funeral is this evening at half-past five o'clock.

Peekskill, N Y, Jun 25. This afternoon the gravel train was thrown from the track, killing C B Wheeler, the conductor, & 3 laborers, & wounding several others.

New Albany [Ind] Ledger, 29th. Yesterday 3 men entered the house of Jos Woodward, residing about 2 miles from Orangeville, & killed Woodward, his wife, & his sister, & attempted to kill Woodward's mother, an old lady, inflicting upon her wounds from which it is thought she cannot possibly recover. The old lady was alive at 10 o'clock this morning & said there were 2 or 3 men, one of whom was a tall, heavy man, & had on a large blue overcoat. They were disguised. The murderers left the premises, & no trace of them has since been obtained. They were there to obtain a sum of money which it was thought Woodward possessded. [Jul 3rd newspaper: David Woodward & his family consisted of himself, his wife, 3 children, sister, & mother, resided upon a farm in Northwest township, Orange Co, 8 miles from Orangeville. They were very poor, but hard working & honest. Wm Sanders, [the murderer of the Woodwards,] to get revenge on another neighbor had his daughter fire his neighbor's house, & after doing the deed, passing Woodward's, she told him what she had done. He made the fact public & Sanders & his daughter were arrested & held to bail. On Jun 19th Sanders went to the door of Woodward's house, rapped loudly upon it, & Woodward got out of bed, went to the door, opened it, & Sanders immediately struck him in the face with the edge of an axe, stabbed him 5 times, producing almost instant death. The murderer went to the bed in which Mrs Woodward was lying & stabbed her 9 times; he stabbed Woodward's sister 7 times & she fell dead at his feet. Sanders then attacked the old lady, Woodward's mother, stabbing her in the breast. She sank to the floor, & supposing her dead, the murderer left the house. Sanders did not see the infant or the little girl that ran out of the house. Woodward's mother had the little girl go to a neighbor's a half mile down the road to tell them that they had all been murdered. Sanders was captured on Wed.]

Forty persons poisoned by eating cheese: in Fayetteville, in the town of Manlius, Onondaga Co, during the present week. The cause was traced to some cheese sold by a merchant in the village, & made at private manufactory. Mrs Scollard died on Thu, & another, name unknown, died the same night. Dr Wm Manlius Smith, of Manlius, is making an analysis of the cheese. Seven persons in the Scollard family are sick.

Rochester [N Y] Express: on Wed at York Centre, Livingston Co, Hugh McGregor, a man about 33, who had had some difficulty with his brother Greger, was literally butchered by him. The murder was committed with a common axe. The brothers had been together the evening previous at their residence. After they parted, their sister Eliza heard Hugh shout, & found him on the floor bleeding. She went to the house of brother Thomas, so he returned with her, finding Hugh alive, but unable to speak. The murderer was captured near Genesee yesterday, & declared that he had premeditated this murder for some time.

The people of Raleigh, N C, propose to erect a monument over the grave of Andrew Johnson's father, who is buried in that city.

Canadian forces mustered out. Gen Napier, cmder of the Canadian forces, on Friday issued an order mustering out the volunteers called to arm to repel the late Fenian invasion.

Boarding at White Point, Westmoreland Co, Va. Board per day $2.
–Henry B Gouldman, proprietor

Public sale of the **Oak Hill Farm**: marshal, trustee, etc, vs Marshall, adm, in Chancery. Decree in this case granted by the County Court of Fauquier Co, Va, appointing special com'r to make sale of a certain portion of the real estate of the late Thos Marshall, deceased. Sale on Aug 1, on the premises: entire tract of land known as **Oak Hill Farm**, containing 650 acres, divided in proper proportions into Meadow, Upland, & Timber Land. Improvements are a fine large dwlg house with all necessary out-bldgs including a blacksmith shop, mill site, & the lower walls of a mill. Most of the fencing destroyed during the war has been restored. **Oak Hill** lies upon Manasses Gap railroad, within 2½ miles of one depot & 4 of another depot. Mr Shumate, upon the place, will show it.
–W S Barton, special com'r, or R T Barton, Atty at Law, Winchester, Va.
[Sep 21st newspaper: Sale was postponed until Oct 26, 1866.]

Chancery sale on Jul 12, 1866, by decree of the Supreme Court of D C, in equity, dated Jun 20 1866, passed in the cause of Frayser et al vs Crome, No 700-Equity. I shall offer for sale lot 11 & part of lot 12 in square 199, with improvements. Also part of lot 12 in square 454, with improvements. –Asbury Lloyd, trustee
–W L Wall & Co, aucts

Dept of the Interior, U S Patent Ofc, Wash, Jun 23, 1866. Ptn of Wanton Rouse, of Taunton, Mass, praying for the extension of a patent granted to him on Nov 2, 1852, for an improvement in Self-Acting Mules, for 7 years from the expiration of said patent, which takes place on Nov 2, 1866. –T C Theaker, Com'r of Patents

Dept of the Interior, U S Patent Ofc, Wash, Jun 23, 1866. Ptn of L Q C Wishart, of Phil, Pa, praying for the extension of a patent granted to him on Oct 25, 1859, for an improvement in Design for Ornamenting Bottles, for 7 years from the expiration of said patent, which takes place on Oct 25, 1866.
–H C Theaker, Com'r of Patents

The amount of the defalcation of A P Stone, who, while Collector of Internal Revenue in Columbus, Ohio, committed suicide in Aug last, has just been ascertained to be $102,400. Of this the Gov't will lose but $2,400, the sureties of the defaulter being good, collectively, for $100,000, the amount of Mr Stone's bond.

Danl Waldron, Homoeopathic Physician: ofc-400 F st, below 7th. Hours: 8 to 11 A M; 4 to 7 P M.

THU JUN 28, 1866
Volunteer ofcrs mustered out: The Sec of War has order the muster out of the following: Assist Quartermasters:
Col Geo W Lee
Capts:

Danl Stinson	J B Dexter
Chas R Tyler	John B Campbell
Peter Heirtand	John B Whitcomb
J H Tighe	D D Bullock
Thos J Coxe	D H Lentz
Nelson P Plato	F O Sawyer
Chas H Gallagher	A E Comstock
Jas R Delveechie	W J Colburn
G W Wells	C E Bliven
Chas Darrow	Jas R Gilmore
L Whitney	M H Alberger
Wm H D Cochran	Rufus K Case
T W Fry, jr	E B Boyd
Gilbert L Parker	Saml D Childs
A M Cummings	John C Gerard
Ersine M Camp	Henry W Johnson
Patrick Flanigan	Isaac N Mason
Stafford G Lynch	John P Rutherford
W S Gross	W S How
J C Van Duzer	Buell C Carter
R C Clowry	A S Flagg
Robt G Staples	Robt S Lacy
Jas L Trumbull	T F P Crandon
Wm L Wainwright	Stuart Barnes
Edwin J Smith	Horatio A Du Puy

Commissaries of Subsistence:
Capts

H A Darling	John W Bond
G B Newton	Geo C Almey
Chas S Langden	Wm R Tracey
Geo F Thompson	Geo T Barrett

Ofcrs of the Engineers Corps:
Capts: 3
Saml M Eaton   O H Howard
Saml Batchell
1st Lts: 3
Henry Ayers,   Henry W Howgate
J L Holopeter
2nd Lts: 4
Jas H Connelly   A R Taylor
Wm Quinton   Henry Mayell

Judge Advocates:
Majors:
John P Knox
Seth C Farrington
Henry E Bingham
Wm H Coyle

B B Keeler
Wm M Hall
De Witt Clinton

Assist Adj Generals:
Majors:
Finley Anderson
Robt H Ramsey

Wickham Hoffman
Capt L J Lambert

Additional Paymasters:
Majors: Chambers; Baird; G P Sanford

Aide de Camp: Capt F W Gilbreth

List of the graduating class of midshipmen who graduated in Jun, 1866. The names are arranged according to the merits of the graduates:

S N Kane, R I
A L Sprague, N Y
W Maynard, Tenn
R W Cutts, D C
H W Lyon, Mass
J H Dayton, Ind
A Walker, N Y
M E S Mackenne, N J
G M Totten, N J
C S Sperry, Conn
F Curtis, Calif
W Watts, N Y
W W Reisinger, Md
J C Rich, Dwla
Wm S Burwell, Mo
J J Hunker, Ohio
J C Soley, Mass
H C Wisner, Mich
W N Little, N Y
M B Field, N Y
F Harfard, N Y
D Robbin, Ohio
R N Griffen, Pa
G A Baldy, Mich
F W Crocker, Mass
R N Berry, Ky
D A Stewart, Mo
A A Blair, Mo
S W Very, Mass

E W Davis, Pa
T S Williams, Iowa
C H Judd, N Y
R B Peck, Mo
Thos C Ferrell, Ind
G A Bicknell, Ind
J M Taft, R I
S F Clarkson, N Y
M S Day, Mass
N N Manney, Minn
H R Wilson, N J
F McCormick, Md
C L Phillips, Pa
J E Moore, Mass
C C Todd, Ky
R Waterman, R I
G A Norris, Maine
R Phelan, Pa
W J Moore, Va
W H Parke, Va
D S Richards, Pa
Isaac T Morris, N Y
H W McKee, Ky
Frank Turnbull, New Mexico
J G Talbot, Ky
J N Hemphill, Ohio
A B B Lillie, N Y
W R Swissburne, R I
E Woodman, N H

A R Carter N J
H Whelan, Iowa
L W Housel, Pa
E McCormack, Ohio
W H Emory, D C
C T Hutchins, Pa
S M Ackley, Mass
E M Lisle, Pa

B McIlvain, Pa
C B Gill, N H
G W Costar, N Y
W W Gillpatrick, Kansas
Isaac I Yates, N Y
S S Spaulding, at large
C F Arnold, N Y

Criminal Court-Judge Cartier, Jun 27, 1866.
1-Ann Hogan , indicted for grand larceny, found guilty, sentenced to 1 year in the penitentiary. 2-Emma J Cole, colored, convicted of a similar offence, same sentence. 3-In the case of Geo Smith & others, indicted for assault & battery, a nolle prosequi was entered. 4-Mary Boston, colored, pleaded guilty to an indictment charging her with grand larceny. Sentenced to 1 year in the penitentiary. 5-Robt McPherson was acquitted of a charge of assault & battery. 6-Robt Warner was sentenced to 1 year in the penitentiary, convicted of assaulting a colored man.

Circuit Court-Judge Olin, Jun 27, 1866. The libel case of Thos D Anderson vs Thos U Walter, is still being tried.

Fatal railroad accident yesterday, as the train to Newark was passing through Bergen Cut, the fireman Jas Houghton, accidentally fell from the engine railing & broke his neck. He had been oiling the machinery near the front of the engine. He was not missed until the train had passed a long distance beyond the spot. Houghton was only 20 years of age, & unmarried. –N Y Herald

Albany Argus of Tue: Hon Gardner Stow, one of the most honored citizens of Troy, died yesterday. Mr Stow had filled many stations of public trust, & was a man the death of whom Troy will long deplore. His age was 77.

Maj Wm A Hall was arrested a few days ago, by the ofcrs of the secret service division of the Treasury Dept, on the charge of forging the name of Capt W A Snyder, late of the 10th N Y volunteers, to a Treasury draft for $200, or with having aided or abetted to the commission of the forgery. Maj Hall called but one witness, who testified that the endorsement of Snyder's name on the draft was not in Hall's handwriting. Judge Clayton reserved his decision. [Jun 30th newspaper: Maj Hall honorably acquitted.]

J C McGuire & Co, sold lot 7 in square 974, 10th & I sts, to Adam Gaddis, jr, for 6 cents per foot; a 3 story brick dwlg on 12th st between N Y ave & I st, to John L Voigt, for $9,000; lot 20 in squar 451, with brick dwlg, on H st, between 6th & 7th sts, to J C McKelden, for $1,700; lot in square 974, corner 10th & I sts, with a brick dwlg, to Adam Gaddis, for $3,650.

Mrd: on Jun 27, by Rev Dr Sunderland, Geo H Wheeler, of Burlington, Vt, to Miss Lois H McKuen, of Irvington, N J.

Mrd: on Jun 26, at St Aloysius' Church, by Rev Fr Lynch, S J, J Converse Webb, of St Paul, Minn, to Bettie, youngest daughter of the late Eli Duval, of Md. [Balt papers please copy.]

Died: on Jun 27, Thomas Walter, aged 1 year & 2 days, infant son of Cornelia Isabella & Jas T Clark. His funeral will be from the residence of his parents, 7th & D sts, Island, at 4½ o'clock, Thursday afternoon.

Died: on Jun 27, Thos W Burch, aged 49 years, a native of Wash City. His funeral will be from his late residence, 5th st, between G & H sts, at 9½ o'clock A M, on Jun 29.

Died: on Jun 27, infant son of Hon John W & Gertrude A Leftwich, of Memphis, Tenn, aged 2 weeks & 2 days. His funeral is today at 4 o'clock P M, at 394 I st, by Rev Dr Brown.

Admiral Lennock, who recently died in England, at the age of 91, entered the British Navy as capt's servant on board the frigate **Blanche**.

Two weeks ago John Bates & Frank Dunn were arrested in Western Missouri, on suspicion of having been connected with a recent murder. They were both acquitted, but on the same day that they were released a mob of men seized them, & as they have not been heard from since, the supposition is that they were hung. Buchnan Co was the scene of this outlawry, & the greatest indignation is expressed by the community.

Hudson River railroad accident on Jun 26, resulting in the following being killed: C B Wheeler, conductor; Wm Adams, laborer; John McLoughlin, laborer; & Chas Caseles, laborer. Martin Lee, fireman & John Dumiken, badly injured.

Rochester Union of the 22nd: a Minister, *Lindsley, [is the monster's name,] whipped to death his 3 year old, for not saying his prayers. Lindsley justifies his horrid work. He thinks it was his duty to punish the child until his will was broken & he obeyed. Lindsley was arrested & committed to jail in Albion. The citizens of Medina wanted to lynch him on the spot. The murder is the all absorbing topic of Orleans Co. [Jul 2nd newspaper: Mr Lindsley was released on $10,000 bail & was not allowed to stay at his brother-in-law's house, fearing his house will be torn down by an excited mob. The miserable man has against taken up his quarters in the jail at Altion, voluntarily, to escape the public.]
[Oct 2nd newspaper: Mr *Lindsey, the preacher who whipped his daughter so severely that she died, had been indicted for murder in Albion, N Y. He plead not guilty.] [*Note: Two spellings of the name Lindsley/Lindsey.]

Com'r sale of valuable real estate in Culpeper Co, Va. By decree of the Circuit Court of Culpeper, made at June Term, 1866, in the case of Nelson, guardian, vs Nelson, etc. Public auction on Jul 31, the very valuable farm known as *Mulberry Green*, containing 489 acres & 16 poies, in said county, adjoining the Brandy station. –Jas Barbour, Jas W Green, aucts

Grafton Tyler, an old & well-known citizen of Trinity parish, PG Co, Md, died on Friday. His death was communicated to Loudoun by a faithful slave, about the same age, who immediately declared that he would die too, "now massa was gone." He threw himself upon his bed & was found dead a few minutes afterwards. Master & slave, or rather gentleman & freeman, were both buried on Sunday last, being 2 of the oldest inhabitants of the said parish.

FRI JUN 29, 1866

Porf Reuben D Mussey, M D, LL D, died last Thu, in Boston, at the residence of a son-in-law, at age 86, after an illness of 2 years, during the larger part of which time he had been confined to his room. Prof Mussey was a native of N H, & one of the most learned & respected surgeons in New England. He was a member of Rev Dr Webb's Church. -Boston Transcript, Jun 25

Mr Erskine S Allin, U S Armorer at Springfield, Mass, has invented a plan for altering the old-fashioned Springfield musket to a breech-loader.

Dr Robt B Lyne, well known in Richmond, died suddenly at his residence, 23rd & Broad sts, Church Hill, yesterday. Yesterday after talking with his son, at his front door, he returned to his chamber, fell over, & died in a few minutes. His demise is supposed to have been caused by the sudden interruption of the circulation of blood through the heart. Dr Lyne was for a number of years a practising physician; but for a number of years past he pursued the real estate agency & collecting business.

A brilliant wedding took place on Wed in Chicago, at the residence of Stiles Burton, his only daughter being married to Ira Holmes, cashier of the Third Nat'l Bank, by Bishop Clarkson. There were 6 bridesmaids & groomsmen, & the guests exceeded 2,000 in number. The presents were over $10,000 in value. [Daughter's name not given.]

Mr Thos W Burch, for several years past the Assessor of the Fourth Ward, died on Wed at his residence in Wash City. He was 50 years of age.

Capt Philip R Forney, 14th U S infty [a son of Col John W Forney,] was recently tried by court martial at San Francisco, Calif, & dismissed the service. The charges of which Capt Forney was found guilty were disobedience of orders & conduct unbecoming an ofcr & a gentleman. The sentence of the court has been confirmed by the commanding general.

A laborer named Boughman, was found guilty of stealing from the Naval Ordnance Yard. The only excuse he had was that his wages of $2 per day, were too small to live on. Justice Cull committed him to jail for court.

Died: on Jun 28, Willie B T, infant son of Chas H & Sarah V Ker, aged 8 months. His funeral will take be from the residence of his grandparents, 252 7th st, Sat, at 10 o'clock.

Columbian College Commencement: the name of J Howard Goodrich should have been mentioned as the youth entitled to the first prize in the first class; an honor gained by him for 3 successive years.

Gtwn Heights: the northern part of *Tudor Place*, having a front on Congress st of 175 feet, & extending back to Valley st, 334 feet, is offered for sale. It is a rare opportunity for those who desire to erect a residence on these celebrated heights. Application to be made at *Tudor Place*.

Public auction on Jul 25, 20 lots of land, varying from 3 to 10 acres, being a subdivision of the farm of John F Clark, now residing in Balt. Call on Green & Williams, aucts.

Trustee's sale: public auction Jul 12 next, on the premises, by deed of trust from Wm P Wood to me, dated Sep 20, 1865, recorded in Liber R M H, No 14, folios 335 thru 338, on the land records in Wash Co, D C: lot 1 in square D; corner of 4½ st west & Md ave. –Ira Goodenow, trustee -Green & Williams, aucts

Trustee's sale of valuable real estate in Chas Co, & of valuable real estate & personal property in St Mary's Co, Md. By decree of the Circuit Court for St Mary's Co, dated Jun 20, 1866, the trustee will offer at public sale, at the Court House door in Port Tobacco, Chas Co, on Jul 24, tract of land known as part of *Marshall Hall*, containing 398 acres, more or less. This land lies directly opposite to *Mount Vernon*; the bldgs are in good order; the land is level, well adapted to grazing & farming. Sat, Jul 28 next, one tract of land called *Swann's Adventure*, & *Pt Compton's Purchase*, containing 160 acres, more or less. The dwlg house is in good order. One tract of land called *Part of Westham*, & *Westham's Support*, & *Swamp Forest*, containing 240 acres, more or less. Located near the village of *Charlotte Hall*, adjoins the estates of Messrs Posey & Barber; the bldgs consist of a first class barn, & 2 houses suitable for tenants. Also, on lot of land, called *Part of Barber's Inclosure*, containing 40 acres, more or less. –F Stone, trustee

House of Reps: 1-The joint resolution for the relief of Eliz Woodward & Geo Chorpenning was returned from the Senate with amendments, reducing the amounts in one instance from $38,000 to $32,000, & in the other instance from $30,000 to 28,000.

Elias Howe, the inventor & patentee of the sewing machine needle, has declared his purpose not to apply for an extension of his patent, which runs out this year, on the ground that he has made a million & a half dollars on it already, which he regards as fortune enough for one man.

SAT JUN 30, 1866

Judge Lowell, U S District Court at Boston, on Monday, awarded $2,000 each to John B Sheridan & Chas Kelley, who assisted in the capture of the steamer **Deer**, in Charleston harbor, during the rebellion. This decision was given on the ground that though the men did not belong to the navy, & were thus not entitled by the prize laws to their share as captors, still their services were sufficiently meritorious to deserve a generous reward. The case of the steamer **Planter**, which was run out of Charleston harbor by Robt Small, was made the precedent for the decision.

Died: on Jun 29, Charlie N J, the only child of Capt E A & Fannie Ellsworth, aged 13 months. His funeral will take place this afternoon at 4 o'clock, from the residence of his grandfather, S J Diggs, 609 M st.

Com'rs sale of 9 houses, by decree of the Supreme Court of D C, dated Jun 15, 1866, passed in the cause of Foote et al vs Phillips, No 668, Equity: sale on Jul 17 next. -Thos Lewis, Job W Angus, Jos F Hodgson, John T Garner, Wm Dixon, com'rs. -Lloyd & Wilson, solicitors -Green & Williams, aucts

$500 reward for the apprehension & conviction of the murderer of David H White, which murder was committed at Patapsco Bridge, Howard Co, Md, on Jun 10, 1866. -Geo Mattingly Balt Sun will please copy & send bill to me

St Vincent's Orphan Asylum & School-Annual Commencement took place on Thu, Rev Fr Walter & Fr McCarthy, of St Patrick's Church, & Fr Bokel, of St Dominic's, distributed the medals & premiums. Medals were awarded to:

Miss Mary Drane	Julia Green	Kate Reilly
Miss Molly Daly	Annie Green	Anna Becker
Miss Helen Boisean	Minnie Finkman	Jennis McGuigan
Addie Gettie	Margaret Mitchell	Eva Clark
Mary Murray	Mary Rapetti	Rebecca Hunt
Rose Keickhoeffer	Betty Jones	Mary Peak
Anna Claxton	Alice Kirk	Ella Miller
Alice Russell	Emma Herold	Minerva Miller
Maria Lawlor	Estelle Stewart	Annie Carroll
Mary Ennis	Lellia Sheckleford	Cora Waterhouse
Mary Tuttle	Kate Holoham	Frances Daly
Margaret Cleary	Lulia Boone	Johanna Claxton
Mary Crolly	Ida Cherry	Alice Payton
Rose Marll	Josphine Peyton	Maria Drane
Augusta Mead	Teresa Drane	Annie McNeil

Annie Doyle
Mary Riggles
Mary Sullivan
Kate Kickens
Lizzie Coombs
Eva Robinson
Annie Berry
Hilda Lawler
Molly Oyster
Mary Duhamel
Lellia Gray
Ella Clemens
Lullia Sutton
Fanny Payton
Ella Cherry
Fanny Moor
Annie Daly
Eva Little
Margaret Carrol
Mary Perry
Ida Keickhoeffer
Bell Oyster
Nettie Schlosser
Ann M Phillips
Ella McCloskey
Kate Lawlor
Mary Shaw
Agnes Cahill
Lizzie Dove
Bridget Carroll
Mary Schutter
Anna McDevitt
Eva McCarthy
Lotty Kelleher
Clara Harvey
Mary Rollins
Sallie Moore
Bridget Roach
Minnie Shehen
Margaret Nolan
Sarah Offutt
Alice Murphy
Mary A Mack
Mary Bush
Mary Oakes
Lizzie Harris

Margaret Buckley
Fanny Ball
Kate Nolan
Ella Buckley
Margaret Bolan
Emily Jenkins
Teresa Mohony
Alice Russell
Annie Claxton
Jessie Boyd
Mary Crolly
Rose Marll
Laura Whyte
Mary Seibel
Betty Payton
Estella Stewart
Jennie Newmeyer
Ida Cherry
Josephine Payton
Helen Scheckels
Mary Zimmerman
Kate Reilly
Kate Holohan
Agnes Cahill
Annie Becker
Mary Shaw
Kate Lawler
Jennie McGuigan
Julia Keickhoeffer
Eva Clark
Mary Peak
Kate Flanagan
Cora Waterhouse
Anna Carroll
Eva Robinson
Fanny Daly
Maria Drane
Anna Wasney
Margaret Thompson
Mary Venable
Anna Doyle
Mary Newton
Mary Sullivan
Annie McNeil
Hilda Lawler
Kate Richards

Eva McCarthy
Annie McDevitt
Mary Duhamel
Mary Sullivan
Kate Griffin
Emma Ryder
Ella Clemens
Kate Sutton
Mary M Stewart
Julia Darby
Rose Horning
Margaret Keys
Minnie Calvert
Alice Rutherford
Jennie Van Riswick
Jennie Byrnes
Mary Ready
Jessie Boyd
Betty Payton
Mary Seibel
Emma Herold
Estelle Stewart
Sarah Murphy
Mary Murphy
Kate Reilly
Marion Williamson
Agnes Cahill
Cora Waterhouse
Eva Clark
Rose Edmonston
Kate Flanagan
Mary Duffy
Eva Robinson
Joanna Claxton
Annie Berry
Mary Newton
Emma Forney
Florence Speak
Kate Dickens
Mary Mankel
Adelia Schlosser
Betty Finkman
J Lockey
Estelle Schutter
Mary Keys
Margaret Keys

Ella Gusler	Netty Schlosser	Joanna Burk
Jennie Byons	Mary Rollins	Mary Carroll
Emma Hurdle	Mary Coyle	Mary Bush
Mary Edmonston	Sally Moore	Margaret Nolan
Genevieve Golden	Maggy Shields	Charlotte Ball
Alice Emby	Kate Murphy	Ella Gaunt
Dovey Forney	Mary Pugney	Ella Lloyd
Susan Brown	Mary Rietor	Mary Ockes
Jennie Leslie	Maggy Duffy	Ella Buckley
Laura Davis	Lizzie Golden	Eliza Hennon
Mary Kelly	Ellen Murphy	Alice Shipmen
Anna Loutner	Sarah McGrain	S Goodwin
Edith McPherson	Mary Higgins	Emma Corcoran
Adelia March	Teresa Mohoney	Bridget Dwyer
Clara Rollins	Mary A Sharkey	Honora Madigan
Clara Harvey	Annie Malay	Catharine Farritan
Fanny Moore	Molly Kelly	Katie Cahill
Eulalia Keickhoeffer	Margaret Droyne	Winnie Cahill
Frances Cowling	Mary A Heming	Fanny Gaitley
Ella McCloskey	Katie Cahill	Mary Corbit
Katie Wasney	Kate Moore	Susie Flemming
Mary Connor	Mary I Murry	Mary Boothe
Bridget Morgan	Margaret Towhey	Mary Dacy
Minnie Failes	Annie Flanagan	Dixie Clark
Lizzie Bender	Ella Harrison	Dollie Louisiana
Mary Perry	Mary Mooney	Fanny Gaitley

Mrd: on Jun 20, by Rev Bernard A Maguire, president of Gtwn College, Maj Henry Goodfellow, U SA, to Eleanor, daughter of the late Robt Y Brent.

MON JUL 2, 1866
Hon Robert Burns, formerly a Rep in Congress from the Third N H District, died in Plymouth on the 20th ult.

Orphans Court-Judge Purcell, Jun 30, 1866.
1-The will of the late Mitchel H Miller, which was executed on Mar 31 last, was filed, fully proven, & admitted to probate. The will bequeaths his property to his wife, Sallie C Miller, & children, & also nominates her as executrix. 2-Letters of administration were issued to Saml Norment on the estate of Sophia Harvey; bond $1,000. 3-Jos H Fletcher was appropriated guardian to the orphan of John J Kidwell; bond $1,000. 4-The first & final account of the execs of Eliza G Moreland & Jas V Shields were approved & passed.

Died: on Jun 30, _bert Graham, aged 11 months & 23 days, only __ of Robt H & Sarah E Watkins. His funeral will be this morning at __ o'clock, from the residence of A H Pickrell, 46 3rd st, Gtwn, D C. [Paper was creased.]

Circuit Court-Judge Olin, Jun 30, 1866. 1-The case of Eliz Kelly & Sara Jane Stanley against John H Sessford & Jos Sessford was taken up yesterday. The case arose out of the will of the late Julia Sessford, who bequeathed her entire property to her daughter, Mrs Kelly, with the exception of a legacy of $500, which she bequeathed to her niece, Miss Stanley. The sons of the testatrix fixed a caveat to the will to the effect that it was made with undue influence, & that the testatrix was not of sound mind at the time the will was made. The propounders claimed that the testatrix was of perfectly sound mind at the time she made the will, & denied that there was any undue influence whatever in the matter. A considerable amount of testimony was given on both sides. The case was then fully argued by the Messrs Bradley for the propounders & Mr Norris for the caveators, & his Honor having charged the jury, they returned into court, after a brief deliberation, with a verdict for the propounders.

Circuit Court-Judge Olin, Jun 30, 1866. W H Earness vs Jas Jackson. In this case, which was a suit for goods sold & delivered, a motion was made by Mr Bradley, jr, under the new attachment law, to quash the writ on the ground of its not being within the provisions of the statue. Messrs Jones & Ashford, on the other side, opposed the motion, & in the course of their arguments contended that sufficient notice had not been given of such a motion, & that under the act they should at least have three days notice. The Court granted the motion & the writ was accordingly quashed.

Criminal Court-Judge Cartier, Jun 29, 1866. 1-Richd Jones, alias Richd Grandison, colored, was indicted for grand larceny, having, as alleged, stolen the sum of $52 from an old Frenchman, Stephen Preneau. During the hearing, Mr H C Gooding applied for the prisoner's discharge on the ground of a flaw in the indictment, the prosecutor's name being Preneau, while in the indictment it was Treneau. His Honor left the matter to the jury, who acquitted the prisoner.
2-In the case of Edw Gotchill, indicted for an assault & battery, a nolle prosequi was entered.

Green & Williams, aucts, sold the estate of the late Com Wadsworth, 12th & K sts, [**Franklin Row**,] a brick dwlg & lot, to E Green, for $17,000; brick house & lot, 8th & Md ave, to Ferdinand Lambrick, for $5,975; a 2 story brick house & lot on N J ave, between F & G, to L Fleming, for $1,850; small frame house on D st, between 3rd & 4th sts, to H T Litchfield, for $1,035; small frame house, 1st & N st, to John Forrest, for $480; 2 story small brick house, in Oregon alley, to Thos Dunawin, for $1,007; 2 story brick house on B st, between N J ave & 1st st, to R W Bruff, for $2,050; part of lot 10 in square 813, on G st, between 5th & 6th sts, to John H Gordon, for 19½ cents per foot; east part of same to A D Collingsworth, at 13 cents per foot.

Died: on Jun 30, Louis, wife of Jacob Veihmeyer, in her 42nd year. Her funeral will take place from 531 13th st, [Island,] on Jul 2 at 11 o'clock.

Died: on Jul 1, after a painful illness, Mary Eliz, 2nd daughter of Capt Frank H & Susan Denin Barroll. Her funeral is today at 4 P M, from 298 Pa ave.

Alfred Tonant, a well known fireman, & extraman of the Franklin steam fire engine, No 2, was drowned yesterday, in the Potomac, off Glymount, when he attempted to leap from a sloop into the yawl behind, but missed his footing & fell into the water. After some difficulty he was rescued. He againt attempted the leap, struck against the boat, injured himself, & he sunk to rise no more. Mr John Magaw could only clutch the hair of Tonant's head; Patrick Riley leaped into the water to rescue Tonant's body. Tonant was about 24 years of age, a native of Wash, & resided on D st, between 14th & 15th.

Last night N Lewis, an extra conductor on the Avenue line, attempted to leap from the front platform of the car & was caught between the wheels, one wheel passing over his stomach. Lewis expired in about a half an hour. Lewis was a married man & resided in Purdy's court, near 1st & Pa ave. He had been sick & was yet very weak. At first the man's name was given out as Davis, & Mrs Davis was conveyed the information, after which caused a possible bad effect, as she is in delicate health.

An alleged gift enterprise swindle. A man named Nathan A Dyar, a trader in this city, was brought before the Police Court a day or two ago, by complaint of John G Wallace, on the charge of embezzling 14 pianos, valued at $5,000, belonging to Mrs Mary M Ladd, admx of the estate of Albert W Ladd. A draft of $5,000 was marked good on the back, & signed & accepted by one of the alleged partners of Dyar, Geo W Chadwick, of Hoboken, Vice Pres of the bank. The pianos were delivered, some to the Fitchburg depot. The prosecution assert that they have ample evidence that the North River bank is wholly bogus, & that within the past 30 days hundreds of thousands of dollars of these drafts have been accepted by Chadwick & issued by Dyar, in payment for any kind of merchandise. Decision reserved until tomorrow. –Boston Herald, Fri

Died: on Jun 30, Jane, wife of Harrison Clay Williams, in her 20th year. Her funeral is today at __ o'clock, from the residence of the family, on C st, between 6th & 7th sts.

Jared Ingersol, of Phil, has pleaded guilty to purloining books from the Mercantile Library of that city, & further admitted that he had robbed other libraries. The books were sold for waster paper. The librarian testified that $10,000 worth of books had been lost in this manner.

A new <u>Catholic Cathedral</u> is about to be erected in Boston. It will occupy the square bounded by Wash & Union Park sts, Harrison ave, & Malden st, & will not be finished for at least 5 years.

Augusta, Ga, Jun 30. Dr H Eaton was murdered by freemen in Camden Co recently. The civil authorities attempted to arrest the murderers, but were successfully resisted by a negro mob. 2-Horrible murder on Wed at Station 15, on the Ga Central railroad. Two freedmen butchered Mrs Rollins, her 2 children, & a negro girl, killing the former, & leaving the three latter without hope of recovery. One of the murderers had been arrested at Macon.

The subscriber, atty for the owner, offers for sale the valuable estate, *Key's Quarter*, in PG Co, Md, containing 773 acres of land; bldgs are new & convenient. –John Brooke, atty, Upper Marlboro, Md.

Buffalo, Jun 29. The Grand Jury presented indictment against the following Fenian prisoners today:

Captured at Buffalo:

Judge O'Niel	Lawrence Shields	John F Geary
Owen Starr	Michl Conlon	John McGuire
John Hoy	Timothy O'Leary	R Fitzpatrick
John Spaulding	Philip H Mundy	P H Tyrrel
Wm Smith	John M Fogarty	Jas H Roche

Captured at Malone:

Michl C Murphy	Jas H Heffernan	Jas T Riley
W H Lindsley	Terence Quinn	Alex'r C Eason

Supreme Court, D C, Equity, 402, Docket 7. Jas M Clayton et ux vs Harriet Williamson et al. Report of the said sale of the said estate be ratified & confirmed. –R J Meigs, clerk [No details given.]

Cleveland, Jun 29. McConnell, the murderer of Mrs Colvin, in Olmstead, Ohio, last spring, has been found guilty of murder in the 1st degree.

Dissolution of copartnership under the firm of Killen & Havenner, 413 H st, by mutual consent. –Geo Killen, C W Havenner. The business will hereafter be carried on at the same place as Havenner & Hyde. –C W Havenner, Hosea Hyde

Miscellaneous Items:
1-Dr John Kenifick, a prominent citizen of Charleston, S C, died of apoplexy on Thu. 2-Mrs Senator Sprague & her sister were presented to Queen Victoria on Jun 9. 3-Jas W Goff heads the list of income in Cincinnati with $1,08,957. 4-M Paul Dupont employs 1,200 people in his Paris printing establishment. 5-The statue of Cleopatra, by W W Story, has arrived in N Y, & will adorn the residence of Paran Stevens. In Fifth ave.

The Pope lately visited the works in progress on *Mount Palatine* to excavate the site of the ancient palace of the Caesars. He expressed a desire to form a large museum of all the objects of art or curiosities which might be secured from the remains.

Miscellaneous Items:
Charlotte Cushman will shortly celebrate her 60th birthday; Fanny Kemble is in her 49th year; Kate Batemen is 24; Julia Dean in 35; Madame Celeste is 61; Mrs John Wood is 36; Julia Bennett Barrow is 41; Ada Isaacs Menken, 27; Avonia Jones, 28; Kate Reigneld, 27. Mrs Vernon is nearly 70; Mrs J H Allen is 22; Madeline Henriques is 20, & is the youngest leading lady on the stage. Parepa is 38; Miss Hosmeris is 26; & Maggie Mitchell is 30.

TUE JUL 3, 1866
Hon Jas H Lane, U S Senator from Kansas, committed suicide yesterday. He shot himself through the head. He was born in Indiana, & was a Rep in Congress from 1853 to 1855; settled in Kansas & took an active part in politics. He had been in ill health for some weeks, & was accorded leave of absence from the Senate for the remainder of the session. It is not, we believe, the only case of the kind in his family. [Jul 4th newspaper: Leavensworth, Jul 2. While riding last evening with his bro-in-law, Mr McCall, & Capt Adams, brother of his son-in-law, he got out of the wagon, which stopped at the gate of the Gov't farm, the residence of McCall, & stepping to the rear, drew a pistol & shot himself in the mouth, the ball passing out through the top of his skull. He is the third member of the family who has committed suicide.] [Jul 5th newspaper: Leavenworth, Jul 5. Hopes are now entertained that Gen Lane will recover. He seemed much better tonight. He is conscious & able to speak.] [Jul 13th newspaper: Leavenworth, Jul 11. Gen J H Lane died at noon today. His remains will be taken to Lawrence for interment. There are 34 candidates for the vacant Senatorship.] [Jul 14th newspaper: Lawrence, Kansas, Jul 13. In consequence to the rapid decomposition of the remains of Gen Lane, the remains were buried today.]

<u>Annual commencement of the Academy of the Visitation took place Jul 2. The President of the U S was present, & aided in the distribution of the premiums.</u>
Premiums to:

Mary Newcomer	Mary Cannon
Anna Abbot	Virginia Cochrane, D C
Mary Conrad	Annie Shirley, D C
Angela Montero	Annie Abbott, D C
Bessir Horner	Annie Lee
Emma Kidwell	Julia Semmes, of Md
Nora Delany	Cora Reid, of Ark
Florence Dooley	Blanche Ashby, of Va
Georgie Brinkler	Nannie Cockerille, Va
Mary Palmer	Florence Moore, of Va
Bertha Honore	Josephine Dowell, of Va
Josie Dickson	Virginia Makall, of Md
Louise Smith	Ella Kent, of Md
Mary Newcomer	Louisa Myrick, of Ga
Emma Cockran	Mary Myrick, of Ga

Capt Richd D Silliman died in Troy, N Y, on Wed, aged 75 years.

Wm W Boyce, Atty at Law: 453 14th st, Wash. [Ad]

Two enlisted men, Patrick Sweeny & Michl McCauley, on Friday last, of the Alleghany Arsenal, in Lawrenceville, Pa, were injured, when a 15 pound percussion shell exploded. Sweeny will doubtless die. There are prospects that McCauley may recover.

Mrd: on Jun 28, at St Aloysius Church, Wash City, by Rev B J Maguire, S J, Maj Henry Goodfellow, U S A, to Eleanor, daughter of the late Robt Y Brent, of Wash.

Mrd: on Jul 1, by Rev R J Keeling, D D, Mr Christopher Florence to Mrs Mary Himmelway, of Wash City.

Died: on Jul 2, after a short & painful illness, Henry Nelson, son of Thos H & Emma R Harper, aged 10 months. His funeral is this afternoon at 3 o'clock, from the residence of his parents, 593 I st, between 4th & 5th sts.

Died: on Jul 2, Charles H, infant son of Dr Charles H & Sydney A Bowen. His funeral is this evening at 6 o'clock P M, from 452 Mass ave, between 6th & 7th sts.

Foreign Items: 1-An autograph of Cromwell at a recent sale in London brought L3, while one of Nell Gwyn brought L1 8s more than Oliver's.

Trustee's sale of valuable real estate in Chas Co, Md, by decree of the Circuit Court for Chas Co, Md: public auction at Patuxent City, on Jul 27, all the real estate formerly owned by Jas T Thomas, consisting of 476 acres of land adjacent to the village of Patuxent; also the store house & lot with a dwlg house thereon, recently built. At the same time & place will be sold the farm called **Simpson's Delight**, containing 330 acres, more or less, with dwlg house & necessary out-bldgs. –R H Edelen, trustee

WED JUL 4, 1866
Hartford Courant, Jun 28. Mrs Ella Walker, residing at 100 Maple ave, English by birth, & her husband, a machinist by trade, resided here for a number of years & have several children. Some months ago a large property, valued at 35 millions of dollars, had fallen to Mrs Walker's father, as a direct heir, & he being dead, that the whole amount belonged to her as his only child. Steps were at once taken to ascertain the truth of this report, & ex-Govn'r T H Seymour was employed to investigate. The result is entirely favorable to Mrs Walker, documents having been received that she will come in possession of this immense property, & she, together with her husband & children, will start for England next week to receive the golden egg.

Annual Commencement of Gtwn College-the first anniversary since peace has come with healing on its wings, & the young men from the east, west, north & south, as in other years, have been permitted to come together for intellectual championship. The list of students at the present time numbers 260, there are but 5 in the graduating class. Order of exercises: Prologue, John T Dickson; Danl F Grant, Michl Wall; Francis J Kieckhoeffer; Chas C Hosmer; Julius Soper; Jos F Edwards; Jose Lanas; Saml M Lawrason; Saml H Anderson; Robt B Wilcox; Noble S Heffar; D Clinton Lyles; Robt M Douglas; Jas V Coleman.

Degree of Master of Arts was conferred on:
Michl Wall, Ireland
Henry Major, A B, N Y
Thos S Rudd, A B, Ky
John W Kidwell, A B, D C
Jas A Murphy, A B, N Y
Dennis R B Sheridan, A B, Mass
Jos A Nolan, D C

Honorary degree of Master of Arts was conferred on:
Henry A Cecil, Ky
Saml J Radcliffe, M D, D C.

The degree of A B was conferred on:
Noble S Hoffar, D C
Louis G Gouley, N Y
Julius Soper, D C
Hugh C Williamson, La
W Tazewell Fox, Va.

Degree of M D conferred on:
Saml A Amery, Md
Adaja Behrend, N Y
Alonzo M Buck, Wisc
Lewellyn A Buck, Maine
Wm M Burchard, jr, Conn
Williams J Henry, Conn
Magnus L Julihn, D C
Richd F Kearney, DC
E S Kimball, Maine
Gillum T Ragan, Ind
Frank Walsh, D C
Columbus J White, D C
R M Whitefoot, Ill
W H Whitely, N J
Thos W Wise, D C
Henry Wheaton, N Y.

Gold & Silver medals or premiums awarded to:
Michl Wall, Ireland
Noble S Hoffar
Louis G Gouley
Julius Soper
Hugh C Williamson
Chas C Homer, Md
Fielder B Chew, D C
Francis J Kieckhoeffer, D C
Jas V Coleman, N Y
Wm F Rudolph, Mo
Algernon C Chalmers, Va
John P Risque, D C
Stephen R Mallory, Fla
Chas A Martin, Ala
Wm A Shorter, Ala
Danl F Grant, Ga
Wm A Hammond, Va
Geo H Fox, N Y
Henry A Seyfert, Pa
Chas S Abell, Md
John B Northrop, Va
Eugene D F Brady, Va;
Chas J Boyle, Mo
Ambrose K Michler, D C
Francis A Cunningham, Pa
Henry B Polkinhorn, D C
Jas W Collins, D C
Chas A Trunnell, D C
Lewis F Wade, Mo
Robt V Simms, D C

Harry Walters, Md
Jas C Ord, Mich
Thos L Oldshue, Pa
Robt M Douglas, Ill
Harry Walters, Md
Chas C Homer, Md
Bladen Forrest, D C
Wm A Hammond, Va
Edw Buckner, Ky
Robt B Willcox, Va
Francis Mix, D C
Alfred N Williams, Va
Stephen R Mallory, Fla
Francis A Cunningham
John M Dickson, Mo
Thos R Allnutt
Henry P Luckett, La
Ambrose K Michler, D C

Fred'k S Williams, Ind
Thos A Badeaux, La
Lewis F Wade, Mo
Henry B Polkinhorn, D C
Jas Clarke, Md
John Lyne, D C
Wm A Hammond, Va
Jas V Coleman, N Y
Thos A Kelley, Pa
Wm A Shorter, Ala
Fendall E Alexander, D C
Jos E Dyer, D C
Lloyd Jones, Miss
Marion B Crownrich, La
Julius Gerring, Va
D Carroll Nicholson, D C
Hugh Caperton, D C

The body of Alfred Tonnet, who was drowned on Sunday in the Potomac, off Glymont, was found yesterday. The flags upon all the engine-houses were at half-mast yesterday.

Last May the headless trunk of a man was found in a forest in Powesheik Co, Iowa, & the head was discovered under a mass of leaves. Last Friday Kirk Vincent was arrested at his home, near Cambridge, Ill, as the murderer. Dr Conway had kept the head in spirits, ready for someone to identify them. He was Claiborne Showers, a former comrade & fellow-traveler of the accused. Vincent was held to bail to await a requisition on Govn'r Oglesby from Govn'r Stone.

Guardian's sale of part of lot 12 in square 80, fronting 20 feet on G st, between 22nd & 23rd sts, on Jul 7. By authority of the Orphans Court of D C, part of the estate of Henry Felson, deceased. –D L Wells & Co, aucts

FRI JUL 6, 1866
Jas W Duncan, late of the Confederate army & in charge of the Andersonville prison, recently tried by a military commission at Savannah, Ga, sentenced to be confined at hard labor for 15 years at **Fort Pulaski**, Ga, for murder in violation of the laws of war.

Mr F A Aiken was arrested a few days ago by Detectives Kelly & Bigly, on a charge of obtaining money from Mr Rudolph Buchly, furniture dealer on 7th st, near H, by false pretences. [Mr J W Clampitt is not now nor has been for months past in partnership with F A Aiken.] Hearing on Saturday.

Died: on Jul 4, Frederick, son of Maria & the late J Fred'k Spencer, aged 12 years & 11 days. His funeral will be from the residence of his mother, 529 11th st, near Ga ave, Navy Yard, this afternoon at 4 o'clock.

Annual Commencement of <u>Gonzaga College</u> last evening. Distribution of Premiums:
Good Conduct: John F Cox; Geo Douglas
Diligence: G Lloyd Magruder; Edw Green
Christian Doctrine: Wm W Boarman; Chas Elliott; Ernest Mudd; Martin O'Connor; Geo Bohn; Fenwick Harvey; John Magee
Premiums to:

W W Boarman	Richd O'Dowd	Geo Repetti
Geo King	John F Cox	Dennis Collins
Geo N Sullivan	John O'Meara	Walter Dennis
Vinton Goddard	John B Brady	Thos A Stephens
Henry Douglas	Henry Bauer	Wm Duhamel
Geo A King	Geo Repetti	Thos A Stephens
Robt Waters	Chas Elliot	Clifford Boarman
John Green	Wm McClosky	Chas Drury
Victor Hyam	Carroll Morgan	Jas Hallinau
Jos Walsh	Adrian Bastianelli	Richd Brown
Patrick O'Sullivan	Wm Tynan	Chas Schaefer
Chas McCardell	Armin Briegleb	Geo Springman

Columbia, S C, Jun 4. Barnwell Rhett, a citizen of this State, was shot yesterday while going to his plantation, near Charleston. About 20 minutes later he fell from his horse dead. A negro man who had expressed strong ammosity against the family is the suspected murderer.

The laying of the corner-stone of the new ***Providence Hospital*** took place yesterday; ceremony by Very Rev Dr Coskery, V G, of Balt, in the absence of Archbishop Spalding, who was unable to be present. Addresses were delivered by Dr Coskery; Grafton, M D; Hon J W Patterson, of N H; Dr Samson, Pres of the Columbian College; Senator Hendricks, of Ind; & Hon B B French, Com'r of Public Bldgs.

Mrd: on Jul 4, by Rev T B McFalls, Mr Thos B Penicks, of Phil, to Miss Sarah J Laurie, the only daughter of John Laurie, of Wash.

Died: on Jul 5, Mr Richd Davis, in his 34th year. His funeral is this afternoon, from the residence of Mr R W Claxton, High st, Gtwn, at 5 o'clock.

Died: on Jul 4, after a long & painful illness of consumption, Isabella V McLane, aged 25 years, 6 months & 15 days, wife of Wm G McLane, & daughter of John & Sarah Holroyd.

Dept of the Interior, U S Patent Ofc, Wash, Jul 2, 1866. Ptn of Lorenzo L Longstroth, of Oxford, Ohio, for the extension of a patent granted to him on Oct 5, 1852, & reissued on May 26, 1863, for an improvement in Bee Hives, for 7 years from the expiration of said patent, which take place on Oct 5, 1866. –T C Theaker, Com'r of Patents

Chancery sale of house & lot near Navy Yard, by decree of the Supreme Court of D C, in the case of Little et al vs Little et al, No 672 equity docket, on May 29, 1866: auction on Jul 26 of part of lot 6 in square 849, fronting 40 feet on Va ave, near T st south, with dwlg thereon. –David A Burr, trustee -Jas C McGuire & Co, aucts

Valuable farm & country seat in the District at auction: that beautiful farm belonging to Capt W A T Maddox, known as **Glen Echo**: contains 101 acres; with a fine roomy dwlg house & kitchen detached, with all necessary out-bldgs, including ice-house. It adjoins the farms of Messrs Pickerd, Ritchie, & Weaver. -Green & Williams, aucts

SAT JUL 7, 1866

Maj Gee, of the rebel army, had charge of the military prison at Salisbury. He was paroled with Johnston's command, but was arrested by the U S authorities, &, after 9 months' imprisonment, was brought to trial before a military court, on the charge of violating the laws of war, in cruel treatment of the Federal prisoners. After a protracted trial, in which many witnesses were examined on the part of the Gov't, Maj Gee was acquitted. Charleston Courier, remarking upon this result, has the following:
1-It was probably true that there was great suffering & mortality at Salisbury; but, as has been state, it was fully established:
First. That every officer connected with that post & prison made every possible effort to supply the prisoners. Second: That they were supplied to the full extent of the ability of the country & the Gov't. Third: That at no time, in no way, was there ever made any difference as to the quantity & quality of supplies furnished them & the Confederate soldiers who guarded them: & Fourth: That their sufferings were caused by the failure of their Gov't to furnish them with proper supplies, by its refusal to exchange them, & by its hostile operations, which rendered it impossible to select a proper place for a prison depot.

Edwin G Webb, formerly editor of the Pennsylvanian, in Phil, died in that city on Wed. At the time of his death he held the office of internal revenue assessor.

Mr Milton Glasgow, a conductor on the train of the Orange & Alexandria railroad, on Wed, at Madison Run Station, while jumping from the cow catcher to adjust a switch, slipped, fell upon the track, & one of his legs was run over & horribly mangled. He was carried to Gordonsville, 4 miles distant, when the leg was amputated, but where he died in the evening.

The Paris papers announce the death of Jos Mery, the celebrated writer, at age 68 years. He was born in Aygulates, near Marseilles, Jan 21, 1798, & made his first appearance as an author in 1820.

Hudson, N Y, Jul 5. On Jul 4, while a party was going to Rogers Island on a picnic excursion in small boats, one of them swamped & Mr Fred'k Gifford, jr, of this city, & Miss Louisa Manlay, of Ottawa, ill, were drowned. Mr Gifford was a respected young business man.

Criminal Court-Judge Cartier. 1-Philip Hyde was found guilty of assault & battery & sentenced to 30 days in prison; he also had 2 other indictments against him for the same offence-one had expired, & the other, he was sentenced to 30 additional days in prison. 2-John Davis was found not guilty of burglary. 3-Catherine Dunne was acquitted for larceny.

Trustee's sale: by decree passed by the Supreme Court of D C, in Equity No 502, in which Zephaniah Jones is cmplnt & Horace Stringfellow & others are dfndnts, dated Jul 3, 1866: sale on Jul 31, on the premises, parts of lot 1 & 12 in square 432, with improvements, well known as the Avenue House. –A Thos Bradley, Wm Y Fendall, trustees -Green & Williams, aucts

Supreme Court of D C, in Equity, Docket 7, No 678. A C Winn vs Mary P Winn et al. Trustees report they have sold to A Gaddis, jr, lot 7, of square 874, for 6 cents per square foot, & lot 6 in said square, with improvements, for $3,650.
–R J Meigs, clerk

Supreme Court of D C, No 500, Chancery. Middleton et al vs Berry et al. Sale reported by John A Middleton & Thos W Berry, to be ratified & confirmed.
–R J Meigs, clerk [No details of sale given.]

Orphans Court of Wash Co, D C. In the case of William Bell, excx of Jas M Smith, the executor & Court have appointed Jul 28 next, for the final settlement of the personal estate of the said deceased, of the assets in hand.
-Z C Robbins, Reg/o wills

Lower Marlboro County. Mr Jeremiah Logan was passing through his oat field when he suddenly trod on a copperhead snake, one of the most venomous species of reptiles found in the State, & in an instant its fangs were embedded in his right leg, causing at the time only a slight tingling pain. The snake then slid out of sight. About an hour later Mr Logan went to his residence because the pain was becoming annoying. Late in the night he died in the most agonizing manner, his leg & his whole person very much swollen, wild & delirous.

Paymaster Paulding has been found guilty of the charges preferred against him, & sentenced to be cashiered, to pay a fine of $5,000, & be imprisoned for 1 year.

Dr Paul Beck Goddard, one of the most eminent physicians of the country, died in Phil on Thursday.

MON JUL 9, 1866
The remains of Rev Theodore Clapp will be removed from Louisville to New Orleans, & a monument erected over them.

The largest income in Chicago is that of G Schuttler, wagon manufacturer, which amounts to $190,771. The second is that of C H McCormick, reaper manufacturer, $153,135.

The N Y Herald of Sat: Eleanor A Jones, a woman who has been living at the house of Mr Ziess, 206 East 10th st, with a Dr August Von Frech, as his wife, committed suicide yesterday by shooting herself with a pistol on the steps of the house 447 Second st. It appears that Dr Frech had taken another wife & deserted Eleanor, refusing to see her or have any explanation with her. Yesterday she was again refused admission, & maddened with jealousy, took her own life. It is believed that it was her intention to kill the Doctor if she could have seen him.

On Sat Mr Saml Wood, one of the drivers employed by the Nat'l Express Co, was delivering leather from his wagon at the door of Thos G Ford's leather store, on 7th st, between G & H sts, when he suddenly fell from the wagon, his head striking the wheel & pavement. He was taken into Mr V Harbaugh's drugstore, where he died in 5 or 10 minutes. His body was removed to the residence of the family of the deceased, on 11th st between O & P sts. He was subject to disease of the heart, that may have been the cause. Dr Eliot, who examined the deceased, found that the fall had broken his spinal cord.

Timothy O'Neal, aged about 24 years, drowned in the Potomac. He had taken some horses to wash them, & afterwards, he entered the river for a bath, when he drowned. The body was recovered & turned over to his relatives, who reside in Oregon alley, between M & N & 6th & 7th sts. An inquest was not deemed necessary.

Green & Williams, aucts, sold a frame bldg & lease of lot at 14th & C sts, to Frear Schmidt, for $700; lot 17 in square 263, on B st, part to J Viehmeyer, for 41 cents per foot-part to Wm Martin, for 45½ cents; a 2 story frame house & lot on 5th st, to Wm T Jones, for $_070; house & lot on 13th st, to John T Coombs, for $2,500; lots 30 & 31, in square 873, on C st, to Danl Atkins, for 15 cents per foot; lots 10 & 11 in square 551, on Q st, to Theodore I Lamb, for 10¾ & 7¾ cents. On Sat J C McGuire & Co, aucts, sold lot 17 in square 567, on N J ave, between F & G sts, to Jas Clark, for 30 cents per foot.

Died: on Jul 5, at his residence in N Y, Geo Bruce, aged 85 years. His funeral will be from Grace Church on Monday afternoon.

Died: on Jul 7, at Culpeper Court House, Va, Francis De Sales, only child of Francis D & Lizzie Cleary, aged 8 months & 8 days.

Died: on Jul 8, Emma E, youngest daughter of Theodore & Ella Wamsley, in her 4th year. Her funeral will be on Jul 9 at 4 o'clock P M, from her father's residence, 278 4th st west.

Mr Geo Bruce, the well-known type-founder, died in N Y on Thu, at age 85 years.

Matthew Gibson & John Stevens were arrested yesterday by Ofcr Coomes on suspicion of being concerned in the robbery of Mr Wheeler's hardware store, on Jul 4.

Orphans Court-Judge Purcell, Jul 7, 1866.
1-Margaret E Sipes was appointed guardian to the orphan children of Henry N Sipes, late of Wash. Bond $6,000; Wm Dixon & Wm Powell co-securities.
2-It was ordered on application that Margaret Sipes be allowed $200 per annum for the board of her ward, Sarah E Sipes. 3-The decree for the sale of the real estate of Dennis Dunn, passed on Jun 30th last, was ratified & confirmed.
4-On application an order was issued authorizing Harriet A Lee, guardian to the orphans Henry & Eliz Felson, to dispose of the rights, titles, interests, & estate of said orphans.

The will of the late Gen Cass had been filed in the Probate ofc. All the property, real & personal, is divided equally among his four surviving children, Lewis Cass, jr, Mrs Mary S Ledyard, Isabella Van Limberg, & Matilda Ledyard; excepting the following specified legacies to former & late personal attendants & confidential business agents. All the furniture in his house to his daughter, Mrs Canfield, & also $10,000 more to this lady, his constant attendant of late years, than to any other of his children; to Wm Foxen, $8,000 in real estate, & $1,000 in cash; to G S Grost, real estate valued at $3,000; to John E Bunt, his brother-in-law, $2,000 in real estate; to Jas C Fitzpatrick & Marcella Blight, $800 each. There are also minor bequests of keepsakes to sons-in-law & grandchildren. His son, L Cass, jr, is appointed executor, & Hon C C Trowbridge & Geo S Frost are designated to divide the property among the heirs.

Balt, Jul 8. The corner-stone of the Church of the Holy Cross was laid today by the Roman Catholic Archbishop Spalding.

Phil, Jul 7. Judge Garrick Mallery, the oldest member of the Phil bar, died yesterday, aged 80 years.

Brookeville Academy, Montg Co, Md: J Durlin Parkinson, A B. Formerly Foundation Scholar of Jesus College, Cambridge, Principal. The school commences on the first Monday in Sept.

Trustee's sale of valuable Wash City lot: by decree of the Supreme Court of D C, in Equity, in the case of White vs McGuire's heirs & others, No 697: sale on Jul 20, of all the right, title, estate of the heirs of John McGuire, deceased, & others interested in & to the following parcel of ground, being part of lot 17 in square 70, in Wash City, with improvements thereon. –Jas Maguire, trustee
-Green & Williams, aucts

Celebration of the Fourth at Hartford, Conn, resulted in the shooting of a daughter of Prof & Mrs Harriet Beecher Stowe, by an unknown boy. The ball passed between the 2 bones of the forearm, half-way between the hand & the elbow, severing a nerve, & very narrowly missed two children of Maj Chapman, who had that moment got out of the same street car. Dr Ellsworth attended the case. Miss Stowe suffered greatly all night, & the doctor says her entire right side was paralyzed on Thu morning. Nobody can tell who fired the shot.

San Francisco, Jul 6. Chang Wow, the first Chinaman ever executed in San Francisco, was hung today for murder.

Dept of the Interior, U S Patent Ofc, Wash, Jul 3. Ptn of D D Allen, of Adams, Mass, praying for the extension of a patent granted to him on Oct 19, 1852, for an improvement in Tool for Cutting Pegs out of Boot Soles, for 7 years from the expiration of said patent, which takes place on Oct 19, 1866.
–T C Theaker, Com'r of Patents

Volunteer officers mustered out under the provisions of Gen Orders No 79, May 1, 1865, from the War Dept, the services of the following named officers being no longer required, they are ordered to be honorably mustered out of the service of the U S, to take effect from the dates set opposite their names:
Aides-de-Camp:
Maj Walter Cutting, Jul 1, 1866
Maj Wm H Lawrence, [brvt brig gen,] Jul 10, 1866
Capt John P Willard, [brvt maj,] Jul 10, 1866
Capt Sanford C Kellogg, [brvt maj,] Jul 10, 1866
Capt W E Blake, [brvt maj,] Jul 10, 1866
Capt Richd F Falstead, [brvt lt col,] Jul 10, 1866
Capt Michl V Sheridan, [brvt maj,] Aug 1, 1866
Capt S W Taylor, [brvt maj,] Jul 10, 1866
Capt Hugh G Brown, [brvt lt col,] Jul 10, 1866
Capt Wm P Wilson, [brvt lt col,] Jul 10, 1866
Maj Oscar A Marks, Jul 1, 1866
Maj Edmund C Bainbridge, Jul 1, 1866
Capt F Ed Crosby, Aug 1, 1866
Assist Adj Generals:
Maj Gustavus M Bascom, [brvt col,] Jul 1, 1866
Maj C C Charlot, [brvt lt col,] Jul 10, 1866
Maj Jas E Montgomery, Jul 10, 1866

Maj Wm Redwood Price, [brvt brig gen,] Jul 10, 1866
Maj C W Armuren, [brvt col,] Aug 1, 1866
Maj T W C Moore, [brvt lt col,] Aug 1, 1866
Capt Theo McGervar, [brvt lt col,] Aug 1, 1866
Capt John Green, [brvt lt col,] Aug 15, 1866
Capt John Williams, Jul 10, 1866
Capt Wm A La Motte, [brvt lt col,] Jul 10, 1866
Capt John S Telford, Jul 10, 1866
Capt Herman A Ulffers, Jul 10, 1866
Capt Martin Norton, Jul 1, 1866
Additional Aides-de-Camp:
Maj Ernest P Toppman, Jul 5, 1866
Maj Verplanck Van Antwerp, [brvt brig gen,] Jul 1, 1866
Capt Geo S Shaw, [brvt maj,] Jul 10, 1866
Capt Wm Korrak, Jul 10, 1866
Capt Adam Badeau, [brvt col,] Jul 1, 1864

Among the American artists at Rome was Wm H Rinehart, sculptor, of Balt. Mr Rinehart left here last in 1858 for the Eternal City, & returned only last week on a visit to his family & friends. He is a native of Carroll Co, where his father now resides. His work of the "Sleeping Children" adorns the lot of Mr Sisson in *Greenmount Cemetery*, & in *Loudon Park Cemetery* a very fine monumental group, composed of four figures, the work of his hands, has been recently erected for Mr Fitzgerald, a well-known & liberal merchant. His "Night and Morning," "Descending to the Bath," & "Indian Girl,' are in possession of patrons of art in N Y. His "Woman of Samaria," perhaps his finest work, is in possession here of a well known art patrion, Wm T Walters, for whom he has also modelled a life-sized figure, now in Munich, to be cast in bronze, & placed in out beautiful *Greenmount*.

TUE JUL 10, 1866
Criminal Court-Judge Cartier, Jul 10, 1866.
1-Chas H Jones was convicted of assault & battery; sentenced to 30 days imprisonment. 2-Milton Kurtz pleaded guilty to larceny: sentenced to the penitentiary for a year. 3-John Weston pleaded guilty to petit larceny: sentenced to 10 days' imprisonment. 4-Julius Wallace, assault & battery: fined $30.

Billard match: champion cue. Mr J H Davis will play at Match Game of Billards, 500 points, carom, with Mr F C Collinsworth, champion amateur of the D C, for A S Brady & Co's champion cue, now held by the latter, at Brady's Gymn, Billard, & Bowling Rooms, La ave, Jul 10. Gentlemen are respectfully invited.

Senate: 1-Cmte on Contingent Expenses of the Senate, reported the resolution to pay to the legal reps of the late Wm Hickey, Chief Clerk of the Senate, $300, to pay his funeral expenses & balance of his salary for the year in which he died: passed.

A duel was fought on Sat last between Maj H C Wall, of the Adj Gen's dept of the late Confederate States Gov't, & Mr D C Mayo, also of the same branch. Maj Schermerhorn, of Henrico, acted in the capacity of a friend for Maj Wall, & Col D W Vowles, of Mo, maintained a like position towards Mr Mayo. They met on the line of the York River railroad, near Richmond. Only one exchange of shots took place, & neither party was wounded, though Mr Mayo, in stepping back after firing, caught his foot in some wiregrass, which tripped him up & threw him down, thereby creating the impression in Maj Wall's mind that he had killed him. The parties then arranged their difficulties amicably & returned to the city in the same hack. –Richmond Times, Jul 9

Mr Geo De Mott, of West Hoboken, died of hydrophobia on Friday. He was bitten by a dog seven weeks ago, & the animal was killed.

Elisha Peek, capt on the reserved list-U S Navy, has just deceased at age 76 yrs.

Died: on Jul 9, after a long & painful illness, Isaac Trunnell, in his 74th year. His funeral will be from the residence of his son, on N st, near 17th, Tue at 2 P M.

Died: on Jul 7, in Hartsville, Bucks Co, Pa, Wm H P Gurley, late of Davenport, Iowa. Mr Gurley was the eldest son of Rev R R Gurley, of Wash City.

Died: at Berkeley Springs, Va, at 8:15 P M, Perry McDonald, son of Mr Perry & Mrs Mary Fuller, aged 3 months & 21 days. [No death date given.]

Died: on Jul 9, in Montg Co, Md, Fannie Wilson, infant daughter of Trner W & Aiwell Wilson. Her funeral will take place from the residence of her grandmother, Mrs Wm E Stubbs, on Jul 10, at 4 o'clock P M.

Awarding of medals & distribution of premiums of the public schools of the 4th District; Mayor Wallach presided. Scholars who received medals & premiums:

Medal Scholars:
Chas E West	Susie Mockabee	Jerry Hepburn
Bettie Robinson	Chas Wright	Harriet Halliday
Willie A Johnson	Chas Sheck	Susie Porter
Belle Halliday	Theodore W Noyes	Wm Hickey
Alceina Brothers	Nellie Lazenby	Barbara Myers
Wmma Wallingsford	Annie Atkins	

Premiums for Best Written Examination:
Thos McArdle	Ellie Dunn	Sarah Baker
Thos W Cridler	Lizzie Riley	Bettie Hazzard
Willia A Korts	Willie S Breck	Ida Barron
Bettie Lynch	Frank Bild	

Premiums for Exemplary Conduct and Punctuality:
Giles Heilprin	Geo W Connor	Geo M Davis
G C Abell	Willie F Dunn	A W Dutton

Lizzie Henning	Sarah Noyes	Morris Wealch
Maggie Pumphrey	Ida Jacobs	Willie Yonson
Katie Wise	Amenia Brown	Henry Butts
Ida Rowe	Clarence Noyes	Jas Thomas
Helen McQueen	Jas Fraser	Willie Barnes
Ellen Halliday	Chas Hoover	Willie Hill
Willie T Wood	Hugo Richter	J Washington
Thos F Taylor	John Taylor	Bradburn
Robt W Hinton	John Davis	Laura Skidmore
Henry Bradley	Willie Luff	Jas Posey
Patrick Reardon	Geo Hutchingson	Chas Muddiman
Jos Charlton	Walter Stumph	Lillie Farmer
Cora Brown	Oliver Veihmeyer	John Mister
Clara Johnson	Jas Ford	Martena Randall
Jane A Adams	Frank Hendley	Sallie Kersey
Emma Fraser	Geo Dunn	Josephine Howe
Fannie Conner	Alfred Yeatman	Geo Toombs
Alice Conksey	Christopher Shreve	Walter Cooksey
Emily Lycett	Harry Davis	Alfred Taylor
Mollie McDevitt	Chauncey Dutton	John Williams
Kate Perkins	Jos Williams	Nelson Page
Clara Cassell	Lillie Clear	Albert Winfield
Florence Hinton	Marian Spates	Michl O'Hare
Josephine Baker	Nettie Robinson	Miliard Thompson
Maggie Emory	Lavinia Selby	Dennis Hickey
Lizzie Corcoran	Joanna Carter	Mary Green
Mary Wallingsford	Minnie Clear	Sallie Bell
Annie Whitemore	Catharine Sayers	Sallie Adams
Sarah King	Mary Fegan	Mary Boyle
Mary Law	Helen Halley	Katie Wolfe
Fennio Tatspaugh	Martha Clarvoe	Ida Rabbit
Sophia Lippharde	Lucy Brothers	
Emma Whitemore	Emma Wise	

Premiums for attention to Study & Improvement:

Eddie Hay	Maggie Boswell	Thos Fry
Robt C Cassell	Ella Grant	John Carrol
John H Yonson	Christiana Smith	Willie Otto
Ida Pumphrey	Laura Vernon	Jas McCook
Maggie Garrett	Kate McArdle	Eugene Snook
Louisa Strobel	Dora Miller	Percy Hall
David W Cridler	Margaret Zauner	Kate Lewis
Francis M Hunter	Oma Dorman	Clara Wilson
Willie McQueen	Fannie Dent	Alphretta Binnix
Anna Ragan	Jas Chappel	Lalla Herron
Sallie McDevitt	Wm Hughes	Maggie Maloney
Mary J McArdle	Simon Imrie	Ida Reeves

Geo McDermott
Orpheus Budlong
Orsemus Budlong
Ida Neale
Jas Skidmore
Fletcher Skidmore
Willie Jones
John Tatspaugh
Mary Stroman
Charlie Walker
Willie Knight
Tommy Bell
Alice Elmore
Annie Frazier
Erminie Bamberger

Premiums for Improvements in Penmanship:
Willie R Hoctor
Delia Gray
Harry McArdle
Mary Gambrill
Ida Willey
Kate Maguire
Ella Traver
Frank Lomax
John Robey
Geo Spransey
Mary Stephens
Martha West
Willie Mitchell
Emma Thomas
Chas Clarke
Albert L Martin
Emma Green

Premiums for Neatness:
Geo W Leesnitzer
Melinda Thomas
Jas E Donaldson
Lizzie Hutchinson
Kate Davidson
Lizzie Bowen
Eliza Barnaclo
Silas Mitchell
Frank Yeatman
Jos Small
Willie Whitemore
Sallie Graham

Premiums for Improvement in Vocal Music:
Thos McArdle
Mary Ward
Chas F Mitchell
Jane A Adams
Aliceana Brothers
Mollie Davis
Kate Kleindeinst
Wm Brennan
Willie Luff
Geo Dunn
Lavinia Selby
Julia Miller
Louis Dentinzer
Jennie Neale
Henry Davis
Wm Connington
Ida Sherwood

Honorably Mentioned:
Mary Maguire
Sarah Shields
Maggie Williams
Agnes Strobel
Laura Snooks
Sarah Reeves
Mary Roach
Emeline Leland
Harry Langley
Henry Demaine
David O'Connell
Alex'r Rogers
Eddie Williams

Supreme Court of D C, Esau & Adolphus H Pickrell against Johanna Grant & Richd P Jackson. By order of the court, passed Jul 5, 1866, I am directed to state the account of R P Jackson, trustee in said cause, & to give notice weekly for 4 months before Dec term of the court, 1866, notifying the heirs-at-law of Jas Kennedy, deceased, late of Wash City, & before his emigration, of the county of Kilkenny, Ireland, to apepar & establish their right to the proceeds of the sale made by the trustee, otherwise they will be forever foreclosed from all interest therein. –W Redin, auditor.

E H McGinnis, a teacher at Louisville, recently chatised a son of Dr Roberts for refusal to participate in gymnastic exercises, & the boy was dismissed from the school. Roberts published a bitter letter in the Democrat, & McGinnis met him & stabbed him, in the back, probably fatally.

Hartford, Ct, Jul 9. Lightning struck the house of Chas Whitney, in Forestville, Bristol, instantly killing Mr Whitney & son & seriously injuring Mrs Whitney.

Surrogate Tucker, of N Y, having summoned Gen Benj F Butler to account for his administration of the estate of the late Col Andrew J Butler, the Gen on Friday obtained an extension of the time until Jul 23, when his accounts of receipts & disbursements is to be rendered. Among the claims filed in the Surrogate's ofc is one for $75,000, for cotton, sugar, carriages, etc, to that amount, alleged to have been seized by Col Butler from one Robt W Bayne, of New Orleans, during the military occupancy of that city. Other claims are awaiting, the adjudication of which is expected to involve some interesting questions.

WED JUL 11, 1866
Orphans Court-Judge Purcell. 1-Yesterday an exemplified copy of the will of W B Richmond & letters of administration w a to Marian Stalker, of Shelby Co, Tenn, were filed & admitted to probate & record. 2-Letters of administration were issued to Treadwell Moore on the estate of Mrs Rose Greenhow; bond $5,000.

Died: on Jul 10, Mary Forsyth Antisell, aged 22 mos, infant daughter of Thos & Marion S Antisell. Her funeral will be at 5 p m today from 21 First st, Gtwn.

Base-Ball: the Gymnastic Base-ball Club have elected the following ofcrs: Pres, Aner S Brady; V Pres, Frank Myers; Sec, Amos W Abbott; Treasurer, Thos B Nolan, Directors: Thos C Lebo, Geo A Schriver, & Frank B Keys.

Paymasters to be mustered out. An order from the War Dept was promulgaged on Monday, relieving from duty in the Division of Referred Claims, Pay Dept, Lt Col R P Dodge, in charge of Division, Col W H Jameson, & Col G B Ely, & directing the muster-out of service of these ofcrs on Jul 20. It is understood that these paymasters are relieved & ordered out of service because, in the evidence they gave at the trial of Lt Col Paulding, they testified to having transferred funds deposited to their credit from one bank to another, as they did not construe the order from the Paymaster Genr'l in the sense of forbidding such transfers in certain cases, thus tending to justify Col Paulding in his breach of the order in question. Col J L Hodge, who had been discharging the duties of Chief Paymaster of the District of Wash since the arrest of Col Paulding, has been assigned to the position, & Col W R Gibson, Inspector of the Pay Dept has been assigned to the position of Chief of the Referred Claim Division, formerly occupied by Lt Col Dodge. Lt Col Taylor has been directed to relieve Lt Col W H Jameson.

Distribution of Medals & Premiums to the pupils of the 3rd District, Wash, yesterday, Mayor Wallach presiding.
Medal Scholars:

Sidney Van Riswick	Clayton Downs	Mary Sanderson
Henry Simpson		Inez Goodrich

Franklin Schott
Henrietta Bates
Chas Henshaw
Julia Stomberger
Redmond Walsh
Mary Nolan

Richd McAnley
Julia Henning
Estelle Willis
Saml Gill
Lillie J Clarke
Richad H Burch

Nellis Dyer
Edw L Kolb
Lizzie Steinle
Johnny Douhey
Thos Killafoyle

Premiums for the Best Written Examination:

Edw Cranch
Thos Stuart
Jas Somerville
Amelia Walborn

Kate Stewart
Mary Robinson
John Daly
John Gordon

Gustave Forsberg
Sallie Thompson
Isabella Kelser
Maggie Bean

Premiums for Exemplory Conduct & Punctuality:

Frank Davis
Geo Stewart
Thos Smith
Hoel I McQueen
Richd Hamilton
Wm T Hutchinson
Mary McNantz
Henrietta Walborn
Annie Ober
Ida Notingham
Eliza Aikin
Lizzie Felger
Wesley Berkley
Jas Brown
Vincent Fields
Chas Emmerich
John Dougherty
Jas Hutchinson
Mary Marshal
Jennett Russell
Mary Woodfield
Bell Stockett
Agnes Simpson
Alice Edelin
Mary Cross
Martha McCutcheon
Annie Bohlayer
Zora Parker
Nellie Krafft
Lizzie Stromberger
Eldoras Smith
Willie Wood
Willie Matthews
Henry Wagner

Chas Barricks
John Howard
Emma Marks
Lillie Arnold
Kate Klinehance
Leila Price
Annie Coogan
Kate Scott
Frank Cross
Leonard Bradley
Harry Berry
L Van Reswick
Henry Speisser
Jas Pegg
Georgeanna Jarboe
Ida Wilkerson
Linnie Nelson
Ida Arnold
Elvie Fletcher
Mary Wilkerson
Chas Felger
Jno Harrison
Saml Gardner
Wm Miller
Franklin Addison
Geo Fisher
Emma Spaulding
Kate Donelly
Carrie Skirving
Sarah Meredith
Ella Conner
Julia Fry
Frank Hickey
Bayne Arnold

Jos Champion
Michl Killafoyle
Robt Brown
Danl Foley
Sarah Taylor
Laura Callaghan
Louisa Simonds
Ida Holt
Kate Doyle
Jane Hart
Ellen O'Neill
Emma Little
Julia Tucker
Katy Wood
Fannie Herold
Minnie Ruff
Geo Crawford
Willie Wilkerson
Geo Nelson
Milliard Peake
Saml Nelson
Willie Moreland
Rhoda Ratrie
Alice Bean
Mary A Ratrie
Miranda Y Luckett
Catherine T O'Leary
Ellen H Luckett
Francis M Smith
M Edwin Bright
Chas J Kuhrist
Jos C Johnson
Alfred T Newman
Henry Seidel

Lizzie Ferguson	Geo W Hill	Willie Mahew
Jennie Baxter	Willie T Hill	Michl Chambers
Kate Sage	Amanda Gottachalk	Johnny Clarke
Annie Beers	Lillie Miller	Timmy Douhey
Eliza McLaine	Alice King	Harry Scott
Annie Schietlin	Rosa Steinle	Geo August
Geo A McCathran	Mary Westhorpe	Saml Crawford
Chas Peake	Eliza Miller	Dennis Callahan
John R Saxton	Willie Cox	Albert Bright
J Homer Altemas	Robt Barrett	Forney Queen

Premiums for Attention to Study & Improvements:

Wm Stromberger	Christopher Kroft	Chas Axe
Jas Wheatley	Wm Shelton	Margaret F O'Leary
J Brown	Cora Buckingham	Clara Cawill
Rose Dyer	Emma Nally	Laura V Bradley
Susie Langley	Mary Holmes	Wm W Kelser
Ida Bean	Jos Szmanoskie	Chas M Nicholson
Wm McFadden	Chas Shelton	Jas F Milstead
Lemuel Lusby	Edgar Jenkins	Katie Somers
Wm Leitch	Maggie Wagner	Kate Andrews
Alice Guinand	Teresa Kaugman	Mattie Smith
Annie Young	Mollie Williamson	Bennie Swain
Mary Langley	Frank Connor	Saml Burgess
Jessie Brown	Fred Souder	Jos Ockert
Emma Scarff	John Souder	Laura Gray
Mary Harman	Mary Garat	Amelia Jueneman
Willie McNally	Hannah Arnold	Monica Morgan
David Leslie	Alice Simpson	Andrew Kiddle
Jas Harbin	Margaret Slinghand	Geo Nash
Lizzie Davis	Susie Howard	Jas Brown
Mary Frost	Margaret Coffey	Albert Morgan
Carrie Everson	Allie Kidwell	Saml Mundell
Andrew Kell	Harry Frost	John Speiden

Premiums for Improvement in Penmanship:

Robt R Langle	Ella Tarrey	Chas C Carroll
Mary Wilkerson	Wm Newman	Lowrie Tolson
Albert Thomas	Emma Minehart	Chas Blanch
Lillian Evans	Wm Mahoney	Bridget Dwyer
Ella Everson	Mary Kealey	Charley Cox
Willie Jordan	Annie Briggs	Benj Mundell
Mary Blosser	Jas Jarboe	
Wm Kerper	Sarah V Maddox	

Premiums for Neatness:

John Holroyd	Josephine Eaton	Annie Everly
Louisa Hopkins	Nellis Scott	Danl Kelly
Edw Padgett	Jas Stockett	Mary Harrington

Edw Sniffen	Walter Walsh	Annie Ward
Julia Stephens	Annie E Teachem	Richd Bruff
Jos Greenwell	Isaac Jacobs	Wm Furguson
Sarah Leslie	Maggie Murphy	
Mary McFarland	Geo W Weber	

Premiums for Vocal Music:

Cornelius Emmerich	Rose Riley	Frank Brown
Jennie Ruff	Frank Dixon	Margaret Beers
Frank Claveloux	Fannie McLain	Jos S Larizzi
Mary Sanderson	Geo Chambers	Ella Carpenter
Annie Hayre	Kate Hart	Wm Kauler
Chas Guinand	Ida Johnston	Wm Fox
Delpha Jenkins	Walter Gates	
Frank Walborn	Martha W Marshall	

Honorably Mentioned:

Lizzie Childs	Delilah S Gunther	Mary Flynn

Senate: Bill introduced to incorporate the Wash & Gtwn Ferry Co: referred to the Cmte on the Dist of Col. The incorporation named are Martin H Cassell, Jos H Parish, Chauncey D Spaids, John B Clark, jr, & Henry W Morrison. It empowers the company to maintain a steam ferry to run from Gtwn to any point except the foot of 4½ & 6th sts in Wash, carrying passengers at seven cents, & freight at the same rate as Wash & Alexandria Co. Capital stock $200,000, in shares of $100.

At Tiffany's, in N Y, there is on exhibition a very handsome gold goblet, bearing this inscription: "From Barney Williams to Mr Charles Gaylor, author of the "Connie Soogah."

Charleston, Jul 10. In return to the writ of habeas corpus granted to the U S Court in the case of Michl Costello, confined in the Charleston jail, the ofcr refused to obey, saying that the prisoner was held under the Pres' proclamation of Sep 15, 1863. He also produced an order from Sec Stanton, instructing him not to deliver up the prisoners on a writ of habeas corpus. The Court granted a continuance of the case for another day. Gen Sickles made the following endorsement on the writ of attachment served on him by the U S Marshal at Charleston this morning for contempt: In compliance with orders from superior authority, I decline to be arrested. Danl E Sickles, Maj Gen Commanding. Gen Sickles received the marshals courteously, & told him that he had telegraphed Wash for instructions. The reply of Sec Stanton endorsed the course of Gen Sickles, & ordered him not to be arrested, & if force was used, to resist with whatever force was necessary. The action is taken in accordance with Pres Lincoln's proclamation of 1863. Judge Bryan has ordered all the proceedings to be laid before the President.
[Jul 13th newspaper: The writ of habeas corpus was to procure the bodies of four persons who were convicted & sentenced to death by a court martial, on the charge of killing a non-commissioned ofcr & two of the private soldiers of a military guard. From a trustworthy source-the Pres will direct Gen Sickles to

answer the writ & surrender the parties to the court. –Associated Press Despatch]

Annapolis, Jul 10. Last night a party of seven, composed of five priests & two students, left Annapolis on a pleasure trip down the bay, when at *Thomas Point*, Fr Classens was lost, & while endeavoring to save him the boat capsized, & the remaining ones, Frs Bradley, *Gerdemann, & students F F Henny & Runge were lost. The two others remained clinging to the boat, & drifted ashore on *Thomas Point*, & then walked to the city, arriving this mornng. A party was sent in search of the bodies, but failed as yet. A liberal reward has been offered for the recovery of the bodies. [Jul 11th newspaper: The body of Rev Fr *Gendemann, one of the priests who drowned, was recovered this P M. He was from Cumberland, Md. The students were John Kenny, of Rochester, N Y, & John Bunge, of Pittsburgh, Pa. [*Two spellings of Gerdemann/Gendemann.]

Dept of the Interior, U S Patent Ofc, Wash, Jul 9, 1866. Ptn of Olden Nichols, of West Roxbory, Mass, for the extension of a patent granted to him Oct 12, 1852, to which additional improvements were annexed Mar 30, 1854, for an improvement in Grinding Mills, for 7 years from the expiration of said patent, which expires on Oct 12, 1866. -Thos Harlan, Acting Com'r of Patents

Gen Sir John Macdonald died in Perthshire, Scotland, on Jun 24, aged 76 years. He joined the British army in 1803, & served in South America, Buenos Ayres; Peninsula; & in the south of France. He devoted his later years to the improvement of the condition of those living on his Highland estates.

Notice to Free People of Color. If Israel & Enoch Briggs, or either of them, will apply at the Intelligencer, they will hear of something which will interest them. The above-named men are free-born natives of Nansemond Co, Va, & removed during the war.

THU JUL 12, 1866
The Board of Visitors of the Va Military Institute have made the following appointments: Thos Fairfax, Richmond; F G Hays, Alexandria; L N Buck, Warren; C Randolf, Fauquier; F Y Menefee, Rappahannock; L Norris & W C Powell, Loudoun.

Criminal Court-Judge Cartier, Jul 11, 1866.
1-John Bowman, guilty of larceny, sentenced to 1 year in the penitentiary.
2-Christopher Fearson, charged with assault & battery, failed to appear, & his recognizance was also forfeited.
3-Jas Wheatley was fined $5 on being convicted of an assault & battery.

On Sat lightning struck the dwlg of Geo Fairbanks, in Hudson, Mass, killing his daughter, Emma, aged 13, & prostrating other members of the family, but not fatally. Several cattle in the neighborhood were also killed.

Annual distribution of Medals & Premiums in the Second District, Wash, yesterday, Mayor Wallach presiding.

Medal Scholars:

Wm Crews	Mary John Taylor	Kate Eckloff
Eliza Caton	Donald Stuart	Sallie Thorn
Henry Smith	Addie Foster	Jas Everett
Kate J Brown	Mary E Thumlert	Eugene Walter
Lucy Bishop	John Shiner	Alice Brown
John Taylor	Frank Ward	Galusha A Riggles
Donald Stuart	Gertrude Eggleston	Lizzie S Hazzelton
Addie Foster	Willie Lawrenson	

Premiums for Best Written Examination:

John Judd	Julia Moran	Horace Kenney
Geo Compton	Amanda East	Jeanette Tabler
Chas Connell	Geo Hedrick	Ida C Adams
Ellen M Wade	Edie Canfield	Louisa Sipe

Premiums for Exemplary Conduct & Punctuality:

Azariah Dennison	Carrie Bliss	John Boss
Jerome Andrews	Abraham Cook	Walter Wright
Frank Compton	John Clokey	Mary Knester
Cornelius Wells	Frank Woodward	Flora Brereton
Willie Vaughn	Jas McDonald	Jessie Warfel
Geo Riggles	Leroy Finney	Alice Skippon
Lizzie Haslup	Saml Turner	Hattie Clayton
Alice L Hern	Ida Jordon	G Cookman Flenner
Nellie Lemon	Mary Williamson	Chapman Lord
Laura Simpson	Adelia Burdine	Willie Wade
Annie Given	Josephine Kennedy	Chas Ward
Mary Tyssowski	Ada Stewart	Albert Donaldson
Andrew Caulwell	Saillie Jackson	Chas Stephens
John Ford	Mary Cassiday	Saml Carpenter
Wm Freas	Ella Frazier	Josephine Prather
Geo Caton	Carrie Cassiday	Emma Davis
Fenton Brewer	Ella White	Emma Schiffner
Wm Richard	Kate Birth	Louisa Schiffner
Marian J Lewis	Mary Johnson	Ella Columbus
Ella J Brown	Stephen Clements	Emma Rowe
Laura C Creaser	Henry Hobbs	Emma Woltz
Anna R Dorsey	Chas Cole	Lillie Foster
Mollie Birth	Willie Daly	Emma Henderson
Susan Smithson	Willie McKnew	Mary J Scott
Annie Patterson	Streeper Freas	Lizzie Clayton
Mary K Davis	Worthington Owen	Julia Parker
Emma Bond	Jos Caspar	Geo Folk
Annie Kallusowski	Jos Burch	Ellwood Johnson
Millie Klopfer	Chas Ourand	Jas Johnston

Eddie Smith
Jos Barkel
Augustus Perrie
Charlie W Downing
Harry Bevins
Frrank Hoffman
Charlie Scott
Charlie Rogers
Geo Harrison

Mary Gallagher
Hattie Garnett
Clara Ball
Ida Prosise
John Richardson
Willie Gamer
Albert T Coumbe
Oscar O Coumbe
Chas W Riggles

Wm C Sword
Wm Jordan
Chas W Sharretts
Mary A Fitzgerald
Sarah Williams
Jennie Quigley
Lizzie Nichols
Maggie McCleary
Annie L Hazzleton

Premiums for Attention to Study & Improvements:

Chas Lusk
Chas Ford
Jacob Doyle
Emma W Stokes
Sarah Stokes
Addie Randall
Geo Greenleaf
Chas Drager
Washington Danenhower
Alice Harrison
Mary D Mowbry
Mary Prather
Susie Collins
Martha Rohrer
Ella Briggs
Jacob Fechtig
Lambert Bergman
Craig Finney
Henrietta Stewart

Elmira Garner
Hattie Wise
Cornelia Ellis
Mollie Fechtig
Alice Prather
Edw Thomas
Andrew Rawlings
Jas Clarkson
Jas Scaggs
Harry Middleton
Enos Crews
Alice Davis
Josephine Kirby
Ida Cook
Willie Miller
Walter Fowler
Eddie Hodgkin
Ada Frazier
Cora Dennison
Gertrude Truman

Ida Vanarsdale
Emma Weaver
Emma Reese
Jos Harbaugh
August Kuester
John Shedd
John Goheens
Henry Rady
Henry Rogers
Cicely A Reamer
Florence Ball
Ellen Pierce
Geo Yeager
Jas Hayes
Edw O Chambers
Ida M Deland
Ida Polgiase
Mary Farnkoph

Premiums for Improvement in Penmanship:

Edw E Morcoe
Jennie Boss
Howard Nyman
Alice Pipher
Louisa Donn
Frank Jackson
Lizzie Robinson

Flora Conover
Prattby Golden
Saml Amiss
Florence Bamberger
Edson Briggs
Cora Pumphrey
Mary Dusenberry

John Jackson
Eugene Golden
Ada Creamer
Thos Adams, jr
Minnie Kolb

Premiums for Neatness:

Wm Chedal
Emma Garner
Marian Bowen
Ida Prather
Willie Curran
Ada Cavis

Lizzie Balt
Ewell Dicks
Willie Nally
Lillie Lavender
Morris Lambdin
Kate Wools

Mary Miller
Edwin Boss
John Bottomly
Clara Haines
Geo Statford
Gussie Nichols

Premiums for Improvement in Vocal Music:
Albert Wise
Rose E Sewell
Marshall Larner
Ella Eckloff
Lucy Bishop
Abraham Cook
Addie Foster
Martha Kirby
Andrew Rawlings
Chas Crocker
Annie Robeds
Preston Moses
Annie Lambdin
Jetta Sardo
Willie Buckley
Willie Rose
Christiana Rainier
Worthington G
Sharretts
Mary L Pettit

Honorably Mentioned:
Fannie Bellman
Laura Klopfer
Randall Lincoln
Chas Canfield
Wm Stuart
Capston McDonald
Henry McDonald
Arthur Folks
John Kaiser

Died: on Jul 10, at Wildwood, Md, Edith, infant daughter of F L & C V Moore. Her funeral services will be at *Oak Hill Cemetery*, Gtwn, D C, at 10½ o'clock Thu, July 12. Friends of the family are invited to attend.

Meadville Republican: on Sat last Hon C Culver took up his lodgings in the Venango county jail, that seeming to be the only way he could escape the relentless persecution waged against him by 3 or 4 of his creditors. Mrs Culver accompanied her husband, & shares his cell with him.

The Com'r of Pensions yesterday appointed the following named examining surgeons of the Pension Ofc: Dr N Udell, Centreville, Iowa; Dr Ira Shedd, Arcade, N Y; & Dr J R Burgess, Webster City, Iowa.

FRI JUL 13, 1866
Large French-plate mirrors & parlor suite at public auction on Jul 14. Were bought by Caroline Johnson on Feb 20, 1866, & a deposit made on them, for which, if they are not called for by the above day, will be sold to pay storage & balance on them. -Green & Williams, aucts

Criminal Court-Judge Cartier, Jul 12, 1866.
1-Rufe Watson, colored boy, 15, convicted of an assault & battery, & also of an indecent assault: sentenced to 2 years in the penitentiary. 2-Cornelius Gladwin not guilty of assault & battery. 3-Thos Ryan & John Williams found guilty of larceny, & sentenced to 1 year in the penitentiary. 4-Chas Snyder, guilty of grand larceny, picking a gentleman's pocket & robbing him of a considerable sum of money in one of the Navy Yard railroad cars, a plumber by trade, & previously of good character, sentenced to 2 years in the penitentiary instead of 5 years.
5-Christopher C Keaton guilty of assault & battery, was fined $50 & costs.

For sale: lots 1, 2 & 3, containing from 6 to 10 acres each situated on the turnpike road, 4½ miles from Wash, adjoining the farms of Allen Dodge, the late John C Rives, & John W Morsell. Address J W Veitch, Atty at Law, Brookville, Md.

Annual distribution of Medals & Premiums of the First District yesterday, May Wallach presided. Gen Garfield delivered a very beautiful address. The gold medal, offered by Mr Rhees, trustee, to the best speller in all the schools, was presented to Miss Hattie E Gove, by Prof Richards.

Medal Scholars:

Clayton A Hoover	Annie C Clark	Sallie Childs
Mary F Hill	ChasJ Wetzel	Eddie Hood
Edw Hunt	Mary C Blackiston	Felix Chism
Matilda Raff	Willie H Nash	Jenie V Stewart
Fannie McHenry	Annie E Seymour	
Benj W Brown	Mary Oliver	

Premiums for the Best Written Examination:

Jas E Bangs	Alfaretta Parker	David McNair
Edw A Newman	Ella McMahon	Hattie Gove
Wm E Tute	Wm Witzel	Fannie Julien
Addie Fuller	Frank Baer	Annie Grubb

Premiums for Exemplary Conduct & Punctuality:

Lewis Denham	Jessie Zoller	Jas Griffin
Geo Lane	Herman A Blan	Willis W Waite
Sam Shedd	Jos Brown	Joanna Carey
Charlie Clarke	Augustus Goodno	Ida M Jewell
Charlie Harkness	Saml Sherwood	Emma McGee
John Graham	Harry Bartle	Emma Belfast
Amanda France	Richd Hoover	Leda Hunter
Jane Murphy	Mary Sanner	Augusta Grubb
Annie Trumbull	Annie B Turton	Lillie Finckel
Sarah Yeatman	Mary Smart	Joanna Oliver
Mida Riggles	Grace Hurdle	Hattie Davis
Kate Rawlings	Geneva Burrows	Maggie Mitchell
Frank Douglass	Florence Thompson	Clara Kraft
Frank Wilkins	Geo Johnson	Katie Sterling
Chas Bishop	Jas Larry	Manie Sharo
Hiram Biddle	Chas Collins	Lidie Hoover
Jas Watt	Eugene Jewell	Clara Heald
Fielder Hunter	Chas Douglass	Ruth Pocock
Odessa Pierce	Ernest Taylor	Marcel Wroe
Jamie Turton	Eliz Furse	Alice Ritter
Katie Hawkins	Susie Jackson	David Lusk
Minnie Blackiston	Kate Davis	John Everett
Emmie Collins	Annie E Blackiston	Hiram Doyle
Fannie Sothoron	Mary J Kelly	Saml Everett
Ida Reiss	Christiana A Brown	Francis Lang
Janie King	Henry Webber	Jas Wheeler
Mary Yeatman	Jas Conroy	Jas Finch
Alice Bowie	Josephine Brown	Bernard Cumberland
Susie Kenney	Lewis Collins	Thos Cavanaugh

Wm Byram
Chas Davis
Robt Stacey
Ida Grenasher
Annie L Sioussa
Kate H Smith
Margaret Hill
Lizzie Dutton
Martha Kuhn

Premiums for Attention to Study & Improvement:

W R Brown
Lewis T M Cowie
Chas Lewis
Libbie C Kelly
Ella May Marsh
May Wilson
Edgar Frazier
Perkins Squier
John Greason
Clara Bliss
Katie Hurst
Miretta Thorne
Clara Wilson
Mary McCarthy
Ella Whildin
Frank P Atkinson
Saml C Smoot
Harry Williams
Ella F Bruff
Carrie C Davis
Annie L Harkness
Morris Urich
John Adams
Erastus Barnard
Katie Shea
Mary V Brown
Theresa McGill
John Griffin
John Dyer
Harry Brandelbury
Alice Parkington
Cecilia Mulldoon
Jennie Byram
Marion Serrins
Agnes O'Donnogue
Katie O'Donnogue
Sallie Vessey
Ida Bowen
Ella Lindsay
Arthur Taylor
Eddie Kaiser
Patrick Harrington
Simon Beard
John Keefe
Robt Perrott
Emma V Troxell
Isabella Meany
Dora Dutton

Premiums for Penmanship:

Howard Hawkins
Emma J McGrew
Jas Platt
Katie Goodall
Alice Williams
Maximilian Georgii
Emma J Sourbier
Jas Payne
Mary D A Poole
Alfred C Hill
Lizzie Ledwich
Katie McSweeny
Annie Bolger
Henry Sands
Eugene Atchison
Mary J Buchanan

Premiums for Vocal Music:

Lewis T M Cowie
Mary Riess
Jos Hurdle
Cora Adams
Sallie Swaze
Hermen A Blau
Annie Clarke
John A Jewell
Dora Johnson
Jas Woods
Alice S Barnes
Maggie Peugh
Mildard Lashorn
Saml Fowler
Annie J Calvert

Premiums for Neatness:

Durbin Ourand
Lizzie L Campbell
Squier Taylor
Alice Collins
Clara Fitzgerald
Lockett Benedict
Katie Melling
Chas Davis
Maggie Aiman
Johnnie B Turton
Nettie Higby
Annie Towers
Eva McCuen
Stewart Boss
John Stacey
Lizzie M Lusk

Honorably Mentioned:

H D Baird
W M Newman
Mary E Rose

Premium for Regular Attendance & Punctuality:

Jos F Hurdle, of Male Intermediate School, who has been punctually present at every session for 5 years.

Book: History of the Life & Times of Jas Madison by Wm C Rives. Vol II. Boston: Little, Brown & Co, 8vo, pp. 658. Jas Madison was the eldest of a family of 4 sons & 3 daughters, who attained years of maturity; the issue of the marriage of Col Jas Madison, of Orange Co, in Va, with Eleanor Conway. He was born on Mar 16, 1751, at the house of his maternal grandmother, in King Geo Co, during a visit of his mother to her ancestral home. His father died at an advanced age in 1801, his mother in 1829, when she had touched her 99th year. Thus both parents lived till their son had gained an imperishable fame; one to see him twice elected Pres of the U S, & for 12 years after the close of his public life, not less honored by his country in his retirement than when he was at the head of her Gov't.
[Peyton Randolph, whose name stood first on the list of delegates from Va to the Continental Congress, having died in Oct, 1775, Richd Henry Lee, as next in order, on Jun 7, 1776, moved, under the instructions of the Va Legislature, the resolutions for declaring independence.]

Dept of the Interior, U S Patent Ofc, Wash, Jul 11, 1866. Ptn of Linus Yale, jr, of N Y, N Y, for the extension of a patent granted to him on Oct 19, 1852, for an improvement in Burglar-proof Plates for Door Safe Walls, Vaults, etc, for 7 years from the expiration of said patent, which takes place on Oct 12, 1866.
–Thos Harlan, Acting Com'r of Patents

Supreme Court, D C. John D Wells & wife against Chas G Baylor & wife, & Helen M & Alex'r Wadsworth. The parties named, the guardian of the minor dfndnts, & the trustees, are hereby notified that on Aug 4 next, at my ofc, City Hall, Wash, I shall state the trustee's account & the distribution of the fund. If there be any creditors of the late Mrs Louisa J Wadsworth, they must file their claims with me forthwith. –W Redin, auditor

SAT JUL 14, 1866
Capt Jasper S Keller, one of the oldest & most respected citizens of Albany, died in that city on Thu, at the age of 85 years. What is remarkable in his life is, that he was never sick a day until within the past 2 weeks, & he was the first of his family to die. His wife, who is 83 years of age, & 9 children are surviving him.

A marble statue of Washington Irving is to be erected in the vestibule of the church erected as a memorial to him in *Sleepy Hallow*.

Tommy Nelson, an old negro, formerly a servant in the Washington family died at Suffolk, Va, recently. He was 94 years old. He helped to cut a canal leading from the western margin of the Dismal Swamp to Drummond's Lake, an enterprise projected by Gen Washington.

Memphis, Jul 12. Duel today on the Mississippi line, between Alonzo Greenlow & A B Taylor, of this city. Taylor was killed at first fire.

Mrd: on Jul 13, by Rev Dr Sunderland, Mr G R Cooper, of Stafford Co, Va, to Miss Bettie Taliaferro, of Orange Co, Va.

Died: on Jul 9, at Balt, Edward, son of Edward & Ellen C Hartley, formerly of Wash City, aged 18 months.

Died: on Jul 12, at Balt, of an affection of the heart, Mr Danl Bixby, who has been for some 8 years clerk of the Avenue House. He was much known to the public & was greatly respected for his genial, gentle, & other most excellent qualities.
+
Obit-died: on Jul 12, Mr Danl Bixby, of this city. He had gone on a brief visit to Balt, was suddenly seized with a severe attack of chronic troubles, & Mr King, the landlord of the Avenue House, had barely time to reach Balt, to answer to a telegram in season to see him alive. He was 31 years of age, & his remains will be conveyed to Litchfield, N H, his native place. He was unmarried.

The old 74-gun ship **Delaware**, one of the war vessels sunk at the Gosport Navy Yard at the outbreak of the war, has been raised. She will be cut up for the purpose of obtaining the immense amount of copper & iron contained in her.

Dept of the Interior, U S Patent Ofc, Wash, Jul 12, 1866. Ptn of Peter Geiser, of Greencastle, Pa, praying for extension of a patent granted him Oct 19, 1852, for an improvement in Grain Separators, for 7 years from expiration of said patent, which takes place on Oct 19, 1866. –Thos Harland, Acting Com'r of Patents

Orphans Court of Wash Co, D C, Jul 10, 1866. In the case of J Carter Marbury, exc of Edw Chapman, deceased, the executor & Court have appointed Aug 4 next, for the final settlement of the personal estate of the said deceased, of the assets in hand. -Z C Robbins, Reg/o wills

Crackers for the Million. Metropolitan Patent Steam Bakery, 347 C st, between 4½ & 6th sts. –Thos Havenner

Hon J H Reagan, late Confederate Postmaster General, was married on Jul 31 to Miss Mollie F Taylor, of Anderson Co, Texas.

MON JUL 16, 1866

Died: on Sunday, of disease of the heart, Mrs Danl A Brosnan. Her funeral will take place at 10 o'clock this morning, from St Patrick's Church. A requiem mass will be offered for the repose of her soul.

Died: on Jul 13, Oliver J Ruger, formerly of Syracuse, N Y, in his 45th year. His funeral will be from his late residence, 440 I st, Jul 16, at 4 o'clock.

Died: on Jul 8, at South Amboy, N J, after a few days' illness, Dr John Eccleston March, formerly of Kent Co, Md, aged 46 years. Chestown papers please copy.

Mr Wm Lyles, of Auburn, near Piscataway, Md, was brutally murdered on Jul 14. Four persons entered the house, & he was shot while in bed. His wife escaped from the room & raised the alarm, but the murderers did not leave until they had found some money, & in their haste they dropped several pieces of gold on the floor. The people of the vicinity are greatly shocked by the terrible crime. A reward of $500 is offered for the murderer or murderers. [Jul 18th newspaper: Five negroes, Thos Davis, Wm Henry Jones, Wm Plater, Henry Sackett, & Henry Richards, have been arrested at Alexandria on suspicion of being the murderers of Mr Lyles. Jones was formerly his carriage driver, & Plater confessed that they committed the crime-plunder being the object. They got $220 in gold, $1,500 in Va money, & other currency. One waited at the river to watch the boat while the other four committed the deed.] [Sep 7th newspaper: the trial of Wm Plater, Henry Luckett, Wm Henry Jones, & Thos Davis, who are charged with the murder of Mr Wm Lyles, at Auburn, PG Co, Md, on Jul 14 last, was commenced at Upper Marlboro on Wed, before Judge Saml H Berry. Edw W Belt, prosecuting atty, & C C Magruder & Jos Roberts, conducted the defense. The jury, in 10 minutes, returned a verdict of "Guilty of murder in the first degree."]

The wife of Maj Gen Jeff C Davis fell overboard from the Louisville mail-boat lately, & narrowly escaped drowning. The General sprang in & saved her.

TUE JUL 17, 1866
Elmore A Studley, a clerk in the post ofc at New Bedford, Mass, for the past 2 years, has been arrested, charged with robbing the mails. He confessed his guilt.

Information received from Mare Island Navy Yard that Saml Welles, constructing engineer of that yard, was fatally injured Jul 10th by the explosion of the boiler of a portable steam engine, & died that day. He was a nephew of the Sec of the Navy, & was previous to going to Calif, stationed at the Wash Navy Yard. He was on the point of returning East to be married, when the event occurred.

Two deliberate murders were committed in Cleveland Friday night. Edwin Hortpence, from Gordon, was murdered for his money, & a laborer Kelly, by a neighbor for revenge.

From the City of Kansas Advertiser, Jul 7. We learn that great excitement was brought about at Cape Girardeau by the repetition of an arrest of some of the Sisters of Charity of nuns, attached as teachers to the convent of a Catholic academy at that point for their not taking the oath prescribed by the new constitution. The matter was compromised by those offenders against the new constitution giving bond for their appearance at the next Circuit Court of Cape Girardeau Co, for their appearance to answer the criminality of the offence of acting in the capacity of teachers without taking the convention oath.

Gen Robt E Lee has been invited to spend his summer vacation in Ky, but says, in declining, that his parole will not allow him to leave Va.

The Boston Commonwealth states that Wm Lloyd Garrison is suffering severely from two falls upon the ice last winter, & is unable to use a pen, & consequently his work on the history of anti-slavery cause is wholly retarded.

Ex-Pres Fillmore & wife returned in the ship **Persia**.

Naval Ofcrs Commissioned: The Sec of the Navy yesterday sent to the Pres for his signature the commission of the following naval ofcrs, which have been prepared in conformity to their confirmation by the Senate, viz: Lt Cmder, B P Smith; Masters, Wm B Hoff, Chas V Gridley, & Geo W Coffin; Surgeon, S Oberley; Assist Surgeon, Wm F Ferry; 1st Lt of Marines, Geo B Haycock; Paymasters, E Bellows, H S Wait, Arthur Burtis, E Putnam, C S Perley, C E Chenery, Wm S Darling, G R Martin, Wm H Andrews, W N Watmough, W Goldsborough, G F D Barton, W R Windlow, H P Tuttle, F H Hinman, C F Guild, J E Tolfree, S G Billingsand, G F Hamilton; Passed Assist Paymasters, C P Thompson, Francis H Swan, & S F Browne.

Appointments on Maj Gen Hooker's Staff: 1st Lt Wm W Tompkins, 3rd U S artl, & Brvt Capt Jas M Lancaster, 1st Lt 3rd U S artl, have been appointed aides-de-camp on the staff of Maj Gen Hooker, commanding the Dept of the East.

Mrd: on Jun 4, by Rev Fr J S O'Neil, at the residence of the bride's mother, Mr Frank D Orme, of Wash City, to Miss Fannie McCullough, of Bloomington, Ill.

Mrd: on Jul 5, at the residence of Mr G W Eaheart, by Rev Mr Crouse, Edw L Dawson, of Wash, to Miss Maggie Clark, of Balt.

Mrd: on Jul 10, in Wash City, by Rev Dr Sunderland, St Clair Morgan, U S N, to Miss Martha V Wroe, daughter of S C Wroe, of Wash City.

Died: on Jul 16, suddenly, Julia M R, wife of Peter Von Essen, in her 77th year. Her funeral will be this evening at 5½ o'clock, from her late residence 38 Congress st, Gtwn, D C.

Died: on Jul 15, in PG Co, Md, Alice, infant daughter of Rv R J & Eliz B Keeling, of Wash City. Norfolk papers copy.

Died: on Jul 15, Henry Thomas, eldest son of B H & Lewellen Clements, aged 13 years & 11 days. His funeral will be from their residence, 278 H st, Jul 17, 5 P M.

Died: on Jul 15, Ann, beloved wife of Hugh Murray, in her 41st year. Her funeral will take place on Tue at 4½ o'clock, from her late residence, Pa ave & 24th st.

Phil, Jul 16. Capt Henry S Stellwagen, U S Navy, died yesterday at Cape Island.

Supreme Court of D C, in Equity, No 718. Constantine Dresler vs Teresa Dresler. The petition of the cmplnt, Constantine Dresler, having been filed on Jul 22, 1866, praying for a divorce, a vinculo matrimonil from the said Teresa Dresler for adultery, committed in D C subsequent to her marriage with the said Constantine Dresler, & other good causes alleged in his said petition, & it appearing to the satisfaction of the Court that a subpoena was duly issued on June 22, 1866, & returned non est, & it further appearing, by the affidavit, of disinterested witness filed in this cause, that the said Teresa Dresler, is a non-resident of D C, & she has been absent therefrom for 6 months, it is ordered that said dfndnt, Teresa Dresler, be requested to appear in person or by solicitor to answer said petition of the cmplnt, & abide the further order of the court in this matter. –R J Meigs, clerk

Orphans Court of Wash Co, D C. In the case of N Carroll Mason, exc of Wm T T Mason, deceased, the executor & Court have appointed Aug 7 next, for the final settlement of the personal estate of the said deceased, of the assets in hand. -Z C Robbins, Reg/o wills

WED JUL 18, 1866
Prof Ferdinand Engel, for nearly 10 years connected with the U S Coast Survey, died on Jul 12 last, at Tremont, N Y, where he had been residing. He was one of the coryphees of mathematical science, &, as far as descriptive geometry is concerned, he was, both here & in Europe, considered to have no superior. For many years he was a resident of Berlin, Prussia, the seat of learning & classical education.

Dept of State: Wash, Jul 14, 1866. Information received from Mr Thos P Smith, the Consul of the U S at La Rochelle, France, of the death, on Jun 23rd ult, at the Ille de Ree, of Mr F Baudin, aged 82 years, and who, for nearly 50 years, has been U S Consular Agent at the place of his decease.

On Sunday Henry Foster was found dead in his room at the Clarendon Hotel; he was about 40 years of age, & has a wife & children in N Y, & relatives in Toledo, Ohio. The deceased having been a Mason, his body was taken charge by them, who will have it embalmed & placed in a vault, to await the action of his family.

Henry Burden, of Troy, returns $176,795 income; John A Griswold, $159,657, & J F Winslow, $123,568.

Mr U H Painter, of the Phil Inquirer, was assaulted & severely beaten in the Capitol yesterday by B F Beveridge, formerly of the Capitol police, in a dispute concerning a charge against Mr Sloanaker, collecter of internal revenue for the 3rd District of Pa, whose confirmation, it is understood, Mr Painter opposed. A cmte of the House was appointed to investigate the case.

Died: on Jul 17, Agnes Wiber, in her 63rd year. Her funeral will be this evening at 3 o'clock, from 523½ K st, between 4th & 5th sts.

Deaths from sun-stroke yesterday. 1-Judge Wagner, residing at 301 D st, was found dead in his bed yesterday. It is believed death resulted from exposure to the rays of the sun. 2-Thos Hughes died of sun-stroke. He returned home & lay down on his bed & died. 3-Michl Coleman fell down on N st, & was taken to his house on the Island. He died almost immediately after he reached there. His death was caused by sun-stroke.

Mrd: at Wrightsville, Pa, by Rev J M Lantz assisted by Rev J J Lane, Hugh A Curran, Prof of Natural Sciences & Modern Languages in Dickinson Seminary, Wmsport, Pa, to Miss Sarah L, daughter of Geo Harris, of Wrightsville. [No marriage date given-current item.]

Died: on Jul 15, at the Convent of the Visitation, Gtwn, D C, Sister Mary Gaudalupe Clinton. Va papers please copy.

Died: Sarah Ella, only daughter of Marcus & Divi McNeal, aged 7 years, 11 months & 11 days. Her funeral will be from the residence of her parents, 578 Md ave, between 9th & 10th sts, Jul 18, at 5 P M. [No death date given.]

Trustee's saleof fine cottage sites contiguous to Wash City on the high grounds between **Kalorama** & **Meridian Hill**, on Jul 20, lot 4 of the tract known as **Widow's Mite**, subdivided in 9 cottage sites, of about 4 acres each; adjoins the valuable place of Mr Little. –Wm Nourse, trustee -Jas C McGuire & Co, aucts

Fortress Monroe: the beautiful **soldiers' cemetery**, about 1½ miles from the fortress, has been laid out & arranged the past 6 months, & is rapidly approaching completion. About 4,000 bodies of the soldiers of many of the Northern regts, which participated in many of the various campaigns, on the Peninsula & on the banks of the James river, have been gathered together in this cemetery from the different burial places at Big Bethel, Newport News, or those attached to the hospitals. These bodies have been reinterred in such a systematic manner that no difficulty will be experienced by relatives & friends at any future period in reclaiming them. Neat headboards, inscribed with the name of the soldier, regt, State, etc, have been procured, & placed at the head of each grave. About $8,000 have been subscribed for a monument.

John F Lane, the oldest brother of the late Senator Lane, of Kansas, also committed suicide, & under peculiar circumstances. He graduated at West Point in 1828, & in 1836, during the Florida war, in which he was actively engaged, he was promoted to the command of a regt of Indians. Shortly after his promotion, directly after going into camp one evening, after a day's march, he placed the hilt of his sword on the ground & the point in his eye, & threw himself on it. No cause for this suicide was ever known or conceived of.

THU JUL 19, 1866
Sidney Everett, son of Edw Everett, was lately married to Miss Fay, of Boston.

Rev Jas King has donated property in Bristol, Tenn, valued at $16,000, to the Holston Presbytery, for the purpose of a theological seminary.

We are indebted to Mr Jno F Ellis, music dealer, 306 Pa ave, for a copy of a beautiful song by J Wm Pope, entitled "The Eyes and Voice of my Loved One."

Capt H N Pellet, late of the 146th N Y V, has been appointed Consul to the Republic of Colombia.

Horatio Bolster, of prize ring notoriety, was yesterday arrested on suspicion of having fired the stable of King & Keyes, & the residence of Mr Nailor, on Tue. He was held to bail in $2,000, & will have a hearing before Justice Walter at 10 o'clock this morning.

Sunstroke. 1-Rev Patrick Donelan, a Catholic priest from Fredericksburg, Va, died from sunstroke yesterday on board the steamer **Vanderbilt**, lying at the 6th st wharf. The friends of the deceased took the body to St Dominic's Church, were it remained previous to interment. 2-David Barry & Wolfgard, also died of sunstroke in Wash City yesterday.

Supreme Court, D C, in Equity, No 559. John Purdy vs Isaac D Surratt et al. Wm Y Fendall, trustee, reported on Jun 26 he sold part of lot 20 in square 454, for $4,700 to John C McKelden, who has complied with the terms of sale.
–Andrew Wylie -R J Meigs, clerk

Balt, Jul 18. Among the deaths from sunstroke were the following well known & highly respected citizens, Wm Spear, insurance agent, & Capt Jas Frazier. Capt W Predham, who commanded a Gov't transport during the war, died from sunstroke today.

Despatch from Helena, Ark, dated Jul 14: Mrs Henrietta W Davenport has just been notified that she has fallen heir to an estate worth $2,000,000, in Scotland, through her uncle, Robt Bruce Blackburn, recently deceased, who was one of the heaviest manufacturers in Europe. Mrs Davenport is the only surviving child of his only sister, &, with her mother, moved to this country in 1848, & located in northern Georgia, where she married. Since the war she & her mother moved here. They have two children. The whole family will proceed to N Y early next month, on their way to Scotland to take possession.

A warrant was issued yesterday for the arrest of a young man, Baker Johnston, on a charge of having committed an assault & battery upon his mother.

FRI JUL 20, 1866
On Tue, while bathing in the river at Great Falls, Miss Stone & Miss Maddox were drowned. The mother of Miss Maddox, who went to their rescue, was also drowned. She leaves a family. The bodies were recovered about 4 hours later.

Mr Bonner, the proprietor of the N Y Ledger, has returned an income for the past year of $165,609.65.

The clerks of the Pension Ofc, pursuant to instructions from Dr H C Lock, Acting Com'r of Pensions, assembled to pay last respects to the memory of their much beloved departed confrere, Rev E S Barrett, late of the Pension Ofc, & brother of Hon Jos H Barrett, Com'r of Pensions. [Edw S Barrett died on Jul 18, after a brief illness.]

Pastor John P Donelan, pastor of the Roman Catholic Church at Rockford, Ill, died at that place on Sunday last. He was born in Boston, Mass, & was about 60 years of age; educated for the priesthood in Balt; & appointed pastor of St Patrick's Church in Wash City. He built, in 1838-39, St Mathew's Church, just n e of the Pres' Square, of which he was made pastor. He was transferred from here to Balt, & then to the West. Rev Jas P Donelan, brother of the deceased, also well known in Wash City, is pastor at the Cathedral in Dubuque.

A despatch from Mr Cyrus W Field, from Valentia, dated Jul 7, states that the shore end of the Atlantic cable was successfully laid on that day.

Household & kitchen furniture at auction on Jul 25, at the residenc of Hon Jas Speed, late Atty Gen, at 284 H st, between 17th & 18th sts.
-Jas C McGuire & Co, aucts

Died: on Wed, after a week's illness, Mrs Lydia A Weber, aged 31 years & 9 months, wife of Louis Weber. Her husband & children have cause to mourn a devoted wife & fond mother. Her funeral is tomorrow at 10 o'clock, from the residence, 569 7th st, between G & I sts, Navy Yard.
+
Mrs Lydia A Weber, wife of the well-known music teacher, Prof Louis Weber, of the Marine Band, who died suddenly on Wed, it is supposed from fever caused by the excessive heat. She had been removed down stairs after confinement, & during the prevalence of the storm was taken with convulsions & died almost immediately.

SAT JUL 21, 1866
Died: on Jul 20, Cornelia M Griffin, daughter of the late Peter & Hannah C Griffin, in her 38th year.

A negro woman, Ann Lee, a particular & intimate friend of Henry Richardson, one of the murderers of the late Mr Lyles, was arrested this morning in the yard of Mrs Eveleth, on South Fairfax st, into which she had jumped from a second story window, when she saw the officers coming for her. On her was a dress identified as belonging to Mrs Lyles. She had a lot of silver spoons marked E P in her pocket, the property of Mrs Palmer, of PG Co, Md, who was robbed some time ago.

Trustee sale of First-class bldg lots on Conn ave, between H & I sts, on Jul 26, on the premises, lots 16 & 17, in square 165, adjoins the residences of Admiral Shubrick & Sec McCulloch. –Chas S Carrington, trustee -Nathl Wilson, solicitor -Green & Williams, aucts

Trustee's sale of valuable real estate on Md ave, by deed of trust from Philip Wagner: sale on Jul 30, of lots 14 & 15 in square 915, improved by a large brick dwlg house. Immediate possession given. After the above sale will be sold lots 8 & 9 in square 893, improved by 3 newly built 2 story frame houses. –Chas H Utermehle, Fred'k Schmidt, Saml L Phillips, Trustees -Green & Williams, aucts

Appointments of Examining Surgeons: Drs H L Bryan, of Covington, Ga, & Wilson H Glass, of Booneville, Ky, have been appointed examining surgeons by the Com'rs of Pensions.

Horatio Ames, of Falls Village, Conn, lately received a liberal offer from the Emperor of Russia, to manufacture extensive quantitites of his patent gun, for the use of the Russian army. The offer was declined on account of a lack of proper facilities in iron & labor in that country.

Oak Hill Cemetery, its origin, history, character, & condition. There has been a wonderful revolution taking place in the last 20 years in the care bestowed upon the resting places of the dead in our country. **Mount Auburn**, dedicated in 1831, has the honor or leading in this ennobling movement, & afterwards came **Laurel Hill**, about the size of **Oak Hill**, with **South Laurel Hill** added, & more than doubling the territory; & in 1842 came **Greenwood Cemetery**, in Brooklyn, originally embracing 175 acres, since increased to 350 acres. **Oak Hill Cemetery**, it is well known, originated in the enlarged benevolence of Wm W Corcoran, whose name is identified with all that is most exalted in benefactions to the cause of religion, humanity, science, & art in Wash City & District. In Jun, 1848, in pursuance of a design which had followed him from the dreams of his boyhood, he purchased 15 acres of land on **Dunbarton Hill**, Gtwn Heights, of the late Geo C Washington, for the sum of $3,000, & on Apr 7, 1849, at the first meeting of the association which had been through his instrumentality organized for that purpose, he notified them that he was ready to transfer the property to their custody, & that the sum of $2,000 was deposited to their credit in the banking house of Corcoran & Riggs as a fund from which to draw for current expenses. The records of the association have been imperfectly kept, & the history to be drawn from them is very unsatisfactory. At the first meeting under the act of incorporation, Apr 7, 1849, there were present, J Marbury, L Thomas, Geo Poe, Edw M Linthicum, Mr Marbury being chosen president, & Mr Thomas secretary & treasurer. The record makes no mention of the choice of directors, but says the board of directors met the same day, & that the deed of conveyance of the land & the notice of the deposit of the $2,000 was received from Mr Corcoran on that occasion. We learn from inquiries that the directors were those who were present at the first meeting of the association. Henry C Matthews was chosen in place of

Mr Poe, resigned. The following items are all that the records furnish, pertaining to the special preparation of the grounds. May 8. Voted to enclose the grounds with a substantial board fence. May 15. Capt Geo F De la Roche employed as engineer at a yearly salary of $500. June 15. Voted to build a bank wall along Rock Creek, 7 feet high, which was actually built 15 feet high. Sep 10. The location of the receiving vault, originally designated on the slope north of the chapel, changed to its present site, the property holders near the original site objecting to having such a vault so near them. Oct 1. Borrowed $1,000 from the banking house of Corcoran & Riggs, which Mr Corcoran, on returning from abroad soon afterwards, promptly paid as an addition to his contributions. Amount of expenditures up to Jan 19, 1850, reported to have been $4,500. The records during the year 1850 comprised little else than meetings & votes appropriating money. The engineer's survey & plan were reported Aug 26, 1851, which, with some small changes, are subsequently what the cemetery now presents. The names of the avenues were "Eastern," Middle," Western," & "Cross" avenues, & it was voted to name the paths after trees, shrubs, & flowers. The lots were offered at auction Oct 17, forty cents per square foot being fixed as the basis, & the purchasers on this basis to bid for choice. Lot Nos 1 to 15, inclusive, selected for a family monument by Mr Corcoran, reserved from sale, as also lots 50, 121, 125, which had been already actually occupied with interments respectively by Geo C Washington, E Chapman, & F Dodge. John A Blundon, Oct 4, selected superintendent, & Walter Cox elected secretary & treasurer, the salary of the latter being fixed at $150. Oct 21, a burial lot voted to the engineer in recognition of the value of his services, another presented to Evan Lyons, in consideration of his having allowed the use in the back wall of a large mass of stone belonging to him & laying in Rock creek, the remnants of the two stone dams which had successively been swept down by the floods. No records from Oct 8, 1852, till Dec, 1853, when the price of the "Circles" in the southern portion of the grounds was fixed at $360 each. No record from this date till Dec, 1855, when the salary of the superintendent was fixed at $600 after Jan 1, 1856. The ofc of the association was Jul 12, 1856, located in the rooms of the Potomac Ins Co, where it has since remained, & Henry King at the same time chosen secretary & treasurer, in place of Walter Cox, resigned. Mar 13, 1857, salary of superintendent fixed at $800, from Apr 1, 1857. From 1857 to 1861 inclusive, there was no quorum at the annual meetings, & officers held over. Jun 7, 1860, lot 388 presented to John A Blundon "for his judicious services in laying out & constructing the eastern section of the cemetery. At a meeting of the lot-holders, Jun 19, 1862, John Marbury, T A Lazenby, C A Buckey, & W W Corcoran were chosen "managers." At a meeting, Mar 19, 1863, as all the lots had been sold, it was proposed, but voted down, to use some of the lawns for lots. The matter was subsequently investigated, & in June, 1863, it was voted thus to use certain portions of the lawns & avenues-the lots to be, as near as practical, 300 feet in area, & at 70 cents per foot. Salary of secretary & treasurer at this time fixed at $300, & Apr 14, 1864, salary of superintendent fixed at $1,000, from Apr 1 of that year. An annual meeting, June 6, 1864, W W Corcoran, T A Lazenby, G W Beall, & John Marbury were chosen managers, & June 14, salary of superintendent raised to $1,200, from Jul 1, 1864, & a present of $500 voted him for his judicious services in laying out the southern side of the cemetery. Records show nothing of the kind, for the purchase of the 6 acres of land adjoining the cemetery, of Mr Chas Dodge. At the last meeting the purchase of this tract for $8,000 was approved, & the superintendent ordered to enclose & lay out the same. Sep 15, 1865, J W Deeble elected secretary & treasurer in place of Mr Henry King, who had filled the place since 1856, & who, by reason of failing powers, been incapable of doing its duties. Dec 5, 1865, voted to allow Fred'k C Crowly to quarry on the newly purchased tract for 10 years at $2,000 a year, & a contract was accordingly made with him allowing him to take stone from the tract from Rock Creek, 100 feet back upon the land, at that price, in semi-annual payments. He is furnishing the paving stones for this city from this source at the present time. The new grounds were ready for the market on Apr 4, 1866, & it was voted to fix the price of the circle on the highest part of the new grounds at not less than $1,000, the other lots not circles to be sold at from $1 to $1.50 per foot. The magnificent site embraced in the circle above specified was selected by Mrs General Reno before the grounds were laid out, & it is the most magnificent spot in the entire cemetery, commanding a full view of the Capital, a fit resting-place for one of the noblest of the great military leaders who fell for their county in American rebellion. J Marbury elected president of the board Jun 4, 1866. The total assets of the association amount to $58,821,87. Unfortunately , $24,500 is invested in Southern stocks & securities which return no income, though it is believed these securities & stocks will ultimately prove good. May 16-action taken to relieve the receiving vault of the bodies which had accumulated in that temporary receptacle, some of which had been there a very long period, with no prospects that they would ever be removed by the family friends. The superintendent was ordered to bury the bodies in such places as he might select, & to institute legal proceedings for the collection of the vault rent, in cases where the parties liable were able to pay. It was voted to require a deposit of $10 for every body placed there, with a limit of 6 months for a body to be retained in the vault, & beyond that period, $5 per month. On Jun 7, 1848, Mr Corcoran purchased the 15 acres comprising the original grounds of Geo C Washington, & his son, Lewis W Washington, for $3,000, & on Mar 3, 1849, he succeeded in procuring a charter for the cemetery from Congress. Survey was made by Capt De La Roche. A massive iron fence was erected on the front line at an expense of some $8,000; the handsome Superintendent's Lodge at an expense of several thousand dollars, & the exceedingly beautiful stone chapel, costing some $5,000, both planned & executed by Jas Renwick, jr, of N Y, a well known artist. Wooden fences were placed on the east & west lines, & the solid stone bank wall erected on the river line, the whole expense thus incurred & paid by Mr Corcoran amounting to not less than $56,000. It was deeded to the company by Mr Corcoran May 1, 1849. The oldest inhabitants of Gtwn remember the **Oak Hill** grounds when they were known as **Parrott's Woods**, where the orators flourished their eloquence on the Fourth of July, & other famous days, & where all sorts of gay times were celebrated long, long ago. Parrott, who owned the Woods, & his ropewalk, which long flourished nearly on the spot where now the superintendent's lodge is located, have passed away, but the remembrance of high & joyous days still linger. Aqueduct water & fountains have been established. There is one peculiarity in the monumental decorations of this cemetery which detracts essentially from it artistic beauty & the pleasing impression. "There is no variety in the material." It is an endless repetition of white marble, a sameness wearisome, as it is unusual, to behold. There is one handsome granite monument in these grounds, the well-executed memorial, designed somewhat after Scipio's tomb at Rome, to the memory of Col John Harris, commandant Marine Corps. There is but one granite shaft of any description at **Oak Hill**, a plain obelisk, inscribed, 'Walter R Johnson, born at Leominster, Massachusetts, 1794; graduated at Harvard, 1819; died in Washington, 1852. The vault of Admiral Jos Smith, has a handsome bronze anchor on the door: he was instantly killed by a shell, standing undismayed at his post, in the fierce conflicts with the rebel ram **Merrimac**, in Hampton Roads: Lt Jos Bryant Smith, U S N. Born Dec 29,1826. Killed in battle while in command of the U S frig **Congress**, Mar 8, 1862. By the side of this is a handsome Fearson vault. You will find side by side the very chaste & richly finished granite vaults of Alex'r Ray, Wm M Boyce, Wm Thos Carroll, Gen S Churchill, Marshall Brown, & Dr Chas Worthington. The tombs Carroll & Marshall Brown were decorated with flowers. Exquisite sculptured memorial is that to the memory of Mary Bell, the little daughter of "William M and Mary E Gwin," who died in Washington in 1852, at the age of 11 years. In a beautifully arched Gothic canopy stands the figure of a little child, with hands clasped before the face, which is directed towards the form of a dove lying at its feet. It is a gem. The Cutts monument, large, similar in design, is fine, but inferior, we think, to this one. An exquisite memorial bears a monogram of the family name; upon one only of the tablets is there an inscription-"Our Children," formed in a graceful crescent, & beneath it, one under the other, are Grayson Page, Mary Jane, Isabel, the names of three little ones who early found their homes in this spot. This charming memorial bears the name of M W Galt. The family vault of Wm W Corcoran, was erected at a cost of $13,000, after a design by Thos U Walter, the architect of the Capitol. Near this stands a massive pillar in the Roman style-to Thomas Corcoran and wife, parents of the foregoing; & in the same vicinity-to the memory of a brother-Thomas Corcoran & wife. There are 2 elegant obelisks-one inscribed Horatio Berry, & the other Thomas C Mathews. Mr Mathews was a director in the cemetery association from its organization till his death in 1852. There is a massive pillar inscribed: John H Eaton, of Tennessee; born June 18, 1790, died November 17, 1853; was U S Senator from the State of Tennessee for eighteen years; Secretary of war; Governor of the State of Florida, and Minister to the Court of Madrid. This monument, in connection with the singular, melancholy history of the wife he left behind him, & her family, awakens gloomy reflections, enforcing, as the history does, the truth of the maxim that " truth is often stranger than fiction." A fine piece, the first in bronze by Fisk Mills, who, inherited a fine genius from his father, Clark Mills, mournfully notes: Lieut John Rogers Meigs, U S Engineers, Chief Engineer of the Army of the Shenandoah, born 9th February, 1842, killed 3d October, 1864." Mr Mills has at his studio, in the basement of the Capitol, another work, which is due to adorn these grounds. It is a life-size female figure, the likeness of her above whose slumbering dust the statue is to stand, the model, which Mills is himself to complete in marble, is to be seen at his studio. The woman is kneeling by the side of a cross, which is clasped by her left arm; the attitude is strikingly graceful; the hair, waving about the forehead, falls in loose ringlets over the shoulders, & the uplifted face is radiant with the celestial illumination of hope & faith. It is to be placed over the grave of Mrs S E Black, of Wash City. We notice a fine memorial to the memory of Brig Gen Jos B Plummer, U S A, a distinguished soldier, who died of wounds received on the field, Aug 9, 1862; a marble pillar, to Henry W Kingsberry, another noble soldier, who was killed in battle at Antietam, Sep 17, 1862, in his 26th year of his age, while in command of the 11th regt of Connecticut volunteers on that memorable day. Elaborate family monument of F A Lutz; marble pillar to H H Chapman; lofty fluted broken column, with anchor wrought in full relief at its base, to Thomas T Houston, U S Navy; Gothic family monument to John Wilson, of Washington; memorial inscribed Rebecca Power Tillinghast, relict of Hon Joseph T Tillighast; obelisk inscribed Leonidas Knowles; elaborate shaft to John Crumbaugh; massive pillar to the memory of Commodore Charles Morris, who died, with honors upon his name, in 1856. Obelisk to Major George Bender, & another to Charles B Fisk; mausoleum to Samuel Whitall, born in New Jersey & died in Gtwn; memorial of Cornelius Baker, with the row of headstones near, of five little ones who died in the space of one month of scarlet fever. Two tombs, one to Maj John Adlum, of Pa, a soldier of the Revolution, & the other of his wife. A broken shaft, with sculpture in ivy, to Dr James S Snyder; heap of stones, decorated with taste, inscribed Charle C Smoot; pretty pillar to the memory of Fannie A, wife of Albert Yerby, & infant son; marble pillar to the memory of the wife of Col Robert E Clary, U S A, with a son not long since, & now again the son's wife; their only children, brought hither to slumber by the mother's side; massive pillar inscribed Alfred V Scott. Memorial in this cemetery, a graceful Doric column of bluish variegated European marble, cut at Stockholm, & erected here by the order of the Emperor of Russia, & inscribed: "Sacred to the memory of Alexander de Bodisco, Chamberlain, Private Counsellor of his Majesty the Emperor of all the Russias, his Envoy Extraordinary and Minister Plenipotentiary to the United States. Born at Moscou the 18-30, October, 1786. Died at Georgtown, 11-23, January, 1856." It will be remembered that Mr Bodisco married a young lady of Gtwn, of great beauty & accomplishments; & it may be added that she is now the wife of an officer of the English army, in India. The family monument of Judge Andrew Wylie is a superbly wrought pillar. In the valley is the final resting place of that grand old soldier, Gen Thos S Jesup, with his wife, & no memorial whatever marks his honored memory. There is an elaborate memorial to Wm Marbury & wife; & another to Wm Carter. The memorials to Geo C Washington & wife, with that of a daughter between, will interest those who remember that when he died Hon Geo C Washington, who had for many years been a representative in Congress from Md, was the oldest & nearest surviving male relative of his grand-uncle Gen Washington. There is a Gothic memorial to Jos Fowler, a native of Md, who after spending many years in

New Orleans, & amassed great wealth there, embarked for a visit to his native place, & dying on his passage thither, & being unmarried, his property fell to his connections here, who raised this structure to his memory. There is a solid handsome marble pillar to Brevet Major General Nathan Towson, Paymaster, U S A. Nor will we forget that very beautiful spot on the hillside, so dear to a mother's heart. A modest marble pillar, crowned with graceful cushion & draped in the hightes taste, bears upon its front "Our Willie," surrounded with a wreath of flowers, & the word "Translated." By the side of this, on another grave, is the marble figure of a child, with hands uplifted & clasped as in prayer, & upon the pedestal is the word "George." It is the lot of W P S Sanger.

MON JUL 23, 1866

The murderers of Dr Webb & son, at Little Rock, a few weeks since, have been arrested. A gold watch taken from Dr Webb was recognized & betrayed them. One was a colored hostler & two colored soldiers. One of them has confessed.

Sale of the U S Marine Hospital & grounds, on Franklin st, Charleston; sold under orders of Collector at Auction yesterday, by Wm Wm M Pelot, auctioneer, was bid off by Mr John Hanckel for the Board of Missions to the colored people & freedmen of the Protestant Episcopal Church of South Carolina for $9,500.
–Charleston Courier

Mrd: on Jul 19, in Gtwn, D C, by Rev J R Nourse, Richd D Dodge, U S N, to Annie W Nourse, eldest daughter of the officiating clergyman.

Died: on Jul 22, Mr Jas Lusby, long a resident of Wash City, D C, & formerly of Annapolis, Md, aged 63 years & 18 days. His funeral will be on Jul 24 at 4 o'clock, corner of 6th & K sts.

H J Coates, postmaster at Albany, Green Co, Wisc, & his wife, have been arrested for robbing the mail at their ofc. Mrs Coates plead guilty, & has been committed to jail in default of $1,000. No evidence being found to implicate Mr Coates, he was released, but has been removed as postmaster. The depredations have been in progress some time.

Bills affecting interests in the District of Columbia have passed on both Houses of Congress. 1-Bill to incorporate the Wash Land & Bldg Co of D C: enacts John M Brodhead, N P Chipman, Wm Orme, Stephen Flanagan, Moses Kelly, Saml P Brown, Jas M Flanagan, Wm W Harding, Wm S Allen, Henry Simons, Thos M Plowman, Jos F Brown, Benj B French, Chas D Gilmore, Wm W Danenhower, Wm B Shaw & D C Forney, their present & future associates, shall be constituted a body politic & corporate, by the name & style aforesaid, & by same name shall have perpetual succession. 2-Act to grade East Capitol st from 3rd to 11th st, & to cause the square at the intersection of said st with Mass, N C, Tenn, & Ky aves, between 11th & 12th sts, to be enclosed with a wooden fence, to be known as **Lincoln Square**. 3-Act to incorporate "The Soldiers' & Sailors' Union, of Wash,

D C: B A Hall, W C Porter, Will A Short, Jas Cross, J H Nightingale, D S Curtiss, L Edwin Dudley, G M Van Buren, Wm S Morse, Lawrence Wilson, Wm L Bramhall, F E Drake, B P Cutter, W H H Bates, H N Rothery, S G Merrill, Chas A Appel, O A Lukenbaugh, J S Fieman, John H Simpson, Geo W De Costa, L J Bryant, J H Gray, Lyman S Every & A I Bennett, & their successors in office, are made a body politic & corporate, by the name aforesaid. 3-Bill to incorporate the **General Hospital of D C**: Jos Henry, Jas C Hall, Amos Kendall, Thos Miller, Richd Wallach, Geo W Riggs, Grafton Tyler, Henry D Cooke, D W Middleton, Chas Knap, Benj B French, Jas C McGuire, Chas H Nichols, Wm B Todd, Wm Gunton, Edw Simms & Thos Young, & their successors in office, are declared a corporation & body politic, in law & in fact, under the name & style of the Directors of the General Hospital of the District of Columbia. 4-Bill to incorporate the **Washington Temperance Society** of the city of Washington, D C: John S Hollingshead, Wm G Flood, Christopher Cammack, sr Asbury Lloyd, John B Wheeler, Zach B Brooke, Ros A Fish, Geo W Maher, Wm P Drew, Wm H Nalley, Thos B Marche, Oscar Alexander, Wm Dixon, & others who now are or may hereafter become members, & their successors, are declared to be one community & body corporate by the name, style, & title aforesaid. 5-Act in incorporate "The **Nat'l Soldiers' & Sailors' Orphan Home**." Mrs Julia B Grant, Mrs Ellen E Sherman, Mrs H D Cooke, Mrs Margaret Fahnestock, Mrs Kathleen Carlisle, Miss Charlotte Taylor, Mrs Jane Speed, Mrs Mary J Welles, Mrs A C Harlan, Mrs Jane L Smith, Mrs Mary K Lewis, Mrs Jane Farnham, Mrs Eliza M Morris, Mrs Cecilia S Sherman, Mrs Ellen Boyer, Mrs Eliz A Howard, Mrs Kate C Sprague, Mrs Eliza B Nye, Mrs Annie Rouse, Mrs Kate L Plants, Mrs Eliz G Todd, Mrs Abby E Hale, Mrs J M Trumbull, Miss Sarah Wood, Mrs Jane Anne Pirtle, Miss Eliz Howard, & their successors, are consitituted a body corporate in D C, by the name aforesaid. 6-Bill to incorporate the **Wash Co Horse Railroad Co** in D C: this bill enact that Saml P Brown, Francis Mattingly, Noble D Larner, Marshall Brown & Jos L Pearson, & their associates & assigns be, & they are hereby, created a body corporate, under the name aforesaid.

Troy, Jul 21. 1-Hon Jas S Thorn, member of Assembly from this city in the last Legislature, died at the residence of his father this morning, of consumption. Mr Thorn was one of the associate editors of the Times of this city. 2-Abram Fonda, associate editor of the Times of this city, fell from the 3rd story of the Phoenix Hotel, at Lansingburg, yesterday, & died at 4 o'clock this morning.

Poughkeepsie, Jul 20. Rev J C Richmond, while standing in his meadow, in the suburbs of this city, today, was struck by a man named Richd Levies & killed. The affair has created considerable excitement, as Mr Richmond was well known & had many friends. [Jul 24th newspaper: Rev Jas Cook Richmond, of the Episcopal Churh, whose death by violence was recorded yesterday, was a native of Providence, R I, & a graduate of Harvard Univ; studied abroad at the Univ of Gottingen for 3 years. On his return to America, he took orders in the Episcopal Church. On the breaking out of the war, he came to Wash as chaplain to a Wisc regt, & after making a campaign in Va, received an appointment as chaplain to St

Eliz Hospital, in this vicinity. He remained for some months; when, manifesting symptoms of insanity, he was removed to the Insane Asylum of this District. On his recovery, he returned to Poughkeepsie where his family resided, & assumed the charge of a parish in Ulster Co. Mr Richmond married a Miss Seaton, of British West Indies, & leaves a large family, one of whom is attached to the War Dept, & is superintendent of the Sunday school of St John's Church.]

The name of P Butterfield is withdrawn from the firm of Vincent Butterfield & Co, he having at no time any interest in said firm. –P Butterfield

Application will be made to the Register of Wash City, D C, for the renewal of 4 tax certificates for lots 1 thru 3 in square 90; sold May 22, 1862, in the name of John Douglass. Also, for lot 8 in square 467, sold May 4, 1864, in the name of Geo Page, the same having been lost or mislaid. –Jas Fraser, jr

On Wed, Mr Geo Raymond, of Woodbury, N J, formerly commercial agent at Belize, & editor of the Whig, in Blair Co, Pa, was brutally murdered on his farm by some persons unknown.

Supreme Court, D C, in Equity No 558. John Purdy against Isaac D, John H, & Anna E Surratt, heirs of John H Surratt, Edw W Belt, his adm de bonis non, John T Given, & Jas S Harvey. The parties above & all creditors of the late John H Surratt, are to meet on Aug 14 next, at my ofc, City Hall, Wash. I shall state the account of the trustee & distribute the funds arising from the sale of the real estate of Surratt. –W Redin, auditor

Barney Van Arsdall & Jas Lemmons, 19 & 20 years of age, were executed at Springfield, Ill, on Friday last. They were convicted in April last, of the murder of John Saunders, at Pawnee. Owing to their youth, the citizens made great efforts to secure a respite or commutation of their sentence, but without avail.

TUE JUL 24, 1866
The Senate yesterday rejected the nomination of Govn'r Holden, of N C, as Minister to San Salvador. Judge Stanbury was confirmed as Atty General. The nomination of Govn'r Randall as Postmaster General was not acted upon.

Despatch from Eliz, N J, dated Jul 22: Harlan G Knapp, age 20 years, of respectability & good family, residing at this place, committed suicide yesterday by shooting himself through the heart & lungs with a 7 barrelled revolver, on the cemetery grounds attached to the First Presbyterian Church, of which he was a member. He had been a regular attendant of labors. No papers or letters were found on the body.

For sale: a very desirable residence in Charlestown, Jefferson Co, West Va: the dwlg is a large 2 story, front & wing, & contains 9 rooms. Possession can be given at once. -D Smith Eichelberger, Charlestown, Jeff Co, West Va.

Obit-died: on Jun 26, at Shepherdstown, Jefferson Co, Va, Mrs Susan E Gordon, wife of Col David Gordon, formerly of Mississippi, but more recently of the cities of Wash & Balt. She was the daughter of Capt Saml Fisher & was born in 1798, & reared near Warrenton, Fauquier Co, Va. She was exceedingly devoted to the study of history. After a tedious & exhausting complication of disease, this lovely woman wound up the career of life on Jun 26, 1866, in her 68th year.

Chancery sale of a valuable improved real estate on Mass ave between 4th & 5th sts west: by decree of the Supreme Court of D C, dated Jul 16, 1866, passed in a cause wherein Thos H Scott et al are cmplnts, & Eliz Clagett et al are dfndnts- Equity No 536. Public auction on Aug 17 next. –Wm Jno Miller, trustee -Green & Williams, aucts

Frederick Female Seminary, Fred'k, Md, will commence its 24th Scholastic year on the first Monday in Sept. Address Rev Thos M Cann, A M, President.

Supreme Court of D C, Equity 691-Docket 7. John D & Annie L Wells vs Chas G Baylor et al. Wm F Mattingly, trustee, reported he sold the real estate in said cause mentioned, at public auction, to Edwin Green for $17,000, & that Green had paid the entire purchase money. –R J Meigs, clerk

To my friends & the public generally. In view of making a change in my business, I offer my entire stock of goods at cost for cash for the next 45 days. –Wm Tucker, Merchant Tailor, 426 Pa ave, between 4½ & 6th sts.

Peter E Blow, one of the oldest & most prominent merchants of St Louis, & a brother of Hon Henry T Blow, died on Thu. He was extensively identified with the mining interests of Missouri.

Dr Wm A Carrington, formerly Medical Director of Va in the Southern army, died in Charlotte Co, Va, a few days ago, in his 37th year.

WED JUL 25, 1866
Mr Jas M Buff, of the firm of John W Buff & Co, one of the heaviest dry-goods houses in Balt, died in that city on Monday, after a brief illness of congestion of the heart.

Dumbarton: under a deed of trust from John F Clark: I will sell, on the premises, Jul 25, twenty lots, from 3 to 10 acres of land, adjoining the District line, on the road to Bladensburg; being a subdivision of the farm of John F Clark, now residing in Balt. A portion of the land has a comfortable dwlg. Mrs Gales' & Thos Berry's is only a mile distant. -Green & Williams, aucts, Wash.

Among the graduates at Kenyon College, Ohio, this year, was John J McCook, the youngest of nine brothers who served in the late war, three of them, as well as their venerable father, having been killed.

Mr Chas Bates, a well-known citizen of Richmond died on Monday.

The Surgeon Gen has received official notice of the death of Assist Surgeon & Brvt Major J T Calhoun, U S army, at the depot at Hart's Island, N Y harbor, on Jul 19. Surgeon Calhoun died of cholera, which he contracted while in the performance of arduous & exhausting duty.

Died: on Jul 24, Hoply Y Werekmuller, a native of Norfolk, Va, but for the last 25 years of N Y. His funeral will take place from St Patrick's Church, at 10 A M, Jul 26. Norfolk, Va, & N Y papers please copy.

Dept of the Interior, U S Patent Ofc, Wash, Jul 21, 1866. Ptn of Albert Gardner, for himself & as administrator of Wm J Hunter, of Cincinnati, Ohio, praying for the extension of a patent granted to the said Gardner, as said administrator, & to himself, Oct 26, 1852, for an improvements in Ploughs, for 7 years from the expiration of said patent, which takes place on Oct 26, 1866.
–T C Theaker, Com'r of Pensions

Supreme Court, D C. Desmond against Radcliffe et al. I shall state the trustee's account & distribute the fund among the heirs of the late Dennis Desmond.
–W Redin, auditor

Supreme Court, D C. McDonald & wife vs Geo W & Henry C Prather. I shall state the trustee's account & distribute the fund among the heirs of the late Overton J Prather. –W Redin, auditor

Orphans Court of Wash Co, D C. In the case of Eliz A Beall, admx of Horatio Beall, deceased, the administratrix & Court have appointed Aug 18 next, for the final settlement of the personal estate of the said deceased, of the assets in hand.
-Z C Robbins, Reg/o wills

Orphans Court of Wash Co, D C. In the case of Catharine Baumann, excx of Paul Baumann, deceased, the executrix & Court have appointed Aug 18 next, for the final settlement of the personal estate of the said deceased, of the assets in hand.
-Z C Robbins Reg/o wills

Orphans Court of Wash Co, D C. Letters of administration on the personal estate of Abigail E Evans, late of said county, deceased. –Chas M Matthews, adm

Public Resolution-No 47. A resolution for the restoration of Lt Cmder Richd L Law, U S Navy, to the active list from the reserved list, & restore him to his original rank in the grade of Lt Cmder. Approved: Jun 22, 1866.

The Pres has granted a pardon to Lawrence Rousseau, of New Orleans, La, formerly a capt in the U S Navy, who resigned & entered the rebel service, on the recommendation of Admiral Shubrick, the Govn'r of the State, & Atty Gen Speed.

THU JUL 26, 1866
The Senate yesterday confirmed Hon A W Randall as Postmaster Gen, Jos S Wilson, Com'r of the Land Ofc, Lt Gen Grant as general of the armies of the U S, & Vice Admiral Farragut as admiral of the naval forces.

The Sec of the Navy was yesterday notified of the confirmation of the following persons to be passed assist paymasters & assist paymasters in the navy.
Passed Assist Paymasters:
Robt W Allen, Mass
Henry W Meade, N Y
Frank Clarke, R I
Edw Sherwin, Mass
Albert D Bache, Pa
Dominick B Batvine, Nevada
W F A Torbet, Md
Edw H Cushing, N H
Leonard H Frailey, D C
John H Stevenson, N Y
Thos L Tullock, N H
Jason W Fairfield, Mass
Edw M Hart, N Y
Geo E Honder, Mass
Milton B Cushing, N Y
J Henry Bulkley, Pa
Robt B Rodney, Pa
Gilbert A Robertson, N Y
To be Assist Paymasters:
H A Thompson, jr, Pa
Albert W Bacon, Pa
F Clarence Imlay, N Y
Rufus S McConnell, Ohio
Chas D Mansfield, Ohio

Jas L Girard, D C
Saml G Wood, jr, N Y
Francis J Painter, Pa
Geo L Mead, N Y
Wm J W Woodhull, N Y
Geo R Watkins, Md
Danforth P Wight, Iowa
Henry T Wright, Iowa
Danl A Smith, jr, N H
Chas W McDaniel, Ohio
Frank H Ames, Conn
John Fivey, N Y
Jared Linsley, jr, N Y
Francis T Gillete, Ind
Geo W Griffing, Md
Emanuel Mellock, N J
Jas H Mulford, jr, N Y
Geo W Brown, Maine

Henry F Skilding, Conn
Chas W Slamm, N Y
J Appleton Berry, Pa
Jos Foster, N J

A cemetery for the Union dead at Culpeper, Va, is being laid out on the farm of Mr Hill, & will embrace 6 acres. The remains of those buried between the Rappahannock river & Gordonsville areas are to be interred in this cemetery, including those who fell in the battle of *Cedar Mountain*.

Mrd: on Jul 24, at St Aloysius Church, by Rev Fr Stonestreet, Mr Ralph Jefferson to Miss Emma Wyman, both of Wash.

Mrd: on Jul 24, at the residence of & by Rev Wm Burris, of Wash, D C, Mr Wm W Pace to Miss E Jane Cooke, both of Richmond, Va.

Orphans Court-Judge Purcell.
1-At the last session the will of the late Marcelia Riley, late Spalding, was partially proven. 2-Letters of administration were issued to Mary Washington, on the estate of Geo Washington; bond $1,000; & to Chas M Matthews, on the estate of Abigail E Evans; bond $300. 3-The first & final account of Jos Cross was approved & passed.

The painting of the battle of Gettysburg, by the artist Rothermel, to be placed in the Capitol of Pa, is not to be less than 30 feet long & 15 feet high. It is to embrace a landscape view, with a battle scene in large figures, embodying some great epoch in the terrible fight which it is to represent. It must be historically true, & must be finished 3 years from this date. The design for the principal painting is to be executed in a study 6 feet long by 5 feet wide, & is to be finished in a year. The principal painting will be the grand rebel charge on Hancock's corps, Jul 3, the subsequent defeat, & the great struggle of the whole battle.

Miss Fanny Forrest, a niece of Gen Forrest, was burned fatally a few days since by the explosion of a can from which she was pouring coal oil at the time upon some burning wood, in order to kindle the fire more rapidly. She lived only a few hours after the accident. Miss Forrest was about 19 years old, & was residing in the family of Dr E W Ayres, near Hannibal, Missouri.

The Marquis of Lunsdowne died on Jul 5, of paralysis. He was the third marquis of the title, & was born in 1780, a son of Lord Shelburne, created marquis in 1784.

FRI JUL 27, 1866
Despatch from Mobile of the 19th says: T J Chandler this morning at daylight fought a duel with L Holcombe. At the second fire Chandler received a ball through the chest, living about 25 minutes. Holcombe was formerly a soldier in the Federal army, & Chandler in the rebel army. The difficulty originated in disputing whether Columbia S C, was burned by Gen Sherman's order or by orders of the Confederate generals.

On Jul 5 the Princess Helena Augusta Victoria, third daughter of her Majesty, was united in marriage to his Royal Highness Prince Christian, of Schleswig-Holstein-Sonderbourg Augustenburg. The ceremony was performed in the private chapel attached to the royal apartments of Windsor Castle.

Mrd: on Jul 24, at St Aloysius Church, by Rev Fr Stonestreet, S J, Ralph Jefferson, of Wash City, to Miss Emma J Nyman, formerly of Wash Co, Md.

Mrd; on Jul 19, in Roxborough, Phil, by Rev David Spencer, Mr Hamilton K Gray, of Wash, D C, to Miss Virginia L Knowlton, daughter of the late Curtis Knowlton.

Mrd: on Jul 25, by R J Keelling, D D, at the residence of Dr Bradisa, Anne Arundel Co, Md, Dr A S Linthicum, of said county, to Mrs Antoinette O Crain, of Richfield Sp___. N Y. [Paper not clear.]

Income Tax-names of tax-payers whose incomes amount to $2,000 & upwards. A list of incomes for the past year has been completed by the Internal Revenue Assessor for this District, Mr Pearson, & the Collector, Mr Clephane, is prepared to receive the tax on the same. Ofcs on 7th st, opposite the Post Ofc bldg.

Isaac Alexander, $5,283
P H Allabach, $3,511
G W Adams, $3,217
R J Atkinson, $6,098
Chris Andrews, $4,634
John Alexander, $7,413
Com J H Aulick, $7,932
Wm Arhends, $5,200
Nicholas Acker, $7,757
Sebastian Aman, $3,785
Jas Adams, $11,112
John G Adams, $3,761
Columbus Alexander, $4,876
C H Baker, $3,881
Ferd Butler, $4,000
D J Bishop, $5,120
S P Belt, $2,611
Benj Beall, $5,393
D W Brown, $2,047
S H Bacon, $2,700
W D Baldwin, $4,392
Henry Baldwin, $3,283
Thos J Barnes, $3,700
J W Bulkley, $3,574
J G Bathel, $2,263
Geo A Bailey, $6,614
Richd Barry, $2,820
Constantine Brumidi, $3,100
Saml Bacon, $6,314
H A Brewster, $2,271
Andrew Baldwin, $2,072
Mary J Blair, $4,573
Chas Bradley, $2,580
J H Browning, $4,037
C W Boteler, $6,688
M W Beveridge, $8,206
W H Baldwin, $2,000
Ed Baldwin, $2,000
Peter F Bacon, $5,714
C W Boteler, $2,520
Jos Borrows, $4,563
Jos Bryan, $5,491
John M Boteler, $6,123
M V B Bogan, $5,599
Philip Berry, $4,386
Thos S Brown, $3,400
L Botsch, $2,000
Jas G Berret, $2,240
Marshal Brown, $22,522
John F Bridget, $2,200
John P Barrett, $2,910
Mrs M M Boyce, $13,844
J R Burroughs, $2,987
Wilson E Brown, $2,270
John A Baker, $4,380
Jos F Brown, $7,029
Anthony Best, $2,365
Jas L Barbour, $5,918
Jos W Barker, $4,002
J Russell Barr, $2,157
Mrs Susan M Barche, $2,795
John H Blondin, $2,122
Wm C Bestor, $3,021
Buckner Baylis, $2,243
H S Benson, $25,230
J P Bartholow, $27,812
J B Blake, $3,053
W A Bradley, $6,811

Fred Bates, $5,071
John N Barry, $4,200
Jos H Bradley, $6,161
Val Blanchard, $6,195
Thos Blagden, $12,666
W H Clagett, $4,252
Mrs McL Cripps, $2,750
C Christiani, $2,547
Arch Campbell, $27,083
R D Cutts, $2,882
G W Cockran, $14,633
R Cohen, $4,789
W H Campbell, $4,608
Mrs E Cropley, $2,485
W H Campbell, $3,515
Mary A Clark, $2,216
John T Cochran, $2,886
J W Colley, $4,603
D B Clarke, $6,601
W E Chandlee, $4,998
Fitzhugh Coyle, $5,086
Leonidas Coyle, $2,591
H A Chadwick, $28,305
Dr R C Croggon, $2,769
Dr P Croghan, $3,144
W D Colt, $2,765
W W Corcoran, $20,390
E C Carrington, $6,705
Robt Campbell, $3,289
Jas M Carlisle, $10,441
Henry D Cooke, $188,735
Mrs L M Closs, $4,950
John B Clagett, $2,616
S DeVaughn, $8,406
Dan Ruben, $2,117
W W Danenhower, $8,022
Columbus Denham, $2,508
Jas Y Davis, $16,443
Geo T Dearing, $2,288
Jos B Dobson, $4,756
E C Dyer, $2,986
G G Duvant, $2,721
P W Dorsey, $2,334
John Dickson, $9,502
Richd Delafield, $15,847
R H Duvall, $2,375

W C Dodge, $2,580
Jacob Dyser, $2,449
W D Dawson, $4,000
Henry S Davis, $3,683
John A Dahlgren, $4,677
Thos J Davis, $5,594
W H Dougal, $3,401
Dr G M Dove, $8,736
Wm Dixon, $7,338
Lewis J Davis, $18,759
W D Davidge, $7,017
P M Dubant, $7,269
Cornelia Dikeman, $6,376
Wm R Dikeman, $2,281
Jona Dennison, jr, $2,780
Col Justin Dimick, $5,518
Frank Etchison, $3,524
John F Ellis, $7,310
John R Elvans, $19,011
Chas Edmonston, $4,039
Gregory Ennis, $2,508
Dr Johnson Eliot, $3,132
Thos Ewing, $3,370
H N Easby, $2,798
Lucia Ela, $2,749
Chas F English, $2,240
Robt Earl & Son, $2,087
Jas L Edwards, $2,552
John O Evans, $6,063
M G Emery, $8,367
Anthony Eberly, $3,199
John Ferguson, $3,353
S C Ford, $2,300
Jos N Fearson, $2,016
N B Fugitt, $2,838
W G Freeman, $23,233
R W Fenwick, $6,000
G E B French, $7,270
Y G Ford, $2,672
R Fullalove, $4,400
J Fugitt, $2,566
J Follansbee, $3,026
P Fegan, $3,244
General J B Fry, $2,886
Dr C M Ford, $2,382
S Fowler, $5,933

Mrs Jane Farnham, $2,008
Elisha Falconer, $3,412
Wm Guinand, $4,821
Mrs Emma Gibbs, $2,232
Wm A Gray, $3,260
L A Gobright, $2,300
B E Gittings, $3,652
Edwin Green, $6,158
H Gasch, $3,050
Mrs S Graves, $4,896
Jno Goldin, $2,002
Chas T Gardner, $2,191
Michl Green, $5,458
Jos Gawler, $2,425
Lemuel Gaddis, $4,269
Wm Gunton, $12,407
E W Grey, $4,918
R H Graham, $2,059
John Grinder, $3,348
E M Grinder, $3,256
Adam Gaddis, jr, $4,524
John T Given, $2,657
Miss Romaine Goddard, $3,846
Vinton Goddard, $4,411
G F Gulick, $4,472
W H Godey, $2,232
M W Galt, $8,857
W Galt, $6,693
Amon Green, $7,285
Alex Gardner, $2,006
Geo Gibson, $2,147
Z C Gilman, $3,400
F W Gieseking, $2,618
W Chandler Gregg, $3,586
Jas Holt, $2,792
Geo P Hamblin, $2,102
Chas Herring, $6,279
Isaac Hackett, $2,193
Saml Heilbrun, $2,439
Lewis Heilbrun, $2,139
Johnson Hellen, $3,595
C Herzber, $2,943
I Herzberg, $4,701
L H Hopkins, $3,538
G C Henning, $2,960
P A Hoover, $4,216

J P Hilton, $4,011
J B Hutchinson, $15,189
F J Heiberger, $6,688
T M Hanson, $3,660
John Hitz, $3,785
Mrs M B Hoban, $2,476
W W Hough, $3,001
Gen D Hunter, $3,944
Peter H Hoe, $3,167
Jos Henry, $3,900
E G Handy, $2,045
Rev C H Hall, $2,401
Jas C Hall, $5,167
T H Havenner, $2,020
Thos Havenner, $3,082
W H Harrover, $2,645
Geo Hill, $3,000
John H Hamilton, $3,078
A J Harvey, $2,051
S H Hable, $2,128
S H Howell, $2,956
A Hyde, $2,139
Bernard Hayes, $3,000
T M Harvey, $2,970
W S Huntington, $11,052
Miss Susan Ireland, $9,370
H C Joy, $2,458
John L Johnson, $3,158
Walter Johnson, $6,463
John Joliffe, $2,145
Lewis Johnson, $13,252
Ed Jordan, $4,657
A J Joyce, $7,269
John M Johnson, $2,962
R P Jackson, $2,290
Geo I Johnson, $7,418
Dr W P Johnston, $14,850
H I King, $3,840
Henry King, $2,061
A F Kimmell, $4,760
Jas Keleher, $2,349
Horatio King, $3,452
Chas Kloman, $4,782
John E Kelly, $11,986
Mose Kelly, $5,426
John C Kennedy, $4,227

A B Keyser, $2,500
Z H P King, $2,070
J B Kibbey's estate, $3,010
W B Kibbey, $7,564
Wm King, $5,944
A Koch, $4,915
A T Keeckhoefer, $17,552
Geo E Kennedy, $3,079
John L Kidwell, $3,282
S H Kauffman, $6,979
Amos Kendall, $15,318
Jacob Lowenthal, $4,500
John Lane, $5,300
P W Lowe, $2,741
Evans Lyons, $2,690
Geo A Lane, $2,636
J W H Lovejoy, $2,001
Dr H Lindsay, $4,441
G Lansburg, $2,782
Dr C H Leiberman, $8,202
John T Lehman, $9,511
John W Lewis, $3,635
Chas H Lane, $2,483
Dr H Lindsley, guardian, $3,946
G Lowry, $6,642
Jos Libbey, jr, $15,350
Ed Linthicum, $8,394
W Linton, $3,010
F A Lutz, $8,219
P Lawrence, $13,603
B Lawrence, $13,784
DeWitt C Lawrence, $5,516
Max Lansburg, $3,682
Jos Libbey, $15,350
J H Lathrop, $6,631
A H Lee, $2,346
Thos Lewis, $3,848
John Little, $2,915
Jos C Lewis, $2,138
Mrs Anna Lindsley, $3,119
C Mades, $2,250
H D Mears, $8,978
John McDermott, $2,627
John R Murray, $7,551
Thos P Morgan, $3,416
F Mohun, $11,170

J C McKelden, $2,581
John Markriter, $2,930
T A McLaughlin, $3,442
D McFarland, $3,344
F B Mohun, $6,129
C A Murphy, $5,100
W McLean, $3,538
Rev W McLain, $2,499
W B Morrison, $2,395
D L Morrison, $9,800
W G Metzerott, $5,180
John R Major, $2,486
Douglass Moore, $3,398
Thos McGill, $6,982
Hora Moran, $3,276
John T Mitchell, $6,798
Thos Miller, $4,050
John S Maxwell, $2,202
J W Morsell, $3,132
Chas Mason, $5,557
Jas C McGuire, $10,108
F B McGuire, $2,132
S A H Marks, $3,258
B R Mansfield, $3,403
B Miller, $2,531
John Marbury, jr, $2,155
B E Murray, $2,645
F McGhan, $5,955
W S Mitchell, $4,269
Lloyd Moxley, $2,548
John Moore, 4,889
Dr Jas E Morgan, $5,031
A McCathran, $3,061
Dr L Mackall, $2,473
C M Matthews, $2,394
D W Middleton, $4,400
M S Miller, $2,266
P McNamara, $2,563
J J May, $5,352
W D C Murdock, $3,370
H Magruder, $4,911
L J Middleton, $3,411
Geo Mattingly, $10,303
Dr S A H McKim, $6,241
Jere McCarthy, $2,194
Mrs E M Mosher, $3,378

John Marbury, trustee, $8,225
John Marbury, $5,423
Richd Mohun, $6,208
Philip May, $2,049
Harvey North, $6,650
J W Nairn, $3,447
W H Nalley, $2,522
S Norment, $12,550
Dr W G H Newman, $2,593
G O Noyes, $5,032
Allison Nailor, $5,201
T A Newman, $2,911
V Niles, $14,280
J G Nailor, $3,700
Col Naylor, $2,013
L Oppenheimer, $5,642
John Ogden, $2,317
W C O'Meara, $4,014
Mrs Otterback, $4,311
Wm Orme, $7,411
Martin O'Donohue, $2,500
S W Owen, $3,684
Edw Owen, $4,586
Jos L Pearson, $2,220
A R Potts, $37,964
K F Page, $6,229
A Pollock, $2,986
J J Peabody, $2,769
A E Perry, $6,014
C B Pearson, $3,447
Peter Parker, $6,611
Geo Parker, $7,411
T J S Perry, $6,048
R W Pearson, $3,178
H Polkinhorn, $2,084
W H Philip, $7,193
Esau Pickrell, $4,089
A H Pickrell, $4,193
Thos Parker, $2,727
R Patterson, $9,072
A Provost, $10,141
W G Palmer, $5,346
Franklin Philp, $11,624
Mrs Ann Pickrell, $4,915
N Phelan, $4,015
L F Perry, $3,331

G H Plant, $9,099
W S Ringgold, $2,804
W B Rochester, $2,640
W Richards, $5,329
H K Randall, $4,128
S Redfern, $4,469
G A W Randall, $3,342
Chris Ruppert, $3,240
F C Richenbach, $2,200
Geo Rhinehart, $3,416
I Rosenthal, $3,181
John Riggles, $2,124
W J Rhees, $3,487
W S Roose, $2,952
C F E Richardson, $4,920
Alex Ray, $19,562
A Ross Ray, $4,655
T A Richards, $4,321
A Richards, $4, 545
John Roves, $2,553
W R Riley, $2,654
R J Ryan, $3,022
G W Riggs, $54,581
Mary Alice Riggs, $16,208
Bush Robinson, $3,321
L J Rothrock, $2,666
W H Rapley, $10,730
Dr Josh Riley, $4,072
J A Ruff, $2,284
Gen D G Ramsay, $2,090
Z C Robbins, $5,303
Wm Redin, $10,799
W W Russell, $2,860
Albert Ray, $4,350
Jos Shillington, $2,774
J W Selby, $2,329
J H Snyder, $2,300
Geo Savage, $3,133
Mrs A Simpson, $6,201
W M Shuster, $11,999
W J Sibley, $11,806
W D Shepherd, $2,236
H C Shuster, $8,482
J J Shedd, $3,303
A B Staughton, $6,815
H C Swain, $3,217

Admiral J Smith, $5,587
J T Stevens, $2,475
A T Shriver, $3,552
A Schneider, $2,783
F Schneider, $2,252
Chas Stott, $2,529
S R Savage, $3,154
J C Smith, $2,808
B H Stimentz, $15,070
H Clay Stewart, $2,297
S Stinemetz, $2,683
M H Stevens, $9,290
Mrs H M Sullivan, $2,468
Jas G Smith, $5,486
Dr S C Smoot, $3,695
Ed Simmons, $4,067
S Simmons, $9,241
W R Snow, $3,580
Mrs E D E N Southworth, $4,300
R A Shinn, $39,285
C Stewart, $4,271
I B Semmes, $6,016
A S Solomons, $6,860
G L Sheriff, $3,400
T A Stephens, $4,385
Adeline Sargent, $2,634
A R Shepherd, $3,359
Walter Stewart, $2,646
D Smith, $3,525
John H Smoot, $3,540
W F Seymour, $3,006
J H Shreve, $3,455
W J Stone, jr, $3,443
R L Smith, $2,321
A Straus, $2,535
H Semkin, $4,602
Mrs W J Stone, $6,145
E F Simpson, $2,380
W E Spalding, $7,900
L H Schneider, $2,635
John H Semmes, $8,168
J A Stephenson, $2,987
J W Sears, $2,206
A Small, $3,496
Saml Stott, $2,618
Jos Travers, $4,337

Jenkin Thomas, $2,137
W S Thompson, $2,327
Gen Z H Tower, $2,978
Owen Thorn, $7,221
Hudson Taylor, $10,031
W B Todd, $7,869
Saml Tilston, $4,400
Enoch Tucker, $2,088
Franck Raylor, $6,523
Jas S Topham, $6,692
Graftn Tyler, $2,005
Jas Towles, $2,203
B Ogle Tayloe, $6,525
Poulus Thyson, $3,974
J W Thompson, $5,195
W S Teal, $3,873
Elias Travers, $3,028
Michl Talty, $3,037
Z Tobriner, $2,481
G W Utermehle, $4,590
Ulysses Ward, $4,362
W D Wyvill, $2,918
E E White, $3,000
Capt H A Wise, $2,978
F E Weston, $2,302
Geo Wilney, $4,858
Ellen F Woodhull, $3,234
W H Wheatley, $2,409
Jas S Welch, $16,692
Jas H Welch, $3,804
Edwin P Welch, $4,785
Rosina Welch, $3,786
John F Webb, $11,854
John W Wetherall, $3,478
Ellen Wolfe, $2,729
Amanda Wilton, $2,000
Jos Walsh, $2,284
G M Wight, $2,004
Frank Wolfe, $4,480
J C Willard, $15,745
C Woodward, $8,800
W B Webb, $3,471
John B Ward, $3,007
Theo Wheeler, $9,512
F S Walsh, $3,017
John Q Willson, $4,283

R H Willett, $2,343
Wm Wilson, $7,812
Michl Willian/William. $3,572
J M Witherow, $6,982
H P Welch, $2,326
Jas Wallace, $2,301
Hon G Welles, $2,610
N Wilson, $4,466
E Wallach, $3,193
Geo Waters, $4,538
John G Worthington, $6,975
John A Wills, $7,618
C C Willard, $7,059
John Webster, $3,952
W Williams, $4,937
W H Ward, $5,708
David Walker, $12, 443
P White, $4,280
F Wheatley, $8,763
Jackson Yates, $2,722
Mark Young, $3,447
Geo W Young, $6,552

St Aloysius Church bells. Just completed at the foundry of Mr Joshua Regester, Holliday st, near Saratoga, three large church bells for the Roman Catholic Church of St Aloyisus, Wash, D C, which will be sent there in a few days. They are of pure bell-metal, consisting principally of copper & tin. No 1 weighs, including stopper, 3,600 pounds; No 2, 1,669 pounds; & No 3, 915 pounds. On one side is an inscription of the name of the manufacturer, Joshua Regester, Balt, 1866. All three will be rung by the mode of swinging, & have been placed on substantial frames. –Balt American [Aug 11th newspaper: The bells were presented to the church by Alex'r Provest, Jas S Harvey, & Geo Savage, of Wash City. They will be placed in the tower of the church about Sep 1. On the bell presented by Alexander Prevost is: IESV. SERVATORIS. CORDI SANTISSIMO. ALEXANDER PROVEST, ANNO. MDCCCLXVI. VT. WASHINGTONIANO. SANCTI. ALOISH TEMPLO. DECVS. ET. COMMODUM. ACCEDAT." Translation: To the most sacred heart of Jesus the Saviour-Alexander Provest, in the year 1866-that glory and advantage may accrue to the temple of St Aloysius at Washington." On the bell presented by Mr Harvey: "HONORI. MARIAR. AVGVSTAE. AB. ORIGINE IMMACVLATAE. JACOLL S. HARVEY. SOMTIDVS AES CONFLATVM. AN MDCCLXVI WAHINGTONIL AD SANCTI ALOISII. AEDES. CVETVS. APPELLO." Translation: to the honor of the august Mary, always immaculate-at the cost of James S Harvey, this monument is made, in the year 1866, at Washington, at the church of St. Aloysius. I call the people." On the bell presented by Mr Savage: TIBI. ALOISI. COELES. TIS. PATRONE. GEORGIVS. SAVAGE. CLIENTVBVS. AES. HOE SACEVM AVSPENDIT. WASHINGTONII. AN. MDCCCLXVI. VTI. [The rest in latin is unreadable.] Translation: To the Aloysius, Heavenly patron, I, George Savage, become a client. He hangs up this sacred brass at Washington, in the year 1866, as stated hours to be rung. It indicates the sacred rights of thy Church."]

On Wed Rudolph Buchley, of Wash City, bought 53 acres of ground with a dwlg house, barn, & stables, on the south side of Columbian turnpike, in Alexandria, Va, for $4,550. At the same time & place J M Young bought 34 acres of ground, with a dwlg-house thereon, quarter of a mile from the above, for $3,300.

For rent: desirable house in Smith's Row, First st, Gtwn; 4 story brick house, containing 14 rooms with a fine yard & good stabling. Inquire of Edw J Shoemaker, Real Estate Agent, 35 First st, Gtwn.

Brick laying in all its branches. Orders left at 169 I st, Wash, or 119 High st, Gtwn, will be promptly attended to. –J V Collins

SAT JUL 28, 1866
There is a rumor that the bark **Trieste**, on which Mr Dan Setchell took passage for Austrailia, had foundered at sea. The vessel had been out over 100 days at last accounts from San Francisco.

For sale: *Enfield Chase*, a plantation of about 600 acres, in PG Co, Md, nearly intermediate between the cities of Balt, Wash, & Annapolis; with a comfortable dwlg & usual out-bldgs. Public auction at Collington on Aug 30 next. Address the undersigned, [living on the premises,] Collington post ofc, PG Co, Md, or Danl Clarke, atty-at-law, Upper Marlboro, Md. –Nich's H Shipley

Mrd: on Jul 26, at St Anne's Church, Annapolis, Md, by Rev Pinkney Hammond, Capt McLane Tilton, U S Marine Corps, to Anne *Maine/Marie Wells, daughter of the late Dr J B Wells, all of Annapolis. No cards. [*Appears to be Maine; but could be Marie.]

Died: on Jul 27, H W Tilley, in his 74th year. His funeral is on Sunday at 4½ o'clock P M, from his late residence, corner of 21st & H sts, Wash, D C.

Trustees of the Wash Academy, at Princess Anne, Somerset Co, Md, desire to employ a Principal Teacher, for the ensuing scholastic year, beginning on the second Monday of Sept, 1866; salary $800 for the scholastic year.
–Isaac L Jones, Pres of Board of Trustees

Bladensburg Academy [Md] will be opened on Sep 3, 1866. Principal, Rev John B Ross.

Trustee's sale of valuable improved real estate of A st, between 1st & N J ave: by deed of trust, dated jul 27, 1863, recorded in Liber N C T No 9, folios 383-385; auction on Sep 10 next, of lot 15 in square 688, improved by a large commodious, & well built brick house, which is known as the *Casparis Hotel*. –R S Davis, Chas H Utermele, trustees
-Green & Williams, aucts

For sale: beautiful farm known as *Glenallen*, the former residence of Capt W A T Maddox; contains 101½ acres of ground. -Green & Williams, aucts, 7th & D sts

Thos F Corry, clerk of the Spencer House, at Cincinnati, was shot on Monday by a lawyer of that city, J C Healey. Corry died on Tuesday.

Prisoners of War of either side held & that died during the war. Sec of War makes the following report: number of Union prisoners South, 26,940; number of rebel prisoners North, 200,000; number of Union prisoners died 22,576; number of rebel prisoners died, 26,436.

MON JUL 30, 1866
Messrs John R Ridge & Elias C Boudinot have been elected delegates to the Phil Convention from the Third Congressional District of Arkansas.

Heart's Content, Jul 28. We are in telegraphic communication with Ireland. The cable is in perfect order. –Cyrus W Field

The following is a list of the Directors of the N Y, Newfoundland, & London Telegraph Co: Peter Cooper, Cyrus W Field, Moses Taylor, Marshal O Roberts, & Wm G Hunt. The ofcrs of the company are: Peter Cooper, Pres; Cyrus W Field, Vice Pres; Moses Taylor, Treasurer; & Robt W Lowber, Secretary.

Died: on Jul 28, in Wash, D C, Mrs Margaret G Rhees, aged 65 years & 9 months, after an illness of 10 weeks.

Home School for Young Ladies: Mrs David H Burr will be prepared to receive at her country home, *Elmwood*, on the Wash Branch railroad, Howard Co, Md, a limited number of pupils who will have the advantage of a thorough French & English education. -Principal, Laurel Post Ofc, PG Co, Md.

I will sell at public auction on Aug 13 next, my late residence in Leesburg, Loudoun Co, Va; bldgs embrace the dwlg, a house for servants, & numerous out-bldgs; adapted for a Female Academy, or a Private Boarding House; & a 5 acre lot. Call upon Horatio Trondle, living in the dwlg, who will show the same. – Chas H Nourse, West River, Md

Orphans Court of Wash Co, D C, Jul 28, 1866. In the case of Mary M Turner, excx of Henry Stark, deceased, the executrix & Court have appointed Aug 21 next, for the final settlement of the personal estate of the said deceased, of the assets in hand. -Z C Robbins, Reg/o wills

Circuit Court of Talbot Co, in Equity, May Term, 1868. Anna M Powdle, assignee of Wm M Bayne vs Thos J Bayne. The object of this bill is to ascertain whether Thos J Bayne, the dfndnt, who has been absent from Talbot Co for more than 20 years, & from whom no tidings have been had for more than 12 years, be alive or not, & to procure a decree or order of Court directing the payment due to cmplnt, of certain proceeds of real estate, under the last will & testament of Rev Thos Bayne, deceased. The bill states that Rev Thos Bayne, of Talbot Co, departed this life some time in Jan, 1862, having first made & executed his last will & testament, in due form of law, dated Apr 23, 1860, duly admitted to probate, in which he devised his entire real estate in said county, to his son, Wm

M Bayne, with a provisio in case his son, Thos J Bayne, then absent, & whether alive or not, he states in said will & testament he knows not, should return, then he devised by certain metes, bounds, & descriptions a portion of said real estate to said Thos J Bayne. The bill further states, that no tidings or news of said Thos J Bayne had been had by his deceased, father, Rev Thos Bayne, for about 16 years before his death, which occurred in Jan, 1862, & no account or tidings have since been heard or had of him by the family to the present time. That the last accounts received of him, some 20 years since, represented him as residing in the State of Ga or Ala. The bill further states, that the personal estate of Rev Thos Bayne, in due course of administration, had been found insufficient to pay & satisfy his debts, & that the real estate of the said testator had been sold by the trustees appointed by said circuit court, sale ratified & confirmed by said Court, & purchase money paid; & after payment of deficiency or balance due on debts, the surplus distributed by Auditor's report, also duly ratified & confirmed by said Court, to said Wm M Bayne & Thos J Bayne, the proportion awarded to said Thos J Bayne being $5,889.95. That the said Wm M Bayne, entitled under the will & testament of his father, Rev Thos Bayne, to the portion of his real estate, devised, as before stated, to his brother, Thos J Bayne in case he never should return, & claim to said share or proportion of Thos J Bayne, his brother, as ascertained & allotted by said Auditor's report, to the cmplnt, Anna M Bowdle, of Talbot Co, Md; & that said Thos J Bayne, if alive, resides out of the State of Md. Absent dfndnt to appear in this Court in person, or by solicitor, on or before Feb 14 next. -Henry H Goldsborough -Sam T Hopkins, Clerk Circuit Court for Talbot Co

TUE JUL 31, 1866
Rev John Early, late president of Gtwn College, has been appointed to the presidency of Loyola College, Balt, Md, a position which he formerly occupied with great distinction.

The wife of Wm Cullen Bryant, the poet & editor of the N Y Evening Post, died at Roslyn, L I, on Jul 27, aged 70 years.

Yesterday the corner stone of the new Episcopal Church was laid; services by Rev Messrs Tillinghast, of St John's Church, Williams, of Christ Church, Chew, of St Alban's, & Rev J Eastburne Browne, with the trustees of the Mission Chapel, [now Grace Church,] repeating the 122nd Psalm. The church is to be free; to be built of blue gueiss stone, & have fine accommodations for its Sunday school. The church will be mainly built through the liberality of Mr H D Cooke, of Gtwn.

Yesterday near 3rd & A st, Capitol Hill, a child of Geo R Kendricks' & a child of Eugene Cavazier were playing in the street with other children, when a child of Cavazier took a box away from Kendrick's child; an affray then occurred between the fathers. Cavazier shot Kendricks through the thigh. Ofcr Sprague arrested them; Kendricks held to bail for court, Cavazier fined $25 for carrying a concealed weapon, & also held to bail.

New Orleans, Jul 30. The outside riot is suspended. The police have surrounded the Convention bldg. The bldg is full of the members of the Convention & negroes. The police are trying to get them out, but the populace is very belligerent. Dr A P Dostie & John Henderson, jr, were brought out dead & carried off in carts. It is doubtful if many will get out alive.
+
New Orleans, Jul 30. Gen Baird has issued a proclamation declaring martial law. Richd Cerus, the only child of Dr Cerus, was killed accidentally, & was the only white person killed. All the rest were negroes. [Aug 13th newspaper: Dr Dostie died on Aug 7, per the Picayune of the Aug 7. No one witnessed his last moments but the nurses in charge of the Hotel Dieu. Dr H Horton also died from his wounds last night, & John Henderson, jr, we learn, is sinking fast. The remains of Dr Dostie were carried to their final resting place yesterday; there were but 15 persons in attendance: 4 ladies, 2 Federal ofcrs, 7 citizens, & 2 negroes. The hearse, 5 carriages, a cab, & a buggy formed the funeral cortege.]

A convention of the soldiers & sailors of Lancaster Co, Pa, was held at Lancaster on Sat last; called to order by Col P S Pyfer; Capt John Wise, 9th Pa cavalry, chosen chairman. Ofcrs elected: Vice Presidents: Private Jos Albright, East Donegal; Lt Geo W White, Manheim Bor; Private John N Muller, Lancaster; Sgt Jacob H Smith, Warwick; Sgt Geo A Pinkerton, Lancaster; Sgt John Garber, Lancaster; Private Wm Brehm, Mount Joy Bor.
Secretaries: Lt C A Lichtenhaler, Warwick; Capt Owen Rice, Lancaster.
Gentlemen elected delegates to the State Convention:

Lt J S Roath, East Donegal	Sgt G A Pinkerton, City
Corp Henry Shireman, Marietta	Pvt Francis Kilburn, City
Corp J Benson Clepper, Columbia	Pvt Casper Weitzel, City
Pvt A J Eby, Manheim Bor	Capt John M Amweg, City
Pvt Wm Brehm, Mt Joy	Capt John Wise, City
Lt John Bitzer, Salisbury	Lt R A Smith, City
Pvt Wm Johnson, Salisbury	Pvt J H Hegener, City
Lt Chas A Lichtenthaler, Warwick	Pvt John Sheaffer, East Donegal
Drum Maj Geo Dyer, Conoy	Pvt John Appold, Marietta
Capt H A Haines, East Donegal	Sgt Hiram Snyder, City
Lt Geo Conrad, Pequea	Pvt Jas Strachem, City
Col Fred S Pyfer, City	Sgt Geo W Kecher, City
Lt E Scheaffer Metzger, City	Pvt F A Houseal, Maytown
Pvt John N Miller, City	Pvt J C Gundaker, City

Orphans Court-Judge Purcell. 1-On Sat the will of the late Marcella Spalding was proven & admitted to probate & record. Augustus M Sprague & Richd H Clarke, executors named, renounced the appointment, & letters of admin with the will annexed were issued to Augustus M Sprague; bond $500. 2-Letters of administration were issued to Mary Washington, on the estate of the late Geo Washington; bond $1,000. 3-Mary Jane Kidwell appointed guardian to the orphan of John J Kidwell, deceased; bond $300.

Geo P Chase, the murderer of Jos F Clark, a warden of Joliet, Ill, penitentiary, was hung at that place on Friday. He had murdered Clark while a convict in the penitentiary. John Kennedy, the last of the trio who committed the murder of Mr Maloney at Sand Ridge, Ill, was also hung at Wankegan on Friday. The murder was a most horrible affair, & two men had already been executed for its commission, Kennedy being the third.

Generals of the U S Army. The generals of the regular army now rank in the order of their names in the following list:

Gen Ulysses S Grant
Lt Gen Wm T Sherman
Maj Gen Henry W Halleck
Maj Gen Geo G Meade
Maj Gen Philip H Sheridan
Maj Gen Geo H Thomas
Maj Gen Winifield S Hancock
Brig Gen Irwin McDowell
Brig Gen Wm S Rosecrans
Brig Gen St Geo Cooke
Brig Gen John Pope
Brig Gen Jos Hooker
Brig Gen John M Schofield
Brig Gen Oliver O Howard
Brig Gen Alfred H Terry
Brig Gen E O C Ord

Of all these, Gen Terry, the captor of *Fort Fisher*, is the only officer drawn from civil life. All the others were educated at West Point; but Grant, Sherman, Hooker, Howard, & Halleck were in civil life when the war broke out, having resigned from the army after the Mexican war.

Wm B Astor, of N Y, returns an income for the last year of $1,153,459; Cornelius Vanderbilt, $623,250; & Horace H Claflin $1,290,000 or $4,000 per day.

The Com'r of Pensions yesterday made the following appointments of examining surgeons: Dr Henry J Churchman, Chillicothe, Mo; Dr Geo W Farron, Ironton, Mo, & Dr Alfred Edlin, Corning, N Y.

Beautiful farm & valuable county seat near Wash, D C, for sale: *Ashland*, the estate of Robt Clark, containing 600 acres; with a handsome brick dwlg & suitable out-bldgs. Apply on the premises, or to John Glenn & Co, 52nd st, Balt, Md.

WED AUG 1, 1866
Hon Henry Stanbery, the present Atty Gen'l of the U S, was born in N Y C in 1803; but since 1814 he has constantly resided in the West, his father having emigrated there. Hon Stanbery was an 1819 graduate of Wash College, Pa. Mr Stanbery's residence is about 3 miles from Cincinnati, in the beautiful & fertile country on the Ky side of the Ohio river, behind Newport. He is now, & has been since 1815, a citizen of Ky.

Died: after a painful illness of 21 months, John L Anderson, in his 63rd year. A native of Phil, but for the last 40 years a resident of Wash City. His funeral will take place tomorrow at 4 o'clock P M, from his residence, 378 13th st.
[No death date given.]

Balt, Jul 31. Explosion at the Light st wharf this morning of the steamer **Henry L Gay**, of the canal line. The cook, Eliza Giles, was killed. Richd Wood, of Balt, fireman, was severely injured. Frank King, of Chesapeake City, was slightly injured.

Heart's Content, Jul 28, via Aspy Bay, Jul 30. C W Field says that the ships **Medway & Albany** will leave on Monday to grapple for the lost cable. The ship **Great Eastern** will leave next Sat for the lost cable. The **Medway** will lay the cable across the Gulf of St Lawrence, & also between Prince Edwards Island & Newfoundland, after the cable is recovered.

Meeting of the honorably discharged soldiers of Butler Co, Pa, was held in the borough of Butler on the 26th ult. John Bulford, of the 102nd regt, co H, called to the chair; John P Orr, John Lowal, John M Sluddybaker, Saml A Davis, Saml Miller, R B Maxwell, Abram Slayter, & Philip Vogel appointed vice presidents; David W Humphreys & J B McQuistion appointed secretaries. Wilson K Potts, W A Lowry, & Augustus Martin were appointed to draft suitable resolutions. Capt S G Bartley, J P Orr, W K Potts, J B M Quistion, Saml A Davis, Harlan Book, Augustus Martin & John Lawal appointed from this Convention to the State Convention at Harrisburg, on Aug 1st next.

A correspondent of Denver, Colo, writes from *Fort Halleck* that, on the 18th ult, as a btln of the 18th U S volunteers, under command of Lt Col Mizener, was crossing the North Platte, the rope attached to the ferryboat broke & 4 men were drowned. The names of the drowned are not given. One was a sgt.

THU AUG 2, 1866
John Ross, the well-known chief of the Cherokee nation, died in Wash City yesterday. He married a lady, we believe, in Delaware, & leaves a numerous family connection. He could not have been much less than 75 years of age at the time of his death. Same paper: Died: on Aug 1, at Joy's Hotel, Wash, John Ross, Principal Chief of the Cherokee Nation.

Died: on Jul 31, in St Mary's Co, Md, Sarah Greeves, infant daughter of Dr J Ford & Marion V Thompson. Her funeral is on Aug 2 at 10 o'clock, from the residence of Mrs S A Greeves, 357 9th st, corner of Mass ave.

Mr Chas Palmer & Mr Wm Booth, of Richmond, Va, died in that city on Tue, the former age 72 years & latter 68 years.

Jas Black, colored, & a faithful porter in Col Sam Owen's store for a number of years, accidentally drowned in the Potomac, a few Sabbaths since. He was a reliable man.

Gen Hancock promoted to the major generalship vacated by the promotion of Gen Sherman, & Gen Ord succeeds Hancock as brig general of the regular army.

Orphans Court-Judge Purcell. 1-Yesterday the will of the late Benj C Freeman, bequeathing his estate to his wife, Mary Jane Freeman, who is also nominated as executrix, was filed & fully proven. 2-The will of the late John O Braxten, bequeathing his estate to his widow & children, was also filed & fully proven, & letters testamentary were issued to Mrs Mary J Braxten, bond 8,000, & also letters of guardianship, bond $4,000.

Mount De Sales Academy for Young Ladies, conducted by The Sisters of the Visitation, near Catonsville, 5 miles west of Balt, Md, will commence on the first Monday of Sept, & ends about Jul 1. Address Mount De Sales, Catonsville Post Ofc, Balt, Md.

FRI AUG 3, 1866
Meeting of the Oldest Inhabitants, on Wed, Col P G Washington in the chair, & Dr A McD Davis secretary. Cmte appointed for the Washington Nat'l Monument: C Bestor, D Hines, Dr Wm B Magruder, A J Joyce, J R Barr, J C Stewart, Lewis Johnson, Seraphim Masi, Maj Thos Donoho, Dr A McD Davis, Ed F Brown, Ed Simms, Geo F Oulick, Robt Bea__, B B French, Michl Nash, Dr F Walsh, Geo A Bohrer, Jeremiah Hepburn, Jas Birch, E J Middleton, Thos Blagden, Henry Naylor, Thos Brown, Richd Petit, & Peter O'Donoghue. Early recollections of Mr Chas Vincent were read by Mr J C Brent.

On Wed, Jas T Harmer, ex-alderman & assessor of the 2nd Ward of Phil, while in the public house of J S Peck & Son, was shot and later died. He was in a political discussion with 6 or 7 other men.

Yesterday at 25th st, near the Pa ave, Mr Harrison Fosdick committed suicide with a large revolver, which was found near him. He was a married man with no children. He was about 51 years of age & had served in the 5th regular cavalry.

State Convention at Harrisburg yesterday. A convention of honorably discharged soldiers favorable to the restoration policy of Pres Johnson & the election of Hon Hoister Clymer for Govn'r of Penn. Gen Sweitzer addressed the convention. Temporary secretaries were chosen:

Capt Jeremiah J Sullivan, 115th regt
Arthur C Greenland, 49th regt
Lt John Hart, 115th regt
Cmte appointed:
Capt C B Brockway, 1st Penn artl
Capt C D Rousch, 6th Pa Reserves
Capt I W Ahl, 201st regt
Maj H M Moody, 183rd regt
Col Oen Jones, 1st Pa cavalry
Sgt F L Coar, 10th Reserves
Dr Jas Kerr, of Pittsburgh

Sgt Maj Israel B Rocker, 4th Pa Reserves
Adj Israel Uneufer, 11th Regt

Lt C F Eldred, 14th N Y cavalry
Pvt J W Connard, 3rd U S artl
Cpl J A Haines, 150th regt
Col Jos Jack, 168th regt
Capt Moulton Goundio, 2nd heavy artl
Adj J H Odell, 30th Ohio regt

Ofcrs of the Convention:
Gen Wm McCandless, of Phil
Vice Presidents:
Gen Peter Lyle, Phil
Col Wm A Leech, Phil
Gen John F Ballier, Phil
Col A H Tippen, Phil
Capt J M C Savage, Chester
Pvt J Wagner, Montgomery
Pvt Danl Kreader, Bucks
Col T H Good, Lehigh
Col John O Neil, Berks
Sgt Geo Bierman, Schuykill
Capt H Thayer, Wayne
Col H B M Kean, Bradford
Capt J W Gregory, Luzerne
Maj C Ryan, Tioga
Col S Wilson, Lycoming
Pvt H Whitemen, Columbia
Pvt J A Stoher, Dauphin
Lt John A Stober, Dauphin
Lt John A Bitzer, Lancaster
Col Levi Meish, York
Cat A Ferguson, Franklin
Capt John H Hite
Pvt Geo W Daisy, Centre
Col B H Morrow, Blair
Sgt A D McPherson, Jefferson
Capt David Banker, Clarion
Maj Kas A Lowry, Alleghany
Col Robt Anderson, Alleghany
Capt P A English, Beaver
Sgt S K McGinnis, Lawrence
Col John P Linton, Cambria
Cpl Geo M Kinney, Berks
Capt John Hart, Montgomerry
Capt J P Newell, Venango
Lt J Lynn, Carbon
Lt A J Smith, Luzerne
Capt C F Maguire, Phil
Lt Wm Fullwood, Alleghany
Surg Abraham Stout, Northampton
Dr Wm Church, Crawford
Capt John A Corcoran, Bucks
Col B McDermott, Camigia
Capt Jeremiah Hoffman, Lebance
[Some names were too light to copy.]

Mrd: on the 31st ult, at the residence of Mrs F J Jones, by Rev Dr Pinkney, Geo Loring Andrews, of Boston, to Mary, 3rd daughter of the late Geo H Jones, of Va. [Richmond & Petersburg papers please copy.]

Died: on Aug 2, Wm Gadsby, in his 59th year. His funeral will take place at 5 P M from his late residence, 212 I st, Wash.

Died: in Wash City, on Aug 1, Emily S, the beloved wife of John T Given, in her 43rd year. Her funeral will take place from the E st Baptist Church, today, 4 P M.

Disastrous flood in Ky: Mr Noel and his wife & 6 other persons of his family were drowned & his house lost. Mr W R Ennis, mail contractor, lost $1,500 he had stored in his house. Louisville Journal

Bishop Early, in a letter to his brother, dated Lynchburg, Va, Jul 21, says: I suffer much less now than when I first left Richmond 2 weeks ago, but am too weak to do much. I am planning yet again to preach.

The largest income reported in Batavia, N Y, is that of Dean Richmond, of $109,721.

It was feared that Dan Setchell, the comedian, had been lost at sea on his voyage to Australia. It is good news that he has safely arrived at Melbourne.

SAT AUG 4, 1866
Dutchess Co, N Y, Aug 2. 1-The only daughter of Mr Henry Wagner, aged 20 years, was accidentally killed at Blue Stone, Columbia Co, yesterday, when she was struck by the handle or sweep, while with her father engaged in pressing hay. 2-At Canaan Four Corners, Columbia Co, the son of Dr Selden Cady was accidentally killed by the discharge of a revolver he was going to use to shoot a troublesome animal.

Edmund Brick was born in 1830, in Phil, his youth passed during a stage in his father's fortunes which afforded him both the opportunities & incentives of an elegant society. His education was of the best; he embraced the legal profession; studied for two years with Anson V Parsons; in 1860 admitted to the Phil bar; came to Wash & became the secretary of Maj Gen Hitchcock in the Bureau of Exchange; accepted the post of U S Consul to Valencia in Spain, but it was too late. A trip to Florida with his sister & aunt, who took the place of his mother, long since deceased, was the last stage of his journey. At St Augustine, on Mar 23rd last, he died of consumption.

Yesterday as Ofcr Peter Becker was arresting a bricklayer named Thos Sutton, on Mass ave, Patrick Scanlon appeared & threw a brick at him with such violence that it glanced off the ofcr's face & went straight into the face of the prisoner, & both were wounded. Ofcr Becker having got a knowledge of wounds in the army, lost no time recovering himself & went to the assistance of Dr Herbert, who dressed the wounds & set the broken bones of the nose. It is fear he will be disfigured for life, as the bones in the nose were actually smashed to pieces. The prisoner's face is also badly injured. Scanlon held to bail in $500 for his appearance at the Criminal Court.

Maj T T Eckert on Wed tendered his resignation as Assist Sec of War, to take effect at once, to accept the position of Gen Superintendent of the eastern division of the American Western Union & U S [consolidated] telegraph lines. He is a practical electrician, & during the war had charge of U S military telegraph lines centering at Wash.

Despatch dated Aug 1, from St Louis to the Cincinnti Commercial. The Radicals, on Sunday, killed S S Headlee, presiding elder of the Methodist Church, in the Springfield District, because he insisted upon preaching without taking the oath. He was shot 3 times & died that night.

Gtwn, Aug 4. The Misses Fitzhugh will resume the duties of their school on the first Monday in Sept.

The friends of the late John P Donolan, who was the first pastor of St Matthew's Church, propose to erect to his memory a handsome monument which shall be placed on the church lot.

Yesterday, at 283 L st, Mr Eugene L Fleury attempted to commit suicide by shooting himself. He was alive throughout the day & up to the time of going to press, but he was in a very precarious condition. The cause of the act is unknown.

Died: on Aug 3, at her residence, on K st, Mrs Rebecca Ord Ketchum, consort of Gen W Scott Ketchum, U S A. Her funeral is Sunday at 4 o'clock P M, from the Church of the Epiphany.

N Y, Aug 3. Gen Santa Anna was arrested & held to bail in the sum of $30,000, charged by Mi_ Montgomery with acting maliciously in having him arrested & imprisoned. He lays his damages at $25,000.

Stafford Co, Va, Jul 26, 1866. There was a picnic at the house of Sandy Davis, in Prince Wm Co, on Jul 19, & some became sick on their way home or the next morning. The principal suffers were the family of Mr Davis, G M Weedon, P T Weedon, Chas Nelson, Walter Keys, the family of Mr Mortimer Lynn, & others. Drs Hore, Wheat, Ford, Stone, & Leavy who traveled night & day, attributed the morbus to the lemonade, made up in a whiskey-barrell; others to the fresh meat & the hot weather. Suspicions rest on no one.

Fort Snelling, Minn, is no longer to be used as a military rendezvous. Efforts are being made, it is said, to secure it from the Gov't as an asylum for disabled soldiers.

Supreme Court, D C, No 451-in Equity. Chas *O'Neal, Thos O'Neale, J Hollingsworth & wife, J C Harkness & wife, E M Spedden & wife, J N Davis & wife, & Eliza J O'Neale against Horatio O'Neale & Robt M Beale, his guardian ad litem, Godfrey Koontz, Calvin Page, & Geo Hoskins. The parties above & creditors are notified that on Aug 26, at my ofc, City Hall, Wash, I shall state the trustee's account & shares of the parties in the fund.
-W Redin, auditor [*Only one without an e.]

Dept of the Interior, U S Patent Ofc, Wash, Jul 30, 1866. Ptn of Jas Greenhalgh, of Woonsocket Falls, R I, praying for the extension of a patent granted to him on Nov 2, 1852, for an improvement in Mode of Counter-balancing Barnesses in Looms, for 7 years from the expiration of said patent, which takes place on Nov 2, 1866. -T C Theaker, Com'r of Patents

Dept of the Interior, U S Patent Ofc, Wash, Aug 1, 1866. Ptn of Lemuel C Jenks, of Boston, Mass, praying for the extension of a patent granted to him on Nov 2, 1852, for an improvement in Machines for Drilling Stones, for 7 years from the expiration of said patent, which takes place on Nov 2, 1866.
-T C Theaker, Com'r of Patents

A man named Dotzler, 60 years of age, employed in the tannery of Gray, Clark & Co, of Chicago, was drowned a few days since by accidentally falling into a vat of the establishment while walking on a plank from one vat to another.

Wm Ringgold Cooper, an acting ensign in the navy, & quite recently on duty in the Ofc of Detail, Bureau of Navigation, Navy Dept, was arrested for forgery upon the Navy & Treasury Depts, by means of which he came into possession of $60,000 of Gov't money. Cooper was married on Thu to a young lady of high standing & well known in the higher circles of Wash society. He with his bride were on their way to N Y, where they were to take the next steamer for Europe on a bridal tour. The detectives followed him on the train & concluded to arrest him upon their arrival in Phil. He was accordingly arrested at the depot in Phil. Of the $60,000 fraudulently obtained by him, about $57,500 was found upon his person.

The funeral of John Ross, Chief of the Cherokee Nation, took place yesterday from Joy's Hotel, 8th st; services conducted by Rev Dr B P Brown, of the Foundry Methodist Episcopal Church, Rev Dr Septimus Tusting, of the Presbyterian Church, & Rev A D Gillette, who also delivered a beautiful address. Hon D N Cooley, Com'r of Indian Affairs was present. The following members of the deceased were also present: both his daughters, Mrs Jane Nane & Miss Annie Ross, & Miss Staple, sister-in-law; Messrs John & Robt B Ross, son & grandson, & Mr T Ross, nephew. A beautiful bouquet was placed upon the coffin by Mrs Hall, niece of Gen Burnett. The body was taken to the hearse by the following pall bearers: Capt Jas McDaniel, White Catcher, Huston Binge, Danl H Ross, John Jones, & Smith Christy. The funeral procession passed down the avenue & the body is now enroute for Wilmington, Dela, where the wife of the deceased is buried, from whence it will be taken to the Cherokee Nation for interment. The following Indians accompanied the procession: Gen Cooper, of the Choctaw Nation; P P Pitchlynn, Chief of the Choctaws, & Col Richd Fields, of the southern portion of the Cherokee Nation. The deceased was a member of the Methodist Church.

MON AUG 6, 1866
Hon Ezekiel Whitman, formerly member of Congress from Maine, & subsequently Chief Justice of the Supreme Court of that State, died at his residence in Bridgewater, Mass, on Aug 1, in the 91st year of his age.

Died: on Jul 29, in Rome, after a brief illness, Gen M L Smith, late C S A.

The old Moyamensing Hall, in Christian st, below 10th st, Phil, used during the war by the Gov't as a hospital, & recently taken possession of by the Board of Health for cholera purposes, was set on fire Sat & almost entirely destroyed. It is supposed that it was set on fire by the residents of the vicinity, who objected to its being used by the Board of Health for the treatment of cholera patients.

Five soldiers [of the 1st U S Artl, stationed at *Fort Schuyler*,] & a civilian, on Wed night, in Westchester Co, N Y, quarrelled with Alex'r Elliott in a bar room & clubbed him. He ran for his life, & was compelled to jump out of the window of his house to escape them as they battered down the door. He aroused the police & while searching for Elliott at his home, came across his cousin, Miss Ellen Hicks, whom they shot & killed. The murderers were arrested yesterday. -N Y Herald

Col John Rutherford, who presided at the recent meeting of the State Central Cmte at Richmond, died suddenly in that city on Friday night, at an advanced age. He was for several years Lt Govn'r of the State.

Miscellaneous Items: 1-Prof Agassiz & lady arrived in N Y on Friday, by the steamship **South America**, from Rio Janeiro. 2-Maj Gen Steedman & Brig Gen Fullerton arrived at N Y on Friday. 3-Ristori has gone to Italy to take leave of her mother previous to visiting the U S. 4-Miss Sedgwick is to return to the Haymarket, the scene of her first London triumph. 5-A D Davenport, the comedian, better known as Dolly, arrived in N Y from Europe on Friday. 6-Mr David Currie, one of the oldest & most influential merchants of Richmond, died suddenly on Friday. He was 49 years of age. 7-Rev Mr Milburn, popularly known as the "blind preacher," was on Sunday last installed as pastor of Trinity Episcopal Church in Chicago. 8-Capt Semmes has been awarded the contract for transporting 200 tons of army supplies from St Louis to *Fort Sully* & *Fort Rice*, at two cents per pound. 9-Byron Sprague, a wealthy & prominent citizen of Providence, R I, formerly of the house of A & W Sprague & Co, died suddenly on Monday night. 10-Jacob Kramer, employed at Harrisburg, Pa, by Adams Express Co as night driver, was arrested on Friday on the charge of stealing packages.

New Orleans Times of Jul 31: riot in that city, police attacked by the Conventionists. List of white men under arrest: S C Blanchard, C W Bridge, E Tooth, A D Mitchell, Michl Caulfield, John McCann, R F Dannoy, L Louis, Geo Howes, [badly wounded,] E Legion, M Cameron, S S Fish, [two serious wounds,] I W Horton, [minister, badly wounded,] A Obre, W H Waters, R King Cutler, W H Nelson, S H Hurst, [badly wounded,] Michl Hahn, [slightly wounded,] T Cook, Dr W H Hire, [seriously wounded,] E Auguste, Jos Dupaty, B Osnard, Dr Pique, W Orr, W R Fish, Alfred Shaw, [shot in the back,] E Sinclair, John Henderson, jr, [several wounds, dying,] C P Duplessis, Mr Waples, [brother of Rufus Waples.] Many of the above give themselves out as spectators arrested by mistake. Dr Dostie received 5 shots & was at one time reported dead. Policeman Mark Sokolowsky was lying at the station suffering from a pistol shot in the groin, & is not expected to recover. Michl Hahn was covered in blood, more scared than hurt. Glendy Burke was wounded in the side. Edgar Cenas, a medical student, only son of one of our most respected citizens, was shot whilst stepping out of the Medical College. He was mortally wounded. Ofcr Jas Henry is said to be mortally wounded. Lawrence Duffy, employed in the foundry, Claiborne & St Louis sts, is said to be mortally wounded in the head.

+

Another list of whites arrested: S C Planchard, C W Bridge, P Footh, Ned Reed, Michl Canfield, Jas McCann, H B Douroy, L Lewis, Geo Howes, P Legion, Mr Cameron, S S Fish, Rev I W Horton, A Obi, W H Waters, W H Nelson, S H Hurst, W Houston, T Cook, W H Hire, G C Pupatty, Ben Osnard, Dr J Pique, N Mandeville, E Auguste, L B Aren, W Orr, W R Fish, Alfred Shaw, E E Sinclair, J Henderson, jr, H Turnbull, D F Beaurgard, Jas Duane, R King Cutler, Michl Hahn, G B Duplessis, assist sec convention.

+

Death of two of the instigators. New Orleans, Aug 5. Dr Dostie & Rev Mr Horton, the officiating minister of the late convention, died this evening.

Tribute by the Third Auditor's Ofc on Aug 3, to the memory of the late Wm Gadsby, late fellow clerk. Cmte: L L Tilden, Henry Sherman, B A Janvier, A L Hazelton, Wm H Gardner; Mr A M Granger, called to the chair; Mr J F Jones, sec.

The laying of the corner stone of the new colored edifice of the *Asbury M E Church*, at K & 11th sts, took place yesterday. Rev Benj Brown, presiding elder, assisted by Rev Richd P Bell, pastor of the church; Rev John Brice, pastor of the Sharp St Church, Balt; Rev Stephen Tasker, of the Orchard St Church, Balt; Rev Nathl Carrell, Mount Zion Church, Gtwn; Rev Robt H Robinson, Ebenezer Church, Capitol Hill; Rev John M Brown, A M E Church, Rev Hyland Garnett, First Presbyterian; Rev Singleton Jones & Rev Jas A Jones, of the Western M E Church. The new church is to be raised upon the site of the old Asbury Church, which was built about 30 years ago; cost is estimated at $15,000, to be finished by Dec 1; $6,000 has already been collected.

Erroneous statements have been published concerning the death of R C Bessan/Hessan, with the impression that he had committed suicide. He was found mortally wounded by a fall upon the pavement in the rear of his boarding house, but the fall might have taken place from a flat roof that projects from beneath the window of his room, or from a high flight of back stairs. For several days he had suffered from a high fever, & had not taken food nor slept for 4 or 5 days. He had been for some time employed as a clerk in the Post Ofc Dept, & was greatly beloved by all who knew him. He was a devout member of the Methodist Episcopal Church, & a teacher in Foundry Sunday School. His mother & brother, who had been written to on Thu by Mr J W Cox, arrived on Sat from their home in Phil, about 2 hours after his decease.

Mrd: on Jul 26, at the Church of the Epiphany, by Rev G L Machenhimer, Dr Richd F Kearney, of Wash, to Rosa, daughter of Maj Geo Calvert, of PG Co, Md. Upper Marlboro & Rockville papers please copy.

Died: on Aug 4, Eugene Louis Fleury, son of the late L A Fleury, in his 31st year. His funeral will take place at 3 P M, from his late residence, 383 L st.

Died: on Aug 4, Miss Sallie M McNeir, daughter of Thos S & Emily R McNeir, in her 18th year. Her funeral will be today at 4 o'clock P M, from the Congressional M E Church, on M st, between 9th & 10th sts.

Died: on Aug 5, after a protracted illness, Mrs Mary Weller, in her 75th year. Her funeral will take place from the residence of her son-in-law, Wm Pope, 228 6th st, between M & N sts, this afternoon at 4 o'clock.

Gen R B Mitchell was inaugurated Govn'r of New Mexico, at Santa Fe, on the 16th ult.

Capt John Shallcross, a veteran steamboat man, died in Louisville on Fri night.

Farm & country residence at public sale on Aug 14, the farm on which I reside in PG Co, Md, adjoining the farms of G W Riggs, W Sibley, & W Gibson; contains 103 acres; with a comfortable dwlg house & numerous out-bldgs. Will also sell stock, implements, & crop, as I have made arrangements to move to Va. Apply to the subscriber or to the firm of Messrs Sibley & Guy, 322 D st, between 10th & 11th sts. –Thos J Barclay, Hyattsville Post Ofc, Md. –E Vowles, auctioneer

Orphans Court of Wash Co, D C. Letters of administration on the personal estate of Thos Chessem, late of Wash, D C, deceased. –Jas Fulton, adm

TUE AUG 7, 1866
Personal. 1-A P Gorman has been removed from the position of Postmaster of the U S, his dismissal to take effect on the 1st proximo. 2-Brig Gen W A Nichols has been assigned to duty as chief of staff to Lt Gen Sherman. 3-Col Delaware Kemper, of Alexandria, who has been associated with Mr W D Stuart in a properous school in that city, has been appointed professor of mathematics in Hampden Sidney College, in Va.

Carlo Luigi Farini, whose death is announced in a despatch from Europe, was an Italian political writer of some distinction. He was born in the Papal States, Oct 22, 1822, & studied medicine in Bologna, but while yet a young man became involved in revolutionary projects, & was several times banished from the Papal States. His chief work, Il Stato Romano, is a history of the Roman States from 1815 to 1850.

Richd Whitfield, an old citizen of Richmond, died Sat: over 80 years of age.

Confiscation of the estate of Don Antonio Lopez de Santa Anna by Maximillian, Emperor of Mexico. –the Palace, in Mexico, Jul 12, 1866: Maximillian

Albert R Sloanaker, on Sat, entered upon his duties as Collector of the First Internal Revenue District, Phil, in place of Col J H Taggart, removed.

Appointments by the Pres:
Jas Lowry, jr, to be Surveyor of Customs, Pittsburgh, Pa.
Moses H Eliott, to be Physician of the Marine Hospital, Pittsburgh, Pa.
Ferdinand V Boitz, to be Collector of Internal Revenue for the 22nd District of Pa.
Wm G McCandless, to be Collector of Internal Revenue for the 23rd Dist of Pa.
Alfred P Lloyd, to be Assessor for the 23rd District of Pa.
Gen Benj Parkridge, to be Assessor for the 6th District of Mich.
John V Hayes, to be Assessor for the 20th District of Pa.
Alonzo Tenner, to be Assessor for the 20th District of N Y.
John W Hunter, to be Collector of Internal Revenue for the 12th District of Ohio.
Austin H Brown, to be Collector of Internal Revenue for the 6th Dist of Indiana.
Wm C Wilson, to be Assessor for the 18th District of Indiana.
Jas P Foster, to be Collector of Customs in Wilmington, N C.

It was reported on Sat that Isaac W Dean, residing at 141 West 21st st, & a salesman in the employ of the N Y Steam Sugar Refining Co, was a defaulter to the extent of from $80,000 to $120,000, & that he has escaped by the last Calif steamer. Dean leaves a wife & 5 children behind. –N Y Sun

Died: on Aug 6, after a long & protracted illness, Sarah W, 2nd daughter of the late Jas Jack, of Wash City. Her funeral will take place this afternoon at 4 o'clock, from the residence of her brother, 653 3rd st, near Va ave. Balt & N Y papers please copy.

Died: on Aug 6, Mrs Catharine Ann Claxton, wife of Mr Richd W Claxton, & only daughter of the late Capt Ignatius Luckett, of Chas Co, Md, aged 54 years & 9 months. Her funeral will be from her late residence, 60 High st, Gtwn, this afternoon, at 3:30 P M.

Died: on Aug 1, at Glen Cove, N Y, in his 18th year, Richmond, eldest son of Jas Mandeville Carlisle.

A despatch from New Orleans states that Lt Butts, of the Freedmen's Bureau, has been murdered by highwaymen in Jackson parish.
[No death date given-current item.]

Guardian's sale of valuable real estate on G st between 21st & 22nd sts, at public auction, on Aug 29, by order of the Orphans Court of Wash Co, D C, approved by the Supreme Court of D C, in Equity: sale of part of lot 12 in square 80, in Wash City. –Harriet Ann Lee, guardian. -Green & Williams, aucts

Appointments of Graduates of the Military Academy. The following order was promulgated yesterday: War Dept, Adj Gen'r Ofc, Wash, Aug 4, 1866. The following named Cadets, graduates of the Military Academy, have been appointed in the Army of the U S by the Pres, by & with the consent of the Senate, with the rank endicated below, to date from Jun 18, 1866: All to be 2nd Lt:

Corps of Engineers: to be 2nd Lt, to fill an original vacancy:
1-Cadet Henry M Adams
2-Cadet Jas Mercur
3-Cadet Chas E L B Davis
4-Cadet Benj D Greene
5-Cadet John H Weeden, jr
6-Cadet Geo M Wheeler
7-Cadet Eugene A Woodruff
8-Cadet Jas B Quinn, vice Handbury, promoted
9-Cadet Danl W Lockwood, vice Post promoted.

Ordnance Dept: to be 2nd Lt:
10-Cadet Wm P Butler, vice Michaelis, promoted.
11-Cadet Frank Soule, jr, vice Winebrenner, promoted.
12-Cadet Edw M Wright, vice Prince, promoted.

2nd Regt of Cavalry:
36-Cadet Albert J Neff, to be 2nd Lt, vice Norton, promoted. Co B.

3rd Regt of Cavalry:
40-Cadet John C Thompson, vice Campbell, promoted. Co B.

4th Regt of Cavalry:
39-Cadet Will I Moberley, vice Taylor, declined.

5th Regt of Cavalry:
32-Cadet J Scott Payne, vice Ruggles, promoted. Co G.

6th Regt of Cavalry:
21-Cadet Wm P Dixon, vice Tolman, promoted, Co E

1st Regt of Artillery:
15-Cadet Hiero B Herr, vice Lee, transferred to the Corps of Engineers. Co F
18-Cadet Abner H Merrill, vice MacMurray, promoted. Co H.
22-Cadet Chas King, jr, vice Hillenbach, promoted. Battery K.

2nd Regt of Artl:
17-Cadet Chas E Kilbourne, vice Ring, promoted. Co E.
23-Cadet Jas E Eastman, vice Handbury, transferred to the Corps of Engineers. Co G

3rd Regt of Artl:
16-Cadet Jas O'Hara, vice Smith, dropped. Co L.
24-Cadet Isaac T Webster, vice Porter, declined. Co K

4th Regt of Artl:
13-Cadet Richd C Churchill, vice Fuger, promoted. Co C.
14-Cadet Chas S Smith, vice Wilkeson, resigned. Co H.
19-Cadet Henry H C Dunwoody, vice Marr, resigned. Co K.
20-Cadet Robt Craig, vice Ennis, promoted. Co G.

5th Regt of Artl:
25-Cadet Wm H Upham, vice Carroll, promoted. Co E
26-Cadet Solon Orr, vice Lee, transferred to the 1st artl.
27-Cadet Elbridge R Hills, vice Fessenden, promoted. Co H.
28-Cadet Jos G Swift, vice McDonald, promoted. Battery F.
29-Cadet Francis L Hills, vice Simons, promoted. Co E.
3rd Regt of Infty:
38-Cadet Chas L Umbstaetter, vice Belger, promoted. Co K.
4th Regt of Infty:
39-Cadet Geo O Webster, vice Hendricks, declined. Co F
31-Cadet Rufus P Brown, vice Simonton, promoted. Co C
5th Regt of Infty:
34-Cadet Quinton Campbell, vice McDonald, promoted. Co E.
6th Regt of Infty:
37-Cadet Wm W Fleming, vice Long, promoted. Co K.
10th Regt of Infty:
35-Cadet John F Stretch, vice Davis, promoted. Co D
II-The General Regulations allow 3 months' leave of absence to the graduates of the Military Academy on entering service. In accordance with the regulation, all the graduates above named, unless hereafter otherwise ordered, will report in person at their proper stations on Sep 30th next.
III-The graduates assigned to the Corps of Engineers & to the ordnance will, on the receipt of this order, immediately report by letter to the chiefs of their respective corps in this city. –E D Townsend, Assist Adj Gen

WED AUG 8, 1866
The Acting Com'r of Pensions has just made the following appointments of Pension Notaries: E M White, Morristown, N J, & Jeduthan Wells, Albion, Pa.

Changes in the Post Ofc Dept: Col R C Washington, appointed chief clerk of the Appointment Ofc; Dr R A Lacy promoted to principal clerkship in the same ofc; J H Marr promoted from a 1st to a 3rd class, & A D Hazon appointed 1st class clerk.

By order of the Sec of War, Capt Edw J Harrington, assist adj gen, has been mustered out of service, to date from Aug 4, 1866.

Mr Saml Harvey, of Pittsylvania Co, Va, recently fell down in front of his own saw mill, & was cut almost into 2 pieces before rescued. He did not live long.

The following income returns were made in N Y: A T Stewart, $4,071,256; Francis Warden, $478,349; Wm E Dodge, $212,808; Wm E Dodge, jr, $124,150; Paran Stevens, $176,383; Geo Bliss, $223,108; E D Morgan, $154,500; Jas Gordon Bennett, $158,648.

A son of Mr Robt Macey, of Preston Hollow, Albany Co, N Y, was struck by lightning Jul 28th & instantly killed. He was an only son & only 15 years of age.

Forty-third Commencement of ***Columbian College***, Wash, D C, was held on Jun 27, & was not covered due to the illness of our reporter. Orations were delivered by A B Duvall, of D C; S H Walker, of Md; H A Duncanson, of D C; John Kurtz, of D C; J Holdsworth Gordon, of D C; Jas Nelson, of Va; Woodbury Wheeler, of N C; D G Gillette, of N Y; & Chas P Harmon, of Va. Distribution of prize medals to: J H Gordon, D C; Woodbury Wheeler, N C; John Kurtz, D C; Jas Nelson, Va; John Kurtz, D C; H A Duncanson, D C; A B Duvall, D C. Degree of Bachelor of Arts was conferred on J Holdsworth Gordon, of D C; Jas Nelson, of Va, & Woodbury Wheeler, of N C. Degree of Master of Arts was conferred on : Danl Gano Gillette, Wm A Gordon, jr, Richd B Cook, of Pa, Jos F Deans, of Va; Wm E Edmonson, of D C; Chas B Harmon, of Va Abner Y Leech & Benj G Lovejoy, of D C. Honorary degree of A M was conferred on: Hiram C Sparks, of N Y C, & on Rev Walter W Williams, of Gtwn, D C; & the honorary degree of D D on Rev J W M Williams, of Balt, Md, & on Rev R J Keeling, at Wash, D C. The honorary degree of LL D was conferred on Geo Peabody, of England.

A row of 6 unfinished frame dwlg-houses on 23rd st, owned by Mr John L Kidwell, were burned last night. Mr Kidwell, supposing that he would have no further use for a private watchman, whom he had employed while the houses were in process of erection, had dismissed him.

Orphans Court-Judge Purcell, Aug 7, 1868.
1-The will of Julia Sessford, which was filed in Sept, 1865, was fully proven & admitted to probate & record; & Eliz Kelley gave bond in the sum of $800 as admx of said estate c t a, with J F Halliday & Geo A M Randall as sureties.
2-Laura V Elan, qualified as admx of the personal estate of Jos A Blan, deceased. Bond, $1,000; sureties, Robt W Groggin & John B Lord.

Died: on Aug 6, in Wash City, Maj Geo T Howard, of San Antonio, Texas, in his 52nd year. His funeral will take place on Wed at 4 o'clock P M, from the residence of his father-in-law, 394 4th st west.

On Monday one of the swings at the 7th st Park was so overladen with young ladies, that it broke down. Miss Mary A Dimond, who resides on G, between 2nd & 3rd sts, had her hand badly cut; Miss Hannah Donohue & Mrs Hedrick were very severely bruised. Dr Cannon was called & dressed their wounds, & they were conveyed to their residence.

Mrs Winifred Gallagher, a native of Ireland, died in Detroit on Friday, aged 106 years.

Adm's sale of the personal effects of the late Thos Chessem, deceased; by order of the Orphans Court of D C, on Aug 11, in front of our auction-rooms, 7th & D sts. By order of the Administrator. -Green & Williams, aucts

Orphans Court of Wash Co, D C. Letters of administration on the personal estate of Julia Sessford, late of Wash, D C, deceased. –Eliz Kelly

Orphans Court of Wash Co, D C. In the case of Walter Scott, exc of Chas M Williams, deceased, the executor & Court have appointed Sep 1 next, for the final settlement of the personal estate of the said deceased, of the assets in hand. -Z C Robbins, Reg/o wills

THU AUG 9, 1866
New appointments: The Pres yesterday signed the commissions for the following:
Arthur P Gorman, collector of Internal Revenue for the 5th District of Md.
John W Frazier, assessor of the 1st District of Pa.
Alex'r H Wallis, reappointed collector of the 5th District of N J.
Archer M Martin, assessor of the 7th District of Pa.
Alonzo Tenner, assessor of the 30th District of N Y.
Mr Gorman has long been a resident of Wash, though a native of Md.

Assist Surgeon Webster Lindsley, U S A, died in this city yesterday morning.

Maj Gen Hunter, upon his own application, colonel 6th U S cavalry, having served over 40 years, has been, by direction of the Pres, retired from active service, & his name will be entered on the retired list of ofcrs of the grade to which he belongs, in accordance with section 15, act approved Aug 3, 1861. This order to take effect Jul 31,1866.

A board of ofcrs to consist of Brvt Col J B Brown, surgeon U S army, Brvt Lt Col H R Wirtz, U S army, Brvt Lt Col Anthony Heger, surgeon U S army, & Brvt Maj Warren Webster, assist surgeon U S army, been ordered by the Sec of War to assemble at N Y C, on Sep 20, or as soon there after as practicable for the examination of assist surgeons for promotion, & of applicants for admission into the medical staff of the U S army.

Medical Ofcrs: Brvt Maj Jos P Wright, assist surgeon U S A, has been relieved from duty in the Dept of the Cumberland & ordered to relieve Brvt Capt Edw Cowles, assist surgeon U S A, in his duties at *Fort Independence*, Boston Harbor. Assist Surgeon Cowles is ordered to duty in the Dept of Louisiana. Assist Surgeon W S Tremaine, U S A, has been ordered to duty in the Dept of Cumberland, vice Assist Surgeon Wright. Surgeon Geo Taylor, U S A, has been relieved from duty in the Dept of the Ohio, & ordered to duty in the Dept of Texas, to relieve Brvt Lt Col E P Vollum as medical director of that dept. Brvt Lt Col Vollum is ordered to duty in the Dept of the East.

Edgar Snowden, sr, editor of the Alexandria Gaz, has been elected as delegate to the Phil Convention. A better selection could hardly have been made, as he is one of the most conservative men in the South.

Acting Com'r of Pensions appointed S W King, of La Harpe, Ill, pension notary.

Died: Aug 5, at the residence of his grandfather, in Upperville, Fauquier Co, Va, A Oscar, 2nd son of A L & Mary S Yerby, of Gtwn, D C, aged 6 years & 4 mos.

Died: on Aug 8, at the residence of his father, Brvt Maj Webster Lindsly, M D, U S A, only son of Dr Harvey & Emeline C Lindsly. His funeral will Friday next, at 11 A M, from 370 C st.
+
Medical Society of D C. Dr Webster Lindsly was a native of Wash City, & son of Dr Harvey Lindsly, one of our oldest & most esteemed practitioners. As a tribute to his memory, as a body, we will attend his funeral. –Drs Wm P Johnston, J M Toner, J W H Lovejoy, Cmte -A F A King, Md, Rec Sec. [Aug 11th newspaper: The funeral of Brvt Major & Assist Surgeon Webster Lindsly took place yesterday. The funeral services were conducted by Rev Dr Sunderland, of the 4½ st Presbyterian Church, after which the remains were placed in the hearse & the coffin was covered with the American flag; & under an escort of a battalion of the 12 U S infty, preceded by the regimental band, & followed a long line of carriages along Pa ave to **Oak Hill Cemetery**, in Gtwn, where the remains were interred. The pall-bearers were Capt Netterville & Lt Hutton, 12th U S infty, & Assist Surgeons P C Daws, W A Bradley, C J Wilson, & J Simms Smith, of the U S army. All along the route of procession crowds assembled to witness the passing cortege, & the utmost respect was shown the memory of the deceased.] [Aug 14th newspaper: Webster Lindsly passed his infancy & childhood in companionship with loving sisters, all of whom are present now amid the solemnities of these funeral rites.]

Household furniture, desks, bedding, school books, benches, etc, at auction on Aug 10, at the Gtwn Female Seminary, Washington & Gay sts. –Sarah T Dougherty, excx -Thos Dowling, auct

Wm H Prince was arrested by Ofcr Sprague, of the 8th Precinct, on a charge of stealing a water coller & rubber coat from W G Starkweather. He was held to bail for court by Justice Handy. Malachi Trail, formerly of Baker's detective force, was yesterday brought before Justice Walter on a charge of obtaining money under false pretences. [He borrowed $25 from Mr A Leadingham, giving him an I O U, to be drawn from his monthly pay. He drew his full pay, however, & thereby deprived the cmplnt of the $25 which, it was alleged, he borrowed. He was sent to jail for court.]

Fire Dept: Board of Fire Com'rs, Messrs J W Thompson, Thos Berry, C I Canfield, & J T C Clark, on Monday night, the appointments of ofcrs & men of the fire companies were made, as required by law. The list of appointments are as follows: Steamer No 1, Union: W W Goddard, foreman; Chas G Griffin, engineer; Jos Parris, fireman; Richd Hill, hosteler; Chas Davis, Chas Weber, Fred'k Mohler, J F Moore, F S Herbert, Wm Davis, extramen; Geo Spellman,

Jacob Turner, Wm Reed, Geo Edwards, supernumeraries. Steamer No 2, Franklin: John F Maddox, foreman; Wm A Shedd, engineer; Thos Martin, fireman; John Holbrook, hostler; Harry C Jones, Geo W Bauer, Fred'k Fridley, Geo St Clair, John D Birch, M J Ridgeway, extramen; John N Moulder, Chas Dawes, Jacob Coddington, Frank Myers, Louis W Dorsey, Wm Brown, supernumeraries. Steamer No 3, Columbia: Jas Lowe, foreman; Danl Barron, engineer; John W Smoot, fireman; Michl Keenan, hostler. Jacob Dyser, Frank Lewis, Jasper Smith, P H Smith, Edw Reynolds, Edw Gatton, extramen; C Kaufman, Jos Platz, Jas Martin, Thos Martin, Thos Robinson, Wm Murray, W P Hicks, supernumeraries. Hook & Ladder No 1, Metropolitan. J T Chancey, foreman; Saml Mackey, tillerman; Henry Lewis, hostler; Chas Merilatt, C F Holbrook, W S Scott, E H Sipe, W A Ringgold, F H Harper, extramen; F D Bennett, G H Noyes, Jas Bush, L P Seibold, Wm Brooks, Jas A Smith, Geo Lewis, C McDermott, supernumeraries.

Members of the Medical Association of the District of Columbia: Drs-

Chas Allen
Saml A Amery
Thos Antisell
S B Blanchard
M V B Bogan
S W Bogan
Saml S Bond
Jos Borrows
Wm B Butt
Carlos Carvallo
Josiah Adams Chamberlin
H W Combs
Jas G Coombe
H F Condict
B F Craig
Chas H Craigin
R C Groggon
Patk A M Croghan
A McD Davis
G M Dove
Wm Bev Drinkard
W J C Du Hamel
Lewis Edwards, U S A
Johnson Eliot
Warwick Evans
G P Fenwick
J M Fotty, U S N
C M Ford
Alex Y P Garnett
D R Wagner

Jas C Hall
Th Hansman
J W Herbert
Flodardo Howard
J T Howard
Richmond Johnson
Wm P Johnston
Wm Jones
John B Keasbey
B King, U S A
A F A King
Alfred H Lee
Wm Lee
C H Leibermann
N S Lincoln
Harvey Lindsly
J W H Lovejoy
W B Magruder
Hezekiah Magruder
John Fred'k May
Louis Mackall, jr
J M McCalla
Chas McCormick, U S A
Chas McCormick
Geo B McKnight, U S N
Geo McCoy
J H J McClery
Wm Marbury
Thos F Maury
Frank W Mead

Ephraim C Merriam
J V D Middleton, U S A
H P Middleton
Thos Miller
A W Miller
Jas E Morgan
W Gray Palmer
G I Pancoast
B J Perry
Armistead Peter
Jas Phillips
T Purrington
S J Radcliff
Jas R Kelley
Joshua Riley
John C Riley
Joshua C Ritchie
H A Robbins
W E Roberts

Jos Scholl
S C Smoot
R H Speake
Robt King Stone
J Ford Thompson
S J Todd
J M Toner
H B Trist
W McK Tucker
Grafton Tyler
Saml E Tyson
Jos Walsh
Bodisco Williams
Thos W Wise
Henry E Woodbury
N Young
Wm P Young
Jas T Young
-J W H Lovejoy, M D, sec

FRI AUG 10, 1866
Police matters. 1-Wm & Francis Fitzgerald, 12 & 16 years of age, were arrested on a charge of burglary, in having 2 weeks ago entered the house of Mr Lewis Baker, on 14th st, & robbed it of from $8 to $10. They were arrested 3 weeks ago on several charges & escaped the station. 2-Ofcr Peter A Becker, who was dangerously wounded some time past by a man named Sullivan, is now quite recovered. 3-Wm B Clarke, dealt out very light bread, & was fined $6. 4-Jas Canlin, a soldier, appropriated to his own use a pair of shoes belonging to Danl Mullen, for which he was arrested & sent to jail for court. 5-N G Starkweather, U S architect, was brought up yesterday charged with stealing Gov't property valued between $5,000 & $6,000 dollars. Wm H Prince could be implicated in the same matter & there will be a further investigation.

Mrs John C Calhoun, the widow of the South Carolina great statesman, died at Pendleton, S C, on Jul 25. –Charleston Courier

The site of the Naval Hospital comprises the entire square No 948, bounded by Pa ave, E st south, & 9th & 10th sts east, & will contain about 31,320 feet within the enclosure of its fence, which is to be of iron, of suitable design. The bldg is 90 by 44 feet, & fronts on E st. The following master mechanics & artisans have been employed: bricklayers, Messrs Kinsley & Clarkson; stonecutter, Nicholas Acker; carpenter, Chas Edmondson; plasterer, Chas Sioussa; plumber & gas-fitter, Alex'r R Shepherd; slaters, Mathew Waite & Co; tinners, Mack & Stromberger; painter & glazier, Geo R Crossfield; ironwork, Messrs Ellis & Brother & J H Mead; heating apparatus, by Hayward & Bartlett, of Balt; cooking apparatus, by Collins & Heath, of Balt; most of the grading done by J Fitzpatrick; the gutter, edgestone,

& sidewalk paving by Henry Burch. The iron fence around the site is being done by F & A Schneider. The original general design & drawings of the hospital bldg were made under the direction of the late Wm Whelan, then chief of the Bureau of Medicine & Surgery, Navy Dept, by E S Friedrick, & completed Sep 17, 1864. Oct 14, 1864, Am__l B Young was appointed the superintendent for the construction of the bldg. The bldg will be ready for occupancy on Oct 1, under the charge of Surgeon K D Maxwell, of the navy, a gentleman of ability & much experience in hospital matters.

Died: Aug 9, at Gtwn, D C, Mrs Margaret Taylor, aged 86 years, 6 mos & 9 days.

Died: on Aug 5, in Balt, J Edw Neale, aged 2 years, elder son of J W & Glovina Anderson.

St Anna's Hall-a school for young ladies, near Brookville, Montg Co, Md. The bldgs are new & specially adapted to the purposes of School. This school opens on Sep 10. -Rev O Hutton, A M, Brookville, Md.

Mrs Anne J Mitchell will open a Boarding & Day School for Young Ladies at her residence, 122 Gay st, Gtwn, D C, on Sep 10, 1866.

Balt, Aug 9. Geo R Dodge, a wealthy citizen, died here today. He was selected from among the loyal citizens of Balt, at the commencement of the rebellion, to organize a provisional police force to succeed that of Marshal Kane, & was appointed Provost Marshal by Gen Banks when he assumed command. He rendered important service.

Trustee's sale of valuable real estate in Chas Co, Md, at the Court house door, in Port Tobacco, Md, on Sep 11, the real estate of which the late Leonard Jarrall died seized, called **Locust Hill**, containing 370 acres, more or less. The dwlg house is large & comfortable, with numerous out bldgs. –F Stone, R H Elder, trustees

SAT AUG 11, 1866
Rev Overton Bernard was found dead on the floor of his room last night. He lived on the **Tarrant Farm**, about 2 miles from Washington. He was a minister of the Methodist Episcopal Church, & for some years had been an ofcr in the Bank of Va, in Portsmouth. He was about 70. –Norfolk Day Book, 6th.

Alex H Newton was yesterday arrested & taken to the Central Guard-house, & fined $20 for peddling watermelons without a license.

Mrd: on Jul 24, in Christ Church, Lexington, Ky, by Rev J S Shipman, Ben K Green, of Whitfield Co, Ga, to Miss Lizzie, daughter of Thos H Waters.

Died: on Aug 10, after a brief & painful illness, Eliz, consort of Saml M Bootes, in her 61st year. Her funeral will be from her late residence, 43 First st, Gtwn, today at 4 P M.

Cincinnati Times of Tue. Yesterday, the steamer **Gen Lytle**, one of the finest & fastest boats plying the Ohio river, exploded one of her boilers. Those who survived the disaster were rescued by the packet **St Charles**, of the People's Line. Capt Godman, of the **Lytle**, had just laid down to rest at the time, & was instantly killed. His body, with 7 others, was recovered. Capt Godman's remains were taken to the residence of his brother-in-law, Col S B Seving, at Madison. Mr Chas Davou, pilot, was thrown high in the air & came down in the water uninjured. Mr Chas Boucha, the other pilot, was seriously injured, & his recovery is doubtful. Inquest has been held on the following persons: Jas Green, colored, Cincinnati; Burbon, colored, Cincinnati; C Graciani, white, Covington, Ky; Andrew Slate, white, Madison, Ind; Richd Harbenrother, barkeeper, Madison; Wm Moore, white, Hibernia, Scott Co, Ind; H Godman, capt, Jeffersonville, Ind; M Garriety, Madison, Ind; Paul Murray, Miss Brasher, of Cincinnati; Dick Berry, of Adams Co, Ohio, badly scalded; J Luse, of Green River, Ky, badly scalded. John W Reed, white, of Va, is lying with cholera. –Jno A Crozier

MON AUG 13, 1866
Mrs Sarah R Cobb, mother of Hon Howell Cobb, formerly Sec of the Treasury, died recently at Atlanta, Ga, in her 74th year. She was spoken of as a highly accomplished lady, & for nearly half a century a zealous member of the Baptist Church.

Henry C Bowen, publisher of the N Y Independent, has been removed from the collectorship of internal revenue in the Third District of N Y, [Brooklyn,] Calvin E Pratt, it is stated, has been appointed in his place.

Hon John B Alley, member of Congress from Mass, declined to be a candidate for re-election.

Yesterday an alarm was sounded that the tailor shop of Mr Edw Linney was on fire. When the firemen arrived Mr Linney told the them about his loss of $7,000 worth of property. On examination, there was no sign that cloth or other articles had been on fire. Mr Linney was arrested & held to bail for a hearing on Tues.

Police matters. 1-John P Lee, a restaurant keeper, was arrested on Sat by Ofcr Leech, for keeping open after hours. He was fined $30 by Justice Bates.
2-Martha Pullen, age about 16, was charged by Capt Fisher with stealing from him some wearing apparel & a gold ring, valued at about $50. She had been a domestic in his service & had left. She was arrested & sent to jail for court.

On Sat, a man named E Hamlain was garroted at 4½ st canal bridge, by 2 negroes & a white man, & robbed of 4 linen sheets marked W & a valise. No clue to the perpetrators.

Died: on Aug 12, after a painful illness, Charles C, youngest daughter of Kate & Chas C Langley, aged 11 months & 27 days.

On Sat, Jas Hill, age about 20 years, was shot & dangerously wounded in Gtwn. He got into a dispute with a colored man, Saml J Briggs. Wm S Levy had a billard saloon nearby, & objected to the dispute, & came outside firing a shot from a pistol, the ball taking effect in Hill's neck below the right ear. Levy was committed to jail for court.

Sale of Real Estate. Green & Williams, aucts, sold a 2 story brick house & lot on F st, between 5th & 6th sts, to Mary Arnold, for $1,400; undivided half of lot 16 in Holmead's addition to Gtwn, to Peter McIntyre, for $750; lot 3 in square 511, to Matthew Lynch, for 14½ cents per foot; lot 18, in Wiltberger's subdivision of Sq 441, to Mary C Santer, at 25 cents per foot; lot 9 in square 548, to Wm Buckley, at 20 cents per foot; lot 11 in square 743, improved, to John T Ashford, for $650.

Died: on Aug 12, Mr Peter Von Essen, at his residence, in Gtwn, D C, 38, corner of Congress st & the Canal. His funeral will take place at 4 o'clock P M tomorrow. The public is invited to attend.

Woman assassinated in Phil on Aug 10. The victim's name was Mary Carney, a native of Mount Holly, N J, & the murderer called himself Newton Champion, late an ex-assistant engineer in the navy. He was charged with killing the girl, [in a disreputable house,] & had kept company with the victim. He is about 20 years old. He has been identified by the sister of the deceased & others as keeping company with Mary Carney several weeks, & quarrelling with her frequently. Two weeks since he attempted to strangle her.
[Aug 14th newspaper: The prisoner's answer to questions: I am Newton Champion, age 26 years, resided at 1,223 Ogden st; I am an engineer; I am single. He served on board the sloop-of-war **Pawnee** & other vessels; after resigning the service, he later enlisted as a private in the army; he was drafted back into the navy; did not remain long in the service. Some who served with him said that his conduct was so strange at times as to induce a belief of insanity.]

For sale, a country seat, with 10 acres of ground, a good log house with 10 rooms & a good brick chimney; 6 miles from the Eastern Branch Bridge. Inquire of Mrs Jessie Anderson on the premises.

Augusta, Ga, Aug 12. The British ship **Tampedo**, from Mobile to Savannah, was lost on Wassaw bar on Sat. The capt & crew were saved. She was owned by J F DeWolf & Co, of Liverpool, & was partially insured.

Orphans Court of Wash Co, D C. Letters of administration on the personal estate of Jas Lusby, late of Wash, D C, deceased. –Adeline Lusby

Petersburg Index: last Sat Wm Crawford, of the firm of Dunlop & Crawford, of that city, while on his way from N Y, by the steamship **Hatteras**, fell overboard below Sandy Hook, & was drowned before assistance could reach him.

Paris correspondent says: Jenny Lind, who was formerly the idol of the public, may be said to have assisted in her own funeral, as an artist, in having unfortunately again come before the public long after her voice was no more. She was hissed by a great part of the audience. This is a lesson to all those who will not retire in time; this is a warning to Grisi, Mario, & the Keans; we hope they will profit by it.

Dept of the Interior, U S Patent Ofc, Wash, Aug 7, 1866. Ptn of Jos J Couch, formerly of Phil, Pa, now of Brooklyn, N Y, praying for the extension of a patent granted to him on Nov 23, 1852, for an improvement in Machines for Drilling Stone, for 7 years from the expiration of said patent which takes place on Nov 23, 1866. –T C Theaker, Com'r of Patents

TUE AUG 14, 1866
The resignation of John S Keyes, U S marshal for the District of Massachusetts, tendered several weeks since, was accepted by the President yesterday.

On Friday night as Mrs Johanna Cook, a white lady, was passing along N st, near 7th, to meet her husband, she was seized by 2 negroes, one of whom took her child from her arms & held it, while the other threw her down. She screamed & when Mr Tilp came out of his house, the villains ran off. They were caught by Ofcr S B Clements, & Wm Smith, colored, was identified & arrested & committed to jail for court.

Mrd: on Apr 25, in Wash City, Thos A Tibbs, of Appomattox, Va, to Miss O S Mason.

Mrd: on Aug 2, at Independence, Texas, by Rev Wm Carey Crane, D D, Jos C Styles Morrow, of Gtwn, Texas, to Miss Nannie E Houston, eldest daughter of Gen Saml Houston, deceased.

Mrd: Aug 7, in Wash City, at the residence of Wm H Ward, by Rev Fr Walter, Mr Edgar A Sheble, of St Louis, Mo, to Miss Nannie M Noyes, eldest daughter of the late Geo S & Ellen Noyes, of Wash City. No cards. St Louis papers please copy.

Detroit, Aug 12. The schnr **America**, of Milwaukee, capsized & abandoned, was found near Grand Haven, Lake Michigan, today. The crew are supposed to have been lost.

Dept of the Interior, U S Patent Ofc, Wash, Aug 9, 1866. Ptn of Stephen C Mendenhall, of Richmond, Ind, & Obed King & Ezra King, of Salem, Iowa, praying for the extension of a patent granted to them on Nov 9, 1852, for an improvement in Hand Looms, for 7 years from the expiration of said patents, which takes place on Nov 9, 1866. -T C Theaker, Com'r of Patents

Dept of the Interior, U S Patent Ofc, Wash, Aug 9, 1866. Ptn of Stephen C Mendenhall, of Richmond, Ind, praying for the extension of a patent granted to him on Nov 9, 1852, for an improvement in Mode of Throwing Shuttles in Looms, for 7 years from the expiration of said patents, which takes place on Nov 9, 1866. -T C Theaker, Com'r of Patents

A despatch from Newark, Ohio, states that C B Griffin, postmaster at that place, was removed on Friday last.

$100 will be paid for the delivery, or information which will lead to the recovery of 4 large bay mules with a wagon & harness, which mules strayed or were stolen, with wagon & harness, from 14th st Park, near Long Bridge on Aug 9. Said Mules were branded & wagon marked "U S." -Jas Hunsberry, Sup't 14th st Park.

WED AUG 15, 1866
Muster-out of Veteran Reserve Ofcrs. The Sec of War has ordered the muster out of the following named ofcrs, their services being no longer required.
Brvt Brig Gen Edw P Fyffe, colonel 7th regt.
Brvt Brig Gen Oscar V Dayton, colonel 19th regt.
Maj David T Foley, 18th regt.
Brvt Col Robt Avery, major 7th regt.
Brvt Maj Geo B Russell, capt 7th regt.
Brvt Maj W K Haviland, capt 4th regt.
Brvt Maj H A Yates, capt 14th regt.
Brvt Capt w S Johnson, 1st Lt 9th regt.

Richd C McCormick took the oath of ofc as Govn'r of Arizona on Jul 9.

Two men were killed in tearing down the old wall of a Catholic Church at Portland, Ind, last Wed. Instantly killed were John Kelsar & Martin Davin, workmen.

Cmdor R B Hitchcock, for some time cmder of the Gosport Navy Yard, has been relieved by Rear Admiral Stephen C Rowan.

St Paul, Minn, Aug 13. Thos Holmes' train of Idaho emigrants was attacked by Indians on the Missouri river. Several of the emigrants were killed.

Mrd: on Aug 14, at St John's Church, by Rev Mr Trimble, Wm Van_ Ingen Mercer to Sophia Letitia, daughter of Wm Hogan.

Died: on Aug 14, at his residence in Gtwn, D C, Dr Henry King, formerly a resident of St Louis, & late Examiner of the U S Patent Ofc, in his 62nd year. His funeral will be from Trinity [Catholic] Church, Gtwn, on Aug 16, at 3 P M.

Mr T B Harrison, a highly respected citizen of Richmond, died on Sunday.

The subscriber offers at private sale *Sharon*, formerly the residence of the late Com Thos Ap C Jones; in Fairfax Co, Va, with a stone dwlg house, & numerous other out-bldgs. Contains 24_ acres. Thos R Love, atty at Law, Fairfax Court House is authorized to sell. -Mark E Jones, exc

U S steamer **Canicus** at public sale on Aug 23, at anchorage, south side of basin, Balt, Md. –G W Bradley, Col & Chief Quartermaster, Middle Military Dept.

A telegraphic despatch from Nice announces the death of Michl Garigaldi, brother of the General.

Mr Francis Hall, formerly the publisher of the N Y Commercial advertiser, died at his residence, in that city, on Sat, at age 82 years. He was a native of England.

THU AUG 16, 1866

Executive Appointments made on Tuesday. Wm B Taylor, to be Register, & Austin Morgan, Receiver of the Land Ofc at Jackson, Miss. Lafayette Porter, Surveyor of Public Lands for the district of Idaho; H A McKelver, to the Assessor of the 2nd Collection Distrist of Iowa; Wm E Bond, to be Collector of Internal Revenue for the First District of N C; Richd H Jackson, to be U S Dist Atty for the Dist of New Mexico; O S Baker, to be Justice of the Peace for Wash Co, N C; C S Eyster, to be Associate Justice of the Supreme Court for the Territory of Colorado.

Jas M Lincoln, editor of the Bath Sentinel, died at Farmington Tuesday afternoon.

Marshall Lefferts, of N Y, has accepted the appointment of Engineer of the Consolidated American & Western Union Telegraph Lines.

Improvements in the vicinity of St Aloysius Church, on I st, near North Capitol. A few years ago, with the exception of the church, there were not many substantial bldgs in that vicinity. Last year Mr Peter Gallant erected 2 fine brick dwlgs, one for Pontius Thyson, & the other for Miss Mary Lynch. Another was erected for Mr Jas S Harvey, & another for Mr Gallant himself. In the same row the *Sisters of Mercy* are making an addition to their academy for young ladies; on the opposide of the street, Mr Calvert is about to erect a substantial dwlg.

Obit-died: on Jul 17, at Auburn, Wm Lyles, in his 58th year. As a citizen, husband, friend, & neighbor, he deserved a high rank, & will long be affectionately remembered. [Jul 16th newspaper: account of the murder of Mr Wm Lyles.]

Died: on Aug 14, of cholera, at St Louis, Mo, Miss R Amelia Ross, aged 17 years, eldest daughter of John A & Emeline A Ross, of Gtwn, D C.

Died: on Aug 15, Rebecca Maria, infant daughter of Mary L & the late Peter C Howle, aged 2 months.

Trustee's sale of valuable square of ground, by deed of trust from S A Douglas & H M Rice, dated Apr 6, 1857, recorded in Liber J A S, No 13, folio 310, of the land records for Wash Co, D C: sale on the premises on Thu, of square 360.
–Wm B Todd, Wm H Ward, trustees. -Green & Williams, aucts

Died: on Aug 15, Paul Percy, infant son of John S & Rosalie Bradford, aged 10 months & 17 days.

Trustees of Public Schools, on Tue, appointed the following teachers for the school year:

S John Thomson	Mary E Rowe	Eliza Sympson
Miss Annie E Evans	Susie E Tilley	Mary Aukward
Amelia M Kirk	Adele Tait	Mary A Hill
Helen E Williams	Miss Maria Davis	Mary Armistead
Fannie E Hoover	Miss Maggie Flenner	Alice Martin
Miss E P Redmond	Ellen Wade	Eliza Wheatley
Mrs Mary J White	L Parker	Alberta Bright
Miss Seraphina Brown	L M Lewis	J E Thompson
	H T Free	Mrs M A Amidon
Mrs Maria E Rodier	Rose Sewall	Miss S A Reed
Miss Octavia Israel	E Wilson	Miss S E Eckloff
Kate A McMahon	Miss Eliza Caton	Miss A M Adams
Emily Robinson	Wm McCathran	Miss M A Lee
Ella C Bates	Mary E Ramsey	Miss M E Martin
Oceana A Walker	Chas Roys	Mrs M A Bowen
Miss N D Stabler	Hattie Thompson	Miss Alice Adams
Maria L Allen	I H Johnson	Miss H J Magee
Belle W Marsh	Lucy Davis	Miss A M Bailey
Miss Addie Fuller	E A Allen	Miss J A Lee
Mrs E Myers	Josephine Bird	Miss A Van Horn
Miss E Billings	L Lusby	Miss E P Morse
Miss M E Fletcher	Kate Murphy	Mrs M E Stratton
Miss H M Morse	Lizzie Hinton	Miss A Milburn
Miss Jane Thomas	A J Donnelly	Miss J E Peyton
Miss Julia A Brown	Jane Moss	Miss R Garrett
Mary Tucker	Victoria L Krouse	Miss M E Gray

The execution of Albert Starkweather, the murderer, whose case has elicited so much interest in Connecticut, & many strenuous appeals for his pardon, is set for Fri next.

Celebrate restaurant for sale: Welcker's Restaurant, Wash, D C. For terms & particulars apply to John Welcker, 322 Pa ave, between 9th & 10th sts.

Bailiff's sale of household furniture on Friday next, at G & 12th st, by writ of distress, issued at the suit of John H Smith, of Wash City, D C, against the goods & chattels of Maria N Abby, of the same place. –Jos F Kelley, Bailiff

Tipton, Mo, Aug 5. On Jul 28th Rev Harvey Chapin, Presbyterian minister, aged 60 years, & late of Michigan, was burned to death by the accidental catching fire of his dwlg house. Himself & 3 children were at one time safe from danger, but in his anxiety to reach a trunk at the head of the stairs, containing a small amount of gold, he fell with the burning steps, & in a moment the entire roof fell upon him. His children are now orphaned.

Robt S Giles, of Omaha, Nebraska, has been appointed to a first class clerkship in the Second Auditor's ofc.

FRI AUG 17, 1866

Mrs Jefferson Davis writes to a friend in Charleston, S C: "Mr Davis is slowly but surely wasting away, and I look forward to his Maker's release, if man does not soon afford him one. It is very kind of you to ask what he wants; but beyond cigars & a little Madeira or sherry wine he seems to desire nothing."

Died: on Aug 15, Martha D Duncanson, relict of the late J A M Duncanson, deceased, of Wash City. Her funeral will take place from her late residence, 478 H st, between 9th & 10th sts, on Aug 17, at 4 o'clock P M.

Local: 1-Martha O'Conner was fined $3 for profanity by Justice Morsell. 2-John Dorsey was arrested for fast driving. 3-A German, Constantine Deelar, was taken before Justice Miller by Ofcr Thompson for having used threats of violence towards his wife, Theresa Deelar. He was required to give security to keep the peace. 4-John Collon was arrested on a charge of attempted robbery, & held for a hearing.

C R Bishop, Dealer in Paper-hangings, Window-shades, Fire-screens, Cord, & Tassels. 517 9th st, three doors above Pa ave, Wash, D C.

Trustee's sale of valuable real estate in St Mary's Co, Md, by decree of the Circuit Court of St Mary's Co, in Equity; sale at the Courthouse door in Leonardtown, on Sep 18, that splendid estate in said county, called *Pt of Notley Hall*, containing about 415 acres; part of the real estate of the late Govn'r Jas Thomas, & has been divided into 3 lots. Lot 1 contains 140 acres, & has on it a dwlg house, 2 barns, stables, & other out-houses. Lot 2 contains about 140 acres, & has on it a very good dwlg house, barn, & other out-bldgs. Lot 3 contains about 140 acres, & is without houses. The lots will be shown by H W Thomas.
-F Stone, trustee

SAT AUG 18, 1866

Mrs Jefferson Davis arrived in N Y, from Wash City, on Wed.

Gen Edw Shriver, of Fred'k, the newly appointed postmaster at Balt, entered upon the discharge of his duties on Thursday. Col Purnell held the position for about 6 years, & retires with the kindest regards of his many friends.

The Pres yesterday signed the commissions of the following named appointees: Nath S Howe, to be Collector of Internal Revenue for the 6th District of Mass; Danl A Carpenter, to be Assessor of Internal Revenue for the 2nd District of Tenn.

The Sec of the Navy awarded medals of honor to the following, who have distinguished themselves by extraordinary heroism in the line of their profession, or by other commendable qualities. 1-John Brown, capt of the after guard, Richd Bates, seaman, Thos Burke, seaman, of the U S ship **De Soto**. Heroic conduct in rescuing from drowning Jas Rose & John Russell, seaman, of the U S ship **Winooski**, off Eastport, Maine, May 10, 1866. Thos Robinson, capt of the after guard of the U S S ship **Tallspoosa**. Heroic effort to save from drowning Wellington Brocar, landsman of the **Tallapoosa**, off New Orleans, Jul 15, 1866.

Hon Edw Wade, brother of Senator Wade, of Ohio, died in East Cleveland a few days ago.

The work of making the bldg known as ***Ford's Theatre*** fire-proof was completed some time ago, & it required only a few finishing touches to put it in a condition to be turned over to the Surgeon Gen for the uses of his dept. The front wall was not secure & other work had to be done. The whole work is being done, & has been done, under the direction of Gen C H Tompkins, U S army. The architect is Mr Edw Clark; Mr John A Foos, superintends the masonry, & bricklaying, by Mr Saml Fries the carpenter work, & Mr John Lincoln the plumbing & gasfitting. The front wall of the theatre will be rebuilt of pressed brick, & finished, painted, & sanded to imitate brownstone. The 1st & 2nd floor are intended for ofcs of the Surgeon Gen & his clerks; the 3rd floor will be used for the preservation of the scientific specimens, already collected & in the medical museum, & others to be collected. The 1st & 3rd floors are tiled; the 2nd story is floored with N C flooring of the best quality. The bldg will be turned over to the Surgeon Gen's Dept about Nov 1.

Rev Mr Gubitosi, Prof of Moral Philosophy in Gtwn College, & temporarily in charge of St Mary's Church, in Wash City, was accidentally shot in the mouth this morning, while gunning on the other side of Hunting Creek. He was attended by Dr Lewis, & was able to proceed to the college this afternoon.

Died: on Aug 17, Wm Morgan, son of John B & S J Morgan, aged 25 years. His funeral will take place from 338 K st, on Sunday at 2 P M. N Y papers please copy.

N Y, Aug 17. Bar_ey Friery was executed in N Y C at 11 A M today.

Dept of the Interior, U S Patent Ofc, Wash, Aug 15, 1866. Ptn of Erasmus A
Pond, of Rutland, Vt, praying for the extension of a patent granted to him Dec 7,
1852, for an improvement in Pill-making Machines, for 7 years from the
expiration of said patent, which takes place on Dec 7, 1868.
–T C Theaker, Com'r of Patents

Hartford, Aug 17. Albert Starkweather was executed at 1 o'clock today, for the
murder of his mother & sister.

MON AUG 20, 1866
Important to enlisted men: Gen Orders No 65, from the War Dept, dated Aug 16.
Enlisted men who may dispose of, or lose through their own carelessness, in the
State of Texas, the Spencer carbine or Colt's or Remington's army revolvers, will
hereafter have charged against them upon the muster rolls the price of the former
at $100, & of the latter at $50, in each case.

Henry Ames, one of the wealthiest citizens of St Louis died at Minneapolis, Iowa,
on Monday night.

The steamer **Samuel L Brewster** & the steamer **Smith Briggs** have been sold at
Gov't sale at Norfolk, the former bringing $1,675, & the latter $750.

Miss Mary Ingalls, one of the oldest inhabitants of Salem, Mass, died there
recently, at the advanced age of 91 years, of paralysis of the brain. Miss Ingalls
was born on the day the battle of Bunker Hill was fought, Jun 17, 1775, in the
house in which she died, & resided there until the day of her death.

Mr Jos Jefferson had arrived safely in N Y on Sunday last, in the ship **Sunrise**,
from Liverpool. He is accompanied by his wife & 3 children, Miss Maggie
Jefferson, Mr Chas Jefferson, & Master T Jefferson. Mr Jefferson, it is said, will
pay his friends in this city a visit, appearing at the Holliday St Theatre, the scene
of his early histrionic triumph. -Balt Sun

Police matters: 1-Henry Miller, alias Patty Miller, was arrested for being drunk
& disorderly, & fined $2.50. 2-Henry Middleton, keeper of a restaurant on 9th st,
was yesterday brought before Justice Morsell charged for keeping his house open
after hours on the previous night, & fined $20.50. 3-A Miller, keeper of the
establishment known as Teutonia Hall, between 9th & 10th sts, was charged with
selling liquor after hours, & was fined $20.50.

Mr Walter Harris, an old & respected citizen of this city, & one who had filled
many ofcs of trust, fell in an apolectic fit on Friday last, while sitting in front of
his store, on King st, between Payne & West, & died in a few minutes.
–Alexandria Gaz

Extensive sale of real estate in Chas Co, Md, by decree of the Circuit Court, in Equity; sale at the Court-house door in Port Tobacco, Md, on Sep 11 next, the real estate of which the late Raphael H Boarman died seized & possessed. Four farm: *Locust Grove* & part of *Chunn's Swamp*, containing about 500 acres, more or less, on the Wicomico river, with necessary bldgs. A farm called *Part of Pennslvania*, containing about 120 acres, more or less, on Cuckhold's Creek, with necessary bldgs. Farm called *Boarman's* **Meadows**, & *Boarman's Rest*, containing about 400 acres, more or less, on Zachia Swamp, with necessary outbldgs. Farm called *Part of Calvert's Hope*, adjoining *Boarman's Meadows*, containing 200 acres, more or less, with necessary improvments.
–F Stone, R H Edelen, trustees

Orphans Court-Judge Purcell. 1-The will of the late Geo H Edmonds was fully proved, & letters testamentary were issued to Olive C Edmonds, bond $1,600. 2-The will of the late Patrick Quigley, bequeathing his property to his children, was filed & fully proven. 3-The first & final account of executor of Christopher Weber, & account of personal estate of the same, & 2nd & 3rd executor of Antoine Smidley, were approved.

Trustee's sale of valuable real estate in Chas Co, Md, by decree of the Circuit Court of St Mary's Co, dated Jun 20, 1866; public sale at the Court-house door, in Port Tobacco, on Sep 11 next, being the parcel or land known as *Part of Marshall Hall*, containing 198 acres; with a small dwlg & out-bldgs. This farm having been once offered & withdrawn, the creditors of L W B Hutchins are notified to attend the sale if they wish to prevent a sacrifice of the property, as the sale will be peremptory. –F Stone, trustee

Trustee's sale of valuable real estate in Chas Co, Md, by decree of the Circuit Court of Chas Co, in Equity; sale on Sep 11 next, at the Court-house door, in Port Tobacco, the farm of the late Alex'r Hamilton died seized generally called *Thos & Henry, Hard Bargain & Small Profit*, containing about 240 acres, with every improvement necessary or convenient for a farm. –F Stone, trustee

Trustee's sale of valuable real estate in Chas Co, Md, by decree of the Circuit Court of Chas Co, in Equity; sale on Sep 11 next, at the Court-house door, in Port Tobacco, land called *Boswell's Enclosure;* about 100 acres, more or less, formerly belonging to John Spalding, decid. Also, a small farm-100 acres, near lands of Walter Mitchell; has all the necessary improvements. –F Stone, trustee

Sale of valuable estate in PG Co, M, by decree of the Circuit Court of PG Co, Md, in Equity; public sale on Aug 30 next, of the estate of which the late Walter A Edelen died seized & possessed, & which is now decreed to be sold for the purpose of partition between his heirs at law: the fine estate known as the *Hermitage*, containing 525 acres, in the valley of *Tinker's Branch*; with a comfortable dwlg house, in good repair; with necessary out-bldgs.
–Edw W Belt, trustee

Mrs Carrie Russel, daughter of the late Jos Eaches, of Alexandria, died with cholera at St Louis on Thursday.

TUE AUG 21, 1866
Appointments by the Pres: Wm C Talley, to be Collector of Internal Revenue for the 7th District of Pa; Geo B Arnold, to be Assessor of Internal Revenue for the 13th District of Pa; Thos G Halley, to be Assessor of the 21st District of N Y; Wm B McCreery, to be Assessor of the 6th District of Michigan. S Ferguson Beach has been re-appointed Surveyor of Customs for the port of Alexandria, Va.

J S Dalzell appointed to a first class clerkship in the Ofc of the Com'r of Customs.

Chicago, Aug 19. Railroad disaster at Hollisville, Ind, this morning, when the train was thrown off the track by a cow. Wounded: Moses Reinaman, cattle dealer of Chicago, arm broken; Mr Street, of Buffalo, slightly injured; L P Hart, of Bath, N Y, Pres of the Ohio River Coal Co, slightly injured; S A Freeman, of Boston, head cut; G Edmonds, of Ill, slightly injured; S W Hough, of Albany, cut over the eye; Mr Lawrence, of Albany, slightly injured; C Fitzsimmons, of Rochester, N Y, slightly injured.

Mrd: on Aug 16, by Rev J H Wingfield, Dr G L Simpson, U S N, to Miss Mary E, daughter of R A F Young.

Died: on Aug 20, at Bladensburg, Md, Nina S, infant daughter of Emily E & Henry L Johnson, aged 19 months.

San Francisco, Aug 20. Honolulu advices to Jul 22nd report the death of a princess who is an aunt of Queen Emma.

Reopening of St John's College, Annapolis, Md, one of the oldest institutions in the State, will open on Sep 18 next, with an entire reorganization. Faculty:
Principal, Henry Barnard, LL D   Wm Steffin, A M
Rev G W McPhail, D D   David N Camp, A M
Geo W Atherton, A M   Zalmon Richards, A M
E P Scammon, A M   Rev Wm L Gage, A M
Hiram Corson, A M   S S Haldeman, A M
Rev Julius M Deshiell, A M   Wm H Hopkins, A M
-Thos Swann, Govn'r of Md. Ex-Off Pres of the Board of Visitors

WED AUG 22, 1866
Appointments by the Pres: A Hyatt Smith to be assist assessor of 2nd District of Wisc; J Peter Bonesteel, assessor of the 4th Dist of Wisc; & Geo C Ginty, to be Collector of Internal Revenue for the 5th District of Wisc.

Appointments of examining surgeons. Com'r of Pensions made the appointments yesterday: Dr Lewis Humphreys, South Bend, Ind; & Dr G Erdman, Danville, Ill.

Police Matters: 1-Francis Brandner, a hotel keeper, was fined $20 yesterday for keeping his establishment open on Sunday. He took an appeal from the decision of the Justice.

Improvements: Mr Saml Herman is finishing a large & beautiful store & dwlg at the corner of 4½ st & Va ave; J Henderson, carpenter & builder. On C st, Mr Saml Norment has just completed 4 very pretty 3 story bldgs; E Brickerd, carpenter & builder.

Died: on Monday, Howard, infant son of Lt Col Jas P & Alice Martin, U S A, aged 10 months. His funeral will take place today at 4 o'clock P M, from the residence of his grandfather, 439 E st.

Wm Gronart, a wine & liquor merchant doing business in N Y C, jumped from a train while in motion on the Harlem railroad, near Mott Haven, in Morrisania, N Y, on Sat last, & was so severely injured that he died soon after.

Leavensworth, Kansas, Aug 20. Indian outrages on the Plains. Letter dated at *Fort Reno*, Jul 31, reports of the hostilities of the Indians, & the entire inefficiency of the military force now there to protect the route. Mr Flood, of Leavenworth, was killed, his head cut off, & set up on the side of the road. Persons killed on Reno creek: Geo L Joelsberger, co A, 2nd btln, 8th infty; Jas Donaldson, Pierce Gassonett, Wm Donare, Henry Arizon, Mass; Wagonmaster Dillon, on Crazy Woman's Ford; Lt N H Daniels & Cpl Cullery, 18th infty, on Dry Ford; Geo H Moore, S Carr, Carlinville, Ill; Wm H Dearborn, Stoughton, Wis; Hiram H Chambell, Champion, N Y; Chas H Barton, Council Bluffs, Iowa; Jack Hustid, Muscatine, Iowa; John Little, Arkansas; Stephen Carson, Howard Co, Mo; Wm Hockwell, Montreal, Canada; John Slose, residence unknown. The massacre occurred between Jul 17th & 18th.

Wheeling [Va] Intelligencer, Aug 14: terrible thunderstorm in West Va, on Sat. On the island, a man named H H Laup, living in a small house on the grounds of Henry Moore, was instantly killed. The entire Robinson family, [man, wife, & 5 children,] living on a branch of Wheeling Creek, on the Ohio side, were drowned, & their bodies swept away.

Beautiful residence in Bladensburg at public auction, on the premises, on Aug 28, the former residence of the late Dr Penn, at Marlborough & Bladensburg roads; contains 23 acres; with a spacious frame dwlg, & other necessary out-bldgs. Title indisputable. -Green & Williams, aucts

U S Marshal's sale, by writ of fieri facias, on Aug 28, of a small brown mare mule, seized & levied upon as the goods & chattels of Wm Ellis, which will be sold to satisfy execution No 1662, in favor of Edmund Carmack against Wm Ellis. –David S Gooding, U S Marshal, D C

Gtwn Academy, Henry Whitall, Principal; Benj Naylor, Prof of Mathematics. Will reopen on Sep 3 over Mr Candall's Bookstore, 128 Bridge st, Gtwn, D C.

THU AUG 23, 1866
Police Matters. Fred'k Ochmed & Saml Owings were arrested last night for attempting to steal a horse at the market. They were both held for a hearing.

The Messrs Schneider & others have recently purchased the property of the late Jesse B Haw, just beyond the Wash City limits, between 7th st & *Mount Pleasant* farm of the late Wm J Stone, & having divided it into bldg sites, they intend to erect country seats. The family residence on the place has recently been fitted up & the grounds improved. Mr C G Schneider has already contracted with Mr W G Phillips for a fine cottage house, to be erected on the highest point of the land. Mr S P Brown recently has divided a portion of his land on 14th st, sites of 1 & 2 acres each, the price obtained for one being $650 per acre, & for the another lot $1,000. Mr H R Searle, architect, has made plans of handsome cottage residences, costing on an average $3,300 each, for the purchasers of the ground, Messrs Delano, Turner, Pratt, Davis, Sturtevant, Baldwin, & Carpenter, & they are now under contract, Mr Isaiah Moran having six of them, & Mr Chas E Walker the other.

Appointments in the Regular Army. To be colonels of white infty: Gen Gordon Granger, capt 3rd cavalry; Gen Alvin C Gillem, capt & A Q M; Gen Geo Stoneman, major 4th cavalry; Gen Jno Gibbon, capt 4th artl; Gen Geo Crook, major 3rd infty. To be colonels of the Veteran Reserve regts: Gen J L Robinson, major 2nd infty-lost a leg; Gen Thos G Pitcher, major 16th infty; Gen Danl E Sickles, lost a leg; major gen volunteers, & one other not yet fixed upon. Of these Gen Pitcher has already received his appointment. To be colonels of cavalry regts: Gen A J Smith, major 1st cavalry; Gen Benj H Grierson, brig gen volunteers; Gen John P Hatch, major 4th cavalry. To be majors of cavalry regts: Gen Jas W Forsythe, capt 18th infty; Gen Lewis C Forsyth, capt & assist quartermaster. To be colonels of colored infty: Gen Wm D Hazen, capt 8th infty; Gen Jos A Mower, capt 1st infty. To be lt colonels of Veteran Reserve regts; Gen John B McIntosh, capt 1st infty; Gen T F Bodenbaugh, capt 2nd cavalry.
Memoranda: Apr, 1866. Maj Gen Geo H Thomas, comanding Military Division of the Tenn, under discretionary authority, ordered the muster out of all volunteers, both white & colored, in his division. May 18, 1866: The Commanding Generals of the Military Divison of the Gulf Dept of N C, & Dept of S C, were directed to muster out all remaining white volunteers in their respective commands. Jul 11, 1866. Maj Gen W S Hancock, commanding First Army Corps, was directed to muster out the remaining ofcrs & men of that corps. Aug 18, 1866. The Commanding Generals of the Dept of the East, Dept of the Lakes, & Dept of Wash, were directed to muster out all remaining troops of the Veteran Reserve Corps. –E D Townsend, Assist Adj Gen

Scranton, Pa, Aug 22. Rev Dr Brainerd, the venerable pastor of the old Pine st Church, Phil, died suddenly last night.

Pottsville, Pa, Aug 22. Rev Dr Huntington declines the Episcopate of Maine, to which he was recently elected.

Died: on Aug 22, Mary Ella, infant daughter of George J & Mary E Suter, aged 7 weeks & 5 days. Her funeral is this afternoon at 5 o'clock, from the residence of her parents, 584 I st, between 4th & 5th sts.

Mrs J A Kesley will open a School for Young Ladies & Misses on Sep 3, at 117 south side of Pa ave, between 19th & 20th sts.

Died: Aug 22, George Lowry, infant child of George H B & Frances V White, aged 11 mos & 26 days. His funeral is today at 2:30 P M, from 371 9th st.

Died: on Aug 22, Sarah Ellen, aged 9 mos & 24 days, daughter of Jacob D & Joanna Bontz. Her funeral will be this evening at 4 o'clock, from the residence, 595 N st, between 6th & 7th sts.

FRI AUG 24, 1866

T W Ustick, one of the oldest & most esteemed citizens of St Louis, died on Thu; 20 years ago, one of the publishers of the Commercial Bulletin of that city.

City Improvements: A handsome residence is almost completed by Messrs Cluss & Kammerhueber, architects, of this city, for John R Elvans, near the corner of 10th & M st. Further down on the same street a new house is being built for Mr Utermehle-intended to be a large drugstore. Mr H Blan, n w corner of B & 14th st, has erected a fine 3 story brick front residence. Mr Z Richards, of the Treasury Dept, is improving his large 2 story brick house, at N Y ave & 14th st, by raising it 2 stories higher. Mr Carsen is the contractor. Dr McFarlan, dentist, is having erected a residence of 4 stories, N Y ave & 14th st; Mr Henry Wilson, contractor. Mrs Virginia Walker is having built a commodious 3 story brick front residence on 14th st, between H & I; contractors are, Messrs Kingsley & Claxton, bricklayers; Mr Cissel, carpenter, & Messrs Cruit & Campbell, plumbers. Mr M W Galt, jeweller, is have a residence of beautiful modern design erected on H st, between 14th & 15th sts; contractors are, Jerome Digges, bricklayer; Baldwin & Brothers, carpenters. Mr Geo H Plant, architect & builder, is having erected a large bldg at N Y ave & 15th st: Mr Downey is the bricklayer, & Mr Entwisle & Barron the carpenters. Mr J G Naylor, builder, constructed the Orphan Asylum on 14th st, between R & S, a fine, large brick bldg.

Police Matters. 1-Augustus Hassler & Augustus R Nixon were yesterday arrested on a charge of assault & battery with intent to kill, Martin J Manning, the cmplnt. Both prisoners were held to bail for court. 2-Alice Harris was charged with assault upon a woman named Annie Hamilton, & fined $5. 3-Thos Steward was required to give bail to appear in court for assault & battery on a man named Maywood.

Laura Smith alias Annie Martin was before Justice Morsell yesterday, to answer the charge of murdering her infant, about 4 months ago. The principal witness against her was a woman name Fanny Mitchell, in whose house the accused lodged at the time of the alleged occurrence. The prisoner was remanded for a further hearing. She is apparently 22 or 23 years of age, & a stranger in the city.

Died: on Aug 23, after a painful illness, Clara, daughter of Henry N & Marian Rothery. Her funeral will be from her parents' residence, 403 7th st, between H & I sts, this evening, at 5 o'clock.

Died: on Aug 23, Maggie Amanda, aged 2 years, 5 months & 2 days, only child of Robt C & Maggie A Seip

I shall open at High School at my residence, 15 miles west of Lynchburg, on Oct 1. Post Ofc, Lynchburg. –Jas P Holcombe

Santa Fe, N M, Aug 12. Ex-Gov Connelly died today.

SAT AUG 25, 1866
The Widow Chicquot, famous throughout the world as the introducer of the Clicquot champagne, died recently in France.

Madame de Thouvenal, the wife of the Senator, died recently in Paris.

Died: on Aug 24, in Gtwn, D C, Jos Libbey, born in Dover, N H, but for about 50 years a resident of the District of Columbia, in his 74th year. His funeral will take place on Sunday evening next, at 4 P M. Constitutional Union & Evening Star please copy.

Maj H A Hall will collect bounties under the new law for 5% on the amount received. Blanks furnished free on application, personally or by letter. Ofc: 525 H st, between 6th & 7th sts, Wash, D C.

Claymount Preparatory Schook for boys will commence Sep 1, 1866, & will close Jun 20, 1867. The School is situated in Jefferson Co, in the valley of Va.
–J S Blackburn
References: The Faculty of the Univ of Va
John B Dangerfield, Alexandria, Va
Wm B Stanard, Dover Mils, Goochland Co, Va
John Davidson, Gtwn, D C
Rev Joshua Peterkin, Richmond, Va
Rev H Suter, Berryville, Va
Rev C W Andrews, Shepherdstown, Jefferson Co, West Va

Leesburg Academy, a Classical & Mathematical School, will begin on Sep 3. Address J Packard, jr, Leesburg, Loudoun Co, Va.

A Balt correspondent states that Madame Bonaparte, she who was Miss Patterson & the wife of Jerome Bonaparte, has for a long time been engaged in writing her autobiography or memoirs, & has them nearly completed. They will cover the history of more than half a century. She resided in her early life, nearly 30 years abroad, & was closely acquainted with many of the European literati, such as Madame de Stael, Byron, Tom Moore, & others. She is finely educated & writes with vigor & grace.

The law firm of Browning & Ewing is dissolved by mutual consent. The unfinished business of the firm will be attended to by Mr Ewing.
–Orville H Browning, Thos Ewing, jr, Wash, Aug 20, 1866.

Dept of the Interior, U S Patent Ofc, Wash, Aug 21, 1866. Ptn of Danl Tainter, of Worcester, Mass, praying for the extension of a patent granted to him on Nov 30, 1852, for an improvement in Rotary Knitting Machines, for 7 years from the expiration of said patent, which takes place on Oct 23, 1866.
–T C Theaker, Com'r of Patents

Simon Batchelder, noted counterfeiter, who has been circulating large amounts of counterfeit in State of Maine, was arrested & taken to Portland for trial on Wed.

MON AUG 27, 1866
Hon David Burnet has been elected U S Senator from Texas.

To Voters of the 5th Congressional District of Md. I respectfully offer myself as a candidate for the next Congress of the U S. I regard it as the solemn duty of every true & patriotic citizen to unite in sustaining the course of Pres Johnson in his efforts to restore the States lately engaged in civil war to their proper consitutional relations to the Gov't. -Thos F Bowie, Upper Marbloro, Aug 3, 1866.

Died: on Aug 25, after a short & painful illness, F N Holtzman, aged 25 years. His funeral will take place on Tue at 9 o'clock A M, from his late residence on L st, between 23rd & 24th sts. Dearest brother, thou has left us, We thy loss do deeply feel; But tis God that has bereft us. He can all our sorrows heal. –M H

Orphans Court of Wash Co, D C. Letters of administration on the personal estate of Wm W Seaton, late of Wash, D C, deceased. –Malcolm Seaton

Farm for sale in Fairfax Co, 330 acres, at Bailey's Cross Roads; dwlg house is nearly new, beautifully located, designed for a summer boarding house, & has accommodations for 100 persons. Numerous out-bldgs. Apply to the subscriber on the premises, Lewis Bailey, or by mail through the Wash City Post Ofc.
–Lewis Bailey

Funeral of Joseph Libbey. Early in the morning the bodies of men in regalia were seen marching toward the house corner of First & Market sts, where Mr Libbey long resided, & at 4 o'clock the procession moved thence to the Methodist Protestant Church, on Congress st, of which he was for many years a member. The ball bearers were Francis Wheatley, Esau Pickrell, Geo Lowry, J D Cathell, Wm Laird, & Henry Addison-Mayor of the city. The coffin was furnished by Wm King, of Wm, undertaker. It was of walnut, covered with black cloth, & silver mounted, on the lid of which was the insignia of the order of Odd Fellows, to which he belonged, & a beautiful wreath of japonicas. Scriptures & prayers were read by Rev Dr Edwards, Rev Mr Shermer, Rev Mr Reeves, & by Rev Mr Barry-[of Rockville, Md.] The Sunday school, which was founded by the deceased, sang a hymn with fine effect. The Odd Fellows, Sons of Temperance, Sunday school, choir, & congregation then passed around the corpse, & somewhat in this order the funeral was thence attended to *Oak Hill Cemetery*, where Rev Mr Swett, on behalf of the Order of Odd Fellows, pronounced a panegyric on Mr Libbey. It was quite dark before the last said rites were concluded, but it is some time since the people of Gtwn has been called to mourn the loss of so public spirited & universally esteemed a man as Joseph Libbey.

TUE AUG 28, 1866
Prof John A Porter, of New Haven, died on Sat, aged 43 years. He was a native of Catskill, N Y: was from 1852 to 1864 Professor of Chemistry at Yale College.

Appointments by the Pres:
Abel Longworth, Collector for the 6th Dist of Ill
David Sitler, Collector for the 8th Dist of Ill.
Solon Chase, Collector for the 2nd Dist of Maine
W M Hamilton, Collector for the 2nd Dist of Mo
Church Howe, Collector for the 8th Dist of Mass
Jas A Greason, Assessor for 2nd Dist of Mo
Robt R Towner, Assessor for 13th Dist of Ill
Jos G Lamb, Assessor for 3rd Dist of Conn
G C Broadhead, Assessor for 5th Dist of Mo
A M Brown, Assessor for 12th Dist of Mo
Wm M Chambers, Assessor for 7th Dist of Ill
John E Cummins, Assessor for 4th Dist of Ohio
C M Zulick, Assessor Internal Revenue for 5th Dist of N J
John Hancock, Assessor for 4th Dist of Pa
___ Stiles, Collector for the 4th Dist of Pa
*Antonio Marrero, Appraiser of Merchandise at Savannah, Ga;
Richd W King, Collector of Customs at Newbern, N C
J Sallade, Postmaster at Wmsbport, Pa [*Aug 28th newspaper: correction-Marrero was appointed for New Orleans, La, not Savannah, Ga.]

Brvt Col Wm J Sloan, Surgeon, U S A, has been assigned to duty as chief medical ofcr at N Y C.

Maj Gen Hooker, lately assigned to duty in command of the Dept of the Lakes has announced the following-named ofcrs as composing his staff: Brvt Brig Gen Geo D Ruggles, assist adj gen; Brvt Capt J M Lancaster, 1st lt 3rd artl, A D C; 1st Lt W W Tompkins, 3rd artl, A D C; Col C H Hoyt, brvt brig gen U S volunteers, chief quartermaster; Capt C B Atchison, A A D C, brvt col U S Volunteers, assist inspector gen; Surgeon C S Tripler, major & brvt col U S army, medical director; Capt J H Gilman, C S, brvt lt col U S army, chief commissary; Capt C F Robe, V R C, acting judge advocate.

Maj Gen Thomas, who was recently assigned to duty in command of the Dept of the Tennessee, has appointed the following ofcrs as composing his staff: Brvt Brig Gen Wm D Whipple, major & A A G, assist adj gen; Capt Geo W Howard, U S vols, assist adj gen; Brvt Maj J P Willard, U S vols, 1st lt 18th infty, A D C; Brvt Maj J C Kellogg, 1st lt 18th infty, A D C; Brvt Col A Von Schrader, assist inspector gen; Brvt Maj Gen J T Donaldson, colonel & quartermaster U S army, chief quartermater; Maj J E Summers, surgeon U S army, medical director; Brvt Maj Gen R W Johnson, major 4th cavalry, acting judge advocate; Brvt Lt Col A L Hough, capt 19th infty, chief commissary of musters.

The Gov't has refused the request of Govn'r Marshall, of Minn, that **Fort Snelling** might be turned over to the State authorities for an asylum for indigent & disabled soldiers. The fort will be used as a storehouse for supplies for the forts in that district.

Mr W A Beach, jr, son of Mr W A Beach, a distinguished lawyer of Troy, N Y, accidentally shot himself on Sat, while gunning at Saratoga Springs. He died a few hours afterwards.

Dean Richmond died this morning, after a brief but severe illness, at the house of Mr S J Tilden, in this city. He had severe complication of internal disorders, greatly aggravated by his unsparing labors to being about the successful result recently attained in the Nat'l Convention at Phil. His wife & family were with him to the last, & he received the best medical ability in the city, Drs Blakeman, Alonzo Clarke, Wm H Van Buren, Metcalfe, Willard Parker, & Flint, being in constant consultation over his case. Mr Richmond was born in Woodstock, Vt, Mar 31, 1801, & just entered his 63rd year. –N Y World

Post Ofc Appointments:
Jos Candu, Buffalo, N Y
Jas McQuade, Utica, N Y
A G Clark, Toledo, Ohio
Thos Kinsella, Brooklyn, N Y
W R Lockwood, Quincy, Ill

H A Starr, Milwaukie, Wisc
E B Allen, Terre Haute, Ill
Henry Barnes, Detroit, Mich
C H Taylor, Grand Rapids, Mich

School of the Immaculate Conception Church, corner of 8th & N sts, under the direction of the Sisters of Charity, will open Sep 3, 1866.

Sale. Attention of the public: the beautiful country seat belonging to Cmdor Harwood, in the suburbs of Bladensburg, will take place today, Aug 28, at 5 o'clock P M. Residence has 23 acres. –Green & Williams, aucts

By decree of the Supreme Court, D C, passed in Equity No 1,421, the subscriber will offer for sale, Sep 7th, square 174, being in the immediate vicinity of *Meridian Hill*, the spot most favorably considered for the new Presidential Mansion. –J Carter Marbury, trustee -W L Wall & Co, aucts

Dept of the Interior, U S Patent Ofc, Wash, Aug 24, 1866. Ptn of John Pepper, of Lake Village, N H, praying for the extension of a patent granted to him on Dec 5, 1854, patented in England Nov 22, 1852, & reissued to said Pepper, Oct 27, 1863, for an improvement in Knitting Machines, for 7 years from the expiration of said patent, which takes place on Nov 2, 1866. –H C Theaker, Com'r of Patents

Dr & Mrs Caulfield will resume their professional duties Sep 3. Their course of instruction embraces: Organ, Piano, & Singing. Address at the music stores. P S. Dr Caulfield is open to an engagement as Organist & Mrs Caulfield is an alto in a church choir.

WED AUG 29, 1866

Appointments by the Pres of internal revenue ofcrs: 1-Collectors: Matthew W Stickler, 9th Dist of Pa; John R Campbell, 18th Dist of Pa; Wm Penn Lloyd, 15th Dist of Pa; Robt C Sinclair, 4th Dist of Mich. Assessors: John W Stokes, 4th Dist of Pa; John C Sanborn, 6th Dist of Mass; Davis A Brown, 9th Dist of Pa; Wm R Judson, 27th Dist of N Y; Wm C Binney, 5th Dist of Mass. 2-John Hastings has been appointed Surveyor of Customs at Albany, N Y, vice T M Stevens, removed.

Artificial limbs to Soldiers. The Surgeon Genr'l has furnished the soldiers of the regular & volunteer force, [both white & colored,] from the commencement of the war up to May 11, 1866, 2,131 artificial arms; 3,784 artificial legs; 44 artificial hands; 9 artificial feet; & 104 trusses & other apparatus for the relief of wounded soldiers. The cost to the Gov't for the furnishing of these limbs was $357,728.

Brvt Col Thos A McCarlin, surgeon U S army, has been assigned by the Sec of War to duty as Medical Director, Dept of the Gulf, & is ordered to report to the commanding general of the Dept accordingly. Brvt Lt Col E T Vollum, surgeon U S army, is ordered to turn over to Brvt Col Thos A McCarlin, surgeon U S army, Medical Director Dept of the Gulf, the records of the Medical Director's ofc, Dept of Texas, & then to report in person to the Medical Director Dept of the East for assignment for duty.

Mr M A Hanks, from Chicago, who has been spending the summer at the Mansion House, in St Paul, Minn, on Thu accidentally shot & killed his wife, while cleaning a revolver in their room. A servant of the house was in the room at the time. The husband & wife were newly married.

Significant endorsement of the Pres: continued ovation on the route of his excursion; large gathering in Balt, & in Phil. Full list of the Pres' party who are travelling upon the same train: Pres Johnson & servant; Gen Grant & Gen Rawlings, his chief of staff; Admiral Farragut & servant; Sec Seward & servant; Sec Welles & lady; E F Wells; Gen D C McCallum; H A Chadwick; Maj G S Koontz; M Romero, Mexican Minister; Surgeon Gen Barnes; Senator D T Patterson & wife; D S Gooding, Marshal of D C; J McGinnis, jr, & lady; Postmaster Gen A W Randall; Lt McGinley; Rear Admiral Radford; Surgeon Norris, U S A; Col W G Moore & R Morrow, Secs of the Pres; Mr Cadwalader, N Y Herald, formerly confidential secretary of Gen Grant; L A Gobirght, Associated Press; Edw Potts, of the Balt & Ohio railroad; R S Spofford, J R Doolittle, J Donaldson, & W W Warden, reps of the press.

In memoriam of Miss Sallie M McNeir, who died on Aug 4, in her 18th year. Seldon has home been darkened by the shadow of death under more affecting circumstances. Her life was marked by those gentle, modest, & lovely qualities that endear & win a lasting place in the heart. –E P N

Serious railway accident new New Brunswick, N J, on Aug 27, from a dirt train hitting a cow, throwing the dirt train off the track, killing the conductor Nicholas de Hart, a well known resident of Elizabeth, & a conductor on the road for 20 years past. The brakeman was killed, & 14 laborers on the rear car, were wounded.

Some days since, in removing public property in the U S Quartermaster's Dept storehouse, on East Bay, two strange packages came to light, which, on examination, proved to be boxes containing the <u>remains of two Federal soldiers,</u> marked as follows: Private H J Hall, company B, 3rd N H vols; Private Albert Flint, company D, 4th N H vols. The former died on Jul 19, & the latter on Aug 8, 1863, & have been stowed away as merchandise for over a year.
-Charleston Courier, 23rd.

Sale of the Seminary Bldgs, Gtwn, D C, late the property of Miss L S English, at private sale until Sep 25 at which time, if not previously sold, it will be offered at public auction. The property occupies the greater part of the square, fronting 180 feet on Wash, 240 on Gay, 90 on Green, & 30 on Dunbarton sts. Improvements consist of a 3 story brick bldg with out houses, containing 67 rooms, some of them very large with Gas, Water, & Baths. For many years used & occupied as a boarding & day school by its former owner, & became celebrated & known throught the U S. Apply to Mr S T Dougherty, on the premises, or to W D Cassin, Gtwn, D C. –Thos Dowling, auct

THU AUG 30, 1866
The Sec of War has ordered the muster-out of Capt Chas B Atchison, [brvt colonel,] additional aide-de-camp, to take effect Sep 1, 1866.

The corner stone of the New York Museum was laid in N Y C on Tuesday.

Our distinguished fellow-citizen, Gen A M Stout, late colonel of the 17th Ky volunteers, has been appointed Chief Clerk of the Land Ofc, Wash, vice Jos Wilson, promoted to the Commissionership. Gen Stout is an amialbe & excellent gentleman; a Union man, every inch of him; supported the Union candiate in the late contest here; was wounded during the war, & is the right man to be appointed to ofc. We congratulate him & the Administration upon all such appointments.

The Com'r of Pensions yesterday made the following appointments of examining surgeons of the Bureau of the Interior Dept: Dr Chas Duerron, Mount Sterling, Ky; Dr Wm E Smith, Sioux City, Iowa; Dr Wm H Gibbon, Chariton, Iowa; & Dr Jeremiah Dunn, Lodi, N Y.

Jas C Vandyke, U S Dist Atty at Phil in Gen Pierce's administration has died. He was much known here in other days, as a most determined Democrat, & a fast adherent to Mr Buchanan. [No death date given, current item.]

Mr Thos Kinsella, editor of the Brooklyn Eagle, has been appointed Postmaster of Brooklyn, vice Geo B Lincoln, removed.

A man named Nelson Little, employed in the Hoboken Ferry Co, was murdered on Tue at the ferry. An altercation ensued between Little & a harper named Michl Courey, & Little was stabbed in the stomach, which produced almost instant death. Others had joined in the altercation, but suspicion fell on Michl Courey who had a large pocket-knife on him.

Died: on Aug 27, in Wash City, F W Thomas, aged 56 years. He was the author of "Clinton Bradshaw," & several other works of fiction.

Meadville, Aug 28. The Corry train on the Atlantic & Great Western Railroad, while standing at Panama, was run into by the extra train following it, & the conductor, Jas Clancey, & a newsboy were killed. The engineer, Peter Murphy, was badly hurt.

Rev John Pierpont was found dead in his bed on Monday morning, at Medford, at age 81 years. He was born in Litchfield, Conn, Apr 6, 1785, & was graduated at Yale College in 1804; in 1818 entered the Cambridge Divinity School, & within a year succeeded the celebrated Dr Holley as pastor of the Hollis St church.
–Boston Journal

Musical Instructions, based upon scientific principles. Saml Carusi will resume the duties of his profession Sep 3, in its various branches-singing, pianoforte, harp & guitar. Also, violin & other stringed instruments, flute, etc. Residence: 462 M st, between 12th & 13th sts.

Revolt at Sing Sing Prison on Aug 27, 1866: Edw Stafford, the ringleader, was killed instantly. Jas McLoughlin, a convict, called to the men in a loud voice to come out & pass that way. The whole crowd, some 27 in number, responded to McLoughlin's call, & came rushing out of the augur shop. They were armed with clubs & long knives. Wm G Gale, guardsman, could not get his gun to shoot. A man named Haff, formerly a guard, died suddenly of disease of the heart soon after the affair was over. Jas McLoughlin received May 5, 1863, from Brooklyn, robbery 1st degree, 5 years, aged 17 years; gunshot- flesh wound, ball extracted. Andrew Yates, May 31, 1865, Brooklyn, murder, life; superficial gunshot wound of scalp. Jas Morse, King's Co, robbery, 1st degree, Oct 9, 1865, 10 years; gunshot wound on back; ball not extracted. Isaac Brennan, alias Peter Butler, Richmond Co, Oct 17, 1865, burglary, 4 years; flesh wound left leg. Edw Stafford, alias Duffy, Jan 20, burglary, 1st degree, aged 24 years, was sentenced to 15 years & 6 months, confinement from Dutchess Co; gunshot wound back of head: dead. McMulligan, who was sentenced at the same time as Stafford, for the same offence, was already to join the conspirators, but his plans were frustrated. One of the inmates, Jas Cunningham, escaped from the prison on Monday, & has not been retaken.

Richmond, Aug 28. Ex-Govn'r John W Morehead, of N C, died yesterday at Rockbridge Alum Springs, Va.

FRI AUG 31, 1866
Wm J Stone, of the Washington bar, died yesterday, at his home, near *Mount Pleasant*, after a severe illness, which he bore with much fortitude. He was 42 & 43 years of age. He leaves a widow & 7 children, & a large circle of friends, to mourn his loss.

Mr Jas Spaulding, late Com'r of the Second Ward, died yesterday, after an illness of several week, of consumption. He leaves a large number of friends to mourn his untimely end.
+
Died: on Aug 30, in Wash City, Jas W Spaulding, aged 34 years. His funeral services will be at the residence of his mother, 11th & L sts north, on Sep 2 at 2 o'clock P M.

Died: on Aug 30, after a short but painful illness, Richard D, third son of Richard & Sarah Wimsatt, in his 14th year. His funeral will be from St Dominic's Church, on Sat at 9 o'clock A M.

Died: on Aug 25, at Berkeley Springs, Edmund Strother, son of Jas L & Emily S S Randolph, aged 11 years.

Died: on Aug 30, after a short but painful illness, Dennis Hogan, aged 28 years. His funeral will be from his late residence on First st, near B st, this evening at 3 o'clock P M.

Mrd: on Aug 28, at Norfolk, Va, at the residence of the bride's uncle, N W Parker, by Rev Mr Okerson, Rev G L Mackenheimer to Miss Carrie P, eldest daughter of Capt J C Jones, of Montg Co, Md.

Supreme Court of D C, in Equity No 513, Docket 7. Dalton, adms, vs Dalton, et al. Wm Y Fendall, trustee, reported that on Jul 16 he sold lot 8, in Todd's subdivision, & lots 6 & 7 in square 537, for $1,550 to John Cameron; & lot 9, in Todd's subdivision, to Matthew Pepper, for $842.13; & both purchasers have complied with the terms of sale. -Geo P Fisher, Justice Supreme Court D C -R J Meigs, clerk

Supreme Court, D C, No 513, Equity. Wm N Dalton against Susan Dalton, John R Dalton, et al. On Sep 22, at my ofc, City Hall, I shall state the trustee's account & the distribution of the fund, of the late John Dalton. -W Redin, auditor

Horrible railroad accident at the junction of the Northern railroad of N J & the Erie railray, on the southern side of Bergen Hills, in Hudson Co, N J, last night. Dr Frank Hasbrook, son of old Dr Hasbrook, of Nyack, Rockland Co, N Y, who is one of the widely known physicians of the Hudson river counties, was killed instantly, his body terribly mangled. It appears he attempted to get off of the train, & fell under the cars. He was about 25 years of age, & was married.
–N Y Post

Suicide in Richmond. On Tue last, some of the relatives of Mr Sidmund Grady, an old citizen of Richmond, discovered that he had taken a large dose of laudanum. Being unwilling to live dependent upon his relatives, he preferred to die. He lost everything in the war & it weighed heavily upon his mind.
–Richmond Dispatch

In St Louis, Mo, last week, Geo Kingsland, age 12 years, playing in a room in his father's house, suspended a long towel from a roller & it became twisted about his neck, & he hung struggling until some one entered the room & released him. He soon after died.

Gustavus Limerick & his wife, both about 60 years each, were both murdered on Sat night, near Walker Roy's old residence, in Stafford, about 1½ miles from Fredericksburg. His wife's remains were found in the ashes of their house, which was burned that night. It is supposed the old people, who were both misers, were murdered for their money. -Fredericksburg Herald

SAT SEP 1, 1866
Mr Wm Macfeely, who has been so long a resident of Wash City in the capacity of railroad agent & telegraphist, is about to leave permanently for the West. He has the best wishes of the many who know him, & appreciate his abilites.

Rear Adm Joshua R Sands relieved from light-house duty; placed on waiting orders.

Muster out of volunteer ofcrs: order from the War Dept: Adj Gen's Ofc, Wash, D C, Aug 28, 1866. Special orders No 429.
Additional Aides-de-Camp: Brvt Brig Gen Anson Stager; Brvt Lt Col Hunter Brooke, Brvt Maj John D Pratt, Sep 1, 1866. Brvt Maj Douglass Pope, Oct 1, 1866.
Aides-de-Camp: Brvt Lt Col Jas McCoy, Brvt Lt Col Miles W Keogh, Brvt Lt Col Jacob DeGress, Brvt Lt Col Geo Meade, Capt Thos L Hayden, Sep 1, 1866.
Assist Adj Gen's: Brvt Brig Gen Chas Mundee, Brvt Brig Gen J A Campbell, Brvt Lt Col John Hancock, Brvt Col Wm H Sinclair, Brvt Col Roswell M Sawyer, Brvt Col Seth B Moe, Brvt Brig Gen Wm Redwood, Brvt Col Thos L Motley, Brvt Col Danl D Wheeler, Brvt Lt Col L M Dayton, Brvt Lt Col Chas H Graves, Brvt Col Alex Von Schrader, Brvt Col Wm A Wiegel, Brvt Col David G Swaine, Sep 1, 1866. Maj Murray Davis & Maj David C Wager, Oct 1, 1866.
Brvt Col Clinton A Cilley, Brvt Col Cornelius Cadle, jr, Maj Thos H Bradley, Brvt Col Chas H Whittlesey, Brvt Col Marcus P Bostow, Brvt Lt Col Robt Chandler, Brvt Lt Col Henry W Smith, Brvt Col Jesse E Jacobs, Capt Byron Porter, Capt Fred'k Speed, Brvt Lt Col Eddy D Mason, Brvt Maj Saml L McHenry, Brvt Lt Col Wm A La Motte, Brvt Maj Wm W Deane, Capt Jas Johnson, Capt Augustine F Hayden, Capt Henry Mahicken, Brvt Maj A R Ninninger, Brvt Maj Oliver D Kinsman, Brvt Col E B Harlan, Brvt Maj Dennis H Williams, Brvt Maj Hubert S Brown, Capt Geo W Howard, Brvt Maj Chas E Howe, Brvt Maj L Porter, Sep 1, 1866. Capt W J Sanbern, Oct 1, 1866.

The Assist Sec of the Navy appointed the following ofcrs inspectors of lighthouses: Cmder John C Carter, Cmder John C Calhoun, Cmder A K Huger, & Cmder T H Stevens.

On Aug 29, Ofcr Miller, of the 3rd Ward, picked up a man named Michl Kane, in an insensible condition. Dr Dorsey was called to attend him, & prescribed for him. The patient lingered until Thu when he expired. He had been a soldier in a N Y regt, & has relatives living in the District. The inquest decided that he died by natural causes, hastened by intemperance.

The Cmte of Pensions yesterday made the following appointments of examing surgeons: Dr A E Turner, Crestline, Ohio, & Dr W G Hunter, Burkesville, Ky.

Died: on Aug 30, in Wash City, Jas W Spaulding, aged 34 years. His funeral will be at St Aloysius Church, on Sep 2, at half past two o'clock P M.

Died: on Aug 31, Alex'r B McFarlan, a native of Perthshire, Scotland, & for a long series of years a resident of Wash City, in his 71st year. His funeral will be from the Fourth Presbyterian Church, 9th st, on Sep 2, at 4 P M. [Sep 8th newspaper: tribute to the memory of Mr A B McFarlan, by the St Andrew's Society of Washington; Mr Wm R Smith, president; Jas Clephane spoke, as did Mr F D Stuart. –Alex Gardner, sec]

Died: on Aug 30, Jane, widow of the late Thos Cookendorfer, in her 72nd year. Her funeral is this afternoon at 4 o'clock, from the residence of her son-in-law, L D Castleman, Pa ave & 26th st west.

Died: on Aug 30, at *Mount Pleasant* farm, after an illness of 10 weeks, Wm J Stone, jr, in his 42nd year. His funeral will take place on Sunday at 3 P M, from the Ascension Church, on H st, near 9th, & from thence will proceed to *Rock Creek burial ground*. [Balt & Richmond papers please copy.]

Died: on Aug 30, at Quincy, Ill, of typhoid fever, Sidney S Babcock, son-in-law of Hon Amos Kendall. His funeral procession will leave the Calvary Baptist Church, 8th & H sts, on Sep 3 at 5 o'clock, to meet the remains at the Balt & Ohio railroad depot, from which they will be taken to *Glenwood Cemetery*.
-Chron & Star

Hampton Woodruff, a prominent St Louis politician, died of cholera on Friday.

Maj Gee, whose long trial before a military commission in Raleigh, N C, recently ended in his acquittal, has returned to his home in Quincy, Fla, & has resumed the practise of medicine, his old profession.

MON SEP 3, 1866
Gen Grant's father-in-law had a shock of paralysis, attended with convulsions at 12 M yesterday. Dr Duhamel, who was in the vicinity of Gen Grant's residence, was prompt in rendering medical aid, & Dr Notson, U S A, & Dr Brennerman, of Gen Grant's staff, & family physician, were also present. At a late hour last evening he was doing better.

Mrd: on Aug 30, in Wash, by Rev P D Gurley, D D, Brvt Maj Wm R King, Capt U S Corps of Engineers, to Virginia Southard, daughter of Lt Col J C Woodruff, U S Corps of Engineers.

Orphans Court of Wash Co, D C. Letters testamentary on the personal estate of Peter Van Essen, late of Gtwn, D C. –Wm King, Geo W Beall, Jenkin Thomas

Supreme Court of the U S, No 10, Dec Term, 1865. In error to the Circuit Court of the U S for the Eastern District of Louisiana. Thos H Newell, plntf in error, vs Richd Nixon. Mr Johnson, of counsel for the plntf in error, having suggested the death of Richd Nixon, the dfndnt in error in this cause, moved the court for an order under the 15th rule of court to make the proper representives parties. It is here ordered by this court, that unless the proper representatives of the said Richd Nixon as aforesaid shall voluntarily become parties within the first 10 days of the ensuing term of this court, the plntf in error shall be entitled to open the record in said cause & to have the same heard, & the judgment therein reversed if erroneous. –D W Middleton, Clerk

Died: on Sep 1, after a long & painful illness, Miss Nancy Owens, aged 61 years & 6 months. Her funeral will take place on Sep 3, at 10 o'clock, from the residence of her brother, Mr Benj Owens, 73 north A st, Capitol Hill.

St Joseph's Academy for Young Ladies, conducted by the **Sisters of Charity**, near Emmittsburg, Fred'k Co, Md, will begin on Aug 28th & Jan 28th.
–Mother Superior, St Joseph's Academy

War Dept, Ofc of the Claims Commission, Wash, D C, Aug 31, 1866. Statement of claims filed before the claims commission during the current month.
1-Claim of R Bonnevall, for property seized & confiscated by Gen Butler; filed Aug 15, 1866. T E Lloyd, Atty.
2-Claim of Allen Valentine, for saving train of army wagons, etc; filed Aug 15, 1866. A S Cox & Co, Attys.
3-Claim of Walter J Dobbin, for losses sustained when Gen Sherman's army entered Columbia S C; filed Aug 15, 1866, through British Embassy.
4-W O Jones, for damage sustained in bldg *Fort Morton*; filed Aug 15, 1866, in person.
5-Mary Cassin, for cotton alleged to have been destroyed; filed Aug 15, 1866, through British Embassy.
6-J C Badger, for services in ferretting out cotton frauds; filed Aug 15, 1866, in person.
7-R D Beans, for horses, etc, alleged to have been taken from him in Va by the U S army; filed Aug 15, 1866, in person.
8-Alfred Farrar, S H Hornbeck, & Jas A Pickett, for services under orders of the Provost Marshal General of the Dept of Missouri; filed Aug 15, 1866. J F Benjamin, Atty.
9-Claim of Sam Worthington & Dr Wm W Worthington, for cotton & other property alleged to have been taken by the Quartermaster's Dept; filed Aug 15, 1866. John Jolliffe, Atty.
10-Claim of John A Cean/Clean, for horses & bridles, alleged to have been taken from him at Natchez; filed Aug 15, 1866, in person.
11-Claim of P S Fayssoux, for value & services of the steamer **Fancy Natchez**; filed Aug 15, 1866. L H Rousseau, Atty.
12-Claim of B F Logan, for restoration of property at Shreveport, La; filed Aug 15, 1866, in person.
13-Claim of Jeffrey Moriarty, for the alleged seizure of property in Va; filed Aug 15, 1866, through the British Embassy.
14-S G Cabell, for rebel property collected by him & turned over to the U S authorities; filed Aug 15, 1866, in person, through the Treasury Dept.
15-Claim of Edward & Davenport for rent of wharf at Richmond, Va; filed Aug 15, 1866. W W Beckwith, Atty.
16-Claim of Elias Shipman, surviving partner, etc, for rent of property at Norfolk, Va; filed Aug 15, 1866, in person, through Treasury Dept.
17-Claim of Indiana H Slaughter, for land taken for a *National Cemetery* at Cold Harbor, Va; filed Aug 15, 1866, Ezekiel S Talley, guardian, etc.

18-Claim of A Morrill, for railroad material alleged to have been taken for military purposes; filed Aug 17, 1866. K F Page, Atty.
19-Julius Hesse & Co, for transportation of paroled prisoners; filed Aug 17, 1866. Wm W Boyce, Atty.
20-Claim of John A Brown, for restoration of certain drafts; filed Aug 18, 1866. Chas F Blake, Atty.
21-Claim of Elsberg & Amsberg, & Jas Hunter, for supplies alleged to have been furnished to the New Mexico militia in 1862; filed Aug 18, 1866. J J McCarty, Atty.
22-Claim of Angelo Miazzo, for the alleged use of ware houses by the U S army; filed Aug 18, 1766, through the Italian Embassy.
23-Claim of Eugene Lodomir Riquet, for property alleged to have been taken from him in 1864; filed Aug 18, 1866, in person.
24-Claim of R S Hipkins, for damages to his property; filed Aug 18, 1866, in person.
25-Claim of Eliza Knighton, for property alleged to have been destroyed by U S troops, filed Aug 18, 1866, through British Embassy.
26-Claim of Chas Nagelin, for cattle alleged to have been seized by the U S military authorities; filed Aug 18, 1866, in person.
27-Claim of L E Babcock, for losses sustained & services rendered; filed Aug 18, 1866, in person.
28-Claim of S D Freeman, L J Polk, & others, trustees of Columbia Female Institute, for repairs to bldg, grounds, etc; filed Aug 18, 1866, in person.
29-Claim of Saml R Jacobs, for vouchers given Wm S Stevens for haversacks; filed Aug 18, 1866. Chipman, Hosmer, Gilmon & Brown, Attys.
30-Claim of Geo S Kausler, for rent of cotton press & yards; filed Aug 18, 1866, in person.
31-Claim of A G Adams & R G Thorne, for 11,550 bushels of sale; filed Aug 18, 1866. Owen & Wilson, Attys
32-Claim of John Brownson, jr, for proceeds of a crop on Black Water plantation; filed Aug 18, 1866. J V Bogett, Atty.
33-Claim of S T Suit, for metal alleged to have been seized by Provost Marshal; filed Aug 21, 1866, in person.
34-Claim of H S Saunders, for damages to property alleged to have been done by the U S troops; filed Aug 21, 1866, in person.
35-Claim of Mary R Kent, for property alleged to have been taken by U S soldiers after Lee's surrender; filed Aug 21, 1866, in person.
36-Claim of Mary Ann Peora, for property alleged to have been taken by U S troops; filed Aug 18, 1866, through the Interior Dept.
37-Claim of Wm J Minor, for sugar & molasses alleged to have been taken by the U S Sequestration Commission; filed Aug 22, 1866. John Jolliffe, Atty.
38-Claim of Mrs C H Halsey, for property alleged to be held by the U S officials; filed Aug 22, 1866. C C Suydam, Atty.
39-Claim of Hugh F Smith, for damages to property at Bowling Green; filed Aug 22, 1866, in person.

40-Claim of J Z Chutkowski, for forage alleged to have been taken by U S troops; filed Aug 22, 1866, in person.
41-Claim of Jos Hamlin, for services at the Soldiers' Rest; filed Aug 22, 1866. Simon Cameron, Agent.
42-Claim of John H Wardwell, for supplying muskets to the Excelsior brigade; filed Aug 22, 1866, in person.
43-Claim of Susan Shacklett, for stoves alleged to have been taken by U S troops; filed Aug 23, 1866, in person.
44-Claim of Thos Cassidy, for services as clerk at headquarters, N Y; filed Aug 23, 1866, in person.
45-Claims of E D Judd & J S Herrick, paymasters, for commutation of quarters; filed Aug 25, 1866, in person.
46-Claim of Michl Fitzimmons, for rent of property by the U S; filed Aug 29, 1866. Hugh L Bond, Atty.
47-Claim of John R G Hotz, for saving arms for the U S; filed Aug 29, 1866. G W Z Black, Atty.
48-Claim of John Sheldon, for pay as guide; filed Aug 29, 1866. Boswell & Kean, Attys.
49-Claim of C S Snead, for cannon alleged to have been seized by order of Maj Gen Nelson; filed Aug 31, 1866, in person. –De Witt Clinton, Bvt Lt Col & Judge Advocate, Recorder

TUE SEP 4, 1866
Mrd: on Jul 30, by Rev Dr Pinckney, Maj Addison Barrett to Marion, 2nd daughter of th late Lt Horace N Harrison, U S N.

Died: on Sep 3, Susan Annette, daughter of Simon Towle, aged 20 years.

On Sat last, a farmer named Kilpatrick, residing near Chattanooga, was shot & killed by a negro with whom he had a previous difficulty. The murdered man was just recovering from a fever, & at the time of the tragedy, was taking a walk, leaning on his wife's arm.

Buffalo, Sep 2. John Hollister's house was entered today by robbers while the inmates were at church, & $23,800, mostly in Gov't bonds, stolen.

Lt Col Jas McElhone, 14th U S infty, died in Phil, on Monday last, from the effects of wounds received in the battle of Gaines' Mills, in 1862. He entered the army at the outbreak of the rebellion, in 1861, as a 2nd lt, & was brevetted a lt colonel for bravery in battle. He was one of the youngest ofcrs of his rank in the regular service. At the terrible battle of Gaines' Mills he had an important command, although wearing the uniform of a lt, & on this & other occasions he distinguished himself by his bravery & his sterling military qualities. Col McElhone was a brother of John McElhone, the eminent phonographic reporter of the Congressional Globe. -Republican

The officials of the Treasury have been informed that John D Eighme was recently tried at Albany, N Y, for smuggling in that district, & fined $500 & to be imprisoned for 6 months. His associates in crime turned State's evidence to save themselves.

Springfield Republican, Sep 1. A heavy defalcation, amounting to not less than $27,000, from the First Nat'l Bank at Greenfield, has lately been discovered. I C Tenney, the teller of the bank, abstracted the money at various times. He is a native of Orange, & employed in the bank for several years. He has been a protege of Rep Washburn & an imate of his family, & so strong was Mr Washburn's paternal interest in the young man that he was affected to tears on hearing of his great crime.

Despatch from Buffalo: Dean Richmond has left an estate valued at a million & a half of dollars. To his 5 sons & daughter he gives $50,000 each, & transferred from himself to his wife the care of the balance of his estate. Of his abundant income from fifteen to twenty thousand a year was dispensed for beneficial objects & in charities. Three of the sons of Mr Richmond are young men, but only one of them is in business. The daughter is unmarried.

Orphans Court of Wash Co, D C. Letters of administration on the personal estate of Jos Libbey, late of Gtwn, D C, deceased. –Louisa Libbey, admx Jos Libbey, jr, & J Edw Libbey are authorized to collect & receipt for all sums due to the estate of Jos Libbey, deceased, & all persons indebted to said estate are requested to settle their indebtedness without delay.

WED SEP 5, 1866
A *Fortress Monroe* despatch says the impression gains ground that Jeff Davis will be released on a conditional parole, on the ground of his continued ill-health.

Mrd: on Sep 4, at the Church of the Epiphany, by Rev Dr Hall, Thos Russell to Florence, youngest daughter of the late John Sergeant, all of Wash City.
[Balt Sun please copy.]

Mrd: on Sep 4, by Rev Mr McFalls, Francis H Heyer, of Wisc, to Miss Martinette E Peck, at the residence of the bride's father, Col Jos Peck, of Wash City.
No cards.

Mrd: on Sep 4, at the Church of the Epiphany, by Rev Chas H Hall, D D, Wm D Baldwin to Margaret Fitzhugh, daughter of Gen Wilham Maynadier, U S A.

Died: on Sep 2, at Norristown, Pa, of typhoid fever, A Thos Smith, counsellor at law, of Wash City, & late naval judge advocate, aged 57 years. His funeral will be today at 3 o'clock P M, from the New Jerusalem Church, on North Capitol st, between B & C sts.

Died: on Sep 3, in Wash City, Mary Hamlin, consort of Jos Hamlin, in her 43rd year. Her remains will be taken from the residence of the family, La ave & 6th st, a 10:30 A M, today, & proceed to Balt for interment.

Orphans Court-Judge Purcell. 1-The following wills were filed, fully proven, & admitted to probate & record: of Cornelia Wittenver, letters testamentary were issued to Rev Mathias Alig as sole executor, in bonds of $2,000; & of Peter Von Essen, letters testamentary issued to Wm King, Geo W Beall, John T Mitchell, & Wm C Magee, in bonds of $16,000. After making ample provision for his widow, children, & grandchildren, the will of Mr Von Essen provides that if there be any surplus it shall be paid to the Corp of Gtwn for the benefit of the white free schools. Also, in case of the death of his children without issue, certain bequests to them shall be paid to the Corp of Gtwn for the same purpose. 2-The will of Martha D Duncanson was fully proven & admitted to probate. 3-The will of Secily Carroll was filed & partially proven. 4-Letters of administration upon the personal estate of the late Jos Libbey were issued to Louisa Libbey, his widow, in bonds of $70,000. 5-An inventory of the personal estate of Jas R Wood was returned by executor; & of the personal estate of Jonas Glick, by the executrix. 6-Martha V McDonald, daughter of the late Jas W McDonald & Nora E McDonald, was bound as an apprentice to Asa Whitney until she is 16 years of age. 7-The following guardians gave the bonds required by the court: Benj F Bittinger, as guardian to Chas Bittinger, orphan son of Catherine Malvina Bittinger; Jesse Jenkins, guardian to Clarence M & Richd H Winemiller, orphans of John C Winemiller; Appolonia Stuntz, guardian to Mary, orphan of Alex'r & Cornelia Wittenver; & Patrick Collins, guardian of Sarah M Nester & Margaret A Nestor, orphans of John Nestor, late of Balt.

The story that Jenny Lind was hissed abroad is declared to be a fabrication by Manager Jarrett, who has just returned from England, & who saw & heard her.

On Friday, during the picnic of the Clinton Park Sabbath School at Presque Isle, 3 miles below Toledo, Ohio, a party of 5 young persons were crossing the river, when their small boat swamped, & all but one, Bennett Holman, aged 15, were drowned. Those drowned were Everett G Isherwood, about 15, Florence Rhodes, Fanny Underwood, & Georgiana Reed, 11, 13, & 14 years of age respectively.

Columbia Gardens, corner 12th st & Ohio ave. Every night concert & performances. For particulars look at our handbill. –Carrie Bentley, proprietress

Auction on Oct 6 next, by deed of trust from John Milburn & wife, dated Jan 25, 1859, recorded in Liber J A S No 169, folio 18 etc, of the land records of Wash Co, D C, near Broad Branch Road, about 7 acres, 3 roods, & 9¼ perches, [except 2 acres heretofore sold to Thos Harris.] This property is near the residence of Col Belt & others. -Robt G Thrift, trustee -K F Page, auct

Dept of the Interior, U S Patent Ofc, Wash, Aug 29, 1866. Ptn of John R Moffitt, of Chelsea, Mass, formerly of Piqua, Ohio, praying for the extension of a patent granted to him on Nov 30, 1853, for an improvement in Grain Separators, & reiussed on May 17, 1859, in 3 divisions, A, B, & C, numbered 715 thru 717; this ptn being for the extension of the reissue B, numbered 716, for 7 years from the expiration of said patent which takes place on Nov 30, 1866. –H C Theaker, Com'r of Patents

Effingham Heights, on the 7th st road, just beyond the Wash City limits, will be sold in lots of from half an acre to one or more acres. Also, the large frame house near the Park Hotel, suitable for a hotel. Apply to John A Smith, 399 C st, between 4½ & 3rd sts.

THU SEP 6, 1866
The Conservative Army & Navy Union held a called meeting on Tue in the Council Chamber, City Hall, the vice pres, Col Jas A Tait, presiding. Lt H C Gooding reported the following as additional vice presidents: Brvt Capt A C Warner, Ill; Sgt John H Thompson, Ohio; Lt J W Richmond, Maine; Lt H Clay Gooding, Ind; Capt E D Tallman, Wisc; Lt Col D Farley, N J; Capt J H Tall, Pa; Capt Jas McConnell, N Y; Capt P Young, Mass; Lt Sidney J Wailes, Md; Lt D F Stiles, N C; Capt A W Chilton, Vt; Assist Surgeon W Craigen, West Va. Also elected: Capt C W Rudyeard, Rec Sec; Engineer J C Mockabee, Cor Sec; Sgt D J O'Connor, Financial Sec; Sgt Fitch J Porter, Treasurer. Delegates to represent this association in the Clevleand Convention: Capt P Young, of Mass; Lt H O Gooding, of Ind; Capt W H Nalley, of D C; Capt Geise, of Pa; Col J R O'Beirne, Col Jas Tait, of D C; Capt W J Gary, of Va; Capt J R McConnell, of N Y; Lt S J Wailes, of Md; Dr Craigen, of West Va; Capt McKean, of Calif; Sgt J H Thompson & Engineer Mockabee. Appointed a cmte on finance: Capt N C Warner, Dr Craigen, & Capt O Hogan. Lt E D Tallman, Capt B Austin, & Engineer Mockabee were appointed the Cmte on Credentials.

Jacob Hess was arrested by Ofcr Sprague for interfering with a Corp contractor who was grading North Capitol st, & it was necessary to cut down some large trees in front of Hess' dwlg. Mr Hess did not approve & became very boisterous to the police, who arrested him. He was fined $5 for disorderly conduct, & held to bail for peace.

Died: on Sep 5, John Allen, in the *7_th year of his age, for the last 50 years a resident of Wash City. His funeral will be this afternoon at 4 o'clock, from his late residence, at Mrs C Boyd's, 314 D st, between 10th & 11th sts. [*There was no number after the 7_.]

First class house & furniture for rent, Pa ave & 25th st, n w corner, at present occupied by Maj Gen O O Howard. Apply to Wm T Steigler, Room No 134 Gen Land Ofc, or address Box 544 City Post Ofc.

Geo M Weston has been nominated for Congress from the 4th District of Maine.

For rent or lease, the house in which I now reside, 501 11th st, containing 15 rooms, besides a dry, well lighted basement, 80 feet deep, in 2 rooms, with gas & Potomac & cistern water. –Edwin Green

We hereby give notice that we are authorized to collect & receipt for all rents due to the undivided real estate of Jos Libbey, deceased, & to institute all legal proceedings necessary in connection with the same.
+
We have for rent 2 large houses in Gtwn, D C; one on the Heights, & 3 small houses in the First Ward of Wash, D C. –Jos & J E Libbey, 27 Water st, Gtwn, D C.

The subscriber is authorized to sell the Farm belonging to the heirs of the late Saml Tayman, in Nottingham District, PG Co, Md. It contains 160 acres & has upon it a good dwlg house, & a convenient Storehouse & Warehouse; also a large new Barn, & other necessary Out-houses, with a pump of good water in the yard. It lies on the main road leading from Upper Marlboro to Brandywine, & the Balt & Potomac railroad will run through the place. Apply to Geo W Wilson, Upper Marlboro, or the subscriber, whose address is Croom Post Ofc. –Jas H Tayman

Supreme Court of D C, Sep 4, 1866; in Equity No 536. Thos B Scott, Ellen R Scott, Ann H Scott, Mary C E Scott, Mary Augusta DeCamp Scott, E B Smith, Judson Smith, J S Smith, & Tyler Smith, vs Alfred Claggett, Eliz Claggett, Ellen C Claggett, & all other heirs at law of Eliz C Scott & Martha E C Scott & Benj S Bayly, adm of Martha E C Scott. Order that the sale made & reported by Wm J Miller, trustee, appointed in this cause for the sale of the real estate of Eliz C & Martha E C Scott, deceased, be ratified & confirmed. –R J Meigs, clerk

Orphans Court of Wash Co, D C, Jul 21, 1866. In the case of Josiah Dent, adm of Wm S Nichols, deceased, the administrator & Court have appointed Oct 2nd next, for the final settlement of the personal estate of the said deceased, of the assets in hand. -Z C Robbins, Reg/o wills

Orphans Court of Wash Co, D C, Sep 1, 1866. In the case of Wm B Hill, exc of Catharine Smith, deceased, the executor & Court have appointed Sep 29 next, for the final settlement of the personal estate of the said deceased, of the assets in hand. -Z C Robbins, Reg/o wills

FRI SEP 7, 1866
Dept of the Interior, U S Patent Ofc, Wash, Aug 31, 1866. Ptn of Jearum Atkins, of Mokena, Ill, praying for the extension of a patent granted to him on Dec 21, 1852, for an improvement in Rakes to Grain Harvesters, for 7 years from the expiration of said patent, which takes place on Dec 21, 1866.
–T C Theaker, Com'r of Patents

Reverend Mother Angela, Superior of St Vincent's Hospital of the Sisters of Charity, died at the hospital in 11th st, yesterday. She was a sister of the late Archbishop Hughes, & was born at her father's farm, near Augner, county Tyrone, Ireland, in 1806. She came to this country with her mother in 1818, her father having emigrated to Pa two years previously. The family settled at Chambersburg, & Ellen was educated in a convent at Fred'k, Md. She joined the sisterhood of charity at age 22 or 23, assuming the name of Angela. She superintended at various schools & charitable institutions in the city & State of N Y. The headquarters of the congregation of N Y, N J, & the New England States was established at Mount St Vincent, within the present limits of Central Park. Mother Angela was chosen Superior & retained that ofc for 6 years, the longest period allowed by the rules. For the last 7 years she has been Director of the hospital in 11th st.

The Com'r of Pensions yesterday appointed Dr S J Radcliffe, of Gtwn, to be a Pension Notary.

Lynchburg News of Tue. An affray occurred at Buckingham Court-house on Sat last, between a lawyer named Jas Leach & Anthony Walton & his son, which resulted in the death of the elder Walton & mortally wounding his son. The affair was settled at the Court-house, but on Sat the son & Mr Leach met on the street, & were discussing the affair, when an officious friend went to the elder Walton's house & told him that his son was having difficulty. The elder proceeded with a pistol & fired at Leach; Leach returned the fire and shot the elder Walton and mortally wounded the son, who was also firing at Leach. Leach was unhurt & surrendered himself to the ofcrs of the law, was tried & acquitted upon the ground of having acted in self-defence. The parties were all highly respectable, & its tragical results are most deeply deplored by the entire community.
[Mr Walton's son's name was not given.]

The city of Chicago has been thrown into a state of intense excitement by the murder of Geo Trussell by a female. Trussell was born in Danville, Vt, where he lived until 1849. He came to Kenosha, was employed in a grocery store; in 1860 he came to Chicago, & was employed by the Richmond & Co. He commenced gambling & soon became proprietor of one of the largest faro banks in the city, & in his profession has amassed over $100,000. He became enamored of a beautiful chambermaid at the American House, Cleveland, between whom several quarrels have occurred in the past few years. While in a fit of jealousy & partial intoxication she sought him, on Tue, & shot him more than once & killed him. Her name was Millie & she has a son, a little boy, who was at school. [Sep 13th newspaper: Mollie Trussell, who killed Geo Trussel, is in close confinement in the county jail, awaiting her trial for murder. She appears to be preparing for her trial by becoming insane.] [Dec 17th newspaper: The trial of Mollie Trussell was concluded at Chicago on Sat. The jury returned a verdict of manslaughter, & she was sentenced to one year in the penitentiary.]

Died: on Sep 5, of cholera infantum, Henry Given, infant son of Harry & Fannie Burr, aged 11 months & 10 days. His funeral will take place from the residence of John T Given, 445 I st, between 9th & 10th sts, on Sep 7 at 10 o'clock.

Capt Albert Smith, chief of the Clothing Bureau of the Navy Dept, is lying in a very low & sinking condition in Boston. He was in command of a ship in the early part of the war, from which duties he was relieved on account of his failing health. He is the only surviving son of Admiral Smith. His only brother, Lt Jos Smith, was killed instantly, by a shell, while at his post as cmder of the U S frig **Congress**, in the conflict with the rebel ram **Merrimac**, in Hampton Roads, in 1862.

SAT SEP 8, 1866

Some 4 or 5 months ago a young man, Saml Paris, employed in the Riggs & Co's Bank, suddenly disappeared from Wash City; & at the same time Robt Holtzman disappeared. They both are suspects in the disappearance of $27,000 in bonds. Both had left the area, Paris went to the West & Southwest, & Holtzman to New Orleans. Paris was arrested & Detective Kelley, armed with the warrant, was despatched to New Orleans to arrest Holtzman.

Geo Peabody has purchased ex-Mayor Maservey's residence in Salem, Mass, for $18,000.

Blessing of the Bells of St Aloysius' Church, on Sep 9, at 4 o'clock P M. Procession will proceed along I st to 10th; thence to Gonzaga College, to Pa ave, to 3rd st, up 3rd to C, along C to the Railroad Station, & after receiving the Archbishop of Balt, out N J ave to I, thence to the Church, where the ceremony will be performed.
Order of Procession: Chief Marshal, T H Parsons; Assist Marshals: A O Shaw & Jas Keleher. Band. Aids, H G Thyson, J C Lay, Thos Thyson.
B F Wiget, Literary Society
St Aloysius' Sunday School
Orphan Boys, St Joseph's Asylum
Orphan Girls, St Vincent's Asylum
Band.
Sunday School of the Holy Trinity, Gtwn
Sunday School-St Patrick's, St Peters, St Matthew's, St Dominick's, Immaculate Conception, & St Mary's. St Joseph's Benevolent Society, [German]
St Aloysius' Society, [German]
Band
Young Catholics' Friend Society
Temperance Association of Wash & Gtwn.
St Vincent de Paul Society
Band
Sodalities of the Blessed Virgin Mary

Died: on Sep 6, at Marietta, Lancaster Co, Pa, Archibald Alex'r Ker, in his 27th year. His funeral will be tomorrow, the Sabbath, at 3 o'clock P M, from the residence of his brother, 503 K st, between 4th & 5th sts.

The Boston Advertiser, in referring to Mr Edwin Booth's return to the stage, & his reception at the Boston Theatre on Monday night, says: "Perhaps never in our theatrical history, certainly not in recent years, has Boston given to any dramatic artist such an ovation as that accorded last night to Edwin Booth.

For rent: a 3 story brick house, with basement & fine large yard, on Pa ave, between 21st & 22nd sts. Inquire of B H Stinemetz, 234 Pa ave, between 12th & 13th sts.

MON SEP 10, 1866

Capt W M Mew, formerly in charge of the Mint branch of the Treasury, has been promoted to the position vacated by the death of Mr Wm Matthews, in charge of the administration of the laws relative to inspection of steamships.

Edmund Blunt, widely known & respected citizen of N Y, died on Sunday, after a lingering illness, at age 67. Mr Blunt had a natural taste for practical mathematics, & became a surveyor. At the age of 17 he surveyed the harbor of N Y; in 1833 he was appointed in the U S Coast survey service.

Origin & Use of bells. The primitive Church used no public signal to call the faithful to her religious assemblies. An ecclesiastic named cursor, runner or messenger, went from house to house, to notify the Christians privately of the day & hour when the Divine office was to be celebrated. On the accession of Constantine, in the 4th century, the Church permitted the use of trumpets. Many authors maintain that bells were invented in the 4th century, at Nola, a city of Campania. Hence they are called Noloe & Campanoe. Some authors give credit to St Panlinus, of Nola, in the 5th century; others insist that Pope Sabinian, in the 7th century, ordered them to be used in the services of the Church. But St Gregory, of Tours, who died in 506, tells us that even before his day bells were rung to mark the hours of the Divine offices. St John Climaens compares them to spiritual trumpets.

The fact that certain citizens of Delhi, Mich, had lynched an octoroon, John Taylor, for attempting the murder of a family named Buck, has been reported by telegraph. He confessed the crime with which he was charged.

Supreme Court, D C, in Equity No 536. Thos A Scott & others against Alfred Clagett & others, heirs of Eliz C Scott & Martha E C Scott & Benj S Baily, adm of said Martha. The parties named & creditors of said Eliz C & Martha C Scott & notified, that on Sep 29 next, I shall state the account of the trustee & the distribution of the fund in said cause. -W Redin, auditor

Rochester, N Y, Sep 5. Railroad accident near Rochester today, when the train which left Albany was thrown from the track by a switch, which was carelessly left open. List of those killed: David Creighton, Newtown, C E; Leroy Shaughnessy, Rochester, railroad employe; Lucius Owen, brakesman, Clyde, N Y; Mr Smith, Gloversville, N Y; Mr Somers, Rosenbloom, N Y. Wounded: A H Stone, Oppenhim, N Y, Mr & Mrs Wm Somers, Decatur, N Y, slightly; Mrs Downing, Rome, N Y, head severely; H Harrington, 19 Maiden La, N Y, slightly; Mrs P J Parker, Buffalo, slightly; W L Vail, Fla, N Y, slightly; W F Mitts, Murray, N Y, slightly; Jas Aspell, Seneca Falls, brakesman; Mr & Mrs A Seymour, Lebanon, N Y, badly bruised; C S Feeters, Syracuse; H C Peters, injured in arms & head; Michl Daley & son, Utica, both slightly; W F Lantry, Oneida, slightly; A F Whartley, Kalamazoo, jaw broken; A DeForest, Ann Arbor, Mich, slightly; David Taylor, Jersey City, [of the firm of Colgate & Co, N Y,] internally; Aaron Stone & wife, slightly; Thos Oliver, Fordham, N Y, slightly; Mrs W W Thomas & son, Belort, Wis, slightly; J A Chapman, Belort, Wis, slightly; J O Johnson, East Saginaw, slightly; E Derby, Courtland, slightly; Mrs Manna, Rochester, head & arm; Andrew Tracy, N Y, slightly; Jas Gould, fireman, Palmyra; John Sapple, Detroit, leg injured; Jas Elliott, N Y; John Pacer, London, C W, ribs boken; C Demeter, Gloverville, N Y, seriously; Wm Rice, Oswego, shoulder blade broken; J W Swan, Medina, N Y; Mrs Swan, hand & arm broken; Susan Page, Binghamton, slightly wounded; Mrs Newell, Calif, slightly; Mr Newell, slightly; Mrs N Somers, Otsego, badly injured; Horace Hoyt, Decatur, internally; Frank Frazier, engineer, slightly; W J McDonald, Calif, slightly. The latter was extricated from the wreck by his 2 sisters. Wm Ryan, of Rochester, slightly wounded. The bodies of Shaughnessy & Owen were left in the wreck, as they could not be immediately removed.

In Equity, before Judge Fisher, Sep 6, 1866. 1-Jas K Clayton et ux. vs. Harriet Williamson et al. This was a proceeding for the sale of the real estate of Benj Williamson, deceased, for the purpose of distribution amongst the heirs of the deceased, & the Court passed a final order ratifying the Auditor's report on the distribution of the proceeds, & ordering distribution to be made accordingly. M Thompson solicitor for cmplnts. 2-Sep 7, 1866. Jas W Gibson vs Eliz Gibson et al. This was a proceeding for the sale of the real estate of Joshua Gibson, deceased, for the purpose of distribution among the heirs. A final decree was passed ratifying the sale of the said estate, & the Auditor's report as to the distribution of the proceeds of the sale of the estate amongst the widow & heirs, & the distribution ordered accordingly. M Thompson solicitor for cmplnts.

Orphans Court of Wash Co, D C. In the case of Edw Shoemaker & Geo Shoemaker, adms of Geo Shoemaker, deceased, the administrators & Court have appointed Oct 6 next, for the final settlement of the personal estate of the said deceased, of the assets in hand. -Z C Robbins, Reg/o wills

London, Sep 8. Lord Northbrooke, formerly Sir John Baring, died today.

Died: on Sep 8, in Boston, Mass, Cmder Albert N Smith, U S N, Chief of the Bureau of Equipment & Recruiting, Navy Dept, in his 44th year. His funeral is on Tue afternoon, at 4 o'clock, from the residence of his father, Rear Admiral Jos Smith, 348 9th st west. [Sep 11th newspaper: Cmder Smith entered the service on Oct 28, 1828; he had been employed on nearly all the stations, but for the past 8 years has been attached to the ship **Independence**, in the Pacific, & special service on the ship **Brooklyn**, then commanded by Admiral Farragut. Upon the breaking out of the rebellion he was selected to command the ship **Wissahickon**, & in that vessel passed the forts at New Orleans on the memorable Apr 25, 1862. He was a gentleman, a devoted son, a warm friend, & a gallant officer.]
[Sep 12th newspaper: The funeral of Cmder A N Smith, took place yesterday; the beautiful services of the Episcopal Church was read by Rev Dr Trimble, of St John's, after which the pall bearers, Acting Sec of the Navy, Wm Faxon, Cmdor Smith, Cmdor Jenkins, Cmder H A Wise, Lt Cmder Wm Mitchell, & Mr W Denby, conveyed the body to the hearse. The funeral cortege, the most imposing we have witnessed for some time, then took up its march to *Oak Hill Cemetery*, where, after the concluding service was read, the remains were deposited in the beautiul vault belonging to the family. A detachment of the Marine Corps, under the command of Major Graham, fired 3 volleys over the tomb. Among the most prominent on the part of the navy, were Rear Admirals Wm B Shubrick, Chas H Davis, & John A Dahlgren, & Cmdor A A Harwood, Maj Gen Meigs & Maj Gen Townsend, of the army, were also present. Cmder Smith entered the U S navy in 1838, & was held in high esteem by all the officers of the service.]

Died: on Sep 1, in Wash City, of dysentery, Ellen Webster, infant daughter of Jas M & Eliza G Follansbee.

Teacher is wanted for the Male Grammar School of the 2nd District, 3rd & 4th Wards, Wash City, D C. The salary is $1,375 per annum. Apply, with references, to W J Rhees, W R Woodward, B F M Hurley, Sub Board.

TUE SEP 11, 1866
The police are looking up offenders under the liquor law, & Jas McGraw & Jas Clancy have been arrested, & each fined $20.44. Geo Kraft, arrested by Ofcr Warwick, was fined $20 for keeping open house on Sunday.

Died: on Sep 9, at his father's residence, in PG Co, Md, Augustus Hill, son of Chas Hill, in his 24th year.

Died: on Sep 10, in Wash, after a short illness, Mrs Eliza Lamb, in her 67th year. Her funeral will take place from her late residence, opposite Willard's Hotel, on Wed morning, at 10 o'clock A M.

For sale or rent, my dwlg at Md & Va aves, between 7th & 8th sts; the house is 54 feet front by 40 feet deep; the lot is 100 feet front by 214 feet deep, embracing one half of lot 434. –Jno H Semmes, Seaton House

Orphans Court-Judge Purcell. 1-On Sat the will of the late Wm Miley, of the Marine Corps, bequeathing $40 to Rev Fr Boyle, & the balance of his property to Sgt Maj Edw Dana, of the Marine corps, who he appoints exec, was fully proven & admitted to probate as regards personality. 2-Also, the will of the late Wm J Stone, jr, bequeathing all his estate & property to his wife, Mary F Stone, whom he nominates as sole exec & guardian to the children. 3-An exemplified copy of the will of the late Saml C Edes, of Balt, was received & admitted to probate. 4-The will of the late Jemima B Conner, bequeathing her property, all of which is personal to her friend, C W Lansdale, of Montg Co, Md, for the sole use of her sister, Mrs Eliza Hunter, was filed. 5-The will of the late Nancy Jackson, bequeathing her property to her eldest sister, Amanda, & her mother-in-law, Teresa Jackson, was filed. 6-Letters of adminitration were issued to Jas T Small, on the estate of Jacob Small; bond $3,000; & to Eliz Schroedel, on the estate of Fred'k Schroedel; bond $100. 7-John E Libbey was appointed guardian to Franklin Libbey, orphan of Jos Libbey; bond $25,000. 8-The balance & distribution of the personal estate of Thos Conner, with the first & final account of the administrator, & also the first & final account of the collector of the estate of Jacob Small, deceased, were approved & passed.

The undersigned wishes to sell a valuable estate in Fauquier Co, Va, containing 788 acres; divided at present into 13 fields; improvements consist of a plain dwlg house for a small family, well built barn, & other necessary out-bldgs. Address me at Salem, Fauquier Co, Va, or refer to R Taylor Scott, Warrenton, Va, or Messrs Thos Branch & Co, Richmond, Va. –Richd H Carter, Salem, Fauquier Co, Va.

Despatch from Little Rock, Ark, on Thu a duel was fought with swords, between Weller Cogswell, postmaster at Wayne, & J T Wright, editor of the Wayne Gaz- the cause, jealousy. Both were frightfully mangled; both will die.

Hon J Hanselton Read died at Charleston, S C, on Sep 2. He was the grandson of Dr Wm Read, of Revolutionary fame, a surgeon in the Continental army & Pres of the Cincinnati Society. Deceased entered the Legislature in the winter of 1844, as rep from Prince George Wi_yah, & continued to be elected unremittingly ever since.

Mrs Saml Hoar, of Concord, Mass, died on Wed. She was the last surviving child of Roger Sherman. Her age was 85. Judge Hoar, her husband, who died about 5 years ago, was well known as having been sent away from Charleston, S C, some years since, for attempting to defend the rights of Massachusetts sailors before the courts of that State. Many of her relatives reside in N Y C.

WED SEP 12, 1866
Fred O Berkline, a member of the Ohio Legislature, & member of the City Council, died on Monday.

Jas J Barclay, a clerk in the Com'r of Customs Ofc of the Treasury, called upon the Assit Sec of the Treasury yesterday, & informed him that he commenced his 63rd year in that Dept yesterday morning. He entered the Dept at age 14, & therefore is 77 years old.

W G W Gray, the murderer of old Mr Gray, of Fayette Co, Ohio, in Oct, 1864, has been found guilty, & sentenced to be hung on Nov 13.

The wife of Geo Archer, proprietor of the Patterson House at Elmira, N Y, died on Friday from the effects of poison administered by herself.

The telegraph announces the death of Hon C C Clay, sr, of Alabama, once U S Senator from Alabama. [No death date given-current item.]

Miss Evans, the author of "Felix Holt, the Radical," the daughter of of a dissenting clergyman in Derbyshire, England, is 46 years old, & besides English, is complete mistress of 3 foreign languages, German, French, & Italian. She has written 6 novels in 10 years.

Mrd: on Sep 10, at Riverview, D C, Brvt Capt Josiah Slick, U S vols, to Miss Carrie Ferris, of Riverview, D C.

Mrd: on Sep 10, by Rev Evan Reese, P S Garretson, of East Millstone, N J, to Emma R Lamb, of Wash, D C.

The body of Peter Williamson, co H, 1st btln, 12th U S infty, was found floating in the Potomac river. Papers were found on his body. His neck was broken & the jury returned a verdict that the cause of his death is unknown.

Josiah Randall, one of the oldest members of the Phil bar, died at his residence, in this city, yesterday, in his 78th year. He was born on Jul 21, 1780. He was much beloved by his family, who will keenly feel his loss. He was the father of Hon Saml J Randall, who now represents the First District of this state in Congress. – Phil Ledger, Sep 11

Orphans Court of Wash Co, D C. Letters testamentary on the personal estate of John M Williams, late of Gtwn, D C, deceased. –Richd W Williams, Richd M Williams, excs

U S Marshal's sale: by writ of fieri facias, I will sell at public sale, for cash, on Oct 1, all of Geo Page's right, title, claim, & interest in & to Lot 15, in Geo Page's subdivision of square 467, in Wash City, with all & singular improvements thereon, seized & levied upon as the property of Geo Page, & will be sold to satisfy fieri facias No 343, trials Oct term 1855, in favor of Oliver Van Every, use of John Van Riswick. –D S Gooding, U S Marshal, D C.

David J Clark, postmaster at Manchester, N H, & brother of Hon Danl Clark, late U S Senator from N H, died on Monday of disease of the lungs.

THU SEP 13, 1866
The Com'r of Pensions appointed the following pension officers: Joel N Angier, Titusville, Pa, to be Pension Notary; Jas G McPherson, Charlestown, West Va, & John Severgood, Lancaster, Pa, to be Examining Surgeons.

The will of Rev John Pierpont is published in the Newton [Mass] Journal. He leaves portraits of himself to his daughters; his tools to his step-son, Mr Fowler; his literary property to his son John, to dispose of as he sees fit; his homestead & the other propery that he died possessed of he leaves to his surviving wife & his unmarried daughter, Mary Eliz.

Hon Stephen Fairbanks, a merchant of Boston, died on Monday, aged 83 years. He was at one time a member of the State Senate, & has filled many other offices of honor & trust in the State of Mass.

Orphans Court-Judge Purcell. 1-At the last session an exemplified copy of the will of the late John M Williams, of Gtwn, D C, made in Montg Co, Md, was filed & admitted to probate; Richd W & Richd M Williams, the excs named, qualifying by entering into $5,000 bond. The property, consisting of real estate in Gtwn & Montg Co, is bequeathed to his wife, children, & grandchildren. 2-Letters of administration were issued to Catherine Morgan on the estate of Bernard Morgan, deceased; bond, $1,500. 3-Eliza Foster was appointed guardian to the orphans of Chas Shafer; bond, $1,000; & Eliz Brown to the orphans of Alex'r Brown, deceased; bond, $6,000. 4-The first account of the guardian to the orphan of Levi Mitchell was approved & passed.

Died: at *Oakley*, the residence of her mother, of typhoid fever, Anne Louisa Kervand, daughter of Anne [*K Mabeth] & the late L Kervand. Her funeral will be from St Alban's Church, on Sep 13, at 4 o'clock P M. [*Possible name. Print is very light. No death date given.]

One of the oldest women in America is Mrs Porch, who lives in the mountains of East Tenn, & is aged 121 years. She is blind, but, being quite hearty, walks without assistance. Her memory is unimpaired, & she can recount many of the events of the Revolution with great accuracy.

Supreme Court of D C, in Equity No 451, Docket 7. O'Neal et al vs O'Neal et al. The trustees have reported they sold part of lot 3 in square 368, in Wash City, to Geo Varnell for $6,325.50, & that said Varnell had assigned his purchase to John C Harkness, & that Harkness had complied with the terms of sale; & also that he sold part of lot 8 in square 286 to W L Waller, for $4,000, & that Waller had complied with the terms of sale. -Andrew Wylie -Geo P Fisher, Justice Supreme Court D C -R J Meigs, clerk

FRI SEP 14, 1866
Gen O B Wilcox, of Michigan, has been made a colonel in the regular army, & assigned to the 29th infty.

Despatch from Albany gives further particulars of the explosion of the saw & planing mill of S & G Rork in that city, announced yesterday. Killed: John Cullen, engineer; had a wife & 4 or 5 children; age 49 years. John Hoffman, age 22; John Rork, a cousin of the owners, age 25; leaves a widowed mother; Jas O'Neill, age 15 or 16 years old, was driving in front of the engine house; he buried his mother a few days ago; John Fenmore, fireman, age 38, married, & had 6 or 7 children; & Cornelius Beye, a German, aged 49 years, married, & had several children.

Gen G A Custer has written a letter, declining to be a candidate for Congress from the First District of Michigan.

Died: on Aug 18, in Gettysburg, Pa, of consumption, Chas C Mason, of Loudoun Co, Va, formerly a resident of Wash City. For more than 12 months the hand of death had been upon him, & he knew it, & made his peace with God.

Died: on Sep 14, Blanche Wilhelmina, daughter of Fred'k W & Annie Storch, aged 1 year & 8 months. Her funeral is on Friday at 4 o'clock P M, from the residence of the parents, 54 Second st, Gtwn, D C.

Members of the Masonic Lodge No 1, two Lodges of Knights of Pythias, Harmony Lodge No 9, I O O F, & Associated Shipwrights, accompanied by the Marine Band, paraded yesterday afternoon to attend the funeral of Mr Geo Sherwood, a well-known employe of the ship-carpenter's dept of the Navy Yard.

A man named De Canine was accidentally run over by a train, at the Elizabeth depot, N J, on Wed last, & was mangled in so shocking a manner that his heartrending solicitations to be put out of the world were complied with, & he was shot through the head. The injuries he had received were past surgical aid.

Supreme Court of D C, No 672, in Equity, Docket 7. Jos F Little et al vs Mary E Little. David A Burr, trustee, reported he sold parts of lot 6 in square 8_9, for $375, by J H Shekel, who had complied with the terms of sale. –Geo P Fisher, Justice Supreme Court D C. –R J Meigs, clerk

SAT SEP 15, 1866
Mrd: on Sep 6, at Castleton, Vt, by Rev J W Diller, D D, of Brooklyn, N Y, Wm C Kent to Lizzie F Ellery, 2nd daughter of Capt Frank Ellery, U S N.

Mrd: on Sep 13, in Wash, at the residence of the bride's father, by Rev Dr Gillette, Thos F Dolan, of Portland, Maine, late Adj & Brvt Major 8th U S V V, 1st Army Corps, to Miss Rebecca O'Brien, of Wash, D C.

Died: on Sep 13, Sydney A Robinson Bowen, wife of Dr Chas H Bowen, & oldest daughter of Mr J & Mrs A M Robinson, aged 23 years, 5 months & 26 days. Her funeral will be from the residence of her husband, Dr Bowen, 452 Mass ave, between 6th & 7th sts, on Sat evening, at 3 o'clock. "O Jesus, take her to your arms."

Obit-died: on Mar 29, 1866, at Wash, D C, at age 30 years, Fanny L, wife of Col H Clay Wood, U S Army, a devoted Freemason. Mrs Wood was the daughter of Tobias Lord, of Steep Falls, Maine, & graduated at Gorham Seminary, Maine. She was a faithful wife & devoted mother. She accompanied her husband in all his travels in the discharge of his arduous duties, both in the States & on the more remote frontier, enduring the hardships of camp life; in Texas, the Indian Territory, Kansas, & Missouri, & over rough mountains, having become a soldier's wife, she willingly shared a soldier's fortunes. Mrs Wood has left behind her two very young & deeply interesting children, & a bereaved husband.

Supreme Court, D C, in Equity, No 500. John A Middleton et al against Eliza T Berry et al. The parties above & trustees are to be at my ofc, City Hall, on Oct 6 next, where I shall state the trustees' account & distribute the fund.
–W Redin, auditor

Supreme Court, D C, in Equity. Morris Earle, Alex'r M Earle & Morris D Earle, vs Rebecca Williams, Brooke B Williams, Wm Williams, Lloyd A Williams, Edw Williams, Alex'r B Williams, Harriet Scott, Douglas Scott, Jonathan H Carter, John E Carter, Wm G Busey, Isaac J Barrett, & John T Meem. The above cause is referred to me, as special auditor, to state the indebtedness of Edw Williams to the cmplnts & all other creditors, & all liens & incumbrances on the property described in the bill, at the intersection of Congress & Road sts, Gtwn, & on the interest of said Edw Williams in the same. Meeting on Sep 24 next in my ofc, Washington, at 11 A M. –Walter S Cox, spec auditor

Supreme Court, D C, in Equity No 560, Docket 7. John H Ingle et al vs Eliza B Ingle et al. John C Kennedy & Wm B Webb, trustees, reported to the Court they sold to Benj Beall parts of lots 16 thru 18 in Revervation B, for $3,500; part of lots 1 & 2 in square 458, to Owen Thorn, for $12,550; lots 20 thru 24 in Kennedy & Webb's subdivision of part of lot 1 in square 518, to Benedict Millburn, for $264; lots 26 thru 30 in same, to John B Lord, for $2,425; parts of lots 5 & 6 in square 690, to Grafton D Hanson, $8,300; lot 4 thru 12, 35 thru 39, in square 732, to Fred'k W Jones, for $6,734.24; lots 2, 3, 9 thru 13, in square 1,059; part of lot 1 in square 1,060; part of lot 2 in square 1,060; lots 9, 10, & 13 in square 1,060; lots 2 thur 4 in square 1,063, to Wm B Todd, for $2,399.81½; lot 27 in Reservation C, to S C Magruder, for $362.50; lots 11 & 12 in square 1,063, & lots 8 & 9 in square 835, to Richd Berry, $491.39; lots 1 thru 3 in Kennedy & Webbs subdivision of lot 1 in square 690, to R Morgan, for $357; & said purchasers have complied with the terms of sale. –Geo P Fisher, Justice Supreme Court D C
-M J Meigs, clerk

MON SEP 17, 1866
Archibald Gamble, one of the oldest citizens of St Louis, is dead.
[No death date given-current item.]

Mr J M Winfree, of Richmond, died there on Friday, of cholera.

Dr A A Gould, Pres of the Mass Medical Society, & widely known physician, died at Boston on Saturday.

Gonzales & Pellicier, convicted of the murder of Senor Otero in Brooklyn, in Nov last, have been sentenced to be hanged on Oct 12 next.

The funeral of Surgeon B B F Vanderkieft, late of the U S army took place at Balt on Friday. As Surgeon in charge of the Annapolis Genr'l Hospital during the war, he became widely known & highly esteemed.

Train accident at Johnstown, Pa, on Friday, killed John Parvet, outright; Mrs Welch, crushed to death; Margaret Davis, instantly killed; Mrs Kerk, dying; Nathl Duncan, killed; Lizzie Srobert, crushed to death; Saml Mansell, dying; Lettie Cannon, killed; Mrs Martha Montrie, cannot recover; John Marsh, & a little girl unknown, crushed to death.

Mrd: on Sep 11, at St Ignatius Church, Balt, by Rev B F Wiget, S J, Pres of Gonzaga College, Wash, D C, assisted by Rev Edw McNerhany, S J, of Loyola College, Mr John P Brophy, of Wash, D C, to Miss Bettie W Tyler, niece of the late Pres Tyler, of Va. Southern papers please copy.

Died: on Sep 15, at his late residence, **Granby Farm**, PG Co, Md, Lewis A Tarlton, only son of the late Merritt Tarlton, in his 49th year. His funeral will take place from Providence Chapel on Wed at 3 o'clock P M. Balt Sun please copy.

Died: on Sep 16, Wm C Piggott, in his 38th year, son of the late Mason A Piggott. He served his country in various capacities long, faithfully, & well on the Pacific coast, & returned but a short time since to the scenes of his boyhood to have his bones mingle in the dust of the earth with the others of his kindred who had gone before. His funeral is today from the residence of A Proctor, 468 17th st, at 3 P M.

Died: on Sep 15, in Wash City, Mrs Lillie C, wife of A J Bentley, of the Treasury Dept, late from Ohio. Her funeral will take place from residence 323 9th st, between L & M sts, at 4 o'clock this afternoon. For 4½ months the deceased had been prostrated with disease, which defied the skill of the most distinguished medical aid to remove or to check. She was a loving wife & a devoted mother. Her departure brings sorrow to her afflicted husband & son. Phil & Cincinnati papers please copy.

Adolph Prayer, a dealer in furnishing goods, in Boston, on Sat, was shot in 3 places by one of his clerks, Frank W Rounds. The cause is unknown.

N Y, Sep 10. The Herald's Cape Haytien correspondence says Gen Salnave had been captured by Gen Calval, & was soon to be executed by order of Pres Geffrard. It was conceded that his death would not in any way impede the revolutionary movement, which is merely to depose Geffrard, who has assumed dictatorial powers, & elect a new president by universal suffrage.

<u>Police matters.</u> 1-John O'Brien & John Carroll, were arrested on a charge of malicious mischief; throwing stones against the house & windows of Cornelius Bresshan, without any apparent cause. They were each fined __ dollars by Justice Walter. 2-Thos E Williams, formerly a Gov't detective, was arrested last night on a charge of horse stealing; from a man named Hilton. The case will be tried today. 3-John Shields, a restaurant keeper, was arrested, charged with selling liquor to minors. He was acquitted on the charge of keeping a gambling house, & fined $20 for selling liquor to minors. 4-Lewis Jones was obliged to find security to keep the peace for assaulting his wife, Sarah Jones, & also for using threats against her. 5-John Smith, Wm Hinson, Ed James, Jos Hopkins, & Ed Brown, all employes of the Navy Yard, were each fined $3 by Justice Walter for malicious mischief-upsetting stands, etc, along the streets.

Household & kitchen furniture at auction on Sep 20, at the residence of the late Alex'r Lee, 475 6th st, between D & E sts. -Jas C McGuire & Co, aucts

TUE SEP 18, 1866
In Cincinnati, on Sunday, a young man, Henry Brunning, called on his sweetheart, a young lady named Miss Ellinger, residing at 5th & Baum sts. He picked up a gun, supposedly to be unloaded, pointed it at her & the next moment her brains were scattered all over the room. The man rushed to the Ohio river & tried to drown himself, but was rescued & handed over to the police.

Miss Spurgeon, who accompanied Queen Emma on her late visit to this country, is a daughter of the celebrated Baptist preacher, Rev Mr Spurgeon, of London.

Rev Fr J L Mullen, pastor for nearly 40 years of St Patrick's Church in New Orleans, died on Sep 9, in his 74th year. For a number of months previous to his death he had been confined at his residence by the effects of a paralytic stroke. His funeral took place on the following Monday, & was attended by a large concourse of people. His remains were laid in state in the church & visited by thousands. He went to New Orleans in 1833; two years afterward he commenced the erection of St Patrick's Church, of which he was pastor, we believe, uninterruptedly until the hour of his death.

Died: on Sep 16, at the Soldiers' Home, Lucy Waldron, daughter of Col O A & Kate Kimick Mack, aged 11 <u>years</u>. [Sep 19th newspaper has the age 11 <u>days</u>.]

Died: on Monday, Walter Scott Denis, son of Felix Denis, aged 18 months & 7 days. His funeral will be from his father's residence, 588 D st, between 7th & 8th sts, this morning at 10 o'clock A M.

Mollie Trussel attempted to commit suicide, two times, each time by hanging. It is stated that Mollie Trussel is almost insane with grief & remorse, now that her "George" is dead.
+
The estate of Geo Trussell, who was lately murdered by a woman in Chicago, has been appraised at $75,000.

Orphans Court of Wash Co, D C. Letters testamentary on the personal estate of Wm J Stone, jr, late of Wash, D C, deceased. –Mary F Stone

The widow Clicquot. Barbe Nicole Ponsardin was born in Rheims, in Sep, 1777, & was the daughter of Baron Ponsardin, for many years Mayor of that city. She was married on Jun 11, 1798, to Mons Francois Clicquot, a half-pay ofcr, whose wounds unfitted him for further service in the army. He set out making champagne & their wines improved & they made very good sales. In 1805 Mons Clicquot died, & his widow, only 27 years old, took her husband's business into her own hands & carried it on with great success. She died recently at the age of 89 years. Her property was valued from $6,000,000 to $8,000,000. -Boston Journal

WED SEP 19, 1866
Ireland claims the invention of the needle gun. Capt Jas Whitley is named as the inventor, having had a breech-loading needle gun made in 1823, in Dublin. Discouraged by the indifference shown at Woolwich to Capt Nortan's elongated shot, Capt Whitley did not carry out the design of patenting his invention.

Appointments of Hospital Stewards. The Sec of War has appointed the following to be hospital stewards in the regular army: A S Pierce, L M Soper, Edgar W Robinson, Winfield Scott Oliver, W B Pomeroy, W J C Keate, Chas Kuhn, Geo A Sanders, Chas Ambrook, Herman Schmidt, & Thos W Hurst.

Naval Changes. Assist Surgeon Wm F Ferry detached from the Wash Navy Yard & ordered to the Naval Academy. Lt Cmders Beatty P Smith & Henry S Johnson detached from ordnance duty at the Wash Navy Yard & ordered to the Naval Academy. Cmdor Melancton Smith, Exec Ofcr of the Wash Navy Yard, has been detached & made Chief of Bureau of Equipment & Repair, in place of Cmder Smith, deceased.

Appointed pension agents: 1-Mr Wm Walker at Dover, Dela, vice D F Burton, removed. 2-A new pension agency has been established at Bangor, Maine, & Gideon Mayo appointed pension agent.

Mrd: on Aug 29, in Brooklyn, N Y, by Rev E E L Taylor, D D, Rev T R Howlett, of Wash, D C, to Miss Cornelia L Fellows, of Brooklyn.

Died: on Sep 18, Willie, youngest son of John & Rose Clarvoe, aged 1 year, 3 months & 12 days. His funeral will take place at 3 o'clock this afternoon, from his father's residence, 677 7th st, [Island.]

The Alexandria Gaz states that the famous "Pitcher portrait" of Gen Washington, which was taken in the early days of the war from the family seat of the late John Augustine Washington, by Maj Atwood, of the Michigan U S volunteers, was returned on Monday last through the Nat'l Express Co, to its rightful owner, R B Washington. This picture is pronounced to be the best likeness of the Father of his Country extant, & additionally interesting from the fact of its having been in his possession at the time of his death.

Chancery sale of valuable property on Louisiana ave, by decree of Circuit Court of D C, in Equity, No 1,537, wherein Peter F Brown was cmplnt & Edw Swann & others were dfndnts; public auction on Oct 9, of part of lot 14 in square 490, near Copp's Bowling Saloon; with the appurtenances. –W A Maury, trustee -J C McGuire & Co, aucts

Dept of the Interior, U S Patent Ofc, Wash, Sep 10, 1866. Ptn of Warren W Dutcher, of Milford, Mass, & Sarah Dutcher, admx of the estate of Elihu Dutcher, of Waukesha, Wisc, praying for the extension of a patent granted to the said Warren W Dutcher & Elihu Dutcher on Dec 28, 1852, for an improvement in Temples for Looms, for 7 years from the expiration of said patent, which takes place on Dec 28, 1866. -H C Theaker, Com'r of Patents

At a contemplated charivarl at Madison, Wisc, last Monday night, in honor of the marriage of an old man, named Williams, to the young daughter of David Holton, of Blue Mounds, Holton discharged a gun full in the face of a young lad, Theron Dryden, son of Natt Dryden, before any offensive demonstrations had been made. The lad was badly hurt, & not expected to recover.

Maj Gen W W Orme died recently at Bloomington, Ill, of consumption.

Col Geo Moody, a prominent lawyer of Port Gibson, Miss, was assassinated in his ofc on Sat evening.

The will of Matthias W Baldwin, lately deceased in Phil, leaves all his property, after the payment of his debts, to his family.

Chas V Holt, a son of V S Holt, a prominent public man of Cambridge, Mass, committed suicide by shooting himself, on Thu night.

During a firemen's riot in Phil on Sunday, Henry Walters, a member of the Shitller Hose Co, was shot & instantly killed.

Gladwin, the forger & letter-stealer, was sentenced at New Haven, on Friday, to 7 years & 6 months imprisonment on the charge of letter stealing, & 7½ years on the other.

The most venerable <u>Dominica Sister</u>, Head of the Order of the "<u>Sisters of the Poor</u> of St Francis," for the U S, died at the Convent of the Sisterhood in Cincinnati, on Sep 11, of cholera. [No name given.]

Hon Francis Woodbury, ex-Senator, died at Savannah, Ga, on Sep 13, of hydrophobia, having been bitten some 2 months ago by a lady's lapdog. Not supposing the animal to be mad, he had paid no attention to the bite.

The Springfield [Mass] Republican says the lady whom Senator Sumner, now for over 50 years a bachelor, is about to marry, is Mrs Sturgis Hooper, daughter-in-law of Rep Hooper, of Boston, a beautiful & accomplished lady.

The Pres had made the following appointments for Phil: Chas M Hall, postmaser; J R Flanigan [editor of the News,] Naval Ofcr; Thos C McDowell, Deputy Surveyor; Wm Milward, Dir of the Mint; Col Chambers McKibben, Treas of the Mint; & Jos Taylor, melter at the mint.

John C Braine, the Confederate Lt who seized the steamer **Chesapeake** on Dec 5, 1863, while she was on her passage from N Y to Portland, was arrested in N Y on Sat, on a charge of murder. The cmplnt is Jas Johnston, 1st engineer of the **Chesapeake**, who was wounded during the capture of the vessel, his assistant, Oran Shafer, being shot.

THU SEP 20, 1866
Dedication of <u>St Lawrence's Catholic Church</u>, at Jessup's Cut, Md, on Sep 23, the Most Rev Archbishop will officiate. Tickets for round trip, $1.50, can be had by application to Fr Walter or Fr Kane, at St Patrick's Church, Fr McCarthy, pastor of the Immaculate Conception, & Fr Wiget, of St Aloysius; the principal bookstores, & at the depot. Fr De Wolf, is the worthy pastor of St Lawrence's Church. Citizens are invited.

Homer [Champion Co] Journal. A few days since Michl L Sullivant sold his farm of 22,000 acres, lying 6 to 10 miles south of this place, to Mr Alexander, of Morgan Co, for $17 per acre, or $374,000, cash. Mr Alexander also bought the stock, grain, hay, & farming utensils on the place, which made the whole amount of purchase money nearly $500,000. Mr Sullivant has yet a place of 45,000 acres in Iroquois Co, beside old land. Mr Alexander will immediately stock the farm with 3,000 or more head of cattle. He will ship 500 head per week to market from this point.

Appointments by the Pres: 1-Chas A Gilman, of Minn, to be receiver of public moneys-St Cloud, Minn. 2-John F Wielandy, of Missouri, to be register; Edw B McPherson, of Missouri, to be receiver of public moneys at Booneville, Missouri.

Foreign Consuls in the U S. The Pres has recognized:
Werner Dresel as Consul of Hanover at Balt, Md.
Hermann Theophilus Plate, Consul for Saxony, at Phil.
Chas E Wunderlich, Consul for Bremen, at Charleston, S C.
Francisco Parraga, Consul for the U S of Columbia, at N Y.
Jean Marier Perrier, Consular Agent of France, at Newport, R I.
L Westergaard, Consul of the Netherlands, at Phil.
G C Johnson, Consul General of Sweden & Norway, at San Francisco, Calif.
Chas E Wunderlich, Consul of the Netherlands, at Charleston, S C.
David Tandy, Consular Agent for the Kingdom of Italy, at St Louis, Missouri.
Pierre Jean Esnard, Vice Consul of Portugal, at Charleston, S C.
Jose Antonio de Lavalle, Consul of Spain, at Phil
J W Currier, Consul General for the Dominican Republic, in N Y.

Post Ofc Appointments. The Pres has appointed W H Harper P M at Lima, Ohio. The Postmaster General has ordered the establishing of a post ofc at Fullersville, Md, S A Lawrence, P M; & the re-establishing of the ofc of Campbell Court House, Va, J S Elder, P M; & the ofc of West Point, Va, Miss C J Hughes, P M.

Orphans Court-Judge Purcell.
1-Last court day the will of the late Wm J Stone, jr, was admitted to probate, & Mary F Stone qualified as excx; bond $6,000, & guardian, bond $10,000. 2-The will of Geo Thos Howard was admitted to probate & record. 3-Francis Lamb obtained letters of administration on the estate of Eliza Lamb; bond $7,000. 4-Mary E Langley was appointed guardian of the orphan of Thos J & Mary J Glazebrook; bond $500; & Cassandra Buck to the orphan of Benj A & Margaret Buck; bond $10,000. 5-The first & final account of the exec of Geo T Smith; of the administrator of Jane E Dannscome, deceased; & the first account of Sallie H Burns; were approved & passed. 6-The case of the will of Sarah Edelin, deceased, filed several months since, in which a caveat was filed by Mary J Harris & Thos J Edelin, brother & sister of the deceased, was decided by Judge Purcell in favor of the will. 7-W M Dangerfield was appointed guardian to a minor child; bond 1,000. 8-Yesterday the Court decided the case of the administratorship of the estate of Mrs Olny P Anderson, the widow of an old Revolutionary soldier, who died in Tenn sometime since, where letters of administration were issued to Thos A Anderson, a son. An amount of money was due her from the Gov't, & her son obtained letters & drew the money. Mr Fuller appeared for the former, & moved that the letters here lie revoked, & Mr Lloyd, with Mr Anderson, resisted the motion. The Judge refused to grant the motion, holding that the letters issued here were good to draw money from the Treasury, but directed that the administrator at once proceed to the distribution, citing the act of Congress of 1840, & several decisions of the Atty General, in support of his decision.

Dennis Sullivan was arrested on Tue by Ofcr Noble, for selling liquor without having complied with the new regulation in obtaining his license.

Died: on Sep 18, Thomazine M, wife of Greenberry Rowzee, & daughter of the late Saml & Mary A Lewis. Her funeral will be this afternoon, at 3 o'clock, from the residence of her husband, 248 P st north, between 14 & 15th sts.

Died: on Sep 19, in Wash City, Mrs Mary F Aulick, wife of Cmdor John H Aulick, U S N, aged 71 years. His funeral will be from his late residence, I & 18th sts, on Sep 22 at 2 P M.

Died: on Sep 18, at Hagerstown, Md, Mrs Eliza Shafer, in her 70th year. Her funeral will take place from the residence of her son, C A Shafer, 485 12th st, today at 10 A M.

Richmond, Sep 19. Mrs Sillo A Harlow was instantly killed at Haxall's flour mill this afternoon by being drawn in between two cogswheels.

John J Donaldson, an old & respected citizen of Balt, died on Tue, aged 78 years.

Hon A H Rice has written a letter declining a nomination for re-election to Congress from the Third Congressional District of Mass.

In addition to the Phil appointments announced yesterday, are Col Wm A Gray, chief cointer of the Mint, & Gustavus Hoy, appraiser at large.

John Guilford died at Portland, on Thu, from over doses of morphine which he had taken to allay pain, by order of his physician.

Rev Mr Law, a Methodist clergyman, died in the pulpit while preaching at Mosherville, Mo, on Sep 16.

David Clark, of Hartford, Conn, does well by his nephews who were disabled in the war against rebellion. Some time since he gave three of them $5,000, & recently he has served two more in like manner.

The first sale of new cotton arrived at Petersburg on Fri last. It was raised by Col Wm H Cheek, of Warren Co, N C, who realizes the handsome price of 40 cents per pound for it, [weight, 365 pounds,] & a premium of $50.

Kate Sibley, age 5 years, was lately whipped to death at Sarnia, C W, on the alleged provocation of refusing to say her prayers. Both father & mother had beat her terribly. The perpetrators of the fiendish cruelty are both under arrest.

I shall open a High School at my residence, 15 miles west of Lynchburg, on Oct 1. -Jas P Holcombe

FRI SEP 21, 1866

The Pres made the following appointments yesterday: M S Perkin, to be U S Atty for West Tenn; Saml Walker, U S Marshal for West Va, & Michl Donn, to be Deputy Postmaster at *Fort Leavenworth*, Kansas. The Medical Staff: Brvt Lt Col R S Satterlee, surgeon U S army, appointed Chief Medical Purveyor, U S army, to be stationed at N Y C. Brvt Cols C McDougall, E H Abadie, Robt Murray, & Chas Sutherland, surgeons U S army, have been appointed Medical Purveyors, U S army. Assist Surgeons J H Bill, De Witt D Peters, Chas Allen, Warren Webster, & John Vanzant have been appointed Surgeons, U S army.

Distressing accident yesterday in Haxall's flour mills, by which Mrs Lillie Ann Harlow, wife of Mr John P Harlow, shipper at 3 mills, was visiting the establishment with 2 lady friends, & were viewing machinery attended by Mr Curtis Taylor, when Mrs Harlow turned to go down the steps, the back portion of her dress was caught in the cog wheels of the flour-conveyor, & she was drawn in between the ponderous wheels & instantly crushed to death. The distress of her husband on hearing of the awful catastrophe may be better imagined than described. Mrs Harlow was a sister of Mr Jas Eddins, of this city, & was highly esteemed by her acquaintances. Her funeral services will be held this morning, at the Broad st Methodist Church. –Richmond Despatch, Sep 26.

Capt Saml Child, of Balt, died on Wed, in the 75th year of his age.

Capt T J Cox, A Q M, brother of Hon S S Cox, late of Ohio, died of cholera, at Nashville, on Thursday.

Hon Henry Grider, member of Congress from Ky, died at his residence in Warren Co, Ky, on Friday last.

Mr Henry Manning, a well-known butter merchant of Balt, while passing along Balt st on Wed, suddenly fell to the pavement & died immediately. The jury rendered a verdict of death from unknown cause. He leaves a wife & 9 children.

In a quarrel at Henderson, Ky, Sat, between Sterling Prince & Richd Allen, Prince drew a knife & advanced on Allen, who shot him with a Derringer, killing him instantly.

Died: on Sep 13, at his residence, in Bloomington, Ill, in his 35th year, Gen Wm Ward Orme, a native of Wash City. He had attained a prominent position in the legal profession & served with distinction in the Union army during the late revolution. May he rest in peace!

Died: on Sep 20, Emme Agnes, aged 16 days, daughter of T A & M L Stephens. Her funeral will be from the residence of the parents, 462 12th st, between G & H tomorrow, at 4 P M.

Died: on Sep 19, in Wash City, Mrs Mary F Aulick, wife of Cmdor John H Aulick, U S N, aged 71 years. Her funeral will take place from her late residence, I & 18th sts, on Sep 22, at 2 P M.

On Wed, says the Phil Ledger, Mrs Eliz Miller, who, with her husband, Milo M Miller, & her sister, Hetty Owens, occupied the 2 story brick dwlg, 924 Buttonwood st, was found in the back room, lying in a pool of blood, with her throat cut from ear to ear. Lying by her right hand was an old razor belonging to her husband with which the deed was evidently done. On further examination it was found that she had head wounds of such a character as to leave no doubt that she was murdered. Mrs Miller was about 60 years old; she had, with her husband, occupied the residence; she never had children. The murderer is unknown. Phil, Sep 20. Second despatch: the murderer is believed to be Gottleib Williams, [age 38,] a miserable pauper, with his left side paralyzed, causing him to walk slowly, supported by a stick. His father formerly owned the house where the deceased lived, & was well acquainted with the locality. He had been in the habit of visiting the house, & the deceased was kind to him, frequently giving him victuals. Detectives are in search of him. Williams record was well known; on Feb 20, 1844, age about 16, he stabbed & killed a boy named Peter Doescher. Through the intercession of the father, Willams was soon pardoned. [Sep 22nd newspaper: supposed murderer of Mrs Miller, Gottleib Williams, has been arrested. –Phil, Sep 21.]

Geo W Lane, superintendent of the U S Mint at Denver, Colo, the only surviving brother of the late Senator Jas H Lane, of this State, says that there is a mistake in saying that his suicide was the third in the family who has thus destroyed himself. It is true that his older brother, John Foot Lane, came to his death under peculiar circumstances, that he had fallen purposely on his own sword, but examination found it was accidental. -From the Atchison Champion.

Comr's sale of valuable real property, in Chancery, Marshal, Trustee, etc, vs Marshall's adm. Sale on Oct 26, the ***Oak Hill Farm***

SAT SEP 22, 1866
Maj Gen Couch has been appointed by the Pres, Collector of the Port of Boston, vice ex-Vice Pres Hamlin, resigned.

Died: on Friday after a protracted illness, Edw Hall, aged 53 years. His funeral will take place from his late residence, 426 F st, on Sep 23, at 2 o'clock P M. [Star & Con Union]

Old Relic. The old bell of Wm & Mary College has been brought down from the college at Wmsburg to be taken North for recasting. It is an old colonial relic. It rang out its peals summoning the college students to prayers & studies & meals long years before the American Revolution.

W S Lincoln was nominated for Congress by the Republicans of the 26th District of N Y.

Oliver H Paine has been nomiated by the Democrats for Congress from the 18th District of Ohio.

Robt Ould, in a card to the people of Richmond, announces his willingness to be a candidate to fill the present Senatorial vacancy.

On Sunday the engine of a train going west, on the Hannibal & St Jos railroad, was thrown off the track into a ditch 20 miles this side of St Jos, killing the fireman, Albert Kennam, & severely injuring the engineer, Kennaman, & injuring mortally the brakeman.

Two farms for sale one mile from Wash City: *Le Grove*, containing 60 acres, with comfortable cottage; *Bealeroy*, containing 100 acres, without dwlg. Price for *Le Grove*, $8,000; for *Bealeroy*, $12,000. Inquire of D T Sheriff, in person, adjoining the premises, or address Jas E S Hollyday, Brandywine, PG Co, Md.

A private despatch received in this city yesterday announced that Col Geo V Moody, of Port Gibson, was assassinated on Sat at his house in Port Gibson. He was sitting in his ofc alone, when he was fired upon from a window, 19 buckshot entering his head & neck, killing him instantly. Mrs Moody accompanied him North, & was to leave that city in a few days to rejoin her husband at Port Gibson. –Jackson Clarion, Sep 11.

MON SEP 24, 1866
Col Geo H Walker, one of the founders of Milwaukee, died on Thursday.

Chas S Gilmor, a highly esteemed citizen of Balt, died on Friday, at age 48 years.

Hon Philip Dorsheimer has been removed as Collector of Internal Revenue for the Buffalo [N Y] District, & Nelson K Hopkins appointed in his place.

Gen R C Vaughn has been appointed assessor of internal revenue for the 6th district of Missouri, vice Joshua Shorn, [Radical,] removed.

The funeral of the Catholic Bishop J M Young took place at Erie, Pa, on Friday. Bishop Dominic, of Pittsburgh, preached the funeral discourse. Over 1,500 people followed the body to the grave.

Gen Sandford, on Friday, received an order relieving him from the command of the first division of the N Y militia. It is said that a number of other ofcrs will be removed from command.

Prof John M Watson, of the Tenn Medical College, died of cancer of the stomach, in Nashville, on Wednesday.

Gills' Hotel, Chicago, was burned Tuesday, & the lodgers had barely time to escape. A little boy, age 7 years, son of Mrs Kate Williams, late of Phil, perished in the flames.

Despatch from St Louis. Mrs Sarah Ellen Hastings, of Springfield, Mo, has arrived, with 2 sick children. She reported to the Mayor that she had been to Southern Ill, & on arriving at Salem had given her trunk in charge of a man whom she supposed was a baggage man, & had not been able to recover it. It contained $350 in gold & silver, in an iron box, $600 in promissory notes, & clothing valued at $3,000.

On Sat, Justice Thompson fined hucksters, B C Talbert, Jas Chamberlain, Catharine Delany, Alfred Jones, Chas Brown, Mary Hines, & M J Motten, the sum of $10 each. They were arrested for purchasing produce of country dealers, contrary to the city ordnance. The practise of hucksters buying up country produce & then combining to keep up prices should be stopped, & we are glad that the law is being enforced.

The Postmaster Genr'l has since Thu, made about 150 changes of postmasters, & of 25 route agents, the latter principally in the West. In addition the Pres has appointed the following postmasters, & has removed their immediate predecessors, namely:

John B Bass, Quincy, Mass
Carleton B Davis, Milton, Pa
Davis H Missemer, Pottstown, Pa
Henry Quilliman, Norristown, Pa
Benj A Giffith, Monmouth, Ill
Harvey S Weeks, Lockport, Ill
Jas F Copp, Rock Island, Ill

Isaac W Webster, Kenosha, Wis
Craig B Beebee, Bever Dam, Wis
Edmund R Barden, Hamilton, N Y
Henry V Colt, Genesee, N Y
Linus Birdsey, Meriden, Conn
Wm H Woodrow, Hillsboro, Ohio

A post ofc has been established at Taverner' Woods, Talbot Co, Md, Wm H Collier appointed postmaster.
The post ofc at Taylorsville, Carroll Co, Md, has been changed to Franklinville.
Appointments in Pa: Franklin B Lancks, assessor, 8th District.
Wm Quail, assessor, 24th District.
The Pres has appointed Jas R Hood, of Tenn, to be Sec of Colorado Territory.
S F Crawford appointed collector of customs at Wilmington, Dela.
Appointments made by the Pres on Sat:
Geo W Dent, of Calif, to be superintendent of Indian Affairs for Arizona; Wm Byers, of Arkansas, to be superintendent of Indian affairs for the Southern superintendency, & E W Wynkoop to be agent for the Arapahoes, Cheyennes, & Apaches.

Postmaster at Boston. Mr Geo H Kingsbury, one of the deputy collectors of the Boston Custom-House, has been appointed postmaster of that city, vice Mr Palfrey.

On Sat, as Judge Purcell & Mr J B W Stewart were taking a ride near the Smithsonian grounds, their horse became frightened at the cars & ran upon an embankment, upsetting the buggy. Judge Purcell jumped out & was slightly bruised about his head & face, but Mr Stewart had his right leg broken.

Died: on Sep 23, of croup, at River View, D C, Mollie E, daughter of B T & Sallie Bryan Swart, aged 4 years & 10 days.

Died: on Aug 23, in St Louis, Mo, of cholera, Michl Flanegan, in his 41st year, only son of the late Garrett Flanegan, of Wash City.

Died: on Sep 23, after a protracted & severe illness, Jas F Martin, in his 34th year. His funeral will take place from the residence of his brother-in-law, Jos T Mitchell, on 6th & D sts, tomorrow, Sep 25, at 3 o'clock P M, & proceed to St Peter's Church, Capitol Hill.

Fatal affair at Memphis, Tenn, on Sep 18, which ended in the death of Mr Frank Cummings, at the hands of Alderman Grace. Quarrel over some articles that Cummings had dictated concerning Grace.

Orphans Court of Wash Co, D C, Sep 18, 1866. In the case of Geo W Young & John Carroll Brent, admx of Norah Digges, deceased, the administrators & Court have appointed Oct 13 next, for the final settlement of the personal estate of the said deceased, of the assets in hand. -Z C Robbins, Reg/o wills

The Pres has authorized the pardon of A V Harlow, convicted at the Oct Term, 1864, of the U S District Court for the District of Rhode Island, of embezzling letters from the post ofc, & sentenced to two years imprisonment. The pardon is issued in view of the ill health of the prisoner, with other mitigating circumstances, & the recommendation of Hon Wm Sprague & other respectable citizens.

The Platte City, Mo affair: Sep 15 the Radicals held a county convention in this city for nominating county ofcrs. A disturbance occurred after the meeting & Wm Callahan, Conservative, & Jas Heath, Radical, were killed. Mortally wounded: Saunders McComas, radical; John Heath, Radical. Wounded: N P Ogden, Radical, sheriff of Platte Co, slightly in the wrist; John Foley, Conservative, slightly; Richd Bush, Conservative, severely in the thigh; Jonathan Todd, Conservative, dangerously through thigh & hip; Frank Cates, Conservative, severely in arm; Henry Todd, boy, Conservative, slightly; Thos Donegan, Radical, the originator of the difficulty, severely in the groin.

Orphans Court of Wash Co, D C. Letters of administration on the personal estate of Eliza Lamb, late of Wash, D C, deceased. –Francis Lamb, adm

TUE SEP 25, 1866
Orphans Court-Judge Purcell. 1-On the last court day letters of administration were issued to Chas Romseau on the estate of Eva Ruppert; bond $1,000. 2-Wallis Young was appointed guardian to his minor child & heir of Rachel Young; bond $1,000. 3-The first & final account of Wm Anderson, administrator of Mrs Only P Anderson, deceased, was approved & passed, & the balance ordered to be distributed among the heirs.

Appointments by the Pres:
Jno S Tully, of Louisiana, to be register of the land ofc at New Orleans, La. Henry Vanderlinden, of Louisiana, to be register of public moneys for the district of lands subject to sale at New Orleans, La. Abel Keyes, of Wisc, to be register of the land ofc at Menasha, Wis. Wm B Franklin, of Ohio, to be register of the land ofc at Chillicothe, Ohio. Jas Rowe of Ohio, to be receiver of public moneys for the district of lands subject to sale at Chillicothe, Ohio. Hiram A Rood, of Mich, to be receiver of public moneys for the district of lands subject to sale a Traverse City, Mich. Jno J Humphreys, of Tenn, to be agent for the Indians of the Shawnee agency in Kansas. Theodore T Dwight, of Nebraska Territory, to be superintendent of Indian affairs for the State of Nevada. Henry Orman, jr, of Calif, to be agent for the Indians at the Smith River Reservation. Forrest R Page, of Kansas, to be agent for the Indians of the Kansas Agency.

Miscellaneous:
Capt Jno Brenard, an old steamboat man of Louisville, cut his throat at Paducah on Thu. He is expected to recover.
Seward Randall, brother to Hon S J Randall, died at Phil on Sunday, after a short illness. His father died only a little over a week ago.
Geo Bishop, who was convicted at the June term, 1866, of the U S Circuit Court for the Eastern District of Mich, of murder & sentenced to death, has been pardoned by the Pres.
On Sunday Mrs Eliz Mousley committed suicide by cutting her throat with a razor at her residence, 57 North Moore st, N Y. She had been an invalid for a number of years, & it is supposed that she committed the act under a temporary fit of insanity.
Gen C C Washburne, of Minn, was severely injured at the Falls of St Anthony on Sep 17, by a workman who tipped a load of broken rock upon him. His head & right foot were very badly injured, & his body was bruised in several places.
Thos G Wright, Co E, 2nd Btln, 19th U S Infty, was convicted of murder by a court martial at Little Rock, Ark, Sep 8, & sentenced to forfeit all pay due him, to be dishonorably discharged the service, & to be confined at hard labor in the Penitentiary, at Columbus, Ohio, for the term of 12 years.

Mrd: on Sep 20, at Weston, Mass, by Rev E E Strong, of Waltham, Wm J Rhees, of Wash, D C, to Romie F Ellis, daughter of the late John S Ellis, of Boston.

Fire on Sunday in N Y C in a 4 story tenement house at the corner of avenue A & 13th st. Philip Hartz, wife, & 4 children occupied the 4th floor, & as the flames got closer, Mr Hartz dropped his children, one by one, onto a bed below; Mrs Hartz jumped, followed by Mr Hartz. Philip Hartz was severely injured; Mrs Kate Hartz, aged 36, badly burned about the face & upper body; Amelia Hartz, aged 12 years, badly injured by jumping from a window; Edw Hartz, aged 9 years, badly burned & limbs fractured; Adolph Hartz, aged 4 years, badly burned about the body. Mr Hartz is a German, & followed the occupation of a sailor. Another child escaped uninjured.

Boston, Sep 27. Jas Quigg [aged 20] was murdered today at Newton Corners, by Bernard McSherry. McSherry has been arrested & committed for trial for murder.

WED SEP 26, 1866
Hon Henry May, who has deceased in Balt of typhoid fever, is, with the exception of Dr Fred'k May, the eminent surgeon, the last of the brothers of the distinguished May family of Washington. His death is a great loss to society.
[No death date given-current item.]

Changes of Naval Paymasters' Stations: Acting Assist Paymaster C A Downe is relieved from the U S steamer **Don**, & is succeeded by Assist Paymaster H G Colby. Passed Assist Paymaster Henry M Mead is ordered to relieve Acting Assist Paymaster Geo W Morton, of the ship **Juniata**. Passed Assist Paymaster W Lee Darling to relieve Paymaster Thos C Marton, on the ship **Macedonian**. Passed Assist Paymaster E N Whitehouse to relieve Assist Paymaster Henry T Skelding, on the ship **Corwin**. Passed Assist Paymaster H T Wright to relieve Acting Assist Paymaster G L Hoodlass, on the ship **Estrella**. Passed Assist Paymaster J H Stevenson to relieve Passed Assist Paymaster A D Bache, on the ship **Tacony**. Paymaster R H Douglas to relieve Acting Assist Paymaster H Le Roy Jones, on the ship **Savannah**. Passed Assist Paymaster J R Carmody to relieve Passed Assist Paymaster M B Cushing, on the ship **Chocura**. Passed Assist Paymaster John Ferry to relieve Passed Assist Paymaster Geo W Browne, on the ship **Yucca**. Passed Assist Paymaster Wm J Thompson to relieve Assist Paymaster A W Bacon, on the ship **Yantie**. Passed Assist Paymaster Geo R Watkins to relieve Acting Assist Paymaster T S Dabney, on the ship **Monongo**.

Fort Monroe, Sep 25. The quarantine steamer **City of Albany** reports having spoken off the Capes this morning the steamer **E C Knight**, from Wilmington, N C, bound to Balt, which reported a large steamer ashore on Body Island, 70 miles south of Cape Henry, signalling in distress. Owing ot the heavy sea & the breakers, the **E C Knight** was unable to render her any assistance.

On Monday a soldier entered the ofc of Paymaser Potter, 15th & F sts, & attempted to draw back pay, bounty, money due on clothing account & travelling allowance said to be due him, he exhibiting a discharge & descriptive list purporting to be signed by the ofcrs of his company & regt. Capt Potter's clerk discovered the forgeries, & the soldiers proved to be Pvt Michl Haggerty & Pvt Offus, of Co A, 1st btln 12th U S infty. Offus has for some time past been acting in the capapcity of company clerk, & was well posted in the manner of filling out discharge papers. They amount they attempted to obtain by fraudulent measures was $260.

Poughkeepsie, Sep 24. Mr John B Steele, of Kingston, N Y, who represented the 13th District of the State in the 37th & 38th Congress, & who was at one time county Judge of Ulster Co, was killed at Kingston today by being thrown from a wagon. The horse took fright & took off at a violent rate, hurling Mr Steele from the vehicle. He leaves a wife & one child.

New Orleans, Sep 24. A few days ago Col McIver, ex-Confederate army ofcr, was arrested by order of Gen Sheridan & imprisoned. It is understood that he is at the head of a filibustering expedition against Mexico, although it is impossible to learn anything from military authorities. Important papers were found upon him.

Louisville, Sep 25. Dr Ferris, U S mail agent, who was arrested at Warsaw a few day ago on the charge of having executed 2 men during the war, while acting as provost marshal, has been released from confinement on giving $25,000 bail for his appearance on Feb 25, before the U S Court.

Mrd: on Sep 25, at the residence of L F Clark, by Rev Fr McNally, Jas V Galt to Emma Cissel.

Died: on Tue, in Balt, Henry May, in his 50th year. His funeral will take place on Sep 27, at 10 o'clock, from the Cathedral.

Copartnership formed today under the name of Campbell & Godfrey, for the purpose of carrying on the Wholesale & Retail Wine Business. –C W Campbell, Chas G Godfrey, 298 E st, Wash.

Raphael Semmes has purchased a third interest in the Mobile Gaz, & is now editorially connected with that paper.

Victor Emmanuel possesses the largest emerald extant. It is six inches in length, four in breadth, & three in thickness.

Hon John Moore, of Springfield, Ill, age 72 years old, died in the City Hospital at Boston on Monday, where he had been under treatment for several months for a severe illness.

Despatch from Memphis: Gen Forrest, having sold his plantation, announces himself a cotton factor & commission merchant.

The Balt papers report the mysterious disappearance of Mr Jas Graham, the cashier of the First Nat'l Bank at Elkton, Md. When he left Elkton it was his intention, as his friends believe, to go to Lockhaven, Pa, to purchase lumber.

The Titusville Herald states that on Wed last a terible accident occurred at *Tarr Farm*, resulting in the instant death of the engineer, Fred Wygant, & the fatal injury of Mr A Jones. The accident occurred at the Chrisman Well, lease No 126, when the boiler exploded. It is thought that Mr Jones cannot survive.

Handsome farm in Montg Co, Md, at public auction, by deed executed by John G Garland, jr, recorded in Liber E B P, No 2, folios 285, of the land records of said county: sale on Nov 3 next, the farm now occupied by said Garland, containing 90 acres, & handsomely improved by a residence, barn, tenant house, & other outbldgs. -John B Moore, trustee

THU SEP 27, 1866

A despatch to the N Y Times states that a son of the Marquis de Montholon, [French Minister,] an ofcr of the Imperial Guard of the French army in Mexico, has been captured & shot by the Mexican Liberals.

Jos S Gitt has been appointed chief engineer of the Western Md Railroad, vice Col Taylor, resigned. –Hagerstown Torchlight

The Pres has made the following appointments:
Hugh Ewing, of Kansas, to be minister Resident at the Hague
W J Valentine, of Mass, to be a Com'r to the Paris Exposition of 1867
Benj F Montgomery, Receiver of Public Moneys for the district of lands subject to sale at La Crosse
M W Quackenbush, Receiver of Public Moneys at East Saginaw, Mich
Isaac G Walton, Register of Land Ofc at East Saginaw, Mich
Albert Tuxbury, Receiver of Public Moneys at Nebraska City
Edw S Reed, Register of Land Ofc at Nebraska City
Chas A Rofflo, agent for the Chippewas of the Mississippi & Lake Winnebago bands, & the Indians of Red Lake & Pembina.
Thos J McKenney, of Iowa, Superintendent of Indian Affairs for the Territory of Wash
Abelard Guthrie, of Kansas, agent for the Indians of the Shawnee agency in Kansas.
Stephen J Dallas, of Ill, principal clerk of surveys in the Gen Land Ofc
John J Humphries, of Tenn, agent of the Cherokee Indians.

Edw Cruft, the oldest merchant in Boston, died on Sunday.

Rev Noah Porter, D D, of Farmington, Conn, died on Sep 24, after a short & comparatively painless illness, in his 85th year.

Dr Chas S Sweet, of Kennebunk, Maine, was poisoned with morphine & died on Sunday night. His wife has been arrested for the crime.

Michl Fitzgibbons has challenged Mike McCool, champion prize fighter of America, who whipped Bill Davis, near St Louis, the other day, to fight for $1,000 & the belt on Oct 12.

John L Scripps, for many years one of the editors & proprietors of the Chicago Tribune, afterwards for 4 years postmaster at Chicago, died at Minneapolis, Minn, on Friday last, aged 48 years.

Elisha C Sprague, of Chicago, has had an action commenced against him for breach of promise, by a Cincinnati lady. Sprague is worth $500,000, & $50,000 damages are claimed. The lady has been for 6 years a teacher in the Newport Seminary.

Mrd: on Sep 26, at the Church of the Epiphany, in Wash City, by Rev C H Hall, D D, John Jay Washburn to Miss Hannah S, daughter of the late Wm R Wanton, of Louisville, Ky. Louisville & St Louis papers please copy.

Mrd: on Sep 25, by Rev R J Keeling, D D, Mr Wm M Johnson, of Green Co, N Y, to Miss Susan Fugitt, of Wash City.

Mrd: on Sep 26, in Trinity Church, by Rev R J Keeling, D D, Mr Harry C Sherman to Miss Susan McConnell, both of Wash City.

Jas C McGuire & Co, aucts, sold brick dwlg house & lot on M st north, near 4th st west, to Thos R Bird, for $2,755; also, small brick house, of 2 stories, on 4th near M, to A Krautner, for $2,200; & 3 story brick house & lot on N J ave, between L & M sts, to W W Danenhower, for $2,000.

The race at Chicago on Sat last, Sep 23, 1866, between Cooley & Butler, terminated in the death of Wm McKeever, the driver of the latter horse. McKeever was running his horse some rod or more ahead of Cooley, when the wheel of the sulky, he thought, struck the fence, & McKeever was thrown out upon the track. The crowd yelled: Was he hurt? Was he dead? McKeever was about 29 years old, born in N Y, where he was brought up to the business of a butcher, which he followed till a few years ago, when he became enamored with the turf, & commenced to handle horses. [Oct 8th newspaper: Coroner's jury concluded that McKeever's death came from injuries inflicted with a board in the hands of person or persons unknown. The plot was to prevent the horse Butler from winning the race.]

Died: on Sep 18, in Paducah, Ky, after an illess of 21 hours, David Alex'r Baird, aged 61 years. He was for many years a resident of Wash City. N Y Herald please copy.

Phil Inquirer: On Monday an inquest was held on the body of Ellen Josphine Sherman, aged 21 years, who died suddenly on Sat last, at 18 north 11th st, in a room she rented with a Mr Arnold, who said the lady was his wife. Arnold despatched a letter to her parents in Bridgeport, Conn about her death. According to the father, his daughter had left home a year ago without any provocation whatever, & was not heard from until 6 months ago, when she called to see him when he was in N Y. She said she was married to Arnold. Parties in N Y knew her by the name of Lacey, & she was employed in a hoop-skirt establishment. Arnold became acquainted with Miss Sherman when he resided in Winsted. When the coroner was called Arnold left for parts unknown. The coroner thought foul play was involved. It is reported the fugitive has a wife & family living in N Y. The father of the deceased is well known in Bridgeport, & an honest & industrious man.

Geo H Dean & Edw Goodfellow, ofcrs of the U S Survey, have gone to Newfoundland to make some scientific experiments with the Atlantic cable, & have with them some of the best astronomical & telegraphic instruments, which have been recently constructed for this special work.

Trustee's sale of valuable real estate, by decree of the Circuit Court of PG Co, Md, passed in a cause in which John D Corse is cmplnt & Edw S Plummer & others are dfndnts; public sale in the village of Piscataway, on Oct 4 next, the tract of land which is on the Potomac river, opposite *Mount Vernon*, of which the late Rebecca A M Plummer, wife of Edw S Plummer, died seized & possessed: 250 acres; the portion of the real estate of the late Wm Bryan, of Richd, which was allotted in the division of his real estate to his daughter, the late Rebecca A M Plummer, wife of said Edw S Plummer. Improvements consist of a barn, corn, & tobacco houses, & some quarters. –Saml B Hance, trustee

FRI SEP 28, 1866
Solomon J Joseph, formerly of the firm of Jos Brothers, a leading banking-house in Wall st, which failed in 1836, died on Wednesday.

Appointments by the Pres: 1-Hugh J Anderson, of Maine, Auditor of the Treasury for the Post Ofc Dept, [commonly denominated the Sixth Auditor,] in place of Hon Isaac N Arnold, resigned. 2-John J Humphreys, of Tenn, agent for the Indians of the Cherokee Agency.

Mrd: on Sep 25, at St John's Church, by Rev Lorenzo Russell, Edw Mullins, jr, of Phil, to Josephine G, daughter of Henry King, of Gtwn, D C. No cards.

Mrd: on Sep 27, by Rev J Vaughan Lewis, rector of St John's Episcopal Church, Dr E de W Breneman, U S army, to Marion, daughter of Wm Wilson, of Wash, D C.

A despatch from Memphis states that Col Galloway, of the Avalanche, is sick with cholera, & not expected to live.

Wm C Fields, of Otsego, N Y, was nominated by the Republicans on Wed for Congress from the 19th District.

Maj Gen Danl E Sickles has been appointed colonel of the 42nd U S infty, one of the new regts recently authorized by Congress.

John Williams, alias Cannon, was convicted of forgery in the Criminal Court of Boston on Wed. He obtained several thousand dollars from Boston banks, in Jan last, on forged checks.

On Sat a quarrel occurred between Peter Funari, an Italian image maker, & Alex'r Urene, one of his workmen, at the shop of the former, 145 Elm st, N Y, when Urene drew a revolver & shot his employer in the left breast, inflicting a fatal wound. He then ran out into the street, but being closely pursued by Ofcr Hyndes, of the 14th Precinct, he placed the revolver to his head & blew out his brains, causing instant death.

Phil Ledger: Hon John P Hale will be recalled from Madrid as soon as a suitable successor can be appointed. The rotary principle is to be applied to him, as it will be soon to others of our representatives abroad.

Mr Harry Gorbutt, s e corner of 8th & E sts, is acquiring an enviable reputation for his restaurant. Personal attention is given to his establishment. A free lunch to be procured every day between the hours of 11½ & 1 o'clock.

For sale: 100 barrels of Old Rye & Bourbon Whiskey; pure Old Sherry Wine; pure Old Port Wine. By Richad J Ryon, 481 9th st, between D & E sts.

By deed of trust to me from Henry De Mariel & wife, dated Mar 15, 1866, recorded in Liber R M H, No 10, page 414, land records for Wash Co, D C, I will sell, upon the premises, by public auction, on Oct 31 next, in Wash Co, D C, all that tract called **Long Meadows**, bounded on the south by the lands of Henry Douglass; on the north by the lands of Alex'r B Abercrombie, & on the west by Wm W Corcoran & John A Bertroff containing 96 acres, more or less. Also, all that other part of **Long Meadows**, near the land of John A Bertroff & the land of Henry Douglass, on main public road leading east from the 3rd boundary stone of Wash City, D C, to the Eastern Branch. -Henry O Hood, trustee -Green & Williams, aucts

Episcopal High School of Va, near Alexandria, Va, will open its 27th School year on Oct 3, 1866, & ends Jul 17, 1867. Principal, Rev Wm F Gardner, Theological Seminary P O, Fairfax Co, Va.

Rt Rev J M Young, Catholic Bishop of the diocese of Erie, died suddenly on Wed, at his pastoral residence in Oil City, Pa. He has been bishop there since 1854, having been consecrated in Apr, 1854. He was an earnest & faithful laborer in the cause of his church, his field of duty extending over the counties of Mercer, Verango Clarion, Jefferson, Potter, & Cameron. His loss will be deeply felt.

SAT SEP 29, 1866

Appointments of Army Surgeons under the recent Act of Congress: appointments by the Sec of War: Assist Surgeon C C Byrne, to be surgeon, vice Sutherland, promoted Medical Purveyor. Assists Surgeons Clinton Wagner, J P Wright, C C Gray, & Wm E Spencer, to be surgeons U S Army, to date from Jul 28, 1866, to fill vacancies created by the act of Congress approved Jul 28, 1866.

Rev Francis L Hawks died on Thu at his residence in N Y C, in his 79th year. His health had been very indifferent for some time past. The deceased was born in Newbern, N C, Jun 10, 1798; graduated at the Univ of N C in 1815; studied law & was admitted to the bar at age 21. He was later led to the ministry in the Protestant Episcopal Church, & ordained in 1828.

A close examination made into the affairs of Mr C C Flint, properietor of the Old Dominion newspaper, shows that he had victimized the following: Nat'l Bank of Norfolk, $6,000; First Nat'l Bank of Norfolk, $3,600; Ins Trust Co, of Norfolk, $6,200. The forgeries were mostly upon Gov't bills & vouchers. No clue to his whereabouts.

The obsequies of the late Hon Henry May took place yesterday from the residence of his brother-in-law, Gen Geo D Wise, U S Army where Mr May drew his last breath. After the religious ceremonies by Rev Dr Thos Foley, by whom Mr May was received into the bosom of the Catholic Church, the funeral train, consisting of the immediate family of the deceased, with many relatives & friends, proceeded to the Cathedral, the pall being borne by Robt J Brent, Geo M Gill, John S Gittings, Richd Norris, jr, Wm G Harrison, Wm Meade Addison, Philip R Fendall, of Wash, & Gen T B Andrews, U S Army. The solemn Mass was sung by Rev Dr Foley, there being in the sanctuary, Very Rev Dr Coskery, Rev Fr Gibbons, & Rev Frs Early, King, & Clarke, from Loyola. The Most Rev Archbishop, after the elevation, came into the sanctuary. Dies ira was sung by the choir, under the leadership of Mr Jos Gegan. On Rev Dr Foley's last visit to Mr May, he said, I have studied your faith in my own family; I was educated by the Jesuit fathers, & I now wish to receive the rites of the church. The cortege proceeded to the **Cathedral Cemetery**, under the charge of Messrs Jas Garvey & H W Jenkins, where Henry May was consigned to the earth to await the last trump. –Balt Sun, 28

General Orders No 80, from the Navy Dept, promulgated yesterday, are as follows: "Wm Ringgold Cooper, late an acting ensign in the navy, having been convicted of defrauding the Gov't of large sums of money, by means of forged papers, will be considered as dishonorably discharged from the service by his arrest for the said offence."

The Nashville papers announce the sudden death by cholera, in that city, of Lt Col Thos J Cox, an elder brother of Hon S S Cox, of Ohio. At the beginning of the war Col Cox was appointed capt & assist quartermaster, & for his efficiency, was promoted to lt colonel in that Dept, in which, on account of his valuable services, he was among the last of the volunteer ofcrs retained in service. He was a native of Zanesville, Ohio, where his family still reside.

On hearing the alarm of fire, caused by the burning of the cooper shop attached to Welch's mills, Thos Cooper, master of canal boat **Communipaw** went out upon the tressel work of the Cumberland Coal & Iron Co, & not noticing that the hatches were open, fell through one of them to the street, a distance of 28 feet. He was injured internally & his back & right arm were broken. He expired about 12 o'clock.

Thos Dowling, auct, on Tue, sold the Seminary property on Greene st-two lots to R A Payne & one to J A Vanderwerken, for $27 per front foot. A house & lot on Dunbarton st, to Anthony Hyde, for $1,500. The Seminary bldg was withdrawn at $19,000. A small bldg lot, fronting 16 feet on 2nd st, near Gtwn College, sold to Mr Magruder for $205.

Balt, Sep 28. H Rives Pollard had a preliminary examination today on the charge of shooting Fred'k Hipkins, on Wed, & was released on $5,000 bail. Hipkins' wound is serious, though not dangerous.

Signor Baragli, the new tenor engaged by Maretzek, arrived at N Y from Europe on Thu.

Mr Cornelius Vanderbilt is spoken of as the most promient candidate for the Presidency of the N Y Central Railroad, vice the late Dean Richmond.

Williams, the supposed murderer of Mrs Miller, of Phil, admits that he was at her house at an early hour in the morning.

Gen D Leadbeater, late of the Confederate army, died of apoplexy, at Clifton, Canada West, on Wed. He belonged at Mobile, & left a considerable sum of money, & valuable effects, where he died.

John Price was convicted of murder in the 2nd degree at Balt, on Thu, for killing Clinton James, at the Balt Museum, last May. This is the third time that Price has been convicted of murder.

Geo M Snow, for over 20 years commercial editor of the N Y Tribune, died suddenly in N Y on Thu, of heart disease, in his 55th year. He was connected with the Tribune from its start until 1863, when he went to Europe to recover his health, since which he has not been engaged upon that paper.

Appointments by the President yesterday of internal revenue ofcrs:
Moses W Black, collector 6th Dist Missouri
Andrew De Forest, collector 3rd Dist Mich.
Wm W Warren, assessor 7th Dist Mass.
John Pitcher, assessor 1st Dist Indiana.
Wm P Wells, assessor 1st Dist Mich.
Thos Allen, assessor 3rd Dist Pa.
John R Finn, collector 14th Dist Ohio.
Chas Glans, assessor 11th Dist Pa.
Andrew G Fulton, assessor 15th Dist Pa.
Jas Mackin, assessor 12th Dist N Y.
Alfred B Getty, assessor 22nd Dist N Y.
Jos E Beebe, assessor 3rd Dist Mich.
Walter B Beckwith, collector 2nd Dist Mich
John M Glover, collector 3rd Dist Missouri

Public sale by decree of the Circuit Court for PG Co, Md, in Equity; on Oct 18 next, of the real estate of the late Jas F Brown died seized & possessed, containing about 196 acres in Spalding's Dist, PG Co. By recent survey, is divided into two lots: one contains about 96 acres; lot 2 contains about 105½ acres. The land adjoins the lands of Jas L Addison, Nathan Masters, & others, & is about ½ mile from **Silver Hill** post ofc. -C C Magruder, jr, trustee

The New Haven Historical Society has Benedict Arnold's account book, & the sign of the store in which he did business before the Revolution. The inscription on it reads: "B. Arnold, druggist, bookseller, etc, from London: Sibi, totique."

Pardoned by the Pres: Peter Ripp, convicted at the Sept term, 1865, of the U S Circuit Court for the northern Dist of Ohio, of passing counterfeit currency, & sentenced to one year in prison. The pardon has also been ordered of Benj F Clark, convicted at the Apr term of the U S Dist Court for the Dist of Delaware, of pasing counterfeit money, & sentenced to one year in prison.

MON OCT 1, 1866
On the 21st ult, at Wyandotte, Kansas, Mr & Miss Baum, of Pleasant Hill, got off the train for supper, & not noticing the train in motion, Miss Baum was run over by one of the cars, mangling her in a terrible way. She expired the next day. They were on their return from Kansas, where they had been looking after the affairs of a brother, who had recently been murdered at Green Point, west of Lawrence.

Died: on Sep 29, at his residence, in Wash City, Dr S C Smoot, aged 48 years & 7 months. His funeral will take place from Calvery Baptist Church, H & 8th sts, at 12 o'clock on Oct 2. [He died at his residence on Pa ave near 20th st. During the past summer he was afflicted with hemorrhage of the lungs, which was followed by asthma, & finally with dropsy of the chest, which had confined him to his house for the last 5 weeks preceding his death.]

Died: on Sep 30, after a long & painful illness, John McDuell, aged 78 years, having been a resident of Wash for nearly 50 years, being one of the oldest & most respected citizens. His funeral will be on Wed at 2 o'clock P M, at the residence of his daughter, 422 14th st. Wash & Boston papers please copy.

Died: on Sep 30, at the residence of his son, Jas A McDevitt, H st, between 7th & 8th sts, John McDevitt, in his 75th year of his age, a native of the county Donegal, Ireland, but for the last 50 years a resident of Balt & Wash. His funeral services will take place at St Dominic's Church, on Tue next, at 9 o'clock, when a solemn requiem mass will be offered up for the repose of his soul. The remains will be taken thence to the Balt depot.

Died: on Sep 3, at the residence of D F Slaughter, in Culpeper Co, Va, Col John B Dade, in his 85th year. He leaves his grief stricken widow & daughter to mourn his loss.

John Pitts was drowned a few miles below Cumberland, Md, on Sat. He attempted to ford the Potomac with a horse & buggy, but the river being very high the current carried them down stream, drowning both the man & the horse.

Brvt Maj C R Greenleaf, assist surgeon, was on Sat relieved from duty in the Dept of Wash & assigned to duty in the Dept of the Tennessee.

Walter P Watson was hung at Newport, Ky, Friday, for the murder of Capt Mentor.

Only $1,500 was found in the possession of Adolph Bernard, who was recently arrested for embezzling some $10,000 from the Memphis & Charleston railroad.

Dr J O Shipman, a well-known physician of large practise in Syracuse, died of cholera. He had on Saturday attended a stranger affected with symptoms of cholera; was slightly affected on Monday; became alarmingly ill during the day, & died on Tuesday.

Trustee's sale of a desirable lot of ground on 14th st west between P & Q sts north; by deed of trust from *Costallo Hosmer & wife, to me, recorded in N C T, No 60, folio 130, of the land records for Wash Co, D C; public auction on Oct 11 next, on the premises, lot 23 in square 241. –W Y Fendall, trustee -Jas C McGuire & Co, aucts [*POSSIBLY Costallo Hosmer—very light print.]

Gen Chas H Peaslee, who for some quarter of a century was one of the conspicuous public men of N H, died on Sep 20, of apoplexy, at St Paul, Minn, aged 62 years. He was born in N H, & in 1804, graduated at Dartmouth College in 1824; settled in Concord, the capital of that State. He was a State rep from 1833 to 1837; Adj Gen from 1839 to 1847; member of the Nat'l House of Reps from 1847 to 1853. He was appointed Collector of Customs at Boston, by Pres Pierce, a position which he filled 4 years with eminent ability. Since 1857 he resided in Portsmouth. His mother, more than 80 years of age, survives him in his native town, & he leaves a wife, one brother, & several sisers, & a wide circle of friends. Maj Gen Dana, of St Paul, is a son of Gen Peaslee's wife, by a former marriage, & it is at his residence, doubtless, that he died.

TUE OCT 2, 1866

Criminal Court-Judge Fisher, Oct 1, 1866. 1-John Jones & Chas Smith, indicted for larceny; Simon White, larceny; Jas Housewright, John Crawford, Robt Magee, & Jas P Ellicott, keeping gaming table; Ann Nolan, bawdy house; Henry Chatain, bawdy house; David E Smith, assault & battery. 2-Eliz Brown, keeping a bawdy house-no guilty. 3-Moses Black, larceny-guilty. Motion for a new trial.

Appointments by the Pres: 1-Maj Gen W W Averill, to be U S Consul General at Montreal, Canada. 2-Owen Thurston, of Kansas, to be Register of the Land Ofc at Humboldt, Kansas. 3-Timothy J Carter, of Ill; Chas T Sherman, of Ohio; Geo Ashmun, of Mass; Springer Harbaugh, of Pa; & Jesse L Williams, at Indiana, to be Directors on the part of the U S Gov't of the Union Pacific Railroad Co until the first Wed in Oct, 1867.

Under an order from the Pres, the household effects left at the *Arlington Mansion* by Gen Lee, or rather the fragments that were remaining of them, were yesterday delivered to the party authorized by Gen Lee to receive them. It appears that nearly everthing of any value had been stolen. Many valuable heirlooms, including some of the family portraits, had been purloined. The portraits were taken from the frames, packed in boxes, & stored in the upper loft of the mansion for safety, in 1861. These boxes had been broken open & everything of value taken away, & the letters & private papers of Gen Lee scattered over the loft. A lady friend of the family, with Mrs Gray, the old & faithful household servant, were yesterday looking over the effects, & gathering up the fragments worth preserving. The only thing remaining there from *Mount Vernon* were 3 book cases & a carved hall chair.

E L Palmer, of Baring, Maine, was appointed by the Pres first lt of the 43rd regt U S infty.

Mrd: on Sep 25, by Rev Mr Lemon, Walter E Fowler to Miss Jenni Danforth.

Mrs Daniels, wife of a prominent merchant of Worthington, Iowa, drowned herself a few days since, while laboring under temporary insanity.

Chas Alexander, one of the oldest journalist, & in his time one of the most extensive publishers of the U S, died at his residence, 112 Wistar st, this morning, after a protracted illness, in his 70 year. He was born in Phil in 1796, & at age 16 was bound an apprentice to the late Zachariah Pouison, to learn the printing business. Later he commenced business for himself at the old printing ofc used by Benj Franklin, in this city, at the s w corner of 7th & Market sts, number 53. He used the old press & type formerly belonging to Franklin. He started the Sat Evening Post with Mr Louis A Godey, his life-long friend. We are sorry to say Mr Alexander died in circumstances beneath his deserts. He was poor.
–Phil paper

The death of Hermann Goldschmidt, a German astronomer of celebrity, is announced. He was born at Frankfort-on-the-Main, Jun 17, 1802. He studied painting in Paris, under Schmorr & Cornelius, &, in 1836 began to devote himself to astronomy. [No death date given-current item.]

War Dept, Wash, D C, Sep 30, 1866. Statement of Claims filed with the Claims Commission during the month of Sept, 1866.
85-L Pierce, jr, late U S Consul at Matamoras, for moneys expended in aiding Union refugees.
86-Jas Millinger, of the firm of R McClay & Co.
87-Lewis Grantham & 14 others, for compensation as witnesses before a military commission at Harper's Ferry. Jas Fullerton, atty
88-Wm Hairgrove for compensation as detective in the District of the Border.
89-Otto Sle, for property destroyed in bldg a fort. Wm Helmick, atty.
90-L S Campbell, for carpenter's tools abandoned for want of transportation.
91-Claim of the owners of the steamer **Wm H Young**, for servics of the steamer.
92-Claim of the owners of the brig **Madeira**, for the loss of said brig, sunk by the U S steamer **Clyde**. The British Minister, through the State Dept.
93-J Bigler, for detention of the brig **Blackfish** at Hilton Head.
94-Adolph Tiensch, for quartermaster's stores taken in Tenn.
95-Eugene Bourcy, for sugar taken by the U S authorities.
96-Robt A Gray, for forage furnished the U S army.
97-Henry Holt, for the destruction of a factory by the U S forces.
98-Geo B Simpson, late paymaster, for commutation of quarters, etc.
99-John T Armstrong, lumber & rent of wharf at Alexandria, Va. John H McMurdy, atty
100-Albert Flagler, for forage furnished to U S troops
101-Mrs E W Turner, for rent of property in New Orleans, La. Geo Taylor, atty
102-J W Pomfrey, for services as a detective.
103-Jas Dearing, for ice seized for the use of the U S Hospital.
104-Geo Lang, for locomotives seized by order of the Sec of War. Rejected.
105-Hugh E Phillips, for damages to his property by Union troops.
106-Wm H Manning, for blacksmith tools taken & used by the Gov't. Saml B Parris, atty
107-Mary J Holland, for rent of house in New Orleans, La. L A Holland, atty

108-Danl Nolan, for liquors seized by Provost Marshal. Chas F McGill, atty
109-Richd Norris & Son, for additional compensation for furnishing locomotives.
110-G H C Rowe, for the use of a church for hospital purposes.
111-Mrs M Lotz, for damages to property by U S forces.
112-W M Lamson, for losses sustained at the hands of U S troops.
113-Webster M Raines, for property said to have been destroyed by U S troops.
114-Mrs Paschall, for damages to her house, alleged to have been occasioned by the explosion at the Washington Arsenal. S York AtLee, atty.
115-Geo W Moody & Robt T Williams, for compensation for the capture of the rebel steamer **Governor Troop**. A W Stone, atty.
116-Thos Greer, for services as teamster at *Fort Smith*, Ark, & for the use of team.
117-J Moulder, Michl Amos, Chas Amos, Ambrose Nelson, C Grant, L T Johnson, J M Fleming, Jas Byrum, C R Patty, Abel Conway, W R Hughes, & C P Yaden, for services as laborers at *Fort Smith*, Ark. M Delany, atty for 116 & 117.
118-Leo Bruger, for services as teamster in the Dept of the Tenn. M Delany, atty.
119-John Isen, A Deny, J A R Forgey, & Bird Jameson, for commissary stores. M Delany, atty.
120-Benj Roach, for cotton. John Jolliffe, atty.
121-Joel Bargdol, for services as blacksmith. M Delany, atty.
122-F K Everhart, for rent of office for Provost Marshal's Dept. M Delany, atty.
123-R N Pollock, A O Reed, & Alanson S Hall, for services in the Provost Marshal's Dept. M Delany, atty.
124-Sgt Garret Tieman, for transportation of prisoners in Provost Marshal's Dept. M Delany, atty.
125-Asa Booher, for boarding two female prisoners. M Delany, atty.
126-Jos West, for keeping contraband horses. M Delany, atty.
127-Dawson Hook, for services as a dectective for the Army of the Frontier. M Delany, atty.
128-J M Hiatt, for services as Asist Provost Marshal. M Delany, atty.
129-Newton White, Wm Harris, Streeter & Strickler, & Timothy Mannon, for quartermaster stores. M Delany, atty.
130-John Davidson, for rent of & damages to property at New Orleans, La, by U S troops. S H Sweetland, atty.
131-Paran Moody, for rent of property at Jacksonville, Fla. No atty.
132-Martin Connor & Jas O Day, for property destroyed by U S troops. No atty.
133-Jas M Hager, for towage on the ship **Ida Lilly**. No atty.
134-Jas Aberdeen, for property seized by U S troops. Presented by the British Minister.
135-Wm A Dean, for money deposited in the First Nat'l Bank of Harrisburg, Pa, by Lt W F Arnold. Robt L Merrick, atty.
136-Michaelis Wood, for five barrels of turpentine. W M Tileston, atty.
137-R A Francis, for kersey furnished to the U S. No atty.
138-Jas T Mason, for rent of Lawson Hospital Bldg. A L Merriman, atty.

139-J H Maddox, for tobacco taken by U S Gov't. J S Black & Lewis E Parsons, attys.
140-John G Taylor, for property taken by U S troops. Jas H Embry, atty.
141-Catholic Church at Fredericksburg, Va, for damages to the church bldg by the U S forces. Jas O Farule.
142-Jules Perrodin, for cotton. John Jolliffe, atty.
143-Adam Kling, for the use of land near Callipolis, Ohio, by U S troops. Allan & Latsoe, attys.
144-Dominique Leave, for horses & cattles taken by U S troops. Aug Berg, atty.
145-Sarafine Welati, for money taken by Provost Marshal at Balt, Md. A S Cox & Co, attys.
146-John H McKee, for cattle, etc, taken by U S troops. John Jolliffe, atty.
147-Methodist Episcopal Church South, of Warrenton, Va, for damages to church edifice by U S troops. J D Blackwell, agent.
148-Gustave Cavnot, for carrying mail under military orders. L G Hine, atty.
149-Louisa Keegan, for losses sustained under orders of Gen Butler. State Dept for the British Minister.
150-John Lockwood, for the use of *Vidella Plantation*, La, by the Freedmen's Bureau. No atty.
151-Richd Berry, for property destroyed by order of Gen Palmer. Chipman & Hosmer, attys.
152-Convent of the Holy Cross, at Plaquemine, La, for losses sustained at the hands of
U S troops. Mary of St Bernard, superior.
153-T Kennedy, late capt, for expenses incurred in raising his company. Tucker & Se'ls attys.
154-Andrew McDaniel, for procuring recruits for the 78th Ohio Volunteer Infty. C E Bishop, atty.
155-E R Hert, for axes furnished to the U S. No atty.
156-Reuben Williams, for furnishing rations, etc. W H Randall, atty.
157-Columbus Reid, for the return of money in the hands of the Provost Marshal's Dept. Wm S DeZeng, atty.
158-John Manwaring, for mules & lumber taken by the U S military authorities. British Minister through State Dept.
159-Danl J Flynn, for loss of furniture. No atty.
160-John McDowell, for forage taken by U S troops. Peter J Sullivan, atty.
161-F A Metcalfe, adm, etc, for the proceeds of cotton. John Jolliffe, atty.
162-Francis Capella, for cotton seized & destroyed by the U S authorities. R McAllister, atty.
163-Jenry Polkinhorn, jr, for property taken by the U S authorities. John Jolliffe, atty.
164-Morris Cohen, for commutation of quarters & fuel. No atty.
165-Celia A Grove, for cotton, etc, taken by the U S authorities. John Jolliffe, atty.
166-Mrs Edw King, for destruction of property by U S troops. State Dept for the British Minister.

167-Mrs Bradley & children, for restoration of the Bradley Iron Works, at Macon, Ga. John T Croxton, atty.
168-Jas K Skinker, for cattles seized by U S authorities. Downman & Green, attys
169-Rebecca Tomlinson, for property destroyed by U S soldiers. No atty.
170-Jas Pearce, for losses sustained at the hands of the U S troops. State Dept for the British Minister.
171-Julius Witkowski & Simon Witkowski, for cotton taken by U S authorities. John Jolliffe, atty.
172-O N Cutler, for cotton seized by U S authorities. R B Carpenter, atty.
173-John Metcalf, for cotton taken by U S Authorities. John Jolliffe, atty.

Statement of claims filed during the month of Aug last, & acted upon during the present month:
1-Claim of: R Bonneval; Allen Valentine; W P Jones; Mary Cassin; S G Cabell; Elias Shipman, [surviving partner;] Angelo Niazza; Chas Nagelin; Saml R Jacobs; E H Jeanjaquet; E M Anderson; C E Brook & Co; Wm J Minor; E Linder; Mrs C H Halsey; Jos Hamlin; John H Wardwell; Thos Cassidy; Chas Willey; Jos Anderson; Eugene Sullivan; Jas Syme; Maria Josefa Cadazos; John Sheldon; & C S Snead: continued for further proof.
2-Claim of: Walter J Dobbin; R D Beans; John A Coan; Benj F Logan; Jeffry Moriarty; Eugene L Riquet; R S Hipkins; Eliza Knighton; Geo S Kausler; John Brownson, jr; Given Watts & Co; H S Saunders; Mary R Kent; Jos Devnoodt; E G Wood; I A Chutkowski; Susan Shacklett; H H Mathias; John R G Hotz; Mat J Williams; & Luke Clarke: rejected.
3-Claim of: J C Badger; John A Bowen; L H Babcock; Mary Ann Peoria; H A Swut; Hugh F Smith [in part;] Washington Saunders; J F Newton; & Michl Fitzsimmons: allowed.
4-Claim of Indiana H Slaughter; returned to War Dept.
5-Claim of A Morell, Esberg & Ambsburg & Jas Hunter; returned to claimant's atty.
6-Claim of: Julius Hesse & Co; returned to claimants.
7-Claim of S D Freeman & others, trustees, etc: returned to Adj Gen of the army.
8-Claim of S T Suit: allowed in part.
9-Claim of Marcus Walker: continued at the requet of claimant's atty.
10-Claim of: John H Grady; John Haskins; Thos J Dunbar & Co, & Jacob F Eaton; M W Baldwin & Co: held under advisement.
11-Claim of H H Wells, Wm H Dungan, & others, leases of the Alexandria canal; claim of David W Lamb & A S Johnson, trustees, etc: stricken from the calendar, it having been placed there by mistake.
-Dewitt Clinton, Brvt lt Col, Recorder.

The claims of: Walter J Dobbins; R D Beans; John A Coan; R S Hipkins; Eliza Knighton; H S Saunders; I Z Chutkowski; Susan Shacklett; Mat J Williams; rejected for want of jurisdiction, or because Congress has failed to make provision for their payment.

Despatch from *Fort Laramie*, dated Wed. On Sep 14 the Indians killed & badly mutilated Pvt Johnson & Ridgeway Glover, an artist for Frank Leslie's paper.

West Point & its graduates. Gen Cullum's Register of the Ofcrs & Graduates of the U S Military Academy at West Point. Class of 1820: John H Winder, eleven in a class of thirty; his infamous records show he did not improve after graduation. Class of 1822: J K F Mansfield was second: maintained his prominence as an engineer ofcr during a long & honorable career. Twenty five & twenty six in his class were David Hunter & Geo A McCall. 1823-Alfred Mordecai, first honors; held a prominent position in the Engineer Corps. Lorenzo Thomas, late Adj Gen of the army, ranked sixteen files below him. Dennis H Mahan, since better known as Prof Mahan, stood number one in the class of 1824. Dixon H Miles was twenty-seventh in the same class, & kept his position well. In the class of 1825 Alex'r T Bache took the highest honors, & in a long career of scientific usefulness has held his own. Benj Huger, of S C, was number eight, & made an efficient ofcr in the Confederate army. Robt Anderson, of *Fort Sumter* fame, was number fifteen, & Chas F Smith, once called Paducah Smith, but regarded by many old ofcrs as the most accomplished soldier in the army, was four files below. As the first men seem to have run to scientific pursuits, it is not strange that Wm H C Bartlett, the first graduate of the class of 1826, have followed the example of Mahan & Bache. T Jefferson Cram, one of the highest of our engineer ofcrs, stood number four in the same class, while Albert Sydney Johnson, in whom the South lost their best field general, was number eight. Silas Casey, Tactics Casey, & S P Heintzelman were also in this class. In the class of 1827 Napoleon B Buford, in whom we lost one of our best cavalry leaders, was number six, & Leonidas Polk number eight. Albert E Church, another scientific first man, carried off the highest honors of the class of 1828. Number 23 in this class was "President" Davis of the late Confederacy. The second on the roll of the class of 1829 was Robt E Lee, in whose class Jos E Johnston was thirteen; O M Mitchell, fifteen; Edw R Long, thirty-nine, & Benj W Brice, now Paymaster Gen-number forty. The first name of note in the class of 1830 is Wm J Pendleton, a prominent general in Lee's army, who was number five. John B Magruder was eleven files below him, & sank a good many more after graduation. Henry Clay, jr, the gifted, gallant, & favorite son of old "Harry of the West," killed in Mexico, was the second man of the class of 1831. Saml E Curtis, of Pea Ridge Fame, was number twenty-seven in this class, Andrew A Humphreys, number thirteen, & Wm H Emory, fourteen. Benj S Ewell, Stonewall Jackson's right arm, was three in the class of 1832. Erasmus D Keyes was ten, & Randolph B Marcy twenty-nine. In the class of 1833 Jonathan G Barnard was twenty-two, & has kept his position among the first ranks of the scientific graduates. Geo W Cullum, a distinguished engineer ofcr, was just below. John M Hartindale stood number three in the class of 1835. In his class Geo Meade stood number nineteen. The last cmder of the Army of the Potomac has made a considerable advance in his relative position since then. In the class of 1836 Montgomery C Meigs stood number five. Below him were Thos W Sherman, ["Port Royal,"] number eighteen, & John W Phelps, ["Proclamation Phelos,"] number twenty-four. Henry

W Benham led the class of 1837. After him were Braxton Bragg, five; Edw D Townsend [Adj Gen of the army,] sixteen; Jubal A Early, [Apple Jack Early,"] eighteen; B H Hill, twenty-one; Wm H French, twenty-two; John Sedgwick, twenty-four; John C Pemerton, twenty-seven; Jos Hooker, twenty-nine; Wm H T Walker, [first Confederate Sec of War,] forty-six. The talent of that class was certainly not monopolized by its "first men." In the class of 1838, the second name is P G T Beauregard. Number seventeen was Wm F Barry, McClellan's & Sherman's able chief of artl. Below them were Irwin McDowell, twenty-three; Wm J Hardee, twenty-six; Robt S Granger, twenty-eight; & Andrew J Smith, thirty-six. At the head of the class of 1839 was Isaac J Stevens, since known as Govn'r & as Gen Stevens, whose early loss during the war ended untimely a career which would have been a brilliant one. Henry W Hallock stood number three; Jas B Rickett, sixteen; Edw O C Ord, seventeen; Jenry J Hunt, nineteen; & Edw R S Canby, thirty. In the class of 1840 Wm T Sherman stood six; below him were Geo H Thomas, twelve; Richd S Ewell, thirteen; Geo W Getty, fifteen. Horatio G Wright was number two in the class of 1841; below him were Amiel W Whipple, five; Nathl Lyon, eleven; Schuyler Hamilton, twenty-four; Jas Totten, twenty-five; John F Reynolds, twenty-six; Don Carlos Buell, thirty-two; Alfred Sully, thirty-five; & Wm F H Brooks, forty-six. In the class of 1854 Henry L Eustis, since known as Prof Eustis, of Harvard Univ, heads the list; below him were John Newton, two; Geo W Rains, three; Wm S Rosecrans, five; Gustavus W Smith, eight; Mansfield Lovel, nine; John Pope, seventeen; Abner Doubleday, twenty-four; Lafayette McLaws, forty-eight; Earl Van Dorn, firty-two; & Jas Longstreet, fifty four. It will be seen that three noted Confederate cmders, the last one of the most efficient, were at the foot of this class. In the class of 1843 Wm B Franklin heads the list; below him were Isaac F Quinby, six; John J Peck, eight; Jos J Reynolds, ten; Christopher C Augur, sixteen, Ulysses S Grant, twenty-one; Fred'k Steele, thirty; & Rufus Ingalls, thirty-two. In the class of 1844 Alfred Pleasanton was seven, & below him were Simon B Buckner, eleven; Winfield S Hancock, eighteen, & Alex'r Hays, twenty. In the class of 1845, Wm F Smith, ["Baldy Smith,] was four; below him were Thos J Wood, five; Chas P Stone, seven; Henry Coppee, eleven; John P Hatch, seventeen; Gordon Granger thirty-five; Henry B Clitz, thirty-six, & David A Russell, thiry-eight. In the class of 1846 Geo B McClellan, was number two; below him were John G Foster, four; Jesse L Reno, eight; Darius N Couch, thirteen; Thos J Jackson ["Stonewall,"] seventeen; Geo Stoneman, thirty-two; Dabney H Maury, thirty-seven; Geo H Gordon, forty-three; & Geo E Pickett, fifty-nine. In the class of 1847 Orlando B Wilcox was number eight; below him were Jas B Fry, fourteen; Ambrose P Hill, jr, fifteen; Ambrose E Barnside, eighteen; Richd H Long, nineteen; Romeyn B Ayres, twenty-two; Chas Griffin, twenty-three; & Henry M Black, twenty-four. In the class of 1849, Quincey A Gillmore was first; below him were John G Parke, number two; & Rufus Saxton, jr, eighteen. We give the above as interesting statistics in the history of the army of West Point. We have merely made a selection sufficiently thorough to answer the purpose of this article.
—Army & Navy Journal

WED OCT 3, 1866
Appointments by the Pres. Caleb P Johnson, U S Marshal, Dist of Delaware.
Jas H Parsons, U S Atty, District of Rhode Island.
Benj F Tracy, U S Atty, Eastern District of N Y.
Francis L Dallon, U S Marshal, Western Dist of N Y.

Com'r of Pensions appointed yesterday: Dr John B Johnston, Evansville, Ind; Dr H E Bowles, Hammonton, N J; Dr J F Grant, Pulaski, Tenn; & Dr Eben J Russ, Benzining, Pa.

Among the passengers in the Royal mail steamship **China**, which sailed on Wed from Boston for Liverpool, was Miss Frances Jane MacLeod, of Wash.

The jury came to the verdict that the deceased, Eliza M Miller, came to her death at the hands of Gottleib Williams, in her house, 924 Buttonwood st, on Sep 19, 1866. The coroner committed Williams for trial.

Mrd: on Oct 2, at the Church of the Epiphany, by Rev C H Hall, D C, E Mason Cooper, of Quincy, Ill, to Mary Fiora, daughter of Henry Baldwin, of Wash City.

Mrd: on Oct 2, at the Church of the Ascension, by Rev Dr Pinckney, J G Trimble, U S A, to Miss Mary N Nichols, all of Wash, D C.

Mrd: on Sep 30, by Rev Fr McNally, Mr Wm K Tucker to Miss Susannah Powell, all of Wash, D C.

Died: on Sep 8, at Glencove, Long Island, at the temporary residence of her son-in-law & grandchildren, Mrs Richmond Margaret Inglis Macleod, widow of Alex'r Norman Macleod, of Marris, in her 67th year.

Meeting of the Union War Prisoners' Association [late prisoners of war in the South during the late war,] was held last night, at the City Hall, Col B F Fisher presided, & Capt J P Perley acted as sec. Brig Gen Lasselle made a report on a constitution & by laws. Lt Harris & Lt Williams appointed to report nominations for a regular organization.

The funeral of the late Dr S C Smoot took place from the Calvary Baptist Church yesterday; the corpse was encased in a handsome mahogany coffin, furnished by Jos Gawler, undertaker. The services were conducted by Rev Dr Howlett, pastor, assisted by Rev Dr Gray. Pall bearers were Dr Hagner & Dr J C Riley, Capt Fillebrown, & Messrs D G Ridgeley, Frank Stickney, & Wm Norton. The remains were interred in the **Congressional Cemetery**. Dr Smoot was at the time of his death a member of the faculty of Columbian College, & the exercises of that institution were suspended in order that the president & professors might attend the funeral in a body.

We should like to hear Senator Wilson tell Gen Custer, to his face, that he "sold himself for unmerited promotion."

Capt W M Mew, of the ofc of the Sec of the Treasury, was the recipient of a surprise party at his residence, where his parlors had been taken possession of by a formidable party, presenting to the Capt & his wife, various useful articles of household & kitchen furniture suitable to the entry of a young couple upon the domestic duties of life.

Orphans Court-Judge Purcell 1-Yesterday David Gordon obtained letters of administration with the will annexed on the estate of Susan E Gordon; bond $1,000. Also, letters of administration to Susan L Hall, on the estate of Edw Hall; bond $125,000; to Catherine Frommell, on the estate of Francis Frommell; bond $10,000; to Franklin Little, on the estate of Jas Little: bond $700.
2-Jas Harris was appointed guardian to the son of Jas Snyder: bond $700.
3-The first & final account of the administrator of Wm S Venable; the fourth general account of the guardian to the orphans of Robt Farnham, with the third & supplementary of the surviving administrator of same, & fourth general as guardian to Caroline Farnham, were approved & passed.

Brvt Maj J Jones, Superintendent of the Freedmen's Bureau for Northern Ala, is at the Metropolitan Hotel, & returns to his post in a few days, with his wife. He says that the people of that section of Alabama are anxious for a peaceful settlement of all national difficulties, & accept the present condition of affairs in good faith. Their treatment of the freedmen is humane & honorable.

Signor G G Garobodi, of Buffalo, has been selected to fresco the N Y Academy of Music.

Mr Danl Drew contributes ground & bldgs for a Methodist College in N Y C, a donation amounting to $250,000.

On Sat, at Pittsfield, Mass, Dr Robt Campbell, an old & highly esteem citizen of Pittsfield, & a director of the Western [Mass] railroad, shot himself through the head. He had been suffering intense agony for sometime from disease of the kidneys, & being impatient to pain, has thus unexpectedly terminated his life. He was about 70 years old.

The trial of Sarah Rubens just concluded at Lockport, on the charge of poisoning her husband with strychnine. The were married in Jul, 1865, but in Sept following he died, after a painful illness, with symptoms of poisoning. A post morten examination devoloped strychnine. The jury were not satisfied of the guilt of the accused & she was acquitted.

Judge Toler, of Kansas City, died on Thursday.

Mrs Robt Walker was killed by a freight train on Friday night while crossing the track of the Michigan Southern railroad, at Detroit.

The funeral of Wm McKeever, who was killed while driving the horse Butler, at Chicago, on Sep 22, took place at N Y on Monday, & was largely attended.

Jas N Palmer, of New Haven, for many years Surgeon Gen of Conn, & a civil engineer of eminent ability, died at Hartford, on Saturday.

Pittsburgh, Oct 1. Richd Thairwell, who murdered Jas Houseman, on Apr 4 last, was executed today at Uniontown, Fayette Co. He died, he said, a Christian, hoping for forgivemess.

Valuable estate for sale: **Gordonsdale**, in Fauquier Co, Va, containing 600 acres, more or less; dwlg house is of brick, large & well built. –Robt E Peyton, Plains Post Ofc, Va.

THU OCT 4, 1866

Appointments by the Pres yesterday: 1-Albert G Lawrence, of Rhode Island, U S Minister resident at Costa Rica. 2-Madison E Hollister, of Ill, U S Consul at Buenos Ayres. 3-Chas Dougherty, of Pa, U S Consul at Londonderry.

Cold blooded murder on Monday, on the Centreville Race-Course, L I, the victim being Mr Robt Walker, the well & favorably known trainer & driver of trotting horses; proprietor of the Centreville Hotel, [adjoining the track,] & came to this country some years since from Ireland. About 3 years ago kept a livery stable at Newark, N J. The murder took place within less than a half mile of his residence, while driving a horse & wagon around the course. He was shot in the right temple. The horse was found near the house. Some employees of the hotel then started out looking for Mr Walker. B W Curtis, Coroner of Queens Co, empannelled a jury & proceeded to collect all the available. Chas Yetter, being sworn, deposted that on Oct 1, 1866, he was in the employe of the deceased; saw Mr Walker who went out to exercise a horse on the track; saw a boy bring the horse & wagon into the stable yard; deceased was found lying on the course shot through the head. Leonard I Brown testified that on Oct 1, he was crossing the fields on his way to work;when he found deceased who was still alive, gasping. Mr Yetter & I conveyed the body to the house. The supervisors of Queens Co yesterday offered a reward of $500 for the apprehension of the guilty parties.
–N Y Herald

Mrd: Oct 3, at the Foundry M E Church, by Rev Bishop Scott, of Delaware, Mr Frank A Springer, of Chicago, Ill, to Miss Annie Virginia Bates, of Wash City.

Died: on Oct 2, after a long & painful illness, Miss Lavinia Boyle, eldest daughter of the late John Boyle. Her funeral will be from St Patrick's Church, on Oct 5, 9 o'clock A M.

On Monday, Mrs Ackers, residing at 434 L st, near 10th, was attacked with cholera, & Dr D W Bliss pronounced it a case of Asiatic cholera. The patient was safely convalescent in 12 hours, & is now entirely well. The Dr's opinion was this case was caused by eating something deleterious. -Star

Death of Gen Muravieff: not only a member of one of the oldest & proudest Russian families, but he was also prominent in his own right. He was born in 1793, served in the army, was in the Persian war of 1828 & the Polish war of 1831; defeated Ibrahim Pasha when moving on Constantinople; commanded the army of the Caucasus in 1855; & captured Kars from Gen Williama. [No death date given-current item.]

Long Island, in Princess Anne, Va, recently purchased by Hon Ben Wood, of N Y, contains 1,900 acres; cost-$7,200. He intends to build there.
–Norfolk Virginian

Thos Reed committed suicide in Phil on Tues, by shooting himself with a pistol.

Prigg's Dollar Jewelry Store, 438 Pa ave, offers great attractions to our lady readers, having just received silver-plated spoons, forks, goblets, cups, call-bells, etc, & any article can be had for only a dollar.

The Prince of Wales has recently bought the estate of **Harewood**, 12 miles s e of Lanceston, in Cornwall, for L26,000.

Mr Miller, a saloon keeper at Shelbyville, was shot, on Sep 26, by his son-in-law. The boy, on returning home, rapped on the door for admission & Mr Miller came to the door & spoke some pretty short words to the boy about entering at such a late hour of the night. The boy became angry & took his revolver & shot & killed Miller. The boy was arrested & lodged in jail for trial. [Boy's name not given.]

FRI OCT 5, 1866
Capt & Brvt Maj Gen A T A Torbert, U S A, well known as one of the most efficient cavalry division cmders during the war, has resigned his position in the regular army, & retires to private life.

Monthly meeting of the Oldest Inhabitants was held on Wed at the **Analostan Mansion**. Wm A Bradley, proprietor of the island, a member of the association, presided at the elegant dinner. This island was originally owned by Gen John Mason, who built the mansion in 1782, upon the site of his original mansion, which was destroyed by fire, the colored gardener, who alone occupied the house, being consumed at the time. David Hepburn, father of John Hepburn, born on this island, was the chief gardener there for 6 years, superintending all the improvements for Gen Mason. Dr A McD Davis, rec sec, was present. The following gentlemen were admitted to membership: Jas Buckley, Geo Harvey, Wm H Stanford, G H Phillips, Walter Pomeroy, Lewis Thomas, Robt White,

Eben G Brown, Fielder Magruder, Chas Dean, John P Hilton, John McClelland, John Bradley, a soldier in the war of 1812, David E Irving, Jas M Towers, John Tretler, & R H Stewart. It was voted to accept the invitation of Jenkin Thomas, of Gtwn, & hold their meeting in Market House Hall, in that city. The following are the names of those who entered this arena: Noble Hurdle, John D Clark, Wm A Bradley, Michl Nash, Thos Wells, G W Young, Jas Bowen, C Bestor, 78, a lt in the army in 1812; John W Martin, Saml Stettinius, D E Irving, Peter O'Donoghue, & John F Callan. [The island, which, prior to the settlement of Gen Mason upon it, was known under the Indian name of *Analostan*, was, during his day, called *Mason's Island*, & since then it has resumed its ancient name. However, it was *Analostan Point*, as it did not become an island till about 1780. Down to the spring of that year there was a small rivulet formed from the water coming from the "*High Hills of Coony*," as the bluffs of *Arlington* were then called, running through the ravine at the foot of the hills, in that spring an unparralleled freshet, succeeding a winter of intense severity, sweeping down ice, forest trees torn from the banks along the way, & especially about Little Falls, obstructed the Potomac here so much as to lift the ice, uproot trees, & drive it down through the ravine thus ploughing out a deep gorge, opening a broad stream, & transforming *Analostan Point* into an island.] The following are names of the association present, together with their respective ages:

Noble Hurdle, 85	F B Lord, sr, 75	Edw Deeble, 76
Jesse Lipscomb, 70	Louis Baker, 56	Robt Widdicombe, 67
Willard Drake, 82	Wm Knowles, 80	
F R Dorsett, 73	J Carroll Brent, 51	John N Young, 59
John W Martin, 57	Gen Peter Force, 76	Simeon Matlock, 82
Chauncey Bestor, 78	J M Towers, 52	Jas Clephane, 76
John F Webb, 68	John G Robinson, 69	E B Stelle, 60
Robt Harrison, 73	Chas Hunt, 71	John F Callan, 55
Henry Tilley, 69	W J Wheatley, 53	Saml Stettinius, 63
Michl Nash, 61	Jenkin Thomas, 60	Peter O'Donoghue, 71
Wm A Bradley, 72	A McD Davis, 58	
John D Clark, 74	Wm Cooper, 68	Geo Savage, 66
Sereno Masi, 64	Saml Magee, 67	John Johnson, 70
Saml Wells, 86	Jas Bowen, 55	A Rothwell, 65
G W Young, 70	John N Ford, 64	
J H Plant, 55	Edw Simms, 72	

The ceremony of installing Rev Dr Boynton as pastor of the First Congregational Church of Wash City took place last evening in the Baptist Church. The grand organ was played with marked skill by Prof Harden, of Sunderland's church.

A few days since Mr J C Willard purchased the lot adjoining the Ebbitt House, on F st, & it was stated yesterday that he also completed a bargain with Mrs Farnham for her lot on 14th st, by which purchase he almost surrounds the Ebbitt House, & thereby prevents hereafter the bldg of a large hotel in that locality.

Mr Donald McCathran, of the 6th Ward, appointed a justice of the peace for D C.

Rear Admiral Francis H Gregory died in N Y C, Oct 4, of inflammation of the bowels, after an illness of a few hours. He honorably served his country for more than 57 years. He was born at Norwalk, Conn, on Oct 9, 1789; warranted as midshipman by Pres Jefferson on Jan 16, 1809; had been in the merchant service previously from Mar, 1802; entered the navy after having escaped from British imprisonment. His first service was on board the schnr **Revenge**, commanded by Lt O H Perry; transferred to the ketch **Vesuvius**, & went to New Orleans in 1809. In 1811 promoted to an acting master; in 1821 Lt Gregory was appointed to command of the schnr **Grampus**. He was commissioned rear admiral Jul 16, 1862, & was age 77 st the time of his death.

Appointments by the Pres yesterday: 1-Francis A Hall, Register of Land Ofc at Monroe, La. 2-Jas F McGuire, Receiver of Public Moneys, at Monroe, La. 3-Saml T Williams, of Md, U S consul at Hamburg.

Died: on Wed, in Wash City, Ebenezer Moore, in his 58th year.

Mr Adolph Eisenbeiss, of the firm of Eisenbeiss & Seitz, beer brewers, on Pa ave, near 13th st, was shot & killed yesterday. He had gone gunning with his son, age 9 or 10, & handed his gun to his son, giving him the stock. Unfortunately the gun was cocked, & the boy, in reaching for it, put his finger upon the trigger, causing the gun to explode, the charge taking effect in Mr Eisenbeiss' groin, causing death in about 3 minutes. He was about 38 years of age, & leaves a wife & 4 children to mourn their loss. [Oct 8th newspaper: The funeral of Mr Eisenbeiss took place yesterday & was attended by our German citizens & by Odd Fellows generally, Mr Eisenbeiss being a member of Oriental Lodge.]

Gtwn, Oct 1, 1866. Young Catholics' Friend Society of Gtwn: letter to Rev Alphonsus Charlier, S J, who is leaving Gtwn for another assignment by the Church. Tribute to Rev Charlier was signed Jas J Kane, Richd Pettit, & Peter O'Donoghue, cmte

Chas Kuntzner, a soldier belonging to **Fort Foote**, was firing a small cannon when the cartridge prematurely discharged, burning him about the face & hands. He was removed to the hotel immediately, & it is thought he should recover, but will loss one or both eyes.

Wm Lilley, atty at law, 468 6th st, has recently been appointed Com'r for the State of Calif.

Yesterday two ebony damsels, Jane Thomas & Mary King, went to Yates & Selby's dry goods store, on Pa ave, Wash, & were arrested for stealing clothes from the store. Both were committed to jail for court.

Col Chas Kingsbury, late assist adj general on Gen Sheridan's staff, died at Maysville, Ky, last week, of cholera.

Mary Cosgriff, better known as Mollie Trussell, was arraigned in the Supreme Court at Chicago on Monday, for the murder of Geo Trussell. Her bail was fixed at $5,000, which had not been given at last accounts.

Miss Mary Marshall, daughter of Mr Horace Marshall, residing near Clarksville, Tenn, on Tue last committed suicide by hanging herself.

At Fairmount Park, on Tue, Wm Edward, residing at 17 South Franklin st, was killed when 5 drunken outlaws drove down a hill, their wagon stricking Mr Edwards. He was hurled from the road; death was instanteous. –Phil News

Old **Fort Defiance** was erected one year previous to the war; located on C st-100 feet, & 125 feet on 11th st, & covers 12,000 feet of ground.

SAT OCT 6, 1866
The Pres made the following appointments yesterday; 1-H L Taylor, of Ill, agent for the Indians of the Shawnee agency. 2-J M Zerback, of Iowa, register of the land ofc at Sioux city.

The Pres has appointed Rolfe S Saunders, of the Memphis Daily Commercial, collector of internal revenue for the 8th district in Tenn.

Rev Michl Slattery, pastor of St Joseph's Catholic Church, in this city, died yesterday, at the clerical residence on Barre st, near Howard. He was a native of Ireland, but, coming at an early age to this country, was educated at St Mary's Seminary, in this city. In Feb last he had an attack of paralysis, since which time he has been in feeble health. His funeral is on Friday, at 9 A M. After a solemn High Mass his remains will be interred in the **Cemetery of the Holy Cross**, on the Hartford road. –Balt Sun, Oct 4.

The Cholera. Mrs Herzberg, residing on C st near 4½ st, was taken with the cholera & recovered. Mr Ebenezer Moore, aged 58, a clerk in the ofc of the Register of the Treasury, who resided at 469 C st, near 2nd, died on Thu from cholera.

Criminal Court-Judge Fisher, Oct 5, 1866. 1-Gustavus Peters: assault & battery: guilty. Fined $20. 2-Robt Ward: assault & resisting an ofcr: guilty. Motion for a new trial. 3-Josiah Burchead: assault & battery: guilty.

Mrd: on Oct 4, at Foundry M E Church, by Rev B P Brown, Mr Thos L Miller, of the Surgeon Gen's Ofc, to Miss Florence E Brandebury, daughter of Hon L G Brandebury.

Judson Palmer eloped with a daughter of Archibald Stephens, of Coeyman's Hollow Albany Co, N Y, & was pursued by the latter. They met on Thu, & commenced firing upon one another, when Stephens was killed & Palmer wounded. He managed to escape with the daughter.

A spiritualist, Richd Ayres, committed suicide on Sat in Pittsburgh, Pa, by hanging himself to the balustrade of the stairway in the 2nd floor of his residence. He leaves his wife, who found him hanging, quite dead.

The wife of John D Wager, of Ghent, committed suicide on Wed by hanging herself in an outhouse. She had been laboring under depression of spirits for some time. –Hudson, N Y

Appointment of Examing Surgeons: Dr Julien H Axelett, Tureola, Mich, & Dr Jas Wise, Cattlettsburg, Ky, have been appointed examining surgeons of pensioners.

New Light at **Sharp's Island**, Chesapeake Bay, Md: a new structure on piles has been erected in 7½ feet water, mean tide; it will be lighted for the first time on Oct 20, 1866; the iron work of the foundation is painted red-the superstructure is painted white.

John P McDermid, aged 25 years, committed suicide on Wed last, in Skowhegan, Me, by discharging a gun into his mouth.

Miss Caroline Brewer, aged about 70 years, died in the almshouse at Portland, Me, on Friday last. She had been an inmate there for the last 35 years. She had not spoken an intelligible word in all that time. Having been disappointed in love, she made a vow never to speak another word.

Moses B Williams,sr, of Boston, wholesale liquor dealer, shot himself at his residence in Brookline, & died on Thursday.

Mr Chas Billings, of Cincinnati, while laboring under a temporary fit of insanity, attempted to commit suicide by cutting her throat with a razor. She is not expected to recover.

Fred'k Bickmann, the first comic actor in Germany, died recently at Vienna.

John R Wigham, a clerk in the N Y post ofc, was arrested on Thu for abstracting registered letters from the mail bags. He had been under surveillance for some time.

Household & kitchen furniture at auction by order of the Orphans Court of D C, on Oct 10, the effects of the late Eliza Lamb. Sale of the contents of the 3 houses, being 203, 307, & 309, south side Pa ave, between 14th & 15th sts.
–Francis Lamb, adm -Jas C McGuire & Co, aucts

On Oct 15, we shall sell, on the premises, the beautiful private residence of John H Semmes, at the intersection of Md & Va aves, between 7th & 8th sts, [Island.] Also, bldg lots on 8th st; & on C st south. -Green & Williams, aucts

Supreme Court, D C. Jos Walsh against the widow & heirs of Jas H Fletcher. On Oct 15 next, I shall state the trustee's account & distribute the funds in hand. —W Redin, auditor

Supreme Court, D C. Henry E Gross & wife against Rosina Stiner & others, heirs of John A Smith. On Oct 15 next, I shall state the trustee's account & distribute the funds in hand, of said John A Smith. —W Redin, auditor

MON OCT 8, 1866

The Pres appointed Hon Lewis V Bogy, of St Louis, Com'r of Indian Affairs, vice Hon D N Cooley, who has resigned, to take effect Nov 1, 1866.

Orphans Court-Judge Purcell, Oct 6, 1866. 1-The will of the late John McDuell was filed & partially proven. He bequeathes his residence & furniture to his wife, & after her death to two of his daughters; another house to a third daughter, & nominated his wife as executrix. 2-The will of the late Michl Murphy, sailor, bequeathing the prize money due him, after the payment of his debts & funeral expenses, to Rev F X Boyle, & nominating John Carroll Brent as executor, was filed. 3-The nephews & heirs-at-law of Jemima Camer prayed the Court that there be sent to the Supreme Court the issues whether the said Jemima Camer was of sound mind at the time of executing the said paper; whether the same is the last will & testament of the deceased; whether undue influences were exerted upon the mind of the deceased to induce her to execute the said will. 4-Letters of administration were issued to Chas W Davis on the estate of Julia Catalane; bond $3,000. To Lucy Ann Johnson on the estate of Isaac Johnson; bond $300. 5-The first & final account of the admx of John T Meem, & an account of the personal estate of John T Meem, deceased.

Green & Williams, aucts, sold a 2 story frame dwlg, with back bldg attached, F & 4½ st, to P Cullinan, for $2,260; & a 2 story frame dwlg & lot on N J ave, between N & O sts north, to Ellen Olean, for $1,550.

Criminal Court-Judge Fisher, Oct 6, 1866. 1-In the cases of John Morgan, charged with assault & battery, & John Davis in two cases of larceny, a nolle pros was entered. 2-John Davis plead guilty to stealing $30 worth of clothing from Owen O'Hare & was sentenced to the Penitentiary for 1 year. 3-John Morgan, indicted for an assault & battery on Lavinia Pallen. Jury discharged: being unable to agree. 4-Henry Miller, indicted for the larceny of a silver pitcher from Margaret J Harrover, was convicted, & sentenced to 18 months in jail. 5-Wm Adams was convicted of an assault & battery, & received a nominal sentence.

Louis Gozlan, one of the best novel writers in France, died suddenly, a few weeks since, aged 63.

A despatch from Chicago says that on Thu the wife of Robt Simms, a farmer, living in Lenawee Co, Mich, took her 4 children into the barn & cut their throats with a razor, afterwards cutting her own throat with the same weapon. Three of the children & the woman are dead, & the fourth child cannot recover. The woman is supposed to be insane. [Oct 10th newspaper: Medina, Mich, Oct 4. On Oct 3, on the farm of Mr Robt F Simms, a wealthy farmer, residing in a beautiful homestead, lived the family of Mr Simms, his wife & 4 children. For several years past Mrs Simms has been afflicted with temporary fits of melancholy & would shut herself up in her apartment refusing to admit anyone, even her children. A few months ago she started to beat her infant with a poker, but a servant rescued the child. The murdered children were: a boy age 9, & 2 girls aged 4 & 7 years, & an infant.]

A little boy, 4 years of age, the child of Mr Moses Tapley, accidentally overturned a stove, containing fire, yesterday, in his father's house, on Water st, & was so severely burned that he died last night.

On Nov 6, 1789, Pope Pius VI founded the See of Balt, & appointed Rev John Carroll archbishop. The first synod was attended by 21 priests; first priest ordained in the U S was Stephen Theodore Badin. On May 25, 1793, Bishop Carroll died at age 80 years. In 1829 Archbishop Whitfield held a provincial council at Balt. The prelates who assembled there were Rt Rev Benedict Jos Flaget, bishop of Bardstown, Ky; Rt Rev John England, bishop of Charleston; Rt Rev Edw Fenwick, bishop of Cincinnati; Rt Rev Rosati, bishop of St Louis, & Rt Rev Benedict Fenwick, bishop of Boston. The second Provinical Council was convened by Archbishop Whitfield, on Oct 20, 1833. The following prelates were present: Rt Rev John B David, coadjutor of Bardstown, Ky; Rt Rev John England, bishop of Charleston; Rt Rev Rosati, bishop of St Louis; Rt Rev Benedict Fenwick, bishop of Boston; Rt Rev John Dubois, bishop of N Y; Rt Rev Michl Portier, bishop of Mobile; Rt Rev Francis P Kenrick, coadjutor of Phil; Rt Rev Fred'k Rese, bishop of Detroit; Rt Rev John Purcell, bishop of Cincinnati. The fourth Provincial Council was held at Balt in 1840, & was convened by Most Rev Saml Eccleston, archbishop of Balt, & attended by 11 prelates. The fifth Provincial Council was held at Balt in 1843, & was convoked by Archbishop Eccleston, & attended by 16 prelates. The sixth Council, May 10, 1846, & the seventh Council, May 6, 1849, were both convened by Most Rev Archbishop Eccleston in Balt.

Balt, Oct 7. On Sat a shooting affray in a public house resulted in the death of a man named Benj F Jones, & the wounding of Geo Goodrich & John Betz, the latter seriously. Wm S Richardson gave himself up as the party who fired the pistol, claiming to have done so in self defence. The coroner's jury discharged him. The affray grew out of political excitement.

Chicago, Oct 5. Augustus Dickens, brother of Chas Dickens, the novelist, lately in the land dept of the Illinois Central Railroad, died here today, of dysentery.

Police Matters: 1-Nathan Brown & Wm Henry, two American citizens of African descent, were arrested by Ofcrs Leech & Frazier on a charge of stealing 2 valuable steers belonging to Mr Z Shaw, of Bladensburg. The steers were sold for $75 each, & the accused were held for a further hearing. 2-Michl Ledam proposed to prepare for cold weather by stealing coal from one of the wharves in Gtwn. Ofcr Harper arrested him. 3-Geo Wilder, better known as Curley George, arrested in Wash for an offence in Alexandria some days ago, & who was delivered to a Virginia ofcr, on a requisition from the Govn'r, escaped from the ofcr on his way to Alexandria. Last night he was re-arrested by Ofcrs Warwick & Miles; he will be conveyed to Alexandria for trial.

Albany, Oct 5. Last evening two young ladies, Miss Hattie Hewitt & Mrs Theresa Heath, were struck by the steamboat express train, at the street crossing in Amsterdam. They were stending on the track waiting for a freight train passing West. Miss Hewitt had both her feet crushed off & was otherwise seriously injured. Mrs Heath is not badly hurt.

Chas Tucker, a stranger, from Detroit, Mich, was robbed in N Y on Tue night of $3,000 out of $5,000, which he had brought there to invest in Gov't securities. Mary Jane McDougal, the daughter of respectable parents, her father being a member of the metropolitan police force, was arrested on suspicion of having committed the theft.

Balt, Oct 7, 1866, opening of the grand Nat'l Council of the Catholic Church of the U S; Most Rev Archbishop Spalding invited the members of the hierarchy to convene here. Mitred Abbots: Rt Rev Boniface Wirner, abbott of St Vincent's; Rt Rev Maria Benedict, abbot of La Trappe; Rt Rev Ephesus McDonnell, abbot of the Cistercian abbey of La Trappe.
Province of Balt:
Diocese of Balt: Most Rev Martin John Spalding, D D, consecrated Sep 10, 1848; translated to this diocese Jul 31, 1864.
Diocese of Charleston: Rt Rev P N Lynch, D D, consecrated Mar 14, 1858.
Diocese of Phil: Rt Rev Jas E Wood, D D, consecrated-Apr 26, 1857.
Diocese of Pittsburgh: Rt Rev Michl Domene, D D, consecrated Dec 9, 1860.
Diocese of Richmond: Rt Rev John McGill, D D, consecrated Dec 10, 1850.
Diocese of Savannah: Rt Rev Augustine Verot, D D, consecrated Apr 25, 1858; translated to this see in 1861.
Diocese of Wheeling: Rt Rev Richd V Whelan, D D, consecrated Mar 21, 1841; translated to this see in 1850.
Vicariate Apostolic of East Florida: Rt Rev Augustine Verot, D D.
Province of Cincinnati:
Diocese of Cincinnati: Most Rev John B Purcell, D D, consecrated Oct 13, 1833. Rt Rev S Rosecrans, auxiliary bishop.

Diocese of Cleveland: Rt Rev Amadeus Rappe, D D, consecrated Oct 10, 1847.
Diocese, of Covington: Rt Rev Geo A Carroll, D D, consecrated Nov 1, 1853.
Diocese of Detroit: Rt Rev Peter P Lefevre, D D, administrator, consecrated Nov 21, 1841.
Diocese of *Fort Wayne*: Rt Rev John H Luers, D D, consecrated Jan 10, 1858.
Diocese of Louisville: Rt Rev P J Lavialle, D D, consecrated Sep 24, 1865.
Diocese of Saut Sainte Marie: Rt Rev Fred'k Barags, D D, consecrated Nov 1, 1853; translated to this see Jan 9, 1847.
Diocese of Vincennes: Rt Rev Maurice de St Palais, D D, consecrated Jan 14, 1849.

Province of New Orleans:
Diocese of New Orleans: Most Rev John M Odin, D D, consecrated Mar 6, 1842; translated to this diocese in 1861.
Diocese of Galveston: Rt Rev M Dubois, consecrated Nov 23, 1862.
Diocese of Little Rock: vacant.
Diocese of Mobile: Rt Rev John Quinlan, D D, consecrated Dec 5, 1859.
Diocese of Natchez: Rt Rev Wm H Elder, D D, consecrated May 3, 1857.
Diocese of Natchitoches: Rt Rev Augustus Martin, D D, consecrated Nov 30, 1853.

Province of N Y:
Diocese of N Y: Most Rev John McCloskey, D D, consecrated Mar 10, 1844; translated to this diocese Aug 21, 1864.
Diocese of Albany: Rt Rev John J Conroy, D D, consecrated Oct 15, 1865.
Diocese of Boston: Rt Rev John B Fitzpatrick, D D, consecrated Mar 24, 1844; translated to this see Aug 11, 1845.
Diocese of Brooklyn: Rt Rev John Laughlin, D D, consecrated Oct 30, 1853.
Diocese of Burlington: Rt Rev Louis De Goesbriand, D D, consecrated Oct 30, 1853.
Diocese of Hartford: Rt Rev Francis P McFarland, D D, consecrated Mar 14, 1858.
Diocese of Newark: Rt Rev Jas R Bayley, D D, consecrated Oct 30, 1853.
Diocese of Portland: Rt Rev David W Bacon, D D, consecrated Apr 22, 1855.

Province of Oregon:
Diocese of Oregon: Most Rev Francis N Blanchet, D D, consecrated Jul 23, 1845.
Diocese of Nesqually: Rt Rev Augustine M A Blanchet, D D, consecrated Sep 27, 1846; translated to this see Jul 28, 1850.
Diocese of Vancouver's Island: Rt Rev Modest Demers, D D.
Vicariate Apostolic of Columbia: Rt Rev Aloysius Jos d'Herbomez, D D, bishop of Metropolis, in partibus infidetium.

Province of St Louis:
Diocese of St Louis: Most Rev Peter R Kenrick, D D, consecrated Nov 30, 1841.
Diocese of Alton: Rt Rev Henry D Juncker, D D, consecrated Apr 26, 1857.
Diocese of Chicago: Rt Rev Jas Dugan, D D, consecrated May 3, 1857; tranlated to this see Aug 21, 1859.
Diocese of Dubuque: Rt Rev Hennessy.
Diocese of Milwaukie: Rt Rev John M Henni, D D, consecrated Mar 19, 1844.

Diocese of Nashville: Rt Rev P A Feehan, D D, consecrated Oct 1, 1865.
Diocese of Santa Fe: Rt Rev John Lamy, D D, consecrated Nov 21, 1850.
Diocese of St Paul: Rt Rev Thos L Grace, D D, consecrated Jul 20, 1859.
Vicariate Apostolic of the Indian territory, east of Rocky Mountains: Rt Rev John B Miege, D D, bishop of Messenia in part, consecrated Mar 25, 1851.
Vicariate Apostolic of Nebraska: Rt Rev Jas O'Gorman, consecrated May 5, 1859.

Province of San Francisco:
Diocese of San Francisco: Most Rev Jos S Alemany, D D, O S D, consecrated bishop to Monterey Jun 10, 1850; translated to this see Jul 29, 1853.
Diocese of Los Angelos: Rt Rev Thaddeus Amat, D D, consecrated Mar 1, 1854.
Vicariate apostolic, Marysville: Rt Rev Eugene O'Connel, D D, consecrated Feb 3, 1861.

TUE OCT 9, 1866
U S Marshal's sale: by writ of fieri facias isued from the clerk's ofc of the Supreme Court of D C: public sale on Oct 25, of part of lot 10 in square 431, fronting on E st; also, part of lot 9 in square 431, on 8th st, & all of said lot 9 not heretofore conveyed to W W Seaton to Nathan Smith by deed, dated Aug 13, 1822, recorded in Liber W B No 6, folio 165; seized & levied upon as the property of W W Seaton, & will be sold to satisfy execution in favor of John F Coyle, use of Henry S Davis, against W W Seaton, surviving partner of Jos Gales. –D S Gooding, U S Marshal

Criminal Court-Judge Fisher, Oct 8, 1866. 1-Mary Lyle: larceny: verdict, guilty. Sentence: 18 months in Albany penitentiary. 2-Louis Martin: guilty of stealing meal valued at $4.80. Sentence: 7 days in jail. 3-Jas Hudson: not guilty of assault & battery with intent to kill. 4-Josiah Burchead: heretofore convicted. Sentence: 24 hours in the county jail. 5-R H Rousseau: guilty of assault.

In Equity Court yesterday Judge Wylie granted a decree divorcing Victoria A J Forrest from the bonds of matrimony with Zachariah Forrest. The custody of the children are given to cmplnt, Mr Forrest, & she is allowed to resume her maiden name of Wooster. The cost are to be paid by the dfndnt. M Thompson, for cmplnt.

Died: on Oct 1, suddenly, at his residence, **Eagle's Nest**, in King Geo Co, Va, Thos J J Grimes, in his 42nd year. An affectionate husband, indulgent father, & friendly neighbor. Mr Grimes died as he had always lived, without an enemy on earth.

Augusta, Oct 8. A stranger named Mr McAuley was assassinated & robbed here on Sat night. John Geo Harley, of Little Rock, Ark, was committed to jail on suspicion of having committed the deed.

Boston, Oct 7. First Nat'l Bank of Yarmouthport was robbed of $75,000, & the crime was perpetrated by a son of the cashier of the bank. The father, Amos Otis, discovered the money missing; the son, Geo Otis, was arrested at Plymouth the next day. The father is a respected citizen of Vermouthport. It is probable that young Otis, about 21, an employe in the bank, will be held to bail.

Princeton, N J, Oct 8. Cmdor Stockton died here last night. His funeral takes place at 2 o'clock Wednesday afternoon.

John S Rarey, the horse trainer, died suddenly at Clevelandon Oct 4. Last Dec he had a stroke of paralysis; on Thu he left the *Waddell House* for a walk, but soon returned, complaining of a pain in the head. He died an hour later. Mr Rarey was a native of Franklin Co, Ohio, where he was borne in 1828. His remains were taken for burial to Groveport, Ohio, where he resided on a fine stock farm which he owned near there.

The N Y World of yesterday: fire destroyed the entire of **St Patrick's Cathedral** in N Y C. All priests of the church, with great bravery during the whole time the bldg was burning, entered the edifice in search of the vessels after the roof had begun to fall through. Work on the Cathedral was commenced in 1811, & was not completed until 1817, when it was opened with great pomp & ceremony. Bishop Culcannon was appointed by the Pope to preside over this diocese, but never lived to see the city, he having died before reaching this country. Bishop Dubois, Archbishop Hughes, & Bishop McClosky have each in turn officiated in the Cathedral. Bishop Hughes enlarged the Cathedral in 1838-39, & it was capable of seating 3,000 persons; it was the second oldest Catholic church in the metropolis. Sheriff Kelley said the loss on the bldg will not fall short of $150,000; there is insurance of $40,000; the organ, erected in 1853, valued at $12,000, was totally destroyed, insured for $6,000. All the vestments, chalices, plates & books were removed before the flames could reach them. There were about 500 men, women, & children during the progress of the fire engaged in bringing out the movable articles. There was no distubance to the burial vaults underneath the structure, wherein lie the venerated remains of three eminent prelates.

The copartnership existing between the late W E Stubbs & C B Bayly, under the name of C B Bayly & Co, was dissolved on Sep 21, by mutual consent. Chas B Bayly will continue the boot & shoe business at the old stand, 278 Pa ave, between 11th & 12th sts.

Home School: Under the care of Miss Eliza C Adam, will be opened on Wash & Prince sts, Alexandria, Va, on Sep 20. Boarders will be limited to 8, & no day scholars received. Every home comfort will be provided: $250 per annum, payable semi-annually in advance. Miss Eliza C Adam

Fortress Monroe, Oct 8. The British steamer **Queen Victoria** foundered at sea on Oct 4. The passengers & crew were picked up yesterday by the brig **Pomfret**, from N Y, & 35 were transferred this morning to the steamer **James Gary**, from Wilmington, for Balt, which arrived in the Chesapeake Bay this afternoon. The engineer died from exposure, & the mate was washed overboard. [No names.] The storm commenced on Oct 2, & the steamer sprung a leak on Oct 3. The ship **H Braband**, 56 days from Bremen, with 320 emigrants, bound for Balt, arrived in the Chesapeake today. All well.

Gen Beauregard arrived in Balt on Sunday.

First Lt H B Beecher, son of Rev Henry Ward Beecher, has resigned his commission in the 4th regt regular artl.

A little daughter of Judge John H Little, of Springfield, Ohio, fell into a hogshead of water on Friday morning, & was drowned before her absence from the house was discovered.

Obit-died: on Sep 29, in Wash, D C, in his 49th year, Dr Saml Clement Smoot. He was born in Wash City, Feb 3, 1818; in 1835 he graduated at the Columbian College. As a husband & father, as a brother & friend, few men are called to so extended responsibility as Dr Smoot assumed. His younger brother, Chas Henry, died in Dec, 1845, & soon after he was publicly baptised & united with the E st Baptist Church. In May, 1846, he married Miss Emma Smallwood.

Dept of the Interior, U S Patent Ofc, Wash, Oct 2, 1866. Ptn of Robt W Andrews, of Staffordville, Conn, praying for the extension of a patent granted to him on Jan 18, 1853, for an improvement in operating the Treadles of Looms, for 7 years from the expiration of said patent, which takes place on Jan 18, 1867.
–T C Theaker, Com'r of Patents

Orphans Court of Wash Co, D C. Letters of administration on the personal estate of Julia Catalaro, late of Wash, D C, deceased. –Chas W Davis, adm

WED OCT 10, 1866
Meeting of the Soldiers & Sailors who have been Prisoners in the south Society was called to order by Col B F Fisher, pres, pro tem. Cmte on Nominations reported the following ticket: for Pres, Col B F Fisher, by ballot; vice Pres, Maj Henry J Nowlan Thompson; rec sec, Capt Jas P Perley; cor sec, Capt S S Stearns; marshal, L Weiser, viva voce. On motion Brig Gen Lasselle, Capt Harris, & Capt Michener were appointed a cmte to examine & report as to suitable room for purposes of association.

Criminal Court-Judge Fisher, Oct 9, 1866. 1-Wm C Snowden: assault & battery with intent to kill: verdict guilty. Sentenced to 2 years in Albany penitentiary. 2-Fred'k Mahoney, Jas Becket, & Cornelius Banks: riot & affray: not guilty.

Messrs Kilbourn & Latta, real estate brokers, 7th & F sts, sold brick house & lot at 19th & G st, to Clement Hill, for $11,350 cash. Lot 15 in sq 629, on L st, between No Capitol & 1st sts west, for $255 cash, to Salena Cook. Green & Williams, aucts, sold part of lot 30 in sq 117, L st, between 20th & 21st sts, to W B Todd for 12 cents per foot.

Equity Court-Judge Wylie, Oct 5, 1866. Johanna McCarthy vs Dennis McCarthy. This is an application for divorce a vinculo matrimonii. The ptn sets forth that the parties were married in the county of Cork, in 1848; that they lived togethere there until 1853 when the dfndt sailed for America. He wrote her one letter about 10 months afterwards, & until recently, she ascertained that about 10 years ago he married another woman in Richmond; that he is now, & has been for the last 3 or 4 years, living & cohabiting with the said woman as his wife, in this city, & by her he has 3 or 4 children. The Court granted a rule to be served upon the dfndt to show cause why he should not pay the petitioner alimony, pendente lite, also her counsel fees, & expenses of the suit, & also why he should not be restrained by injunction from selling, assisting,or otherwise disposing of his property, [amounting it is alleged in the ptn, to about $10,000,] until the further order of the Court. On last Sat, while detained in the ofc of Justice Handy upon a charge of bigamy, the petitioner & her daughter & 2 sons of a former deceased husband appeared & confronted him, whereupon the Justice held him to bail in the sum of $3,000 for his appearance at the Criminal Court to answer the charge of bigamy. J M Thompson & C C Callan solicitors for the petitioner.

Orphans Court-Judge Purcell, Oct 9, 1866. 1-First & final account of Ann Kelly, admx of the estate of Patrick Kelly, deceased, was approved & passed. 2-First account of J B H Smith, exc of the estate of Anna M Thornton, deceased, was approved & passed. 3-Rosa Eisenbeiss qualified as the admx of the estate of Adolph Eisenbeiss, deceased. Bond $2,000. Sureties, John Vogt & Jos Whitman. The same party also gave bond in the sum of $1,500, with the same sureties, as guardian to Bertha & Emma, minor daughters of Adolph Eisenbeiss, deceased. 4-Nicholas Callan was appointed administrator of the estate of Nathl J Lynde, deceased, & qualified by giving bond in the sum of $1,000. Sureties: Thos Woodward & Tobias Boudinot. 5-Maria E _ King qualified as admx of the estate of Henry King, late of Gtwn, deceased. Bond $600. Sureties: John L Kidwell & Wm F Howard. 6-Emma Smoot qualified a admx of the estate of Saml C Smoot, deceased. Bond $6,000. Sureties: Danl R Hagner & Geo W Samson. Mrs Smoot also qualified as guardian of Kenneth R & Matilda, orphans of S C Smoot, deceased. Bond $4,000. Same securities.

Appointments by the Pres: 1-John Seys, of Ohio, to be Minister Resident & Consul General of the U S to the Republic of Liberia. 2-Chas Seymour, of N Y; Wm A B Budd, of N Y; & Enoch R Mudge, of Mass, to be Com'rs to the Paris Exposition.

Died: on Oct 4, at his late residence, Prospect Hill, PG Co, Md, John H Stine, formerly of St Mary's Co, in his 47th year.

Thanksgiving. Proclamation issued by the Pres of the U S. Almighty God, our heavenly Father, has been pleased to vouchsafe to us as a people another year of that national life which is an indispensable condition of peace, security, & progress. The civil war that so recently closed among us, has not been anywhere reopened. Now, therefore, I, Andrew Johnson, Pres of the U S, do hereby recommend that Thursday, Nov 20th next, be set apart & be observed everywhere in the several States & Territories of the U S by the people thereof, as a day of thanksgiving & praise to Almight God. –Andrew Johnson, Pres of the U S -Wm H Seward, Sec of State

Mr Alonzo Mays, a young man employed as a fireman on one of the locomotives of the Orange & Alexandria Railroad, in jumping from the train on Sat, in Lynchburg, slipped, & falling upon the track, was run over & almost instantly killed.

From a private letter from Memphis, we learn that young Mr Oliver Crook, who left here this fall for that city, died there last week of Asiastic cholera. All who contemplate visiting Memphis are urgently advised to postpone their trip until the entire disappearance of that disease.

Train on the Illinois Central Railroad thrown off the track yesterday, at Little Muddy, 18 miles below Centralia: Alonzo George, engineer, was killed. Henry Cunningham, fireman, was severely scalded. –Chicago Times, Oct 4.

N Y Tribune: from Topeka, Kansas, dated Friday. Frank Kilby & Chas Smith, stock tenders for Holladay's Overland State Co, were murdered by Indians on Sat last at Chalk Bluffs, a station on the Smoky Hill route, 100 miles west of **Fort Ellsworth**. After the Indians demanded something to eat, & were given it, they went off. Later they returned & shot one with a revolver, & killed the other with a lance.

Female Bookkeepers in New England. The Shoe & Leather Reporter says: we notice a majority of young ladies employed as bookkeepers & accountants. They are more generally reliable than the other sex, careful correspondents, are not liable to have loafers in the counting room, smoking their employer's cigars during his absence, & last, perhaps not least, don't spend his money playing billiards, drinking or driving fast horses.

The late Ebenezer Moore, who died on Oct 3, was a graduate of Bowdoin College in 1832; admitted to the bar in his native State, Maine; removed to Illinois & commenced the practise of law; accumulating by his professional labors a handsome property. He was a liberal & consistent member of the Episcopal communion, & long filled the ofc of vestryman in his native parish.

Mr Wilkie Collins, who is reported to be threatened with consumption, is travelling in the south of Europe for his health.

On Tue of last week the house of Jas M Pinneger, of Greenwich, R I, was entered by a rogue, who robbed a trunk there of $4,600, & successfully escaped.

Savannah, Oct 9. During the gale in which the schnr **Veto** was damaged, B S Miller, of Long Island, [second ofcr,] was washed overboard & lost.

Chambersburg [Pa] Repository. Mrs Mary Andrews died at Strasburg, this county, on 22nd ult, at the advanced age of 105 years. What a long, long, weary pilgrimage!

Orphans Court of Wash Co, D C. Letters of administration on the personal estate of Saml C Smoot, M D, late of Wash, D C, deceased. –Emma Smoot

Orphans Court of Wash Co, D C, Oct 9, 1865. In the case of Walter S Cox, adm w a of Mary Stevenson, the administrator w a & Court have appointed Nov 3 next, for the final settlement of the personal estate of the said deceased, of the assets in hand. -Z C Robbins, Reg/o wills

For sale: valuable tract of wood land, containing 551 acres, in PG Co, adjoining the estates of Mr Lemuel I Middleton & Mr Wm Rozier. –W I Beall, Upper Marlboro, PG Co, Md.

THU OCT 11, 1866
Pardons of the following named persons have been ordered by the Pres: 1-Jas W Addison, convicted at the Mar Term, 1866, of the U S Dist Court for the Dist of Mass, of stealing letters from the post ofce, & sentenced to 10 years in prison. 2-J R Rickoly, convicted at the Dec term, 1866, of the U S Dist Court for the Southern Dist of N Y, of presenting for payment false & fraudulent vouchers of the U S, & sentenced to 1 year in prison.

The following appointments of revenue ofcrs were made yesterday: Anthony Rickles, assessor for the 2nd Dist of N J; Jas G Knight, assessor for the 3rd Dist of Wisc; Jesse J Alexander, collector for the 7th Dist of Indiana.

Criminal Court-Judge Fisher, Oct 10, 1866. 1-Walter Smith: larceny: verdict-guilty of stealing shoes valued at $4.50. Sentence: 1 day in jail the accused having been incarcerated 3 months. 2-Henry May: assault & battery: verdict-guilty. 3-Danl Kreamer: larceny: verdict-not guilty. 4-Peter Brady: renting a house for disorderly & baudy purposes: verdict-not guilty. 5-Catharine Downs: larceny: verdict-guilty. Sentenced to 18 months at Albany Penitentiary. 6-Courtney Moore: assault & battery: verdict guilty. Sentence: fined $25, & 20 days imprisonment.]

Rev Arthur Waring, of this State, a missionary of the Baptist Church, died suddenly in this city yesterday. He was in church the day before.

Mrd: on Oct 9, by Rev Fr Hitselberger, S J, at the residence of Capt J H Goddard, in Wash City, Mr John B Simmons, of Rhode Island, to Miss Maggie A Shaw, of Wash City.

Mrd: on Oct 9, at Rocheaumont Park, on the Hudson, the residence of the bride's father, by Rev A J F Behrends, Mr Jas L Hatch, of Rochester, N Y, to Miss Nellie, daughter of Dr Edw Maynard, formerly of Wash, D C. No cards.

Died: on Oct 5, in Gtwn, D C, of typhoid fever, Dr Ellis Hughes, formerly of Annapolis, Md, & son of the late Jeremiah Hughes, of Balt. He was at one time demonstrator of anatomy in the Univ of Md.

Died: on Oct 4, at his late residence, **Prospect Hill**, PG Co, Md, John H Stine, formerly of St Mary's Co, in his 47th year.

On Monday last Eugene Jacobs, colored, aged 15 years, died at his father's residence, in <u>Blagden's alley</u>, in the square between 9th & 10th & M & N sts. He left a younger brother home to visit an acquaintance, Henry Harris, the capt of a wood-boat plying between this city & Occoquan, who entertained a liking for Eugene, & frequently took him with him down the river. While unloading the boat with his friend, Eugene became ill & took 2 pills given to him by Harris. He then began to rave & was thrown into a stupor from which he never recovered. He was carried home & died that evening. The druggist who it is alleged sold the pills asserted that such as he sold contained nothing but quinine; & he seemed to doubt that he had sold the pills given by Harris to the deceased. Further investigation will be done to settle the cause of the boy's death.

Wash Improvements: a handsome, modern built brick house, the property of S A H Marks, of the Quartetmaster's Dept, Marine Corps, is about being finished at 398 south G st east, by Geo A Barr, bldr & contractor. The ornamental plaster work is designed by John Keiler, plasterer; plumbing by Messrs Brown & Powers. The bldg is entirely separated from the kitchen, &, alone will cost about $13,000.

Police Items. 1-Justice Drury fined Harrison Bunday, cart driver, $1.50 for obstructing Pa ave, by unloading bricks carelessly. 2-Dennis Burns, keeper of a tavern & grocery store at 27th & K sts, was fined $30 for keeping his place of business open & selling liquor on Sunday. 3-John Garner, a notoriously bad boy, was arrested at the instance of Michl McCormick, a newsboy, who charges the accused with stealing about $50 from his person while asleep at the Chronicle ofc. About $44 of the money, which Garner had taken home, was recovered. The accused was committed to answer.

Boston Commercial: Maria Cavanaugh & Hannah McLaughlin, each about 20, attempted suicide by jumping into the water from Cragle's Bridge. Jos Bradley & John Barrett, seamen, who were in the schnr **Valor**, immediately picked them up. Drs Richardson & McDonald were called, who, after considerable difficulty, succeeded in the resuscitation of the McLaughlin girl, who is slowly recovering. The body of Maria Cavanaugh was taken to the Dead House.

N Y Herald, Oct 10. Disaster-loss of the steamship **Evening Star**. Many experienced seamen express grave doubts as to the truth of the disaster to the **Evening Star**. Capt Knapp had been long time known, but had not been in active service for 2 years-retired, but providing for the family necessitated his return to his old profession. His wife dreaded some accident would happen to him while at sea. The capt's last request at the ofc was that when they heard from the vessel they would telegraph his wife; she lives in Springfield, Conn. Only two of the 6 lifeboats have been heard of at Savannah. List of passengers: Gen H C Palfrey, lady, child, & servant; Miss Palfrey, Miss Sloo, Mrs E Vansickle, Mrs J T Mason, Frank R Dennis, Mr Haborow, Mr Rockwell, John Touro, Mrs John J Adams, Mrs W H Robbins, Miss Lilly Parker, Miss Minnie Taylor, Miss Addie Norton, Miss Rosa Burns, Miss S Sterrett, Mrs J King, Mrs G T Philbin, Miss Julia Munroe, Miss A Clibband, A Goett & wife, Mrs S F Gordon, Mrs Spangenberg & 3 servants, Alex'r & Alfred Landlors, Mrs Henry Newell & daughter, Geo Hillman & son, Miss Margaret Hillman, D Pretto & wife, Mrs Gillespie & daughter, Jas Golifer &wife, Mr Ehenest, Mr Tapain & wife, Miss Tapain, O Destorbuy & wife, Miss Lagnement, Miss H Straus, Miss J Posonby, Henry T Crocheron, Miss Belinda Meserole, Mrs Severa, T Coignard & S Robert, Mr Solomon Myers, Miss G L Conme, Mrs S C Fraser & aunt, Jonathan Havens & lady, C C Ackerman, J Poiglars, J J Hercoy, F T Fontaubleau, S J Depeirris, Herman Spader, Chas T Low, G T Whit, J M Davidson, J Monroe Pell, S M Barlow, Frank Dennison, T Mery, Mr & Mrs N G Vila, Jas Harkness, jr, Geo Fisher, Capt Wm Chipman, S E Smith, Harry H Register, Martin T Hall, Isaac Harper, Jas McGuire, Miss Caillant, Miss L de Monpierre, Miss Amelia Ferne, Miss Josephine Campana, Messrs J Mindbled, C Fisher, Miss Destorbuy, Miss Eva Krepps, Miss Nellie Levere, Miss Mary Hudson, Mrs Elodie Girard, Miss G Ferney, Miss E Durand, Mrs J Darnery, Miss J M Ster, Mrs T Masic, Miss T Campana, T Dessormes, Miss T Aorel, Miss Celine Cayot, Mr & Mrs Codpim, Mr & Mrs Caillant, Ch Alnaya & lady, Mrs Chenup, S Francis, Mrs G Thomas, Henry Smith, Miss Quatorse, V Michel, Mrs N Frontier, H Humboldt, Miss H Jeremol, Mr LaFontaine, Mr & Mrs P Polydor, G Harrison, Miss Jane T Moran, Miss Helen Pomeroy, J H Dupasseur, John T Martin, Miss T Clotain, Miss H Renout, Miss G Reed, Miss T Benidetti, J C Envry, S M Parigot, T Buvan, Mrs N Doyle, H D Heartnes, John Perchal, S Morenschelager, T Laquenment, J L Stram, John Gelser, Ferd H Stutt, Harrison Quinan, Jas Bonffe, S Ferne, Geo Sandal, John Harper, Jeremiah Franconia, Geo Estell, Miss Emily Devlin, D B Small, Miss Mary Duvall,Leopold Schwerin, John J Reed, Paul Julien, H F Ninage, Chas Puckdeschel & daughter, Jos & Theresa Ulrich, Mrs S Geiser & child, Mrs N Doyle, Miss Caroline Glanner, Miss Mary Lyman, Barbara & Julia Cornia, Edw

O'Brien & child, Franklin Smith, Harvey Crowther.

Storage Passengers: Mrs A F Spanginberg's 2 servants, Mrs Geiser & child, Caroline Glanner, Maria Julian, Theresa Ulrich, Barbara Fortzer, Frederika Shaffer, Ellen Heron, Wm Hotley, Mr Berthold, Miss Mary Farley, Catharine Galligan, Dr Johnson, Mrs Johnson, Peter Rosmassen, E F Corning, A Crampton, Catharine McGinn, Edw Martin, L Hawkings, W H Roucher.

List of the crew of that vessel: Wm Knapp, capt; David Burr, mate; Wm Goldie, 2nd mate; Thos Fitzpatrick, boatswain; E L Allen, purser; Frank Gill, Chas Spencer, John Powers, Lewis Jago, Jas Howe, Jas Hogan, Frank Groge, Thos Higgins, John Campbell, Geo Smith, Matthew Golder, & John Dempsey, seamen; Patrick Sutherwood, mess boy; Robt Finger, engineer; L Finger, 1st assist engineer; Andrew McMahon, 2nd do; John Lang, John H Cole, & Jas P Russell, water-tenders, Saml Duffy, Franck Meerchan, Wm Sempsey, Wm Rogers, Patrick Gary, & John Cavanagh, firemen; Gustaye Aclone, Fred'k Schaffer, John Schaffer, Geo Newman, Wm Sterling, Frank Andersack, Thos Ryan, Frank Miller, & Henry Heron, coal-passers; Geo Lawlor, messman; Diley, steward; P Lee, 2nd do; Mary Hazzle, John Wynkoop, cooks; John Perry, 2nd cook; Wm Roberts, 3rd cook; Jas Fitzpatrick, pastry cook; Wm Jones, pantryman; Wm Driscoll, 2nd do; Simeon Fanning, porter; August Geizelburst, storekeeper; Martin Brett, butcher; Matthew Graham, Dennis Gannon, Wm Lawrence, Ed Potter, Ed Trevelin, Henry Vaughan, John Haywood, Dennis Graham, Isaac Cox, Ronald Stevens, waiters; Chauncey Mason, steerage steward.

Among the prominent passengers was Gen H W Palfrey, long & favorably known as a real estate auctioneer in New Orleans, & occupying the rank of General in the Louisiana State Militia. With him were his wife & child. Miss Soo, was the daughter of Thos Sloo, Pres of the Sun Mutual Ins Co, of New Orleans, & niece of the gentleman to whom the original grant across the Isthmus of Nicaragua was made. D Pretto was a member of the firm of Wolf & Co of N Y, & of New Orleans. He had just returned from Europe, & was proceeding home with his wife, who had come to N Y for the purpose of accompanying him on the trip back. The New Orleans Opera Troupe: Among the passengers was the opera troupe of Mr Paul Alhaiza, comprising 59 signers, artistes, & musicians, whom the manager had engaged in Paris. Mr Alhaiza & his company reached this city on Thu, the 27th ult, by the steamer **Ville de Paris**. Having put up at a hotel to await the departure of the **Evening Star**, the following persons took passage for New Orleans on Sat following their arrival in N Y: Mr Cuesnest, Mr Tapian, wife & child, O D'Esterbeco, wife & child, Mme Elodie Girard, Mr & Mrs Ferne, Miss E Durand, Miss J M Sten, Mrs Mario, Miss Marita Campana & servant, Miss Bord, Mr Raymond, Mr & Mrs Coppini, Mr Chas Alhaiza, Miss T Clovam, Miss Renoug, Miss G Read, Miss Benedetti, Miss Lacquement, Miss Strausse, Miss A Ferne, Mr G Saverac, Mr T Coignard, Mr S Robert, Mr & Mrs V G Volla, Mr & Mrs Cailland, Mrs Caillot, Mr G Fischer, Mr T Baban, & some 29 others, whose names do not appear on the list of passengers at the company's ofc. Mr Paul Alhaiza, the manager, was strongly advised to convey his artist to New Orleans by rail, but fearing that the voyage would prove too fatiguing for the ladies of the troupe, he decided not, however, secured his own berth on board, but proceeded to New Orleans by land, thus avoiding a sad fate. While in Paris Mr Alhaiza received the news of his father's death, & loss of a brother 2 weeks later. His second brother, Mr Chas Alhaiza, was one of the passengers by the **Evening Star**. Dr Spaulding's Circus Co, numbering about 30 persons, was also on board. 97 girls between the ages of 15 to 22 were among the unfortunates. These had been engaged for sundry houses of ill-game in New Orleans. The **Evening Star** was the sister of the boat **Morning Star**.

Ofcr John Hipwell, of the 45th Precinct, was shot at his post about 3 o'clock A M yesterday, & by an unknown hand, & expired almost immediately. Hipwell was in his 42nd year of his age; a native of N J; & leaves a wife & 4 children.
–N Y Times

Capt Alonzo Greenlaw, of Memphis, who recently killed a young man named Taylor in a duel, attempted to commit suicide on Sat by shooting himself in the breast. He has a severe though not a fatal wound. Remorse, he says, is the cause.

Gen Frank Blair attempted to address a meeting at Cape Girardeau, Missouri, on Sat, but was driven from the stand with stones, & followed to the hotel with hooting. The windows on the side where Gen Blair was known to be were all broken.

FRI OCT 12, 1866
Cmdor Robt Stockton died at his residence, Princeton, N J, on Monday last. He was a grandson of Richd Stockton, one of the signers of the Declaration of Independence, & was born in Princeton, in 1796. He entered the navy at 15, while a college student, & was assigned to the Pres, under Cmdor Rogers, & received honorable mention for gallantry for several engagements. Princeton, N J, Oct 10: the funeral of Cmdor Stockton took place at 3 o'clock today.

Appointments by the Pres yesterday: Wickman Hoffman, of La, Assist Sec of Legation of the U S at Paris; Geo F Kettell, of N Y, U S Consul at Rhenish Bavaria.

The Marquis de Boissy, an eccentric Frenchman, whose hatred of la perfide Albion is proverbial, died recently in Paris. He was the representative of a noble family. His wife is the celebrated La Guiccioli, the friend in former years of Lord Byron, & she still lives.

Mrd: on Oct 10, by Rev Dr P D Gurley, Mr Wm D Colt to Miss Susie Gideon, daughter of Mr Geo S Gideon.

Died: on Oct 10, Capt Wm Ramsay, U S N. His funeral is on Oct 12 at 2 o'clock P M, from St John's Church.

Criminal Court-Judge Fisher, Oct 11, 1866. 1-John Mahoney: larceny: verdict-guilty. Sentence: 1 year in the Albany Penitentiary. 2-Courtney Moore: assault & battery, with intent to kill Noah Fields: verdict-not guilty. 3-Randall Bowie: assault & battery: verdict-guilty. Sentence: 60 days in the county jail. 4-John Tolson, Patrick Reynolds, & John Evans: robbery. Reynold & Evans only were arraigned. The parties were accused of garoting Maj Geo B Ely while the latter was passing through the Capitol Grounds, & robbing him of a watch & money. The case is still on trial.

During the storm on Wed night, Mr W G Parkhurst, residing at 178 4th st, left home to go to the wharf to meet his little daughter, who was expected to arrive on the steamer **Express**. Since then nothing has been heard of him, & the family is in great distress. Mr Parkhurst was chief of the Stamp Division of the Internal Revenue Dept, & had the keys of the mail-bag & the safe in his pocket. He was formerly a short-hand reporter in the U S Senate. He was a Mason in high standing, having served last year as High Priest of the Grand Lodge.

Messrs Kilbourn & Latta, real estate brokers, sold a 3 story brick house & 2 lots in square 185 on 16th st, between I & K sts, to Wm E Prutt, of Pa, for $13,000. Also, lot F, in square 620, on L st, between North Capitol & 1st st west, to Americus Brown, for $235.

Police Matters: 1-Dennis Burns, tavern keeper, was arrested for keeping his place of business open on Sunday: fined $30. 2-Martin Hampton, colored, was arrested for the larceny of a shawl, the property of John McCarty: prisoner was sent to jail for court. 3-Thos Hines, blacksmith, working in the Navy Yard, was fined $10 for insulting ladies in the 7th st cars.

Supreme Court of D C, in Equity No 640-Docket 7. Henry E Gross & wife vs Rosina Stiner et al. Chas H Utermehle, trustee, reported he made sale of the real estate of John A Smith, deceased. –R J Meigs, clerk [No other details.]

Charleston, Oct 10. The schnr **Morning Star**, from Cardenas, has arrived at Quarantine. She picked up 7 additional persons who were abroad the steamer **Evening Star**. Their names are: Jas W Lyon, pilot; John Berry, cook; Andrew McMahon, assist engineer; A Sauza, passenger; E A Van Sickles, passenger; Minnie Taylor, passenger; Mollie Wilson, passenger. The following named persons were lost out of the boat in which the above were picked up: John Kavanaugh, fireman; Martin Bret, butcher; & a lady & gentleman whose names are unknown.

Mr Adolph Prayer, who was shot by his clerk, Frank W Rounds, at his store on Wash st, Boston, some 3 weeks ago, died at the Massachusetts Hospital Monday. Rounds is waiting in prison for trial.

SAT OCT 13, 1866
Chicago, Oct 11. Dr Danl Brainard, an old & eminent physician of this city, died here last night of cholera. He was founder & president of Rush Medical College, & had lately returned from a vacation tour in Europe.

The body of Mr W G Parkhurst who had gone to the wharf to meet his daughter, & was missing, was found near the wharves on 6th st. Jurors proceeded to hold an inquest, viz: Noble D Larner, Robt T Campell, Robt B Donaldson, Edw B Macgrotty, Henry O Noyes, Justus H Rathbone, Anthony Buckley, Fred'k White, John C Proctor, Oscar K Parris, John J Hall, & Solomon Herbert. His umbrella was found in the water, & his coat was buttoned up close, & all the valuables & money that he had about his person were untouched; his watch had stopped at 12 minutes past 7 P M, & even his hat & spectacles were found. The jury concluded that there was no light upon the wharf & in walking about the wharves he had lost his way & got into the slip. The Masonic friends of the deceased took charge of his remains. He had been W M of Harmony Lodge, R W S G W of the Grand Lodge, Past High Priest of Wash Chapter of Masons, & Capt Gen of Columbia Commandery of Knights Templar. He will be buried with Masonic honors, from his late residence, on 4th st, on Sunday.

Detectives McDevitt & Clarvoe arrested a young man, Ashbury Thompson, a clerk in the inspector's division of the Navy Yard, in Wash City, on a charge of robbing the Gov't of goods valued at between $14,000 & $15,000. He has been employed at the yard since 1861. Some two weeks ago Paymaster Jas Fulton received information to the effect that extensive thieving operations were going on in the Clothing Inspector's Bureau. Thompson is 28 years old & married.

Mrd: on Oct 9, in Emanuel Church, Warrenton, N C, by Rev Wm Hodges, D D, Mr John L Edwards, of Wash, D C, to Miss Caroline Seymour, daughter of the officiating clergyman.

Died: Oct 2, at New Castle, Dela, Reynolds Driver, first assist engineer, U S N, in his 27th year. He was ill only 5 days, & he died with calm fortitude & earnest faith of the consistent Christian. Steadfast, immovable, always abounding in the work of the Lord.

N Y, Oct 12. Gonzales & Pellicer were executed shortly after 10 o'clock today in Raymond st jail, Brooklyn, within a few blocks of the murder of Senor Otero. They made a full confession. Their necks were not broken by the fall.

Dept of State, Wash, Oct 6, 1866. Information has been received at this Dept from Mr Jos C Matteini, the Vice Consul Gen of the U S at Florence, Italy, of the death, on Sep 3, at the above named place, of Mr B Leoni Kirschel, a resident of San Francisco, Calif.

$50 reward for return of my pocketbook, containing currency & a certificate of deposit from Messrs Jay Cooke & Co, for $3,800, to any person who returns it to me, as I am inclined to think I dropped it in the crowd near the ticket ofc. I can be found at the Mexican Legation, K & 13th sts, or at 402 13th st, betwee G & H.
–Ignacio Mariscal

Dept of the Interior, U S Patent Ofc, Wash, Oct 10, 1866. Ptn of Pinckney Frost, of Springfield, Vt, praying for extension of a patent granted to him Jan 11, 1853, & reissued Feb 9, 1858, for an improvement in Seythe Fastenings, for 7 years from the expiration of said patent, which takes place on Jan 11, 1867.
–T C Theaker, Com'r of Patents

MON OCT 15, 1866
Equity Court-Judge Wylie, Oct 13. 1-Steuart & Thomas vs Austin. Order for judgment of condemnation. 2-Steuart & Thos vs Briget & King. Appeal allowed.

Police Affairs. 1-Sgt Robinson yesterday arrested Francis Lee for threats of violence on his wife & sister. Lee's father went his security to keep the peace. 2-Ofcrs Harper & Cunningham, on Sat night, arrested Jas & Mary Kimble for disorderly conduct. They were fined $2.44 each, which was paid. 3-Jas Becket was arrested at the market house, for assault & battery on Ed Johnson. He was committed to jail. 4-John O'Connor was arrested for drunkenness & disorderly conduct. He paid a fine of $5. It has not been long since he was released from the penitentiary. 5-Timothy Gleason & Bridget, his wife, were arrested at 20th & L sts for drunkenness. They paid the fine & were dismissed.

Criminal Court-Judge Fisher, Oct 13 1866. 1-Mary Moriarty was convicted of larceny & sentenced to 10 days in the common jail. 2-Wm Lee was convicted of larceny & sentenced to 1 year in the Albany Penitentiary. 3-Martha Tydings, indicted for assault & battery, submitted her case, & was sentenced to 10 days in the common jail. 4-Thos Johnson, convicted of larceny, was sentenced to 1 year in the Albany Penitentiary.

At a sale of pictures belonging to the late Hon Dr Wellesley, a very small pen & ink sketch by Raphael was purchased for the British Museum for L600.

Mrd: on Oct 11, at Fairfield, Conn, at the residence of Andrew Thorp, by Rev Dr Osgood, Maj S B Phinney, editor of the Barnstable [Mass] Patriot, to Miss Lucia Green, daughter of the late Hon Isaiah L Green, of Barnstable. No cards.

Died: on Sat, at Bladensburg, in her 76th year, Mrs Wm Noyes, consort of the late Wm Noyes, of Gtwn, D C.

Louisville, Oct 13. The indictment for treason against L F Bullet in the U S Circuit Court was quashed today, the U S atty entering a nolle pros.

Woman Candidate. Mrs Eliz Cady Stanton announces herself a candidate for Congress in the Eighth N Y District.

TUE OCT 16, 1866
J M Binckley has been appointed Law Clerk of the Atty Gen's Ofc. The salary is $2,500.

John R Young, managing editor of the N Y Tribune, is now in Wash City upon a brief visit to his family. He is undoubtedly the youngest member of the editorial profession occupying so important a position as that now devolved upon him.

Naval: John G Ayres appointed an assist surgeon in the navy. Paymaster Jas Fullerton has been detached from the Wash NavyYard & is succeeded by Paymaster Wm B Baggs.

Mr Thos A Hall, stage manager of the Holliday St Theatre, in Balt, received a despatch from Mr Frank Rivers, agent, who says: The Fowler sisters, Millie & Clara, were on board the steamer **Evening Star**, with their sister Louisa & Millie's band, Mr Wm M Dawson. The Fowler sisters recently completed an engagements at the Nat'l Theatre in Wash City.

Nat'l Theatre. Mrs Gen Lander, [better known to fame as Jean M Davenport,] makes her first appearance here this evening as Pauline in the "Lady of Lyous." The entire press of N Y C, where she just had an engagement, represents her as reviving her former triumphs, & as unsurpassed in all that makes the finished artist by any lady upon the American stage.

Death of Prominent Citizens of Richmond. 1-Dr Francis W Hancock, Pres of the Board of Health of Richmond, died there on Friday, aged 45 years. 2-Mr Jas Caskle, an old & respected citizen of Richmond, died there on Thursday, in his 75th year.

Two eminent Chicago physicians, Drs Hoph & Winter, died of cholera on Thu night.

Messrs Kilbourne & Latta, real estate brokers, sold a frame house & lot, on 7th st, between M & N sts, for $3,000 cash, to Jos Anthony.

Orphans Court of Wash Co, D C. Letters of administration on the personal estate of Michl Flanagan, late of Wash, D C, deceased. –Stephen M Curran, adm. All persons having claims will present the same to Wm H Ward, atty for adm.

On Thu last Mrs Mildred Allport, residing near Bowling Green, Caroline Co, Va, was gored to death by a vicious cow, which she was in the act of milking. At last accounts the unfortunate lady was alive, though her death was hourly expected. She was upwards of 65 years of age, & highly respected throughout the county.

Mr Wendell Snyder, a highly respectable citizen residing at 188 Orleans st, has a family of 6 daughters, varying in age from 10 years to 22. About 10 days since the 13 year old died on Oct 7 of something that resembled diptheria. In a day or two the 20 & 22 year olds were taken in the same way. Two other daughters are now ill of the same disease. We console most sincerely with the heart-broken parents. –Balt Commercial

Jas E Fitch, Real Estate Agent, corner of 7th & G sts, Wash. [Ad]

Trustee's sale of Confectionary Stock on 6th st west, between G & H sts, at public auction, by deed of trust dated Mar 31, 1866, recorded in Liber R M H, No 2, folios 171 thru 173, of the land records of Wash Co, D C, the establishment formerly known as Jos Shaffield's, being 386 6th st. –Chas H Utermehle, trustee -Green & Williams, aucts

WED OCT 17, 1866

Police matters: 1-Frank Owen was committed to jail for stealing, during the freshet, a double barrel shot gun, 2 pairs of pants, a box of cigars, & a basket of apples from Chas Henert, on Eldorado Island, opposite 17th st. Owen had deposited the articles with one Philip Smith for sale keeping. 2-Emelius & Sina Pearson, mulattoes, had a cross-action, each accusing the other of bad treatment. Justice Drury fined them each $3.00. 3-John Reed, colored, was arrested for having burglarized the house of Mrs Mary A Givens, 2nd & E sts, & robbing it of silver spoons, forks, etc. Reed was committed to jail for court.

Orphans Court-Judge Purcell, Oct 16, 1866. 1-First & final account of Wm O Nixon, guardian of Alfred Vernon Scott, orphan of Alfred V Scott, was approved & passed. 2-W Albert King & Thos Dowling were appointed to appraise the personal property of Henry King, late of Gtwn, deceased. 3-The will of John McDuell, late of Wash, was filed & partially proven. 4-Robt Fox, upon giving bonds to the amount of $35,000, was appointed administrator of Sidney S Babcock, late of Adams Co, Ill. 5-Mrs Sarah Parkhurst gave bond in the sum of $8,000 & was appointed administratrix upon the estate of Wm G Parkhurst, late of Wash, deceased.

Criminal Court-Judge Olin, Oct 16, 1866. 1-Leopold Hoffman: forgery: he was a claim agent, & Dr J H Allen, a surgeon in the army, having lost a horse in the service put in his claim in the hands of Hoffman, at the suggestion of the latter, giving a power of atty to another of the same firm to receive the draft. After waiting a considerable time, & being informed that the claim had not been allowed, he inquired direct at the Dept, & was informed that the claim had been allowed & the draft was paid. The endorsement proved to be a forgery; Hoffman was arrested. Verdict of the jury-guilty. 2-Maurice Decons: assault & battery: verdict-guilty. 3-Geo McAll: larceny: verdict-not guilty.

Justice Thompson placed warrants in the hands of Ofcrs Ellis & Markwood for the following to come forward & pay their dog tax: Chas Fenton, W Irwin, Eliz Martin, Fred Bentz, Robt Brooks, Alice Weiz, Henderson Beton, Walter D Wyville, & Philip Robison. The authorities intend fully in forcing the law relating to dogs.

Jas T Jones was shot by Mr Marcus W Bayley, in Fauquier Co, Va, on Tuesday last. The difficulty originated during the war. Mr Jones was the grand nephew of the late Chief Justice Marshall, & gentleman of talent & ability. He leaves a wife & 8 children to mourn their untimely loss. Jones died the next morning. Bayley made his escape.

Gtwn: 1-Michl Ledum was fined $3.44 for disorderly conduct towards his wife, which he paid. 2-R McGuire was arrested for drunkenness & disorder; fined $2.50. McGuire was also charged with using threats of violence towards his wife; for this he was held to bail. 3-John W Jett was fined $2.25 for neglecting to take out his corporation license.

Savannah, Oct 15. Gouldsby, second mate of the ill-fated steamer **Evening Star**, arrived there, having left the steamer with a boat load of lady passengers, all but two of whom were lost before getting near the shore. In landing the latter were lost, one named Annie, from Rhode Island, & the other Rosa Howard, of N Y. Both became insane from want & starvation. Their bodies were washed ashore, that of the latter being nearly devoured by the sharks. The mate is barely alive.

A young man from this city, John H Devaughn, U S assessor for Culpeper Co, was arrested at the Culpeper Court-House, on Thu last, for shooting Mr Robt Roberts, of that county, &, in default of bail to the amount of $2,500 for his appearance at the next term of the court, was committed to jail. The shot took effect, but will not inflict a serious wound.

Thos Dowling, auct, sold a bldg on the north side of Prospect, next west of Market st, 62 feet front, with a depth of 72 feet, to Dr L W Ritchie, for $26 per front foot.

N Y, Oct 16. John Van Buren died two days since on board of the steamship **Scotia** at sea. His body has been brought on here.

Appointment of Examining Surgeons by the Com'r of Pension. Dr C J Neff,Lima, Ohio; Dr J R Cutter, Charleston, S C; Dr Wm A Wilcox, Independence, Mo; & Dr G A Griswold, Fulton, Ill

Thos Ewing, jr, & Clifton Hellen: Attys & Counsellors-at-law. Ofc: 274 F st, Wash, D C.

Orphans Court of Wash Co, D C. Letters of administration on the personal estate of Sidney S Babcock, late of Adams Co, Ill, deceased. –Robt C Fox, adm

The British bark **Ambrosine**, of Plymouth, England, Wm Owen, master, which sailed from Cardiff, England, Apr 27, for Vera Cruz, foundered in a gale off the Florida coast, on Oct 2. The capt, 2nd mate, & 3 of the hands were saved, after passing 36 hours on a raft. The following were rescued: Wm Owen, master; John Neal, 2nd mate; Edw Hazard, seaman; Peter McCougal, seaman; Jas Welsh, steward. The remainder of the ship's company, ten in number, are supposed to be lost. The **Ambrosine** was an old vessel, formerly the ship **Chattanooga**, of N Y, & was owned by R G Dogger, of Plymouth, England. Both vessel & cargo were insured.

Mrd: on Oct 16, at the Church of the Epiphany, by Rev John V Dervis, Frank _ Stores, of N Y, to Kittie, youngest dght of the late Wm M Thompson, of Balt, Md.

Mrd: on Oct 16, at McKendree Chapel, by Rev W Krebs, Wm Kinkead, of St Cloud, Minn, to Miss Laura A Harkness, of Wash, D C. No cards.

Mrd: on Oct 16, at McKendree Chapel, by Rev W Krebs, Wm E Spedden to Miss Marie S Davis, daughter of Jas N Davis, all of Wash, D C. No cards.

Mrd: on Oct 16, at the residence of the bride's father, by Rev Mr Williams, Geo Braxton Whiting, to Nannie Harrison, daughter of Evan Lyons, of Wash, D C.

Died: on Sep 27, at London, in her 81st year. Mrs Mary Osborne Macdaniel, widow of the late John Macdaniel, of Wash, D C.

Died: on Oct 12, at West Point, N Y, Fannie Belfield, daughter of Brvt Maj L Lorain, U S A, aged 1 year & 3 monthsl

Augusta [Ill] Cor Chicago Tribune. A day or two since Jesse Rose was murdered by his son, Jas Rose, aged about 19, & the young man confessed the parricide, & implicated his mother in the crime. Jesse Rose has been in the habit of drawing the money his sons had earned by their labor in the neighborhood, & said he was going to draw some $45 due the eldest son, who is 19 years old, on Friday last. His son told him if he did he would kill him. The father went to a spelling school that day, but, it appears, did not get the money. The son, supposing he had got it, by his mother's instigation, with his younger brother, hid behind a stump near some bushes by which the father would return. The younger brother became frightened & fled. As Rose passed the stump the older son struck him with the axe he had with him, knocking his brains out, & then cut his throat with a butcher knife, leaving the body lying until morning. The mother & both sons were arrested, & the eldest immediately confessed the deed. Rose was a lazy, shiftless sort of fellow, & the mother has not borne a good name for some time.

Died: on Oct 16, at her father's residence, Upper Marlboro, Md, after a few hours' illness, Sarah Eleanor Hardesty, youngest child of Eleanor D & Edw W Belt, aged 20 months, lacking 3 days.

Trustee's sale of 190 acres of land, by decree of the Circuit Court for Montg Co, sitting as a court of equity, passed in a cause in said court wherein John H Hunter & others are cmplnts & Susannah G K Hunter & others are dfndnts: public sale in from of Mr John Mullican's blacksmith shop, on the Frederick road, 2 miles north of Rockville, on Nov 16. One parcel of the land contains 100 acres, & adjoins the land of Geo W Graff/Craff; with a frame dwlg & out-bldgs & out-houses. The other portion of said land lies to the west of the dwlg, & adjoins the lands of the late Addison Belt, Jas W Anderson, & Richd Ricketts. This land is unimproved.
–Susannah G K Hunter, trustee

THU OCT 18, 1866

Equity Court, Judge Wylie, Oct 17, 1866. B I Neale & wife vs John E Neale. The bill in this asks that certain property on H st north, between 4th & 5th sts, be deeded to the wife of the plntf, alleging that the ground was given to the wife as a bridal present, & that her money went towards bldg the house erected thereon. The dfndnt alleges that the house was given upon conditions to the son, which were by him violated, & that he had contributed toward the erection of the house, & that the son, at the time he failed in business, was owing him a large sum of money, & that the plntf had no right to call on him for a deed. The evidence was taken before J J Johnson, Com'r, & was very voluminous, its reading occupying an entire day. A decision is expected to be made shortly.

Criminal Court-Judge Fisher, Oct 17, 1866. 1-Henry Harvey & Albert Martin: larceny: guilty as to Martin. 2-Alice Williams: larceny: verdict-guilty.

Gtwn affairs. Mr Plowman, architect, has in course of erection, on the east side of High st, below the canal, a Gothic structure, to be called **Grace Church**, [Episcopal.] The bldg is the gift of Mr HenryD Cooke, of the banking firm of J Cooke & Co, to the congregation. The bldg is expected to be finished in Apr next, & will cost about $12,000. Mr J H Hutchins superintends the mason work.

Mary Jane Phoenix, age 14 to 15 years old, was arrested & committed to jail yesterday on the charge of murdering her infant child. She formerly lived at Bishop Johns' near the Seminary. The girl's brother, Richd Phoenix, who buried it in **Penny Hill burying ground**, asserts that he was unable to find it this morning, as it had been removed from the place in which he had depostied it.

Died: on Oct 13, at the residence of her son-in-law, Rev John C McCabe, D D, rector of St Matthew's parish, Bladensburg, Mrs Mary Noyes, relict of the late Capt Wm Noyes, of Gtwn, D C, in her 77th year. Her remains rest in the same grave with her husband, in **Oak Hill Cemetery**, Gtwn, D C.

Hon John Van Buren died at sea on the steamer **Scotia**, Cmdor Jenkins commanding, on Oct 13. Last May Mr Van Buren resolved upon a short tour of the United Kingdom & the continent. Later that month, accompanied by his daughter, Miss Van Buren, & his niece, Miss Nellie Van Buren, & the daughter of his eldest brother, Col Abraham Van Buren, now residing at 46 East 21st st, he embarked on the **Scotia** for Liverpool. Towards the latter part of Sep it became necessary for Mr Van Buren to arrange for his return to the U S. Before final departure he concluded to accept the warm invitation of his friend, Lord Dulhousie, that he should visit him at his seat in the Highlands. Several days were spent with extreme pleasure. On Sep 28 Mr Van Buren & the Misses Van Buren were received at Durculich House, Perthshire, Scotland, by Mr Alex'r Duncan, friend of the distinguished gentleman. It was at his mansion that Mr Van Buren was apparently seized with his fatal illness, which is stated to have had its seat in an affection of the kidneys, inducing general prostration of the system. On Oct 5 Mr Van Buren arrived at Liverpool, his condition was then extremely weak. He had to be borne on a cot to his stateroom. On Oct 6th the **Scotia** weighed anchor & lifted out of the Mersey. Dr Crane, of this city, also a passenger on the **Scotia**, was called in for professional consultation on the case. His friends, Mmr Carrol Livingston & Mr Marbury, of N Y, who were on board, did much to alleviate the tedium of his illness. He opened his mind freely & frequently to them. He said he had been in the world 56 years, but I always say I am 80 years old, for there has been a least that much of living crammed into me. While Dr Price, the surgeon, was with him, & just as his daughter & niece entered, Mr Van Buren's head fell back upon the pillow & died without a struggle. The body of the deceased was properly & promptly laid out & placed in a temporary coffin. On arrival in N Y the body was delivered to Mr Isaac Brown, of Grace Church. For the present the remains are in vault at the church, where the funeral services will occur at 10½ A M on Friday, Oct 19; final interment at the family ground at **Kinderhook**. [Oct 22nd newspaper: The coffin of Mr Van Buren had a silver plate, bearing in Roman letters the simple inscription: John Van Buren. Born February 8, 1810. Died October 13, 1866. A wreath of japonicas & camelias, studded with white roses & relieved by a border of dark green myrtle, encircled the inscription. N Y Herald, Sat.]

Mrd: on Oct 16, in St Luke's Church, Bladensburg, by Rev Dr McCabe, Jas L White, of Wash, D C, to Fannie E, third daughter of Woolman Gibson, of PG Co, Md. Balt & PG Co papers please copy.

Died: on Oct 16, Sarah V Zimmerman, beloved wife of H F Zimmerman, in her 36th year. Her funeral will be this afternoon at 3½ o'clock P M, from M St Methodist Church, between 9th & 10th sts.

Augusta, Oct 17. Dr R W Gibbs, a prominent citizen & journalist of South Carolina is dead. [No death date given-current item.]

Marshall's sale-Oct 23, of one black horse, seized by me under attachment 2,712, Wm H Carrico against John H Burgess. –D S Gooding, U S marshal, Dist of Col.

Guardian's sale of real estate, by order of the Orphans Court of D C., passed on Sep 11, 1866, approved by the Supreme Court of D C on Oct 2, 1866, the undersigned as guardian of the minor children of the late Wm McDermott, will sell, at public auction, on the premises, on Nov 2, all the following property, situated on the south side of I st, lying east of & adjacent to the dwlg house on lot 20 in square 105, which was owned by the late Wm McDermott, save & except 4 feet adjacent to & east of said dwlg, with a depth equal to the depth of said lot 20. –Jas McDermott, guardian -Jas C McGuire & Co, aucts

Marshall's sale on Oct 23, of one black horse, seized by me under attachment 2,712, Wm H Carrico against John H Burgess. –D S Gooding, U S marshal, Dist of Col.

FRI OCT 19, 1866

Criminal Court-Judge Olin, Oct 18, 1866. 1-Wm Hawkins: assault & bettery: verdict-guilty. 2-Jas Conlan: larceny: verdict-guilty. Sentence: 1 year in the Albany Penitentiary. 3-Henry Freeman: larceny: verdict-guilty. Sentence: 1 year in the Albany Penitentiary. 4-Alice Williams, alias Jane Carter: larceny: verdict-guilty. Motion for a new trial. 5-Leopold Hoffman: convicted of forgery. Sentence: 2 years in the Albany Penitentiary. 6-John Williams & Chas Longston: convicted of larceny: sentence: each to 2 years in the Albany Penitentiary.

In Gen Orders the Quartermaster Gen announces the death of a brother ofcr, Brvt Col T J Cox, assist quartermaster, U S Volunteers, who died of cholera at Nashville, Tenn, on Sep 17, 1866. He entered the service as capt & assist quartermaster of volunteers on Jun 11, 1862. He leaves a bereaved family.

Yesterday the Pres appointed Saml H Jones to be Marshal for the Western District of Tenn, & Robt S Chilton, of D C, to be Com'r of Emigration in the State Dept, vice H N Conger.

Dr Marsh, Paymaster of the Wash Aqueduct & Capitol Extension, has been removed, & Mr Kendig, his clerk, appointed in his place.

Hon Chas Cook died at Auburn, N Y, on Tue, of apoplexy, in his 66th year.

M Alexandre Dumas, sr, has agreed to write the libretto of an opera on an episode from his novel of "Le Comte de Bragelonne," [the heroine of which is M'lle de Lavalliere, who was slightly lame,] expressly for M'lle Carlotta Patti. Flotow is to compose the music.

Mr Addison Davis, late moulder in the Navy Yard, died yesterday of cholera.

Improvements: 1-Mr McGrann is finishing a 3 story brick house at N J ave & First st, at a cost of about $5,000: 25 x 32 feet. Hammond & Davis are the builders; Carson & Sourbier, plasters. 2-Geo Calvert is putting up a 3 story brick house on I st, near First, south side; cost will probably be $8,000: 32 x 40 feet. 3-Peter Gallant is finishing a modern built bldg, of brick, for Geo A Birch; cost about $8,000; I & 1st sts. 4-On D st north & east of 2nd, Mr Wm Wadder is having a convenient 7 room brick house built, costing about $6,000. Mr Dant is bricklayer; Mr Carroll, carpenter, & John Davis, painter. 5-On Pa ave, near 1st st, W H Falconer is bldg a large store for W W Cochran, to be 3 stories high, & cost about $9,000.

Police matters: 1-Richd Williams was arrested for creating a disturbance in his mother's house at 20th & M sts, & was sent to the workhouse for 90 days, as he was unable to pay a fine of $10.58. 2-Chas Hunter, a lad, arrested for disorderly conduct: fined $5.58. 3-Lorrin Cole & John Donoho arrested for drunkenness & disorderly conduct: each fined $3. 4-John Johnson, a deserter from his regt, was arrested & turned over to the military authorities. 5-R L Hide arrested for drunkeness: fined $3.00

On Thu a scaffold at the stable course of erection for Mr Galt, in the rear of his residence, on 9th st, between G & H, broke down, & several of the bricklayers fell to the ground 26 feet. Mr Saml Lewis, residing on I st, between 4th & 5th sts, was severely injured in the back, & is supposed internally. Others escaped with bruises.

Superior household & kitchen furniture at auction on Oct 25, at the residence of Judge Chipman, 470 7th st, between E & F sts. -Jas C McGuire & Co, aucts

Trustee's sale by virtue of 2 deeds of trust from Francis Fromwell, one ot S S Williams & Chas Walter, dated Feb 2, 1863, recorded in Liber N C T No 2, folio _51,of the land records of Wash Co D C; the other to Wm F Mattingly, dated Jul 15, 1865, recorded in Liber N C T No 60, folio 22 et seq, of said records. Public auction on Nov 9, of lots 2 & 3 in square 844, & part of lot 4, in said square. This property is located on D st, between 5th & 6th sts, with a large 2 story brick bldg, that has been used as a lager beer brewery. Also for sale, the personal effects connected with the brewery. –Chas Walter, surviving trustee; Wm F Mattingly, trustee; Wm L Dunlop, trustee -Green & Williams, aucts

Orphans Court of Wash Co, D C, Oct 16, 1866. In the case of Sophie A Ailer, admx of Geo Ailer, deceased, the administratrix & Court have appointed Nov 10 next, for the final settlement of the personal estate of the said deceased, of the assets in hand. -Z C Robbins, Reg/o wills

Boston, Oct 17. Train from Portland was thrown off the track at Haverhill this morning, by a broken rail, & Isaac Horne, engineer, was killed. Andrew Blodgett, fireman, is supposed to be fatally injured.

Mrd: on Oct 16, at St John's [P E] Church, Gtwn, D C, by Rev J Eastburn Brown, Henry J Kopper, of N Y, to Louisa, daughter of the late Gen T T Wheeler, of Md. No cards.

Died: on Oct 17, Nannie Kin_, aged 20 years & 5 months. Her funeral will take place at 3 o'clock P M, today, from the residence of her father, 18 Congress st, Gtwn.

Died: on Oct 18, Mary M, consort of Lucius S Allyn, in her 54th year. Her funeral will be on Oct 20 at 3 o'clock, from her late residence, 603 M st north.

Boston Journal, Oct 9. Amos Spear, a respectable citizen of Saco, Me, was murdered near the covered bridge which crosses the Saco river between Biddeford & Saco, by 3 notorious Biddeford roughs, R Hartley Lewis, Chas E Edgerly, & Chas Watkins. Lewis has turned State's evidence, & says he & Edgerley & Watkins concealed themselves, & as Spear approached, Watkins struck him with a large club on the head, & repeated the blows several times. They all stamped upon his body until he was nearly dead, & found a small amount of currency in his pocket. Mr Spear worked in one of the York mills & was paid off on Friday. He and his wife went to Biddeford to shop for groceries. Mrs Spear, having an infant 3 months old, hurried home first, leaving her husband to finish the marketing. He was a quiet man 25 years old, & leaves a wife & one child.

SAT OCT 20, 1866

Police Affairs: 1-At the Island station house, yesterday, Justice Hancy fined Lucinda Phillips $5.90 for using abusive language toward Alex S Whiteside, letter-carrier. 2-John Dainhardt, a drover, was arrested on Wed for buying stolen mules. The mules were stolen from the 14th st Park. 3-Nicholas Harris was sent to the workhouse for violating the water law. Housekeepers & others would do well to have their servants & employes using water on the public way know that the law limits the use of water for washing pavements, carriages, etc, to 15 minutes at a time, & to be used between the hours of 4 & 7 A M, & 6 & 7 P M at this season of the year. 4-Jas O'Day & Thos Walsh were each fined $10.90 for a dispute they had in which Walsh picked up a brick to throw at O'Day. 5-Jeff Johnson was fined $5 yesterday for driving a two horse wagon across the pavement at C st & Pa ave. 6-Fred Hall was fined $1 for drunkenness. 7-Andrew Balman was sent to the workhouse for disorderly conduct. This young man caused a great deal of trouble to his family, & is on the road to ruin. Gtwn: 6-Jacob Little & Solby Pride, sailors, each fined $3.50 for fighting on Water st. The capt of their vessel paid the fine. 7-Robt Gates was fined $2.44 for disorderly conduct.

Yesterday the new & second-hand clothing store of Michl McDevitt, 21st & I sts, was robbed of a quantity of clothing valued at $150. The police are tracing the stolen goods.

Belle Boyd's husband was among the lost by the steamer **Evening Star**.

The N Y Herald of yesterday says it is rumored that Cmdor Vanderbilt has purchased St John's Park for $1,000,000, or thereabouts. It could possibly be donated for a philanthropic object.

Improvements in the Wash City. 1-W Letourneau is having a frame, 16 x 36, erected on N C ave, between 4th & 5th sts; cost about $1,700; Bright & Humphreys, builders. 2-A two story frame on Pa ave, near 7th, is nearly completed by Geo Scroggin for Jno Easeman: 16 x 32, cost, about $1,100. 3-Mr Barrett, grocer, last month completed a 2 story brick at 392 2nd st, costing about $3,300; size 20 x 64. 4-Opposite St Peter's Church, 2nd st, below C south, Henry Keirle, carpenter, is putting up a neat & plain 2 story frame residence for Jas Gulick, at a cost of about $2,500; size 21 x 32. 4-Capt Grant, architect & contractor, is erecting at 2nd & D st south, a commodious bldg for the Sisters of Charity in charge of *Providence Hospital*. The bldg now under way is L shaped, 130 feet front on D st, running back 100 feet, is 4 stories high, & but half the size of the hospital when entirely built. It was commenced Sep 5, & will be ready for occupancy about Feb. Martin & Foos, bricklayers. Cost, about $45,000.

Among the improvements in Gtwn is the remodelling & enlarging of Henry D Cooke's residence, corner of Wash & Stoddard sts, at the foot of the Heights. The entire improvements will cost probably $30,000. The bldg contains about 2,000 feet of cornice, over 500 feet of tin flues, & 85,000 cubic feet. It is heated by Morns, Tasker & Co's hot water apparatus. The bldg is in Italian style. Plowman, architect; J McElroy, superintendent.

Mrd: on Oct 18, at St Aloysius' Church, by Rev B F Wiget, S J, Mr Geo W Dove to Miss Mary A, eldest daughter of the late Chas F Lowrey, all of Wash City.

Died: on Oct 18, Christopher Yeabower, aged 52 years. His funeral will take place from his late residence, 330 High st, Gtwn, Sunday afternoon at 3 o'clock.

N Y, Oct 19. Frank Ferris, otherwise known as Francisco Ferrero, the wife murderer, was executed this morning in the jail yard in this city this morning. While under the gallows the condemned sung a hymn, during the pauses of which he fervently kissed a crucifix & recited a prayer. He said he was about to die, but was innocent. His hand was guilty, but his heart was pure.

The marriage of Miss Kate Bateman to a young English surgeon, formerly connected with the Havre line of steamships is announced. Miss Bateman retires from the stage, which thus loses one of its brightest ornaments.

A handsome monument has been erected at Flatbush, L I, to Senor Otero, the wealthy Cuban, who was murdered in Brooklyn last winter.

Theodore Dwight, a well known citizen, died at his house in Brooklyn, aged 70 years. He was the son of the late Hon Theodore Dwight, formerly member of Congress from Conn, & afterwards for many years editor of the Daily Advertiser in this city. He was able to converse with readiness in French, Spanish, Italian, German, Greek, & to some extent in Hebrew. On Monday last he accompanied his married daughter to Jersey City, where she took the train to rejoin her husband in the South. As he took leave of her in the car he found the door fastened, & before it could be opened the train had begun to move, so that in leaping out he was thrown down & severely bruised. His daughter saw him fall & entreated that the train might stop but without effect until she had been carried a considerable distance. The conductor consented to set her out upon the track, & with her two children, one a babe, she was able to reach her father, & found him alive, conscious, & peaceful. He lived to be brought home, to greet & comfort his family, & then departed before the break of day. –N Y Express

MON OCT 22, 1866

The Pres has recognized Jose Augustin Quintero as consul of Costa Rica at New Orleans, La; & the following as vice consuls for Sweden & Norway: Martin Lewis, of Balt; Wm M Perkins, at New Orleans; C Schwarzkopp, at Norfolk; & S Valm, at Austin, Texas.

Maj M O Van Horn is said to have ridden on horseback from Huntsville, Ala, to Delaware, Ohio, to vote at the late election.

Died: on Oct 20, in Wash City, Geo P Williamson, of Lebanon, Ohio, aged 64 years. Southern Ohio papers please copy.

Police matters: 1-Mary Miller, Mary Brophy, Barney Brophy, Timothy Hurlahay, & Murtagh McCarty got up a family row in Swampoodle. They were all arrested & held to bail to keep the peace by Justice Walter. 2-Zorah Neale was arrested for stealing a coat from Whitfield Johnson; garment found in Neale's possession: committed to jail for court.
3-Jas Rhodes was arrested for carrying concealed weapons & threatening to shoot Miller therewith: fined $20. 4-Geo Nash, Sam Booth, & Andrew Webster, 3 negroes from Gtwn, were arrested on Sat for boisterous conduct & swearing on the street: each fined $5.58. Neither being able to pay the fine, they were all sent to the workhouse for 30 days.

Catharine Murphy escaped from the Insane Asylum on Sat, & was found wandering about the streets, & returned to her old quarters by Ofcr Yeatman, of the 7th Ward.

The removal of the remains of soldiers from the old grave yard to the **Crown Hill Cemetery**, at Indianapolis, was commenced on Friday.

Mr Jas Derrickson, son of the senior member of the firm of Derrickson & Bartlett, paper dealers, of N Y, was drowned at Chittenden's mills, in Shockport, on Thu. He had visited the mill on business, & in surveying the premises walked out one of the bulkheads, when he tripped & fell over the water-wheel into the flume. He was 21 years of age.

Chancery sale of very valuable house & business stand on Pa ave; by decree of the late Circuit Court, passed in cause No 1,496, in Equity, Kibbey at al against Campbell' heirs, etc: public auction, on Nov 13th, of part of lot 6 in square 491, on Pa ave; property is a few doors east of the Nat'l Hotel, being 396 Pa ave.
–Wm R Woodward, trustee -Jas C McGuire & Co, aucts

David Bartlett, Edw Watson, alias Edw McGuire, alias Fairy McGuire, & Oren Simms, alias Rory Simms, all of whom are notorious burglars, were arrested in N Y on Fri, charged with robbing the Nat'l Village bank of Bowdoinham, Me, on Jun 22 last.

TUE OCT 23, 1866
N Y World: Gladiateur's celebrated rider is dead-found dead underneath his dog cart, in a ditch. The name of Harry Grimshaw was so well known by all-turfists & no turfists, that a word on the subject of his death may not be misplaced. He attended Northampton races on Wed to ride Count Lagrange's Atalante in the Harleston Nursery, which he won. On Thu he was found dead under his trap, & his servant, insensible, close by. Grimshaw was about 26 years of age, & had been married but 8 months. Count Lagrange was extremely attached to Grimshaw, a faithful & valuable servant.

Hon Chas Sumner was married in Boston on Wed to Mrs Alice Hooper, daughter of Jonathan Mason, of that city. The nuptial ceremonies were performed by Bishop Eastburn. The honeymoon is to be passed in Newport.

Mj Wm Henderson & Capt Chas Henderson, of the 15th N Y Volunteer Engineers, were honorable discharged the service of the U S, as per special order No 518, Adj Gen's Ofc.

Appointments made by the Pres yesterday: Wm B Thornburg, to be Surveyor Gen U S for the State of Nevada; Joshua D Giddings, Assist Treasurer U S at Charleston, S C; Chas R Goodwin & O F Winchester, Com'rs to the Paris Exposition in 1867; Eli P Norton, Solicitor of the U S to represent the Gov't before the Court of Claims; Thos D Hodgsin & Geo W Larner, Justices of the Peace for Wash Co; Wm H Hoyt, Deputy Postmaster at Burlington, Vt; Geo E Goodrich, do, at Fitchburg, Mass; Ezra Reade, at Terre Haute, Ind; Edw Hicks, at Green Bay Wis; Lyman G Wilcox, Register of Land Ofce at Traverse City, Mich.

Died: Oct 20, in Wash City, Geo P Williamson, aged 64 years. His funeral will take place today at 2 P M, with funeral services at the Calvary Baptist Church.

Supreme Court, D C; in Equity No 532. Geo Presbury against Nannie Haw, Marshall Brown, Geo Prentiss, & Emily Wiley, heirs of Jesse B Haw. On Nov 3, at City Hall, I shall state an account of the personal estate of said Jesse B Haw.
–W Redin, auditor

East Washington improvements. 1-East Capitol st, from 3rd to 11th, is being graded under the supervision of Andrew Gleason. Lincoln Square is being laid out by supervisor Job Angus. A Gaddis, jr, at 10th & I sts, is thoroughly repairing his house & garden. 2-The Parochial School of St Peter's Church, [Rev Fr Boyle,] is being as rapidly pushed forward as good workmanship will permit; it is 45 feet front by 115 feet deep, with basement & 2 stories; the bldg will be fire-proof. The iron columns which support the first floor will also convey hot or cold air from the basement to assist heating or ventilating the upper story. Estimated cost: $15,000. C B Clusky, architect; W B McCullum, bricklayer; Barr, plasterer. 3-J Trumble is bldg a 2 story brick bldg, cost $2,800, on 4th at S C ave. 4-J D O'Donnell, druggist, is about finishing a fine store & dwlg at 589 8th st. It is 3 stories high, 30 feet front, 45 feet deep; cost about $7,000. 5-Lloyd Pumphrey has nearly completed a 2 story frame, 16 x 28, on E st, near 8th. 6-T H Denham is erecting a 2 story frame, 14 x 30, on 9th near G; cost $6,000. 7-Wm Hutchinson is bldg 3 frames on 10th st, near G, at a cost of about $1,600. J Brown, carpenter. 8-A Frederick is bldg a double 2 story brick residence, 40 feet front, at 91 East Capitol st, to cost $7,000.

Police Affairs: 1-Louis Betz; & Chas Klotz; were each fined $20 & costs yesterday, for keeping their restaurants open on Sunday. Both have saloons on G st, between 17th & 18th sts. 2-Griffin Bagley was fined $10.90 yesterday, for disorderly conduct. Bagley, about 15 years old, was arrested for throwing stones & cutting a boy, Geo Butler, very badly in the head. The dispute arose over a ball. 3-John Gettner was fined $5 for disorderly conduct. 4-Chas Charleston was fined $20 for selling some 60 hams without a license. The police traced up the case & found the hams had been stolen.

Blenheim, the seat of the late Andrew Stevenson, 9 miles from Charlottesville & the Univ of Va, in Albemarle Co, Va, will be offered at public auction on Nov 6 next; contains 975 acres; with a beautiful house. **Blenheim**, the ancient seat of the Carters, was for many years the residence of the late Hon Andrew Stevenson, [at one time the Minister to the Court of St James.] -Benson & Bro, aucts, Charlottesville, Va

Died: on Oct 21, in Gtwn, after a painful illness, Mrs Mary, consort of Francis Gross, in her 63rd year. Her funeral will take place on Wed morning at 10 o'clock, from Trinity Church, Gtwn.

Died: on Oct 21, in Wash City, suddenly, Annie C, wife of T P Martinez, [Surgeon Gen's Ofc,] & daughter of the late Rev Jehiel Talmage, of N J. Her funeral will be from their residence, 23 14th st west, this afternoon at 1½ o'clock.

Died: on Oct 21, John T Cochrane, in his 54th year. His funeral will take place from his late residence, 383 12t^h st, on Wed, Oct 24, at 2 o'clock P M.

Augusta, Oct 22. Arthur Williams, his wife, & 2 daughters were murdered near Rome, Ga. Two freedman, who committed the murder, were arrested. One confessed, after wounding Mrs Williams, he ravished her. His accomplice killed Mr Williams & the daughters. The object of the outlaws was to obtain money, & they found none.

Chancery sale of valuable improved & un-improved property in Wash City, by decree passed by the Supreme Court of D C, in a cause depending therein, #560, in Equity, in which John H Ingle & others are cmplnts, & Eliza B Ingle & others are dfndnts. Sale on Nov 15th next of lot 25 in Reservation B, on Pa ave, with a substantial brick house. Also, lot 30 in Reservation B, on Pa ave, with a substantial brick house. On Nov 16 next; the east half of lot 3 in Revervation 11. On Nov 17 next, the interest of the late John P Ingle, in lot 5, of John P Ingle's subdivision of lot 7 in square 518, having a front on the alley running through the said square of 20 feet, & a depth, with that width 90 feet. Lot 18 in Reservation C. Lot 1 in square 1,002. Lots 2 & 3 in square 1,002. Lot 1 in square 971.
–John C Kennedy, Wm B Webb, trustees -Jas C McGuire & Co, aucts

Gtwn Bldg Improvements: on 8th st, near High, Col J D Kurtz is adding a neat green house to his residence. At Fayette & Prospect sts Dr Kidwell is having a laboratory, 40 x 24 feet, built by C F Willett. On Vallet st, near Rodes, back of the reservoir, 2 small frames, costing about $400, are being built by E Dyer. On 5th st, between Market & High, Robt Cunningham is having a frame 26 square feet, built by Easton & Custard. The material is old Gov't lumber, which makes the cost of the bldg only $500. On Water st, between Wash & Jefferson, Michl Moran is having a 2 story brick, 22 x 45, built by Jos Collins, bricklayer, & F P Waivall, carpenter; cost about $2,000. At Fred'k & Prospect, Mr Seymour is having a substantial brick residence built by W J Dyer, at a cost of some $12,000. On Bridge st, above Wash, Chas Uberhoff, tobacconist, is having two 3 story bricks, 17 x 63 feet each, built, & expects to have them ready for occupancy by Nov 15. The ground floors are arraigned for stores. Jas V Yates, carpenter; Jos Chicks, plasterer; cost $8,000. At Dunbarton & Congress sts, Frank Dodge is having his residence greatly remodeled by the addition of a 3rd story & a back bldg of 60 feet. W J Duer, carpenter; Henry Barbour, bricklayer; cost about $15,000. Walter S Cox is having a conservatory added to his residence, Gay & Congress sts; E J Shoemaker, carpenter. John R Dickson is bldg a two story frame bldg on Second st, above High, costing $1,000. R A Shins is about finishing the most extensive improvements that have been made in Gtwn this season. They consist of 7 new bldgs on Wash st, a new weiss-beer brewery on Green st, & the reconstruction of two dwlgs & a hotel on Bridge st. The hotel is 4 stories high, with French roof. The basement, at the corner of Bridge & Wash sts, is for a restaurant.

Com'r Cooley, of the Indian Bureau, yesterday received from Alex'r Cummings, Govn'r & ex efficio Superintendent of Indian Affairs of Colorado Territory, a communication, enclosing two letters from Kit Carson & A J Alexander, giving the particulars of the outbreak of the Ute tribe of Indians in the southern part of the Territory, which occurred on Oct 1. Thirteen of the Indians were killed & two of our soldiers were wounded in a skirmish.

WED OCT 24, 1866
The Pres yesterday appointed Jarvid Russell U S Marshal for the District of N H.

Brvt Brig Gen Amos Beckwith has been assigned to duty as chief commissary of the Det of the Gulf.

Gov Fanton, of N Y, has appointed Thur, Nov 29, as a day of Thanksgiving.

Died: on Oct 20, near Bladensburg, Miss, Mary Lucas, only child of Maj J M Lucas, formerly of Illinois. Thus has a gentle spirit passed away.

It is known to many that Mr Geo Bartlett, of the firm of Bartlett Bros, under the Sherman House, has been for some time insane, & was taken about a year ago for treatment to the State Asylum at Jacksonville. He lately escaped & returned to Chicago. It was determined by his friends to take him back to the asylum. He manifested the most intense opposition to this when it was discussed, & continued to do so until he was safely on the train. During the night Mr Bartlett jumped off the back platform of the train while it was moving at about 30 miles an hour, while his guardians were asleep. This was about 5 miles this side of Lincoln. Mr Willard & Mr Huntington, his guardians, proceeded on foot up the track for 12 miles, but without finding a single trace of the insane man. The search on Thu was continued under the superintendence of the lunatic's brother, Mr Wm Bartlett, & northing has been found of him. Mr Bartlett has an insurance of $101,000 on his life, which makes the question of his safety a matter of great pecuniary interest to the life insurance companies. -Chicago Republican, Sat

Titusvile [Pa] Herald of Oct 18. Accident on the express train Oct 17, due at Corry, that ran off the track a few miles east of Union. The entire train was precipitated down an embankment. Injured: Mrs W Y Dumont, N Y, slightly; G H Cashel, Corry, do; C H Lathrop, Vincennes, Ind, do; Rev Mr Broughton & wife, N Y, do; Mrs Eliz Rivers, Vincennes, Ind, head badly bruised & internally injured; Marvin Babcock, Frewsberg, N Y, arm broken & head cut; A Hard, Norwalk, Ohio, slightly; Richd Illingworth, Corry, head cut; Wm F Rowe, Huntington, Ohio, slightly; Lt J C Carroll, 14th N Y Infty, face badly cut; G T Pierce, Elinville, N Y, hand bruised; W D Miller, Corry, bruised; Frank Howard, Springfield, Mass, face cut; J Williams, Corry, slightly; Lt E R Hills, 5th U S Artl, bruised; G H Swift, formerly of the American House, residence Cuba, N Y; leg bruised; Mrs G H Swift, Cuba, N Y; slightly. One of the sufferers, a lady with 5 children, it is thought cannot survive. Her children escaped with slight bruises.

Railroad accident yesterday on the North Pa railroad, by which the engineer, Richd Dolday, & a passenger, Chas Slack, were seriously injured. Mr Slack resided at 1311 Vine st, but was removed to the Episcopal Hospital by Mr J B Wickeraham, one of the passengers. The locomotive struck a cow & the force of the blow turned the engine over upon its side. –Phil Ledger, Tue

Orphans Court of Wash Co, D C. Letters of administration on the personal estate of Peter W Magruder, late of Gtwn, D C, deceased. –Geo Magruder, adm

Admx's sale of excellent household & kitchen furniture at auction on Oct 26, by order of the Orphans Court of Wash Co, D C., the personal effects of the late Edw Hall, deceased, at his late residence on F st, between 6th & 7th sts. By order of the admx. -Green & Williams, aucts

THU OCT 25, 1866
Appointment of Internal Revenue Ofcrs-yesterday: Walter G Beckwith, Collector for the 2nd Dist of Mich; John C Hay, Assessor for the 10th Dist of Pa.

Gtwn: on Tue a well dressed man was found drowned in the canal at Green st. Mr P Emerick identified the body as that of Chas Rupprecht, a member of Oriental Lodge No 19, I O O F, of Wash City. Verdict-the deceased must have accidentlly fallen into the canal-time & place unknown. The body was taken in charge by Mr Burch, the undertaker, to be embalmed.

<u>Improvements in Wash City</u>: 1-A new Roman Catholic Church of ordinary dimensions, built of brick, is being erected at Pa ave & 25th st. 2-Wm H Burch is bldg a large livery stable & carriage house on 14th st, between D & E; 3 stories high; cost $15,000. W Chappin, carpenter & superintendent; W Downey, bricklayer. It is the intention to made a large & desirable hotel for farmers. 3-C Demonett, confectioner, is bldg a store & dwlg on Pa ave, between 17th & 18th sts, 3 stories high, about 26 feet front by 78 feet deep, & will cost $14,000; Entwisle & Barron, contractors & carpenters; B Hutchins & Jas Lewis, bricklayers. 4-On south G st, near 21st, S Bache, contractor, is bldg 2 first class 3 story frame bldgs for W B Todd, costing about $19,000; size of each about 20 x 70 feet. 4-McKinney, at 22nd & G sts, has built a 2 story brickstore & dwlg, costing about $2,500. 5-On 22nd st, near Pa ave, Jas Chapman is bldg two 3 story brick houses, costing about $4,000. 6-J James, carpenter, is bldg a 2 story frame, on I st, between 22nd & 23rd sts, costing about $1,500. 7-<u>St Dominic's Roman Catholic</u> Church, 6th & E sts, is of granite from Port Deposit, with edgings of Seneca redstone, pure Gothic style; front of 115 feet, including the chapels, & a depth of 200 feet. The tower will be some 208 feet high, & contain a large bell. It will be under roof early next year. P C Keeley, architect; Foley, superintendent. 8-A beautiful fountain has been erected in front of the executive bldg of the Depot of Army clothing & Equipage, on 7th st, near Md ave. It was made by G W Goodall, of Wash City, & cost $170. 9-John Lincoln has built a fine 3 story brick house [store & dwlg] at 651 7th st; 25 feet front by 60 feet deep; cost $7,000. G W

Gates keeps a dry goods & fancy notion store on the ground floor. Mr Lincoln is also erecting two 1 story stores adjoining, each costing about $1,000. 10-Thos E Lloyd, Pres of the Board of Alderman, is having a modern built 3 story brick house erected at 11th & C sts, by Moses Merrill, bricklayer, & Bird & Baker, carpenters, at a cost of $7,000; it is 22 feet front by 53 feet deep.

Liverpool Post of Oct 10: the famous Confederate cruiser **Shanandoah** was quietly given up to the Fed authorities at Liverpool on the termination of the civil war in America. The U S Consul at Liverpool had her fitted up & despatched to N Y, but she was driven back disabled to the Mersey in a succession of gales. After lying for many months in the Liverpool docks, she came under the notice of Messrs Smith & Fleming, of London, who were on the look-out for a vessel suitable for the requirements of the Sultan of Zanzibar. This potentate now owns the famous cruiser, the purchase this week having been finally effected by Messrs Stoddart Brothers, of Liverpool.

Hartford Courant, Oct 23. Luther G Thompson was murdered on Sat, in Farmington, by a man who came to his door telling him he needed his help because his wagon had broken. Mr Thompson lived with his mother & a young sister about 16 years of age, on the road leading to Talcott mountain. Mr Thompson went with him to help & was later found dead under a willow tree. [The name of the murderer was not given.]

Gottleib Williams was arraigned in Phil on Monday for the alleged murder of Mrs Miller, & pleaded not guilty. Mr Thos J Worrell, his counsel, said that a very important witness had not yet been found. A reward had been offered for him, & it was intended to increase the reward. The trial date was fixed for Thu, Nov 1.

Dept of Wash: Gen Order No 62, headquarters Dept of Wash, Oct 19, anounces the following assignment of troops in this dept:
Garrison of Wash: Brvt Maj Gen W H Emory, colonel 5th U S cavalry, commanding; 1st & 3rd btlns 12th U S infty, 44th regt U S [Veteran Reserve] infty, & detachment 5th U S cavalry-at Sedgwicks Barracks, in this city.
Fort McHenry, Md: Brvt Brig Gen H Brooks, colonel 4th U S artl, commanding; co I, & headquarters 4th U S artl.
Fort Washington, Md: Brvt Lt Col F M Follett, capt 4th U S artl, commanding; companies A & D, 4th U S artl.
Fort Whipple, Va: Maj Jos Stewart, 4th U S artl, commanding; companies C & H, 4th U S artl.
Battery Rogers, Alexandria, Va: Brvt Col C L Best, capt 4th U S artl, commanding; co F, 4th U S artl.
Fort Foot, Md: Brvt Lt Col M P Miller, capt 4th U S artl, commanding; co E, 4th U S artl.

Died: Oct 24, in Wash City, Morven J McClery, U S Coast Survey, aged 44 years. His funeral will be from his late residence, N Y ave, near 15th, Oct 26 at 10 A M.

Jurors for the Circuit Court-Wash-selected yesterday:

Chas Robinson	John J Lewis	Jas B Moore
Wm Sibley	S C Mickum	L B Bradley
Jas O'Bryan	A M Hoover	John Wise
Thos Miller	W H Baldwin	Geo H Gaddis
Wm Bagnam	J G Dudley	W W Parker
John W Rogers	S A Gordon	Thos Thornley
A J Bell	H S Benson	Ed Hartley
Terrence Drury	Francis Miller	Arch White
Jas Daley	Alex Forrest	

Mrd: on Oct 23, by Rev Chas J White, Jasper Smith to Emily de [*Fl aniere] Kieckhoefer, daughter of A T Kieckhoefer, all of Wash City. [*Letter missing.]

Mrd: on Oct 22, by Rev Dr Keeling, Maj Jas Haggerty, U S A, to Mrs Kate Appleton, of Wash City.

Mrd: on Oct 23, by Rev Dr J Keeling, Capt Chas Howard, U S Marine Corps, to Miss Carrie Bacon, daughter of Saml Bacon.

Died: on Oct 24, in Wash City, Morven J McClery, U S Coast Survey, aged 44 years. His funeral will take place from his late residence, on N Y ave, near 15th, on Oct 26 at 10 o'clock A M.

The cable despatches announce the death, at Paris, on Oct 19, of M Ednonard Antoine Thouvenel, the precedessor of Drouyn de Lhuys in the ofcr of French Minister of Foreign Affairs. We announced about a month ago the death of his wife, a sister of Crevilliers Fleury, one of the proprietors of the Debats of Paris, & a former tutor in the Orleans family. M Thouvenel was born at Verdon, Nov 11, 1818.

The train on the Memphis & Charleston road, returning from a tournament at Tuscumbia, met with an accident near Burnsville, on Oct 18. The rear truck of the express car broke. Forty persons injured, 3 seriously; Gen Beauregard & Gen Forrest escape unhurt.

Farm for rent in Alexandria Co, Va, 2½ miles from Gtwn, containing 66 acres, well watered, a dwlg house in a fine oak grove; will be rented for 1 or 2 years. Apply to Mrs M A Hayes, on the premises, or to Z D Gilman, Druggist, 350 Pa ave, Wash.

Admx's sale of a bay horse, leather top buggy, & harness at public auction, on Oct 27, by order of the Orphans Court of D C, belonging to the estate of the late Edw Hall, deceased. Terms cash. By order of the adms.
-Green & Williams, aucts

FRI OCT 26, 1866

Police matters: 1-Fred'k Dowling was yesterday fined $50 for keeping a gambling saloon at Ohio ave & 10th st. 2-Justice Handy fined Richd Callahan $20.90 for selling liquor without a license. 3-Justice Cull yesterday had Catherine Fitz, David Rawlins, & Ann Bohlayer before him for driving wagons without a license. They took out license, & their cases were dismissed. 4-Joshua Edelin, colored, was fined $2 for letting his dog follow him into the market house.

Mrd: on Oct 18, at Wm Kilgours, by Rev Fr Maguire, assisted by Rev Fr McCarty, Mr John J McCollum to Miss Olivia M Queen, all of Wash City.

Died: on Aug 26, near Vicksburg, Miss, of congestive fever, Wm H Allen, aged 31 years & 6 months. Mr Allen was formerly a resident of Wash City, son of Hon John W Allen, of Cleveland, Ohio.

Died: on Oct 24, Mrs Isabella M Hall, aged 26 years. Her funeral will be on Sat at 11 o'clock A M, from the residence of her mother, Mrs M S Rich, 467 9th st.

Tournament in St Mary's Co, Md, on Friday last, at Leonardtown; the horsemanship was admirable. The Maids of Honor selected were Miss Mary Ferguson, of Chas Co, as first Maid; Miss Alice Waring; Miss Maria Garner, of Chaptico, & Miss Kate Colton, of Longworth Point, also chosen Maids. The "Knight of Thornley:" Mr F X Simms; Mr J Harris; Mr A Jarboe;Mr G R Garner; Mr J Waring; & Mr W Hammett, were Knights. The chief marshal of the occasion was Mr G Fred Maddox. Assist marshals: Geo Barber John Davis, J T M Raley, & Dr L J Sutton. Herald: Wm A Kirk. Judges: Col John F Dent, Oscar Hayden, & John H Waters.

San Francisco, Oct 23. Capt Townsend, of the U S steamer **Wachusett**, died on Aug 15 at Shanghai.

Yesterday two men, Pedeste Carlow, an Italian, & Henry Jovell, went to the Marsh Market & priced some corn of an old colored man, Jas Patterson, who lives with Mr Lodgers, near the Chain Bridge, saying that they would give him 50 cents in addition to the price of the corn if he would carry it to their home, but a few squares from the market, to which the old man consented. When a distance from the Market, Carlow & Jovell proceeded to choke & rob Patterson of $4.16. The cries of Patterson were heard when Col Clark Mills, Mr Johnson & others from **Fort Lincoln** pursued & captured the robbers. They are held to bail for court.

The Navy Dept has received despatches from Cmder Carter, commanding the U S steamer **Monocacy**, announcing the arrival of that vessel at Bridgetowne, Barbadoes, on Sep 24. The **Monocacy** put into Barbadoes in consequence of the illness & subsequent death of Lt Cmder J C Chaplain, the executive ofcr of that vessel. He died on the 23rd ult, of remittant fever, after an illness of 4 days.

The funeral of Mr Chas Rupprecht, who was found drowned in the canal, took place yesterday from Odd Fellows' Hall; services conducted by Rev P H Sweet, & the remains were interred in *Prospect Hill Cemetery*.

Boston, Oct 25. 1-At Lawrence, Geo A Kinnerton, one of the Beverly burglars, who engaged in an affray with the State constable at Chelsea beach some time ago, was sentenced to the State prison for 20 years. 2-The ship chandlery shop of Wm G Goodhue, in Salem, took fire today from the ignition of kerosene oil. Wm Gray was smothered to death, & Geo Davison was badly burned.

N Y, Oct 25. The presentation of medals to veteran soldiers & sailors of Kings Co took place today at Brooklyn. The following were present: Gov Fenton, Admiral Farragut, Rear Admiranl Bell, Gens Morton, Vogdes, Delacey, Irvine, Duryea, Roberts, Smith Cook, & others. The medals were presented by Mayor Booth, of Brooklyn, & received on behalf of the soldiers by ex-Mayor Wood. Admiral Farragut was surprised with a beautiful gold medal. A letter was received from Gen Grant regretting his inability to be present.
[Names of those who received medals was not given.]

Soldiers' Cemetery on the Va Peninsula. A despatch from *Fortress Monroe* says: the ofcrs constituting the Soldiers' Monument Board, organized 15 months ago to solicit subscriptions to locate a soldiers' cemetery, have completed their labors, aided by Miss D L Dix. It will be gratifying to the relatives of the fallen soldiers to learn that their remains are resting where they can at any time be reclaimed.

Extensive household & kitchen furniture at auction on: Nov 1, at the residence of John H Semmes, fronting on Va ave, between 7th & 8th sts, Island. Also, on the same day, the residence consisting of a fine built brick house. Also, 7 handsome bldg lots 20 x 100 feet deep. -Green & Williams, aucts

SAT OCT 27, 1866
The *Stonewall Cemetery* was dedicated at Winchester on Thu, in the presence of 5,000 people. The remains of Gen R Ashley & Capt Dick Ashley, & of Col Marshall & Col Thompson, were transferred & buried under the auspices of the Masonic Lodges of the valley, after which an oration was delivered by ex-Govn'r Henry A Wise.

The pardon of Geo A Trenholm, who was the rebel Sec of the Treasury, was granted at the special request of Maj Gen O O Howard, Chief of the Freedmen's Bureau; Maj Gen Danl E Sickles, commanding in S C; Maj Gen Dix, & a number of other persons of similar military & political prominence.

Le Roy Tuttle has been appointed Assist Treasurer of the U S.

Orphans Court-Judge Purcell, Oct 23. 1-The will of the late Levi Neale was filed & fully proven & letters testamentary were issued by Geo S White; bond $400.

2-Letters testamentary were issued to Eliza McDuell on the estate of the late John McDuell. 3-Wm Keenan was appointed guardian to the orphans of P W Byrne; bond $2,000. 4-Letters of administration were issued on the estate of Peter W Magruder to Geo Magruder; bond $6,000.

Criminal Court-Judge Fisher, Oct 26, 1866. 1-Eliza Bryant & Jane Brown: larceny. Brown was placed on trial: verdict-not guilty. 2-Armistead Holmes, assault & battery with intent to kill; verdict-guilty. Sentence: 2 years in the Albany Penitentiary. 3-John Ashby & Lawrence Royal: burglary: verdict-guilty. Sentence: 3 years each in the Albany Penitentiary. 4-Robt Butler: larceny: verdict-guilty. Sentence: 1 year in the Albany Penitentiary. 5-Geo Fries: larceny: accused plead guilty. Sentence: 1 year in the Albany Penitentiary. 6-Betsey Glascoe: larceny: verdict-guilty. Sentence: 1 year in the Albany Penitentiary. 7-John Turner: larceny: verdict-not guilty. 8-John C Buehler: larceny: verdict-not guilty.

On Thu an affray in front of Butler's restaurant, 14th st, resulted in the shooting of Cornelius Driscoll, a soldier of the 4th artl, stationed near Alexandria. H C Leo was arrected upon a charge of shooting with intent to kill. Mr Leo had delivered himself up to the authorties for further investigation. Driscoll was also wounded in the face by the heel of a boot.

The funeral of the late Morven J McClery took place yesterday, from his late residence, on N Y ave, & was attended by a large number of our most respected citizens. Rev Dr Hall officiated. The remains were interred in *Congressional Cemetery*.

Mrd: on Oct 25, by Rev Dr Pinkney, Jas F Allen, of Bradford, N H, to Julia A, 2nd daughter of the late Jesse E Dow, of Wash City.

Grand Organ Concert at Foundry M E Church, corner of 14th & G sts, on Tue evening, Oct 30, 1866. Geo W Morgan, Organist, Grace Church, N Y, will preside, assisted by the talent of this city, Madame Kretshhmar, Mrs Butts, Dr Caulfield, Mr W Burnett, & others. Tickets, $1, for sale at the princiapl Music & Book stores.

Troy, Oct 21. Hiram Coon, the murderer of Mary Larkin, in South Petersburg, Rensselaer Co, was arrested in Bennington, Vt, this afternoon, coming into this State from Vt of his own accord. Mary Larkin, whose head Coon split open with an axe, cannot possibly survive.

Toronto, Oct 26. It is rumored that an attempt will be made to rescue Col Lynch, who was yesterday sentenced to be hanged for taking part in the Fenian raid.

Gen Logan is seriously ill at Olney, Ill.

Gov Wise now resides in Richmond, in the house formerly the residence of Chief Justice Marshall.

New Orleans, Oct 25. Matthew Gibson, a citizen charged with murdering Sgt Shuck, of the 6th U S Cavalry, in Park Co, Texas, has been arrested by the civil authorities & held for trial under bonds. He was afterwards arrested by a military order from Gen Heintzelman. The was then brought by habeas corpus before Dist Judge Goode, who decided that the military had no jurisdiction of his offence, he being a citizen.

San Francisco, Oct 24. Dr John King Robinson, formerly assist surgeon at Camp Douglas, was decoyed from his home on Monday, under pretext of his services being required, & murdered within half a block of his own house. His funeral took place today under the direction of the Order O Odd Fellows. An investigation has elicited nothing.

Mrs Cunningham, who figured in the Burdell murder case in N Y, some years ago, was among the lost of the steamer **Evening Star**, as was also Wylde Hardings, who resigned from the U S Navy to marry Belle Boyd, the actress.

The following missionaries embarked at Boston on Wed under the auspices of the American Baptist Missionary Union: Rev J J Stoddard, wife, & one son; & Rev M B Camfort & wife, for Assam; Rev J N Cushing & wife, & Miss M A Cottries & Miss A R Gage, for Burmah.

Supreme Court of D C, in Chancery; No 831-Equity. Columbus Alexander vs Antonio Buckignani, Margaret Buckignani, Henrietta & Wm Pendleton, Mary & Beverly Randolph, John E Evans, & Wm T Evans. The bill states that Rhoda O'Neal in her lifetime sold to Wm Douglas square 135 in Wash City, D C, & upon full payment did convey the same in fee simple to the said Douglas, his heirs & assigns, forever, & that before the said deed was recorded it was lost or destroyed. The object of this bill is to procure a deed from the heirs of Rhoda O'Neal of square 135 to the cmplnt in this cause, to whom the said Douglas heretofore conveyed all his right, title & interest to the same.
-R J Meigs, clerk

MON OCT 29, 1866
Kilbourne & Latta, real estate brokers, 7th & F sts, sold a 3 story brick house & lot on square 247, on 13th st, between L st & Mass ave, to Hon A G Riddle, for $10,800.

Letters of administration on the personal estate of John T Cochrane, late of Wash, D C, deceased. –Jas D McPherson, exc

Louisville, Oct 27. Geo D Prentiss, editor of the Journal, is seriously ill with bronchitis. His recovery is doubtful.

Trustee's sale of valuable property in Gtwn; by decree made by the Supreme Court of D C, on Sep 25, 1866, in equity case 1,807. Judson Mitchell et al vs Virginia Nicholls et al, the undersigned trustee will offer for sale, on the premises, at public auction, on Oct 29, the following real estate in Gtwn, D C, viz: 1-Property known as the residence of the late Wm S Nicholls, of Gtwn, containing 227 front feet on the west side of Congress st, 180 front feet on the north side of West st, 304 front feet on the east side of Valley st, & 492 feet along the northern boundary of said property running from Congress to Valley st, on which stands a large & substantial brick mansion. 2-Lot of ground in Gtwn, the west part of lot 92, in Beall's additon to Gtwn, containing 30 feet front on the north side of Beall st, by 120 in depth. 3-Lot of ground, the middle part of lot 209, in Beatty & Hawkins' addition to Gtwn, fronting 25 feet on the west side of Market st, running back that width 70 feet. 4-Lot of ground, the s w part of lot 4, in Old Gtwn, fronting 25 feet, 2¼ inches on the north side of Bridge st, & running back that width 269 feet, with a 3 story brick bldg thereon. –Josiah Dent, trustee

On Oct 29, after the sale of the *Nicholls' Mansion*, I will sell that desirable business stand, No 60 High st, near Bridge st. The lot fronts 29½ feet with a depth of 202 feet; with a large 3 story brick store & dwlg with back bldg. After which I will sell a 3 story brick store & dwlg, 55 High st, near Bridge, now occupied by Wm R Wallace, as a confectionery store.
–Thos Dowling, auct, Gtwn, D C

Nashville Despatch, Oct 23. Yesterday Chas H W Bent, for some 8 or 9 years past a resident of the city, was shot in Cherry st, by a young man named Hugh McGavock. The affair was the result of a bit of scandal which transpired in Louisville, & was published in the papers of that city about a week ago, implicating the mother of the latter in connection with Mr Bent. McGavock shot Bent with a pistol on the street. Bent ran to the corner, accelerated his pace, & fell dead. McGavock was taken into custody.

Orphans Court-Judge Purcell, Oct 27, 1866. 1-The will of the late John T Cochrane was filed & fully proved, & admitted to probate. The will bequeathes his estate to his wife & sister, & nominates John D McPherson, exc. 2-Letters testamentary were issued on the estate of Mr McPherson, who gave bond in the sum of $25,000. 3-The will of Michl Murphy, heretofore filed, has been fully proven. 4-The will of the late Julia Catilino, bequeathing her property to Virginia P Norwood, was fully proved. 5-Letters of administration were issued to Sarah Odrick, on the estate of Jos H Odrick: bond $1,000; to Mary Ann Stone on the estate of Woodford Stone; bond $10,000; to Mary _ Spencer on the estate of John F Spencer: bond $20,000. 6-Virginia Hollingsworth was appointed guardian to the orphan of Jas H Doughty, late of Brooklyn: bond $10,000. 7-The first account of Francis Weilhelm, guardian to the orphan of M P Mohun, was approved & passed.

Supreme Court of D C; in Equity No 802-Docket 8. Thos C Wilson vs Geo H, Fred'k, Nathl, Gibson, Wallace, & Alex'r Terrett, Amelia Hunter, Geo H Paine, & Margaret H Fillebrown. Orris S Paine, being seized of part of lots 16 thru 18 in square 127, in Wash City, on Aug 17, 1846, conveyed the same to Washington Terrett, his heirs & assigns, in trust for Mary A, wife of the said Orvis S Paine, her heirs & assigns, & to convey the same to such person or persons & for such uses & interests as the said Mary A Paine, under her hand & seal may direct; that the said Washington Terrett, on Oct 28, 1853, by deed acknowledged before one magistrate in Charleston District, State of S C, reconveyed said parcel of land unto the said Orris S Paine, that the said Orris S Paine died intestate, & his widow & heirs at law conveyed a part of said & unto Thos A McLaughlin & Thos C Wilson, cmplnt, in fee simple as tenants in common, that said Thos A McLaughlin conveyed all his interest in said parcel of land to the cmplnt on Apr 1, 1861; & that the remainder thereof became vested in the said cmplnt by conveyance; that the said Washington Terrett died intestate & without issue, leaving said dfndnts his heirs at law, in whom the bill avers the bare legal title to said parcel of land is vested; & that all of said dfndnts, except the said Geo H Paine & Margaret H Fillebrown, are non-residents of D C. The object of the bill of complnt is to have the legal title to said parcel of land vested in the cmplnt. Non resident dfndnts are to appear in the Clerk's ofc in the Supreme Court of D C, on the first Tues in Mar, 1867. –R J Meigs, clerk
-Wm F Mattingly, solicitor

Rochester, N Y, Oct 27. Josiah Rogers, a blacksmith of this city, aged 48 years, was murdered last night near the County Fair Grounds. He had been to a horse race, & after leaving the track, was stuck by a slung shot, which caused his death in a few hours. The murderer is still at large. The motive is unknown.

Died: on Oct 28, in her 23rd year, Kate E, wife of Thos W Bevan, & daughter of the late John Sergeant. Her funeral will take place from the residence of her mother, 404 E st, on Tuesday at 11 o'clock.

Died: on Oct 26, Ann Douglas, aged 65 years, beloved wife of Wm Douglas, sr. Her funeral will take place this morning at 11 o'clock, from her late residence 358 11th st.

Died: on Oct 18, at St Georges, Dela, Jery Lee Page, formerly of Salem, Mass, & late of Fairfax Co, Va, at age 87 years. Capt Page was for several years a resident of Wash City, & was one of the two only survivors of the pioneers in the East India trade.

Died: on Oct 28, at Alexandria, Va, Mrs Marian Speiden, wife of the late Paymaster Wm Speiden, U S Navy, aged 56 years & 7 months. Her funeral will be from the Baptist Church, Alexandria, Va, tomorrow, Tuesday, at 1 o'clock, from whence the remains will be conveyed to the *Congressional Cemetery*, Wash, D C.

Typhoid fever at Bladensburg last week. Miss Lucas, the only daughter of Maj Lucas, was one of the victims. On Sunday her body was embalmed, previous to its conveyance to Illinois, of which State her father was a resident.
–Marlboro Gaz [No death date given.]

TUE OCT 30, 1866
Mr Frank Henry, a well known citizen of Wash, & who has for years been connected with the Wash & N Y press, died at Easton, Pa, on Oct 29, at the residence of J L Mingle. He has been suffering all the summer from a complication of diseases, but it was not until about 2 months ago that his malady assumed a serious firm. He went to Easton about a month ago, thinking that a change of air might be beneficial. He died at the age of 35 years, in the arms of his wife. The remains of the deceased will be brought to this city. [Nov 1st newspaper: Mr Frank Henry was buried today from his late residence, on C st, between 2nd & 3rd sts. His remains were received at the depot by a large number of his friends. He was so much emaciated from sickness that his best friends could hardly recognize him.]

Yesterday a woman named Johnanna Deely died at her residence, 2nd & F st, & a few moments thereafter her brother, Edw P Walsh, preferred a complaint against Patrick Deely, the husband of the deceased, charging him with having caused her death by abuse & ill treatment. Dr Jas Reilley testified that he was called to see the deceased on Sat & found her purging & vomiting freely. She appeared to be in much pain. John Shanahan, a brother-in-law of deceased, was sworn, & testified that on Sat, a week ago, deceased came to his house. He saw blood oosing from her ear, & she said Patrick [her husband] had struck her with a board & she was unable to sleep since then. Edw P Walsh, the brother of deceased, testified he visited his sister one week ago last Sat, & she complained of ill treatment by her husband. Deely is possessed of some valuable real estate & a store, but it is understood that most of the property was in his wife's name, & his brother-in-law, Walsh, claims that he is proper protector of his sister's children. There is something very curious about the whole case, & much litigation may yet arise from it.

Mr Jacob Lowenthal, well known here as claim agent, & as head of the Union Claim Agency, on Pa ave, near 15th st, died last night at his boarding house on Pa ave. He took ill yesterday. His death resulted from cholera or cholera morbus, most probably the latter. He was about 40 years of age.

Executive appointments. The following ofcrs of the internal revenue were commissioned yesterday: John S Williams, collector for the 8th Dist of Ind; H W Harrington, collector of the 8th Dist of Ind; Davis H Wilson, collector for the 9th Dist of Ind; Owen D Downey, assessor for the 2nd Dist of West Va; Wm D H Hunter, assessor for the 4th Dist of Mo.

Died: Oct 29, Miss Frances Adeline Seward, only daughter of Wm H Seward. Her funeral will be Wed next, at 3:30 P M, at St John's Church. [Since the death of his wife, Mr Seward's affections have clung most closely & fondly to his daughter.] [Nov 1st newspaper: The following gentlemen were pallbearers: Baron Von Gerolt, Admirals Chas H Davis & Jas A Dahlgren, Maj Generals M C Meigs & E D Townsend, Judge Olin, Chas Knap, & Mr Peale. Clergymen in attendance: Rev John Vaughn Lewis, Rector, St John's Church; Dr C H Hall, Rector of the Church of the Epiphany; Dr J Trimble, Assist of St John's; Rev Augustus Jackson, Missionary, Wash City Convocation; Rev R W Lowrie, Rector of the Church of the Incarnation. Funeral arrangements by Mr Harvey, undertaker, 410 7th st, aided by Mr Alonzo Marr. Maj G S Koontz accompanies the funeral from this city in a special car provided by the Balt & Ohio Railroad Company.]

Mrd: on Oct 10, in St Paul's Church, Salem, N Y, by Rev H M Davis, Rector, Mr Geo B McCartee, of Wash, D C, to Miss Caroline Allen, daughter of the late Geo Allen, M D, of the former place. No cards.

Died: Oct 29, Jane Harrison Scott, relict of the late Capt I D Scott, of Gtwn, D C, & daughter of the late Maj Thos Beatty, of the former place. Her funeral will be from her former residence, 549 13th st, between B & C, [Island]Wed at 10 A M.

Police matters. 1-Dennis Barrett & Henry Hall trespassed upon the property of Jas Crutchett & took gravel therefrom, whereupon Ofcr O'Callaghan arrested them, & Justice Walter fined them $10 each. 2-Jas Carter broke the Sabbath by pitching cents. He was fined $1. 3-Violators of city ordinances have a hard road to travel. The following were fined: Geo Carson, wagon without number; John Paton, Jas Bostane, Chas Huaise, T S Denham, wagons without license, $5 each; E L McDaniel, cart unlicensed, $2.50; Michls Burns was arrested for fast driving & fined $20 & committed to the work house for 10 days in default of payment. Wm Harrington & Lawrence McMahon were fined $5 each for a violation of the law relative to the keeping of hogs. Jeremiah Lynch was fined $2 for violating the cow law. John Clarke & John Sullivan, two masons working on the new church on High st, Gtwn, yesterday got rather high-spirited by putting spirits down: each fined $3.44. Baldassarro Maraughi was fined $20 for violating the law in reference to selling on Sunday. He keeps a fruit & candy store on Pa ave.

Louisville, Oct 28. 1-On the authority of Col Starr, commanding the late Fenian expedition, now here, we state that Col Lynch, who was convicted & sentenced to be hung at Toronto, was a bookkeeper in a mercantile house of this city, & was sent with the Finian expedition by his employers. He had no rank & did not belong to the organization. He accompanied it merely as an adventurer to report to his employers. Col Starr offered Lynch a commission, which he refused to accept. 2-W O Summerville,of Charlestown, West Va, was found dead Sat on board the steamer **Prima Donna**. He evidently died from cholera. A check drawn at Marietta for $1,200 was found on his person.

Randolph Macon College. Col Thos O Johnson, a graduate of this institution, & a native of Va, though recently of Alabama, has been elected President.

Mississippi Cotton Plantation for sale: 480 acres of land, frame house & all necessary out-houses, in Noxubee Co. Address Dr R K Hinton, Brooksville, Miss. I will trade the farm for a farm in Md or Pa.

I certify that I have no connection with the Drug Store, 231 N Y ave, between 4th & 5th sts. Mr Chas E Edwards is sole proprietor & owner of said store.
–C Miller, M D

Dept of the Interior, U S Patent Ofc, Wash, Oct 24, 1866. Ptn of Wm Stratton & Matthias Stratton, of Phil, Pa, praying for the extension of a patent granted to them on Feb 1, 1823, for improvement in Portable Gas Apparatus, for 7 years from the expiration of said patent, which takes place on Feb 1, 1867.
–T C Theaker, Com'r of Patents.

Supreme Court of D C; No 738 Equity, Docket 8. Sallie Laforge vs Saml F Laforge. The ptn of the cmplnt having been filed on Jul 28, 1866, praying for a divorce a mensa et thoro from the said Saml F Laforge for brutal neglect, & ill treatment, committed in the District of Col, subsequent to his marriage with the said Sallie Laforge, & other good causes assigned in her said ptn, & it appearing to the satisfaction of the Court that a subpoena was duly issued on Jul 28, 1866, & returned non est, & it further appearing, by the affidavit of a disinterested witness in this cause, that the said Saml F Laforge is a non-resident of D C. Said dfndnt is to appear in person or solicitor to answer said ptn of the cmplnt in this matter. –R J Meigs, clerk -J Carter Marbury, solicitor

WED OCT 31, 1866
Presidential appointments. The following Postmasters were yesterday appointed: John P Mitchell, at LeRoy, N Y; C L Shrewsburg, at Madison, Ind; A E Day, reappointed at Webster, Mass. H B Denman, of Kansas, was appointed Superintendent of Indian Affairs for the Northern Superintendency.

<u>Wash City Improvements.</u> 1-A new bldg on 6th st, between L & M sts, for the congregation of the German Evangelical Church, Rev Dr Hetzell, is being finished by Chas Just, contractor & carpenter; cost $16,000. Conredis & Walston, bricklayers; John Keiler, plasterer; Walter & Hendricks, painters. 2-A new bldg for the parochial school of St Mary's Roman Catholic Church, on 5th near H st, is being built, occupancy by Nov 10. John Keiser, contractor & builder. 3-Adam Kiesecher is making an addition to his bldg at 6th & H sts. 4-John Flaherty is bldg a residence on 5th st, below C, costing about $1,500. 5-John McMurray has built for himself, on H about 3rd st, a 3 story brick, 17 x 40, including back bldg, costing about $3,200. 6-Jos Prather, butcher, is bldg a handsome pressed brick front dwlg, with stable, on M st, near 4th, costing about $8,000. Jos Mockabee, carpenter & builder, Wm McCollum, bricklayer, Stewart & Shuit, plasterers.

7-Mrs Greaves has built three 2 story brick stores & dwlgs on 7th st, below L, costing about $7,000. 8-J H Darrow has built himself a new carpenter shop, 16 x 80, on K st, below 7th. 9-**Carroll Hall**, on G st, between 9th & 10th sts, is rapidly approaching completion, under the direction of the Christian Brothers; 54 front x 113 feet deep.

Orphans Court-Judge Purcell, Oct 30, 1866. 1-The will of the late Christopher Yeabower was filed for probate & record. The estate is bequeathed to his widow, who is nominated excx as also guardian to the children. 2-Mary L Spesser was appointed guardian to the orphans of John D Spesser; bond $1,500.

Coroner Grover, of N Y, held on inquest upon the body of Emil Moth, who had committed suicide in his apt, 19 Allen st, by inhaling charcoal gas. He left 3 letters, in one stating that he died by his own hand; the other was to his wife, & the third to Mr Chas H Palmer.

Mrd: on Oct 30, at the residence of the bride's father, by Rev Mr Hamilton, G E Dalton, M D, of Phil, to Sallie E Cohen, of Wash, D C. No cards.

Mrd: on Oct 30, at the E st Baptist Church, by Rev Dr Gray, Henry C Johnson, of Ill, to Martha Washington, daughter of A Rothwell, of Wash City.

Died: on Oct 29, at New Orleans, of yellow fever, in her 23rd year, Lizzie, younger daughter of the late Col Jas Thatcher, of St Anthony, Minn.

Died: on Oct 12, at **Fort Union**, New Mexico, of pneumonia, John T S Whiting, formerly of Wash City, in his 24th year of his age.

Thos Dowling, auct, sold the large brick mansion & grounds, on West st, known as the **Nicholls property**, to F W Hanewinckel, of Richmond, Va, for $26,000. Also, a 3 story brick store & dwlg on Bridge st, to F W Geisezing, for $5,150; brick store & dwlg on High st, to H J Baker, for $1,975.

Another prominent actor in the last war has passed away. Dr Chas S Tripler died of cancer on Oct 20 at Cincinnati, where he had gone to be under the care of his friend, Dr Blackburn. He was born in N Y C in Aug, 1806, & was in his 61st year. He was promoted to be surgeon on Jul 2, 1838; stationed at different times at Detroit, **Fort Gratiot**, & Mackinaw. Dr Tripler received the rank of colonel, & was brevetted brig general for his arduous services in behalf of his country.
–Detroit Free Press

In Syracuse, on Sat last, Mrs Samantha Hall, wife of Mr Hall, of the firm of Hall & Rice, died suddenly as she was about to step into her carriage to ride out.

Wm S Halabird, son of ex-Lt Gov'n'r Halabird, of Conn, was accidentaly killed while carelessly handling a gun on Tuesday.

Dr Geo Edw Lynch Cotton, Bishop of Calcutta, was recently drowned in the Ganges, while landing from a steamboat. The bishop's diocese had an area of 301,102 square miles, but the number of clergy under him was only 200.

Harrisburg, Oct 29. A man named Martin Tate, living in Cumberland Co, died last night of hydrophobia. He had been bitten by a rabid dog 9 weeks ago.

THU NOV 1, 1866
Alexandria: Since Sunday two old residents of this city, Mr Wm Atwell & Mrs Catherine Ward, have departed this life.

Criminal Court-Judge Olin, Oct 31, 1866. 1-Danl Stewart: assault & battery with intent to kill: jury unable to agree upon a verdict & was discharged. 2-Gabriel Cachot: rape. The accused, a Frenchman, & the prosecutrix is his own daughter. It appears that the father, mother, & daughter lived all together in one room in a tenement house, & the unnatural father after several attempts, at last succeeded in accomplishing his incestuous purpose. Evidence was clear, pointed, undeniable, & the jury rendered a verdict of conviction. Accused has not yet been sentenced.

Dept of the Interior, Ofc Indian Affairs, Oct 31, 1866. Letter to Hon Dennis N Colley, expressive of their feelings towards him, on his voluntary retirement as Com'r of Indian Affaris. Signed:

Chas E Mix	Lewis S Hayden	C G Cutting
W H Watson	Geo W Scriver	Arthur Moffatt
Wm B Waugh	E F Ruth	Lonsville Twitchell
Micajah P Smith	French F Mix	G F Jocknick
Geo Lewis	Gideon Burkhart	Jos M Wilson
Louis T Brennan	John H Smoot	Wm P Copeland
Jas M Davidson	H R Clum	Jas H Bell
C S Mattoon	J C Kretschmar	Geo H Holtzman
W E Fuller	Boon Chambers	Thos E McGraw
C C Royce	Chas Herzog	Stephen A Dole
Alex'r Johnston	Jas H Eby	Walter R Irwin

Appointments by the Pres yesterday:
Solomon T Clark, U S Atty for the Eastern Dist of Ark.
John E Rozetto, U S Atty for the Southern Dist of Ill.
John T C Clarke, Justice of the Peace for D C.
John A Miller, of Mo, Register of the Land Ofc at Ironton, Mo.
Lewis Lowry, of Nebraska Agent for the Indians of the Omaha Agency.
Chas Bogy, [brother of Hon Louis V Bogy, Com'r of Indian Affairs] Purchasing Agent to buy ponies for the Arapahoes & Cheyennes.
John Williams, of Kansas, Register of the Land Ofc at Junction City, Kansas.
Col Jas T Abernethey, Collector of Internal Revenue for the Second Dist of Tenn.
Jas N Patterson, Postmaster at Jeffersonville, Ind.
Jas M Graham, Postmaster at St Jos, Mo.

Mrs Barton, whose illness had been reported, died on Tuesday of a genuine case of cholera. We hear it started again by the sanitary police that she had eaten beans on Saturday, cabbage on Sunday, & on Monday had eaten salt fish.

Police matters. 1-Jos Payton stole a frock coat & other articles from John W McCray, who is employed at Rush Barracks. He was committed to jail for court. 2-Henry Young, colored, stole $7 in pennies, & a pistol, from the junk shop of Mrs Sarah Fenkes, on Bridge st, between Market & Fred'k. Ofcr Paxson arrested him, & Justice Buckey committed him for court.

Mrd: on Oct 30, at the residence of the bride's father, by Rev W V Lewis, rector of St John's, Edmund Pendleton Gaines to Frances, daughter of Wm Hogan.

Boston, Oct 31. Rev Sylvanus Cobb, a well known Universalist clergyman, died today, aged 68 years.

At 377 Sedgwick st in Chicago on Sunday, where a number of young men reside, Reuben T Bryant, from Council Bluffs, Iowa, confined to the house for several days by sickness, drank from a bottle labeled blackberry cordial. After swallowing a mouthful, he realized it was not what it was supposed to be. He had accidentally drank nitric acid. He was still alive Monday, but not a particle of hope for his recovery was entertained. He must either die of ulceration of the bowels, or else more lingeringly & painful of starvation.

Solomon L Hull, a prominent member of the N Y bar & president of the Union Dime Savings Bank, of that city, died recently at St Paul.

Marius Baker, a well known conductor on the Old Colony railroad, died on Tue, at Boston, from injuries received by being run over by a freight train a few days since.

Mr J L Babson, jr, a prominent citizen of Gloucester, Mass, & well known throughout the State, was accidentally & fatally shot by his brother while out gunning a few days since.

Geo Calvert, clerk in the employ of C C Parks, 34 New st, N Y, on Tuesday absconded with $40,000 in gold checks belonging to his employer. $10,000 of the amount has been cashed; payment on the rest has been stopped.

A wrecking company has lately been engaged in saving portions of the cargo of the steamer **Andrew Johnson**, recently wrecked on the N C coast. Capt R Haley, of the wrecking service, who has been attending to the operations, recently returned to Norfolk, having been successful in recovering cargo to the amount of some $30,000. The cargo saved is now in Norfolk ready for shipment to N Y.

A copartnership has this day been formed by Messrs J E Fitch & R C Fox, of Wash City, & the business conducted by Fitch will be carried on in their joint names. General Agency for the purchase & sale of Real Estate, Collection of Rents, care of property, etc.

Trustee's sale, by decree of the Supreme Court of D C, in chancery, wherein Wm H Terrett et al are cmplnts, & Wm W Terrett et al are dfndnts. Public auction on Nov 8, of lot 5 & part of lot 6 in square 315, located at K & 11th st, with a 3 story brick dwlg, with side lot. –Wm F Mattingly, trustee -Green & Williams, aucts

FRI NOV 2, 1866
Noah M Gould, a promiment citizen of Lincolnville, Me, was killed Tuesday night by a board blown from his barn during a storm.

Henry U Fleetwood was yesterday appointed postmaster at St Johnsburg, Vt.

Today Wm Plater, Wm H Jones, Thos Davis, & Henry Luckett, all colored men, will suffer the extreme penalty of the law, at Marlborough, for crimes of which they have been duly convicted. The crime for which they are to be executed was the murder of Mr Wm Lyles, of PG Co, Md, on Jul 14. The residence of Mr Lyles was on the south bank of Piscataway creek, near its junction with the Potomac, & nearly opposite **Fort Washington**. It was formerly improved by a fine brick mansion, which was destroyed by fire early in the war. For this arson several of Mr Lyles' own negroes were indicted, but escaped from jail before trial, among them one of the parties implicated in the murder. After the fire Mr Lyles & his wife lived in a small cabin originally built as a servant's quarter, consisting of one room only on the first floor, entered by two doors. Opposite each other in the front & rear. The night of the murder, after Mr & Mrs Lyles had retired, there was loud knocking at the rear door, when Mr Lyles demanded what was wanted. In reply the travellers stated that they were travellers, from Port Tobacco, & supposing the house to be occupied by colored persons, had called to ask for lodging & directions as to obtaining employment. Mr Lyle directed them to another quarter near by, where they could remain for the night, & in the morning would see what could be done. Mr & Mrs Lyles fell asleep. Sometime afterwards the door was suddenly burst in by main force, & the negroes burst in, firing toward the bed as they entered. Mrs Lyles immediately aroused, & not finding Mr Lyles in bed & supposing he had escaped, unlocked the front door & went out, endeavoring to secure herself. She was overtaken by the ruffians & brought back. Being asked where her husband was, she replied she knew not. They then demanded to know where the money & keys were, & required a light to be furnished. The negroes allowed a small servant girl to go, & get a lamp. They stole $1,200 to $1,500 in Va currency, & upwards of $200 in gold & some silver coins. Mrs Lyles managed to hide behind a tree & eluded further harm. The dead body of Mr Lyle was found lying on the floor, in a narrow space between one side of the bed & the secretary. Under his body was a pistol of his own, which usually lay upon a shelf near the bed. He was struck by the first fire as they entered the room, the pistol shot entered the right cheek bone & proceeded upward through the brain. He did not groan or make a sound when he fell to the floor. Mr Lyles was nearly 58 years of age, of fine personal presence & in vigorous health. [Wm Plater, born in Chester, Pa, lived in Alexandria; Henry Luckett was from the neighborhood of Warrenton, Fauquier Co, Va. Wm Henry Jones was formerly a slave of Mr Lyles; age about 30. Thos Davis, mulatto, age 19 years, belonged to Col Jennings, near Piscataway. Wm Jones, a 5th party who was to be executed, was convicted of the commission of a rape on the person of Mrs Anderson, near *Silver Hill*, but was respited until Nov 14.]

Hon Wm Wright, one of the U S senators from N J, died yesterday. He was a native of Rockland Co, N Y, & removed to N J in 1794. [A similar announcement was prematurely made on May 23 last.]

The gale last Tuesday at Providence, R I, blew down a large drying shed connected with Walsh's waste bleaching at Dry Book, near this city, & killed Thos Ferguson, an employe & injured two or three others.

Wedding: Capt Alfred Mordcai, U S A, was married at the Church of the Epiphany, yesterday, to the daughter of Gen Maynadier, of the Ordnance Dept, Rev Dr Hall officiating. [Bride's name not given.]

Police Affairs: 1-Two hackmen, John Simmons & Saml Rainey, were fined $1 each for driving their hack across the line at the Balt depot, & crowding among the passengers as they came out of the station. 2-Danl Hurley was fined $50 for dealing in lottery policies, & fined $2 for getting drunk . 3-Chas Brown & K H Lambell were fined $5 each for driving wagons without license. 4-Danl Raidy was fined $30, & Geo Bradley $40, for selling liquor on Sunday.

Mrd: on Oct 31, at Gtwn, by Rev Mr Williams, Walter S Cox to Margaret L Dunlop, only daughter of Jas Dunlop.

Mrd: on Nov 1, by Rev R J Keeling, D D, Robt E Taylor, of Poughkeepsie, N Y, to Miss Virginia S, daughter of Franck Taylor, of Wash City.

Died: Oct 26, at Mobile, Ala, Mrs Louisa R Zantainger, 73, a native of N Y.

Died: on Oct 16, at San Antonio, Texas, of cholera, Mrs Fanny Yorke Bailey, wife of Lt Fred W Bailey, of the 17th regt, U S infty. Her death was followed on the evening of the same day by that of her son aged 1 month. Mrs Bailey was the only daughter of S Yorke AtLee, of Wash City.

Died: on Nov 1, in Wash City, of diptheria, in his 52nd year, John M Speed, of Lynchburg, Va. His friends will be gratified to know that in the full possession of his faculties he resigned himself to his Maker with full faith & humble confidence. –M F P

Died: on Nov 1, Maria L, wife of Dr J W H Lovejoy, & daughter of Wm A Greene, of Brooklyn, N Y. Her funeral will take place from the residence of her husband, 9th & F sts, on Nov 3 at 2 o'clock P M.

Troy, Oct 31. Mrs Maj Gen Wool was struck with paralysis at the old headquarters of this Dept in this city today. Her entire right side was paralyzed, & the attack will probably prove fatal. Gen Wool was telegraphed to at Balt & will probably reach here tomorrow night. Mrs Wool is a daughter of the late Howard Mouiton.

The Pres has directed the issue of warrants for the pardon of W H McCown & John S Kelly, who were convicted upon a joint indictment at the Dec term, 1865, of the U S Dist court for the southern dist of N Y of defrauding the Gov't, & sentenced to imprisonment, the former for 18 months, & the latter for 1 year.

Jas Lewis, who is confined in jail in Poughkeepsie, charged with the murder of Rev J C Richmond, attempted to commit suicide in his cell on Oct 30, with a razor. He now lies in a critical condition.

Antietnam Nat'l Cemetery, Thos A Boullt, sec & treasurer of the Association. A burial corps has been sent to the cemetery by the Gov't with a train of wagons, etc. The men of this corps disinter the bodies from the many trenches & graves around the neighborhood of the battle-field, place them in coffins, & deliver them to Dr Biggs, superintendent of the cemetery. Trenches have been excavated in the divisions of the cemetery set apart for each State, & as the bodies are received they are interred in their respective trenches; the coffins are placed exactly 8 inches apart. There are trenches excavated for 16 States. After all the bodies around the battle field are interred, the burial corps will proceed to gather & transport to the cemetery those lying at different points in the county, Keedysville, Boonsobro, Funkstown, Hagerstown, & other places, together with those who fell at South Mountain. –Hagerstown Torchlight

War Dept, Rooms of Claims Div, Wash, D C, Oct 31, 1866. Claims filed during Oct, 1866-claim of:
Julia Armstead, property destroyed by Union troops.
A H Mann, horses impressed into the U S service. Wm G Sneethen, atty.
Moses Mills, services as teamster. Wm C Wood, atty
A Anstele, for tobacco taken by U S authorities.
Patrick McCormick, for iron seized by the U S Gov't. Saml V Niles, atty.
Martin Hammers, late capt 98th regt, Pa infty, for subsisting his command. Johnson, Brown Co, atty.
Bernard Escole, property damaged in the bombardment of Donaldsonville, La.
Sabina Peacher, property destroyed by U S troops.
C T Venniegerholz, for one half of the value of the steamer **St Mary**. J W Denver & O F Peck, attys.

Geo Hume, for sugar seized by U S authorities. A S Fuller, atty.
Charlotte Moore, for the occupation of property by U S authorities. Mary Thos McSwiggin, assignee. No atty.
Fontain F Freeman, for mules taken by U S troops. Henry & Walker, attys.
A Davidson, sutler, etc, for stores taken for hospital purposes.
Thos C Kelsey, Henry J Thompson, John H Bingham, Jonathan Oldham, Otis Phillips & J H Hunt, & Jas G Davis; for services as scouts. Gregory & Jones, attys.
J F Newlon, for services as assist provost marshal. Gregory & Jones, attys.
Henry Williams, Wm Satchell, David C Pignette, & Gideon E Coldren; for services as special officers. Gregory & Jones, attys.
Jas D Rowland, for services as blacksmith. Striblen & Simpson, attys.
Frank Day for quartermaster stores furnished to the U S military authorities. Do.
Milton Jackson, for quartermaster stores. Do.
R J Stringfellow, for rent & compensation of property by U S authorities. Do.
W J Sharp, for services as special ofcr in the Army of the Cumberland. Parsmon, Sowers & Co, atty.
C Hector Durward, for pay as lt & aide-de-camp. No atty.
S B Bowen, sutler, etc, for property taken by U S soldiers. Do.
John Westover, & J M Randkin, for services as scouts. John Higginbotham, atty.
Rosalie D Kelley, for services in communicating information to the U S authorities. No atty.
Jas G Hamilton, for use of the steamer **St Maurice**, John Joliffe, atty.
Mrs J W Woolfork, for the destruction of property. No atty.
Jules Courche, for rent of property. Do
Mrs Asoline Fay, for property taken & destroyed by U S soldiers. State Dept for the French Minister.
Mrs Josephin Gosselin, for cattle taken by U S authorities. No atty.
Mrs Philomine Sigur, for property taken & destroyed by U S authorities. Do
Montgomery Hunt, for balance on contract for oats furnished to the U S, W G Sneethen, atty.
E D Wheeler, for cotton taken for the fortifications around Nashville, Tenn. A L Merriman, atty.
Sarah A Snowden, for rent of property at Nashville, tenn. Striblen & Simpson, attys.
J L Hurst, for rent of property at Loudon, Tenn. Do.
Isaac Burton, for quartermaster stores. Do.
John L & Wm Usrey, for cotton taken by U S troops. Do.
Aaron Weeks, for fees as a witness in Missouri. Cr_c_er & Bramhall, attys.
Francis Segura, for cotton, John Jollife, atty.
John Wayman, for quartermaster & commissary stores. R W Downman, atty
Juliet Hannah Baker, for quartermaster stores. Do.
M C Brickley, for services as detective in Provost Marshal Dept. W C Goodloe, agent.
J R Hall, for services as a detective. Jas H Birdsel & Co, attys.
John C Dawson, for money taken by Gov't detective. Daniels & Sherwood, attys.

Alexis & Eugene Tuenit, for property taken for the use of the U S army. John Jolliffe, atty.

Thos Niles, for damages to lands used for miitary purposes. Gardiner Tufts, agent.

Bennett M Bird, for services, etc, as superintendent of Fletcher Farm, Va. No atty.

Saml M Johnston, for rent of property in Tenn. Striblen & Simpson, attys

F W Dermon, J Mullery, G A Valentine, L Richard, Jim Coole, Alfred Beary, Jim Light, John Hill, W Henry, Ch Anderson, L James, S Sponier, D Richards, J Douglas, Perry Moore, A Sappington, W Roan, J Chambline, G Jefferson, B Moore, J Forthuse, A Freizor, J Rollins, W Merrick & H Jackson, for services at the forts around St Louis, Mo. M Delany, atty.

A Beary, W Richards, Jas Cooley, Louis Richards, Louis James, Sam Spencer, W Richard, D Richard, W Chapman, G Duncan, J Coleman, J H Haley, John Hall, J Mullery, Wm Schillingman, & Ch Johnson, for services at the forts around St Louis, Mo. M Delany, atty.

Fendal Carpenter, for proceeds of the sale of cotton. Horatio King, atty.

Wm Burey, for hay taken for the use of the army. A S Cox & Co, attys.

Jordan Y Cummings, for forage, etc, taken by U S troops. Peter J Sullivan, atty.

Wm Jones, for corn, horses, & mules taken by U S troops. Do.

Martin W Guy, for forage, horses, & mules taken by U S troops. Do.

Michl Ryan, for money & property taken by U S authorities. Chas F & Geo W McGill, attys.

Carl U Henricks, consul, etc, for property taken by U S troops. State Dept.

J R Dickerson, for rent of property, etc, occupied by the Gov't. Chas F & Geo W McGill, attys.

Jos de Filipi, for destruction of property by U S troops. State dept for the Italian Minister.

R M Richards, for property taken by the Provost Marshal at Nashville, Tenn. A S Cox & Co, attys.

Fred'k Schraag, for services as engineer. Clifton Hellen, atty.

H Harvey McKee, for pay as 2nd lt. Edw N Wood, atty.

Jas H Gibbens, for cotton used the U S forces. A Barg, atty.

Michl O'Day, for property taken by U S troops. State Dept for the British Minister.

David Young, Michl Kreis, A Dolphy, & M Lynch, for tobacco seized by order of Maj Gen Sherman at Atlanta, Ga. North, Rohrer & Co, attys.

Thos L Pleasants, for horse taken by U S army. No atty.

Caleb S Hallowell, for damages to property by U S troops. R P Jackson, atty.

Jas Jett, for forage. Downman & Magruder, attys.

Dr B Maas, for services as a member of a board of enrollment in Louisiana. John Jolliffe, atty.

Wm J Sexton, for services as scout. A L Merriman, atty.

Fritz Johnson, for money taken from him at Soldiers' Rest, Wash, D C. No atty.

_ M A Huff, for rent of property at Mason, Ga. Do.

Louis Paul Cayer, for damages to his property. Do.

Isaac Fisher, for quartermaster & commissary stores. Downman & Magruder, attys.
Robt H White, for services as clerk in the Quartermaster Dept. Jas Fullerton, atty.
Thos C Case, for quartermaster' stores. S F Primrose & others, attys.
Miss Manora Sayre, for damages to property. No atty.
Wm Barnes, for services during the war. Do.
John Holleran, for horses & carriage. Do
John B Griffin, for services as sepcial ofcr. Ayres & Bishop attys.
R P Kirkpatrick, for property. No atty.
Sam M Johnson, for damages to property. Do.
John Bigham, Seaborn, Skinner, & Duncan Graham, ,for quartermaster & commissary stores. Downmann & Magruder, attys.
P B Burroughs, John Parsons, Jas M Salter, Wm H Stevens, Lloyd Mitchell, & John R Silver, for quartermaster stores. Do.
Henry G Jones, for commissary stores. Do.
Wm Low, for sugar. State Dept for the British Minister.
Henry G Jones, for commissary stores. Downman & Magruder, attys.
Asop Buck for services in the Provost Marshal's Dept. Saml Niles, atty
John M Tracy, for property destroyed. No atty.
Reuben Smith, for services as assist provost marshal. J Higginbotham, atty.
John J Trittman, for cotton. State Dept for Swiss Consul Gen.
Chas C Walcutt, warden of the Ohio penitentiary, for keeping military prisoners. No atty.

SAT NOV 3, 1866
Mrs Experience C Fiske, of Warwicke, Mass, left property valued at $10,000 to $15,000 to the American Bible Society, & her heirs are endeavoring to break the will.

Mrd: Nov 1, at the Parsonage of the Church of the Immaculate Conception, Wash, D C, by Rev Fr McCarthy, Jas W Drane to Emily J Lowe, both of Wash City.

Mrd: on Oct 30 last, at St Aloysius Church, Wash City, by Rev Nicholas D Young, Mary B, youngest daughter of Geo W Young, to Hampton B Denman, of Leavenworth, Kansas. Kansas papers please copy.

Mrd: on Oct 30, in Balt, at the residence of Prof N R Smith, by Rev D Foley, Dr N S Lincoln, of Wash, to Nannie M Smith, daughter of the late Col Saml Moale, of Balt.

Mrd: on Nov 1, at the Church of the Epiphany, by Rev Chas H Hall, D D, Brvt Lt Col Alfred Mordecai, Capt U S Ordnance Corps, to Sally Sanford, daughter of Gen Wm Maynadier, U S A.

The only place in town where Artists' materials can be had, C S Whittlesey's, 528 7th st.

Wm Plater, Henry Luckett, Wm Jones, & Henry Davis yesterday suffered the extreme penalty of the law at Marlboro, Md. They were convicted of the murder of Mr Wm Lyles, near Piscataway. The roads to Marlboro were thronged with people who were desirous of witnessing the hanging. Wm Henry Jones, who was charged with rape, & who it was expected would also be hung, was respited by Govn'r Swann, the testimony in his case being doubtful, & some evidence existing of his innocence. The courier arrived at Marlborough, with a respite for Jones, on Thursday, the respite being for 6 weeks. Jones at first did not understand the respite until Mr Brooke, the clerk of the court, explained to him that he was not to be hung until Dec 14. Jones remarked,: Well, I'll have a good time of it." On Monday last the undertaker took the measures for their coffin. Plater seemed somewhat moved & his eyes moistened for a moment. The others showed no emotion whatever. The graves of the prisoners were dug in the jail yard, where the new jail is erected. On Thu, the wife of Plater, & the wife & friend of Luckett, visited them, & took their final farewell. Plater exhibited little feeling but Luckett, was very affectionate kissing his child again & again. On Friday, Rev Mr Kershaw, the Episcopal Minister, visited them. At 11 o'clock the prisoners appeared, clad in white shrouds, in the following order: Plater, Jones, Davis, & Luckett. After they had hung 10 minutes they were lowered & examined by Dr John H Mundell, physician to the jail. In the conversation with Mr Kershaw, Plater & Davis acknowledged that they were concerned with Frank Dixon in the burglary of the house of the Misses Palmer last spring. A man named Ova_y Slater is now in the penitentiary for this crime. Luckett confessed to being connected with Richards & John Parker in robbing McCracken's store, in Alexandria. Plater & Davis acknowledged in conjunction with Frank Dixon & Richards, that they had robbed the place at **Eckington**, when a most brutal murder was committed. Luckett says he remembers shooting on the occasion referred to, but he doubts whether he killed anyone.

Galveston, Nov 2. The gang of marauders which infested certain portions of the State have been captured, shot or hung. Col Young, their leader, formerly a chief of scouts, was hung by the rancheros.

Died, at the Wash Arsenal, on Nov 1, Sgt Thos Vickers, of the Ordnance Dept U S army, in his 79th year. He was born in Shadlow, England, Aug 22, 1788; enlisted in the Goldstream Guards Sep 19, 1806; in 1831 he enlisted in the U S army, & served in the 1st artl during the Florida war, & as Cpl Vickers, was commended in the official report for gallantry in the affair of **Fort Drane**, Jun, 1836; the same year he joined by enlistment the Ordnance Dept, at Wash. Sgt Vickers was in faith an Episcopalian, & a member & communicant of Grace Church, Island, from which church his funeral will take place on Sunday next at 2 o'clock P M.

MON NOV 5, 1866
Oak Hill Farm, the ancient seat of Chief Justice Marshal, in Fauquier Co, Va, has been sold to Wm Knight, of Cecil Co, Md, for $51.25 per acre.

A man named Chas Plato met with a fearful death at Niagara Falls on Thu. He was employed in a saw-mill, & was in the act of oiling some of the machinery, when he became entangled therein, & his body was horribly mutilated. His head was cut off.

Surgeon Warren Webster, now stationed at Boston, has been promoted to the rank of lt colonel for his faithful services during the prevalence of the cholera last summer among the troops on Hart's & David's Islands, in N Y harbor.

Mr Jerre Ketchum, of Buffalo, has promised to donate land in that city for the Normal School in case the State Com'rs decide to locate in that city one of the 4 schools of this class provided for by the Legislature at its last session. The city has appropriated $45,000 for the erection of suitable bldgs.

Mrs Eleanor Anna Scott, who resides on B st south, near 6th st, committed suicide on Sat by cutting her throat with a razor. It is said that for some time past she has been laboring under a derangement of mind, produced by deep study on religious matters. He husband noticed a change in her manner several days since, bu did not apprehend any serious consequences. In the morning, all at once, Mrs Scott went into the back yard & cut her throat; her husband ran to her & carried her to bed. He ran for Dr Croggon, but before he returned she had died.

Col Jas R O'Beirne has been appointed Reg of Wills of the Dist of Col, vice Mr Z C Robbins, removed. Col O'Beirne entered upon the discharge of his duties Sat.

Danl D Home, the celebrated medium, has written letters to his friends in Norwich stating that a very wealthy lady named Lyon, in England, has adopted him & made him her sole heir on condition of his taking her name. This he consented to do, & signs himself Danl D Home Lyon.

Died: on Sunday, John Cullum, in his 71st year. His funeral is this morning from 18 Market Space, between 8th & 9th sts, at 10 o'clock.

Died: at his residence at Newark, N J, Hon Wm Wright, U S Senator.

Fortress Monroe, Nov 3. The parole granted Jeff Davis some months ago, giving him the privilege of the fortress during the day, has been extended through Executive clemency in removing all surveiliance over him, & the guards from his rooms in Carroll Hall at night. Instructions to this effect have been sent from Washington to Gen Benton, commandant of the fort, thus divesting his imprisonment of anything like severity, & paving the way for his final parole & release. He now enjoys perfectly untrammelled liberty. He has expressed great gratification at this action of the Gov't, & already contemplates the vacating Carroll Hall, & taking up his residence with Mrs Davis in the casemates assigned her shortly after her arrival here.

Toledo, Nov 4-double murder in Michigan. At Coldwater, Mich, last night, Ebenezer Searle met his wife walking with Geo C Brown, a young lawyer, & shot them both dead. Cause, jealousy.

The funeral of Chas A Hecksher, a distinguished merchant of N Y C, took place Sat, & was largely attended.

A man named Jas Thompson & three of his children were drowned at Oldtown, Maine, on Friday, by the upsetting of a boat.

By the recent death of Col Saml Swett, Mr Isaac Lincoln is left the sole survivor of the Harvard class of 1800.

Washington Irving's old summer house was lately sold at auction for $10.

A young man named Chas U Burt came to his death at Elmira on Friday. On Sat he played ball & soon after complained of pain & swelling on his lip. Physicians were summoned from N Y & Albany, & his disease was pronounced a peculiar form of erysipelas, produced by some poisonous matter from the ball. The deceased was a step-son of Hon Lucius Robinson, late Comptroller of the State.

A handsome monument of marble has been erected in **Mount Olivet Cemetery**, Balt, to the memory of Rev Robt Strawbridge, the first preacher & founder of Methodism in Md. A memorial tablet records, among other matters, that
He Built
The Log Meeting House
In Frederick County, Maryland,
1764,
The First in America.
He Died in peace
In 1781,
At Mr John Wheeler's, Baltimore County,
Whither He Had Gone to Preach.

TUE NOV 6, 1866
Criminal Court-Judge Fisher. 1-Gilbert Vanderwerken, charged with assault & battery on Mr Geo Hill, jr; Mr Vanderwerken was indicted in 1861-jury failed to agree. Mr Hill rented a house to Mr Vanderwerken, retaining the room below as a store-room. There was an area back leading to the cellar, under the dwlg. They has a contest about this area. Hill barricaded it. Vanderwerken tore it down. [Vanderwerken has a son, Chas.] Mr Chas Vanderwerken swears Hill fired the first shot, & Hill was slightly wounded. The jury returned a verdict finding the accused guilty of assault & battery, & he was fined $150. 2-Yesterday the case of Milburn Hunter was taken up-the accused was arrested on the charge of the murder of Beniah W Luckett, in Feb last, on 7th st, near L, & was tried about

Jun 1, when after the D A had withdrawn the charge, claiming a verdict for manslaughter, the jury failed to agree, & were discharged. No new facts were elicited yesterday.

Orphans Court-Judge Purcell. 1-The will of the late Geo Barton was admitted to probate. 2-The will of the late Christopher Yeabower was partially proven. 3-The will of the late Marion Speiden was fully proven, & letters testamentary issued to the daughter, Mariana Speiden; bond $30,000. 4-The will of the late Jacob Loewenthal, bequeathing his entire agency business to J B Hutchinson, in payment of a debt, & the balance of his estate, after satisying the debt, to his wife & mother. Mr J B Hutchinson, of this city, & John Kelly, of N Y, are nominated as executors. 5-Letters of administration were granted to Eliz C Ferguson on the estate of Jas R Ferguson; bond $1,000. She was also appointed guardian to the children; bond $800. 6-Letters of administration were granted to Johanna Koppel on the estate of Frank Koppel; bond $600. 7-Jos R Keene was appointed guardian to the orphans of Jos R Keene; bond $1,000. 8-Eliza Ann Taylor was appointed guardian to the orphans of Thos B Taylor, sr; bond $300.

Mrd: on Oct 30, at St James' Cathedral, Wheeling, Va, by Rt Rev R V Whelan, D D, Alex'r Loughborough, of D C, to Mariana, daughter of the late Ebenezer Zane, of Wheeling, Va.

Mrd: on Nov 5, at the Seaton House, in Wash City, by Rev H M Paynter, D D, of Richmond, Va, A C Steger, of Cumberland Co, Va, to Miss Virginia E, daughter of the late Judge Seymour Lynn, of Prince Wm Co, Va. –Richmond papers please copy.

Died: on Nov 5, Charles Eugene, only child of Richd F & Seville Boiseau, aged 11 months & 12 days. His funeral will take place Tuesday afternoon, at 2 o'clock, from the residence of J T Boiseau, 9th & G sts.

Died: on Nov 3, Martha R, wife of Dr G W Woodley, in her 46th year. Her funeral will take place today at 3 o'clock P M, from 495 7th st, between D & E sts. Mrs Woodley won for herself, during her sojourn in Wash, a large circle of friends, & leaves behind an affectionate husband to mourn her loss.

Nagle & Co, aucts, sold lot 7 in square 184, with improvements, to Mr H Rundlett, for $1,575; & lot 17 in square 116, to J Platz, for 50 cents per foot.

Police Affairs: 1-Richd Kane, a lad, was arrested yesterday near M & 9th sts, for playing ball on the highway, & fined $3. Playing ball on the streets has become a nuisance, & the police are determined to break up the practise. 2-John Ross was arrested for stealing a buffalo robe from a carriage near 13th & P sts, while the driver, Wm Johnson, was taking his horses into the stable. 3-Chas Johnson, alias Wm Mockabee, was arrested yesterday for cutting a tassel off of the dress of a lady walking along Pa ave, near 6th st. He was fined $2.58 for his sharp work.

Dept of the Interior, U S Patent Ofc, Wash, Oct 29, 1866. Ptn of Harvey Murch, of Labanon, N H, praying for the extension of a patent granted on Jun 14, 1853, for an improvement in Mop Heads, for 7 years from the expiration of said patent, which takes place on Jun 14, 1867. –T C Theaker, Com'r of Patents

N Y, Nov 5. Simeon Draper died today of paralysis of the right side. [Nov 7th newspaper: He was long a leading merchant & popular auctioneer; collector of the port of N Y, receiving his appointment from Pres Lincoln after removal of Mr Barney; later he was removed & the place given to ex-Senator King, of St Lawrence Co. At the time of his death he was U S Cotton agent, & had charge of all the cotton received at this port. He leaves a family & hosts of attached friends to mourn his loss. –N Y Express, 5th.

[Nov 7th newspaper-same paper as above: The announcement of the death of Simeon Draper was premature. He died this morning.]

Mrs Leach, wife of the postmaster at Joliet, Ill, set fire to her clothing while lighting a lamp on Thursday, & was so badly burned that she died the next morning.

Geo Smith, age 17, was found dead in his bed at the Putnam County House, in 4th ave, N Y, on Sat last. His two brothers, Ephraim & Danl occupied the same room, & on Sat Geo was found dead, & his 2 brothers in an insensible condition. The flue was undoubtedly the cause of Geo's death. The two survivors are in a critical condition.

Ex-Confederates in Mexico. Letter from Cordova, Mexico, says: Gen Sterling Price & family are here; also Gen J O Shelby's family-he is at present in the City of Mexico. Govn'r I G Harris, of Tenn, is living at Carlotta, about 8 miles from here. Gen P C Hindman, of Ark, is at Orizaba, as is Judge C H Randolph, of Texas, formerly State Treasurer of that State, but I learn he goes back with his family soon, because we have no schools where he can educate his children. This will be remedied when we can get enough of good working men with families to settle here.

Last week, in Marshall Co, Miss, during a difficulty between Mr Logan Walker & a Mr James, the superintendent of Mr Walker's farm, the latter was killed by a shot from a pistol, in the hands of Mrs Bradley, a sister of Walker.

Extensive sale of household & kitchen furniture at auction on Nov 14, at the residence of K F Page, 469 6th st, between D & E sts. Also, an elegant family carriage, made by Jacobs, Area st, Phil; horses, harnesses, & saddles. -Green & Williams, aucts

Trustee's sale of 3 farms at Laurel, Md: 127 acres; 132 acres; & 120 acres. Apply to M Bannon, trustee, 32 St Paul's st, Balt, Md.

WED NOV 7, 1866

Washington bldg improvements. The foundation of the First Congregational Church, 10th & H sts, is nearly completed. The U S Army Medical Museum & Surgeon General's Ofc [which **Ford's Theatre** had been converted into,] is nearly complete. The entire front wall had been rebuilt, & 40 carpenters, under the direction of John S Slater, are hard at work finishing the specimen cases & record shelves. Should be in order by Dec 10,1866. On N st, between 13th & 14th sts, a Lutheran church & parsonage are in course of erection. Mr Eames has built a large brick residence at 14th & H sts, 4 stories high, with 24 rooms, costing about $22,000. Matthew Galt has built a spendid 3 story house, brownstone front, costing about $60,000. Franklin square is being laid out according to plans of B B French, jr, the work being done under the direction of Jas Nokes, public gardener, & superintendent Jas Stone. A fountain is to be placed in the centre. Sec McCulloch has built a dwlg on H st, between 16th & 17th sts, costing about $22,000. At 16th & I, Chas Knap has refitted his residence with a new French roof & fine brown stone front steps. Rev S Tustin, Presyterian Minister, has built a residence on 16th, between H & I sts, costing some $3,000. At 15th & N Y ave, Geo H Plant is erecting a large bldg to be used for ofcs & stores; will cost about $33,000.

Orphans Court-Judge Purcell. 1-Col Jas R O'Beirne, recently appointed Register of Wills, vice Mr Z C Robbins, yesterday appeared before Judge Purcell, & took the oath of ofc & entered upon his duties. 2-Benj Freeman qualified as administrator of the estate of Martha Ingersoll, deceased, late of Cumberland Co, Maine, & gave bond in the sum of $250. Sureties, Wm G Whittlesey & Harris C Hamlin. 3-Louis Wehn, the next of kin, & legatee of Catharine Redeger, deceased, renounced her right to administer in said estate, & petitioned for the appointment of Christian Lederer as administrator. 4-Mary L Speisser qualified as guardian to the orphans of John F Speisser, deceased, by giving bond in the sum of $1,500. Sureties, Edw McKenney & Benj H Bryan. 5-Henry C Noyes gave bond in the sum of $1,000 as administrator of the estate of Mary Noyes, deceased, late of Gtwn. Sureties, John J Beall & Jas Gozler. 6-Chas G Page gave bond in the sum of $1,000 as administrator of the estate of Jerry L Page, deceased. Sureties, Anthony Potlock & Zenas C Robbins. 7-Christian Lederer gave bond in the sum of $7,000 as administrator c t a of the estate of Catharine Redeger, deceased. Sureties, Geo Lantner & Florian Frederick.

Criminal Court-Judge Fisher. 1-Milburn Hunter, accused with the murder of B W Luckett in Feb last, was found not guilty, & discharged from custody. 2-Jas H Booth alias Martin: assault & battery with intent to kill Oliver May; case not concluded.

Messrs Kilbourn & Latta, real estate brokers, sold lot 11 in square 86, on 20th st, between I & K sts, to Mrs Eliz Houser, for $2,200. Also, lot on L st, near North Capitol st, to G Rogers, for $350. A frame house & lot on 9th st, between P & Q sts, was sold to John M Lewis, for $1,900 cash.

Gen Henry A Wise is lying dangerously sick of cholera at his residence, the old Marshall House, corner of Marshall & 9th sts. He is under the treatment of Dr Haxall. –Richmond Times

The President yesterday appointed Jas B Williams register of the land ofc at *Fort Dodge*, Iowa; T W Bedford, register of the land ofc in Nebraska Territory; Wm H H Taylor, postmaster at Cincinnati; & Wm C Herschberger, postmaster at *Fort Madison*, Iowa.

Benj Parry was tried in the Toronto court on Monday for complicity in the Fenian invasion. He was a mere boy of 15 & was acquitted.

Julia Dean Hayne has secured a divorce at Salt Lake. The divorce was granted in the summer by the Probate Court, but without a hearing from Mr Hayne. After he was heard from the former decree was confirmed.

Mrd: on Nov 1, at *Townshend's Delight*, PG Co, Md, by Rev Mr Chipchase, F O St Clair, of Wash, D C, to Miss Lelia C Dent, of St Mary's Co, Md.

Col Albert J Myer has been appointed Chief Signal Ofcr of the army.

Information wanted of Edw Louis Batteganji or Geo Olsen. Please leave information at Gerhardt's Hotel, Pa ave, between 4½ & 6th sts, Wash.

Cincinnati, Nov 5. Alex'r E V Hirlay, M D, of this city, committed suicide last night by taking morphine. Disappointment in love & intemperance had so unsettled his mind as to induce him to destroy himself.

New Orleans, Nov 6. Rev Dr J P B Wilmer will be consecrated tomorrow as Bishop of Louisiana, in place of Bishop Polk, killed near Atlanta during the war.

Balt, Nov 6. Shooting affray, in which one man, Augustus Talbot, formerly a member of the City Councils, & belonging to the Radical party, was shot, & thought to be fatally wounded.

Orphans Court of Wash Co, D C. Letters of administration on the personal estate of Jerry L Page, late of Wash, D C, deceased. –Chas G Page, adm

THU NOV 8, 1866
Police Matters: 1-Nelly Windsor & Jas Johnson were arrested & fined $5 each for keeping dogs without a license. 2-Emma Kelly, colored, was arrested on a charge of stealing a coat & hat, the property of Mr David M Barr, from his boarding house, 213 Pa ave; the accused was employed in the house. Emma was sent to jail for court.

New Orleans Picayune: Friday, Mr Jas Thompson, a laboring man of Oldtown, went in a boat to a small island on the Milford side to obtain a load of sand, taking all his children with him, three boys from 4 to 10 years old. On their return the boat upset and the father & 3 boys were all drowned. Mrs Thompson mourns the loss of her husband & children.

Association of the Oldest Inhabitants meeting was held at the Gtwn Market house Hall yesterday; P G Washington, Pres, J McDonald Davis, sec; journal of last meeting was corrected by inserting the name of John P Hilton. Mr Jenkin Thomas submitted the following named gentlemen for membership: A Hyde, Dr Magruder, John Marbury, Robt McPherson, Morris Adler, John Meem, E A Eliason, D W Edmunston, & W H Tenny, who were accepted. Mr John F Callan nominated Chas H Wiltberger; Mr J C Brent nominated Thos McDonnell; Dr A McD Davis nominated Dennis Pumphrey; J C Brent nominated Henry Halliday; Mr Young nominated Andrew Hancock; J D Clark nominated Henry Barron; Lewis Johnson nominated Gregory Ennis. On motion of Dr Blake, the rules were suspended, in order to enable Mr J C Brent to read a paper, relating to Gen Ross, of Bladensburg notoriety. It was announced that by a vote passed some months ago, a photograph album had been procured, in which had been placed the photographs of members of the association, the card bearing on the reverse side the date of birth of the members. The photographs have been made by Mr Gardner. The corresponding secretary, John Carroll Brent, has possession of the album. On motion of Mr Nash, Mr Dorsett was requested to furnish the original roll of Capt Stull's company. The roll was furnished by Mr Dorsett with a vote of thanks. A communication was received from Mr Christian Hines, accompanied by 2 copies of his recently published book, entitled "Reminiscences of Washington." Mr Dorsett also presented a copy of a letter to Maj Peter, [commanding the District forces in the war of 1812;] Gen Armsrong, Sec of War.

Judge Wylies has made his decision in the case of B I Neale & Mary, his wife, against John E Neale. The bill is to compel the dfndnt to deed a house & lot to Mary Neale, one of the cmplnts, on the ground that the lot was given to her before her marriage to promote the same & in consideration thereof, & that her money in consequence of this gift was expended in the erection of the house now on the lot & occupied by the dfndnt. The Court being of the opinion that a trustee ought to be appointed to hold the property for the benefit of Mrs Neale, one of the cmplnts, but could make no decree as the case now stands. The Court allowed the cmplnts to Nov 15 to amend their bill on the payment of costs, which are quite large.

Criminal Court-Judge Fisher: 1-Yesterday Jas H Booth alias Martin, indicted for assault & battery with intent to kill Oliver May, was convicted & sentenced to 3 years in the Albany penitentiary. 2-Edw Parker, indicted for the larceny of $130 from R Cromelein, was convicted & sentenced to 18 months in the Albany.

Gen Oliver P Gooding, of Indiana, has been appointed Deputy Marshal for the Dist of Col, in place of Col Jas R O'Beirne, appointed Register of Wills.

A shocking outrage was perpetrated at Bowling Green on last Monday, in the murder of an old lady, Mrs Sill, by 3 negroes. While at a lawyer's ofc the preceding Sat, 3 negroes overheard Mrs Sill tell the lawyer she had $65 at home. On Monday the widow's son, a little fellow, who had been out in the fields, came home to get his shoes & found his mother lying on the floor dead, her head split open by an axe. The 3 negroes were later apprehended & are now in jail at Bowling Green. The negro Lewis wore a pair of shoes that precisely matched the tracks leading from the victim's house. –Nashille Dispatch, 2nd.

The wife of Carpenter Danl Jones, U S N, attached to the Portsmouth Navy Yard, was burned to death on Friday by the explosion of a kerosene lamp.

An old man named John Perkins, who has been watchman of a white-lead factory in Louisville, for 8 years, was detected robbing his employers' safe a few nights ago. He had a false key, & had been stealing small amounts for a long time.

Capt Nimrod M *Baggerly, conductor of a passenger train on the Orange & Alexandria railroad, in attempting to get on the train this morning, at Catlett's Station, accidentaly fell upon the track, & had both his legs mangled by the car-wheels, & is not expected to live. He was originally from Warren Co, Va, but had resided in Wash City for a number of years with his family. –Alexandria Gaz of Tuesday. [Nov 9th newspaper: Capt *Baggarly died a short time after the accident. What remained of his body was coffined by his friends, & sent on the up-train to his wife in Alexandria. He expressed a desire to be buried in Warrenton, which we suppose will be carried out.]
*Two spellings of Baggerly/Baggarly.

It is said that the oldest inhabitant of Alexandria is a colored woman, born in 1755, [which would make her 111 years old] named Anna Carter. We expect she is not as old as this, but her age is very great.

Mrd: on Nov 6, at Church of the Ascension, by Rev Dr Pinkney, Stirling Murray, of Balt Co, Md, to Anna Thornton, daughter of Dr Thos Miller, of Wash, D C. Balt papers please copy.

Orphans Court of Wash Co, D C. In the case of Henry C Noyes, exec of Wm Noyes, deceased, the executor & Court have appointed Dec 1 next, for the final settlement of the personal estate of the said deceased, of the assets in hand. -Z C Robbins, Reg/o wills

Orphans Court of Wash Co, D C. In the case of John G Clarke, adm of Matthew St Clair Clarke, deceased, the administrator & Court have appointed Dec 1 next, for the final settlement of the personal estate of the said deceased, of the assets in hand. -Z C Robbins, Reg/o wills

N Y, Nov 7, Reuben Withers, pres of the Bank of the State of N Y, is dead. [No death given, current item.] [Nov 9th newspaper: Mr Withers was born in Va in 1789, was therefore in his 77th year. On his return from a trip to Europe, in 1818, he married the daughter of Mr David Dunham, & settled in N Y. On the death of Mr Lawrence, Mr Withers was made president of the Bank of the State of N Y, which ofc he filled at the time of his death. –N Y Commercial Advertiser]

FRI NOV 9, 1866
Fairfax H Whiting has been appointed Assist Assessor of Internal Revenue for the Third Division [Fauquier Co] of the 7th Dist of Va, vice Geo A Thatcher, resigned.

Further investigation into the alleged charge of arson & perjury against Emanuel Hoffman: Mr John McKenney, agent of the Park Ins Co, was sworn, testified he knew the dfndnt; saw cotton stuck in the door & match marks on the walls. Mr Henry Seitz, who lived opposite the store, testified that he had seen Hoffman remove some of his goods a day or two previous to the fire. Mr Albert Grupe, the owner of the premises was seen crying at the fire. Justice Bates held the accused to bail for court in the sum of $3,000, Chas Walter, becoming his security.

Installation of Ofcrs of Good Templars-Morning Star Lodge No 3, on Nov 6: A C H Webster, Worthy Chief Templar; Miss Anna S Shuman, Worthy Vice Templar; A R Abbots, Sec; Miss Laura L Wilson, Assist Sec; Wm H Kuhns, Treasurer; Miss M L Williams, Financial Sec; J C Dougherty, Marshal; Olive J Longley, Deputy Marshal; N B Hilliken, Outside Guard; Miss Millie White, Inside Guard; Miss Marion Taylor, Right Hand Supporter; Mrs A C H Webster, Left Hand Supporter; C Storrs, Chaplain; C T Sheppard, Past Worthy Chief Templar.

Police Matters: 1-Alice Jourdan was arrested for selling liquor without license: fined $20. 2-Jas Thyer, an agent, & W J Gray, a peddlar: each fined $20.58 for plying their vocation without a license. 3-Thos Venable, a degenerate son of respectable parents, was sent to the workhouse for drunkenness & disorderly conduct near the NavyYard.

Mrd: on Nov 6, at the residence of the bride's father, by Rev Dr Oulds, Chas H James to Matilda V, daughter of Col Henry Naylor.

Mrd: on Nov 5, in King Geo Co, Va, by Rev Mr Billingsley, P Louis Rodier, of Wash City, to Miss Mary Marmaduke, of King Geo Co, Va.

Mrd: on Nov 7, in Wash City, by Rev Wm Krebs, Jas G Holland to Maggie E, 2nd daughter of Mr Wm Flenner. No cards.

Albert M Van Kluck, for 5 years postmaster at Poughkeepsie, N Y, on Wed night fell, in an apoplectic fit, on Maine st, & died in a few hours afterwards.

Died: on Nov 8, in Balt, Md, after a brief illness, Miss Annie Curran, in her 16th year, youngest daughter of B B Curran, of Wash City. Her funeral will take place this morning at 10 o'clock, from the residence of her sister, 172 Hanover st, Balt. Her estimable parents have been deprived of one of the brightest of ornaments of their household.

Oak Hill, formerly the property of Chief Justice Marshall, has been finally sold, under a decree of the Circuit Court, to Mr Knight, of Md. It contains about 542 acres, & brought $54.25 per acre-$39,403.50.

Gen Sherman arrived at St Louis on Sunday.

Union Hotel for rent or lease; thoroughly remodelled & rebuilt; in Gtwn, D C, on the corner of Bridge & Washington sts; contains 40 rooms. –Riley A Shinn, Greene & Olive sts, Gtwn, D C.

Circuit Court for PG Co, in Equity, No 441. Jos Nessensohn, vs Sophia Vierberchen, admx of John Vierberchen & Margaretta Vierberchen. Ordered that the papers & proceedings in this cause be referred to the Auditor to state an account between the creditors of John Vierberchen, deceased, & the trust fund. –Saml H Berry -Fred'k Sasscer, Clerk

SAT NOV 10, 1866
The Pres yesterday made the following appointments: Cloys B Wilson, postmaster at Finley, Ohio; John J Douglas, at Zanesville, Ohio; Saml B Evans, at Ottumwa, Iowa; J P Evans, deputy postmaster at Waterloo, Iowa; Jos Colwell, do, at Elkton, Md; Andrew J C Wood, do, at Warsaw, Ind; John W Wells, of D C, agent for the Flat Head & other confederated tribes of Indians in Montana Territory; Joel B Bassett, of Minn, agent for the Chippewas of the Mississippi, Pillager, & Lake Winnebagoshish Lands, & the Indians of Red Lake & Pembina.

Mrd: on Nov 8, at St Matthew's Church, by Rev Fr McNalley, Geo P Fenwick, M D, to Miss Mary A, daughter of the late Geo W Stewart, all of Wash City.

Died: on Nov 8, Lemuel Sheriff, in his 24th year, son of Mrs Susan B Sheriff. His funeral will take place from his mother's residence, in Wash Co, this morning at 11 o'clock.

Raleigh, Nov 9. A general court-martial has been commenced at this city, by order of Gen Sickles, for the trial of Maj Alex'r Gosling, A Q M, of Buffalo, & other prisoners. The court is composed of: Gen N Goff, of R I; Col C G Brady, of Conn; Lt Col M R Hogan, Surgeon U S V, of N Y; Brvt Maj E Crawford, of Pa; Capt A M Staffee, of N Y. Brig Gen R Aveny, of N Y, is Judge Advocate. The court will proceed with the trial of Capt E Brown, 37th U S colored troops, of Boston, under charge alleging various fraudulent sales of Gov't property. The case of Maj Gosling is not ready for trial, & will not be taken up for a week.

Foreign Items: Gen Giulay, who commanded the Austrian army at the commencement of the war in 1859, has just been struck with apoplexy.

Geo Alfred Townsend writes of Rossini, the composer: "His face is large, puffy, heavy, but full of a good liver's wrinkles that look like dimples. He wears a black wig, which reduces his age twenty years. His house at Passy, in the environs of Paris, is beautiful. He is happy, as it seems, & much beloved."

Mr Lewis Fox, the celebrated billiard player, was severely wounded on Thursday, at his residence in Rochester, N Y, by the accidental discharge of a pistol in the pocket of his coat. The ball entered the abdomen & lodged in the thigh, beyond the reach of a probe. The surgeons think he will recover.

The Jumel will case was called yesterday, before Judge J F Barnard, & will commence this morning at 10 o'clock. Madame Jumel died in this city on Jul 16, 1865, at age 91 years; left an estate valued at a million dollars or more;-mostly landed property & houses in this city, the bulk of which she bequeathed by will to various charitable institutions, & but little of which was left to her relatives, or those who claim to be her relatives, & lawful heirs. As is usual, the heirs have resolved to contest the will, on the ground the will was made during the last days of the testator, when her mental capacity unfitted her for such an act. M'me Jumel was one of the most remarkable female characters that figured in our Revolutionary era, & was possessed of beauty & accomplishments that would have made their mark in any era. Born at sea, of a mother who died in giving her birth, she was brought up as an orphan, in the quiet town of Newport, R I, until age 17, when she eloped with an English ofcr & came to this city, where her career as a woman of fashion commenced, & where she first came in contact with the distinguished men of the Revolution. Here & in Phil she formed the acquaintance of Washington, of Jefferson, of Benj Franklin, of Lafayette, of Patrick Henry, of Aaron Burr, & others. She allied hereself with a rich French wine merchant of this city, & Miss Capet became Madame Stephen Jumel. The happy pair shifted their residence to Paris. When her husband's exchequer broke down, he became moody & low spirited, & Madame Jumel turned her attention to finance, came back to N Y, & took charge of the remnants of her husband's estate. He joined her & the two lived together until his death, at age 70 years. While a widow she renewed her acquaintance with Aaron Burr, whom she had employed as a lawyer. He offered her his hand & she became Mrs Burr, although she was past 70. The match did not turn out well & the wedded life was of short duration. The lady, taking divorce without opposition, resumed the name Madame Jumel. The leading party who now contests the will is Nelson Chace, a lawyer of this city, whose wife, now deceased, was the daughter of M'me Jumel's sister, & who, with her husband, was adopted by M'me Jumel, & brought up in her family. In addition to his own interests as guardian of his children, he has purchased the interest of all the other heirs, consisting of 4 or 5 persons by the name of Jones, the children of M'me Jumel's sister. The party who is charged with having undue influence over the testator in the matter of the will is Rev John Howard Smith, pastor of a church in Carmansville, to which M'me Jumel belonged, & who was her spiritual adviser some time previous to her death. Among the counsel for the contestants of the will are Chas O'Conor, ex-Judge Pierrepont, B F Dunning, Jas C Carter, & Aaron Vanderpoel. For the executor appear E W Stoughton, A W Bradford, Henry L Clinton, & Martin & Smith, besides others who have been engaged by various parties interested in maintaining the validity of the will. –N Y Times [Boston Journal: a curious incident has come to light in relation to her state of mind. She got an idea that the Prince of Wales would made her a visit, & set out a table elaborately, & would not allow a thing to be removed, being confident that he would come some time. A woman with such hallucinations is not regarded as competent to make a will.]

Mr H H Piper, of Lonaconing, superintendent of Atlantic & George's Creek Coal Co, died suddenly last Friday. He was at a dancing party given at the new mill-Haneycamp & Co. After the first set, he leaned against a friend, placed his hand over his heart, & in an instant was dead. His bereaved widow has the heartfelt sympathy of her very many devoted friends. –Cumberland Civilian, Nov 8.

Orphans Court of Wash Co, D C. Letters of administration on the personal estate of Mary Noyes, late of Gtwn, D C, deceased. –Henry C Noyes, adm

Valuable Potomac land for sale: by decree of the Circuit Court of Westmoreland Co, Va, in the suit of Stuart, trustee, vs Kinzer & others: public auction on Dec 12 next, at the court-house, in said county, of *Longwood*-contains upwards of 1,600 acres of land. The old mansion was burnt some years ago, but there are comfortable dwlg houses in good repair. Address to me at *Edge Hill*, King Geo Co, Va, or to G W Lewis, at *Oak Grove*, Westmoreland Co, Va. The title is unquestionable. –R H Stuart, Com'r & trustee

MON NOV 12, 1866

Green & Williams, aucts, sold a large brewery & bldgs, on D st, between 5th & 6th sts, to Catharine Baumann, for \$8,100;a 3 story brick residence, 61 K st, to Jabez Fox, for \$8,000; 2 story frame dwlg, on Md ave, near 10th, to Geo W Busher, for \$2,400. Messrs Kilbourn & Latta, Real Estate Brokers, sold a house & lot, 435 H st, near 11th, to W B Entwisle, for \$2,500 cash; lot 1, square 786, with 2 story frame dwlg, to Sarah S Benedict, for \$3,120; also lot on L st, near North Capitol st, to Wm G Metzerott, for \$100; also, house & lot on M st, between 14th & 15th sts, for \$2,300 cash.

Phineas S Willard, first salesman in the machinery store of Todd & Rafferty, No 4 Dey st, N Y, was instantly killed on Sat while engaged with other persons in moving a large drill, an iron machine weighing from 2,500 to 3,000 pounds. The machine fell over, striking him on the breast, knocked him to the floor, & crushed & killed him.

Yesterday morning a gloom was cast over many of the old residents of this District by the announcement of the death of Maj Robt Beale. He died on Sat at his residence, on Capitol Hill, of congestion of the brain. Maj Beale was one of the oldest inhabitants of Wash, where he had long occupied a prominent position. He was for several years Sgt at Arms to the U S Senate, & during a portion of the administration of Pres Lincoln was warden of the jail. He was a large property owner, & a genial, social gentleman, whose mansion was the favorite resort of many of the leading public men of the nation. Maj Beale leaves 3 sons & 3 daughters to lament their loss.

+

Died; on Nov 10, of congestion of the brain, Robt Beale, in his 66th year. His funeral will be on Nov 13, from his late residence, on 13th st, at 1 o'clock. [Nov 14th newspaper: The funeral of the late Robt Beale took place yesterday. The services at the house were conducted by Rev Drs Pinckney & Keeling, of the Episcopal Church, & Rev Dr Tustin, of the Presbyterian Church. The remains were interred in *Oak Hill Cemetery*. The pall bearers were Col Alexander, Messrs B B French, G W Riggs, J M Carlisle, J C Brent, J M Broadhead, John H Houston, & Geo Parker.]

Benj C Truman appointed Special Post Ofc Agent for Calif & the Pacific coast.

Orphans Court-Judge Purcell. 1-On Sat Matilda C Roberts qualified as guardian to the orphan children of Chas R Reynolds, deceased. Bond, $6,000. Sureties, Wm E Roberts & John M Roberts. 2-Jos Freundt qualified as guardian of the orphans of Ludwig Grunding, deceased. Bond, $1,000. Sureties, Edw Voight & Wm Frey. 3-Christian Lederer qualified as guardian of the orphans of Wm G Parkhurst, deceased. Bond, $1,000. Sureties, Thos Wood & Smith Pettitt. 4-Chas E Sherman was appointed administrator of the estate of John Snyder, deceased. Bond, $2,000. Sureties, Elger H Sherman & Amos L Merriman.

Sanford Conover, alias J A Dunham, has been indicted for perjury by the grand jury of this District.

Wm Redin, the oldest member of the Washington bar, with the exception of John Marbury, died on Friday at his residence on Gay st, Gtwn. Mr Redin was an Englishman by birth, & was born in Cambridgeshire in 1791. He married in England just previous to his immigrating to this country. He landed at N Y on Sep 5, 1818, & settled in Gtwn, & declared his intentions to become a citizen on Dec 28th following, on which day he was admitted. He was a very able & clear headed lawyer, especially in chancery; punctual in keeping engagements; accurate in dealings. For many years past he has held the position of auditor of the court. He will be buried from his late residence this afternoon.

+

Died: on Nov 10, in Gtwn, D C, Wm Redin, in his 75th year. His funeral will be from his late residence Gay st, Gtwn, on Nov 12 at 10 o'clock.

Died: on Nov 11, in his 51st year, Joseph, son of the late Thos Hughes. His funeral is today at 3 o'clock, from the residence of Mr M Murphy, 69 Wash st, Gtwn, D C.

Died: on Nov 11, in Wash City, Lt Leander W Fogg, 12th U S infty. Ofcrs of the army, navy, marine corps, friends, & acquaintances are invited to attend his funeral, which will take place today at 2 o'clock P M, from the U S A Post Hospital, K & I sts, Wash, D C.

Mrs Garvin & daughter were murdered near Orangeburg, S C, on Thu, by two freedmen. The murderers were arrested. [Nov 13th newspaper: Branchville, S C, Nov 12. The negroes who killed Mrs Garvin & daughter, were hung on Sat by the citizens. The freedmen were so incensed against the perpetrators of the outrage that they wanted to burn the murderers, but were prevented by the whites.]

The Levy Court of Wash Co, D C, have deemed it conducive to the public interest to condemn the following described piece of ground, to wit: being that part or portion known as the Military Road, commencing at the county road near the residence of Geo Collins, & running thence through the lands of Henry Payne, Adam Foutze, John McGee, & Pierce Shoemaker, leading down to Broad Branch at the bridge. Also, that part or portion of land commencing on the east side of Broad Branch, near the new road, between *Chanpell & Smith, running thence easterly through the lands of Fred'k Bowman, ____ Taylor, Henry Bradley, B T Swartz, Pierce Shoemaker, B D Carpenter, ____ Reynolds, ____ Fletcher, & others, as per survey & plat thereof by the county surveyor on file in the ofc of the clerk of the Levy Court. All persons who may have any objection thereto to present them to the court at its next regular meeting. By order of the court, N Callan, Clerk Levy Court. [*Possibly Chanpell—print very light.]

Mr Frank Hellen, a Wall st broker, has been arrested for having in his possession eight one thousand dollar seven thirty bonds, which proved to have been a part of the large amount of securities stolen from Mr Lord some months since.

State of Md, Executive Dept: $500 reward for the apprehension & conviction of Henry Richards, alias Henry Richardson, the fifth named in the murder of the late Wm Lyles, in PG Co, Md. –Thos Swann

Orphans Court of Wash Co, D C. In the case of Wm G Moore, exc of Virginia B Baldwin, deceased, the executor & Court have appointed Dec 4 next, for the final settlement of the personal estate of the said deceased, of assets in hand. –Jas R O'Beirne, Reg/o wills

TUE NOV 13, 1866
Col Geo V Rutherford, for a long time in the service of the Quartermaster's Dept of this city, had been mustered out of service to date from Nov 10.

Col Christopher Andrews died on Nov 12, at his residence in Wash City, from the effects of a severe fall. He was one of our oldest inhabitants, having resided among us, with but short intervals, since 1801, & at the time of his death was in his 77th year. Col Andrews was adjutant of uniformed volunteer troops of this Distrcit mustered in the U S service in 1813; was commanding ofcr of volunteers in 1814; earned great credit for his bravery & gallantry in the field, & for efficient support with his command of Cmdor Perry & Cmdor Porter in their attacks on the British fleet in the Potomac. He entered the regular army, & for years discharged most important service, particularly in Florida & the Mexican war. He resigned his commission when he reached retirement age. His funeral will be from his late residence, 11th & G sts, on Wed next, at 12 o'clock M.

The Pres has appointed Geo Pomeroy additional paymaster U S volunteers, as full paymaster in the regular army, under the act approved Jul 28, 1766. This is the first appointment of paymaster for the regular army that has as yet been made. Paymaster Pomeroy is assigned to duty in N Y C. The Pres yesterday appointed Danl H Newman assessor for the 11th district of Pa, & Thos Miller assessor for the 7th district of Ohio.

Mrs Gleason, who resides near the race-course north of Wash City, was burned very seriously on Wed last. While sitting in from of an open fire, the flame communicated to her hoop skirt, & when she arose from her chair the blaze of the burning dress came over her head. She ran out of the house into the yard where her husband was. By plunging her into a horse trough, he succeeded in extinguishing the flames, but his hands were badly burned by the steel ribs of the crinoline, which were red hot. Mrs Gleason is terribly burned, & it is not known whether she will recover. Mr Gleason will not be able to use his hands for a long time.

Cleveland, Nov 12. Hon Hiram V Wilson, District Judge of the Northern District of Ohio, died on Sunday of consumption.

Toronto, Nov 12. Another Fenian acquitted. Wm Diggan was the only prisoner tried today, & he was acquitted.

The late Wm Redin was buried from his late residence on Gay st, near Wash, yesterday; funeral services were of the Episcopal Church, read by Rev Mr Williams, of Christ Church. The pall bearers, with one exception, were selected by Mr Redin himself a year ago. He had selected young men, the sons of old friends. They were: Wm Dunlop, son of Judge Dunlop; J Carter Marbury, C M Matthews, Walter S Cox, P R Fendall, an old friend; Wm J Stone, Walter D Davidge, & John P Ennis. Mr Stone dying before Mr Redin, the latter became the former's pall-bearer, & for the occasion of yesterday, Mr Wm B Webb was selected pall-bearer by the family. The remains were taken to **Oak Hill Cemetery**, where they were temporarily deposited, & whence they will shortly be removed to **Rock Creek Church** for interment.

Dry Tortugas. Revolting treatment of prisoners & private soldiers by the Military Authorites, from the N Y World. *Fort Jefferson*, Sep 12. The first case of cruelty occurred on Aug 10, when the prisoners were unloading the steamer **St Mary** & the brigantine **Rebecca Sheppard**, & became drunk, with the armed guard placed over them, from the liquor given them by the crews of the vessels. Jas Dunn, prisoner, was lifted on his feet for 2 hours, & then fell heavily to the ground by breaking of the rope, which rendered him insensible. He was again ordered to carry a 46 pound shot but was too weak to perform the task, & was again tied up by the thumbs & left suspended in mortal agony for 4 hours. When released he was conveyed to the hospital, where he still remains. He lost his right thumb & his left hand. Capt C McConnell, the ofcr of the day, & Sgt Donelly, both of the 5th U S artl, are the agents of this misfortune & suffering. John Fiedenbach, of Co D, 5th U S artl, was also drinking & was tied up by the wrist. John Brown, prisoner confined for desertion on Sep 11, refused to carry a shot while suffering from an attack of diarrhoea; his hands were tied behind his back & pushed into the water. Brvt Maj Ritterhouas, 5th U S artl, & 2 privates, watched the fun. Ritterhaus pushed Brown under the water 3 times until he made a gesture that he would carry the shot. One man, named Kelly, had his finger cut off by Sgt Murphy, with his sword, because his hand was not held in the proper place. Private Gosuie, of Co I, age 17, was made to march in the hot sun with his musket & 16 bricks in his knapsack, & when he gave out he was beaten with a club until he was black & blue. The ofcrs are charged with starving & cheating the soldiers & prisoners. The post commissary, Maj Ritterhaus, is accused of selling to Lt Peoples, acting quartermaster, 15 barrels of flour economized in the bakery, for $16 per barrel, & pocketing the proceeds.

Mrd: Oct 28, at Church of the Epiphany, by Rev Chas H Hall, D D, rector, Robt V Elliot, of Wash, D C, to Emily Theresa, 2nd daughter of the late Jas H Lake, of Falmouth, England.

Nashville Despatch, Nov 9. Yesterday the train from Louisville to Nashville, speeding at a rapid rate, when suddenly the watchful eye of the engineer, Jim Stewart, discovered an obstruction ahead on the track, but because of the speed of the train, was unable to stop the train plunged into a pile of cross-ties & rails placed there by a band of thieves & outlaws, who coolly waited for the train to stop & then commenced the work of pillage & plunder. The party consisted of 10 or 12 men who went through the coaches demanding money & valuables. The robbers then disappeared into the woods. Capt W H Sutherland, from Louisville, a passenger, crawled under one of the lower bunks of the sleeping car, where he remained undiscovered until the robbers had disappeared. Capt H H Cushing, of Louisville, saved a splendid gold watch by hanging it down his back inside his shirt. Capt S B Brown, of Louisville, found his carpet-bag with $10,000 worth of vouchers & photographs, some 2 miles from the railroad. R K Dunkaison, of N Y, had his pocket book taken, containing about $80. J C Goetz, agent of the Lousiville brewery in this city, had a fine gold watch & $100 taken.

Died: on Nov 12, in Wash City, Kate B Sutherland, wife of Dr Chas Sutherland, U S A. Her funeral will take place from 160 G st, on Nov 14 at 11 o'clock.

Jas L France & Henry Olive were arrested for dealing in lottery policies, keeping a gambling house, & selling liquor without a license, etc. The prosecuting witness, Geo H Jarboe, failing to appear, the cases were continued until Wednesday morning.

Arthur Baker, living on the corner of Montgomery & Dunbarton sts, was taken last Wed with symptoms of cholera, & though every remedy was applied by his physician, he died Sunday night.

WED NOV 14, 1866
Trustee's sale of fixtures belonging to a brewing establishment, by deed of trust from Francis Frommel, dated Oct 10, 1865, recorded in Liber R M H, No 6, folio 151, of the land records of Wash Ci, D C, at the Brewing Establishment of said late Francis Frommel, on D st south, between 5th & 6th sts, on Nov 16. —W L Dunlop, trustee -Green & Williams, aucts

Navy Bulletin: 1-Resigned, Nov 6-Passed Assist Paymaster Gilbert A Anderson. 2-Appointments revoked, Nov 6. Acting Master Henry Taylor, of the **Connemaugh**, & Acting ensign Henry D Whittemore. 3-Ordered, Nov 6: Chief Engineer John H Long, to duty as a member of a board to witness the contract trial of the **Madawaska**; Midshipman John M Taft, to the ship **Susquehanna**; Passed Assist Surgeon Frank S Du Bois, to the ship **Jamestown**, as an assist to Surgeon Duvall. 4-Detached, Nov 6: Assist Surgeon Fred'k Krecker, from the **Jamestown**, & ordered North; Lt Cmder Henry Erben, from duty at the Navy Yard, N Y, & ordered to the ship **Vermont**; Acting Master John V Cook, from the **Susquehanna**, & ordered to the ship **Tacony**; Lt Cmder A E K Benham, from the **Vermont**, & ordered to the **Susquehanna**; 2nd Assist Engineer John D Toppin, from duty at League Island, & granted sick leave of abence. 5-Order Revoked, Nov 6: Midshipman Geo A Baldy to the **Susquehanna**, & granted sick leave of absence.

Mr H O Hood, jeweller, purchased of Mr T M Harvey, his property at the n w corner of Pa ave & 11th st, paying for it the large sum of $35,000; the lot contains 1,675½ square feet, & has a front on the avenue of 20 feet. It is improved by a small 2 story frame. -Star

On Monday evening, Mrs Sophia A Crooks, with her 2 daughters & some gentlemen friends, visited 7th st wharf to see Capt Buch, & while walking upon the wharf, Mrs Crooks missed her footing & fell overboard & was drowned. The body was soon recovered, & Lt Gessford & Sgt Vernon took it to the late residence of the deceased, on D st, between 8th & 9th sts.

The following are among the most important changes in postmasters during the week ending Nov 10, 1866:

Kenner post ofc, Jefferson parish, La, re-established, & Miss Mary Long appointed postmistress.

Vidalia post ofc, Concordia parish, La, Christian Rush appointed postmaster, vice W P Galion.

Jefferson post ofc, Jefferson parish, La, re-established, & Robt H Brown appointed postmaster.

Bayou Barbary post ofc, Livingston parish, re-established, & W C Opdenweyer appointed postmaster.

Mayport Mills post ofc, Duval Co, Fla, Miss Mary E Brown appointed postmistress, vice H H Phillips, resigned.

Forked river post ofc, Ocean Co, N J, Luther Bradley, appointed postmaster, vice Jacob Vaughn, declined.

Petroleum Centre, Venango Co, Pa, Henry E Blackmore appointed postmaster, vice Geo Winson.

Hills View post ofc, Westmoreland Co, Pa, John Hasinger appointed postmaster, vice Hannah M Wiley, resigned.

Sewickleyville post ofc, Alleghany Co, Pa, Jas Rankin appointed postmaster, Baldwin Grey, removed.

Bakerstown post ofc, Alleghany Co, Pa, Jas White appointed postmaster, vice Andrew Harper, removed.

New post ofcs have been established at Oil Rock & Calif House, Wirt Co, West Va, C D Henderson is appointed to the former & Wm N West to the latter ofc.

The post ofc at Richland, Butler Co, Ky, has been discontinued.

West Liberty post ofc, Morgan Co, Ky, Jas H Morgan appointed postmaster, vice L T Griggs, declined.

Sherburne Mills post ofc, Fleming Co, Ky, John H Wrenchy appointed postmaster, vice Isaac Wrenchy, deceased.

London post ofc, Laurel Co, Ky, H G Litton appointed postmaster, vice Miss J E Ramsey resigned.

Warburg post ofc, Calloway Co, Ky, Saml Williams appointed postmaster, vice B Rosenstein, resigned.

Zanesville, Ohio, John J Douglass appointed postmaster, vice W C Morehead, removed.

Pinley post ofc, Hancock Co, Ohio, C B Wilson appointed postmaster, vice J B Rothschilds, removed.

New post ofc at Houcktown, Hancock Co, Ohio, Israel Simpson appointed postmaster.

Eagle post ofc, Hancock Co, Ohio, B D Evans appointed postmaster, vice J W Williams, removed.

Handy post ofc, Hancock Co, Ohio, Emanuel Binkley appointed postmaster, vice P Bendy, removed.

Arcadia post ofc, Hancock Co, Ohio, Wm Karns appointed postmaster, vice J Peters, resigned.

East Shadrack, Rensselaer Co, N Y, Harris B Howard appointed postmaster, vice J C Brown, resigned.
Greenville, Wash Co, N Y, Alfred Buckley appointed postmaster, vice B F Otterson, removed.
North Branch, Lapeer Co, Mich, Jacob Gallinger appointed postmaster, vice A S Scott, resigned.
L Duftin, Clinton, Mich, Jas Tucker appointed postmaster, vice S R Dewistoe, removed.
London, Monroe Co, Mich, Wm Ostrander appointed postmaster, vice J Kingsley, removed.
Athens post ofc, Calhoun Co, Mich, Saml R Culp appointed postmaster, vice S S Ware, removed.
Lesington post ofc, Mich, L M Brown appointed postmaster, vice H N Ninis, removed.
Poland, Mahoning Co, Ohio, E J Clark appointed postmaster, vice Geo Allen, removed.
Greenford, Mahoning Co, Ohio, Wm Shafnecker appointed postmaster, vice N S Griffiths, removed.
New Springfield, Ohio, John Peters appointed postmaster, vice G Smith, removed.
Rockland Station, Hamilton Co, Ohio, John H Sheehan appointed postmaster, vice Wm S Bacon.
Fort Madison, Lee Co, Iowa, Wm C Hershberger appointed postmaster, vice B Hugel, removed.
Ottumwa Wapelleo Co, Iowa, Saml B Evans appointed postmaster, vice John M Hidneck.
Louisiana, Pike Co, Mo, Chas Murray appointed postmaster, vice Augustus Owing, removed.

The Madame Jumel suit came to trial on Monday, says the N Y Herald, in the Supreme Court, Circuit, before Justice Jos F Barnard. The case had been actually settled between the parties before coming into court, & the trial was only gone through as a necessary formality. It is understood that under this settlement, $88,500 is to be paid by Mr Nelson Chase, of which $10,000 goes to the Rev J Howard Smith, $10,000 to the church at Carmansville; the various religious & charitable societies are to the sums respectively assigned to them in the will, & the balance is to be divided up among the lawyers. The heirs-at-law get $40,000, & the estate passes into the possession of Mr Nelson Chase.

The Charleston Courier reports the murder of Elliot, of Co F, 6th Infty, by Harrison, of Co C, of the same infty. The affair occurred on Saturday, & caused much excitement.

Mrs Gray, residing on K st, between 3rd & 4½ sts, died on Monday, as is supposed, of cholera.

New Grocery Store: Israel Deming, 485 9th st, between D & E sts.

Died: on Nov 13, at his residence, in Wash City, Rev Saml M Dickson, of the M E Church, Balt Conference. His funeral will take place at the residence of his father, in Gtwn, corner of Green & Stoddard sts, Nov 15 at 10 o'clock.

Orphans Court-Judge Purcell. 1-Yesterday a copy of the will of Patrick Neligan, of Benicia Solano Co, Calif, certified to by the clerk of the Orphans Court of said county, was filed for probate & record. It nominates Maurice Neligan, of this city, executor, & bequeaths to him lot 15 in square 567, of Wash City. 2-The will of Julia Catilino, bequeathing her property to Virginia E Norwood, was finally admitted to probate & record. Virginia E Norwood qualified as admx c t a of the estate of Julia Catilino, deceased. Bond, $3,000. Sureties: Jos S Norwood, Thos Rich, & Augustus Davis. 3-John D McPherson qualified as adm of the estate of Chas F Robertson, deceased. Bond, $2,000. Sureties: David P Moore & Danl Wormer. 4-The will of Christopher Yeabower, deceased, was fully proven & admitted to probate & record. 5-The will of Laviny Whitaker was filed & partially proven. The property is bequeathed to the children of the deceased. 6-Lelia M Talbert & Duncan S Walker qualified as co-adms of the estate of Jas W Brown, deceased. Bond, $1,200. Sureties: Chas D Gilmore & Addison A Hosmer. 7-Susan Cooper qualified as admx of Henry D Cooper, deceased. Bond, $600. Sureties: John T Suter & John Y Donn. 8-Ellen Daily qualified as admx of the estate of Dominick Daily, deceased. Bond, $1,000. Sureties: Thos Castello & Chas Calvert.

Police matters. 1-Thos Crumpin & Rudolph Lamar were arrested & put down on the police blotter as thieves. In default of payment of fines they were committed to the workhouse. 2-Nathl Hines & Henry O Parker, two colored barbers, were charged with obtaining 40 bushels of oysters from David Barkley by false representations. These fellows are colored sharps, & it is not the first time they have been engaged in swindling operations. 3-Albert Washington, a porter, fined $20 for driving through a funeral procession. 4-Thos Harron was committed to jail for stealing 75 cents. 5-Martha Votry, colored, had a good home with Mr Amos C Tabor, but being of a lazy disposition, she resorted to purloining articles from her employer, for which she was arrested & committed to jail. 6-John Cook, alias Jack Diamond, a notorious denizen of Murder Bay, whipped Nancy Garett because she remonstrated with him on account of his vagabond, & inconstant habits, & fined him $3 for disorderly conduct, & as his fist deprived Nancy of 2 or 3 of her teeth, he was sent to jail for assault.

Mrd: on Nov 8, at St Aloyisus Church, by Rev Chas Stonestreet, P Croghan, M D, to Cornela, daughter of Peter F Bacon.

A son of Reuben Stanford, of Burlington, Vt, who went out hunting last week, but did not return, the next day was found in the woods, shot through the head, probably by accidental explosion of his gun.

Col Robt Y Brown died at New Orleans, on Oct 15, after a brief illness, in his 26th year. He was born at Gallatin, Miss, on Oct 8, 1811, the elder of two children of Hon Albert G Brown, formerly Govn'r of that State. The mother of the deceased, a daughter of the late Gen Robt Young, of Alexandria, Va, was well known in the social circles of Wash before & during the service of her husband in the U S Congress. He was her first born. His classical education was completed at Gtwn College, D C; he was a pupil in the law dept. He was a combatant of many a bloody field, was twice severely wounded, & was twice made prisoner. A few months before his death he established himself in New Orleans, in the practise of his profession. He leaves his parents in unspeakable agony.

Chicago, Nov 10. A terrible occurrence is said to have taken place near New Quincy, in this State. Mrs McClure was supposed to have died on Sunday last, & on Monday was buried in a vault belonging to the family. On Wed groans were heard from the vault by children of the buried woman & an old lady who was with them. The husband & neighbors broke open the door, opened the coffin, & found the woman alive. She had torn her hair & wounded her fingers in vain efforts to escape from her narrow prison. She was taken home, & is said to be now in a fair way to recover.

A large & brilliant wedding took place on Thu last at Galena, Ill: Gen O E Babcock, of Gen Grant's staff, married Miss Annie E Campbell, daughter of B H Campbell. The groomsmen were Maj Gen Upton, of N Y; Col Adam Badeau, of Gen Grant's staff; A S Campbell, A B Campbell, & Lt B H Campbell. The bridesmaids were Miss Hattie Campbell & Miss Jennie Drummond, of Chicago; Miss Louisa Jones, of Dubuque, & Miss Augusta Scot, of Wash. There were some 300 guests present, including Gen Washburne, Hon E B Washburne, Judge Drummond, Gen Chetlain, Gen Rowley, & Gen Duen. Gen Grant had promised to be present, but could not come.

Balt, Nov 13. Gen Grant is in town to attend the horse fair. He is the guest of Judge Bond.

A young man, Chas Ross, was arrested in Cincinnati on Sunday, charged with shooting with intent to kill, & slightly wounding, Bishop Rosecrans of the Catholic Church of that city.

John Bradley, a prominent citizen of Vt, & for the last 20 years connected with the railroad enterprises of New England, expired at his residence, in Poultney, on Sunday last. His remains will be taken to Burlington on Wed next for interment.

Orphans Court of Wash Co, D C. Letters of administration on the personal estate of Jas W Brown, late of Wash, D C, deceased. –Lilia M Talbert, Duncan S Walker, admx

THU NOV 15, 1866

The funeral of Mary Cecelia Emen took place in N Y on Tue. She was a prominent actress at the Old Park Theatre in its palmy days.

The late Mr Wm Redin; was born & educated, & admitted to the bar in England. He came to this country a married man in 1818; he came directly to Gtwn & settled there & resided there till his death. In 1848 he was appointed to succeed Clement Cox, as auditor in chancery, & held that ofc till his death.

Col J P Marston, U S A, who has been in charge of the Cavalry Bureau in Wash City for nearly 2 years, has been relieved & ordered to join his regt in Florida.

Eighteen months have nearly elapsed since Jefferson Davis was made a state prisoner. He had previously been publicly charged by the Pres of the U S with conspiring to assassinate Pres Lincoln, & $100,000 offered for his capture thereupon. The capture was promptly made & the money duly paid; yet, up to this hour, there has not been even an attempt made by the Gov't to procure his indictment on that charge. He has also been popularly, if not officially, accused of complicity in the virtual murder of Union soldiers, while prisoners of war, by subjecting them to needless, inhuman exposure, privation & abuse; but no official attempt has been made to indict him on that charge. He has been indicted for simple treason; & even this indictment has not been obtained at the instance of the Gov't. Repeated attempts have been made by the prisoner's counsel to bring his case to trial; but to no purpose. The upshot of all this is, that the prisoner is not tried, nor likely to be; & that, if tried, he is morally certain not to be convicted; if convicted, not to be punished. There are many persons who would like to have him executed; but there is not one intelligent man on earth who has the faintest notion that he ever will be. If Mr Davis is even probably guilty of complicity with Booth, he should long since have been indicted & tried for that crime.

Tournament at Surrattsville, PG Co, Md, on Tuesday; Capt B F Gwynn, assisted by Dr P H Heiskell & Henry Tolson, acted as marshals. The "charge" was delivered to the knights by W B Rooker, in an eloquent manner. The judges were F M Bowie, C S Middleton, F Tolson, Wm A Jarboe, W P Griffin, & A P Hill. W A Jarboe crowned the Queen of Love & Beauty, Miss Nettie Heiskell; W A Edelin, crowned the First Maid of Honor, 2nd Maid, Miss Maggie Pumphrey; 3rd Maid, Miss M J Gardner; Jesse R Edelin crowned 4th Maid, Miss Mary Hunter; & Knight of Moorfield, Wm Barry. 5th Maid, Miss Emma Hopkins. The knights were T S Tolson, Thos W Berry, & R S Bryan. During the day the Holly Hill Band, of Gtwn, discoursed in sweetest strains, several appropriate airs.

Yesterday a man, Jos Winfield, a watchman employed at the Gov't warehouse near the depot, tried to commit suicide by cutting his throat with a razor. His wife said that whenever he gets on a spree he assumes the name of Patrick Winer. The cause for the rash act seems to have been drink. Winfield is between 30 & 35 yrs of age & resides on G st, between 9th & 10th sts. He has a wife, but no children.

Zachariah Thomas, Thos Fogarty, & Patrick Brannon, 3 soldiers, were arrested yesterday for the robbery of a watch & money from a comrade, Jas Dolan. The accused were committed to jail. Dolan, the cmplnt, was turned over to the military authorities as a deserter, he having been confined on that charge at the time of the robbery.

Henry Moore, a colored man, died yesterday, in the 7th Ward, a victim of Asiatic cholera

Navy Bulletin: Honorably Discharged, Nov 7. Acting Assist Paymaster W J Henly, from Nov 2, 1865; Acting Ensign & Pilot Wm La Mee, from Oct 30, 1866; Acting Master Saml Hanes, from Oct 30, 1866; & Acting Ensign Geo Stein, from Nov 6, 1866. Detached, Nov 7. Gunner A F Thompson, from the ship **Macedonian** & placed on waiting orders.

The Pres yesterday made the following appointments: John M Waldron, of Minn, register of the land ofc at Greenleaf, Minn; Henry Hill, of Minn, receiver of public moneys for the district of lands subject to sale at Greenleaf, Minn; Danl Chaplin, of Oregon, to be receiver of public moneys of the district of lands subject to sale at Le Grand, Oregon; Saml W Black, of Oregon, to be receiver of public moneys at Le Grand, Oregon.

Rt Rev F A Rutledge, Bishop of Fla, died in Tallahassee on Nov 6, in his 68th year of his age & the 44th of his ministry. We believe his death was occasioned by a cancer in the mouth. He was a native of S C, & the earlier years of his ministry were spent in there. He was educated at Yale College. His father was the venerable Chancellor Rutledge.

The Pres has directed the issue of a warrant for the pardon of Zeno Kelley, convicted at the Oct term, 1863, of the U S Circuit Court for the Dist of Mass, of fitting out a vessel for the slave trade, & sentenced to 4 years' imprisonment, & to pay a fine of $1,000. The pardon has also been ordered of John Walker, convicted at the May term, 1865, of the U S District Court for the Southern Dist of Fla, of an attempt to defraud the U S & sentenced to 2 years' imprisonment.

Died: on Nov 10, at Selma, near Leesburg, Va, Col Wm B Beverley, of Blandfield, Essex Co, Va, aged 72 years. His remains were deposited in the cemetery at Leesburg for the present. The death of Col Beverley will be regretted by a large number of friends in the Dist of Columbia, Va, & Ala.

Died: on Nov 8, at Athens, Ga, Mrs Harriet M Kennard, in her 37th year, wife of Joel S Kennard, & daughter of the late Isaac Hanson, of Wash.

Died: on Nov 12, at Cornwall, Pa, Col Wm G Freeman, of Wash, D C.

Phil, Nov 14. In the homicide case of Maggie Baer, who was murdered in 1864, in the Continental Theatre, the jury returned a verdict of manslaughter in the 2nd degree. The prisoner, throughout the trial, gave real or simulated symptoms of insanity. This verdict will give the Court an opportunity to send him to an insane asylum. [The murderer's name is not given.]

The **National Cemeteries**: *Arlington Cemetery* has seen much improvement in the last 6 months; the Mansion has been brushed up externally, but internally bears the aspect of hard usage. The fragments of furniture belonging to the Lee family were piled together on the lower floors, bruised, broken, & worthless; fragments of private letters & papers were scattered upon the floor in the upper unfinished loft of the Mansion. Under the orders of Gen Whipple, in whose death the country lost a lofty Christian soldier, while in command there at the opening of the war, the valuable papers, paintings, & family relics were all carefully packed & placed under lock & key in the attic. After he was called to the field the vandalism was perpetrated. The bedstead upon which Washington died was not among the plundered relics. It was carried away by curiosity hunters years ago, in small pieces, from the room in which Washington died, at *Mount Vernon*. Mr E L McLean, is the superintendent of the cemetery. Within a dozen rods of the *Arlington Mansion* is a circular pit, 20 feet deep & the same in diameter, has been sunk by the side of the flower garden cemented & divided into compartments, & down in this gloomy receptacle are cast the bones of such soldiers as perished on the field & either were not buried at all or were so covered up as to have their bones mingle indiscriminately together. At the time we looked into this gloom cavern, a literal Golgotha, there were piled together skulls in one division, legs in another, arms in another, & ribs in another, what were estimated as the bones of 2,000 human beings. They were dopping fragmentary human skeletons into this receptacle almost daily, & at that time was half full. The first thought in looking down upon this revolting scene was that now such disposition should have been planned for these bones, that there was land enough & they should have been buried as others were, in parcels as nearly those of a human body as possible, & marked as unknown soldiers. We have not changed our mind upon subsequent reflection. This plan subserves very well the purpose of erecting a monument, which it is said Gen Meigs contemplates. There had been up to the first of this month about 6,800 bodies of white soldiers & about 3,300 bodies of contrabands, soldiers & others, deposited in this cemetery. The white section is located on the top of the bluffs in the rear of the mansion, some 25 acres have been occupied. The purpose of the superintendent, Lt Col Jas M Moore, A Q M, U S A, is evidently to surround the spot with beauty. The colored section, down the heights on the n e corner of the 200 acres, is the farthest possible from the white. The whole number of interments thus far in this Dept, including the Dist of Col, Va, & Ga, is, in round numbers, 100,000 bodies, of which 46,000 are identified, & 54,000 belong to the great & solemn roll of the unknown. The "Roll of Honor" at Col Moore's ofc, embracing only his dept of the burial service, contains already 37,000 names, to which additions are daily added. During the last year 12 nat'l cemeteries have been opened, of which 7 have been completed. Selling soldiers bodies: many attempts have been made to speculate upon the bodies of soldiers buried on the field. Individuals at first started out in Va & elsewhere, & finding, or pretending to find, the bodies which they knew the friends anxiously desired, made them pay the most exorbitant prices for the bodies, which in many cases were not the remains they purported to be after all. This system has been broken up. No persons are allowed to meddle with a body at all. The *Military Asylum Cemetery*, at the Soldiers' Home, in this District, is full, containing 5,717 bodies; *Battle Cemetery*, containing the 40 Union soldiers who fell in repelling Early's attack upon this city, is also completed, as also is *Union Cemetery*, which contains 1,012 contrabands. *Harmony Cemetery*, 1½ miles n e of the Capitol, contains 3,630. The following in Va are also full & closed: *Cold Harbor Cemetery*, 9 miles from Richmond, containing 1,930 bodies; *Glendale Cemetery*, near Malvern Hill, about 3,000; *Seven Pines Cemetery*, 10 miles from Richmond, 1,356; *Fort Harrison Cemetery*, 8 miles from Richmond, about 3,800. The estimated expenses of the bureau for the next fiscal year are $4,000,000, & the estimated expense of removing all the bodies scattered in private cemeteries & temporary resting places in every section of the country, from Maine to Texas, & from the Atlantic to the Pacific, into the nat'l cemeteries, is $3,000,000. In the territory under the charge of Col Moore, of the 100,000 bodies that have been found, 52,006 have been re-interred, & 47,994 remain to be yet taken up & transferred to the permanent nat'l cemeteries. The cost to re-inter a soldier, including the wooden headboard, has been, $8; average daily removals for the year, about 65 bodies. The *National Cemetery* at Fredericksburg, when completed, will contain some 15,000 bodies. The cemeteries at Chancellorsville, at Spottsylvania Court House, & at the Wilderness have been closed. The bodies in them all are to be transferred to Fredericksburg. The Rebel List is made up with the same care as is the Union List, Roll of Honor. The names of the prisoners of war taken at *Fort Donelson*, & who died at *Camp Douglas*, 3,525 in number, have recently been received, & the clerks are placing them upon the records. The following are the larger cemeteries also under Col Moore's care, *City Point Cemetery*, 5,463; *Poplar Grove Cemetery*, 4,210; *Yorktown Cemetery*, 2,150. These are not yet full. The *Winchester Cemetery* contains 3,605, & when full will contain 5,700. Alexandria has 3,601; Annapolis, Md, 2,630; Hampton, Va, 3,141; Andersonville, 12,912. All the cemeteries through the country, & the number of soldiers buried in each, including private cemeteries in which soldiers are deposited away from friends. They are scattered. The following are some of the largest collections, viz: New Orleans, 3,193; Indianapolis, Ind, 1,306; *Camp Butler*, Ill, 977; Mound City, Ill, 1,270; Cincinnati, 754; Paducah, Ky, 564; *Camp Dennison*, 1,151, of which 38 are Confederates; Chicago, 1,919; Baton Rouge, La, 2,152; Newbern, N C, 1,352; *Fort Brown*, Brownsville, Brazos Santiago, etc, Texas, 845; Raleigh, N C, 229; Ship Island, Miss, 232; Barrancas, Fla, 507; Madison, Wisc, 266; Columbus, Ohio, 368; Springfield, Mo, 566; Quincy, Ill, 268; Moorhead, N C, 160; Portsmouth Grove, R I, 305; *Fort Leavenworth*, 223; *Fort Kearney*, 11; *Fort Pillow*, Tenn, 41; *Fort Snelling*, Minn, 96; *Fort Laramie*,

Dakota Territory, 18; New Haven, Conn, 345; Little Rock, Ark, 978; Beaufort, S C, 1,363; City Point, Va, & vicinity, 1,796; around Petersburg, Va, 1,502; Danville, Va, 1,280; Hilton Head, 1,028; Duvall's Bluff, Ark, 501; *Fort Bridger*, Neb, 9; Camden, Ark, 449; N Y C, 346; Jefferson barracks, St Louis, 2,985; *Wellegan Cemetery*, St Louis, 3,947; *Small-pox Cemetery*, St Louis, 404; Christ Church, St Louis, 389; *Camp Chase*, Ohio, 2,072 rebels. The Roll of Honor is the list of the soldiers who fell in the rebellion & are buried in national cemeteries. There have been 6 successive pamphlets issued by the Quartermaster's Dept, embracing these names as they have been collected. The 1st list embraced the Dist of Col, the 2nd, Alexandria, 3rd Wilderness & Spottsylvania, 4th Andersonville, Ga, 6th the Dept of Texas. Embraces all who are buried in Maine, Minn, Md, Pa, R I, Ark, Miss, La, & Colorado Territory. This last list alone contains not less, upon a rough estimate, we should say, 60,000 names, of which some thousands are colored soldiers. Recent survey by Mr Clark, engineer at the Capitol, shows *Arlington Cemetery* embraces about 260 acres. The cemetery was first open on May 13, 1864, the first interments being made in the corner which is designated the colored section. In June, 1864, about a month later, when the dead came in such multitudes from Gen Grant's battles, the grounds were opened for the white soldiers upon the plateau near the *Arlington Mansion*. Some white soldiers have since been taken up from the colored section. The colored section now has 1,032 white soldiers, & 3,366 colored soldiers. There are 1,012 colored buried in *Union Cemetery*, exclusively. In *Harmony Cemetery* [small pox] are buried some 4,000, mostly colored. There are no headboards to the graves of the colored people in any of the cemeteries.

Guardian's sale of bldg lot on Dec 6, on the premises: lot 3 in square 184, fronting 33 feet on north K st, between 16th & 17th sts. –Julia H Addison, Guardian of Chas Morris Addison. -Jas C McGuire & Co, aucts

Salt Lake Vedetto of Oct 25: Dr John King Robinson was assassinated here on Oct 22, within a half block of his residence. Dr Robinson was roused from his sleep by a man who came to his residence & informed him that John Jones, an acquaintance of the Dr, had broken his leg & required surgical aid immediately. The Dr's young wife objected to his going out so late, as threats had been made against his life, in anonymous letters. Mrs Robinson was unable to prevail on her husband to shirk the call of humanity, & the murderer & his victim passed out into the night. A very few minutes after, a shot was heard. Mr Chas King, J Wimmer, & Col Kahn were sitting in their room conversing, in their house nearby, when looking out the window, they saw 3 men running down the street. On further investigation they discovered Dr Robinson, still breathing, but insensible. Dr Robinson breathed his last about 3 A M, in the presence of his friends & horror stricken family.

Orphans Court of Wash Co, D C. Letters of administration on the personal estate of Julia Catilino, late of Wash, D C, deceased. –Virginia E Norwood, admx w a

Capt T S Hardee has been appointed State Engineer to Mississippi.

John H Rixley has sold his *Silver Spring* farm, containing 300 acres, near Salem, to Mr W S Callahan, of Wash Co, Pa, for $35 per acre. We understand that the same purchaser offered B F Rixey $70 per acre for his farm of 1,000 acres, & Mr Rixey declined the proposition. -Warrenton Index

Erie, Pa, Nov 13. Express train thrown off the track this afternoon. Workmen has been employed in repairing the track about a mile east of Wealeyville, & had removed two rails. Aware that the N Y express train was due, they took no precaution to warn the train. The train was instantly thrown down an embankment, some 10 to 15 feet. The dead as far as can be learned were Dr Wheeler, of Milwaukee, & his little grandchild; a man named Hunt, who was dressed in the garb of a soldier, from Danville, N Y; & an elderly man, named Harlan, residence unknown. The child's mother was severely injured & is not expected to recover. Some 40 or 50 others were wounded, most of them slightly. Mr M Brown, of Rochester, bruised; his son, age 12 or 13, has his right foot badly sprained. Francis Moran, from Austin, head cut. Patrick Rounce, from N Y, very badly hurt about the head. W B Grafton, for Worthington, Ohio, scalp cut & foot strained. John Oakeson, Murney, Ind, collar bone broken. Robt Lynch, N Y, scalp cut & face badly mutilated. John Donahoe, N Y, face cut & body injured. Margaret Gerrynote, Rochester, injured in hand; her little son has his scalp cut. Chas Bocherah, Plymouth, Rich Co, Ohio, had his leg hurt slightly.

Col Stodare, who for the past 2 years has performed at the Egyptian Hall, London, died suddenly on Oct 23 from the rupture of a blood vessel. It was he who first introduced the "mystery of the Sphynx," & several other clever deceptions.

Boston, Nov 13. The trial of Jas Brown, a colored seamen, for the murder of Jas Foster on board the bark **Atlantic**, in May last, resulted this afternoon in a verdict of guilty.

Boston, Nov 14. Rev Dr Jenks, a well known clergyman, died yesterday, aged 83. He graduated at Harvard in 1797, & of his graduating class Hon Horace Binney, of Phil, is the only survivor.

Estray dark red Cow came to the subscriber, north of Columbian College. Owner is to call, prove property, pay charges, & take her away. –Jas Eslin

FRI NOV 16, 1866
Dr A C Stewart died at Quitman, Miss, recently.

The Savannah papers say that the ordnance stores at *Hilton Head* are being rapidly removed North, the quartermasters have all gone. *Fort Willis* is being dismantled.

Austin City, Oct 30, 1866. The inhabitants of this city or county have no right to burial in the *State Cemetery*. The grounds were set apart as a place of sepulture for the heroes, patriots, & states-men of the Stateof Texas. Many of there heroes & patriots of the revolution of 1835 & 1836 are buried there. Nearly all the statesmen who have died in the last 20 years are buried in the *State Cemetery*. No other class of men have ever been buried there until a detachment of the Federal army stationed here commenced burying the soldiers indiscriminately among the illustrious dead of the State. Putting soldiers of the army between those heretofore buried, when only sufficient space was left to erect suitable monuments to each was much regretted. –F F Foscue [A knoll now affords an inhospitable resting place for the remains of Burleson, Lipscomb, Hemphill, McLeod, & McCulloch, who, having devoted themselves to the service of the common-wealth, were honored in life by their fellow-citizens.
–N G Shelley, for the Cmte.]

Chicago, Nov 13. John Sheahan was walking along the track of the Pittsburgh & *Fort Wayne* railroad, near Burlington Crossing, & run over by the passenger train. He was instantly killed.

Cincinnati, Nov 15. The Society of the Army of the Tenn re-assembled this morning, & the following ofcrs were elected for the ensuing year: Pres, Gen J A Rawlings; vice presidents, Maj Gen's J A Logan, F Blair, R J Oglesby, G A Smith, Brvt Brig Gens W W Belknap & Fairchild; recording secretary, Col L M Dayton; corr sec Brig Gen A Hickenlarfer; treasurer, Maj Gen M P Force. The greater portion of the proceedings were occupied in discussing the proposed monument to Maj Gen McPherson.

New Orleans, Nov 13, The steamer **Henry Von Phul**, with 3,800 bales of cotton, was burned this morning, above Donaldsonville. The fire was caused by the pipe of deck hand, & was soon underway. Nearly all the 101 passengers escaped, except for one passenger who was burned & several were drowned. The passengers lost all their baggage, many of them having only their nightclothes. Among them were Col Fisher & lady, of Memphis, who were on a bridal trip to New Orleans.

Died: on Thu, in his 74th year, Louis Vivans, a native of France, but for the past 42 years a citizen of Wash City. His funeral will take place from St Matthew's Church, this morning, at 11 o'clock, where his friends & the St Vincent de Paul Society are invited. [Nov 17th newspaper: The funeral of the late Louis Vivans: the remains were interred in *Mount Olivet Cemetery*. The pall-bearers were Messrs Nicholas Callan, J Carroll Brent, Gregory Ennis, John J Joyce, Jas Ryon, & Henry Rochat.]

Sale of a small lot of wines & dinner & dessert service glassware, etc, of Hon A Hume Burnby, English Legation, at the auction rooms on Nov 20.
-Jas C McGuire & Co, aucts

Gtwn Academy: Edwin Arnold, sr, LL D, Principal; Edwin Arnold, jr, Assist. Dr Arnold was formerly of Wash & principal & proprietor of Rugby Institute, Mount Wash, Md. He had just returned to the District & has taken the room over the bookstore of Mr Crandell, 128 Bridge st, Gtwn, lately occupied by Prof Whithall, where he will receive the sons of his old friends & others after Nov 14th. When formerly here, among his pupils were the sons of Col J L Edwards, Hon Jos S Wilson, Hon John Wilson, Postmaster Gen Wickliffe, Gen Roger Jones, Com Thos Ap Catesby Jones, Hon John M Brodhead, Gen Jesup, Col W W Seaton, Rev Mr Hawley, Rev Dr Pyne, G M Davis, & John D Wilson. Many of these have passed away.

SAT NOV 17, 1866
Court of Appeals of Md, Oct Term, 1866, Annapolis, Nov 15, 1866.
Jos T Gough & wife vs Ida C Manning et al. Appleal from the Circuit Court for St Mary's Co in equity. This case was argued & concluded by Thos G Pratt for the appellants & Thos S Alexander for the appellees. Nov 16. John L Budd vs Peter Williams & wife. Appeal from the equity side of the Circuit court for Chas Co. Argued & concluded by Levin Gate & V Brent for the appellant, & Thos G Pratt for the appelles.

Suicide on Thu at the residence of Mr Francis Esputa, 511 E st, Navy Yard. Lt Milstead & Sgt Harbin found that Mr Esputa, who is over 71 years of age, shot himself in the forehead with a revolver, death ensuing in about 5 minutes. Mrs Esputa was asleep at the time. The deceased has been slightly deranged for some time. He left a letter written in Spanish. He was a native of Barcelonia, Spain; came to this country over 30 years ago; had been employed most of the time as a musician in the Marine Band. He leaves his wife & 4 grown children.

Police matters: 1-John J Frier, a miller, took a horse from a farmer in Fred'k Co, Va, named L S Loux, & disposed of him for $10 in Winchester. He was arrested & committed to await the requisition of the Govn'r of Va. 2-Frank Owens stole some socks from the store of Mr John A Pierson, 22nd & H sts; he was committed to court. 3-Ferdinand Berry & John G Fowler ran their wagons without a license, & were muleted in fines of $5 each. 4-Robt Battrie & E M Botler were arrested for keeping dogs without a license: each fined $5. 5-Andrew Balman was sent to the work house fo 60 days for vagrancy, being found by Ofcr Hurdle in Lafayette Square, sleeping among the bushes. 6-Two bootblacks, Dan Conner & John Key, were yesterday arrested & locked up for a few hours for obstructing the entrance to the Metropolitan Hotel.

Kate Simmons, proprietress of a sink of iniquity, was yesterday charged with enticing to & harboring in her den a girl of 15 years of age, the child of respectable parentage. Her aged father was almost heart-broken at the recital of his daughter's shame. It is impossible to conceive of a punishment too severe for a wretch who thus deliberately sets about to accomplish the ruin & degradation of almost mere children.

Capt Ayers, of Mound City, Ill, was on Tuesday drowned by the capsizing of a sail-boat.

The Pres yesterday appointed Jas S Shrigley, of Ark, register of the land ofc at Clarksville, Ark.

A well in the rear of 229 South 2nd st, Phil, fell in Thur, killing a young man, Chas Hollmann, & severely injuring Peter Rittimeyer.

Boston papers record the death on Wed, of Mrs Sarah Preston Hale, widow of the late Hon Nathan Hale, & sister of the late Hon Edw Everett, at her residence in Brookline.

Louisville, Nov 16. Hon Timolan Craven, a prominent politician of Southern Ky, died at Columbia on Wed.

E D Slate, of Tompkins Co, N Y, operator in the employ of the Western Union Telegraph Co, at Boyd Farm, Pa, was run over by a train on Tuesday & died the next morning.

Sister Mary, of St Martin, a professed religieuse in the *Convent of the Good Shepherd*, in Balt, died on Nov 3. Her family name was Rapi_r. She was a native of Ky, & in her 29th year of her age, & the 4th of her religious profession.

Mrs Ann Kirby Barnum, widow of the late David Barnum, died at the City Hotel yesterday, in her 92nd year. She was born in Litchfield, Conn, on Jul 4, 1774; her maiden name was Kirby, she being a younger sister of Col Ephraim Kirby, who was conspicuous in New England during the struggle for American independence. During the many years since the death of the elder Mr Barnum, his widow has always made the City Hotel her home. Mr Geo Peabody, one of her old familiar friends, visited with her a week or two since. For an hour he sat beside her bed talking of the scenes of the past. The deceased was an aunt of the late Zenos Barnum, who so long conducted the City Hotel. Her honored grave will be bedewed with the tears of children, grandchildren, & great grandchildren.
-Balt Sun

Edw Bartholomew, who lately died at Harwinton, Conn, aged 95, purchased his coffin 14 years since, & bound the dealer of whom he bought it to trim it when needed for $2. Four years since he attempted to have his grave dug in the fall in the apprehension that he should die before the winter was over but in this he was overruled by his family. He never made an explanation of his singular proceedings.

Mr Tuft, of Norfolk, Va, is reported as having fallen heir to two millions of dollars by the death of a relative in England.

Changes in postmasters & post ofcs made by the Postmaster Gen since Nov 10th:
Aully P O, Sonora Co, Calif, re-established, Geo Henehett appointed postmaster.
Live Oak, DeWitt Co, Texas, re-established, Elisha B Davis, appointed postmaster.
Camden, Seward Co, Neb, Winfield S Roper postmaster, vice H Martin, resigned.
Richland, Fillmore Co, Minn, Williams T Steens postmaster, vice H Miller, delinquent.
Rice Lake, Dodge Co, Minn, Amasa T Minor postmaster, vice J P Green, removed.
Canton Mower Co, Minn, Walter Fuller postmaster, vice H Marsh, resigned.
Minnesota City, Winona Co, Minn, Edgar Chapman, vice Robt Pike, resigned.
Cherry Grove, Fillmore Co, Minn, John H Bonsteel, vice John E Haskins, delinquent.
Fillmore, Fillmore Co, Minn, Francis H Bartlett, vice Chas Conkey, resigned.
Troutville, Clearfield Co, Pa, Mrs Caroline Weaver, vice J M McHendry, resigned.
Burnside, Clearfield Co, Pa, Matthew L Irwin, vice Wm C Irwin, resigned.
Laughlintown, Westmoreland Co, Pa, Miss Rachel Shaeffer, vice John G Armor, resigned.
Bradford, McKean Co, Pa, E A Newell, vice B F Thompson, resigned.
New Era, Bradford Co, Pa, E Brock, vice J Battles, resigned.
Colosse, Oswego Co, N Y, C H Harvey, vice R F Avery, removed.
Kinderhook, Coluumbia Co, Pa, Lawrence Van Boten, vice L Pruyn, not confirmed.
Kidare, Juneau Co, Wisc, P O'Reilly, vice J Ramsey, removed.
Island Pond, Essex Co, Vt, D S S_orrs, vice A L Robinson, resigned.
New Castle, Henry Co, Ind, Chas J Morrisson, vice W H Elliot, declined.
Wilton, Franklin Co, Maine, Sewall Crane, vice R R Fulton, removed.
Waupaca, Waupaca Co, Wisc, Winfield Scott, vice S Strickland, removed.
Defere, Brown Co, Wisc, Robt Beattie, vice A Maeller, removed.
Wantoma, Waushara Co, Wisc, A D McIntire, vice D Lockerly, removed.
Colfax, Placer Co, Calif, N R D Traphagen, vice V W Cleveland.

Presidential appointments of postmasters:
Portsmouth, Sciota Co, Ohio, Wm R Smith, vice John Row, removed.
Wooster, Wayne Co, Ohio, R B Spink, vice Enos Foreman, removed.
Poughkeepsie, Dutchess Co, N Y, Henry C Smith, vice A Van Kleeck, deceased.
Circleville, Ohio, H H Sage, vice Wm H P Denney, removed.
Wilkesbarre, Pa, Wm Pursell, vice H H Chase.
Scranton, Pa, Wm H Pier, vice A H Courrea.
Chicago, Ill, Robt A Gillmore, vice T O Osborne.

Mrd: on Nov 8, at Mexico, Mo, by Rev R S Symington, Walter S McFarlan, formerly of Wash City, to Mary E, youngest daughter of Col Peter B Petrie, formerly of Madison Co, N Y.

Died: on Nov 15, Geo S Caton, in his 32nd year. His funeral is this afternoon at 3 o'clock, from his parents' residence, 361 5th st.

J Gatto, 325 7th st, between N Y ave & L st: Hair Dressing, Shaving, Shampooing, & Hair Dyeing. Shaving 3 times a week & hair cutting once a month, $1.25; single shave, 10 cents; shampooing 25 cents; children's hair cutting, 20 cents; hot & cold baths, 25 cents, or 5 tickets for $1.

MON NOV 19, 1866

Nashville Despatch, Nov 13. Maj Wm B Lewis, one of the oldest & most highly esteemed citizens of this county, died at his residence, near Nashville, yesterday. We believe he was about 82 years of age. He came to this county at an early day & has witnessed the growth of Nashville from a small village to a comparatively large & wealthy city. He was the intimate friend of Gen Jackson, & there was no man in the State so thoroughly acquainted with the history of political parties during the administration of the old hero. He had served with Gen Jackson during the war of 1812, & the Indian wars of that period, & upon the election of the latter to the Presidency, Maj Lewis repaired to Wash with him, & was his trusted friend & confidential adviser during his administration. With the retirement of Gen Jackson, Maj Lewis returned to his home on the banks of the Cumberland. Maj Lewis, disgusted with the course of the dominant part in the Legislature, resigned the seat to which he had been elected.

Brookhaven [Miss] Journal of Nov 10th: Jasper Decell was murdered some weeks since by an unknown assassin, & his son narrowly escaped. In the same neighborhood, Mr Joel Norton was fired upon by a concealed assassin while out on his gallery getting a drink of water. Six balls entered his body & caused almost instant death. His sister found him lifeless on the floor. In entering the bed chamber of the little children to disclose to them the said tidings of the death of their uncle, lo! it was found that one of the innocent little creatures was murdered by one of the balls. Mr Norton was a peaceful man & bore malice to no one. His death will be regretted by a host of friends.

The body of John W Gear, an artist, of Boston, was discovered in the *Mount Auburn Cemetery* at Cambridge, Mass, on Thu last. He committed suicide.

Died: on Nov 15, at the residence of her mother, Miss Eliza Lee Thomas, 2nd daughter of the late Dr John M Thomas. Her funeral will take place on Monday at 11 o'clock, at St Matthew's Church, on H st.

The funeral of Geo S Caton, [32] son of M Caton, one of our oldest & most highly esteemed fellow-citizens, took place on Sat. The Columbia Typographical Society, of which he was a member, turned out with the Marine Band. The remains were interred in *Mount Olivet Cemetery*. The pall bearers were Messrs D Harbaugh, Maurice Murphy, John Birch, John T Chauncey, Jas Smith, & Geo Brawner.

Navy Bulletin. Placed on Sick Leave, Nov 10. First Assist Engineer Louis J Allen. Appointed, Nov 10: Acting Assist Surgeon Geo F Fife, an assist surgeon in the navy. Resigned, Nov 10: 3rd Assist Engineer Jas D Lee.

Orphans Court-Judge Purcell. 1-On Sat the will of the late Robt Beale was filed for probate. It directs the excs to collect the rents due, & keep the estate intact until his children have arrived at the age of 21 years, & nominates Mary D Beal & his son, Robt M, [who has deceased since the execution of the will] as executors. 2-The will of the late Wm Redin, of Gtwn, was filed & fully proven. It nominates his daughter, Catharine, & his friend, Wm L Dunlop & John Marbury, as excs, & bequeathes his estate to his daughters. A codicil of the will substitutes the name of his son-in-law, W R Woodward, for his daughter, as one of the execs. 3-The will of Martha R Wooley, bequeathing her property to her sister, H A Rubendale, of *Fort Wayne*, Ind, & nominating Henry Whitea_l as exec, was filed & fully proven. 4-John Kelly, of N Y, once of the excs named in the will of the late Jacob Lowenthal, renounced the right to the appointment, & letters testamentary were issued to J B Hutchinson; bond, $30,000. 5-Letters of administration were issued to Martha Burke, on the estate of John Burke; bond, $1,000. 6-Mary E Keefe was appointed guardian to the orphan of Robt Devereux; bond, $500. 7-The first & final accounts of the adm of the estate of J M Roberts, & the excs of Mary E Allen, were approved & passed.

A few mornings since the police came across a man in a coffin, who appeared to be a genuine corpse, the jaws being bandaged, fingers clasped, & the usual copper cents enclosed in paper on the eyes, until he snored. When woken up, Mot Varnum, the "corpse" swore never to drink again. It appears that some citizens attempted to carry him to the station, & seeing the coffin in a yard, they decided to play this practical joke on him. –Sunday Herald

Police matters. 1-Thos C Brosman was arrested & held to bail for court to answer the charge of assaulting Mary C Williams, a colored woman. The accused is a capt of a tug boat upon which Mary Williams is employed as a cook, & the allegations is that in a dispute about some groceries Brosnan choked her. 2-Chas Parker was arrested on a charge of stealing a lot of clothing from Mrs Margaret Horner. The stolen property was recovered & Parker was committed to jail for court. 3-Patrick Foley was fined for driving through a funeral procession. 4-Chas H Steele & Wm H Gardner were accused by Mr John Mills of obtaining money from him by false representations. 5-Wm Walker was arrested on the complnt of Henry Mickings, who charges him with assaulting him with a brick. Mickings was sent to jail for court.

The Sec of War has ordered the muster-out of Hospital Chaplain John C Jacobi, Capt Lazarus L Moore, assist quartermaster, U S Vols, & Surgeon Caleb W Harner, brevet lt colonel, U S Vols.

Hon J Z Goodrich has been elected president of the Housatonic Railroad, in place of Chas Hunt, resigned.

Orphans Court of Wash Co, D C. Letters of administration on the personal estate of John Burke, late of U S Army, deceased. –Martin Burke, adm

Pittsburgh, Nov 18. Rev Dr Jas Presley, recently suspended from relations with the United Presbyterian Church, on the charge of cruelty to his wife & family, & indecent & blasphemous language, & maintaining improper relations with females, delivered his farewell address today to his congregation, while disclaiming any complaint against the action of the Presbytery, who acted upon the positive testimony of 3 witnesses, while the testimony in his behalf of his aged father, kind brother, & affecionate children, was only negative, & necessarily to no avail. He thanked God he had not been found guilty of adultery. Mrs Presley has petitioned for divorce.

Chancery sale of valuable house & grounds at G & 18th sts, belonging to the estate of the late Edw Everett; by decree passed by the Supreme Court of D C, in Chancery, in cause #651, wherein H Sidney Everett & others are cmplnts & Helen C Everett & others are dfndnts: public auction on Dec 6 of part of square 169, improved by a first class 3 story double house, one of the most desirable residences in Wash City. –Wm H Phillip, trustee -Jas C McGuire & Co, aucts

Supreme Court of D C, No 800-Equity. Louisa Warren vs Jane R Brent & Eliza Miller. The above cause which is a creditor's suit, is referred to me, to take proof of the claims of the cmplnt & other creditors of Caroline Hill, deceased, who may file their claims, & to inquire into the probable value of the real estate described in the proceedings. Parties interested are to appear before me, to be heard in the premises, on Nov 25, at my ofc. -Walter S Cox, auditor

TUE NOV 20, 1866
Postmasters appointed by the Pres:
Henry C Kelsey, at Newton, N J
Albert H Stamborough, Morristown, N J.
Geo H Hall, St Jos, Mo.
Henry N Merrill, Havermille, Mass.
Jas H Barker, Milford, Mass
Patrick McGuire, Cold Spring, N Y
Alfred Buckhart, Sing Sing, N Y
John H Beale, Lewisberg, Pa
Danl Brewster, Montrose, Pa
G Ashman Miller, Huntington, Pa
Henry Gliebe, Hazleton, Pa
Jas Hoyle, Xenia, Ohio
Wm C Morehead, Zanesville, Ohio
W W McNair, Minneapolis, Minn

Richd Besham, deputy postmaster at Ann Harbor, Mich.
The Pres yesterday appoint D M Leatherman, of Tenn, Com'r on the part of the U S to the Paris Exhibition.

Col Wm G Moore, one of the Pres' private secretaries, has been appointed a paymaster in the regular army, with the rank of major.

Robt Adrain, of New Brunswick, son of the late Prof Adrain, of Rutgers College, surrogate of Middlesex Co, N J, & one of the eminent members of the bar of that State, died of apoplexy on Nov 11, at age 56 years.

Mary Wright was found guilty of the murder of her newborn infant colored male child, soon after its birth, a few days ago, in the 10th precinct. A colored woman gave police the information.

Navy Bulletin: Detached, Nov 12. Lt Cmder Edw C Graften from the command of the ship **Yantie**, & placed on waiting orders. Acting Ensign Sidney Hall, from the **Yantie**, & granted leave of absence. Midshipman C B Gill, B McIlvaine, & S M Ackley, from the **Yantie**, & ordered to the ship **Rhode Island**. Acting Volunteer Lt Var_alls, from the **Yantie** & ordered to the ship **Tacony**. First Assist Engineer Wm W Smith, 2nd Assist Engineers Oscar B Mills & Henry F Loveaire, from the **Yantie**, & placed on waiting orders. Acting Ensigns C H Beckstaf_, J F Churchill, J C Lord, Acting Assist Surgeon Geo L Simpson, Acting Second Assist Engineer Brye_ Wilson, & Acting Third Assist Engineer Geo Hilton, from the **Yantie**, & placed on waiting orders. Assist Paymaster Wm J Thomson, from the **Yantie**, & ordered to settle his accounts. Promoted, Nov 12. Cmdor Thos F Craven to rear admiral, from Oct 10. Resigned, Nov 12. Midshipman Chas J Bates, of the Naval Academy.

The N Y Commercial says that Mr Jas Buchan, of Rochester, N Y, has in his possession the original parchment deed of the property in N Y C that was granted by Queen Anne, of England, 200 years ago to Aneke Jans. The deed is described as a rare old relic of the olden time, & is certainly just now an object of great interest to the vestry of Trinity Church that holds the property, & no less so the heirs of the prolific Mrs Jans, whose descendants so multitudiously abound in these parts.

A negro, Jas Robertson, said to be from Providence, R I, entered the house of Rev David A Wasson, in Somerville, Mass, on Friday & demanded money. Mrs Wasson, being alone, refused, & he offered her violence. The frightened lady promised him whatever he wanted to take away. He stole a pistol & $5, inflicted personal violence upon her, & departed. The police are on his track.

Mrd: on Oct 29, by Rev T B McFalls, Mr Geo F Taylor to Miss Henrietta B, only daughter of the late John Clagett, both of PG Co, Md.

Galveston, Texas, Nov 14, via New Orleans, Nov 19. On Nov 10 Gen Tapia died from cholera.

Dr Wm F Townsend, a well known physician of Boston, died of cholera on Sat. The disease was contracted from attending upon a colera patient whose case terminated in death a few days since.

Balt, No 19. Insane mother attempts to kill all her children. Horrible affair at the residence of Mr Jesse Marsden, on East Balt st; Mrs Geo Clogg, a daughter of Mr Marsden, residing with the family, while under a fit of insanity, attacked her own children & those of her sister, Mrs Eichman, with a common table knife, & cut the throat of a son of Mrs Eichman, aged 4 years, cutting the jugular vein causing almost instant death.. She then attempted the life of her youngest child, a daughter, aged 4 years, wounding it severely, after which she endeavored to kill her eldest child, age 6, but it escaped. The parties are highly respectable. Second despatch: It appears that Mrs Clogg did not succeed in inflicting serious injury on her children, but only attempted to do so; seeing her kill the little boy, they made their escape from their mother unharmed. The unhappy woman was removed to an insane asylum shortly after the sad affair. [Nov 21st newspaper: Mr Geo S Clogg, is a shoe-dealer on South Calvert st; Mrs Clogg has been residing at her father's residence for the past month, 123 E Balt st, & has shown signs of mental derangement, but considered harmless. Geo Eichman, the murdered child, was the son of Mr Julius Eichman, tailor, on Charles st. Mrs Clogg was sent to Mount Hope Insane Asylum. -Balt Commercial, 20th.]

Linwood & rich Jersey lands for sale: losses of property & my sons, with a desire to close business & pay my debts, has induced me to convey, by deed in trust in all my property to Alfred Hargrave, of Lexington, N C, which will be sold by him, & conveyances made on Dec 11, 1866, at *Linwood* first, & Lexington next, from day to day until all is sold, consisting of *Linwood*, 1,649 acres, with mill, cottage, & numerous bldgs. Tract of 200 acres of Woodland near Lexington. *Trentham Place*, constituting a part & adjoining the town of Lexington, highly improved. Also, my interest in the houses & lots on which I live, in all, 9 acres, with a fine Mansion House. Also, the bloodied stallion Medley; North Devon Cattle; Down Sheep; wagons, family carriage, & carts. –W R Holt, Lexington, N C [Interest discounted for cash over sums of $10. –Alfred Hargrave.]

Sidney Tompkins, a wealthy farmer of Stillwater, Wash Co, N Y, met with his death on Friday. Upon visiting his cattle yard, he discovered one of his cows in great distress with a potato lodged in the throat. Mr Tompkins thrust his arm partially down the throat & the cow pressed its head downward, & suddenly elevated Mr Tompkins, throwing him into a picket which entered his neck, severing one of the arteries, from which he bled to death in a few moments.

On Oct 31, during the passage of the steamship **Pereire** from Havre to this port, the Very Rev Etienne Roussellon, Vicar Gen of the Catholic diocese of New Orleans, La, a passenger on board the vessel., in going on deck, slipped & fell backwards, injuring himself severely. The **Pereire** arrived on Nov 6, & he was conveyed to St Vincent's Hospital, where it was found he had a fracture of the neck of the left thigh bone. He continued to fail & died; he was 66 yrs of age, & a native of Leon, France. His remains will be taken to New Orleans for interment. He was the senior member of the Archiepiscopal Council of the New Orleans diocese. His sucessor will be Rev N J Porche, his former assistant. –N Y Herald

The San Antonio Herald announces the arrest & imprisonment of Jonathan & Antoine Lindley, father & son, charged with the murder of Tom Duncan, a citizen of Bell Co. The murder was supposed to have been prompted by revenge for the hanging of one of the sons of the old man for horse-stealing.

U S Marshal's sale on Nov 21, of 209 bushels of sweet potatoes & 97 bushels Irish potatoes, seized & levied upon as the goods & chattels of John Naigley, & will be sold to satisfy attachment 3,211, Supreme Court, D C, in favor of John C Johnson & Co. -D S Gooding, U S Marshal D C

Thos Kyle, late of Balt City, bequeathed by his last will to the trustees of the Orphans' Home of Balt City, attached to St Patrick's Roman Catholic Church, $500; to the trustees of St Vincent's Male Orphan Asylum, attached to St Vincent de Paul's Roman Catholic Church, $700; to the trustees of St Mary's Female Orphan Asylum on Franklin st, $800, & also his gold watch & chain. The interest on 56 shares of the stock of the Farmers' & Planters' Bank, upon certain contingencies, to the trustees of St Vincent de Paul's Church, in trust, for the use & benefit of the pastor of said church.

WED NOV 21, 1866
Navy Bulletin: Dropped, Nov 13. Guner Geo W Allen, Oct 30, 1865.
Orders Revoked, Nov 13: Acting Master John V Cook, to the ship **Tacony**, & placed on sick leave of absence; Midshipman Robt M Berry, to the ship **Susequehanna**, & he is ordered to the ship **Sabine**.
Honorably Discharged, Nov 13. Acting 3rd Assist Engineer Alex'r D Renshaw, from Nov 8.
Detached, Nov 13. Lt Cmder N F Crossman, from temporary duty at the N Y Navy Yard, & ordered to the ship **Ossipee**.

Mustered out: Hospital Stewards E H Packard & Saml Johnson, U S army, by order of the Sec of War.

The Navy Dept yesterday received information of the death in N Y C, of Capt Wm M Walker, U S N.

Brvt Col Wm S King, surgeon U S army, has been assigned to duty as Medical Director of the Dept of the Lakes.

Dept of Dakota. Maj Gen Alfred H Terry, commanding the Dept of Dakota, announces the following appointments of ofcrs on his staff: Surgeon J E Summers, U S A, as medical director; Brvt Lt Col S H Gilmore, capt & C S, U S A, as chief commissary of subsistence. The duties of judge advocated to the dept will for the present be discharged by 1st Lt Chas H Graves, A D C, & the duties of assist inspector general by 2nd Lt J G Telford, A D C.

John Wilson Osborne, the oldest representative of the Indiana press, died at the residence of his son-in-law, Solomon Claypool, in Greencastle, on Nov 12.

The suit of the city of Providence against the bondsmen of its dishonest treasurer, Maurinus W Gardner, to recover the amount of his defalcation, $12,000, after a lengthy trial in the Supreme Court there, was decided on Thu by a verdict of $2,487 for the city.

Mrs Sarah E Newell, who resided on First st east, between H & I sts, died of cholera on Monday, aged 42 years. She had been ill only a few days.

Mrd: on Nov 20, at the residence of the bride's parents, by Rev Mr Krebs, Mr Augustus Donath, of Boston, to Miss Emily Lewis, of Wash, D C.

Died: on Nov 19, at *The Cedars*, Gtwn Heights, in her 54th year, Ellen Louisa, wife of Wm D C Murdock, & daughter of the late Chas A Burnett, of Gtwn. Her funeral will be from her late residence this afternoon at half past 4 o'clock.

Died: on Nov 20, Isaac De Reamer. His funeral will take place from his residence, 60 Pa ave, near 22nd st, on Thu morning at 10 o'clock.

Savannah, Ga, Nov 19. A citizen, Augustus McLean, was shot yesterday, by a freedman, in a dispute about ten cents. The verdict of the jury was wilful murder.

Louisville, Nov 19. The coroner's jury which examined the remains of Mrs Ben Powell, reports that no traces of poison were found in her stomach, & consequently exonerated her husband & every one else from suspicion. The recent report of the arrest of Mr Powell, in reference to this matter, was incorrect.

Richmond, Nov 20. Rev Jacob James, a colored preacher, was shot last night by another colored man, Thornton Holmes. James died this morning. Holmes also shot his wife who will recover. He was arrested & acknowledged the deed.

Public auction on Nov 26, of the entire stock in the store of K F Page, 502 7th st; boots, bedspreads, guns, rifles, hosiery, clocks, hats, trunks, valises, watches & jewelry. -Green & Williams, aucts

Orphans Court of Wash Co, D C. Letters testamentary on personal estate of Wm Redin, late of Gtwn, D C, deceased. –Wm R Woodward, Wm L Dunlop, John Marbury, jr, excs

Orphans Court of Wash Co, D C. Letters of administration on the personal estate of Francis Espiuta, late of Wash City, deceased. –Jos Espiuta, adm

Orphans Court of Wash Co, D C. Letters testamentary on the personal estate of Jacob Lowenthal, late of Wash City, deceased. –John B Hutchinson, exc

THU NOV 22, 1866
Navy Bulletin: 1-Ordered, Nov 14. Capt Danl Ammen & Cmder K Randolph Breese, to duty as members of the examining board at Hartford, Conn. 2-Detached, Nov 14: Cmder Walter W Queen, from ordnance duty at Reading, Pa, & ordered to duty as a member of the examining board at Hartford, Conn; Second Assist Engineer David Hardie, from the ship **Susquehanna**, & granted sick leave of absence.

Whilst the Peruvian war steamer **Putumayo** was recently exploring the river Pachitea, a tributary of the Amazon, some Caribbean Indians came down to the bank where the vessel was anchored, & by friendly demonstrations induced Capt Tavara, Lt Albert West, & some sailors to go on shore. The savages killed the two ofcrs, & the sailors barely saved their lives by running to the ship. There appears little doubt that the unfortunate ofcrs were eaten by the savages, as no traces could be found of their remains.

Jos Jefferson: the first member of this family of genius who distinguished himself on the stage was the contemporary & fellow actor of Garrick. He was manager of the Plymouth [England] theatre at the time of his death, & died greatly respected. His wife died singularly, when thrown into a fit of uncontrollable laughter, which resulted in convulsions, from a comic feat at a dramatic performance, from which she never recovered. Jos Jefferson the son of the above, arrived in Boston in 1796; short time later he went to N Y, & was a favorite there, sharing the comic honors with Hodgkisson, the first comic actor of the time. In 1803 he became a member of the Phil stage, & continued so during the remainder of his professional life. He retired from the stage before his death, in failing health & spirits, from attacks of gout, inherited from his father. He went to Harrisburg, performing there occasionally, & closed his honored life in that city in 1832. His remains were buried in St Stephen's Protestant Episcopal Church of that place, & remained without the slightest memorial till 1843, when the late Judge Gibson & Judge Rogers, of that State, placed a handsome marble slab over his grave. The inscription follows:
Beneath this Marble
Are deposited the Ashes of
Joseph Jefferson,
An actor whose unrivalled powers took in the whole
range of comic character,
From pathos to soul-shaking mirth.
His coloring of the part was that of Nature, warm, pure, and fresh;
But of Nature enriched with the finest conceptions of
Genius.
He was a Member of the Chestnut street Theatre, Phila-
delphia,
In its most high and palmy days.
And the compeer
Of Cooper, Wood, Warren, Francis,

And a long list of worthies,
Who, Like himself,
Are remembered with admiration and praise.
He was a native of England,
With an unblemished reputation as a man,
He closed a career of professional success,
In calamity & affliction,
At this place,
In the year 1832.
"I knew him, Horatio;
A fellow of infinite jest and most excellent fancy."
Jos Jefferson the 3rd in succession, is well remembered; he married Mrs Burke, a lady distinguished for her musical powers, whose first husband was a gifted comic actor, & whose son, Charlie Burke, died early in his professional career. Jos Jefferson, the 4th in succession was a fruit of this second marriage. This Jos Jefferson, is a first cousin of Warren, the well-known Boston comedian, cannot be yet 35 years of age. He recently filled a protracted engagement at the Theatre Royal, in Liverpool.

John W Patton has become an associate with Col Vann in the publication of the Copiahan, at Hazlehurst.

Mrd: on Oct 24, by Rev Septimus Tustin, D D, H Rowland to Miss Amelia J Donnelly, both of Chester Co, Pa.

Died: on Nov 20, at N Y, Capt Wm M Walker, U S Navy. His funeral will be from the residence of his mother, 261 I st, at 2 o'clock this afternoon.

Died: on Nov 20, in N Y C, Estwick Evans, of this city, & formerly of Portsmouth, N H, aged 80 years. His funeral will be from Ascension Church, on Nov 23, at 2 o'clock.

Died: on Nov 21, David Hines. His funeral is today at 2½ o'clock, from his late residence, 110 Pa ave, corner of 20th st.

Died: on Nov 21, in Wash City, D C, Mr Saml C Worthington, of Wash Co, Miss, in his 77th year. His remains will be taken to Mississippi for interment.

Fred'k Weed, late of the 2nd Calif Volunteer Cavalry committed suicide on Sat last, by taking an ounce of laudanum. It was premediated as a letter was found under his pillow. He had confessed to his friends that insanity prevailed in his family. Mr Weed was the nephew of Thurlow Weed, of N Y, & was well known. He entered the service in 1861, as a private in the 2nd cavalry of Calif volunteers, & accompanied Gen Conner to Utah. His letter ends with: " I take my leap into the unknown future without misgiving. I am tired-I am discouraged."
–Frederick Weed

Cmdor Vanderbilt has bought an Abdallah colt for $5,000.

Improvements in Wash City: A R Shepherd is putting up 14 dwlg-houses, 3 on M st, each 3 stories high; 3 others of like appearance on N st, between 9th & 10th sts. Mr J H Darrow is bldg two 3 story houses on 9th st, between O & P sts. N J ave & 1st st, Mr McGraim is finishing a 3 story brick house, 25 x 32 feet, costing $5,000. On I north near 1st st, Geo A Birch is having a modern residence built, which will cost at least $8,000. On I st south, near 1st st, Geo Calvert is erecting a 3 story brick house, 32 x 40 feet, costing $8,000. At D & 2nd sts, Mr Wm Wadder is having a pretty brick residence built, costing $6,000. Mass ave, between 13th & 14th sts, a magnificent 4 story pressed brick front, brownstone finish, 40 x 60 feet, with 2 story back bldg, for a private residence, is being erected by Mr W B Jackson. It will be one of the finest houses in the city, & will cost $40,000.

Yesterday, at 1:30 P M, Sylvanus Hartshorne, in his 73rd year, died of disease of the heart, & his sufferings were but short; for he departed in half an hour after he was first taken. About 3 o'clock he was followed to the land of spirits by his beloved wife, who, like himself, was perfectly well in the morning; but when she had lost her dear husband of her youth, the shock was so terrible that nature gave way, & she sank under the awful blow. They have left not one single enemy behind in all Norfolk. –Norfolk Old Dominion, 20th.

T F Crane, son of Edw Crane, a well known railroad man, was accidentally killed on the train at Southbridge, Mass, Nov 20.

FRI NOV 23, 1866
The Pres appointed Andrew J Gerritson assessor of internal revenue for the 12th Dist of Pa, & Geo B Dickson, assessor for the District of Delaware.

Navy Bulletin: Appointment revoked, Nov 12. Mate John Sinnot, of Vt. Dismissed, Nov 15: Acting Ensign Aloysius J Kane.
Ordered, Nov 15: 1st Assist Engineer Chas E De Valin, to the naval rendezvous at N Y; Lt Cmder Francis M C Bunce. to duty at the Boston Navy Yard on Dec 16.

New appointments by the Postmaster General, of postmasters since Nov 18:
Kansas: Monrovia, Atchison Co, Jas Kirkpatrick, vice S J H Snyder, resigned; Grenada, Nemaha Co, N H Rising, vice J Sherrin, resigned.
Minnesota: Riceford, Houston Co, C H Brown, vice W H Birdsell, removed; Sterling, Blue Earth Co, Wm Russell, vice Josiah Russell, resigned; Belle Plan, Scott Co, Ambrose B Walker, vice H W Stone, removed; Hamilton station, Scott Co, Martin Quinn, vice L M Williams, resigned; Cedar Lake, Scott Co, C O Conner, vice M Phelan, removed; Shakopee, Scott Co, Chas Hartman, vice D L Horn, removed; Stockton, Winona Co, Geo Little, vice Jas Floyd, declined; Concord, Dodge Co, Thos L Wright, vice E L Wright, resigned.
Calif: Wood Valley, Puebla, H Q Jamison, vice E B Sutherland, resigned.

Oregon: St Helen, Columbia Co, B Giltner, vice B M Wats, resigned.
Wisc: Randolph Centre, Columbia Co, E B Finney, vice J M Bay, resigned; Cross Plains, Dane Co, John Baer, vice R Pickhard, removed; La Fayette, Chippewa Co, Jos Barnum, vice J H Brown, resigned.
N Y: Lavonia station, Livingston Co, C Brown, vice W H Patterson, resigned; Bristol, Ontario Co, G Francis, vice P Hicks, resigned; New Hamburgh, Dutchess Co, F Myers, vice S F Jones, resigned; Hyde Park, Dutchess Co, J L Richard, vice V Angerine, removed; Windsor, Broome Co, A J Butts, vice J R Balden, removed; Cross River, Westchester Co, E Merritt, vice W Hunt, removed; Chateaugay Lake, Franklin Co, J B Bart, vice G L Havers, resigned; Bedford, Westchester Co, J S Knox, vice R J Simmeson, removed; Round Ridge, Westchester Co, J D Bishop, vice A Monroe, removed; Rhinebeck, Dutchess Co, John M Keese, vice S Gillender, removed; Union Springs, Cayuga Co, T J Merserau, vice J B Clark, removed; Weedspott, Cayuga Co, J Kernan, vice C C Adams.
Michigan: Portage, Kalamazoo Co, D Lathrop, vice A E Lathrop, resigned.
Ohio: Geneva, Ottawa Co, David C Stewart, vice A B Ruder, resigned; Ontario, Richland Co, G B Thralkell, vice D A Hacksom, resigned; Oak Harbor, Ottawa Co, H H Mylandie, vice H L Bull, absconded; Flat Rock, Seneca Co, S Harner, vice W J Heisle; Wertville, Champagne Co, J Snyder, vice R R McLaughlin, resigned; Agersville, Defiance Co, Isaac Odell, vice J W Tate, resigned; Malaga, Monroe Co, Geo Ketterar, vice Miss Mary J Beacher; Newburgh, Cuyahoga Co, A P Leland, vice M Fish, removed.
North Carolina: Childsville, Yancey Co, Miss N M Wiseman, vice C C Wise; Dallas, Gaston Co, Miss E C Morris, vice V S Tremberger, resigned; South River, Rowan Co, C Zarahart, vice A M Miller, resigned.
Pennsylvania: New Bedford, Lawrence Co, S Price, vice A Holland, resigned.
West Va: Raymond City, Putnam Co, T Verner, vice H F Averill, resigned; Calif House, Wirt Co, T Boulware, vice W A West.
Maine: Smithfield, Somerset Co, N D Smith, vice J H Patce, removed.
Vt: Rochester, Windsor Co, G S Guernelsey, vice Chas Morgan, removed.
Mass: Mansfield, Bristol Co, W D Durham, vice W Robinson, removed; Arrabet, Middlesex Co, A G Haynes, vice J R Harreman, resigned.
Conn: Forrestville, Hartford Co, C H Alpress, vice S E Greene, removed; South Coventry, Tolland Co, J A Spalding, vice W A Loomis, resigned.
Ky: Wilsonville, Spencer Co, J W Day, vice T G Dale, resigned; Bridgeport, Franklin Co, J W Jackson, vice W Wiggs, resigned; Lynn, Granup Co, T Bartlett, vice S B Callons, resigned; Whitesburgh, L_tcher Co, L W Field, vice S S Reid, resigned; Banson, Franklin Co, J W Coots, vice John Sheets, removed.
New Jersey: Hightstown, Mercer Co, Saml Holcomb, vice C Keeler, removed; Clinton Station, Hunterdon Co, J Cole, vice T H Risley, resigned.
Tenn: Dyersburgh, Dyer Co, W B Tipton, vice L H Silsby, declined; Lewisburgh, Marshall Co, M C West, vice J L Reed, declined; Smeedville Station, Dixon Co, S S Donegan, vice J C Donegan, resigned.
Indiana: Hobbieville, Greene Co, W B Evans, vice A A Evans; Half Way, Jay Co, M Bader, vice H O Current, resigned.

Missouri: Holden, Johnson Co, W M Coventry, vice W W Rose, resigned; Dundee, Franklin Co, J C McDonald, vice S S Bailey, resigned; Walnut Grove, Greene Co, W C Wardlow, vice B Lemmon, resigned; College Mound, Mason Co, L Wisdom, vice J W Jones, resigned; Granby, Newton Co, F R Sweet, vice S H Hargrove, resigned; Caruthersville, Pumircolt Co, J Snow, vice F Bell, resigned; Perryville, Perry Co, V P Tucker, vice J E Doare, resigned; Ridge Prairie, Saline Co, J W Wallace, vice J R Lewis, resigned; Stanford, Texas Co, P M Greene, vice J Farris, resigned; Smithton, Worth Co, J Carlon, vice J W Watson.

Virginia: Harsely's Landing, Nelson Co, S Phelps, vice M Harding, declined; Shirando, Augusta Co, V Bare, vice D Balslay.

Illinois: Zif, Wayne Co, L A Sharp, vice L T E Johnson, resigned; Hutton, Coles Co, V McGohan, vice C H Rice; Dayton, La Salle Co, G W Makinson, vice O W Trumbo, resigned.

Iowa: Dayton Centre, Chickasaw Co, N B Silsbee, vice S S Potter, declined; Pleasant Grove, Des Moines Co, G Zion, vice J Stricker, resigned; Bethel, Fayette Co, E M Aiken, vice Ira Burbank, resigned; Clifton, Louisa Co, C F Butler, vice Geo Haywood, resigned; Eveland Grove, Mahaska Co, E Baker, vice J H Nowles, resigned; Athica, Marion Co, J A Welch, vice W Thomas, resigned; White Cloud, Mills Co, J Galbreth, vice J Wilber, resigned.

Appointments ordered by the Pres yesterday: Edw Uhl, of N Y, U S Consul at Guatemala; Jos T K Plant & Wm H Frazier, Justices of Peace, Wash Co, D C.

Pottsville Miner's Journal: on Sat last, one of the boilers exploded at the Wm Kear & Co, Mine Hill Gap, killing 8 boys, slate-pickers, whose ages ranged from 12 to 18 years of age: killed were Geo H Clemens, Wm Edwards, Richd Welsh, Michl Welsh, Jas Ryan, E Lawler, & John Welsh. The engineer, named Good, was seriously wounded.

Mrs Isaac Taylor, who died recently at Racine, Wis, by her will, after making numerous bequests to her relatives & friends, left $65,000 to Racine College, $5,000 to Nashota Seminary, in Wakesha Co, & the residue of her property to trustees to found an orphan asylum for the orphans of Racine Co, to be named in honor of her husband. The amount will be from $130,000 to $150,000.

Mr Tripp, the original oil man, well known in the city of Buffalo, & throughout Canada, died suddenly from congestion of the brain a few days since in New Orleans, La. He brought specimens of oil & earth from the vicinity of Enniskillen, Canada, & endeavored to interest capitalists in this city & in N Y to bore wells for oil, to manufacture gas from the soil which was impregnated with oil. –Buffalo Courier

Mr Chas Gautier, jr, has returned to Wash City after a very protracted tour in Europe, mainly upon business connected with the establishment of his father in this city.

Miss Jennie Page, of Rochester, N Y, aged 16 years, committed suicide by drowning, on Monday.

Mr N P Willis has had a paralytic stroke, & is in a very critical condition.

Miss Anna Morrison fell from a ferryboat, at the Carr st landing, St Louis, on Friday, & was drowned.

Capt Henry W Pattesson, 4th U S infty, was married on Oct 25 to Miss Louisa C Dawson, daughter of Hon John L Dawson, of Pa.

Danl Shaver, member of Assembly elect from Schoharie Co, N Y, died on Wed.

A Yacht Club was organized at Boston on Wed; club consists of 90 members; Dexter H Follet elected commodore.

A movement is under way at Panama to secure the erection of a monument on the Isthmus to the memory of W H Aspinwall, J L Stephens, & H Chaunce.

San Francisco, Nov 22. It is rumored that Gen Vega, who went to assist Corona, was really employed by Ortega, & having disobeyed Juarez' orders was shot as a traitor by order of Corona.

Augusta, Ga, Nov 22. 1-Geo Meyer, Assist U S Internal Revenue Assesor, was shot & killed at Blackville, S C, by 2 men named Sanders, who surrendered to the sheriff. 2-A locomotive exploded on the Georgia railroad today, killing fireman Martin & wounding engineer Berry.

A few days since, Miss Sarah Van Sickle was thrown from her horse while riding on the Nat'l road, near Uniontown, Pa, & her foot holding in the stirrup, she was dragged some 400 yards. Her injuries caused death in a few hours.

Died: on Nov 22, Admiral French Forrest, formerly of the U S Navy, late of the Confederate States Navy, in his 71st year. His funeral will be from the residence of his brother, Bladen Forrest, 78 1st st, Gtwn, at 1 o'clock P M, Sat. Balt Gaz please copy. [Nov 24th newspaper: Admiral Forrest died after a short but painful illness of typhoid fever. He fought bravely in the war of 1812; was in the naval engagement under Cmdor Perry; fought valiantly in the Mexican war; he was appointed at that time adj general of the land & naval forces, & the responsible duty devolved upon him of having the forces transported into the interior of Mexico. When Va seceded, he joined the fortunes of the Southern Confederacy, & was given the position of cmder-in-chief of the naval forces of Va, & commanded at the Norfolk Navy Yard, & afterwards appointed to the command of the James River Squadron, & then Acting Assist Sec of the Navy. He was a kind & affection husband & father, loved & respected by all who knew him.]

SAT NOV 24, 1866
Jurors for the criminal court-Wash:
Grand Jurors:

Benj G Prather	T Sheckells	John C Clary
Wm Acton	H Burns	Thos Murphy
H B Curtis	A R Shepherd	John Hammond
Geo W Keating	Geo Baker	John P Hilton
Cline C Lineweaver	Geo Bogus	Wm Wetzell
J Buchanan	F I Fugitt	Thos Mosher
Geo E Mattingly	Saml M Evans	Hugh Murray
D V Burr	Jas Bradshaw	

Petit Jurors:

Richd Dove	C Cammack	Valentine Connor
I Herzberg	John W Mead	John Mullen
W W Birch	C G Klopfer	E O Sanderson
R Polkinhorn	Zach Baker	Minor Gibson
Jabez Wheeler	Jas Osburne	Geo J Johnson
Theo Frasher	C W Hancock	A T Pumphrey
Saml Adams	Decius Edmonston	John Ardesser
J T Jenkins	Z D Gilman	Chas Kloman
Chas F Creamer	Henry M Knight	

Washington real estate. Near the new State Dept, lots have been taken by wealthy citizens, who are preparing to build fine mansions. Mr Joshua Pierce has just sold a square between Q & R, & 15th & 16th sts, for $25,000.

Larkin G Mead, jr, the Vermont sculptor, sailed for Italy last Sat, to be gone 4 years. He has orders that will occupy him for 3 years.

Richd Lawrence, who made an attempt to assassinate Gen Jackson in 1835, still lives, & is an inmate of the Md Lunatic Asylum.

Dept of the Tenn. Maj Gen Thomas, commanding the Military Dept of the Tenn, announces in general orders that the following named ofcrs comprise his staff: Brvt Maj Gen Wm D Whipple, major & A A G, U S A, assist adj gen; Brvt Lt Col A L Hough, capt 19th infty, U S A, acting assist adj gen, & chief commissary of musters; 1st Lt J P Willa_d, 17th infty, U S A, brvt colonel U S volunteers, aide de camp; 1st Lt S C Kellogg, 18th infty, U S A, brevet colonel U S volunteers, aide de camp; Brvt Brig Gen D B Sacket, U S A, inspector general; Brvt Brig Gen A Von Schrader, major & A A G, U S volunteers, acting assist inspector general; Brvt Maj Gen R W Johnson, major 4th cavalry, U S A, acting judge advocate; Brvt Brig Gen Thomas Swords, colonel & assist quartermaster general, U S A, chief quartermaster; Brvt Maj S R Hamill, capt & A Q M, U S volunteers, in charge of military railroads, & staff quartermaster; Brvt Col M P Small, capt & C S, U S A, chief commissary of subsistence; Brvt Col J Simpson, surgeon U S A, medical director.

Police Matters: 1-Jas Coleman, on the cmplnt of C G Roland, was arrested & charged with grand larceny. He was committed to jail for further hearing. 2-Wm Dacher & Benj Stannell were both fined $5 yesterday for violation of the license relative to the numbering of carts. 3-Wm Woodward, a merchant, was fined $5 yesterday for keeping an unlicensed dog.

Navy Bulletin: Ordered, Nov 16: Passed Assist Paymaster Jared Lindsly to the ship **Osceola**. Detached, Nov 16: Acting Ensign Andrew Jackson, from the ship **Newbern**, & ordered to the ship **Constellation**; Cmder Jas P Foster, from command of the ship **Tacony**, & ordered to command of the ship **Osceloa**; Lt Cmder Edwin M Shephard, Midshipmen Wm J Moore, Edw Woodman, Benj S Richards, A H Carter, Louis V Howsel, Jos N Hemphill, 1st Assist Engineer W B Clark, 2nd Assist Engineers Geo E Towers, Henry C Blye, Passed Assist Surgeon Edw Kershner, Acting Volunteer Lt J G Vassalls, Acting Master C F R Wappenhaws, Acting Ensigns Hugh Jones, Norman McLeod, & Acting 3rd Assist Engineers Jas C Vestes & Wm Holland, from the **Tacony**, & ordered to the **Osceola**; Passed Assist Paymaster A D Bache, from the **Tacony**, & ordered to settle his accounts. Resigned, Nov 16: 1st Assist Engineer T B Cunningham & 2nd Assist Engineer Geo W Hall.

The Pres appointed Jos Severns surveyor of the port of Phil, & that gentleman yesterday gave bonds for entering upon the discharge of his duties.

The silver wedding of A S Barnes, the prominent book publisher of N Y, was celebrated on Sat week. Mrs Barnes received from her husband a magnificent breastpin, whose central stone was a diamond, representiing the wife & mother; around this ten pearls were set, representing the 10 children; these in turn were encircled by 25 garnets, indicating the years of married life, & the outer circlet of 50 diamonds signified the age of the husband. On the reverse were inscribed the dates of the engagment, marriage, & silver wedding.

Promotion: Jas P Tustin has been promoted to a 4th class clerkship in the Pension Ofc, at a salary of $1,800 per annum.

Died: on Nov 22, Mrs Addie Hart, in her 19th year. Her funeral will be from her mother's [Mrs Mary Daly,] residence, Mass ave, near 4th st, on Nov 24 at 2 P M.

Died: on Nov 23, after 2 days illness, Mrs Ann Rothwell, wife of A Rothwell, aged 54 years. Her funeral will be tomorrow at 2 o'clock P M. at the E st Baptist Church.

A notorious character, Thos Killduck was arrested yesterday on the charge of committing an assault upon a negro, Henry Clay. The man arrested is reputed to be a Balt rough. He was fined $5 for assault & battery.

The funeral discourse of the late Mr Bessan, to be delivered at Foundry M E Church tomorrow.

Household & kitchen furniture, vegetables, carriage & harness, cow & farming implements, at auction on Nov 30, at **Greenwood**, the residence of Gen B S Alexander, Gtwn Heights, on the Tennallytown road. –Thos Dowling, auct

Greenberry Point Farm for sale: contains 30½ acres, on the north side of the Severn river, half a mile from Annapolis, Md; with an old-fashioned brick dwlg, with 8 rooms, & numerous out-bldgs. Henry C Middleton, on the place, will show it. Letters to Clarksburg, Harrison Co, West Va, will meet attention. –Henry O Middleton

Hon Andrew D Norton, of Syracuse, N Y, has been elected president of Cornell Univ.

John B Chapman, a prominent member of the Phil bar, died suddenly on Thursday.

Mr Leutze is here painting a protrait of the late Miss Fannie Seward, from photographs, aided by the recollections of her relatives.

Mr Wm J Romyn, a prominent member of the St Louis bar, died on Nov 19. He was, we believe, a native of Balt, Md.

Wm A Willard, of Worcester, Mass, has commenced to paint a portrait of the late Pres Lincoln, for the State House at Boston.

Montreal, Nov 23. Jas Mack, the murderer of Alfred Smith, of the Royal Artl, was hung today. The Catholic priest administered the sacrament. The prisoner confessed his crime & said he was ready to die.

Jas Brewster, one of the oldest & most prominent citizens of New Haven, died in that city on Thursday, aged 78 years.

This morning a locomotive boiler exploded at Newburg, killing Fred'k Gardener, the engineer, & Jas T Green, the fireman. The top of Mr Gardener's head was blown off & his body was thrown about 150 feet, while that of Mr Green was thrown 500 feet. Thos Boardman, conductor, was struck by a piece of the engine, his leg broken, & amputation may be necessary. Mr Brimfield, brakeman, was slightly wounded. Both Gardener & Green leave wives & children to lament their sad death. Gardner has 2 children & Green has one child. Green was an extra fireman, & was filling the place for a few days of the regular fireman, a nephew of Gardener.

MON NOV 26, 1866
The Fremont Journal says the family of Gen McPherson have finally decided that the body shall remain at Clyde. All talk of removal of the remains of Gen McPherson to West Poinst is at an end. The Monument Association will push the work of raising subscriptions with all possible vigor.

Navy Bulletin, Detached, Nov 17. Surgeon J D Miller, from duty connected with the medical board at Phil, & ordered to the steamer **Rhode Island**, & to duty as fleet surgeon of the North Atlantic Squadron; Carpenter Geo W Elliott, from the ship **Michigan**, & placed on waiting orders. Ordered, Nov 17. Surgeon Edwin R Denby, to duty as recorder of the medical board at Phil. Disgracefully Discharged, Nov 17. Boatswain Chas A Bragdon, from Oct 10, 1866.

On Sat last the body of Wm F Gude was found, but it appears he shot himself on Thursday. He was an agent for the firm of Drost & Sutro, fancy goods merchants of Balt, & did business on the 2nd floor of 487 8th st west, between D st & Market space. He occupied a small room in the back as a sleeping apt. For some time he has been troubled with a complicated disease, which seriously affected his mind. Nicholas Mayard resided nearby & distinctly heard the report of a pistol on Thu. Wm Poulton, who resided nearby, heard a shot on Thurs. Gude was 23 years of age. The body was removed to Balt, on Sat, where he had many friends. His parents reside at Egg Harbor, N Y.

Gilbert Cameron, the builder of the Smithsonian Institute, died at his residence, Washington Cottage, Greenock, on Nov 6, from a severe illness which began on Nov 5. He was 57 years of age. Mr Cameron leaves a widow but no family. He was the builder of the Metropolitan Hotel, Trinity Church, the Poor House, & other bldgs. He was for many years president of St Andrew's Society.

The Old Bowery Theatre, at N Y, was on Sat sold at auction under mortgage. It was sold to Mr J W Dimmick for $100,700.

Sixth Auditor's Ofc: changes for the Post Ofc Dept: J Emond Mallet, of N Y; J B Patterson, of Pa, & John H Dixon, of the Dist of Columbia, from first-class [$1,200] to second class [$1,400] clerkships. Benj E McGrew promoted from a messenger to a first class clerkship.

Orphans Court-Judge Purcell. 1-On Sat the will of the late Wm G Freeman, bequeathing his estate to his wife, was fully proven, & letters testamentary were issued to Margaret C Freeman; bond $100,000. 2-Letters testamentary were issued to Mary D Beale on the estate of the late Robt Beale; bond, $20,000. To Henrietta Andrews on the estate of the late Christopher Andrews; bond, $50,000. To Henry Whitall, on the estate of Martha R Wooley; bond $600. 3-The first & final account of the administrator with the will annexed of Otho Boswell, on account of the estate, was approved & passed.

Fatal affray on Nov 20 near Bladensburg, between a white man, Geo L Bridewell & Geo Wilson, a negro. In a scuffle the negro got the white man down, & fearing for his life, he drew a pistol & fired, killing the negro. Harrison Wallis, acting coroner, summoned a jury of inquest, & rendered a verdict of justifiable homicide. Young Bridewell gave himself up to await the action of the grand jury. –Prince Georgian

Orphans Court of Wash Co, D C. Letters of administration on the personal estate of Christopher Andrews, late of Wash, D C, deceased. –Henrietta M Andrews

Lot 17 in square 56, on I st north, between 2nd & 3rd sts west, with a 2 story frame dwlg on the front & 2 tenements on the rear, were sold to Wm Clagett, for $4,775.

TUE NOV 27, 1866
Mr P H Herbert, the agent of the Ghioni & Susini Opera Troupe, died suddenly at New Orleans on Tuesday. He was perfectly well on Monday night, at which time he returned from the Opera House to the St Chas Hotel, partook of some oysters, & retired. The New Orleans Picayune thinks that his death was caused by a cold, followed by indigestion.

Internal Revenue: The Pres yesterday appointed Edw O Perrin assessor of internal revenue for the 1st District of N Y, & Thos H Benton assessor for the 6th District of Iowa.

Navy Bulletin. Ordered, Nov 19. Mates S H Richardson, F A Haskell, Wm H Harland, & Jas Heron, to duty in the Gulf Squadron; 2nd Assist Engineer Oscar B Mills, to duty in the Novel Iron Works, N Y C. Detached, Nov 19. Lt Cmder Wm H Dana, from the ship **Ossipee**. Honorably Discharged, Nov 19: Acting Volunteer Lt Cmder E F Devens, from date. Dismissed, Nov 19: Midshipmen John S Hart & Chas E Soule, of the Naval Academy.

Announced: 1st Lt Wm Ennis, 4th U S artl, has been announced as aide-de-camp on the staff of Maj Gen Schofield, commanding the Dept of the Potomac. Brvt Maj J R Myrick, 3rd U S artl, is announced as acting judge advocate of the Dept of the South.

Brvt Maj Geo W Cullum, of the Corps of Engineers, & late Superintendent of the U S Military Academy, has been detailed as a member of the board to consider the subject of the modification of the existing coast fortifications. Gen Cullum will be stationed in Wash City.

The entire evaluation of the estate of the late Senator Wm Wright, of N J, was one million dollars, & the will required revenue stamps to the value of $500 when it was admitted to probate. All his property, except $1,000, is devised to his family, & the bulk of it goes to his widow & his son & daughter.

Count Montholon, the Minister of France, with his lady, left Wash City Sunday for St Louis, via the cities of interior Pa & the Northwest.

Last Sunday week, in Clay Co, Mo, a young man, Jacob I Harmon, returned from church wearing a pair of revolvers. His father reprimanded him for carrying his pistols, especially on the Sabbath. The son fired a revolver at his father & missed him. The father procured a double-barrelled shot-gun, & shot his son dead.

Police Matters. 1-Martha Grish was found guilty of commtting a nuisance & fined $1.25. 2-Philip J Ennis was apprehended on the charge of malicious mischief. The cmplnt was by Dr Ray. Case to be continued. 3-Mary Mitchell, age 40, was apprehended on Nov 25 charged with vagrancy: fined $3, & went on her way rejoicing. 4-Wm R Dorgan, unable to pay the fine for vagrancy, was kindly permitted to leave Wash City.

Mrd: on Nov 20, by Rev J D Powell, at the residence of the bride's father, in Goochland Co, Va, S H Cutts to Miss M S, daughter of J W DeKrafft.

Mrd: on Nov 26, at the M P Church, Gtwn, D C, by Rev Wm B Evans, A M, Andrew Van Buren Robey, of Robeysville, Md, to Miss Alice M DeVaughn, of Gtwn, D C.

Died: on Nov 11, in Waynesville, Warren Co, Ohio, Gideon Davis, a native of Loudoun Co, Va, in his 84th year. For many years he was a residence of Gtwn, D C, where he was largely engaged in the manufacture of agricultural implements, & was one of the pioneers of their improvement in the U S. He rests from his labors.

St Paul, Nov 23. The Chippewa Indians, on hunting expeditions, are molesting the settlers along the frontier. A party consisting of David Ellis, Mrs Barker, two young ladies, names unknown; an elderly lady, name unknown, & a little boy, who left Knoxville, Iowa, in Oct, for the purpose of crossing the plains, were captured, & all but the ladies murdered by the redskins.

Detroit, Nov 24. The steamship **Milwaukie** & the Lake Superior propeller **Lac la Belle** came into collision last night in the St Clair river, the propeller sinking in 5 minutes. The engineer, Jas Evans, & a colored waiter, name unknown, were drowned.

Col John Hay, Sec of Legation at Paris, has sent in his resignation.

Despatch from Stonington, Conn, states that Ralph Rodman, of Peacedale, R I, mate of the schnr **Elizabeth B**, of Newport, was killed Friday by Nelson Dewey, of that city. Dewey had received a severe blow over the eyes, when he took a gun & shot Rodman. He delivered himself to the authorities.

At Providence on Friday, Robt Crowe was convicted of murdering Wm H Roberts, of Wmsburg, L I, mate of the brig **Ocean Wave**, on the high seas.

Boucicault has made $75,000 out of "Arrah-na-Pegue" in Paris.

Judah P Benjamin, it is said, is writing for a London newspaper.

Jas Lackey, Merchant Tailor: 462 7th st, opposite Post Ofc. [Ad]

Public sale of a large stock of fat cattle, milch cows, work oxen, farm horses, hogs, reaper & mower, carts, hay & corn, lot of wood, farming implements, on Dec 3, at the residence of Theodore Mosher, known as *Nonsuch*, on the Marlboro road, 2 miles from the Navy Yard bridge, & ajoining *Fort Baker*.. A flag near *Good Hope* willdesignate the farm. -Green & Williams, aucts

WED NOV 28, 1866

Orphans Court-Judge Purcell. 1-In the Orphans Court yesterday Jos Redfern qualified as admistrator of the estate of Louis Vivans, deceased; bond, $15,000; sureties, Saml Redfern & Saml Wilson. 2-The fourth account of Christopher Cammack, sr, guardian to the orphans of Michl Connington, deceased, was approved & passed. 3-Mrs Emily Douglas Forrest, widow of French Forrest, deceased, renounced her right to administer on the estate of her deceased husband, & petitioned the court to appoint her son, Douglas French Forrest, administrator.

Mr Chas A Dana has bought up the old material of the N Y Herald, types, presses, etc, for his new Radical paper.

Police Matters. 1-Mrs Barbara Wall, the proprietress of a tavern, was arrested on Nov 26 & fined $5 for permitting a ball to be given in her house without first obtaining the proper license. 2-Nathan Goodhelp, a merchant & owner of a wagon, was fined $5 yesterday for not having it numbered. 3-Thos Coolrich was arrested for violating the water law: fined $2. 4-John Erhernt, Wm Galt, & Richd Bonds, were arrested & fined $5 to $10 each for disregarding the wagon & cart law, in regard to numbering vehicles. 5-John McNally, a restaurant keeper, was arrested twice on Monday last for selling liquor without a proper license: fined $2 each time.

Information has been received that Henry Parks, a canal boatman, had accidentally fallen overboard near the aqueduct & was drowned.

Mrd: on Nov 27, in Wash City, by Rev E B Prettyman, C D Gardette, of Phil, to Eulalie, daughter of the late Cmdor Z F Johnston, U S navy.

Died: on Nov 26, of pneumonia, in his 3rd year, Walter Lee, son of Wm H & Adele Clagett. His funeral will take place today at 11 o'clock A M.

Harriet Drew died on Nov 26, from taking apple-peru leaves mixed with the thoroughwort, rendering the tea made thereform deadly poisonous. Mrs Drew had swalled a little, but recovered. She had been suffering from a cold.
–Boston Journal

Navy Bulletin. Ordered, Nov 20. Passed Assist Paymaster W F A Torbett, to the ship **Newbern**; Lt Cmder Edw C Grafton, to the ship **Gettysburg**; Lt Cmder John H Rowland, Assist Paymaster Chas A Cable, 1st Assist Engineer E A Du Plaine, Midshipmen R B Peck, T C Ferrell, Saml T Clarkson, D A Stewart, & T J Williams to the ship **Gettysburg**; Acting Volunteer Lt H W Grinnell, Acting 3rd Assist Engineers Bryce Wilson & Geo Holton, to the **Gettysburg**. Detached, Nov 20. Passed Assist Paymaster E H Cushing, from the **Newbern**, & ordered to settle his accounts; Passed Assist Paymaster John H Stevenson, from the ship **Tacony**, & ordered to settle his accounts; Midshipman Robt M Berry, for the ship **Sabine**, & ordered to the **Gettysburg**. Cashiered, Nov 20. 2nd Assist Engineer Wm H Kelly, of the U S steamer **Frolic**.

Bangor, Me, Nov 27. This evening an attack was made on Geo W Whitney, keeper of the jail, by 8 or 10 prisoners. During the melee one prisoner was severely shot in the shoulder. None escaped.

Richmond, Nov 27. A soldier named Fleming, of the 11th U S infty, garrisoned near this city, was murdered by a comrade yesterday.

Trustee's sale of valuable land, by deed of trust, dated Aug 9, 1865, recorded in liber E B P, No 2, folio 241, of the land records for Montg Co. Public sale on Dec 13, part of a tract of land called *The Second Resurvey on Partnership*; part of a tract called *Brightwell's Hunting Quarter*, part of a tract called *Sugar Bottom*; part of a tract called *Dublington*, & part of a tract called *Sipe* containing 398 acres of land, more or less. The whole of this land borders on the Chesapeake & Ohio canal & on the river road, about 3 miles above Seneca Mills, being the farm owned by Geo W Peter. Improvements consist of a plain dwlg & necessary outbldgs. –Geo Peter, trustee

Trustee's sale of 271 acres of land, by decree of the Circuit Court for Montg Co, in Equity, in a case wherein Philip Stone & others are cmplnts, & Lloyd Hill & others are dfndnts: public sale, on the premises, at the house of Mr John Mormoyle, on Dec 1 next, the following real estate, of which John Hill, late of said county, died seized & possessed. This land borders on the Chesapeake & Ohio canal, about 2½ miles below the Great Falls on the Potomac.
–Geo Peter, Philip Stone, trustee

Supreme Court of D C, in Equity, No 1,253. Armand Jardin et al vs Albertine Favier et al. Statement of the trustee's account & distribution to the parties interested, on Dec 8, in City Hall. –Wm R Woodward, Special Auditor

Supreme Court of D C, in Equity, No 1,807. Judson Mitchell et al vs Virginia Nicholls et al. Statement of the trustee's account on Dec 7, in City Hall. –Wm R Woodward, Special Auditor

Orphans Court of Wash Co, D C. Letters of administration on the personal estate of Louis Vivan, late of Wash City, D C, deceased. –Jos Redfern

Orphans Court of Wash Co, D C. Letters testamentary on the personal estate of Robt Beale, late of Wash, D C, deceased. –Mary D Beale, excx

Orphans Court of Wash Co, D C. Letters testamentary on the personal estate of Wm G Freeman, late of Wash, D C, deceased. –Margaret C Freeman, excx

Orphans Court of Wash Co, D C. In the case of Andrew Rothwell, exc of Eliza Henning, deceased, the executor & Court have appointed Dec 22 next, for the final settlement of the personal estate of the said deceased, of the assets in hand. -Jas R O'Beirne, Reg/o wills

Supreme Court of D C, in Equity No 1,253, Docket 5. Armand Jardin & wife vs Albertine Favier et al. The trustee reported he sold lots 2 & 3 in square 160, being lots 2 to 11, both inclusive of the recorded subdivision, to Wm H Philip, for $3,285.46, & the purchaser has complied with the terms of sale. –A B Olin -R J Meigs, clerk

Supreme Court of D C, in Equity, No 1,807, Docket 6. Judson Mitchell et al vs Virginia Nichols et al. The trustee reported that he had sold the residence of Wm S Nichols to F W Havewinckel, for $26,000; the west 30 feet of lot 92 in Beall's addition to Gtwn, to W H Godey, for $1,005; the middle part of lot 209, in Beatty & Hawkins' addition to Gtwn, fronting 25 feet on Market st, to F W Havewinckel, for $225, & the s w part of lot 4, of old Gtwn, fronting 25 feet 2¼ inches on Bridge st, to F R Gieseking, for $5,150; & the purchasers have complied with the terms of sale. –A B Olin -R J Meigs, clerk

THU NOV 29, 1866
Hon Cave Johnson, of Clarksville, Tenn, died on Friday last. He was a native of the State of Tenn, born in 1793, when it was almost exclusively an unsettled wilderness. At the time of Pres Polk's election Mr Johnson was re-elected by that ofcr as his Postmaster General, & served until Mar 3, 1849.

Albert Bierstadt, the artist, was married in Waterville, N Y, on Nov 21, to Miss Rosalie Osborn, of N Y C.

Mrd: on Nov 13, by Rev Fr Keane, of St Patrick's Church, Jas Columbus Seitz, of Wash City, to Altona Hinton Forster, daughter of Thos Gales Forster, formerly of Cincinnati. Cincinnati papers please copy.

Mrd: on Nov 22, at Cape Girardeau, Mo, by Rev P M O'Regan, Henry S Merrill, of Wash, D C, to Miss Eliza Caroline Petingale, daughter of Thos Petingale, of the Treasury Dept.

Mrd: on Nov 28, in the Church of the Epiphany, Wash City, by Rev Chas H Hall, D D, Carrington H Raymond, of N Y, to Rebecca M, daughter of the late Capt Jas M Gilliss, U S Navy.

Died: on Nov 28, Mrs Mary E Will, wife of Jos B Will. Her funeral will be on Friday next at 11 A M, from his residence, n w corner of 6th & L sts.

Messrs Wm Duvall & Co, contractors for bldg the new bridges across the canal, are progressing finely with the work. The bridges at Congress & Green sts will be done inside of a month. The work of removing the old stone bridges was a very tedious job, especially the one at Congress st, which took nearly a month, with a large number of hands for its removal. The new iron bridges are built remarkably strong, & look as if they might stand for centuries. The life or draw-bridges are an ingenious arangement, & reflect great credit on the inventor, Mr Wm Duvall, who is one of the finest mechanics in the country.

Jas Stephens has disappeared. He left his ofc in N Y, a few days ago, in company with 4 men who had lately arrived from Ireland. He took leave of his friends, assuring them he should never be seen again in the office.

Navy Bulletin. Ordered, Nov 21. Carpenter H M Lowry, to the ship **Michigan**, on Dec 1_; Acting passed Assist Surgeon Geo L Simpson, to the ship **Gettysburg**. Detached, Nov 21. Acting Master Wm L Howorth, from the ship **De Soto**, & permitted to return North. Honorably Discharged, Nov 21. Acting Volunteer Lt A W Muldaur, from Nov 19; Mate W H Mott, from Nov 21.

Brvt Lt Col H S S Schell, assist surgeon U S A, has been relieved from duty in the Dept of the Tenn, & assigned to duty at *Fort Laramie*, Dakota Territory.

Naval Intelligence. Despatches have been received at the Navy Dept from Cmder J C Febiger, commanding the U S steamer **Ashu**____, announcing his arrival at Port Louis, island of Mauritius, Indian Oean, on Oct 2: all well.

Providence, Nov 28. 1-In the U S Circuit Court today Robt Crowl was convicted of murder on the high seas & sentenced to be hanged on Mar 1. As Rhode Island abolished capital punishment many years ago, this sentence may be carried into effect at *Fort Adams*, on the Dutch Island territory, under the exclusive jurisiction of the U S. 2-Henry H Wightman, a deaf man, was killed near East Greenwich last evening, while walking on the railroad track.

Geo Grove, of the firm of Grove & Brother, extensive manufactures of linseed oil, died suddenly in Phil on Tuesday.

Duffin's Creek, C W, Nov 28. The schnr **Swallow**, from Highland Creek, for Toronto, capsized & drifted ashore near Etsbicok creek. It is supposed the crew was lost. The capt, Wm Hutchinson, was a well-known skipper on the lakes.

Phil, Nov 28. Alfred Teufel was arrested here, charged with the murder of Capt Jos Wiley, on a canal boat, near Frenchtown, Bucks Co, on last Sat. He will be sent to Doylestown to await an investigation of the case.

FRI NOV 30, 1866
Mr J B Auld, private secretary to Mayor Hoffman, of N Y, died on Wednesday.

Rev Sylvester Holmes, one of the oldest clergymen in Mass, died in New Bedford on Tuesday, aged 78 years. He was for many years a leading man in the Orthodox Congregational denomination in the Southeastern part of the State. [Nov 30th newspaper gives his age as 77 years.]

Buffalo Courier: accident on the Buffalo & Erie railroad last week; Mrs West, of Milwaukie, lost her child, & was trapped in the wreckage. The pressure was so crushing that her eyeballs were forced from their sockett & hung down on the cheeks, & the face swollen by the congestion or rupture of blood vessels to more than twice its proper size. The body of the babe, beneath her, being soft & yielding, was perhaps the only thing that saved her life. Miss West, her niece, had her left hand crushed. When Mrs West was released she dictated a telegram to her husband at Milwaukee: "Your babe is dead, your wife severely injured; Uncle Wheeler killed, & Emma slightly hurt." She was carried to the house of Mr Chambers; the surgeons arrived & attended to replacing the eyes in the sockets. She still remains there & is improving rapidly. The surgeons declare that they never saw its parallel.

Police Matters. 1-Mary Williams, Margaret Grant, & Jas Peakman were arrested on Nov 28, charged with false swearing. Mary Williams was dismissed & the other two were to give security & appear at court for trial. 2-Henry Johnson, a negro servant, was arrested on the cmplnt of Mr Jas Packson, who alleges that the negro stole something from him. Johnson was committed to jail on the charge of grand larceny. 3-John Sprightly & Robt Bean got into a dispute yesterday. Sprightly threatened to revenge himself upon the person of Bean. Sprightly was bound over to keep the peace. 4-Michl Welch, a young vagrant, was charged with the larceny of several bottles of wine from the Franklin House. He was committed to jail to await the trial by the court. 5-Michl Burke was fined $3 yesterday for drunkenness. 6-John Lilley, a negro sailor, was arrested for stealing a coat & a revolver. He was committed for trial.

Cincinnati, Nov 29. W Y W Smith, who was to have been hung for murder on Nov 30, at Wash Court House, Ohio, has been respited for 2 weeks, during which time Gov'r Cox will decide on his application for commutation of sentence.

N Y, Nov 28. N Y Herald says that among the steamer **San Francisco** passengers, detained by accident at *Fortress Monroe*, was found & arrested Edw Nevins, late confidential clerk of Adams, Horley & Co, of N Y. He is charged with embezzling $5,000.

Maj Geo E Glenn, U S Paymaster, was robbed at *Fort Boise*, last Friday of his treasure box for money, containing $59,000 in legal tenders & $58,000 of vouchers he had paid out in camps lately visited. Maj Glenn, with several others, arrived at *Fort Boise* Friday night, & alighted from the ambulance at the headquarters of Maj Marshall. The baggage was taken from the ambulance & laid close to the steps of the door, & the treasure box placed on the top of the baggage. There being no one about the house at the time, Maj Glenn walked up to the next quarters, a few yards distant, & went to Capt Eckerson's about three-quarters of an hours, long enough to take supper, & on his return found the treasure box gone.

Died: on Nov 29, Carrie Augusta, youngest child of Jas G & Carrie A Wilmarth, aged 11 months & 19 days. Her funeral will take place this Friday at 12 o'clock, from the residence of Mr John Coburn, H & 13th sts.

Died: on Nov 29, Jemima Mulloy, consort of the late John Mulloy, aged 76 years, a native of Va, & a resident of Wash City for 60 years. Her funeral is today at 3 o'clock, from St Peter's Church, to proceed to *Mount Olivet Cemetery*.

Henry Ward Beecher is writing a story for the N Y Ledger.

Fort Rawlings, just below Vicksburg, is to be demolished, by order of Gen Grant. It took 2,000 men 60 days to erect the works.

SAT DEC 1, 1866
The Pres yesterday appointed Thos E Hayden, of Nevada, U S Atty for the District of Nevada.

In the Equity Court, yesterday, Judge Olin granted a decree divorcing Lucy A Nicholson from bed & board with Jas Nicholson, giving her the custody of her child, & awarding alimony of $30 per month. The petition filed May 9 last, sets forth that she was married to the respondent in Oct, 1863, she then being but 16 years of age; that she has had two children by him, one now dead, & charges that he has frequently ill-treated & beat her, driving her away from the house.

Toronto Globe of Tues: A telegraph operator, H A Bogardus, now in this city, has fallen heir to $2,300,000 through the death of relatives who held an interest in the Trinity Church property in N Y. The claim is in the hands of Messrs Bostwick, Seward, & Griswold, of N Y C.

The Pres yesterday appointed Geo S Woods Assessor of Internal Revenue for the Second District of Minnesota.

Navy Bulletin. Ordered, Nov 22. Gunner Geo Edmonds, to the ship **Sabine**; Acting Ensigns J F Churchill, John C Lord, & C H Beckshaffe, & Acting 3rd Assist Engineer John W Briggs, to the ship **Newbern**.
Resigned, Nov 22: 1st Assist Engineer Wm W Hopper.
Appointment Revoked, Nov 22. Acting 3rd Assist Engineer Jos V Howe, of the **Newbern**.
Detached, Nov 22: Capt Reedwerden, for the command of, & Lt Cmder Henry B Seely, from the ship **Bienville**, & placed on waiting orders; Lt Cmder W F Stewart, Surgeon C J Cleborne, Carpenter O H Gerry, Acting Boatswain Henry Peters, Acting Master Henry C Neilds, Acting Ensigns Walter M Smith & John Bishop, for the **Bienville**, & ordered to hold themselves in readiness for duty on board the ship **Iroquois**; Acting Assist Surgeon Chas W Knight, Acting 1st Assist Engineer Chas W Pennington, Acting 2nd Assist Engineers M C Heath & John T Buckley, Acting 3rd Assist Engineers Wm C Woods, Walter S Jarboe, & Chas Euggoier, from the **Bienville**, place on waiting orders.
Placed on Leave, Nov 23: Cmder A J Drake, sick, & Acting 2nd Assist Engineer Jos Graffin, awaiting discharge.

On the last Sabbath, in this county, Mr Jas Skinner, a farmer living on the plantation of Maj Lee, for want of sufficient out-bldgs, stored some of his cotton in a portion of his dwlg. Mr Skinner & his wife took a walk, leaving their children, a boy aged 4 or 5 years, & an infant about 9 months old, by the fire in the house. They were gone but a short time when their dwlg was in flames. The little boy by some means had set fire to the cotton, & alarmed he ran from the house. The distressed parents arrived too late to rescue their infant, who perished in the flames, with all their household goods, leaving them nothing but the clothing they were wearing. –Covington [Ga] Examiner

Miss Effie Germon has returned to the stage in Phil, after an absence of 3 months, caused by severe illness.

Gen McClellan, at last accounts, was at the baths of St Moritz, Switzerland, & Mrs McClellan's health had much improved.

Hon Jacob Fry, ex-Auditor Gen'l of Pa, died at his residence, in Montg Co, on Wed.

In the Supreme Court of N Y, on Monday, Judge Sutherland decided that the question of color, embracing also the question of how much African blood is necessary to determine whether a man is colored or not, was a case to be decided by a jury.

Mr Jas Chaplin, boss roller at the Lochiel Iron Works near Harrisburg, Pa, was killed on Tue, when his clothing caught in the belting & his head was suddenly forced between the rollers. He was killed almost instantly. He leaves a large family.

Vicksburg Times, Nov 26. Last Sunday pistol shots were heard, by a sentry stationed near the quarters of Lt Neal, of the U S Army, lately on duty at this post. On repairing to his room, Lt Neal was discovered in bed, having committed suicide, by shooting himself. By his bedside was found a memorandum of the addresses of various friends & a brief statement of his business affairs. He was an Englishman by birth, served during the whole war, & we understand, was a brave & honorable soldier. While in the army he was shot in the right eye, the sight of which was destroyed, & the ball came out of the ear on the same side. This made a very deep impression on his mind, & he frequently alluded to the probabiltiy of committing suicide.

New Orleans Crescent. Vicksburg Times of Nov 21. The lessor mentioned is the venerable & venerated elder brother of Jefferson Davis, & *Brierfield* was formerly the home of the latter. The disposition made of these plantations is undoubtedly such as would be approved by the latter, between whom & his brother there were, from the greater age of the Jos E Davis, almost the relations of father & son, & the most tender mutual confidence & agreement. To the colored people: The undersigned have secured for a term of years the *Hurricane* & *Brierfield* plantations, in Warren Co, in this State, from Jos E Davis, the proprietor thereof, proposes on Jan 1, 1867, to organize a community, composed exclusively of colored people, to occupy & cultivate said plantations, & invites the cooperation of such as are recommended by honesty, industry, sobriety, & intelligence, in the enterprise. –B T Montgomery, colored. Formerly a slave, & one of the business managers of Jos E Davis, on the part of the association. Vicksburg, Miss, Nov 19, 1866.
+
Jos E Davis, having been pardoned by his Excellency the Pres, & an order having been issued to restore to Mr Davis the possession of his property, the *Hurricane* & *Brierfield* plantations, the same will be done at the close of the present year. –T J Wood, Brvt Maj Gen U S A, commanding.

Louisville Journal-lynching of 3 robbers in Lebanon, Ky. On Nov 24, a number of men broke into the jail. After some parleying, 5 men marched into the dungeon & called for Clem Crowdus, Wm Goode, & Tom Stephens, who delivered themselves up. The mob left the city in the direction of *Grimes' Hill* with the prisoners. On Sunday, Nov 25, Crowdus was hung first, followed by Wm Goode & Tom Stephens.

A suit has been commenced before the Supreme Court of N Y, by John H Lester, against Gen Butler, charging him with false imprisonment, [damages laid at $100,000,] & with fraudulent conversion of property, [damages $50,000.] Lester received a free pass from Sec Stanton during the war, to bring his family North. Gen Butler disregarded the permit, & imprisoned him.

MON DEC 3, 1866
Navy: appointed, Nov 24. Jos B Parker, an assist surgeon of the navy.

Died: Nov 11, 1866, at Laplace, Macon Co, Ala, Mrs Saphronia F Thompson, daughter of John Mount, of Wash City, in her 35th year of her age. Her house & heart were always open to the Ministers of the Gospel, & her purse to the church & the poor. Her end was peace.

Last Sat night at the Delmonico Houe, on 11th st, between E & Pa ave, Mr W A Curran entered the restaurant, went into the parlor & conversed with a friend, & then walked into the yard. Accidentally stumbling over a barrel, he fell down into the cellar, a distance of 5 feet, & broke his neck. Yesterday the body was found by one of the servants of the house. A telegram was sent to Dr Curran, the father of the deceased, residing at Annapolis. The deceased was about 32 years of age, a claim agent by occupation, & doing business in Wash City. He came from Indianapolis, Ind, where his parents reside; he was unmarried, but was a member of a large family. He had been in Wash City for about 2 years, much beloved by those who knew him, intelligent & active, & much respected.

Police Matters. 1-Martha E Ferguson was apprehended on Sat last charged with assault & battery with intent to kill Mary Cissel. Mrs Ferguson went into the home of Mrs Cissel, & while there the two became implicated in a quarrel, caused by jealousy. Mrs Ferguson drew a revolver on Mrs Cissel & assaulted her. Mrs Ferrguson gave security to appear for trial at the Criminal Court. 2-Edw Burke & John Smith, two gay shopkeepers, were arrested yesterday charged with selling liquor without a license. Burke was fined $30.90 & Smith $20.

Obit-death of a lovely lady. We are pained to record the death, in New Orleans, by yellow fever, on Nov 18, of Mrs Mary Grover, a most estimable lady, wife of our young friend, Hiram J Grover, & daughter of Saml M Semmes, of Cumberland, Md, & a niece of Admiral Semmes. She was but in the hay day of wedded life; her noble husband had just established himself successfully in the practise of law, when death sadly intervenes, to impose on him the mournful mission of transporting to her parents the empty casket of her noble soul, & the nuturing of an infant boy, born but a few brief months ago. A younger sister, already on the way from Md to pay her a bridal visit, will find her sister a corpse.

Brvt Brig Gen E B Comstock, A D C to Gen Grant, in a letter to the Sec of War, states that while he was treasurer of the U S Military Academy he issued checks on the Assist Treasurer at N Y in favor of Cadets John O'Brien & Pierce Butler Young in Feb & May, **1867**, amounting in the aggregate of $118.88. These checks were sent by mail to the cadets, who left the Academy to go to their homes in the South. Since the close of the war they have been returned to Gen Comstock through the Dead Letter Ofc. The Sec of War now directs the checks to be cancelled & the money returned to the fund whence derived, & that a similar course be pursued in all cases of a like character.

Wm Robinson Whittingham, bishop of the diocese of Md, arrived here today from Europe.

Despatches received at the Navy Dept from Capt Wm Reynolds, commanding the U S steamer **Lackawanna**, dated Montevideo, Oct 15, announcing his arrival at that place. Officers & crew all well.

Quarantine Station, Staten Island, Dec 2. The ship **Kate Dyer**, of Portland, Capt Leavitt, 84 days from Callao, on Dec 1 was run into by the steamship **Scotland** hence for Liverpool, striking the **Kate Dyer** on the starboard bow, cutting her completely through, & causing her to sink in an instant. Thirteen of the crew went dow with the ship. The **Kate Dyer** had a pilot on board at the time, Mr Michl Collins, who says, as does Capt Leavitt, that they saw the steamer about 15 minutes before she struck them, & had she kept her course the collision would have been avoided. The following of those lost on the **Kate Dyer**: Paul Bodice, mate, of Antwerp; Frank Jones & Fred Smith, boys, of Portland; Wm Blanchard, sailmaker, of London; Fred Jenkins, carpenter, of Hamburg; Wm Rollins, colored, steward, of N Y; Wallace Cox, colored, of N J; seamen Wm Harris, of Balt; Jones, of N Y; Robt Barber, Robt Bounce, of London; Henry Johnson, of N J; John Quirk, of Ireland.

Geo Brumback has sued the city of Louisville, for $25,000, alleging that the death of his daughter & wife from cholera, last summer, was caused by negligence on the part of the city in grading 10th st so that the yards of houses were overflowed, which overflow, he claims, produced pestilence.

Col J C Groom, of Cecil Co, Md, who died in Elkton on Sat, was a prominent politician, & some years ago ran on the Democratic ticket for Govn'r against the late Senator Hicks.

Rev Benj T Brooks, a well known Episcopalian minister of this city, has received a call from a congregation in Memphis, Tenn.

Dissolution of the copartnership existing between J P Bartholow & John A Baker, as the firm of J P Bartholow & Co, is this day, Dec 3, dissolved by mutual consent. The business will hereafter be continued under the style of J P Bartholow. -J P Bartholow, Jno A Baker

For sale-valuable lands in Howard Co, Md, by deed of trust from the owners, the undersigned trustees will expose to sale, by public auction, on Dec 13, that valuable farm, with improvements, 2 miles from Laurel, within less than 300 yards from Savage Station, containing 72¾ acres, more or less, being part of a tract known as **Snowden's New Birmingham Manor**, & formerly owned by Wm A Purdy, & lately occupied by Florence McCarthy. The farm adjoins the farm of the late Dr Waters, now called **Burrows**. The farm is improved by a substantial brick dwlg with the necessary out-houses. Also, all the farming utensils will be sold. At the same time & place, a small tract, containing 4 acres, more or less, on which a tavern formerly stood, known as **Reilley's Tavern** or the **Sixteen-Mile-House**. –John J Snyder, Wm Shepard Bryan, trustees -Saml H Gover, auct

Orphans Court of Wash Co, D C. Letters of administration on the personal estate of French Forrest, late of Wash City, D C, deceased. –Douglas F Forrest, adm. Ofc of Chas S Wallach, Atty-at-Law, 42 La ave.

Orphans Court of Wash Co, D C. Letters of administration on the personal estate of Michl Costello, late of Wash Co, deceased. –Jeremiah Costello, adm

TUE DEC 4, 1866
The Gov't had information as long ago as last winter that John H Surratt had gone to Europe. On Sunday Sec Seward received a despatch by Atlantic cable as follows: I have arrested John H Surratt, one of the Pres Lincoln's assassins. No doubt of his identity. -Hale, U S Consul Gen, Alexandria, Egypt

John McNamara, a citizen of St Louis, on Sunday, accidentally shot his wife & then tried to kill himself.

On Sat, at Richmond, a white man, Marquis L Murray, was shot by a negro, Henry Norris, & instantly killed. There was some altercation about a boat, during which the negro seized an Enfield musket & fired the fatal shot.

Balt, Dec 3. Josiah O Baylies, Most Worthy Grand Master of the Grand Lodge of Md I O of O F, & Most Worthy Grand Patriarch of the Grand Encampment of the same Order, died last night. He was an old & useful citizen.

Julia Dean, whose name revives a grateful memory of a graceful & admirable actress, has left the stage after a series of triumphs on the Pacific coast, & will reside in N Y. Ten years ago, or more, she married Dr A P Hayne, of Charleston, son of Robt G Hayne, whose Senatorial debate with Webster on nullification has become historic. Last Year Mrs Hayne obtained a divorce from her husband, on the ground of failure to support. She is now the wife of Mr J G Cooper, of this city, & the charming centre of that circle of friends which had not forgotten the brilliant Julia Dean of a past season. –N Y Tribune

Supreme Court of the U S, Dec 3, 1866, present: Hon Salmon P Chase, Chief Justice
Associate Justices:
Hon Jas M Wayne   Hon Neah H Swayne   Hon Stephen J Field
Hon Saml Nelson   Hon Saml F Miller
Hon Nathan Clifford   Hon David Davis

Orphans Court of Wash Co, D C. Letters of administration on the personal estate of Christian Henry Munck, of Wash City, D C, deceased. –Carlotte L Munck

Orphans Court of Wash Co, D C. Letters of administration on the personal estate of Wm M Walker, late of the U S navy, deceased. –A Thos Bradley, adm c t a

WED DEC 5, 1866

Appointments by the Pres yesterday: John C Carroll, of Idaho, receiver of public moneys for the district of lands subject to sale at Boise City, Idaho; Robt H Brown, of Idaho, register of land ofc at Boise City, Idaho.

The brevet of brig general in the regular army has been conferred upon Col John H Eaton, the efficient assist of the Paymaster General, & author of the Paymaster's Manuel.

Sir Henry Holland, who passed his summer vacation in America, was bereaved of his wife a few days after his return to London. She had passed the summer at a water-side cottage, was seized with apoplexy the day after her arrival at home. She survived but 48 hours in an unconscious state. The attack was unexpected. Lady Holland was a daughter of Sydney Smith.

Miss Anna E Dickinson is seriously ill at Rockford, Ill.

Mrd: on Oct 27, by Rev A T Fullerton, of Springfield, Ohio, at the residence of the bride's mother, Gen Durbin Ward to Miss Elizabeth, youngest daughter of the late Rev John Probasco, both of Lebanon, Ohio. No cards.

Died: on Dec 3, at the residence of Thos Woodward, at Gtwn, D C, T Woodward Israel, in his 23rd year. His funeral will take place this afternoon at 3 o'clock.

Florence [Nov 14] correspondence of London Post. It is stated that J H Surratt [one of the persons charged with complicity in the assassination of the late Pres of the U S Abraham Lincoln] has been serving for some time past in the Papal Zouves, his company being quartered at Veroli, one of the frontier towns of the Appenines, near Frosinon. He had assumed the name of John Watson.

Mr N P Willis, who has been an invalid for some years, is now lying dangerously ill at his home, *Idlewild*, on the Hudson. Mrs Willis writes, dated Nov 29, that he fails every day. I feel that he may die at any moment. Mr Willis was born in Portland, Maine, in 1807, & is consequently in his 60th year.

Zanesville, Dec 4. A portion of the Eastern bound passenger train due here, fell through the iron bridge at this place. Jesse Hill, of Pleasant Valley, was killed. Wounded: Levy Claypool, of Nashport, Ohio, slightly; Jas Haviland, of Gaines' Station, Mich, slightly; Mr Hart, of N J, slightly, Benj Shipley, engineer of the freight train, injured in the back; Silas Higgins, fireman of the freigth train, slightly; Geo Thompson, slightly; Patrick Smith, engineer, slightly. It will require several days to repair the bridge.

N Y, Dec 4. Missing & supposed to have perished in the Walker st fire last night: John Birmingham, Adam MacLizer, Henry Dean, & Geo Robinson.

Oil City, Dec 3. Fire broke out in the dwlg of John Donovan, a small frame house, ignited from an oil lamp. The following were burned to death: Wm Donovan, aged nearly 100 years; Jerry Donovan, aged 11 years; & Mr Carrigan, aged 30 years.

Orphans Court of Wash Co, D C. Letters of administration on the personal estate of John Forrest, late of Wash City, D C, deceased. –Julia Ann Forrest

Important order-*Organization of New Regts*. Main points of this order are as follows:
First. The two additional regts of cavalry, composed of white men, will be known as the 7th & 8th regts of cavalry, & their chief field ofcrs are:
7th cavalry: Col, Andrew G Smith; Lt Col Geo A Custar; Majs, Alfred Gibbs, two vacancies; station of regt; Military Div of Missouri.
8th cavalry: Col, John T Gregg; Lt Col Thos C Devin; Majs, Wm Gamble, Wm R Price, one vacancy; station, Military Div of the Pacific.
The two additional regts of cavalry, composed of colored men, will be the 9th & 10th regts of cavalry & their chief ofcrs are:
9th cavalry: Col, Edw Hatch; Lt Col, Merritt; Majs, Andrew S Alexander, Jas F Wade, & Jas A Forsyth; station, Dept of the Gulf.
10th cavalry: Col, Benj H Grierson; Lt Col, Chas C Walcot; Majs, Jas W Forsyth, two vacancies; station, Military Div of the Missouri.
Second: The 10 old regts of infty will retain their designation. The first btlns of the 3 btln regts will retain the designation of the regts to which they belonged, & under the new organization will be the 11th thru 19th regts of infty. The chief ofcrs of these regts are:
11th infty, Col, Wm S Ketchum; Lt Col, Robt S Granger; Maj, Daniel; headquarters, Richmond, Va.
12th infty: Col, C C Augur; Lt Col, Geo W Wallace; Maj, Henry E Maynadier; headquarters, Wash, D C.
13th infty: Col, Isaac V D Reeve; Lt Col, Geo L Andrews; Maj, Wm Clinton; headquarters, *Fort Rice*, Dakota.
14th infty: Col, Chas S Lovell; Lt Col, Henry D Wallace; Maj, Lewis C Hunt; headquarters, Arizona Territory.
15th infty: Colm Oliver L Shepherd; Lt Col, Julius Hayden; Maj, Edw McR Hudson; headquarters, Macon, Ga.
16th Infty: Col, Caleb C Sibley; Lt Col, G R Giddings; Maj, vacant; headquarters, Savannah, Ga.
17th infty: Col, Saml P Heintzelman; Lt Col, Abner Doubleday; Maj, vacant; headquarters, Galveston, Texas.
18th infty: Col, Henry B Carrington; Lt Col, Henry W Wessels; Maj, Jas Van Voart; headquarter, *Fort Kearny*, Dakota Territory.
19th infty: Col, Saml R Dawson; Lt Col, Delancy Floyd Jones; Maj, Pinkney Lugenheel; headquarters, *Fort Gibson*, Indian Territory.

The second btlns of the same regts will, under the new organization, become the 20th thru the 28th regts of infty. The chief ofcrs of those regts are as follows:
20th infty: Col, Fred'k Steele; Lt Col, Louis D Watkins; Maj, Thos H Neill; headquarters, Richmond, Va.
21st infty: Col, Geo Stoneman; Lt Col, vacant; Maj, Dickinson Woodruff; headquarters, Petersburg, Va.
22nd infty: Col, David S Stanley; Lt Col, vacant; Maj, Hiram Dryer; headquarters, **Fort Randall**, Dakota Territory.
24th infty: Col, Alvan C Gillem; Lt Col, Adelbert Ames; Maj, Nathan A M Dudly; headquarters, Vicksburg, Miss.
25th infty: Col Gordon Granger; Lt Col, Emory Upton; Maj, Peter T Swaine.
26th infty: Col, Jos J Reynolds; Lt Col, vacant; Maj, Levi C Bootes; headquarters, Austin, Texas.
27th infty: Col, John E Smith; Lt Col, vacant; Maj, vacant; headquarters, **Fort Kearny**, Dakota Territory.
28th infty: Col, Chas H Smith; Lt Col, R B Ayres; Maj, Chas C Gilbert; headquarters, Camden, Ark.
The 3rd btlns of the same regts will, under the new organization, become the 29th thru the 37th regts of infty. The chief ofcrs of these regts are:
29th infty: Col, Orlando B Wilcox; Lt Col, vacant; Maj, Lyman Bissell; headquarters, Norfolk, Va.
30th infty: Col, John D Stevenson; Lt Col, Jos H Porter; Maj, S Dodge; headquarters, Wash, D C.
31st infty: Col, Regis de Trebriand; Lt Col, R H Bowerman; Maj, Jos N G Wissler; headquarters, **Fort Rice**, Dakota.
32nd infty: Col, Thos L Crittenden; Lt Col, vacant; Maj, S Chapin; headquarters, **Fort Goodwin**, Arizona.
33rd infty: Col, Thos H Buger; Lt Col, Chas R Woods; Maj, John D Wilkins; headquarters, Macon, Ga.
34th infty: Col, vacant; Lt Col, August V Kuntz; Maj, Wm P Carlin; headquarters, Nashville, Tenn.
35th infty: Col, Chas Griffin; Lt Col, Jas H Wilson; Maj, John S Mason; headquarters, San Antonio, Texas.
36th infty: Col, Geo W Getty; Lt Col, John R Brook; Maj, vacant; headquarters, **Fort Riley**, Kansas.
[37th infty-no information.]
Third. 4 regts of infty, to be composed of colored men, will be 38th thru 41st regts of infty.
38th infty: Col, Wm B Hazen; Lt Col, Cuvler/Cuvier Grover; Maj, Henry C Merriam; station, Military Div of the Missouri.
39th infty: Col, Jos N Mowers; Lt Col, Frank Wheaton; Maj, vacant; station, Dept of the Gulf.
40th infty: Col, Nelson A Miller; Lt Col, E W Henks; Maj, C E Compton; station, Dept of Washington.

41st infty: Col & Lt Col, vacant; Maj, Geo W Schofield; station, Dept of the Gulf.
Fourth. The 4 regts of infty to be officered by wounded ofcrs & soldiers of volunteers & of the regualr army will be 42nd thru 45th of infty, [Veteran Reserve Corps.] The field ofcrs of these regts are:
42nd: Col, Danl E Sickles; Lt Col, John B McIntosh; Maj, T F Redenbaugh; station, Dept of the East.
43rd infty: Col, John C Robinson; Lt Col, J B Koddoo; Maj, Martin D Hardin; station, Dept of the Lakes.
44th infty: Col, Thos G Pitcher; Lt Col, Alex'r S Webb; Maj, Fred'k E Trotter; station, Dept of Washington.
45th infty: Col, Wager Swayne; Lt Col, Geo A Woodward; Maj, Benj P Bunkle; station, Dept of the Tenn.
The relative rank of the new colonels is as follows: Steele, Stoneman, A J Smith, Robinson, Getty, Pitcher, Stanley, Gibbon, Griffin, Granger, Davis, Hazen, Gregg, Gillem, Mower, Crittenden, Sickles, Reynolds, Grierson, Swayne, Miles, Willcox, Stevenson, J E Smith, Ruger, De Trobriand, Hatch, & C H Smith.

Navy Bulletin: Resigned, Nov 26: Passed Assist Paymaster J H Mulford, jr.
Honorably Discharged, Nov 26: Acting Ensign W W Duly, from Nov 25, 1866.
Ordered, Nov 26: Cmdor J B Hull, as president, & Cmders J P McKinstry & J B Marchant, as members of an examination board for the promotion of ofcrs of the U S navy in pursuance of an act approved Apr 21, 1864, to meet at the Phil NavyYard Dec 3, 1866. Detached, Nov 27: Cmdor Fred'k Engle, from the Retiring Board at the Naval Asylum in Phil, & waiting orders; Cmdors Henry A Adams & Chas Lowndes, from duty as members of the Retiring Board at Phil, & waiting orders; Acting Ensign J W Chandler, from duty in connection with ironclads in ordinary, & placed on leave for discharge. Resigned, Nov 27: Assist Surgeon Leslie D Frost, of the Chelsea Hospital, Mass; 1st Assist Engineer W C F Reichenbach.

Trustee's sale, by decree of the Circuit Court for PG Co, in equity, passed in a cause wherein Geo Forbes is cmplnt, & Jas I Bowie & Catharine Bowie are dfndnts, the undersigned, as trustee, will sell at public sale, at Croom P O, near the premises, on Dec 20 next, all that part or portion of the real estate of the late Robt W Bowie, called **Mattaponi**, which was assigned & laid off to Catherine Bowie as & for her dower, containing 300 acres, more or less, & being the same land the reversion in fee of which was purchased by Jas I Bowie of Caleb C Magruder & Wm H Tuck, trustee, & is more particularly described in a deed of the reversionary interest of the same from Wm H Tuck & C C Magruder, trustees, to Jas I Bowie, bearing the date of May 31, 1856. This farm adjoins the lands of C C Magruder, Dr John T Eversfield, & others. There is a large & commodious Brick Mansion with all necessary out-bldgs for a first class farm.
–Danl Clark, trustee

Orphans Court of Wash Co, D C. Letters of administration on the personal estate of John Forrest, late of Wash City, D C, deceased. –Julia Ann Forrest

THU DEC 6, 1866

Wm H Bliss has sued the city of Brooklyn for $50,000 damages, for infringement of his patent for fire hose couplings.

In order to prevent any possibility of escape, John H Surratt, arrested for complicity in the assassination of the late Pres Lincoln, is to be brought here by water, an order having been telegraphed per Atlantic cable to Admiral Goldsborough, commanding the pacific squadron, to send a gunboat to Alexandria, Egypt, to bring him to this city direct.

Mr J W Noyes, formerly a well known conductor on the Wash & Gtwn railroad was yesterday appointed on the Capitol police force by Hon B B French, Com'r of Public Bldgs.

Navy Bulletin. Ordered, Nov 28. Assist Surgeon Geo S Fife to duty at the naval hospital at Chelsea, Mass. Detached, Nov 28. Assist Paymaster Chas D Mansfield from the U S Coast Survey schnr **Arago**, & ordered to settle his accounts; Acting First Assist Engineer John H Padgett from the U S Coast Survey schnr **Arago**, & placed on the leave for discharge; Acting Ensign F A S Bacon from the U S Coast Survey schnr **Arago**, & waiting orders; mate A M Bergner from the U S Coast Survey schnr **Arago**, & ordered to the ship **Massachusetts**.
Appointed, Nov 28. John B Parks, as assistant surgeon U S navy.
Honorably Discharged, Nov 28. Mate Jos W Fox from Aug 27, 1865.

Orphans Court-Judge Purcell. 1-On Tues, the will of the late Gilbert Cameron, bequeathing his estate to his wife, & also making provision for his mother & brothers & sisters, was filed. 2-The will of the late Conrad Sherry, bequeathing his estate to his wife during her life, & afterwards to his sons, was filed & fully proven. 3-Letters testamentary were issued to Christiana Hines, John A Rheem, & Saml Duvall on the estate of the late David Hines; bond, $8,000. Letters of administration to Julia Ann Forrest on the estate of the late John Forrest; bond, $1,600. Mrs Forrest was appointed guardian to the orphan children; bond, $800. Charlotte L Munck was appointed guardian to the orphans of the late C H Munck; bond, $5,000. 4-The first & final accounts of the executor of Dolly Ann Williams, & of the executor of Eliza Reaves, were approved & passed.

Residences of the Judges of the Court of Claims of the U S:
Hon Jos Carey, 388 C st
Hon Edw G Loring, 303 I st
Hon David Wilmot, 4 A st, Capitol Hill
Hon Ebenezer Peck, 385 C st
Hon Chas C Nott, 184 F st

Mark Shinbone, a noted bank robber, escaped from the State prison at Concord, N H, on Tuesday.

Alexandria-accident on Tues on a railroad train, when near Four Mile run, it was discovered that Thos Mortimer, of Wash City, for some time past employed by Mr Jos Thorton, as a wood train hand, was found lying bleeding from injuries on the head on the road. His injuries were examined by Dr J B Johnson, & not considered to be of a serious character. It appears he was knocked from the train when passing under the bridge.

Died: after a painful illness of 14 months, Thos S Smith, in his 47th year. His funeral is on Dec 7 at 10 o'clock, from the residence of his brother, 271 4th st, between Mass ave & I st. [No death date given-current item.]

Obit-died: on Nov 15, Eliza Lee, second daughter of the late Dr John M Thomas, of Wash City. Thirteen years she was like a martyr, witnessing indeed, by patience under continuous disease. No one except myself, said her physician, knew how much she suffered, yet a smile lingered on her sweet sad face. The sacrament of the dying was administered to her, & an innocent soul seemed to shine in delicately chiseled features.

Hon E McCook, U S Minister resident at Hawaii, arrived at San Francisco in the U S steamer **Vanderbilt** on Monday. He returns on account of his wife's health, which is very poor.

Mr Leonard W Jerome, of N Y, has arranged with Maretzek to give a series of operatic performances at his private theatre, in 26th st, two nights in each week, until the Academy of Music is finished.

Mr C White, a wealthy citizen of Kingston Springs, about 25 miles from Nashville, Tenn, was murdered Thursday by a man named Paterson. The murderer assaulted Mr White with an axe just as he was entering the door of his house & killed him instantly. The object of the murderer was undoubtedly plunder.

Phil, Dec 5. 1-Frank Lewis, of Fred'k City, Md, was robbed in that place, at a dance, of $695, & some $2,000 in promissory notes. A girl known as Maggie Gowan, alias Continental Mag, was arrested tonight in this city, charged with committing the theft. 2-The walls of Austin's old brewery, near Haddington, fell this afternoon, & Geo Morris, aged 67 was killed, & 4 men were badly injured.

War Dept, Rooms of Claims Commission, Wash, D C, Nov 30, 1866. Statement of claims filed during the month of Nov, 1866.
Claim of John Kennarty, property taken by U S Troops. Britton, Gray & Pitcher, attys.
Peter Gilbam, for quartermaster's stores. J E Pollock, atty.
Geo W Seward & Geo Wells, for destruction of saw mill. Stewart, Riddle & Co, attys
W H Irwin, for appropriations of property by U S troops. R J Atkinson, atty.

Geo G Lott, for commutation of fuel & quarters. Justine I McCarty, atty.
Peter Paul, for property destroyed. Swiss Counsul Gen, through the State Dept.
Isaac Lane, for services as a scout. Saml Wells, atty.
Mrs Eliza A Clark, for horses & mules. No atty.
Chas W Taylor & Dr McNair, for rent of property. H H Wells, atty.
Wm Sagar, for damages to property. No atty.
Wm T Brown, for horses, etc. No atty.
Mrs Julianne Hobbie, for use & occupancy of the Cliffbourne property. No atty.
Lewis Shots, for quartermaster's & subsistence stores. Wm Kilgour, atty.
Ben J Grubb, for commissary stores. Gregory & Jones, attys.
J M Conner, for quartermaster's stores. Stribler & Simpson, attys.
Robt W Carter, for quartermaster's & subsistence stores. Wm Kilgour, atty.
Jas A Stewart, for use & value of flouring mills. Stribler & Simpson, attys.
J M Conner, for commissary stores. Lloyd D Simpson, atty.
Aldridge James, for quartermaster's stores. Downman & Magruder, attys.
Julius Frank, for sutler's goods. Tucker & Sells, attys.
Jas H Gaskins, for commissary stores. Downman & Magruder, attys.
John W Hall, do. Wm Kilgour, atty.
Mrs Eliz A Belt, for commissary stores. Wm Kilgour, atty.
Geo Hamilton, for quartermaster's stores. Downman & Magruder, attys.
Henry Holt, do; do.
Mrs Frances Johnson, do; do.
Mrs Maria D Orme, for property destroyed. No atty.
Wm Faux: [No readable information.]
Thos Ratcliffe, for return of tax assessed upon cotton. Chipman, Hosmer & Co, attys.
Edw Swann, for property taken & destroyed. No atty.
John D Minns, for quartermaster's stores. Chinman, Hosmer & Co, attys.
John M Hunt & others, for taking up & keeping Gov't horses in the track of Morgan's raid in Ohio. Horatio King, atty.
John W Alver, for damages to property. Wm Fitch & Co, attys.
Mrs Margaret Knight, for pay due her husband. Patterson & Dietz, attys.
Joshua Rhodes & Wm Bagley, trustees for the creditors of McCluskey Cosgrove & Co, for quartermaster's stores. Wm Fitch & Co, attys.
Clayborne Ladenson, for services in Quartermaster's Dept. Chas M Fay, atty.
Jos Black, for tobacco & cotton taken by U S troops. R J Atkinson, atty.
Antonio Caire, for cotton. John Jolliffe.
E C Dewey, for property taken. No atty.
John Ford, for property destroyed by U S troops. British Minister through the State Dept.
Jas Keenan, for whiskey seized by U S authorities. No atty.
John Slattery, for transportation of troops. Horace J Gray, atty.
Jas A Stewart, for the use & value of property. Stribles & Simpson, attys.
Thornton Adlman, for services as pilot. No atty.
Mrs Anne J Pendleton & Philip Pendleton, for use of bldgs & grounds. No atty.

A W Hurlbut, for damages to property. Stewart Biddle & Co, attys.
Richd Lawton, for bounty due deceased son. No atty.
Jo J Prom & Co, for alcohol seized by the U S. Robt J Atkinson, atty.
P K O'Donnell & others, for services in the Provost Marshal General's Dept of Missouri. John P Camp, atty.
Mrs Margaret Bilbian, for bagging & rope furnished for packing captured cotton. No atty.
Jas Tongue, for lumber seized by the U S forces. No atty.
Wm B Comstock, for property used by the U S. Albert Stickney, atty.
Peter Swartzwalder, for quartermaster's stores & rent of property. Jas Fullerton, atty.
Cornelius Halpin, for quartermaster's & commissary stores. Jas Fullerton, atty.
Jos Zeringue & D Hyme, for rent. Robt J Atkinson, atty.
Towankinkpeota, [Indian] for services. No atty.
Wm Hand & Jas F Bailey, for reimbursement of money alleged to have been taken by an ofcr of the Provost Marshal's Dept. John H Johnson, atty.
C H Mastin, for rent of Levert Hospital. No atty.
Mrs Flora A Darling, for property seized. No atty.
Mrs Ann Craig, for services. E J Searle, atty.
Thos Keddy, for sugar & molasses taken. No atty.
Mrs Louisa E Segur, for property & supplies for U S Army. Robt J Atkinson, atty.
Jacob Augustine, for rent. Robt J Atkinson, atty.
Jas E Price & Chas H Gordon, for payment for a vessel destroyed the the U S authorities. P C Ellmaker, atty.
Geo Searight & F Furman, for sugar seized by U S. No atty.
C H Hugely & Jas G Bowen, for horses taken by the military authorities. Saml V Niles, atty.
John A Rollins, for wood. No atty.
Jacob Bird & others, for services rendered. No atty.
John B Dearing, for property taken & injuries received at the hands of guerillas. No atty.
Mrs Nancy Lear, for compensation for subsistence stores. C W Bennett, atty.
Gardner Green & R B Gibbs, for compensation as witnesses. Striblen & Simpson, attys.
Allan Pearce, for property destroyed. No atty.
Mary Irwin, for the use & occupation of a lot of ground. No atty.
Joel T Compton, for payment for secret service. No atty.
G A Lillendahl, for payment of a draft lost in transit. Chipman Hosmer & Co, attys.
Wm J Poitevant, for damage to & use of a steamer. Geo Taylor, atty.
Moses Simon, for property used & destroyed. John S Slater, atty.
John B Sweet, for services as a detective. S H Sweetland, atty.
Moses Simon, for rent. A K Browne, atty.
John F Javens, for a horse taken by U S troops. Britton, Gray & Pitcher, attys.
M Oglesby, for damages to property. No atty.

Mrs B A Offutt, for fuel & forage taken by U S. R Bruce, atty.
Wm A Orman, for saddles. Chipman, Hosmer & Co, attys.
Thos Sherlock, for the use of a steamer. No atty.
D R Godwin & A F Cochran, for sugar seized by U S. W S Hodge, atty.
J R Hollowbush, late Capt & A Q M, for reimbursement of moneys expended in the Quartermaster's Dept. No atty.
John Caldwell, for quartermaster's stores. A Dunford, atty.
Thos Neal, for quartermaster's stores. Robt J Atkinson, atty.
Jacob Hirsch, for cotton. Aug Barg, atty.
Robt A Phillips, for wood sold by the U S. No atty.
John A King, for services in saving Gov't property. Jas Fullerton, atty.
Thos Kehoe, for iron seized by Gov't. John Danby, atty.
Matthew Pepper, for liquors seized by U S. Chipman, Hosmer & Co, attys.
J B Baverdy & others, for bldgs taken & used by the Gov't. No atty.
Amherst W Stone, for iron sage. Saml B Parris, atty.
R A McComb, for leather furnished the U S. No atty.
Statement of the action had on claims during the present month.
Continued-claim of: R Bonneval; Allen Valentine; Angelo Miazzo; Chas Nagelin; Saml R Jacobs, M H Jeanjacquet; C E Brooke & Co; Maraus Walker; Jas Syme; Maria Josepa Cadazoo; A J Richardson; John Sheldon; C S Snead; L Pierce, jr; Jas Millegan; owners of the steamer **W H Young**; owners of the brig **Maderia**; Adolph Teusch; Eugene Bonney; Robt A Gray; John T Armstrong; Mrs E W Turner; J W Pomfrey; McDonald & Fuller; Mary J Holland; Benj Roach; Pannon Moody; R A Francis; J H Maddox; John Wells & Son; Jules Perrodin; Dominque Levet; John M McKee; Gustave Caynot; E E Hart; John McDowell; Henry Polkinghorn, jr; Celia A Grove; Mrs Edw King; O N Cutler; A Anstelle; C T Venniegerholtz; Geo Hume; Ober, Atwater & Co; Mrs J W Woolfold; Jules Conche; Montgomery Hunt; E D Wheeler; Francis Segura; M C Buckley; J R Hall; Thos Niles; & Bennett M Bird.
Allowed-claim of: W P Jones; A G Adams & R G Thorne; H Barnes; John Haskins; Jas Dearing; John Davidson; John G Taylor; Reuben Williams; Martin Hammers; A Davidson, jr; Henry J Thompson; Thos C Kelsey; John B Bingham; Jonathan Oldham; Curtis Phillips & J H Hunt; Jas G Davis; J F Newton; Henry Williams; Wm Satchell; David C Piquette; Gideon E Coldren; W J Sharp; John Westover; J M Rankin; Aaron Weeks; & John C Dawson.
Rejected-claim of: J Chambline & others; F W Dermon & others; Alexis & Eugene Tircuit; Mrs Philomene Sigur; Josephine Gosselin; Mrs Azoline Fay; Rosalie B Kelley; S B Bowen; C Hector Durward; Sabina Peacher; Bernard Escole; Patrick McCormick; A H Minn; John Metcalf; Jas Pearce; Rebecca Tomlinson; Jas A Skinker; Morris Cohen; Francis Capella; Danl J Flynn; John Manwaring; Columbus Reid; Louisa Keegan; Seratino Velati; Geo Olney; Michelis Wood; Wm A Dean; Jas Abendeen; Mrs Paschall; Wm W Lampson; & M V Baldwin & Co.
Held under advisement-claim of: A Morrell; Wm J Miner; Richd Berry; Jas G Hamilton;

Awaiting further proof-claim of: Jos Anderson
Returned to claimant-claim of: Adam Kling; R Kennedy; Andrew McDaniel; Fontain P Freeman; Jas D Rowland; Frank Day; Milton Jackson; R J Stringfellow, adm, etc; John Wayman; Mrs Juliet A Corbin; Mrs Hannah Baker; & Saml M Johnson.
De Witt Clinton, Brvt Lt Col, Recorder
Forwarded to Adj Gen: claim of J L Hurst; of Isaac Burton; & of John L & Wm Usrey.

FRI DEC 7, 1866
Maj Gen Howard yesterday issued an order censuring Brig Gen Whittlesey, late Assist Com'r of the Freedmen's Bureau for the State of N C, in accordance with the sentence of the military commission before whom he was recently tried, at Raleigh, N C.

Mr Geo W Brunner, age about 25 years, committed suicide in a fit of mental aberration, yesterday, at his lodgings, 400 E st, near 5th, by cutting his throat with a razor. He had breakfast & went back to his room, members of the family having advised him not to go out. A letter was left for him & was taken to his room, but the door was locked. A ladder was procured & his room entered by the window. He was found dead on the floor with an ugly gash on the left side of his neck. Brunner came from Phil, where his parents & a sister & brother reside. S M Barrows was a room-mate of the deceased. The deceased was a graduate of a High School, in Pa, & came here in Apr, 1864, taking a position of a phonographic clerk in the War Dept. He had received the degree of bachelor of arts; left the War Dept about Mar 1 last; occupied the position of departmental reporter on the Star newspaper of Wash City, & was highly esteemed. The brother of the deceased was telegraphed & arrived here last night & took charge of the remains.

Mrd: on Dec 6, at the Church of the Epiphany, by Rev Dr Ball, Chas A Bell, of Nashville, to Evelina F Evans, daughter of the late Evan Evans, of Wash, D C.

Jas C McGuire & Co, on Thu, sold lot 5 in square 170, on 18th st west, near F st, with a small brick house jupn it, to C H Winder, for $900. The same gentlemen sold a house at G & 18th sts, belonging to the estate of Edw Everett, to Chas Knap, for $18,750.

Senate: Dec 6. 1-Memorial from W S Adams, Collector of Customs of the Dist of Oregon, praying to be relieved from liability for money stolen en route to San Francisco: referred to the Cmte of Claims.

A Card: the undersigned will be necessarily absent from the city for a few months. All persons having business matters with him will please address him at York, Pa, or communicate through Nicholas Callan, Notary Public, 448 15th st.
–Thos A McLaughlin

Appointments in the Quartermaster's Dept: Brvt Brig Gen R E Clary & Brvt Maj Gen Rufus Ingalls, lt colonels & deputy quartermaster generals, U S army, have been appointed colonels in the Quartermaster's Dept. Brvt Brig Gen M S Miller, Maj Alex'r Montgomery, Brvt Brig Gen L C Easton, Brvt Maj Gen S Van Vliet, Brvt Col R W Kirkham, Brvt Brig Gen J C McFarrad, Brvt Brig Gen Fred Myers, majors & quartermasters, U S army; & Brvt Brig Gen S B Halabird, Brvt Maj Gen R C Tyler, Brvt Brig Gen C H Tompkins, & Brvt Brig Gen J A Ekin, captains & assist quartermasters, U S army, have been appointed lt colonels in the Quartermaster's Dept.

The funeral of the late Jas Welch, whose mysterious disappearance, while on a visit to Balt to attend the laying of the corner-stone of the new Masonic temple, has already been noticed, took place yesterday afternoon from the Unitarian Church. The body was encased in a handsome mahogany coffin, upon which were displayed the emblems of the Masonic order, of which deceased was a prominent member. The remains were interred in the ***Congressional Cemetery***.

Wilmington, N C, Dec 6. The steamship **Suwanee**, Capt Cotbarine, from N Y for Brazos Santiago, foundered at sea, 45 miles s w of Frying Pan Shoals, on Dec 3. Three boats containing all on board, left the ship; one boat arrived here with the capt, & his wife & 2 children; Dr Hadden, of Jersey City; assist engineer A P Smith; steward J N Wine; a Mexican passenger, & seamen Thos Brook & W Smith, & 4 firemen. The other boats, containing the 1st & 2nd mates, & 13 others, have not been heard from

Phil, Dec 6. Capt Julius, of the ship **Tonawanda**, from Liverpool, arrived today at this port. He reports that on Nov 18 he saw a dismantled vessel; proved to be the brig **Jacques,** Capt Fontaine, of Granville, from St Pierre, N F. The **Tonawanda** brought away 67 passengers besides her crew. Dr D W Harry, of the **Tonawanda** attended those injured; on Dec 5, Jean Theffaine, of St Veran Ese de Nord, died from his injuries; on Dec 1, Thos Carrigan, seamen, of St John, N B, fell overboard & was drowned.

It gives us pleasure to state that Mr H J McLaughlin, 353 7th st, between I & K sts, has now in store a large & varied assortment of fancy & useful articles. Mr McLaughlin makes a speciality of fine dress & cloak trimming, etc, etc, & has taken great pains & evinced fine taste in selecting his goods, & brought them in the best markets, & at the lowest figures; he has marked them down & is determined to sell.

John Scott, Geo Cutler, & Dr Wilder, of the commission house of Scott, Cutler & Co, of Kansas city, have been arrested, charged with setting fire to their own store, which was destroyed. It is said the proof is positive. Mr Cutler, while under arrest, tried to commit suicide by jumping out of a window. Two clerks lost their lives by this fire.

Dept of the Interior, U S Patent Ofc, Wash, Nov 28, 1866. Ptn of Robt Waddell, of Liverpool, Kingdom of Great Britain, praying for the extension of a patent granted to him Jun 6, 1854, antedated to Apr 27, 1853, in England on Mar 2, 1853, for an improvement Balancing Side Valves of Steam Engines, for 7 years from expiration of said patent, which takes place on Apr 27, 1867.
–T C Theaker, Com'r of Patents

J H McVeigh offers for rent his commodious & handsome residence, 217, corner of Cameron & St Asaph sts, Alexandria, Va. Apply at 117 Queen st, Alexandria, Va.

SAT DEC 8, 1866
Following is a list of the ofcrs of the 12th U S infty, now stationed in Wash City:

Col, Christopher C Augur	Capt B R Perkins
Lt Col, Geo W Wallace	Capt R C Parker
Maj, Henry E Maynadier	Capt M H Stacy
Capt, Henry R Rathbone	Capt H C Egberrt
Capt P W Stanhope	Capt R H Pond
Capt W J L Nicodemus	

1st Lts:

A Thieman	E Hunter
J E Putnam	C A Tripler
J H May	A B MacGowan
J L Rathborn	J L Voven

2nd Lts:

Wm E Dove	L Nolen
A Trolinger	D J Cragie
D W Applegate	W A Coulter
S L Hammon	S B M Young

On Wed night, an toxicated man was conveyed to the Central Guard-house, & then he made himself known as Noah Gill, ex-police commissioner & ex-councilman of Balt. His pockets were searched & $417 taken from them. $10 was then returned to him, & he was released & shown to a hotel. Not long afterward Ofcr McElfresh arrested him again for being drunk in the street, & he was conveyed to the police station. This time the search brought to light $51, & he was locked up for the night. On Thu Gill, with $450 about him, was in the saloon of John Rooney, C & 13th sts, & he soon discovered that his money had been stolen. Two thieves, well known, Robt J Miller & Michl Cooley were arrested; the case has not yet been disposed of.

The **Sisters of the Visitation** recently purchased of Mr Nathl Carusi, square 162, bounded by L, M, & 17th sts & Conn ave, for $65,000, on which they propose to erect, next spring, a splendid seminary for young ladies.

Mrd: on Dec 6, by Rev Dr Keeling, David Blair, H S, U S A, to Miss Sarah Eberle, of Phil. Phil & N Y papers please copy.

Mrd: on Dec 4, at Phil, by Rev A C Mercer, D D, Carlile Boyd, chaplain U S A, to Maria, 2nd daughter of S A Mercer, of Phil. No cards.

Geo D Taff, Merchant Tailor, 399 7th st, between H & I sts. [Ad.]

S W Owen, successor to E Owen & Son, Military & Naval: Merchant Tailor, Pa ave, between 14th & 15th sts, Wash City. [Ad.]

Richmond, Dec 6. The trial of Henry Bird Lewis, one of the nearest living relations of Gen Washington, is progressing in King Geo Co. He is charged with the murder of Dr Rose, during the late war. Eminent counsel are engaged in the defence. [Dec 27th newspaper: Henry Byrd Lewis was convicted on Sat, at King Geo's Court House, Va, of voluntary manslaughter, in killing Dr Rose, some 5 years ago. He was sentenced to 3 years & 6 months in the penitentiary.]

Terre Haute, Ind, Dec 7. Railroad accident on the St Louis, Alton, & Terre Haute railroad, between the construction & gravel trains. Jno Bryon was killed outright; Wm Foully, fireman, laborer, was mortally wounded.

Memphis, Dec 7. Railroad accident this afternoon 12 miles south of Clarksville, when the train was precipated through the trestle, killing Jas McGuire, express messenger.

MON DEC 10, 1866

A woman named Liebman, at Cairo, Ill, on Sat, attempted to kill her 2 children with an axe; she afterwards cut her own throat & died. One of the children will probably die.

Orphans Court-Judge Purcell. 1-On Sat Wm H Watson received letters of administration on the estate of Lavinia Boyle; bond, $1,260; Bridget Cullinane on the estate of Michl Cullinane; bond, $14,000; Simon Fentwell on the estate of Lawrence Conroy, sometimed called Frank Hale; bond, $1,600. 2-Margaret Fuller was appointed guardian to the orphans of Philip K & Mary Jane Bailey, of Balt; bond, $800; Osceola C Green to the orphans of Jas B Leach; bond, $50,000. 3-The will of the late John McDuell was fully proved. 4-The first & final account of the administratrix of Geo F Huguely; an account of personal estate of same; first general & individual accounts of same; & an account of the personal estate of Henry C Baldwin by the executors, were approved & passed.

Hiram Powers has executed at Elorance a figure of "Eve after the fall," a work said to be finer than his:"California" or his "Greek Slave."

Real estate sales: part of the land in Wash Co, known as *White Haven*, the property of Dennis Donn, deceased, to H Gutshall, for $1,500. Frame house & lot on O st, between 12th & 13th sts, to Mrs P Duffy, for $710. Lot 3 in square 504, with a 4 story brick house, on P st, between 4½ & 6th sts, to Mrs M L Porschall, for $1,500. Two story brick house & lot on 8th st west, between P & Q sts, to C H Griggs, for $2,300 cash.

Navy Bulletin: Detached, Dec 1. Cmder Wm D Whiting, from navigation duty at N Y, & ordered to temporary duty at the N Y Navy Yard; Lt Cmder Jas G Maxwell, from duty at Bay Point, S C, & ordered to temporary duty at the N Y Navy Yard; Lt Allan B Browne, from the ship **Rhode Island**, & ordered to the ship **Unadilla**; Lt Cmder Francis H Baker, from duty at the Norfolk Navy Yard, & ordered to the command of the ship **Unadilla**; Lt Cmder La Rue P Adams, from duty at the N Y Navy Yard, & ordered to the ship **Peoria** on Dec 15; Master Wm K Wheeler, from the **Rhode Island**, & ordered to the ship **Huron** on Jan 1; Capt W B Woolfrey, from duty at the Naval Observatory, Wash, & ordered to command the ship **Pawnee** on Jan 1; Ensigns Royal B Bradford, Arthur H Fletcher, & Josiah M Wilson, from the **Rhode Island**, & ordered to the ship **Iroquois** on Jan 1; Cmder Oscar C Badger, from ordnance duty at Pittsburgh, Pa, on the reporting of his relief, & ordered to command the **Iroquois**, on Jan 1; Lt Cmder Alfred T Mahan, from ordnance duty at Wash, D C, & ordered to the **Iroquois**, on Jan 1; Acting 2nd Assist Engineer Chas W Clift, from the N Y Navy Yard, & ordered to the Unadilla; Acting Passed Assist Surgeon Francis V Greene, from duty at the Naval Laboratory at N Y, & ordered to the ship **Aroostook**; Acting 3rd Assist Engineer Jas H Sleeper, from the ship **Palas**, & ordered to the ship **Penobscot**; 1st Assist Engineer G L M Maccarty, from the ship **Guerriere**, & ordered to the **Penobscot**; Acting 3rd Assist Engineer John Grimes, from the ship **Pilgrim**, & ordered to the **Penobscot**; 1st Assist Engineer John Grimes, from the **Pilgrim**, & ordered to the **Penobscot**; 1st Assist Engineer E J Whittaker, from the **Guerriere**, & ordered to the **Unadilla**; Acting 2nd Assist Engineer Jas Patterson, from the ship **Chattanooga**, & ordered to the **Penobscot**; Acting 3rd Assist Engineer Geo H Chesney, from duty at Bay Point, S C, & ordered North. Ordered, Dec 1. Lt Cmder Wm H Dana, to the ship **Pawnee**, on Jan 1; Cmdor Wm Rogers Taylor, to temporary ordnance duty at Pittsburgh, Pa; Acting 3rd Assist Engineers Wm J Faul, John H Blake, & 2nd Assist Engineer John Miller, to the **Unadilla**; Acting Passed Assist Surgeon John E Parsons, to the **Penobscot**; Master John C Kennett, to the **Rhode Island**; Master W S Dana, to the **Aroostook**; Acting Assist Surgeon Henry C Eckstein, to the ship **Huron**, on Jan 1; Master N Ludlow, to the **Iroquois**, on Jan 1; Lt Cmder I A Beardslee, to the command of the **Aroostook**; Acting Assist Surgeon L Fussell, to the **Unadilla**; Passed Assist Paymaster A D Bache, to the **Iroquois**, on Jan 1; Acting Volunteer Lt Geo R Durand, to the **Penobscot**; lt Cmder Chas E Fleming, to command the **Penobscot**; Assist Paymaster W J Thompson, to the **Unadilla**; Lt Cmder H B Erben, to command the **Huron**; Assist Paymaster Chas W Slamm, to the **Penobscot**.

Army appointments: Brvt Brig Gen Jas A Ekin, U S volunteers, & Brvt Brig Gen C H Tompkins, U S volunteers, to be Deputy Quartermasters General, with the rank of lt colonels in the regular army. Both of these ofcrs have been on duty in Wash City for some years past.

The Pres has appointed N W Brown, now Deputy Paymaster Gen, & Danl McClure, of Indiana, to be Assist Paymasters Gen under the new army. John P McGrath, of Missouri, & Wm H Johnson, of Ohio, have been appointed paymasters in the regular army.

A whole family was poisoned at Berlin, Conn, on Friday: Mr Peck, his wife & mother, & son & daughter, 15 & 17 years of age, were stricken down in the night so severely & at nearly the same time that they were unable to send for assistance. Mr Peck's mother died on Sunday, & his wife & servant are not expected to recover. The poison was arsenic. There are property complications & a law suit, in which the Peck family are witnesses. About a year since Mr Nelson Taylor, brother-in-law to Mrs Peck, died suddenly, & it is now thought he may have been poisoned. His remains will be analyzed. The family relatives know more than they tell. Later-the servant girl, Eliza Fox, is still living & there is thought that Mr Peck & his wife, & the son & daughter will recover. [Dec 13th newspaper: There is some hope that Eliza Fox will survive; the body of Nelson Taylor revealed the presence of arsenic in it; Mr & Mrs Peck, the son & daughter, are somewhat better. –Hartford Times, Sat]

Norfolk, Dec 8. Accident off the mouth of the Rappahannock river this morning, on board the steamer **Kelso**-the chimney exploded. The wounded, as far as ascertained, are: R S Osborne, Oxford, N C, seriously; C U Nixon, Edenton, N C, seriously; Wm McGee, Norfolk, slightly; Maj Carter, U S army, painfully; Chas Reeder, chief engineer, painfully; Wm D Wilson, 2nd engineer, seriously; John Rowan, fireman, seriously; Stephen S Hayes, Newark, N J, seriously; John Thomas, colored waiter, seriously; Harman Botts, fireman, mortally. Mr S Honey, one of the engineer ofcrs, is reported to have behaved most heroically in cutting off the steam. Later: List of victims killed: Chief Engineer, Rider; assist engineer, Willson; M Waldron, baggage master; Wm Hall, fireman, & John Rowans, Capt Cralle, & 3 firemen were badly scalded. Passengers badly scalded: Rev J Cowling, Geo Rickett, Mrs Southampton, Edw Bachler, L Sangtell, Maj Carter, 18th infty; Jos Davis, Stephen Hayes, & Chas Nixon. The **Kelso** was towed to this city. Her injured passengers have been taken to the naval hospital.

Chancery sale of valuable improved property on N J ave & south B st, Capitol Hill: by decree of the Supreme Court of D C, in Equity, pronounced Dec 6, in cause No 806, wherein Chas T Iardella et al are cmplnts & Lawrence A Iardella et al are dfndnts: public auction on Dec 24 next, of part of lot 11 in square 690, in Wash City. Separate sale will be made of a parcel of ground & 3 story brick dwlg-house, on B st. –Jas E Williams, John N Oliver, trustees
-Green & Williams, aucts

Pittsburgh, Dec 9. Young Montgomery, the son of Hon Wm Montgomery, who murdered a man, Dinsmore, in Wash Co, recently, & for whose capture a reward of $1,000 was offered, was captured yesterday at Wellsurg, West Va.
+
On Tuesday 2 men visited the residence of Mr Dinsmore, on the Middletown road, about 6 miles from Wash, Pa, & shot & stabbed him. He died a few hours afterwards. A man named Fogler has been arrested. He is reported to have made a confession implicating another man named Montgomery, still at large. Robbery was the motive. [Dec 13th newspaper: Taylor & Pollard had no connection with the murder; two young men, Fogler & Montgomery, have been arrested & identified as the perpretrators of the murder. Folger confessed & stated that Wm Montgomery, age about 18, son of Hon Wm Montgomery, was his accomplice. –Pittsburgh Republic, Dec 8.]

N Y, Dec 9. Hon Wm Pollock, of Pittsfield, Mass, one of the most prominent & wealthy woollen manufacturers in Mass, died at the Fifth Ave Hotel this morning, aged 59 years. His remains will be taken to Pittsfield for interment on Tues next.

Orphans Court of Wash Co, D C, Dec 8, 1866. In the case of Louisa K Keach, admx of Jas B Leach, deceased, the administratrix & Court have appointed Jan 7, 1867, for the final settlement of the personal estate of the said deceased, of the assets in hand. -Jas R O'Beirne, Reg/o wills

David H Lane, of Sullivan Co, Missouri, on going to bed Thursday night, at the Revere House, in Chicago, blew out the gas, instead of turning it off, & was found dead in his bed the following morning.

Orphans Court of Wash Co, D C. Letters of administration on the personal estate of Michl Cullinane, late of Wash, D C, deceased. –Bridget Cullinane, Patrick Cullinane, adms

Executor's sale of real estate at public auction: on Dec 11, on the premises, that portion of land belonging to the late Eliz Butler, deceased, lying on the south side of Milk-house Ford Road, at Piney Branch road, & near **Fort Stevens**, containing several acres, to be sold in two or more lots. Call on J S McChesney, at **Brightwood**, who will show the property. Title perfect. Terms cash. –Alfred Ray, exc -Green & Williams, aucts

TUE DEC 11, 1866
Capt Saml Phillips, a well known citizen of Balt, aged 43 years, & his wife, aged 41 years, were both attacked with sudden illness on Sat, & the Capt died during the night & his wife died the latter Sunday. He owned & commanded some of the finest clipper schnrs trading between Balt & Charleston, & at the time of his death was concerned in the ownership of a number of coasting vessels.

Navy Bulletin. Resigned, Dec 3. Acting Ensign Saml L Griffin, of the ship **Onward**. Ordered, Dec 3. Midshipmen Geo A Morris, Jas L Morse, Geo A Baldy, & Frank Courtis, to the ship **Pawnee** on Jan 1; Midshipmen Horatio R Wilson, John R Pholan, Wm Watts, & Wm H Emory, to the ship **Iroquois**, on Jan 1. Detached, Dec 3. Lt Cmder Henry Erben, from the N Y Navy Yard, & ordered to command of the ship **Huron**, on Jan 1. Lt Cmder B J Cromwell, Lt Geo W Coffin, Master Wm B Hoff, passed Assist Surgeon D R Bannan, 1st Assist Engineer R J Talbot & 2nd Assist Engineers John Lowe, W J Montgomery, & J M Emanuel, from the ship **Shawmut** & placed on waiting orders; Cmder Geo U Morris, from command of the **Shawmut**, & placed on waiting orders; Acting Assist Paymaster Jas C Graves, from the **Shawmut**, & ordered to settle his accounts; Acting Master T N Meyer, Acting Ensign Otis A Thompson, Mates S O'Brien & G W Pratt, from the **Shawmut**, & placed on waiting orders; Acting Ensign J H Chapman, from the **Onward**, from Sep 20 last, & granted leave of absence. Mscl: Jos J Harvey, whose appointment as an acting assist paymaster was revoked on Apr 13 last, has had his resignation accepted from that date.

U S steamer **Shenandoah**: Capt J R Goldsborough, commanding the **Shenandoah**, reports to the Sec of the Navy, under date of Nov 1st, his arrival at Point de Gailo, Island of Ceylon, after a pleasant voyage from Bombay, which place he left on Oct 20.

Postmaster Genr'l has made the following changes in postmasters since Dec 5.
Md: Greenwood, Balt Co, Geo W Burton, vice Jas Barton, jr, moved away.
New Offices established:
Maine: Biddeford Pool, York Co, Wm P Goldthwait appointed postmaster.
Ark: Eglantine, Van Buren Co, Wm K Bradford appointed postmaster.
N J: Smithville, Burlington Co, John Sagine appointed postmaster.
N C: Hay Store, Wake Co, W H Page appointed postmaster.
Tenn: Duck River Station, Maury Co, Elis Harris appointed postmaster.
Minn: Elk River Station Sherburne Co, J Q A Nickers, appointed postmaster.
S C: Allison's Store, York Co, R Wiley appointed postmaster.
Texas: Somerset, Ataxora Co, W Carothers appointed postmaster.
Missouri: Edgar Springs, Phelps Co, Jas Lamar appointed postmaster.
Offices re-established:
Va: New London, Campbell Co, W Lyle, postmaster; Dickinson's, Franklin Co, Geo W Brown, postmaster. Missouri: Barbois, Franklin Co, Henry E Green, postmaster. Tenn: Jefferson, Rutherford Co, Jas W Waller, postmaster.
Ark: North Creek, Phillips Co, Mrs M Armstrong, postmistress; Saline, Levacca Co, L A Smith, postmaster. Louisiana: Stony Point, East Baton Rouge, Parson Philip Spiller, postmaster; Bienville Co, H Shaw, postmaster. Fla: Orlando, Orange Co, Miss Mary A McGinnis, postmistress; **Fort Taylor**, Hernando Co, Miss E Avery, postmistress; Abe Spring, Calhoun Co, E Richards, postmaster.

The late Capt Wm M Walker, was born on Sep 2, 1813, & died on Nov 20, 1866; entered the navy as a midshipman on Nov 1, 1827, when that branch of the service was under the administration of Hon Saml L Southard. He passed through his novitiate in the Naval School at Norfolk, from which he graduated with honor; warranted as a passed midshipman from Jun 10,1833; service in the Mediterranean & in the waters of the West Indies; was appointed in 1838 to take part in the famous exploring expedition committed to the direction of Capt Wilkes, & in which young Walker signalized his seamanship & deservedly won for him the promotion of the Dept & the admiration of his comrades. Commanded at one time the U S schnr **Flying Fish**. During 39 years of his official life, more than 16 were spent in arduous sea service & more than 10 in shore duty. At the date of his death he was inspector of lighthouses in the Third Dist of N Y.

Miss Glooma Jennings, the only heiress to the Duke of Marlborough's estate of one hundred million pounds, leaves Alabama next month for England to claim her property, Sam Jennings, of Conn, & other heirs having transferred their claim to her.

Vienna, C W, Dec 10. Fire yesterday destroyed the post ofc, telegraph ofc, & stores of Suffel & Co, Francis Jewell, & Saml Brasher. Robt McKay, a much respected citizen was burned to death.

Emrich's Restaurant, 355 Pa ave, near 6th st: P Emrich keeps on hand oysters fresh every day, prepared in every style. His wines & liquors cannot be surpassed. [Ad.]

Reported that yesterday Col Paulding, the paymaster who lost a large amount of Gov't funds by the failure of the Merchants' Nat'l Bank, of his city, & who was sentenced to pay a fine of $5,000, & be imprisoned for one year, has been released by order of the Pres, & the fine remitted.

Farm for rent in Alexandria Co, Va, 2½ miles from Gtwn; 66 acres, a dwlg house, & is well watered. Will be rented for one or two years. For terms apply to Mrs M A Hayes on the premises, or to Z D Gilman, Druggist, 350 Pa ave.

Orphans Court of Wash Co, D C. Letters of administration on the personal estate of Lavinia Boyle, late of Wash City, D C, deceased. –Wm H Watson

WED DEC 12, 1866
Appointments by the Pres: Cmdor C K Garrison, formerly Mayor of San Francisco, & principal owner of the line of steamers to Calif, has been appointed Com'r on the part of the U S to the grand Universal Exposition at Paris. A T Stewart, the eminent merchant of N Y, has also been appointed in the same capacity.

Capt Francis Gallagher died in this city yesterday, at the residence of John B O'Donnell, on German st. He died of consumption, the result of his services in the late war, in his 51st year of his age. He commenced his career in life as a mechanic, adopted the profession of the law, was a Douglas Democrat, entered the army at an early period as an ofcr of Md cavalry & continued until the rebellion was suppressed in the field. -Balt American, Tues

Examining Surgeons: The Com'r of Pensions yesterday appointed Dr J F Redfield, at **Fort Scott**, Kansas; R Putnam, Fayetteville, Ark, & Geo W Foote, of Galesburg, Ill, examining surgeons of pensioners.

Assignments: Brvt Maj Gen Robt Allen, Acting Quartermaster Gen, has been announced as chief quartermaster of the Military Div of the Pacific. Brvt Col E B Babbitt, Deputy Quartermaster Gen, appointed chief quartermaster of the Dept of Columbia. Brvt Col R W Kirkham assigned to duty as chief quartermaster of the Dept of Calif.

Navy Bulletin. Ordered, Dec 4. Acting Assist Engineer John T Buckley to the ship **Glance**; Cmder Thos Patterson to the Norfolk [Va] Navy Yard; Midshipman Geo A Bicknell to the ship **Iroquois** on Jan 4. Detached, Dec 4. Gunner Geo Sirian, from the naval magazine, **Fort Norfolk**, & ordered to ordnance duty in that year; Gunner John Gaskins, from ordnance duty at the Norfolk Navy Yard & ordered to duty at the naval magazine at **Fort Norfolk**; Acting Third Assist Engineer John H Hutton from the **Glance**, & ordered to the ship **Aroostook**. Lt Cmder Milton Horton, from duty at the naval rendezvous, N Y, & ordered to the ship **Vermont**; Acting Third Assist Engineer H C Barrows, from the ship **Snowdrop** & ordered to the **Aroostook**. Honorably Discharged, Dec 4. Acting Chief Engineers J McCausland, from Dec 1, & John Germain, from Dec 2; Acting First Assist Engineer

Mustered out: Surgeon Wm Carroll, brvt lt colonel, U S V, has been mustered out of service by order of the Sec of War.

Mrd: on Dec 6, at Christ Church, Alexandria, by Rev A M Randolph, Henry T Wight, of Goochland Co, to Miss Harriot W, daughter of Francis A Dickins, of Fairfax Co, Va.

Mrd: ON Dec 5, at the residence of the bride's father, in Liberty, Va, by Rev John Austin Wharton, Mr Rowland D Buford to Miss Sarah A Bell, daughter of Alfred A Bell.

Died: on Dec 11, Mrs Ann Roberts, in her 80th year. Her funeral will be from her late residence, 433 G st south, btwn 7th & 8th sts east, Navy Yard, Dec 13 at 2 PM.

Wm Montgomery, son of Hon Wm Montgomery, the murderer of Mrs Densmore, near Wash, Pa, for whose arrest $1,000 reward was offered, was arrested on Sat at Wellsbury, West Va.

Orphans Court of Wash Co, D C. Letters of administration on the personal estate of Eliza J Schenig, late of Wash, D C, deceased. –Geo R Schenig, exc

Public sale of valuable real estate, by decree of the Circuit Court of PG Co, in Equity, public sale on Jan 1, 1867, a part of the real estate which the late Dr A S Magruder died seized & possessed. The property is known as the ***Twenty Acre Lot***, in said county, about 1 mile from Ellaville; adjoins the lands of O C Duffy & W F Deakins, contains 20 acres by survey. -C C Magruder, jr, trustee

THU DEC 13, 1866
Brvt Maj Gen Frank Wheaton has been promoted to the rank of lt colonel in the 39th colored infty. Gen Wheaton entered the army from civil life on Mar 3, 1855, receiving the appointment of 1st lt in the 2nd U S cavalry. He is but 33 years of age, & has been in 42 battles.

Jas S Weatherby, an old citizen of Cincinnati, died on Sunday, aged 76 years.

Navy Bulletin. Honorably Discharged, Dec 5. Acting Master Oliver Colburn, Dec 4; Mate W F Warnick, Dec 6. Ordered, Dec 5. Assist Surg Jos B Parker, to the Naval Academy; Surg Jas Suddards, to duty as a member of a board in Phil, presided over by Surg Dillard; & Assist Paymaster Henry T Skelding, to the ship **Gettysburg**. Resigned, Dec 5. Assist Paymaster Chas A Cable. Detached, Dec 5. Surg J S Ramsey, from the Naval Academy, & placed on waiting orders.

Despatch dated Rome: The man who gave the information which led to the arrest of John H Surratt is a French Canadian, named St Marie. He was formerly a Union soldier, & served in the Papal Zouaves. Both he & Surratt were in love with the same lady in Washington, & St Marie betrayed Surratt through jealousy.

Nathl Pascall, senior editor of the Missouri Repulican, died Dec 12, aged 64. He commenced the printing business as an apprentice in the Republican ofc, 52 years ago, & was the oldest editor west of the Mississippi river, if not of the Alleghany mountains, & regarded as one of the best & most influential citizens of St Louis.

N Y, Dec 12. Meeting of the wool trade today at the store of Messrs Lawrence, Wright & Co, to express sorrow at the death of Mr John W Smythe. Resolutions of condolence with the family were passed.

At Franconia, N H, on Sat last, Geo Maxwell, a farmer living alone, was brutally murdered & his house robbed by some person unknown. His neck was nearly severed with an axe. The Selectmen have offered a $100 reward for the murderer.

John W Garrett was yesterday re-elected president of the Balt & Ohio railroad, & John King, late auditor of the company, was chosen vice president.

Geo Custis Lee, son of Gen Lee, has been elected president of the Md Agricultural College.

The dwlg of Jas Miller, of Rock Island, Ill, was destroyed by fire on Sunday. His mother, aged 70 years, & two of his sons were burned to death. Another son was so badly burned that he is not expected to live.

Robt Weire, Sr, formerly proprietor of the Montreal Herald, died in Scotland recently at the advanced age of 83 years.

Mr E J Roberts, a merchant at Church Hill, Queen Anne's Co, Md, was murdered on Sat night last. It appears that he closed his store at the usual house & started for his residence, only about 40 paces distant. As he failed to reach home, his wife, who had retired to bed, got up & proceeded across the yard, when she discovered him hanging across the railing which enclosed his residence. He was bleeding copiously from a severe head wound. He died in a few hours. All the money he had about him was gone.

Mrd: on Dec 11, at Trinity Church, by Rev Dr Keeling, Mr Jas B Wimer to Miss Mary Molan, daughter of Mr Jas Molan. [Phil Ledger & Inquirer & N Y Herald please copy.]

Died: on Dec 12, after an illness of 2 days, Ethie Reeves, aged 6 months & 2 days, youngest daughter of John E & Ethie A O'Brien. Her funeral will take place from the residence of her parents, 493 L st, between 9th & 10th, this afternoon at 3 o'clock.

Died: on Dec 12, William David, infant son of Dr Jos T & Cizzie M Howard. [Salem, N J, Sunbeam & Lansing, Iowa, papers please copy.]

Died: on Dec 12, Jos Follansbee, a native of Mass, & for the last 50 years a resident of Wash City, aged 73 years & 11 months. His funeral will take place on Dec 13, at 2 P M, from his late residence on H st, between 6th & 7th sts.

M Losano, Merchant Tailor, 9th & D sts, Wash; Mr R Hardon, associate. [Ad.]

Dept of the Interior, U S Patent Ofc, Wash, Dec 7, 1866. Ptn of Wm Coleman & Stephen G Coleman, of Providence, R I, praying for the extension of a patent granted to them Mar 15, 1853, for an improvement in supporting the tapping-lift & peak-halyard block of sail vessels, for 7 years from the expiration of said patent, which takes place on Mar 15, 1867. -H C Theaker, Com'r of Patents

Shaffield's French Confectionary & Ladies' Ice-Cream & Dining Saloons. Business resumed at 246 Pa ave, between 12th & 13th sts. –Jos H Shaffield
+
Having disposed of our establishment to Mr Jos Shaffield, so favorably known as a confectioner, we respectfully request our friends to entend their favors to him, knowing they will not regret it. –Jewell's

FRI DEC 14, 1866

House of Reps: 1-Memorial of Wm McGeraham, relative to his claim to certain land-grants: referred to the Cmte on Private Land Claims. 2-Bill for the relief of Hugh Worthington, of Metropolis City, Ill: referred. 3-Bill for the relief of Almanson Eaton, receiver of public moneys at Stevens Point, Wisc: referred. 4-Cmte on Private Land Claims: bill releasing to Francis S Lyon the interest of the U S in certain lands, & recommended its passage. 5-Cmte on Naval Affairs: bill for the relief of Geo Henry Preble, a cmder in the U S navy, & recommended its passage. [The bill provides that he be allowed pay for the time during which he was suspended the same as if the order discharging him had never been issued.]

Died: on Dec 13, Mary E Warrington, daughter of the late Wm M Scott. Her funeral will be from the residence of her mother, 183 H st, between 19th & 20th sts, on Dec 15 at 1 o'clock.

Died: on Dec 12, in Rockville, Md, Mrs Anne E Matlack, wife of S A Matlack, formerly of Wash City. [Star please copy.]

Navy Bulletin. Appointment Revoked, Dec 6. Acting Ensign Henry Clay Serlie. Order Revoked, Dec 6. Surgeon C J Cleborne to the ship **Iroquois**, & placed on waiting orders. Ordered, Dec 6. Passed Assist Surgeon E D Payne, to the Naval Hospital, Wash, D C; Surgeon T W Leach, Assist Surgeon H N Beaumont, Sailmaker Josiah E Crowell, Carpenter O H Gerry, & Acting Boatswain Herman Peters, to the **Iroquois** on Jan 1; Boatswain Zachariah Whitmarsh & Carpenter Josiah D Palmer, to the ship **Peoria**; Cmder A W Weaver, to the command of the ship **Tallapoosa**; 1st Assist Engineer Wm S Smith, to duty at the Norfolk, Va, Navy Yard, as assist to Chief Engineer Newell; Surgeon Wm Johnson, jr, 2nd Assist Engineers Geo W Greene, Wm H Mintzyer, John F Bingham, Carpenter Wm F Laughton, Boatswain Thos Smith, & Sailmaker B B Blydenburg, to the ship **Pawnee** on Jan 1; 2nd Assist Engineer H L Slosson, to special duty on the ship **Franklin**. Detached, Dec 6. Passed Assist Surgeon C H Giberson & 2nd Assist Engineer H S Rose from the N Y Navy Yard, & ordered to the **Peoria**; Chief Engineer Geo S Bright from special duty at Phil, & ordered to the **Pawnee**; Lt Cmder W P McCann from the command of the **Tallapoosa**, on the reporting of his relief, & granted leave of absence; 2nd Assist Engineer John H Gardner from duty at League Island, & ordered to the **Peoria**; 1st Assist Engineer John Purdy, 2nd Assist Engineers W Lane, & R L Webb from special duty at Boston & ordered to the **Peoria**.

For rent: the corner store & the one adjoining, on La ave & 6th st, eligibly situated for drug & grocery business. Apply to Mrs A Simpson, 4 La ave.

SAT DEC 15. 1866

The Frenchman who was engaged with Weichman in teaching on 19th st, & who furnished the information leading to the arrest of John H Surratt, is Santa Farara- at least, that is the name by which he then passed. He is a tall, good-looking man, with black hair & moustache, & manners somewhat dignified.

Cmder H Rolando, commanding the U S steamer **Florida**, under date of St Croix, West Indies, Nov 25, reports the death of Lt Cmder Morean Forrest, of that vessel, on the 24th ultimor, of yellow fever, after an illness of 7 days. His body was buried at sea in consequence of the refusal of the civil authorities to allow him to be interred on shore. In compliance with the orders of Admiral Palmer, Cmder Rolando proceeded to the Island of St Thomas, there to await the arrival of the Admiral; but owing to the prevalence of cholera, yellow fever, & small pox on the island, he was compelled to return to St Croix.

Navy Bulletin for Dec 7. Ordered. Acting 2nd Assist Engineer Marcellus C Heath, to the tug **Patos**. Detached: Acting 2nd Assist Engineer R K Morrison, from the **Patos**, & ordered to the ship **Don**; Mate Jas Oliver, from the ship **Bienville**, & placed on waiting orders; Acting 3rd Assist Engineer Thos Clarke, from the ship **Maria**, & order to the ship **Unadilla**; Acting 2nd Assist Engineer H F Hayden, from the **Don**, & ordered to the ship **Massachusetts**; Acting 3rd Assist Engineer Wm J Fant, from the **Unadilla**, & ordered to the **Maria**.

On Dec 11th, Mrs John Hinesley, keeper of the Russell House, on Pa ave, between 10th & 11th sts, was selling her furniture at auction, with a view of leaving the city, when she noticed a gold watch, valued at $275, a breast pin valued at $175, missing. Geo Farr was suspected & arrested. He was committed to jail for further hearing. [Dec 19th newspaper: Geo Farr: Evidence being insufficient to justify a commitment for the court, the case was dismissed.]

Orphans Court of Wash Co, D C. Letters of administration on the personal estate of Lawrence Conroy, [sometimes called Frank Hall,] late of Wash, D C, deceased. -Simon Fennell, adm

Supreme Court of D C, in Equity No 553-Docket 7. D R Hagner vs A M Smith. Trustee reported he sold to Thos W Riley lots 13 thru 16 in sq 355, & lot 11 in an unrecorded subdivision of part of said square, on 11th st, for the sum of $4,351.40, & the purchaser has complied with the terms of sale. –R J Meigs, clerk

Orphans Court of Wash Co, D C, Dec 11, 1866. In the case of John Chandler Smith, adm c t a of Hamilton J Smith, deceased, the administrator c t a & Court have appointed Jan 8, 1867, for the final settlement of the personal estate of the said deceased, of the assets in hand. -Jas R O'Beirne, Reg/o wills

Balt, Dec 13. This morning at the Mount Clare depot, on the Balt & Ohio railroad, in Hooper's shop, while repairing a tank, Robt McKenzie entered a tank with a lamp in his hand, when it exploded, killing him instantly & burning Francis Thompson, in a shocking manner. It is feared Thompson will die. Thos Smith was also badly burned.

The celebrated caricaturist Gavarni, whose real name was Sulpice Paul Chevelier, died in Paris on Nov 24, aged 65 years.

Mrs Julia Thoman, formerly Miss Julia Pelby, a well-known actress, committed suicide at her residence in Cambridge, Mass, Sat, by taking laudanum. She recently returned from professional engagements in Calif.

MON DEC 17, 1866
The wife of Senator Fowler, of Tenn, died here on Friday night.
+
The funeral of Mrs M L Fowler, who died at the Seaton House on Friday last, after a short but painful illness, was held yesterday. She had been an invalid during the latter part of her life, but at times was well enough to attend to her family duties. The exertion made by her for Thanksgiving aggravated her complaint. The funeral service was in the parlor of the Seaton House, due to the inclemency of the weather-they were to have been held at the E st Baptist Church. The remains will be taken to Lexington, Ky, today, for interment in the cemetery at that place.

There is but one Revolutionary pensioner left of that band of patriots to whose persistent courage & sagacious wisdom we are indebted for our freedon, Saml Downing, of Saratoga Co, N Y.

Green & Williams, aucts, sold a portion of the land on the Milk House Ford road, at Piney Branch road, near **Fort Stevens**, belonging to the late Eliz Butler, divided into lots of about 7 acres, as follows: lot 1, to Pierce Shoemaker, for $170.50 per acre; lot 2 to Arch White, for $135 per acre; & lot 3 to Enos Ray, $135 per acre.

Orphans Court-Judge Pursell. 1-Geo Cudewia gave bonds in the sum of $5,000, & was appointed executor of Emma Boscow, deceased. 2-Marlow Falconer gave bond in the sum of $800 as guardian to his minor children.

Criminal Court-Judge Fisher. 1-In the case of Timothy Middleton, indicted for larceny, a nolle pros was entered by the Dist Atty. 2-In the case of Carlo Rederto & Henry Ivill, indicted for larceny, a motion for a new trial was made.

Balt, Dec 16. Hon Silas Morris Cochran, Associate Justice of the Court of Appeals of this State, died here today. Gov Swann has power of appointing a successor until the next State election.

In the Orphans Court of Wash Co, D C. on Sat, the case of Dr G W Woolley vs Henry Whitail, executor of the estate of Martha R Woolley, deceased, was argued at length. It seems that Dr Woolley & Martha R Woolley some years ago made a written agreement in the State of N Y to live together as man & wife. They moved to this city a few years since, & about 4 months ago Mrs Woolley died. She bequeather her personal effects to her sister, & the Doctor protested against the execution of the will on the ground that she had no legal right to dispose of her property in this manner. The dfndnt claims that they were never legally married, & in addition, that the Doctor had a wife at the time the agreement was made between him & the deceased. The court rejected the latter statement, as it was not contained in the answer of the respondent. The case now rests on the legality of the marriage relation. According to the laws of N Y, where the agreement was made, the marriage is valid. Judge Purcell will give his decision tomorrow. Fred Schmidt for petitioner, R S Jackson for respondent. [Dec 19th newspaper: The Judge sustained the petition, & introduced an authority which neither counsel had offered or referred to in this case; 4th Mumford & Hellen, Supreme Court of Va. The Court ruled that as they had lived together as man & wife for years, & acknowledged each other as such, & were so known in all their intercourse with society, living happily together, & that as she had signed this will as Mrs Woolley on her dying bed as the wife of the petitioner, it was not competent for claiming under her to deny the fact; & as there was no evidence to contradict this fact, & as they had offered no evidence to contradict the above facts, he should order that the probate of Martha Woolley should be set aside & the will annulled. Col M Thompson asked for a rehearing of the case.]

Patrick Fitzgerald was arrested on Thu for assaulting & beating Margaret Kingsley, a woman near 70 years of age, & also for assault & battery with intent to kill Thos Ragan, her son-in-law. Fitzgerald struck Ragan with a stone upon his head, indicting a serious, if not mortal wound & struck him also across the loins with a club or ax, severely injuring him. Fitzgerald has been committed for a hearing when Ragan's wounds are known.

Larcenies. 1-Wm J Martin was arrested for larceny of 2 pairs of pants from the store of A Kauffman, Wall's Opera House. The property was found in the possession of the prisoner, who was sent to jail for court. 2-Wm Brown & John Hart, 13 & 15 years of age, were arrested for petty larceny of meat, the property of Wm Hess: they were sent to jail for court. 3-Edw Hoover was arrested as an accomplice in the larceny of the barrel of syrup from Thos M Cassell: held to bail for court. 3-Emanuel Werner was arrested for larceny for various articles of harness, belonging to T T Fowler; the articles were sold to W B Mills, who keeps a junk shop. Werner was sent to jail for court for larceny, & Mills was held to bail for buying the goods. 4-Timothy Regan, Jas Crokes, & Andrew Bowman were arrested for larceny of a chain & collar; they were sent to jail for court.

Rev Geo W Whally, of the Methodist Church South, one of the pioneers of Methodism in the West, died at Urbana, Ohio, on Friday.

Fred'k W Hewitt, who has been found guilty of several confidence operations in the vicinity of Boston, was on Sat sentenced to one year in the House of Corrections.

Phil, Dec 16. The frig **New Ironsides**, once proud & gallant, which during the war of the rebellion, performed such invaluable service, is now a mass of smouldering ruins. Last night a watchman from the iron-clad fleet at League Island, on the Delaware river, near this city, informed the ofcr of the day at the navy yard that the frig was burning. The naval tug **Pilgrim** & the tug **Glance**, under the orders of Capt W H Macomb, U S navy, & a company of marines, under Lt H C Cochrane, U S Marine Corps, were immediately sent to the island, but unable to save her because of strong winds & great headway made by the flames.

The Phil train for N Y, when a little north of that city, ran over a carriage containing a man named Thos Watt, his wife & child. The child was killed, & the wife had her arm & leg broken. Mr Watt was slightly injured.

Last night at the Clark St M E Church, a Roman Catholic priest, Rev Fr Kenny, of Dubuque, arose & formally renounced his faith in presence of the congregation. Fr Kenny will proceed to N Y. –Chicago Tribune, Thu

Orphans Court of Wash Co, D C, Dec 15, 1866. In the case of Mrs Mary Cornelia Cook, exc of Abraham Cook, deceased, the executrix & Court have appointed Jan 5 next, for the final settlement of the personal estate of the said deceased, of the assets in hand. -Jas R O'Beirne, Reg/o wills

Orphans Court of Wash Co, D C, Dec 15, 1866. In the case of Rebecca S Parker, excx of Henry S Parker, deceased, the executrix & Court appointed Jan 5 next, for final settlement of the personal estate of the said deceased, of the assets in hand. -Jas R O'Beirne, Reg/o wills

TUE DEC 18, 1866
Gen Grant has purchased the old Dent homestead, of 280 acres, 10 miles from St Louis.

Rev Stephen Williams, a well-known clergyman of the Presbyterian Church, died on Sat at his residence in Balt, of heart disease, aged nearly 84 years.

Dr J Fales, the oldest resident physician in East Boston, died on Saturday of heart disease, aged 68 years.

Lt Col Jas A Cunningham has been appointed Adj Gen of Mass, in place of Gen Schouler, removed. By law of the last State Legislature, the appointment lasts for one year, & the possessor of it is entitled to the rank of major general.

Died: in Phil, at the residence of her son-in-law, Edw Olmsted, Clarissa Cohen Nisbet, widow of the late Michl Nisbet, of that city, in her 75th year.
[No death date given-current item.]

Died: on Dec 16, Lincoln, infant son of Jas S & Ann M M Topham, aged 1 year, 10 months & 18 days. His funeral will take place on Tue at 2 o'clock, from the residence of his parents, 180 4th st, between L & N Y ave.

Peremptory Pawnbroker sale of unredeemed pledges. Isaac Herzberg & Son, being desirous of closing out their entire stock before the close of the year, will sell without reserve, on Dec 20. -Green & Williams, aucts

Orphans Court of Wash Co, D C, Dec 8, 1866. Ordered, on application, that the admx of Christian H Munck, deceased, sell at public auction, for cash, the personal estate belonging to said deceased. –Jas R O'Beirne, Reg/o Wills
+
In compliance with the above order, I will expose for sale on Dec 22, for cash, the fixtures, stock, tools, & the safe, at the old established stand of the late C H Munck, Gun & Locksmith, 6th st, between Pa ave & Missouri ave.

WED DEC 19, 1866
Navy Bulletin. Detached from Dec 8 to 11. Acting Past Assist Surgeon Thos K Chancler, from Wash NavyYard & ordered to the ship **Penobscot**; 2nd Assist Engineer Henry F Bradford, from the Boston Navy Yard, & ordered to the ship **Aroostook**; Acting Master Nicholas Pratt, from the ship **Ohio**, & granted leave of absence; Lt Cmder W Green, from the ship **Chicopee**, & placed on waiting orders; Acting Masters W W Wood, Saml Very, jr, Acting Ensigns Robt Elder, J A H Willmuth, Acting Assist Surgeon R Smith, & Acting 3rd Assist Engineer D A Bandall, from the ship **Chicopee**, & ordered to the ship **Marblehead**; Cmder W F Spicer, from the command of the **Chicopee**, & placed on waiting orders; Acting Ensign R S M Jones, from the ship **Vermont**, & ordered to the **Penobscot**; 1st Assist Engineer Robt Potts, 2nd Assist Engineers E Sarus, R N Ellis, & 3rd Assist Engineer C F Nagle, from the **Chicopee**, & ordered to the **Marblehead**; Mate J A Belcher, from the **Chicopee**, & order to the ship **Peoria**.
Honorably Discharged, Dec 10. Acting Ensign N G Iverson, from Dec 6.
Resigned, Dec 9. Acting Passed Assist Surgeon John E Parsons, of the **Penobscot**; Assist Paymaster H A Thompson, jr.
Ordered, from Dec 9 to 11. 1st Assist Engineer Louis J Allen to duty at the Naval Rendezvous, Phil; Lt Cmder LeRoy Fitch, to command the **Marblehead**; Assist Paymaster Jos Foster, to the **Marblehead**; Mate Jas Oliver, to the **Peoria**.

Orphans Court-Judge Purcell. 1-The 12th & final account of Catharine E Evans, guardian to the orphan of Evan Evans, deceased, settled. 2-The 2nd & supplemental account of Wm H Baldwin & Edw Baldwin, excs of Henry Clay Baldwin, deceased, was settled.

Brvt Maj A H Smith, surgeon U S army, assigned to duty at Hunt's Island, N Y Harbor.

Criminal Court-Judge Fisher. 1-Wm Linkin was fined $25 for an assault on Catherine Shugrue. 2-Edw Neason, for an assault & battery on John Clancy, with intent to kill, sentenced to 1 year hard labor in the Albany Penitentiary for 2 years. On Dec 2, Neason broke a large pitcher over Clancy's head, & then cut his body with the handle, inflicting a number of ugly but not dangerous wounds. 3-Benj Pickett was sentenced to the Albany Penitentiary for 1 year for stealing a gun. 4-Geo Lanber & Leonard Luber, indicted for an assault & battery, were found not guilty. 5-Ellen Sorrell, indicted for an assault & battery, was found guilty.

Brvt Maj J Howard Carlisle, U S army, died on Dec 16, at the residence of Mrs John L Griffith, near Aberdeen, Harford Co, Md, in the 45th year of his age.

Hon Alex R Boteler, of Va, recently sold 13 acres of land near Shepherdstown, containing water-lime, for $35,000.

Caspar Vanah, a German butcher, was on Monday convicted at Newark, N J, for selling diseased horse meat & fined $25.00.

Chas R Ruh, of Hudson Co, N Y, was sentenced on Monday [the Supreme Court having overruled the objections] to one year in the State prison. Mr Ruh had been convicted of bribery in the Legislature of 1866.

The wife of Senator Conness, of Calif, died at the residence of her parents, in McHenry Co, Ill, on Nov 9, in her 44th year. Mrs Conness had been a confirmed & helpless invalid for a number of years past, & her death was not unexpected by her relatives & friends.

Dept of the Interior, U S Patent Ofc, Wash, Dec 13, 1866. Ptn of Moses Marshall, of Lowell, Mass, praying for the extension of a patent granted to him Mar 15, 1853, for an improvement in Knitting Machines, for 7 years from the expiration of said patent, which taked place on Mar 15, 1867.
–T C Theaker, Com'r of Patents

Dept of the Interior, U S Patent Ofc, Wash, Nov 21, 1866. Ptn of Jas E A Gibbs, of "Steel's Tavern," Va, praying for the extension of a patent granted to him Feb 21, 1860, for an improvement in Design for a Sewing Machine, for 7 years from the expiration of said patent, which takes place on Feb 21, 1867.
–T C Theaker, Com'r of Patents.

Orphans Court of Wash Co, D C. Letters testamentary on the personal estate of Emma Boscow, late of Wash, D C, deceased. –Geo Clendenin, exc

THU DEC 20, 1866
Mrd: on Dec 18, by Rev Wm R Evans, A M, at Dr Gurley's Church, N Y ave, Mr Tolbert Lanston to Miss Bettie Hurdle, both of Gtwn, D C. No cards.

Mrd: on Dec 18, in Wash, D C, by Rev John Vaughn Lewis, John Marshal Brown, of Portland, Maine, to Miss Alda, daughter of the late Hon W T Carroll, of Wash.

Died: on Dec 19, Mrs Emiline Willet, widow of the late Beniah Willet, aged 58 years. Her funeral will be from her late residence, 473 13th st, tomorrow at 2½ o'clock. Waterford [N Y] Sentinel please copy.]

Navy Bulletin for Dec 12. Ordered: Assist Surgeon Fred'k Kr_eker, to the ship **Constellation**; Lt Cmder Wm F Stewart, to the ship **Iroquois**; 2nd Assist Engineer Henderson, at the Boston Navy Yard; 2nd Assist Engineer Wm J Montgomery, to duty as an assist to Chief Engineer King, at the N Y Navy Yard. Detached: Assist Surgeon Adam Fran, from the Navy Asylum at Phil, & ordered to the Naval Hospital at Norfolk, Va; Surgeon Newton L Bates, from the Naval Laboratory at Norfolk, Va, & placed on waiting orders; Assist Surgeon Ernest D Martin, from the **Constellation**, & ordered to the Naval Hosp at N Y; Surgeon Edw S Bogert, from duty at the Naval Hosp at Norfolk, Va, & ordered to the Naval laboratory at N Y. Honorably Discharged: Actg Ensigns Sydney Hall & John Bishop.

Public sale of valuable real estate in Culpeper Co, Va: by decree of the Circuit Court, Nov term, in the suits of Miller & others vs Miller & others, & Barbour, etc, vs Barbour, etc: public auction of the Farm of which Henry Miller, deceased, died possessed, known as *Fleetwood*, containing 1,500 acres. This is one of the finest farms in the State of Va. -J Y Menefee, J C Gibson, Com'rs

Catherine Bexford has recovered $7,500 in an action against a N Y horse railroad for the loss of one of her limbs by the negligence of one of defendents' conductors in starting the car while she was getting into it, & thus causing the injury which compelled the amputation of the limb.

Boots & Shoes-new store. Geo B Wilson, 502 7th st, under Odd Fellows Hall. The New Cheap Store, formerly K F Page's store.

Supreme Court of D C; in Equity no 1,471, Docket 6. The Potomac Ins Co vs Chas H Van Patten et al. J Carter Marbury, trustee, sold lot 1 in square 174 to Jas W Reddick, for the sum of $605; & lots 2 thru 6 in same square, to Wm B Todd, for $2,659.51; the purchasers have complied with the terms of sale.
–R J Meigs, clerk

FRI DEC 21, 1866
Boston, Dec 20. Fred'k Marsh, a well-known newspaper man, died today from the rupture of a blood vessel.

Criminal Court-Judge Fisher. 1-Geo Rollins guilty of assault & battery with intent to kill Peter Duffey: sentenced to the Albany penitentiary for 5 years. In a case of robbery he was convicted & sentenced to 3 years in addition to the sentence above. 2-Edw Letcher, a colored soldier, was arraigned on the charge of assault with intent to kill Ofcr David J Cunningham, of Gtwn, on Oct 31 last, by Letcher & Thos Giston, also a colored soldier, but who failed to appear for trial. Letcher remanded to jail. [Dec 22nd newspaper: Letcher: the jury was out but a few minuted & returned a verdict of guilty. G H Day, counsel for the prisoner gave notice that he would file a petition for a new trial.]

Memphis, Dec 19. The confectionery establishment of Jos Specht, 3 Madison st, took fire & about 25 persons were asleep in the 3rd & 4th stories of the bldg. Fourteen persons were suffocated in their rooms, or lost their lives by leaping from the windows. The killed were: Wm Jehle & wife, the latter a daughter of Mr Specht, both suffocated; Wm C Honke, killed by leaping from a window; Frank Rudelhulber, a German pastrycook; Mucinda Ringwold, colored, & 2 children; a German cook named Philip; Dolly Flint, colored; John German, confectioner; Fred A French, cook; one white & one colored man, both waiters, & a colored woman, name unknown. An infant child of Mr & Mrs Jehle was found alive in the room with them, the only one saved of those remaining in the room. Mr Specht saved himself by tying curtains together & climbing down the balustrade on the 2nd floor. Jos Barthol jumped from the 4th story into a mudhole in the alley & saved his life. Mr Walter & clerk leaped from the 4th story & caught on a window shutter of the 3rd story, where they held themselves until rescued by the firemen. [Dec 24th newspaper: Mrs Yarbry, mother of Mrs Jehle, Miss Sallie Lee, & 2 children, owe their lives to the firemen; Mr Jos Barthol was hurt but no danger to his life; Victor Scwarburg, bookkeeper, & Louis Correll, salesman, escaped by the ladder, assisted by the firemen. Mr Wm Jehle was about 25 years old, came to Memphis from St Louis about 3 years ago, & had been married over 2 years; his wife, Nannie J, was about 18 years old, raised in Memphis; Atienne Tres, a Frenchman, a cook, came here from St Louis a few months ago, & leaves a wife & 2 children in that city; he lived at 1562 Colondalett ave, & was the son-in-law of a gentleman named Kline. Augustus Mienhauser was quite a young man, & was the only support of an old & blind mother. Augustus will be well remembered as a newsboy a few years ago. J C Huck, was once a fireman, & his death was a terrible one indeed; finding himself enveloped in hot smoke, he jumped from the 4th story. Mr Hauck's wife died on Sep 10 last, & he leaves 3 small children friendless in the world. Frank Ridlehuber has some relatives in Chelsea. Mr & Mrs Jehle were in a room in the 3rd story, & Capt Phil Teaffe ordered his ladder to that point, & Will Crosby mounted up to the rescue. The smoke was so hot that he had to retire. Mr Waldraven went up & reached the couple, but fell powerless, Mrs Jehle being too heavy for the strength of the fireman. Her babe, about 5 weeks old, was taken to safety. Mr Jehle expired before he got to the ground.

Naylor-Naylor. Mrd: on Dec 20, at the residence of the bride's father, by Rev Mr M L Olds, Thos I Naylor to Lizzie P S, eldest daughter of Col M Naylor.

Post Ofc Dept: the Postmaster Gen has made the following changes since Dec 16: Md-Upper Trappe, Somerset Co, H T Toadvine, vice W F Allen, resigned. Va: Berryville, Clark Co, C Bowson, vice G W Koonce, resigned; Aspen Wall, Charlotte Co, R A Baldwin, vice Mrs S E Morrison, resigned; Irisburg, Henry Co, R A Major, vice J H Wade, failed to bond. West Va: Graham Station, Marion Co, E C Hopkins, vice J H Rider, resigned; Mercer's Bottom, Mason Co, J M Hanley, vice J S Hanley, resigned; Anderson's Store, Lewis Co, W H McNulty, vice J Anderson, resigned; Lindside, Monroe Co, C McNeer, vice Mrs J M Ballard, ineligible. Minn: Young America, Carver Co, L B Brant, vice J Slocum, jr, removed; Farmington, Dakota Co, J E Andrews, vice N E Slack, resigned; Lakeville, Dakota Co, G F Ackley, vice D C Johnson, removed; Alexandria, Douglas Co, R F Caving, vice R Wynan, removed; Winnebago City, Fairbault Co, C A Cottrell, vice G K Moulton, removed; Chatfield, Fillmore Co, W L Bailey, vice M McLarty, removed; Freeborn, Freeborn Co, D Southwick, vice J Boward, removed; Albert Lea, Freeborn Co, F B Forbes, vice S Eaton, removed; Moscow, Freeborn Co, J Dysslin, vice E Morgan, removed; Pine Island, Goodhue Co, S S Worthing, vice C R White, removed; Torah, Stearns Co, H Broker, vice H Brunning, removed; Lake City, Wabashaw Co, M R Merrill, vice E Porter, removed.

Miles Greenwood appointed treasurer of Hamilton Co, Ohio, vice Gen Parry, deceased.

Oil has been struck in the neighborhood of Munson's Hill, Va. Josiah Milliard, of Alexandria, has discovered surface indications of oil on his farm near Manassas.

Orphans Court of Wash Co, D C. In the case of Walter S Cox, adm w a of Jas R Young, deceased, the administrator & Court have appointed Jan 5 next, for the final settlement of the personal estate of the said deceased, of the assets in hand. -Jas R O'Beirne, Reg/o wills

SAT DEC 22, 1866
Mrd: on Dec 19, in Staunton, Va, by Rev Jas Latane, Jos D McGuire, of Howard Co, Md, to Anna, daughter of Alfred Chapman, of Staunton, Va.

Died: on Dec 19, in Wash City, Hattie Ashton, wife of Strafford Evans. Her funeral will be from her late residence, on Dec 22, at 12 o'clock.

The Com'r of Pensions yesterday made the following appointments of examining surgeons of pensioners: Dr Philip P Silvernail; Candon, Ind; Dr Jas H McGrew, Shelbyville, Tenn; Dr Wesley Wright, Stockbridge, Mich, & Dr Henry B Johnson, of Bel__t, Wisc.

F W Bennet & Co Peremptory sale of valuable lands in Allegany Co, Md: Glade Lands, Timber, Coal, & Mineral Lands: public auction on Jan 17th next, at the Exchange sales room, in Balt City:
Lochiel, 5,980¾ acres
Common Sense: 1,279 acres
Residue of the **Rights of Man**, 2,251 acres
Residue of **Park**: 1,607 acres
Riverside: 312½ acres
Addition to **Paradise**: 1,472 acres
Residue of **Paradise**: 587½ acres
Residue of **Chance**: 658 acres.
Residue of the **Royal Charlotte**: 1,362½ acres
Resurvey on **Kindness**: 1,817½ acres.
Stony Ridge: 388½ acres
Part of the **Promised Land Resurveyed**: 85 acres
Milk & Honey: 2,756 acres
Herrington Manor: 2,307 acres
[**Herrington Manor**-part whereof will be reserved by the owner]
White Oak Point: 286 acres
The **Oak & Farm**, including **Mount Oakland**: 481½ acres
Six **Soldiers' Lots**, 2,611, 2,612, 2,613, 2,614, 1,110, & 1,763, each containing 50 acres.
Part of **Republic**: 2,171 acres
Parts of tracts called **Park**, First Part of **Rights of Man**, 2 pieces of the tract **Pink Allegany**, & **Soldiers' Lots** 1,782, & 3,021, the whole of which tract is fully described in a deed from Benj Stoddert & Wm Marbury to Robt Oliver, John Alton, & Jas McHenry, dated on or about Mar 4, 1808, & recorded among the land records of Allegany Co, & contains about 2,959 acres.
Soldiers' Lots 3,882,32,884, 3,885, 3,886, 2,018, 2,109, 11,755, 2,022, 3,833, containing each 50 acres.
The titles are indisputable & every parcel will be sold free from any incumbrances. **Lochiel** is represented to contain the finest body of timber in the State. **Common Sense**, **Rights of Man**, & the **Park**, are all heavily timbered. Addition to **Paradise**, **Riverside**, **Chance**, & **Royal Charlotte**, lie on & near the Northwestern Va Turnpike. **Milk & Honey** & **Herrington Manor** are universally conceded to be the finest estates in the Glades. **Stony Ridge** is rough, but is valuable for its timber & coal. **White Oak Point** is well timbered. The sale will be continued from day to day.
As owner of the property, I add this note to say that the sale is advertised as peremptory with my consent. I had hoped that I would have been able, within a period designated by myself, to pay off all liens & emcumbrances. As that period has elapsed, & some of the creditors are urgent for payment of their claims, I have no right to object to an immediate sale-to such extent, at least, as may be necessary to satisfy all claims. I may possibly be in error as to the real value of this property, but I believe most confidently that it is the most desirable property in Md for profitable investment. –Wm Schley

Dept of the Potomac: Brvt Brig Gen J M Schofield has added the counties of Southampton, Isle of Wight, Nansemon, Norfolk, & Princess Anne to the District of *Fortress Monroe*, Brvt Brig Gen H S Burton commanding. Brvt Maj Gen Geo Stoneman, colonel 21st U S infty, has been assigned to command the District of Petersburg, to comprise that part of Va which lies west of the James river, & is not embraced in the Districts of Lynchburg & *Fortress Monroe*. Headquarters at *Fortress Monroe*. Col O B Wilcox, 29th U S infty, has been assigned to the command of the District of Lynchburg, comprising the counties of Bath, Rockbridge, Amherst, Appomattox, Campbell, & Pittsylvania. Headquarters at Lynchburg. The following ofcrs now comprise Gen Schofield's staff: Brvt Col S F Chaflin, A A G; Brvt Brig Gen A P Blunt, chief quartermaster; Brvt Col Geo B H __, chief commissary of subsistence; Brvt Col Geo Gibson, jr, A A inspector general; Brvt Maj C E Layton, acting judge advocate; Brvt Maj Edw R Perry, commissary of musters; & 1st Lts J S Rathbone & Wm Ennis, aides de camp.

Navy Bulletin for Dec 14. Ordered: Assist Paymaster A W Bacon, to the ship **Aroostook**. Placed on Furlough: Paymaster Thos C Marten. Appointment Revoked: Acting 3rd Assist Engineer Jas H Sleeper, of the ship **Penobscot**. Detached: 1st Assist Engineer Robt Potts, from the Naval School, & placed on waiting orders; Surgeon Wm S King, from Hartford, placed on sick leave of absence.

Mustered out: Hospital Stewards Henderson, Hayward, & Henry W Heartt, U S A, have been mustered out of service by order of the Sec or War.

The largest Confectionery Establishment, 466 Pa ave, between 3rd & 4½ sts, north side, Wash City. –S Simmons

Died: on Dec 20, after a short illness, Henrietta, beloved wife of Thos M Cassell, & the youngest daughter of Lazareth & Henrietta Wetzel, in her 26th year. Her funeral will be Dec 22 at 9 o'clock, from her late residence, C st south, between 6th & 7th sts west.

Obit-died: on Dec 11, Addie Padgett, only daughter of Mrs Adelaide R & the late Jonathan T Padgett, in Port Tobacco, within a few days of the 7th year of her age. Lovely in life, lovely in death, she is an angel in Heaven.

MON DEC 24, 1866
Green & Williams, aucts, sold a 4 story brick dwlg house, 12th & G sts, to O Tweedy, for $10,000; a 4 story brick dwlg on G st, between 12th & 13th, to Julia E Waters, for $7,000; 2 frame dwlgs on Wash st, for $1,000 & $800, to A T Donn.

Green & Williams, aucts, sold a 4 story brick dwlg house, 12th & G sts, to O Tweedy, for $10,000; a 4 story brick dwlg on G st, between 12th & 13th, to Julia E Waters, for $7,000; 2 frame dwlgs on Wash st, for $1,000 & $800, to A T Donn.

Orphans Court-Judge Purcell. 1-The fourth & final account of Andrew Rothwell, exc of Eliza Henning, deceased, was settled. 2-The will of Josephine Follansbee was received, but there being a caveat filed against the same, it was postponed. 3-The will of Jacob Snyder, deceased, was fully proven, & letters testamentary were issued to Fred'k Volk, who, upon giving bond in the sum of $4,000, was appointed executor. 4-The question of rehearing the case of the late Martha R Woolly, which was annulled on the last court day, on the ground of the testatrix being a married woman & having no separate estate, was argued by Mr Thompson for the executor, & by F Schmidt for Dr Woolly, the court reserving his decision until the first Saturday in January.

Naval Bulletin for Dec 15. Ordered-Passed Assist Surgeon D R Bannan to duty in the N Y Navy Yard. Miscellaneous-the unexecuted portion of the sentence of a naval general court martial, in the case of Capt Richd W Meade, has been remitted, & he is placed on waiting orders.

In the fight with the Sioux Indians, near **Fort Phil Kearny**, Dec 6, Lt H S Bingham, 2nd U S cavalry, & Sgt Bowen, 18th infty, were killed, & Sgt Aldridge & 4 privates of the 18th infty were wounded.

Gtwn affair: during the war the porperty of Richd S Cox, near Gtwn, was taken possession of by the managers of the Home for Colored Women & Children, by direction of the Sec of War-the owner then being in the South. After his return, he was pardoned, & commenced proceedings & succeeded in regaining possession, the managers of the Home, with their proteges, leaving the premises. The managers, during their occupancy, obtained from the Gov't, through the Quartermaster Gen, it is said, the use of certain lumber & other materials, with which they constructed a temporary frame bldg adjoining the brick mansion. Friday, Gen O O Howard, of the Freedmen's Bureau, issued an order to have this frame structure torn down, & the materials, the property of the Gov't, removed to Wash City, & to use military force to carry out the order if necessary. T C Collins, formerly in the military service & now a Gov't agent, was sent to execute this order, & employed Mr Edw J Shoemaker, a carpenter & bldr of Gtwn, to tear down the bldg. In the afternoon they commenced work, & took out the doors & windows & removed the roof. Mr Shoemaker was arrested on the charge of trespassing, on a warrant issued by Justice Buckey, on Friday night, & at the instance of Mr Wm H Rohrer, the agent of Mr Cox. Mr Shoemaker stated that he was employed by Mr Collins, when Mr Rohrer also had a warrant issued for his arrest, charging him with forcibly & maliciously breaking open the dwlg house, & bldg attached, of Richd S Cox, & carrying away a part of the same. The case will come up today before Justice Buckey.

Prof Henry Vethake, LL D, of the Polytechnic College, died on Sunday, at his residence in this city, after a short illness, in his 75th year. –Phila Ledger

T Ellicott, one of the most esteemed merchants of Balt, died on Sat.

In the Senate of the U S yesterday, Mr Wade presented a petition of J W Phelps, for the reannexation of Alexandria Co to the Dist of Columbia. He states he has been for many years an owner of real estate in the city & county of Alexandria, & has no confidence in the administation of law & justice in the State of Va, & therefore prays for the restoration of said city & county to the Dist of Columbia, from which it has, as he believes, been violently & unconstitutionally disserved. That Mr Phelps is a non-resident of this city is evident from the fact of his being unaware of some of the late verdicts rendered in our courts. —Alex Gaz, 17th.

Trustee's sale of land in St Mary's Co, by decree of the Circuit Court there, in Equity, in the case of G K Kane vs Jas B Thomas: sale on Jan 2, 1867, at the Court House door, in Leonardtown, a Farm called *Point of Hampstead*, containing 228¼ acres, lying in *Cedar Point*, on Chesapeake Bay, adjoining the lands of Messrs Thompson & Carroll & Col John D Freeman. It has a comfortable dwlg & other necessary bldgs. –A B Hagner, trustee -Annapolis, Dec 3, 1866.

Trustee's sale of valuable improved real estate, by deed of trust made by Job W Angus to Chas H Winder, dated Jul 22, 1865, recorded in Liber R M H, No 9, folios 63 etc, to secure the payment of a promissory note drawn by said Angus in favor of Sarah Edelin, & by her endorsed, bearing even date with said deed of trust, for $6,000, with interest from date till paid. Public auction on Jan 8 next, of lots 13 thru 18 in square 625, according to Jos S Cabot's subdivision thereof, with a commodious frame dwlg & gardener's house thereon, also frame.
–Ch H Winder, trustee -J C McGuire & Co, aucts

Eliza Newton, the N Y actress, has married an Englishman of rank.

Bjursten, the famous German song writer, lately committed suicide.

Supreme Court of D C, in Equity, No 671, Docket 8. H Sidney Everett et al vs Helen C Everett et al. The trustee reported he sold lot 8 & 9, & west half of lot 10, in square 169, with improvements, to Chas Knap, who has assigned the same to Henry A Wise, for $18,750, & that he has complied with the terms of sale.
–R J Meigs, clerk

TUE DEC 25, 1866
Yesterday Mr Jos T Walker, superintendent of the burial corps under Col Moore, died at his father's residence, Montg & Olive sts, & it was supposed to be cholera. Mr Walker was very highly esteemed by his numerous acquaintances in Gtwn.

John Clare, charged with the murder of H B Grove, photographer, in Balt a year ago, was on Thu convicted of murder in the first degree by the court at Towsontown, Balt Co, Md.

Sunday night the 13 year old daughter of Mr W H Hollingsworth, residing on Va ave, near 7th, died from the effects of medicine giver her. She complained of severe pain in her side and the family physician, Dr A W Miller prescribed for her. The prescription was put up at the drug store of Jas Walsh. She took the medicine & died in a few hours. Dr Miller, in writing out the prescription, the chief ingredient of which should have been one drachm elixir of opium, not an officinal prepartion, but known as McMann's preparation of opium, & recognized by the medical profession for its soothing qualitles. The Dr in writing the prescription abreviated the world "elixir," as he claims "exl," but the son of Dr JasWalsh read it "ext" & so compounded it. Dr Miller admitted that it was the extract that caused the child's death, but claimed the drug clerk should have read it elixir. [Dec 27th newspaper: Jos Walsh, M D, states that neither he nor his son had anything to do with this sad occurrence. I never attended the young lady or even knew of her sickness. –Jos Walsh, M D, 403 E st south, Navy Yard.]

Died: on Dec 19, in Phil, Mrs Eliz Vermillion, relict of the late Richd Vermillion, formerly of Norfolk, Va. Norfolk & Portsmouth papers please copy.

Stephen Elliot, Bishop of Georgia, died at his residence in Georgia, on Friday. He died doubtlessly died from heart disease. He was born in Beaufort, S C, in 1806; graduated at Harvard College in 1824; was ordained a deacon of the Protestant Episcopal Church in 1835, & a priest in the following year. He was elected Bishop of the diocese of Georgia, & in Feb, 1841, was consecrated. He was age 60 years at the time of his death.

Balt, Dec 24. 1-Geo Kohler fell into the dock this evening & was accidentally drowned. 2-The death of Justice Cochran was announced in the Court of Appeals, at Annapolis, on Sat.

Trustee's sale of valuable improved property & water power, near Gtwn, D C, at auction: by deed of trust from John S Berry & Co to the subscriber, dated Feb 23, 1856, recorded in Liber J A S No 111, folio 303, amongst the records in D C: public auction, on the premises, on Jan 17 next, that portion of the old Foundry property lying west of Gtwn, situated between the Chesapeake & Ohio canal, & the Potomac river, [excepting, however, the section including the two stone mills assigned to D L Shoemaker & Brother, by articles of agreement recorded amongst said records in Liber J A S No 147, folio 305, & the extreme eastern angle conveyed by John Corcoran, by deed recorded in Liber J A S No 203, folio 35.] There is upon the property to be sold a very valuable Distillery & fixtures, with good water power from the canal, as well as from the stream known as Mill Branch. I will also sell, by deed of trust from John Ehrmantraut to the subscriber made Dec 13, 1858, all that part of the original Foundry property lying north of said canal. –Hugh Caperton, trustee -Thos Dowling, auct

Griffin Taylor, a prominent citizen of Connecticut, died on Saturday.

On May 19, 1854, & May 16, 1857, 38 pieces of U S Revolutionary land bounty scrip, Nos 4,673 to 4,703, both inclusive, & Nos 8,158 to 8,164 both inclusive, amounting in the aggregate of 2,666 2/3 acres, were issued by the Dept of the Interior, under the act of Congress of Aug 31, 1852, in satisfaction of Va military land warrants Nos 8,913, 8,914, 8,932, 8,933, & 9,591, granted for the services of John Carson, a lt in the Va Continental Line in the War of the Revolution; & whereas all of said scrip was stolen from one John McCulloch, the agent of the heirs of said Lt John Carson, deceased, & has not been recovered, & is therefore lost to said heirs. On Feb 21, 1867, application will be made to the Com'r of the Gen Land Ofc, at Wash City, D C, for the issue of certified copies in lieu of said stolen & lost scrip was issued, & the present lawful owner of a part thereof. –Chas S Bekem, for self & other heirs of Lt John Carson, deceased.

All the jurors in the trial of Mollie Trussell have signed a petition to the Govn'r for her pardon. The judge & the prosecuting atty refused to sign it.

THU DEC 27, 1866

Navy Bulletin for Dec 18 & 19. Ordered: Actig Mstr F N Prayer, to the ship **De Sota**; 1st Assist Engr Henry B Nones, to the ship **Iroquois**; Cmder C P Williams, to temporary ord duty at Boston Navy Yard; Gunner A F Thompson, to ord duty at the N Y Navy Yard; Actg 3rd Assist Engr J H Chesney, to the **Iroquois**; Actg 3rd Assist Engr Chas H Enggren, to the ship **Sorrel**. Honorably Discharged: Actg Assist Surg Alex'r Mackenzie. Detached: Acting Mstr C H Brantingham, from duty at N Y Navy Yard, & granted leave of absence; Assist Paymaster A W Bacon, from the ship **Aroostook**, & ordered to the ship **Marblehead**; Ensign Wm A Eilliot, from the ship **Rhode Island**, & ordered to the ship **Huron**; Assist Surg Robt A Whedon, from duty at the Naval Hospital at N Y, & ordered to duty at the Naval Rendezvous, N Y; Cmder J C P De Kraft, from ord duty at the Phil Navy Yard, & placed on waiting orders; 2nd Assist Engr W W Heaton, from special duty at N Y, & ordered to the **Iroquois**; Actg 2nd Assist Engr A M Clements, from the ship **Ascutney**, & ordered to the ship **Nina**; 2nd Assist Engr Minor N Knowlton, from special duty at the N Y Navy Yard, ordered to the **Iroquois**; Actg Ensign Wm F Kilgore, from duty at the Norfolk Navy Yard, ordered to the **Nina**; Actg 2nd Assist Engr Jas H Finn, from the ship **Sorrel**, & ordered to the **Huron**; Gunners Thos Robinson, Jos Swift, & Stephen Young, from duty at Norfolk Navy Yard, & placed on waiting orders; Gunner Geo W Oxenseller, from ord duty at the Phil Navy Yard, & placed on waiting orders; Gunner Peter Barrett, from ord duty at the Boston Navy Yard, & placed on waiting orders; Gunners Geo L Albro & Jas Hutchinson, from ord duty at Norfolk Navy Yard, & placed on waiting orders; Gunner Jas Hays, from ord duty at Jefferson Barracks, Mo, & placed on waiting orders; Actg 3rd Assist Eng Peter Smith, from ship **Michigan**, & ordered to the **Huron**. [ord-ordnance/engr-engineer]

Phil, Dec 26. Horace Martin, a well known newspaper editor & telegraph correspondent died in this city on Sunday. He was highly esteemed, & his loss is deeply lamented.

Maj Gen Sheridan, commanding the Dept of the Gulf, announces the following names of persons deserving of honorable mention for faithful & meritorious services rendered in the Sedgwick U S Gen Hospital, near New Orleans, as nurses & attendants during the prevalence of cholera there: Robt Tinker, citizen employe; Stephen Van Norman, private Co E, 6th U S cavalry; Geo Cahill, hospital steward, & Chas Ayre, citizen employe.

Yesterday as Private Jos Williams was going his rounds, he noticed two suspicious characters, & ordered them to stop. As he was walking toward them, one of them fired at the ofcr, the ball striking a button of his coat. Ofcr Shea, hearing the report of the pistol, found Ofcr Williams lying on the sidewalk in an helpless condition. He was taken to the residence of Fr McCarthy, of the Church of the Immaculate Conception. Surgeons Dorsey & Prentiss were called & they dressed the wound, & he was removed to his home, on 8th st, near E. Ofcr Shea is a married man, with a family of small children. The ball has not been extracted, & it is impossible to tell where it has lodged.

The Sec of the Interior received yesterday a telegram announcing the death, by apoplexy, at Council Bluffs, of Gen Saml R Curtis, one of the com'rs appointed to inspect the finished work upon the Union Pacific railroad. Gen Curtis was born in Ohio, Feb 3, 1807, while his parents were emigrating Westward from Conn. He graduated at the U S Military Academy at West Point in 1831, & was appointed a lt of infty, but resigned in 1832. He studied & practised law in Ohio, but subsequently devoted himself to engineering in Ohio & Iowa, & from 1837 till 1840 was engineer in charge of the Muskingum Works. During the Mexican war he commanded one of the regts of the Ohio volunteers. He was elected to the 36 & 37th Congress. He left his seat to accept the position of brig gen of volunteers, & served in Mo & Ark, & was made maj gen.

Col J M Moore, A Q M, in charge of the U S burial corps, & recently from Saulsbury, N C, obtained the record of the Union prisoners who died at this place during the war, as well as a part of those who died in Florence & Columbia, S C, & a partial list of those who died at Richmond, in all about 5,000 names. This information the Col got from various sources, mainly from surgeons & ofcrs of the Confederate army. These records are invaluable aids, as they will be received as such, & enable those who have back pay & bounty falling to them to collect the same. Many who had been recorded as missing will be found on this list.

Mr Augustus Wells, a citizen of East Pipe Run township, Pa, a few days since came to his death by poison alleged to have been administered by Mrs Mary E Crum_onie, an adopted daughter of the deceased. She was arrested & is in the Wash Co jail awaiting trial.

Eliz Williams, who resided in First st, Brooklyn, was seized in the machinery at Patterson's saw mill, on Monday, & mutilated in such a shocking manner, that her life was immediately crushed out.

Fort Laramie, Dec 26. A terrible massacre is reported to have occurred on Dec 22, near ***Fort Phil Kearney***. Brvt Col Filleman, Capt Brown, & Lt Grammond, of the 18th infty, with 80 enlisted men of the 2nd cavalry & 18th infty, were surrounded by Indians, & every ofcr & man killed. [Dec 29th newspaper: Reports confirm the massacre of 3 ofcrs of the U S army & 91 men near ***Fort Phil Kearney***, [not ***Fort Laramie***, as has been stated.] Col H B Carrington, who commands at ***Fort Phil Kearney***, telegraphs to Gen Grant that his men were attacked near the fort by about 3,000 Indians, who succeeded in killing Brvt Lt Col Fetterman, Capt H H Brown, & Lt Grummond, with 91 privates. After the massacre Col Carrington succeeded in recovering & bringing to the fort all the bodies.]

On Dec 11, Lt Egbert Olcutt, of the 29th U S infty, shot Private Geo King, Co D, of the same regt, through the head with a revolver, while on the road from Yorktown to Warwick Court House, killing him instantly. King had been ordered by Col Shipman to be the driver. Olcutt, after drinking freely, wanted a negro they saw on the road, who knew the way to Warwick, to drive. King refused to let him. Olcutt shot King so close to the head that his face blackened. The murdered man was dragged to the side of the road, his head beaten with rails, & his jugular vein severed with a knife. As thus he lay he was buried.

Saml P Hanes, an old resident of Richmond, died on Monday.

Lt H H Wilson, 6th U S cavalry, son of Senator Wilson, of Mass, died on Monday at Austin, Texas.

Col R A Wainright, of the U S ordnance corps, committed suicide at Benecia Barracks, San Francisco, on Sunday.

New Orleans: Miss Dora Hendricks, a young lady of unusual beauty, who boarded in the family of Mr McLinn, & was attending school in the city, was struck behind the ear with a blunt instrument, from the effects of which she died.

Trustee's sale, by decree of the Circuit Court for PG Co, in Equity, passed in the cause of Jas B Dodson & others vs John T Fenwick, adm de bonus non of John F Carter & others, I will expose to public sale, at the late residence of the said Carter, on Jan 15 next, ***Melrose***, the tract of land which he died seized & possessed, containing about 199 acres. Also, a parcel of land adjoining containing about 12 acres. Also a tract of land containing about 125 acres. ***Melrose*** is about 2 miles from Hyattsville Station; & the improvements consist of a first class frame dwlg & a commodious barn. –N C Stephen, trustee

FRI DEC 28, 1866
Phil, Dec 27. John Logan, about 35, was instantly killed this morning by the falling of a wall while engaged in tearing out the burned bldg at 12th & Market sts.

Navy Bulletin for Dec 20. Detached. Assist Paymaster J Appleton Berry, from the ship **Suwanee**, on the reporting of his relief, & ordered North; Passed Assist Paymaster F G Painter, from the ship **Tuscorora**, on the reporting of his relief, & ordered North; 3rd Assist Engineer Henry C Christopher, from special duty connected with the ship **Franklin**, & granted sick leave of absence; Paymaster Chas W Abbott, from duty as member of the Board of which Paymaster Pettit is president, & placed on waiting orders; Acting 3rd Assist Enginer Pliney H Fales, from the ship **Michigan**, & ordered to temporary duty on board the ship **Chattanooga**; Mate Geo Rogers, from the ship **Potomac**, & order North. Resigned: Mate Richd W Wallace, of Ohio. Ordered: Passed Assist Paymaster M B Cushing, to the **Suwanee**; Passed Assist Paymaster G W Brown, to the **Tuscorcra**; Acting 1st Assist Engineer Chas W Penington, to temporary duty on board the **Franklin**. Miscellaneous: Paymater J D Murray will perform duty as a member of the Examining Board, of which Paymaster Pettit is president, in addition to his current duties.

Balt, Dec 27. Jas Glosson has been arrested at Wmsport, Md, charged with killing Clinton Rench, of that place, in the spring of 1861. The difficulty grew out of politics. Glosson was a Unionist, served in the army during the war, & since its close has been living at Wmsport. He has been released on bail.

Criminal Court-Judge Fisher. 1-Edw Miles, convicted of larceny & sentenced to Albany penitentiary for 1 year. 2-Henry Knorr, convicted of an asault & battery, the motion for a new trial was overruled, & he was sentenced to pay a fine of $10. 3-Amanda Matthews, was convicted of keeping a bawdy house & sentenced to 6 days in jail. 4-Emila Dorsey was convicted of a like offense & received a similar sentence. 5-Phillip Lancaster alias Chas Ford, indicted for larceny, was convicted. 6-Saml Dyson, indicted for an assault & battery with intent to kill Cecilla Williams, was found guilty of an assault & battery, & sentenced to 5 days in jail. 7-Richd Tinsley, was found not guilty of larceny. 8-Stephen Washington & Levi Butler, were convicted of larceny & sentenced to 1 year each in the penitentiary. 9-A nolle pros was entered in the case of Fanny Hall, indicted for larceny.

Police Items. 1-Josephine Lawrence, colored was arrested for selling liquor without a license: fined $21.87. 2-August Koch, a German restaurant keeper was arrested & charged with keeping his bar open on Sunday for the sale of liquors: fined $28.50. 3-Francis Butler was arrested for a similar offence: fined $21.27. 4-Rebecca Harris, a negro servant, was arrested upon complaint of Mrs Jane Field, charging her with petit larceny. She was committed to jail for court.

Orphans Court of Wash Co, D C., Dec 22, 1866. In the case of Frances Blanchard, excx of Valentine Blanchard, deceased, the executrix & Court have appointed Jan 19, 1867, for the final settlement of the personal estate of the said deceased, of the assets in hand. -Jas R O'Beirne, Reg/o wills

Chancery sale of brick house & store at N & 4th st; by decree of Supreme Court of D C, in cause 665, in Equity, docket 7, wherein Wm M Galt is cmplnt & Frank J O'Brien & others dfndnts: public auction on Jan 9, the leasehold estate for 99 years from Jan 1, 1864, in part of lot 26 in square 513, in Wash City; improved by a comparatively new Brick House, with Store & back bldg.
–W Y Fendall, trustee -Jas C McGuire & Co, aucts

Jesse Murphy, the well known proprietor of Jackson Park trotting Course, was murdered on Christmas Day, at the Chesterfield Park, in Chesterfield Co. When Murphy found there was some difficulty as to whether or not the race would come off, he began cursing everybody generally. Jos Kelly remonstrated with him, when Murphy informed him he could whip his or any other scoundrel on the ground. Kelly drew his pistol, fired, the shot taking effect in Murphy's back. As Murphy turned, Kelly again fired. He then dealt him several severe blows upon his head & face with the butt of his pistol. Kelly was arrested at an early hour of the evening. He was committed to the jail of Chesterfield to await a further examination.

There seems to be no longer room for doubt that M Danl E Setchell has perished at sea. Nearly a year has elapsed since he sailed from San Francisco, bound to Auckland, New Zealand, where he made an engagement to play. The actor left on the vessel **Trieste**, an old craft. Mr Setchell was about 30 years of age. Peace be with him, wheresoever he rests. –N Y Tribune

Supreme Court of D C: 429 Equity Docket 7. Catharine Dyer vs Edw C Dyer, Geo F Dyer, John I Dyer & Josephine Dyer, John C Dyer & Robt Dyer, heirs at law of Robt W Dyer. The bill states that the late Edw Dyer, of Wash City, D C, in his lifetime, to wit; Jan 9, 1845, made his deed of trust of that date, where he conveyed in fee to Robt W Dyer, since dead, lot 7 in square 305, fronting on 12th st, with bldgs & improvements, upon the following trusts: First: That if, at any time therafter, Richd H Dyer, one of the children of John R Dyer, deceased, [the said Richd, from his long absence from D C, being presumed to be dead,] should personally appear in Wash City & claim of said Edw Dyer, or his heirs or personal reps, any portion of his father's estate, that the said Robt or his heirs, or his, the said Richd so appearing in proper person, & making such claim, & on his executing to the said Edw Dyer & his heirs, a receipt in full for his share of said estate, shall by a valid deed release & convey the aforesaid lot with the bldgs & premises unto him, the said Richd H Dyer, & his heirs in fee simple. Upon further trust, until such time to hold said lot in substance for the use of the cmplnt, during her natural life, with power to the cmplnt to dispose of the same in fee by last will & testament, & in default of such will or testament, then to the heirs at law of said cmplnt, subject, in either case, however, to the above mentioned claim of the said Richd H Dyer, & so also in trust to receive rents & profits & pay over the same, less taxes & charges, to said cmplnt, her devisees or heir, subject to said

Richd's aforesaid claims. The bill further charges that a long time ago, in the lifetime of said Edw, & long before he executed said deed of Jan 9, 1845, the said Richd wrote a letter to said Robt W Dyer, requesting & directing said Edw to pay over to the cmplnt for her own use absolutely, said Richd's share of his father's, John R Dyer-estate, then or to coaxe into the hands of said Edw & which said letter was seen & read by his widow, now Mrs Henrietta H Boone, that after her first husband's [said Edw Dyer] death the said letter, with other papers not thought material to be preserved, was destroyed by Mrs Boone, which facts are attested by the affidavit of Mrs Boone attached to the bill. The letter & its contents had also been made known to cmplnt's brother, Edw C Dyer, in the lifetime of their uncle, the said Edw Dyer. The bill charges that the letter was a gift to complainant of her brother Richd's share of his father's estate, & a valid assignment to her of the same, which the said Edw Dyer was bound to recognize & obey, & entitled her to stand in Richd's place in equity, in demanding a conveyance in fee of said lot 7 in square 315, or the proceeds of its sale. Cmplnt also claims said letter to be a testamentary bequest to her of said Richd's share of his father's estate, & to entitle her, in equity, to a conveyance of said lot, or the proceeds of it's sale. The bill charges that said Richd has been absent & unheard of more than 20 years, & must be presumed to be dead; presumed in law to be dead, his heirs at law, in addition to cmplnt are her brothers, Edw C Dyer, of Wash City, Geo F Dyer, of Calif; John I Dyer, of Md, & the following children of Robt W Dyer, her deceased brother, & trustee in said deed of Jan 9, 1845, to wit: Josephine, of full age, & John C Dyer & Roberta Dyer, minors all said children residingin Wash City, all of whom are made dfndnts, & required to appear & answer said bill. The bill further prays that the said lot may be sold, & a suitable trustee for that purpose appointed by the court, & sold disincumbered of the trusts of said deed, & the proceeds brought into court & paid over to cmplnt. The bill avers the only relief of cmplnt to be in equity, & prays process of subpoena against the resident dfndnts, & publication against the non-resident dfndnts. The non-resident dfndnt, Geo F Dyer, resides in Calif, & John I Dyer, in Md; same absent dfndts are to appear in the Clerk's ofc on the first Tue of May, 1867. –R J Meigs, clerk -Wm L Dunlop, solicitor for cmplnt

SAT DEC 29, 1866
Navy Bulletin, Dec 21. Appointed: Acting Master Wm Burditt, & acting boatswain in the regular navy. Detached: Lt Cmder Chas H Green, from the ship **Monongahela**, & placed on waiting orders. Honorably Discharged: Acting Master Wm Burditt.

Police Items: 1-John Bitzer, a German huckster, was arrested on cmplnt of Howard Brooks, another huckster, charging him with personal violence: fined $5. The accused was held to security to keep the peace. 2-Danl W Bates, a jeweller, was arrested & charged with threats of violence towards his wife, the cmplnt. The accused was required to give security to keep the peace. 3-C C Willard, hotel-keeper, was arrested for violating the law by selling liquor on Sunday: fined $20.58.

Mr A D Renshaw, who was arrested upon cmplnt of Geo Hammond, had a hearing & was honorably acquitted. The charges preferred were entirely without foundation, & the result a mistake.

The body of ___ Fitzpatrick, a U S marine, attached to the corps at the Navy Yard, was found dead in the canal. A verdict rendered that the deceased accidentally fell into the canal & froze to death.

Died: on Dec 18, of pneumonia, Mrs Mary W Eveleth, wife of Eben Eveleth, in her 67th year. Her funeral will be this afternoon at 1 o'clock, from her late residence, 333 G st, corner of 12th st.

Richmond, Va, Dec 28. Saml Rowlett, clerk in a store at Meherrin, was murdered this morning. No clue to the murderer has been found.

Austin, Texas, Dec 27. T Adj Gen U S A, Wash. Lt Wilson was at my quarters apparently well & in good spirits on Dec 22nd. Later in the day he complained a little, & the surgeon took charge of him, & next morning had him removed to the hospital. On Dec 24 he was taken with a hemorrhage of the stomach & bowels, & died at 10 o'clock. His remains were carefully embalmed, & this morning started for Wash in charge of Col Johnson & Acting Assist Surgeon Kirk, & will reach Wash in 8 or 9 days. Col Crittenden has taken an inventory of his effects, & will forward immediately as directed. –S Q Sturgis, Brig Gen

Orphans Court of Wash Co, D C. Letters of administration on the personal estate of John Lange, late of Wash City, D C, deceased. –Zachariah F Borland, adm

Supreme Court of D C, in Equity No 761, Docket 8. Saml C Smoot et al vs John M Turley et al. Wm F Mattingly, trustee, reported he sold at public auction part of lots 25 & 26 in square 197, Wash City, to John A Gray, for $1,000, & he had complied with the terms of sale. –A B Olin -R J Meigs, clerk

Richmond, Dec 28. John W McKiel & Juan Pizzini, old citizens, died here yesterday.

MON DEC 31, 1866
Navy Bulletin for Dec 22. Ordered: Passed Assist Paymaster John H Stevenson, to the ship **Pawnee**, on Jan 1; 2nd Assist Engineer John Lowe, to the ship **Madawaska**. Granted Sick leave of Absence: Paymaster Geo A Sawyer. Resigned: 2nd Assist Engineer Owen Jones, & Past Assist Paymaster Edw Sherwin. Detached: 2nd Assist Engineer Oscar Lewis, from the **Madawaska**, & ordered to the ship **Huron**.

The copartnership existing between L J Middleton & W W Russell will expire by its own limitation on Dec 31, 1866. The affairs of the late copartnerhsip will be wound up by the undersigned. –L J Middleton

Orphans Court-Judge Purcell. 1-Sat the will of the late Clara Nesbit was partially proven. 2-August Schroeder qualified as administrator of the estate of Rita Triay, giving bonds in $2,000, & was also appointed guardian to the children, giving a $1,000 bond. 3-Julia Grimes qualified as administratrix of the estate of Lewis Grimes, giving bonds in $300. 4-Lydia Nixon was appointed guardian to the orphans of R T & S A Nixon. 5-E C Morgan was appointed guardian to the orphans of Wm Walker.

The wife of Sgt Geo T Sears, a member of the police of Balt, committed suicide on Thursday by cutting her throat with a razor. She had been taken from the Md Hospital for the Insane to spend Christmas at home, where she committed the act.

Supreme Court of D C, No 1,453 in Equity, Docket 5. Wordin vs Wordin. Wm Y Fendall, trustee, reported that he sold part of lot 2 in square 513, to John H Johnson, for the sum of $1,995.80, & he has complied with the terms of sale. –A B Olin, Justice -R J Meigs, clerk

Orphans Court of Wash Co, D C, Dec 29, 1866. In the case of Wm Y Fendall, adm of Chas A Henderson, deceased, the administrator & Court have appointed Jan 26 next, for the final settlement of the personal estate of the said deceased, of the assets in hand. -Jas R O'Beirne, Reg/o wills

Surratt is expected to arrive here about Jan 20th.

A

Abadie, 411
Abbey, 116
Abbot, 288
Abbots, 504
Abbott, 12, 53, 288, 302, 596
Abby, 368
Abell, 71, 146, 270, 290, 299
Abendeen, 565
Abercrombie, 94, 422
Aberdeen, 132, 429
Aberdeeser, 55
Abernethey, 487
Acker, 39, 44, 332, 360
Ackerman, 453
Ackers, 437
Ackley, 278, 530, 587
Aclone, 454
Acton, 540
Adam, 447
Adams, 7, 20, 34, 56, 71, 73, 74, 94, 96, 98, 104, 111, 121, 126, 132, 144, 146, 158, 192, 206, 210, 246, 252, 254, 267, 270, 273, 279, 288, 300, 301, 307, 308, 311, 332, 350, 354, 367, 388, 442, 453, 537, 540, 551, 560, 565, 566, 570
Adamson, 59, 80
Addison, 13, 38, 43, 61, 221, 303, 378, 423, 425, 451, 521
Adler, 22, 46, 502
Adlman, 563
Adlum, 324
Adrain, 530
African blood, 552
Agassiz, 350
Agnew, 267
Agnue, 197
Ahl, 345
Ah-Moose, 93
Ahrens, 160
Aiken, 71, 245, 291, 538
Aikin, 303

Ailer, 466
Aiman, 311
Akers, 28
Alberger, 276
Albert, 26
Albion, 455
Albright, 342
Albro, 593
Alcorn, 108
Alden, 234
Aldeo, 67
Aldridge, 590
Alemany, 446
Alexander, 48, 52, 62, 74, 126, 200, 257, 291, 326, 332, 408, 428, 451, 473, 480, 508, 524, 542, 558
Alger, 28
Alhaiza, 454, 455
Alig, 92, 391
Allabach, 332
Allan, 63
Allen, 28, 34, 48, 57, 62, 106, 114, 123, 140, 183, 192, 193, 205, 233, 234, 237, 240, 252, 253, 288, 297, 325, 330, 359, 367, 379, 392, 411, 425, 454, 460, 477, 479, 484, 514, 528, 532, 575, 583, 587
Alley, 199, 362
Allin, 280
Allison, 41
Allport, 459
Allston, 67, 132
Allyn, 467
Alman, 100
Almey, 106, 276
Almy, 104
Alnaya, 453
Alpress, 537
Alston, 102
Altemus, 54
Alton, 588
Alver, 563
Aman, 332
Amat, 446

Ambrook, 406
Ambsburg, 431
American Cousin, 147, 242
American Methodism, 164
Amery, 97, 224, 290, 359
Ames, 171, 320, 330, 370, 559
Amidon, 367
Amiss, 308
Ammen, 149, 203, 534
Amos, 18, 429
Amsberg, 388
Amweg, 342
Analostan, 438
Analostan Mansion, 437
Analostan Point, 438
Andersack, 454
Anderson, 48, 62, 104, 126, 202, 207, 222, 234, 251, 269, 277, 278, 290, 343, 346, 361, 363, 409, 416, 421, 431, 432, 463, 490, 493, 512, 566, 587
Anderton, 228
Andrews, 5, 43, 77, 161, 182, 304, 307, 315, 332, 346, 376, 423, 448, 451, 510, 543, 544, 558, 587
Angerine, 537
Angier, 401
Angus, 282, 591
Anna, 239, 348
Anstele, 491
Anstelle, 565
Anthony, 72, 125, 126, 459
Antietnam Nat'l Cemetery, 491
Antisell, 302, 359
Antoine, 141
Antonio, 409
Aorel, 453
Appel, 326
Applegate, 102, 568
Appleton, 150, 219, 476
Appointments by the Pres, 353, 372, 378, 380, 409, 416, 421, 427, 434, 436, 439, 449, 455, 487, 557, 574
Appold, 342
Arbuthnot, 47
Archer, 400

Ardeeser, 59, 224
Ardesser, 540
Aren, 351
Arhends, 332
Arizon, 373
Arlington, 216, 438
Arlington & the Nat'l Cemetery, 216
Arlington Cemetery, 218, 519, 521
Arlington Mansion, 427
Armistead, 367
Armor, 526
Armsrong, 502
Armstead, 491
Armstrong, 94, 101, 106, 110, 112, 131, 206, 428, 565, 573
Armuren, 298
Arnold, 59, 104, 105, 126, 198, 234, 278, 303, 304, 363, 372, 421, 425, 524
Arson, 7
Arter, 72
Arthur, 101, 261
Artificial limbs, 380
Artman, 159
Asboth, 75
Asbury M E Church, 351
Ashbury, 100
Ashby, 288, 479
Ashford, 126, 188, 249, 285, 363
Ashland, 31, 343
Ashley, 5, 38, 478
Ashmun, 427
Ashton, 587
Aspell, 397
Aspinwall, 131, 539
Astor, 7, 51, 223, 343
At Lee, 271
Atchison, 311, 379, 381
Atherton, 372
Atkins, 40, 234, 295, 299, 393
Atkinson, 311, 332, 562, 563, 564, 565
Atlantic cable, 319, 421, 561
AtLee, 429, 490
Attocha, 149

Atwater, 233, 565
Atwell, 215, 487
Atwood, 99, 113, 407
Aue, 65
Augur, 171, 235, 262, 433, 558, 568
August, 304
Auguste, 350, 351
Augustine, 270, 564
Aukward, 367
Auld, 550
Aulick, 332, 410, 412
Austin, 126, 392, 458
Avego, 229
Aveny, 505
Averill, 427, 537
Avery, 365, 526, 573
Axe, 304
Axelett, 441
Ayer, 22, 54
Ayers, 276, 525
Ayre, 594
Ayres, 105, 171, 331, 433, 441, 459, 494, 559

B

Baban, 454
Babbington, 168, 174
Babbitt, 575
Babcock, 170, 386, 388, 431, 460, 462, 473, 516
Babson, 488
Bache, 330, 417, 432, 474, 541, 570
Bachelor, 72
Bachler, 571
Bachus, 159
Bacon, 61, 79, 118, 149, 162, 176, 183, 214, 235, 330, 332, 417, 445, 476, 514, 515, 561, 589, 593
Badder, 148
Badeau, 165, 298, 516
Badeaux, 291
Baden, 98
Bader, 537
Badger, 203, 229, 387, 431, 570
Badin, 443
Baer, 263, 310, 519, 537

Baggarly, 503
Baggerly, 503
Baggett, 48
Baggs, 459
Bagley, 471, 563
Bagnam, 476
Bailey, 6, 15, 77, 104, 106, 134, 154, 197, 236, 253, 332, 367, 377, 454, 490, 538, 564, 569, 587
Bailey's Cross Roads, 377
Baily, 122, 396
Bainbridge, 103, 297
Baird, 171, 311, 342, 421
Baker, 8, 18, 21, 27, 39, 48, 59, 131, 159, 176, 181, 206, 224, 231, 245, 250, 251, 253, 255, 299, 300, 324, 332, 358, 360, 366, 438, 475, 486, 488, 492, 512, 538, 540, 555, 566, 570
Balch, 186
Balden, 537
Baldwin, 38, 74, 77, 101, 105, 174, 332, 374, 375, 390, 407, 431, 434, 476, 509, 565, 569, 583, 587
Baldy, 277, 512, 573
Ball, 26, 78, 119, 158, 178, 259, 270, 283, 284, 308, 566
Ballantine, 104, 195
Ballard, 68, 587
Ballenger, 39, 181, 190
Ballier, 346
Ballinger, 185
Ballou, 167
Balman, 467, 524
Balslay, 538
Balt, 308
Bamberger, 301, 308
Bancker, 31
Bancroft, 199
Bandall, 583
Bangs, 63, 310
Bank, 260
Banker, 346
Bankhead, 106
Banks, 361, 448
Bannan, 573, 590

Bannon, 151, 499
Bansfield, 116
Baragli, 424
Barags, 445
Barber, 102, 104, 151, 281, 477, 555
Barbour, 10, 59, 123, 134, 152, 154, 164, 176, 188, 238, 280, 332, 472, 585
Barche, 332
Barclay, 136, 179, 352, 400
Bard, 104
Barden, 414
Bare, 538
Barg, 493, 565
Bargdol, 429
barge **Rose**, 214
Baring, 397
bark **Ambrosine**, 462
bark **Atlantic**, 522
bark **B Sewell**, 5
bark **Diadem**, 30
bark **M and E Robbins**, 30
bark **Trieste**, 339
Barkel, 308
Barker, 39, 46, 88, 123, 148, 332, 529, 545
Barkley, 515
Barlow, 13, 15, 160, 453
Barnaclo, 84, 301
Barnam, 16
Barnard, 26, 77, 171, 311, 372, 432, 506, 514
Barnes, 58, 107, 109, 112, 125, 153, 201, 207, 227, 276, 300, 311, 332, 379, 381, 494, 541, 565
Barnett, 91
Barney, 499
Barnhart, 111
Barnhill, 183, 184
Barnside, 433
Barnum, 75, 525, 537
Baron de Witzieben, 212
Baronn, 170
Barr, 86, 110, 120, 176, 253, 332, 345, 452, 471, 501
Barrand, 20, 240

Barranger, 197
Barraud, 182
Barrell, 219
Barrett, 9, 92, 267, 276, 304, 319, 332, 389, 403, 453, 468, 484, 593
Barricks, 303
Barroll, 286
Barron, 181, 299, 359, 375, 474, 502
Barrow, 288
Barrows, 566, 575
Barry, 115, 123, 196, 200, 239, 318, 332, 333, 378, 433, 517
Bart, 537
Barthlomew, 33
Barthol, 586
Bartholomew, 525
Bartholow, 332, 555
Bartle, 310
Bartlett, 71, 92, 101, 140, 360, 432, 470, 473, 526, 537
Bartley, 344
Barton, 91, 228, 275, 315, 373, 488, 498, 573
Bascom, 297
baseball, 259
Base-Ball, 302
Base-Ball Club, 199
Bass, 414
Bassett, 505
Bastapool, 177
Bastianelli, 292
Bastine, 229
Batchelder, 143, 377
Batchell, 276
Batelle, 259
Bateman, 468
Batemen, 288
Bates, 39, 40, 103, 139, 233, 279, 303, 326, 329, 333, 362, 367, 369, 436, 504, 530, 585, 598
Bathel, 332
Batteganji, 501
Battle Cemetery, 218, 520
battle of Gettysburg, 331
Battles, 526
Battrie, 524

Batvine, 330
Baucher, 17
Baudin, 316
Bauer, 292, 359
Baugher, 168, 170
Baum, 271, 425
Baumann, 329, 507
Baumgarten, 152
Baverdy, 565
Baxter, 50, 63, 304
Bay, 537
Bayard, 66
Bayer, 104
Bayley, 1, 59, 82, 445, 461
Baylies, 556
Baylis, 332
Bayliss, 126
Baylor, 245, 312, 328
Bayly, 393, 447
Bayne, 17, 33, 211, 230, 232, 302, 340
Bea__, 345
Beach, 172, 372, 379
Beacher, 537
Beal, 237
Beale, 31, 126, 242, 348, 508, 528, 529, 543, 548
Bealeroy, 413
Beales, 11
Beall, 7, 9, 13, 14, 62, 79, 92, 126, 160, 321, 329, 332, 386, 391, 403, 451, 500
Beall's Fancy, 122
Bean, 14, 15, 35, 158, 201, 204, 228, 303, 304, 550
Beans, 387, 431
Beard, 210, 223, 311
Beardslee, 570
Beary, 493
Beasley, 84
Beasly, 64
Beatie, 164
Beattie, 526
Beatty, 3, 484
Beaumont, 106, 578
Beaureard, 24

Beauregard, 433, 448, 476
Beaurgard, 351
Beck, 222
Becker, 255, 282, 283, 347, 360
Becket, 448, 458
Beckman, 100
Beckshaffe, 552
Beckstaf_, 530
Beckwith, 171, 387, 425, 473, 474
Bedford, 501
Beebe, 425
Beebee, 414
Beecher, 10, 23, 135, 147, 297, 448, 551
Beers, 181, 304, 305
Behrend, 290
Behrends, 452
Bekem, 118, 593
Belcher, 83, 259, 583
Belfast, 310
Belfield, 462
Belger, 355
Belknap, 523
Bell, 1, 31, 35, 68, 78, 106, 138, 153, 176, 294, 300, 301, 323, 351, 476, 478, 487, 538, 566, 575
Bellefontaine Cemetery, 219
Bellman, 309
Bellows, 315
Belt, 33, 314, 327, 332, 371, 391, 463, 563
Bender, 284, 324
Bendy, 513
Benedetti, 454
Benedict, 23, 311, 444, 507
Benham, 4, 107, 171, 433, 512
Benidetti, 453
Benjamin, 59, 268, 387, 546
Benner, 15
Bennet, 588
Bennett, 39, 82, 100, 105, 159, 273, 326, 355, 359, 564
Benning, 27
Benser, 178
Bensinger, 158
Benson, 23, 104, 332, 471, 476

Bent, 271, 481
Bentley, 391, 404
Benton, 46, 257, 496, 544
Bentz, 461
Beremund, 165
Berg, 105, 430
Bergen, 14, 102
Berger, 14, 40, 93, 122, 142
Bergess, 210
Bergman, 308
Bergner, 561
Berkley, 303
Berkline, 399
Bernard, 189, 361, 426
Berrada, 213
Berret, 62, 126, 332
Berry, 33, 59, 61, 68, 80, 116, 125, 126, 143, 161, 165, 171, 198, 266, 277, 283, 294, 303, 314, 323, 328, 330, 332, 358, 362, 403, 430, 456, 505, 517, 524, 532, 539, 547, 565, 592, 596
Berthold, 454
Bertroff, 422
Besham, 529
Bessan, 351, 542
Best, 248, 332, 475
Bestor, 332, 345, 438
Beton, 461
Betts, 144, 240
Betz, 443, 471
Bevan, 126, 482
Bevans, 33
Beveridge, 13, 316, 332
Beverley, 518
Bevins, 308
Bexford, 585
Bexley, 203
Bey, 172, 178, 179
Beye, 402
Bias, 138
Bibb, 247
Bickely, 101
Bickmann, 441
Bicknell, 277, 575
Biddle, 310, 564

Bidwell, 238
Bierman, 346
Biershing, 151
Bierstadt, 548
Bigelow, 71, 196
Bigger, 105
Biggs, 6, 491
Bigham, 494
Bigler, 135, 428
Bigley, 182
Bigly, 291
Bilbian, 564
Bild, 299
Bill, 411
Billings, 367, 441
Billingsand, 315
Billingsley, 504
Binckley, 103, 459
Binge, 349
Bingham, 100, 277, 492, 565, 578, 590
Binkley, 513
Binney, 380, 522
Binnix, 300
Birch, 39, 79, 133, 345, 359, 466, 527, 536, 540
Bird, 108, 126, 367, 420, 475, 493, 564, 565
Birdsall, 220
Birdsel, 492
Birdsell, 536
Birdsey, 414
Birmingham, 557
Birth, 307
Bishop, 106, 307, 309, 310, 332, 368, 416, 430, 494, 537, 552, 585
Bissell, 559
Bittinger, 221, 391
Bitzer, 342, 346, 598
Bixby, 313
Bjursten, 591
Black, 30, 104, 126, 234, 324, 344, 389, 425, 427, 430, 433, 518, 563
Blackburn, 34, 318, 376, 486
Blackestone, 126
Blackford, 89, 253

Blackiston, 310
Blackistone, 165
Blackmore, 513
Blackwell, 430
Blagden, 264, 333, 345
Blagden's alley, 452
Blair, 26, 73, 182, 277, 332, 455, 523, 569
Blake, 8, 61, 79, 88, 241, 297, 332, 388, 502, 570
Blakely, 3
Blakeman, 154, 379
Blaker, 102
Blan, 310, 356, 375
Blanch, 304
Blanchard, 1, 2, 3, 44, 183, 228, 333, 350, 359, 555, 596
Blanchet, 445
Blanding, 199
Blau, 311
Bleak House, 151
Blenheim, 471
Blessing of the Bells, 395
Blevins, 205
Blight, 296
Bliss, 111, 307, 311, 355, 437, 561
Bliss,, 259
Bliven, 276
Blodgett, 111, 228, 466
Blondin, 332
Blosser, 304
Blount, 5, 29, 258
Blow, 328
Blundon, 321
Blunt, 4, 25, 396, 589
Blydenburg, 578
Blye, 541
Boardman, 65, 542
Boarman, 292, 371
Boarman's **Meadows**, 371
Boarman's Rest, 371
boat **Calumet**, 188
boat **Morning Star**, 455
boat **W J Shreve**, 210
Bocherah, 522
Bodenbaugh, 374

Bodice, 555
Bodisco, 324
Bogan, 96, 209, 332, 359
Bogardus, 551
Bogert, 585
Bogett, 388
Boggs, 71, 165
Bogle, 76
Bogue, 10, 155
Bogus, 126, 540
Bogy, 442, 487
Bohlayer, 303, 477
Bohler, 133
Bohn, 292
Bohnner, 67
Bohrer, 146, 271, 345
Boisean, 282
Boiseau, 498
Boitz, 353
Bokel, 282
Boker, 236
Bolan, 283
Boland, 65
Bolger, 311
Bolster, 148, 318
Bolton, 193
Bonaparte, 377
Bond, 67, 276, 307, 359, 366, 389, 516
Bonds, 546
Bonesteel, 372
Bonffe, 453
Bonifant, 87, 117
Bonner, 319
Bonnet, 5
Bonneval, 431, 565
Bonnevall, 387
Bonney, 108, 565
Bonsteel, 526
Bontz, 57, 375
Booch, 72
Booher, 429
Book, 344
Boon, 167
Boone, 282, 598
Boose, 9

Bootes, 258, 361, 559
Booth, 59, 72, 159, 172, 202, 230, 242, 262, 344, 396, 469, 478, 500, 502, 517
Boothe, 284
Bord, 454
Borland, 27, 599
Borley, 6
Borrows, 57, 332, 359
Borume, 196
Boscow, 580, 584
Boss, 133, 135, 147, 159, 307, 308, 311
Bostane, 484
Boston, 278
Bostow, 385
Bostwick, 551
Boswell, 22, 28, 214, 300, 389, 543
Boswell's Enclosure, 371
Bosworth, 161
Boteler, 3, 17, 25, 43, 49, 61, 70, 79, 84, 87, 132, 140, 143, 170, 200, 332, 584
Botler, 242, 524
Botsch, 332
Bottomly, 308
Botts, 571
Bouch, 80
Boucha, 362
Boucher, 10, 126
Boucicault, 546
Boudinot, 340, 449
Boughman, 281
Bouic, 245
Boulden, 140
Boullt, 491
Boult, 151
Boulware, 537
Bounce, 555
Bourcy, 428
Bourne, 242
Boursh, 57
Boutelle, 122
Boutwell, 159
Boward, 587
Bowditch, 219, 223

Bowdle, 341
Bowen, 23, 168, 174, 181, 289, 301, 308, 311, 362, 367, 403, 431, 438, 492, 564, 565, 590
Bower, 186
Bowerman, 559
Bowers, 77, 79, 129
Bowie, 76, 79, 266, 310, 377, 456, 517, 560
Bowles, 434
Bowling, 56, 407
Bowman, 85, 306, 509, 581
Bowson, 587
Boyce, 29, 46, 162, 289, 323, 332, 388
Boyd, 59, 91, 181, 223, 224, 276, 283, 392, 468, 480, 569
Boyden, 168
Boyer, 326
Boyett, 260
Boyle, 26, 60, 111, 126, 174, 177, 211, 224, 271, 290, 300, 399, 436, 442, 471, 569, 574
Boynton, 438
Brabbham, 245
Brace, 214
Brackett, 230
Bradburn, 300
Bradford, 36, 58, 93, 107, 367, 507, 570, 573, 583
Bradisa, 332
Bradley, 31, 44, 61, 74, 75, 85, 90, 102, 105, 172, 189, 215, 269, 285, 294, 300, 303, 304, 306, 332, 333, 358, 366, 385, 431, 437, 438, 453, 476, 490, 499, 509, 513, 516, 556
Bradshaw, 540
Brady, 18, 60, 72, 159, 222, 241, 290, 292, 298, 302, 451, 505
Bragdon, 543
Bragg, 433
Brainard, 24, 457
Braine, 408
Brainerd, 375
Bramhall, 326, 492
Branch, 399

Brand, 15, 94
Brandebury, 440
Brandelbury, 311
Brandner, 373
Brannan, 171
Brannon, 518
Bransell, 156
Brant, 587
Brantigam, 47
Brantingham, 593
Brasher, 106, 362, 574
Brave, 237
Brawner, 527
Braxten, 345
Brayton, 46, 82
Breck, 108, 299
Breckinridge, 50
Breese, 107, 534
Brehm, 342
Bremer, 33
Brenard, 416
Breneman, 422
Brengle, 268
Brennan, 301, 383, 487
Brennerman, 386
Brent, 12, 30, 43, 79, 116, 156, 167, 174, 178, 262, 284, 289, 345, 415, 423, 438, 442, 502, 508, 523, 524, 529
Brentwood, 116
Brereton, 307
Bresshan, 405
Bret, 456
Brett, 94, 454
Brewer, 307, 441
Brewster, 332, 529, 542
Brice, 227, 234, 351, 432
Brick, 135, 347
Brickerd, 373
Brickley, 492
Bridewell, 544
Bridge, 39, 350, 351
Bridges, 101
Bridget, 332
Briegleb, 292
Brierfield, 553

brig **Blackfish**, 428
brig **Cyclone**, 145
brig **Jacques**, 567
brig **Madeira**, 428
brig **Maderia**, 565
brig **Ocean Wave**, 546
brig **Pomfret**, 448
brig **Star of Hope**, 145
brigantine **Rebecca Sheppard**, 511
Briget, 458
Briggs, 53, 180, 304, 306, 308, 363, 552
Bright, 165, 195, 303, 304, 367, 468, 578
Brightwell's Hunting Quarter, 547
Brightwood, 572
Brimfield, 542
Brinkler, 288
Brinsmade, 28
Brinton, 24
Brisbois, 47
Briscoe, 1, 48, 126, 189, 227
Britt, 72, 178
Britton, 99, 231, 562, 564
Broadhead, 126, 378, 508
Broadus, 179
Broatch, 102
Brocar, 369
Brock, 526
Brockerton, 96
Brockway, 345
Brodhead, 13, 325, 524
Brodie, 198
Brogan, 178
Brokenbrough, 23
Broker, 587
Bronson, 5
Brook, 431, 559, 567
Brooke, 11, 19, 39, 57, 125, 287, 326, 385, 495, 565
Brooks, 72, 111, 231, 359, 433, 461, 475, 555, 598
Broom, 2
Brophy, 404, 469
Brosman, 528
Brosnan, 80, 313, 528

Brothers, 64, 299, 300, 301
Broughton, 473
Brown, 6, 34, 39, 51, 61, 64, 68, 73, 74, 87, 88, 101, 111, 125, 161, 174, 175, 177, 178, 189, 198, 205, 210, 221, 222, 223, 234, 250, 264, 267, 279, 284, 292, 297, 300, 303, 304, 305, 307, 310, 311, 312, 323, 325, 326, 330, 332, 345, 349, 351, 353, 355, 357, 359, 367, 369, 378, 380, 385, 388, 405, 407, 414, 425, 427, 436, 438, 440, 444, 452, 456, 464, 467, 471, 479, 490, 491, 497, 505, 511, 513, 514, 515, 516, 522, 536, 537, 563, 571, 573, 581, 585, 595, 596
Browne, 238, 315, 341, 417, 564, 570
Browning, 30, 62, 73, 75, 103, 155, 176, 332, 377
Brownson, 388, 431
Bruce, 136, 139, 142, 295, 296, 565
Bruff, 285, 305, 311
Bruger, 429
Brumback, 555
Brumidi, 332
Bruner, 144, 154
Brunner, 566
Brunning, 405, 587
Brunt, 106
Bryan, 18, 22, 37, 65, 176, 227, 305, 320, 332, 421, 500, 517, 555
Bryant, 51, 53, 152, 155, 235, 236, 237, 255, 326, 341, 479, 488
Bryon, 569
Bubb, 102
Buch, 512
Buchan, 530
Buchanan, 11, 17, 24, 27, 90, 96, 226, 230, 311, 382, 540
Buchannan, 171
Buchley, 338
Buchly, 291
Buck, 108, 184, 290, 306, 396, 409, 494
Buckey, 321, 488, 590

Buckhart, 529
Buckignani, 480
Buckingham, 4, 183, 304
Buckley, 14, 77, 181, 283, 284, 309, 363, 437, 457, 514, 552, 565, 575
Buckner, 126, 291, 433
Budd, 56, 107, 449, 524
Budlong, 301
Buehler, 479
Buel, 58, 70
Buell, 276, 433
Buena Vista, 151
Buff, 328
Buford, 432, 575
Buger, 559
Bulford, 344
Bulkley, 330, 332
Bull, 26, 92, 537
Bullet, 458
Bullmand, 155
Bullock, 276
Bulwinkle, 152
Bunce, 536
Bunday, 452
Bunge, 306
Bunkle, 560
Bunt, 296
Bunyan, 92
Burbank, 171, 205, 538
Burbon, 362
Burch, 12, 59, 69, 224, 248, 279, 280, 303, 307, 361, 474
Burchard, 290
Burche, 126
Burchead, 440, 446
Burchell, 3, 32, 37, 60, 113, 129
Burdell, 176, 480
Burden, 316
Burdette, 126
Burdine, 307
Burditt, 598
Burey, 493
Burgess, 107, 168, 173, 230, 253, 255, 304, 309, 465
Burgoyne, 103
Burgundy, 142

Burham, 222
Burk, 6, 109, 284
Burke, 112, 120, 194, 197, 271, 351,
 369, 528, 529, 535, 550, 554
Burkhart, 487
Burks, 209
Burleson, 523
Burley, 114, 185
Burlingame, 269
Burnby, 523
Burness, 104
Burnet, 377
Burnett, 55, 179, 349, 479, 533
Burnham, 196, 243
Burnhart, 111
Burnley, 90
Burns, 112, 117, 200, 231, 253, 255,
 270, 284, 409, 452, 453, 456, 484,
 540
Burnstenbender, 171
Burnstenbinder, 215
Burnt Mills, 245
Burr, 55, 96, 223, 242, 293, 340,
 395, 402, 454, 506, 540
Burris, 331
Burroughs, 332, 494
Burrows, 165, 167, 228, 310, 555
Bursher, 231
Burt, 128, 191, 497
Burtis, 315
Burton, 251, 280, 406, 492, 566,
 573, 589
Burwanger, 226
Burwell, 277
Busch, 221
Busey, 119, 126, 403
Bush, 6, 72, 110, 234, 271, 283, 284,
 359, 415
Busher, 507
Busk, 95
Busteed, 5, 260
Butler, 4, 8, 29, 40, 44, 53, 65, 66,
 68, 90, 101, 147, 180, 181, 267,
 302, 332, 354, 383, 387, 420, 430,
 471, 479, 538, 553, 572, 580, 596
Butt, 125, 255, 359

Butterfield, 192, 327
Butts, 210, 300, 353, 479, 537
Buvan, 453
Buzer, 93
Byers, 414
Byons, 284
Byram, 177, 311
Byrne, 110, 423, 479
Byrnes, 283
Byron, 377, 455
Byrum, 429

C

Cabell, 387, 431
Cable, 547, 576
Cabot, 591
Cachot, 487
Cadazoo, 565
Cadazos, 431
Cadle, 385
Cadman, 126
Cadwalader, 381
Cadwallader, 197
Cady, 347
Caesars, 287
Caffay, 200
Cahill, 100, 283, 284, 594
Cahilll, 284
Cailland, 454
Caillant, 453
Caillot, 454
Caire, 563
Caldwell, 20, 107, 111, 565
Calhoun, 56, 329, 360, 385
Callaghan, 59, 165, 241, 303, 484
Callahan, 6, 80, 101, 126, 241, 304,
 415, 477, 522
Callan, 33, 62, 69, 76, 115, 124, 126,
 175, 187, 213, 262, 438, 449, 502,
 509, 523, 566
Callihan, 206
Callons, 537
Callum, 234
Calval, 405
<u>Calvary Baptist Church</u>, 210

Calvert, 43, 216, 264, 283, 311, 352, 366, 466, 488, 515, 536
Calvert's Hope, 371
Calvo, 165
Camer, 442
Cameron, 119, 131, 350, 351, 384, 389, 543, 561
Camfort, 480
Cammack, 164, 326, 540, 546
Camp, 39, 103, 276, 372, 564
Camp Barry, 173
Camp Butler, 520
Camp Chase, 521
Camp Dennison, 520
Camp Douglas, 480, 520
Camp Lincoln, 206
Campana, 453, 454
Campbell, 4, 5, 7, 32, 48, 64, 77, 78, 88, 90, 93, 105, 111, 184, 247, 267, 276, 311, 333, 354, 355, 375, 380, 385, 418, 428, 435, 454, 470, 516
Campell, 457
canal boat **Communipaw**, 424
Canby, 433
Candall, 374
Candu, 379
Canfield, 103, 296, 307, 309, 351, 358
Canlin, 360
Cann, 328
Cannon, 89, 180, 288, 356, 404, 422
Capella, 430, 565
Caperton, 62, 240, 291, 592
Capet, 506
Carberry, 74
Carbery, 254
Card, 231
Car-drivers, 163
Carey, 101, 190, 255, 310, 561
Carleton, 168, 171
Carley, 113
Carlin, 559
Carlisle, 68, 79, 189, 216, 326, 333, 353, 508, 584
Carll, 50

Carlon, 538
Carlow, 477
Carlyle, 194
Carmack, 373
Carman, 265
Carme, 114
Carmichael, 246
Carmody, 417
Carney, 363
Carolin, 105
Caroll, 171
Carothers, 573
Carpenter, 24, 40, 100, 105, 209, 305, 307, 369, 374, 431, 493, 509
Carr, 20, 100, 107, 171, 373
Carrell, 351
Carrico, 164, 465
Carrier, 72, 142
Carrigan, 558, 567
Carrington, 9, 30, 35, 80, 137, 202, 205, 320, 328, 333, 558, 595
Carrol, 36, 283, 300
Carroll, 103, 126, 181, 185, 190, 282, 283, 284, 304, 323, 355, 391, 405, 443, 445, 466, 473, 557, 575, 585, 591
Carroll Hall, 486
Carsen, 375
Carson, 373, 466, 473, 484, 593
Carter, 56, 68, 77, 96, 104, 114, 120, 197, 229, 276, 278, 300, 324, 385, 399, 403, 427, 465, 477, 484, 503, 507, 541, 563, 571, 595
Carters, 471
Cartier, 91, 278, 285, 294, 298, 306, 309
Carusi, 79, 93, 382, 568
Caruthers, 27
Carvallo, 359
Cary, 56, 90, 141, 148
Case, 276, 494
Caseles, 279
Casey, 52, 204, 432
Casgrove, 126
Cashel, 473
Cashill, 64

Caskle, 459
Caspar, 307
Casparis Hotel, 339
Cass, 260, 262, 272, 296
Cassel, 193
Cassell, 45, 96, 181, 272, 300, 305, 581, 589
Cassiday, 307
Cassidy, 389, 431
Cassin, 13, 14, 25, 126, 381, 387, 431
Casswell, 268
Castel, 79
Castell, 14, 15
Castello, 515
Castigan, 126
Castlemaine, 216
Castleman, 386
Castor, 196
Catalane, 442
Catalaro, 448
Catcher, 349
Cateley, 104
Cates, 415
Cathedral Cemetery, 423
Cathell, 378
Catholic Cathedral, 286
Catholic Church edifice, 181
Catholic colored Chapel, 50
Catilino, 481, 515, 521
Caton, 185, 307, 367, 527
Caulfield, 350, 380, 479
Caulwell, 307
Causin, 60
Causir, 139
Cavada, 111
Cavanagh, 454
Cavanaugh, 310, 453
Cavazier, 341
Caving, 587
Cavis, 308
Cavnot, 430
Cawill, 304
Cawood, 226
Cayer, 493
Caynot, 565

Cayot, 453
Cazenove, 126, 263
Cean, 387
Cecil, 290
Cedar Hill Cemetery, 236
Cedar Mountain, 330
Cedar Point, 591
Celeste, 288
Cemetery for Union dead, 191
Cemetery of the Holy Cross, 440
Cenas, 351
Centralia, 257
Centre City, 257
Cerus, 342
Cervantes, 206
Chace, 506
Chadbourne, 72
Chadwick, 201, 286, 333, 381
Chaffee, 22
Chaflin, 589
Chalmers, 11, 290
Chambell, 373
Chamberlain, 15, 85, 122, 414
Chamberlin, 359
Chambers, 36, 304, 305, 308, 378, 487, 550
Chambline, 493, 565
Champion, 2, 303, 363
Chance, 588
Chancellor, 126
Chancey, 359
Chancler, 583
Chandlee, 333
Chandler, 39, 73, 126, 331, 385, 560
Chaney, 119
Chanpell, 509
Chapin, 69, 71, 74, 118, 368, 559
Chaplain, 477
Chaplin, 518, 552
Chapman, 16, 89, 111, 225, 297, 313, 321, 324, 397, 474, 493, 526, 542, 573, 587
Chappel, 300
Chappin, 474
Chapston, 272
Charbonnean, 214

Charles II, 216
Charleston, 471
Charlier, 161, 190, 439
Charlot, 297
Charlotte Hall, 281
Charlton, 300
Chase, 41, 124, 131, 193, 247, 343, 378, 514, 526, 556
Chatain, 427
Chatham, 1, 23
Chatlit, 120
Chaunce, 539
Chauncey, 527
Chaves, 126
Chedal, 308
Cheek, 410
Cheeklay, 123
Cheeseman, 46, 107
Chenery, 315
Cheney, 211
Chenup, 453
Cherry, 282, 283
Chesney, 570, 593
Chessem, 352, 356
Chestar, 101
Chestnut, 139
Chetlain, 516
Chevelier, 580
Chew, 138, 264, 290, 341
Chickering, 49
Chicks, 472
Chicquot, 376
Child, 411
Childs, 48, 197, 243, 276, 305, 310
Chilson, 103
Chilton, 392, 465
Chinman, 563
Chipchase, 501
Chipman, 202, 235, 325, 388, 430, 453, 466, 563, 565
Chisholm, 154
Chism, 310
Chittenden, 470
Choisy, 103
Choppin, 148
Chorpenning, 281

Christ, 241
Christian Brothers, 486
Christiani, 333
Christopher, 596
Christy, 349
Chrysler, 145
Chunn's Swamp, 371
Church, 235, 236, 346, 432
Church of the Holy Cross, 296
Churchill, 104, 267, 273, 323, 354, 530, 552
Churchman, 343
Churn, 43
Chutkowski, 389, 431
Cilley, 100, 385
Cinnamond, 52
Ciroux, 43
Cissel, 181, 375, 418, 554
Cissell, 210
Cissell's Quarries, 210
City Point Cemetery, 520
Civil Rights, 207
Clafflin, 66
Claflin, 23, 343
Clagett, 60, 118, 252, 254, 328, 333, 396, 530, 544, 546
Claggett, 393
Clampitt, 62, 245, 291
Clancey, 382
Clancy, 398, 584
Clapp, 72, 102, 189, 295
Clare, 15, 591
Clarey, 168, 170
Claridge, 48
Clark, 1, 13, 22, 23, 39, 56, 65, 78, 92, 94, 126, 167, 181, 212, 231, 279, 281, 282, 283, 284, 295, 305, 310, 315, 328, 333, 343, 349, 358, 369, 379, 401, 410, 418, 425, 438, 487, 502, 514, 521, 537, 541, 560, 563
Clarke, 3, 33, 61, 73, 95, 97, 101, 102, 104, 118, 126, 146, 171, 198, 234, 254, 256, 291, 301, 303, 304, 310, 311, 330, 333, 339, 342, 360, 379, 423, 431, 484, 487, 503, 579

Clarkson, 32, 277, 280, 308, 360, 547
Clarvoe, 29, 73, 135, 300, 407, 457
Clary, 107, 264, 324, 540, 567
Classens, 306
Clatlin, 264
Claudius II, 51
Claveloux, 305
Claxton, 282, 283, 292, 353, 375
Clay, 31, 103, 132, 160, 190, 223, 400, 432, 541
Claypool, 533, 557
Clayton, 17, 62, 148, 164, 173, 253, 278, 287, 307, 397
Clean, 387
Clear, 300
Cleary, 126, 282, 296
Cleborne, 552, 578
Clemens, 104, 283, 538
Clement, 196
Clements, 53, 75, 113, 118, 126, 156, 307, 315, 364, 593
Clendenin, 271, 584
Cleopatra, 287
Clephane, 8, 79, 183, 332, 385, 438
Clepper, 342
Cleveland, 526
Clews, 66
Clibband, 453
Clicquot, 376, 406
Cliffbourne, 563
Clifford, 104, 556
Clift, 570
Climaens, 396
Clinch, 262
Cline, 259
Clinton, 277, 317, 389, 431, 507, 558, 566
Clitz, 433
Clogg, 531
Clokey, 307
Closs, 333
Clotain, 453
Cloud, 68
Cloudland, 6, 135
Clovam, 454

Clowes, 138, 139
Clowry, 276
Cluley, 102
Clum, 487
Clusky, 471
Cluss, 181, 375
Cluster, 101
Clymer, 124, 345
Coan, 431
Coar, 345
Coates, 325
Cobb, 113, 247, 262, 362, 488
Coburn, 25, 551
Cochran, 118, 242, 276, 333, 466, 565, 580, 592
Cochrane, 22, 24, 288, 472, 480, 481, 582
Cockerille, 288
Cockey, 212
Cockran, 288, 333
Cockrill, 33
Codding, 103
Coddington, 359
Codpim, 453
Coenzler, 104
Coffey, 304
Coffin, 168, 315, 573
Coffinberry, 272
Coffman, 105
Cogan, 132
Coggins, 178
Cogswell, 399
Cohen, 333, 430, 486, 565, 583
Coignard, 453, 454
Colburn, 24, 276, 576
Colby, 72, 108, 417
Cold Harbor Cemetery, 520
Coldin, 108
Coldren, 492, 565
Cole, 165, 196, 278, 307, 454, 466, 537
Colebrooke, 38
Coleman, 74, 103, 224, 253, 255, 290, 291, 317, 493, 541, 577
Coles, 12
Colesville, 245

Colgate, 397
Colley, 333, 487
Collier, 37, 414
Collingsworth, 232, 285
Collins, 36, 40, 66, 103, 107, 143, 144, 147, 153, 155, 196, 202, 290, 292, 308, 310, 311, 339, 360, 391, 451, 472, 509, 555, 590
Collinsworth, 298
Collon, 368
Colman, 111
colored regts, 16
Colt, 136, 199, 236, 333, 414, 455
Colt's or Remington's, 370
Colt's pistol factory, 136
Coltman, 7, 82, 92, 96, 126
Colton, 126, 477
Columbia Hospital for Women, 207
Columbian College, 281, 356, 434
Columbian College Law School, 253, 255
Columbus, 307
Colvin, 287
Colwell, 505
Combs, 73, 162, 359
Common Sense, 588
Compston, 101
Compton, 157, 307, 559, 564
Comstock, 140, 171, 276, 554, 564
Conant, 272
Conche, 565
Condict, 359
Cone, 13
Conger, 159, 465
Congressional Burying Ground, 166
Congressional Cemetery, 13, 15, 85, 88, 93, 121, 206, 208, 262, 434, 479, 482, 567
Conkey, 526
Conkling, 157
Conksey, 300
Conlan, 175, 465
Conlin, 47
Conlon, 287
Conme, 453

Connard, 345
Connell, 307
Connelly, 102, 276, 376
Connemaugh, 512
Conner, 59, 200, 221, 300, 303, 368, 399, 524, 535, 536, 563
Conness, 251, 584
Connington, 164, 301, 546
Connor, 159, 167, 178, 284, 299, 304, 429, 540
Conovan, 265
Conover, 308, 508
Conrad, 265, 288, 342
Conrad's Tavern, 194
Conredis, 485
Conroy, 90, 107, 195, 310, 445, 569, 579
Constantine, 396
Conte, 189
Convent of the Good Shepherd, 525
Convent of the Holy Cross, 430
Convent of the Visitation, 317
Converse, 71, 103
Conway, 80, 100, 291, 312, 429
Conyngham, 103
Coogan, 303
Cook, 12, 27, 48, 151, 200, 214, 222, 307, 308, 309, 350, 351, 356, 364, 449, 465, 478, 512, 515, 532, 582
Cooke, 24, 51, 61, 79, 170, 215, 326, 331, 333, 341, 343, 458, 463, 468
Cookendorfer, 386
Cooks, 98
Cooksey, 300
Coole, 493
Cooley, 21, 103, 349, 420, 442, 473, 493, 568
Coolidge, 30, 32, 39, 101
Coolrich, 546
Coombe, 359
Coombs, 126, 162, 283, 295
Coomes, 82, 232, 296
Coon, 126, 479
Cooper, 66, 91, 102, 105, 138, 184, 185, 191, 208, 246, 313, 340, 349, 424, 434, 438, 515, 534, 556

Coots, 537
Copeland, 487
Copp, 407, 414
Coppee, 433
Coppinger, 23, 110
Coppini, 454
Corbett, 159
Corbin, 566
Corbit, 284
Corcoran, 59, 127, 183, 204, 224, 284, 300, 320, 321, 323, 333, 346, 422, 592
Corkery, 35
Cornelius, 428
Cornia, 453
Corning, 255, 454
Cornish, 256
Corona, 539
Correll, 586
Corry, 339, 382
Corse, 421
Corson, 372
Corwin, 23, 247
Cosby, 118
Cosgriff, 440
Cosgrove, 563
Coskery, 292, 423
Costar, 278
Costello, 305, 556
Costigan, 126
Cotbarine, 567
Cotes, 43
Cotter, 6
Cottingham, 56, 74
Cotton, 487
Cottrell, 587
Cottries, 480
Couch, 364, 412, 433
Coulter, 568
Coumbe, 308
Counselman, 100
Courche, 492
Courey, 382
Courrea, 526
Courtenay, 169
Courtis, 573
Courtney, 145, 175
Coutts, 33
Coventry, 538
Cover, 212
Covert, 248
Cowan, 271
Cowgill, 17
Cowie, 111, 311
Cowles, 357
Cowling, 215, 284, 571
Cox, 28, 39, 48, 64, 81, 138, 152, 158, 175, 182, 232, 265, 292, 304, 321, 351, 387, 403, 411, 424, 430, 451, 454, 465, 472, 490, 493, 510, 517, 529, 550, 555, 587, 590
Coxe, 32, 189, 276
Coyle, 1, 8, 43, 62, 73, 154, 183, 277, 284, 333, 446
Craff, 463
Cragie, 568
Cragle, 453
Craig, 267, 354, 359, 564
Craigen, 392
Craigin, 359
Crain, 332
Cralle, 571
Cram, 104, 432
Cramer, 56
Crampton, 204, 454
Cranch, 139, 303
Crandell, 524
Crandon, 276
Crane, 192, 364, 464, 526, 536
Craufurd, 34, 38
Craven, 28, 525, 530
Cravens, 7
Crawford, 38, 40, 58, 62, 171, 247, 303, 304, 363, 414, 427, 505
Creamer, 308, 540
Creaser, 55, 307
Creighton, 397
Crele, 47
Crenshaw, 256
Cresswell, 72
Creswell, 5, 167
Crews, 307, 308

Cridier, 73
Cridler, 73, 299, 300
Cripps, 126, 333
Crittenden, 559, 560, 599
Crocheron, 6, 453
Crocker, 60, 277, 309
Croggon, 333, 496
Croghan, 333, 359, 515
Crokes, 581
Crolly, 282, 283
Crome, 275
Cromelein, 502
Cromlein, 178
Cromwell, 289, 573
Crook, 171, 374, 450
Crooks, 512
Cropley, 62, 333
Crosby, 7, 102, 107, 154, 297, 586
Crosier, 108
Cross, 18, 25, 29, 45, 82, 161, 271, 303, 326, 331
Crossfield, 360
Crossman, 532
Crouse, 315
Crowdus, 553
Crowe, 546
Crowell, 262, 578
Crowl, 549
Crowley, 88, 161
Crowly, 322
Crown, 8, 9, 23, 134
Crown Hill Cemetery, 469
Crownrich, 291
Crowther, 454
Croxton, 431
Crozier, 87, 362
Cruft, 419
Cruikshand, 271
Cruikshank, 253
cruiser **Shanandoah**, 475
Cruit, 375
Crum_onie, 594
Crumbaugh, 126, 152, 155, 158, 324
Crumfels, 9
Crump, 65
Crumpin, 515

Cruse, 108
Crutchett, 85, 484
Cudden, 255
Cudewia, 580
Cudlipp, 123
Cuesnest, 454
Cuiverwell, 220
Culbertson, 105
Culcannon, 447
Cull, 281, 477
Cullen, 237, 341, 402
Cullery, 373
Cullinan, 442
Cullinane, 569, 572
Cullum, 238, 432, 496, 544
Cully, 172
Culp, 514
Culpeper, 216
Culver, 309
Culverwell, 8
Cumberland, 310
Cumming, 22, 155
Cummings, 7, 150, 276, 415, 473, 493
Cummins, 378
Cunliff, 250
Cunningham, 128, 150, 159, 176, 290, 291, 383, 450, 458, 472, 480, 541, 582, 586
Curley, 3
Curlin, 171
Curran, 62, 91, 140, 308, 317, 459, 505, 554
Current, 537
Currie, 350
Currier, 409
Curry, 42
Curtain, 39, 233
Curtin, 93
Curtis, 63, 101, 235, 250, 270, 277, 432, 436, 540, 594
Curtiss, 326
Cushing, 107, 257, 330, 417, 480, 511, 547, 596
Cushman, 220, 288
Custar, 558

Custard, 472
Custer, 171, 214, 402, 435
Custis, 126, 216
Cutler, 259, 350, 351, 431, 565, 567
Cutter, 326, 461
cutter **Northerner**, 188
cutter **Sirius**, 112
Cutting, 297, 487
Cutts, 277, 323, 333, 545

D

D'Esterbeco, 454
d'Herbomez, 445
Dabney, 417
Dacher, 541
Dacy, 284
Dade, 426
Dahlgren, 106, 203, 333, 398, 484
Dailey, 81
Daily, 167, 515
Daingerfield, 25
Dainhardt, 467
Dainies, 126
Daisy, 346
Dale, 537
Daley, 397, 476
Dall, 246
Dallam, 56
Dallas, 247, 419
Dallon, 434
Dalton, 1, 43, 249, 384, 486
Daly, 74, 233, 282, 283, 303, 307, 541
Dalzell, 372
Dana, 111, 117, 224, 232, 399, 427, 544, 546, 570
Danby, 565
Dance, 251
Danenhower, 308, 325, 333, 420
Danforth, 427
Dangerfield, 376, 409
Daniel, 45, 120, 558
Daniels, 72, 105, 196, 228, 373, 427, 492
Dannoy, 350
Dannscome, 409

Dant, 466
Darby, 283
Darling, 131, 276, 315, 417, 564
Darnall, 268
Darnell, 59
Darnery, 453
Darrah, 148
Darrell, 6, 19, 57
Darrow, 276, 486, 536
Daugherty, 264
Davenport, 318, 350, 387, 459
David, 189, 443, 496
Davidge, 93, 143, 172, 333, 510
Davidson, 59, 99, 126, 128, 171, 301, 376, 429, 453, 487, 492, 565
Davies, 196, 234
Davin, 365
Davis, 1, 8, 26, 39, 41, 43, 46, 47, 59, 62, 72, 76, 79, 87, 91, 96, 102, 105, 108, 126, 131, 159, 165, 166, 171, 176, 180, 181, 183, 185, 191, 195, 196, 197, 200, 203, 204, 208, 211, 215, 219, 222, 229, 230, 243, 244, 246, 256, 261, 262, 267, 268, 277, 284, 286, 292, 294, 298, 299, 300, 301, 303, 304, 307, 308, 310, 311, 314, 333, 339, 344, 345, 348, 354, 355, 358, 359, 367, 368, 374, 385, 390, 398, 404, 414, 420, 432, 437, 438, 442, 446, 448, 462, 465, 466, 477, 484, 489, 492, 495, 496, 502, 515, 517, 524, 526, 545, 553, 556, 560, 565, 571
Davison, 478
Davou, 362
Daw, 181
Dawes, 359
Daws, 358
Dawson, 59, 152, 315, 333, 459, 492, 539, 558, 565
Day, 98, 133, 168, 277, 429, 485, 492, 537, 566, 586
Dayton, 5, 171, 277, 365, 385, 523
de Beaumont, 180
De Canine, 402
De Compte, 126

De Costa, 56, 326
de Filipi, 493
De Forest, 425
De Goesbriand, 445
De Hass, 230
De Kraft, 593
De La Roche, 322
de Lavalle, 409
de Lhuys, 476
de Marguerrites, 269
De Mariel, 422
de Monpierre, 453
de Montholon, 419
De Mott, 299
De Normandie, 175
De Reamer, 533
De Sales, 296
De Schiele, 14
de St Palais, 445
de Stael, 377
de Thouvenal, 376
de Trebriand, 559
De Trobriand, 560
De Valin, 536
De Voss, 126
dead chieftain, 93
Deakins, 576
Deal, 67
Dean, 288, 353, 421, 429, 438, 556, 557, 565
Deane, 167, 385
Deans, 356
Dearborn, 110, 373
Dearing, 333, 428, 564, 565
Death-bed marriage, 54
Decell, 527
Decons, 460
Deeble, 15, 41, 60, 322, 438
Deelar, 368
Deely, 483
Deems, 46
DeEntron, 180
Deeordy, 196
Deering, 141, 145, 148, 153, 181, 190, 253, 255
DeForest, 397

DeGress, 385
Degu, 108
Dehass, 240
Deihl, 212
DeKrafft, 545
Delacey, 478
Delafield, 227, 234, 333
Delancy, 17
Deland, 308
Delaney, 134
Delano, 108, 124, 374
Delany, 288, 414, 429, 493
Delius, 65
Dellinger, 119
Delly, 178
Delveechie, 276
Demaine, 301
Demar, 181
Dement, 227
Demers, 445
Demeter, 397
Deming, 176, 515
Demonett, 474
Dempsey, 454
Denby, 398, 543
Denham, 72, 310, 333, 471, 484
Denier, 251
Denis, 406
Denison, 125
Denman, 485, 494
Dennbond, 273
Denney, 526
Dennis, 65, 189, 246, 292, 453
Dennison, 108, 271, 307, 308, 333, 453
Densmore, 576
Dent, 165, 300, 393, 414, 477, 481, 501, 582
Dentinzer, 301
Denver, 491
Deny, 429
Depeirris, 453
DePutron, 182
Derby, 103, 397
Dermon, 493, 565
Derrickson, 470

Dervis, 462
DeSaussure, 22
Deshiell, 372
Desmond, 329
Desohart, 221
Dessormes, 453
Destorbuy, 453
Detmold, 66
DeTocqueville, 180
Deuel, 43
Devaughn, 461
DeVaughn, 333, 545
Devens, 544
Devereaux, 72
Devereux, 528
Devin, 558
Devine, 59, 102, 107
Deviney, 178
Devlin, 453
Devnoodt, 431
Devoe, 159
Dewey, 545, 563
Dewistoe, 514
DeWitt, 335
DeWolf, 363
Dexter, 150, 247, 276
DeZeng, 430
Diamond, 515
Dibble, 103, 105
Dick, 131
Dickens, 125, 137, 283, 444
Dickerson, 493
Dickins, 575
Dickinson, 4, 51, 145, 146, 557
Dickman, 136
Dicks, 308
Dickson, 126, 288, 290, 291, 333, 472, 515, 536
Didier, 165
Dietz, 563
Diggan, 510
Digges, 62, 235, 375, 415
Diggins, 248
Diggs, 10, 139, 282
Dignan, 5
Dikeman, 333

Dill, 9, 14, 59
Dillard, 576
Dille, 264
Dillenbach, 100
Diller, 402
Dillingham, 121
Dillon, 76, 373
Dimick, 123, 233, 333
Dimmick, 543
Dimond, 50, 356
Dinsmore, 572
Dittrich, 136
Divine, 43
Dix, 247, 478
Dixon, 61, 79, 121, 144, 167, 180, 221, 250, 267, 282, 296, 305, 326, 333, 354, 495, 543
Doare, 538
Dobbin, 387, 431
Dobbins, 431
Dobler, 87
Dobson, 333
Dodd, 61
Doddridge, 56
Dodge, 62, 66, 81, 101, 169, 253, 302, 309, 321, 322, 325, 333, 355, 361, 472, 559
Dodson, 595
Doescher, 412
Dogger, 462
Doherty, 159, 172
Dolan, 130, 141, 148, 402, 518
Dolday, 474
Dole, 487
<u>Dollar Jewelry Store</u>, 437
Dolphy, 493
Domene, 444
<u>Dominica Sister</u>, 408
Dommer, 22
Don, 94
Donahoe, 522
Donaldson, 59, 111, 210, 259, 301, 307, 373, 379, 381, 410, 457
Donare, 373
Donath, 533
Donegal, 342

Donegan, 415, 537
Donelan, 318, 319
Donelly, 57, 99, 303, 511
Donn, 272, 308, 411, 515, 570
Donne, 231
Donnell, 253
Donnelly, 65, 68, 82, 174, 193, 367, 535
Donney, 22
Donoghue, 86, 183, 438, 439
Donoho, 82, 109, 155, 345, 466
Donohue, 336, 356
Donolan, 348
Donovan, 90, 180, 181, 558
Dooley, 288
Doolittle, 381
Doran, 96
Doremus, 47
Dorgan, 545
Dorman, 56, 300
Dornan, 241
Dorsch, 49
Dorsett, 438, 502
Dorsey, 31, 307, 333, 359, 368, 385, 594, 596
Dorsheimer, 413
Dost, 101
Dostie, 342, 350, 351
Dotzler, 349
Doubleday, 94, 433, 558
Dougal, 22, 333
Dougherty, 77, 177, 303, 358, 381, 436, 504
Doughty, 29, 481
Douglas, 30, 131, 201, 220, 290, 291, 292, 367, 417, 480, 482, 493, 505, 575
Douglas Place, 30
Douglass, 1, 15, 103, 126, 310, 327, 422, 513
Douhey, 303, 304
Douroy, 351
Dove, 65, 102, 283, 333, 359, 468, 540, 568
Dow, 479
Dowell, 288

Dowling, 77, 83, 104, 136, 143, 175, 194, 237, 240, 358, 381, 424, 460, 461, 477, 481, 486, 542, 592
Dowman, 33
Downe, 417
Downer, 126
Downes, 107
Downey, 375, 474, 483
Downing, 166, 197, 210, 222, 308, 397, 580
Downman, 33, 139, 431, 492, 493, 494, 563
Downmann, 494
Downs, 118, 127, 139, 200, 265, 302, 451
Doyle, 46, 73, 156, 283, 303, 308, 310, 453
Drager, 308
Drake, 101, 326, 438, 552
Dramond, 57
Drane, 19, 200, 244, 282, 283, 494
Draper, 66, 108, 211, 268, 499
Dresel, 409
Dresler, 316
Dresser, 66, 161
Drew, 79, 100, 111, 326, 435, 547
Driggs, 102
Drinkard, 198, 199, 359
Driscoll, 101, 454, 479
Driver, 457
Drost, 543
Droyne, 284
Drummond, 312, 516
Drury, 46, 126, 165, 292, 452, 460, 476
Drybergh, 112
Dryden, 407
Dryer, 96, 559
Du Bois, 512
Du Plaine, 547
Du Puy, 276
Duane, 171, 247, 351
Dubant, 333
Dublington, 547
Dubois, 443, 445, 447
Duchet, 3

Duckery, 221
Dudley, 69, 115, 137, 196, 326, 476
Dudly, 559
Duen, 516
Duer, 472
Duerron, 382
Duffey, 586
Duffie, 266
Duffield, 272
Duffy, 141, 283, 284, 351, 383, 454, 570, 576
Dugan, 82, 101, 445
Duggan, 227
Duhamel, 62, 75, 283, 292, 386
Duke, 212
Duke of Hesse Darmstadt, 136
Duke of Marlborough, 574
Dukehart, 48
Dukes, 126, 250
Dukin, 101
Dulhousie, 464
Duly, 560
Dumas, 465
Dumbar, 88
Dumbarton, 328
Dumiken, 279
Dumont, 129, 473
Dunawin, 285
Dunbar, 180, 431
Dunbarton Hill, 320
Duncan, 75, 154, 291, 404, 464, 493, 532
Duncanson, 53, 244, 356, 368, 391
Dunford, 565
Dungan, 431
Dunham, 504, 508
Dunkaison, 511
Dunlop, 62, 363, 466, 490, 510, 512, 528, 533, 598
Dunn, 102, 197, 202, 222, 279, 296, 299, 300, 301, 382, 511
Dunne, 14, 294
Dunning, 507
Dunnington, 126
Dunwood, 267
Dunwoody, 354

Dupasseur, 453
Dupaty, 350
Duplessis, 350, 351
Dupont, 106, 287
Durand, 453, 454, 570
Durant, 162, 170
Durham, 188, 537
Durns, 260
Durward, 492, 565
Duryea, 64, 478
Dusenberry, 308
Dutcher, 48, 407
Dutton, 299, 300, 311
Duval, 279
Duvall, 2, 34, 245, 333, 356, 453, 512, 549, 561
Duvant, 333
Dwight, 416, 469
Dwyer, 284, 304
Dyar, 286
Dyer, 13, 14, 59, 62, 78, 158, 179, 227, 259, 264, 270, 291, 303, 304, 311, 333, 342, 472, 597, 598
Dyott, 242
Dyser, 333, 359
Dyson, 596
Dysslin, 587

E

Eaches, 372
Eagle's Nest, 446
Eagleston, 263
Eaheart, 315
Eames, 105, 185, 500
Earl, 333
Earle, 403
Earls, 42
Early, 249, 250, 341, 346, 423, 433, 520
Earness, 285
Easby, 127, 204, 333
Easeman, 468
Easley, 205
Eason, 287
East, 307
Eastburn, 470

Eastlake, 25
Eastman, 13, 267, 354
Easton, 79, 140, 472, 567
Eaton, 41, 107, 227, 276, 287, 304, 323, 431, 557, 578, 587
Ebbitt, 37, 60, 438
Ebel, 158
Eber, 35
Eberle, 569
Eberly, 333
Eby, 342, 487
Eccleston, 313, 443
Eckerson, 21, 551
Eckert, 347
Eckhardt, 97, 119
Eckington, 116, 495
Eckington House, 240
Eckles, 104
Eckloff, 307, 309, 367
Eckstein, 570
Eckton, 116
Eddins, 411
Edelen, 289, 371
Edelin, 147, 164, 303, 409, 477, 517, 591
Edes, 42, 119, 125, 181, 399
Edge Hill, 507
Edgerly, 467
Edie, 63
Edilin, 12
Edlin, 343
Edmond, 33, 184
Edmonds, 152, 371, 372, 552
Edmondson, 360
Edmonson, 356
Edmonston, 62, 88, 116, 270, 283, 284, 333, 540
Edmunds, 53
Edmunston, 502
Edward, 440
Edwards, 15, 89, 102, 105, 156, 159, 290, 333, 359, 378, 440, 457, 485, 524, 538
Eells, 214
Effects of tobacco, 54
Effingham Heights, 392

Egan, 100, 176
Egberrt, 568
Egenolf, 234
Eggemeyer, 102
Eggleston, 307
Ehenest, 453
Ehrmantraut, 592
Eichelberger, 327
Eichman, 531
Eighme, 390
Eilliot, 593
Eisenbeiss, 439, 449
Eisley, 188
Ekin, 567, 571
Ela, 333
Elan, 356
Elder, 361, 409, 445, 583
Eldred, 345
Eldridge, 153
Elgish, 92
Eliason, 74, 98, 112, 502
Eliot, 83, 183, 295, 333, 359
Eliott, 353
Elizabeth Mills, 65
Elkinton, 6
Ellenborough, 216
Ellery, 259, 402
Ellicott, 144, 427, 590
Ellicott's Mills, 37
Ellinger, 405
Elliot, 153, 292, 511, 514, 526, 592
Elliott, 71, 100, 103, 127, 171, 292, 350, 397, 543
Ellis, 6, 41, 49, 54, 103, 241, 308, 318, 333, 360, 373, 417, 461, 545, 583
Ellmaker, 564
Ellmyer, 76
Ellsworth, 88, 94, 282, 297
Elmore, 301
Elmwood, 340
Elmwood Cemetery, 272
Elorance, 569
Elsberg, 388
Elvans, 33, 333, 375
Ely, 74, 302, 456

Emanuel, 573
Embree, 259
Embry, 430
Embury, 164
Emby, 284
Emen, 517
Emerick, 474
Emerson, 127, 253, 255
Emery, 13, 176, 333
Emmanuel, 418
Emmerich, 303, 305
Emory, 109, 171, 278, 300, 432, 475, 573
Emoss, 109
Emperor of France, 78
Emrich, 574
Enals, 176
Enfield Chase, 339
Engel, 316
Enggren, 593
England, 443
Engle, 104, 560
English, 17, 56, 67, 77, 86, 107, 118, 132, 158, 221, 264, 333, 346, 381
Ennis, 3, 14, 62, 66, 93, 168, 265, 282, 333, 346, 354, 502, 510, 523, 544, 545, 589
Entwisle, 375, 474, 507
Envry, 453
Episcopal Church, 341
Erben, 512, 570, 573
Erdman, 372
Erhernt, 546
Ericsson, 183
Erwin, 6
Esberg, 431
Eschenburg, 103
Escole, 491, 565
Esdaile, 225
Eslin, 522
Esnard, 409
Espey, 137
Espiuta, 533
Esputa, 524
Essinger, 60
Estell, 453

Etchison, 79, 333
Etien, 214
Etting, 127
Euggoier, 552
Eustis, 433
Evans, 46, 64, 79, 91, 113, 118, 119, 174, 176, 179, 185, 208, 230, 261, 304, 329, 331, 333, 359, 367, 400, 456, 480, 505, 513, 514, 535, 537, 540, 545, 566, 583, 585, 587
Eveleth, 170, 319, 599
Everett, 20, 127, 307, 310, 317, 525, 529, 566, 591
Everhart, 429
Everly, 304
Eversfield, 560
Eversfield's Map of Italy, 266
Everson, 304
Every, 326
Ewalt, 130
Ewell, 48, 308, 432, 433
Ewers, 105
Ewing, 30, 104, 220, 247, 333, 377, 419, 461
Exchange Hotel, 258
Eyster, 366

F

Fagan, 34, 99, 165
Fague, 19
Fahey, 57
Fahnestock, 61, 79, 326
Failes, 284
Fainter, 46
Fairbanks, 306, 401
Fairchild, 523
Fairfax, 306
Fairfield, 112, 330
Falconer, 43, 93, 334, 466, 580
Fales, 582, 596
Fall, 231
Falstead, 297
Faltoute, 215
Falvey, 100
Fanning, 80, 454
Fant, 155, 183, 579

Fanton, 473
Farara, 579
Farini, 352
Farley, 144, 392, 454
Farmer, 49, 300
Farnham, 79, 195, 326, 334, 435, 438
Farnkoph, 308
Farnsworth, 102
Farnum, 204
Farquhar, 107
Farr, 579
Farragut, 106, 234, 255, 262, 330, 381, 398, 478
Farrand, 202
Farrar, 387
Farrington, 277
Farris, 232, 538
Farrish, 7
Farritan, 284
Farron, 343
Farule, 430
Fassett, 228
fast driving, 134
Faul, 570
Faulkner, 124, 156
Faux, 563
Favier, 152, 547, 548
Favier's Square, 152, 208
Fawsett, 152, 155, 158
Faxon, 268, 398
Fay, 70, 91, 196, 317, 492, 563, 565
Fayman, 129
Fayssoux, 387
Fearson, 306, 323, 333
Febiger, 107, 549
Fechtig, 308
Feehan, 446
Feeters, 397
Fegan, 300, 333
Felger, 303
Felix Holt, the Radical, 400
Fellows, 407
Felson, 291, 296
Female Bookkeepers, 450

Fendall, 1, 2, 61, 62, 175, 182, 249, 254, 263, 294, 318, 384, 423, 426, 510, 597, 600
Fendell, 240
Fenian Sisterhood, 50
Fenkes, 488
Fenmore, 402
Fennell, 579
Fenner, 195
Fennimore, 130
Fenton, 105, 461, 478
Fentwell, 569
Fenwick, 12, 41, 53, 59, 64, 86, 181, 292, 333, 359, 443, 505, 595
Fergurson, 477
Ferguson, 45, 304, 333, 346, 490, 498, 554
Ferne, 453, 454
Ferney, 453
Ferre, 92
Ferrell, 277, 547
Ferrero, 227, 468
Ferris, 400, 418, 468
Ferry, 315, 406, 417
Fessenden, 4, 40, 168, 191, 247, 355
Fetterman, 595
Fiedenbach, 511
Field, 41, 102, 151, 260, 277, 319, 340, 344, 537, 556, 596
Fielder, 10
Fields, 48, 303, 349, 422, 456
Fieman, 326
Fife, 528, 561
Fill, 197
Fillebrown, 434, 482
Filleman, 595
Fillmore, 199, 252, 315
Filson, 74
Finch, 58, 310
Finckel, 56, 310
Findlay, 182
Finger, 454
Finkman, 282, 283
Finn, 425, 593
Finney, 221, 307, 308, 537
first prayer, 3

Fischer, 454
Fish, 66, 125, 326, 350, 351, 537
Fisher, 6, 13, 18, 31, 36, 39, 80, 85, 88, 89, 91, 94, 97, 127, 136, 138, 144, 147, 153, 156, 159, 163, 168, 172, 174, 177, 180, 181, 185, 190, 192, 236, 254, 303, 328, 362, 384, 397, 401, 402, 403, 427, 434, 440, 442, 446, 448, 451, 453, 456, 458, 463, 479, 494, 497, 500, 502, 523, 580, 584, 586, 596
Fisk, 34, 159, 200, 324
Fiske, 204, 494
Fitch, 104, 460, 489, 563, 583
Fitz, 477
Fitzgerald, 6, 80, 100, 102, 127, 174, 176, 298, 308, 311, 360, 581
Fitzgibbons, 420
Fitzhugh, 31, 62, 78, 217, 218, 348, 390
Fitzimmons, 389
Fitzpatrick, 47, 52, 81, 153, 195, 287, 296, 360, 445, 454, 599
Fitzsimmons, 372, 431
five cent coin, 232
Fivey, 330
Flaget, 443
Flagg, 121, 276
Flagler, 428
Flaherty, 485
Flanagan, 283, 284, 325, 459
Flanegan, 415
Flanigan, 276, 408
Flannery Brothers, 211
Flasson, 31
Fleetwood, 489, 585
Fleming, 47, 56, 102, 195, 267, 285, 355, 429, 475, 547, 570
Flemming, 284
Flenner, 307, 367, 504
Fletcher, 96, 100, 166, 178, 196, 222, 228, 249, 251, 262, 284, 303, 367, 442, 493, 509
Fleury, 348, 352, 476
Fling, 127
Flinn, 61

Flint, 379, 381, 423, 586
Flood, 326, 373
Florence, 211, 289
Flotow, 465
Floyd, 101, 136, 536
Flynn, 177, 204, 233, 305, 430, 565
Foeley, 138
Fogarty, 287, 518
Fogg, 509
Fogler, 572
Foley, 99, 168, 177, 244, 303, 365, 415, 423, 474, 494, 528
Folk, 307
Folks, 309
Follansbee, 59, 333, 398, 577, 590
Follet, 539
Follett, 475
Fonda, 326
Fontaine, 250, 567
Fontaubleau, 453
Foos, 369, 468
Foot, 117, 121, 412
Foote, 72, 74, 137, 202, 282, 575
Footh, 351
Forbes, 32, 52, 104, 560, 587
Forbis, 164
Forbush, 163
Force, 62, 166, 265, 438, 523
Ford, 20, 40, 91, 112, 121, 127, 147, 155, 156, 295, 300, 307, 308, 333, 344, 348, 359, 438, 563, 596
Ford Theatre, 21, 162
Ford's Theater, 238
Ford's Theatre, 242, 369, 500
Foreman, 526
Forgey, 429
Forney, 40, 280, 283, 284, 325
Forrest, 23, 186, 285, 291, 331, 419, 446, 476, 539, 546, 556, 558, 560, 561, 579
Forsberg, 303
Forster, 548
Forsyth, 9, 62, 302, 374, 558
Forsythe, 374
Fort, 111, 157
Fort Abercrombie, 94

Fort Adams, 549
Fort Atkinson, 198
Fort Baker, 546
Fort Boise, 551
Fort Bridger, 521
Fort Brown, 520
Fort Defiance, 440
Fort Delaware, 213
Fort Dodge, 253, 501
Fort Donelson, 520
Fort Drane, 495
Fort Ellsworth, 450
Fort Fisher, 171, 343
Fort Foot, 475
Fort Foote, 439
Fort Gibson, 131, 558
Fort Goodwin, 195, 206, 214, 559
Fort Grant, 169, 195
Fort Gratiot, 486
Fort Halleck, 96, 344
Fort Harrison, 171
Fort Harrison Cemetery, 520
Fort Independence, 357
Fort Jefferson, 511
Fort Kearney, 520
Fort Kearny, 558, 559
Fort Laramie, 432, 520, 549, 595
Fort Larned, 96
Fort Leavenworth, 411, 520
Fort Lincoln, 477
Fort Madison, 501, 514
Fort McAllister, 171
Fort McHenry, 475
Fort Monroe, 160, 188, 202, 417
Fort Morgan, 88
Fort Morton, 387
Fort Norfolk, 575
Fort Phil Kearney, 595
Fort Phil Kearny, 590
Fort Pillow, 520
Fort Pulaski, 130, 154, 291
Fort Randall, 559
Fort Rawlings, 551
Fort Reno, 373
Fort Rice, 350, 558, 559
Fort Riley, 559

Fort Schuyler, 350
Fort Scott, 575
Fort Smith, 429
Fort Snelling, 348, 379, 520
Fort Steedman, 171
Fort Stevens, 218, 572, 580
Fort Sully, 350
Fort Sumter, 17, 24, 71, 432
Fort Taylor, 573
Fort Union, 486
Fort Vancouver, 21
Fort Wadsworth, 94
Fort Wagner, 171
Fort Washington, 475, 489
Fort Wayne, 161, 170, 220, 445, 523, 528
Fort Whipple, 475
Fort Willis, 522
Forthuse, 493
Fortress Monroe, 25, 138, 145, 162, 185, 191, 203, 208, 215, 218, 219, 229, 246, 255, 256, 269, 317, 390, 448, 478, 496, 551, 589
Fortune, 66, 173
Fortzer, 454
Forward, 247
Foscue, 523
Fosdick, 345
Foster, 77, 171, 269, 307, 309, 316, 330, 353, 401, 433, 522, 541, 583
Fotty, 359
Foulkes, 37, 74
Foully, 569
Foutze, 509
Fowble, 212
Fowle, 142
Fowler, 61, 62, 200, 266, 268, 308, 311, 324, 333, 401, 427, 459, 524, 580, 581
Fox, 7, 87, 222, 231, 290, 305, 460, 462, 489, 506, 507, 561, 571
Foxen, 296
Fragrett, 67
Frailey, 330
Fran, 585
France, 89, 310, 512

Frances, 255
Francesco, 210
Francis, 23, 429, 453, 534, 537, 565
Francisco, 222
Franconia, 453
Frank, 563
Franklin, 10, 24, 38, 141, 262, 416, 428, 433, 506
Franklin Row, 285
Franks, 53, 102
Fraser, 300, 327, 453
Frasher, 540
Frayser, 275
Frazier, 221, 259, 268, 301, 307, 308, 311, 318, 357, 397, 444, 538
Freas, 307
Frech, 295
Frecke, 22
Freddburg, 105
Frederick, 471, 500
Free, 367
Freeland, 23, 156
Freeling, 109
Freeman, 179, 333, 345, 372, 388, 431, 465, 492, 500, 518, 543, 548, 566, 591
Freer, 224
Freizor, 493
Fremont, 219, 248
French, 6, 17, 98, 102, 198, 224, 228, 234, 292, 325, 326, 333, 345, 433, 500, 508, 561, 586
Freundt, 508
Frey, 508
Frick, 52
Fridley, 359
Friedrick, 361
Friel, 234
Friend, 228
Friendship, 194
Frier, 524
Friery, 369
Fries, 369, 479
frig **Congress**, 323, 395
frig **New Ironsides**, 582
frigate **Blanche**, 279

Frink, 11
Frisbee, 108
Frisbie, 26
Fritz, 171
Frommel, 512
Frommell, 435
Fromwell, 466
Frontier, 453
Frost, 149, 296, 304, 458, 560
Fry, 225, 276, 300, 303, 333, 433, 552
Fuger, 354
Fugitt, 333, 420, 540
Fullalove, 333
Fuller, 38, 57, 76, 242, 267, 299, 310, 367, 409, 487, 492, 526, 565, 569
Fullerton, 350, 428, 459, 494, 557, 564, 565
Fullwood, 346
Fulton, 352, 425, 526
Fulton Market, 236
Funari, 422
Fuqua, 54
Furguson, 305
Furman, 564
Furse, 310
Fuseli, 25
Fussell, 60, 570
Fyffe, 365

G

Gaburri, 5
Gaddis, 59, 127, 266, 278, 294, 334, 471, 476
Gadsby, 26, 36, 346, 351
Gage, 372, 480
Gageby, 105
Gaines, 488
Gaitley, 284
Galbreth, 538
Gale, 383
Gales, 116, 240, 260, 328, 446, 548
Galion, 513
Gall, 45

Gallagher, 98, 103, 253, 276, 308, 356, 575
Gallaher, 77
Gallant, 366, 466
Gallatin, 247
Galligan, 454
Galliger, 153
Gallinger, 514
Galloway, 94, 422
Galt, 8, 17, 61, 62, 119, 212, 214, 264, 323, 334, 375, 418, 466, 500, 546, 597
Galvin, 138
Gamble, 404, 558
Gambrill, 301
Gamer, 308
Gannon, 454
Gantt, 29
Garat, 304
Garber, 342
Gardener, 542
Gardette, 546
Gardiner, 4, 122
Gardner, 16, 127, 151, 205, 234, 303, 329, 334, 351, 385, 423, 502, 517, 528, 533, 542, 578
Garett, 515
Garfield, 310
Garigaldi, 366
Garland, 105, 419
Garner, 127, 282, 308, 452, 477
Garnett, 207, 308, 351, 359
Garobodi, 435
Garrard, 171
Garretson, 99, 400
Garrett, 300, 367, 577
Garrick, 534
Garriety, 362
Garrish, 168
Garrison, 19, 315, 574
Garry, 166
Garthwaite, 215
Gartland, 145
Garvey, 423
Garvin, 509
Gary, 55, 62, 392, 454

Gasch, 334
Gaskill, 138
Gaskings, 135
Gaskins, 153, 179, 254, 563, 575
Gass, 152
Gassonett, 373
Gaston, 238
Gate, 524
Gates, 103, 105, 201, 305, 467, 475
Gatewood, 116, 135, 138, 147, 153
Gatto, 527
Gatton, 36, 359
Gauler, 148
Gaunt, 284
Gaunter, 141, 142, 148
Gautier, 222, 538
Gavarni, 580
Gawler, 15, 334, 434
Gay, 232
gay shopkeepers, 554
Gayle, 260, 268
Gaylor, 56, 305
Gaylord, 66
Gayrand, 114
Gear, 167, 527
Geary, 287
Gebhard, 234
Gee, 142, 227, 258, 273, 293, 386
Geffrard, 405
Gegan, 423
Geise, 392
Geiser, 313, 453, 454
Geisezing, 486
Geizelburst, 454
Gelong, 167
Gelser, 453
Genan, 19
General Hospital of D C, 326
Geo, 358
George, 444, 450
Georgii, 311
Geralds, 119
Gerard, 276
Gerdemann, 306
Gerhardt, 501
Germain, 575

German, 586
Germon, 552
Gerring, 291
Gerritson, 536
Gerry, 552, 578
Gerrynote, 522
Gessford, 512
Gettie, 282
Gettings, 151
Gettner, 471
Getty, 171, 425, 433, 559, 560
Gherardi, 107
Ghioni, 544
Gibbens, 493
Gibbon, 171, 374, 382, 560
Gibbons, 37, 41, 197, 423
Gibbony, 260
Gibbs, 108, 133, 334, 464, 558, 564, 584
Giberson, 578
Gibson, 39, 60, 84, 99, 104, 134, 158, 187, 192, 234, 240, 244, 248, 258, 296, 302, 334, 352, 397, 464, 480, 534, 540, 585, 589
Giddings, 470, 558
Gideon, 61, 455
Giesboro Point, 77
Gieseking, 334, 548
Giffith, 414
Gifford, 294
Gilbam, 562
Gilbert, 559
Gilbreath, 103
Gilbreth, 122, 277
Giles, 97, 117, 344, 368
Gilford, 195
Gill, 161, 278, 303, 423, 454, 530, 568
Gillem, 374, 559, 560
Gillen, 154
Gillender, 537
Gillespie, 453
Gillete, 330
Gillett, 8, 100
Gillette, 9, 13, 196, 207, 349, 356, 402

Gilliland, 103
Gillingham, 196
Gillis, 268
Gilliss, 549
Gillmore, 171, 433, 526
Gillpatrick, 278
Gills, 414
Gilman, 38, 334, 379, 409, 476, 540, 574
Gilmon, 388
Gilmor, 413
Gilmore, 276, 325, 515, 532
Gilpatric, 228
Gilpin, 19
Gilston, 182
Giltner, 537
Gimmill, 159
Gingall, 175
Ginty, 372
Girard, 330, 453, 454
Girton, 129
Giston, 586
Gitt, 419
Gittings, 334, 423
Giulay, 506
Given, 22, 47, 153, 154, 307, 327, 334, 346, 395
Givens, 59, 460
Glachett, 161
Gladiateur, 470
Gladke, 161
Gladmon, 127
Gladwin, 309, 408
Glanner, 453, 454
Glans, 425
Glascoe, 479
Glasgow, 293
Glass, 165, 320
Glazebrook, 409
Gleason, 458, 471, 510
Glen Echo, 293
Glenallen, 339
Glendale Cemetery, 520
Glenn, 30, 343, 551
Glennon, 177
Glenwood Cemetery, 143, 200, 386

Glick, 391
Gliebe, 529
Glisson, 106
Glossbrenner, 47
Glosson, 596
Glover, 425, 432
Gobright, 334
Goddard, 62, 77, 110, 146, 292, 295, 334, 358, 452
Godey, 34, 59, 253, 334, 428, 548
Godfrey, 146, 418
Godgin, 215
Godman, 101, 362
Godon, 183
Godwin, 565
Goett, 453
Goetz, 511
Goff, 287, 505
Goheens, 308
Golden, 134, 176, 284, 308
Golder, 454
Goldie, 454
Goldin, 334
Golding, 127
Goldsborough, 57, 106, 175, 198, 219, 315, 341, 561, 573
Goldschmidt, 428
Goldsmith, 172
Goldstein, 63
Goldthwait, 573
Golifer, 453
Gonzaga College, 292
Gonzales, 27, 34, 251, 404, 457
Good, 346, 538
Good Hope, 546
Goodall, 255, 311, 474
Goode, 480, 553
Goodenow, 281
Goodfellow, 284, 289, 421
Goodhelp, 546
Goodhue, 478, 587
Gooding, 41, 80, 85, 90, 285, 373, 381, 392, 400, 446, 465, 502, 532
Goodloe, 492
Goodman, 234
Goodno, 310

Goodrich, 209, 281, 302, 443, 470, 529
Goodrick, 87, 194
Goods, 1, 39
Goodwin, 107, 284, 470
Gool, 141
Gorbutt, 422
Gordon, 12, 35, 36, 188, 209, 237, 253, 285, 303, 328, 356, 433, 435, 453, 476, 564
Gordonsdale, 436
Gorman, 352, 357, 446
Gosling, 505
Gosnell, 233
Gosselin, 492, 565
Gosuie, 511
Goszler, 40
Gotchill, 285
Gottachalk, 304
Gotthold, 178
Gough, 524
Gould, 234, 397, 404, 489
Gouldman, 275
Gouldsby, 461
Gouley, 290
Gov't bldgs, 84
Gove, 310
Gover, 257, 555
Gow, 259
Gowan, 562
Gozlan, 443
Gozler, 500
Grabel, 234
Grace, 415, 446
Grace Church, 463
Graciani, 362
Grady, 144, 192, 384, 431
Graff, 91, 463
Graffin, 552
Graften, 530
Grafton, 98, 207, 271, 280, 292, 522, 547
Graham, 4, 24, 28, 47, 120, 188, 214, 229, 284, 301, 310, 334, 398, 419, 454, 487, 494
Grammer, 179, 264

Grammond, 595
Gran, 222
Granby Farm, 242, 404
Grandison, 285
Granger, 167, 171, 202, 351, 374, 433, 558, 559, 560
Grant, 24, 34, 42, 44, 59, 66, 79, 87, 122, 129, 134, 165, 170, 211, 214, 215, 238, 243, 261, 290, 300, 301, 326, 330, 343, 381, 386, 429, 433, 434, 468, 478, 516, 521, 550, 551, 554, 582, 595
Grantham, 428
Grassland, 139
Gratiot, 56
Gravel, 169
Graven, 167
Graves, 334, 385, 532, 573
Gray, 51, 55, 62, 74, 167, 225, 246, 271, 283, 301, 304, 326, 332, 334, 349, 367, 400, 410, 423, 427, 428, 434, 478, 486, 504, 514, 562, 563, 564, 565, 599
Graynor, 191
Grayson, 8, 266
Greason, 109, 112, 311, 378
Great Cavalry Depot of the U S, 77
Greaves, 486
Greeley, 243
Green, 8, 20, 33, 59, 61, 69, 84, 97, 103, 107, 111, 114, 115, 130, 132, 134, 137, 139, 143, 146, 251, 267, 282, 292, 298, 300, 301, 328, 334, 361, 362, 393, 431, 458, 526, 542, 564, 569, 573, 583, 598
Green Mountain Farm, 12
Greenberry Point Farm, 153, 201, 542
Greene, 4, 5, 71, 106, 130, 354, 491, 537, 538, 570, 578
Greenhalgh, 348
Greenhow, 302
Greenland, 345
Greenlaw, 455
Greenleaf, 308, 426
Greenleaf Point, 75

Greenlow, 312
Greenman, 6
Greenmount Cemetery, 298
Greenwell, 305
Greenwood, 233, 272, 542, 587
Greenwood Cemetery, 320
Greer, 429
Greeves, 344
Gregg, 48, 100, 111, 334, 558, 560
Gregory, 64, 169, 346, 439, 492, 563
Grenasher, 311
Gressman, 163
Grevemeyer, 268
Grey, 48, 334, 513
Grider, 411
Gridley, 315
Grier, 41
Grierson, 374, 558, 560
Griest, 103
Griffen, 277
Griffin, 103, 171, 283, 310, 311, 319, 358, 365, 433, 494, 517, 559, 560, 573
Griffing, 330
Griffith, 3, 15, 22, 30, 68, 140, 584
Griffiths, 514
Griggs, 513, 570
Grilley, 20
Grimes, 136, 217, 446, 570, 600
Grimes' Hill, 553
Grimes' Tavern, 33
Grimshaw, 470
Grinder, 16, 22, 27, 334
Grinnell, 66, 72, 257, 547
Grish, 545
Grisi, 364
Griswold, 66, 155, 316, 461, 551
Groge, 454
Groggin, 356
Groggon, 359
Gronart, 373
Groom, 555
Grophard, 133
Gross, 276, 442, 456, 471
Grossman, 66
Grost, 296

Groux, 43
Grove, 430, 549, 565, 591
Grover, 29, 61, 131, 171, 187, 192, 242, 486, 554, 559
Groves, 37
Grubb, 310, 563
Grubbs, 45
Grunding, 508
Grupe, 19, 504
Gtwn College, 290
Gubitosi, 369
Gude, 543
Gudgen, 204
Gudgin, 215
Guernelsey, 537
Guest, 223
Guiccioli, 455
Guild, 189, 315
Guilford, 410
Guinand, 304, 305, 334
Gulick, 36, 334, 468
gunboat **Quinebaug**, 124
Gundaker, 342
Gunnell, 127
Gunter, 259
Gunther, 305
Gunton, 98, 326, 334
Gurk, 139
Gurley, 45, 197, 299, 386, 455, 585
Gurney, 225
Gurowski, 185
Gusler, 284
Gustaff, 183
Guthrie, 102, 247, 262, 419
Gutshall, 570
Guy, 266, 352, 493
Gwin, 209, 323
Gwyn, 289
Gwynn, 517

H

Hable, 334
Haborow, 453
Hackett, 30, 209, 334
Hacksom, 537
Hadden, 567

Haff, 383
Hagan, 6, 102, 241
Hager, 429
Hagerts, 164
Haggerty, 418, 476
Hagins, 203
Hagner, 121, 124, 188, 434, 449, 579, 591
Hahn, 350, 351
Haines, 105, 308, 342, 345
Hair, 81
Hairgrove, 428
Hake, 188
Halabird, 486, 567
Haldeman, 372
Hale, 104, 175, 326, 422, 525, 556, 569
Hales, 70
Haley, 104, 488, 493
Haliday, 62
Hall, 36, 45, 53, 60, 63, 66, 74, 79, 98, 121, 124, 139, 142, 145, 147, 150, 151, 174, 175, 176, 181, 188, 200, 207, 211, 219, 233, 262, 268, 277, 278, 300, 326, 334, 349, 359, 366, 376, 381, 390, 408, 412, 420, 429, 434, 435, 439, 453, 457, 459, 467, 474, 476, 477, 479, 484, 486, 490, 492, 493, 494, 511, 529, 530, 541, 549, 563, 565, 571, 579, 585, 596
Halleck, 7, 133, 214, 343
Halley, 300, 372
Halliday, 299, 300, 356, 502
Hallinane, 127
Hallinau, 292
Hallock, 17, 23, 433
Hallowell, 28, 493
Halpin, 564
Halsey, 215, 388, 431
Halstead, 262
Hambleton, 60, 231
Hamblin, 334
Hambrick, 48
Hambright, 202
Hamel, 359

Hamer, 54
Hamill, 540
Hamilton, 10, 60, 101, 152, 158, 176, 206, 231, 234, 247, 273, 303, 315, 334, 371, 375, 378, 433, 486, 492, 563, 565
Hamlain, 362
Hamlin, 72, 228, 389, 391, 412, 431, 500
Hammack, 172
Hammer, 105
Hammers, 491, 565
Hammett, 477
Hammon, 568
Hammond, 7, 138, 185, 252, 254, 290, 291, 339, 466, 540, 599
Hampton, 141, 162, 456
Hance, 421
Hanckel, 325
Hancock, 24, 80, 155, 171, 331, 343, 344, 374, 378, 385, 433, 459, 502, 540
Hancy, 467
Hand, 272, 564
Handbury, 354
Handley, 8, 98, 112
Handy, 65, 96, 118, 129, 203, 334, 358, 449, 477
Hanes, 518, 595
Hanewinckel, 486
Hanford, 20
Hanger, 231
Hanks, 380
Hanley, 147, 153, 587
Hanna, 67, 260
Hannet, 157
Hannum, 108
Hanscom, 152
Hanselton, 399
Hansman, 359
Hanson, 13, 20, 77, 98, 111, 256, 334, 403, 518
Harbach, 102
Harbaugh, 69, 77, 170, 295, 308, 427, 527
Harbenrother, 362

Harbin, 304, 524
Harbour, 255
Harbuck, 259
Hard, 473
Hard Bargain & Small Profit, 371
Hardee, 433, 522
Harden, 438
Hardesty, 463
Hardie, 99, 534
Hardin, 560
Harding, 53, 108, 132, 325, 538
Hardings, 480
Hardon, 577
Hardwick, 273
Hardy, 83, 156
Harewood, 437
Harfard, 277
Hargrave, 104, 531
Hargrove, 538
Harkins, 101
Harkness, 66, 148, 251, 264, 310, 311, 348, 401, 453, 462
Harlan, 24, 79, 105, 306, 312, 326, 385, 522
Harland, 313, 544
Harley, 129, 446
Harlow, 410, 411, 415
Harman, 304
Harmer, 345
Harmon, 72, 196, 253, 356, 545
Harmony, 124
Harmony Cemetery, 218, 520
Harned, 111
Harner, 528, 537
Harnett, 90
Harold, 105, 201
Harper, 38, 39, 77, 160, 233, 234, 262, 289, 359, 409, 444, 453, 458, 513
Harreman, 537
Harrington, 80, 100, 304, 311, 355, 397, 483, 484
Harrinway, 38
Harris, 69, 100, 109, 131, 143, 154, 229, 231, 283, 317, 323, 370, 375,

391, 409, 429, 434, 435, 448, 452, 467, 477, 499, 555, 573, 596
Harrison, 13, 35, 57, 65, 97, 104, 118, 120, 126, 127, 196, 203, 263, 284, 303, 308, 365, 389, 423, 438, 453, 462, 514
Harron, 217, 515
Harrover, 59, 244, 334, 442
Harry, 186, 189, 238, 567
Hart, 25, 127, 143, 211, 224, 303, 305, 330, 345, 346, 372, 381, 496, 541, 544, 557, 565, 581
Harte, 215
Hartell, 103
Hartenstein, 146
Hartindale, 432
Hartley, 313, 467, 476
Hartman, 164, 536
Hartright, 136
Hartshorne, 536
Hartsuff, 17, 171
Hartz, 417
Harvard class, 497
Harvey, 57, 112, 117, 133, 169, 283, 284, 292, 327, 334, 338, 355, 366, 437, 463, 484, 512, 526, 573
Harwood, 20, 149, 380, 398
Hasbrook, 384
Hasinger, 513
Haskell, 544
Haskins, 29, 431, 526, 565
Haslup, 307
Hassler, 38, 101, 214, 375
Hastings, 120, 193, 235, 380, 414
Hatch, 55, 374, 433, 452, 558, 560
Hathaway, 159
Hatting, 207
Hatton, 110
Hauptan, 39
Hauptman, 127
Haven, 72, 86
Havenner, 8, 43, 287, 313, 334
Havens, 71, 453
Havermans, 190
Havers, 537
Havewinckel, 548

Haviland, 235, 245, 365, 557
Haw, 265, 374, 471
Haw Hill, 70
Hawkings, 454
Hawkins, 94, 111, 310, 311, 465
Hawks, 423
Hawley, 251, 524
Haxall, 410, 411, 501
Hay, 41, 127, 300, 474, 545
Haycock, 315
Hayden, 50, 385, 477, 487, 551, 558, 579
Haydon, 6
Hayes, 100, 102, 228, 308, 334, 353, 476, 571, 574
Hayne, 501, 556
Hayner, 134, 143
Haynes, 210, 537
Hayre, 305
Hays, 129, 132, 170, 306, 433, 593
Hayward, 250, 360, 589
Haywood, 454, 538
Hazard, 462
Hazel, 178
Hazelton, 351
Hazen, 171, 374, 559, 560
Hazleton, 159
Hazon, 355
Hazzard, 299
Hazzelton, 307
Hazzle, 454
Hazzleton, 308
HcHugh, 50
Heacock, 231
Head, 111, 202, 257
Headlee, 347
Heal, 188
Heald, 109, 221, 310
Healey, 339
Healy, 127
Heard, 59, 224
Hearn, 104
Heartnes, 453
Heartt, 589
Heath, 213, 215, 360, 415, 444, 552, 579

Heaton, 186, 593
Hebb, 38
Heck, 164
Hecksher, 497
Hedrick, 307, 356
Heffar, 290
Heffernan, 287
Hegener, 342
Heger, 357
Heiberger, 334
Heilbrun, 176, 334
Heilman, 104
Heilprin, 299
Heiner, 102
Heintzelman, 432, 480, 558
Heirtand, 276
Heiskell, 111, 517
Heiskill, 15
Heisle, 537
Heitzelberger, 139
Helfstean, 251
Hellen, 208, 334, 461, 493, 509, 581
Helmick, 45, 428
Hemenway, 255
Heming, 284
Hemphill, 277, 523, 541
Hempstead, 3
Henderson, 1, 2, 65, 77, 103, 131, 260, 307, 342, 350, 351, 373, 470, 513, 585, 589, 600
Hendley, 114, 300
Hendricks, 101, 292, 355, 485, 595
Henehett, 526
Henert, 460
Henks, 559
Henley, 10
Henly, 518
Hennessy, 445
Henney, 146
Henni, 445
Henning, 39, 300, 303, 334, 548, 590
Hennon, 284
Henny, 306
Henrahan, 29
Henricks, 493
Henriques, 121, 288

Henry, 24, 80, 90, 98, 102, 138, 205, 290, 326, 334, 351, 444, 483, 492, 493, 506
Hens, 196
Henshaw, 303
Henton, 72
Hepburn, 1, 257, 299, 345, 437
Herbert, 1, 3, 15, 83, 153, 174, 198, 201, 204, 347, 358, 359, 457, 544
Hercoy, 453
Herdon, 238
Herman, 226, 373
Hermitage, 173, 371
Hern, 307
Herold, 159, 189, 221, 282, 283, 303
Heron, 454, 544
Herr, 172, 267, 354
Herrick, 78, 389
Herring, 33, 334
Herrington Manor, 588
Herron, 273, 300
Herschberger, 501
Hershberger, 514
Hert, 430
Hertzberg, 153
Herzber, 334
Herzberg, 81, 153, 334, 440, 540, 583
Herzog, 487
Hess, 10, 102, 392, 581
Hessan, 351
Hesse, 388, 431
Hesselberger, 101
Hetzell, 485
Hewett, 114
Hewitt, 444, 582
Heydon, 149, 230
Heyer, 390
Hiatt, 429
Hick, 75
Hickenlarfer, 523
Hickey, 3, 9, 11, 12, 28, 33, 125, 298, 299, 300, 303
Hickok, 75
Hicks, 350, 359, 470, 537, 555
Hide, 466

Hidneck, 514
Hieder, 175
Higby, 311
Higginbotham, 109, 492, 494
Higgins, 51, 174, 242, 251, 284, 454, 557
High Hills of Coony, 438
Highland, 67
Hildt, 234
Hilgard, 273
Hill, 20, 34, 42, 62, 79, 81, 86, 120, 127, 136, 140, 214, 215, 300, 304, 310, 311, 330, 334, 358, 363, 367, 393, 398, 433, 449, 493, 497, 517, 518, 529, 547, 557
Hillenbach, 354
Hilliken, 504
Hillman, 66, 453
Hills, 267, 355, 473
Hilton, 173, 245, 334, 405, 438, 502, 530, 540
Hilton Head, 522
Himmelway, 289
Hindman, 499
Hine, 430
Hines, 8, 28, 30, 126, 200, 414, 456, 502, 515, 535, 561
Hinesley, 579
Hinks, 29
Hinman, 103, 315
Hinson, 405
Hinton, 300, 367, 485, 548
Hipkins, 388, 424, 431
Hipwell, 455
Hire, 350, 351
Hirlay, 501
Hirsch, 565
Hitchcock, 127, 215, 227, 347, 365
Hite, 346
Hitselberger, 452
Hitz, 69, 115, 137, 334
Hitzelberger, 149, 173
Hoach, 188
Hoag, 186
Hoar, 399
Hoban, 334

Hobbie, 563
Hobbs, 253, 307
Hobson, 251
Hobzer, 127
Hockwell, 373
Hoctor, 301
Hodge, 61, 302, 565
Hodges, 43, 117, 236, 269, 457
Hodgkin, 110, 308
Hodgkins, 108, 123, 196
Hodgkisson, 534
Hodgsin, 470
Hodgson, 1, 84, 282
Hodsdon, 122
Hoe, 334
Hoff, 315, 573
Hoffar, 290
Hoffman, 19, 127, 153, 210, 245, 277, 308, 346, 402, 455, 460, 465, 504, 550
Hogan, 103, 118, 147, 159, 248, 278, 365, 383, 392, 454, 488, 505
Hoge, 101
Hogeman, 14
Hoister, 345
Holbrook, 359
Holcomb, 537
Holcombe, 331, 376, 410
Holden, 327
Holdsworth, 356
Holladay, 66, 450
Holland, 85, 138, 210, 273, 428, 504, 537, 541, 557, 565
Holleck, 24
Holleran, 127, 494
Holley, 382
Hollidge, 80, 210
Hollingshead, 43, 226, 326
Hollingsworth, 348, 481, 592
Hollister, 389, 436
Hollman, 234
Hollmann, 525
Holloran, 80
Holloway, 165, 167
Hollowbush, 565
Hollyday, 13, 413

Holman, 17, 391
Holmes, 18, 280, 304, 365, 479, 533, 550
Holoham, 282
Holohan, 283
Holopeter, 276
Holroyd, 292, 304
Holt, 39, 45, 47, 50, 159, 227, 303, 334, 407, 428, 531, 563
Holton, 407, 547
Holtzman, 377, 395, 487
Holzshire, 57
Home, 496
Home Place, 210
Homer, 270, 290, 291, 304
Honder, 330
Honey, 571
Honke, 586
Honore, 288
Hood, 106, 115, 130, 151, 227, 310, 414, 422, 512
Hoodlass, 417
Hooe, 142, 172, 226
Hook, 92, 429
Hooker, 24, 26, 171, 315, 343, 379, 433
Hooper, 408, 470, 580
Hoose, 174
Hooton, 103
Hoover, 61, 62, 99, 300, 310, 334, 367, 476, 581
Hoph, 459
Hopkins, 13, 21, 32, 57, 104, 108, 114, 140, 210, 258, 304, 334, 341, 372, 405, 413, 517, 587
Hopper, 552
Hore, 348
Horig, 181
Horley, 551
Horn, 91, 536
Hornbeck, 387
Hornbrook, 72
Horne, 466
Horner, 288, 528
Horning, 283
Hornsly, 159

Horraghan, 22
Horseman, 48, 75, 132, 213
Horton, 28, 105, 342, 350, 351, 575
Hortpence, 314
Horwitz, 52
Hoskins, 348
Hosmer, 235, 290, 388, 426, 430, 515, 563, 564, 565
Hosmeris, 288
Hotley, 454
Hotsenpiller, 104
Hotz, 389, 431
Hough, 55, 59, 127, 135, 144, 153, 254, 334, 372, 379, 540
Houghtling, 29
Houghton, 112, 278
Houseal, 342
Housel, 278
Houseman, 436
Houser, 93, 500
Housewright, 138, 144, 427
Houston, 26, 324, 351, 364, 508
How, 276
Howard, 23, 24, 35, 62, 79, 89, 92, 112, 116, 136, 159, 160, 171, 174, 179, 186, 190, 191, 195, 204, 227, 276, 303, 304, 326, 343, 356, 359, 379, 385, 392, 409, 449, 461, 473, 476, 478, 514, 566, 577, 590
Howe, 282, 300, 369, 378, 385, 454, 552
Howell, 100, 127, 241, 334
Howes, 350, 351
Howgate, 276
Howison, 181
Howland, 41, 104
Howle, 55, 367
Howlett, 192, 407, 434
Howorth, 108, 549
Howsel, 541
Hoy, 287, 410
Hoyle, 529
Hoyt, 66, 227, 234, 379, 397, 470
Huaise, 484
Hubbard, 109, 199
Hubbell, 7, 239

Huck, 586
Hudson, 19, 35, 104, 159, 197, 446, 453, 558
Huff, 493
Hugel, 514
Hugely, 564
Huger, 385, 432
Hugg, 109
Huggins, 100
Hughes, 49, 50, 62, 155, 217, 255, 300, 317, 394, 409, 429, 447, 452, 509
Hugo, 251
Huguely, 569
Huguenot French, 78
Hulbert, 265
Hull, 44, 51, 242, 263, 488, 560
Humboldt, 453
Hume, 90, 160, 176, 187, 492, 565
Humphrey, 95, 103, 171, 261
Humphreys, 104, 150, 344, 372, 416, 421, 432, 468
Humphries, 419
Humpton, 154
Hungerford, 184, 225
Hunker, 277
Hunsberry, 365
Hunt, 23, 66, 107, 125, 171, 178, 282, 310, 340, 433, 438, 492, 522, 529, 537, 558, 563, 565
Hunter, 55, 59, 85, 107, 135, 171, 189, 224, 231, 300, 310, 329, 334, 353, 357, 385, 388, 399, 431, 432, 463, 466, 482, 483, 497, 500, 517, 568
Hunting, 101
Huntington, 23, 43, 48, 61, 73, 75, 102, 235, 334, 375, 473
Hunton, 32
Hurd, 41, 228
Hurdle, 284, 310, 311, 438, 524, 585
Hurlahay, 469
Hurlbut, 564
Hurley, 74, 76, 398, 490
Hurricane, 553

Hurst, 159, 311, 350, 351, 406, 492, 566
Hussey, 5, 228
Hustid, 373
Hutchingson, 300
Hutchins, 29, 278, 371, 463, 474
Hutchinson, 61, 144, 195, 235, 301, 303, 334, 471, 498, 528, 533, 550, 593
Hutton, 127, 172, 174, 187, 358, 361, 575
Huyck, 17, 61, 232
Hyam, 44, 292
Hyatt, 102, 135
Hyde, 62, 83, 127, 287, 294, 334, 424, 502
Hyland, 56, 137
Hyme, 564
Hyndes, 422
Hynes, 16, 101

I

Iardella, 160, 571
Idlewild, 557
Iglehart, 14
Illingworth, 473
Imlay, 330
Immaculate Conception Church, 379
Imrie, 300
Ingalls, 72, 104, 234, 370, 433, 567
Ingersol, 286
Ingersoll, 221, 500
Ingham, 247
Ingle, 73, 98, 115, 127, 172, 174, 194, 403, 472
Ingleside, 110, 115
Inglis, 434
Ingram, 8
Ireland, 334
Irvine, 478
Irving, 312, 438, 497
Irwin, 83, 100, 461, 487, 526, 562, 564
Isaacs, 230
Isbell, 71
Isen, 429

Isherwood, 391
Israel, 367, 557
Iverson, 583
Ives, 40
Ivill, 580

J

Jack, 103, 345, 353
Jacks, 35
Jackson, 2, 9, 28, 48, 49, 62, 75, 77, 91, 96, 102, 104, 110, 115, 136, 151, 156, 172, 173, 207, 225, 233, 263, 270, 285, 301, 307, 308, 310, 334, 366, 399, 432, 433, 484, 492, 493, 527, 536, 537, 540, 541, 566, 581
Jacobi, 528
Jacobs, 35, 200, 212, 300, 305, 385, 388, 431, 452, 499, 565
Jacques, 205
Jago, 454
James, 153, 198, 405, 424, 474, 493, 499, 504, 533, 563
Jameson, 302, 429
Jamison, 266, 536
Janes, 262
Janney, 65
Jans, 530
Janvier, 351
Jarboe, 127, 303, 304, 477, 512, 517, 552
Jardella, 119
Jardin, 152, 547, 548
Jarolomon, 116
Jarrall, 361
Jarrett, 391
Jarvis, 199
Javens, 564
Jayne, 76, 100
Jeanjacquet, 565
Jeanjaquet, 431
Jecobaman, 116
Jefferson, 191, 330, 331, 370, 439, 493, 506, 534
Jeffries, 269
Jehle, 586

Jenkins, 56, 181, 193, 222, 283, 304, 305, 391, 398, 423, 464, 540, 555
Jenks, 349, 522
Jennings, 490, 574
Jeralman, 185
Jeremol, 453
Jerome, 66, 214, 562
Jersey, 116
Jesup, 324, 524
Jett, 461, 493
Jewell, 3, 66, 127, 237, 310, 311, 574, 578
Jewett, 102
Jillard, 173
Jocelyn, 101
Jocknick, 487
Joelsberger, 373
Johns, 6, 19, 463
Johnson, 2, 8, 23, 25, 31, 39, 48, 56, 58, 61, 63, 67, 69, 71, 72, 74, 78, 87, 88, 90, 96, 101, 109, 117, 119, 122, 125, 127, 137, 152, 156, 158, 161, 171, 176, 180, 185, 190, 193, 203, 211, 228, 238, 253, 262, 269, 271, 274, 276, 299, 300, 303, 307, 309, 310, 311, 323, 334, 342, 345, 359, 365, 367, 372, 377, 379, 381, 385, 386, 397, 406, 409, 420, 429, 431, 432, 434, 438, 442, 450, 454, 458, 463, 466, 467, 469, 477, 485, 486, 491, 493, 494, 498, 501, 502, 532, 538, 540, 548, 550, 555, 562, 563, 564, 566, 571, 578, 587, 599, 600
Johnston, 17, 24, 38, 40, 52, 69, 90, 105, 121, 132, 134, 171, 173, 191, 207, 293, 305, 307, 318, 334, 358, 359, 408, 432, 434, 487, 493, 546
Joliffe, 334, 492
Jollife, 148, 492
Jolliffe, 387, 388, 429, 430, 431, 493, 563
Jones, 3, 4, 8, 15, 61, 69, 91, 97, 111, 127, 135, 138, 139, 142, 145, 153, 156, 158, 177, 185, 220, 228, 230, 268, 282, 285, 288, 291, 294, 295,

298, 301, 314, 339, 345, 346, 349,
351, 359, 366, 384, 387, 403, 405,
414, 417, 419, 427, 431, 435, 443,
454, 461, 465, 489, 490, 492, 493,
494, 495, 503, 506, 516, 521, 524,
537, 538, 541, 555, 558, 563, 565,
583, 599
Jonesboro, 241
Jordan, 16, 188, 304, 308, 334
Jordon, 205, 307
Joseph, 421
Jost, 211
Jouett, 107, 230
Jourdan, 504
Jovell, 477
Joy, 334, 349
Joyce, 42, 43, 81, 98, 112, 114, 165, 169, 334, 523
Juarez, 539
Judah, 23
Judd, 166, 170, 277, 307, 389
Judson, 162, 380
Jueneman, 304
Julian, 454
Julien, 310, 453
Julihn, 290
Julius, 567
Jumel, 506, 514
Juncker, 445
Jung, 257
Just, 178, 485
Justin, 153

K

Kaestner, 84
Kahlert, 206
Kahn, 521
Kaiser, 59, 101, 119, 309, 311
Kallusowski, 307
Kalorama, 317
Kammerhueber, 181, 375
Kandler, 65
Kane, 90, 201, 243, 277, 361, 385, 408, 439, 498, 536, 591
Karney, 110
Karns, 513

Kasson, 83
Kauffman, 148, 335, 581
Kaufman, 359
Kaugman, 304
Kauler, 305
Kausler, 388, 431
Kavanaugh, 456
Kay, 249
Kaye, 178
Keach, 572
Kealey, 304
Kean, 34, 166, 346, 389
Keane, 46, 548
Keans, 364
Kear, 538
Kearney, 54, 172, 290, 352
Keasbey, 359
Keate, 406
Keating, 540
Keaton, 309
Kecher, 342
Keckeler, 244
Keddy, 564
Keeckhoefer, 335
Keefe, 39, 96, 238, 311, 528
Keegan, 430, 565
Keeler, 277, 537
Keeley, 474
Keeling, 12, 58, 93, 103, 129, 174, 289, 315, 356, 420, 476, 490, 508, 569, 577
Keelling, 332
Keen, 124
Keenan, 24, 34, 99, 359, 479, 563
Keene, 147, 194, 265, 498
Keese, 86, 537
Keeshan, 197
Kehl, 75
Kehoe, 565
Keickhoeffer, 282, 283, 284
Keif, 15
Keiler, 77, 452, 485
Keirle, 468
Keiser, 485
Keleher, 334, 395
Kell, 304

Kelleher, 283
Keller, 59, 146, 312
Kelley, 120, 153, 259, 282, 291, 356, 360, 368, 395, 447, 492, 518, 565
Kellogg, 104, 105, 200, 297, 379, 540
Kelly, 7, 25, 115, 127, 182, 233, 284, 285, 291, 304, 310, 311, 314, 325, 334, 357, 449, 491, 498, 501, 511, 528, 547, 597
Kelsar, 365
Kelser, 79, 303, 304
Kelsey, 492, 529, 565
Kelton, 199
Kemble, 288
Kemon, 9
Kemper, 352
Kempff, 107
Kendall, 44, 62, 98, 104, 127, 183, 192, 238, 271, 326, 335, 386
Kendall Green Park, 164
Kendall Meadow, 122
Kendig, 465
Kendricks, 341
Kenedy, 8
Kengla, 175
Kenifick, 287
Keniston, 48
Kennally, 127
Kennam, 413
Kennaman, 413
Kennard, 518
Kennarty, 562
Kennedy, 51, 89, 91, 115, 174, 176, 194, 234, 249, 250, 301, 307, 334, 335, 343, 403, 430, 472, 566
Kennett, 570
Kenney, 127, 307, 310
Kennicott, 105
Kenny, 306, 582
Kenrick, 443, 445
Kent, 233, 288, 388, 402, 431
Keogh, 385
Kephart, 65
Kepler, 230
Ker, 281, 396

Kerby, 33
Kerfoot, 32
Kerk, 404
Kernan, 537
Kerns, 273
Kerper, 304
Kerr, 149, 345
Kerrigan, 240
Kersey, 300
Kershaw, 495
Kershner, 541
Kervand, 401
Kesley, 375
ketch **Vesuvius**, 439
Ketchum, 2, 103, 348, 496, 558
Kettell, 205, 455
Ketterar, 537
Key, 17, 244, 524
Key's Quarter, 287
Keyes, 102, 318, 364, 416, 432
Keys, 283, 302, 348
Keyser, 335
Keyworth, 176, 182
Kibbey, 127, 335, 470
Kickens, 283
Kiddle, 304
Kidwell, 62, 69, 81, 98, 196, 284, 288, 290, 304, 335, 342, 356, 449, 472
Kieckhoefer, 476
Kieckhoeffer, 290
Kieffer, 116
Kiesecher, 485
Kilbourn, 449, 456, 500, 507
Kilbourne, 267, 354, 459, 480
Kilburn, 342
Kilby, 4, 450
Kile, 15
Kilgore, 593
Kilgour, 80, 563
Kilgours, 477
Killafoyle, 303
Killduck, 541
Killen, 287
Kilpatrick, 171, 389
Kimball, 253, 255, 290

Kimble, 458
Kimmell, 37, 74, 334
Kin_, 467
Kinderhook, 464
Kindness, 588
King, 3, 6, 17, 37, 47, 59, 79, 95, 96, 99, 102, 118, 127, 131, 145, 155, 163, 167, 171, 182, 185, 202, 204, 208, 212, 214, 267, 292, 300, 304, 310, 313, 318, 321, 334, 335, 344, 354, 358, 359, 364, 365, 378, 386, 391, 421, 423, 430, 439, 449, 453, 458, 460, 493, 499, 521, 532, 563, 565, 585, 589, 595
King of Prussia, 136
Kingsberry, 324
Kingsbury, 415, 440
Kingsland, 384
Kingsley, 375, 514, 581
Kinkead, 462
Kinne, 253
Kinnerton, 478
Kinney, 346
Kinnie, 255
Kinsella, 379, 382
Kinsello, 113
Kinsley, 360
Kinsman, 385
Kinzer, 507
Kinzie, 50, 244
Kirby, 101, 308, 309, 525
Kirk, 127, 282, 367, 477, 599
Kirkham, 567, 575
Kirkman, 28, 104
Kirkpatrick, 494, 536
Kirkwood, 59
Kirschel, 457
Kitchan, 59
Kitchen, 17
Klein, 35
Kleindeinst, 301
Kline, 586
Klinehance, 303
Kling, 430, 566
Kloman, 62, 334, 540
Klopfer, 307, 309, 540

Klotz, 39, 471
Knap, 61, 98, 326, 484, 500, 566, 591
Knapp, 7, 30, 48, 453, 454
Knappp, 327
Kneller, 217
Knester, 307
Knight, 153, 239, 259, 301, 451, 495, 505, 540, 552, 563
Knighton, 388, 431
Knoll, 28
Knorr, 596
Knowles, 181, 324, 438
Knowlton, 332, 593
Knox, 11, 21, 99, 105, 277, 537
Koch, 335, 596
Koddoo, 560
Kohler, 592
Kolb, 303, 308
Kolecki, 266
Koonce, 587
Koones, 115
Koontz, 212, 348, 381, 484
Koppel, 120, 498
Kopper, 467
Korrak, 298
Korts, 299
Kr_eker, 585
Kracke, 174
Krafft, 3, 303
Kraft, 86, 251, 310, 398
Krake, 158
Kramer, 120, 350
Krause, 105
Krautner, 420
Kreader, 346
Kreamer, 451
Krebs, 104, 177, 462, 504, 533
Krecker, 512
Kreis, 493
Krepps, 453
Kretschmar, 12, 487
Kretshhmar, 479
Kris, 169
Kroft, 304
Krouse, 367

Kubel, 127
Kuchling, 181
Kuehling, 160
Kuester, 308
Kuhl, 137
Kuhn, 311, 406
Kuhns, 504
Kuhrist, 303
Kumlers, 243
Kumles, 79
Kuntz, 559
Kuntzner, 439
Kurtz, 92, 298, 356, 472
Kussmaul, 20
Kyle, 104, 532

L

La Fontaine, 250
La Mee, 518
La Motte, 298, 385
Lacey, 80, 178, 421
Lackey, 113, 546
Lacquement, 454
Lacy, 276, 355
Ladd, 286
Laden, 261
Ladenson, 563
Lafayette, 506
Lafebvre, 214
LaFontaine, 453
Laforge, 485
Lagnement, 453
Lagrange, 470
Laird, 244, 378
Lake, 160, 511
Lakeman, 93
Lakenan, 95
Lamar, 26, 122, 515, 573
Lamb, 160, 201, 295, 378, 398, 400, 409, 416, 431, 441
Lambard, 122
Lambdin, 308, 309
Lambell, 140, 490
Lambert, 34, 47, 80, 97, 98, 120, 129, 146, 277
Lambrick, 285

Lamon, 30, 62, 141, 162
Lamphere, 233
Lampson, 565
Lamsden, 168
Lamson, 429
Lamy, 446
Lanas, 290
Lanber, 584
Lancaster, 101, 167, 315, 379, 596
Lancet, 129
Lancks, 414
Land, 6
Lander, 459
Landlors, 453
Landon, 105
Landsdale, 51
Lane, 6, 17, 24, 77, 90, 105, 108, 175, 255, 270, 288, 310, 317, 335, 412, 563, 572, 578
Lang, 89, 135, 310, 428, 454
Langden, 276
Lange, 599
Langford, 139
Langle, 304
Langley, 35, 79, 148, 301, 304, 362, 409
Lanman, 107
Lansburg, 335
Lansdale, 399
Lanston, 585
Lantner, 500
Lantry, 397
Lantz, 317
Lanum, 180
Laquenment, 453
Lardner, 106
Larizzi, 305
Larkin, 160, 479
Larned, 127
Larner, 61, 309, 326, 457, 470
Larocque, 214
Larrabee, 102
Larry, 310
Lashhorn, 230
Lashorn, 311
Laskey, 25, 45, 82, 93, 159

Lasselle, 434, 448
Latane, 587
Latham, 179
Lathrop, 66, 335, 473, 537
Latimer, 202
Latrobe, 23
Latsoe, 430
Latta, 449, 456, 459, 480, 500, 507
Laub, 37
Laughlin, 445
Laughton, 578
Laup, 373
Laurel Hill, 320
Laurie, 179, 292
Lavalliere, 465
Lavender, 308
Lavialle, 445
Law, 127, 216, 300, 329, 410
Lawal, 344
Lawer, 109
Lawler, 75, 283, 538
Lawlor, 132, 282, 283, 454
Lawrason, 290
Lawrence, 62, 109, 129, 140, 167, 297, 335, 372, 409, 436, 454, 504, 540, 576, 596
Lawrenson, 110, 261, 307
Laws, 270
Lawson, 20, 99, 100, 102, 108, 113
Lawton, 22, 97, 564
Lay, 92, 104, 212, 395
Layton, 589
Lazarus, 250
Lazenby, 299, 321
Le Grove, 413
Lea, 152, 587
Leach, 18, 148, 154, 168, 394, 499, 569, 572, 578
Leadbeater, 424
Leader, 229
Leadingham, 358
Leahy, 100
Leakin, 3
Lear, 564
Learned, 101
Leas, 111

Leatherman, 529
Leave, 430
Leavitt, 555
Leavy, 348
Lebo, 302
Leckner, 167
Ledam, 444
Lederer, 500, 508
Ledum, 461
Ledwich, 311
Ledyard, 105, 296
Lee, 2, 4, 15, 68, 74, 105, 106, 127, 133, 137, 171, 172, 177, 214, 217, 270, 276, 279, 288, 296, 312, 314, 319, 335, 353, 354, 355, 359, 362, 367, 388, 405, 427, 432, 458, 519, 528, 552, 577, 586
Leech, 73, 121, 346, 356, 362, 444
Leesnitzer, 301
Leet, 129
Lefevre, 445
Lefferts, 366
Leftwich, 125, 279
Legg, 128
Legion, 350, 351
Lehman, 335
Lehne, 40
Leiberman, 200, 335
Leibermann, 359
Leifried, 152
Leighton, 234
Leishear, 37
Leitch, 304
Leland, 301, 537
Leman, 105
Lemby, 71
Lemmon, 68, 538
Lemmons, 327
Lemon, 307, 427
Lenman, 89, 148
Lennock, 279
Lent, 63
Lentz, 276
Leo, 479
Leonard, 46, 146
Leslie, 284, 304, 305, 432

Lester, 100, 221, 255, 553
Letcher, 209, 586
Letourneau, 468
Leuitze, 542
Leuven, 189
Levere, 453
Leverett, 5
Levering, 55
Levet, 565
Levies, 326
Levy, 38, 202, 363
Lewenthal, 156
Lewis, 6, 79, 100, 103, 127, 161, 200, 216, 233, 264, 282, 286, 300, 307, 311, 326, 335, 351, 359, 367, 369, 410, 422, 466, 467, 469, 474, 476, 484, 487, 488, 491, 500, 507, 527, 533, 538, 562, 569, 585, 599
Liambias, 237
Libbey, 71, 227, 335, 376, 378, 390, 391, 393, 399
Liber, 91
Lichtenhaler, 342
Lichtenthaler, 342
Liddell, 105
Lieberman, 194
Liebman, 569
Light, 493
Lillendahl, 564
Lilley, 439, 550
Lillie, 277
Lilly, 31
Limerick, 384
Lincoln, 23, 36, 83, 104, 121, 146, 147, 162, 170, 180, 202, 209, 226, 244, 260, 268, 305, 309, 359, 366, 369, 382, 413, 474, 475, 494, 497, 499, 508, 517, 542, 556, 557, 561
Lincoln Square, 325
Lind, 105, 207, 364, 391
Linder, 431
Lindley, 532
Lindon, 1
Lindsay, 311, 335
Lindsey, 279
Lindsley, 82, 115, 279, 287, 335, 357

Lindsly, 358, 359, 541
Lineweaver, 540
Link, 105
Linkin, 584
Linkins, 127
Linney, 362
Linsley, 330
Linthicum, 62, 240, 320, 332, 335
Linton, 188, 335, 346
Linwood, 531
Lippharde, 300
Lipscomb, 146, 438, 523
Lisle, 278
Lister, 149
Litchfield, 233, 285
Little, 103, 105, 160, 183, 242, 277, 283, 293, 303, 312, 317, 335, 373, 382, 402, 435, 448, 467, 536
Littlejohn, 203
Litton, 513
Livingston, 464
Lloyd, 3, 25, 62, 134, 202, 239, 275, 282, 284, 326, 353, 380, 387, 403, 409, 475
Lochiel, 588
Lock, 319
Locke, 79
Lockerly, 526
Lockey, 283
Lockrey, 98
Lockwood, 127, 267, 354, 379, 430
Locust Grove, 371
Locust Hill, 361
Locust Shade, 151
Lodge, 151
Lodgers, 477
Loewenthal, 498
Logan, 29, 65, 101, 220, 294, 387, 431, 479, 523, 595
Lomax, 301
London Telegraph Co, 340
Long, 6, 40, 72, 75, 81, 111, 127, 171, 242, 259, 355, 432, 433, 512, 513
Long Island, 437
Long Meadows, 422

Longley, 504
Longston, 174, 465
Longstreet, 433
Longstroth, 293
Longwood, 507
Longworth, 378
Lonpay, 159
Loomis, 103, 234, 256, 537
Loosley, 103
Lorain, 462
Lorch, 219
Lord, 82, 103, 196, 307, 356, 403, 438, 509, 530, 552
Lord Baltimore, 149
Lord Shelburne, 331
Loretta l'Indovina, 210
Loring, 52, 71, 561
Losano, 153, 577
Lott, 563
Lotz, 429
Loucks, 100
Loudon Park Cemetery, 298
Loudoun Park Cemetery, 67
Loughborough, 139, 498
Louis, 350
Louisiana, 284
Loutner, 284
Loux, 524
Love, 366
Loveaire, 530
Lovejoy, 249, 253, 272, 335, 356, 358, 359, 360, 491
Lovel, 433
Lovell, 558
Low, 87, 453, 494
Lowal, 344
Lowber, 340
Lowe, 335, 359, 494, 573, 599
Lowell, 282
Lowenthal, 335, 483, 528, 533
Lower, 171
Lowler, 221
Lowndes, 560
Lowrey, 85, 468
Lowrie, 13, 264, 484

Lowry, 138, 335, 344, 346, 353, 375, 378, 487, 549
Luber, 584
Lubey, 60
Lucas, 50, 473, 483
Luce, 224, 232
Luckett, 55, 59, 63, 85, 224, 291, 303, 314, 353, 489, 495, 497, 500
Ludington, 6
Ludlow, 570
Luers, 445
Luff, 300, 301
Lugenheel, 558
Luhn, 101
Lukenbaugh, 326
Lundt, 108
Lusby, 304, 325, 363, 367
Luse, 362
Lusk, 38, 308, 310, 311
Lutz, 192, 264, 324, 335
Lycett, 300
Lydecker, 204
Lyle, 346, 446, 573
Lyles, 127, 290, 314, 319, 366, 489, 495, 509
Lyman, 146, 198, 326, 453
Lynch, 9, 30, 69, 115, 137, 140, 159, 229, 233, 265, 276, 279, 299, 363, 366, 444, 479, 484, 493, 522
Lynde, 449
Lyne, 280, 291
Lynn, 76, 346, 348, 498
Lyon, 103, 111, 277, 433, 456, 496, 578
Lyons, 85, 183, 321, 335, 462

M

Maas, 493
Mac Gill, 161
Macalester, 24
Maccarty, 570
Macdaniel, 462
Macdonald, 306
Macey, 355
Macfeely, 384
MacGowan, 102, 568

Macgrotty, 457
Machenhimer, 352
Mack, 181, 283, 360, 405, 542
Mackall, 335, 359
Mackenheimer, 384
Mackenne, 277
Mackenzie, 89, 238, 593
Mackey, 104, 359
Mackie, 236
Mackin, 425
Mackubin, 12, 264
Maclay, 100
Macleod, 434
MacLeod, 434
MacLizer, 557
MacMurray, 354
Macomb, 4, 582
Macy, 46, 72
Madawaska, 512
Madden, 100, 104
Maddox, 84, 163, 260, 293, 304, 318, 339, 359, 430, 477, 565
Madeira, 105
Maden, 181
Mades, 189, 335
Madigan, 100, 284
Madison, 132, 312
Maeller, 526
Maenner, 203
Magaw, 286
Magee, 97, 144, 292, 367, 391, 427, 438
Magraw, 19, 131, 262
Magruder, 10, 18, 43, 61, 143, 155, 221, 232, 257, 266, 292, 314, 335, 345, 359, 403, 424, 425, 432, 438, 474, 479, 493, 494, 502, 560, 563, 576
Maguire, 61, 156, 175, 232, 284, 289, 301, 346, 477
Magurder, 158
Mahaffy, 172
Mahan, 35, 104, 432, 570
Maher, 173, 271, 326
Mahew, 304
Mahicken, 385

Mahon, 102, 120
Mahoney, 304, 448, 456
Mahorn, 46
Main, 198
Maine, 35
Mairn, 158
Major, 190, 290, 335, 587
Majtheny, 100
Makall, 288
Makinson, 538
Malay, 284
Malden, 71, 130
Malibran, 207
Mallery, 296
Mallet, 543
Mallette, 214
Mallison, 193
Mallory, 103, 104, 290, 291
Malloy, 110
Malone, 167, 234, 287
Maloney, 127, 300, 343
Mandeville, 351
Maneret, 178
Mank, 5, 155
Mankel, 283
Mankin, 48, 75, 125, 132
Manlay, 294
Mann, 7, 173, 263, 491
Manna, 397
Manney, 277
Manning, 130, 243, 375, 411, 428, 524
Mannoghue, 39
Mannon, 429
Mansell, 404
Mansfield, 133, 190, 330, 335, 432, 561
Mantz, 79
Manwaring, 430, 565
Mapes, 13
Maraughi, 484
Marbury, 18, 22, 60, 121, 123, 232, 313, 320, 321, 324, 335, 336, 359, 380, 464, 485, 502, 508, 510, 528, 533, 585, 588
Marceron, 62, 211

March, 284, 313
Marchant, 106, 560
Marcy, 127, 432
Maretzek, 424, 562
Marie Amelie, 157
Mario, 364, 454
Mariscal, 458
Markriter, 335
Marks, 123, 297, 303, 335, 452
Markwood, 72, 461
Marll, 282, 283
Marlow, 136
Marmaduke, 504
Marquis de Boissy, 455
Marquis of Lunsdowne, 331
Marr, 101, 255, 354, 355, 484
Marrero, 378
Marschall, 22
Marsden, 531
Marsh, 24, 186, 227, 257, 311, 367, 404, 465, 526, 585
Marshal, 303, 495
Marshall, 138, 229, 275, 305, 379, 440, 461, 478, 480, 505, 584
Marshall Hall, 77, 281, 371
Marston, 517
Marten, 589
Martin, 15, 57, 67, 108, 120, 125, 129, 156, 169, 213, 221, 233, 290, 295, 301, 315, 344, 357, 359, 367, 373, 376, 415, 438, 444, 445, 446, 453, 454, 461, 463, 468, 500, 502, 507, 526, 539, 581, 585, 593
Martindale, 48
Martinez, 471
Marton, 417
Marvin, 167, 248
Mary, 127
Mary of St Bernard, 430
Masely, 162
Maservey, 395
Masi, 44, 345, 438
Masic, 453
Mason, 22, 109, 127, 195, 253, 255, 276, 316, 335, 364, 385, 402, 429, 437, 453, 454, 470, 559

Mason's Island, 438
Massenet, 189
Massey, 48
Massie, 181
Mast, 101
Masters, 221, 425
Mastin, 564
Masy, 72
Mather, 108
Mathews, 82, 96, 120, 233, 323
Mathias, 431
Mathison, 246
Matlack, 578
Matlock, 69, 438
Mattaponi, 560
Matteini, 457
Matthews, 39, 62, 270, 303, 320, 329, 331, 335, 396, 510, 596
Mattingly, 8, 42, 70, 81, 118, 122, 125, 137, 146, 220, 234, 243, 245, 282, 326, 328, 335, 466, 482, 489, 540, 599
Mattoon, 487
Maupin, 96
Maurice, 100
Maury, 17, 61, 62, 174, 186, 203, 359, 407, 433
Maximillian, 353
Maxwell, 102, 335, 344, 361, 570, 576
May, 102, 335, 336, 359, 417, 418, 423, 451, 500, 502, 568
Mayard, 543
Mayell, 276
Mayer, 204
Mayfield, 17
Mayherr, 188
Maynadier, 22, 390, 490, 494, 558, 568
Maynard, 53, 205, 253, 277, 452
Mayo, 299, 406
Mays, 103, 450
Maywood, 376
McAll, 460
McAllister, 7, 430
McAnley, 303

McArdle, 299, 300, 301
McArthur, 55, 104, 192
McAuley, 446
McBlair, 36
McBride, 91
McCabe, 231, 463, 464
McCafferty, 100
McCaffery, 99
McCall, 288, 432
McCalla, 359
McCallum, 381
McCandless, 346, 353
McCann, 89, 91, 107, 350, 351, 578
McCardell, 292
McCarlin, 380
McCartee, 484
McCarthy, 25, 59, 69, 126, 167, 236, 282, 283, 311, 335, 408, 449, 494, 555, 594
McCarty, 388, 456, 469, 477, 563
McCaskey, 103
McCathran, 304, 335, 367, 439
McCauley, 63, 107, 177, 289
McCausland, 575
McCeney, 136
McChesner, 70
McChesney, 572
McClay, 428
McCleary, 308
McClellan, 253, 255, 433, 552
McClelland, 130, 272, 438
McClermont, 100
McClery, 359, 475, 476, 479
McCloskey, 234, 283, 284, 445
McClosky, 292, 447
McCloug, 192
McClure, 516, 571
McColgan, 177
McCollum, 477, 485
McComas, 415
McComb, 228, 565
McConihe, 103
McConnell, 206, 287, 330, 392, 420, 511
McCook, 96, 98, 111, 135, 171, 300, 328, 562

McCool, 420
McCord, 182
McCorkle, 255
McCormack, 278
McCormick, 55, 91, 223, 277, 295, 359, 365, 452, 491, 565
McCougal, 462
McCown, 491
McCoy, 14, 172, 359, 385
McCracken, 33, 495
McCray, 488
McCreery, 372
McCrone, 113
McCuen, 311
McCulloch, 70, 109, 118, 188, 247, 320, 500, 523, 593
McCullough, 41, 315
McCullum, 471
McCutcheon, 158, 303
McDaniel, 330, 349, 430, 484, 566
McDermid, 441
McDermott, 160, 301, 335, 346, 359, 465
McDevitt, 29, 135, 283, 300, 426, 457, 467
McDonald, 262, 299, 307, 309, 329, 355, 391, 397, 453, 502, 538, 565
McDonnell, 444, 502
McDonough, 143, 168
McDougal, 444
McDougall, 411
McDowell, 24, 98, 171, 343, 408, 430, 433, 565
McDuell, 249, 426, 442, 460, 479, 569
McElfresh, 568
McElhone, 389
McElrath, 259
McElroy, 242, 468
McFadden, 304
McFalls, 292, 390, 530
McFarlan, 375, 385, 526
McFarland, 7, 305, 335, 445
McFarrad, 567
McGavock, 481
McGee, 129, 310, 509, 571

McGeraham, 578
McGervar, 298
McGhan, 335
McGill, 8, 127, 158, 311, 335, 429, 444, 493
McGinley, 381
McGinn, 454
McGinnis, 36, 301, 346, 381, 573
McGinniss, 103, 161
McGlan, 192
McGohan, 538
McGowan, 229
McGraim, 536
McGrain, 284
McGrann, 466
McGrath, 571
McGraw, 17, 398, 487
McGregor, 274
McGrew, 311, 543, 587
McGuigan, 282, 283
McGuiggan, 17
McGuire, 9, 40, 44, 61, 75, 82, 90, 98, 119, 121, 131, 132, 147, 153, 164, 194, 200, 228, 264, 287, 297, 326, 335, 439, 453, 461, 470, 529, 569, 587
McHendry, 526
McHenry, 310, 385, 588
McHugh, 68
McIlvain, 278
McIlvaine, 530
McIlvains, 32
McIndoe, 231
McIntee, 77
McIntire, 90, 526
McIntosh, 69, 114, 115, 137, 167, 171, 374, 560
McIntyre, 178, 363
McIver, 418
McKay, 92, 574
McKean, 96, 106, 392
McKee, 277, 430, 493, 565
McKeever, 104, 420, 436
McKelden, 140, 155, 278, 318, 335
McKelver, 366
McKenly, 6

McKenney, 152, 200, 228, 419, 500, 504
McKenzie, 89, 580
McKibben, 408
McKibbin, 103
McKiel, 599
McKildoe, 52
McKim, 101, 133, 179, 206, 335
McKinney, 474
McKinstry, 560
McKivron, 183
McKnew, 45, 83, 118, 125, 176, 232, 307
McKnight, 3, 359
McKuen, 279
McLain, 23, 63, 305, 335
McLaine, 304
McLane, 153, 247, 292
McLarty, 587
McLaughlin, 62, 163, 175, 214, 335, 453, 482, 537, 566, 567
McLauren, 257
McLaws, 433
McLean, 179, 188, 335, 519, 533
McLeod, 523, 541
McLinn, 595
McLoughlin, 104, 279, 383
McMahan, 188
McMahon, 90, 145, 256, 310, 367, 454, 456, 484
McMann, 592
Mcmanue, 254
McManus, 132
McMaster, 100
McMath, 71
McMichael, 111, 129, 141
McMillan, 204, 234
McMulligan, 383
McMurdy, 428
McMurray, 100, 485
McNair, 310, 529, 563
McNalley, 505
McNally, 26, 37, 304, 418, 434, 546
McNamara, 335, 556
McNantz, 303
McNeal, 6, 34, 149, 248, 317

McNeer, 587
McNeil, 6, 282, 283
McNeir, 62, 352, 381
McNerhany, 5, 404
McNulty, 587
McPhail, 372
McPherson, 27, 68, 122, 172, 177, 230, 268, 278, 284, 346, 401, 409, 480, 481, 502, 515, 523, 543
McQuade, 91, 129, 379
McQueen, 69, 300, 303
McQuistion, 344
McRoberts, 174
McSherry, 417
McSweeny, 311
McSwiggin, 492
McVeigh, 568
McWhorter, 193
McWilliams, 127
Mead, 224, 282, 330, 359, 360, 417, 540
Meade, 24, 171, 330, 343, 385, 423, 432, 590
Meador, 142
Meadows, 198
Meagher, 103
Means, 158
Meany, 164, 311
Mears, 335
Mechlin, 27
Meehan, 241
Meem, 15, 403, 442, 502
Meerchan, 454
Meigs, 6, 16, 58, 86, 219, 227, 264, 323, 398, 432, 484, 519
Meinhold, 100
Meish, 346
Melcher, 251
Meline, 235
Melling, 311
Mellock, 330
Mellon, 33
Melrose, 595
Mendenhall, 7, 364, 365
Meneely, 15
Menefee, 306, 585

Menke, 188
Menken, 288
Mente, 32
Menter, 240, 251, 260
Mentz, 188
Mercer, 26, 186, 365, 569
Mercott, 242
Mercur, 267, 354
Meredith, 116, 211, 247, 303
Meridian Hill, 317, 380
Merilatt, 359
Meritt, 11
Merriam, 360, 559
Merrick, 30, 56, 81, 167, 172, 253, 429, 493
Merrilat, 240
Merrill, 219, 267, 326, 354, 475, 529, 549, 587
Merriman, 429, 492, 493, 508
Merritt, 171, 537
Merserau, 537
Merwin, 63
Mery, 294, 453
Meserole, 453
Messer, 73
Metcalf, 31, 431, 565
Metcalfe, 379, 430
Metropolis View, 143
Metropolitan Mills, 7
Metzerott, 97, 335, 507
Metzger, 342
Metzgher, 164
Mew, 396, 435
Meyenberg, 128
Meyer, 85, 102, 539, 573
Miazzo, 388, 565
Michaelis, 354
Michel, 67, 453
Michener, 448
Michler, 290, 291
Mickings, 528
Mickler, 237
Mickum, 476
middle name, 49
Middleton, 8, 41, 65, 90, 93, 98, 127, 143, 153, 183, 198, 201, 231, 245,

294, 308, 326, 335, 345, 360, 370,
386, 403, 451, 517, 542, 580, 599
Miege, 446
Mienhauser, 586
Milburn, 69, 350, 367, 391
Mildrum, 108
Miles, 3, 10, 202, 219, 385, 432,
444, 560, 596
Miley, 399
Military Asylum Cemetery, 520
Military Cemetery, 16
Military Road, 509
Milk & Honey, 588
Millburn, 403
Millegan, 565
Miller, 41, 53, 60, 71, 80, 96, 98,
102, 104, 112, 114, 118, 119, 139,
156, 168, 169, 179, 189, 207, 231,
253, 263, 265, 268, 282, 284, 300,
301, 303, 304, 308, 326, 328, 335,
342, 344, 360, 368, 370, 385, 393,
412, 424, 434, 437, 440, 442, 451,
454, 469, 473, 475, 476, 485, 487,
503, 510, 526, 529, 537, 543, 556,
559, 567, 568, 570, 577, 585
Milliard, 587
Millinger, 428
Mills, 99, 122, 253, 323, 477, 491,
528, 530, 544, 581
Millsager, 224
Millward, 35
Milnor, 60
Milstead, 304, 524
Miltimore, 100
Milward, 408
Mimmack, 102
Mindbled, 453
Minehart, 304
Miner, 565
Mingle, 483
Minn, 565
Minns, 563
Minor, 82, 164, 388, 431, 526
Minsingerode, 222
Mintzyer, 578
Misnering, 197

Missemer, 414
Mister, 300
Mitchell, 4, 11, 20, 39, 61, 69, 75,
104, 105, 124, 127, 163, 179, 204,
229, 238, 268, 282, 288, 301, 310,
335, 350, 352, 361, 371, 376, 391,
398, 401, 415, 432, 481, 485, 494,
545, 548
Mitts, 397
Mix, 291, 487
Mizener, 344
Moale, 494
Moberley, 354
Moberly, 267
Mockabee, 299, 392, 485, 498
Moe, 385
Moffatt, 487
Moffit, 77
Moffitt, 392
Mohler, 358
Mohoney, 9, 284
Mohony, 236, 283
Mohun, 1, 37, 44, 68, 235, 335, 336,
481
Molan, 577
Moler, 155
Mollison, 144
Molyneux, 273
Monahan, 100
Monroe, 30, 73, 132, 228, 537
Monteith, 100
Monterean, 93
Montero, 288
Montgomery, 114, 158, 168, 297,
348, 419, 553, 567, 572, 573, 576,
585
Montholon, 545
Montrie, 404
Moody, 191, 345, 407, 413, 429, 565
Mooney, 284
Moons, 228
Moor, 283
Moore, 5, 16, 25, 31, 45, 58, 69, 75,
84, 89, 105, 134, 149, 177, 189,
191, 201, 218, 265, 277, 283, 284,
288, 298, 302, 309, 335, 358, 362,

373, 377, 381, 418, 419, 439, 440,
450, 451, 456, 476, 492, 493, 509,
515, 518, 519, 520, 528, 529, 541,
591, 594
Moran, 110, 161, 307, 335, 374, 453, 472, 522
Morcoe, 8, 308
Mordcai, 490
Mordecai, 432, 494
Morehead, 383, 513, 529
Moreland, 227, 284, 303
Morell, 431
Morenschelager, 453
Morgan, 34, 81, 113, 114, 159, 181, 183, 229, 235, 284, 292, 304, 315, 335, 355, 360, 366, 369, 401, 403, 442, 479, 513, 537, 563, 587, 600
Moriarty, 73, 387, 431, 458
Moriatta, 94
Mormon bishop, 138
Mormons, 237
Mormoyle, 547
Morns, 468
Moroney, 103
Morrell, 565
Morrill, 98, 228, 388
Morris, 5, 32, 62, 79, 127, 210, 243, 277, 324, 326, 537, 562, 573
Morrison, 92, 122, 129, 156, 200, 248, 305, 335, 539, 579, 587
Morrisson, 526
Morrow, 75, 124, 229, 346, 364, 381
Morse, 64, 108, 251, 326, 367, 383, 573
Morsell, 13, 14, 176, 193, 238, 252, 309, 335, 368, 370, 376
Mortimer, 562
Morton, 11, 99, 417, 478
Mosby, 42
Moses, 309
Mosher, 116, 335, 540, 546
Moss, 205, 367
Moth, 486
Mother Angela, 394
Motley, 385
Mott, 549

Motten, 414
Mouiton, 491
Moulder, 53, 359, 429
Moulton, 587
Mount, 101, 554
Mount Auburn, 320
Mount Auburn Cemetery, 527
Mount De Sales Academy, 345
Mount Oakland, 588
Mount Olivet Cemetery, 12, 53, 230, 497, 523, 527, 551
Mount Palatine, 287
Mount Pleasant, 188, 374, 383, 386
Mount Pleasant Cemetery, 215
Mount Vernon, 216, 217, 427, 519
Mountford, 196
Mourton, 101
Mousley, 416
Mowbry, 308
Mower, 171, 374, 560
Mowers, 559
Moxley, 140, 335
Moyamensing Hall, 350
MrGuire, 97
MrWaldraven, 586
Mudd, 75, 76, 292
Muddiman, 300
Mudge, 449
Muir, 9
Mulberry Green, 280
Mulcheary, 223
Muldaur, 549
Mulford, 100, 330, 560
Mullaney, 107
Mulldoon, 311
Mullen, 195, 360, 405, 540
Muller, 342
Mullery, 493
Mullican, 463
Mulligan, 127
Mullikin, 101
Mullins, 421
Mulloy, 551
Mumford, 72, 172, 581
Munck, 556, 561, 583
Mundee, 385

Mundell, 304, 495
Mundy, 287
Muneret, 167, 170
Munford, 175
Munroe, 2, 156, 159, 453
Murat, 78
Muravieff, 437
Murch, 499
Murdoch, 187
Murdock, 101, 335, 533
Muriwell, 206
Murlock, 151
Murphy, 6, 39, 69, 109, 111, 158, 159, 181, 283, 284, 287, 290, 305, 310, 335, 367, 382, 442, 469, 481, 509, 511, 527, 540, 597
Murray, 12, 134, 166, 212, 240, 261, 282, 315, 335, 359, 362, 411, 503, 514, 540, 556, 596
Murry, 284
Murtagh, 134
Musgrove, 110
Mussey, 280
mustered out, 16
Myer, 501
Myers, 51, 52, 53, 88, 143, 180, 251, 299, 302, 359, 367, 453, 537, 567
Mygatt, 30, 119
Mylandie, 537
Myrick, 288, 544

N

N J Historical Society, 211
Nadal, 13
Nagelin, 388, 431, 565
Nagle, 60, 68, 80, 498, 583
Naigley, 532
Nailor, 59, 202, 252, 254, 318, 336
Nairn, 18, 61, 69, 336
Nalley, 221, 326, 336, 392
Nally, 304, 308
Names, 177
Nane, 349
Nanmann, 220
Napier, 275
Napoleon, 78

Napoleon III, 31
Nash, 8, 304, 310, 345, 438, 469, 502
Nat'l Cemeteries, 218
Nat'l Cemetery, 217
Nat'l Intellgencer newspaper, 260
Nat'l Soldiers' & Sailors' Orphan Home, 326
Nathans, 152, 248
National Cemeteries, 519
national cemetery, 211
National Cemetery, 387, 520
Naval Hospital, 360
naval magazine, 206
Navy Bulletin, 512, 518, 528, 530, 532, 534, 536, 541, 543, 544, 547, 549, 552, 560, 561, 570, 573, 575, 576, 578, 579, 583, 585, 593, 596, 598, 599
Naylor, 227, 336, 345, 374, 375, 504, 587
Neal, 462, 553, 565
Neale, 221, 301, 361, 463, 469, 478, 502
Nealy, 102
Neason, 584
Neenan, 269
Neff, 267, 354, 461
Neil, 346
Neilds, 552
Neill, 4, 145, 303, 402, 559
Neilson, 261
Neligan, 515
Nelms, 29
Nelson, 11, 41, 103, 280, 303, 312, 348, 350, 351, 356, 389, 429, 556
Nepper, 146
Nesbit, 73, 600
Nesmith, 86, 234
Nessensohn, 505
Nester, 391
Nestor, 391
Netterville, 358
Nevell, 191
Nevin, 24
Nevins, 551

Nevitt, 50
new Catholic church, 232
New Haven Historical Society, 425
New York Museum, 382
Newbern, 90
Newbold, 101
Newcomer, 288
Newell, 346, 386, 397, 453, 526, 533, 578
Newgarten, 159
Newkirk, 101
Newland, 208
Newlin, 102, 103
Newlon, 492
Newman, 9, 250, 255, 303, 304, 310, 311, 336, 454, 510
Newmeister, 78
Newmeyer, 283
Newton, 8, 129, 152, 171, 249, 276, 283, 361, 431, 433, 565, 591
Niazza, 431
Nicholas, 158
Nicholls, 127, 481, 548
Nicholls property, 486
Nicholls' Mansion, 481
Nichols, 56, 66, 98, 160, 168, 243, 306, 308, 326, 352, 393, 434, 548
Nicholson, 4, 181, 201, 291, 304, 551
Nickers, 573
Nickerson, 103
Nicodemus, 568
Niemeyer, 20
Nightingale, 120, 326
Niles, 34, 336, 491, 493, 494, 564, 565
Ninage, 453
Ninis, 514
Ninninger, 209, 385
Nisbet, 583
Nixon, 375, 386, 460, 571, 600
Noah, 254
Noble, 104, 127, 410
Noel, 346
Noerr, 77, 181, 208
Nokes, 500

Nolan, 100, 129, 283, 284, 290, 302, 303, 427, 429
Noland, 48
Nolen, 568
Nones, 593
Nonsuch, 546
Noonan, 81, 116, 255
Norment, 179, 284, 336, 373
Normile, 253, 255
Norris, 35, 41, 42, 43, 45, 62, 63, 215, 236, 277, 285, 306, 381, 423, 429, 556
Norse, 41
Nortan, 406
North, 336, 493
Northbrooke, 397
Northrop, 290
Norton, 71, 177, 253, 298, 354, 434, 453, 470, 527, 542
Norwood, 100, 255, 481, 515, 521
Notingham, 303
Notley Hall, 368
Notson, 386
Nott, 36, 37, 75, 561
Nourse, 183, 317, 325, 340
Nowlan, 448
Nowland, 196
Nowles, 538
Noyes, 114, 299, 300, 336, 359, 364, 457, 458, 463, 500, 503, 507, 561
Null, 156
Nutt, 189
Nye, 157, 161, 326
Nyman, 308, 331

O

O'Beirne, 75, 85, 392, 496, 500, 502, 509
O'Brien, 14, 66, 87, 100, 117, 173, 196, 250, 253, 402, 405, 454, 554, 573, 577, 597
O'Bryan, 476
O'Callahan, 5, 152
O'Connel, 446
O'Connell, 140, 168, 253, 255, 301

O'Connor, 57, 100, 140, 168, 212, 219, 292, 392, 458
O'Conor, 222, 507
O'Day, 467, 493
O'Donnell, 127, 471, 564, 575
O'Donnogue, 311
O'Donoghue, 345
O'Dowd, 292
O'Hara, 267, 354
O'Hare, 81, 114, 300, 442
O'Harra, 207
O'Leary, 175, 287, 303, 304
O'Mahony, 50
O'Meara, 292, 336
O'Neal, 119, 295, 348, 401, 480
O'Neal Tract, 186
O'Neale, 6, 127, 348
O'Neil, 142, 235, 238, 315
O'Niel, 287
O'Regan, 549
O'Shea, 118
Oak, 168
Oak & Farm, 588
Oak Grove, 507
Oak Hill, 505
Oak Hill Cemetery, 185, 266, 309, 320, 358, 378, 398, 463, 508, 510
Oak Hill Farm, 275, 412, 495
Oakes, 111, 283
Oakeson, 522
Oakley, 401
O'Beirne, 548
Obenchain, 158
Ober, 303, 565
Oberley, 315
Obi, 351
Obre, 350
Ochmed, 374
Ockert, 304
Ockes, 284
Oddie, 187
Odell, 172, 180, 253, 261, 262, 345, 537
Oden, 52
Odin, 445
Odrick, 481

Offenbacher, 253
Offus, 418
Offutt, 10, 283, 565
Ogden, 260, 336, 415
Ogdensburg Cemetery, 212
Ogilive, 259
Ogle, 79
Oglesby, 291, 523, 564
Ogleton, 109, 112
Ohrt, 27
Okerson, 384
Olcott, 159
Olcutt, 595
Old Capitol, 98, 173
old Foundry burial-ground, 208
Old Relic, 412
Oldest Inhabitants, 8, 43, 79, 139, 183, 261, 262, 437, 502
oldest man, 47
Oldest newspaper, 265
Oldham, 492, 565
Olds, 82, 587
Oldshue, 291
Ole Bull, 151
Olean, 442
Olin, 109, 112, 114, 124, 125, 132, 140, 146, 152, 155, 156, 158, 168, 172, 174, 181, 187, 194, 278, 285, 460, 465, 484, 487, 548, 551, 599, 600
Olive, 512
Oliver, 96, 104, 174, 181, 289, 310, 397, 406, 571, 579, 583, 588
Olmstead, 102, 105, 155
Olmsted, 583
Olney, 565
Olsen, 501
one Revolutionary pensioner, 580
Opdenweyer, 513
Opdyke, 66
Openheimer, 127
Oppenheimer, 336
Ord, 14, 171, 291, 343, 344, 348, 433
Organization of New Regts, 558
Origin & Use of bells, 396

Orman, 416, 565
Orme, 315, 325, 336, 407, 411, 563
Orphans Court, 1, 2, 3, 10, 12, 13,
  14, 18, 20, 22, 24, 25, 27, 28, 29,
  33, 34, 36, 37, 39, 40, 41, 43, 44,
  45, 47, 49, 57, 64, 68, 74, 76, 77,
  82, 84, 86, 92, 96, 98, 113, 118,
  119, 120, 125, 126, 138, 139, 154,
  156, 157, 158, 163, 164, 166, 167,
  170, 172, 174, 176, 178, 179, 181,
  189, 192, 201, 204, 205, 215, 220,
  221, 224, 234, 238, 250, 251, 256,
  264, 266, 268, 270, 272, 273, 284,
  291, 294, 296, 302, 313, 316, 329,
  331, 340, 342, 345, 352, 353, 356,
  357, 363, 371, 377, 386, 390, 391,
  393, 397, 399, 400, 401, 406, 409,
  415, 416, 435, 441, 442, 448, 449,
  451, 459, 460, 462, 465, 466, 474,
  476, 478, 481, 486, 498, 500, 501,
  503, 507, 508, 509, 515, 516, 521,
  528, 529, 533, 543, 544, 546, 548,
  556, 558, 560, 561, 569, 572, 574,
  576, 579, 580, 581, 582, 583, 584,
  587, 590, 596, 599, 600
Orr, 267, 344, 350, 351, 355
Orrell, 154
Ortega, 539
Ortell, 195
Osbon, 83
Osborn, 70, 181, 269, 548
Osborne, 526, 533, 571
Osburne, 540
Osgood, 143, 458
Osnard, 350, 351
Ossinger, 180
Osterman, 41
Ostrander, 42, 105, 229, 514
Otego, 34
Otero, 27, 251, 404, 457, 468
Otis, 447
Otterback, 39, 181, 336
Otterson, 514
Otto, 133, 156, 300
Ould, 30, 79, 413
Oulds, 504

Oulick, 345
Our Willie, 325
Ourand, 307, 311
Overby, 250
Overend, 225
Overly, 250
Owen, 5, 35, 53, 62, 64, 79, 153,
  272, 307, 336, 344, 388, 397, 460,
  462, 569
Owens, 5, 115, 117, 173, 387, 412,
  524
Owing, 68, 514
Owings, 374
Owner, 264
Oxenseller, 593
Oye, 68
Oyster, 283

P

Pace, 250, 251, 331
Pacer, 397
Packard, 168, 180, 182, 377, 532
packet **St Charles**, 362
Packson, 550
Paddock, 83
Padgett, 304, 561, 589
Page, 16, 66, 127, 162, 168, 186,
  255, 259, 300, 323, 327, 336, 348,
  391, 397, 400, 416, 482, 499, 500,
  501, 533, 539, 573, 585
Page property, 99
Page's Rest, 266
Paine, 413, 482
Painter, 316, 330, 596
Paison, 165
Palfrey, 415, 453, 454
Pallen, 442
Palmer, 1, 80, 111, 119, 159, 201,
  234, 239, 288, 319, 336, 344, 360,
  427, 430, 436, 441, 486, 495, 578,
  579
Palmerston, 54
Pancoast, 63, 222, 360
Papal Zouaves, 576
Papal Zouves, 557
Paradise, 588

Pareja, 27
Parepa, 288
Parigot, 453
Paris, 395
Parish, 305
Park, 588
Parke, 171, 212, 216, 277, 433
Parker, 62, 74, 81, 87, 127, 136, 152, 176, 180, 182, 245, 276, 303, 307, 310, 336, 367, 379, 384, 397, 453, 476, 495, 502, 508, 515, 528, 553, 555, 568, 576, 582
Parkhurst, 456, 457, 460, 508
Parkington, 311
Parkinson, 104, 296
Parkridge, 353
Parks, 546, 561
Parnell, 100
Parraga, 409
Parris, 9, 358, 428, 457, 565
Parrott, 107, 229, 322
Parrott's Woods, 322
Parry, 29, 89, 104, 140, 144, 501, 587
Parsmon, 492
Parsonins, 94
Parsons, 49, 347, 395, 430, 434, 494, 570, 583
Part of Barber's Inclosure, 281
Part of Pennslvania, 371
Part of Westham, 281
Partello, 74
Partridge, 108
Parvet, 404
Pascall, 576
Paschal, 103
Paschall, 429, 565
Pasha, 437
Patce, 537
Patch, 115
Paterson, 562
Paton, 484
Patrick, 245
Patten, 234
Patterson, 2, 13, 73, 75, 79, 82, 101, 102, 105, 158, 183, 253, 255, 292, 307, 336, 377, 381, 477, 487, 537, 543, 563, 570, 575, 594
Pattesson, 539
Patti, 207, 465
Patton, 535
Patty, 429
Paul, 93, 104, 563
Paulding, 206, 235, 294, 302, 574
Paxson, 488
Paymasters, 7, 56, 167, 277, 302, 315, 330, 417, 571
Payne, 1, 20, 159, 260, 267, 311, 354, 424, 509, 578
Paynter, 498
Payton, 3, 282, 283, 488
Peabody, 10, 172, 193, 205, 251, 259, 336, 356, 395, 525
Peacher, 491, 565
Peak, 282, 283
Peake, 303, 304
Peakman, 550
Peal, 100
Peale, 484
Pearce, 431, 564, 565
Pearson, 116, 326, 332, 336, 460
Peaslee, 427
Peat, 246
Peck, 52, 84, 103, 110, 272, 277, 345, 390, 433, 491, 547, 561, 571
Peek, 299
Pegg, 166, 303
Peirce, 41, 52
Peiree, 28
Pelby, 580
Pell, 453
Pellet, 318
Pellicer, 34, 251, 457
Pellicier, 404
Pelot, 325
Pemerton, 433
Pendergrass, 114
Penderson, 139
Pendleton, 138, 209, 226, 432, 480, 488, 563
Penicks, 292
Penington, 596

Penn, 138, 191, 373
Pennington, 76, 552
Penny Hill burying ground, 463
Peoples, 511
Peora, 388
Peoria, 431
Pepper, 8, 68, 380, 384, 565
Perchal, 453
Percy, 28
Perdue, 231
Perego, 262
Perham, 239
Perkin, 411
Perkins, 51, 102, 126, 127, 240, 300, 469, 503, 568
Perley, 315, 434, 448
Perrell, 224
Perrie, 176, 308
Perrier, 409
Perrin, 544
Perrodin, 430, 565
Perrott, 311
Perry, 62, 103, 111, 230, 252, 283, 284, 336, 360, 439, 454, 510, 539
Perryman, 248
Person, 64
Persons, 161
Peter, 360, 502, 547
Peterkin, 376
Peters, 12, 166, 182, 212, 397, 411, 440, 513, 514, 552, 578
Peterson, 83, 104, 139
Petingale, 549
Petit, 345
Petrie, 526
Petriken, 101
Pettee, 99
Petter, 199
Pettit, 32, 36, 54, 103, 309, 439, 596
Pettitt, 508
Peugh, 1, 311
Peyton, 282, 367, 436
Pfinger, 175
Pheatt, 3
Phelan, 114, 174, 254, 277, 336, 536

Phelps, 17, 47, 56, 105, 432, 538, 591
Philbin, 453
Philip, 208, 336, 548, 586
Philippe, 157
Phillip, 529
Phillips, 9, 44, 62, 127, 131, 136, 143, 144, 156, 158, 159, 202, 205, 264, 265, 277, 282, 283, 320, 360, 374, 428, 437, 467, 492, 513, 565, 572
Philp, 193, 336
Phinney, 458
Phoenix, 463
Pholan, 573
Pickerd, 293
Pickerell, 160
Pickett, 183, 387, 433, 584
Pickhard, 537
Pickrell, 62, 284, 301, 336, 378
Pier, 526
Pierce, 76, 77, 95, 130, 193, 226, 308, 310, 382, 406, 427, 428, 473, 540, 565
Pierie, 122
Pierpont, 185, 382, 401
Pierrepont, 507
Pierson, 524
Piggott, 404
Piggott Tract, 186
Pignette, 492
Pike, 147, 153, 165, 190, 526
Pillsbury, 23
Pinckney, 160, 165, 244, 262, 264, 389, 434, 508
Pinckneys, 32
Pink Allegany, 588
Pinkerton, 213, 342
Pinkney, 51, 53, 57, 346, 479, 503
Pinneger, 451
Piper, 37, 234, 507
Pipher, 308
Pique, 350, 351
Piquette, 565
Pirtle, 326
Pise, 223, 234, 270

Pitcher, 374, 425, 560, 562, 564
Pitcher portrait, 407
Pitchlynn, 349
Pitts, 426
Pizzini, 599
Planchard, 351
Plant, 61, 73, 136, 336, 375, 438, 500, 538
Plants, 326
Plantz, 140
Plate, 409
Plater, 314, 489, 495
Plato, 276, 496
Platt, 9, 35, 127, 193, 311
Platz, 359, 498
Pleasanton, 171, 433
Pleasants, 99, 493
Plowden, 11
Plowman, 325, 463, 468
Plummer, 99, 324, 421
Plunkett, 259
Plymouth Church, 23
Pocock, 310
Poe, 18, 171, 190, 320, 321
Pohler, 177
Pohlman, 105
Poiglars, 453
Point Lookout, 6, 218
Point of Hampstead, 591
Poitevant, 564
Poitevin, 214
Polgiase, 308
Polglass, 206
Polk, 146, 241, 388, 432, 501, 548
Polkinghorn, 565
Polkinhorn, 62, 117, 290, 291, 336, 430, 540
Pollak, 40
Pollard, 55, 179, 223, 424, 572
Pollock, 103, 336, 429, 562, 572
Polly, 219
Polydor, 453
Pomeroy, 127, 406, 437, 453, 510
Pomfrey, 428, 565
Pond, 370, 568
Ponsardin, 406

Poole, 109, 311
Poor, 270
Poorks, 177
Pope, 24, 56, 94, 171, 177, 245, 287, 318, 343, 352, 385, 433
Pope Julius, 51
Pope Pius VI, 443
Pope Sabinian, 396
Poplar Grove Cemetery, 520
Poplar Hill, 25
Porch, 401
Porche, 531
Porschall, 570
Porter, 17, 31, 44, 56, 101, 106, 108, 234, 299, 326, 354, 366, 378, 385, 392, 420, 510, 559, 587
Porterfield, 209
Portier, 443
Posey, 281, 300
Posonby, 453
Post, 32, 354
Post Ofc Appointments, 379, 409
Potlock, 500
Potter, 18, 58, 108, 137, 147, 155, 171, 231, 234, 418, 454, 538
Potts, 35, 182, 336, 344, 381, 583, 589
Pouison, 428
Poulson, 73
Poulton, 543
Powdle, 340
Powell, 10, 24, 64, 123, 205, 234, 244, 296, 306, 434, 533, 545
Power, 104, 167
Powers, 29, 452, 454, 569
Prather, 127, 307, 308, 329, 485, 540
Pratt, 102, 111, 362, 374, 385, 524, 573, 583
Prayer, 405, 456, 593
Preble, 578
Predham, 318
Preneau, 285
Prentice, 152
Prentis, 72
Prentiss, 79, 471, 480, 594
Pres Lincoln died, 83

Pres of the U S, 450
Presburg, 265
Presbury, 471
Presley, 529
Preston, 58, 86, 115, 265, 525
Pretto, 453, 454
Prettyman, 546
Prevost, 338
Price, 100, 198, 223, 229, 298, 303, 424, 464, 499, 537, 558, 564
Pride, 467
Pridham, 221
Prigg, 437
Primrose, 494
Prince, 136, 192, 354, 358, 360, 411
Prince Christian, 38, 331
Prince of Wales, 437, 507
Princess Helena, 38
Princess Mary, 273
Princeton, 234
Prisoners of War, 340
Pritchard, 5, 159, 165
privateer **Royal Yacht**, 230
Probasco, 179, 557
Probst, 142, 153, 181, 190, 241, 247
Proby, 59
Proctor, 263, 404, 457
Prom, 564
Promised Land Resurveyed, 588
propeller **Lac la Belle**, 545
Prosise, 308
Prospect Hill, 450, 452
Prospect Hill Cemetery, 478
Protzman, 151
Prout, 127, 187, 236
Provest, 62, 338
Providence Hospital, 121, 292, 468
Provost, 336
Prutt, 456
Pruyn, 526
Pt Compton's Purchase, 281
Puckdeschel, 453
Pugh, 37, 222
Pugney, 284
Pulford, 105
Pullen, 362

Pumphrey, 64, 84, 139, 224, 265, 300, 308, 471, 502, 517, 540
Pupatty, 351
Purcell, 1, 14, 18, 22, 28, 40, 43, 61, 64, 68, 74, 77, 82, 86, 92, 96, 113, 118, 126, 138, 156, 164, 167, 178, 189, 192, 201, 204, 215, 221, 234, 238, 250, 272, 273, 284, 296, 302, 331, 342, 345, 356, 371, 391, 399, 401, 409, 415, 416, 435, 442, 443, 444, 449, 460, 478, 481, 498, 508, 515, 528, 543, 546, 561, 569, 581, 583, 590, 600
Purcells, 186
Purdy, 57, 61, 65, 215, 254, 286, 318, 327, 555, 578
Purindon, 159
Purnell, 111, 222, 369
Purrington, 360
Pursell, 526, 580
Putnam, 72, 102, 315, 568, 575
Pyfer, 342
Pyne, 524
Pywell, 215

Q

Quackenboss, 107
Quackenbush, 419
Quail, 414
Quantrell, 114
Quatorse, 453
Queen, 12, 62, 84, 304, 477, 534
Queen Anne, 530
Queen Emma, 372, 405
Queen of the French, 157
Queen Victoria, 218, 251, 287
Quigg, 417
Quigley, 308, 371
Quigly, 57
Quilliman, 414
Quinan, 453
Quinby, 103, 433
Quinlan, 445
Quinn, 109, 112, 164, 267, 287, 354, 536
Quintard, 66

Quintero, 469
Quinton, 276
Quirk, 555
Quistion, 344

R

Rabadon, 108
Rabbit, 300
Rabe, 66
Rabus, 112
Radcliff, 46, 360
Radcliffe, 37, 290, 329, 394
Radford, 381
Rady, 308
Raff, 310
Rafferty, 507
Raftery, 253, 255
Ragan, 77, 90, 290, 300, 581
Raidy, 490
Raines, 429
Rainey, 161, 490
Rainier, 309
Rains, 433
Ralchild, 148
Raley, 477
ram **Merrimac**, 323, 395
ram **Merrimack**, 236
Ramsay, 336, 455
Ramsey, 167, 173, 277, 367, 513, 526, 576
Randall, 101, 300, 308, 327, 330, 336, 356, 381, 400, 416, 430
Randkin, 492
Randolf, 306
Randolph, 12, 217, 312, 383, 480, 499, 575
Rankin, 38, 513, 565
Ranson, 107
Ransone, 20, 182, 240
Rapetti, 282
Raphael, 458
Rapley, 128, 245, 336
Rappe, 445
Rarey, 447
Ratcliffe, 167, 563
Rathbone, 147, 457, 568, 589

Rathborn, 568
Ratrie, 303
Rau, 68
Raw, 65
Rawdon, 55
Rawlings, 308, 309, 310, 381, 523
Rawlins, 24, 477
Ray, 6, 59, 128, 175, 323, 336, 545, 572, 580
Raylor, 337
Raymond, 74, 327, 454, 549
Raynor, 253, 255
Rea, 135
Read, 6, 11, 31, 399, 454
Reade, 470
Ready, 283
Reagan, 313
Reamer, 308
reannexation of Alexandria Co, 591
Reardon, 300
Reaves, 561
Red House Field, 266
Reddick, 585
Reddy, 129
Redeger, 500
Redenbaugh, 560
Rederto, 580
Redfern, 336, 546, 548
Redfield, 575
Redin, 6, 98, 301, 336, 508, 510, 517, 528, 533
Redmond, 101, 367
Redwood, 298, 385
Reed, 51, 68, 91, 94, 101, 102, 180, 222, 237, 242, 351, 359, 362, 367, 391, 419, 429, 437, 453, 460, 537
Reeder, 2, 150, 571
Reedle, 172
Reedwerden, 552
Reedy, 103
Reese, 72, 127, 212, 308, 400
Reeside, 128
Reeve, 558
Reeves, 40, 178, 181, 300, 301, 378, 577
Regan, 581

Regester, 338
Register, 453
Reichel, 211
Reichenbach, 560
Reichhelm, 89
Reid, 105, 135, 288, 430, 537, 565
Reider, 109
Reifsnider, 212
Reigneld, 288
Reiley, 23
Reilley, 483
Reilley's Tavern, 555
Reilly, 101, 282, 283, 526
Reily, 44
Reinaman, 372
Reinhard, 146
re-interment, 16
Reisinger, 277
Reiss, 96, 310
remains of two Federal soldiers, 381
Remington, 159
Rench, 596
Rencher, 207
Renett, 245
Reno, 235, 322, 433
Renoug, 454
Renout, 453
Renshaw, 532, 599
Rentz, 245
Renwick, 322
Repetti, 292
Republic, 588
Rese, 443
Resurvey on part of the James & Mary, 174
Resurvey on the Grove, 174
Reville, 108
Reynold, 128
Reynolds, 86, 165, 359, 433, 456, 508, 509, 555, 559, 560
Reynor, 73
Rheam, 34
Rheem, 34, 77, 561
Rhees, 310, 336, 340, 398, 417
Rhett, 292
Rhinehardt, 226

Rhinehart, 336
Rhodes, 391, 469, 563
Ricaud, 36
Rice, 41, 104, 129, 189, 342, 367, 397, 410, 486, 538
Rich, 73, 127, 277, 477, 515
Richard, 237, 307, 493, 537
Richards, 59, 81, 116, 129, 134, 140, 145, 146, 162, 189, 272, 277, 283, 310, 314, 336, 372, 375, 493, 509, 541, 573
Richardson, 41, 135, 193, 225, 228, 308, 319, 336, 443, 453, 509, 544, 565
Richenbach, 336
Richie, 119
Richleim, 89
Richmond, 302, 326, 347, 379, 390, 392, 424, 491
Richter, 300
Rickett, 433, 571
Ricketts, 463
Rickford, 159
Rickles, 451
Rickoly, 451
Riddle, 167, 172, 480, 562
Ridenour, 86, 128
Rider, 86, 158, 571, 587
Ridge, 340
Ridgeley, 434
Ridgely, 106, 244, 248
Ridgeway, 359
Ridgewood, 120
Ridlehuber, 586
Ridout, 244
Riess, 311
Rietor, 284
Rigby, 25
Riggles, 283, 307, 308, 310, 336
Riggs, 61, 73, 98, 116, 162, 320, 326, 336, 352, 395, 508
Rights of Man, 588
Riley, 40, 52, 55, 64, 69, 97, 121, 167, 168, 190, 207, 269, 286, 287, 299, 305, 331, 336, 360, 434, 579
Rinehart, 298

Ring, 354
Ringgold, 336, 349, 359, 424
Ringwold, 586
Rinker, 65
Ripley, 4, 54, 159
Ripp, 425
Riquet, 388, 431
Rising, 536
Risley, 537
Risque, 290
Ristori, 222, 350
Ritchie, 33, 74, 220, 259, 293, 360, 461
Rittenhouse, 42, 61, 238
Ritter, 310
Ritterhaus, 511
Ritterhouas, 511
Rittimeyer, 525
Rivers, 80, 245, 459, 473
Riverside, 588
Rives, 75, 309, 312
Rixey, 522
Rixley, 522
Roach, 283, 301, 429, 565
Roan, 493
Roath, 342
Robbin, 277
Robbins, 10, 39, 41, 74, 96, 100, 200, 239, 336, 360, 453, 496, 500
Robby, 47
Robe, 379
Robeds, 309
Robert, 453, 454
Robert's Choice, 122
Roberts, 45, 66, 108, 127, 240, 301, 314, 340, 360, 454, 461, 478, 508, 528, 546, 575, 577
Robertson, 107, 152, 179, 330, 515, 530
Robey, 301, 545
Robins, 102
Robinson, 19, 102, 150, 171, 176, 190, 228, 231, 241, 259, 265, 283, 299, 300, 303, 308, 336, 351, 359, 367, 369, 373, 374, 406, 438, 458,
476, 480, 497, 521, 526, 537, 557, 560, 593
Robison, 461
Roccoford, 12
Rochat, 523
Roche, 128, 239, 287, 321
Rochester, 336
Rock Creek burial ground, 386
Rock Creek Church, 510
Rockburne, 13
Rocker, 345
Rockford, 102
Rockwell, 453
Rodebaugh, 184
Roder, 101
Rodgers, 106, 107, 157, 231, 249
Rodier, 35, 367, 504
Rodman, 545
Rodney, 71, 330
Roemmele, 77, 119
Rofflo, 419
Rogan, 181
Roger, 92
Rogers, 92, 98, 129, 132, 159, 180, 294, 301, 308, 454, 455, 476, 482, 500, 534, 596
Rohrer, 308, 493, 590
Roland, 541
Rolando, 579
Rollings, 43
Rollins, 13, 37, 228, 283, 284, 287, 493, 555, 564, 586
Rolte, 75
Roman, 103
Romero, 129, 381
Romisarow, 236
Romseau, 416
Romyn, 542
Rood, 416
Rooker, 517
Rooney, 568
Roosa, 248
Roose, 336
Roosevelt, 205
Root, 199
Roper, 526

Rork, 402
Rosati, 443
Rosch, 159
Rose, 143, 309, 311, 369, 462, 538, 569, 578
Rosecrans, 24, 343, 433, 444, 516
Rosenstein, 513
Rosenthal, 336
Rosmassen, 454
Ross, 100, 101, 224, 236, 339, 344, 349, 366, 498, 516
Rossecrans, 169
Rosser, 20
Rossini, 245, 506
Roswell, 101, 385
Roth, 190, 244
Rothermel, 331
Rothery, 326, 376
Rothrock, 336
Rothschilds, 148, 513
Rothwell, 438, 486, 541, 548, 590
Roucher, 454
Rounce, 522
Rounds, 405, 456
Rousch, 345
Rouse, 275, 326
Rousseau, 169, 205, 330, 387, 446
Roussellon, 531
Routh, 120
Roves, 336
Row, 526
Rowan, 365, 571
Rowans, 571
Rowe, 300, 307, 367, 416, 429, 473
Rowell, 228
Rowland, 18, 192, 234, 492, 535, 547, 566
Rowlett, 599
Rowley, 122, 516
Rowzee, 410
Rowzer, 89
Roy, 384
Royal, 479
Royal Charlotte, 588
Royce, 487
Royell, 228

Roys, 367
Rozetto, 487
Rozier, 451
Ruben, 333
Rubendale, 528
Rubens, 435
Rucker, 35, 84, 238
Rudd, 290
Rudelhulber, 586
Ruder, 537
Rudolph, 290
Rudyeard, 392
Ruff, 303, 305, 336
Ruger, 313, 560
Rugg, 101
Ruggles, 111, 234, 354, 379
Ruh, 584
Rullman, 179
Rundlett, 498
Runge, 306
Ruppert, 336, 416
Rupprecht, 474, 478
Rush, 247, 513
Russ, 5, 434
Russel, 372
Russell, 64, 79, 100, 105, 148, 167, 211, 282, 283, 303, 336, 365, 369, 390, 421, 433, 454, 473, 536, 599
Ruth, 487
Rutherford, 145, 276, 283, 350, 509
Rutledge, 518
Ryan, 2, 143, 190, 191, 273, 309, 336, 346, 397, 454, 493, 538
Ryder, 283
Ryer, 100
Ryon, 37, 176, 422, 523

S

S_orrs, 526
Sabin, 167
Sacket, 540
Sackett, 314
Safford, 7
Sagar, 563
Sage, 102, 223, 304, 526
Sagine, 573

Sallade, 56, 378
Salnave, 405
Salter, 245, 494
Sambour, 21
Sample, 111
Sampson, 45, 84, 159
Samson, 6, 33, 107, 292, 449
Samuels, 114, 133
Sanbern, 385
Sanborn, 380
Sanchez, 175
Sandal, 453
Sandborn, 197
Sanders, 245, 274, 406, 539
Sanderson, 79, 181, 302, 305, 540
Sandford, 47, 273, 413
Sands, 4, 106, 311, 384
Sanford, 66, 86, 88, 103, 494
Sanger, 325
Sangtell, 571
Sanner, 310
Sanno, 101
Santa Anna, 353
Santer, 363
Sappington, 493
Sapple, 397
Sardo, 235, 309
Sargent, 161, 199, 337
Sarkint, 19
Sarus, 583
Saschell, 171
Sasscer, 267, 505
Satchell, 492, 565
Satterlee, 234, 411
Saul, 119
Saunders, 9, 327, 388, 431, 440
Sauntry, 68
Sauza, 456
Savage, 62, 103, 123, 140, 193, 336, 337, 338, 346, 438
Saverac, 454
Savoy, 122
Sawyer, 80, 233, 276, 385, 599
Saxton, 222, 304, 433
Sayder, 175
Sayers, 300

Sayre, 494
Sayres, 185
Scaggs, 27, 308
Scammon, 372
Scanlon, 234, 347
Scarff, 304
Schaad, 129
Schade, 62
Schaefer, 292
Schaffer, 26, 454
Schall, 104
Scheckels, 283
Schell, 24, 549
Schenck, 178, 229
Schenig, 576
Schermerhorn, 299
Schetz, 57
Schff, 29
Schietlin, 304
Schiffler, 104
Schiffner, 307
Schillingman, 493
Schindel, 101
Schley, 588
Schlosser, 283, 284
Schmidt, 3, 85, 217, 264, 273, 295, 320, 406, 581, 590
Schmorr, 428
Schneider, 242, 258, 337, 361, 374
schnr **America**, 364
schnr **Americus**, 25
schnr **Arago**, 561
schnr **Christiana**, 18
schnr **Clara Coward**, 184
schnr **Elizabeth B**, 545
schnr **Emeline**, 80
schnr **Flying Fish**, 574
schnr **General S Van Vliet**, 161
schnr **Grampus**, 439
schnr **J L Diess**, 157
schnr **John Boynton**, 4
schnr **John C Henry**, 145
schnr **Morning Star**, 456
schnr **Pacific**, 145
schnr **Revenge**, 439
schnr **Rhodella**, 25

schnr **Swallow**, 550
schnr **Valor**, 453
schnr **Veto**, 451
schnr **West Wind**, 80
schnr **William Carleton**, 168
schnr **Witch of the Wave**, 145
schnr **Wm Cousins**, 145
Schofield, 24, 171, 343, 544, 560, 589
Scholfield, 271
Scholl, 360
Schoolcraft, 29, 129
Schott, 303
Schouler, 4, 582
Schraag, 493
Schreiner, 102
Schreyer, 100
Schriver, 227, 302
Schroedel, 399
Schroeder, 91, 181, 600
Schutter, 283
Schuttler, 295
Schwan, 102
Schwartz, 102
Schwarzkopp, 469
Schwarzman, 222
Schwerin, 453
Scipio, 323
Scollard, 274
Scollay, 93, 117
Scolley, 93
Scot, 516
Scott, 19, 31, 45, 66, 76, 106, 134, 225, 226, 227, 234, 303, 304, 307, 308, 324, 328, 348, 357, 359, 393, 396, 399, 403, 436, 460, 484, 496, 514, 526, 567, 578
Scovell, 229
Scoville, 92
Scripps, 9, 420
Scrivener, 69, 98, 115, 137
Scriver, 487
Scroggin, 468
Scwarburg, 586
Se'ls, 430
Seaborn, 200, 494

Seabright, 123
Seabrook, 245
Seago, 214
Searight, 564
Searle, 374, 497, 564
Sears, 43, 116, 229, 255, 337, 600
Seaton, 8, 58, 183, 259, 261, 262, 327, 377, 446, 524, 580
Sebastian, 90
Second Resurvey on Partnership, 547
Sedgwick, 350, 433
See of Balt, 443
Seeley, 75
Seely, 552
Sefton, 273
Segur, 564
Segura, 492, 565
Seibel, 283
Seibold, 95, 359
Seidel, 303
Seip, 376
Seiss, 91
Seitz, 189, 439, 504, 548
Selby, 27, 300, 301, 336, 439
Selden, 53, 62, 231
Sellhausen, 93
Sells, 563
Semkin, 337
Semmes, 10, 36, 61, 132, 179, 201, 209, 270, 288, 337, 350, 398, 418, 442, 478, 554
Sempsey, 454
Senac, 69
Senack, 69
Senec, 69
Seney, 149
Sergeant, 390, 482
Serlie, 578
Serrin, 128
Serrins, 311
Sessford, 8, 160, 285, 356, 357
Setchell, 339, 347, 597
Seven Pines, 191
Seven Pines Cemetery, 520
Severa, 453

Severgood, 401
Severns, 541
Seving, 362
Sewall, 128, 367
Seward, 90, 99, 139, 381, 450, 484, 542, 551, 556, 562
Sewell, 309
sewing machine, 282
Sexton, 230, 493
Seyfert, 290
Seymour, 33, 171, 289, 310, 337, 397, 449, 457, 472
Seys, 449
Shackelford, 151
Shacklett, 389, 431
Shadd, 128
Shaeffer, 526
Shafer, 152, 401, 408, 410
Shaffer, 224, 454
Shaffield, 460, 578
Shafnecker, 514
Shallcross, 352
Shanahan, 164, 483
Shannon, 128
Sharkey, 284
Sharo, 310
Sharon, 366
Sharp, 94, 165, 492, 538, 565
Sharp's Island, 89, 441
Sharretts, 308, 309
Shaughnessy, 397
Shaver, 539
Shaw, 21, 133, 144, 174, 212, 245, 283, 298, 325, 350, 351, 395, 444, 452, 573
Shea, 134, 219, 222, 311, 594
Sheaffer, 342
Sheahan, 523
Sheble, 364
Sheck, 299
Sheckelford, 39
Sheckells, 540
Sheckels, 31, 77
Sheckleford, 282
Sheckles, 151
Shedd, 192, 308, 309, 310, 336, 359

Sheehan, 257, 514
Sheehy, 133
Sheets, 67, 537
Shehan, 99
Shehen, 283
Sheherd, 99
Shekel, 402
Shelby, 499
Sheldon, 7, 111, 154, 389, 431, 565
Shelley, 191, 523
Shellman, 226
Shelton, 304
Shepard, 102
Shephard, 541
Shepherd, 73, 122, 156, 336, 337, 360, 536, 540, 558
Sheppard, 504
Sherburne, 4
Sheridan, 16, 17, 24, 56, 100, 182, 282, 290, 297, 343, 418, 440, 594
Sheriff, 337, 413, 505
Sherlock, 565
Sherman, 24, 44, 58, 61, 62, 73, 79, 105, 132, 171, 209, 239, 253, 255, 326, 331, 343, 344, 351, 352, 387, 399, 420, 421, 427, 432, 433, 473, 493, 505, 508
Shermer, 378
Sherrin, 536
Sherry, 561
Sherwin, 330, 599
Sherwood, 6, 39, 54, 180, 182, 233, 240, 301, 310, 402, 492
Shetaline, 152
Shetman, 171
Shields, 22, 128, 163, 166, 284, 287, 301, 405
Shillington, 336
Shinbone, 561
Shiner, 307
Shinn, 258, 337, 505
Shins, 472
ship **Africa**, 252
ship **Aroostook**, 570, 575, 583, 589, 593
ship **Ascutney**, 593

ship **Bienville**, 552, 579
ship **Brooklyn**, 398
ship **Chattanooga**, 462, 570, 596
ship **Chicopee**, 583
ship **Chocura**, 417
ship **Constellation**, 541, 585
ship **Corwin**, 417
ship **De Sota**, 593
ship **De Soto**, 369, 549
ship **Don**, 579
ship **E W Seyburn**, 139
ship **Estrella**, 417
ship **Franklin**, 578, 596
ship **Gettysburg**, 547, 549, 576
ship **Glance**, 575
ship **Great Eastern**, 344
ship **Guerriere**, 570
ship **H Braband**, 448
ship **Hartford**, 255
ship **Huron**, 570, 573, 593, 599
ship **Ida Lilly**, 429
ship **Independence**, 398
ship **Iroquois**, 552, 570, 573, 575, 578, 585, 593
ship **Jamestown**, 512
ship **Juniata**, 417
ship **Kate Dyer**, 555
ship **Macedonian**, 417, 518
ship **Madawaska**, 599
ship **Marblehead**, 583, 593
ship **Maria**, 579
ship **Massachusetts**, 561, 579
ship **Michigan**, 543, 549, 593, 596
ship **Monongahela**, 598
ship **Monongo**, 417
ship **Newbern**, 541, 547, 552
ship **Nina**, 593
ship **Ohio**, 583
ship **Onward**, 573
ship **Osceola**, 541
ship **Ossipee**, 532, 544
ship **Palas**, 570
ship **Pawnee**, 570, 573, 578, 599
ship **Penobscot**, 570, 583, 589
ship **Peoria**, 570, 578, 583
ship **Persia**, 315
ship **Pilgrim**, 570
ship **Potomac**, 596
ship **Pyramus**, 151
ship **Rhode Island**, 530, 570, 593
ship **S H Sharp**, 25
ship **Sabine**, 532, 547, 552
ship **Savannah**, 417
ship **Shawmut**, 573
ship **Snowdrop**, 575
ship **Sorrel**, 593
ship **Sunrise**, 370
ship **Susequehanna**, 532
ship **Susquehanna**, 512, 534
ship **Suwanee**, 596
ship **Tacony**, 417, 512, 530, 541, 547
ship **Tallapoosa**, 578
ship **Tallspoosa**, 369
ship **Tampedo**, 363
ship **Tonawanda**, 567
ship **Tuscorora**, 596
ship **Unadilla**, 570, 579
ship **Vermont**, 512, 575, 583
ship **Winooski**, 369
ship **Wissahickon**, 398
ship **Yantie**, 417, 530
ship **Yucca**, 417
Shipley, 339, 557
Shipman, 361, 387, 426, 431, 595
Shipmen, 284
ships **Medway & Albany**, 344
ship**Tacony**, 532
Shireman, 342
Shirk, 109
Shirley, 288
Shivas, 227
Shoemaker, 37, 59, 77, 128, 156, 191, 253, 254, 339, 397, 472, 509, 580, 590, 592
Shorkley, 103
Shorn, 413
Short, 28, 133, 140, 326
Shorter, 290, 291
Shots, 563
Showacre, 203
Showers, 291

Shreeve, 43
Shreve, 3, 300, 337
Shrewsburg, 485
Shrigley, 525
Shriver, 337, 369
Shroder, 39
Shryock, 230
Shubrick, 105, 320, 330, 398
Shuck, 480
Shugrue, 584
Shuit, 485
Shull, 212
Shultz, 136
Shuman, 238, 504
Shumate, 275
Shuster, 336
Sibley, 42, 125, 336, 352, 410, 476, 558
Sickles, 165, 197, 305, 374, 422, 456, 478, 505, 560
Sigourney, 23
Sigston, 60
Sigur, 492, 565
Sill, 503
Silliman, 289
Silsbee, 538
Silsby, 537
Silver, 494
Silver Hill, 425, 490
Silver Spring, 522
Silvernail, 587
Simmeson, 537
Simmons, 35, 59, 120, 128, 239, 245, 337, 452, 490, 524, 589
Simms, 8, 12, 55, 80, 98, 290, 326, 345, 438, 443, 470, 477
Simon, 564
Simonds, 303
Simons, 101, 241, 325, 355
Simonton, 101, 355
Simple, 104
Simpson, 32, 33, 35, 48, 75, 132, 172, 213, 253, 302, 303, 304, 307, 326, 336, 337, 372, 428, 492, 493, 513, 530, 540, 549, 563, 564, 579
Simpson's Delight, 289

Sinclair, 350, 351, 380, 385
Sing Sing, 64
Singleton, 196
Sinnot, 536
Sioussa, 176, 311, 360
Sipe, 307, 359, 547
Sipes, 296
Sirian, 575
Siskut, 232
Sister Loretto Riley, 121
Sister Mary, 525
Sister Mary Gaudalupe, 317
Sisters of Charity, 52, 121, 207, 314, 379, 387, 394, 468
Sisters of Mercy, 15, 220, 366
Sisters of the Poor, 408
Sisters of the Visitation, 345, 568
Sitler, 378
Sixteen-Mile-House, 555
Skau-ba-wis, 93
Skelding, 417, 576
Skidmore, 29, 30, 300, 301
Skilding, 330
Skinker, 431, 565
Skinner, 77, 91, 105, 146, 180, 494, 552
Skippon, 80, 307
Skirving, 47, 154, 303
Skriving, 47, 153, 154
Slack, 149, 474, 587
Slamm, 330, 570
Slate, 362, 525
Slater, 150, 495, 500, 564
Slattery, 440, 563
Slaughter, 387, 426, 431
Slayman, 188
Slayter, 344
Sle, 428
Sleeper, 570, 589
Sleepy Hallow, 312
Sletor, 105
Slicer, 128
Slick, 400
Slinghand, 304
Sloan, 101, 243, 378
Sloanaker, 166, 316, 353

Slocum, 587
Slomon, 141
Sloo, 453, 454
sloop-of-war **Pawnee**, 363
Slose, 373
Slosson, 578
Sluddybaker, 344
Small, 282, 301, 337, 399, 453, 540
Small-pox Cemetery, 521
Smallwood, 210, 249, 448
Smart, 310
Smedberg, 21, 103
Smidley, 371
Smith, 3, 5, 22, 23, 28, 31, 33, 35, 42, 45, 50, 53, 55, 58, 64, 65, 66, 75, 78, 79, 81, 100, 101, 102, 104, 105, 107, 108, 111, 114, 118, 120, 121, 124, 128, 136, 138, 140, 159, 161, 168, 170, 171, 172, 174, 177, 180, 181, 190, 193, 213, 214, 225, 230, 231, 237, 238, 239, 246, 250, 252, 253, 256, 260, 261, 262, 267, 268, 272, 274, 276, 278, 287, 288, 294, 300, 303, 304, 307, 308, 311, 315, 316, 323, 326, 330, 337, 342, 346, 349, 352, 354, 358, 359, 364, 368, 372, 374, 376, 382, 385, 388, 390, 392, 393, 395, 397, 398, 405, 406, 409, 427, 431, 432, 433, 442, 446, 449, 450, 451, 453, 454, 456, 460, 475, 476, 487, 494, 499, 507, 509, 514, 523, 526, 527, 530, 537, 542, 550, 552, 554, 555, 557, 558, 559, 560, 562, 567, 573, 578, 579, 580, 583, 584, 593
Smith's Row, 339
Smithson, 307
Smoot, 2, 96, 98, 166, 169, 252, 311, 324, 337, 359, 360, 426, 434, 448, 449, 451, 487, 599
Smull, 2
Smyth, 138
Smythe, 66, 70, 262, 576
Smyzer, 207
Snead, 389, 431, 565
Sneed, 80

Sneethen, 491, 492
Snicker's Gap, 186
Sniffen, 305
Snook, 300
Snooks, 301
Snow, 1, 62, 337, 425, 538
Snowden, 167, 196, 357, 448, 492
Snowden's New Birmingham Manor, 555
Snyder, 10, 128, 261, 271, 278, 309, 324, 336, 342, 435, 460, 508, 536, 537, 555, 590
Sohl, 128
Sokolowsky, 350
soldiers' cemetery, 317
Soldiers' Cemetery, 478
Soldiers' Lots, 588
Soley, 277
Solger, 17, 26
Solomons, 193, 337
Somers, 304, 397
Somerville, 303
Soo, 454
Soper, 290, 406
Sorrell, 584
Sothoron, 310
Souder, 304
Soule, 154, 267, 354, 544
Sourbier, 311, 466
South Laurel Hill, 320
Southal, 174
Southampton, 571
Southard, 386, 574
Southwell, 49
Southwick, 587
Southworth, 159, 337
Sowers, 492
Spader, 453
Spadetta, 210
Spafford, 94
Spaids, 305
Spalding, 51, 61, 71, 86, 173, 177, 221, 245, 292, 296, 331, 337, 342, 371, 444, 537
Spalding's Dist, 425
Spangenberg, 453

Spanginberg, 454
Sparks, 88, 120, 217, 356
Spates, 154, 300
Spaulding, 278, 287, 303, 383, 385, 455
Speak, 283
Speake, 173, 360
Spear, 318, 467
Specht, 586
Spedden, 348, 462
Speed, 79, 319, 326, 385, 490
Speiden, 304, 482, 498
Speisser, 303, 500
Spence, 123, 157
Spencer, 25, 46, 53, 102, 111, 247, 262, 269, 292, 332, 423, 454, 493
Spencer carbine, 370
Sperry, 277
Spesser, 486
Spicer, 583
Spignul, 74, 118
Spiller, 573
Spilman, 151
Spink, 526
Spinner, 27, 259
Spofford, 381
Sponier, 493
Spooner, 145
Sprague, 124, 131, 135, 149, 277, 287, 326, 341, 342, 350, 358, 392, 415, 420
Spransey, 301
Spraul, 172
Sprigg, 94
Sprightly, 550
Spring Hill, 114
Spring Hoop Skirt, 90
Springer, 170, 233, 237, 436
Springman, 292
Sproul, 167
Spurgeon, 405
Squibbs, 265
Squier, 311
Srobert, 404
St Aloysius Church, 366
St Aloysius Church bells, 338

St Aloysius' Church, 395
St Anna's Hall, 361
St Augustin's Cemetery, 52
St Charles Borromeo Cemetery, 130
St Clair, 137, 359, 501
St Dominic's Roman Catholic, 474
St Germain, 93
St Gregory, 396
St Joseph's Academy, 387
St Marie, 576
St Marius, 51
St Panlinus, 396
St Peter's Cemetery, 177
St Valentine, 51
St Vincent's Hospital, 394
Stabler, 367
Stacey, 311
Stacy, 568
Staffee, 505
Stafford, 383
Stager, 385
Stake, 62
Stalker, 302
Stamborough, 529
Stanard, 376
Stanber, 159
Stanbery, 343
Stanbury, 327
Standish, 214
Standley, 72
Stanford, 437, 515
Stanhope, 162, 202, 568
Stanley, 102, 171, 285, 559, 560
Stannell, 541
Stansbury, 151
Stanton, 17, 162, 237, 305, 459, 553
Staple, 349
Staples, 102, 276
Staplis, 108
Stark, 340
Starke, 121
Starkweather, 38, 358, 360, 367, 370
Starr, 163, 214, 287, 379, 484
State Cemetery, 190, 523
Statford, 308
Staub, 9

Staughton, 336
steam ram **Stonewall**, 168
steamboat **C H Hayner**, 134
steamboat **Charles H Hayner**, 143
steamboat **Electra**, 161
steamboat **Financier**, 148
steamboat **Lion**, 214
steamboat **St Patrick**, 231
steamboat **Winchester**, 67
steamer **Adelaide**, 89, 185
steamer **Alpha**, 154
steamer **Andrew Johnson**, 488
steamer **Ashu___**, 549
steamer **Augusta**, 114
steamer **Bostona**, 241
steamer **Britannia**, 5
steamer **C W Thomas**, 234
steamer **Canicus**, 366
steamer **Chesapeake**, 408
steamer **City of Albany**, 417
steamer **City of Memphis**, 231
steamer **City of Norwich**, 161
steamer **City of Washington**, 198
steamer **Clinton**, 205
steamer **Clyde**, 428
steamer **Coeur de Leon**, 114
steamer **Colorado**, 19
steamer **Commonwealth**, 4
steamer **Constitution**, 186
steamer **Continental**, 186
steamer **Cuba**, 166
steamer **Cunard**, 131
steamer **Dean Richmond**, 248
steamer **Deer**, 282
steamer **Don**, 417
steamer **E C Knight**, 417
steamer **England**, 151, 184
steamer **European**, 165
steamer **Evening Star**, 456, 459, 461, 468, 480
steamer **Express**, 456
steamer **Fancy Natchez**, 387
steamer **Florida,**, 579
steamer **Frolic**, 547
steamer **Gen Lytle**, 362
steamer **General Hooker**, 110

steamer **Governor Troop**, 429
steamer **Henry Ames**, 38
steamer **Henry L Gay**, 344
steamer **Henry Von Phul**, 523
steamer **Herman Livingston**, 229
steamer **Hillman**, 66
steamer **Ida Handy**, 241
steamer **Indian River**, 6
steamer **James Gary**, 448
steamer **James Raymond**, 241
steamer **James T Brady**, 229
steamer **John Sylvester**, 256
steamer **Kelso**, 571
steamer **L J Cannon**, 25
steamer **Lackawanna**, 555
steamer **Liberty**, 145
steamer **London**, 39
steamer **Louisa Moore**, 6
steamer **Marblehead**, 30
steamer **Margaret**, 120
steamer **Miami**, 38
steamer **Missouri**, 37, 39, 41
steamer **Monocacy**, 477
steamer **Nannie Byers**, 66
steamer **New York**, 59
steamer **Planter**, 282
steamer **Pocahontas**, 142
steamer **Prima Donna**, 484
steamer **Princeton**, 183
steamer **Propontis**, 198
steamer **Putumayo**, 534
steamer **Queen Victoria**, 448
steamer **Resaca**, 128
steamer **Rhode Island**, 543
steamer **Saginaw**, 19
steamer **Samuel L Brewster**, 370
steamer **San Francisco**, 551
steamer **Santee**, 230
steamer **Scotia**, 464
steamer **Shenandoah**, 573
steamer **Smith Briggs**, 370
steamer **St Andrew**, 214
steamer **St Mary**, 491, 511
steamer **St Maurice**, 492
steamer **Swatara**, 269
steamer **Vanderbilt**, 318, 562

steamer **Ville de Paris**, 454
steamer **W H Young**, 565
steamer **W R Carter**, 41
steamer **Wachusett**, 477
steamer **Wm H Young**, 428
steamship **China**, 434
steamship **Constitution**, 6
steamship **Evening Star**, 453
steamship **Fairfax**, 5
steamship **Hatteras**, 363
steamship **London**, 38
steamship **Milwaukie**, 545
steamship **New York**, 38
steamship **Pereire**, 531
steamship **Scotia**, 461
steamship **Scotland**, 555
steamship **South America**, 350
steamship **Suwanee**, 567
steamship **Vanderbilt**, 236
Stearns, 448
Stebbins, 66
Steedman, 350
Steele, 5, 103, 171, 418, 433, 528, 559, 560
Steelhammer, 104
Steens, 526
Steffin, 372
Steger, 498
Steiger, 136
Steigler, 392
Stein, 91, 518
Steinle, 303, 304
Stelle, 438
Stellwagen, 315
Sten, 454
Stephen, 187, 595
Stephens, 45, 135, 140, 152, 215, 292, 301, 305, 307, 337, 411, 441, 539, 549, 553
Stephenson, 69, 97, 188, 337
Ster, 453
Sterling, 128, 310, 454
Sternbery, 158
Sterrett, 453
Stettinius, 438
Steuart, 107, 165, 458

Stevens, 75, 104, 111, 173, 215, 261, 287, 296, 337, 355, 380, 385, 388, 433, 454, 494
Stevenson, 330, 417, 451, 471, 547, 559, 560, 599
Steward, 126, 375
Stewart, 7, 14, 19, 39, 48, 60, 63, 65, 103, 245, 262, 277, 282, 283, 303, 307, 308, 310, 337, 345, 355, 415, 438, 475, 485, 487, 505, 511, 522, 537, 547, 552, 562, 563, 574, 585
Sthelon, 200
Stickler, 380
Stickney, 210, 434, 564
Stiles, 280, 378, 392
Stimentz, 337
Stinchcomb, 170
Stine, 450, 452
Stinemetz, 181, 212, 337, 396
Stiner, 442, 456
Stinson, 234, 276
Stober, 346
Stockett, 303, 304
Stockton, 100, 447, 455
Stodare, 522
Stoddard, 480
Stoddart, 475
Stoddert, 588
Stoher, 346
Stokes, 308, 380
Stomberger, 303
Stone, 37, 64, 128, 147, 181, 197, 224, 234, 275, 281, 291, 318, 337, 348, 360, 361, 368, 371, 374, 383, 386, 397, 399, 406, 409, 429, 433, 481, 500, 510, 536, 547, 565
Stoneman, 124, 171, 374, 433, 559, 560, 589
Stonestreet, 12, 330, 331, 515
Stonewall, 433
Stonewall Cemetery, 478
Stony Ridge, 588
Storch, 402
Stores, 462
Storrs, 148, 258, 261, 504
Story, 104, 239, 253, 255, 287

Stothard, 108
Stott, 128, 337
Stough, 103
Stoughton, 507
Stout, 346, 382
Stover, 2, 75
Stow, 278
Stowe, 297
Stowers, 169
Straaffstockett, 165
Strachem, 342
Stram, 453
Stratton, 68, 235, 236, 367, 485
Straub, 54, 152
Straus, 337, 453
Strausse, 454
Strawbridge, 497
Street, 372
Streeter, 429
Stretch, 267, 355
Striblen, 492, 493, 564
Stribler, 563
Stricker, 538
Strickland, 526
Strickler, 429
Stringfellow, 294, 492, 566
Stringham, 4, 106
Strobel, 300, 301
Stroman, 301
Stromberg, 163
Stromberger, 303, 304, 360
Strong, 3, 5, 101, 251, 252, 417
Strother, 201, 383
Stuart, 217, 303, 307, 309, 352, 385, 507
Stubbs, 74, 299, 447
Studley, 50, 57, 82, 314
Studwell, 262
Stull, 502
Stumph, 300
Stuntz, 391
Sturgis, 408, 599
Sturtevant, 374
Stutman, 246
Stutt, 453
Styles, 105

Suago, 209
Suddards, 576
sue in her own name, 187
Suffel, 574
Sugar Bottom, 547
Suit, 388, 431
Sullivan, 46, 77, 93, 283, 292, 337, 345, 360, 410, 430, 431, 484, 493
Sullivant, 408
Sully, 171, 433
Sultan of Zanzibar, 475
Summers, 256, 379, 532
Summerville, 484
Sumner, 104, 261, 408, 470
Sunday Herald, 133
Sunderland, 26, 54, 117, 149, 279, 313, 315, 358, 438
Surbrug, 33, 115
Surburg, 192
Surratt, 215, 254, 318, 327, 556, 557, 561, 576, 579, 600
Susini, 544
Suter, 83, 375, 376, 515
Sutherland, 84, 104, 273, 411, 423, 511, 512, 536, 552
Sutherwood, 454
Sutro, 543
Sutter, 220
Sutton, 54, 283, 347, 477
Suydam, 47, 388
Swain, 12, 304, 336
Swaine, 385, 559
Swainson, 165
Swamp Forest, 281
Swan, 315, 397
Swann, 16, 128, 233, 372, 407, 495, 509, 563, 580
Swann's Adventure, 281
Swart, 39, 62, 415
Swartz, 6, 509
Swartzwalder, 564
Swayne, 13, 41, 556, 560
Swaze, 311
Swazey, 108
Sweeney, 221
Sweeny, 240, 241, 254, 289

Sweet, 420, 478, 538, 564
Sweetland, 429, 564
Sweetzer, 128
Sweitzer, 345
Swett, 378, 497
Swetting, 241
Swift, 70, 111, 233, 257, 267, 355, 473, 593
Swinghammer, 128
Swinton, 193
Swissburne, 277
Swisshelm, 28
Sword, 308
Swords, 540
Swut, 431
Sycles, 95
Sykes, 61, 171
Syle, 187
Sylvester, 8, 47, 62, 221, 228
Syme, 431, 565
Symington, 526
Sympson, 367
Szmanoskie, 304

T

Tabler, 307
Tabor, 515
Taff, 569
Taft, 40, 277, 512
Taggart, 166, 353
Tainter, 377
Tait, 367, 392
Talbert, 32, 414, 515, 516
Talbot, 277, 501, 573
Talbott, 37, 72, 118
Talburtt, 24
Taliaferro, 313
Talks, 80, 210
Tall, 392
Tallburt, 18
Talley, 208, 372, 387
Tallman, 392
Talmage, 471
Taltavull, 59, 79, 271
Talty, 337
Tandy, 409

Taney, 247
Tapain, 453
Tapia, 530
Tapian, 454
Tapley, 443
Tappan, 11
Tarlton, 404
Tarr Farm, 419
Tarrant Farm, 361
Tarrey, 304
Taskatt, 207
Tasker, 351, 468
Tate, 128, 487, 537
Tatspaugh, 300, 301
Tatum, 45
Tavara, 534
Taverner, 414
Tavigne, 155
Tayloe, 62, 79, 128, 175, 183, 337
Taylor, 2, 8, 17, 33, 34, 38, 41, 54, 65, 79, 81, 82, 95, 97, 100, 101, 111, 118, 119, 128, 129, 140, 156, 157, 162, 163, 190, 196, 236, 276, 297, 300, 302, 303, 307, 310, 311, 312, 313, 326, 337, 340, 354, 357, 361, 366, 379, 396, 397, 407, 408, 411, 419, 428, 430, 440, 453, 455, 456, 490, 498, 501, 504, 509, 512, 530, 538, 563, 564, 565, 570, 571, 572, 592
Tayman, 393
Teachem, 305
Teaffe, 586
Teal, 337
Teaton, 143
Tebbs, 65
Teel, 70
Teichman, 257
telegraph line, 114
Telford, 298, 532
Templeton, 105
Ten Broeck, 21
Tenbrook, 109, 112
Tenner, 353, 357
Tenney, 166, 390
Tenny, 502

Terrett, 128, 482, 489
Terrill, 154
Terry, 24, 117, 171, 343, 532
Teufel, 550
Teusch, 565
Tew, 270
Tewksberry, 53
Thairwell, 436
Thanksgiving, 450
Tharp, 79
Thatcher, 14, 106, 212, 486, 504
Thaw, 51
Thayer, 116, 255, 346
The Cedars, 533
Theaker, 7, 86, 348, 377
Theffaine, 567
Thian, 161
Thibodeaux, 106
Thieman, 568
Thom, 91
Thoma, 8
Thoman, 580
Thomas, 20, 24, 53, 62, 69, 84, 92, 101, 106, 128, 130, 138, 144, 150, 156, 171, 179, 198, 227, 247, 289, 300, 301, 304, 308, 320, 337, 343, 367, 368, 374, 379, 382, 386, 397, 432, 433, 437, 438, 439, 453, 458, 502, 518, 527, 538, 540, 562, 571, 591
Thomas Point, 306
Thomason, 86
Thompson, 5, 8, 30, 35, 36, 37, 41, 51, 69, 74, 75, 76, 79, 84, 86, 87, 101, 104, 108, 109, 110, 115, 118, 121, 128, 137, 143, 148, 169, 188, 207, 244, 253, 258, 267, 268, 276, 283, 300, 303, 310, 315, 330, 337, 344, 354, 358, 360, 367, 368, 392, 397, 414, 417, 446, 448, 449, 457, 461, 462, 475, 478, 492, 497, 502, 518, 526, 554, 557, 565, 570, 573, 580, 581, 583, 590, 591, 593
Thomson, 79, 367, 530
Thorn, 59, 186, 307, 326, 337, 403
Thornburg, 470

Thorne, 103, 311, 388, 565
Thornley, 476
Thornly, 178
Thornton, 158, 180, 190, 193, 233, 449, 503
Thorp, 458
Thorton, 562
Thos & Henry, 371
Thouvenel, 476
Thralkell, 537
Thrift, 391
Thruston, 128
Thumlert, 307
Thurlow, 198, 228
Thurston, 427
Thyer, 504
Thyng, 100
Thyson, 337, 366, 395
Tibbs, 364
Tiber creek, 85
Tieman, 114, 429
Tiensch, 428
Tiernan, 168
Tighe, 276
Tilden, 173, 351, 379
Tileston, 429
Tilley, 7, 339, 367, 438
Tillinghast, 324, 341
Tillman, 7
Tillson, 270
Tilp, 364
Tilston, 337
Tilton, 145, 339
Tilts, 6
Tinker, 594
Tinker's Branch, 371
Tinsley, 196, 596
Tippen, 346
Tipton, 203, 537
Tircuit, 565
Toadvine, 587
Tobin, 128
Tobriner, 337
Todd, 34, 56, 61, 63, 79, 98, 127, 128, 179, 223, 264, 277, 326, 337,

360, 367, 403, 415, 449, 474, 507, 585
Todd's subdivision, 384
Toldon, 198
Toler, 435
Tolfree, 315
Toll, 128
Tolman, 354
Tolson, 62, 304, 456, 517
Tomlinson, 431, 565
Tompkins, 3, 103, 222, 315, 369, 379, 531, 567, 571
Tonant, 286
Toner, 358, 360
Tongue, 564
Tonnet, 291
Toombs, 300
Toomey, 18
Tooth, 350
Topham, 337, 583
Toppin, 512
Topping, 220
Toppman, 298
Toppon, 195
Torbert, 134, 171, 437
Torbet, 330
Torbett, 547
Torrey, 103
Tossell, 196
Totten, 104, 168, 277, 433
Touro, 453
Towankinkpeota, 564
towboat **Nick Hughes**, 188
tow-boat **Tigress**, 186
Tower, 337
Towers, 18, 128, 181, 311, 438, 541
Towhey, 284
Towle, 105, 389
Towles, 337
Towner, 378
Townes, 229
Townsend, 84, 98, 105, 159, 215, 227, 355, 374, 398, 433, 477, 484, 506, 530
Townshend's Delight, 501
Towson, 325

Tracey, 276
Tracy, 397, 434, 494
Trail, 358
transport **Star**, 235
transport **Thorn**, 154
Traphagen, 526
Trapier, 24
Traver, 301
Travers, 337
Travis, 48, 75, 213
Treadway, 111
Treat, 159, 248
Tredick, 175
Tremaine, 167, 357
Tremberger, 537
Trenchard, 107
Treneau, 285
Trenholm, 478
Trentham Place, 531
Tres, 586
Tretler, 224, 438
Trevelin, 454
Trevor, 100
Triay, 600
Trimble, 365, 398, 434, 484
Tripler, 379, 486, 568
Tripp, 214, 538
Trist, 360
Tristran, 56
Trittman, 494
Trolinger, 102, 568
Trondle, 340
Trook, 96, 113, 118, 119
Trotler, 250
Trott, 119, 138, 139, 156
Trotter, 251, 560
Trowbridge, 296
Troxel, 104
Troxell, 311
True, 74
Truman, 308, 508
Trumble, 162, 471
Trumbo, 538
Trumbull, 217, 276, 310, 326
Trunion, 10
Trunnell, 213, 290, 299

Trussel, 394, 406
Trussell, 394, 406, 440, 593
Tuck, 51, 560
Tucker, 87, 94, 128, 164, 180, 213, 228, 255, 263, 302, 303, 328, 337, 360, 367, 430, 434, 444, 514, 538, 563
Tudor, 67, 188
Tudor Hall, 209
Tudor Place, 240, 281
Tuenit, 493
Tuft, 525
Tufts, 493
tug **Glance**, 582
tug **Patos**, 579
tug **Pilgrim**, 582
Tuley, 75
Tulley, 242
Tullman, 18
Tullock, 13, 330
Tully, 197, 416
Tunion, 1
Turley, 599
Turnbull, 23, 277, 351
Turnburke, 75, 125, 255
Turner, 7, 15, 68, 128, 129, 153, 269, 307, 340, 359, 374, 385, 428, 479, 565
Turpin, 183
Turton, 59, 62, 85, 310, 311
Tustin, 55, 500, 508, 535, 541
Tusting, 349
Tute, 310
Tutt, 226
Tuttle, 108, 282, 315, 478
Tutweiler, 241
Tuxbury, 419
Tweedy, 179, 589
Twenty Acre Lot, 576
Twitchell, 487
Tydings, 458
Tyler, 3, 5, 98, 121, 133, 171, 203, 207, 253, 271, 276, 280, 326, 337, 360, 404, 567
Tynan, 292
Tyrrel, 287

Tyson, 69, 360
Tyssowski, 307

U

Uberhoff, 472
Udell, 309
Uhl, 538
Uhlman, 128, 135
Ulffers, 298
Ulke, 147
Ulrich, 453, 454
Umbstaetter, 355
Umstaetter, 267
Unadilla, 570
Underhill, 111, 176
Underwood, 69, 72, 81, 161, 196, 391
Uneufer, 345
Uniac, 159
Union Burial Ground, 218
Union Cemetery, 520, 521
Union dead, 330
Union soldiers, 211
Union War Prisoners, 434
Upham, 267, 355
Upperman, 136, 176
Upton, 171, 253, 255, 516, 559
Urell, 199
Urene, 422
Urich, 311
Usher, 56, 180
Usrey, 492, 566
Ustick, 375
Utermehle, 264, 320, 337, 375, 456, 460
Utermele, 339
Utley, 72
Utter, 17

V

Vail, 397
Valentine, 387, 419, 431, 493, 565
Valliant, 57
Valm, 469
Van Antwerp, 215, 298
Van Arsdall, 327

Van Boten, 526
Van Buren, 111, 326, 379, 461, 464
Van Dorn, 188, 433
Van Duzer, 102, 276
Van Essen, 386
Van Every, 400
Van Hook, 87, 167
Van Horn, 367, 469
Van Horne, 104
Van Kleeck, 526
Van Kluck, 504
Van Limberg, 296
Van Ness, 123
Van Norman, 594
Van Patten, 128, 585
Van Reswick, 303
Van Riswick, 41, 86, 168, 204, 205, 283, 302, 400
Van Sickle, 539
Van Sloe, 108
Van Valkenburg, 56
Van Vliet, 234, 567
Van Voart, 558
Van Winkle, 220
Van Yassel, 33
Vanah, 584
Vanarsdale, 128, 308
Vanbiller, 128
Vance, 80, 105, 107, 228
Vanderbilt, 236, 343, 424, 468, 536
Vanderkieft, 404
Vanderlinden, 416
Vanderpoel, 507
Vanderpool, 215
Vanderwerken, 42, 424, 497
Vandyke, 382
Vanmeter, 67
Vann, 535
Vansickle, 453
Vanzant, 23, 411
Var_alls, 530
Varden, 126
Varnell, 96, 401
Varnum, 528
Vassalls, 541
Vaughan, 454

Vaughn, 307, 413, 513
Vedder, 261
Vega, 539
Veidt, 82
Veihmeyer, 285, 300
Veil, 100
Veirs, 245
Veitch, 309
Velati, 565
Venable, 128, 283, 435, 504
Venniegerholtz, 565
Venniegerholz, 491
Vermann, 103
Vermillion, 592
Verner, 537
Vernon, 103, 138, 163, 260, 288, 300, 512
Verot, 444
Verplanck, 101
Very, 277, 583
vessel **Trieste**, 597
vessel **Wild Gazelle**, 139
Vessey, 311
Vestes, 541
Vethake, 590
Viale, 76
Vickers, 250, 495
Victoria, 331
Vidella Plantation, 430
Viehmeyer, 295
Vierberchen, 505
Vigel, 125
Vigle, 1
Vila, 453
Vinal, 102
Vincent, 262, 291, 345
Vining, 256
Vinson, 72, 155
Vivan, 548
Vivans, 523, 546
Viven,, 102
Vogdes, 478
Vogel, 344
Vogt, 449
Voight, 34, 508
Voigt, 278

Volk, 590
Volla, 454
Vollum, 357, 380
Von Briesen, 134
Von Essen, 315, 363, 391
Von Frech, 295
Von Gerolt, 484
Von Kamecke, 212
Von Schrader, 379, 385, 540
von Teck, 273
Voorhees, 184
Voorhies, 7
Vose, 100
Voss, 182
Votry, 515
Voven, 568
Vowles, 299, 352
Vroom, 100

W

Waddell, 568
Waddell House, 447
Wadder, 466, 536
Wade, 222, 290, 291, 307, 367, 369, 558, 587, 591
Wadsworth, 66, 285, 312
Wager, 154, 385, 441
Wagner, 102, 152, 264, 303, 304, 317, 320, 346, 347, 359, 423
Wagoner, 69
Wailes, 392
Wainright, 595
Wainwright, 86, 276
Wait, 315
Waite, 101, 197, 310, 360
Waivall, 472
Wakeman, 262
Walach, 8
Walborn, 303, 305
Walbridge, 110, 115
Walcot, 558
Walcutt, 494
Walden, 4
Waldron, 275, 405, 518, 571
Wales, 109, 238

Walker, 39, 51, 56, 80, 102, 105, 106, 110, 111, 131, 203, 244, 247, 252, 277, 289, 301, 338, 356, 367, 374, 375, 406, 411, 413, 431, 433, 436, 492, 499, 515, 516, 518, 528, 532, 535, 536, 556, 565, 574, 591, 600
Wall, 36, 38, 91, 99, 100, 119, 126, 173, 183, 275, 290, 299, 380, 546, 581
Wallace, 41, 64, 74, 88, 107, 108, 109, 119, 210, 286, 298, 338, 481, 538, 558, 568, 596
Wallach, 25, 61, 98, 121, 128, 187, 299, 302, 307, 310, 326, 338, 556
Wallbut, 153
Waller, 161, 248, 401, 573
Walleron, 263
Wallingsford, 114, 158, 226, 299, 300
Wallington, 62
Wallis, 13, 130, 357, 544
Walsh, 69, 249, 290, 292, 303, 305, 337, 345, 360, 442, 467, 483, 490, 592
Walston, 485
Walter, 19, 23, 135, 149, 174, 250, 256, 278, 282, 307, 318, 323, 358, 364, 405, 466, 469, 484, 485, 504, 586
Walters, 53, 67, 129, 291, 298, 408
Walton, 228, 394, 419
Waltz, 159
Wamsley, 296
Wandell, 109
Wanless, 100
Wannall, 118
Wanton, 420
Waples, 350
Wappenhaws, 541
war of 1812, 136, 142
War of 1812, 261
Ward, 3, 8, 35, 42, 43, 100, 102, 130, 143, 155, 172, 211, 215, 222, 233, 238, 262, 301, 305, 307, 337, 338, 364, 367, 440, 459, 487, 557

Warden, 355, 381
Wardlow, 538
Wardwell, 132, 196, 389, 431
Ware, 48, 514
Wareland, 31
Warfel, 307
Warfield, 75
Waring, 452, 477
Warner, 65, 191, 278, 392
Warnick, 576
Warren, 94, 171, 188, 234, 253, 255, 425, 529, 534
Warrington, 578
Warthen, 149
Warwick, 35, 342, 359, 398, 444
Wash City Improvements, 485
Wash Co Horse Railroad Co, 326
Wash Gas Light Co, 169
Washburn, 390, 420
Washburne, 416, 516
Washington, 8, 41, 43, 48, 61, 63, 312, 320, 324, 331, 342, 407, 502, 506, 515, 569, 596
Washington bldg improvements, 500
Washington Temperance Society, 326
Wasney, 283, 284
Wasson, 530
Waterbury, 118
Waterhouse, 282, 283
Waterman, 277
Waters, 96, 103, 140, 212, 292, 338, 350, 351, 361, 477, 555, 589
Watkins, 171, 269, 284, 330, 417, 467, 559
Watmough, 107, 315
Wats, 537
Watson, 12, 88, 94, 192, 233, 260, 309, 414, 426, 470, 487, 538, 557, 569, 574
Watt, 40, 142, 310, 582
Watts, 11, 14, 93, 277, 431, 573
Waugh, 487
Way, 212
Wayman, 492, 566
Wayne, 41, 252, 556

Ways, 212
Wayson, 181, 189, 204
Wealch, 300
wearing men's attire, 244
Weatherby, 576
Weaver, 74, 153, 293, 308, 526, 578
Webb, 71, 111, 124, 171, 185, 194, 240, 260, 279, 280, 293, 325, 337, 403, 438, 472, 510, 560, 578
Webber, 196, 310
Weber, 305, 319, 358, 371
Webster, 59, 100, 132, 153, 181, 190, 212, 222, 267, 338, 354, 355, 357, 411, 414, 469, 496, 504, 556
Wedderburn, 142
Weed, 535
Weeden, 267, 354
Weedon, 348
Weeks, 160, 414, 492, 565
Wehn, 500
Weichman, 579
Weightman, 8, 62
Weikel, 247
Weilhelm, 481
Weire, 577
Weiser, 448
Weitzel, 171, 342
Weiz, 461
Welati, 430
Welch, 337, 338, 404, 424, 538, 550, 567
Welcker, 367
Well, 48, 236
Wellegan Cemetery, 521
Weller, 352
Welles, 75, 79, 268, 314, 326, 338, 381
Wellesley, 458
Wells, 43, 48, 80, 111, 153, 159, 192, 195, 237, 245, 276, 291, 307, 312, 328, 339, 355, 381, 425, 431, 438, 505, 562, 563, 565, 594
Welsh, 80, 97, 126, 462, 538
Wemerskerch, 159
Wendell, 61, 159
Wentworth, 99

684

Wentz, 212
Wenzler, 130
Weoden, 5
Werekmuller, 329
Werne, 237
Werner, 581
Werninger, 100
Wessels, 558
West, 43, 44, 52, 63, 68, 90, 96, 107, 155, 215, 299, 301, 429, 513, 534, 537, 550
Westergaard, 409
Western, 103
Westham's Support, 281
Westhorpe, 304
Weston, 262, 298, 337, 393
Westover, 492, 565
Wetherall, 337
Wetherell, 79
Wetzel, 310, 589
Wetzell, 540
Whally, 581
Whartley, 397
Wharton, 35, 93, 575
Wheat, 348
Wheatland, 17, 24
Wheatley, 69, 304, 306, 337, 338, 367, 378, 438
Wheaton, 171, 290, 559, 576
Whedon, 593
Wheelen, 267
Wheeler, 6, 9, 12, 22, 61, 105, 111, 173, 273, 279, 296, 310, 326, 337, 354, 356, 385, 467, 492, 497, 522, 540, 550, 565, 570
Whelan, 100, 278, 361, 444, 498
Wherren, 56
Wherry, 38
Whewell, 98
Whildin, 311
Whilton, 82
Whipple, 51, 76, 79, 205, 259, 379, 433, 519, 540
Whit, 453
Whitail, 581
Whitaker, 105, 116, 515

Whitall, 324, 374, 543
Whitcomb, 22, 113, 276
White, 3, 29, 35, 40, 44, 50, 97, 102, 103, 104, 128, 133, 152, 156, 168, 176, 181, 182, 184, 192, 196, 209, 218, 220, 232, 239, 246, 264, 282, 290, 297, 307, 337, 338, 342, 355, 367, 375, 427, 429, 437, 457, 464, 476, 478, 494, 504, 513, 562, 580, 587
White Haven, 570
White Oak Point, 588
Whitea_l, 528
Whitefoot, 290
Whitehouse, 417
Whitehurst, 162
Whitely, 58, 290
Whitemen, 346
Whitemore, 46, 300, 301
Whiteside, 467
Whitfield, 352, 443
Whithall, 524
Whiting, 20, 21, 31, 261, 462, 486, 504, 570
Whitley, 406
Whitlord, 152
Whitman, 349, 449
Whitmarsh, 578
Whitney, 178, 276, 302, 391, 547
Whiton, 74, 77, 82, 113
Whitside, 100
Whittaker, 570
Whittemore, 104, 512
Whittier, 220
Whittingham, 554
Whittlesey, 36, 88, 89, 161, 385, 494, 500, 566
Whitwell, 176
Whyte, 283
Wiber, 316
Wickeraham, 474
Wickliffe, 524
Widdecombe, 79
Widdicombe, 65, 125, 138, 243, 438
Widow's Mite, 317
Wiegand, 188

Wiegel, 385
Wielandy, 409
Wiget, 12, 175, 395, 404, 408, 468
Wiggins, 228
Wiggs, 537
Wigham, 441
Wight, 63, 330, 337, 575
Wightman, 549
Wilber, 538
Wilcox, 100, 105, 290, 402, 433, 461, 470, 559, 589
Wild, 65
Wilder, 224, 444, 567
Wiley, 100, 250, 471, 513, 550, 573
Wilkens, 71
Wilkerson, 303, 304
Wilkes, 22, 106, 108, 574
Wilkeson, 354
Wilkie, 123
Wilkins, 76, 79, 272, 310, 559
Will, 549
Willa_d, 540
Willard, 20, 104, 158, 168, 297, 337, 338, 379, 438, 473, 507, 542, 598
Willcox, 291, 560
Willet, 585
Willett, 338, 472
Willey, 301, 431
William, 338
Williama, 437
Williams, 11, 17, 20, 25, 30, 32, 46, 47, 62, 64, 77, 79, 80, 81, 87, 97, 99, 101, 109, 114, 122, 128, 132, 134, 137, 139, 140, 144, 149, 154, 155, 156, 168, 171, 181, 183, 184, 185, 190, 192, 193, 200, 233, 235, 236, 238, 240, 243, 255, 257, 261, 264, 265, 266, 272, 277, 286, 291, 298, 300, 301, 305, 308, 309, 311, 338, 341, 356, 357, 360, 367, 385, 400, 401, 403, 405, 407, 412, 414, 422, 424, 427, 429, 430, 431, 434, 439, 441, 462, 463, 465, 466, 472, 473, 475, 483, 487, 490, 492, 501, 504, 510, 513, 524, 528, 536, 547,
550, 561, 565, 571, 582, 589, 593, 594, 596
Williamson, 15, 25, 105, 138, 148, 188, 215, 230, 253, 283, 287, 290, 304, 307, 397, 400, 469, 470
Willian, 338
Willis, 229, 303, 539, 557
Williss, 79
Willmuth, 583
Willoughby, 48
Wills, 74, 136, 338
Willson, 8, 43, 337, 571
Wilmarth, 551
Wilmer, 133, 134, 212, 501
Wilmot, 561
Wilney, 337
Wilson, 6, 12, 26, 27, 34, 42, 55, 59, 69, 73, 105, 114, 123, 140, 149, 152, 156, 167, 171, 174, 176, 186, 201, 202, 213, 221, 277, 282, 297, 299, 300, 311, 320, 324, 326, 330, 338, 346, 353, 358, 367, 375, 382, 388, 393, 422, 435, 456, 482, 483, 487, 504, 505, 510, 513, 524, 530, 544, 546, 547, 559, 571, 573, 585, 595, 599
Wilt, 188
Wiltberger, 12, 502
Wiltberger's subdivision, 363
Wilton, 45, 337
Wiltsof, 155
Wiltsoff, 113
Wimer, 577
Wimmer, 521
Wimsatt, 58, 128, 383
Winans, 152
Winchester, 470
Winchester Cemetery, 520
Winder, 118, 142, 156, 170, 432, 566, 591
Windlow, 315
Windsor, 501
Wine, 567
Winebrener, 101
Winebrenner, 354
Winemiller, 56, 391

Winer, 517
Winfield, 300, 517
Winfree, 404
Wingate, 39, 72, 224, 260
Wingfield, 372
Winn, 230, 294
Winne, 24
Winslow, 99, 167, 273, 316
Winson, 513
Winter, 122, 159, 459
Winters, 5
Wirner, 444
Wirt, 198, 219
Wirtz, 357
Wisdom, 538
Wise, 66, 206, 290, 300, 308, 309, 337, 342, 360, 398, 423, 441, 476, 478, 480, 501, 537, 591
Wiseman, 537
Wishart, 275
Wisner, 277
Wissler, 559
Witherell, 272
Witherow, 338
Withers, 154, 504
Witkowski, 431
Witt, 183
Wittenver, 391
Witz, 75
Witzel, 310
Witzieben, 212
Wm Tell Hotel, 68
Wolbert, 142
Wolcott, 247
Wolf, 41, 408, 454
Wolfe, 97, 241, 300, 337
Wolfgard, 318
Wollard, 128
Woltz, 307
Woman Candidate, 459
Wood, 79, 89, 105, 121, 133, 171, 172, 281, 288, 295, 300, 303, 326, 330, 344, 391, 403, 429, 431, 433, 437, 444, 491, 493, 505, 508, 534, 553, 565, 583
Woodbridge, 120

Woodbury, 247, 356, 360, 408
Woodfield, 303
Woodhouse, 20
Woodhull, 330, 337
Woodland Cemetery, 164
Woodley, 498
Woodman, 277, 541
Woodrow, 414
Woodruff, 199, 267, 354, 386, 559
Woods, 171, 209, 249, 311, 551, 552, 559
Woodson, 232
Woodward, 64, 269, 274, 281, 307, 337, 398, 449, 470, 528, 533, 541, 547, 548, 557, 560
Wool, 491
Woolaston, 217
Woolcocks, 42
Wooley, 39, 528, 543
Woolfold, 565
Woolfork, 492
Woolfrey, 570
Woolley, 581
Woolly, 590
Wools, 308
Woolsey, 165
Wooster, 446
Worden, 234
Wordin, 600
Works, 268
Wormer, 515
Worrell, 475
Worster, 97
Worthing, 587
Worthington, 323, 338, 387, 535, 578
Woster, 224
Wow, 297
Wrenchy, 513
Wright, 55, 66, 80, 103, 129, 171, 215, 225, 233, 253, 255, 267, 299, 307, 330, 354, 357, 399, 416, 417, 423, 433, 490, 496, 530, 536, 544, 576, 587
Wroe, 310, 315
Wunderlich, 409

Wyckoff, 125
Wygant, 419
Wyhe, 134
Wylie, 58, 81, 153, 158, 172, 174,
    219, 224, 244, 253, 254, 318, 324,
    401, 446, 449, 458, 463
Wylies, 502
Wylle, 69
Wyman, 107, 117, 330
Wynan, 587
Wyncoop, 96
Wynkoop, 414, 454
Wyvill, 337
Wyville, 461

X

Xelowski, 172, 178, 179

Y

Yaden, 429
Yale, 312
Yarbry, 586
Yates, 58, 128, 185, 188, 205, 278,
    338, 365, 383, 439, 472
Yeabower, 468, 486, 498, 515
Yeager, 308
Yeatman, 118, 119, 300, 301, 310,
    469
Yelverton, 251
Yerby, 21, 324, 358
Yetter, 436
Yois, 154
Yonge, 150
Yonson, 300

York, 273
Yorke, 490
Yorkshire, 174
Yorktown Cemetery, 520
Yots, 154
Young, 19, 20, 43, 64, 67, 71, 75, 77,
    79, 87, 89, 91, 98, 116, 128, 156,
    157, 158, 165, 176, 194, 237, 304,
    326, 338, 360, 361, 372, 392, 413,
    415, 416, 423, 438, 459, 488, 493,
    494, 495, 502, 554, 568, 587, 593
Youngsborough, 53
Yuille, 209
Yulee, 130, 195

Z

Zalinski, 101
Zane, 498
Zange, 57
Zantainger, 490
Zarahart, 537
Zauner, 300
Zearing, 180
Zerback, 440
Zeringue, 564
Zevely, 13
Ziess, 295
Zimmer, 159
Zimmerman, 68, 183, 185, 283, 464
Zion, 538
Zoller, 310
Zollicoffer, 118
Zulick, 378

Other Heritage Books by Joan M. Dixon:

National Intelligencer *Newspaper Abstracts Special Edition: The Civil War Years Volume 1: January 1, 1861–June 30, 1863*

National Intelligencer *Newspaper Abstracts Special Edition: The Civil War Years Volume 2: July 1, 1863–December 31, 1865*

National Intelligencer *Newspaper Abstracts Jan. 1, 1869–Jan. 8, 1870*

National Intelligencer *Newspaper Abstracts Volume 1866–Volume 1868*

National Intelligencer *Newspaper Abstracts Volume 1840–Volume 1860*

National Intelligencer *Newspaper Abstracts, 1838–1839*

National Intelligencer *Newspaper Abstracts, 1836–1837*

National Intelligencer *Newspaper Abstracts, 1834–1835*

National Intelligencer *Newspaper Abstracts, 1832–1833*

National Intelligencer *Newspaper Abstracts, 1830–1831*

National Intelligencer *Newspaper Abstracts, 1827–1829*

National Intelligencer *Newspaper Abstracts, 1824–1826*

National Intelligencer *Newspaper Abstracts, 1821–1823*

National Intelligencer *Newspaper Abstracts, 1818–1820*

National Intelligencer *Newspaper Abstracts, 1814–1817*

National Intelligencer *Newspaper Abstracts, 1811–1813*

National Intelligencer *Newspaper Abstracts, 1806–1810*

National Intelligencer *Newspaper Abstracts, 1800–1805*